THE PHILOSOPHY OF LANGUAGE

THE PHILOSOPHY OF
LANGUAGE

FIFTH EDITION

Edited by

A. P. Martinich

New York   Oxford
OXFORD UNIVERSITY PRESS
2008

Oxford University Press, Inc., publishes works that further Oxford University's
objective of excellence in research, scholarship, and education

Oxford   New York
Auckland   Cape Town   Dar es Salaam   Hong Kong   Karachi
Kuala Lumpur   Madrid   Melbourne   Mexico City   Nairobi
New Delhi   Shanghai   Taipei   Toronto

With offices in
Argentina   Austria   Brazil   Chile   Czech Republic   France   Greece
Guatemala   Hungary   Italy   Japan   Poland   Portugal   Singapore
South Korea   Switzerland   Thailand   Turkey   Ukraine   Vietnam

Published by Oxford University Press, Inc.,
198 Madison Avenue, New York, NY 10016
http://www.oup.com

Library of Congress Cataloging-in-Publication Data

The philosophy of language / edited by A. P. Martinich.—5th ed.
    p. cm
  Includes bibliographical references.
  ISBN-13: 978-0-19-518830-1 (pbk. : alk. paper)
  1. Language and languages—Philosophy.   I. Martinich, Aloysius.

P107 .P545 2008
401—dc22   2006049362

Printing number: 9 8 7 6 5 4

Printed in the United States of America
on acid-free paper

CONTENTS

NOTE TO THE FIFTH EDITION

As in previous editions, it was easier to identify selections that deserved to be included than to select the ones that would be deleted. One of the omissions was personally painful to me. Much excellent work in the philosophy of language has been done over the last quarter century.

I want to thank my editor, Robert Miller, for encouraging me to produce this edition; Sarah Calabi, associate editor, and Christine D'Antonio, production editor at Oxford University Press, who guided me through the process; and Akeel Bilgrami and Mark Sainsbury, who suggested selections. Cory Juhl, who has often read drafts of my work and has always been willing to discuss philosophy, deserves more general gratitude.

Leslie Martinich helped me secure permissions, and she and Liudmila Inozemtseva were exceptionally helpful in preparing the manuscript for press.

Revisions and additions to the introductions were supported by a Faculty Research Assignment, University of Texas at Austin.

I dedicate my work in this book to Carol, John, and Mary.

Introduction

I

Philosophers and reflective persons in general have been interested in language for a long time and for various reasons. First, since language seems to be characteristic of human beings, to know about language is to know something about being human. Although some anthropologists claim that some of the nonhuman primates can acquire language, most philosophers and linguists disagree. While conceding that these chimpanzees and gorillas have learned to communicate using a symbol system, they deny that what the primates are using counts as a human language. That is, none of the systems the primates use allows for the construction of an infinitely large number of expressions. And it is this feature that philosophers and linguists take to be characteristic of human language.

Second, since certain philosophical problems seem to arise from false beliefs about the structure of language, understanding it may help solve those problems or avoid them altogether. For example, since the sentence "Nothing came down the road" is, at least superficially, grammatically like "John came down the road" and John is something that exists, one might think that nothing is something that exists. But this absurd view would be caused by a misunderstanding of the structure of language.

In *Through the Looking Glass,* Lewis Carroll exploited the difference between the word "nothing" and ordinary proper names, when Alice told the king, "I see nobody on the road," and the king replied, "I only wish I had such eyes to be able to see Nobody! And at that distance too!" What Alice meant is, "It is not the case that I see somebody on the road," while the king understood her to mean, "I see something, namely, Nobody, on the road."

It would also be a mistake, caused by a misunderstanding of how language works, to think that since "Justice is a virtue" is grammatically like "Mary is a lawyer," justice is a concrete, actual thing.

Third, many philosophers have held that language is a reflection of reality, so, if one could understand the structure of language, one could understand the structure of reality. It is not odd to think that the structure of language is the same or similar to the structure of reality. For language is the expression of thought, and, if human thoughts can count as knowledge about the world, thought would seem to be a reflection of reality. This view of language, thought, and reality is very old, at least as old as Plato, who has Socrates explain that this very belief is the strategy behind his own philosophizing. In Socrates' account of his turn away from the physical philosophy of Anaxagoras to his own method, he says that he feared that if he tried to figure out the structure of reality by studying reality directly, he might be intellectually blinded. Thus he resolved to use language as a kind of mirror of reality: "I decided to take refuge in language, and study the truth of things by means of it" (*Phaedo* 99E). The same idea of language as a reflection of reality continued through the middle ages, and through modern philosophy into the twentieth century. One of the most forceful statements of this view of language is Ludwig Wittgenstein's *Tractatus Logico-Philosophicus,* published in 1921. His ideas were dubbed the picture theory of language, and it has been the dominant view during the twentieth century. There is a Kantian variation on this view according to which language is not a reflection of reality, which is inaccessible to human intelligence, but a reflection of our thought about reality. Much of the philosophizing of those who do not accept any version of the picture theory of language consists of little more than criticism.

Fourth, language is, of course, interesting in itself and might be studied profitably for its own sake.

II

Philosophers distinguish three areas of the study of language: syntax, semantics, and pragmatics.

Syntax is the study of the rules that describe what a well-formed or grammatical sentence is in purely formal terms. That is, it describes what a sentence is in terms of rules that specify what sequences of words are permissible. These rules are called concatenation rules, from the metaphor of words being linked together as if in a chain. A syntactic description of language is not allowed to use the concept of meaning or any related concept in order to explain what a grammatical sentence is.

Semantics is the study of the meaning of words and sentences. A semantic theory tries to explain what meaning is, and any theory of meaning will have to describe what is and what is not a meaningful expression as well as the systematic relations between words and what they mean. The principal semantic notions are truth and reference, although pragmatics, too, has much to say about reference.

Pragmatics is the study of what speakers do with language. Speakers do not simply talk. In or by speaking, they promise, marry, swear, forgive, apologize, insult, and enrage, among many other things. Further, what is communicated is not wholly conveyed by what is said; much is implied. The treatment of these and related topics belongs to pragmatics. (Some philosophers have a different and more restrictive notion of pragmatics; they define it as the study of indexical expressions, such as "I," "here" and "now," the reference of which depends upon the context of the utterance.)

In addition to syntax, semantics, and pragmatics, linguists study a fourth aspect of language, phonetics, that is, the science of the sounds of human languages. Each human language uses only a small number of the sounds that people can easily vocalize, and the presence of some sounds in a language excludes, as a matter of fact, the use of certain other sounds that exist in other languages. Phonetics is fascinating, but philosophers have done virtually no work in this area.

The one exception is some work done on contrastive stress. To understand this, we first need to appreciate that there is a normal rhythm to English sentences. For example, indicative sentences have a "falling" intonation at the end of a sentence, while interrogative sentences have a rising one. Listen to the difference between, "Mary left the room," versus, "Did Mary leave the room?" A grammatical indicative sentence can actually be used to ask a question by substituting a rising intonation at the end instead of the normal falling one. (In recent years, I have noticed that some speakers are obliterating the distinction between indicative and interrogative intonation by using rising intonation as the normal one for indicative sentences.)

Contrastive stress is one way of altering the normal pattern of stress in a sentence to communicate something special. For example, if one uses the sentence, "John stole the cookies," to make a simple statement, the stress is distributed fairly uniformly on each word. But now suppose that someone falsely accuses Mary of being the thief. Someone might object to this accusation by putting extra or contrastive stress on "John" in order to convey that it is not Mary, but John who is the thief: *John* stole the cookies. Alternatively, suppose that some cookies are stolen and then eaten. If it is mistakenly thought that John is the one who ate the cookies, one might say, "John *stole* the cookies," indicating that he only stole them and did not eat them. Finally, suppose that John is accused of stealing both cookies and some money but that he stole only the cookies. One might say, "John stole the *cookies*." According to one theory, the three differently stressed sentences have different truth-conditions: "*John* stole the cookies," for example, is true only if someone other than John is thought to have stolen them. The theory is controversial.

III

Several distinctions are presupposed by many of the articles in this anthology and need to be understood. First there is the use-mention distinction. For the most part, words are *used* in such a way that the word itself is not the primary object of interest. Roughly, words are signs that point beyond themselves to other things. However, it is possible for words to be used to *mention* or talk about themselves, to make the very word itself the object of interest. Consider the sentences

(1) Cicero was a Roman senator.
(2) Cicero is a word with six letters.
(3) "Cicero" was a Roman senator.
(4) "Cicero" is a word with six letters.

Sentences (1) and (4) are or can be used to make true statements. Sentence (1) is about the historical person Cicero; the subject expression was *used* to talk about Cicero. Sentence (4) is not about the historical person Cicero; it is about a word, about the proper name of Cicero, and it is that name that was *mentioned* in (4).

Sentences (2) and (3) are false. (2) is false because it claims that the person Cicero was a word, which is absurd; (3) is false because it claims that a word is a person.

This might seem simple and straightforward enough. But now consider this. In sentence (1), the word "Cicero" is used to talk about Cicero. In sentence (4), "'Cicero'" is used to talk about the word "Cicero." Notice that in the preceding sentence, the subject expression contains two sets of quotation marks. The inner (single) quotation marks are used to mention a word; the outer (double) quotation marks are used to mention the mention of a word. These quotation marks can be stacked indefinitely, if necessary, to mention other mentioned expressions.

Instead of double quotation marks, philosophers sometimes use single quotation marks to indicate that a word or phrase is being mentioned. Thus, instead of the sentence

"Cicero" is a word with six letters.

a philosopher might write

'Cicero' is a word with six letters.

This convention has the advantage of distinguishing between when the author is mentioning a word or phrase and when the author is directly quoting the words of someone else.

There are three ways to avoid the quotation mark device of mentioning a word or expression. One is to *display* the mentioned word or expression on a separate line. For example, the word

Cicero

has six letters. In the previous sentence, "Cicero" is mentioned by displaying it on a separate line. (Sometimes it is convenient to display a word or expression immediately following a colon.) The device of displaying an expression has already been used. Sentences (1) through (4) above were displayed. If I had not wanted to display them, I might have mentioned them in this way: Consider the sentences, (1) "Cicero was a Roman senator," (2) "Cicero is a word with six letters," (3) " 'Cicero' was a Roman senator," (4) " 'Cicero' is a word with six letters." Obviously, displaying expressions is often neater.

The second way to mention a word is to name it. Just as one might name an infant or pet, one can name words or expressions (or anything else). Suppose we want to talk about the word "Cicero" extensively. We might name that word "Harry." If we do, then the sentence "Harry is a word with six letters" is true. Question: Is the sentence " 'Harry' has six letters" true or false?

Linguists have a third way of mentioning an expression. They italicize it. Thus, instead of (4), a linguist might write

(4′) *Cicero* is a word with six letters.

IV

The use-mention distinction can be generalized in a certain way to distinguish between using a language and mentioning a language. This is the distinction between metalanguage and object language. Most areas of science and philosophy use language to talk about nonlinguistic phenomena. Linguistics and philosophy of language are unusual in that language is used to talk about language. We can distinguish then between the language used to express the science or philosophy and the language that is being studied. Since the language being studied is the *object* of study, it is called the object language. Since the language used to express the study is in a sense "outside" or "higher" than the language being studied, it is called the metalanguage. The metalanguage of a linguistic researcher will typically be his native language. English-speaking linguists typically use English as their metalanguage to talk about language. If Latin is the object of study, then Latin is the object language. When the metalanguage and the object language are different, there is relatively little risk of confusion. It is not difficult to understand what is meant by " 'Fiat lux' is a Latin sentence, consisting of a verb followed by a noun" and why it is being uttered. Yet, a linguist might take his native language as his object of study. An English-speaking linguistic researcher might take English as his object of study, in which case English is both the metalanguage and the object language. The identity of the metalanguage and object language raises philosophical problems, some of which are discussed by Alonzo Church, Alfred Tarski, and Donald Davidson in their articles in Section I. There is also a kind of practical problem. When the metalanguage and the object language are the same and the discussion involves the meaning of the object language, the results can sound trivial. Philosophers have expended a lot of effort over the sentence

"Snow is white" means snow is white.

and

"Snow is white" is true just in case snow is white.

For Davidson, the truth of this latter, seemingly trivial sentence is crucial to his program for semantics. Other philosophers have called the sentence degenerate. Whatever the truth of the matter, one must keep in mind that the quoted sentence (the one mentioned) is the object of study, while the unquoted clause (the one being used) is part of the metalanguage being used to discuss the object language.

V

In the discussion of the use-mention distinction, the word "sentence" was used loosely and, one might argue, uncritically. For philosophers of language have found it necessary to distinguish between sentences, meanings, statements, and proposition, among other things; and sentences, contrary to my earlier usage, are often held not to be the kinds of things that can be either true or false.

To get a sense of the distinctions involved here, consider these expressions:

(5) I am a bachelor.
(6) John is a bachelor.
(7) John is an unmarried adult male.

(5) through (7) are different sentences in English. None of them has all the same words in the same order as any other. Yet, although (6) and (7) are different sentences, they have the same meaning. Sentences of different languages can have the same meaning. The English sentence "It is raining," the Italian sentence "*Piove*," and the German sentence "*Es regnet*" mean the same thing. Sentence (5) does not have the same meaning as (6) or (7). But suppose sentence (5) is uttered by John. Then (5) seems to be the same as (6) and (7) in some respect. They each express the same proposition: each refers to the same object and predicates the same thing of it. In order to determine whether (5) expresses the same proposition as (6) and (7), it is necessary to know something about the context. In this case, I have stipulated that John asserted the sentence. I have presupposed that the time and place of the utterance of the other sentences as well as the identities of the speakers were appropriate to make them express the same proposition. Many philosophers think this dependence upon context is philosophically significant. Without knowing who uttered (5), it is impossible to know what proposition was expressed. More importantly, without knowing whether the sentence was asserted, or merely used as an example of a sentence of English without anyone committing himself to its truth, (5) is not used to express a proposition at all. On this view, (5) is a sentence and neither true nor false; and, in general, sentences do not have truth-values. Propositions do. Other philosophers do not think the sentence/meaning/proposition

distinction is so important. They think that a proposition can be defined by relativizing a sentence to a context: a proposition is simply an ordered triple consisting of a sentence, a person, and a time of utterance.

Propositions also need to be distinguished from statements. The same proposition can be expressed with different forces. For example, consider these sentences:

I state that John will be at the party.
I promise that John will be at the party.
I question whether John will be as the party.
I order you, John, to be at the party.

All of them can be used to express the same proposition. But only the first has the potential force to make a statement directly. The other sentences, respectively, have the potential force to promise that the proposition will be made true, to question whether it is true and to order that it will be made true. Roughly, the difference between a proposition and a statement is that a proposition has a truth value without any special force attached to it, while a statement is a proposition the truth of which the speaker has committed himself to on the basis of sufficient evidence. This distinction between propositions and statements is explained by John Searle in "The Structure of Illocutionary Acts."

Related to these distinctions is a type-token distinction. Count the number of sentences displayed immediately below.

It is raining.
It is raining.
It is raining.

One might count one or three. There is one sentence-type and three tokens or instances of that one sentence-type. If it seems dubious that there is only one sentence occurring three times, consider that if a teacher says, "Write the sentence 'I will not speak in class' one hundred times" she is using the word "sentence" in the sense of sentence-type. For it is the same sentence that is to be written repeatedly. She wants one sentence written: I will not speak in class. But she wants one hundred tokens of it.

VI

There is another device that philosophers of language use that needs to be mentioned, namely, a pair of matched right angles ($\ulcorner$, $\urcorner$). The device goes by various names: 'corner quotes', 'square quotes', 'quasi-quotes', and sometimes 'Quine corners', after their inventor W. V. Quine. Corner quotes function similarly to quotation marks that are used to mention phrases. The difference is that, whereas quotation marks mention all the symbols inside of them, corner quotes mention symbols selectively; they mention all the words inside of them, but not other symbols (metavariables).

For example, suppose someone wants to talk about every sentence that begins with the word 'The' and ends with the word 'tree', such as

The woodsman cut down a tree.
The dog chased the cat up a tree.
The most beautiful plant is a tree.

Some symbol needs to be used to represent the words between 'The' and 'tree'. Suppose it is the Greek symbol 'Φ' (phi). It would be natural, but incorrect, to represent the three sentences above by writing, 'The Φ tree'. What the symbols within quotation marks represent is the sequence, 'The', followed by 'Φ', followed by 'tree'. That is, the Greek letter Φ is being mentioned. But that was not what was intended. What was intended was the word 'The', followed by some sequence of words, followed by the word 'tree'. In other words, some device is needed that will mention certain words or symbols of the object language but skip over mentioning symbols that are used in the metalanguage to designated words and symbols in the object language. Corner quotes do exactly that. That is, the symbols

⌜The Φ tree⌝

(where 'Φ' is any sequence of words within a grammatical English sentence) can be used to represent the three quoted sentences.

The use of corner quotes will be extremely important in our discussion of syntax.

VII

A formal treatment of a subject is one that is clear, precise, and explicit. Let's apply this idea to that of a grammar for language. A formal grammar consists of two parts: a syntax and a semantics. The syntax itself also consists of two parts: a vocabulary and formation rules. The vocabulary specifies which marks or sounds can appear in sentences. Roughly, the vocabulary consists of words and punctuation marks or whatever would be equivalent to them in the language being treated. The phrase, 'marks or sounds' was used rather than 'symbols' because 'symbol' suggests something that has a meaning, and syntax is not permitted to use any semantic concept. The formation rules either generate sentences out of the items in the vocabulary or they describe them. The semantics consists of two parts: a part that specifies the meanings of the simplest elements of the language, and a part that specifies the meanings of the complex elements of the language. The simplest elements of the language may either be words or sentences, depending on the specific language being studied and the philosophical views of the author of the grammar.

Most research in syntax is currently done by linguists. Nonetheless, something needs to be said about syntax because it is presupposed by most of the articles in this book, because it is important not to confuse syntactic with semantic issues, and because it is interesting in its own right. To think about language syntactically is to think about it as consisting of sequences of sounds or physical shapes without regard to its having any meaning, as if the sentences had no significance, no truth-value, no reference beyond themselves, and no symbolic value at all. This is difficult to do because when people use language, they focus almost exclusively on what the language means. Let me illustrate these points by constructing a syntax for a language that looks very much like a part or fragment of English. We shall call the language 'Languish', and it resembles certain systems used in logic. The number of sentences or well-formed formulas of this language is infinite even though they are relatively simple in syntactic structure. Because the number is infinite, I could not hope to include all of them. For now I shall list only a few.

Adam walks
Beth walks
Adam talks
Beth talks
it is not the case that Adam walks
(it is not the case that Adam walks and Beth talks)
it is not the case that (Adam walks and Beth talks)

Sequences of words that are not sentences include these:

> walks Beth
> Beth walked
> it is not the case that Beth walks and Adam talks

Even from the brief list of sentences that was given, it should be plausible that the complex sentences ("molecular sentences') are formed from the simple sentences ("atomic sentences'). This important fact about language allows us to explain how an infinite number of sentences can be generated from a finite base. (By a "finite base', here, I mean a finite number of vocabulary items [words] and syntactic, generation rules.) Here is a syntax for Languish.

A SYNTAX FOR LANGUISH

Vocabulary

> *Proper names*: Adam, Beth, Carol, David
> *Predicates*: walks, talks, flies, sits, reads
> *Sentential connectives*: it is not the case that, and, or, if, . . . then, if and only if

Formation Rules

1. Where α is any proper name and Φ is any predicate, enter $\alpha\Phi$ as a sentence.
2. Where Φ is any sentence, enter $\ulcorner$it is not the case that $\Phi\urcorner$ as a sentence.
3. Where Φ is a sentence and Ψ is a sentence, $\ulcorner$enter $(\Phi$ and $\Psi)\urcorner$ as a sentence.
4. Where Φ is a sentence and Ψ is a sentence, enter $\ulcorner(\Phi$ or $\Psi)\urcorner$ as a sentence.
5. Where Φ is a sentence and Ψ is a sentence, enter $\ulcorner$(if Φ, then $\Psi)\urcorner$ as a sentence.
6. Where Φ is a sentence and Ψ is a sentence, enter $\ulcorner(\Phi$ if and only if $\Psi)\urcorner$ as a sentence.

Notice that this syntax consists of two parts: a vocabulary (sometimes called 'an alphabet') and formation rules. The vocabulary is divided into categories. These categories are analogous to the parts of speech that you were taught in grammar school. The category of proper names is analogous to the grammatical category of proper nouns. The category of predicates is analogous to the grammatical category of verbs. The category of sentential connectives is analogous to the grammatical category of particles. In school grammars, there are eight parts of speech. In our syntax, there are only three parts of speech. This is not accidental, or wholly due to the simplicity of Languish. In general, philosophers try to explain things using as few categories as possible.

The syntax for Languish generates sentences. A sentence (by stipulative definition) is any line in a generation. 'Generation' is a technical term, which I shall explain in large part by giving examples of it. Here is a generation of the sentence 'Adam walks':

1. Adam walks   Rule 1

In this example, α = 'Adam' and Φ = 'walks'. Here is a generation of the sentence 'Beth talks':

1. Beth talks   Rule 1

In this example, α = 'Beth' and Φ = 'talks'. Here is a generation of the sentence 'it is not the case that (Beth walks and Adam talks)':

1. Beth walks	Rule 1
2. Adam talks	Rule 1
3. (Beth walks and Adam talks)	Rule 3, from lines 1 and 2
4. it is not the case that (Beth walks and Adam talks)	Rule 2, from line 3

In line 3 of the generation, Φ = 'Beth walks', but in line 4 of the generation, Φ = 'Beth walks and Adam talks'.

Notice the following characteristics of this syntax and the generations of sentences: (i) A rule can be used an indefinite number of times. (ii) The complex sentences are formed from the simpler sentences. (iii) The metavariables, α, Φ, and Ψ, can be used for any individual symbol from the category they indicate; thus, α can be 'Adam' in one sentence and 'Beth' in the next. (iv) The parentheses substitute for punctuation marks, such as commas, semicolons, and periods, and for such words as 'either' and 'both'. (v) The placement of the parentheses is very important. The formation rules must be followed precisely. Words and other marks must be put in when and only when they are dictated. (vi) The formation rules can be thought of as being of two kinds. Some rules get the process started by directly generating some sentences, for example, Rule 1. These may be called 'syntactic base rules'. Some rules form new and more complex sentences from simpler sentences that have already been generated, namely, Rules 2–6. These may be called 'syntactic projection rules'.

Here is a final example of a generation:

1. Carol reads	Rule 1
2. Adam talks	Rule 1
3. Beth walks	Rule 1
4. it is not the case that Adam talks	Rule 2, from line 2
5. (it is not the case that Adam talks and Beth walks)	Rule 3, from lines 4 and 3
6. (Carol reads if and only if (it is not the case that Adam talks and Beth walks))	Rules 6, from lines 1 and 5

Because the words 'Adam', 'Beth', 'walks', 'talks', 'and', 'or', and so on are familiar to us, as are the categories of proper names and predicates, it is tempting to think of them as having a semantic value. 'Adam' seems to be the name of Adam or as referring to Adam. The word 'walks' seems to mean something like walking or the concept of walking. However, since we are considering Languish purely syntactically, we must resist the temptation to view words in this way. Considered syntactically, these items of Languish do not have any meaning or representational value at all.

The formation rules of Languish are acceptable syntactic rules in large part because they merely give instructions about what vocabulary items are to be placed next to which other vocabulary items in order to form a sentence. The fact that a syntax does not treat sentences, word-sequences, or formulas as having a meaning can be brought out better if we look at some syntaxes for some very simple systems that genuinely do not have any meaning. For simplicity's sake, we shall refer to the following sets of symbols as languages. (The following treatment is inspired by Noam Chomsky's *Syntactic Structures* [1957].) Consider the language that consists of all and only sequences of 'a's followed by the identical number of 'b's, and sequences of 'b's followed by the identical number of 'a's. In other words, these are some sentences of the language:

ab, ba, aabb, bbaa, aaabbb, bbbaaa.

These are not sentences of the language:

a, b, aab, bba, aabaa, bbab.

Here is a syntax for this language:

Vocabulary: a, b

Formation Rules

1. Enter 'ab' as a sentence.
2. Enter 'ba' as a sentence.
3. If ⌜aΦb⌝ is a sentence, enter ⌜aaΦbb⌝ as a sentence.
4. If ⌜bΦa⌝ is a sentence, enter ⌜bbΦaa⌝ as a sentence.

Since all the vocabulary items are of one type, there is no need to distinguish different categories of vocabulary items. Rules 1 and 2 are base rules; Rules 3 and 4 are projection rules.

Here is a generation of 'aabb':

1. ab	Rule 1
2. aabb	Rule 3, from line 1

In this language, some rules are needed to generate the simplest sentences out of which the more complicated sentences will be generated. Rules 1 and 2 serve this purpose and one of them will always be the first rule applied in a generation. Here is a generation of the sentence 'bbbbaaaa':

1. ba	Rule 2
2. bbaa	Rule 4, from line 1
3. bbbaaa	Rule 4, from line 2
4. bbbbaaaa	Rule 4, from line 3

Exercise: generate 'aaabbb'.

Let's now consider another language that consists of sequences of 'a's and 'b's, followed by the mirror image of 'a's and 'b's. That is, the following are sentences:

aa, bb, abba, baab, aabbaa, ababbaba, aaaa, bbbb

The following are not sentences:

a, b, ab, ba, aba, bab, aab, bba, abab, aaabaaa

Here is a syntax for this language:

Vocabulary: a, b

Formation Rules

1. Enter 'aa' as a sentence.
2. Enter 'bb' as a sentence.
3. If Φ is a sentence, enter ⌜aΦa⌝ as a sentence.
4. If Φ is a sentence, enter ⌜bΦb⌝ as a sentence.

Exercise: Generate 'bbbbbbbb' and 'abbaaaaaabba'.

Now consider a language that consists of some number of 'a's and/or 'b's followed by the identical string of 'a's and/or 'b's. The following are sentences:

aa, bb, abab, baba, aaaa, bbbb, abaaba

The following are not sentences:

a, b, aaa, aba, bbabb, aabb, bbaa

Here is a syntax for this language:

Vocabulary: a, b

Formation Rules

1. Enter 'aa' as a sentence.
2. Enter 'bb' as a sentence.
3. If ⌜ΦΦ⌝ is a sentence, enter ⌜aΦaΦ⌝ as a sentence.
4. If ⌜ΦΦ⌝ is a sentence, enter ⌜bΦbΦ⌝ as a sentence.

Exercise: Generate 'bbbbbb' and 'abaaba'.

Exercise: Write a grammar for a language in which the sentences are all and only strings of alternating 'a's and 'b's. Thus, the following are sentences:

ab, abab, ababab, ba, baba, bababa

The following strings are not sentences:

a, b, aa, bb, aba, bab, aabb, bbaa

In order to provide some additional help in understanding what a syntactic description of a language is, let me introduce several more syntactically very simple languages. Numerals used to designate the natural numbers can be considered a language or quasi language. Implicit in the last sentence is the important distinction between the numerals themselves and the numbers that they represent. In giving a syntactic description, it is important that we focus only on how the numerals themselves are concatenated, and ignore all references to the numbers that they represent. The sentences of the language we are discussing are the following:

1, 2, 3, . . . , 9, 10, 11, 12, . . . , 100, 101, 102, . . .

Strings of numerals that are not sentences of the language include the following:

0, 01, 1.1, 1/4, 2 + 2 = 4

That is, neither the numeral zero nor natural numerals preceded by zero, decimals, fractions, nor equations are sentences. Here is a syntax for this language:

Vocabulary: 1, 2, 3, 4, 5, 6, 7, 8, 9, 0

Formation Rules

1. Enter '1' as a sentence.
2. Enter '2' as a sentence.
3. Enter '3' as a sentence.
4. Enter '4' as a sentence.
5. Enter '5' as a sentence.
6. Enter '6' as a sentence.
7. Enter '7' as a sentence.
8. Enter '8' as a sentence.
9. Enter '9' as a sentence.
10. Where Φ is a sentence and Ψ is a vocabulary item, enter $\Phi\Psi$ as a sentence.

Exercises:

1. Why are there no quotation marks and no Quine corners around '$\Phi\Psi$' in Rule 10?
2. Generate '5', '30', '209', and '2009'.

Both the even numerals and the odd numerals separately can be considered languages in themselves. Thus, one might devise a language in which the following strings of marks are sentences:

$$1, 3, 5, 7, 9, 11, 13, 15, \ldots, 101, 103, \ldots$$

and the following strings of marks are not sentences:

$$0, 2, 10, 12, 102.$$

Exercise: Write a syntax for the language just described.

Similarly, one might devise a language in which the following strings of marks are sentences:

$$2, 4, 6, 8, 10, 12, \ldots, 100, 102, \ldots, 990, \ldots$$

and the following strings are not sentences:

$$0, 1, 3, 5, 7, \ldots$$

Exercise: Write a syntax for this language.

VIII

Semantics is the study of the meaning of words and sentences. The chief ideas used in semantics are reference and truth. It is plausible that the function of language is to connect words with the world. The connection or relation between words and the world is often said to involve reference. Also, if the words of a sentence connect with the world in the right sort of way, then it is plausible that the sentence is true. Every semantics consists of two parts: rules that specify the meanings of the basic elements of the language (either words or the simplest sentences); and rules that specify how the meanings of the complex sentences are determined. In the twentieth century, the most popular formal semantic theory has been what is called 'a referential semantics'. The basic idea behind such a semantic theory is that the meaning of a word or sentence is the object that it refers to or denotes. Such a semantics can be illustrated in connection with the language consisting of all and only the numerals for natural numbers.

Semantic Base Rules

1. '1' refers to the number one.
2. '2' refers to the number two.

.

.

.

9. '9' refers to the number nine.
10. '0' refers to the number zero.

Semantic Projection Rule

11. Where $\Phi\Psi$ is a sentence, Φ is a string of vocabulary items, and Ψ is a vocabulary item, $\Phi\Psi$ refers to ten times the number referred to by Φ, plus the number referred to by Ψ.

Let's look at two examples to see how these rules, especially Rule 11, work.

Sentence	Semantics	Semantic Rule
1. 5	5	Rule 5
2. 58	$10 \times 5 + 8$	Rule 11

The first occurrence of '5' in line 1 is a sentence generated by a syntactic rule. The second occurrence of '5' expresses the meaning of the first occurrence. This may seem odd, because as users of the Arabic numeral system, we already know that '5' means 5. Let's now consider line 2: Φ = '5' and Ψ = '8'. Notice the single quotation marks around the numerals. Making the proper substitutions for Φ and Ψ in Rule 11, we see that '58' refers to $10 \times 5 + 8$. That is, it refers to 58. Here's the second example:

Sentence	Semantics	Semantic Rule
1. 3	3	Rule 3
2. 39	$10 \times 3 + 9$	Rule 11, line 1
3. 396	$10 \times (10 \times 3 + 9) + 6$	Rule 11, line 2
4. 3,967	$10 \times (10 \times (10 \times 3 + 9) + 6) + 7$	Rule 11, line 3

Lines 1 and 2 should be obvious. Now apply Rule 11 to line 3. Since Φ = '39', Φ refers to ten times 39; that is, $10 \times ((10 \times 3) + 9)$. That is, '39' refers to 390, because it precedes another numeral, namely, Ψ. Finally, Ψ = '6' and it refers to 6. Thus, the sentence '396' refers to 396.

Apply Rule 11 again to line 4. Φ = '396'; Φ refers to ten times 396; that is, $10 \times (10 \times (10 \times 3 + 9) + 6)$. That is, Φ refers to 3,960. Finally, Ψ = '7', and it refers to 7. Thus, the sentence '3,967' refers to 3,967.

It is much more complicated to understand the description of the calculations underlying the reference of the numerals than it is to understand the calculations themselves.

Once we understand the compositionality of the method, it is acceptable to simplify the calculations at each stage of the derivation:

Sentence	Semantics	Semantic Rule
1. 3	3	Rule 3
2. 39	$30 + 9$	Rule 11, line1
3. 396	$390 + 6$	Rule 11, line 2
4. 3,967	$3,960 + 7$	Rule 11, line 3

Let's now consider a referential semantics for Languish.

A SEMANTICS FOR LANGUISH

Semantic Base Rules

Proper Names:

'Adam' refers to Adam
'Beth' refers to Beth
'Carol' refers to Carol
'David' refers to David

Predicates:

'walks' refers to the concept of walking
'talks' refers to the concept of talking
'flies' refers to the concept of flying

'sits' refers to the concept of sitting
'reads' refers to the concept of reading

Semantic Projection Rules

1. Where α is any proper name and Φ is any predicate, the sentence αΦ is true if and only if α falls under the concept Φ.

Where Φ and Ψ are sentences:

2. The sentence ⌜it is not the case that Φ⌝ is true if and only if Φ is false; and otherwise it is false.
3. The sentence ⌜(Φ and Ψ)⌝ is true if and only if Φ is true and Ψ is true; and otherwise it is false.
4. The sentence ⌜(Φ or Ψ)⌝ is true if and only if Φ is true or Ψ is true; and otherwise it is false.
5. The sentence ⌜(if Φ, then Ψ)⌝ is true if and only if Φ is false or Ψ is true; and otherwise it is false.
6. The sentence ⌜(Φ if and only if Ψ)⌝ is true if and only if Φ and Ψ are both true or Φ and Ψ are both false; and otherwise it is false.

Instead of defining the predicates in terms of concepts, some philosophers prefer to speak of properties. Thus, one may say that the word 'walks' refers to the property of walking; and Semantic Formation Rule 1 would read:

1′. Where α is any proper name and Φ is any predicate, the sentence αΦ is true if and only if α has the property Φ.

Another possibility is to say that the meaning of a predicate is a set of objects. Given that Adam and Beth walk and that Carol and David do not, the meaning of 'walks' is the set consisting of Adam and Beth:

{Adam, Beth}

On this view of the meaning of predicates, Semantic Formation Rule 1 would be formulated as follows

1″. Where α is any proper name and Φ is any predicate, the sentence αΦ is true if and only if α is a member of the set referred to by Φ.

The semantics sketched so far specifies a meaning for proper names and predicates, and it gives some direction about how to determine the truth-value for the simplest sentences. The simplest sentences are sometimes called 'atomic sentences', and they are defined as those sentences of which no proper part is a sentence. The meanings of the proper names and predicates, together with Semantic Rule 1 are not sufficient to yield the meaning (truth-value) of the atomic sentences. What is also needed is some information about the world.

The truth of the basic or atomic sentences, such as 'Adam walks' and 'Beth reads' is partially determined by the meanings of 'Adam', 'Beth', 'walks', and 'reads'; partially determined by Semantic Rule 1; and partially determined by the way the world is. If it is a fact that Adam walks, then 'Adam walks' is true, and if it is a fact that Adam does not walk, then 'Adam walks' is false.

Also notice that Semantic Rules 2–6 assume that one knows the meaning of the words 'and' and 'or' since those phrases occur in the definiens of the semantic rules. The purpose of the semantic formation rules is primarily to explain how the truth-values of complex sentences are determined by properties of their parts and not to give the intuitive sense of negation, conjunction, disjunction, implication ('if . . . , then'), and equivalence ('if and only if'). Some philosophers think that this is a defect of this sort of semantics.

The intuition behind such a semantics is that to know the meaning of a sentence is to know the conditions under which that sentence is true and the conditions under which it is false. This is quite plausible for declarative sentences. It is less obvious for interrogative, imperative, and exclamatory sentences, but they are not part of our simple language. If they were to be made part of an enriched language, related to Languish, it may be possible to relate their meaning to truth in some manner. For example, an interrogative sentence asks whether the truth-conditions for a certain related sentence are fulfilled. An imperative sentence tries to get the truth-conditions for a certain related sentence fulfilled. Philosophers have argued about whether the Semantic Rules 2–6 accurately capture the meanings of the English words and phrases they purport to define. Most philosophers thought that they did not, until H. P. Grice, in "Logic and Conversation," explained how it is possible to hold that the Semantic Rules 2–6 are accurate but that speakers often use those phrases in conversation to convey additional things that are not part of the meaning of the phrases themselves. Thus Grice distinguishes between what the speaker says in virtue of the meanings of the words he uses and what the speaker implies in virtue of certain contextual features that interact with the meanings of the words.

Let's now apply the semantic formation rules to some of the sentences generated earlier. It is stipulated that the world is such that Adam and Beth walk and that Carol and David do not; and that Adam and Beth talk. Consequently, when Rule 1 is cited, it indirectly depends upon how the world is.

Sentence	Semantics
1. Adam walks	True by Rule 1

Here's another example:

Sentence	Semantics
1. Beth walks	True by Rule 1
2. Adam talks	True by Rule 1
3. (Beth walks and Adam talks)	True by Rule 3, from lines 1 and 2
4. it is not the case that (Beth walks and Adam talks)	False by Rule 2, from line 3

Exercise: Determine the truth value of the sentence '(it is not the case that Beth talks and (Adam walks if and only if Carol walks))'.

The syntactic generation of each sentence can be combined with the semantic computation of the sentences' meaning in the following way:

Sentence	Syntax	Semantics
1. Beth walks	Rule 1	True by Rule 1
2. Adam talks	Rule 1	True by Rule 1
3. (Beth walks and Adam talks)	Rule 3, from lines 1 and 2	True by Rule 3, from lines 1 and 2
4. it is not the case that (Beth walks and Adam talks)	Rule 2, from line 3	False by Rule 2, from line 3

Although an infinite number of sentences can be generated by the grammar of Languish, Languish is quite impoverished in its expressive ability, compared with that of natural languages. Even if thousands of proper names and predicates were added to it, it would lack almost all of the expressive resources of a genuine natural language. My purpose in presenting it is the limited one of illustrating what a rudimentary formal syntax and semantics might look like.

The last language I will present is a version of the predicate calculus, call it 'Predical'. In addition to subject-predicate sentences, it can express relational sentences, and quantified ones (in English such sentences 'Some dog is happy' and 'All dogs are happy'). We introduce some syntactic rules that take a sentence and rather than simply forming a more complex sentence, the rules change parts of that sentence to form a new sentence. Also, we introduce semantic rules that give the sentences meaning in virtue of 'models'. In fact, I will present, as customary, only an outline of a syntax and semantics for such a language. It is not an actual language for at least the following reasons: With regard to its syntax, it contains an infinite number of vocabulary items, contrary to our earlier position that the vocabulary and rules of actual languages are finite. With regard to semantics, it does not specify the meanings of any of the proper names (individual constants), any of the sentence letters, or any of the predicates. Only the meanings of the sentential connectives (words and phrases like 'it is not the case that', 'and', 'if . . . , then _____' and two quantifiers ('there exists an object α such that' and 'for any object α') are specified. As regards semantics, it would be easy enough to give a partial model. For example, we could have 'a' refer to Adam and 'b' refer to Beth, and 'A^1' could mean being the first human. But this would still leave an infinite number of individual constants, predicates, and sentence letters without a meaning.

A SYNTAX FOR PREDICAL

A sentence is any string of vocabulary items that is generated by the Formation Rules. Nothing else is a sentence.

In the Vocabulary below, a superscript indicates how many names the predicate requires in order to be a sentence. See Formation Rule 2.

Vocabulary

Sentence letters: $A^0, B^0, C^0, \ldots, A_1^0, B_1^0, C_1^0, \ldots$
Predicate letters: $A^1, B^1, C^1, \ldots, A_1^1, B_1^1, C_1^1, \ldots$
$A^2, B^2, C^2, \ldots, A_1^2, B_1^2, C_1^2, \ldots$

.

.

.

Proper names: $a, b, c, \ldots s, a_1, b_1, c_1, \ldots s_1, \ldots$
Individual variables: $x, y, z, t, u, v, w, x_1, y_1, z_1, t_1, u_1, v_1, w_1, \ldots$
Sentential connectives (logical constants) $\sim, \&, v, \rightarrow, \leftrightarrow$
Punctuation: (,)

Formation Rules

1. Enter any sentence letter as a sentence.
2. If Φ^n is an n-place predicate and $\alpha_1, \ldots \alpha_n$ a series of proper names, enter $\Phi^n \alpha_1, \ldots \alpha_n$ as a sentence.
3. If Φ is a sentence, enter $\ulcorner \sim\Phi \urcorner$ as a sentence.
4. If Φ and Ψ are sentences, enter $\ulcorner (\Phi \& \Psi) \urcorner$ as a sentence.
5. If Φ and Ψ are sentences, enter $\ulcorner (\Phi \lor \Psi) \urcorner$ as a sentence.
6. If Φ and Ψ are sentences, enter $\ulcorner (\Phi \rightarrow \Psi) \urcorner$ as a sentence.

7. If Φ and Ψ are sentences, enter $\ulcorner(\Phi \leftrightarrow \Psi)\urcorner$ as a sentence.
8. If . . . α ___ is a sentence in which α represents each and every occurrence of some one individual constant, enter $\ulcorner(\exists\beta). . . \beta$ ___$\urcorner$ as a sentence.
9. If . . . α ___ is a sentence in which α represents each and every occurrence of some one individual constant, enter $\ulcorner(\beta). . . \beta$ ___$\urcorner$ as a sentence.

(Concerning Rule 8 and Rule 9, the sentence $(A^2bb \vee C^2ba)'$, for example, could (or would) be transformed into '$((\exists x)(A^2xx \vee C^2bx)$' and '$(x)(A^2xx \vee C^2bx)$' respectively.)

A SEMANTICS FOR PREDICAL

Preliminary Comments

The semantics for Predical is known in formal logic as an interpretation. Interpretations require four elements:

1. A specification of a nonempty universe of discourse (domain). (These are the things that the language talks about.)
2. An assignment of individual constants to individuals. (Individual constants are in effect proper names; each individual constant names one and only one object.)
3. Assignments of predicates of degree n to sets of ordered n-tuples of objects, which are also called 'extensions'. (For example, the predicate 'L^2' might be correlated with $\{<2,1>, <3, 2>, <4, 3>, . . .\}$ and in effect mean the same as 'α is one natural number larger than β'.)
4. Assignments of sentence letters to truth-values. (For example, 'A' may be assigned to truth, and 'B' to falsity. This would be expressed more briefly as '$V(A)=T$' (read: the valuation of 'A' is truth) and '$V(B)=F$' (read: the valuation of 'B' is falsity), respectively.)

The final preliminary is some definitions:

A sentence is *atomic* if and only if it contains no logical constants or quantifiers.
A sentence is *molecular* if and only if it is not atomic.
A *model* for a sentence is an interpretation that makes the sentence true.
A *model* for a *set* of sentences is an interpretation that makes every sentence in the set true.

We are making the following assumptions. Every sentence is either true or false; a universe of discourse (domain) has been given, every sentence letter has been assigned a truth-value, every predicate an extension, and every proper name an individual. Then, we can give the semantics of the sentences of Predical as follows:

1. $V(\Phi^n_{\alpha 1. . .\alpha n}) = T$ if and only if $<\alpha_1, . . . , \alpha_n>$ is a member of the extension of Φ^n.
2. $V(\sim\Phi) = T$ if and only if $V(\Phi) = F$.
3. $V((\Phi \& \Psi)) = T$ if and only if $V(\Phi) = T$ and $V(\Psi) = T$.
4. $V((\Phi \vee \Psi)) = T$ if and only if $V(\Phi) = T$ or $V(\Psi) = T$ or both.
5. $V((\Phi \rightarrow \Psi)) = T$ if and only if $V(\Phi) = F$ or $V(\Psi) = T$.
6. $V((\Phi \leftrightarrow \Psi)) = T$ if and only if $V(\Phi) = V(\Psi)$.
7. $V((\exists\beta)(. . .\beta$ ___$)) = T$ if and only if $V((. . . \alpha$ ___$)) = T$, for some name α and for some assignment of α to an object in the universe of discourse, not necessarily the actual assignment of α. Also, in this and the next rule, $(. . . \beta$ ___$)$ represents every occurrence of a variable β in the open sentence $(. . . \beta$ ___$)$; similarly for α mutatis mutandis.
8. $V((\beta)(. . . \beta$ _____$)) = T$ if and only if $V((. . . \alpha$ _____$)) = T$, for every assignment of α to an object in the universe of discourse.

We could convert the sentences of Predical to sentences of English roughly by introducing (i) 'lexical insertion rules', which would convert the vocabulary to equivalent words and phrases in English, (ii) transformation rules that would invert strings like 'A¹a' to 'aA¹' (or 'is aggressive Adam' to 'Adam is aggressive', and (iii) one or more rules that would tell us when to stop applying the rules. This is harder than it seems, and it would come nowhere close to giving a complete grammatical description of English.

IX

Subject and Predicate

The most fundamental distinction in the philosophy of language is that between subject and predicate. This distinction is closely related to the distinction that goes under the same name in grammar schools; but there are important differences. I will talk about the distinction only as philosophers typically understand it.

Many, if not most philosophers, take sentences like

Socrates sits

and

Napoleon ruled

as instances of the most basic kind of sentence. They can be divided into two parts: a subject expression and a predicate expression. The paradigmatic examples of subjects are proper names, and I am assuming that 'Socrates' and 'Napoleon' are proper names. (Many philosophers would disagree.) Whether noun phrases like 'the philosopher who taught Plato' or 'the greatest French general' are or should be considered genuine subject expressions when they occur as the grammatical subject of a sentence is a hotly debated philosophical topic; Gottlob Frege and P. F. Strawson think they are. Bertrand Russell thinks they are not. The issue is discussed in Section III, "Reference and Descriptions."

The paradigmatic predicate expressions are verbs like 'sits' and 'ruled'. (We will ignore the tense of the verb.) Complex verb phrases like 'sits in a chair' or 'ruled the beautiful country northwest of Italy and across the English Channel from Great Britain' are usually considered to be unproblematic predicate expressions also. Of course, these latter predicates are complex and a complete theory of language would have to explain how their complexity functions. An explanation of the complexity of 'Socrates sits in a chair' is that it consists of three simpler parts: 'Socrates', 'sits in', and 'a chair'. (This is not exactly the way that grammar school grammar would divide it.)

Traditionally, philosophers have not been interested in the distinction between subjects and predicates for its own sake, but because they were interested in the basic structure of reality. And they reasoned that since people generally think about the world correctly and express their thoughts in language, language must reflect the basic structure of reality. If the basic structure of language is subject-predicate, then the basic structure of reality must be something analogous.

If one thinks about the difference between subjects and predicates, one may well come to think that subjects (are used to) pick out individual objects in the world. 'Socrates' and 'Napoleon' (are used to) pick out particulars (objects that have a definite location in space and time). Instead of picking out, philosophers often talk about subjects referring to, mentioning, identifying, or denoting individuals. All of these locutions get at roughly the same idea.

What is the purpose of picking out a particular? The standard answer is that a person does this in order to go on to *say something* about that object. The job of saying something is performed by the predicate. In the sentence, 'Socrates sits', the predicate 'sits' says something about Socrates. What exactly is *saying something* in this sense? A good answer, I think, is that saying something is categorizing something. And categories are general; they group things of the same kind together. Socrates and Napoleon belong to the same category of being human. Thus, we could say correctly,

(1) Socrates is human

and

(2) Napoleon is human.

Now notice an important difference or asymmetry between the function of subjects and predicates. Subjects (are used to) pick out or refer to individual objects. In contrast, predicates (are used to) express something general, something that can belong to or can be common to many things. Only one thing is Socrates, but many things are human. Only one thing is Napoleon, but many things ruled.

This difference is closely connected to the metaphysical distinction between particulars and universals. In other words, subjects pick out particulars and predicates 'pick out' or express universals. Nominalists maintain that however predicate expressions work, there actually are no entities other than particulars. Thomas Hobbes, a staunch nominalist, said that the only universals are words, and by this he meant, predicates, which themselves are particular objects. Realists believe that in addition to particulars, there are entities that are essentially general and are picked out by predicates. These things are called 'universals' and sometimes 'concepts', 'properties', 'features', or 'characteristics'. All of these words serve roughly the same logical role.

As my examples so far have suggested, particulars are objects that have a location in space and time; universals do not. Of course, all sorts of problem cases arise. Given that Socrates and Napoleon are dead, do they exist in space and time? Do fictional characters like Pegasus and Sherlock Holmes exist? Alternatively, are the words 'Pegasus' and 'Sherlock Holmes' able to be used as genuine subjects or not? These questions, for which philosophers have given myriad answers, are touched on in some of the articles in Section III. I shall not discuss them here at all.

Relations

Let's now consider a plausible extension of the distinction between subjects and predicates. In traditional grammars, sentences that have transitive verbs are said to have a subject and a direct object. But one could also say that they have two subject expressions, ordered in a certain way. For example, the sentence

Adam loves Beth

could be analyzed as consisting of two subjects, 'Adam' and 'Beth' with the verb 'loves' being understood as a predicate that categorizes pairs of objects, namely, just those pairs of things in which the first object loves the second. (Do not confuse the use of 'object' here with grammatical term 'direct object'.) If 'Adam loves Beth' is true, then it is because the relation of loving categorizes or groups Adam and Beth together as an ordered pair. The order is important because while 'Adam loves Beth' may be true, 'Beth loves Adam' may be false.

Philosophers love to generalize or to see similar patterns in things that may not immediately look similar. For example, some sentences can be seen as having predicates that group three or four objects together:

Adam is between Beth and Carol
Adam is between Beth and Carol and in front of David.

That is, for the first sentence, a philosopher might take 'α is between β and γ' as the predicate and 'Adam', 'Beth', and 'Carol' as three subjects, ordered in the way indicated by the Greek letters. (These Greek letters also mark the places that need to be filled appropriately in order to create a sentence.) The predicate 'α is between β and γ' expresses a relation that groups three objects together. If the three objects referred to stand to each other in the relation designated by the predicate, then the sentence is true. As regards the second sentence, the predicate 'α is between β and γ and in front of δ' expresses a relation that orders Adam, Beth, Carol, and David. And so on.

Rather than talking about subjects and predicates for these kinds of sentences, it is standard to talk about terms and relations, although the words 'term' and 'relation' are often used ambiguously. 'Term' sometimes is used to mean the name 'Adam' and sometimes the person Adam. 'Relation' sometimes is used to mean the verb or predicate, for example 'α is between β and γ' and sometimes the property, concept or universal of *being between one thing and another*. I too will use 'term' and 'relation' ambiguously and trust the reader to figure out the right meaning of the words from the context.

For the sake of generality, we can assimilate the idea of subject-predicate sentences to the idea of terms and relations by saying that subject-predicate sentences express monadic relations, that is, relations that essentially involve only one term or object. Some people object to the idea of monadic relations on the grounds that by definition a relation requires two individuals. While relations typically relate one object to one or more other objects, that is not always the case. Every true identity statement, for example, 'Cicero is identical with Tully' and 'Hesperus is Phosphorus' relates one object to itself. Whenever an identity statement relates one object to some other object, it is false, for example, 'Cicero is identical with Hesperus'. Or suppose a person loves only herself. Then love relates that person to herself, and only one individual is involved.

Moreover, we are willing to depart from the ordinary conception of relation for the sake of getting a more general explanation of certain phenomena. We begin with the ordinary conception and use it as the basis for constructing a theoretically more useful one. The primary advantage of merging subjects and predicates into the category of relations is that it allows one distinction to do the work of two. This is not an arbitrary move. In the sentence 'Socrates sits', the verb 'sits' intuitively seems to be doing the same thing with one word, 'Socrates', that 'loves' seems to do with two words, say, 'Adam' and 'Beth', in the sentence 'Adam loves Beth', and that 'α is between β and γ' does with three words, say, 'Adam', 'Beth', and 'Carol' in the sentence 'Adam is between Beth and Carol'.

Properties of Relations

Many relations have interesting properties. Let's restrict our discussion to dyadic relations, that is, those relations that hold, roughly, between two objects. Being a sibling of, being adjacent to, and being the same height as someone are symmetric relations. If Adam is a sibling of Beth, then Beth is a sibling of Adam. If Carol is adjacent to David, then David is adjacent to Carol. If Adam is the same height as Beth, then Beth is the same height as Adam. In general, a relation R is symmetric, if the following formula is true for every x and y in the domain or universe of discourse:

Symmetry: If x has the relation R to y, then y has that very same relation R to x.

Being taller, being older, and being younger are transitive relations. If Adam is taller than Beth and Beth is taller than Carol, then Adam is taller than Carol. If Adam is older than Beth and Beth is older than Carol, then Adam is older than Carol. If Adam is younger than Beth and Beth is younger than Carol, then Adam is younger than Carol. In general, a relation R is transitive, if for every x, y and z, in the domain or universe of discourse the following formula is true:

Transitivity: If x has the relation R to y and y has that same relation R to z, then x has R to z.

Weighing the same, and being the same height are reflexive relations. Adam weighs the same as himself and is the same height as himself. The same holds for Beth, Carol, and every other thing. In general, a relation R is reflexive, if the following formula is true for every x in the domain or universe of discourse:

Reflexivity: x has the relation R to x.

Here are definitions of some other properties of dyadic relations with exercises that will help you understand the property:

A relation R is asymmetric just in case for every x and every y, if x has R to y, then y does not have R to x.

Exercise: Identify the relations that are asymmetric: α is taller than β, α is as heavy as β, α is to the right of β, α is numerically greater than β.

A relation R is intransitive just in case for every x, y, and z, if x has R to y and y has R to z, then x does not have R to z.

Exercise: Identify the relations that are intransitive: α is a parent of β, α is as heavy as β, α is perpendicular to β, α is twice as large as β.

A relation R is irreflexive just in case for every x, x does not have R to x (itself).

Exercise: Identify the relation that is not irreflexive: α is taller than β, α is heavier than β, α is to the right of β, α is as tall as α.

Finally, let's introduce three additional properties of dyadic relations.

A relation R is nonsymmetric just in case R is not symmetric.
A relation R is nontransitive just in case R is not transitive.
A relation R is nonreflexive just in case R is not reflexive.

All asymmetrical, intransitive, and irreflexive relations are respectively nonsymmetrical, nontransitive, and nonreflexive; but the converse does not hold. That is, some nonsymmetrical relations are asymmetrical (e.g., being a parent of), some nontransitive relations are intransitive (e.g., being a parent of), and some nonreflexive relations are irreflexive (e.g., being taller than).

Exercises:

1. Suppose that David and Eve are not biologically related. Is the following sentence true? And if so, why?

   If David is a sibling of Eve, then Eve is a sibling of David.

2. Suppose that David weighs fifty pounds, Eve weighs one hundred pounds, and Frank weighs one hundred and fifty pounds. Is the following sentence true? And if so, why?

If David is heavier than Eve, and Eve is heavier than Frank, then David is heavier than Frank.

3. Categorize the relations expressed by the following relational phrases as symmetric, transitive, reflexive, asymmetric, intransitive, and irreflexive, nonsymmetric, nontransitive, or nonreflexive. Use as many of these properties as appropriate. (Assume the domain or universe of discourse is either living human beings or the natural numbers, as appropriate.)

a is heavier than b
a is a cousin of b
a is greater than b
a is divisible without remainder by b
a is identical with b
a is the square of b

4. (a) Are all nonsymmetric relations asymmetric?
   (b) Are all asymmetric relations nonsymmetric?

Relations that are symmetric, transitive, and reflexive are called equivalence relations. They partition objects into groups that do not overlap. For example, suppose arbitrarily that there are ten people who are four feet tall, eleven people who are five feet tall, and twelve people who are six feet tall. The relation of being the same height conceptually groups every one of those ten, eleven, and twelve people, respectively, into distinct groups. Let's call these groups 'equivalence classes', because they are determined by an equivalence relation.

Exercise: Which of the following phrases express equivalence relations?

(a) α is taller than β
(b) α is younger than β
(c) α is congruent with β
(d) α is a spouse of β
(e) α is the same height as of β

Identity

One of the most wonderful, remarkable, and seemingly mysterious relations is that of identity. On the one hand, it seems to be one of the simplest and the most pervasive of relations. Bishop Butler's famous remark, "Everything is what it is, and not another thing," seems tautologous and too weak. Everything has to be what it is. Things could not be anything other than what they are. On the other hand, the relation was not completely understood until Gottlob Frege wrote about it in the late nineteenth century. Many people today do not realize that what is often referred to as equality as in mathematical equations '$(7 + 5 = 12)$' are assertions of identity (the number 12 is identical with the number that is the result of adding seven and five). The kind of identity I am referring to is sometimes called numerical or individual identity, in order to distinguish it from the general identity (identity of species) that can hold between two individual objects of the same kind. ('Adam owns a blue 2006 Nissan Maxima LE and Beth has an identical one.')

Numerical identity is an equivalence relation. For every object, if x is identical with y and y with z, then y is identical with x (symmetry), x is identical with z (transitivity), and x is identical with x (reflexivity).

Exercise: Given what was said in the preceding sentence, is y identical with y? Is z identical with x?

While many relations are equivalence relations, identity has two properties that makes it unique:

The Principle of the Indiscernibility of Identicals: If x is identical with y, then x and y have all the same properties, that is, any property that x has y has also.

The Principle of the Identity of Indiscernibles: If x and y have all the same properties, that is, if any property that x has y has also, then x is identical with y.

By the indiscernibility of identicals, if Cicero is identical with Tully, and if Cicero is a Roman, an orator, and a philosopher, then Tully is a Roman, an orator, and a philosopher. And by the identity of indiscernibility, if Cicero has all of the very same properties as Tully (including, but not restricted to, being a Roman, an orator, and a philosopher), then Cicero is identical with Tully.

There are many problematic cases. The evening star and the morning star are identical. (Each is Venus.) But many people do not know this. And no one knew it until some brilliant astronomer discovered that (other than the sun and moon) the heavenly object that is usually the first to be seen in the night sky and that disappears behind the horizon during the night is identical with the object that appears on the horizon before full daylight and that is usually the last to disappear in the morning. Suppose that John does not know this much astronomy. Since the evening star is identical with the morning star, how could he believe that the evening star is the first celestial body that he sees at night and not believe that the morning star is the first celestial body that he sees at night?

This and related questions are discussed in Section V, "Propositional Attitudes."

X

There are three topics that readers often expect to be treated extensively in a book about the philosophy of language that typically are not: a theory to the effect that language determines how a person perceives the world; a theory that people communicate attitudes or emotions through the way they position their bodies; and the view that males and females communicate in radically different ways.

The first view is sometimes called the Sapir-Whorf hypothesis, after Edward Sapir and Benjamin Whorf, sometimes the thesis of linguistic relativity, and sometimes that of linguistic determinism. There is no entry for it in *The Cambridge Dictionary of Philosophy,* 2d ed. (1999), no entry for it in Blackwell's *Companion to the Philosophy of Language* (1997), and about seventy-five words about it in *The Oxford Companion to Philosophy* (1995). The reason it is absent from standard philosophical handbooks is a combination of two things: either the explanation of it is self-contradictory or it is inconsequential. In its inconsequential form, the hypothesis asserts that the vocabulary for some languages divides the world differently from the way the vocabulary of some other languages does. So there is no exact single word equivalent in Spanish for 'brown' in English; and Eskimos have words for, say, seventeen kinds of snow, whereas English has only one. There is no doubt that each language has many words for which there is no existing word in some other language. It would be strange if this were not the case, given the diversity of conditions, values, and histories accompanying the use of language. However, this thesis is inconsequential because it is consistent with the following two facts: all the distinctions that are made in one language can be made in another language either by using phrases, 'powdered snow', 'wet snow', 'snow with a crust formed by the partial melting and then refreezing of it', etc., or by enriching the language with new words, often some form of the semantically elusive word. That's how words like 'espresso', 'mauve', 'taupe', and thousands of others got into English.

The contradictory version of the hypothesis is something to the effect that languages determine how people perceive reality. And because of this linguistic relativity or determinism, people of one language group or culture conceptualize the world so differently from people of another language group or culture that the one cannot understand the other. The incoherence of this hypothesis emerges as soon as its proponent provides evidence for it. For that evidence consists of explaining in the proponent's own language the very differences that are supposed to be impossible for him and his audience to understand about the world. Consider this passage by Stuart Chase:

In English we say "Look at that wave." But a wave in nature never occurs as a single phenomenon. A Hopi says "Look at that slosh." The Hopi word, whose nearest equivalent in English is "slosh," gives a closer fit to the physics of wave motion, connoting movement in a mass.

"The light flashed," we say in English. . . . The trend in modern physics, however, with its emphasis on the *field*, is away from subject-predicate propositions. Thus a Hopi Indian is the better physicist when he says *Reh-pi*—"flash"—one word for the whole performance, no subject, no predicate, no time element. (Stuart Chase, in *Language, Thought, and Reality,* ed. John B. Carroll [Cambridge: M.I.T. Press, 1956] p. viii)

Notice that Chase has the supposedly inscrutable Hopi speaking English. How is this possible if Hopi thought is so radically different from English thought? And notice that subject-predicate-thinking physicists discovered fields, the structure of which is not subject-predicate. Again, how is this possible if linguisitic determinism is true? Moreover, in addition to understanding his own conceptual scheme and that of people who supposedly have radically different ones, Chase, a subject-predicate-thinking author (his writing is full of subject-predicate sentences) makes authoritative judgments about whether the language of English-speaking nonscientists is nearer to or farther away from that of the scientists. This judgmental stance makes sense only if linguistic categories are not tyrannical, that is, only if the Sapir-Whorf hypothesis is false.

A defender of linguistic determinism may object that Chase only approximated to the meaning that the Hopi and Indian expressed and, more importantly, as a hypothesis, the Sapir-Whorf hypothesis does not need to provide actual evidence. I could reply that Chase is merely following Whorf, who wrote, "We have just seen how the Hopi language maps out a certain terrain of what might be termed primitive physics" (*Language, Thought and Reality,* p. 55). So more than approximation is being claimed. A stronger reply is that it is not the supposed actual evidence that makes the view contradictory. Rather, the problem is that any attempt to explain what the view asserts, as for example by indicating in a general way what the difference is between English-thinking and Hopi-thinking, turns out to be contradictory. Let's say something more about this latter point. If we suppose that it is impossible for, say, an English speaker to translate what a Hopi says, because the Hopi's corresponding conceptual scheme is so radically different, then we do not have enough evidence to judge that the Hopi is even speaking a language. In order to understand something as a language at all, it is necessary to assign beliefs and intentions to the speaker and meanings to the utterances in such a way that something systematic enough to count as a language emerges. Failing to discover such regularities, one cannot judge that the creatures being studied speak a language. (For more on this, see Donald Davidson, "On the Very Idea of a Conceptual Scheme," in *Inquiries into Truth and Interpretation* [Oxford: Clarendon Press, 1984].)

Let me end the consideration of the Sapir-Whorf hypothesis with a simpler objection. The fact that each language contains words in certain categories, say, categories of things animal, vegetable, or mineral, does not determine that a person must see everything as belonging to one of these types, for every language contains some sign of negation, some sign that says an object does not belong to some given category; and this makes it possible to say that something belongs to none of the existing categories. If English contained words for only three kinds of animals—dogs, cats, and squirrels—and an aardvark came on the scene, a speaker could say, "This animal is not a dog, not a cat, and not a squirrel. I will call it an 'aardvark'." (The story goes on that upon being questioned as to why the speaker called it an 'aardvark', she said, "Because it looks like an aardvark.")

The second topic not covered in the articles in this book concerns 'body language', the view that people 'communicate' what they believe and how they feel by the way they position various parts of their bodies during a conversation. A person who crosses his arms is cautious and reserved; a person whose crossed legs point away from his interlocutor does not want to be in the conversation; and so on. Even if there is solid empirical data to support these claims, they would be linguistically uninteresting because these bodily positions lack the most basic characteristics of languages. A language needs to have a syntax by which a person builds up more complicated structures from simpler ones, with no set limit on their ultimate complexity. Also, people assume the bodily positions in question unconsciously; but an utterance of a language needs to be accompanied by a certain kind of intention to communicate. It is easy to mistake 'body language' for language because it makes sense to say, "Arms crossed against one's chest *means* the person is being cautious." However, as H. P. Grice makes clear in "Meaning" in Section I, "Truth and Meaning," this sense of 'mean', what he calls 'natural meaning', is not the relevant sense of 'meaning'. The relevant kind is communicative meaning, which Grice calls 'nonnatural meaning'.

The third issue not treated in the rest of this book concerns the alleged differences between so-called male and female speech. According to the stereotype, males are direct; females are indirect. No doubt there is something to this. My wife comes from a family consisting exclusively of females, except for brief, necessary male presences; and I come from a family consisting exclusively of males, except for the constant and necessary management of a wife and mother. We were on the brink of divorce during the first year of our marriage because we did not understand each other's linguistic conventions. I would come home in the late afternoon and ask, "What time are we having dinner?" intending to get information so that I could plan whether to start another activity or get ready for dinner. My wife took my question to be an indirect criticism, "You should have dinner ready now!" I could tell that she was angry, because she yelled at me —I appreciated that directness—but I did not know why she was angry, because she wouldn't say. I was direct; I said what I meant. She was indirect; what she said meant something else. I should have known that she was offended by my directness, but I didn't. When I came to understand the directness/indirectness differences between my wife and me, I devised the plan of prefacing my questions with the clarifying sentence, "This is a pure interrogative: When are we having dinner?" She interpreted my innocent, if obtuse, tactic as sarcasm.

On other occasions, my wife would be relaxing in the living room. When she saw me enter the kitchen to get a snack, she would ask, "Would you like some tea?" Knowing that she knew that I did not drink tea, I found the question odd, but answered directly: "No, thank you." I would complete my task and leave the kitchen. I could smell an emotional smoldering emanating from my wife, but could not figure out the cause. My wife indirectly had been asking me to get her some tea.

Examples could be multiplied. However, the phenomenon just illustrated is more complicated than the examples suggest. Not all males and females use male and female speech methods, respectively. Also, there are ethnic differences in speech. So female members of ethnic group E are typically more direct than male members of ethnic group F. And members of ethnic group G, male and female, typically interrupt each other more than males of group H typically interupt females of group H. (See Deborah Tannen, *Gender and Discourse* [New York: Oxford University Press, 1996].) The reason that these speech conventions are not a philosophical topic is that they themselves do not clarify or call into question the things that the philosophy of language cares about, namely, the most basic communicative concepts. In philosophy, these include meaning, reference, truth, belief, intentions, and so on. Direct and indirect speech, whether practiced by males or females, people of one culture or another, can be explained by the theory of speech acts, which includes the theory of indirect speech acts. This is not to say that different types of communicative tactics are unimportant or uninteresting, only that they are more properly studied by linguists, sociolinguists, and speech communication theorists.

XI

W. V. Quine argued in "Two Dogmas of Empiricism" that the concept of synonymy, the concept of *x* meaning the same as *y,* cannot justifiably be used in a theory of language because no clear empirical sense can be made of it. Donald Davidson replaces the concept of meaning with that of truth. Instead of asking "What does a sentence mean?" Davidson asks, "What are the truth conditions for a sentence?"

The original 1951 version of "Two Dogmas of Empiricism" is reprinted here rather than the more familiar one published in *From a Logical Point of View.* Analytic philosophers recently have become interested in their twentieth-century origins. So something is gained by looking at Quine's original words, such as his acknowledgment of the work of Morton White. Something is lost in that some clarifications or reconsiderations are missing. One of these that should be noted occurs on page 65, column a, paragraph 2. The sentence beginning "Otherwise, there would be" reads as follows in the 1961 version: "Otherwise there would be a state-description which assigned truth to 'John is a bachelor' and to 'John is married,' and consequently 'No bachelors are married' would turn out synthetic rather than analytic under the proposed criterion." Another is an addition made after page 70, column a, paragraph 2, which reads in part, "It may be instructive to compare the notion of a semantical rule with that of a postulate. Relative to a given set of postulates, it is easy to say what a postulate is: it is a member of the set. Relative to a given set of semantical rules, it is easy to say what a semantical rule is. But given simply a notation, mathematical or otherwise, and indeed as thoroughly understood a notation as you please in point of the translations or truth conditions of its statements, who can say which of its true statements rank as postulates? Obviously the question is meaningless. . . ." The most significant omission from the original article in the 1961 version is the four paragraphs on page 74, column b, beginning with "Imagine, for the sake of analogy . . ."

Section I is devoted to articles about the nature of meaning. Alfred Tarski resurrected the philosophical study of meaning in 1935 with the publication of his article, "The Concept of Truth in Formalized Languages," in which he demonstrated that semantics could be treated with the same formal rigor as syntax. The resurrection was necessary because most philosophers had understood Ludwig Wittgenstein's *Tractatus Logico-Philosophicus* (1921) to have shown that only a syntactic description of language is possible. Today almost all research in syntax is done by linguists. Philosophers are interested in syntax only insofar as it relates to semantics or pragmatics. The articles by Tarski and Alonzo Church sketch a syntactic theory because it is relevant to their views about semantics.

In addition to the meaning that words or sentences have, there is also a sense in which speakers mean things. H. P. Grice gave the first explicit, though tentative, analysis of this concept in his article "Meaning," published in 1957. He extended and revised that analysis, in response to numerous criticisms, in his "Utterer's Meaning and Intentions." Grice's view, utterance, word, and sentence meaning are derivative concepts. That is, an analysis of utterance, word, and sentence meaning will contain the concept of utterer's meaning in the analysans. This view goes against the grain of most work in semantics. Thus, Section I develops two important theories of meaning and touches on a number of related semantic issues.

Section II consists of selections about pragmatics or speech acts. It continues the line of thinking expounded in the article by Grice. If a person has successfully conveyed what he meant by an utterance then he has done something with those words: he has performed a speech act. The founder of speech act theory is J. L. Austin, who constructed a theory from the insights that not all cognitively significant talk is supposed to be true or false and that talking is a kind of doing. Many philosophers have extended Austin's work in various fruitful ways.

Section III concerns the single most discussed issue in the philosophy of language: reference. Reference has the importance that it does because philosophers typically think that the principal way in which language attaches to reality is through reference. This is presupposed in most of the selections in this section. The central issue of debate is whether reference is a semantic or pragmatic notion.

Section IV concerns a topic related to reference: Names and demonstratives are paradigmatic kinds of expressions that refer or are used to refer. What are names? What are demonstratives? How do they attach to reality?

In Section V a different problem is discussed. What people say is often the expression of a belief ("It is raining," or "The cat is on the mat"). Notice however that expressions of belief are not in themselves expressions that someone has a belief. To say that the cat is on the mat is *not to say that anyone believes* that the cat is on the mat. Yet, one does of course often express such beliefs. In the sentences "Mary believes that it is raining" and "Mary believes that the cat is on the mat," the speaker is saying that Mary has certain beliefs. Philosophers have wondered what the objects of belief are. This question can be put in a linguistic mode: they have wondered what the object of "it is raining" and "the cat is on the mat" is when they follow the phrase "believes that." There are puzzles that seem to show that a clause occurring after the phrase "believes that" cannot refer to the same thing as it does when it occurs as the main clause of a sentence. And the same puzzles arise for a large family of words called verbs of propositional attitude, including "know," "think," "desire," and "look for."

Section VI concerns two derivative uses of language. The first is metaphor. The selections by Donald Davidson and A. P. Martinich develop theories that can be considered extensions of the theories of meaning introduced in Section I. The second derivative use of language is the use of names of fictional characters, which, according to Mark Crimmins and Frederick Kroon, involves pretense.

Section VII concerns the nature of understanding what is said. Within most contemporary scholarship, this issue is referred to as interpretation or translation. W. V. Quine has argued that one can come to see that sentences do not have a determinate meaning (the thesis of indeterminacy) if one considers the nature of translation, that is, linguistic understanding. Donald Davidson follows Quine to a large extent and concludes that there is no such thing as language, as philosophers typically have understood it. John Searle thinks that Quine's view is mistaken because he has ignored the legitimacy of the speaker's point of view.

Section VIII deals with one of the most intriguing and elusive issues in the philosophy of language. What is the nature of language? Is it possible for one person to have his own language? Must language be a social phenomenon? Is it a formal system like logic or mathematics? Or a subsystem of the human brain? These issues overlap with the first topic discussed in this book, meaning. So, this is a good topic on which to end a philosophical reflection on language. Or to begin.

I TRUTH AND MEANING

What is meaning? In what terms will meaning be analyzed, and what is the ontological status of these terms? Is it words, sentences, or persons that primarily mean or have meaning? These are the central questions raised and answered in various ways in this section.

The first article, Gottlob Frege's "The Thought," explains his two-tiered theory of meaning. The first tier consists of the senses (*Sinne*) of words, phrases, and sentences. The second tier consists of referents (*Bedeutungen*), the things that the senses pick out. The distinction can be grasped by thinking about the difference between what a linguistic expression talks about and how an expression presents what is talked about to the mind of the user of the language. The way an expression presents an object to a user of a language seems to determine what the expression is about. Suppose that four signs or symbols are written horizontally on a blackboard, say, @, #, *, &. The phrase 'the third symbol from the left' and the phrase 'the second symbol from the right' talk about or refer to the same thing, the asterisk. They have the same *Bedeutung,* the asterisk. But those two phrases present the asterisk to the speaker's mind in different ways. The phrase 'the third symbol from the left' involves thinking of something as related to things to its left. It's possible that nothing is to its right. The phrase 'The second symbol from the right' involves thinking of something as related to things to its right; again, it's possible that nothing is to its left. So the two phrases have different senses. In short, the phrase 'the third symbol from the left' seems to present the asterisk to thought in a different way than the phrase 'the second object from the right' does.

The difference between reference (*Bedeutung*) and sense (*Sinn*), which has just been illustrated with respect to phrases, can be extended to sentences. The sentences 'The third symbol from the left is an asterisk' and the sentence 'The second symbol from the right is an asterisk' both seem to be about the same thing. It is natural to think that those two sentences refer to facts. However, that is not Frege's view. He thinks both sentences refer to the truth. In fact, the truth is the referent of every true sentence. In the same way he thinks that falsehood or the false is the referent of every false sentence. I won't go into his reasons for this, in large part because "The Thought" focuses on the *Sinne* of sentences, the thoughts (*Gedanken*) that sentences present.

The thoughts expressed by the sentence 'The third symbol from the left looks like a star' and the sentence 'The second sentence from the right looks like a star' are different because the mind is presented with two different things (*Sinne*). If this is not already obvious, it should be obvious when one considers that the meaning of a sentence is a function of the meanings of its parts, that is, its words and sentences. Since the two sentences consist of different words, their senses are different.

Philosophers have argued about whether sentences, statements, propositions, or something else is the primary bearer of, or to use a more neutral locution, the associate of, truth. Frege says that the right answer is thoughts (*Gedanken*), the *Sinne* of sentences. True thoughts are facts, so truth is not a correspondence of thoughts to facts. If truth were correspondence between one thing, a sentence or the meaning of a sentence, and something else, a fact, then 'true' would be a relational word, like 'dog'. But it is not. One might object that 'true' is like 'mother'. Although the word 'mother' looks like a nonrelational word in sentences like 'Their mother became a lawyer', it is obvious that a necessary condition for being a mother is being the mother of someone. So a predicate, like 'x is a mother,' has to be dependent on some predicate like 'x is the mother of y'. Similarly, the objection continues, the (apparent) predicate 'x is true' is dependent on the relational predicate 'x is true to y', as in 'Lee was true to Adrian'. Presumably, Frege would object that 'true to' here has the sense of 'faithful to' and that is not the sense in which sentences or statements are true. (The more interesting claim that 'x is true' depends on 'x is true to the facts' will not be considered here.)

Some philosophers hold that true sentences correspond to facts. But, for Frege, a "fact is a thought that is true." Frege thinks that truth is indefinable, because "in a definition certain characteristics would have to be stated." Whatever characteristics were involved, "the question would always arise whether it were *true* that the characteristics were present" [my italics]. Instead of settling the question of truth, the issue of determining whether it is true that the characteristics are present causes the very same question to recur.

There is something else that truth is not. It is not a property of thoughts. According to Frege, 'snow is white' expresses the same thought as 'it is true that snow is white'. In other words, truth adds nothing to a thought. Later philosophers, following Frege, developed the redundancy theory of truth.

Let's set aside the issue of truth and return to Frege's account of what a thought is. He maintains that "thought, in itself immaterial, clothes itself in the material garment of a sentence and thereby becomes comprehensible to us. We say a sentence expresses a thought." The sentences 'The sun set' and 'Clinton was the greatest president' express thoughts. But these examples may be misleading since they give the impression that things like the sun and people like Clinton might be parts of thoughts. They are not. Thoughts are expressed by 'that'-clauses, as in the sentences 'Lee saw *that the sun set*' and 'Lee believed *that Clinton was the greatest president*', not to mention, 'Lee thought *that Clinton was the greatest president*'. Presenting thoughts as what 'that'-clauses refer to helps to diminish the idea that spatio-temporal things are parts of thoughts. Thoughts are immaterial objects.

Nonetheless, thoughts are not ideas. Ideas are private psychological entities that exactly one person can have. Lee's idea or the sense impression that she has when she looks at a rose bush is not the same idea or sense impression that Adrian has when he looks at a rose bush. In contrast, thoughts are public in the sense that they are open to many minds. Many people know the Pythogorean theorem. There is just one theorem, and it is not part of the content of anyone's mind. "[T]houghts are neither things of the outer world nor ideas. A third realm must be recognized. We are not bearers of thought as we are bearers of our ideas."

According to Frege, the sentences 'the door is closed' and 'the door is not closed' both express thoughts because truth is essentially tied to each of them. The thought that the door is closed is the same as the thought that it is true that the door is closed. In contrast, imperative sentences, like 'Close the door', do not express a thought, even though they have a meaning, because the meaning of that sentence is neither true nor false. The goal of an imperative is to have some proposition made true. Sentences like 'Lee wants to own a boat' and 'I request that you close the door' similarly do not express thoughts. Nor do exclamations, 'Oh, no!' nor open questions, 'What did Lee do?' express thoughts.

Another linguistic component that is not part of a thought is the mood, tone, or color of words. 'Lee's a police officer' and 'Lee's a copper' express the same thought but express different moods or tones, so both are true or both false. 'Snow is white and coal is black' expresses the same thought and has the same truth-value as 'Snow is white but coal is black'.

"The Thought" may be the single most remarkable article in the history of the philosophy of language because no other article presents so many seminal thoughts on so many major topics in the philosophy of language, not to mention the relevance of Frege's comments to the philosophy of mind. His views about meaning and truth have already been indicated (see Sections V and VIII). Here's a brief survey of other major topics.

Thoughts need to be distinguished from assertions. The question 'Lee is over sixty-five years old, isn't she?' and the supposition 'Suppose that Lee is over sixty-five years old' both express thoughts, just as 'Lee is over sixty-five years old' does, but only the latter asserts something. Each thought has a different force attached to it. This idea is the forerunner of the distinction between illocutionary and locutionary acts in J. L. Austin's philosophy, and illocutionary force acts and propositional acts in John Searle's philosophy. (See Section II.)

Sentences often do not express complete thoughts. "I am here now' does not itself express a complete thought but must be supplemented by the context of the utterance. (See Section IV.) Frege also considers how the senses of a proper name contribute to the sense of a thought. (See Section III.) Frege's investigation of the possibility that the mind only had contact with its own ideas is in effect a contemplation of the possibility of a private language and a refutation of a Lockean theory of meaning. (See Section VIII.)

The second and third selections of Section I criticize the theory of meaning espoused by logical positivism, which dominated the second quarter of this century and which was moribund shortly into the third quarter, partly because of the kinds of criticisms developed by Carl Hempel and W. V. Quine.

Hempel in "Empirical Criteria of Cognitive Significance: Problems and Changes" discusses the theory of meaning of logical positivism, according to which a sentence is meaningful just in case it is (a) analytic or contradictory or (b) verifiable or confirmable by experience. One purpose of this view was to have a criterion that would exclude from scientific philosophy certain traditional philosophical problems or solutions. As Hempel clearly and cogently shows, the criterion is both too strong and too weak. It excludes some things that the logical positivists wanted to include as philosophy and includes some that they would not want to. Hempel argues "the content of a statement with empirical import cannot, in general, be exhaustively expressed by means of any class of observation sentences." (An observation sentence is a sentence that might be verified or confirmed by some perception.) Further, "the cognitive meaning of a statement in an empirical language is reflected in the totality of its logical relationships to all other statements in that language and not to observation sentences alone." Although Hempel is critical of the standard formulations of the empiricist criterion of meaning, he is sympathetic with the project behind it.

A more unrelenting critique of some aspects of empiricism is W. V. Quine's "Two Dogmas of Empiricism," which is the *locus classicus* for the attack on the alleged distinction between analytic and synthetic (or empirical) propositions. Questions of meaning seem to be different from questions of fact. Questions of meaning concern analyticity, synonymy, and entailment. Questions of fact concern the way the world is, not how we talk about the world. Quine challenges these seemingly unchallengeable views. He claims that there is no firm distinction between fact and meaning. Quine's results do not entail that there can be no theory of meaning, although they do impose restrictions on what will count as an adequate theory.

Two significantly different theories of meaning are represented in this section: a semantic and a pragmatic theory. Tarski's article, "The Semantic Conception of Truth," is an informal presentation of Tarski's technical paper "The Concept of Truth in Formalized Languages," which presented a way of rigorously treating the concept of truth. Tarski's original article was especially significant when it was first published because arguments of the then dominant school of logical positivism seemed to imply that semantics was impossible and that language could be described syntactically also. Tarski's work showed this to be mistaken.

Alonzo Church in "Intensional Semantics" presents a formal semantics for natural languages, which, though an alternative to Tarski's, still satisfies the same rigorous conditions. He modifies Frege's view that an adequate semantics for natural languages must specify both a sense and reference for almost all words.

Donald Davidson extends Tarski's work by asserting that a theory of truth for a language is at the same time a theory of meaning. H. P. Grice's theory of meaning is pragmatic in the sense that he takes as basic the notion of utterer's meaning, what it is for a person to mean something by an utterance. Utterance- or sentence-meaning is derivative in the sense that it will be analyzed in terms of utterer's meaning.

It is also important to distinguish between utterer's meaning and speaker's meaning. Utterer's meaning is the broader notion. It is whatever a person who tries to communicate something to another person means, no matter whether the utterance takes the form of a gesture, a token, or words. Speaker meaning is what a person who tries to communicate something by uttering words means.

One of the chief obstacles to understanding what philosophers of language are doing when they study meaning is the fact that the word 'meaning' is highly equivocal; 'meaning' itself has many meanings or senses. So it is important to distinguish between these various senses in order to be able to focus on those being discussed in this section. Since Grice is particularly interested in explicitly making some of these distinctions, the following discussion will often refer to his article, "Meaning." Grice distinguishes between three senses of "meaning' and he is most interested in contrasting the first two of these.

1. *Natural or noncognitive meaning.* The first kind of meaning that Grice introduces is what he calls 'natural meaning' but which I prefer to call 'noncognitive meaning'. This is the sense that operates in sentences such as 'Smoke means that there is a fire' and 'Those spots mean that Jones has measles'. These sentences can be abbreviated to read 'Smoke means fire' and 'Those spots mean measles', but for our purposes, it is better to use the unabbreviated form. What stands out in these examples is the natural connection that holds between what has the meaning (smoke) and what is meant (that there is fire). Grice mentions five ways of identifying this sense of meaning, but only three need to be explained here.

First, if a sentence of the form 'x means that p' entails 'p', then the natural or noncognitive sense of meaning is operating. That is, the thing that has the meaning guarantees the existence of what is meant. If there should happen to be smoke and there is no fire, then the sentence 'Smoke means that there is a fire' is false. Second, if there is no agent or person that meant something, then the natural or noncognitive sense of meaning is involved. Given that smoke means fire, it is obvious that there is no one that means fire by the smoke. (It is even dubious whether the previous sentence is grammatical.) Third, it is inappropriate to express what is (naturally or noncognitively) meant by using quotation marks. The sentence, 'Smoke means that there is a fire' cannot be paraphrased as 'Smoke means "There is a fire"'. The smoke does not have the capacity for meaning something that is equivalent to the meaning of a sentence.

2. *Nonnatural or communicative meaning*. The principal reason for discussing natural or noncognitive meaning is to ensure that it does not get confused with the sense of meaning that is of most importance to the philosophy of language, namely what Grice calls 'nonnatural meaning' and what I call 'communicative meaning'. My reservation about Grice's term is that it suggests that there is something unnatural about communicative meaning, when nothing is more natural to humans than communication.

The communicative sense of 'meaning' operates in the sentences, 'Smith's hand wave means that she is leaving' and 'By saying her lover is a treasure, she meant that she valued him highly'. The marks of these sentences are just the opposite of the ones for 'natural' or 'noncognitive meaning'. The first involves a certain lack of entailment. The sentence 'Smith's hand wave means that she is leaving' does not entail 'Smith is leaving'. It is quite possible for a person to signal with a hand wave that she is leaving without necessarily leaving. In such a case, the person was either innocently mistaken in what she would do or was being deceptive. But that does not change the fact that she and her hand wave meant that she was leaving. Similarly, a person can mean that she values her lover highly and yet not. What she said was not true, but that does not detract from its being an instance of communicative meaning.

It is obvious that if Smith's hand wave means that she is leaving, then there is someone who meant something by the hand wave. The connection between communicative meaning and people need not be belabored. One further mark of communicative meaning involves quotability. The sentence 'Smith's hand wave means that she is leaving' can be paraphrased as 'Smith's hand wave means "I am leaving"'. The reason is that what Smith meant by the hand wave could have been conveyed using a sentence. Grice's distinctions between utterer's meaning, utterance meaning, and occasion meaning are species of nonnatural or communicative meaning.

Let's now consider whether a third sense of meaning is related to either of the first two main senses.

3. *Intentional or simple cognitive meaning*. In the sentences 'Smith meant to shoot the horse, not the dog' and 'Smith means to go to London', the word 'mean' has the same sense as 'intend', and those sentences would make perfect sense with 'intend' substituted for 'mean'. Grice says that this kind of intentional meaning is a kind of natural meaning. My guess is that his reason for holding this is the following. He ultimately wants to reduce nonnatural (communicative) meaning to natural (noncognitive) meaning because he is a physicalist. (He believes that the physical world is the totality of reality.) He can achieve this goal by analyzing nonnatural meaning in terms of intentions (which is the same as analyzing it in terms of intentional meaning) if intentional meaning is a kind of natural meaning.

The problem with this strategy is that intentional meaning looks less like natural or noncognitive meaning than like nonnatural or communicative meaning. First, the sentence, 'Smith (intentionally) meant to shoot the horse, not the dog' does not entail 'Smith shot the horse'. Second, there obviously is an agent who intends something. Intentional meaning is like natural meaning in that quotability fails. But this fact can be construed simply as indicating that this is the specific difference that distinguishes intentional meaning from communicative meaning.

We can now deal more briefly with several other senses of 'meaning'.

4. *Referential meaning.* Related to communicative meaning is a narrower sense of the word, in which 'meaning' has the same sense as 'refer' as in the sentence 'When Smith said that the most maligned American president recently died, she meant Nixon'. Philosophers who subscribe to referential semantics, take something like this sense as paradigmatic for the philosophy of language.

5. *Meaning as sincerity.* In the sentences, 'Smith said that she would be at the party, but she did not mean it', and 'Smith said that she will prosecute and she meant it', 'mean' has the sense of 'is sincere about' and is replaceable by that phrase. As the second example indicates, meaning in this sense may indicate a high degree of resoluteness. Also notice that a person can both communicatively mean something and not mean that same thing in the sense of being sincere about it. If Smith says that she will be at the party but is insincere, then she (communicatively) means that she will be at the party and does not mean (is not sincere) that she will be at the party.

6. *Meaning as significance.* People sometimes wonder about the meaning of life, the meaning of sports in American culture, or the meaning of some illness that they suffer. What they are wondering about is the significance, implications, and importance of their lives, sports, or illness, respectively. They are wondering about how something (their life, for example) fits into some larger scheme of things, because they hope that their life will seem to be worthwhile if it has a place in some larger scheme. In most cases, this sense of meaning will not be confused with the others. There are some cases, however, in which the possibility of confusion is, I think, prevalent.

Literary critics often discuss the meaning of some work of art. Some have argued that the meaning of *Oedipus Rex* is that every human life is determined by fate and that the meaning of *Hamlet* is the Oedipal complex. These arguments concern the works' meaning in the sense of their significance. What makes this issue difficult is that the relationship of this kind of meaning to the other kinds is not clear. Some critics think that the meaning of a literary work must be the expression of something that the author meant (in the sense of intended) or meant (in the sense of communicated). But there are reasons to doubt that this is a necessary connection. Why couldn't a work of art have a meaning (as significance) that the author did not intend in any sense. The artist would have meant (intended) to write the work, would have communicatively meant each word and sentence of it, and would have meant (been sincere about) all of it; but he or she would not have meant the significance it has. Its significance would be the result of properties it has within the context of literature and culture, because of (semantic) relationships that its sentences have to the sentences of other literary works. Further, these properties would in large part be determined by how that work of art affected its readers, independently of what the author meant (in any sense). This is not to say that what the author meant (in any sense) is irrelevant to understanding the meaning (significance) of the work. Authors are often conscious of what they mean (intend) their work to mean (significance), and it may be helpful to have this kind of information in order to understand or discover the work's meaning (significance). There is no reason to refuse to learn about the author's intentions simply because those intentions do not necessarily determine the work's meaning. (I have used 'meaning' in several senses in this paragraph in order to show how easy it would be to think that only one sense of 'meaning' were involved if I had not also included the disambiguating phrases in parentheses.)

The meaning (significance) of a text is often closely connected with its aesthetic value. Works that have no meaning (significance) are rarely, if ever, aesthetically valuable. But a work may have a meaning (significance), without it having any aesthetic value. Most amateur poets and many unpublished novelists give their works a meaning (significance) but fail to achieve any aesthetic value. As I said earlier, the point of distinguishing these six senses of 'meaning' is to get clear about the one that Grice wants to focus on, namely, the second, nonnatural or communicative meaning. Although what a speaker means and what a word or sentence means are kinds of nonnatural meaning, the most basic kind is 'utterer's occasion meaning', which Grice analyzes in effect as follows:

An utterer U means something on some occasion by uttering T if and only if U intends to induce some effect in an audience H at least in part due to H's recognition that H recognizes that U has this intention.

Utterance occasion meaning can then be defined very simply.

An utterance T means something on some occasion O if and only if U meant something by T on O.

Grice's analysis of utterer's occasion meaning is neutral between what Grice thinks are the two main types of nonnatural meaning: getting someone to believe someone and getting someone to do something.

Once the analysis of utterer's (and utterance) occasion meaning is in place, Grice aims at analysing 'timeless' (or what many would call 'conventional') meaning for some utterance type. But this is still one step away from linguistic meaning, which, in addition to conventionality (or whatever other concept is appropriate) has to account for the compositionality of meaning. (The meaning of the whole is a function of the meaning of the parts.) In "Meaning," he is vague about these issues. In "Utterer's Meaning, Sentence-Meaning, and Word-Meaning," he proffered analyses of these concepts, but most regard them as unsuccessful.

One objection is, I believe, mistaken. John Searle presents the following scenario: Suppose that during the Second World War an American soldier is captured by Italian troops. The soldier would like to tell the Italians that he is German, but he does not know enough Italian or German to do this. Believing that the Italians know no German, the soldier utters the only German he remembers, the sentence, "Kennst du das Land, wo die Zitronen blühen?" The American intends to get his audience to believe he means that he is a German soldier and to produce this effect by means of their recognition of his intention to get them to believe it. Now, according to Searle, this is a counterexample to Grice's analysis because the German sentence uttered does not mean, 'I am a German soldier', but, 'Do you know the land where the lemon trees bloom?'. Searle says, "Meaning is more than a matter of intention, it is also a matter of convention."

I do not think that Searle's counterexample succeeds. He is confusing the timeless utterance meaning of the German sentence, 'Kennst du das Land, wo die Zitronen blühen?' with the soldier's utterance occasion meaning, which is the same as the timeless meaning in German of 'Ich bin ein deutscher Offizier' and in English of 'I am a German soldier'. Although the soldier's utterance is a sentence of German, the soldier does not mean by it what it literally (conventionally) means in German. Since Grice was analyzing utterer's occasion meaning, his analysis fits what the soldier meant. *Pace* Searle, not all meaning is a matter of convention. Nonetheless, Grice's analysis has other problems (too complicated to go into here) and the most promising alternative is the one John Searle presents in his *Intentionality*.

The Thought: A Logical Inquiry

GOTTLOB FREGE

The word "true" indicates the aim of logic as does "beautiful" that of aesthetics or "good" that of ethics. All sciences have truth as their goal; but logic is also concerned with it in a quite different way from this. It has much the same relation to truth as physics has to weight or heat. To discover truths is the task of all sciences; it falls to logic to discern the laws of truth. The word "law" is used in two senses. When we speak of laws of morals or the state we mean regulations which ought to be obeyed but with which actual happenings are not always in conformity. Laws of nature are the generalization of natural occurrences with which the occurrences are always in accordance. It is rather in this sense that I speak of laws of truth. This is, to be sure, not a matter of what happens so much as of what is. Rules for asserting, thinking, judging, inferring follow from the laws of truth. And thus one can very well speak of laws of thought too. But there is an imminent danger here of mixing different things up. Perhaps the expression "law of thought" is interpreted by analogy with "law of nature" and the generalization of thinking as a mental occurrence is meant by it. A law of thought in this sense would be a psychological law. And so one might come to believe that logic deals with the mental process of thinking and the psychological laws in accordance with which it takes place. This would be a misunderstanding of the task of logic, for truth has not been given the place which is its due here. Error and superstition have causes just as much as genuine knowledge. The assertion both of what is false and of what is true takes place in accordance with psychological laws. A derivation from these and an explanation of a mental process that terminates in an assertion can never take the place of a proof of what is asserted. Could not logical laws also have played a part in this mental process? I do not want to dispute this, but when it is a question of truth possibility is not enough. For it is also possible that something not logical played a part in the process and deflected it from the truth. We can only decide this after we have discerned the laws of truth; but then we will probably be able to do without the derivation and explanation of the mental process if it is important to us to decide whether the assertion in which the process terminates is justified. In order to avoid this misunderstanding and to prevent the blurring of the boundary between psychology and logic, I assign to logic the task of discovering the laws of truth, not of assertion or thought. The mean-

Translators' Note: This essay was first published in the *Beiträge zur Philosophie des Deutschen Idealismus* for 1918–19, and was the first of two connected essays, the other being "Die Verneinung," which has been translated into English by Mr. P. T. Geach, and appears in his and Mr. M. Black's *Translations from the Philosophical Writings of Gottlob Frege*. A. M. and Marcello Quinton, Oxford.
Gottlob Frege, "The Thought" *Mind*, vol. 65, 1956, pp. 289–311. By permission of Oxford University Press.

ing of the word "true" is explained by the laws of truth.

But first I shall attempt to outline roughly what I want to call true in this connexion. In this way other uses of our word may be excluded. It is not to be used here in the sense of "genuine" or "veracious", nor, as it sometimes occurs in the treatment of questions of art, when, for example, truth in art is discussed, when truth is set up as the goal of art, when the truth of a work of art or true feeling is spoken of. The word "true" is put in front of another word in order to show that this word is to be understood in its proper, unadulterated sense. This use too lies off the path followed here; that kind of truth is meant whose recognition is the goal of science.

Grammatically the word "true" appears as an adjective. Hence the desire arises to delimit more closely the sphere in which truth can be affirmed, in which truth comes into the question at all. One finds truth affirmed of pictures, ideas, statements, and thoughts. It is striking that visible and audible things occur here alongside things which cannot be perceived with the senses. This hints that shifts of meaning have taken place. Indeed! Is a picture, then, as a mere visible and tangible thing, really true, and a stone, a leaf, not true? Obviously one would not call a picture true unless there were an intention behind it. A picture must represent something. Furthermore, an idea is not called true in itself but only with respect to an intention that it should correspond to something. It might be supposed from this that truth consists in the correspondence of a picture with what it depicts. Correspondence is a relation. This is contradicted, however, by the use of the word "true", which is not a relation-word and contains no reference to anything else to which something must correspond. If I do not know that a picture is meant to represent Cologne Cathedral, then I do not know with what to compare the picture to decide on its truth. A correspondence, moreover, can only be perfect if the corresponding things coincide and are, therefore, not distinct things at all. It is said to be possible to establish the authenticity of a banknote by comparing it stereoscopically with an authentic one. But it would be ridiculous to try to compare a gold piece with a twenty-mark note stereoscopically.

It would only be possible to compare an idea with a thing if the thing were an idea too. And then, if the first did correspond perfectly with the second, they would coincide. But this is not at all what is wanted when truth is defined as the correspondence of an idea with something real. For it is absolutely essential that the reality be distinct from the idea. But then there can be no complete correspondence, no complete truth. So nothing at all would be true; for what is only half true is untrue. Truth cannot tolerate a more or less. But yet? Can it not be laid down that truth exists when there is correspondence in a certain respect? But in which? For what would we then have to do to decide whether something were true? We should have to inquire whether it were true that an idea and a reality, perhaps, corresponded in the laid-down respect. And then we should be confronted by a question of the same kind and the game could begin again. So the attempt to explain truth as correspondence collapses. And every other attempt to define truth collapses too. For in a definition certain characteristics would have to be stated. And in application to any particular case the question would always arise whether it were true that the characteristics were present. So one goes round in a circle. Consequently, it is probable that the content of the word "true" is unique and indefinable.

When one ascribes truth to a picture, one does not really want to ascribe a property which belongs to this picture altogether independently of other things, but one always has something quite different in mind and one wants to say that that picture corresponds in some way to this thing. "My idea corresponds to Cologne Cathedral" is a sentence and the question now arises of the truth of this sentence. So what is improperly called the truth of pictures and ideas is reduced to the truth of sentences. What does one call a sentence? A series of sounds; but only when it has a sense, by which is not meant that every series of sounds that has sense is a sentence. And when we call a sentence true, we really mean its sense is. From which it follows that it is for the sense of a sentence that the question of truth arises in general. Now is the sense of a sentence an idea? In any case being true does not consist in the correspondence of this sense with something else, for otherwise the question of truth would reiterate itself to infinity.

Without wishing to give a definition, I call a thought something for which the question of truth arises. So I ascribe what is false to a thought just as much as what is true.[1] So I can say: the thought is the sense of the sentence without wishing to say as well that the sense of every sentence is a thought. The thought, in itself immaterial, clothes itself in the material garment of a sentence and thereby becomes comprehensible to us. We say a sentence expresses a thought.

A thought is something immaterial and everything material and perceptible is excluded from this sphere of that for which the question of truth arises. Truth is not a quality that corresponds with a particular kind of sense-impression. So it is sharply distinguished from the qualities which we denote by the words "red", "bitter", "lilac-smelling". But do we not see that the sun has risen and do we not then also see that this is true? That the sun has risen is not an object which emits rays that reach my eyes, it is not a visible thing like the sun itself. That the sun has risen is seen to be true on the basis of sense-impressions. But being true is not a material, perceptible property. For being magnetic is also recognized on the basis of sense-impressions of something, though this property corresponds as little as truth with a particular kind of sense-impressions. So far these properties agree. However, we need sense-impressions in order to recognize a body as magnetic. On the other hand, when I find that it is true that I do not smell anything at this moment, I do not do so on the basis of sense-impressions.

It may nevertheless be thought that we cannot recognize a property of a thing without at the same time realizing the thought that this thing has this property to be true. So with every property of a thing is joined a property of a thought, namely, that of truth. It is also worthy of notice that the sentence "I smell the scent of violets" has just the same content as the sentence "it is true that I smell the scent of violets". So it seems, then, that nothing is added to the thought by my ascribing to it the property of truth. And yet is it not a great result when the scientist after much hesitation and careful inquiry, can finally say "what I supposed is true"? The meaning of the word "true" seems to be altogether unique. May we not be dealing here with something which cannot, in the ordinary sense, be called a quality at all? In spite of this doubt I want first to express myself in accordance with ordinary usage, as if truth were a quality, until something more to the point is found.

In order to work out more precisely what I want to call thought, I shall distinguish various kinds of sentences.[2] One does not want to deny sense to an imperative sentence, but this sense is not such that the question of truth could arise for it. Therefore I shall not call the sense of an imperative sentence a thought. Sentences expressing desires or requests are ruled out in the same way. Only those sentences in which we communicate or state something come into the question. But I do not count among these exclamations in which one vents one's feelings, groaning, sighing, laughing, unless it has been decided by some agreement that they are to communicate something. But how about interrogative sentences? In a word-question we utter an incomplete sentence which only obtains a true sense through the completion for which we ask. Word-questions are accordingly left out of consideration here. Sentence-questions are a different matter. We expect to hear "yes" or "no". The answer "yes" means the same as an indicative sentence, for in it the thought that was already completely contained in the interrogative sentence is laid down as true. So a sentence-question can be formed from every indicative sentence. An exclamation cannot be regarded as a communication on this account, since no corresponding sentence-question can be formed. An interrogative sentence and an indicative one contain the same thought; but the indicative contains something else as well, namely, the assertion. The interrogative sentence contains something more too, namely, a request. Therefore two things must be distinguished in an indicative sentence: the content, which it has in common with the corresponding sentence-question, and the assertion. The former is the thought, or at least contains the thought. So it is possible to express the thought without laying it down as true. Both are so closely joined in an indicative sentence that it is easy to overlook their separability. Consequently we may distinguish:

1. the apprehension of a thought—thinking,
2. the recognition of the truth of a thought—judgment,[3]
3. the manifestation of this judgment—assertion.

We perform the first act when we form a sentence-question. An advance in science usually takes place in this way, first a thought is apprehended, such as can perhaps be expressed in a sentence-question, and, after appropriate investigations, this thought is finally recognized to be true. We declare the recognition of truth in the form of an indicative sentence. We do not have to use the word "true" for this. And even when we do use it, the real assertive force lies, not in it, but in the form of the indicative sentence and where this loses its assertive force the word "true" cannot put it back again. This happens when we do not speak seriously. As stage thunder is only apparent thunder and a stage fight only an apparent fight, so stage assertion is only apparent assertion. It is only acting, only fancy. In his part the actor asserts nothing, nor does he lie, even if he says something of whose falsehood he is convinced. In poetry we have the case of thoughts being expressed without being actually put forward as true in spite of the form of the indicative sentence, although it may be suggested to the hearer to make an assenting judgment himself. Therefore it must still always be asked, about what is presented in the form of an indicative sentence, whether it really contains an assertion. And this question must be answered in the negative if the requisite seriousness is lacking. It is irrelevant whether the word "true" is used here. This explains why it is that nothing seems to be added to a thought by attributing to it the property of truth.

An indicative sentence often contains, as well as a thought and the assertion, a third component over which the assertion does not extend. This is often said to act on the feelings, the mood of the hearer or to arouse his imagination. Words like "alas" and "thank God" belong here. Such constituents of sentences are more noticeably prominent in poetry, but are seldom wholly absent from prose. They occur more rarely in mathematical, physical, or chemical than in historical expositions. What are called the human-ities are more closely connected with poetry and are therefore less scientific than the exact sciences which are drier the more exact they are, for exact science is directed toward truth and only the truth. Therefore all constituents of sentences to which the assertive force does not reach do not belong to scientific exposition but they are sometimes hard to avoid, even for one who sees the danger connected with them. Where the main thing is to approach what cannot be grasped in thought by means of guesswork, these components have their justification. The more exactly scientific an exposition is, the less will the nationality of its author be discernible and the easier will it be to translate. On the other hand, the constituents of language, to which I want to call attention here, make the translation of poetry very difficult, even make a complete translation almost always impossible, for it is in precisely that in which poetic value largely consists that languages differ most.

It makes no difference to the thought whether I use the word "horse" or "steed" or "carthorse" or "mare". The assertive force does not extend over that in which these words differ. What is called mood, fragrance, illumination in a poem, what is portrayed by cadence and rhythm, does not belong to the thought.

Much of language serves the purpose of aiding the hearer's understanding, for instance the stressing of part of a sentence by accentuation or word-order. One should remember words like "still" and "already" too. With the sentence "Alfred has still not come" one really says "Alfred has not come" and, at the same time, hints that his arrival is expected, but it is only hinted. It cannot be said that, since Alfred's arrival is not expected, the sense of the sentence is therefore false. The word "but" differs from "and" in that with it one intimates that what follows is in contrast with what would be expected from what preceded it. Such suggestions in speech make no difference to the thought. A sentence can be transformed by changing the verb from active to passive and making the object the subject at the same time. In the same way the dative may be changed into the nominative while "give" is replaced by "receive". Naturally such transformations are not indifferent in every respect; but they do not touch the thought, they do not touch what is true or false. If the inadmissibility of such transformations were generally admitted, then all deeper logical investigation would be hindered. It is just as important to neglect distinctions that do not touch the heart of the matter as to make distinctions which concern what is essential. But what is essential depends on one's purpose. To a mind concerned with what is beautiful in language what is indifferent to the logician can appear as just what is important.

Thus the contents of a sentence often go beyond the thoughts expressed by it. But the opposite often happens too, that the mere wording, which can be grasped by writing or the gramophone, does not suffice for the expression of the thought. The present tense is used in two ways: first, in order to give a date, second, in order to eliminate any temporal restriction where timelessness or eternity is part of the thought. Think, for instance, of the laws of mathematics. Which of the two cases occurs is not expressed but must be guessed. If a time indication is needed by the present tense, one must know when the sentence was uttered to apprehend the thought correctly. Therefore the time of utterance is part of the expression of the thought. If someone wants to say the same today as he expressed yesterday using the word "today", he must replace this word with "yesterday". Although the thought is the same, its verbal expression must be different so that the sense, which would otherwise be affected by the differing times of utterance, is readjusted. The case is the same with words like "here" and "there". In all such cases the mere wording, as it is given in writing, is not the complete expression of the thought, but the knowledge of certain accompanying conditions of utterance, which are used as means of expressing the thought, is needed for its correct apprehension. The pointing of fingers, hand movements, glances may belong here too. The same utterance containing the word "I" will express different thoughts in the mouths of different men, of which some may be true, others false.

The occurrence of the word "I" in a sentence gives rise to some questions.

Consider the following case. Dr. Gustav Lauben says, "I have been wounded". Leo Peter hears this and remarks some days later, "Dr. Gustav Lauben has been wounded". Does this sentence express the same thought as the one Dr. Lauben uttered himself? Suppose that Rudolph Lingens were present when Dr. Lauben spoke and now hears what is related by Leo Peter. If the same thought is uttered by Dr. Lauben and Leo Peter, then Rudolph Lingens, who is fully master of the language and remembers what Dr. Lauben has said in his presence, must now know at once from Leo Peter's report that the same thing is under discussion. But knowledge of the language is a separate thing when it is a matter of proper names. It may well be the case that only a few people associate a particular thought with the sentence "Dr. Lauben has been wounded". In this case one needs for complete understanding a knowledge of the expression "Dr. Lauben". Now if both Leo Peter and Rudolph Lingens understand by "Dr. Lauben" the doctor who lives as the only doctor in a house known to both of them, then they both understand the sentence "Dr. Gustav Lauben has been wounded" in the same way, they associate the same thought with it. But it is also possible that Rudolph Lingens does not know Dr. Lauben personally and does not know that he is the very Dr. Lauben who recently said "I have been wounded". In this case Rudolph Lingens cannot know that the same thing is in question. I say, therefore, in this case: the thought which Leo Peter expresses is not the same as that which Dr. Lauben uttered.

Suppose further that Herbert Garner knows that Dr. Gustav Lauben was born on 13th September 1875 in N.N. and this is not true of anyone else; against this, suppose that he does not know where Dr. Lauben now lives nor indeed anything about him. On the other hand, suppose Leo Peter does not know that Dr. Lauben was born on 13th September 1875, in N.N. Then as far as the proper name "Dr. Gustav Lauben" is concerned, Herbert Garner and Leo Peter do not speak the same language, since, although they do in fact refer to the same man with this name, they do not know that they do so. Therefore Herbert Garner docs not associate the same thought with the sentence "Dr. Gustav Lauben has been wounded" as Leo Peter wants to express with it. To avoid the drawback of Herbert Garner's and

Leo Peter's not speaking the same language, I am assuming that Leo Peter uses the proper name "Dr. Lauben" and Herbert Garner, on the other hand, uses the proper name "Gustav Lauben". Now it is possible that Herbert Garner takes the sense of the sentence "Dr. Lauben has been wounded" to be true while, misled by false information, taking the sense of the sentence "Gustav Lauben has been wounded" to be false. Under the assumptions given, these thoughts are therefore different.

Accordingly, with a proper name, it depends on how whatever it refers to is presented. This can happen in different ways and every such way corresponds with a particular sense of a sentence containing a proper name. The different thoughts which thus result from the same sentence correspond in their truth-value, of course; that is to say, if one is true then all are true, and if one is false then all are false. Nevertheless their distinctness must be recognized. So it must really be demanded that a single way in which whatever is referred to is presented be associated with every proper name. It is often unimportant that this demand should be fulfilled but not always.

Now everyone is presented to himself in a particular and primitive way, in which he is presented to no-one else. So, when Dr. Lauben thinks that he has been wounded, he will probably take as a basis this primitive way in which he is presented to himself. And only Dr. Lauben himself can grasp thoughts determined in this way. But now he may want to communicate with others. He cannot communicate a thought which he alone can grasp. Therefore, if he now says "I have been wounded", he must use the "I" in a sense which can be grasped by others, perhaps in the sense of "he who is speaking to you at this moment", by doing which he makes the associated conditions of his utterance serve for the expression of his thought.[4]

Yet there is a doubt. Is it at all the same thought which first that man expresses and now this one?

A person who is still untouched by philosophy knows first of all things which he can see and touch, in short, perceive with the senses, such as trees, stones and houses, and he is convinced that another person equally can see and touch the same tree and the same stone which he himself sees and touches. Obviously a thought is not one of these things. Now can it, nevertheless, stand in the same relation to a person as does a tree?

Even an unphilosophical person soon finds it necessary to recognize an inner world distinct from the outer world, a world of sense-impressions, of creations of his imagination, of sensations, of feelings and moods, a world of inclinations, wishes and decisions. For brevity I want to collect all these, with the exception of decisions, under the word "idea".

Now do thoughts belong to this inner world? Are they ideas? They are obviously not decisions. How are ideas distinct from the things of the outer world? First:

Ideas cannot be seen or touched, cannot be smelled, nor tasted, nor heard.

I go for a walk with a companion. I see a green field, I have a visual impression of the green as well. I have it but I do not see it.

Secondly: ideas are had. One has sensations, feelings, moods, inclinations, wishes. An idea which someone has belongs to the content of his consciousness.

The field and the frogs in it, the sun which shines on them are there no matter whether I look at them or not, but the sense-impression I have of green exists only because of me, I am its bearer. It seems absurd to us that a pain, a mood, a wish should rove about the world without a bearer, independently. An experience is impossible without an experiment. The inner world presupposes the person whose inner world it is.

Thirdly: ideas need a bearer. Things of the outer world are however independent.

My companion and I are convinced that we both see the same field; but each of us has a particular sense-impression of green. I notice a strawberry among the green strawberry leaves. My companion does not notice it, he is colour-blind. The colour-impression, which he receives from the strawberry, is not noticeably different from the one he receives from the leaf. Now does my companion see the green leaf as red, or does he see the red berry as green, or does he see both as of one colour with which I am not acquainted at all? These are unanswerable, indeed really nonsensical, questions. For when the word "red" does not state a property of things but is supposed to characterize sense-impressions belonging to my consciousness, it is only applicable within the sphere of my consciousness. For it is impossible to compare my sense-impression with that of someone else. For that it would be necessary to bring together in one consciousness a sense-impression, belonging to one consciousness, with a sense-impression belonging to another consciousness. Now even if it were possible to make an idea disappear from one consciousness and, at the same time, to make an idea appear in another consciousness, the question whether it were the same idea in both would still remain unanswerable, it is so much of the essence of each of my ideas to be the content of my consciousness, that every idea of another person is, just as such, distinct from mine. But might it not be possible that my ideas, the entire content of my consciousness might be at the same time the content of a more embracing, perhaps divine, consciousness? Only if I were myself part of the divine consciousness. But then would they really be my ideas, would I be their bearer? This oversteps the limits of human understanding to such an extent that one must leave its possibility out of account. In any case it is impossible for us as men to compare another person's ideas with our own. I pick the strawberry, I hold it between my fingers. Now my companion sees it too, this very same strawberry; but each of us has his own idea. No other person has my idea but many people can see the same thing. No other person has my pain. Someone can have sympathy for me but still my pain always belongs to me and his sympathy to him. He does not have my pain and I do not have his sympathy.

Fourthly: every idea has only one bearer; no two men have the same idea.

For otherwise it would exist independently of this person and independently of that one. Is that lime-tree my idea? By using the expression "that lime-tree" in this question I have really already anticipated the answer, for with this expression I want to refer to what I see and to what other people can also look at and touch. There are now two possibilities. If my intention is realized when I refer to something with the

expression "that lime-tree", then the thought expressed in the sentence "that lime-tree is my idea" must obviously be negated. But if my intention is not realized, if I only think I see without really seeing, if on that account the designation "that lime-tree" is empty, then I have gone astray into the sphere of fiction without knowing it or wanting to. In that case neither the content of the sentence "that lime-tree is my idea" nor the content of the sentence "that lime-tree is not my idea" is true, for in both cases I have a statement which lacks an object. So then one can only refuse to answer the question for the reason that the content of the sentence "that lime-tree is my idea" is piece of fiction. I have, naturally, got an idea then, but I am not referring to this with the words "that lime-tree". Now someone may really want to refer to one of his ideas with the words "that lime-tree". He would then be the bearer of that to which he wants to refer with those words, but then he would not see that lime-tree and no-one else would see it or be its bearer.

I now return to the question: is a thought an idea? If the thought I express in the Pythagorean theorem can be recognized by others just as much as by me, then it does not belong to the content of my consciousness, I am not its bearer; yet I can, nevertheless, recognize it to be true. However, if it is not the same thought at all which is taken to be the content of the Pythagorean theorem by me and by another person, one should not really say "the Pythagorean theorem" but "my Pythagorean theorem", "his Pythagorean theorem" and these would be different; for the sense belongs necessarily to the sentence. Then my thought can be the content of my consciousness and his thought the content of his. Could the sense of my Pythagorean theorem be true while that of his was false? I said that the word "red" was applicable only in the sphere of my consciousness if it did not state a property of things but was supposed to characterize one of my sense-impressions. Therefore the words "true" and "false", as I understand them, could also be applicable only in the sphere of my consciousness, if they were not supposed to be concerned with something of which I was not the bearer, but were somehow appointed to characterize the content of my consciousness. Then truth would be restricted to the content of my consciousness and it would remain doubtful whether anything at all comparable occurred in the consciousness of others.

If every thought requires a bearer, to the contents of whose consciousness it belongs, then it would be a thought of this bearer only and there would be no science common to many, on which many could work. But I, perhaps, have my science, namely, a whole of thought whose bearer I am and another person has his. Each of us occupies himself with the contents of his own consciousness. No contradiction between the two sciences would then be possible and it would really be idle to dispute about truth, as idle, indeed almost ludicrous, as it would be for two people to dispute whether a hundred-mark note were genuine, where each meant the one he himself had in his pocket and understood the word "genuine" in his own particular sense. If someone takes thoughts to be ideas, what he then recognizes to be true is, on his own view, the content of his consciousness and does not properly concern other people at all. If he were to hear from me the opinion that a thought is not an idea, he could not dispute it, for, indeed, it would not now concern him.

So the result seems to be: thoughts are neither things of the outer world nor ideas.

A third realm must be recognized. What belongs to this corresponds with ideas, in that it cannot be perceived by the senses, but with things, in that it needs no bearer to the contents of whose consciousness to belong. Thus the thought, for example, which we expressed in the Pythagorean theorem is timelessly true, true independently of whether anyone takes it to be true. It needs no bearer. It is not true for the first time when it is discovered, but is like a planet which, already before anyone has seen it, has been in interaction with other planets.[5]

But I think I hear an unusual objection. I have assumed several times that the same thing that I see can also be observed by other people. But how could this be the case, if everything were only a dream? If I only dreamed I was walking in the company of another person, if I only dreamed that my companion saw the green field as I did, if it were all only a play performed on the stage of my consciousness, it would be doubtful whether there were things of the outer world at all. Perhaps the realm of things is empty and I see no things and no men, but have only ideas of which I myself am the bearer. An idea, being something which can as little exist independently of me as my feeling of fatigue, cannot be a man, cannot look at the same field together with me, cannot see the strawberry I am holding. It is quite incredible that I should really have only my inner world instead of the whole environment, in which I am supposed to move and to act. And yet it is an inevitable consequence of the thesis that only what is my idea can be the object of my awareness. What would follow from this thesis if it were true? Would there then be other men? It would certainly be possible but I should know nothing of it. For a man cannot be my idea, consequently, if our thesis were true, he also cannot be an object of my awareness. And so the ground would be removed from under any process of thought in which I might assume that something was an object for another person as for myself, for even if this were to happen I should know nothing of it. It would be impossible for me to distinguish that of which I was the bearer from that of which I was not. In judging something not to be my idea I would make it the object of my thinking and, therefore, my idea. On this view, is there a green field? Perhaps, but it would not be visible to me. For if a field is not my idea, it cannot, according to our thesis, be an object of my awareness. But if it is my idea it is invisible, for ideas are not visible. I can indeed have the idea of a green field, but this is not green for there are no green ideas. Does a shell weighing a hundred kilogrammes exist, according to this view? Perhaps, but I could know nothing of it. If a shell is not my idea then, according to our thesis, it cannot be an object of my awareness, of my thinking. But if a shell were my idea, it would have no weight. I can have an idea of a heavy shell. This then contains the idea of weight as a part-idea. But this part-idea is not a property of the whole idea any more than Germany is a property of Europe. So it follows:

Either the thesis that only what is my idea can be the object of my awareness is false, or all my knowledge and perception are limited to the range of my ideas, to the stage of my consciousness. In this case I should have only an inner world and I should know nothing of other people.

It is strange how, upon such reflections, the opposites collapse into each other. There is, let us suppose, a physiologist of the senses. As is proper for a scholarly scientist, he is, first of all, far from supposing the things he is convinced he sees and touches to be his ideas. On the contrary, he believes that in sense-impressions he has the surest proof of things which are wholly independent of his feeling, imagining, thinking, which have no need of his consciousness. So little does he consider nerve-fibres and ganglion-cells to be the content of his consciousness that he is, on the contrary, rather inclined to regard his consciousness as dependent on nerve-fibres and ganglion-cells. He establishes that light-rays, refracted in the eye, strike the visual nerve-endings and bring about a change, a stimulus, there. Some of it is transmitted through nerve-fibres and ganglion-cells. Further processes in the nervous system are perhaps involved, colour-impressions arise and these perhaps join themselves to what we call the idea of a tree. Physical, chemical and physiological occurrences insert themselves between the tree and my idea. These are immediately connected with my consciousness but, so it seems, are only occurrences in my nervous system and every spectator of the tree has his particular occurrences in his particular nervous system. Now the light-rays, before they enter my eye, may be reflected by a mirror and be spread further as if they came from a place behind the mirror. The effects on the visual nerves and all that follows will now take place just as they would if the light-rays had come from a tree behind the mirror and had been transmitted undisturbed to the eye. So an idea of a tree will finally occur even though such a tree does not exist at all. An idea, to which nothing at all corresponds, can also arise through the bending of light, with the mediation of the eye and the nervous system. But the stimulation of the visual nerves need not even happen through light. If lightning strikes near us we believe we see flames, even though we cannot see the lightning itself. In this case the visual nerve is perhaps stimulated by electric currents which originate in our body in consequence of the flash of light-

ning. If the visual nerve is stimulated by this means, just as it would be stimulated by light-rays coming from flames, then we believe we see flames. It just depends on the stimulation of the visual nerve, it is indifferent how that itself comes about.

One can go a step further still. This stimulation of the visual nerve is not actually immediately given, but is only a hypothesis. We believe that a thing, independent of us, stimulates a nerve and by this means produces a sense-impression, but, strictly speaking, we experience only the end of this process which projects into our consciousness. Could not this sense-impression, this sensation, which we attribute to a nerve-stimulation, have other causes also, as the same nerve-stimulation can arise in different ways? If we call what happens in our consciousness idea, then we really experience only ideas but not their causes. And if the scientist wants to avoid all mere hypothesis, then only ideas are left for him, everything resolves into ideas, the light-rays, nerve-fibres and ganglion-cells from which he started. So he finally undermines the foundations of his own construction. Is everything an idea? Does everything need a bearer, without which it could have no stability? I have considered myself as the bearer of my ideas, but am I not an idea myself? It seems to me as if I were lying in a deck-chair, as if I could see the toes of a pair of waxed boots, the front part of a pair of trousers, a waistcoat, buttons, part of a jacket, in particular sleeves, two hands, the hair of a beard, the blurred outline of a nose. Am I myself this entire association of visual impressions, this total idea? It also seems to me as if I see a chair over there. It is an idea. I am not actually much different from this myself, for am I not myself just an association of sense-impressions, an idea? But where then is the bearer of these ideas? How do I come to single out one of these ideas and set it up as the bearer of the rest? Why must it be the idea which I choose to call "I"? Could I not just as well choose the one that I am tempted to call a chair? Why, after all, have a bearer for ideas at all? But this would always be something essentially different from merely borne ideas, something independent, needing no extraneous bearer. If everything is idea, then there is no bearer of ideas. And so now, once again, I experience a change into the opposite. If there is no bearer of ideas, then there are also no ideas, for ideas need a bearer without which they cannot exist. If there is no ruler, there are also no subjects. The dependence, which I found myself induced to confer on the experience as opposed to the experiment, is abolished if there is no more bearer. What I called ideas are then independent objects. Every reason is wanting for granting an exceptional position to that object which I call "I".

But is that possible? Can there be an experience without someone to experience it? What would this whole play be without an onlooker? Can there be a pain without someone who has it? Being experienced is necessarily connected with pain, and someone experiencing is necessarily connected with being experienced. But there is something which is not my idea and yet which can be the object of my awareness, of my thinking, I am myself of this nature. Or can I be part of the content of my consciousness while another part is, perhaps, an idea of the moon? Does this perhaps take place when I judge that I am looking at the moon? Then this first part would have a consciousness and part of the content of this consciousness would be I myself once more. And so on. Yet it is surely inconceivable that I should be boxed into myself in this way to infinity, for then there would not be only one I but infinitely many. I am not my own idea and if I assert something about myself, e.g. that I do not feel any pain at this moment, then my judgment concerns something which is not a content of my consciousness, is not my idea, that is me myself. Therefore that about which I state something is not necessarily my idea. But, someone perhaps objects, if I think I have no pain at the moment, does not the word "I" nevertheless correspond with something in the content of my consciousness and is that not an idea? That may be. A certain idea in my consciousness may be associated with the idea of the word "I". But then it is an idea among other ideas and I am its bearer as I am the bearer of the other ideas. I have an idea of myself but I am not identical with this idea. What is a content of my consciousness, my idea, should be sharply distinguished from what is an object of my thought. Therefore the thesis that only what

belongs to the content of my consciousness can be the object of my awareness, of my thought, is false.

Now the way is clear for me to recognize another person as well as to be an independent bearer of ideas. I have an idea of him but I do not confuse it with him himself. And if I state something about my brother, I do not state it about the idea that I have of my brother.

The invalid who has a pain is the bearer of this pain, but the doctor in attendance who reflects on the cause of this pain is not the bearer of the pain. He does not imagine he can relieve the pain by anaesthetizing himself. An idea in the doctor's mind may very well correspond to the pain of the invalid but that is not the pain and not what the doctor is trying to remove. The doctor might consult another doctor. Then one must distinguish: first, the pain whose bearer is the invalid, second, the first doctor's idea of this pain, third, the second doctor's idea of this pain. This idea docs indeed belong to the content of the second doctor's consciousness, but it is not the object of his reflection, it is rather an aid to reflection, as a drawing can be such an aid perhaps. Both doctors have the invalid's pain, which they do not bear, as their common object of thought. It can be seen from this that not only a thing but also an idea can be the common object of thought of people who do not have the idea.

So, it seems to me, the matter becomes intelligible. If man could not think and could not take something of which he was not the bearer as the object of his thought, he would have an inner world but no outer world. But may this not be based on a mistake? I am convinced that the idea I associate with the words 'my brother' corresponds to something that is not my idea and about which I can say something. But may I not be making a mistake about this? Such mistakes do happen. We then, against our will, lapse into fiction. Indeed! By the step with which I secure an environment for myself, I expose myself to the risk of error. And here I come up against a further distinction between my inner and outer worlds. I cannot doubt that I have a visual impression of green but it is not so certain that I see a lime-leaf. So, contrary to widespread views, we find certainty in the inner world while doubt never altogether leaves us in our excursions into the outer world. It is difficult in many cases, nevertheless, to distinguish probability from certainty here, so we can presume to judge about things in the outer world. And we must presume this even at the risk of error if we do not want to succumb to far greater dangers.

In consequence of these last considerations I lay down the following: not everything that can be the object of my understanding is an idea. I, as a bearer of ideas, am not myself an idea. Nothing now stands in the way of recognizing other people to be bearers of ideas as I am myself. And, once given the possibility, the probability is very great, so great that it is in my opinion no longer distinguishable from certainty. Would there be a science of history otherwise? Would not every precept of duty, every law otherwise come to nothing? What would be left of religion? The natural sciences too could only be assessed as fables like astrology and alchemy. Thus the reflections I have carried on, assuming that there are other people besides myself who can take the same thing as the object of their consideration, of their thinking, remain essentially unimpaired in force.

Not everything is an idea. Thus I can also recognize the thought, which other people can grasp just as much as I, as being independent of me. I can recognize a science in which many people can be engaged in research. We are not bearers of thoughts as we are bearers of our ideas. We do not have a thought as we have, say, a sense-impression, but we also do not see a thought as we see, say, a star. So it is advisable to choose a special expression and the word 'apprehend' offers itself for the purpose. A particular mental capacity, the power of thought, must correspond to the apprehension[6] of thought. In thinking we do not produce thoughts but we apprehend them. For what I have called thought stands in the closest relation to truth. What I recognize as true I judge to be true quite independently of my recognition of its truth and of my thinking about it. That someone thinks it has nothing to do with the truth of a thought. 'Facts, facts, facts' cries the scientist if he wants to emphasise the necessity of a firm foundation for science. What is a fact? A fact is a thought

that is true. But the scientist will surely not recognize something which depends on men's varying states of mind to be the firm foundation of science. The work of science does not consist of creation but of the discovery of true thoughts. The astronomer can apply a mathematical truth in the investigation of long past events which took place when on earth at least no one had yet recognized that truth. He can do this because the truth of a thought is timeless. Therefore that truth cannot have come into existence with its discovery.

Not everything is an idea. Otherwise psychology would contain all the sciences within it or at least it would be the highest judge over all the sciences. Otherwise psychology would rule over logic and mathematics. But nothing would be a greater misunderstanding of mathematics than its subordination to psychology. Neither logic nor mathematics has the task of investigating minds and the contents of consciousness whose bearer is a single person. Perhaps their task could be represented rather as the investigation of the mind, not of minds.

The apprehension of a thought presupposes someone who apprehends it, who thinks. He is the bearer of the thinking but not of the thought. Although the thought does not belong to the contents of the thinker's consciousness, yet something in his consciousness must be aimed at the thought. But this should not be confused with the thought itself. Similarly Algol itself is different from the idea someone has of Algol.

The thought belongs neither to my inner world as an idea nor yet to the outer world of material, perceptible things.

This consequence, however cogently it may follow from the exposition, will nevertheless not perhaps be accepted without opposition. It will, I think, seem impossible to some people to obtain information about something not belonging to the inner world except by sense-perception. Sense-perception indeed is often thought to be the most certain, even to be the sole, source of knowledge about everything that does not belong to the inner world. But with what right? For sense-impressions are necessary constituents of sense-perceptions and are a part of the inner world. In any case two men do not have the same, though they may have similar, sense-impressions. These alone do not disclose the outer world to us. Perhaps there is a being that has only sense-impressions without seeing or touching things. To have visual impressions is not to see things. How does it happen that I see the tree just there where I do see it? Obviously it depends on the visual impressions I have and on the particular type which occur because I see with two eyes. A particular image arises, physically speaking, on each of the two retinas. Another person sees the tree in the same place. He also has two retinal images but they differ from mine. We must assume that these retinal images correspond to our impressions. Consequently we have visual impressions, not only not the same, but markedly different from each other. And yet we move about in the same outer world. Having visual impressions is certainly necessary for seeing things but not sufficient. What must still be added is non-sensible. And yet this is just what opens up the outer world for us; for without this non-sensible something everyone would remain shut up in his inner world. So since the answer lies in the non-sensible, perhaps something non-sensible could also lead us out of the inner world and enable us to grasp thoughts where no sense-impressions were involved. Outside one's inner world one would have to distinguish the proper outer world of sensible, perceptible things from the realm of the non-sensibly perceptible. We should need something non-sensible for the recognition of both realms but for the sensible perception of things we should need sense-impressions as well and these belong entirely to the inner world. So that in which the distinction between the way in which a thing and a thought are given mainly consists is something which is attributable, not to both realms, but to the inner world. Thus I cannot find this distinction to be so great that on its account it would be impossible for a thought to be given that did not belong to the inner world.

The thought, admittedly, is not something which it is usual to call real. The world of the real is a world in which this acts on that, changes it and again experiences reactions itself and is changed by them. All this is a process in time. We will hardly recognize what is timeless and unchangeable as real. Now is the thought changeable or is it timeless? The thought we express by the Pythagorean theorem is surely timeless, eternal, unchangeable. But are there not thoughts which are true today but false in six months time? The thought, for example, that the tree there is covered with green leaves will surely be false in six months time. No, for it is not the same thought at all. The words 'this tree is covered with green leaves' are not sufficient by themselves for the utterance, the time of utterance is involved as well. Without the time-indication this gives, we have no complete thought, i.e. no thought at all. Only a sentence supplemented by a time-indication and complete in every respect expresses a thought. But this, if it is true, is true not only today or tomorrow but timelessly. Thus the present tense in 'is true' does not refer to the speaker's present but is, if the expression be permitted, a tense of timelessness. If we use the mere form of the indicative sentence, avoiding the word "true", two things must be distinguished, the expression of the thought and the assertion. The time-indication that may be contained in the sentence belongs only to the expression of the thought, while the truth, whose recognition lies in the form of the indicative sentence, is timeless. Yet the same words, on account of the variability of language with time, take on another sense, express another thought; this change, however, concerns only the linguistic aspect of the matter.

And yet! What value could there be for us in the eternally unchangeable which could neither undergo effects nor have effect on us? Something entirely and in every respect inactive would be unreal and non-existent for us. Even the timeless, if it is to be anything for us, must somehow be implicated with the temporal. What would a thought be for me that was never apprehended by me? But by apprehending a thought I come into a relation to it and it to me. It is possible that the same thought that is thought by me today was not thought by me yesterday. In this way the strict timelessness is of course annulled. But one is inclined to distinguish between essential and inessential properties and to regard something as timeless if the changes it undergoes involve only its inessential properties. A property of a thought will be called inessential which consists in, or follows from the fact that, it is apprehended by a thinker.

How does a thought act? By being apprehended and taken to be true. This is a process in the inner world of a thinker which can have further consequences in this inner world and which, encroaching on the sphere of the will, can also make itself noticeable in the outer world. If, for example, I grasp the thought which we express by the theorem of Pythagoras, the consequence may be that I recognize it to be true and, further, that I apply it, making a decision which brings about the acceleration of masses. Thus our actions are usually prepared by thinking and judgment. And so thought can have an indirect influence on the motion of masses. The influence of one person on another is brought about for the most part by thoughts. One communicates a thought. How does this happen? One brings about changes in the common outside world which, perceived by another person, are supposed to induce him to apprehend a thought and take it to be true. Could the great events of world history have come about without the communication of thoughts? And yet we are inclined to regard thoughts as unreal because they appear to be without influence on events, while thinking, judging, stating, understanding and the like are facts of human life. How much more real a hammer appears compared with a thought. How different the process of handing over a hammer is from the communication of a thought. The hammer passes from one control to another, it is gripped, it undergoes pressure and on account of this its density, the disposition of its parts, is changed in places. There is nothing of all this with a thought. It does not leave the control of the communicator by being communicated, for after all a person has no control over it. When a thought is apprehended, it at first only brings about changes in the inner world of the apprehender, yet it remains untouched in its true essence, since the changes it undergoes involve only inessential properties. There is lacking here something we observe throughout the order of nature: reciprocal action. Thoughts are by no means unreal but their reality is of quite a different kind from that of things. And their effect is brought about by an act of the thinker without which they would be ineffective, at least as far as we can see. And yet the thinker does not create them but must take them as they are. They can be true without being apprehended by a thinker and are not wholly unreal even then, at least if they could be apprehended and by this means be brought into operation.

NOTES

1. In a similar way it has perhaps been said "a judgment is something which is either true or false". In fact I use the word "thought" in approximately the sense which "judgment" has in the writings of logicians. I hope it will become clear in what follows why I choose "thought". Such an explanation has been objected to on the ground that in it a distinction is drawn between true and false judgments which of all possible distinctions among judgments has perhaps the least significance. I cannot see that it is a logical deficiency that a distinction is given with the explanation. As far as significance is concerned, it should not by any means be judged as trifling if, as I have said, the word "true" indicates the aim of logic.

2. I am not using the word "sentence" here in a purely grammatical sense where it also includes subordinate clauses. An isolated subordinate clause does not always have a sense about which the question of truth can arise, whereas the complex sentence to which it belongs has such a sense.

3. It seems to me that thought and judgment has not hitherto been adequately distinguished. Perhaps language is misleading. For we have no particular clause in the indicative sentence which corresponds to the assertion, that something is being asserted lies rather in the form of the indicative. We have the advantage in German that main and subordinate clauses are distinguished by the word-order. In this connexion it is noticeable that a subordinate clause can also contain an assertion and that often neither main nor subordinate clause expresses a complete thought by themselves but only the complex sentence does.

4. I am not in the happy position here of a mineralogist who shows his hearers a mountain crystal. I cannot put a thought in the hands of my readers with the request that they should minutely examine it from all sides. I have to content myself with presenting the reader with a thought, in itself immaterial, dressed in sensible linguistic form. The metaphorical aspect of language presents difficulties. The sensible always breaks in and makes expression metaphorical and so improper. So a battle with language takes place and I am compelled to occupy myself with language although it is not my proper concern here. I hope I have succeeded in making clear to my readers what I want to call a thought.

5. One sees a thing, one has an idea, one apprehends or thinks a thought. When one apprehends or thinks a

thought, one does not create it but only comes to stand in a certain relation, which is different from seeing a thing or having an idea, to what already existed beforehand.

6. The expression "apprehend" is as metaphorical as "content of consciousness". The nature of language does not permit anything else. What I hold in my hand can certainly be regarded as the content of my hand but is all the same the content of my hand in quite a different way from the bones and muscles of which it is made and their tension, and is much more extraneous to it than they are.

2

Empiricist Criteria of Cognitive Significance: Problems and Changes

CARL G. HEMPEL

1. THE GENERAL EMPIRICIST CONCEPTION OF COGNITIVE AND EMPIRICAL SIGNIFICANCE

It is a basic principle of contemporary empiricism that a sentence makes a cognitively significant assertion, and thus can be said to be either true or false, if and only if either (1) it is analytic or contradictory—in which case it is said to have purely logical meaning or significance—or else (2) it is capable, at least potentially, of test by experiential evidence—in which case it is said to have empirical meaning or significance. The basic tenet of this principle, and especially of its second part, the so-called testability criterion of empirical meaning (or better: meaningfulness), is not peculiar to empiricism alone: it is characteristic also of contemporary operationism, and in a sense of pragmatism as well; for the pragmatist maxim that a difference must make a difference to be a difference may well be construed as insisting that a verbal difference between two sentences must make a difference in experiential implications if it is to reflect a difference in meaning.

How this general conception of cognitively significant discourse led to the rejection, as devoid of logical and empirical meaning, of various formulations in speculative metaphysics, and even of certain hypotheses offered within empirical science, is too well known to require recounting. I think that the general intent of the empiricist criterion of meaning is basically sound, and that notwithstanding much oversimplification in its use, its critical application has been, on the whole, enlightening and salutary. I feel less confident, however, about the possibility of restating the general idea in the form of precise and general criteria which establish sharp dividing lines (a) between statements of purely logical and statements of empirical significance, and (b) between those sentences which do have cognitive significance and those which do not.

In the present paper, I propose to reconsider these distinctions as conceived in recent empiricism, and to point out some of the difficulties they present. The discussion will concern mainly the second of the two distinctions; in regard to the first, I shall limit myself to a few brief remarks.

This essay combines, with certain omissions and some other changes, the contents of two articles: "Problems and Changes in the Empiricist Criterion of Meaning," *Revenue Internationale de Philosophie* 11 (January 1950): 41–63; and "The Concept of Cognitive Significance: A Reconsideration," *Proceedings of the American Academy of Arts and Sciences* 80 (1): 61–77 (1951). Reprinted with permission of the Free Press, a division of MacMillan, Inc. from *Aspects of Scientific Explanation* by Carl F. Hempel. Copyright © 1965 by the Free Press. Copyright © 1950, *Revue Internationale de Philosophie*.

2. THE EARLIER TESTABILITY CRITERIA OF MEANING AND THEIR SHORTCOMINGS

Let us note first that any general criterion of cognitive significance will have to meet certain requirements if it is to be at all acceptable. Of these, we note one, which we shall consider here as expressing a necessary, though by no means sufficient, *condition of adequacy* for criteria of cognitive significance.

(A) If under a given criterion of cognitive significance, a sentence N is nonsignificant, then so must be all truth-functional compound sentences in which N occurs nonvacuously as a component. For if N cannot be significantly assigned a truth value, then it is impossible to assign truth values to the compound sentences containing N; hence, they should be qualified as nonsignificant as well.

We note two corollaries of requirement (A): (A1) If under a given criterion of cognitive significance, a sentence S is nonsignificant, then so must be its negation, $\sim S$.

(A2) If under a given criterion of cognitive significance, a sentence N is nonsignificant, then so must be any conjunction $N \cdot S$ and any disjunction $N \lor S$, no matter whether S is significant under the given criterion or not.

We now turn to the initial attempts made in recent empiricism to establish general criteria of cognitive significance. Those attempts were governed by the consideration that a sentence, to make an empirical assertion must be capable of being borne out by, or conflicting with, phenomena which are potentially capable of being directly observed. Sentences describing such potentially observable phenomena—no matter whether the latter do actually occur or not—may be called observation sentences. More specifically, an *observation sentence* might be construed as a sentence—no matter whether true or false—which asserts or denies that a specified object, or group of objects, of macroscopic size has a particular *observable characteristic,* i.e., a characteristic whose presence or absence can, under favorable circumstances, be ascertained by direct observation.[1]

The task of setting up criteria of empirical significance is thus transformed into the problem of characterizing in a precise manner the relationship which obtains between a hypothesis and one or more observation sentences whenever the phenomena described by the latter either confirm or disconfirm the hypothesis in question. The ability of a given sentence to enter into that relationship to some set of observation sentences would then characterize its testability-in-principle, and thus its empirical significance. Let us now briefly examine the major attempts that have been made to obtain criteria of significance in this manner.

One of the earliest criteria is expressed in the so-called *verifiability requirement.* According to it, a sentence is empirically significant if and only if it is not analytic and is capable, at least in principle, of complete verification by observational evidence; i.e., if observational evidence can be described which, if actually obtained, would conclusively establish the truth of the sentence.[2] With the help of the concept of observation sentence, we can restate this requirement as follows: A sentence S has empirical meaning if and only if it is possible to indicate a finite set of observation sentences, $O_1, O_2, \ldots , O_n$, such that if these are true, then S is necessarily true, too. As stated, however, this condition is satisfied also if S is an analytic sentence or if the given observation sentences are logically incompatible with each other. By the following formulation, we rule these cases out and at the same time express the intended criterion more precisely.

2.1. Requirement of Complete Verifiability in Principle

A sentence has empirical meaning if and only if it is not analytic and follows logically from some finite and logically consistent class of observation sentences.[3] These observation sentences need not be true, for what the criterion is to explicate is testability by "potentially observable phenomena," or testability "in principle."

In accordance with the general conception of cognitive significance outlined earlier, a sentence will now be classified as cognitively significant if either it is analytic or contradictory, or it satisfies the verifiability requirement.

This criterion, however, has several serious

defects. One of them has been noted by several writers:

(a) Let us assume that the properties of being a stork and of being red-legged are both observable characteristics, and that the former does not logically entail the latter. Then the sentence

(S1) All storks are red-legged

is neither analytic nor contradictory; and clearly, it is not deducible from a finite set of observation sentences. Hence, under the contemplated criterion, S1 is devoid of empirical significance; and so are all other sentences purporting to express universal regularities or general laws. And since sentences of this type constitute an integral part of scientific theories, the verifiability requirement must be regarded as overly restrictive in this respect.

Similarly, the criterion disqualifies all sentences such as "For any substance there exists some solvent," which contain both universal and existential quantifiers (i.e., occurrences of the terms "all" and "some" or their equivalents); for no sentences of this kind can be logically deduced from any finite set of observation sentences.

Two further defects of the verifiability requirement do not seem to have been widely noticed:

(b) As is readily seen, the negation of S1

(~S1) There exists at least one stork that is not red-legged

is deducible from any two observation sentences of the type "a is a stork" and "a is not red-legged." Hence, ~S1 is cognitively significant under our criterion, but S1 is not, and this constitutes a violation of condition (A1).

(c) Let S be a sentence which does, and N a sentence which does not satisfy the verifiability requirement. Then S is deducible from some set of observation sentences; hence, by a familiar rule of logic, SvN is deducible from the same set, and therefore cognitively significant according to our criterion. This violates condition (A2) above.[4]

Strictly analogous considerations apply to an alternative criterion, which makes complete falsifiability in principle the defining characteristic of empirical significance. Let us formulate this criterion as follows:

2.2. Requirement of Complete Falsifiability in Principle

A sentence has empirical meaning if and only if its negation is not analytic and follows logically from some finite logically consistent class of observation sentences.

This criterion qualifies a sentence as empirically meaningful if its negation satisfies the requirement of complete verifiability; as it is to be expected, it is therefore inadequate on similar grounds as the latter:

(a) It denies cognitive significance to purely existential hypotheses, such as "There exists at least one unicorn," and all sentences whose formulation calls for mixed—i.e., universal and existential—quantification, such as "For every compound there exists some solvent," for none of these can possibly be conclusively falsified by a finite number of observation sentences.

(b) If 'P' is an observation predicate, then the assertion that all things have the property P is qualified as significant, but its negation, being equivalent to a purely existential hypothesis, is disqualified [cf. (a)]. Hence, criterion 2.2 gives rise to the same dilemma as 2.1.

(c) If a sentence S is completely falsifiable whereas N is a sentence which is not, then their conjunction S·N (i.e., the expression obtained by connecting the two sentences by the word "and") is completely falsifiable; for if the negation of S is entailed by a class of observation sentences, then the negation of S·N is, a fortiori, entailed by the same class. Thus, the criterion allows empirical significance to many sentences which an adequate empiricist criterion should rule out, such as "All swans are white and the absolute is perfect."

In sum, then, interpretations of the testability criterion in terms of complete verifiability or of complete falsifiability are inadequate because they are overly restrictive in one direction and overly inclusive in another, and because both of them violate the fundamental requirement A.

Several attempts have been made to avoid these difficulties by construing the testability criterion as demanding merely a partial and possibly indirect confirmability of empirical hypotheses by observational evidence.

A formulation suggested by Ayer[5] is characteristic of these attempts to set up a clear and sufficiently comprehensive criterion of confirmability. It states, in effect, that a sentence S has empirical import if from S in conjunction with suitable subsidiary hypotheses it is possible to derive observation sentences which are not derivable from the subsidiary hypotheses alone.

This condition is suggested by a closer consideration of the logical structure of scientific testing; but it is much too liberal as it stands. Indeed, as Ayer himself has pointed out in the second edition of his book, *Language, Truth, and Logic*,[6] his criterion allows empirical import to any sentence whatever. Thus, e.g., if S is the sentence "The absolute is perfect," it suffices to choose as a subsidiary hypothesis the sentence "If the absolute is perfect then this apple is red" in order to make possible the deduction of the observation sentence "This apple is red," which clearly does not follow from the subsidiary hypothesis alone.

To meet this objection, Ayer proposed a modified version of his testability criterion. In effect, the modification restricts the subsidiary hypothesis mentioned in the previous version to sentences which either are analytic or can independently be shown to be testable in the sense of the modified criterion.[7]

But it can readily be shown that this new criterion, like the requirement of complete falsifiability, allows empirical significance to any conjunction $S \cdot N$, where S satisfies Ayer's criterion while N is a sentence such as "The absolute is perfect," which is to be disqualified by that criterion. Indeed, whatever consequences can be deduced from S with the help of permissible subsidiary hypotheses can also be deduced from $S \cdot N$ by means of the same subsidiary hypotheses; and as Ayer's new criterion is formulated essentially in terms of the deducibility of a certain type of consequence from the given sentence, it countenances $S \cdot N$ together with S. Another difficulty has been pointed out by Church, who has shown[8] that if there are any three observation sentences none of which alone entails any of the others, then it follows

for any sentence S whatsoever that either it or its denial has empirical import according to Ayer's revised criterion.

All the criteria considered so far attempt to explicate the concept of empirical significance by specifying certain logical connections which must obtain between a significant sentence and suitable observation sentences. It seems now that this type of approach offers little hope for the attainment of precise criteria of meaningfulness: this conclusion is suggested by the preceding survey of some representative attempts, and it receives additional support from certain further considerations, some of which will be presented in the following sections.

3. CHARACTERIZATION OF SIGNIFICANT SENTENCES BY CRITERIA FOR THEIR CONSTITUENT TERMS

An alternative procedure suggests itself which again seems to reflect well the general viewpoint of empiricism: It might be possible to characterize cognitively significant sentences by certain conditions which their constituent terms have to satisfy. Specifically, it would seem reasonable to say that all extralogical terms[9] in a significant sentence must have experiential reference, and that therefore their meanings must be capable of explication by reference to observables exclusively.[10] In order to exhibit certain analogies between this approach and the previous one, we adopt the following terminological conventions.

Any term that may occur in a cognitively significant sentence will be called a *cognitively significant term*. Furthermore, we shall understand by an *observation term* any term which either (a) is an *observation predicate*, i.e., signifies some observable characteristic (as do the terms 'blue', 'warm', 'soft', 'coincident with', 'of greater apparent brightness than') or (b) names some physical object of macroscopic size (as do the terms 'the needle of this instrument', 'the Moon', 'Krakatoa Volcano', 'Greenwich, England', 'Julius Caesar').

Now while the testability criteria of meaning aimed at characterizing the cognitively significant sentences by means of certain inferential connections in which they must stand to some observation sentences, the alternative approach under consideration would instead try to specify the vocabulary that may be used in forming significant sentences. This vocabulary, the class of significant terms, would be characterized by the condition that each of its elements is either a logical term or else a term with empirical significance; in the latter case, it has to stand in certain definitional or explicative connections to some observation terms. This approach certainly avoids any violations of our earlier conditions of adequacy. Thus, e.g., if S is a significant sentence, i.e., contains cognitively significant terms only, then so is its denial, since the denial sign, and its verbal equivalents, belong to the vocabulary of logic and are thus significant. Again, if N is a sentence containing a nonsignificant term, then so is any compound sentence which contains N.

But this is not sufficient, of course. Rather, we shall now have to consider a crucial question analogous to that raised by the previous approach: Precisely how are the logical connections between empirically significant terms and observation terms to be construed if an adequate criterion of cognitive significance is to result? Let us consider some possibilities.

3.1. Requirement of Definability

The simplest criterion that suggests itself might be called the *requirement of definability*. It would demand that any term with empirical significance must be explicitly definable by means of observation terms.

This criterion would seem to accord well with the maxim of operationism that all significant terms of empirical science must be introduced by operational definitions. However, the requirement of definability is vastly too restrictive, for many important terms of scientific and even prescientific discourse cannot be explicitly defined by means of observation terms.

In fact, as Carnap[11] has pointed out, an attempt to provide explicit definitions in terms of observables encounters serious difficulties as soon as disposition terms, such as 'soluble', 'malleable', 'electric conductor', etc., have to be accounted for; and many of these occur even on the prescientific level of discourse.

Consider, for example, the word 'fragile'.

One might try to define it by saying that an object x is fragile if and only if it satisfies the following condition: If at any time t the object is sharply struck, then it breaks at that time. But if the statement connectives in this phrasing are construed truth-functionally, so that the definition can be symbolized by

(D) $Fx \equiv (t)(Sxt \supset Bxt)$

then the predicate 'F' thus defined does not have the intended meaning. For let a be any object which is not fragile (e.g., a raindrop or a rubber band), but which happens not to be sharply struck at any time throughout its existence. Then 'Sat' is false and hence '$Sat \supset Bat$' is true for all values of 't'; consequently, 'Fa' is true though a is not fragile.

To remedy this defect, one might construe the phrase 'if . . . then . . .' in the original definiens as having a more restrictive meaning than the truth-functional conditional. This meaning might be suggested by the subjunctive phrasing 'If x were to be sharply struck at any time t, then x would break at t.' But a satisfactory elaboration of this construal would require a clarification of the meaning and the logic of counterfactual and subjunctive conditionals, which is a thorny problem.[12]

An alternative procedure was suggested by Carnap in his theory of reduction sentences.[13] These are sentences which, unlike definitions, specify the meaning of a term only conditionally or partially. The term 'fragile', for example, might be introduced by the following reduction sentence:

(R) $(x)(t)[Sxt \supset (Fx \equiv Bxt)]$

which specifies that if x is sharply struck at any time t, then x is fragile if and only if x breaks at t.

Our earlier difficulty is now avoided, for if a is a nonfragile object that is never sharply struck, then that expression in R which follows the quantifiers is true of a; but this does not imply that 'Fa' is true. But the reduction sentence R specifies the meaning of 'F' only for application to those objects which meet the "test condition" of being sharply struck at some time; for these it states that fragility then amounts to breaking. For objects that fail to meet the test condition, the meaning of '*F*' is left undetermined. In this sense, reduction sentences have the character of partial or conditional definitions.

Reduction sentences provide a satisfactory interpretation of the experiential import of a large class of disposition terms and permit a more adequate formulation of so-called operational definitions, which, in general, are not complete definitions at all. These considerations suggest a greatly liberalized alternative to the requirement of definability.

3.2. Requirement of Reducibility

Every term with empirical significance must be capable of introduction, on the basis of observation terms, through chains of reduction sentences.

This requirement is characteristic of the liberalized versions of positivism and physicalism which, since about 1936, have superseded the older, overly narrow conception of a full definability of all terms of empirical science by means of observables,[14] and it avoids many of the shortcomings of the latter. Yet, reduction sentences do not seem to offer an adequate means for the introduction of the central terms of advanced scientific theories, often referred to as theoretical constructs. This is indicated by the following considerations: A chain of reduction sentences provides a necessary and a sufficient condition for the applicability of the term it introduces. (When the two conditions coincide, the chain is tantamount to an explicit definition.) But now take, for example, the concept of length as used in classical physical theory. Here, the length in centimeters of the distance between two points may assume any positive real number as its value; yet it is clearly impossible to formulate, by means of observation terms, a sufficient condition for the applicability of such expressions as 'having a length of $\sqrt{2}$ cm' and 'having a length of $\sqrt{2} + 10^{-100}$ cm'; for such conditions would provide a possibility for discrimination, in observational terms, between two lengths which differ by only 10^{-100} cm.[15]

It would be ill-advised to argue that for this reason, we ought to permit only such values of the magnitude, length, as permit the statement of sufficient conditions in terms of observables. For this would rule out, among others, all irrational numbers and would prevent us from assigning, to the diagonal of a square with sides of length 1, the length $\sqrt{2}$, which is required by Euclidean geometry. Hence, the principles of Euclidean geometry would not be universally applicable in physics. Similarly, the principles of the calculus would become inapplicable, and the system of scientific theory as we know it today would be reduced to a clumsy, unmanageable torso. This, then, is no way of meeting the difficulty. Rather, we shall have to analyze more closely the function of constructs in scientific theories, with a view to obtaining through such an analysis a more adequate characterization of cognitively significant terms.

Theoretical constructs occur in the formulation of scientific theories. These may be conceived of, in their advanced stages, as being stated in the form of deductively developed axiomatized systems. Classical mechanics, or Euclidean or some non-Euclidean form of geometry in physical interpretation, present examples of such systems. The extralogical terms used in a theory of this kind may be divided, in familiar manner, into primitive or basic terms, which are not defined within the theory, and defined terms, which are explicitly defined by means of the primitives. Thus, e.g., in Hilbert's axiomatization of Euclidean geometry, the terms 'point', 'straight line', 'between' are among the primitives, while 'line segment', 'angle', 'triangle', 'length' are among the defined terms. The basic and the defined terms together with the terms of logic constitute the vocabulary out of which all the sentences of the theory are constructed. The latter are divided, in an axiomatic presentation, into primitive statements (also called postulates or basic statements) which, in the theory, are not derived from any other statements, and derived ones, which are obtained by logical deduction from the primitive statements.

From its primitive terms and sentences, an axiomatized theory can be developed by means of purely formal principles of definition and deduction, without any consideration of the empirical significance of its extralogical terms. Indeed, this is the standard procedure employed in the axiomatic development of uninterpreted mathematical theories such as those of abstract groups or rings or lattices, or any form of pure (i.e., noninterpreted) geometry.

However, a deductively developed system of this sort can constitute a scientific theory only if it has received an empirical interpretation[16] which renders it relevant to the phenomena of our experience. Such interpretation is given by assigning a meaning, in terms of observables, to certain terms or sentences of the formalized theory. Frequently, an interpretation is given not for the primitive terms or statements but rather for some of the terms definable by means of the primitives, or for some of the sentences deducible from the postulates.[17] Furthermore, interpretation may amount to only a partial assignment of meaning. Thus, e.g., the rules for the measurement of length by means of a standard rod may be considered as providing a *partial* empirical interpretation for the term 'the length, in centimeters, of interval i', or alternatively, for some sentences of the form 'the length of interval i is r centimeters'. For the method is applicable only to intervals of a certain medium size, and even for the latter it does not constitute a full interpretation since the use of a standard rod does not constitute the only way of determining length: various alternative procedures are available involving the measurement of other magnitudes which are connected, by general laws, with the length that is to be determined.

This last observation, concerning the possibility of an indirect measurement of length by virtue of certain laws, suggests an important reminder. It is not correct to speak, as is often done, of "the experiential meaning" of a term or a sentence in isolation. In the language of science, and for similar reasons even in prescientific discourse, a single statement usually has no experiential implications. A single sentence in a scientific theory does not, as a rule, entail any observation sentences; consequences asserting the occurrence of certain observable phenomena can be derived from it only by conjoining it with a set of other, subsidiary, hypotheses. Of the latter, some will usually be observation sentences, others will be previously accepted theoretical statements. Thus, e.g., the relativistic

theory of the deflection of light rays in the gravitational field of the sun entails assertions about observable phenomena only if it is conjoined with a considerable body of astronomical and optical theory as well as a large number of specific statements about the instruments used in those observations of solar eclipses which serve to test the hypothesis in question.

Hence, the phrase, 'the experiential meaning of expression E' is elliptical: What a given expression "means" in regard to potential empirical data is relative to two factors, namely:

(1) *The linguistic framework L to which the expression belongs.* Its rules determine, in particular, what sentences—observational or otherwise—may be inferred from a given statement or class of statements.

(2) The theoretical context in which the expression occurs, i.e., the class of those statements in L which are available as subsidiary hypotheses.

Thus, the sentence formulating Newton's law of gravitation has no experiential meaning by itself; but when used in a language whose logical apparatus permits the development of the calculus, and when combined with a suitable system of other hypotheses—including sentences which connect some of the theoretical terms with observation terms and thus establish a partial interpretation—then it has a bearing on observable phenomena in a large variety of fields. Analogous considerations are applicable to the term 'gravitational field', for example. It can be considered as having experiential meaning only within the context of a theory, which must be at least partially interpreted; and the experiential meaning of the term—as expressed, say, in the form of operational criteria for its application—will depend again on the theoretical system at hand, and on the logical characteristics of the language within which it is formulated.

4. COGNITIVE SIGNIFICANCE AS A CHARACTERISTIC OF INTERPRETED SYSTEMS

The preceding considerations point to the conclusion that a satisfactory criterion of cognitive significance cannot be reached through the second avenue of approach here considered, namely by means of specific requirements for the terms which make up significant sentences. This result accords with a general characteristic of scientific (and, in principle, even prescientific) theorizing: Theory formation and concept formation go hand in hand; neither can be carried on successfully in isolation from the other.

If, therefore, cognitive significance can be attributed to anything, then only to entire theoretical systems formulated in a language with a well-determined structure. And the decisive mark of cognitive significance in such a system appears to be the existence of an interpretation for it in terms of observables. Such an interpretation might be formulated, for example, by means of conditional or biconditional sentences connecting nonobservational terms of the system with observation terms in the given language; the latter as well as the connecting sentences may or may not belong to the theoretical system.

But the requirement of partial interpretation is extremely liberal; it is satisfied, for example, by the system consisting of contemporary physical theory combined with some set of principles of speculative metaphysics, even if the latter have no empirical interpretation at all. Within the total system, these metaphysical principles play the role of what K. Reach and also O. Neurath liked to call *isolated sentences:* They are neither purely formal truths or falsehoods, demonstrable or refutable by means of the logical rules of the given language system; nor do they have any experiential bearing; i.e., their omission from the theoretical system would have no effect on its explanatory and predictive power in regard to potentially observable phenomena (i.e., the kind of phenomena described by observation sentences). Should we not, therefore, require that a cognitively significant system contain no isolated sentences? The following criterion suggests itself.

4.1

A theoretical system is cognitively significant if and only if it is partially interpreted to at least such an extent that none of its primitive sentences is isolated.

But this requirement may bar from a theoretical system certain sentences which might well be viewed as permissible and indeed desirable. By way of a simple illustration, let us assume that our theoretical system T contains the primitive sentence

$$(S1) \quad (x)[P_1x \supset (Qx \equiv P_2x)]$$

where 'P_1' and 'P_2' are observation predicates in the given language L, while 'Q' functions in T somewhat in the manner of a theoretical construct and occurs in only one primitive sentence of T, namely $S1$. Now $S1$ is not a truth or falsehood of formal logic; and furthermore, if $S1$ is omitted from the set of primitive sentences of T, then the resulting system, T', possesses exactly the same systematic, i.e., explanatory and predictive, power as T. Our contemplated criterion would therefore qualify $S1$ as an isolated sentence which has to be eliminated—excised by means of Occam's razor, as it were—if the theoretical system at hand is to be cognitively significant.

But it is possible to take a much more liberal view of $S1$ by treating it as a partial definition for the theoretical term 'Q'. Thus conceived, $S1$ specifies that in all cases where the observable characteristic P_1 is present, 'Q' is applicable if and only if the observable characteristic P_2 is present as well. In fact, $S1$ is an instance of those partial, or conditional, definitions which Carnap calls bilateral reduction sentences. These sentences are explicitly qualified by Carnap as analytic (though not, of course, as truths of formal logic), essentially on the ground that all their consequences which are expressible by means of observation predicates (and logical terms) alone are truths of formal logic.[18]

Let us pursue this line of thought a little further. This will lead us to some observations on analytic sentences and then back to the question of the adequacy of 4.1.

Suppose we add to our system T the further sentence

$$(S2) \quad (x)[P_3x \supset (Qx \equiv P_4x)]$$

where 'P_3', 'P_4' are additional observation predicates. Then, on the view that "every bilateral reduction sentence is analytic,"[19] $S2$ would be analytic as well as $S1$. Yet, the two sentences jointly entail nonanalytic consequences which are expressible in terms of observation predicates alone, such as[20]

$$(O) \quad (x)[\sim(P_1x \cdot P_2x \cdot Px_3 \cdot \sim P_4x) \cdot$$
$$\sim(P_1x \cdot \sim P_2x \cdot P_3x \cdot P_4x)]$$

But one would hardly want to admit the consequence that the conjunction of two analytic sentences may be synthetic. Hence if the concept of analyticity can be applied at all to the sentences of interpreted deductive systems, then it will have to be relativized with respect to the theoretical context at hand. Thus, e.g., $S1$ might be qualified as analytic relative to the system T, whose remaining postulates do not contain the term 'Q', but as synthetic relative to the system T enriched by $S2$. Strictly speaking, the concept of analyticity has to be relativized also in regard to the rules of the language at hand, for the latter determine what observational or other consequences are entailed by a given sentence. This need for at least a twofold relativization of the concept of analyticity was almost to be expected in view of those considerations which required the same twofold relativization for the concept of experiential meaning of a sentence.

If, on the other hand, we decide not to permit $S1$ in the role of a partial definition and instead reject it as an isolated sentence, then we are led to an analogous conclusion. Whether a sentence is isolated or not will depend on the linguistic frame and on the theoretical context at hand: While $S1$ is isolated relative to T (and the language in which both are formulated), it acquires definite experiential implications when T is enlarged by $S2$.

Thus we find, on the level of interpreted theoretical systems, a peculiar rapprochement, and partial fusion, of some of the problems pertaining to the concepts of cognitive significance and of analyticity: Both concepts need to be relativized; and a large class of sentences may be viewed, apparently with equal right, as analytic in a given context, or as isolated, or nonsignificant, in respect to it.

In addition to barring, as isolated in a given context, certain sentences which could just as well be construed as partial definitions, the criterion 4.1 has another serious defect. Of two logically equivalent formulations of a theoretical system it may qualify one as significant while barring the other as containing an isolated sentence among its primitives. For assume that a certain theoretical system T1 contains among its primitive sentences S', S'', . . . exactly one, S', which is isolated. Then $T1$ is not significant under 4.1. But now consider the theoretical system $T2$ obtained from $T1$ by replacing the two first primitive sentences, S', S'', by one, namely their conjunction. Then, under our assumptions, none of the primitive sentences of $T2$ is isolated, and $T2$, though equivalent to $T1$, is qualified as significant by 4.1. In order to do justice to the intent of 4.1, we would therefore have to lay down the following stricter requirement.

4.2

A theoretical system is cognitively significant if and only if it is partially interpreted to such an extent that in no system equivalent to it at least one primitive sentence is isolated.

Let us apply this requirement to some theoretical system whose postulates include the two sentences $S1$ and $S2$ considered before, and whose other postulates do not contain 'Q' at all. Since the sentences $S1$ and $S2$ together entail the sentence O, the set consisting of $S1$ and $S2$ is logically equivalent to the set consisting of $S1$, $S2$, and O. Hence, if we replace the former set by the latter, we obtain a theoretical system equivalent to the given one. In this new system, both $S1$ and $S2$ are isolated since, as can be shown, their removal does not affect the explanatory and predictive power of the system in reference to observable phenomena. To put it intuitively, the systematic power of $S1$ and $S2$ is the same as that of O. Hence, the original system is disqualified by 4.2. From the viewpoint of a strictly sensationalist positivism as perhaps envisaged by Mach, this result might be hailed as a sound repudiation of theories making reference to fictitious entities, and as a strict insistence on theories couched exclusively in terms of observables. But from a contemporary vantage point, we shall have to say that such a procedure overlooks or misjudges the important function of constructs in scientific theory: The history of scientific endeavor shows that if we wish to arrive at precise, comprehensive, and well-confirmed general laws, we have to rise above the level of direct observation. The phenomena directly accessible to our experience are not connected by general laws of great scope and rigor. Theoretical constructs are needed for the formulation of such higher-level laws. One of the most important functions of a well-chosen construct is its potential ability to serve as a constituent in ever new general connections that may be discovered; and to such connections we would blind ourselves if we insisted on banning from scientific theories all those terms and sentences which could be "dispensed with" in the sense indicated in 4.2. In following such a narrowly phenomenalistic or positivistic course, we would deprive ourselves of the tremendous fertility of theoretical constructs, and we would often render the formal structure of the expurgated theory clumsy and inefficient.

Criterion 4.2, then, must be abandoned, and considerations such as those outlined in this paper seem to lend strong support to the conjecture that no adequate alternative to it can be found; i.e., that it is not possible to formulate general and precise criteria which would separate those partially interpreted systems whose isolated sentences might be said to have a significant function from those in which the isolated sentences are, so to speak, mere useless appendages.

We concluded earlier that cognitive significance in the sense intended by recent empiricism and operationism can at best be attributed to sentences forming a theoretical system, and perhaps rather to such systems as wholes. Now, rather than try to replace 4.2 by some alternative, we will have to recognize further that cognitive significance in a system is a matter of degree: Significant systems range from those whose entire extralogical vocabulary consists of observation terms, through theories whose formulation relies heavily on theoretical constructs, on to systems with hardly any bearing on potential empirical findings. Instead of dichotomizing this array into significant and nonsignificant systems it would seem less arbitrary and more promising to appraise or compare different theoretical systems in regard to such characteristics as these:

(a) the clarity and precision with which the theories are formulated, and with which the logical relationships of their elements to each other and to expressions couched in observational terms have been made explicit;

(b) the systematic, i.e., explanatory and predictive, power of the systems in regard to observable phenomena;

(c) the formal simplicity of the theoretical system with which a certain systematic power is attained;

(d) the extent to which the theories have been confirmed by experiential evidence.

Many of the speculative philosophical approaches to cosmology, biology, or history, for example, would make a poor showing on practically all of these counts and would thus prove no matches to available rival theories, or would be recognized as so unpromising as not to warrant further study or development.

If the procedure here suggested is to be carried out in detail, so as to become applicable also in less obvious cases, then it will be necessary, of course, to develop general standards, and theories pertaining to them, for the appraisal and comparison of theoretical systems in the various respects just mentioned. To what extent this can be done with rigor and precision cannot well be judged in advance. In recent years, a considerable amount of work has been done towards a definition and theory of the concept of degree of confirmation, or logical probability, of a theoretical system;[21] and several contributions have been made towards the clarification of some of the other ideas referred to above.[22] The continuation of this research represents a challenge for further constructive work in the logical and methodological analysis of scientific knowledge.

NOTES

1. Observation sentences of this kind belong to what Carnap has called the thing-language, cf., e.g. (1938), pp. 52–53. That they are adequate to formulate the data which serve as the basis for empirical tests is clear in particular for the intersubjective testing procedures used in science as well as in large areas of empirical inquiry on the common-sense level. In epistemological discussions, it is frequently assumed that the ultimate evidence for beliefs about empirical matters consists in perceptions and sensations whose description calls for a phenomenalistic

type of language. The specific problems connected
with the phenomenalistic approach cannot be discussed here; but it should be mentioned that at any
rate all the critical considerations presented in this
article in regard to the testability criterion are applicable, *mutatis mutandis*, to the case of a phenomenalistic basis as well.

2. Originally, the permissible evidence was meant to be
restricted to what is observable by the speaker and
perhaps his fellow beings during their lifetimes.
Thus construed, the criterion rules out, as cognitively meaningless, all statements about the distant
future or the remote past, as has been pointed out,
among others, by Ayer (1946), chapter 1; by Pap
(1949), chapter 13, esp. pp. 333ff.; and by Russell
(1948), pp. 445–47. This difficulty is avoided, however, if we permit the evidence to consist of any
finite set of "logically possible observation data",
each of them formulated in an observation sentence.
Thus, e.g., the sentence S_1, "The tongue of the
largest dinosaur in New York's Museum of Natural
History was blue or black" is completely verifiable
in our sense; for it is a logical consequence of the
sentence S_2, "The tongue of the largest dinosaur in
New York's Museum of Natural History was blue";
and this is an observation sentence, in the sense just
indicated.

  And if the concept of *verifiability in principle* and
the more general concept of *confirmability in principle,* which will be considered later, are construed as
referring to *logically possible evidence* as expressed
by observation sentences, then it follows similarly
that the class of statements which are verifiable, or at
least confirmable, in principle include such assertions as that the planet Neptune and the Antarctic
Continent existed before they were discovered, and
that atomic warfare, if not checked, will lead to the
extermination of this planet. The objections which
Russell (1948), pp. 445 and 447, raises against the
verifiability criterion by reference to those examples
do not apply therefore if the criterion is understood
in the manner here suggested. Incidentally, statements of the kind mentioned by Russell, which are
not actually verifiable by any human being, were
explicitly recognized as cognitively significant
already by Schlick (1936), part V, who argued that
the impossibility of verifying them was "merely
empirical." The characterization of verifiability with
the help of the concept of observation sentence as
suggested here might serve as a more explicit and
rigorous statement of that conception.

3. As has frequently been emphasized in the empiricist
literature, the term "verifiability" is to indicate, of
course, the conceivability, or better, the logical possibility, of evidence of an observational kind which,
if actually encountered, would constitute conclusive
evidence for the given sentence; it is not intended to
mean the technical possibility of performing the
tests needed to obtain such evidence, and even less
the possibility of actually finding directly observable
phenomena which constitute conclusive evidence

for that sentence—which would be tantamount to
the actual existence of such evidence and would thus
imply the truth of the given sentence. Analogous
remarks apply to the terms "falsifiability" and "confirmability". This point has clearly been disregarded
in some critical discussions of the verifiability criterion. Thus, e.g., Russell (1948), p. 448 construes
verifiability as the actual existence of a set of conclusively verifying occurrences. This conception,
which has never been advocated by any logical
empiricist, must naturally turn out to be inadequate
since according to it the empirical meaningfulness of
a sentence could not be established without gathering empirical evidence, and moreover enough of it to
permit a conclusive proof of the sentence in question! It is not surprising, therefore, that his extraordinary interpretation of verifiability leads Russell to
the conclusion: "In fact, that a proposition is verifiable is itself not verifiable" (l.c.). Actually, under the
empiricist interpretation of complete verifiability,
any statement asserting the verifiability of some sentence S whose text is quoted, is either analytic or
contradictory; for the decision whether there exists a
class of observation sentences which entail S, i.e.,
whether such observation sentences can be formulated, no matter whether they are true or false—that
decision is a purely logical matter.

4. The arguments here adduced against the verifiability
criterion also prove the inadequacy of a view closely
related to it, namely that two sentences have the
same cognitive significance if any set of observation
sentences which would verify one of them would
also verify the other, and conversely. Thus, e.g.,
under this criterion, any two general laws would
have to be assigned the same cognitive significance,
for no general law is verified by any set of observation sentences. The view just referred to must be
clearly distinguished from a position which Russell
examines in his critical discussion of the positivistic
meaning criterion. It is "the theory that two propositions whose verified consequences are identical have
the same significance" (1948), p. 448. This view is
untenable indeed, for what consequences of a statement have actually been verified at a given time is
obviously a matter of historical accident which cannot possibly serve to establish identity of cognitive
significance. But I am not aware that any logical
empiricist ever subscribed to that "theory."

5. Ayer (1936, 1946), chapter I. The case against the
requirements of verifiability and of falsifiability, and
in favor of a requirement of partial confirmability
and disconfirmability, is very clearly presented also
by Pap (1949), chapter 13.

6. Ayer (1946), 2d ed., pp. 11–12.

7. This restriction is expressed in recursive form and
involves no vicious circle. For the full statement of
Ayer's criterion, see Ayer (1946), p. 13.

8. Church (1949). An alternative criterion recently suggested by O'Connor (1950) as a revision of Ayer's
formulation is subject to a slight variant of Church's
stricture: It can be shown that if there are three

observation sentences none of which entails any of the others, and if S is any noncompound sentence, then either S or $\sim S$ is significant under O'Connor's criterion.

9. An extralogical term is one that does not belong to the specific vocabulary of logic. The following phrases, and those definable by means of them, are typical examples of logical terms: 'not', 'or', 'if . . . then', 'all', 'some', '. . . is an element of class. . . .' Whether it is possible to make a sharp theoretical distinction between logical and extra-logical terms is a controversial issue related to the problem of discriminating between analytic and synthetic sentences. For the purpose at hand, we may simply assume that the logical vocabulary is given by enumeration.

10. For a detailed exposition and critical discussion of this idea, see H. Feigl's stimulating and enlightening article (1950).

11. Cf. Carnap (1936–37), especially section 7.

12. On this subject, see for example Langford (1941); Lewis (1946), pp. 210–30; Chisholm (1946); Goodman (1947); Reichenbach (1947), chapter VIII; Hempel and Oppenheim (1948), part III; Popper (1949); and especially Goodman's further analysis (1955).

13. Cf. Carnap, loc. cit. note 11. For a brief elementary presentation of the main idea, see Carnap (1938), part III. The sentence R here formulated for the predicate 'F' illustrates only the simplest type of reduction sentence, the so-called bilateral reduction sentence.

14. Cf. the analysis in Carnap (1936–37), especially section 15; also see the briefer presentation of the liberalized point of view in Carnap (1938).

15. (Added in 1964.) This is not strictly correct. For a more circumspect statement, see note 12 in "A Logical Appraisal of Operationalism" and the fuller discussion in section 7 of the essay "The Theoretician's Dilemma."

16. The interpretation of formal theories has been studied extensively by Reichenbach, especially in his pioneer analyses of space and time in classical and in relativistic physics. He describes such interpretation as the establishment of *coordinating definitions* (Zuordnungsdefinitionen) for certain terms of the formal theory. See, for example, Reichenbach (1928). More recently, Northrop [cf. (1947), chapter VII, and also the detailed study of the use of deductively formulated theories in science, ibid., chapters IV, V, VI] and H. Margenau [cf., for example, (1935)] have discussed certain aspects of this process under the title of *epistemic correlation*.

17. A somewhat fuller account of this type of interpretation may be found in Carnap (1939), §24. The articles by Spence (1944) and by MacCorquodale and Meehl (1948) provide enlightening illustrations of the use of theoretical constructs in a field outside that of the physical sciences, and of the difficulties encountered in an attempt to analyze in detail their function and interpretation.

18. Cf. Carnap (1936–37), especially sections 8 and 10.

19. Carnap (1936–37), p. 452.

20. The sentence O is what Carnap calls the *representative sentence* of the couple consisting of the sentences $S1$ and $S2$; see (1936–37), pp. 450–53.

21. Cf., for example, Carnap (1945)1 and (1945)2, and especially (1950). Also see Helmer and Oppenheim (1945).

22. On simplicity, cf. especially Popper (1935), chapter V; Reichenbach (1938), 42; Goodman (1949)1, (1949)2, (1950); on explanatory and predictive power, cf. Hempel and Oppenheim (1948), part IV.

REFERENCES

Ayer, A. J., *Language, Truth and Logic* (London: 1936) 2d ed. 1946.

Carnap, R., "Testability and Meaning," *Philosophy of Science*, 3 (1936) and 4 (1937).

Carnap, R., "Logical Foundations of the Unity of Science," in *International Encyclopedia of Unified Science*, I, 1 (Chicago: 1938).

Carnap, R., *Foundations of Logic and Mathematics* (Chicago: 1939).

Carnap, R., "On Inductive Logic," *Philosophy of Science*, 12 (1945). Referred to as (1945)1 in this article.

Carnap, R., "The Two Concepts of Probability," *Philosophy and Phenomenological Research*, 5 (1945). Referred to as (1945)2 in this article.

Carnap, R., *Logical Foundations of Probability* (Chicago: 1950).

Chisholm, R. M., "The Contrary-to-Fact Conditional," *Mind*, 55 (1946).

Church, A., Review of Ayer (1946), *The Journal of Symbolic Logic*, 14 (1949), 52–53.

Feigl, H., "Existential Hypotheses: Realistic vs. Phenomenalistic Interpretations," *Philosophy of Science*, 17 (1950).

Goodman, N., "The Problem of Counterfactual Conditionals," *The Journal of Philosophy*, 44 (1947).

Goodman, N., "The Logical Simplicity of Predicates," *The Journal of Symbolic Logic*, 14 (1949). Referred to as (1949)1 in this article.

Goodman, N., "Some Reflections on the Theory of Systems," *Philosophy and Phenomenological Research*, 9 (1949). Referred to as (1949)2 in this article.

Goodman, N., "An Improvement in the Theory of Simplicity," *The Journal of Symbolic Logic*, 15 (1950).

Goodman, N., *Fact, Fiction, and Forecast* (Cambridge, Mass.: 1955).

Helmer, O. and P. Oppenheim, "A Syntactical Definition of Probability and of Degree of Confirmation." *The Journal of Symbolic Logic*, 10 (1945).

Hempel, C. G., "A Logical Appraisal of Operationalism," in *Aspects of Scientific Explanation* (New York: 1965).

Hempel, C. G., "A Theoretician's Dilemma: A Study in the Logic of Theory Construction," in *Aspects of Scientific Explanation* (New York: 1965).

Hempel, C. G. and P. Oppenheim, "Studies in the Logic of Explanation," *Philosophy of Science*, 15 (1948).

Langford, C. H., *Review in The Journal of Symbolic Logic*, 6 (1941), 67–68.

Lewis, C. I., *An Analysis of Knowledge and Valuation* (La Salle, Ill.: 1946).

MacCorquodale, K. and P. E. Meehl, "On a Distinction Between Hypothetical Constructs and Intervening Variables," *Psychological Review*, 55 (1948).

Margenau, H., "Methodology of Modern Physics," *Philosophy of Science*, 2 (1935).

Northrop, F. S. C., *The Logic of the Sciences and the Humanities* (New York: 1947).

O'Connor, D. J., "Some Consequences of Professor A. J. Ayer's Verification Principle," *Analysis*, 10 (1950).

Pap, A., *Elements of Analytic Philosophy* (New York: 1949).

Popper, K., *Logik der Forschung* (Vienna: 1935).

Popper, K., "A Note on Natural Laws and So-Called 'Contrary-to-Fact Conditionals'," *Mind*, 58 (1949).

Reichenbach, H., *Philosophie der Raum-Zeit-Lehre* (Berlin: 1928).

Reichenbach, H., *Elements of Symbolic Logic* (New York: 1947).

Russell, B., *Human Knowledge* (New York: 1948).

Schlick, M., "Meaning and Verification," *Philosophical Review*, 45 (1936). Also reprinted in Feigl, H. and W. Sellars, eds. *Readings in Philosophical Analysis* (New York: 1949).

Spence, Kenneth W., "The Nature of Theory Construction in Contemporary Psychology," *Psychological Review*, 51 (1944).

3 Two Dogmas of Empiricism

W. V. QUINE

Modern empiricism has been conditioned in large part by two dogmas.[1] One is a belief in some fundamental cleavage between truths which are *analytic,* or grounded in meanings independently of matters of fact, and truths which are *synthetic,* or grounded in fact. The other dogma is *reductionism*: the belief that each meaningful statement is equivalent to some logical construct upon terms which refer to immediate experience. Both dogmas, I shall argue, are ill-founded. One effect of abandoning them is, as we shall see, a blurring of the supposed boundary between speculative metaphysics and natural science. Another effect is a shift toward pragmatism.

I. BACKGROUND FOR ANALYTICITY

Kant's cleavage between analytic and synthetic truths was foreshadowed in Hume's distinction between relations of ideas and matters of fact, and in Leibniz's distinction between truths of reason and truths of fact. Leibniz spoke of the truths of reason as true in all possible worlds. Picturesqueness aside, this is to say that the truths of reason are those which could not possibly be false. In the same vein we hear analytic statements defined as statements whose denials are self-contradictory. But this definition has small explanatory value; for the notion of self-contradictoriness, in the quite broad sense needed for this definition of analyticity, stands in exactly the same need of clarification as does the notion of analyticity itself.[2] The two notions are the two sides of a single dubious coin.

Kant conceived of an analytic statement as one that attributes to its subject no more than is already conceptually contained in the subject. This formulation has two shortcomings: it limits itself to statements of subject-predicate form, and it appeals to a notion of containment which is left at a metaphorical level. But Kant's intent, evident more from the use he makes of the notion of analyticity than from his definition of it, can be restated thus: a statement is analytic when it is true by virtue of meanings and independently of fact. Pursuing this line, let us examine the concept of *meaning* which is presupposed.

We must observe to begin with that meaning is not to be identified with naming, or reference. Consider Frege's example of "Evening Star" and "Morning Star." Understood not merely as a recurrent evening apparition but as a body, the Evening Star is the planet Venus, and the Morning Star is the same. The two singular terms *name* the same thing. But the meanings must be treated as distinct, since the identity "Evening Star = Morning Star" is a statement of fact established by astronomical observation. If "Evening Star" and "Morning Star" were alike in meaning, the identity "Evening Star = Morning Star" would be analytic.

Again there is Russell's example of "Scott" and "the author of *Waverley*." Analysis of the

W. V. Quine, "Two Dogmas of Empiricism." *Philosophical Review* 60 (1951).

meaning of words was by no means sufficient to reveal to George IV that the person named by these two singular terms was one and the same.

The distinction between meaning and naming is no less important at the level of abstract terms. The terms '9' and 'the number of planets' name one and the same abstract entity but presumably must be regarded as unlike in meaning; for astronomical observation was needed, and not mere reflection on meanings, to determine the sameness of the entity in question.

Thus far we have been considering singular terms. With general terms, or predicates, the situation is somewhat different but parallel. Whereas a singular term purports to name an entity, abstract or concrete, a general term does not; but a general term is *true* of an entity, or of each of many, or of none. The class of all entities of which a general term is true is called the *extension* of the term. Now paralleling the contrast between the meaning of a singular term and the entity named, we must distinguish equally between the meaning of a general term and its extension. The general terms "creature with a heart" and "creature with a kidney," e.g., are perhaps alike in extension but unlike in meaning.

Confusion of meaning with extension, in the case of general terms, is less common than confusion of meaning with naming in the case of singular terms. It is indeed a commonplace in philosophy to oppose intension (or meaning) to extension, or, in a variant vocabulary, connotation to denotation.

The Aristotelian notion of essence was the forerunner, no doubt, of the modern notion of intension or meaning. For Aristotle it was essential in men to be rational, accidental to be two-legged. But there is an important difference between this attitude and the doctrine of meaning. From the latter point of view it may indeed be conceded (if only for the sake of argument) that rationality is involved in the meaning of the word "man" while two-leggedness is not; but two-leggedness may at the same time be viewed as involved in the meaning of "biped" while rationality is not. Thus from the point of view of the doctrine of meaning it makes no sense to say of the actual individual, who is at once a man and a biped, that his rationality is essential and his two-leggedness accidental or vice versa.

Things had essences, for Aristotle, but only linguistic forms have meanings. Meaning is what essence becomes when it is divorced from the object of reference and wedded to the word.

For the theory of meaning a conspicuous question is the nature of its objects: what sort of things are meanings? They are evidently intended to be ideas, somehow—mental ideas for some semanticists, Platonic ideas for others. Objects of either sort are so elusive, not to say debatable, that there seems little hope of erecting a fruitful science about them. It is not even clear, granted meanings, when we have two and when we have one; it is not clear when linguistic forms should be regarded as *synonymous*, or alike in meaning, and when they should not. If a standard of synonymy should be arrived at, we may reasonably expect that the appeal to meanings as entities will not have played a very useful part in the enterprise.

A felt need for meant entities may derive from an earlier failure to appreciate that meaning and reference are distinct. Once the theory of meaning is sharply separated from the theory of reference, it is a short step to recognizing as the business of the theory of meaning simply the synonymy of linguistic forms and the analyticity of statements; meanings themselves, as obscure intermediary entities, may well be abandoned.

The description of analyticity as truth by virtue of meanings started us off in pursuit of a concept of meaning. Bun now we have abandoned the thought of any special realm of entities called meanings. So the problem of analyticity confronts us anew.

Statements which are analytic by general philosophical acclaim are not, indeed, far to seek. They fall into two classes. Those of the first class, which may be called *logically true,* are typified by:

(1) No unmarried man is married.

The relevant feature of this example is that it not merely is true as it stands, but remains true under any and all reinterpretations of "man" and "married." If we suppose a prior inventory of *logical* particles, comprising "no," "un-," "not," "if," "then," "and," etc., then in general a logical truth is a statement which is true and remains true under all reinterpretations of its components other than the logical particles.

But there is also a second class of analytic statements, typified by:

(2) No bachelor is married.

The characteristic of such a statement is that it can be turned into a logical truth by putting synonyms for synonyms; thus (2) can be turned into (1) by putting "unmarried man" for its synonym "bachelor." We still lack a proper characterization of this second class of analytic statements, and therewith of analyticity generally, inasmuch as we have had in the above description to lean on a notion of "synonymy' which is no less in need of clarification than analyticity itself.

In recent years Carnap has tended to explain analyticity by appeal to what he calls state-descriptions.[3] A state-description is any exhaustive assignment of truth values to the atomic, or noncompound, statements of the language. All other statements of the language are, Carnap assumes, built up of their component clauses by means of the familiar logical devices, in such a way that the truth value of any complex statement is fixed for each state-description by specifiable logical laws. A statement is then explained as analytic when it comes out true under every state description. This account is an adaptation of Leibniz's "true in all possible worlds." But note that this version of analyticity serves its purpose only if the atomic statements of the language are, unlike "John is a bachelor" and "John is married," mutually independent. Otherwise there would be a state-description which assigned truth to "John is a bachelor" and falsity to "John is married," and consequently "All bachelors are married" would turn out synthetic rather than analytic under the proposed criterion. Thus the criterion of analyticity in terms of state-descriptions serves only for languages devoid of extralogical synonym-pairs, such as "bachelor" and "unmarried man"—synonym-pairs of the type which give rise to the "second class" of analytic statements. The criterion in terms of state-descriptions is a reconstruction at best of logical truth, not of analyticity.

I do not mean to suggest that Carnap is under any illusions on this point. His simplified model language with its state-descriptions is aimed primarily not at the general problem of analyticity but at another purpose, the clarification of probability and induction. Our problem, however, is analyticity; and here the major difficulty lies not in the first class of analytic statements, the logical truths, but rather in the second class, which depends on the notion of synonymy.

II. DEFINITION

There are those who find it soothing to say that the analytic statements of the second class reduce to those of the first class, the logical truths, by *definition*; "bachelor," for example, is *defined* as "unmarried man." But how do we find that "bachelor" is defined as "unmarried man"? Who defined it thus, and when? Are we to appeal to the nearest dictionary, and accept the lexicographer's formulation as law? Clearly this would be to put the cart before the horse. The lexicographer is an empirical scientist, whose business is the recording of antecedent facts; and if he glosses "bachelor" as "unmarried man" it is because of his belief that there is a relation of synonymy between those forms, implicit in general or preferred usage prior to his own work. The notion of synonymy presupposed here has still to be clarified, presumably in terms relating to linguistic behavior. Certainly the "definition" which is the lexicographer's report of an observed synonymy cannot be taken as the ground of the synonymy.

Definition is not, indeed, an activity exclusively of philologists. Philosophers and scientists frequently have occasion to "define" a recondite term by paraphrasing it into terms of a more familiar vocabulary. But ordinarily such a definition, like the philologist's, is pure lexicography, affirming a relation of synonymy antecedent to the exposition in hand.

Just what it means to affirm synonymy, just what the interconnections may be which are necessary and sufficient in order that two linguistic forms be properly describable as synonymous, is far from clear; but, whatever these interconnections may be, ordinarily they are grounded in usage. Definitions reporting selected instances of synonymy come then as reports upon usage.

There is also, however, a variant type of definitional activity which does not limit itself to the reporting of pre-existing synonymies. I have in mind what Carnap calls *explication*—an activity to which philosophers are given, and scientists also in their more philosophical moments. In explication the purpose is not merely to paraphrase the definiendum into an outright synonym, but actually to improve upon the definiendum by refining or supplementing its meaning. But even explication, though not merely reporting a pre-existing synonymy between definiendum and definiens, does rest nevertheless on *other* pre-existing synonymies. The matter may be viewed as follows. Any word worth explicating has some contexts which, as wholes, are clear and precise enough to be useful; and the purpose of explication is to preserve the usage of these favored contexts while sharpening the usage of other contexts. In order that a given definition be suitable for purposes of explication, therefore, what is required is not that the definiendum in its antecedent usage be synonymous with the definiens, but just that each of these favored contexts of the definiendum, taken as a whole in its antecedent usage, be synonymous with the corresponding context of the definiens.

Two alternative definientia may be equally appropriate for the purposes of a given task of explication and yet not be synonymous with each other; for they may serve interchangeably within the favored contexts but diverge elsewhere. By cleaving to one of these definientia rather than the other, a definition of explicative kind generates, by fiat, a relation of synonymy between definiendum and definiens which did not hold before. But such a definition still owes its explicative function, as seen, to pre-existing synonymies.

There does, however, remain still an extreme sort of definition which does not hark back to prior synonymies at all: namely, the explicitly conventional introduction of novel notations for purposes of sheer abbreviation. Here the definiendum becomes synonymous with the definiens simply because it has been created expressly for the purpose of being synonymous with the definiens. Here we have a really transparent case of synonymy created by definition; would that all species of synonymy were as intelligible. For the rest, definition rests on synonymy rather than explaining it.

The word "definition" has come to have a dangerously reassuring sound, owing no doubt to its frequent occurrence in logical and mathematical writings. We shall do well to digress now into a brief appraisal of the role of definition in formal work.

In logical and mathematical systems either of two mutually antagonistic types of economy may be striven for, and each has its peculiar practical utility. On the one hand we may seek economy of practical expression—ease and brevity in the statement of multifarious relations. This sort of economy calls usually for distinctive concise notations for a wealth of concepts. Second, however, and oppositely, we may seek economy in grammar and vocabulary; we may try to find a minimum of basic concepts such that, once a distinctive notation has been appropriated to each of them, it becomes possible to express any desired further concept by mere combination and iteration of our basic notations. This second sort of economy is impractical in one way, since a poverty in basic idioms tends to a necessary lengthening of discourse. But it is practical in another way: it greatly simplifies theoretical discourse *about* the language, through minimizing the terms and the forms of construction wherein the language consists.

Both sorts of economy, though prima facie incompatible, are valuable in their separate ways. The custom has consequently arisen of combining both sorts of economy by forging in effect two languages, the one a part of the other. The inclusive language, though redundant in grammar and vocabulary, is economical in message lengths, while the part, called primitive notation, is economical in grammar and vocabulary. Whole and part are correlated by rules of translation whereby each idiom not in primitive notation is equated to some complex built up of primitive notation. These rules of translation are the so-called *definitions* which appear in formalized systems. They are best viewed not as adjuncts to one language but as correlations between two languages, the one a part of the other.

But these correlations are not arbitrary. They are supposed to show how the primitive notations can accomplish all purposes, save brevity and convenience, of the redundant language. Hence the definiendum and its definiens may be expected, in each case, to be related in one or another of the three ways lately noted. The definiens may be a faithful paraphrase of the definiendum into the narrower notation, preserving a direct synonymy as of antecedent usage; or the definiens may, in the spirit of explication, improve upon the antecedent usage of the definiendum; or finally, the definiendum may be a newly created notation, newly endowed with meaning here and now.

In formal and informal work alike, thus, we find that definition—except in the extreme case of the explicitly conventional introduction of new notations—hinges on prior relations of synonymy. Recognizing then that the notion of definition does not hold the key to synonymy and analyticity, let us look further into synonymy and say no more of definition.

III. INTERCHANGEABILITY

A natural suggestion, deserving close examination, is that the synonymy of two linguistic forms consists simply in their interchangeability in all contexts without change of truth value—interchangeability, in Leibniz's phrase, *salva veritate*. Note that synonyms so conceived need not even be free from vagueness, as long as the vaguenesses match.

But it is not quite true that the synonyms "bachelor" and "unmarried man" are everywhere interchangeable *salva veritate*. Truths which become false under substitution of "unmarried man" for "bachelor" are easily constructed with the help of "bachelor of arts" or "bachelor's buttons"; also with the help of quotation, thus:

"Bachelor" has less than ten letters.

Such counterinstances can, however, perhaps be set aside by treating the phrases "bachelor of arts" and "bachelor's buttons" and the quotation "bachelor" each as a single indivisible word and then stipulating that the interchangeability *salva veritate* which is to be the touchstone of synonymy is not supposed to apply to fragmentary occurrences inside of a word. This account of synonymy, supposing it acceptable on other counts, has indeed the drawback of appealing to a prior conception of 'word' which can be counted on to present difficulties of formulation in its turn. Nevertheless some progress might be claimed in having reduced the problem of synonymy to a problem of wordhood. Let us pursue this line a bit, taking 'word' for granted.

The question remains whether interchangeability *salva veritate* (apart from occurrences within words) is a strong enough condition for synonymy, or whether, on the contrary, some heteronymous expressions might be thus interchangeable. Now let us be clear that we are not concerned here with synonymy in the sense of complete identity in psychological associations or poetic quality; indeed no two expressions are synonymous in such a sense. We are concerned only with what may be called *cognitive* synonymy. Just what this is cannot be said without successfully finishing the present study; but we know something about it from the need which arose for it in connection with analyticity in Section I. The sort of synonymy needed there was merely such that any analytic statement could be turned into a logical truth by putting synonyms for synonyms. Turning the tables and assuming analyticity, indeed, we could explain cognitive synonymy of terms as follows (keeping to the familiar example): to say that "bachelor" and "unmarried man" are cognitively synonymous is to say no more nor less than that the statement:

(3) All and only bachelors are unmarried men

is analytic.[4]

What we need is an account of cognitive synonymy not presupposing analyticity—if we are to explain analyticity conversely with help of cognitive synonymy as undertaken in Section I. And indeed such an independent account of cognitive synonymy is at present up for consideration, namely, interchangeability *salva veritate* everywhere except within words. The question before us, to resume the thread at last, is whether such interchangeability is a sufficient condition for cognitive synonymy. We can quickly assure ourselves that it is, by examples of the following sort. The statement:

(4) Necessarily all and only bachelors are bachelors

is evidently true, even supposing "necessarily" so narrowly construed as to be truly applicable only to analytic statements. Then, if "bachelor" and "unmarried man" are interchangeable *salva veritate*, the result:

(5) Necessarily all and only bachelors are unmarried men

of putting "unmarried man" for an occurrence of "bachelor" in (4) must, like (4), be true. But to say that (5) is true is to say that (3) is analytic, and hence that "bachelor" and "unmarried man" are cognitively synonymous.

Let us see what there is about the above argument that gives it its air of hocus-pocus. The condition of interchangeability *salva veritate* varies in its force with variations in the richness of the language at hand. The above argument supposes we are working with a language rich enough to contain the adverb "necessarily," this adverb being so construed as to yield truth when and only when applied to an analytic statement. But can we condone a language which contains such an adverb? Does the adverb really make sense? To suppose that it does is to suppose that we have already made satisfactory sense of "analytic." Then what are we so hard at work on right now?

Our argument is not flatly circular, but something like it. It has the form, figuratively speaking, of a closed curve in space.

Interchangeability *salva veritate* is meaningless until relativized to a language whose extent is specified in relevant respects. Suppose now we consider a language containing just the following materials. There is an indefinitely large stock of one- and many-place predicates, mostly having to do with extralogical subject matter. The rest of the language is logical. The atomic sentences consist each of a predicate followed by one or more variables; and the complex sentences are built up of atomic ones by truth functions and quantification. In effect such a language enjoys the benefits also of descriptions and class names and indeed singular terms generally, these being contextually definable in known ways. Such a language can be adequate to classical mathematics and indeed to scientific discourse generally, except insofar as the latter involves debatable devices such as modal adverbs and countrary-to-fact conditionals. Now a language of this type is *extensional*, in this sense: any two predicates which *agree extensionally* (i.e., are true of the same objects) are interchangeable *salva veritate*.[5]

In an extensional language, therefore, inter-changeability *salva veritate* is no assurance of cognitive synonymy of the desired type. That "bachelor" and "unmarried man" are interchangeable *salva veritate* in an extensional language assures us of no more than that (3) is true. There is no assurance here that the extensional agreement of "bachelor" and "unmarried man" rests on meaning rather than merely on accidental matters of fact, as does the extensional agreement of "creature with a heart" and "creature with kidneys."

For most purposes extensional agreement is the nearest approximation to synonymy we need care about. But the fact remains that extensional agreement falls far short of cognitive synonymy of the type required for explaining analyticity in the manner of Section I. The type of cognitive synonymy required there is such as to equate the synonymy of "bachelor" and "unmarried man" with the analyticity of (3), not merely with the truth of (3).

So we must recognize that interchangeability *salva veritate,* if construed in relation to an extensional language, is not a sufficient condition of cognitive synonymy in the sense needed for deriving analyticity in the manner of Section I. If a language contains an intensional adverb "necessarily" in the sense lately noted, or other particles to the same effect, then interchangeability *salva veritate* in such a language does afford a sufficient condition of cognitive synonymy; but such a language is intelligible only in so far as the notion of analyticity is already understood in advance.

The effort to explain cognitive synonymy first, for the sake of deriving analyticity from it afterward as in Section I, is perhaps the wrong approach. Instead we might try explaining analyticity somehow without appeal to cognitive synonymy. Afterward we could doubtless derive cognitive synonymy from analyticity satisfactorily enough if desired. We have seen that cognitive synonymy of "bachelor" and "unmarried man" can be explained as analyticity of (3). The same explanation works for any pair of one-place predicates, of course, and it can be extended in obvious fashion to many-place predicates. Other syntactical categories can also be accommodated in fairly parallel fashion. Singular terms may be said to be cognitively synonymous when the statement of identity formed by putting "=" between them is analytic. Statements may be said simply to be cognitively synonymous when their biconditional (the result of joining them by "if and only if") is analytic.[6] If we care to lump all categories into a single formulation, at the expense of assuming again the notion of 'word' which was appealed to early in this section, we can describe any two linguistic forms as cognitively synonymous when the two forms are interchangeable (apart from occurrences within 'words') *salva* (no longer *veritate* but) *analyticitate*. Certain technical questions arise, indeed, over cases of ambiguity or homonymy; let us not pause for them, however, for we are already digressing. Let us rather turn our backs on the problem of synonymy and address ourselves anew to that of analyticity.

IV. SEMANTICAL RULES

Analyticity at first seemed most naturally definable by appeal to a realm of meanings. On refinement, the appeal to meanings gave way to an appeal to synonymy or definition. But definition turned out to be a will-o'-the-wisp, and synonymy turned out to be best understood only by dint of a prior appeal to analyticity itself. So we are back at the problem of analyticity.

I do not know whether the statement "Everything green is extended" is analytic. Now does my indecision over this example really betray an incomplete understanding, an incomplete grasp of the 'meanings', of "green" and "extended"? I think not. The trouble is not with "green" or "extended," but with "analytic."

It is often hinted that the difficulty in separating analytic statements from synthetic ones in ordinary language is due to the vagueness of ordinary language and that the distinction is clear when we have a precise artificial language with explicit 'semantical rules'. This, however, as I shall now attempt to show, is a confusion.

The notion of analyticity about which we are worrying is a purported relation between statements and languages: a statement S is said to be *analytic for* a language L, and the problem is to make sense of this relation generally, that is, for variable "S" and "L." The point that I want to make is that the gravity of this problem is not

perceptibly less for artificial languages than for natural ones. The problem of making sense of the idiom "S is analytic for L," with variable "S" and "L," retains its stubbornness even if we limit the range of the variable "L" to artificial languages. Let me now try to make this point evident.

For artificial languages and semantical rules we look naturally to the writings of Carnap. His semantical rules take various forms, and to make my point I shall have to distinguish certain of the forms. Let us suppose, to begin with, an artificial language L_0 whose semantical rules have the form explicitly of a specification, by recursion or otherwise, of all the analytic statements of L_0. The rules tell us that such and such statements, and only those, are the analytic statements of L_0. Now here the difficulty is simply that the rules contain the word "analytic," which we do not understand! We understand what expressions the rules attribute analyticity to, but we do not understand what the rules attribute to those expressions. In short, before we can understand a rule which begins "A statement S is analytic for language L_0 if and only if . . . ," we must understand the general relative term "analytic for"; we must understand "S is analytic for L" where "S" and "L" are variables.

Alternatively we may, indeed, view the so-called rule as a conventional definition of a new simple symbol "analytic-for-L_0," which might better be written untendentiously as "K" so as not to seem to throw light on the interesting word "analytic." Obviously any number of classes K, M, N, etc. of statements of L_0 can be specified for various purposes or for no purpose; what does it mean to say that K, as against M, N, etc., is the class of the 'analytic' statements of L_0?

By saying what statements are analytic for L_0 we explain "analytic-for-L_0" but not "analytic," not "analytic for." We do not begin to explain the idiom "S is analytic for L" with variable "S" and "L," even if we are content to limit the range of "L" to the realm of artificial languages.

Actually we do know enough about the intended significance of "analytic" to know that analytic statements are supposed to be true. Let us then turn to a second form of semantical rule, which says not that such and such statements are analytic but simply that such and such statements are included among the truths. Such a rule is not subject to the criticism of containing the un-understood word "analytic"; and we may grant for the sake of argument that there is no difficulty over the broader term "true." A semantical rule of this second type, a rule of truth, is not supposed to specify all the truths of the language; it merely stipulates, recursively or otherwise, a certain multitude of statements which, along with others unspecified, are to count as true. Such a rule may be conceded to be quite clear. Derivatively, afterward, analyticity can be demarcated thus: a statement is analytic if it is (not merely true but) true according to the semantical rule.

Still there is really no progress. Instead of appealing to an unexplained word "analytic," we are now appealing to an unexplained phrase "semantical rule." Not every true statement which says that the statements of some class are true can count as a semantical rule—otherwise *all* truths would be 'analytic' in the sense of being true according to semantical rules. Semantical rules are distinguishable, apparently, only by the fact of appearing on a page under the heading "Semantical Rules"; and this heading is itself then meaningless.

We can say indeed that a statement is *analytic-for-L_0* if and only if it is true according to such and such specifically appended 'semantical rules', but then we find ourselves back at essentially the same case which was originally discussed: "S is analytic-for-L_0 if and only if. . . ." Once we seek to explain "S is analytic for L" generally for variable "L" (even allowing limitation of "L" to artificial languages), the explanation "true according to the semantical rules of L" is unavailing; for the relative term "semantical rule of" is as much in need of clarification, at least, as "analytic for."

It might conceivably be protested that an artificial language L (unlike a natural one) is a language in the ordinary sense *plus* a set of explicit semantical rules—the whole constituting, let us say, an ordered pair; and that the semantical rules of L then are specifiable simply as the second component of the pair L. But, by the same token and more simply, we might construe an artificial language L outright as an ordered pair whose second component is the class of its analytic statements; and then the analytic state-

ments of L become specifiable simply as the statements in the second component of L. Or better still, we might just stop tugging at our bootstraps altogether.

Not all the explanations of analyticity known to Carnap and his readers have been covered explicitly in the above considerations, but the extension to other forms is not hard to see. Just one additional factor should be mentioned which sometimes enters: sometimes the semantical rules are in effect rules of translation into ordinary language, in which case the analytic statements of the artificial language are in effect recognized as such from the analyticity of their specified translations in ordinary language. Here certainly there can be no thought of an illumination of the problem of analyticity from the side of the artificial language.

From the point of view of the problem of analyticity the notion of an artificial language with semantical rules is a *feu follet par excellence*. Semantical rules determining the analytic statements of an artificial language are of interest only in so far as we already understand the notion of analyticity; they are of no help in gaining this understanding.

Appeal to hypothetical languages of an artificially simple kind could conceivably be useful in clarifying analyticity, if the mental or behavioral or cultural factors relevant to analyticity—whatever they may be—were somehow sketched into the simplified model. But a model which takes analyticity merely as an irreducible character is unlikely to throw light on the problem of explicating analyticity.

It is obvious that truth in general depends on both language and extralinguistic fact. The statement "Brutus killed Caesar" would be false if the world had been different in certain ways, but it would also be false if the word "killed" happened rather to have the sense of "begat." Hence the temptation to suppose in general that the truth of a statement is somehow analyzable into a linguistic component and a factual component. Given this supposition, it next seems reasonable that in some statements the factual component should be null; and these are the analytic statements. But, for all its a priori reasonableness, a boundary between analytic and synthetic statements simply has not been drawn.

That there is such a distinction to be drawn at all is an unempirical dogma of empiricists, a metaphysical article of faith.

V. THE VERIFICATION THEORY AND REDUCTIONISM

In the course of these somber reflections we have taken a dim view first of the notion of meaning, then of the notion of cognitive synonymy, and finally of the notion of analyticity. But what, it may be asked, of the verification theory of meaning? This phrase has established itself so firmly as a catchword of empiricism that we should be very unscientific indeed not to look beneath it for a possible key to the problem of meaning and the associated problems.

The verification theory of meaning, which has been conspicuous in the literature from Peirce onward, is that the meaning of a statement is the method of empirically confirming or infirming it. An analytic statement is that limiting case which is confirmed no matter what.

As urged in Section I, we can as well pass over the question of meanings as entities and move straight to sameness of meaning, or synonymy. Then what the verification theory says is that statements are synonymous if and only if they are alike in point of method of empirical confirmation or infirmation.

This is an account of cognitive synonymy not of linguistic forms generally, but of statements.[7] However, from the concept of synonymy of statements we could derive the concept of synonymy for other linguistic forms, by considerations somewhat similar to those at the end of Section III. Assuming the notion of 'word', indeed, we could explain any two forms as synonymous when the putting of the one form for an occurrence of the other in any statement (apart from occurrences within 'words') yields a synonymous statement. Finally, given the concept of synonymy thus for linguistic forms generally, we could define analyticity in terms of synonymy and logical truth as in Section I. For that matter, we could define analyticity more simply in terms of just synonymy of statements together with logical truth; it is not necessary to appeal to synonymy of linguistic forms other than statements. For a statement may be described as ana-

lytic simply when it is synonymous with a logically true statement.

So, if the verification theory can be accepted as an adequate account of statement synonymy, the notion of analyticity is saved after all. However, let us reflect. Statement synonymy is said to be likeness of method of empirical confirmation or infirmation. Just what are these methods which are to be compared for likeness? What, in other words, is the nature of the relation between a statement and the experiences which contribute to or detract from its confirmation?

The most naive view of the relation is that it is one of direct report. This is *radical reductionism*. Every meaningful statement is held to be translatable into a statement (true or false) about immediate experience. Radical reductionism, in one form or another, well antedates the verification theory of meaning explicitly so called. Thus Locke and Hume held that every idea must either originate directly in sense experience or else be compounded of ideas thus originating; and taking a hint from Tooke[8] we might rephrase this doctrine in semantical jargon by saying that a term, to be significant at all, must be either a name of a sense datum or a compound of such names or an abbreviation of such a compound. So stated, the doctrine remains ambiguous as between sense data as sensory events and sense data as sensory qualities; and it remains vague as to the admissible ways of compounding. Moreover, the doctrine is unnecessarily and intolerably restrictive in the term-by-term critique which it imposes. More reasonably, and without yet exceeding the limits of what I have called radical reductionism, we may take full statements as our significant units—thus demanding that our statements as wholes be translatable into sense-datum language, but not that they be translatable term by term.

This emendation would unquestionably have been welcome to Locke and Hume and Tooke, but historically it had to await two intermediate developments. One of these developments was the increasing emphasis on verification or confirmation, which came with the explicitly so-called verification theory of meaning. The objects of verification or confirmation being statements, this emphasis gave the statement an ascendency over the word or term as unit of significant discourse. The other development, consequent upon the first, was Russell's discovery of the concept of incomplete symbols defined in use.

Radical reductionism, conceived now with statements as units, set itself the task of specifying a sense-datum language and showing how to translate the rest of significant discourse, statement by statement, into it. Carnap embarked on this project in the *Aufbau*.[9]

The language which Carnap adopted as his starting point was not a sense-datum language in the narrowest conceivable sense, for it included also the notations of logic, up through higher set theory. In effect it included the whole language of pure mathematics. The ontology implicit in it (that is, the range of values of its variables) embraced not only sensory events but classes, classes of classes, and so on. Empiricists there are who would boggle at such prodigality. Carnap's starting point is very parsimonious, however, in its extralogical or sensory part. In a series of constructions in which he exploits the resources of modern logic with much ingenuity, he succeeds in defining a wide array of important additional sensory concepts which, but for his constructions, one would not have dreamed were definable on so slender a basis. Carnap was the first empiricist who, not content with asserting the reducibility of science to terms of immediate experience, took serious steps toward carrying out the reduction.

Even supposing Carnap's starting point satisfactory, his constructions were, as he himself stressed, only a fragment of the full program. The construction of even the simplest statements about the physical world was left in a sketchy state. Carnap's suggestions on this subject were, despite their sketchiness, very suggestive. He explained spatio-temporal point-instants as quadruples of real numbers and envisaged assignment of sense qualities to point-instants according to certain canons. Roughly summarized, the plan was that qualities should be assigned to point-instants in such a way as to achieve the laziest world compatible with our experience. The principle of least action was to be our guide in constructing a world from experience.

Carnap did not seem to recognize, however, that his treatment of physical objects fell short of reduction not merely through sketchiness,

but in principle. Statements of the form "Quality q is at point-instant $x;y;z;t$" were, according to his canons, to be apportioned truth values in such a way as to maximize and minimize certain overall features, and with growth of experience the truth values were to be progressively revised in the same spirit. I think this is a good schematization (deliberately oversimplified, to be sure) of what science really does; but it provides no indication, not even the sketchiest, of how a statement of the form "Quality q is at $x;y;z;t$" could ever be translated into Carnap's initial language of sense data and logic. The connective "is at" remains an added undefined connective; the canons counsel us in its use but not in its elimination.

Carnap seems to have appreciated this point afterward; for in his later writings he abandoned all notion of the translatability of statements about the physical world into statements about immediate experience. Reductionism in its radical form has long since ceased to figure in Carnap's philosophy.

But the dogma of reductionism has, in a subtler and more tenuous form, continued to influence the thought of empiricists. The notion lingers that to each statement, or each synthetic statement, there is associated a unique range of possible sensory events such that the occurrence of any of them would add to the likelihood of truth of the statement, and that there is associated also another unique range of possible sensory events whose occurrence would detract from that likelihood. This notion is of course implicit in the verification theory of meaning.

The dogma of reductionism survives in the supposition that each statement, taken in isolation from its fellows, can admit of confirmation or infirmation at all. My countersuggestion, issuing essentially from Carnap's doctrine of the physical world in the *Aufbau*, is that our statements about the external world face the tribunal of sense experience not individually but only as a corporate body.[10]

The dogma of reductionism, even in its attenuated form, is intimately connected with the other dogma—that there is a cleavage between the analytic and the synthetic. We have found ourselves led, indeed, from the latter problem to the former through the verification theory of meaning. More directly, the one dogma clearly supports the other in this way: as long as it is taken to be significant in general to speak of the confirmation and infirmation of a statement, it seems significant to speak also of a limiting kind of statement which is vacuously confirmed, *ipso facto,* come what may; and such a statement is analytic.

The two dogmas are, indeed, at root identical. We lately reflected that in general the truth of statements does obviously depend both upon language and upon extralinguistic fact; and we noted that this obvious circumstance carries in its train, not logically but all too naturally, a feeling that the truth of a statement is somehow analyzable into a linguistic component and a factual component. The factual component must, if we are empiricists, boil down to a range of confirmatory experiences. In the extreme case where the linguistic component is all that matters, a true statement is analytic. But I hope we are now impressed with how stubbornly the distinction between analytic and synthetic has resisted any straightforward drawing. I am impressed also, apart from prefabricated examples of black and white balls in an urn, with how baffling the problem has always been of arriving at any explicit theory of the empirical confirmation of a synthetic statement. My present suggestion is that it is nonsense, and the root of much nonsense, to speak of a linguistic component and a factual component in the truth of any individual statement. Taken collectively, science has its double dependence upon language and experience; but this duality is not significantly traceable into the statements of science taken one by one.

Russell's concept of definition in use was, as remarked, an advance over the impossible term-by-term empiricism of Locke and Hume. The statement, rather than the term, came with Frege to be recognized as the unit accountable to an empiricist critique. But what I am now urging is that even in taking the statement as unit we have drawn our grid too finely. The unit of empirical significance is the whole of science.

VI. EMPIRICISM WITHOUT THE DOGMAS

The totality of our so-called knowledge or beliefs, from the most casual matters of geography and history to the profoundest laws of atomic physics or even of pure mathematics and logic, is a man-made fabric which impinges on experience only along the edges. Or, to change the figure, total science is like a field of force whose boundary conditions are experience. A conflict with experience at the periphery occasions readjustments in the interior of the field. Truth values have to be redistributed over some of our statements. Reevaluation of some statements entails reevaluation of others, because of their logical interconnections—the logical laws being in turn simply certain further statements of the system, certain further elements of the field. Having reevaluated one statement we must reevaluate some others, which may be statements logically connected with the first or may be the statements of logical connections themselves. But the total field is so underdetermined by its boundary conditions, experience, that there is much latitude of choice as to what statements to reevaluate in the light of any single contrary experience. No particular experiences are linked with any particular statements in the interior of the field, except indirectly through considerations of equilibrium affecting the field as a whole.

If this view is right, it is misleading to speak of the empirical content of an individual statement—especially if it is a statement at all remote from the experiential periphery of the field. Furthermore it becomes folly to seek a boundary between synthetic statements, which hold contingently on experience, and analytic statements, which hold come what may. Any statement can be held true come what may, if we make drastic enough adjustments elsewhere in the system. Even a statement very close to the periphery can be held true in the face of recalcitrant experience by pleading hallucination or by amending certain statements of the kind called logical laws. Conversely, by the same token, no statement is immune to revision. Revision even of the logical law of the excluded middle has been proposed as a means of simplifying quantum mechanics; and what difference is there in principle between such a shift and the shift whereby Kepler superseded Ptolemy, or Einstein Newton, or Darwin Aristotle?

For vividness I have been speaking in terms of varying distances from a sensory periphery.

Let me try now to clarify this notion without metaphor. Certain statements, though *about* physical objects and not sense experience, seem peculiarly germane to sense experience—and in a selective way: some statements to some experiences, others to others. Such statements, especially germane to particular experiences, I picture as near the periphery. But in this relation of 'germaneness' I envisage nothing more than a loose association reflecting the relative likelihood, in practice, of our choosing one statement rather than another for revision in the event of recalcitrant experience. For example, we can imagine recalcitrant experiences to which we would surely be inclined to accommodate our system by reevaluating just the statement that there are brick houses on Elm Street, together with related statements on the same topic. We can imagine other recalcitrant experiences to which we would be inclined to accommodate our system by reevaluating just the statement that there are no centaurs, along with kindred statements. A recalcitrant experience can, I have urged, be accommodated by any of various alternative reevaluations in various alternative quarters of the total system; but, in the cases which we are now imagining, our natural tendency to disturb the total system as little as possible would lead us to focus our revisions upon these specific statements concerning brick houses or centaurs. These statements are felt, therefore, to have a sharper empirical reference than highly theoretical statements of physics or logic or ontology. The latter statements may be thought of as relatively centrally located within the total network, meaning merely that little preferential connection with any particular sense data obtrudes itself.

As an empiricist I continue to think of the conceptual scheme of science as a tool, ultimately, for predicting future experience in the light of past experience. Physical objects are conceptually imported into the situation as convenient intermediaries—not by definition in terms of experience, but simply as irreducible posits comparable, epistemologically, to the gods of Homer. Let me interject that for my part I do, qua lay physicist, believe in physical objects and not in Homer's gods; and I consider it a scientific error to believe otherwise. But in

point of epistemological footing the physical objects and the gods differ only in degree and not in kind. Both sorts of entities enter our conception only as cultural posits. The myth of physical objects is epistemologically superior to most in that it has proved more efficacious than other myths as a device for working a manageable structure into the flux of experience.

Imagine, for the sake of analogy, that we are given the rational numbers. We develop an algebraic theory for reasoning about them, but we find it inconveniently complex, because certain functions such as square root lack values for some arguments. Then it is discovered that the rules of our algebra can be much simplified by conceptually augmenting our ontology with some mythical entities, to be called irrational numbers. All we continue to be really interested in, first and last, are rational numbers; but we find that we can commonly get from one law about rational numbers to another much more quickly and simply by pretending that the irrational numbers are there too.

I think this a fair account of the introduction of irrational numbers and other extensions of the number system. The fact that the mythical status of irrational numbers eventually gave way to the Dedekind-Russell version of them as certain infinite classes of ratios is irrelevant to my analogy. That version is impossible anyway as long as reality is limited to the rational numbers and not extended to classes of them.

Now I suggest that experience is analogous to the rational numbers and that the physical objects, in analogy to the irrational numbers, are posits which serve merely to simplify our treatment of experience. The physical objects are no more reducible to experience than the irrational numbers to rational numbers, but their incorporation into the theory enables us to get more easily from one statement about experience to another.

The salient differences between the positing of physical objects and the positing of irrational numbers are, I think, just two. First, the factor of simplification is more overwhelming in the case of physical objects than in the numerical case. Second, the positing of physical objects is far more archaic, being indeed coeval, I expect, with language itself. For language is social and so depends for its development upon intersubjective reference.

Positing does not stop with macroscopic physical objects. Objects at the atomic level are posited to make the laws of macroscopic objects, and ultimately the laws of experience, simpler and more manageable; and we need not expect or demand full definition of atomic and subatomic entities in terms of macroscopic ones, any more than definition of macroscopic things in terms of sense data. Science is a continuation of common sense, and it continues the common-sense expedient of swelling ontology to simplify theory.

Physical objects, small and large, are not the only posits. Forces are another example; and indeed we are told nowadays that the boundary between energy and matter is obsolete. Moreover, the abstract entities which are the substance of mathematics—ultimately classes and classes of classes and so on up—are another posit in the same spirit. Epistemologically these are myths on the same footing with physical objects and gods, neither better nor worse except for differences in the degree to which they expedite our dealings with sense experiences.

The overall algebra of rational and irrational numbers is underdetermined by the algebra of rational numbers, but is smoother and more convenient; and it includes the algebra of rational numbers as a jagged or gerrymandered part. Total science, mathematical and natural and human, is similarly but more extremely underdetermined by experience. The edge of the system must be kept squared with experience; the rest, with all its elaborate myths or fictions, has as its objective the simplicity of laws.

Ontological questions, under this view, are on a par with questions of natural science. Consider the question whether to countenance classes as entities. This, as I have argued elsewhere,[10] is the question whether to quantify with respect to variables which take classes as values. Now Carnap has maintained[11] that this is a question not of matters of fact but of choosing a convenient language form, a convenient conceptual scheme or framework for science. With this I agree, but only on the proviso that the same be conceded regarding scientific hypotheses generally. Carnap[12] has recognized that he is able to preserve a

double standard for ontological questions and scientific hypotheses only by assuming an absolute distinction between the analytic and the synthetic; and I need not say again that this is a distinction which I reject.[12]

Some issues do, I grant, seem more a question of convenient conceptual scheme and others more a question of brute fact. The issue over there being classes seems more a question of convenient conceptual scheme; the issue over there being centaurs, or brick houses on Elm Street, seems more a question of fact. But I have been urging that this difference is only one of degree, and that it turns upon our vaguely pragmatic inclination to adjust one strand of the fabric of science rather than another in accommodating some particular recalcitrant experience. Conservatism figures in such choices, and so does the quest for simplicity.

Carnap, Lewis, and others take a pragmatic stand on the question of choosing between language forms, scientific frameworks; but their pragmatism leaves off at the imagined boundary between the analytic and the synthetic. In repudiating such a boundary I espouse a more thorough pragmatism. Each man is given a scientific heritage plus a continuing barrage of sensory stimulation; and the considerations which guide him in warping his scientific heritage to fit his continuing sensory promptings are, where rational, pragmatic.

NOTES

1. Much of this paper is devoted to a critique of analyticity which I have been urging orally and in correspondence for years past. My debt to the other participants in those discussions, notably Carnap, Church, Goodman, Tarski, and White, is large and indeterminate. White's excellent essay "The Analytic and the Synthetic: An Untenable Dualism," in *John Dewey: Philosopher of Science and Freedom* (New York, 1950), says much of what needed to be said on the topic; but in the present paper I touch on some further aspects of the problem. I am grateful to Dr. Donald L. Davidson for valuable criticism of the first draft.

2. See White, op. cit., p. 324.

3. R. Carnap, *Meaning and Necessity* (Chicago, 1947), pp. 9ff.; *Logical Foundations of Probability* (Chicago, 1950), pp. 70ff.

4. This is cognitive synonymy in a primary, broad sense. Carnap (*Meaning and Necessity*, pp. 56ff.) and Lewis (*Analysis of Knowledge and Valuation*

[La Salle, Ill., 1946], pp. 83ff.) have suggested how, once this notion is at hand, a narrower sense of cognitive synonymy which is preferable for some purposes can in turn be derived. But this special ramification of concept-building lies aside from the present purposes and must not be confused with the broad sort of cognitive synonymy here concerned.

5. See, e.g., my *Mathematical Logic* (New York, 1940; Cambridge, Mass., 1947), sec. 24, 26, 27; or *Methods of Logic* (New York, 1950), sec. 37ff.

6. The "if and only if" itself is intended in the truth functional sense. See Carnap, *Meaning and Necessity*, p. 14.

7. The doctrine can indeed be formulated with terms rather than statements as the units. Thus C. I. Lewis describes the meaning of a term as "*a criterion in mind*, by reference to which one is able to apply or refuse to apply the expression in question in the case of presented, or imagined, things or situations" (op. cit., p. 133).

8. John Horne Tooke, *The Diversions of Purley* (London, 1776; Boston, 1806), I, ch. ii.

9. R. Carnap, *Der logische Aufbau der Welt* (Berlin, 1928).

10. E.g., in "Notes on Existence and Necessity," *Journal of Philosophy*, XL (1943), 113–127.

11. Carnap, "Empiricism, Semantics, and Ontology," *Revue internationale de philosophie*, IV (1950), 20–40.

12. Op. cit., p. 32, footnote.

4

Intensional Semantics

ALONZO CHURCH

We distinguish between a *logistic system* and a *formalized language* on the basis that the former is an abstractly formulated calculus for which no interpretation is fixed, and thus has a syntax but no semantics; but the latter is a logistic system together with an assignment of meanings to its expressions.

As primitive basis of a logistic system it suffices to give, in familiar fashion: (1) The list of primitive symbols or *vocabulary* of the system (together usually with a classification of the primitive symbols into categories, which will be used in stating the formation rules and rules of inference). (2) The *formation rules,* determining which finite sequences of primitive symbols are to be *well-formed* expressions, determining certain categories of well-formed expressions, among which we shall assume that at least the category of *sentence* is included, and determining (in case *variables* are included among the primitive symbols) which occurrences of variables in a well-formed expression are *free* occurrences and which are *bound* occurrences.[1] (3) The transformation rules or *rules of inference,* by which from the *assertion* of certain sentences (the *premisses,* finite in number) a certain sentence (the *conclusion*) may be *inferred.* (4) Certain asserted sentences, the *axioms.*

In order to obtain a formalized language it is necessary to add to these *syntactical rules* of the logistic system, *semantical rules* assigning meanings (in some sense) to the well-formed expressions of the system.[2] The character of the semantical rules will depend on the theory of meaning adopted, and this in turn must be justified by the purpose which it is to serve.

Let us take it as our purpose to provide an abstract theory of the actual use of language for human communication—not a factual or historical report of what has been observed to take place, but a norm to which we may regard everyday linguistic behavior as an imprecise approximation, in the same way that e.g. elementary (applied) geometry is a norm to which we may regard as imprecise approximations the practical activity of the land-surveyor in laying out a plot of ground, or of the construction foreman in seeing that building plans are followed. We must demand of such a theory that it have a place for all observably informative kinds of communication—including such notoriously troublesome cases as belief statements, modal statements, conditions contrary to fact—or at least that it provide a (theoretically) workable substitute for them. And solutions must be available for puzzles about meaning which may arise, such as the so-called "paradox of analysis."

There exist more than one theory of meaning showing some promise of fulfilling these requirements, at least so far as the formulation

Originally published under the title "The Need for Abstract Entities," in the *American Academy of Arts and Sciences Proceedings* 80 (1951): 100–113. Reprinted by permission of the publisher and author.

and development have presently been carried. But the theory of Frege seems to recommend itself above others for its relative simplicity, naturalness, and explanatory power—or, as I would advocate, Frege's theory as modified by elimination of his somewhat problematical notion of a function (and in particular of a *Begriff*) as *ungesättigt,* and by some other changes which bring it closer to present logistic practice without loss of such essentials as the distinction of sense and denotation.

This modified Fregean theory may be roughly characterized by the tendency to minimize the category of *syncategorematic* notations—i.e., notations to which no meaning at all is ascribed in isolation but which may combine with one or more meaningful expressions to form a meaningful expression[3]—and to reduce the categories of meaningful expressions to two, (proper) *names* and *forms,* for each of which two kinds of meaning are distinguished in a parallel way.

A name, or a *constant* (as we shall also say, imitating mathematical terminology), has first its *denotation,* or that of which it is a name.[4] And each name has also a *sense*—which is perhaps more properly to be called its meaning, since it is held that complete understanding of a language involves the ability to recognize the sense of any name in the language, but does not demand any knowledge beyond this of the denotations of names. (Declarative) *sentences,* in particular, are taken as a kind of names, the denotation being the *truth-value* of the sentence, *truth* or *falsehood,* and the sense being the *proposition* which the sentence expresses.

A name is said to *denote* its denotation and to express its sense, and the sense is said to be *a concept of* the denotation. The abstract entities which serve as senses of names let us call *concepts*—although this use of the word 'concept' has no analogue in the writings of Frege, and must be carefully distinguished from Frege's use of 'Begriff'. Thus anything which is or is capable of being the sense of some name in some language, actual or possible, is a concept.[5] The terms *individual concept, function concept,* and the like are then to mean a concept which is a concept of an individual, of a function, etc. A *class concept* may be identified with a *property,*

and a *truth-value concept* (as already indicated) with a proposition.

Names are to be meaningful expressions without free variables, and expressions which are analogous to names except that they contain free variables, we call forms (a rather wide extension of the ordinary mathematical usage, here adopted for lack of a better term).[6] Each variable has a *range,* which is the class of admissible *values* of the variable.[7] And analogous to the denotation of a name, a form has a *value* for every system of admissible values of its free variables.[8]

The assignment of a value to a variable, though it is not a syntactical operation, corresponds in a certain way to the syntactical operation of substituting a constant for the variable. The denotation of the substituted constant represents the value of the variable.[9] And the sense of the substituted constant may be taken as representing a *sense-value* of the variable. Thus every variable has, besides its range, also a *sense-range,* which is the class of admissible sense-values of the variable. And analogous to the sense of a name, a form has a *sense-value* for every system of admissible sense-values of its free variables.[10]

The following principles are assumed[11]: (i) Every concept is a concept of at most one thing. (ii) Every constant has a unique concept as its sense. (iii) Every variable has a non-empty class of concepts as its sense-range. (iv) For any assignment of sense-values, one to each of the free variables of a given form, if each sense-value is admissible in the sense that it belongs to the sense-range of the corresponding variable, the form has a unique concept as its sense-value. (v) The denotation of a constant is that of which its sense is a concept. (vi) The range of a variable is the class of those things of which the members of the sense-range are concepts. (vii) If $S, s_1, s_2, \ldots, s_m$ are concepts of $A, a_1, a_2, \ldots,$ am respectively, and if S is the sense-value of a form F for the system of sense-values $s_1, s_2, \ldots, s_m$ of its free variables $x_1, x_2, \ldots, x_m,$ then the value of F for the system of values $a_1, a_2, \ldots a_m$ of $x_1, x_2, \ldots, x_m$ is $A.$ (viii) If C' is obtained from a constant C by replacing a particular occurrence of a constant c by a constant c' that has the same sense as c, then C' is a constant having the same sense as C.[12] (ix) If C′ is obtained from a constant C by replacing a particular occurrence of a constant c by a constant c′ that has the same denotation as c, then C′ is a constant having the same denotation as C.[13] (x) If C′ is obtained from a constant C by replacing a particular occurrence of a form f by a form f′ that has the same free variables as f, and if, for every admissible system of sense-values of their free variables, f and f′ have the same sense-value, then C′ is a constant having the same sense as C.[12] (xi) If C′ is obtained from a constant C by replacing a particular occurrence of a form f by a form f′ that has the same free variables as f, and if, for every system of values of their free variables which are admissible in the sense that each value belongs to the range of the corresponding variable, f and f′ have the same value, then C′ is a constant having the same denotation as C.[13] (xii) If $x_1, x_2, \ldots, x_m$ are all the distinct variables occurring (necessarily as bound variables) in a constant C, if $y_1, y_2, \ldots, y_m$ are distinct variables having the same sense-ranges as $x_1, x_2, \ldots, x_m$ respectively, and if C′ is obtained from C by substituting $y_1, y_2, \ldots, y_m$ throughout for $x_1, x_2, \ldots, x_m$ respectively, then C′ is a constant having the same sense as C. (xiii) If $x_1, x_2, \ldots, x_m$ are the distinct variables occurring in a constant C, if $y_1, y_2, \ldots, y_m$ are distinct variables having the same ranges as $x_1, x_2, \ldots, x_m$ respectively, and if C′ is obtained from C by substituting $y_1, y_2, \ldots, y_m$ throughout for $x_1, x_2, \ldots, x_m$ respectively, then C′ is a constant having the same denotation as C. (xiv) The result of substituting constants for all the free variables of a form is a constant, if the sense of each substituted constant belongs to the sense-range of the corresponding variable.[12] (xv) The sense of a constant C thus obtained by substituting constants $c_1, c_2, \ldots, c_m$ for the free variables $x_1, x_2, \ldots, x_m$ of a form F is the same as the sense-value of F when the senses of $c_1, c_2, \ldots, c_m$ are assigned as the sense-values of $x_1, x_2, \ldots, x_m$.

To these must still be added principles which are similar to (viii)-(xv), except that substitution is made in forms instead of constants, or that forms and variables as well as constants are substituted for the free variables of a form. Instead of stating these here, it may be sufficient to remark that they follow if arbitrary extensions of the language are allowed by adjoining (as prim-

itive symbols) constants which have as their senses any concepts that belong to sense-ranges of variables in the language, if the foregoing principles are assumed to hold also for such extensions of the language, and if there is assumed further: (xvi) Let an expression F contain the variables $x_1, x_2, \ldots, x_m$; and suppose that in every extension of the language of the kind just described and for every substitution of constants $c_1, c_2, \ldots, c_m$ for the variables $x_1, x_2, \ldots, x_m$ respectively, if the sense of each constant belongs to the sense-range of the corresponding variable, F becomes a constant; then F is a form having $x_1, x_2, \ldots, x_m$ as its free variables.

To those who find forbidding the array of abstract entities and principles concerning them which is here proposed, I would say that the problems which give rise to the proposal are difficult and a simpler theory is not known to be possible.[14]

To those who object to the introduction of abstract entities at all I would say that I believe that there are more important criteria by which a theory should be judged. The extreme demand for a simple prohibition of abstract entities under all circumstances perhaps arises from a desire to maintain the connection between theory and observation. But the preference of (say) *seeing* over *understanding* as a method of observation seems to me capricious. For just as an opaque body may be seen, so a concept may be understood or grasped. And the parallel between the two cases is indeed rather close. In both cases the observation is not direct but through intermediaries—light, lens of eye or optical instrument, and retina in the case of the visible body, linguistic expressions in the case of the concept. And in both cases there are or may be tenable theories according to which the entity in question, opaque body or concept, is not assumed, but only those things which would otherwise be called its effects.

The variety of entities (whether abstract or concrete) which a theory assumes is indeed one among other criteria by which it may be judged. If multiplication of entities is found beyond the needs of the workability, simplicity, and generality of the theory, then the razor shall be applied.[15] The theory of meaning here outlined

I hold exempt from such treatment no more than any other, but I do advocate its study.

Let us return now to our initial question, as to the character of the semantical rules which are to be added to the syntactical rules of a logistic system in order to define a particular formalized language.

On the foregoing theory of meaning the semantical rules must include at least the following: (5) *Rules of sense,* by which a sense is determined for each well-formed expression without free variables (all such expressions thus becoming names). (6) *Rules of sense-range,* assigning to each variable a sense-range. (7) *Rules of sense-value,* by which a sense-value is determined for every well-formed expression containing free variables and every admissible system of sense-values of its free variables (all such expressions thus becoming forms).

In the case of both syntactical and semantical rules there is a distinction to be drawn between *primitive* and *derived* rules, the primitive rules being those which are stated in giving the primitive basis of the formalized language, and the derived rules being rules of similar kind which follow as consequences of the primitive rules. Thus besides primitive rules of inference there are also derived rules of inference, besides primitive rules of sense also derived rules of sense, and so on. (But instead of "derived axioms" it is usual to say *theorems.*)

A statement of the denotation of a name, the range of a variable, or the value of a form does not necessarily belong to the semantics of a language. For example, that 'the number of planets' denotes the number nine is a fact as much of astronomy as it is of the semantics of the English language, and can be described only as belonging to a discipline broad enough to include both semantics and astronomy. On the other hand, a statement that 'the number of planets' denotes the number of planets is a purely semantical statement about the English language. And indeed it would seem that a statement of this kind may be considered as purely semantical only if it is a consequence of the rules of sense, sense-range, and sense-value, together with the syntactical rules and the general principles of meaning (i)–(xvi).

Thus as derived semantical rules rather than

primitive, there will be also: (8) *Rules of denotation,* by which a denotation is determined for each name. (9) *Rules of range,* assigning to each variable a range. (10) *Rules of value,* by which a value is determined for every form and for every admissible system of values of its free variables.

By stating (8), (9), and (10) as primitive rules, without (5), (6), and (7) there results what may be called the *extensional part* of the semantics of a language. The remaining *intensional part* of the semantics does not follow from the extensional part. For the sense of a name is not uniquely determined by its denotation, and thus a particular rule of denotation does not of itself have as a consequence the corresponding rule of sense.

On the other hand, because the metalinguistic phrase which is used in the rule of denotation must itself have a sense, there is a certain sense (though not that of logical consequence) in which the rule of denotation, by being given as a primitive rule of denotation, uniquely indicates the corresponding rule of sense. Since the like is true of the rules of range and rules of value, it is permissible to say that we have fixed an *interpretation* of a given logistic system, and thus a formalized language, if we have stated only the extensional part of the semantics.[16]

Although all the foregoing account has been concerned with the case of a formalized language, I would go on to say that in my opinion there is no difference in principle between this case and that of one of the natural languages. In particular, it must not be thought that a formalized language depends for its meaning or its justification (in any sense in which a natural language does not) upon some prior natural language, say English, through some system of translation of its sentences into English—or, more plausibly, through the statement of its syntactical and semantical rules in English. For speaking in principle, and leaving all questions of practicality aside, the logician must declare it a mere historical accident that you and I learned from birth to speak English rather than a language with less irregular, and logically simpler, syntactical rules, similar to those of one of the familiar logistic systems in use today—or that we learned in school the content of conventional English grammars and dictionaries rather than a more precise statement of a system of syntactical and semantical rules of the kind which has been described in this present sketch. The difference of a formalized language from a natural language lies not in any matter of principle, but in the degree of completeness that has been attained in the laying down of explicit syntactical and semantical rules and the extent to which vaguenesses and uncertainties have been removed from them.

For this reason the English language itself may be used as a convenient though makeshift illustration of a language for which syntactical and semantical rules are to be given. Of course only a few illustrative examples of such rules can be given in brief space. And even for this it is necessary to avoid carefully the use of examples involving English constructions that raise special difficulties or show too great logical irregularities, and to evade the manifold equivocacy of English words by selecting and giving attention to just one meaning of each word mentioned. It must also not be asked whether the rules given as examples are among the "true" rules of the English language or are "really" a part of what is implied in an understanding of English; for the laying down of rules for a natural language, because of the need to fill gaps and to decide doubtful points, is as much a process of legislation as of reporting.

With these understandings, and with no attempt made to distinguish between primitive and derived rules, following are some examples of syntactical and semantical rules of English according to the program which has been outlined.[17]

(1) Vocabulary: 'equals' 'five' 'four' 'if' 'is' 'nine' 'number' 'of' 'planet' 'planets' 'plus' 'round' 'the' 'then' 'the world''—besides the bare list of primitive symbols (words) there must be statements regarding their classification into categories and systematic relations among them, e.g., that 'planet' is a common noun,[18] that 'planets' is the plural of 'planet,'[19] that 'the world' is a proper noun, that 'round' is an adjective.

(2) Formation Rules: If A is the plural of a common noun, then 'the' ⌢ 'number' ⌢ 'of' ⌢ A is a singular term. A proper noun standing alone is a singular term. If A and B are singular terms, then A ⌢ 'equals' ⌢ B is a sentence. If A is a singular term and B is an adjective, then A ⌢ 'is' ⌢ B is a sentence.[20] If A and B are sentences, then 'if' ⌢ A ⌢ 'then' ⌢ B is a sentence.—Here singular terms and sentences are to be understood as categories of well-formed expressions; a more complete list of formation rules would no doubt introduce many more such.

(3) Rules of Inference: Where A and B are sentences, from 'if' ⌢ A ⌢ 'then' ⌢ B and A to infer B. Where A and B are singular terms and C is an adjective, from A ⌢ 'equals' ⌢ B and B ⌢ 'is' ⌢ C to infer A ⌢ 'is' ⌢ C.

(4) Axioms-Theorems: 'if the world is round, then the world is round'; 'four plus five equals nine.'

(5) Rules of Sense: 'round' expresses the property of roundness. 'the world' expresses the (individual) concept of the world. 'the world is round' expresses the proposition that the world is round.

(8) Rules of Denotation: 'round' denotes the class of round things. 'the world' denotes the world. 'the world is round' denotes the truth-value thereof that the world is round.[21]

On a Fregean theory of meaning, rules of truth in Tarski's form—e.g., " 'the world is round' is true if and only if the world is round"—follow from the rules of denotation for sentences. For that a sentence is true is taken to be the same as that it denotes truth.

NOTES

1. For convenience of the present brief exposition we make the simplifying assumption that sentences are without free variables, and that only sentences are asserted.
2. The possibility that the meaningful expressions may be a proper subclass of the well-formed expressions must not ultimately be excluded, But again for the present sketch it will be convenient to treat the two classes as identical—the simplest and most usual case. Compare, however, note 13.
3. Such notations can be reduced to at most two, namely the notation (consisting, say, of juxtaposition between parentheses) which is used in application of a singulary function to its argument, and the abstraction operator λ. By the methods of the Schönfinkel-Curry combinatory logic it may even be possible further to eliminate the abstraction operator,

and along with it the use of variables altogether. But this final reduction is not contemplated here—nor even necessarily the simpler reduction to two syncategorematic notations.

4. The complicating possibility is here ignored of *denotationless names*, or names which have a sense but no denotation. For though it may be held that these do occur in the natural languages, it is possible, as Frege showed, to construct a formalized language in such a way as to avoid them.

5. This is meant only as a preliminary rough description. In logical order, the notion of a concept must be postulated and that of a possible language defined by means of it.

6. Frege's term in German is *Marke*.—The form or *Marke* must of course not be confused with its associated abstract entity, the *function*. The function differs from the form in that it is not a linguistic entity, and belongs to no particular language. Indeed the same function may be associated with different forms; and if there is more than one free variable the same form may have several associated functions. But in some languages it is possible from the form to construct a name (or names) of the associated function (or functions) by means of an abstraction operator.

7. The idea of allowing variables of different ranges is not Fregean, except in the case of functions in Frege's sense (i.e., as *ungesättigt*), the different categories of which appear as ranges for different variables. The introduction of *Gegenstandsbuchstaben* with restricted ranges is one of the modifications here advocated in Frege's theory.

8. Exceptions to this are familiar in common mathematical notation. E.g. the form x/y has no value for the system of values $0,0$ of x, y. However, the semantics of a language is much simplified if a value is assigned to a form for every system of values of the free variables which are admissible in the sense that each value belongs to the range of the corresponding variable. And for purposes of the present exposition we assume that this has been done. (Compare note 4.)

9. Even if the language contains no constant denoting the value in question, it is possible to consider an extension of the language obtained by adjoining such a constant.

10. The notion of a sense-value of a form is not introduced by Frege, at least not explicitly, but it can be argued that it is necessarily implicit in his theory. For Frege's question, "How can a=b if true ever differ in meaning from a=a?" can be asked as well for forms a and b as for constants, and leads to the distinction of value and sense-value of a form just as it does to the distinction of denotation and sense of a constant. Even in a language like that of *Principia Mathematica*, having no forms other than propositional forms, a parallel argument can be used to show that from the equivalence of two propositional forms A and B the identity in meaning of A and B in all respects is not to be inferred. For otherwise how could A ≡ B if

true (i.e., true for all values of the variables) ever differ in meaning from A ≡ A?

11. For purposes of the preliminary sketch, the metalanguage is left unformalized, and such questions are ignored as whether the metalanguage shall conform to the theory of types or to some alternative such as transfinite type theory or axiomatic set theory. Because of the extreme generality which is attempted in laying down these principles, it is clear that there may be some difficulty in rendering them precise (in their full attempted generality) by restatement in a formalized metalanguage. But it should be possible to state the semantical rules of a particular object language so as to conform, so that the principles are clarified to this extent by illustration.

It is not meant that the list of principles is necessarily complete or in final form, but rather a tentative list is here proposed for study and possible amendment. Moreover it is not meant that it may not be possible to formulate a language not conforming to the principles, but only that a satisfactory general theory may result by making conformity to these principles a part of the definition of a formalized language (compare note 12).

12. In the case of some logistic systems which have been proposed (e.g., by Hilbert and Bernays), if semantical rules are to be added, in conformity with the theory here described and with the informally intended interpretation of the system, it is found to be impossible to satisfy (viii), (x), and (xiv), because of restriction imposed on the bound variables which may appear in a constant or form used in a particular context. But it would seem that modifications in the logistic system necessary to remove the restriction may reasonably be considered nonessential, and that in this sense (viii), (x), (xiv) may still be maintained.

In regard to all of the principles it should be understood that nonessential modifications in existing logistic systems may be required to make them conform. In particular the principles have been formulated in a way which does not contemplate the distinction in typographical style between free and bound variables that appears in systems of Frege and of Hilbert-Bernays.

In (x) and (xi), the condition that f′ have the same free variables as f can in many cases be weakened to the condition that every free variable of f′ occur also as a free variable of f.

13. Possibly (ix) and (xi) should be weakened to require only that if C′ is well-formed then it is a constant having the same denotation as C. Since there is in general no syntactical criterion by which to ascertain whether two constants c and c′ have the same denotation, or whether two forms have always the same values, there is the possibility that the stronger forms of (ix) and (xi) might lead to difficulty in some cases. However, (ix) as here stated has the effect of preserving fully the rule of substitutivity of equality—where the equality sign is so interpreted that $[c_1 = c_2]$ is a sentence denoting truth if and only if c_1 and c_2

are constants having the same denotation—and if in some formalized languages, (ix) and (xi) should prove to be inconsistent with the requirement that every well-formed expression be meaningful (note 2), it may be preferable to abandon the latter. Indeed the preservation of the rule of substitutivity of equality may be regarded as an important advantage of a Fregean theory of meaning over some of the alternatives that suggest themselves.

14. At the present stage it cannot be said with assurance that a modification of Frege's theory will ultimately prove to be the best or the simplest. Alternative theories demanding study are: the theory of Russell, which relies on the elimination of names by contextual definition to an extent sufficient to render the distinction of sense and denotation unnecessary; the modification of Russell's theory, briefly suggested by Smullyan [*The Journal of Symbolic Logic,* 13 (1948), pp. 31–37], according to which descriptive phrases are to be considered as actually contained in the logistic system rather than being (in the phrase of Whitehead and Russell) "mere typographical conveniences," but are to differ from names in that they retain their need for scope indicators; and finally, the theory of Carnap's *Meaning and Necessity.*

Though the Russell theory has an element of simplicity in avoiding the distinction of two kinds of meaning, it leads to complications of its own of a different sort, in connection with the matter of scope of descriptions. The same should be said of Smullyan's proposed modification of the theory. And the distinctions of scope become especially important in modal statements, where they cannot be eliminated by the convention of always taking the minimum scope, as Smullyan has shown (loc. cit.).

Moreover, in its present form it would seem that the Russell theory requires some supplementation. For example, "I am thinking of Pegasus," "Ponce de Leon searched for the fountain of youth," "Barbara Villiers was less chaste than Diana" cannot be analyzed as "$(Ec)[x$ is a Pegasus$\equiv_x x=c]$ [I am thinking of c]," "$(Ec)[x$ is a fountain of youth $\equiv_x x=c]$ [Ponce de Leon searched for c]," "$(Ec)[x$ is a Diana $\equiv_x x=c]$ [Barbara Villiers was less chaste than c]" respectively—if only because of the (probable or possible) difference of truth-value between the given statements and their proposed analyses. On a Fregean theory of meaning the given statements might be analyzed as being about the individual concepts of Pegasus, of the fountain of youth, and of Diana rather than about some certain winged horse, some certain fountain, and some certain goddess. For the Russell theory it might be suggested to analyze them as being about the property of being a Pegasus, the property of being a fountain of youth, and the property of being a Diana. This analysis in terms of properties would also be possible on a Fregean theory, though perhaps slightly less natural. On a theory of the Russell type the difficulty arises that names of properties seem to be required, and on pain of read-

mitting Frege's puzzle about equality (which leads to the distinction of sense and denotation in connection with names of any kind), such names of properties either must be analyzed away by contextual definition—it is not clear how—or must be so severely restricted that two names of the same property cannot occur unless trivially synonymous.

15. Here a warning is necessary against spurious economies, since not every subtraction from the entities which a theory assumes is a reduction in the variety of entities.

For example, in the simple theory of types it is well known that the individuals may be dispensed with if classes and relations of all types are retained; or one may abandon also classes and relations of the lowest type, retaining only those of higher type. In fact any finite number of levels at the bottom of the hierarchy of types may be deleted. But this is no reduction in the variety of entities, because the truncated hierarchy of types, by appropriate deletions of entities in each type, can be made isomorphic to the original hierarchy—and indeed the continued adequacy of the truncated hierarchy to the original purposes depends on this isomorphism.

Similarly the idea may suggest itself to admit the distinction of sense and denotation at the nth level and above in the hierarchy of types, but below the nth level to deny this distinction and to adopt instead Russell's device of contextual elimination of names. The entities assumed would thus include only the usual extensional entities below the nth level, but at the nth level and above they would include also concepts, concepts of concepts, and so on. However, this is no reduction in the variety of entities assumed, as compared to the theory which assumes at all levels in the hierarchy of types not only the extensional entities but also concepts of them, concepts of concepts of them, and so on. For the entities assumed by the former theory are reduced again to isomorphism with those assumed by the latter, if all entities below the nth level are deleted and appropriate deletions are made in every type at the nth level and above.

Some one may object that the notion of isomorphism is irrelevant which is here introduced, and insist that any subtraction from the entities assumed by a theory must be considered a simplification. But to such objector I would reply that his proposal leads (in the cases just named, and others) to perpetual oscillation between two theories T_1 and T_2, T_1 being reduced to T_2 and T_2 to T_1 by successive "simplifications" *ad infinitum.*

16. As is done in the revised edition of my *Introduction to Mathematical Logic, Part I.*

17. For convenience, English is used also as the metalanguage, although this gives a false appearance of triviality or obviousness to some of the semantical rules. Since the purpose is only illustrative, the danger of semantical antinomies is ignored.

18. For present illustrative purposes the question may be

avoided whether common nouns in English, in the singular, shall be considered to be variables (e.g., 'planet' or 'a planet' as a variable having planets as its range), or to be class names (e.g., 'planet' as a proper name of the class of planets), or to have "no status at all in a logical grammar" (see Quine's *Methods of Logic,* p. 207), or perhaps to vary from one of these uses to another according to context.

19. Or possibly 'planet' and 's' could be regarded as two primitive symbols, by making a minor change in existing English so that all common nouns form the plural by adding 's.'

20. If any of you finds unacceptable the conclusion that therefore 'the number of planets is round' is a sentence, he may try to alter the rules to suit, perhaps by distinguishing different types of terms. This is an example of a doubtful point, on the decision of which they may well be differences of opinion. The advocate of a set-theoretic language may decide one way and the advocate of type theory another, but it is hard to say that either decision is the "true" decision for the English language as it is.

21. But of course it would be wrong to include as a rule of denotation: 'the world is round' denotes truth. For this depends on a fact of geography extraneous to semantics (namely that the world is round).

5

The Semantic Conception of Truth and the Foundations of Semantics

ALFRED TARSKI

This paper consists of two parts; the first has an expository character, and the second is rather polemical.

In the first part I want to summarize in an informal way the main results of my investigations concerning the definition of truth and the more general problem of the foundations of semantics. These results have been embodied in a work which appeared in print several years ago.[1] Although my investigations concern concepts dealt with in classical philosophy, they happen to be comparatively little known in philosophical circles, perhaps because of their strictly technical character. For this reason I hope I shall be excused for taking up the matter once again.[2]

Since my work was published, various objections, of unequal value, have been raised to my investigations; some of these appeared in print, and others were made in public and private discussions in which I took part.[3] In the second part of the paper I should like to express my views regarding these objections. I hope that the remarks which will be made in this context will not be considered as purely polemical in character, but will be found to contain some constructive contributions to the subject.

In the second part of the paper I have made extensive use of material graciously put at my disposal by Dr. Marja Kokoszyńska (University of Lwów). I am especially indebted and grateful

to Professors Ernest Nagel (Columbia University) and David Rynin (University of California, Berkeley) for their help in preparing the final text and for various critical remarks.

I. EXPOSITION

1. The Main Problem—A Satisfactory Definition of Truth

Our discussion will be centered around the notion[4] of *truth*. The main problem is that of giving a *satisfactory definition* of this notion, i.e., a definition which is *materially adequate* and *formally correct*. But such a formulation of the problem, because of its generality, cannot be considered unequivocal, and requires some further comments.

In order to avoid any ambiguity, we must first specify the conditions under which the definition of truth will be considered adequate from the material point of view. The desired definition does not aim to specify the meaning of a familiar word used to denote a novel notion; on the contrary, it aims to catch hold of the actual meaning of an old notion. We must then characterize this notion precisely enough to enable anyone to determine whether the definition actually fulfills its task.

Secondly, we must determine on what the formal correctness of the definition depends.

From *Philosophy and Phenomenological Research* 4 (1944): 341–375. Reprinted by permission of the publisher.

Thus, we must specify the words or concepts which we wish to use in defining the notion of truth; and we must also give the formal rules to which the definition should conform. Speaking more generally, we must describe the formal structure of the language in which the definition will be given.

The discussion of these points will occupy a considerable portion of the first part of the paper.

2. The Extension of the Term "True"

We begin with some remarks regarding the extension of the concept of truth which we have in mind here.

The predicate "true" is sometimes used to refer to psychological phenomena such as judgments or beliefs, sometimes to certain physical objects, namely, linguistic expressions and specifically sentences, and sometimes to certain ideal entities called "propositions." By "sentence" we understand here what is usually meant in grammar by "declarative sentence"; as regards the term "proposition," its meaning is notoriously a subject of lengthy disputations by various philosophers and logicians, and it seems never to have been made quite clear and unambiguous. For several reasons it appears most convenient to *apply the term "true" to sentences,* and we shall follow this course.[5]

Consequently, we must always relate the notion of truth, like that of a sentence, to a specific language; for it is obvious that the same expression which is a true sentence in one language can be false or meaningless in another.

Of course, the fact that we are interested here primarily in the notion of truth for sentences does not exclude the possibility of a subsequent extension of this notion to other kinds of objects.

3. The Meaning of the Term "True"

Much more serious difficulties are connected with the problem of the meaning (or the intension) of the concept of truth.

The word "true," like other words from our everyday language, is certainly not unambiguous. And it does not seem to me that the philosophers who have discussed this concept have helped to diminish its ambiguity. In works and discussions of philosophers we meet many different conceptions of truth and falsity, and we must indicate which conception will be the basis of our discussion.

We should like our definition to do justice to the intuitions which adhere to the *classical Aristotelian conception of truth*—intuitions which find their expression in the well-known words of Aristotle's *Metaphysics:*

To say of what is that it is not, or of what is not that it is, is false, while to say of what is that it is, or of what is not that it is not, is true.

If we wished to adapt ourselves to modern philosophical terminology, we could perhaps express this conception by means of the familiar formula:

The truth of a sentence consists in its agreement with (or correspondence to) reality.

(For a theory of truth which is to be based upon the latter formulation the term "correspondence theory" has been suggested.)

If, on the other hand, we should decide to extend the popular usage of the term "designate" by applying it not only to names, but also to sentences, and if we agreed to speak of the designata of sentences as "states of affairs," we could possibly use for the same purpose the following phrase:

A sentence is true if it designates an existing state of affairs.[6]

However, all these formulations can lead to various misunderstandings, for none of them is sufficiently precise and clear (though this applies much less to the original Aristotelian formulation than to either of the others); at any rate, none of them can be considered a satisfactory definition of truth. It is up to us to look for a more precise expression of our intuitions.

4. A Criterion for the Material Adequacy of the Definition[7]

Let us start with a concrete example. Consider the sentence "snow is white." We ask the question under what conditions this sentence is true or false. It seems clear that if we base ourselves on the classical conception of truth, we shall say that the sentence is true if snow is white, and that it is false if snow is not white. Thus, if the definition of truth is to conform to our conception, it must imply the following equivalence:

> The sentence "snow is white" is true if, and only if, snow is white.

Let me point out that the phrase "snow is white" occurs on the left side of this equivalence in quotation marks, and on the right without quotation marks. On the right side we have the sentence itself, and on the left the name of the sentence. Employing the medieval logical terminology we could say that on the right side the words "snow is white" occur in *suppositio formalis,* and on the left in *suppositio materialis.* It is hardly necessary to explain why we must have the name of the sentence, and not the sentence itself, on the left side of the equivalence. For, in the first place, from the point of view of the grammar of our language, an expression of the form "X is true" will not become a meaningful sentence if we replace in it 'X' by a sentence or by anything other than a name—since the subject of a sentence may be only a noun or an expression functioning like a noun. And, in the second place, the fundamental conventions regarding the use of any language require that in any utterance we make about an object it is the name of the object which must be employed, and not the object itself. In consequence, if we wish to say something about a sentence, for example that it is true, we must use the name of this sentence, and not the sentence itself.[8]

It may be added that enclosing a sentence in quotation marks is by no means the only way of forming its name. For instance, by assuming the usual order of letters in our alphabet, we can use the following expression as the name (the description) of the sentence "snow is white":

> the sentence constituted by three words, the first of which consists of the 19th, 14th, 15th, and 23rd letters, the second of the 9th and 19th letters, and the third of the 23rd, 8th, 9th, 20th, and 5th letters of the English alphabet.

We shall now generalize the procedure which we have applied above. Let us consider an arbitrary sentence; we shall replace it by the letter 'p.' We form the name of this sentence and we replace it by another letter, say 'X.' We ask now what is the logical relation between the two sentences "X is true" and 'p.' It is clear that from the point of view of our basic conception of truth these sentences are equivalent. In other words, the following equivalence holds:

> (T) X is true if, and only if, p.

We shall call any such equivalence (with 'p' replaced by any sentence of the language to which the word "true" refers, and 'X' replaced by a name of this sentence) an *"equivalence of the form* (T)."

Now at last we are able to put into a precise form the conditions under which we will consider the usage and the definition of the term "true" as adequate from the material point of view: we wish to use the term "true" in such a way that all equivalences of the form (T) can be asserted, and *we shall call a definition of truth "adequate" if all these equivalences follow from it.*

It should be emphasized that neither the expression (T) itself (which is not a sentence, but only a schema of a sentence) nor any particular instance of the form (T) can be regarded as a definition of truth. We can only say that every equivalence of the form (T) obtained by replacing 'p' by a particular sentence, and 'X' by a name of this sentence, may be considered a partial definition of truth, which explains wherein the truth of this one individual sentence consists. The general definition has to be, in a certain sense, a logical conjunction of all these partial definitions.

(The last remark calls for some comments. A language may admit the construction of infinitely many sentences; and thus the number of partial definitions of truth referring to sentences of such a language will also be infinite. Hence to give our remark a precise sense we should have to explain what is meant by a "logical conjunction of infinitely many sentences"; but this would lead us too far into technical problems of modern logic.)

5. Truth as a Semantic Concept

I should like to propose the name "*the semantic conception of truth*" for the conception of truth which has just been discussed.

Semantics is a discipline which, speaking loosely, *deals with certain relations between ex-*

pressions of a language and the objects (or "states of affairs") *"referred to"* by those expressions. As typical examples of semantic concepts we may mention the concepts of *designation, satisfaction,* and *definition* as these occur in the following examples:

> the expression "the father of his country" designates (denotes) George Washington;
> snow satisfies the sentential function (the condition) "x is white";
> the equation "2 · x = 1" defines (uniquely determines) the number 1/2.

While the words "designates," "satisfies," and "defines" express relations (between certain expressions and the objects "referred to" by these expressions), the word "true" is of a different logical nature: it expresses a property (or denotes a class) of certain expressions, viz., of sentences. However, it is easily seen that all the formulations which were given earlier and which aimed to explain the meaning of this word (cf. sections 3 and 4) referred not only to sentences themselves, but also to objects "talked about" by these sentences, or possibly to "states of affairs" described by them. And, moreover, it turns out that the simplest and the most natural way of obtaining an exact definition of truth is one which involves the use of other semantic notions, e.g., the notion of satisfaction. It is for these reasons that we count the concept of truth which is discussed here among the concepts of semantics, and the problem of defining truth proves to be closely related to the more general problem of setting up the foundations of theoretical semantics.

It is perhaps worthwhile saying that semantics as it is conceived in this paper (and in former papers of the author) is a sober and modest discipline which has no pretensions of being a universal patent-medicine for all the ills and diseases of mankind, whether imaginary or real. You will not find in semantics any remedy for decayed teeth or illusions of grandeur or class conflicts. Nor is semantics a device for establishing that everyone except the speaker and his friends is speaking nonsense.

From antiquity to the present day the concepts of semantics have played an important role in the discussions of philosophers, logicians, and philologists. Nevertheless, these con-cepts have been treated for a long time with a certain amount of suspicion. From a historical standpoint, this suspicion is to be regarded as completely justified. For although the meaning of semantic concepts as they are used in everyday language seems to be rather clear and understandable, still all attempts to characterize this meaning in a general and exact way miscarried. And what is worse, various arguments in which these concepts were involved, and which seemed otherwise quite correct and based upon apparently obvious premises, led frequently to paradoxes and antinomies. It is sufficient to mention here the *antinomy of the liar,* Richard's *antinomy of definability* (by means of a finite number of words), and Grelling-Nelson's *antinomy of heterological terms.*[9]

I believe that the method which is outlined in this paper helps to overcome these difficulties and assures the possibility of a consistent use of semantic concepts.

6. Languages with a Specified Structure

Because of the possible occurrence of antinomies, the problem of specifying the formal structure and the vocabulary of a language in which definitions of semantic concepts are to be given becomes especially acute; and we turn now to this problem.

There are certain general conditions under which the structure of a language is regarded as *exactly specified.* Thus, to specify the structure of a language, we must characterize unambiguously the class of those words and expressions which are to be considered *meaningful.* In particular, we must indicate all words which we decide to use without defining them, and which are called *"undefined* (or *primitive) terms"*; and we must give the so-called *rules of definition* for introducing new or *defined terms.* Furthermore, we must set up criteria for distinguishing within the class of expressions those which we call *"sentences."* Finally, we must formulate the conditions under which a sentence of the language can be *asserted.* In particular, we must indicate all axioms (or *primitive sentences*), i.e., those sentences which we decide to assert without proof; and we must give the so-called *rules of inference* (or *rules of proof*) by means of which we can deduce new asserted sentences from other sentences which have been previously asserted. Axioms, as well as sentences deduced from them by means of rules of inference, are referred to as *"theorems"* or *"provable sentences."*

If in specifying the structure of a language we refer exclusively to the form of the expressions involved, the language is said to be *formalized.* In such a language theorems are the only sentences which can be asserted.

At the present time the only languages with a specified structure are the formalized languages of various systems of deductive logic, possibly enriched by the introduction of certain nonlogical terms. However, the field of application of these languages is rather comprehensive; we are able, theoretically, to develop in them various branches of science, for instance, mathematics and theoretical physics.

(On the other hand, we can imagine the construction of languages which have an exactly specified structure without being formalized. In such a language the assertability of sentences, for instance, may depend not always on their form, but sometimes on other, nonlinguistic factors. It would be interesting and important actually to construct a language of this type, and specifically one which would prove to be sufficient for the development of a comprehensive branch of empirial science; for this would justify the hope that languages with specified structure could finally replace everyday language in scientific discourse.)

The problem of the definition of truth obtains a precise meaning and can be solved in a rigorous way only for those languages whose structure has been exactly specified. For other languages—thus, for all natural, "spoken" languages—the meaning of the problem is more or less vague, and its solution can have only an approximate character. Roughly speaking, the approximation consists in replacing a natural language (or a portion of it in which we are interested) by one whose structure is exactly specified, and which diverges from the given language "as little as possible."

7. The Antinomy of the Liar

In order to discover some of the more specific conditions which must be satisfied by languages

in which (or for which) the definition of truth is to be given, it will be advisable to begin with a discussion of that antinomy which directly involves the notion of truth, namely, the antinomy of the liar.

To obtain this antinomy in a perspicuous form,[10] consider the following sentence:

> The sentence printed in this paper on p. 89, column b, ll. 8–9, is not true.

For brevity we shall replace the sentence just stated by the letter 's.'

According to our convention concerning the adequate usage of the term 'true', we assert the following equivalence of the form (T):

> (1) 's' is true if, and only if, the sentence printed in this paper on p. 89, column b, ll. 8–9 is not true.

On the other hand, keeping in mind the meaning of the symbol 's,' we establish empirically the following fact:

> (2) 's' is identical with the sentence printed in this paper on p. 89, column b, ll. 8–9.

Now, by a familiar law from the theory of identity (Leibniz's law), it follows from (2) that we may replace in (1) the expression "the sentence printed in this paper on p. 89, column b, ll. 8–9" by the symbol "'s.'" We thus obtain what follows:

> (3) 's' is true if, and only if, 's' is not true.

In this way we have arrived at an obvious contradiction.

In my judgment, it would be quite wrong and dangerous from the standpoint of scientific progress to depreciate the importance of this and other antinomies, and to treat them as jokes or sophistries. It is a fact that we are here in the presence of an absurdity, that we have been compelled to assert a false sentence [since (3), as an equivalence between two contradictory sentences, is necessarily false]. If we take our work seriously, we cannot be reconciled with this fact. We must discover its cause, that is to say, we must analyze premises upon which the antinomy is based; we must then reject at least one of these premises, and we must investigate the consequences which this has for the whole domain of our research.

It should be emphasized that antinomies have played a preeminent role in establishing the foundations of modern deductive sciences. And just as class-theoretical antinomies, and in particular Russell's antinomy (of the class of all classes that are not members of themselves), were the starting point for the successful attempts at a consistent formalization of logic and mathematics, so the antinomy of the liar and other semantic antinomies give rise to the construction of theoretical semantics.

8. The Inconsistency of Semantically Closed Languages[7]

If we now analyze the assumptions which lead to the antinomy of the liar, we notice the following:

(I) We have implicitly assumed that the language in which the antinomy is constructed contains, in addition to its expressions, also the names of these expressions, as well as semantic terms such as the term *"true"* referring to sentences of this language; we have also assumed that all sentences which determine the adequate usage of this term can be asserted in the language. A language with these properties will be called *"semantically closed."*

(II) We have assumed that in this language the ordinary laws of logic hold.

(III) We have assumed that we can formulate and assert in our language an empirical premise such as the statement (2) which has occurred in our argument.

It turns out that the assumption (III) is not essential, for it is possible to reconstruct the antinomy of the liar without its help.[11] But the assumptions (I) and (II) prove essential. Since every language which satisfies both of these assumptions is inconsistent, we must reject at least one of them.

It would be superfluous to stress here the consequences of rejecting the assumption (II), that is, of changing our logic (supposing this were possible) even in its more elementary and fundamental parts. We thus consider only the possibility of rejecting the assumption (I). Accordingly, we decide *not to use any language which is semantically closed* in the sense given.

This restriction would of course be unaccept-able for those who, for reasons which are not clear to me, believe that there is only one "genuine" language (or, at least, that all "genuine" languages are mutually translatable). However, this restriction does not affect the needs or interests of science in any essential way. The languages (either the formalized languages or—what is more frequently the case—the portions of everyday language) which are used in scientific discourse do not have to be semantically closed. This is obvious in case linguistic phenomena and, in particular, semantic notions do not enter in any way into the subject matter of a science; for in such a case the language of this science does not have to be provided with any semantic terms at all. However, we shall see in the next section how semantically closed languages can be dispensed with even in those scientific discussions in which semantic notions are essentially involved.

The problem arises as to the position of everyday language with regard to this point. At first blush it would seem that this language satisfies both assumptions (I) and (II), and that therefore it must be inconsistent. But actually the case is not so simple. Our everyday language is certainly not one with an exactly specified structure. We do not know precisely which expressions are sentences, and we know even to a smaller degree which sentences are to be taken as assertible. Thus the problem of consistency has no exact meaning with respect to this language. We may at best only risk the guess that a language whose structure has been exactly specified and which resembles our everyday language as closely as possible would be inconsistent.

9. Object Language and Metalanguage

Since we have agreed not to employ semantically closed languages, we have to use two different languages in discussing the problem of the definition of truth and, more generally, any problems in the field of semantics. The first of these languages is the language which is "talked about" and which is the subject matter of the whole discussion; the definition of truth which we are seeking applies to the sentences of this language. The second is the language in which we "talk about" the first language, and in terms of which we wish, in particular, to construct the definition of truth for the first language. We shall refer to the first language as "the object language," and to the second as "the metalanguage."

It should be noticed that these terms "object language" and "metalanguage" have only a relative sense. If, for instance, we become interested in the notion of truth applying to sentences, not of our original object language, but of its metalanguage, the latter becomes automatically the object language of our discussion; and in order to define truth for this language, we have to go to a new metalanguage—so to speak, to a metalanguage of a higher level. In this way we arrive at a whole hierarchy of languages.

The vocabulary of the metalanguage is to a large extent determined by previously stated conditions under which a definition of truth will be considered materially adequate. This definition, as we recall, has to imply all equivalences of the form (T):

(T) X is true if, and only if, p.

The definition itself and all the equivalences implied by it are to be formulated in the metalanguage. On the other hand, the symbol 'p' in (T) stands for an arbitrary sentence of our object language. Hence it follows that every sentence which occurs in the object language must also occur in the metalanguage; in other words, the metalanguage must contain the object language as a part. This is at any rate necessary for the proof of the adequacy of the definition—even though the definition itself can sometimes be formulated in a less comprehensive metalanguage which does not satisfy this requirement.

[The requirement in question can be somewhat modified, for it suffices to assume that the object-language can be translated into the metalanguage; this necessitates a certain change in the interpretation of the symbol 'p' in (T). In all that follows we shall ignore the possibility of this modification.]

Furthermore, the symbol 'X' in (T) represents the name of the sentence which 'p' stands for. We see therefore that the metalanguage must be rich enough to provide possibilities of constructing a name for every sentence of the object language.

In addition, the metalanguage must obviously contain terms of a general logical character, such as the expression "if, and only if."[12]

It is desirable for the metalanguage not to contain any undefined terms except such as are involved explicitly or implicitly in the remarks above, i.e.: terms of the object language; terms referring to the form of the expressions of the object language, and used in building names for these expressions; and terms of logic. In particular, we desire *semantic terms* (referring to the object language) *to be introduced into the metalanguage only by definition.* For, if this postulate is satisfied, the definition of truth, or of any other semantic concept, will fulfill what we intuitively expect from every definition; that is, it will explain the meaning of the term being defined in terms whose meaning appears to be completely clear and unequivocal. And, moreover, we have then a kind of guarantee that the use of semantic concepts will not involve us in any contradictions.

We have no further requirements as to the formal structure of the object language and the metalanguage; we assume that it is similar to that of other formalized languages known at the present time. In particular, we assume that the usual formal rules of definition are observed in the metalanguage.

10. Conditions for a Positive Solution of the Main Problem

Now, we have already a clear idea both of the conditions of material adequacy to which the definition of truth is subjected, and of the formal structure of the language in which this definition is to be constructed. Under these circumstances the problem of the definition of truth acquires the character of a definite problem of a purely deductive nature.

The solution of the problem, however, is by no means obvious, and I would not attempt to give it in detail without using the whole machinery of contemporary logic. Here I shall confine myself to a rough outline of the solution and to the discussion of certain points of a more general interest which are involved in it.

The solution turns out to be sometimes positive, sometimes negative. This depends upon some formal relations between the object lan-

guage and its metalanguage; or, more specifically, upon the fact whether the metalanguage in
its logical part is *"essentially richer"* than the
object language or not. It is not easy to give a
general and precise definition of this notion of
"essential richness." If we restrict ourselves to
languages based on the logical theory of types,
the condition for the metalanguage to be "essentially richer" than the object language is that it
contain variables of a higher logical type than
those of the object language.

If the condition of "essential richness" is not
satisfied, it can usually be shown that an interpretation of the metalanguage in the object language is possible; that is to say, with any given
term of the metalanguage a well-determined
term of the object language can be correlated in
such a way that the assertible sentences of the
one language turn out to be correlated with
assertible sentences of the other. As a result of
this interpretation, the hypothesis that a satisfactory definition of truth has been formulated
in the metalanguage turns out to imply the possibility of reconstructing in that language the
antinomy of the liar; and this in turn forces us to
reject the hypothesis in question.

(The fact that the metalanguage, in its nonlogical part, is ordinarily more comprehensive
than the object language does not affect the possibility of interpreting the former in the latter.
For example, the names of expressions of the
object language occur in the metalanguage,
though for the most part they do not occur in the
object language itself; but, nevertheless, it may
be possible to interpret these names in terms of
the object language.)

Thus we see that the condition of "essential
richness" is necessary for the possibility of a
satisfactory definition of truth in the metalanguage. If we want to develop the theory of truth
in a metalanguage which does not satisfy this
condition, we must give up the idea of defining
truth with the exclusive help of those terms
which were indicated above (in section 8). We
have then to include the term "true," or some
other semantic term, in the list of undefined
terms of the metalanguage, and to express fundamental properties of the notion of truth in a
series of axioms. There is nothing essentially
wrong in such an axiomatic procedure, and it
may prove useful for various purposes.[13]

It turns out, however, that this procedure can
be avoided. For *the condition of the "essential
richness" of the metalanguage proves to be, not
only necessary, but also sufficient for the construction of a satisfactory definition of truth;*
i.e., if the metalanguage satisfies this condition,
the notion of truth can be defined in it. We shall
now indicate in general terms how this construction can be carried through.

11. The Construction (in Outline) of the Definition[14]

A definition of truth can be obtained in a very
simple way from that of another semantic
notion, namely, of the notion of *satisfaction.*

Satisfaction is a relation between arbitrary
objects and certain expressions called *"sentential functions."* These are expressions like "x is
white," "x is greater than y," etc. Their formal
structure is analogous to that of sentences; however, they may contain the so-called free variables (like 'x' and 'y' in "x is greater than y"),
which cannot occur in sentences.

In defining the notion of a sentential function
in formalized languages, we usually apply what
is called a "recursive procedure"; i.e., we first
describe sentential functions of the simplest
structure (which ordinarily presents no difficulty), and then we indicate the operations by
means of which compound functions can be
constructed from simpler ones. Such an operation may consist, for instance, in forming the
logical disjunction or conjunction of two given
functions, i.e., by combining them by the word
"or" or "and." A sentence can now be defined
simply as a sentential function which contains
no free variables.

As regards the notion of satisfaction, we
might try to define it by saying that given
objects satisfy a given function if the latter
becomes a true sentence when we replace in it
free variables by names of given objects. In this
sense, for example, snow satisfies the sentential
function "x is white" since the sentence "snow
is white" is true. However, apart from other difficulties, this method is not available to us, for
we want to use the notion of satisfaction in
defining truth.

To obtain a definition of satisfaction we have
rather to apply again a recursive procedure. We

indicate which objects satisfy the simplest sentential functions; and then we state the conditions under which given objects satisfy a compound function—assuming that we know which
objects satisfy the simpler functions from which
the compound one has been constructed. Thus,
for instance, we say that given numbers satisfy
the logical disjunction "x is greater than y or x is
equal to y" if they satisfy at least one of the functions "x is greater than y" or "x is equal to y."

Once the general definition of satisfaction is
obtained, we notice that it applies automatically
also to those special sentential functions which
contain no free variables, i.e., to sentences. It
turns out that for a sentence only two cases are
possible: a sentence is either satisfied by all
objects, or by no objects. Hence we arrive at a
definition of truth and falsehood simply by saying that *a sentence is true if it is satisfied by all
objects, and false otherwise.*[15]

(It may seem strange that we have chosen a
roundabout way of defining the truth of a sentence, instead of trying to apply, for instance, a
direct recursive procedure. The reason is that
compound sentences are constructed from simpler sentential functions, but not always from
simpler sentences; hence no general recursive
method is known which applies specifically to
sentences.)

From this rough outline it is not clear where
and how the assumption of the "essential richness" of the metalanguage is involved in the
discussion; this becomes clear only when the
construction is carried through in a detailed and
formal way.[16]

12. Consequences of the Definition

The definition of truth which was outlined
above has many interesting consequences.

In the first place, the definition proves to be
not only formally correct, but also materially
adequate (in the sense established in section 4);
in other words, it implies all equivalences of the
form (T). In this connection it is important to
notice that the conditions for the material adequacy of the definition determine uniquely the
extension of the term "true." Therefore, every
definition of truth which is materially adequate
would necessarily be equivalent to that actually
constructed. The semantic conception of truth

gives us, so to speak, no possibility of choice
between various nonequivalent definitions of
this notion.

Moreover, we can deduce from our definition
various laws of a general nature. In particular,
we can prove with its help the *laws of contradiction and of excluded middle,* which are so
characteristic of the Aristotelian conception of
truth; i.e., we can show that one and only one of
any two contradictory sentences is true. These
semantic laws should not be identified with the
related logical laws of contradiction and
excluded middle; the latter belong to the sentential calculus, i.e., to the most elementary part
of logic, and do not involve the term "true" at
all.

Further important results can be obtained by
applying the theory of truth to formalized languages of a certain very comprehensive class of
mathematical disciplines; only disciplines of an
elementary character and a very elementary logical structure are excluded from this class. It
turns out that for a discipline of this class *the
notion of truth never coincides with that of
provability;* for all provable sentences are true,
but there are true sentences which are not provable.[17] Hence it follows further that every such
discipline is consistent, but incomplete; that is
to say, of any two contradictory sentences at
most one is provable, and—what is more—
there exists a pair of contradictory sentences
neither of which is provable.[18]

13. Extension of the Results to Other Semantic Notions

Most of the results at which we arrived in the
preceding sections in discussing the notion of
truth can be extended with appropriate changes
to other semantic notions, for instance, to the
notion of satisfaction (involved in our previous
discussion), and to those of *designation* and
definition.

Each of these notions can be analyzed along
the lines followed in the analysis of truth. Thus,
criteria for an adequate usage of these notions
can be established; it can be shown that each of
these notions, when used in a semantically
closed language according to those criteria,
leads necessarily to a contradiction;[19] a distinction between the object language and the meta-

language becomes again indispensable; and the "essential richness" of the metalanguage proves in each case to be a necessary and sufficient condition for a satisfactory definition of the notion involved. Hence the results obtained in discussing one particular semantic notion apply to the general problem of the foundations of theoretical semantics.

Within theoretical semantics we can define and study some further notions, whose intuitive content is more involved and whose semantic origin is less obvious; we have in mind, for instance, the important notions of *consequence, synonymity,* and *meaning.*[20]

We have concerned ourselves here with the theory of semantic notions related to an individual object language (although no specific properties of this language have been involved in our arguments). However, we could also consider the problem of developing *general semantics* which applies to a comprehensive class of object languages. A considerable part of our previous remarks can be extended to this general problem; however, certain new difficulties arise in this connection, which will not be discussed here. I shall merely observe that the axiomatic method (mentioned in section 10) may prove the most appropriate for the treatment of the problem.[21]

II. POLEMICAL REMARKS

14. Is the Semantic Conception of Truth the "Right" One?

I should like to begin the polemical part of the paper with some general remarks.

I hope nothing which is said here will be interpreted as a claim that the semantic conception of truth is the "right" or indeed the "only possible" one. I do not have the slightest intention to contribute in any way to those endless, often violent discussions on the subject: "What is the right conception of truth?"[22] I must confess I do not understand what is at stake in such disputes; for the problem itself is so vague that no definite solution is possible. In fact, it seems to me that the sense in which the phrase "the right conception" is used has never been made clear. In most cases one gets the impression that the phrase is used in an almost mystical sense

based upon the belief that every word has only one "real" meaning (a kind of Platonic or Aristotelian idea), and that all the competing conceptions really attempt to catch hold of this one meaning; since, however, they contradict each other, only one attempt can be successful, and hence only one conception is the "right" one.

Disputes of this type are by no means restricted to the notion of truth. They occur in all domains where—instead of an exact, scientific terminology—common language with its vagueness and ambiguity is used; and they are always meaningless, and therefore in vain.

It seems to me obvious that the only rational approach to such problems would be the following: We should reconcile ourselves with the fact that we are confronted, not with one concept, but with several different concepts which are denoted by one word; we should try to make these concepts as clear as possible (by means of definition, or of an axiomatic procedure, or in some other way); to avoid further confusions, we should agree to use different terms for different concepts; and then we may proceed to a quiet and systematic study of all concepts involved, which will exhibit their main properties and mutual relations.

Referring specifically to the notion of truth, it is undoubtedly the case that in philosophical discussions—and perhaps also in everyday usage—some incipient conceptions of this notion can be found that differ essentially from the classical one (of which the semantic conception is but a modernized form). In fact, various conceptions of this sort have been discussed in the literature, for instance, the pragmatic conception, the coherence theory, etc.[6]

It seems to me that none of these conceptions have been put so far in an intelligible and unequivocal form. This may change, however; a time may come when we find ourselves confronted with several incompatible, but equally clear and precise, conceptions of truth. It will then become necessary to abandon the ambiguous usage of the word "true," and to introduce several terms instead, each to denote a different notion. Personally, I should not feel hurt if a future world congress of the "theoreticians of truth" should decide—by a majority of votes—to reserve the word "true" for one of the nonclassical conceptions, and should suggest another word, say, "frue," for the conception considered here. But I cannot imagine that anybody could present cogent arguments to the effect that the semantic conception is "wrong" and should be entirely abandoned.

15. Formal Correctness of the Suggested Definition of Truth

The specific objections which have been raised to my investigations can be divided into several groups; each of these will be discussed separately.

I think that practically all these objections apply, not to the special definition I have given, but to the semantic conception of truth in general. Even those which were leveled against the definition actually constructed could be related to any other definition which conforms to this conception.

This holds, in particular, for those objections which concern the formal correctness of the definition. I have heard a few objections of this kind; however, I doubt very much whether anyone of them can be treated seriously.

As a typical example let me quote in substance such an objection.[23] In formulating the definition we use necessarily sentential connectives, i.e., expressions like "if . . . , then," "or," etc. They occur in the definiens; and one of them, namely, the phrase "if, and only if" is usually employed to combine the definiendum with the definiens. However, it is well known that the meaning of sentential connectives is explained in logic with the help of the words "true" and "false"; for instance, we say that an equivalence, i.e., a sentence of the form "p if, and only if, q," is true if either both of its members, i.e., the sentences represented by 'p' and 'q,' are true or both are false. Hence the definition of truth involves a vicious circle.

If this objection were valid, no formally correct definition of truth would be possible; for we are unable to formulate any compound sentence without using sentential connectives, or other logical terms defined with their help. Fortunately, the situation is not so bad.

It is undoubtedly the case that a strictly deductive development of logic is often preceded by certain statements explaining the conditions under which sentences of the form "if p, then q,"

etc., are considered true or false. (Such explanations are often given schematically, by means of the so-called truth-tables.) However, these statements are outside of the system of logic, and should not be regarded as definitions of the terms involved. They are not formulated in the language of the system, but constitute rather special consequences of the definition of truth given in the metalanguage. Moreover, these statements do not influence the deductive development of logic in any way. For in such a development we do not discuss the question whether a given sentence is true, we are only interested in the problem whether it is provable.[24]

On the other hand, the moment we find ourselves within the deductive system of logic—or of any discipline based upon logic, e.g., of semantics—we either treat sentential connectives as undefined terms, or else we define them by means of other sentential connectives, but never by means of semantic terms like "true" or "false." For instance, if we agree to regard the expressions "not" and "if . . . , then" (and possibly also "if, and only if") as undefined terms, we can define the term "or" by stating that a sentence of the form "p or q" is equivalent to the corresponding sentence of the form "if not p, then q." The definition can be formulated, e.g., in the following way:

$$(p \text{ or } q) \text{ if, and only if, (if not } p, \text{ then } q).$$

This definition obviously contains no semantic terms.

However, a vicious circle in definition arises only when the definiens contains either the term to be defined itself, or other terms defined with its help. Thus we clearly see that the use of sentential connectives in defining the semantic term "*true*" does not involve any circle.

I should like to mention a further objection which I have found in the literature and which seems also to concern the formal correctness, if not of the definition of truth itself, then at least of the arguments which lead to this definition.[25]

The author of this objection mistakenly regards scheme (T) (from section 4) as a definition of truth. He charges this alleged definition with "inadmissible brevity, i.e., incompleteness," which "does not give us the means of deciding whether by 'equivalence' is meant a logical-formal, or a nonlogical and also structurally nondescribable relation." To remove this "defect" he suggests supplementing (T) in one of the two following ways:

(T′) X is true if, and only if, p is true,

or

(T″) X is true if, and only if, p is the case (i.e., if what p states is the case).

Then he discusses these two new "definitions," which are supposedly free from the old, formal "defect," but which turn out to be unsatisfactory for other, nonformal reasons.

This new objection seems to arise from a misunderstanding concerning the nature of sentential connectives (and thus to be somehow related to that previously discussed). The author of the objection does not seem to realize that the phrase "if, and only if" (in opposition to such phrases as "are equivalent" or "is equivalent to") expresses no relation between sentences at all since it does not combine names of sentences.

In general, the whole argument is based upon an obvious confusion between sentences and their names. It suffices to point out that—in contradistinction to (T)—schemata (T′) and (T″) do not give any meaningful expressions if we replace in them 'p' by a sentence; for the phrases "p is true" and "p is the case" (i.e., "what p states is the case") become meaningless if 'p' is replaced by a sentence, and not by the name of a sentence (cf. section 4).[26]

While the author of the objection considers schema (T) "inadmissibly brief," I am inclined, on my part, to regard schemata (T′) and (T″) as "inadmissibly long." And I think even that I can rigorously prove this statement on the basis of the following definition: An expression is said to be "inadmissibly long" if (i) it is meaningless, and (ii) it has been obtained from a meaningful expression by inserting superfluous words.

16. Redundancy of Semantic Terms—Their Possible Elimination

The objection I am going to discuss now no longer concerns the formal correctness of the definition, but is still concerned with certain formal features of the semantic conception of truth.

We have seen that this conception essentially consists in regarding the sentence "X is true" as equivalent to the sentence denoted by 'X' (where 'X' stands for a name of a sentence of the object language). Consequently, the term "true" when occurring in a simple sentence of the form "X is true" can easily be eliminated, and the sentence itself, which belongs to the metalanguage, can be replaced by an equivalent sentence of the object language; and the same applies to compound sentences provided the term "*true*" occurs in them exclusively as a part of the expressions of the form "X is true."

Some people have therefore urged that the term "true" in the semantic sense can always be eliminated, and that for this reason the semantic conception of truth is altogether sterile and useless. And since the same considerations apply to other semantic notions, the conclusion has been drawn that semantics as a whole is a purely verbal game and at best only a harmless hobby.

But the matter is not quite so simple.[27] The sort of elimination here discussed cannot always be made. It cannot be done in the case of universal statements which express the fact that all sentences of a certain type are true, or that all true sentences have a certain property. For instance, we can prove in the theory of truth the following statement:

All consequences of true sentences are true.

However, we cannot get rid here of the word "true" in the simple manner contemplated.

Again, even in the case of particular sentences having the form "X is true" such a simple elimination cannot always be made. In fact, the elimination is possible only in those cases in which the name of the sentence which is said to be true occurs in a form that enables us to reconstruct the sentence itself. For example, our present historical knowledge does not give us any possibility of eliminating the word "true" from the following sentence:

The first sentence written by Plato is true.

Of course, since we have a definition for truth and since every definition enables us to replace the definiendum by its definiens, an elimination of the term "true" in its semantic sense is always theoretically possible. But this would not be the kind of simple elimination discussed above, and it would not result in the replacement of a sentence in the metalanguage by a sentence in the object language.

If, however, anyone continues to urge that—because of the theoretical possibility of eliminating the word "true" on the basis of its definition—the concept of truth is sterile, he must accept the further conclusion that all defined notions are sterile. But this outcome is so absurd and so unsound historically that any comment on it is unnecessary. In fact, I am rather inclined to agree with those who maintain that the moments of greatest creative advancement in science frequently coincide with the introduction of new notions by means of definition.

17. Conformity of the Semantic Conception of Truth with Philosophical and Common-sense Usage

The question has been raised whether the semantic conception of truth can indeed be regarded as a precise form of the old, classical conception of this notion.

Various formulations of the classical conception were quoted in the early part of this paper (section 3). I must repeat that in my judgment none of them is quite precise and clear. Accordingly, the only sure way of settling the question would be to confront the authors of those statements with our new formulation, and to ask them whether it agrees with their intentions. Unfortunately, this method is impractical since they died quite some time ago.

As far as my own opinion is concerned, I do not have any doubts that our formulation does conform to the intuitive content of that of Aristotle. I am less certain regarding the later formulations of the classical conception, for they are very vague indeed.[28]

Furthermore, some doubts have been expressed whether the semantic conception does reflect the notion of truth in its common-sense and everyday usage. I clearly realize (as I already indicated) that the common meaning of the word "true"—as that of any other word of everyday language—is to some extent vague, and that its usage more or less fluctuates. Hence the problem of assigning to this word a fixed and exact meaning is relatively unspecified, and

every solution of this problem implies necessarily a certain deviation from the practice of everyday language.

In spite of all this, I happen to believe that the semantic conception does conform to a very considerable extent with the common-sense usage—although I readily admit I may be mistaken. What is more to the point, however, I believe that the issue raised can be settled scientifically, though of course not by a deductive procedure, but with the help of the statistical questionnaire method. As a matter of fact, such research has been carried on, and some of the results have been reported at congresses and in part published.[29]

I should like to emphasize that in my opinion such investigations must be conducted with the utmost care. Thus, if we ask a high-school boy, or even an adult intelligent man having no special philosophical training, whether he regards a sentence to be true if it agrees with reality, or if it designates an existing state of affairs, it may simply turn out that he does not understand the question; in consequence his response, whatever it may be, will be of no value for us. But his answer to the question whether he would admit that the sentence "it is snowing" could be true although it is not snowing, or could be false although it is snowing, would naturally be very significant for our problem.

Therefore, I was by no means surprised to learn (in a discussion devoted to these problems) that in a group of people who were questioned only 15% agreed that "true" means for them "agreeing with reality," while 90% agreed that a sentence such as "it is snowing" is true if, and only if, it is snowing. Thus, a great majority of these people seemed to reject the classical conception of truth in its "philosophical" formulation, while accepting the same conception when formulated in plain words (waiving the question whether the use of the phrase "the same conception" is here justified).

18. The Definition in Its Relation to "The Philosophical Problem of Truth" and to Various Epistemological Trends

I have heard it remarked that the formal definition of truth has nothing to do with "the philosophical problem of truth."[30] However, nobody has ever pointed out to me in an intelligible way just what this problem is. I have been informed in this connection that my definition, though it states necessary and sufficient conditions for a sentence to be true, does not really grasp the "essence" of this concept. Since I have never been able to understand what the "essence" of a concept is, I must be excused from discussing this point any longer.

In general, I do not believe that there is such a thing as "the philosophical problem of truth." I do believe that there are various intelligible and interesting (but not necessarily philosophical) problems concerning the notion of truth, but I also believe that they can be exactly formulated and possibly solved only on the basis of a precise conception of this notion.

While on the one hand the definition of truth has been blamed for not being philosophical enough, on the other a series of objections have been raised charging this definition with serious philosophical implications, always of a very undesirable nature. I shall discuss now one special objection of this type; another group of such objections will be dealt with in the next section.

It has been claimed that—due to the fact that a sentence like "snow is white" is taken to be semantically true if snow is *in fact* white (italics by the critic)—logic finds itself involved in a most uncritical realism.[31]

If there were an opportunity to discuss the objection with its author, I should raise two points. First, I should ask him to drop the words "in fact," which do not occur in the original formulation and which are misleading, even if they do not affect the content. For these words convey the impression that the semantic conception of truth is intended to establish the conditions under which we are warranted in asserting any given sentence, and in particular any empirical sentence. However, a moment's reflection shows that this impression is merely an illusion; and I think that the author of the objection falls victim to the illusion which he himself created.

In fact, the semantic definition of truth implies nothing regarding the conditions under which a sentence like (1):

(1) snow is white

can be asserted. It implies only that, whenever we assert or reject this sentence, we must be ready to assert or reject the correlated sentence (2):

(2) the sentence "snow is white" is true.

Thus, we may accept the semantic conception of truth without giving up any epistemological attitude we may have had; we may remain naive realists, critical realists or idealists, empiricists or metaphysicians—whatever we were before. The semantic conception is completely neutral toward all these issues.

In the second place, I should try to get some information regarding the conception of truth which (in the opinion of the author of the objection) does not involve logic in a most naive realism. I would gather that this conception must be incompatible with the semantic one. Thus, there must be sentences which are true in one of these conceptions without being true in the other. Assume, e.g., the sentence (1) to be of this kind. The truth of this sentence in the semantic conception is determined by an equivalence of the form (T):

The sentence "snow is white" is true if, and only if, snow is white.

Hence in the new conception we must reject this equivalence, and consequently we must assume its denial:

The sentence "snow is white" is true if, and only if, snow is not white (*or perhaps*: snow, in fact, is not white).

This sounds somewhat paradoxical. I do not regard such a consequence of the new conception as absurd; but I am a little fearful that someone in the future may charge this conception with involving logic in a "most sophisticated kind of irrealism." At any rate, it seems to me important to realize that every conception of truth which is incompatible with the semantic one carries with it consequences of this type.

I have dwelt a little on this whole question, not because the objection discussed seems to me very significant, but because certain points which have arisen in the discussion should be taken into account by all those who for various epistemological reasons are inclined to reject the semantic conception of truth.

19. Alleged Metaphysical Elements in Semantics

The semantic conception of truth has been charged several times with involving certain metaphysical elements. Objections of this sort have been made to apply not only to the theory of truth, but to the whole domain of theoretical semantics.[32]

I do not intend to discuss the general problem whether the introduction of a metaphysical element into a science is at all objectionable. The only point which will interest me here is whether and in what sense metaphysics is involved in the subject of our present discussion.

The whole question obviously depends upon what one understands by "metaphysics." Unfortunately, this notion is extremely vague and equivocal. When listening to discussions in this subject, sometimes one gets the impression that the term "metaphysical" has lost any objective meaning, and is merely used as a kind of professional philosophical invective.

For some people metaphysics is a general theory of objects (ontology)—a discipline which is to be developed in a purely empirical way, and which differs from other empirical sciences only by its generality. I do not know whether such a discipline actually exists (some cynics claim that it is customary in philosophy to baptize unborn children); but I think that in any case metaphysics in this conception is not objectionable to anybody, and has hardly any connections with semantics.

For the most part, however, the term "metaphysical" is used as directly opposed—in one sense or another—to the term "empirical"; at any rate, it is used in this way by those people who are distressed by the thought that any metaphysical elements might have managed to creep into science. This general conception of metaphysics assumes several more specific forms.

Thus, some people take it to be symptomatic of a metaphysical element in a science when methods of inquiry are employed which are neither deductive nor empirical. However, no trace of this symptom can be found in the development of semantics (unless some metaphysical elements are involved in the object language to which the semantic notions refer). In particular, the semantics of formalized languages is constructed in a purely deductive way.

Others maintain that the metaphysical character of a science depends mainly on its vocabulary and, more specifically, on its primitive terms. Thus, a term is said to be metaphysical if it is neither logical nor mathematical, and if it is not associated with an empirical procedure which enables us to decide whether a thing is denoted by this term or not. With respect to such a view of metaphysics it is sufficient to recall that a metalanguage includes only three kinds of undefined terms: (i) terms taken from logic, (ii) terms of the corresponding object language, and (iii) names of expressions in the object language. It is thus obvious that no metaphysical undefined terms occur in the metalanguage (again, unless such terms appear in the object language itself).

There are, however, some who believe that, even if no metaphysical terms occur among the primitive terms of a language, they may be introduced by definitions; namely, by those definitions which fail to provide us with general criteria for deciding whether an object falls under the defined concept. It is argued that the term "true" is of this kind, since no universal criterion of truth follows immediately from the definition of this term, and since it is generally believed (and in a certain sense can even be proved) that such a criterion will never be found. This comment on the actual character of the notion of truth seems to be perfectly just. However, it should be noticed that the notion of truth does not differ in this respect from many notions in logic, mathematics, and theoretical parts of various empirical sciences, e.g., in theoretical physics.

In general, it must be said that if the term "metaphysical" is employed in so wide a sense as to embrace certain notions (or methods) of logic, mathematics, or empirical sciences, it will apply a fortiori to those of semantics. In fact, as we know from part I of the paper, in developing the semantics of a language we use all the notions of this language, and we apply even a stronger logical apparatus than that which is used in the language itself. On the other hand, however, I can summarize the arguments given above by stating that in no interpretation of the term "metaphysical" which is familiar and more or less intelligible to me does semantics involve any metaphysical elements peculiar to itself.

I should like to make one final remark in connection with this group of objections. The history of science shows many instances of concepts which were judged metaphysical (in a loose, but in any case derogatory sense of this term) before their meaning was made precise; however, once they received a rigorous, formal definition, the distrust in them evaporated. As typical examples we may mention the concepts of negative and imaginary numbers in mathematics. I hope a similar fate awaits the concept of truth and other semantic concepts; and it seems to me, therefore, that those who have distrusted them because of their alleged metaphysical implications should welcome the fact that precise definitions of these concepts are now available. If in consequence semantic concepts lose philosophical interest, they will only share the fate of many other concepts of science, and this need give rise to no regret.

20. Applicability of Semantics to Special Empirical Sciences

We come to the last and perhaps the most important group of objections. Some strong doubts have been expressed whether semantic notions find or can find applications in various domains of intellectual activity. For the most part such doubts have concerned the applicability of semantics to the field of empirical science—either to special sciences or to the general methodology of this field; although similar skepticism has been expressed regarding possible applications of semantics to mathematical sciences and their methodology.

I believe that it is possible to allay these doubts to a certain extent, and that some optimism with respect to the potential value of semantics for various domains of thought is not without ground.

To justify this optimism, it suffices I think to stress two rather obvious points. First, the development of a theory which formulates a precise definition of a notion and establishes its general properties provides *eo ipso* a firmer basis for all discussions in which this notion is involved; and, therefore, it cannot be irrelevant for anyone who uses this notion, and desires to do so in a conscious and consistent way. Secondly, semantic notions are actually involved in various branches of science, and in particular of empirical science.

The fact that in empirical research we are concerned only with natural languages and that theoretical semantics applies to these languages only with certain approximation, does not affect the problem essentially. However, it has undoubtedly this effect that progress in semantics will have but a delayed and somewhat limited influence in this field. The situation with which we are confronted here does not differ essentially from that which arises when we apply laws of logic to arguments in everyday life—or, generally, when we attempt to apply a theoretical science to empirical problems.

Semantic notions are undoubtedly involved, to a larger or smaller degree, in psychology, sociology, and in practically all the humanities. Thus, a psychologist defines the so-called intelligence quotient in terms of the numbers of *true* (right) and *false* (wrong) answers given by a person to certain questions; for a historian of culture the range of objects for which a human race in successive stages of its development possesses adequate *designations* may be a topic of great significance; a student of literature may be strongly interested in the problem whether a given author always uses two given words with the same *meaning*. Examples of this kind can be multiplied indefinitely.

The most natural and promising domain for the applications of theoretical semantics is clearly linguistics—the empirical study of natural languages. Certain parts of this science are even referred to as "semantics," sometimes with an additional qualification. Thus, this name is occasionally given to that portion of grammar which attempts to classify all words of a language into parts of speech, according to what the words mean or designate. The study of the evolution of meanings in the historical development of a language is sometimes called "historical semantics." In general, the totality of investigations on semantic relations which occur in a natural language is referred to as "descriptive semantics." The relation between theoretical and descriptive semantics is analogous to that between pure and applied mathematics, or perhaps to that between theoretical and empirical physics; the role of formalized languages in semantics can be roughly compared to that of isolated systems in physics.

It is perhaps unnecessary to say that semantics cannot find any direct applications in natural sciences such as physics, biology, etc.; for in none of these sciences are we concerned with linguistic phenomena, and even less with semantic relations between linguistic expressions and objects to which these expressions refer. We shall see, however, in the next section that semantics may have a kind of indirect influence even on those sciences in which semantic notions are not directly involved.

21. Applicability of Semantics to the Methodology of Empirical Science

Besides linguistics, another important domain for possible applications of semantics is the methodology of science; this term is used here in a broad sense so as to embrace the theory of science in general. Independent of whether a science is conceived merely as a system of statements or as a totality of certain statements and human activities, the study of scientific language constitutes an essential part of the methodological discussion of a science. And it seems to me clear that any tendency to eliminate semantic notions (like those of truth and designation) from this discussion would make it fragmentary and inadequate.[33] Moreover, there is no reason for such a tendency today, once the main difficulties in using semantic terms have been overcome. The semantics of scientific language should be simply included as a part in the methodology of science.

I am by no means inclined to charge methodology and, in particular, semantics—whether theoretical or descriptive—with the task of clarifying the meanings of all scientific terms. This task is left to those sciences in which the terms are used, and is actually fulfilled by them (in the

same way in which, e.g., the task of clarifying the meaning of the term "*true*" is left to, and fulfilled by, semantics). There may be, however, certain special problems of this sort in which a methodological approach is desirable or indeed necessary (perhaps, the problem of the notion of causality is a good example here); and in a methodological discussion of such problems semantic notions may play an essential role. Thus, semantics may have some bearing on any science whatsoever.

The question arises whether semantics can be helpful in solving general and, so to speak, classical problems of methodology. I should like to discuss here with some detail a special, though very important, aspect of this question.

One of the main problems of the methodology of empirical science consists in establishing conditions under which an empirical theory or hypothesis should be regarded as acceptable. This notion of acceptability must be relativized to a given stage of the development of a science (or to a given amount of presupposed knowledge). In other words, we may consider it as provided with a time coefficient; for a theory which is acceptable today may become untenable tomorrow as a result of new scientific discoveries.

It seems a priori very plausible that the acceptability of a theory somehow depends on the truth of its sentences, and that consequently a methodologist in his (so far rather unsuccessful) attempts at making the notion of acceptability precise, can expect some help from the semantic theory of truth. Hence we ask the question: Are there any postulates which can be reasonably imposed on acceptable theories and which involve the notion of truth? And, in particular, we ask whether the following postulate is a reasonable one:

An acceptable theory cannot contain (or imply) any false sentences.

The answer to the last question is clearly negative. For, first of all, we are practically sure, on the basis of our historical experience, that every empirical theory which is accepted today will sooner or later be rejected and replaced by another theory. It is also very probable that the new theory will be incompatible with the old one; i.e., will imply a sentence which is contradictory to one of the sentences contained in the old theory. Hence, at least one of the two theories must include false sentences, in spite of the fact that each of them is accepted at a certain time. Secondly, the postulate in question could hardly ever be satisfied in practice; for we do not know, and are very unlikely to find, any criteria of truth which enable us to show that no sentence of an empirical theory is false.

The postulate in question could be at most regarded as the expression of an ideal limit for successively more adequate theories in a given field of research; but this hardly can be given any precise meaning.

Nevertheless, it seems to me that there is an important postulate which can be reasonably imposed on acceptable empirical theories and which involves the notion of truth. It is closely related to the one just discussed, but is essentially weaker. Remembering that the notion of acceptability is provided with a time coefficient, we can give this postulate the following form:

As soon as we succeed in showing that an empirical theory contains (or implies) false sentences, it cannot be any longer considered acceptable.

In support of this postulate, I should like to make the following remarks.

I believe everybody agrees that one of the reasons which may compel us to reject an empirical theory is the proof of its inconsistency: a theory becomes untenable if we succeed in deriving from it two contradictory sentences. Now we can ask what are the usual motives for rejecting a theory on such grounds. Persons who are acquainted with modern logic are inclined to answer this question in the following way: A well-known logical law shows that a theory which enables us to derive two contradictory sentences enables us also to derive every sentence; therefore, such a theory is trivial and deprived of any scientific interest.

I have some doubts whether this answer contains an adequate analysis of the situation. I think that people who do not know modern logic are as little inclined to accept an inconsistent theory as those who are thoroughly familiar with it; and probably this applies even to those who regard (as some still do) the logical law on which the argument is based as a highly controversial issue, and almost as a paradox. I do not think that our attitude toward an inconsistent theory would change even if we decided for some reasons to weaken our system of logic so as to deprive ourselves of the possibility of deriving every sentence from any two contradictory sentences.

It seems to me that the real reason of our attitude is a different one: We know (if only intuitively) that an inconsistent theory must contain false sentences; and we are not inclined to regard as acceptable any theory which has been shown to contain such sentences.

There are various methods of showing that a given theory includes false sentences. Some of them are based upon purely logical properties of the theory involved; the method just discussed (i.e., the proof of inconsistency) is not the sole method of this type, but is the simplest one, and the one which is most frequently applied in practice. With the help of certain assumptions regarding the truth of empirical sentences, we can obtain methods to the same effect which are no longer of a purely logical nature. If we decide to accept the general postulate suggested above, then a successful application of any such method will make the theory untenable.

22. Applications of Semantics to Deductive Science

As regards the applicability of semantics to mathematical sciences and their methodology, i.e., to metamathematics, we are in a much more favorable position than in the case of empirical sciences. For, instead of advancing reasons which justify some hopes for the future (and thus making a kind of pro-semantics propaganda), we are able to point out concrete results already achieved.

Doubts continue to be expressed whether the notion of a true sentence—as distinct from that of a provable sentence—can have any significance for mathematical disciplines and play any part in a methodological discussion of mathematics. It seems to me, however, that just this notion of a true sentence constitutes a most valuable contribution to metamathematics by semantics. We already possess a series of interesting metamathematical results gained with the help of the theory of truth. These results concern the mutual relations between the notion of truth and that of provability; establish new properties of the latter notion (which, as well known, is one of the basic notions of metamathematics); and throw some light on the fundamental problems of consistency and completeness. The most significant among these results have been briefly discussed in section 12.[34]

Furthermore, by applying the method of semantics we can adequately define several important metamathematical notions which have been used so far only in an intuitive way—such as, e.g., the notion of definability or that of a model of an axiom system; and thus we can undertake a systematic study of these notions. In particular, the investigations on definability have already brought some interesting results, and promise even more in the future.[35]

We have discussed the applications of semantics only to metamathematics, and not to mathematics proper. However, this distinction between mathematics and metamathematics is rather unimportant. For metamathematics is itself a deductive discipline and hence, from a certain point of view, a part of mathematics; and it is well known that—due to the formal character of deductive method—the results obtained in one deductive discipline can be automatically extended to any other discipline in which the given one finds an interpretation. Thus, for example, all metamathematical results can be interpreted as results of number theory. Also from a practical point of view there is no clearcut line between metamathematics and mathematics proper; for instance, the investigations on definability could be included in either of these domains.

23. Final Remarks

I should like to conclude this discussion with some general and rather loose remarks concerning the whole question of the evaluation of scientific achievements in terms of their applicability. I must confess I have various doubts in this connection.

Being a mathematician (as well as a logician, and perhaps a philosopher of a sort), I have had the opportunity to attend many discussions between specialists in mathematics, where the problem of applications is especially acute, and I have noticed on several occasions the following phenomenon: If a mathematician wishes to disparage the work of one of his colleagues, say, A, the most effective method he finds for doing this is to ask where the results can be applied. The hard-pressed man, with his back against the wall, finally unearths the researches of another mathematician B as the locus of the application of his own results. If next B is plagued with a similar question, he will refer to another mathematician C. After a few steps of this kind we find ourselves referred back to the researches of A, and in this way the chain closes.

Speaking more seriously, I do not wish to deny that the value of a man's work may be increased by its implications for the research of others and for practice. But I believe, nevertheless, that it is inimical to the progress of science to measure the importance of any research exclusively or chiefly in terms of its usefulness and applicability. We know from the history of science that many important results and discoveries have had to wait centuries before they were applied in any field. And, in my opinion, there are also other important factors which cannot be disregarded in determining the value of a scientific work. It seems to me that there is a special domain of very profound and strong human needs related to scientific research, which are similar in many ways to aesthetic and perhaps religious needs. And it also seems to me that the satisfaction of these needs should be considered an important task of research. Hence, I believe, the question of the value of any research cannot be adequately answered without taking into account the intellectual satisfaction which the results of that research bring to those who understand it and care for it. It may be unpopular and out-of-date to say—but I do not think that a scientific result which gives us a better understanding of the world and makes it more harmonious in our eyes should be held in lower esteem than, say, an invention which reduces the cost of paving roads, or improves household plumbing.

It is clear that the remarks just made become

pointless if the word "application" is used in a very wide and liberal sense. It is perhaps not less obvious that nothing follows from these general remarks concerning the specific topics which have been discussed in this paper; and I really do not know whether research in semantics stands to gain or lose by introducing the standard of value I have suggested.

NOTES

1. Compare Tarski [2] (see Bibliography following Notes). This work may be consulted for a more detailed and formal presentation of the subject of the paper, especially of the material included in sections 6 and 9–13. It contains also references to my earlier publications on the problems of semantics (a communication in Polish, 1930; the article Tarski [1] in French, 1931; a communication in German, 1932; and a book in Polish, 1933). The expository part of the present paper is related in its character to Tarski [3]. My investigations on the notion of truth and on theoretical semantics have been reviewed or discussed in Hofstadter [1], Juhos [1], Kokoszyńska [1] and [2], Kotarbiński [2], Scholz [1], Weinberg [1], et al.

2. It may be hoped that the interest in theoretical semantics will now increase, as a result of the recent publication of the important book Carnap [2].

3. This applies, in particular, to public discussions during the I. International Congress for the Unity of Science (Paris, 1935) and the Conference of International Congresses for the Unity of Science (Paris, 1937); cf., e.g., Neurath [1] and Gonseth [1].

4. The words "notion" and "concept" are used in this paper with all of the vagueness and ambiguity with which they occur in philosophical literature. Thus, sometimes they refer simply to a term, sometimes to what is meant by a term, and in other cases to what is denoted by a term. Sometimes it is irrelevant which of these interpretations is meant; and in certain cases perhaps none of them applies adequately. While on principle I share the tendency to avoid these words in any exact discussion, I did not consider it necessary to do so in this informal presentation.

5. For our present purposes it is somewhat more convenient to understand by "expressions," "sentences," etc., not individual inscriptions, but classes of inscriptions of similar form (thus, not individual physical things, but classes of such things).

6. For the Aristotelian formulation see Aristotle [1], γ, 7, 27. The other two formulations are very common in the literature, but I do not know with whom they originate. A critical discussion of various conceptions of truth can be found, e.g., in Kotarbiński [1] (so far available only in Polish), pp. 123ff., and Russell [1], pp. 362ff.

7. For most of the remarks contained in sections 4 and 8, I am indebted to the late S. Lésniewski who devel-

oped them in his unpublished lectures in the University of Warsaw (in 1919 and later). However, Lésniewski did not anticipate the possibility of a rigorous development of the theory of truth, and still less of a definition of this notion; hence, while indicating equivalences of the form (T) as premises in the antinomy of the liar, he did not conceive them as any sufficient conditions for an adequate usage (or definition) of the notion of truth. Also the remarks in section 8 regarding the occurrence of an empirical premiss in the antinomy of the liar, and the possibility of eliminating this premiss, do not originate with him.

8. In connection with various logical and methodological problems involved in this paper the reader may consult Tarski [6].

9. The antinomy of the liar (ascribed to Eubulides or Epimenides) is discussed here in sections 7 and 8. For the antinomy of definability (due to J. Richard) see, e.g., Hilbert-Bernays [1], vol. 2, pp. 263ff.; for the antinomy of heterological terms see Grelling-Nelson [1], p. 307.

10. Due to Professor J. Łukasiewicz (University of Warsaw).

11. This can roughly be done in the following way. Let S be any sentence beginning with the words "Every sentence." We correlate with S a new sentence $S*$ by subjecting S to the following two modifications: we replace in S the first word, "Every," by "The"; and we insert after the second word, "sentence," the whole sentence S enclosed in quotation marks. Let us agree to call the sentence S "(self-)applicable" or "non-(self-)applicable" dependent on whether the correlated sentence $S*$ is true or false. Now consider the following sentence:

    Every sentence is nonapplicable.

    It can easily be shown that the sentence just stated must be both applicable and nonapplicable; hence a contradiction. It may not be quite clear in what sense this formulation of the antinomy does not involve an empirical premiss; however, I shall not elaborate on this point.

12. The terms "logic" and "logical" are used in this paper in a broad sense, which has become almost traditional in the last decades; logic is assumed here to comprehend the whole theory of classes and relations (i.e., the mathematical theory of sets). For many different reasons I am personally inclined to use the term "logic" in a much narrower sense, so as to apply it only to what is sometimes called "elementary logic," i.e., to the sentential calculus and the (restricted) predicate calculus.

13. Cf. here, however, Tarski [3], pp. 5f.

14. The method of construction we are going to outline can be applied—with appropriate changes—to all formalized languages that are known at the present time; although it does not follow that a language could not be constructed to which this method would not apply.

15. In carrying through this idea a certain technical difficulty arises. A sentential function may contain an

arbitrary number of free variables; and the logical nature of the notion of satisfaction varies with this number. Thus, the notion in question when applied to functions with one variable is a binary relation between these functions and single objects; when applied to functions with two variables it becomes a ternary relation between functions and couples of objects; and so on. Hence, strictly speaking, we are confronted, not with one notion of satisfaction, but with infinitely many notions; and it turns out that these notions cannot be defined independently of each other, but must all be introduced simultaneously.

To overcome this difficulty, we employ the mathematical notion of an infinite sequence (or, possibly, of a finite sequence with an arbitrary number of terms). We agree to regard satisfaction, not as a many-termed relation between sentential functions and an indefinite number of objects, but as a binary relation between functions and sequences of objects. Under this assumption the formulation of a general and precise definition of satisfaction no longer presents any difficulty; and a true sentence can now be defined as one which is satisfied by every sequence.

16. To define recursively the notion of satisfaction, we have to apply a certain form of recursive definition which is not admitted in the object-language. Hence the "essential richness" of the metalanguage may simply consist in admitting this type of definition. On the other hand, a general method is known which makes it possible to eliminate all recursive definitions and to replace them by normal, explicit ones. If we try to apply this method to the definition of satisfaction, we see that we have either to introduce into the metalanguage variables of a higher logical type than those which occur in the object language; or else to assume axiomatically in the metalanguage the existence of classes that are more comprehensive than all those whose existence can be established in the object-language. See here Tarski [2], pp. 393ff., and Tarski [5], p. 110.

17. Due to the development of modern logic, the notion of mathematical proof has undergone a far-reaching simplification. A sentence of a given formalized discipline is provable if it can be obtained from the axioms of this discipline by applying certain simple and purely formal rules of inference, such as those of detachment and substitution. Hence to show that all provable sentences are true, it suffices to prove that all the sentences accepted as axioms are true, and that the rules of inference when applied to true sentences yield new true sentences; and this usually presents no difficulty.

On the other hand, in view of the elementary nature of the notion of provability, a precise definition of this notion requires only rather simple logical devices. In most cases, those logical devices which are available in the formalized discipline itself (to which the notion of provability is related) are more than sufficient for this purpose. We know, however, that as regards the definition of truth just the opposite holds. Hence, as a rule, the notions of truth and

provability cannot coincide; and since every provable sentence is true, there must be true sentences which are not provable.

18. Thus the theory of truth provides us with a general method for consistency proofs for formalized mathematical disciplines. It can be easily realized, however, that a consistency proof obtained by this method may possess some intuitive value—i.e., may convince us, or strengthen our belief, that the discipline under consideration is actually consistent— only in case we succeed in defining truth in terms of a metalanguage which does not contain the object language as a part (cf. here a remark in section 9). For only in this case the deductive assumptions of the metalanguage may be intuitively simpler and more obvious than those of the object-language— even though the condition of "essential richness" will be formally satisfied. Cf. here also Tarski [3], p. 7.

The incompleteness of a comprehensive class of formalized disciplines constitutes the essential content of a fundamental theorem of K. Gödel; cf. Gödel [1], pp. 187ff. The explanation of the fact that the theory of truth leads so directly to Gödel's theorem is rather simple. In deriving Gödel's result from the theory of truth we make an essential use of the fact that the definition of truth cannot be given in a metalanguage which is only as "rich" as the object language (cf. note 17); however, in establishing this fact, a method of reasoning has been applied which is very closely related to that used (for the first time) by Gödel. It may be added that Gödel was clearly guided in his proof by certain intuitive considerations regarding the notion of truth, although this notion does not occur in the proof explicitly; cf. Gödel [1], pp. 174f.

19. The notions of designation and definition lead respectively to the antinomies of Grelling-Nelson and Richard (cf. note 9). To obtain an antinomy for the notion of satisfaction, we construct the following expression:

The sentential function X does not satisfy X.

A contradiction arises when we consider the question whether this expression, which is clearly a sentential function, satisfies itself or not.

20. All notions mentioned in this section can be defined in terms of satisfaction. We can say, e.g., that a given term designates a given object if this object satisfies the sentential function "x is identical with T" where 'T' stands for the given term. Similarly, a sentential function is said to define a given object if the latter is the only object which satisfies this function. For a definition of consequence see Tarski [4], and for that of synonymity, Carnap [2].

21. General semantics is the subject of Carnap [2]. Cf. here also remarks in Tarski [2], pp. 388f.

22. Cf. various quotations in Ness [1], pp. 13f.

23. The names of persons who have raised objections will not be quoted here, unless their objections have appeared in print.

24. It should be emphasized, however, that as regards

the question of an alleged vicious circle the situation would not change even if we took a different point of view, represented, e.g., in Carnap [2]; i.e., if we regarded the specification of conditions under which sentences of a language are true as an essential part of the description of this language. On the other hand, it may be noticed that the point of view represented in the text does not exclude the possibility of using truth-tables in a deductive development of logic. However, these tables are to be regarded then merely as a formal instrument for checking the provability of certain sentences; and the symbols 'T' and 'F' which occur in them and which are usually considered abbreviations of "true" and "false" should not be interpreted in any intuitive way.

25. Cf. Juhos [1]. I must admit that I do not clearly understand von Juhos' objections and do not know how to classify them; therefore, I confine myself here to certain points of a formal character. Von Juhos does not seem to know my definition of truth; he refers only to an informal presentation in Tarski [3] where the definition has not been given at all. If he knew the actual definition, he would have to change his argument. However, I have no doubt that he would discover in this definition some "defects" as well. For he believes he has proved that "on ground of principle it is impossible to give such a definition at all."

26. The phrases "*p* is true" and "*p* is the case" (or better "it is true that *p*" and "it is the case that *p*") are sometimes used in informal discussions, mainly for stylistic reasons; but they are considered then as synonymous with the sentence represented by '*p*'. On the other hand, as far as I understand the situation, the phrases in question cannot be used by von Juhos synonymously with '*p*'; for otherwise the replacement of (T) by (T′) or (T″) would not constitute any "improvement."

27. Cf. the discussion of this problem in Kokoszyńska [1], pp. 161ff.

28. Most authors who have discussed my work on the notion of truth are of the opinion that my definition does conform with the classical conception of this notion; see, e.g., Kotarbiński [2] and Scholz [1].

29. Cf. Ness [1]. Unfortunately, the results of that part of Ness' research which is especially relevant for our problem are not discussed in his book; compare p. 148, footnote 1.

30. Though I have heard this opinion several times, I have seen it in print only once and, curiously enough, in a work which does not have a philosophical character—in fact, in Hilbert-Bernays [1], vol. II, p. 269 (where, by the way, it is not expressed as any kind of objection). On the other hand, I have not found any remark to this effect in discussions of my work by professional philosophers (cf. note 1).

31. Cf. Gonseth [1], pp. 187f.

32. See Nagel [1], and Nagel [2], pp. 471f. A remark which goes, perhaps, in the same direction is also to be found in Weinberg [1], p. 77; cf., however, his earlier remarks, pp. 75f.

33. Such a tendency was evident in earlier works of Carnap (see, e.g., Carnap [1], especially part V) and in writings of other members of Vienna Circle. Cf. Kokoszyńska [1] and Weinberg [1].

34. For other results obtained with the help of the theory of truth see Gödel [2]; Tarski [2], pp. 401ff.; and Tarski [5], pp. 111f.

35. An object—e.g., a number or a set of numbers—is said to be definable (in a given formalism) if there is a sentential function which defines it; cf. note 20. Thus, the term "definable," though of a metamathematical (semantic) origin, is purely mathematical as to its extension, for it expresses a property (denotes a class) of mathematical objects. In consequence, the notion of definability can be redefined in purely mathematical terms, though not within the formalized discipline to which this notion refers; however, the fundamental idea of the definition remains unchanged. Cf. here—also for further bibliographic references—Tarski [1]; various other results concerning definability can also be found in the literature, e.g., in Hilbert-Bernays [1], vol. I, pp. 354ff., 369ff., 456ff., etc., and in Lindenbaum-Tarski [1]. It may be noticed that the term "definable" is sometimes used in another, metamathematical (but not semantic), sense; this occurs, for instance, when we say that a term is definable in other terms (on the basis of a given axiom system). For a definition of a model of an axiom system see Tarski [4].

BIBLIOGRAPHY

Only the books and articles actually referred to in the paper will be listed here.

Aristotle [1]. *Metaphysica*. (*Works*, vol. VIII.) English translation by W. D. Ross. (Oxford: 1908).

Carnap, R. [1]. *Logical Syntax of Language*. (London and New York: 1937).

———.[2]. *Introduction to Semantics*. (Cambridge: 1942).

Gödel, K. [1]. "Über formal unentscheidbare Sätze der *Principia Mathematica und verwandter Systeme*, I." *Monatshefte fur Mathematik und Physik*, XXXVIII (1931), pp. 173–198.

———.[2]. "Über die Lange von Beweisen." *Ergebnisse eines mathematischen Kolloquiums*, vol. VII (1936), pp. 23–24.

Gonseth, F. [1]. "Le Congrès Descartes. Questions de Philosophie scientifique." *Revue thomiste*, vol. XLIV (1938), pp. 183–193.

Grelling, K., and Nelson, L. [1]. "Bemerkungen zu den Paradoxien von Russell und Burali-Forti." *Abhandlungen der Fries'schen Schule*, vol. II (new series), (1908), pp. 301–334.

Hofstadter, A. [1]. "On Semantic Problems." *The Journal of Philosophy*, vol. XXXV (1938), pp. 225–232.

Hilbert, D., and Bernays, P. [1]. *Grundlagen der Mathematik*. 2 vols. (Berlin: 1934–1939).

Juhos, B. von. [1]. "The Truth of Empirical Statements." *Analysis*, vol. IV (1937), pp. 65–70.

Kokoszyńska, M. [1]. "Über den absoluten Wahrheitsbegriff und einige andere semantische Begriffe." *Erkenntnis,* vol. VI (1936), pp. 143–165.

———.[2]. "Syntax, Semantik und Wissenschaftslogik." *Actes du Congrès International de Philosophie Scientifique,* vol. III (Paris: 1936), pp. 9–14.

Kotarbiński, T. [1]. *Elementy teorji poznania, logiki formalnej i metodologji nauk. (Elements of Epistemology, Formal Logic, and the Methodology of Sciences,* in Polish.) (Lwów: 1929).

———.[2]. "W sprawie pojęcia prawdy." (*"Concerning the Concept of Truth,"* in Polish.) *Przeglgd filozoficzny,* vol. XXXVII, pp. 85–91.

Lindenbaum, A., and Tarski, A. [1]. "Über die Beschränktheit der Ausdrucksmittel deduktiver Theorien." *Ergebnisse eines mathematischen Kolloquiums,* vol. VII, (1936), pp. 15–23.

Nagel, E. [1]. Review of Hofstadter [1]. *The Journal of Symbolic Logic,* vol. III, (1938), p. 90.

———.[2]. Review of Carnap [2]. *The Journal of Philosophy,* vol. XXXIX, (1942), pp. 468–473.

Ness, A. [1]. "'Truth' As Conceived by Those Who Are Not Professional Philosophers." *Skrifter utgitt av Det Norske Videnskaps-Akademi i Oslo, II. Hist.-Filos. Klasse,* vol. IV (Oslo: 1938).

Neurath, O. [1]. "Erster Internationaler Kongress für Einheit der Wissenschaft in Paris 1935." *Erkenntnis,* vol. V (1935), pp. 377–406.

Russell, B. [1]. *An Inquiry Into Meaning and Truth.* (New York: 1940).

Scholz, H. [1]. *Review of Studia philosophica,* vol. I. *Deutsche Literaturzeitung,* vol. LVIII (1937), pp. 1914–1917.

Tarski, A. [1]. "Sur les ensembles définissables de nombres réels. I." *Fundamenta mathematicae,* vol. XVII (1931), pp. 210–239.

———.[2]. "Der Wahrheitsbegriff in den formalisierten Sprachen." (German translation of a book in Polish, 1933.) *Studia philosophica,* vol. I (1935), pp. 261–405.

———.[3]. "Grundlegung der wissenschaftlichen Semantik." *Actes du Congrès International de Philosophie Scientifique,* vol. III (Paris: 1936), pp. 1–8.

———.[4]. "Uber den Begriff der logischen Folgerung." *Actes du Congrès International de Philosophie Scientifique,* vol. VII (Paris: 1937), pp. 1–11.

———.[5]. "On Undecidable Statements in Enlarged Systems of Logic and the Concept of Truth." *The Journal of Symbolic Logic,* vol. IV, 1939, pp. 105–112.

———.[6]. *Introduction to Logic.* (New York: 1941).

Weinberg, J. [1]. Review of *Studia philosophica,* vol. I. *The Philosophical Review,* vol. XLVII, pp. 70–77.

6 Meaning

H. P. GRICE

Consider the following sentences:

"Those spots mean (meant) measles."
"Those spots didn't mean anything to me, but to the doctor they meant measles."
"The recent budget means that we shall have a hard year."

(1) I cannot say, "Those spots meant measles, but he hadn't got measles," and I cannot say, "The recent budget means that we shall have a hard year, but we shan't have." That is to say, in cases like the above, *x meant that p* and *x means that p* entail *p*.

(2) I cannot argue from "Those spots mean (meant) measles" to any conclusion about "what is (was) meant by those spots"; for example, I am not entitled to say, "What was meant by those spots was that he had measles." Equally I cannot draw from the statement about the recent budget the conclusion "What is meant by the recent budget is that we shall have a hard year."

(3) I cannot argue from "Those spots meant measles" to any conclusion to the effect that somebody or other meant by those spots so-and-so. *Mutatis mutandis*, the same is true of the sentence about the recent budget.

(4) For none of the above examples can a restatement be found in which the verb "mean" is followed by a sentence or phrase in inverted commas. Thus "Those spots meant measles"

cannot be reformulated as "Those spots meant 'measles'" or "Those spots meant 'he has measles.'"

(5) On the other hand, for all these examples an approximate restatement can be found beginning with the phrase "The fact that . . ."; for example, "The fact that he had those spots meant that he had measles" and "The fact that the recent budget was as it was means that we shall have a hard year."

Now contrast the above sentences with the following:

"Those three rings on the bell (of the bus) mean that the bus is full."
"That remark, 'Smith couldn't get on without his trouble and strife,' meant that Smith found his wife indispensable."

(1) I can use the first of these and go on to say, "But it isn't in fact full—the conductor has made a mistake"; and I can use the second and go on, "But in fact Smith deserted her seven years ago." That is to say, here *x means that p* and *x meant that p* do not entail *p*.

(2) I can argue from the first to some statement about "what is (was) meant" by the rings on the bell and from the second to some statement about "what is (was) meant" by the quoted remark.

(3) I can argue from the first sentence to the conclusion that somebody (viz., the conductor)

From *Philosophical Review* 66 (1957): 377–388. Reprinted by permission of the publisher.

meant, or at any rate should have meant, by the rings that the bus is full, and I can argue analogously for the second sentence.

(4) The first sentence can be restated in a form in which the verb "mean" is followed by a phrase in inverted commas, that is, "Those three rings on the bell mean 'the bus is full.'" So also can the second sentence.

(5) Such a sentence as "The fact that the bell has been rung three times means that the bus is full" is not a restatement of the meaning of the first sentence. Both may be true, but they do not have, even approximately, the same meaning.

When the expressions "means," "means something," "means that" are used in the kind of way in which they are used in the first set of sentences, I shall speak of the sense, or senses, in which they are used, as the *natural* sense, or senses, of the expressions in question. When the expressions are used in the kind of way in which they are used in the second set of sentences, I shall speak of the sense, or senses, in which they are used, as the *nonnatural* sense, or senses, of the expressions in question. I shall use the abbreviation "means$_{NN}$" to distinguish the non-natural sense or senses.

I propose, for convenience, also to include under the head of natural senses of "mean" such senses of "mean" as may be exemplified in sentences of the pattern "*A* means (meant) *to do* so-and-so (by *x*)," where *A* is a human agent. By contrast, as the previous examples show, I include under the head of nonnatural senses of "mean" any senses of "mean" found in sentences of the patterns "*A* means (meant) something by *x*" or "*A* means (meant) by *x* that. . . ." (This is overrigid; but it will serve as an indication.)

I do not want to maintain that *all* our uses of "mean" fall easily, obviously, and tidily into one of the two groups I have distinguished; but I think that in most cases we should be at least fairly strongly inclined to assimilate a use of "mean" to one group rather than to the other. The question which now arises is this: "What more can be said about the distinction between the cases where we should say that the word is applied in a natural sense and the cases where we should say that the word is applied in a non-natural sense?" Asking this question will not of

course prohibit us from trying to give an explanation of "meaning$_{NN}$" in terms of one or another natural sense of "mean."

This question about the distinction between natural and nonnatural meaning is, I think, what people are getting at when they display an interest in a distinction between "natural" and "conventional" signs. But I think my formulation is better. For some things which can mean$_{NN}$ something are not signs (e.g., words are not), and some are not conventional in any ordinary sense (e.g., certain gestures); while some things which mean naturally are not signs of what they mean (cf. the recent budget example).

I want first to consider briefly, and reject, what I might term a causal type of answer to the question, "What is meaning$_{NN}$?" We might try to say, for instance, more or less with C. L. Stevenson,[1] that for *x* to mean$_{NN}$ something, *x* must have (roughly) a tendency to produce in an audience some attitude (cognitive or otherwise) and a tendency, in the case of a speaker, to *be* produced *by* that attitude, these tendencies being dependent on "an elaborate process of conditioning attending the use of the sign in communication"[2] This clearly will not do.

(1) Let us consider a case where an utterance, if it qualifies at all as meaning$_{NN}$ something, will be of a descriptive or informative kind and the relevant attitude, therefore, will be a cognitive one, for example, a belief. (I use "utterance" as a neutral word to apply to any candidate for meaning$_{NN}$; it has a convenient act-object ambiguity.) It is no doubt the case that many people have a tendency to put on a tail coat when they think they are about to go to a dance, and it is also no doubt the case that many people, on seeing someone put on a tail coat, would conclude that the person in question was about to go to a dance. Does this satisfy us that putting on a tail coat means$_{NN}$ that one is about to go to a dance (or indeed means$_{NN}$ anything at all)? Obviously not. It is no help to refer to the qualifying phrase "dependent on an elaborate process of conditioning. . . ." For if all this means is that the response to the sight of a tail coat being put on is in some way learned or acquired, it will not exclude the present case from being one of meaning$_{NN}$. But if we have to take seriously the second part of the qualifying

phrase ("attending the use of the sign in communication"), then the account of meaning$_{NN}$ is obviously circular. We might just as well say, "X has meaning$_{NN}$ if it is used in communication," which, though true, is not helpful.

(2) If this is not enough, there is a difficulty—really the same difficulty, I think—which Stevenson recognizes: how we are to avoid saying, for example, that "Jones is tall" is part of what is meant by "Jones is an athlete," since to tell someone that Jones is an athlete would tend to make him believe that Jones is tall. Stevenson here resorts to invoking linguistic rules, namely, a permissive rule of language that "athletes may be nontall." This amounts to saying that we are not prohibited by rule from speaking of "nontall athletes." But why are we not prohibited? Not because it is not bad grammar, or is not impolite, and so on, but presumably because it is not meaningless (or, if this is too strong, does not in any way violate the rules of meaning for the expressions concerned). But this seems to involve us in another circle. Moreover, one wants to ask why, if it is legitimate to appeal here to rules to distinguish what is meant from what is suggested, this appeal was not made earlier, in the case of groans, for example, to deal with which Stevenson originally introduced the qualifying phrase about dependence on conditioning.

A further deficiency in a causal theory of the type just expounded seems to be that, even if we accept it as it stands, we are furnished with an analysis only of statements about the *standard* meaning, or the meaning in general, of a "sign." No provision is made for dealing with statements about what a particular speaker or writer means by a sign on a particular occasion (which may well diverge from the standard meaning of the sign); nor is it obvious how the theory could be adapted to make such provision. One might even go further in criticism and maintain that the causal theory ignores the fact that the meaning (in general) of a sign needs to be explained in terms of what users of the sign do (or should) mean by it on particular occasions; and so the latter notion, which is unexplained by the causal theory, is in fact the fundamental one. I am sympathetic to this more

radical criticism, though I am aware that the point is controversial.

I do not propose to consider any further theories of the "causal-tendency" type. I suspect no such theory could avoid difficulties analogous to those I have outlined without utterly losing its claim to rank as a theory of this type. I will now try a different and, I hope, more promising line. If we can elucidate the meaning of

"x meant$_{NN}$ something (on a particular occasion)" and
"x meant$_{NN}$ that so-and-so (on a particular occasion)"

and of

"A meant$_{NN}$ something by x (on a particular occasion)" and
"A meant$_{NN}$ by x that so-and-so (on a particular occasion),"

this might reasonably be expected to help us with

"x means$_{NN}$ (timeless) something (that so-and-so),"
"A means$_{NN}$ (timeless) by x something (that so-and-so),"

and with the explication of "means the same as," "understands," "entails," and so on. Let us for the moment pretend that we have to deal only with utterances which might be informative or descriptive.

A first shot would be to suggest that "x meant$_{NN}$ something" would be true if x was intended by its utterer to induce a belief in some "audience" and that to say what the belief was would be to say what x meant$_{NN}$. This will not do. I might leave B's handkerchief near the scene of a murder in order to induce the detective to believe that B was the murderer; but we should not want to say that the handkerchief (or my leaving it there) meant$_{NN}$ anything or that I had meant$_{NN}$ by leaving it that B was the murderer. Clearly we must at least add that, for x to have meant$_{NN}$ anything, not merely must it have been "uttered" with the intention of inducing a certain belief but also the utterer must have intended an "audience" to recognize the intention behind the utterance.

This, though perhaps better, is not good enough. Consider the following cases:

(1) Herod presents Salome with the head of St. John the Baptist on a charger.
(2) Feeling faint, a child lets its mother see how pale it is (hoping that she may draw her own conclusion and help).
(3) I leave the china my daughter has broken lying around for my wife to see.

Here we seem to have cases which satisfy the conditions so far given for meaning$_{NN}$. For example, Herod intended to make Salome believe that John the Baptist was dead and no doubt also intended Salome to recognize that he intended her to believe that St. John the Baptist was dead. Similarly for the other cases. Yet I certainly do not think that we should want to say that we have here cases of meaning$_{NN}$.

What we want to find is the difference between, for example, "deliberately and openly letting someone know" and "telling" and between "getting someone to think" and "telling."

The way out is perhaps as follows. Compare the following two cases:

(1) I show Mr. X a photograph of Mr. Y displaying undue familiarity to Mrs. X.
(2) I draw a picture of Mr. Y behaving in this manner and show it to Mr. X.

I find that I want to deny that in (1) the photograph (or my showing it to Mr. X) meant$_{NN}$ anything at all; while I want to assert that in (2) the picture (or my drawing and showing it) meant$_{NN}$ something (that Mr. Y had been unduly unfamiliar), or at least that I had meant$_{NN}$ by it that Mr. Y had been unduly familiar. What is the difference between the two cases? Surely that in case (1) Mr. X's recognition of my intention to make him believe that there is something between Mr. Y and Mrs. X is (more or less) irrelevant to the production of this effect by the photograph. Mr. X would be led by the photograph at least to suspect Mrs. X even if instead of showing it to him I had left it in his room by accident; and I (the photograph shower) would not be unaware of this. But it will make a difference to the effect of my picture on Mr. X whether or not he takes me to be intending to inform him (make him believe

something) about Mrs. X, and not to be just doodling or trying to produce a work of art.

But now we seem to be landed in a further difficulty if we accept this account. For consider now, say, frowning. If I frown spontaneously, in the ordinary course of events, someone looking at me may well treat the frown as a natural sign of displeasure. But if I frown deliberately (to convey my displeasure), an onlooker may be expected, provided he recognizes my intention, *still* to conclude that I am displeased. Ought we not then to say, since it could not be expected to make any difference to the onlooker's reaction whether he regards my frown as spontaneous or as intended to be informative, that my frown (deliberate) does not mean$_{NN}$ anything? I think this difficulty can be met; for though in general a deliberate frown may have the same effect (as regards inducing belief in my displeasure) as a spontaneous frown, it can be expected to have the same effect only *provided* the audience takes it as intended to convey displeasure. That is, if we take away the recognition of intention, leaving the other circumstances (including the recognition of the frown as deliberate), the belief-producing tendency of the frown must be regarded as being impaired or destroyed.

Perhaps we may sum up what is necessary for A to mean something by x as follows. A must intend to induce by x a belief in an audience, and he must also intend his utterance to be recognized as so intended. But these intentions are not independent; the recognition is intended by A to play its part in inducing the belief, and if it does not do so something will have gone wrong with the fulfillment of A's intentions. Moreover, A's intending that the recognition should play this part implies, I think, that he assumes that there is some chance that it will in fact play this part, that he does not regard it as a foregone conclusion that the belief will be induced in the audience whether or not the intention behind the utterance is recognized. Shortly, perhaps, we may say that "A meant$_{NN}$ something by x" is roughly equivalent to "A uttered x with the intention of inducing a belief by means of the recognition of this intention." (This seems to involve a reflexive paradox, but it does not really do so.)

Now perhaps it is time to drop the pretense that we have to deal only with "informative" cases. Let us start with some examples of imperatives or quasi-imperatives. I have a very avaricious man in my room, and I want him to go; so I throw a pound note out of the window. Is there here any utterance with a meaning$_{NN}$? No, because in behaving as I did, I did not intend his recognition of my purpose to be in any way effective in getting him to go. This is parallel to the photograph case. If on the other hand I had pointed to the door or given him a little push, then my behavior might well be held to constitute a meaningful$_{NN}$ utterance, just because the recognition of my intention would be intended by me to be effective in speeding his departure. Another pair of cases would be (1) a policeman who stops a car by standing in its way and (2) a policeman who stops a car by waving.

Or, to turn briefly to another type of case, if as an examiner I fail a man, I may well cause him distress or indignation or humiliation; and if I am vindictive, I may intend this effect and even intend him to recognize my intention. But I should not be inclined to say that my failing him meant$_{NN}$ anything. On the other hand, if I cut someone in the street I do feel inclined to assimilate this to the cases of meaning$_{NN}$, and this inclination seems to me dependent on the fact that I could not reasonably expect him to be distressed (indignant, humiliated) unless he recognized my intention to affect him in this way. (Cf., if my college stopped my salary altogether I should accuse them of ruining me; if they cut it by 2/6^d I might accuse them of insulting me; with some intermediate amounts I might not know quite what to say.)

Perhaps then we may make the following generalizations:

(1) "A meant$_{NN}$ something by x" is (roughly) equivalent to "A intended the utterance of x to produce some effect in an audience by means of the recognition of this intention"; and we may add to that to ask what A meant is to ask for a specification of the intended effect (though, of course, it may not always be possible to get a straight answer involving a "that" clause, for example, "a belief that . . .").

(2) "x meant something" is (roughly) equiva-
lent to "Somebody meant$_{NN}$ something by x." Here again there will be cases where this will not quite work. I feel inclined to say that (as regards traffic lights) the change to red meant$_{NN}$ that the traffic was to stop; but it would be very unnatural to say, "Somebody (e.g., the Corporation) meant$_{NN}$ by the red-light change that the traffic was to stop." Nevertheless, there seems to be *some* sort of reference to somebody's intentions.

(3) "x means$_{NN}$ (timeless) that so-and-so" might as a first shot be equated with some statement or disjunction of statements about what "people" (vague) intend (with qualifications about "recognition") to effect by x. I shall have a word to say about this.

Will any kind of intended effect do, or may there be cases where an effect is intended (with the required qualifications) and yet we should not want to talk of meaning$_{NN}$? Suppose I discovered some person so constituted that, when I told him that whenever I grunted in a special way I wanted him to blush or to incur some physical malady, thereafter whenever he recognized the grunt (and with it my intention), he did blush or incur the malady. Should we then want to say that the grunt meant$_{NN}$ something? I do not think so. This points to the fact that for x to have meaning$_{NN}$, the intended effect must be something which in some sense is within the control of the audience, or that in some sense of "reason" the recognition of the intention behind x is for the audience a reason and not merely a cause. It might look as if there is a sort of pun here ("reason for believing" and "reason for doing"), but I do not think this is serious. For though no doubt from one point of view questions about reasons for believing are questions about evidence and so quite different from questions about reasons for doing, nevertheless to recognize an utterer's intention in uttering x (descriptive utterance), to have a reason for believing that so-and-so, is at least quite like "having a motive for" accepting so-and-so. Decisions "that" seem to involve decisions "to" (and this is why we can "refuse to believe" and also be "compelled to believe"). (The "cutting" case needs slightly different treatment, for one cannot in any straightforward sense "decide" to be offended; but one can refuse to be offended.)

It looks then as if the intended effect must be something with the control of the audience, or at least the *sort* of thing which is within its control.

One point before passing to an objection or two. I think it follows that from what I have said about the connection between meaning$_{NN}$ and recognition of intention that (insofar as I am right) only what I may call the primary intention of an utterer is relevant to the meaning$_{NN}$ of an utterance. For if I utter x, intending (with the aid of the recognition of this intention) to induce an effect E, and intend this effect E to lead to a further effect F, then insofar as the occurrence of F is thought to be dependent solely on E, I cannot regard F as in the least dependent on recognition of my intention to induce E. That is, if (say) I intend to get a man to do something by giving him some information, it cannot be regarded as relevant to the meaning$_{NN}$ of my utterance to describe what I intend him to do.

Now some question may be raised about my use, fairly free, of such words as "intention" and "recognition." I must disclaim any intention of peopling all our talking life with armies of complicated psychological occurrences. I do not hope to solve any philosophical puzzles about intending, but I do want briefly to argue that no special difficulties are raised by my use of the word "intention" in connection with meaning. First, there will be cases where an utterance is accompanied or preceded by a conscious "plan" or explicit formulation of intention (e.g., I declare how I am going to use x, or ask myself how to "get something across"). The presence of such an explicit "plan" obviously counts fairly heavily in favor of the utterer's intention (meaning) being as "planned"; though it is not, I think, conclusive; for example, a speaker who has declared an intention to use a familiar expression in an unfamiliar way may slip into the familiar use. Similarly in nonlinguistic cases: if we are asking about an agent's intention, a previous expression counts heavily; nevertheless, a man might plan to throw a letter in the dustbin and yet take it to the post; when lifting his hand he might "come to" and say *either* "I didn't intend to do this at all" *or* "I suppose I must have been intending to put it in."

Explicitly formulated linguistic (or quasi-linguistic) intentions are no doubt comparatively rare. In their absence we would seem to rely on very much the same kinds of criteria as we do in the case of nonlinguistic intentions where there is a general usage. An utterer is held to intend to convey what is normally conveyed (or normally intended to be conveyed), and we require a good reason for accepting that a particular use diverges from the general usage (e.g., he never knew or had forgotten the general usage). Similarly in nonlinguistic cases: we are presumed to intend the normal consequences of our actions.

Again, in cases where there is doubt, say, about which of two or more things an utterer intends to convey, we tend to refer to the context (linguistic or otherwise) of the utterance and ask which of the alternatives would be relevant to other things he is saying or doing, or which intention in a particular situation would fit in with some purpose he obviously has (e.g., a man who calls for a "pump" at a fire would not want a bicycle pump). Nonlinguistic parallels are obvious: context is a criterion in settling the question of why a man who has just put a cigarette in his mouth has put his hand in his pocket; relevance to an obvious end is a criterion in settling why a man is running away from a bull.

In certain linguistic cases we ask the utterer afterward about his intention, and in a few of these cases (the very difficult ones, like a philosopher asked to explain the meaning of an unclear passage in one of his works), the answer is not based on what he remembers but is more like a decision, a decision about how what he said is to be taken. I cannot find a nonlinguistic parallel here; but the case is so special as not to seem to contribute a vital difference.

All this is very obvious; but surely to show that the criteria for judging linguistic intentions are very like the criteria for judging nonlinguistic intentions is to show that linguistic intentions are very like nonlinguistic intentions.

NOTES

1. *Ethics and Language* (New Haven: 1944), ch. 3.
2. Ibid., p. 57.

7 Truth and Meaning

DONALD DAVIDSON

It is conceded by most philosophers of language, and recently even by some linguists, that a satisfactory theory of meaning must give an account of how the meanings of sentences depend upon the meanings of words. Unless such an account could be supplied for a particular language, it is argued, there would be no explaining the fact that we can learn the language: no explaining the fact that, on mastering a finite vocabulary and a finitely stated set of rules, we are prepared to produce and to understand any of a potential infinitude of sentences. I do not dispute these vague claims, in which I sense more than a kernel of truth.[1] Instead I want to ask what it is for a theory to give an account of the kind adumbrated.

One proposal is to begin by assigning some entity as meaning to each word (or other significant syntactical feature) of the sentence; thus we might assign Theaetetus to "Theaetetus" and the property of flying to "flies" in the sentence "Theaetetus flies." The problem then arises how the meaning of the sentence is generated from these meanings. Viewing concatenation as a significant piece of syntax, we may assign to it the relation of participating in or instantiating; however, it is obvious that we have here the start of an infinite regress. Frege sought to avoid the regress by saying that the entities corresponding to predicates (for example) are 'unsaturated' or 'incomplete' in contrast to the entities that cor-respond to names, but this doctrine seems to label a difficulty rather than solve it.

The point will emerge if we think for a moment of complex singular terms, to which Frege's theory applies along with sentences. Consider the expression "the father of Annette"; how does the meaning of the whole depend on the meaning of the parts? The answer would seem to be that the meaning of "the father of" is such that when this expression is prefixed to a singular term the result refers to the father of the person to whom the singular term refers. What part is played, in this account, by the unsaturated or incomplete entity for which "the father of" stands? All we can think to say is that this entity 'yields' or 'gives' the father of x as value when the argument is x, or perhaps that this entity maps people onto their fathers. It may not be clear whether the entity for which "the father of" is said to stand performs any genuine explanatory function as long as we stick to individual expressions; so think instead of the infinite class of expressions formed by writing "the father of" zero or more times in front of "Annette." It is easy to supply a theory that tells, for an arbitrary one of these singular terms, what it refers to: if the term is "Annette" it refers to Annette, while if the term is complex, consisting of "the father of" prefixed to a singular term t, then it refers to the father of the person to whom t refers. It is obvious that no entity corre-

From *Synthese* 17 (1967): 304–323. Copyright © 1967 by D. Reidel Publishing Company, Dordrecht, Holland. Reprinted by permission of the publisher.

sponding to "the father of" is, or needs to be, mentioned in stating this theory.

It would be inappropriate to complain that this little theory *uses* the words "the father of" in giving the reference of expressions containing those words. For the task was to give the meaning of all expressions in a certain infinite set on the basis of the meaning of the parts; it was not in the bargain also to give the meanings of the atomic parts. On the other hand, it is now evident that a satisfactory theory of the meanings of complex expressions may not require entities as meanings of all the parts. It behooves us then to rephrase our demand on a satisfactory theory of meaning so as not to suggest that individual words must have meanings at all, in any sense that transcends the fact that they have a systematic effect on the meanings of the sentences in which they occur. Actually, for the case at hand we can do better still in stating the criterion of success: what we wanted, and what we got, is a theory that entails every sentence of the form "*t* refers to *x*" where '*t*' is replaced by a structural description[2] of a singular term, and '*x*' is replaced by that term itself. Further, our theory accomplishes this without appeal to any semantical concepts beyond the basic "refers to." Finally, the theory clearly suggests an effective procedure for determining, for any singular term in its universe, what that term refers to.

A theory with such evident merits deserves wider application. The device proposed by Frege to this end has a brilliant simplicity: count predicates as a special case of functional expressions, and sentences as a special case of complex singular terms. Now, however, a difficulty looms if we want to continue in our present (implicit) course of identifying the meaning of a singular term with its reference. The difficulty follows upon making two reasonable assumptions: that logically equivalent singular terms have the same reference; and that a singular term does not change its reference if a contained singular term is replaced by another with the same reference. But now suppose that '*R*' and '*S*' abbreviate any two sentences alike in truth value. Then the following four sentences have the same reference:

(1) R

(2) $\hat{x}(x=x.R) = \hat{x}(x=x)$

(3) $\hat{x}(x=x.S) = x(x=x)$

(4) S

For (1) and (2) are logically equivalent, as are (3) and (4), while (3) differs from (2) only in containing the singular term '$\hat{x}(x=x.S)$' where (2) contains '$\hat{x}(x=x.R)$' and these refer to the same thing if S and R are alike in truth value. Hence any two sentences have the same reference if they have the same truth value.[3] And if the meaning of a sentence is what it refers to, all sentences alike in truth value must be synonymous—an intolerable result.

Apparently we must abandon the present approach as leading to a theory of meaning. This is the natural point at which to turn for help to the distinction between meaning and reference. The trouble, we are told, is that questions of reference are, in general, settled by extralinguistic facts, questions of meaning not, and the facts can conflate the references of expressions that are not synonymous. If we want a theory that gives the meaning (as distinct from reference) of each sentence, we must start with the meaning (as distinct from reference) of the parts.

Up to here we have been following in Frege's footsteps; thanks to him, the path is well known and even well worn. But now, I would like to suggest, we have reached an impasse: the switch from reference to meaning leads to no useful account of how the meanings of sentences depend upon the meanings of the words (or other structural features) that compose them. Ask, for example, for the meaning of "Theaetetus flies." A Fregean answer might go something like this: given the meaning of "Theaetetus" as argument, the meaning of "flies" yields the meaning of "Theaetetus flies" as value. The vacuity of this answer is obvious. We wanted to know what the meaning of "Theaetetus flies" is; it is no progress to be told that it is the meaning of "Theaetetus flies." This much we knew before any theory was in sight. In the bogus account just given, talk of the structure of the sentence and of the meanings of words was idle, for it played no role in producing the given description of the meaning of the sentence.

The contrast here between a real and pretended account will be plainer still if we ask for a theory, analogous to the miniature theory of reference of singular terms just sketched, but different in dealing with meanings in place of references. What analogy demands is a theory that has as consequences all sentences of the form "*s* means *m*" where '*s*' is replaced by a structural description of a sentence and '*m*' is replaced by a singular term that refers to the meaning of that sentence; a theory, moreover, that provides an effective method for arriving at the meaning of an arbitrary sentence structurally described. Clearly some more articulate way of referring to meanings than any we have seen is essential if these criteria are to be met.[4] Meanings as entities, or the related concept of synonymy, allow us to formulate the following rule relating sentences and their parts: sentences are synonymous whose corresponding parts are synonymous ("corresponding" here needs spelling out of course). And meanings as entities may, in theories such as Frege's, do duty, on occasion as references, thus losing their status as entities distinct from references. Paradoxically, the one thing meanings do not seem to do is oil the wheels of a theory of meaning—at least as long as we require of such a theory that it nontrivially give the meaning of every sentence in the language. My objection to meanings in the theory of meaning is not that they are abstract or that their identity conditions are obscure, but that they have no demonstrated use.

This is the place to scotch another hopeful thought. Suppose we have a satisfactory theory of syntax for our language, consisting of an effective method of telling, for an arbitrary expression, whether or not it is independently meaningful (i.e., a sentence), and assume as usual that this involves viewing each sentence as composed, in allowable ways, out of elements drawn from a fixed finite stock of atomic syntactical elements (roughly, words). The hopeful thought is that syntax, so conceived, will yield semantics when a dictionary giving the meaning of each syntactic atom is added. Hopes will be dashed, however, if semantics is to comprise a theory of meaning in our sense, for knowledge of the structural characteristics that make for meaningfulness in a sentence, plus knowledge of the meanings of the ultimate parts, does not add up to knowledge of what a sentence means. The point is easily illustrated

by belief sentences. Their syntax is relatively unproblematic. Yet, adding a dictionary does not touch the standard semantic problem, which is that we cannot account for even as much as the truth conditions of such sentences on the basis of what we know of the meanings of the words in them. The situation is not radically altered by refining the dictionary to indicate which meaning or meanings an ambiguous expression bears in each of its possible contexts; the problem of belief sentences persists after ambiguities are resolved.

The fact that recursive syntax with dictionary added is not necessarily recursive semantics has been obscured in some recent writing on linguistics by the intrusion of semantic criteria into the discussion of purportedly syntactic theories. The matter would boil down to a harmless difference over terminology if the semantic criteria were clear; but they are not. While there is agreement that it is the central task of semantics to give the semantic interpretation (the meaning) of every sentence in the language, nowhere in the linguistic literature will one find, so far as I know, a straightforward account of how a theory performs this task, or how to tell when it has been accomplished. The contrast with syntax is striking. The main job of a modest syntax is to characterize *meaningfulness* (or sentencehood). We may have as much confidence in the correctness of such a characterization as we have in the representativeness of our sample and our ability to say when particular expressions are meaningful (sentences). What clear and analogous task and test exist for semantics?[5]

We decided a while back not to assume that parts of sentences have meanings except in the ontologically neutral sense of making a systematic contribution to the meaning of the sentences in which they occur. Since postulating meanings has netted nothing, let us return to that insight. One direction in which it points is a certain holistic view of meaning. If sentences depend for their meaning on their structure, and we understand the meaning of each item in the structure only as an abstraction from the totality of sentences in which it features, then we can give the meaning of any sentence (or word) only by giving the meaning of every sentence (and word) in the language. Frege said that only in the context of a sentence does a word have meaning; in the same vein he might have added that only in the context of the language does a sentence (and therefore a word) have meaning.

This degree of holism was already implicit in the suggestion that an adequate theory of meaning must entail *all* sentences of the form "*s* means *m*." But now, having found no more help in meanings of sentences than in meanings of words, let us ask whether we can get rid of the troublesome singular terms supposed to replace '*m*' and to refer to meanings. In a way, nothing could be easier: just write "*s* means that *p*," and imagine '*p*' replaced by a sentence. Sentences, as we have seen, cannot name meanings, and sentences with "that" prefixed are not names at all, unless we decide so. It looks as though we are in trouble on another count, however, for it is reasonable to expect that in wrestling with the logic of the apparently nonextensional "means that" we will encounter problems as hard as, or perhaps identical with, the problems our theory is out to solve.

The only way I know to deal with this difficulty is simple, and radical. Anxiety that we are enmeshed in the intensional springs from using the words "means that" as filling between description of sentence and sentence, but it may be that the success of our venture depends not on the filling but on what it fills. The theory will have done its work if it provides, for every sentence s in the language under study, a matching sentence (to replace '*p*') that, in some way yet to be made clear, 'gives the meaning' of *s*. One obvious candidate for matching sentence is just s itself, if the object language is contained in the metalanguage; otherwise a translation of s in the metalanguage. As a final bold step, let us try treating the position occupied by '*p*' extensionally: to implement this, sweep away the obscure "means that," provide the sentence that replaces '*p*' with a proper sentential connective, and supply the description that replaces '*s*' with its own predicate. The plausible result is

(*T*) *s* is *T* if and only if *p*.

What we require of a theory of meaning for a language *L* is that without appeal to any (further) semantical notions it place enough restrictions on the predicate "is *T*" to entail all sentences got from schema *T* when '*s*' is replaced by a structural description of a sentence of *L* and '*p*' by that sentence.

Any two predicates satisfying this condition have the same extension,[6] so if the metalanguage is rich enough, nothing stands in the way of putting what I am calling a theory of meaning into the form of an explicit definition of a predicate "is *T*." But whether explicitly defined or recursively characterized, it is clear that the sentences to which the predicate "is *T*" applies will be just the true sentences of *L*, for the condition we have placed on satisfactory theories of meaning is in essence Tarski's Convention *T* that tests the adequacy of a formal semantical definition of truth.[7]

The path to this point has been tortuous, but the conclusion may be stated simply: a theory of meaning for a language *L* shows "how the meanings of sentences depend upon the meanings of words" if it contains a (recursive) definition of truth-in-L. And, so far at least, we have no other idea how to turn the trick. It is worth emphasizing that the concept of truth played no ostensible role in stating our original problem. That problem, upon refinement, led to the view that an adequate theory of meaning must characterize a predicate meeting certain conditions. It was in the nature of a discovery that such a predicate would apply exactly to the true sentences. I hope that what I am doing may be described in part as defending the philosophical importance of Tarski's semantical concept of truth. But my defense is only distantly related, if at all, to the question whether the concept Tarski has shown how to define is the (or a) philosophically interesting conception of truth, or the question whether Tarski has cast any light on the ordinary use of such words as "true" and "truth." It is a misfortune that dust from futile and confused battles over these questions has prevented those with a theoretical interest in language—philosophers, logicians, psychologists, and linguists alike—from recognizing in the semantical concept of truth (under whatever name) the sophisticated and powerful foundation of a competent theory of meaning.

There is no need to suppress, of course, the obvious connection between a definition of truth of the kind Tarski has shown how to construct, and the concept of meaning. It is this: the definition works by giving necessary and sufficient conditions for the truth of every sentence, and to give truth conditions is a way of giving the meaning of a sentence. To know the semantic concept of truth for a language is to know what it is for a sentence—any sentence—to be true, and this amounts, in one good sense we can give to the phrase, to understanding the language. This at any rate is my excuse for a feature of the present discussion that is apt to shock old hands: my freewheeling use of the word "meaning," for what I call a theory of meaning has after all turned out to make no use of meanings, whether of sentences or of words. Indeed since a Tarski-type truth definition supplies all we have asked so far of a theory of meaning, it is clear that such a theory falls comfortably within what Quine terms the "theory of reference" as distinguished from what he terms the "theory of meaning." So much to the good for what I call a theory of meaning, and so much, perhaps, against my so calling it.[8]

A theory of meaning (in my mildly perverse sense) is an empirical theory, and its ambition it to account for the workings of a natural language. Like any theory, it may be tested by comparing some of its consequences with the facts. In the present case this is easy, for the theory has been characterized as issuing in an infinite flood of sentences each giving the truth conditions of a sentence; we only need to ask, in selected cases, whether what the theory avers to be the truth conditions for a sentence really are. A typical test case might involve deciding whether the sentence "Snow is white" is true if and only if snow is white. Not all cases will be so simple (for reasons to be sketched), but it is evident that this sort of test does not invite counting noses. A sharp conception of what constitutes a theory in this domain furnishes an exciting context for raising deep questions about when a theory of language is correct and how it is to be tried. But the difficulties are theoretical, not practical. In application, the trouble is to get a theory that comes close to working; anyone can tell whether it is right.[9] One can see why this is so. The theory reveals nothing new about the conditions under which an individual sentence is true; it does not make those conditions any

clearer than the sentence itself does. The work of the theory is in relating the known truth conditions of each sentence to those aspects ('words') of the sentence that recur in other sentences, and can be assigned identical roles in other sentences. Empirical power in such a theory depends on success in recovering the structure of a very complicated ability—the ability to speak and understand a language. We can tell easily enough when particular pronouncements of the theory comport with our understanding of the language; this is consistent with a feeble insight into the design of the machinery of our linguistic accomplishments.

The remarks of the last paragraph apply directly only to the special case where it is assumed that the language for which truth is being characterized is part of the language used and understood by the characterizer. Under these circumstances, the framer of a theory will as a matter of course avail himself when he can of the built-in convenience of a metalanguage with a sentence guaranteed equivalent to each sentence in the object language. Still, this fact ought not to con us into thinking a theory any more correct that entails " 'Snow is white' is true if and only if snow is white" than one that entails instead:

(S) "Snow is white" is true if and only if grass is green,

provided, of course, we are as sure of the truth of (S) as we are of that of its more celebrated predecessor. Yet (S) may not encourage the same confidence that a theory that entails it deserves to be called a theory of meaning.

The threatened failure of nerve may be counteracted as follows. The grotesqueness of (S) is in itself nothing against a theory of which it is a consequence, provided the theory gives the correct results for every sentence (on the basis of its structure, there being no other way). It is not easy to see how (S) could be party to such an enterprise, but if it were—if, that is, (S) followed from a characterization of the predicate "is true" that led to the invariable pairing of truths with truths and falsehoods with falsehoods—then there would not, I think, be anything essential to the idea of meaning that remained to be captured.

What appears to the right of the biconditional in sentences of the form "*s* is true if and only if *p*," when such sentences are consequences of a theory of truth, plays its role in determining the meaning of *s* not by pretending synonymy but by adding one more brush-stroke to the picture which, taken as a whole, tells what there is to know of the meaning of *s*; this stroke is added by virtue of the fact that the sentence that replaces '*p*' is true if and only if *s* is.

It may help to reflect that (*S*) is acceptable, if it is, because we are independently sure of the truth of "snow is white" and "grass is green"; but in cases where we are unsure of the truth of a sentence, we can have confidence in a characterization of the truth predicate only if it pairs that sentence with one we have good reason to believe equivalent. It would be ill advised for someone who had any doubts about the color of snow or grass to accept a theory that yielded (*S*), even if his doubts were of equal degree, unless he thought the color of the one was tied to the color of the other. Omniscience can obviously afford more bizarre theories of meaning than ignorance; but then, omniscience has less need of communication.

It must be possible, of course, for the speaker of one language to construct a theory of meaning for the speaker of another, though in this case the empirical test of the correctness of the theory will no longer be trivial. As before, the aim of theory will be an infinite correlation of sentences alike in truth. But this time the theory-builder must not be assumed to have direct insight into likely equivalences between his own tongue and the alien. What he must do is find out, however he can, what sentences the alien holds true in his own tongue (or better, to what degree he holds them true). The linguist then will attempt to construct a characterization of truth-for-the-alien which yields, so far as possible, a mapping of sentences held true (or false) by the alien onto sentences held true (or false) by the linguist. Supposing no perfect fit is found, the residue of sentences held true translated by sentences held false (and vice versa) is the margin for error (foreign or domestic). Charity in interpreting the words and thoughts of others is unavoidable in another direction as well: just as we must maximize agreement, or risk not making sense of

what the alien is talking about, so we must maximize the self-consistency we attribute to him, on pain of not understanding *him*. No single principle of optimum charity emerges; the constraints therefore determine no single theory. In a theory of radical translation (as Quine calls it) there is no completely disentangling questions of what the alien means from questions of what he believes. We do not know what someone means unless we know what he believes; we do not know what someone believes unless we know what he means. In radical translation we are able to break into this circle, if only incompletely, because we can sometimes tell that a person accedes to a sentence we do not understand.[10]

In the past few pages I have been asking how a theory of meaning that takes the form of a truth definition can be empirically tested, and have blithely ignored the prior question whether there is any serious chance such a theory can be given for a natural language. What are the prospects for a formal semantical theory of a natural language? Very poor, according to Tarski; and I believe most logicians, philosophers of language, and linguists agree.[11] Let me do what I can to dispel the pessimism. What I can in a general and programmatic way, of course; for here the proof of the pudding will certainly be in the proof of the right theorems. Tarski concludes the first section of his classic essay on the concept of truth in formalized languages with the following remarks, which he italicizes:

The very possibility of a consistent use of the expression 'true sentence' which is in harmony with the laws of logic and the spirit of everyday language seems to be very questionable, and consequently the same doubt attaches to the possibility of constructing a correct definition of this expression.[12]

Late in the same essay, he returns to the subject:

the concept of truth (as well as other semantical concepts) when applied to colloquial language in conjunction with the normal laws of logic leads inevitably to confusions and contradictions. Whoever wishes, in spite of all difficulties, to pursue the semantics of colloquial language with the help of exact methods will be driven first to undertake the thankless task of a reform of this language. He will find it necessary to define its structure, to overcome the ambiguity of the terms which occur in it, and finally to split the language into a series of languages of greater and greater extent, each of which stands in the same relation to the next in which a formalized language stands to its metalanguage. It may, however be doubted whether the language of everyday life, after being 'rationalized' in this way, would still preserve its naturalness and whether it would not rather take on the characteristic features of the formalized languages.[13]

Two themes emerge: that the universal character of natural languages leads to contradiction (the semantic paradoxes), and that natural languages are too confused and amorphous to permit the direct application of formal methods. The first point deserves a serious answer, and I wish I had one. As it is, I will say only why I think we are justified in carrying on without having disinfected this particular source of conceptual anxiety. The semantic paradoxes arise when the range of the quantifiers in the object language is too generous in certain ways. But it is not really clear how unfair to Urdu or to Hindi it would be to view the range of their quantifiers as insufficient to yield an explicit definition of 'true-in-Urdu' or 'true-in-Hindi'. Or, to put the matter in another, if not more serious way, there may in the nature of the case always be something we grasp in understanding the language of another (the concept of truth) that we cannot communicate to him. In any case, most of the problems of general philosophical interest arise within a fragment of the relevant natural language that may be conceived as containing very little set theory. Of course these comments do not meet the claim that natural languages are universal. But it seems to me this claim, now that we know such universality leads to paradox, is suspect.

Tarski's second point is that we would have to reform a natural language out of all recognition before we could apply formal semantical methods. If this is true, it is fatal to my project, for the task of a theory of meaning as I conceive it is not to change, improve or reform a language, but to describe and understand it. Let us look at the positive side. Tarski has shown the way to giving a theory for interpreted formal languages of various kinds; pick one as much like English as possible. Since this new language has been explained in English and contains much English we not only may, but I think must, view it as part of English for those who understand it. For this fragment of English we have, *ex hypothesi*, a theory of the required sort. Not only that, but in interpreting this adjunct of English in old English we necessarily gave hints connecting old and new. Wherever there are sentences of old English with the same truth conditions as sentences in the adjunct we may extend the theory to cover them. Much of what is called for is just to mechanize as far as possible what we now do by art when we put ordinary English into one or another canonical notation. The point is not that canonical notation is better than the rough original idiom, but rather that if we know what idiom the canonical notation is canonical *for*, we have as good a theory for the idiom as for its kept companion.

Philosophers have long been at the hard work of applying theory to ordinary language by the device of matching sentences in the vernacular with sentences for which they have a theory. Frege's massive contribution was to show how "all," "some," "every," "each," "none," and associated pronouns, in some of their uses, could be tamed; for the first time, it was possible to dream of a formal semantics for a significant part of a natural language. This dream came true in a sharp way with the work of Tarski. It would be a shame to miss the fact that as a result of these two magnificent achievements, Frege's and Tarski's, we have gained a deep insight into the structure of our mother tongues. Philosophers of a logical bent have tended to start where the theory was and work out towards the complications of natural language. Contemporary linguists, with an aim that cannot easily be seen to be different, start with the ordinary and work toward a general theory. If either party is successful, there must be a meeting. Recent work by Chomsky and others is doing much to bring the complexities of natural languages within the scope of serious semantic theory. To give an example: suppose success in giving the truth conditions for some significant range of sentences in the active voice. Then with a formal procedure for transforming each such sentence into a corresponding sentence in the passive voice, the theory of truth could be extended in an obvious way to this new set of sentences.[14]

One problem touched on in passing by Tarski does not, at least in all its manifestations, have to be solved to get ahead with theory: the existence in natural languages of "ambiguous terms." As long as ambiguity does not affect grammatical form, and can be translated, ambiguity for ambiguity, into the metalanguage, a truth definition will not tell us any lies. The trouble, for systematic semantics, with the phrase "believes that" in English is not its vagueness, ambiguity, or unsuitability for incorporation in a serious science: let our metalanguage be English, and all *these* problems will be translated without loss or gain into the metalanguage. But the central problem of the logical grammar of "believes that" will remain to haunt us.

The example is suited to illustrating another, and related, point, for the discussion of belief sentences has been plagued by failure to observe a fundamental distinction between tasks: uncovering the logical grammar or form of sentences (which is in the province of a theory of meaning as I construe it), and the analysis of individual words or expressions (which are treated as primitive by the theory). Thus Carnap, in the first edition of *Meaning and Necessity*, suggested we render "John believes that the earth is round" as "John responds affirmatively to 'the earth is round' as an English sentence." He gave this up when Mates pointed out that John might respond affirmatively to one sentence and not to another no matter how close in meaning. But there is a confusion here from the start. The semantic structure of a belief sentence, according to this idea of Carnap's, is given by a three-place predicate with places reserved for expressions referring to a person, a sentence, and a language. It is a different sort of problem entirely to attempt an analysis of this predicate, perhaps along behavioristic lines. Not least among the merits of Tarski's conception of a theory of truth is that the purity of method it demands of us follows from the formulation of the problem itself, not from the self-imposed restraint of some adventitious philosophical puritanism.

I think it is hard to exaggerate the advantages to philosophy of language of bearing in mind this distinction between questions of logical form or grammar, and the analysis of individual concepts. Another example may help advertise the point.

If we suppose questions of logical grammar settled, sentences like "Bardot is good" raise no special problems for a truth definition. The deep differences between descriptive and evaluative (emotive, expressive, etc.) terms do not show here. Even if we hold there is some important sense in which moral or evaluative sentences do not have a truth value (for example, because they cannot be 'verified'), we ought not to boggle at "'Bardot is good' is true if and only if Bardot is good"; in a theory of truth, this consequence should follow with the rest, keeping track, as must be done, of the semantic location of such sentences in the language as a whole—of their relation to generalizations, their role in such compound sentences as "Bardot is good and Bardot is foolish," and so on. What is special to evaluative words is simply not touched: the mystery is transferred from the word "good" in the object language to its translation in the metalanguage.

But "good" as it features in "Bardot is a good actress" is another matter. The problem is not that the translation of this sentence is not in the metalanguage—let us suppose it is. The problem is to frame a truth definition such that "'Bardot is a good actress' is true if and only if Bardot is a good actress"—and all other sentences like it—are consequences. Obviously "good actress" does not mean "good and an actress." We might think of taking "is a good actress" as an unanalyzed predicate. This would obliterate all connection between "is a good actress" and "is a good mother," and it would give us no excuse to think of "good," in these uses, as a word or semantic element. But worse, it would bar us from framing a truth definition at all, for there is no end to the predicates we would have to treat as logically simple (and hence accomodate in separate clauses in the definition of satisfaction): "is a good companion to dogs," "is a good 28-year-old conversationalist," and so forth. The problem is not peculiar to the case: it is the problem of attributive adjectives generally.

It is consistent with the attitude taken here to deem it usually a strategic error to undertake philosophical analysis of words or expressions which is not preceded by or at any rate accompanied by the attempt to get the logical grammar straight. For how can we have any confidence in our analyses of words like "right," "ought," "can," and "obliged," or the phrases we use to talk of actions, events, and causes, when we do not know what (logical, semantical) parts of speech we have to deal with? I would say much the same about studies of the 'logic' of these and other words, and the sentences containing them. Whether the effort and ingenuity that has gone into the study of deontic logics, modal logics, imperative and erotetic logics has been largely futile or not cannot be known until we have acceptable semantic analyses of the sentences such systems purport to treat. Philosophers and logicians sometimes talk or work as if they were free to choose between, say, the truth-functional conditional and others, or free to introduce non-truth-functional sentential operators like "Let it be the case that" or "It ought to be the case that." But in fact the decision is crucial. When we depart from idioms we can accomodate in a truth definition, we lapse into (or create) language for which we have no coherent semantical account—that is, no account at all of how such talk can be integrated into the language as a whole.

To return to our main theme: we have recognized that a theory of the kind proposed leaves the whole matter of what individual words mean exactly where it was. Even when the metalanguage is different from the object language, the theory exerts no pressure for improvement, clarification or analysis of individual words, except when, by accident of vocabulary, straightforward translation fails. Just as synonomy, as between expressions, goes generally untreated, so also synonomy of sentences, and analyticity. Even such sentences as "A vixen is a female fox" bear no special tag unless it is our pleasure to provide it. A truth definition does not distinguish between analytic sentences and others, except for sentences that owe their truth to the presence alone of the constants that give the theory its grip on structure: the theory entails not only that these sentences are true but that they will remain true under all significant rewritings

of their nonlogical parts. A notion of logical truth thus given limited application, related notions of logical equivalence and entailment will tag along. It is hard to imagine how a theory of meaning could fail to read a logic into its object language to this degree; and to the extent that it does, our intuitions of logical truth, equivalence, and entailment may be called upon in constructing and testing the theory.

I turn now to one more, and very large, fly in the ointment: the fact that the same sentence may at one time or in one mouth be true and at another time or in another mouth be false. Both logicians and those critical of formal methods here seem largely (though by no means universally) agreed that formal semantics and logic are incompetent to deal with the disturbances caused by demonstratives. Logicians have often reacted by downgrading natural language and trying to show how to get along without demonstratives; their critics react by downgrading logic and formal semantics. None of this can make me happy: clearly, demonstratives cannot be eliminated from a natural language without loss or radical change, so there is no choice but to accommodate theory to them.

No logical errors result if we simply treat demonstratives as constants[15]; neither do any problems arise for giving a semantic truth definition. " 'I am wise' is true if and only if I am wise," with its bland ignoring of the demonstrative element in "I" comes off the assembly line along with " 'Socrates is wise' is true if and only if Socrates is wise" with *its* bland indifference to the demonstrative element in "is wise" (the tense).

What suffers in this treatment of demonstratives is not the definition of a truth predicate, but the plausibility of the claim that what has been defined is truth. For this claim is acceptable only if the speaker and circumstances of utterance of each sentence mentioned in the definition is matched by the speaker and circumstances of utterance of the truth definition itself. It could also be fairly pointed out that part of understanding demonstratives is knowing the rules by which they adjust their reference to circumstance; assimilating demonstratives to constant terms obliterates this feature. These complaints can be met, I think, though only by a fairly far-reaching revision in the theory of truth. I shall barely suggest how this could be done, but bare suggestion is all that is needed: the idea is technically trivial, and quite in line with work being done on the logic of the tenses.[16]

We could take truth to be a property, not of sentences, but of utterances, or speech acts, or ordered triples of sentences, times, and persons; but it is simplest just to view truth as a relation between a sentence, a person, and a time. Under such treatment, ordinary logic as now read applies as usual, but only to sets of sentences relativized to the same speaker and time; further logical relations between sentences spoken at different times and by different speakers may be articulated by new axioms. Such is not my concern. The theory of meaning undergoes a systematic but not puzzling change: corresponding to each expression with a demonstrative element there must in the theory be a phrase that relates the truth conditions of sentences in which the expression occurs to changing times and speakers. Thus the theory will entail sentences like the following:

"I am tired" is true as (potentially) spoken by p at t if and only if p is tired at t.
"That book was stolen" is true as (potentially) spoken by p at t if and only if the book demonstrated by p at t is stolen prior to t.[17]

Plainly, this course does not show how to eliminate demonstratives; for example, there is no suggestion that "the book demonstrated by the speaker" can be substituted ubiquitously for "that book" *salva veritate*. The fact that demonstratives are amenable to formal treatment ought greatly to improve hopes for a serious semantics of natural language, for it is likely that many outstanding puzzles, such as the analysis of quotations or sentences about propositional attitudes, can be solved if we recognize a concealed demonstrative construction.

Now that we have relativized truth to times and speakers, it is appropriate to glance back at the problem of empirically testing a theory of meaning for an alien tongue. The essence of the method was, it will be remembered, to correlate held-true sentences with held-true sentences by way of a truth definition, and within the bounds of intelligible error. Now the picture must be elaborated to allow for the fact that sentences are true, and held true, only relative to a speaker and a time. The real task is therefore to translate each sentence by another that is true for the same speakers at the same times. Sentences with demonstratives obviously yield a very sensitive test of the correctness of a theory of meaning, and constitute the most direct link between language and the recurrent macroscopic objects of human interest and attention.[18]

In this paper I have assumed that the speakers of a language can effectively determine the meaning or meanings of an arbitrary expression (if it has a meaning), and that it is the central task of a theory of meaning to show how this is possible. I have argued that a characterization of a truth predicate describes the required kind of structure, and provides a clear and testable criterion of an adequate semantics for a natural language. No doubt there are other reasonable demands that may be put on a theory of meaning. But a theory that does no more than define truth for a language comes far closer to constituting a complete theory of meaning than superficial analysis might suggest; so, at least, I have urged.

Since I think there is no alternative, I have taken an optimistic and programmatic view of the possibilities for a formal characterization of a truth predicate for a natural language. But it must be allowed that a staggering list of difficulties and conundrums remains. To name a few: we do not know the logical form of counterfactual or subjunctive sentences, nor of sentences about probabilities and about causal relations; we have no good idea what the logical role of adverbs is, nor the role of attributive adjectives; we have no theory for mass terms like "fire," "water," and "snow," nor for sentences about belief, perception, and intention, nor for verbs of action that imply purpose. And finally, there are all the sentences that seem not to have truth values at all: the imperatives, optatives, interrogatives, and a host more. A comprehensive theory of meaning for a natural language must cope successfully with each of these problems.

ACKNOWLEDGMENTS

An earlier version of this paper was read at the Eastern Division meeting of the American Philosophical Association in December, 1966; the main theme traces back to an unpublished paper delivered to the Pacific Division of the American Philosophical Association in 1953. Present formulations owe much to John Wallace, with whom I have discussed these matters since 1962. My research was supported by the National Science Foundation.

NOTES

1. Elsewhere I have urged that it is a necessary condition, if a language is to be learnable, that it have only a finite number of semantical primitives: see "Theories of Meaning and Learnable Languages," in *Proceedings of the 1964 International Congress for Logic, Methodology and Philosophy of Science* (North-Holland Publishing Company, Amsterdam: 1965), pp. 383–394.

2. A 'structural description' of an expression describes the expression as a concatenation of elements drawn from a fixed finite list (for example of words or letters).

3. The argument is essentially Frege's. See A. Church, *Introduction to Mathematical Logic,* vol. I (Princeton: 1956), pp. 24–25. It is perhaps worth mentioning that the argument does not depend on any particular identification of the entities to which sentences are supposed to refer.

4. It may be thought that Church, in "A Formulation of the Logic of Sense and Denotation," in *Structure, Method and Meaning: Essays in Honor of H. M. Sheffer*, Henle, Kallen and Langer, eds. (Liberal Arts Press, New York: 1951), pp. 3–24, has given a theory of meaning that makes essential use of meanings as entities. But this is not the case: Church's logics of sense and denotation are interpreted as being about meanings, but they do not mention expressions and so cannot of course be theories of meaning in the sense now under discussion.

5. For a recent and instructive statement of the role of semantics in linguistics, see Noam Chomsky, "Topics in the Theory of Generative Grammar," in *Current Trends in Linguistics*, Thomas A. Sebeok, ed., vol. III (The Hague: 1966). In this article, Chomsky (1) emphasizes the central importance of semantics in linguistic theory, (2) argues for the superiority of transformational grammars over phrase structure grammars largely on the grounds that, although phrase structure grammars may be adequate to define sentencehood for (at least) some natural languages, they are inadequate as a foundation for semantics, and (3) comments repeatedly on the 'rather primitive state' of the concepts of semantics and remarks that the notion of semantic interpretation "still resists any deep analysis".

6. Assuming, of course, that the extension of these predicates is limited to the sentences of *L*.

7. Alfred Tarski, "The Concept of Truth in Formalized Languages," in *Logic, Semantics, Metamathematics* (Oxford: 1956), pp. 152–278.

8. But Quine may be quoted in support of my usage: ". . . in point of *meaning* . . . a word may be said to be determined to whatever extent the truth or falsehood of its contexts is determined." "Truth by Convention," first published in 1936; now in *The Ways of*

Paradox (New York: 1966), p. 82. Since a truth definition determines the truth value of every sentence in the object language (relative to a sentence in the metalanguage), it determines the meaning of every word and sentence. This would seem to justify the title Theory of Meaning.

9. To give a single example: it is clearly a count in favor of a theory that it entails " 'Snow is white' is true if and only if snow is white." But to contrive a theory that entails this (and works for all related sentences) is not trivial. I do not know a theory that succeeds with this very case (the problem of 'mass terms').

10. This sketch of how a theory of meaning for an alien tongue can be tested obviously owes its inspiration to Quine's account of radical translation in chapter II of *Word and Object* (New York: 1960). In suggesting that an acceptable theory of radical translation take the form of a recursive characterization of truth, I go beyond anything explicit in Quine. Toward the end of this paper, in the discussion of demonstratives, another strong point of agreement will turn up.

11. So far as I am aware, there has been very little discussion of whether a formal truth definition can be given for a natural language. But in a more general vein, several people have urged that the concepts of formal semantics be applied to natural language. See, for example, the contributions of Yehoshua Bar-Hillel and Evert Beth to *The Philosophy of Rudolph Carnap*, Paul A. Schilpp, ed., (La Salle, Ill.: 1963), and Bar-Hillel's "Logical Syntax and Semantics," *Language* 30, 230–237.

12. Tarski, ibid., p. 165.

13. Ibid., p. 267.

14. The rapprochement I prospectively imagine between transformational grammar and a sound theory of meaning has been much advanced by a recent change in the conception of transformational grammar described by Chomsky in the article referred to above (note 5). The structures generated by the phrase-structure part of the grammar, it has been realized for some time, are those suited to semantic interpretation; but this view is inconsistent with the idea, held by Chomsky until recently, that recursive operations are introduced only by the transformation rules. Chomsky now believes the phrase-structure rules are recursive. Since languages to which formal semantic methods directly and naturally apply are ones for which a (recursive) phrase-structure grammar is appropriate, it is clear that Chomsky's present picture of the relation between the structures generated by the phrase-structure part of the grammar, and the sentences of the language, is very much like the picture many logicians and philosophers have had of the relation between the richer formalized languages and ordinary language. (In these remarks I am indebted to Bruce Vermazen.)

15. Quine has good things to say about this in *Methods of Logic* (New York: 1950). See 8.

16. For an up-to-date bibliography, and discussion, see A. N. Prior, *Past, Present, and Future* (Oxford: 1967).

17. There is more than an intimation of this approach to demonstratives and truth in Austin's 1950 article "Truth", reprinted in *Philosophical Papers* (Oxford: 1961). See pp. 89–90.

18. These remarks clearly derive from Quine's idea that 'occasion sentences' (those with a demonstrative element) must play a central role in constructing a translation manual.

SUGGESTED FURTHER READING

Alston, William, "Semantic Rules," in *Semantics and Philosophy,* ed. Milton Munitz and Peter Unger (New York: New York University Press, 1974), pp. 17–48.

Atlas, J. D., *Philosophy without Ambiguity: A Logico-Linguistic Essay* (Oxford: Clarendon Press, 1989)

Bennett, Jonathan, *Linguistic Behavior* (Cambridge: Cambridge University Press, 1976).

Biro, John, "Intentionalism in the Theory of Meaning," *The Monist* 62 (1979): 238–258.

Black, Max, "Meaning and Intention: An Examination of Grice's Views," *New Literary History* 4 (1973): 257–279.

Blackburn, Simon, *Spreading the Word* (Oxford: Clarendon Press, 1984).

Devitt, Michael, *Coming to Our Senses: A Naturalistic Program for Semantic Localism* (Cambridge: Cambridge University Press, 1996).

Dummett, Michael, "What Is a Theory of Meaning?" in *Mind & Language,* ed. Samuel Guttenplan (Oxford: Clarendon Press, 1975), pp. 97–138.

Dummett, Michael, "What Is a Theory of Meaning? (II)" in *Truth & Meaning,* ed. Gareth Evans and John McDowell (Oxford: Clarendon Press, 1976), pp. 67–137.

Field, Hartry, "Tarski's Theory of Truth," *Journal of Philosophy* 79 (1972): 347–375.

Garfield, Jay L. and Murray Kitely, eds. *Meaning and Truth: Essential Readings in Modern Semantics* (New York: Paragon House, 1991).

Grandy, Richard E. and Richard Warner, eds., *Philosophical Grounds of Rationality* (Oxford: Clarendon Press, 1986).

Grice, H. P. and P. F. Strawson, "In Defense of a Dogma," *Philosophical Review* 55 (1956): 141–158.

Grice, H. P., "Utterer's Meaning, Sentence-Meaning and Word-Meaning," *Foundations of Language* 4 (1968): 1–18.

Grice, H. P., "Utterer's Meaning and Intentions," *Philosophical Review* 78 (1969): 147–177.

Grice, H. P., "Meaning Revisited," in *Mutual Knowledge,* ed. N. V. Smith (New York: Academic Press, 1982), pp. 223–243.

Kirkham, Richard L., *Theories of Truth: A Critical Introduction* (Cambridge: MIT Press, 1995).

Larson, Richard, and Gabriel Segal, *Knowledge of Meaning* (Cambridge: MIT Press, 1995).

Linsky, Leonard, *Semantics and the Philosophy of Language* (Urbana, Ill.: University of Illinois Press, 1952).

McDowell, John, "Meaning, Communication, and Knowledge," in *Philosophical Subjects,* ed. Zak Van Straaten (Oxford: Clarendon Press, 1980), pp. 117–139.

Quine, W. V., "Cognitive Meaning," *Monist* 62 (1979): 129–142.

Recanati, F., *Literal Meaning* (Cambridge: Cambridge University Press, 2004).

Searle, John, "The Background of Meaning," in *Speech Act Theory and Pragmatics,* ed. John R. Searle and Ferenc Kiefer (Dordrecht: D. Reidel, 1980), pp. 221–232.

Shiffer, Stephen, *Meaning* (Oxford: Clarendon Press, 1972).

Schiffer, Stephen, *Remnants of Meaning* (Cambridge: MIT Press, 1987).

Soames, Scott, *Understanding Truth* (New York: Oxford University Press, 1999).

Strawson, P. F., "Truth," *Analysis* 9 (1949): 83–97.

Tarski, Alfred, "The Concept of Truth in Formalized Languages," in *Logic, Semantics and Metamathematics* (Oxford: Clarendon Press, 1956), pp. 152–278.

Ziff, Paul, "On H. P. Grice's Account of Meaning," *Analysis* 28 (1967): 1–8.

II SPEECH ACTS

According to Grice, to mean something is first of all for a person to mean something; and, if the person successfully communicates what he means, he has performed a speech act. Although there are hints of speech act theory in earlier philosophers as different as Avicenna and Thomas Hobbes, the first to study the issue explicitly and at length was J. L. Austin. In "Performative Utterances," Austin introduced the idea that to say something is to do something. As Searle was to point out later, this means that a general theory of speech is a part of action theory. Austin's idea is important because people often think that there is an important distinction between talking and doing, as indicated by the fact that people often say, "Don't talk about it; do something."

Austin was originally motivated to explore the nature of performative utterances as part of a project to refute the theory of meaning championed by the logical positivists, primarily during the 1920s and 1930s. According to them, only statements, that is, only sentences that have a truth value, are meaningful. This idea is a result of their belief that philosophy ought to be scientific, that science only describes the world, that all descriptions are either true or false, and hence that only those utterances that try to describe the world, namely, statements, are meaningful. Sentences of ethics ('Murder is evil'), aesthetics ('Michelangelo's *Moses* is beautiful'), and religion ('God is good') were taken to be pseudostatements, neither true nor false. They should not be thought of as attempting to describe the world, because the physical world does not contain values, and the physical world is the only thing that exists. Value-utterances and religious-utterances were in fact designed, according to the logical positivists, either to express emotion or to induce an emotion in the audience.

Austin's strategy for refuting the logical positivists' view was quite straightforward. He would present counterexamples to the claim that only statements were meaningful. In order to get examples that might be persuasive to the positivists themselves, Austin needed sentences that did not contain value-words like 'good', 'evil', 'beautiful', or 'ugly', nor words that purportedly referred to nonempirical entities, such as 'God' and 'transcendent'. The counterexamples were sentences like,

I apologize for stepping on your foot.
I name this ship the *Queen Elizabeth.*
I bet that the Cleveland Indians win the World Series.

These sentences are clearly meaningful, but not true or false. Austin called them 'performative utterances' because their function is not to describe something but to perform an action. Talking is a kind of doing. As John Searle would make explicit later, a general theory of speech is a part of action theory.

Because performative utterances are actions, they can suffer in many of the same ways that other actions can. Some attempts to perform a speech act simply fail. A person who says, 'I bet that the Cleveland Indians win the World Series', without having anyone accept the offer, fails to bet. Although he tried to bet by saying, 'I bet . . .', he failed. Other performatives can succeed but be defective. A person who says, 'I promise to return your book tomorrow' but has no intention of returning the book, does promise; but it is defective, like walking with a bad limp.

Performative utterances seemed to have a paradigmatic grammatical form. The verb was always in the first person singular present nonprogressive tense, active voice, and indicative mood, for example, 'I promise', not 'You (we) promise(d)', or 'I am promising' or 'I am promised' or 'I may promise'.

Yet, as promising as the category of performatives, in contrast with 'statements', seemed to be, Austin discovered that it was ultimately untenable. The sentence, 'I state that the president will not run for reelection' has the characteristics of both a performative and a statement. As a statement, it is true or false, but as a performative it can fail or be defective in various ways. The upshot was that a more sophisticated theory of speech had to be devised.

In *How to Do Things with Words,* Austin distinguished between three kinds of linguistic acts: locutionary, illocutionary, and perlocutionary acts. Austin divides locutionary acts into three subgroups. First, phonetic acts are acts of producing sounds, whether or not these sounds are part of a natural language or used to communicate. Second, phatic acts are acts of producing sounds that both are part of a language and are intended as being construed as parts of a language. The last clause is necessary in order to exclude cases of producing sounds that accidentally or incidentally belong to a language. For example, suppose that the sound of clearing one's throat has a meaning in some language. People who clear their throats do not perform a phatic act unless they intend that sound to be taken as a linguistic object. Third, rhetic acts are acts of using sounds with a certain sense and reference. A person who says, "The cat is on the mat," in order to express that a certain cat is on a certain mat is performing a rhetic act, because he or she is referring to things in the world and saying something about them. It should be obvious that performing a rhetic act involves performing a phatic act, and performing a phatic act involves performing a phonetic act. But the converse relations do not hold.

Illocutionary acts are such things as promising, betting, swearing, and stating. They are the forces that attach to rhetic acts. For example, the rhetic act of saying that a certain bull is about to charge (expressed by uttering the sentence, "That bull is about to charge") could be involved with the performance of various illocutionary acts, depending upon the intentions of the speaker and the circumstances of the utterance. An expert about bulls might *state* that the bull is about to charge or may be *warning* someone about that; an inexperienced observer might *guess* or *conjecture* that the bull is about to charge; someone else may be using the sentence to make a bet. An illocutionary act for Austin is the *force* of a rhetic act. It is an act performed *in* speaking. For example, promising is an illocutionary act, because it makes sense to say, "In saying, 'I promise', the speaker promised."

Austin would consider illocutionary acts conventional acts in contrast with perlocutionary ones, which are nonconventional in the sense of causing some natural condition or state in a person. Boring, harassing, irritating, pleasing, or persuading someone is performing a perlocutionary act. A perlocutionary act is an act performed *by* speaking. For example, irritating is a perlocutionary act, because it makes sense to say, "By reading the *Communist Manifesto* to the Libertarians, the speaker irritated them."

John Searle showed that even Austin's latest version of the theory of speech acts needed important changes. For example, Searle in effect showed that the rhetic act should not be separated from the illocutionary act. Rather, explicit illocutionary acts typically consist of two parts: a force and a proposition. More important than his criticisms are Searle's constructive moves; and he devised the standard theory of illocutionary acts.

In "What Is a Speech Act?" (1965), Searle presented an analysis of promising that he refined in chapter 3 of *Speech Acts* (1969), included in this section. As good as his analysis is, I think that the form can be improved. The primary speech acts that should be analyzed are fully explicit and nondefective ones. While people often promise with such abbreviated utterances as 'I promise' or 'I'll be at the party', and succeed in promising even when they are insincere, the concept of promising comes into clearest focus when promises are made with sentences like 'I promise that I will be at the party'. Let's call such explicit, successful, and nondefective illocutionary acts 'paradigmatic' cases.

A REVISED ANALYSIS OF PARADIGMATIC PROMISING

In uttering a sentence T to an addressee H, speaker S explicitly and nondefectively promises that p if and only if

(N-1) Normal input and output conditions obtain.

(PC-1) S expresses that p in the utterance of T, and thereby S predicates a future act A of S.

(PR-1) H would prefer S's doing A to his not doing A, and S believes H would prefer his doing A to his not doing A.

(PR-2) It is not obvious to both S and H that S will do A in the normal course of events.

(PR-3) S is able to do A.

(SC-1) S intends to do A.

(EC-1) S understands that the utterance of T will place him under an obligation to do A.

(SE-1) S understands that the utterance of T will produce in H a belief that conditions (SC-1)-(EC-1) obtain by means of the recognition of the intention to produce that belief, and he intends that recognition to be achieved by means of the recognition of the sentence as one conventionally used to produce such beliefs.

(SE-2) The semantical rules of the dialect spoken by S and H are such that T is correctly and sincerely uttered if and only if conditions (PC-1)-(SE-1) obtain.

(HU-1) H accepts S's taking on of the obligation mentioned in (EC-1)

The numbering of these conditions is guided by the following categorization:

N = Normal Input and Output Conditions
PC = Propositional Content Conditions
PR = Preparatory Conditions
SC = Sincerity Conditions

EC = Essential Conditions
SE = Semantic Conditions
HU = Addressee Uptake Conditions

Notice that my revised analysis requires that the speaker's addressee understand that the speaker has promised.

If we now consider merely successful promises, that is, ones that may be either inexplicit or defective in various ways, the conditions necessary and sufficient are quite weak.

MERELY SUCCESSFUL PROMISING

In uttering something T to an addressee H, speaker S merely promises that p if and only if

(PC-1) In the utterance of T, S means (expresses or implies) that p in the utterance of T, and thereby expressly or implicitly predicates a future action A of S.

(PR-1) S is able to do A.

(EC-1) S understands or should understand that the utterance of T will place him under an obligation to do A.

(SE-1) S understands or should understand that the utterance of T will produce in H a belief that conditions (PR-1) and (EC-1) obtain by means of the recognition of the *meaning* of T.

(HU-1) H understands that T may be understood to linguistically communicate that (EC-1) obtains.

Notice that T does not need to be a sentence; it can be a word or phrase.

Let's now consider another speech act analysis of an explicit, successful, and nondefective illocutionary act:

PARADIGMATIC COUNSELING

In uttering a sentence T to an addressee H, speaker S explicitly and nondefectively counsels H to do an action A if and only if

(N-1) Normal input and output conditions obtain;

(PC-1) S expresses that p in the utterance of T and thereby predicates a future action A of H;

(PR-1) H believes that S knows what action is in H's best interest;

(PR-2) It is not obvious to S or H that H will do A in the normal course of events;

(PR-3) H is able at the time of the utterance of T to do A at or within the time specified in the proposition that p;

(PR-4) A is in H's best interest;

(SC-1) S believes that A is in H's best interest;

(EC-1) S understands that the utterance of T counts as expressing that A is in H's best interest;

(SE-1) S intends that H will understand that conditions (PC-1)-(EC-1) obtain and in part understands that (PC-1), (PR-1), (PR-3), and (EC-1) obtain by means of S's utterance of T; and

(HU-1) H knows that (PC-1) and (EC-1) obtains at least in part in virtue of hearing S's utterance of T.

It is useful to compare the conditions for paradigmatic counseling with the conditions for paradigmatic promising.

Exercises:

1. Give an analysis of merely successful counseling. (Counseling that may be inexplicit or defective in various ways.)
2. Give speech act analyses for paradigmatic apologizing, commanding, congratulating, and betting.

In *How to Do Things with Words,* J. L. Austin had distinguished between five types of illocutionary acts: verdictives, exercitives, commissives, behabitives, and expositives. In "A Taxonomy of Illocutionary Acts," Searle presents a superior taxonomy, based on his general pattern of analyzing speech acts. Some readers may need help with some of the symbols that Searle uses. Understand 'S' as 'sentence', 'NP' as 'noun phrase', 'VP' as 'verb phrase', 'N' as 'noun', 'V' as 'verb', 'Aux' as 'auxiliary verb', 'Fut' as 'future tense', 'Vol Verb' as 'voluntary verb' (that is, a verb that expresses a voluntary activity), and 'Adv' as 'adverb'. When two or more 'NP's have the same subscript, the noun phrase consists of the same words and refers to the same object in each case.

What is said is just one part of what a speaker communicates. Much, perhaps most, of what is communicated is implied in one way or another. Although this is a kind of commonplace, it had not been incorporated into a theory of meaning until Grice sketched the main types of implication and roughly characterized them in his William James Lectures for 1967, titled "Logic and Conversation." His theory also has substantial applications to traditional philosophical problems.

The central kind of implication is conversational implication. One kind of conversational implication involves indirect speech acts, which are speech acts that result from the performance of some other speech acts. For example, the explicit speech act performed by saying "Can you pass the salt?" is a question ("Are you able to . . . ?"); yet, at a dinner table it is typically used to make a request. The explicit speech act performed by saying "You are standing on my feet" is a statement, yet it too is sometimes used to request that a person get off the speaker's feet. Searle's analysis of these indirect speech acts is an extension of his theory of speech acts and has a place within Grice's theory of conversation.

Grice divides the Conversational Maxims into four categories: Quality, Quantity, Relation, and Manner. They are not adequate as they stand. One problem is that they are not specific enough. This is most obvious for the Maxim of Relation: Be relevant.

Another problem is that the Maxims are too narrow. Grice formulated them with Assertives in mind, that is, speech acts that are designed to convey information, in contrast with, say, Commissives ('I promise to go to the party'), which are designed to impose some obligation on the speaker, or Expressives ('I congratulate you on your victory'), which are designed to express an attitude or feeling. A better, but by no means adequate, set of maxims is the following:

Maxim of Quality: Do not participate in a speech act unless you are able to fulfill the conditions for its successful and nondefective performance.

1. For Assertives, (a) say what is true; (b) have evidence sufficient for the illocutionary act performed. [Stating requires more evidence that guessing, and guessing more than conjecturing.]

2. For Commissives, (a) do not say you will do something that you cannot do; (b) intend to do what you say you will do.
3. For Directives, . . .
4. For Expressives, . . .
5. For Declarations, . . .

Maxim of Quantity: Make your illocutionary act as strong as is appropriate for the occasion.

1. Propositional Quantity: Communicate a proposition that is as strong as is required by the purposes of the conversation. [Do not say "Mary has two children," if she has more than two children.]
2. Force Quantity: Communicate an illocutionary force that is as strong as is required by the purposes of the conversation. [Do not conjecture that p if you can state that p.]

Maxim of Relation: Say something that factually or logically connects with what has been said earlier in the conversation. [Immediately preceding utterances are more relevant than nonimmediate ones.]

Maxims of Manner: Be perspicuous. That is, choose words and syntax that make it easy for your audience to understand what you mean.

1. Choose clear expressions.
2. Avoid ambiguity.
3. Be brief.
4. Be orderly.

   a. Temporal ordering: Report events in the order in which they occurred.
   b. Spatial ordering: If objects, a, b, c, . . . belong together, put their names or descriptions of them together. (See Robert Harnish, "Logical Form and Implicature," in *Pragmatics*, ed. Steven Davis, pp. 338–339.)
   c. The main topic of the sentence should be expressed in the subject; the main idea to be conveyed about the topic should be in the main verb or verb phrase.

Exercise: Improve on these maxims.

Because of its unprecedented character, Grice's statement of his theory in "Logic and Conversation" contains some easily identifiable and easily correctible errors. For example, he distinguishes among four ways in which a conversational maxim can go unfulfilled: (1) by violating a maxim; (2) by opting out of a maxim; (3) by flouting a maxim; and (4) by being faced with a clash of maxims. The first, violating a maxim, is a specific way of not fulfilling a maxim in a broad sense. It is to quietly and unostentatiously not fulfill a maxim. But Grice sometimes mistakenly uses "violate" where he should have used the broader term, "not fulfill." Watch for this.

Also, it is clear that (4) does not belong with (1)–(3). (4) is not a way in which a maxim can go unfulfilled. Rather, it is a reason why a maxim might go unfulfilled. If a speaker is faced with a clash of two maxims, that is, a situation in which he can fulfill one or the other but not both, then he will have to sacrifice one in order to fulfill the other. (Suppose someone is asked to give a brief and complete explanation of Hegel's theory of Absolute Idealism.) Thus, in being faced with a clash, the speaker may violate, opt out of, or flout one of the maxims.

It is plausible that these remaining three maxims need to be supplemented with a fourth. Just as violating a maxim is complemented by flouting a maxim, that is, openly and ostentatiously not fulfilling one, opting out of a maxim seems to have a complement. Opting out of a maxim is temporarily not accepting the force of a maxim. A person might opt out of the maxim of saying as much as is required by an interlocutor when that person must keep a secret. Thus, to the remaining three, we might add *suspending* a maxim, that is, permanently not accepting the force of a maxim in certain situations. For example, because the United States Senate allows filibustering, it suspends the maxim of relevance; and because it also does not allow a senator to be prosecuted for anything he says on the Senate floor, it suspends the maxim of quality: "Say what is true."

In medieval universities, the Maxims of Quality were suspended in an academic exercise called "The Game of Obligation," in which a student would be required to defend some proposition as true, even though it might in fact be false. To counter certain objections against that proposition, the student was allowed to assert any additional proposition, true or false, as long as it was consistent with all the previous propositions to which he had committed himself. The Maxims of Quality were suspended, but not the ironclad rules of logic.

The Maxims of Quality are also suspended while telling a joke and telling (fictional) stories. Coleridge was not far off the mark when he said that poetic faith is that willing suspension of disbelief for the moment.

To these actual examples, we can easily add an invented one that is close to actuality. In the United States, although a person charged with a crime is not required to testify at her trial, if she chooses to testify, then she is required to fulfill the Maxims of Quality, especially, "Do not say what is false." The system could be different. It could require defendants to testify but allow them to say what is false; that is, the Maxims of Quality could be suspended.

Grice's "Logic and Conversation" raises the issue of what the distinction between semantics (what words and sentences mean) and pragmatics (what people do with words) is. There is a tendency for semantics to poach on the territory of pragmatics and vice versa. An example of the first is the view that the meaning of a word or sentence is its use or the rule or rules for its use. One objection to this view is that since some sentences are never used but still have meaning, their meaning cannot be identified with their use. While this objection may have force against an identification of meaning with actual use, it does not seem to have force against the version that identifies meanings with rules of use. Another objection is that the idea of use is too vague. Someone might use "Lee is helpful" (i) to give an example of an English sentence, (ii) to practice his diction, (iii) to say that Lee is helpful, or (iv) to insult Lee. The relevant sense of "use" applies to (iii), but does that clarify the concept of meaning as use?

Pragmatics poaches on semantics in the view that what a speaker says is what her sentence means. That is, if the sentence "It is raining" says or means that it is raining and the speaker says "It is raining," then the speaker says that it is raining. Underlying this view is the idea that what is said is identical with semantics and what is conversationally implied or implicated is identical with pragmatics, in Grice's sense of what is said and what is implicated. I think that this underlying view is not an accurate understanding of Grice. Both what is said and what is implicated belong to pragmatics. Certainly, what is said is constrained by the meaning or semantics of the words the speaker utters, but uttering a sentence is not the same as saying something. Someone singing in the shower, "I dream of Jeannie with the light brown hair," is not saying that he dreams of Jeannie with the light brown hair. It is a mistake, I think, to assert that "It is raining" says or means that it is raining. Although it may look like merely a typographical change, it is closer to the truth to assert that "It is raining" is designed to be used by a speaker to say that it is raining or that "It is raining" means *it is raining*. Concerning the latter disjunct, the italicized words express a meaning without saying how sentence meaning should be analyzed. (See Grice's "Utterer's Meaning, Sentence-

Meaning, and Word-Meaning," in *Studies in the Way of Words*.) But however it should be analyzed, it won't be the case that sentences mean that something. The former disjunct makes clear that it is speakers who say things, not words or sentences except in the derivative, instrumental sense in which one can say that a gun shoots a victim in virtue of the fact that a shooter used a gun to shoot the victim.

A notable attempt to defend a semantic theory that does not poach on pragmatism is that of Herman Cappelen and Ernie Lepore in *Insensitive Semantic*. They argue for two main theses. One is

Speech Act Pluralism: There are many ways to report what a speaker said.

These numerous ways are hardly constrained by the words the speaker actually utters. So if a speaker says "The table is covered with books," true reports of what she said include, depending on the circumstances,

The table with the vase is covered with books.
The piece of furniture in the corner has books on it.
Lee's present to Bo has books on it.

not to mention

The table is covered with books.

In other words, what is said is not a highly regimented locution.

The second and more important thesis is

Semantic Minimalism: There are few context-sensitive expressions in natural languages.

The paradigmatic examples of context-sensitive expressions, such as "I," "she," "this," "that," "here," "there," "now," and "then," and their plural and oblique forms are just about all the context-sensitive expressions that there are. A consequence of Semantic Minimalism is that the context of an utterance has little effect on the "semantic content" of the sentences, after the contributions of the context-sensitive expressions, if any, have been added. According to Cappelen and Lepore, there is no close connection between the semantic content of a sentence and the speech act content. Hence, semantics does not poach on pragmatics.

I think Semantic Minimalism is true if it is meant or expanded as

Narrowly Semantic Minimalism: There are few context-sensitive expressions in natural languages because of their semantics,

but not if it is meant or expanded as

Broadly Semantic Minimalism: There are few expressions in natural languages that are context sensitive in any way.

Broadly Semantic Minimalism is false because many words are context sensitive in virtue of varying criteria of application. These criteria are not however semantic. The meaning of "It is raining" is the same in Tucson, Arizona, and Seattle, Washington—people in both places use the same dictionaries—but the criterion of application is different in each place. The phrase "context sensitive" in Broadly Semantic Minimalism may be misleading because the criterion of application does not apply so much to the kind of object at issue as it does to the interests or desires of the speaker and hearer. A person from Tucson, Arizona, could continue to apply her usual criterion for the sentence "It is raining" when she is in Seattle, Washington. She may do this either because she thinks it is a more sensible criterion or because she is talking to other people from

Tucson, and possibly because she does not know that a different criterion is used by people in Seattle.

One reason for holding that the meaning of a word does not vary with the criterion of application is that words having varying criteria satisfy the normal tests for being univocal. For example, the criteria for being a big dog and a big elephant are different, but these statements are true: Fido and Dumbo are big. Fido is big and so is Dumbo. So-called contextualists in epistemology maintain that sentences of the form "S knows that p" are true or false depending on the criterion appropriate to "know" in that situation. One criterion applies when little or nothing is at stake; another stricter criterion applies when a lot is at stake, as when a person testifies under oath in a criminal prosecution. A standard criticism of this view is that it makes "know" equivocal when it is clearly univocal. I think that epistemic contextualism withstands this objection when the criterion associated with knowledge is nonsemantic. What the distinction between meaning and the criterion of application takes seriously is the idea that in order to use a language, some nonsemantic factual knowledge about the world is needed in addition to semantic knowledge.

Robert Stalnaker describes pragmatics differently from the way I have. For him, pragmatics is "the study of the relation between linguistic expressions and their contexts of use" (*Context and Content,* p. 4). His project in "Assertion" is to explain some of the ways in which the content of a speech act, that is, a proposition, interacts with the context within which it is expressed. The most important concept that he uses is that of possible world, which is basic or "primitive" for him. He uses that concept without defining or explaining it. If enough problems can be explained in terms of possible worlds, then it is a valuable theoretical concept. Propositions, for example, can be analyzed either as the set of possible worlds in which the proposition is true or alternatively as functions from possible worlds into truth-values. However, although he does not give a definition, he does in another place indicate its meaning: "a possible world is a kind of property that the world might have had." Unlike David Lewis's possible worlds, Stalnaker's are not parallel universes and not "essentially linguistic or representational" (ibid., pp. 2–3).

Stalnaker's most important insight is that facts affect propositions in two ways. The first is that if a proposition states a fact, then the proposition is true. The second is that what proposition gets expressed depends on how the world is. This can be illustrated with a sentence like "I am ill." If Lee is the speaker, one proposition is expressed; if Bo is the speaker, a different proposition is expressed. Part of the world determines what proposition gets expressed. A semantics that pays attention to both ways in which the facts affect a proposition is called "two-dimensional" semantics.

In normal communications, the speaker and the hearer share the same beliefs; they presuppose the same possible worlds as their context. As the conversation progresses, each assertion shrinks the number of possible worlds in the context because each assertion eliminates all the possible worlds that are incompatible with it. In abnormal communications, the speaker and hearer do not share the same beliefs, so the hearer mistakes what propositions the speaker is asserting because he presupposes different possible worlds form the context.

BIBLIOGRAPHY

Bach, K., "Conversational Impliciture," *Mind and Language,* 9 (1994), 124–62.
Bach, K., "The Myth of Conventional Implicature," *Linguistic and Philosophy,* 22 (1999), 327–66.
Cappelen, Herman and Ernie Lepore, *Insensitive Semantics* (Malden, Mass.: Blackwell, 2005).
Fotion, Nick, *John Searle* (Princeton: Princeton University Press, 2000).
Stalnaker, Robert, *Context and Content* (New York: Oxford University Press, 1999).

8 Performative Utterances

J. L. AUSTIN

I

You are more than entitled not to know what the word "performative" means. It is a new word and an ugly word, and perhaps it does not mean anything very much. But at any rate there is one thing in its favor, it is not a profound word. I remember once when I had been talking on this subject that somebody afterwards said: "You know, I haven't the least idea what he means, unless it could be that he simply means what he says." Well, that is what I should like to mean.

Let us consider first how this affair arises. We have not got to go very far back in the history of philosophy to find philosophers assuming more or less as a matter of course that the sole business, the sole interesting business, of any utterance—that is, of anything we say—is to be true or at least false. Of course they had always known that there are other kinds of things which we say—things like imperatives, the expressions of wishes, and exclamations—some of which had even been classified by grammarians, though it wasn't perhaps too easy to tell always which was which. But still philosophers have assumed that the only things that they are interested in are utterances which report facts or which describe situations truly or falsely. In recent times this kind of approach has been ques-

tioned—in two stages, I think. First of all people began to say: "Well, if these things are true or false it ought to be possible to decide which they are, and if we can't decide which they are they aren't any good but are, in short, nonsense." And this new approach did a great deal of good; a great many things which probably are nonsense were found to be such. It is not the case, I think, that all kinds of nonsense have been adequately classified yet, and perhaps some things have been dismissed as nonsense which really are not; but still this movement, the verification movement, was, in its way, excellent.

However, we then come to the second stage. After all, we set some limits to the amount of nonsense that we talk, or at least the amount of nonsense that we are prepared to admit we talk; and so people began to ask whether after all some of those things which, treated as statements, were in danger of being dismissed as nonsense did after all really set out to be statements at all. Mightn't they perhaps be intended not to report facts but to influence people in this way or that, or to let off steam in this way or that? Or perhaps at any rate some elements in these utterances performed such functions, or, for example, drew attention in some way (without actually reporting it) to some important feature of the circumstances in which the utterance

From *Philosophical Papers,* 3d ed., J. O. Urmson and G. J. Warnock, eds. (Oxford: Oxford University Press, 1979), pp. 233–252. © Oxford University Press 1961, 1970, 1979. Reprinted by permission of the publisher.

was being made. On these lines people have now adopted a new slogan, the slogan of the "different uses of language." The old approach, the old statemental approach, is sometimes called even a fallacy, the descriptive fallacy.

Certainly there are a great many uses of language. It's rather a pity that people are apt to invoke a new use of language whenever they feel so inclined, to help them out of this, that, or the other well-known philosophical tangle; we need more of a framework in which to discuss these uses of language; and also I think we should not despair too easily and talk, as people are apt to do, about the *infinite* uses of language. Philosophers will do this when they have listed as many, let us say, as seventeen; but even if there were something like ten thousand uses of language, surely we could list them all in time. This, after all, is no larger than the number of species of beetle that entomologists have taken the pains to list. But whatever the defects of either of these movements—the 'verification' movement or the 'use of language' movement—at any rate they have effected, nobody could deny, a great revolution in philosophy and, many would say, the most salutary in its history. (Not, if you come to think of it, a very immodest claim.)

Now it is one such sort of use of language that I want to examine here. I want to discuss a kind of utterance which looks like a statement and grammatically, I suppose, would be classed as a statement, which is not nonsensical, and yet is not true or false. These are not going to be utterances which contain curious verbs like "could" or "might," or curious words like "good," which many philosophers regard nowadays simply as danger signals. They will be perfectly straightforward utterances, with ordinary verbs in the first person singular present indicative active, and yet we shall see at once that they couldn't possibly be true or false. Furthermore, if a person makes an utterance of this sort we should say that he is *doing* something rather than merely *saying* something. This may sound a little odd, but the examples I shall give will in fact not be odd at all, and may even seem decidedly dull. Here are three or four. Suppose, for example, that in the course of a marriage ceremony I say, as people will, "I do"—(sc. take this woman to

be my lawful wedded wife). Or again, suppose that I tread on your toe and say "I apologize." Or again, suppose that I have the bottle of champagne in my hand and say "I name this ship the *Queen Elizabeth*." Or suppose I say "I bet you sixpence it will rain tomorrow." In all these cases it would be absurd to regard the thing that I say as a report of the performance of the action which is undoubtedly done—the action of betting, or christening, or apologizing. We should say rather that, in saying what I do, I actually perform that action. When I say "I name this ship the *Queen Elizabeth*" I do not describe the christening ceremony, I actually perform the christening; and when I say "I do" (sc. take this woman to be my lawful wedded wife), I am not reporting on a marriage, I am indulging in it.

Now these kinds of utterance are the ones that we call *performative* utterances. This is rather an ugly word, and a new word, but there seems to be no word already in existence to do the job. The nearest approach that I can think of is the word "operative," as used by lawyers. Lawyers when talking about legal instruments will distinguish between the preamble, which recites the circumstances in which a transaction is effected, and on the other hand the operative part—the part of it which actually performs the legal act which it is the purpose of the instrument to perform. So the word "operative" is very near to what we want. "I give and bequeath my watch to my brother" would be an operative clause and is a performative utterance. However, the word "operative' has other uses, and it seems preferable to have a word specially designed for the use we want.

Now at this point one might protest, perhaps even with some alarm, that I seem to be suggesting that marrying is simply saying a few words, that just saying a few words *is* marrying. Well, that certainly is not the case. The words have to be said in the appropriate circumstances, and this is a matter that will come up again later. But the one thing we must not suppose is that what is needed in addition to the saying of the words in such cases is the performance of some internal spiritual act, of which the words then are to be the report. It's very easy to slip into this view at least in difficult, portentous cases, though perhaps not so easy in simple cases like apologizing. In the case of promising—for example, "I promise to be there tomorrow"—it's very easy to think that the utterance is simply the outward and visible (that is, verbal) sign of the performance of some inward spiritual act of promising, and this view has certainly been expressed in many classic places. There is the case of Euripides' Hippolytus, who said "My tongue swore to, but my heart did not"—perhaps it should be "mind" or "spirit" rather than "heart," but at any rate some kind of backstage artiste. Now it is clear from this sort of example that, if we slip into thinking that such utterances are reports, true or false, of the performance of inward and spiritual acts, we open a loophole to perjurers and welshers and bigamists and so on, so that there are disadvantages in being excessively solemn in this way. It is better, perhaps, to stick to the old saying that our word is our bond.

However, although these utterances do not themselves report facts and are not themselves true or false, saying these things does very often imply that certain things are true and not false, in some sense at least of that rather woolly word "imply." For example, when I say "I do take this woman to be my lawful wedded wife," or some other formula in the marriage ceremony, I do *imply* that I'm not already married, with wife living, sane, undivorced, and the rest of it. But still it is very important to realize that to imply that something or other is true, is not at all the same as saying something which is true itself.

These performative utterances are not true or false, then. But they do suffer from certain disabilities of their own. They can fail to come off in special ways, and that is what I want to consider next. The various ways in which a performative utterance may be unsatisfactory we call, for the sake of a name, the infelicities; and an infelicity arises—that is to say, the utterance is unhappy—if certain rules, transparently simple rules, are broken. I will mention some of these rules and then give examples of some infringements.

First of all, it is obvious that the conventional procedure which by our utterance we are purporting to use must actually exist. In the examples given here this procedure will be a verbal one, a verbal procedure for marrying or giving

or whatever it may be; but it should be borne in mind that there are many nonverbal procedures by which we can perform exactly the same acts as we perform by these verbal means. It's worth remembering too that a great many of the things we do are at least in part of this conventional kind. Philosophers at least are too apt to assume that an action is always in the last resort the making of a physical movement, whereas it's usually, at least in part, a matter of convention.

The first rule is, then, that the convention invoked must exist and be accepted. And the second rule, also a very obvious one, is that the circumstances in which we purport to invoke this procedure must be appropriate for its invocation. If this is not observed, then the act that we purport to perform would not come off—it will be, one might say, a misfire. This will also be the case if, for example, we do not carry through the procedure—whatever it may be— correctly and completely, without a flaw and without a hitch. If any of these rules are not observed, we say that the act which we purported to perform is void, without effect. If, for example, the purported act was an act of marrying, then we should say that we "went through a form" of marriage, but we did not actually succeed in marrying.

Here are some examples of this kind of misfire. Suppose that, living in a country like our own, we wish to divorce our wife. We may try standing her in front of us squarely in the room and saying, in a voice loud enough for all to hear, "I divorce you." Now this procedure is not accepted. We shall not thereby have succeeded in divorcing our wife, at least in this country and others like it. This is a case where the convention, we should say, does not exist or is not accepted. Again, suppose that, picking sides at a children's party, I say "I pick George." But George turns red in the face and says "Not playing." In that case I plainly, for some reason or another, have not picked George—whether because there is no convention that you can pick people who aren't playing, or because George in the circumstances is an inappropriate object for the procedure of picking. Or consider the case in which I say "I appoint you Consul," and it turns out that you have been appointed already—or perhaps it may even transpire that you are a horse; here again we have the infelicity of inappropriate circumstances, inappropriate objects, or what not. Examples of flaws and hitches are perhaps scarcely necessary—one party in the marriage ceremony says "I will," the other says "I won't"; I say "I bet sixpence," but nobody says "Done," nobody takes up the offer. In all these and other such cases, the act which we purport to perform, or set out to perform, is not achieved.

But there is another and a rather different way in which this kind of utterance may go wrong. A good many of these verbal procedures are designed for use by people who hold certain beliefs or have certain feelings or intentions. And if you use one of these formulae when you do not have the requisite thoughts or feelings or intentions then there is an abuse of the procedure, there is insincerity. Take, for example, the expression, "I congratulate you." This is designed for use by people who are glad that the person addressed has achieved a certain feat, believe that he was personally responsible for the success, and so on. If I say "I congratulate you" when I'm not pleased or when I don't believe that the credit was yours, then there is insincerity. Likewise if I say I promise to do something, without having the least intention of doing it or without believing it feasible. In these cases there is something wrong certainly, but it is not like a misfire. We should not say that I didn't in fact promise, but rather that I did promise but promised insincerely; I did congratulate you but the congratulations were hollow. And there may be an infelicity of a somewhat similar kind when the performative utterance commits the speaker to future conduct of a certain description and then in the future he does not in fact behave in the expected way. This is very obvious, of course, if I promise to do something and then break my promise, but there are many kinds of commitment of a rather less tangible form than that in the case of promising. For instance, I may say "I welcome you," bidding you welcome to my home or wherever it may be, but then I proceed to treat you as though you were exceedingly unwelcome. In this case the procedure of saying "I welcome you" has been abused in a way rather different from that of simple insincerity.

Now we might ask whether this list of infelicities is complete, whether the kinds of infelicity are mutually exclusive, and so forth. Well, it is not complete, and they are not mutually exclusive; they never are. Suppose that you are just about to name the ship, you have been appointed to name it, and you are just about to bang the bottle against the stem; but at that very moment some low type comes up, snatches the bottle out of your hand, breaks it on the stem, shouts out "I name this ship the *Generalissimo Stalin*," and then for good measure kicks away the chocks. Well, we agree of course on several things. We agree that the ship certainly isn't now named the *Generalissimo Stalin*, and we agree that it's an infernal shame and so on and so forth. But we may not agree as to how we should classify the particular infelicity in this case. We might say that here is a case of a perfectly legitimate and agreed procedure which, however, has been invoked in the wrong circumstances, namely by the wrong person, this low type instead of the person appointed to do it. But on the other hand we might look at it differently and say that this is a case where the procedure has not as a whole been gone through correctly, because part of the procedure for naming a ship is that you should first of all get yourself appointed as the person to do the naming and that's what this fellow did not do. Thus the way we should classify infelicities in different cases will be perhaps rather a difficult matter, and may even in the last resort be a bit arbitrary. But of course lawyers, who have to deal very much with this kind of thing, have invented all kinds of technical terms and have made numerous rules about different kinds of cases, which enable them to classify fairly rapidly what in particular is wrong in any given case.

As for whether this list is complete, it certainly is not. One further way in which things may go wrong is, for example, through what in general may be called misunderstanding. You may not hear what I say, or you may understand me to refer to something different from what I intended to refer to, and so on. And apart from further additions which we might make to the list, there is the general overriding consideration that, as we are performing an act when we issue these performative utterances, we may of course be doing so under duress or in some other circumstances which make us not entirely responsible for doing what we are doing. That would certainly be an unhappiness of a kind—any kind of nonresponsibility might be called an unhappiness; but of course it is a quite different kind of thing from what we have been talking about. And I might mention that, quite differently again, we could be issuing any of these utterances, as we can issue an utterance of any kind whatsoever, in the course, for example, of acting a play or making a joke or writing a poem—in which case of course it would not be seriously meant and we shall not be able to say that we seriously performed the act concerned. If the poet says "Go and catch a falling star" or whatever it may be, he doesn't seriously issue an order. Considerations of this kind apply to any utterance at all, not merely to performatives.

That, then, is perhaps enough to be going on with. We have discussed the performative utterance and its infelicities. That equips us, we may suppose, with two shining new tools to crack the crib of reality maybe. It also equips us—it always does—with two shining new skids under our metaphysical feet. The question is how we use them.

II

So far we have been going firmly ahead, feeling the firm ground of prejudice glide away beneath our feet which is always rather exhilarating, but what next? You will be waiting for the bit when we bog down, the bit where we take it all back, and sure enough that's going to come but it will take time. First of all let us ask a rather simple question. How can we be sure, how can we tell, whether any utterance is to be classed as a performative or not? Surely, we feel, we ought to be able to do that. And we should obviously very much like to be able to say that there is a grammatical criterion for this, some grammatical means of deciding whether an utterance is performative. All the examples I have given hitherto do in fact have the same grammatical form; they all of them begin with the verb in the first person singular present indicative active— not just any kind of verb of course, but still they all are in fact of that form. Furthermore, with these verbs that I have used there is a typical

asymmetry between the use of this person and tense of the verb and the use of the same verb in other persons and other tenses, and this asymmetry is rather an important clue.

For example, when we say "I promise that . . . ," the case is very different from when we say "He promises that . . . ," or in the past tense "I promised that . . . ." For when we say "I promise that . . ." we do perform an act of promising—we give a promise. What we do *not* do is to report on somebody's performing an act of promising—in particular, we do not report on somebody's use of the expression "I promise." We actually do use it and do the promising. But if I say "He promises," or in the past tense "I promised," I precisely do report on an act of promising, that is to say an act of using this formula "I promise"—I report on a present act of promising by him, or on a past act of my own. There is thus a clear difference between our first person singular present indicative active, and other persons and tenses. This is brought out by the typical incident of little Willie whose uncle says he'll give him half-a-crown if he promises never to smoke till he's 55. Little Willie's anxious parent will say "Of course he promises, don't you, Willie?" giving him a nudge, and little Willie just doesn't vouchsafe. The point here is that he must do the promising himself by saying "I promise," and his parent is going too fast in saying he promises.

That, then, is a bit of a test for whether an utterance is performative or not, but it would not do to suppose that every performative utterance has to take this standard form. There is at least one other standard form, every bit as common as this one, where the verb is in the passive voice and in the second or third person, not in the first. The sort of case I mean is that of a notice inscribed "Passengers are warned to cross the line by the bridge only," or of a document reading "You are hereby authorized" to do so-and-so. These are undoubtedly performative, and in fact a signature is often required in order to show who it is that is doing the act of warning, or authorizing, or whatever it may be. Very typical of this kind of performative—especially liable to occur in written documents of course— is that the little word 'hereby' either actually occurs or might naturally be inserted.

Unfortunately, however, we still can't possibly suggest that every utterance which is to be classed as a performative has to take one or another of these two, as we might call them, standard forms. After all it would be a very typical performative utterance to say "I order you to shut the door." This satisfies all the criteria. It is performing the act of ordering you to shut the door, and it is not true or false. But in the appropriate circumstances surely we could perform exactly the same act by simply saying "Shut the door," in the imperative. Or again, suppose that somebody sticks up a notice "This bull is dangerous," or simply "Dangerous bull," or simply "Bull." Does this necessarily differ from sticking up a notice, appropriately signed, saying "You are hereby warned that this bull is dangerous"? It seems that the simple notice "Bull" can do just the same job as the more elaborate formula. Of course the difference is that if we just stick up "Bull" it would not be quite clear that it is a warning; it might be there just for interest or information, like "Wallaby" on the cage at the zoo, or "Ancient Monument." No doubt we should know from the nature of the case that it was a warning, but it would not be explicit.

Well, in view of this breakdown of grammatical criteria, what we should like to suppose— and there is a good deal in this—is that any utterance which is performative could be reduced or expanded or analysed into one of these two standard forms beginning "I . . ." so and so or beginning "You (or he) hereby . . ." so and so. If there was any justification for this hope, as to some extent there is, then we might hope to make a list of all the verbs which can appear in these standard forms, and then we might classify the kinds of acts that can be performed by performative utterances. We might do this with the aid of a dictionary, using such a test as that already mentioned—whether there is the characteristic asymmetry between the first person singular present indicative active and the other persons and tenses—in order to decide whether a verb is to go into our list or not. Now if we make such a list of verbs we do in fact find that they fall into certain fairly well-marked classes. There is the class of cases where we deliver verdicts and make estimates and appraisals of various kinds. There is the class where we give undertakings, commit ourselves in various ways by saying something. There is

the class where by saying something we exercise various rights and powers, such as appointing and voting and so on. And there are one or two other fairly well-marked classes.

Suppose this task accomplished. Then we could call these verbs in our list explicit performative verbs, and any utterance that was reduced to one or the other of our standard forms we could call an explicit performative utterance. "I order you to shut the door" would be an explicit performative utterance, whereas "Shut the door" would not—that is simply a 'primary' performative utterance or whatever we like to call it. In using the imperative we may be ordering you to shut the door, but it just isn't made clear whether we are ordering you or entreating you or imploring you or beseeching you or inciting you or tempting you, or one or another of many other subtly different acts which, in an unsophisticated primitive language, are very likely not yet discriminated. But we need not overestimate the unsophistication of primitive languages. There are a great many devices that can be used for making clear, even at the primitive level, what act it is we are performing when we say something—the tone of voice, cadence, gesture—and above all we can rely upon the nature of the circumstances, the context in which the utterance is issued. This very often makes it quite unmistakable whether it is an order that is being given or whether, say, I am simply urging you or entreating you. We may, for instance, say something like this: "Coming from him I was bound to take it as an order." Still, in spite of all these devices, there is an unfortunate amount of ambiguity and lack of discrimination in default of our explicit performative verbs. If I say something like "I shall be there," it may not be certain whether it is a promise, or an expression of intention, or perhaps even a forecast of my future behavior, of what is going to happen to me; and it may matter a good deal, at least in developed societies, precisely which of these things it is. And that is why the explicit performative verb is evolved— to make clear exactly which it is, how far it commits me and in what way, and so forth.

This is just one way in which language develops in tune with the society of which it is the language. The social habits of the society may considerably affect the question of which performative verbs are evolved and which, sometimes for rather irrelevant reasons, are not. For example, if I say "You are a poltroon," it might be that I am censuring you or it might be that I am insulting you. Now since apparently society approves of censuring or reprimanding, we have here evolved a formula "I reprimand you," or "I censure you," which enables us expeditiously to get this desirable business over. But on the other hand, since apparently we don't approve of insulting, we have not evolved a simple formula "I insult you," which might have done just as well.

By means of these explicit performative verbs and some other devices, then, we make explicit what precise act it is that we are performing when we issue our utterance. But here I would like to put in a word of warning. We must distinguish between the function of making explicit what act it is we are performing, and the quite different matter of *stating* what act it is we are performing. In issuing an explicit performative utterance we are not stating what act it is, we are showing or making explicit what act it is. We can draw a helpful parallel here with another case in which the act, the conventional act that we perform, is not a speech act but a physical performance. Suppose I appear before you one day and bow deeply from the waist. Well, this is ambiguous. I may be simply observing the local flora, tying my shoelace, something of that kind; on the other hand, conceivably I might be doing obeisance to you. Well, to clear up this ambiguity we have some device such as raising the hat, saying "Salaam," or something of that kind, to make it quite plain that the act being performed is the conventional one of doing obeisance rather than some other act. Now nobody would want to say that lifting your hat was stating that you were performing an act of obeisance; it certainly is not, but it does make it quite plain that you are. And so in the same way to say "I warn you that . . ." or "I order you to . . ." or "I promise that . . ." is not to state that you are doing something, but makes it plain that you are—it does constitute your verbal performance, a performance of a particular kind.

So far we have been going along as though there was a quite clear difference between our performative utterances and what we have contrasted them with, statements or reports or descriptions. But now we begin to find that this distinction is not as clear as it might be. It's now that we begin to sink in a little. In the first place, of course, we may feel doubts as to how widely our performatives extend. If we think up some odd kinds of expression we use in odd cases, we might very well wonder whether or not they satisfy our rather vague criteria for being performative utterances. Suppose, for example, somebody says "Hurrah." Well, not true or false; he is performing the act of cheering. Does that make it a performative utterance in our sense or not? Or suppose he says "Damn"; he is performing the act of swearing, and it is not true or false. Does that make it performative? We feel that in a way it does and yet it's rather different. Again, consider cases of 'suiting the action to the words'; these too may make us wonder whether perhaps the utterance should be classed as performative. Or sometimes, if somebody says "I am sorry," we wonder whether this is just the same as "I apologize"—in which case of course we have said it's a performative utterance—or whether perhaps it's to be taken as a description, true or false, of the state of his feelings. If he had said "I feel perfectly awful about it," then we should think it must be meant to be a description of the state of his feelings. If he had said "I apologize," we should feel this was clearly a performative utterance, going through the ritual of apologizing. But if he says "I am sorry" there is an unfortunate hovering between the two. This phenomenon is quite common. We often find cases in which there is an obvious pure performative utterance and obvious other utterances connected with it which are not performative but descriptive, but on the other hand a good many in between where we're not quite sure which they are. On some occasions of course they are obviously used the one way, on some occasions the other way, but on some occasions they seem positively to revel in ambiguity.

Again, consider the case of the umpire when he says "Out" or "Over," or the jury's utterance when they say that they find the prisoner guilty. Of course, we say, these are cases of giving verdicts, performing the act of appraising and so forth, but still in a way they have some connection with the facts. They seem to have something like the duty to be true or false, and seem not to be so very remote from statements. If the umpire says "Over," this surely has at least something to do with six balls in fact having been delivered rather than seven, and so on. In fact in general we may remind ourselves that "I state that . . ." does not look so very different from "I warn you that . . ." or "I promise to . . . ." It makes clear surely that the act that we are performing is an act of stating, and so functions just like 'I warn' or 'I order'. So isn't "I state that . . ." a performative utterance? But then one may feel that utterances beginning "I state that . . ." do have to be true or false, that they *are* statements.

Considerations of this sort, then, may well make us feel pretty unhappy. If we look back for a moment at our contrast between statements and performative utterances, we realize that we were taking statements very much on trust from, as we said, the traditional treatment. Statements, we had it, were to be true or false; performative utterances on the other hand were to be felicitous or infelicitous. They were the doing of something, whereas for all we said making statements was not doing something. Now this contrast surely, if we look back at it, is unsatisfactory. Of course statements are liable to be assessed in this matter of their correspondence or failure to correspond with the facts, that is, being true or false. But they are also liable to infelicity every bit as much as are performative utterances. In fact some troubles that have arisen in the study of statements recently can be shown to be simply troubles of infelicity. For example, it has been pointed out that there is something very odd about saying something like this: "The cat is on the mat but I don't believe it is." Now this is an outrageous thing to say, but it is not self-contradictory. There is no reason why the cat shouldn't be on the mat without my believing that it is. So how are we to classify what's wrong with this peculiar statement? If we remember now the doctrine of infelicity we shall see that the person who makes this remark about the cat is in much the same position as somebody who says something like this: "I promise that I shall be there, but I haven't the least intention of being there." Once again you can of course perfectly well promise to be there without having the least intention of being there, but there is something outrageous about saying it, about actually avowing the insincerity of the promise you give. In the same way there is insincerity in the case of the person who says "The cat is on the mat but I don't believe it is," and he is actually avowing that insincerity—which makes a peculiar kind of nonsense.

A second case that has come to light is the one about John's children—the case where somebody is supposed to say "All John's children are bald but John hasn't got any children." Or perhaps somebody says "All John's children are bald," when as a matter of fact—he doesn't say so—John has no children. Now those who study statements have worried about this; ought they to say that the statement "All John's children are bald" is meaningless in this case? Well, if it is, it is not a bit like a great many other more standard kinds of meaninglessness; and we see, if we look back at our list of infelicities, that what is going wrong here is much the same as what goes wrong in, say, the case of a contract for the sale of a piece of land when the piece of land referred to does not exist. Now what we say in the case of this sale of land, which of course would be effected by a performative utterance, is that the sale is void—void for lack of reference or ambiguity of reference; and so we can see that the statement about all John's children is likewise void for lack of reference. And if the man actually says that John has no children in the same breath as saying they're all bald, he is making the same kind of outrageous utterance as the man who says "The cat is on the mat and I don't believe it is," or the man who says "I promise to but I don't intend to."

In this way, then, ills that have been found to afflict statements can be precisely paralleled with ills that are characteristic of performative utterances. And after all when we state something or describe something or report something, we do perform an act which is every bit as much an act as an act of ordering or warning. There seems no good reason why stating should be given a specially unique position. Of course philosophers have been wont to talk as though you or I or anybody could just go round stating anything about anything and that would be perfectly in order, only there's just a little question:

is it true or false? But besides the little question, is it true or false, there is surely the question: is it in order? Can you go round just making statements about anything? Suppose for example you say to me "I'm feeling pretty moldy this morning." Well, I say to you "You're not"; and you say "What the devil do you mean, I'm not?" I say "Oh nothing—I'm just stating you're not, is it true or false?" And you say "Wait a bit about whether it's true or false, the question is what did you mean by making statements about somebody else's feelings? I told you I'm feeling pretty moldy. You're just not in a position to say, to state that I'm not." This brings out that you can't just make statements about other people's feelings (though you can make guesses if you like); and there are very many things which, having no knowledge of, not being in a position to pronounce about, you just can't state. What we need to do for the case of stating, and by the same token describing and reporting, is to take them a bit off their pedestal, to realize that they are speech acts no less than all these other speech acts that we have been mentioning and talking about as performative.

Then let us look for a moment at our original contrast between the performative and the statement from the other side. In handling performatives we have been putting it all the time as though the only thing that a performative utterance had to do was to be felicitous, to come off, not to be a misfire, not to be an abuse. Yes, but that's not the end of the matter. At least in the case of many utterances which, on what we have said, we should have to class as performative—cases where we say "I warn you to . . . ," "I advise you to . . ." and so on—there will be other questions besides simply: was it in order, was it all right, as a piece of advice or a warning, did it come off? After that surely there will be the question: was it good or sound advice? Was it a justified warning? Or in the case, let us say, of a verdict or an estimate: was it a good estimate, or a sound verdict? And these are questions that can only be decided by considering how the content of the verdict or estimate is related in some way to fact, or to evidence available about the facts. This is to say that we do require to assess at least a great many performative utterances in a general dimension of corre-

spondence with fact. It may still be said, of course, that this does not make them very like statements because still they are not true or false, and that's a little black and white speciality that distinguishes statements as a class apart. But actually—though it would take too long to go on about this—the more you think about truth and falsity the more you find that very few statements that we ever utter are just true or just false. Usually there is the question are they fair or are they not fair, are they adequate or not adequate, are they exaggerated or not exaggerated? Are they too rough, or are they perfectly precise, accurate, and so on? 'True' and 'false' are just general labels for a whole dimension of different appraisals which have something or other to do with the relation between what we say and the facts. If, then, we loosen up our ideas of truth and falsity we shall see that statements, when assessed in relation to the facts, are not so very different after all from pieces of advice, warnings, verdicts, and so on.

We see then that stating something is performing an act just as much as is giving an order or giving a warning; and we see, on the other hand, that, when we give an order or a warning or a piece of advice, there is a question about how this is related to fact which is not perhaps so very different from the kind of question that arises when we discuss how a statement is related to fact. Well, this seems to mean that in its original form our distinction between the performative and the statement is considerably weakened, and indeed breaks down. I will just make a suggestion as to how to handle this matter. We need to go very much farther back, to consider all the ways and senses in which saying anything at all is doing this or that—because of course it is always doing a good many different things. And one thing that emerges when we do do this is that, besides the question that has been very much studied in the past as to what a certain utterance *means*, there is a further question distinct from this as to what was the *force*, as we may call it, of the utterance. We may be quite clear what "Shut the door" means, but not yet at all clear on the further point as to whether as uttered at a certain time it was an order, an entreaty, or whatnot. What we need besides the old doctrine about meanings is a new doctrine about all the possible forces of utterances, towards the discovery of which our proposed list of explicit performative verbs would be a very great help; and then, going on from there, an investigation of the various terms of appraisal that we use in discussing speech-acts of this, that, or the other precise kind—orders, warnings, and the like.

The notions that we have considered then, are the performative, the infelicity, the explicit performative, and lastly, rather hurriedly, the notion of the forces of utterances. I dare say that all this seems a little unremunerative, a little complicated. Well, I suppose in some ways it is unremunerative, and I suppose it ought to be remunerative. At least, though, I think that if we pay attention to these matters we can clear up some mistakes in philosophy; and after all philosophy is used as a scapegoat, it parades mistakes which are really the mistakes of everybody. We might even clear up some mistakes in grammar, which perhaps is a little more respectable.

And is it complicated? Well, it is complicated a bit; but life and truth and things do tend to be complicated. It's not things, it's philosophers that are simple. You will have heard it said, I expect, that oversimplification is the occupational disease of philosophers, and in a way one might agree with that. But for a sneaking suspicion that it's their occupation.

9 The Structure of Illocutionary Acts

JOHN R. SEARLE

The ground has now been prepared for a full dress analysis of the illocutionary act. I shall take promising as my initial quarry, because as illocutionary acts go, it is fairly formal and well articulated; like a mountainous terrain, it exhibits its geographical features starkly. But we shall see that it has more than local interest, and many of the lessons to be learned from it are of general application.

In order to give an analysis of the illocutionary act of promising I shall ask what conditions are necessary and sufficient for the act of promising to have been successfully and non-defectively performed in the utterance of a given sentence. I shall attempt to answer this question by stating these conditions as a set of propositions such that the conjunction of the members of the set entails the proposition that a speaker made a successful and non-defective promise, and the proposition that the speaker made such a promise entails this conjunction. Thus each condition will be a necessary condition for the successful and non-defective performance of the act of promising, and taken collectively the set of conditions will be a sufficient condition for such a performance. There are various kinds of possible defects of illocutionary acts but not all of these defects are sufficient to vitiate the act in its entirety. In some cases, a condition may indeed be intrinsic to the notion

of the act in question and not satisfied in a given case, and yet the act will have been performed nonetheless. In such cases I say the act was "defective". My notion of a defect in an illocutionary act is closely related to Austin's notion of an "infelicity".[1] Not all of the conditions are logically independent of each other. Sometimes it is worthwhile to state a condition separately even though it is, strictly speaking, entailed by another.

If we get such a set of conditions we can extract from them a set of rules for the use of the illocutionary force indicating device. The method here is analogous to discovering the rules of chess by asking oneself what are the necessary and sufficient conditions under which one can be said to have correctly moved a knight or castled or checkmated a player, etc. We are in the position of someone who has learned to play chess without ever having the rules formulated and who wants such a formulation. We learned how to play the game of illocutionary acts, but in general it was done without an explicit formulation of the rules, and the first step in getting such a formulation is to set out the conditions for the performance of a particular illocutionary act. Our inquiry will therefore serve a double philosophical purpose. By stating a set of conditions for the performance of a particular illocutionary act we shall have offered an explication of that notion and shall also have paved the way for the second step, the formulation of the rules.

So described, my enterprise must seem to have a somewhat archaic and period flavor. One of the most important insights of recent work in the philosophy of language is that most non-technical concepts in ordinary language lack absolutely strict rules. The concepts of *game,* or *chair,* or *promise* do not have absolutely knock-down necessary and sufficient conditions, such that unless they are satisfied something cannot be a game or a chair or a promise, and given that they are satisfied in a given case that case must be, cannot but be, a game or a chair or a promise. But this insight into the looseness of our concepts, and its attendant jargon of "family resemblance"[2] should not lead us into a rejection of the very enterprise of philosophical analysis; rather the conclusion to be drawn is that certain forms of analysis, especially analysis into necessary and sufficient conditions, are likely to involve (in varying degrees) idealization of the concept analyzed. In the present case, our analysis will be directed at the center of the concept of promising. I am ignoring marginal, fringe, and partially defective promises. This approach has the consequence that counter-examples can be produced of ordinary uses of the word "promise" which do not fit the analysis. Some of these counter-examples I shall discuss. Their existence does not 'refute' the analysis, rather they require an explanation of why and how they depart from the paradigm cases of promise making.

Furthermore, in the analysis I confine my discussion to full blown explicit promises and ignore promises made by elliptical turns of phrase, hints, metaphors, etc. I also ignore promises made in the course of uttering sentences which contain elements irrelevant to the making of the promise. I am also dealing only with categorical promises and ignoring hypothetical promises, for if we get an account of categorical promises it can easily be extended to deal with hypothetical ones. In short, I am going to deal only with a simple and idealized case. This method, one of constructing idealized models, is analogous to the sort of theory construction that goes on in most sciences, e.g., the construction of economic models, or accounts of the solar system which treat planets as points. Without abstraction and idealization there is no systematization.

Another difficulty with the analysis arises from my desire to state the conditions without certain forms of circularity. I want to give a list of conditions for the performance of a certain illocutionary act, which do not themselves mention the performance of any illocutionary acts. I need to satisfy this condition in order to offer a model for explicating illocutionary acts in general; otherwise I should simply be showing the relation between different illocutionary acts. However, although there will be no reference to illocutionary acts, certain institutional concepts, such as e.g."obligation", will appear in the analysans as well as in the analysandum; I am not attempting to reduce institutional facts to brute facts; and thus there is no reductionist motivation in the analysis. Rather, I want to analyze certain statements of institutional facts, statements of the form "X made a promise", into statements containing such notions as intentions, rules, and states of affairs specified by the rules. Sometimes those states of affairs will themselves involve institutional facts.[3]

In the presentation of the conditions I shall first consider the case of a sincere promise and then show how to modify the conditions to allow for insincere promises. As our inquiry is semantical rather than syntactical, I shall simply assume the existence of grammatically well-formed sentences.

3.1. HOW TO PROMISE: A COMPLICATED WAY

Given that a speaker S utters a sentence T in the presence of a hearer H, then, in the literal utterance of T, S sincerely and nondefectively promises that p to H if and only if the following conditions 1–9 obtain:

(1) *Normal input and output conditions obtain.*

I use the terms "input" and "output" to cover the large and indefinite range of conditions under which any kind of serious and literal[4] linguistic communication is possible. "Output" covers the conditions for intelligible speaking and "input" covers the conditions of understanding. Together they include such things as that the speaker and hearer both know how to speak the language; both are conscious of what they are doing; they have no physical impediments to communication, such as deafness, aphasia, or laryngitis; and they are not acting in a play or telling jokes, etc. It should be noted that this condition excludes *both* impediments to communication such as deafness and also parasitic forms of communication such as telling jokes or acting in a play.

(2) *S expresses the proposition that p in the utterance of T.*

This condition isolates the proposition from the rest of the speech act and enables us to concentrate on the peculiarities of promising as a kind of illocutionary act in the rest of the analysis.

(3) *In expressing that p, S predicates a future act A of S.*

In the case of promising the scope of the illocutionary force indicating device includes certain features of the proposition. In a promise an act must be predicated of the speaker and it cannot be a past act. I cannot promise to have done something, and I cannot promise that someone else will do something (although I can promise to see that he will do it). The notion of an act, as I am construing it for the present purposes, includes refraining from acts, performing series of acts, and may also include states and conditions: I may promise not to do something, I may promise to do something repeatedly or sequentially, and I may promise to be or remain in a certain state or condition. I call conditions 2 and 3 the propositional content conditions. Strictly speaking, since expressions and not acts are predicated of objects, this condition should be formulated as follows: In expressing that P, S predicates an expression of S, the meaning of which expression is such that if the expression is true of the object it is true that the object will perform a future act A.[5] But that is rather long-winded, so I have resorted to the above metonymy.

(4) *H would prefer S's doing A to his not doing A, and S believes H would prefer his doing A to his not doing A.*

One crucial distinction between promises on the one hand and threats on the other is that a promise is a pledge to do something for you, not to you; but a threat is a pledge to do something to you, not for you. A promise is defective if the thing promised is something the promisee does not want done; and it is further defective if the promisor does not believe the promisee wants it done, since a non-defective promise must be intended as a promise and not as a threat or warning. Furthermore, a promise, unlike an invitation, normally requires some sort of occasion or situation that calls for the promise. A crucial feature of such occasions or situations seems to be that the promisee wishes (needs, desires, etc.) that something be done, and the promisor is aware of this wish (need, desire, etc.). I think both halves of this double condition are necessary in order to avoid fairly obvious counter-examples.[6]

One can, however, think of apparent counter-examples to this condition as stated. Suppose I say to a lazy student, "If you don't hand in your paper on time I promise you I will give you a failing grade in the course". Is this utterance a promise? I am inclined to think not; we would more naturally describe it as a warning or possibly even a threat. But why, then, is it possible to use the locution "I promise" in such a case? I think we use it here because "I promise" and "I hereby promise" are among the strongest illocutionary force indicating devices for *commitment* provided by the English language. For that reason we often use these expressions in the performance of speech acts which are not strictly speaking promises, but in which we wish to emphasize the degree of our commitment. To illustrate this, consider another apparent counter-example to the analysis along different lines. Sometimes one hears people say "I promise" when making an emphatic assertion. Suppose, for example, I accuse you of having stolen the money. I say, "You stole that money, didn't you?". You reply, "No, I didn't, I promise you I didn't". Did you make a promise in this case? I find it very unnatural to describe your utterance as a promise. This utterance would be more aptly described as an emphatic denial, and we can explain the occurrence of the illocutionary force indicating device "I promise" as derivative from genuine promises and serving here as an expression adding emphasis to your denial.

In general, the point stated in condition 4 is that if a purported promise is to be non-defective, the thing promised must be something the hearer wants done, or considers to be in his interest, or would prefer being done to not being done, etc.; and the speaker must be aware of or believe or know, etc., that this is the case. I think a more elegant and exact formulation of this condition would probably require the introduction of technical terminology of the welfare economics sort.

(5) *It is not obvious to both S and H that S will do A in the normal course of events.*

This condition is an instance of a general condition on many different kinds of illocutionary acts to the effect that the act must have a point. For example, if I make a request to someone to do something which it is obvious that he is already doing or is about to do quite independently of the request, then my request is pointless and to that extent defective. In an actual speech situation, listeners, knowing the rules for performing illocutionary acts, will assume that this condition is satisfied. Suppose, for example, that in the course of a public speech I say to a member of my audience, "Look here, Smith, pay attention to what I am saying". In interpreting this utterance, the audience will have to assume that Smith has not been paying attention, or at any rate that it is not obvious that he has been paying attention, that the question of his not paying attention has arisen in some way, because a condition for making non-defective request is that it is not obvious that the hearer is doing or about to do the thing requested.

Similarly with promises. It is out of order for me to promise to do something that it is obvious to all concerned that I am going to do anyhow. If I do make such a promise, the only way my audience can interpret my utterance is to assume that I believe that it is not obvious that I am going to do the thing promised. A happily married man who promises his wife he will not desert her in the next week is likely to provide more anxiety than comfort.

Parenthetically, I think this condition is an instance of the sort of phenomenon stated in

Zipf's law. I think there is operating in our language, as in most forms of human behavior, a principle of least effort, in this case, a principle of maximum illocutionary ends with minimum phonetic effort; and I think condition 5 is an instance of it.

I call conditions such as 4 and 5 *preparatory conditions*. Though they do not state the essential feature, they are *sine quibus non* of happy promising.

(6) *S intends to do A.*

The distinction between sincere and insincere promises is that, in the case of sincere promises, the speaker intends to do the act promised; in the case of insincere promises, he does not intend to do the act. Also, in sincere promises, the speaker believes it is possible for him to do the act (or to refrain from doing it), but I think the proposition that he intends to do it entails that he thinks it is possible to do (or refrain from doing) it, so I am not stating that as an extra condition. I call this condition the *sincerity condition*.

(7) *S intends that the utterance of T will place him under an obligation to do A.*

The essential feature of a promise is that it is the undertaking of an obligation to perform a certain act. I think that this condition distinguishes promises (and other members of the same family such as vows) from other kinds of illocutionary acts. Notice that in the statement of the condition, we only specify the speaker's intention; further conditions will make clear how that intention is realized. It is clear, however, that having this intention is a necessary condition of making a promise, for if a speaker can demonstrate that he did not have this intention in a given utterance he can prove that the utterance was not a promise. We know, for example, that Mr Pickwick did not really promise to marry the woman because we know he did not have the appropriate intention. I call this the *essential condition*.

(8) *S intends (i-1) to produce in H the knowledge (K) that the utterance of T is to count as placing S under an obligation to do A. S intends to produce K by means of the recognition of i-1, and he intends i-1 to be recog-*

nized in virtue of (by means of) H's knowl-
edge of the meaning of T.

This captures our amended Gricean analysis of what it is for the speaker to mean the utterance as a promise. The speaker intends to produce a certain illocutionary effect by means of getting the hearer to recognize his intention to produce that effect, and he also intends this recognition to be achieved in virtue of the fact that the meaning of the item he utters conventionally associates it with producing that effect. In this case the speaker assumes that the semantic rules (which determine the meaning) of the expressions uttered are such that the utterance counts as the undertaking of an obligation. The rules, in short, as we shall see in the next condition, enable the intention in the essential condition 7 to be achieved by making the utterance. And the articulation of that achievement, the way the speaker gets the job done, is described in condition 8.

(9) *The semantical rules of the dialect spoken by S and H are such that T is correctly and sincerely uttered if and only if conditions 1–8 obtain.*[7]

This condition is intended to make clear that the sentence uttered is one which, by the semantical rules of the language, is used to make a promise. Taken together with condition 8, it eliminates counter-examples like the captured soldier example considered earlier. The meaning of a sentence is entirely determined by the meaning of its elements, both lexical and syntactical. And that is just another way of saying that the rules governing its utterance are determined by the rules governing its elements. We shall soon attempt to formulate the rules which govern the element or elements which serve to indicate that the illocutionary force is that of a promise.

I am construing condition 1 broadly enough so that together with the other conditions it guarantees that *H* understands the utterance, that is, together with 2–9 it entails that the illocutionary effect *K* is produced in *H* by means of *H*'s recognition of *S*'s intention to produce it, which recognition is achieved in virtue of *H*'s knowledge of the meaning of *T*. This condition could always be stated as a separate condition, and if the reader thinks that I am asking too

much of my input and output conditions that they should guarantee that the hearer understands the utterance, then he should treat this as a separate condition.

3.2. INSINCERE PROMISES

So far we have considered only the case of a sincere promise. But insincere promises are promises nonetheless, and we now need to show how to modify the conditions to allow for them. In making an insincere promise the speaker does not have all the intentions he has when making a sincere promise; in particular he lacks the intention to perform the act promised. However, he purports to have that intention. Indeed, it is because he purports to have intentions which he does not have that we describe his act as insincere.

A promise involves an expression of intention, whether sincere or insincere. So to allow for insincere promises, we need only to revise our conditions to state that the speaker takes responsibility for having the intention rather than stating that he actually has it. A clue that the speaker does take such responsibility is the fact that he could not say without absurdity, e.g., "I promise to do *A* but I do not intend to do *A*". To say, "I promise to do *A*" is to take responsibility for intending to do *A,* and this condition holds whether the utterance was sincere or insincere. To allow for the possibility of an insincere promise, then we have only to revise condition 6 so that it states not that the speaker intends to do *A,* but that he takes responsibility for intending to do *A,* and to avoid the charge of circularity, I shall phrase this as follows:

(6a) *S intends that the utterance of T will make him responsible for intending to do A.*

Thus amended (and with "sincerely" dropped from our analysandum and from condition 9), our analysis is neutral on the question whether the promise was sincere or insincere.

3.3. RULES FOR THE USE OF THE ILLOCUTIONARY FORCE INDICATING DEVICE

Our next task is to extract from our set of conditions a set of rules for the use of the indicator of illocutionary force. Obviously, not all of our conditions are equally relevant to this task. Condition 1 and conditions of the forms 8 and 9 apply generally to all kinds of normal illocutionary acts and are not peculiar to promising. Rules for the illocutionary force indicator for promising are to be found corresponding to conditions 2–7.

The semantical rules for the use of any illocutionary force indicating device *Pr* for promising are:

> *Rule 1. Pr* is to be uttered only in the context of a sentence (or larger stretch of discourse) *T,* the utterance of which predicates some future act *A* of the speaker *S.* I call this the *propositional content rule.* It is derived from the propositional content conditions 2 and 3.
>
> *Rule 2. Pr* is to be uttered only if the hearer *H* would prefer *S*'s doing *A* to his not doing *A,* and *S* believes *H* would prefer *S*'s doing *A* to his not doing *A.*
>
> *Rule 3.* Pr is to be uttered only if it is not obvious to both *S* and *H* that *S* will do *A* in the normal course of events. I call rules 2 and 3 *preparatory rules,* and they are derived from the preparatory conditions 4 and 5.
>
> *Rule 4.* Pr is to be uttered only if *S* intends to do *A.* I call this the *sincerity rule,* and it is derived from the sincerity condition 6.
>
> *Rule 5.* The utterance of *Pr* counts as the undertaking of an obligation to do *A.* I call this the *essential rule.*

These rules are ordered: rules 2–5 apply only if rule 1 is satisfied, and rule 5 applies only if rules 2 and 3 are satisfied as well. We shall see later on that some of these rules seem to be just particular manifestations as regards promising of very general underlying rules for illocutionary acts; and ultimately we should be able, as it were, to factor them out, so that they are not finally to be constructed as rules exclusively for the illocutionary force indicating device for promising as opposed to other types of illocutionary force indicating devices.

Notice that whereas rules 1–4 take the form of quasi-imperatives, i.e., they are of the form: utter *Pr* only if *x;* rule 5 is of the form: the utterance of *Pr* counts as *Y.* Thus, rule 5 is of the kind peculiar to systems of constitutive rules which I discussed in chapter 2.

Notice also that the rather tiresome analogy with games is holding up remarkably well. If we ask ourselves under what conditions a player could be said to move a knight correctly, we would find preparatory conditions such as that it must be his turn to move, as well as the essential condition stating the actual positions the knight can move to. There are even sincerity conditions for competitive games, such as that one does not cheat or attempt to 'throw' the game. Of course, the corresponding sincerity 'rules' are not rules peculiar to this or that game but apply to competitive games generally. There usually are no propositional content rules for games, because games do not in general represent states of affairs.

To which elements, in an actual linguistic description of a natural language would rules such as 1–5 attach? Let us assume for the sake of argument that the general outlines of the Chomsky-Fodor-Katz-Postal[8] account of syntax and semantics are correct. Then it seems to me extremely unlikely that illocutionary act rules would attach directly to elements (formatives, morphemes) generated by the syntactic component, except in a few cases such as the imperative. In the case of promising, the rules would more likely attach to some output of the combinatorial operations of the semantic component. Part of the answer to this question would depend on whether we can reduce all illocutionary acts to some very small number of basic illocutionary types. If so, it would then seem somewhat more likely that the deep structure of a sentence would have a simple representation of its illocutionary type.

3.4. EXTENDING THE ANALYSIS

If this analysis is of any general interest beyond the case of promising, then it would seem that these distinctions should carry over into other types of illocutionary act, and I think a little reflection will show that they do. Consider, e.g., giving an order. The preparatory conditions include that the speaker should be in a position of authority over the hearer, the sincerity condition is that the speaker wants the ordered act done, and the essential condition has to do with the fact that the speaker intends the utterance as an attempt to get the hearer to do the act. For assertions, the preparatory conditions include the fact that the hearer must have some basis for supposing the asserted proposition is true, the sincerity condition is that he must believe it to be true, and the essential condition has to do with the fact that the proposition is presented as representing an actual state of affairs. Greetings are a much simpler kind of speech act, but even here some of the distinctions apply. In the utterance of "Hello" there is no propositional content and no sincerity condition. The preparatory condition is that the speaker must have just encountered the hearer, and the essential rule is that the utterance counts as a courteous indication of recognition of the hearer. We can represent such information about a wide range of illocutionary acts in the table shown on pp. 148–149.

On the basis of this table, it is possible to formulate and test certain general hypotheses concerning illocutionary acts:

1. Wherever there is a psychological state specified in the sincerity condition, the performance of the act counts as an *expression* of that psychological state. This law holds whether the act is sincere or insincere, that is whether the speaker actually has the specified psychological state or not. Thus to assert, affirm, state (that *p*) counts as an *expression of belief* (that *p*). To request, ask, order, entreat, enjoin, pray, or command (that *A* be done) counts as *an expression of a wish or desire* (that *A* be done). To promise, vow, threaten or pledge (that *A*) counts as *an expression of intention* (to do *A*). To thank, welcome or congratulate counts as *an expression of gratitude, pleasure* (at *H*'s good fortune).[9]

2. The converse of the first law is that only where the act counts as the expression of a psychological state is insincerity possible. One cannot, for example, greet or christen insincerely, but one can state or promise insincerely.

3. Where the sincerity condition tells us what the speaker *expresses* in the performance of the act, the preparatory condition tells us (at least part of) what he *implies* in the performance of the act. To put it generally, in the performance of any illocutionary act, the speaker implies that the preparatory conditions of the act are satisfied. Thus, for example, when I make a statement I imply that I can back it up, when I make

a promise, I imply that the thing promised is in the hearer's interest. When I thank someone, I imply that the thing I am thanking him for has benefited me (or was at least intended to benefit me), etc.

It would be nicely symmetrical if we could give an account of *saying* in terms of the essential rules, parallel to our accounts of *implying* and *expressing*. The temptation is to say: the speaker *implies* the (satisfaction of the) preparatory conditions, *expresses* the (state specified in the) sincerity conditions, and *says* (whatever is specified by) the essential condition. The reason this breaks down is that there is a close connection between saying and the constative class of illocutionary acts. Saying fits statements but not greetings. Indeed, Austin's original insight into performatives was that some utterances were not sayings, but doings of some other kind. But this point can be exaggerated. A man who says "I (hereby) promise" not only promises, but *says* he does.[11] That is, there is indeed a connection between saying and constatives, but it is not as close as one might be inclined to think.

4. It is possible to perform the act without invoking an explicit illocutionary force-indicating device where the context and the utterance make it clear that the essential condition is satisfied. I may say only "I'll do it for you", but that utterance will count as and will be taken as a promise in any context where it is obvious that in saying it I am accepting (or undertaking, etc.) an obligation. Seldom, in fact, does one actually need to say the explicit "I promise". Similarly, I may say only "I wish you wouldn't do that", but this utterance in certain contexts will be more than merely an expression of a wish, for, say, autobiographical purposes. It will be a request. And it will be a request in those contexts where the point of saying it is to get you to stop doing something, i.e., where the essential condition for a request is satisfied.

This feature of speech—that an utterance in a context can indicate the satisfaction of an essential condition without the use of the explicit illocutionary force-indicating device for that essential condition—is the origin of many polite turns of phrase. Thus, for example, the sentence, "Could you do this for me?" in spite of the meaning of the lexical items and the interrogative illocutionary force-indicating devices is not characteristically uttered as a subjunctive question concerning your abilities; it is characteristically uttered as a request.

5. Wherever the illocutionary force of an utterance is not explicit it can always be made explicit. This is an instance of the principle of expressibility, stating that whatever can be meant can be said. Of course, a given language may not be rich enough to enable speakers to say everything they mean, but there are no barriers in principle to enriching it. Another application of this law is that whatever can be implied can be said, though if my account of preparatory conditions is correct, it cannot be said without implying other things.

6. The overlap of conditions on the table shows us that certain kinds of illocutionary acts are really special cases of other kinds; thus asking questions is really a special case of requesting, viz., requesting information (real question) or requesting that the hearer display knowledge (exam question). This explains our intuition that an utterance of the request form, "Tell me the name of the first President of the United States", is equivalent in force to an utterance of the question form, "What's the name of the first President of the United States?" It also partly explains why the verb "ask" covers both requests and questions, e.g., "He asked me to do it" (request), and "He asked me why" (question).

A crucially important but difficult question is this: Are there some basic illocutionary acts to which all or most of the others are reducible? Or alternatively: What are the basic species of illocutionary acts, and within each species what is the principle of unity of the species? Part of the difficulty in answering such questions is that the principles of distinction which lead us to say in the first place that such and such is a different kind of illocutionary act from such and such other act are quite various (see 8 below).[12]

7. In general the essential condition determines the others. For example, since the essential rule for requesting is that the utterance counts as an attempt to get H to do something, then the propositional content rule has to involve future behavior of H.

If it really is the case that the other rules are functions of the essential rule, and if some of the

others tend to recur in consistent patterns, then these recurring ones ought to be eliminable. In particular the non-obviousness preparatory condition runs through so many kinds of illocutionary acts that I think that it is not a matter of separate rules for the utterance of particular illocutionary force-indicating devices at all, but rather is a general condition on illocutionary acts (and analogously for other kinds of behavior) to the effect that the act is defective if the point to be achieved by the satisfaction of the essential rule is already achieved. There is, e.g., no point in telling somebody to do something if it is completely obvious that he is going to do it anyhow. But that is no more a *special* rule for requests than it is a matter of a special rule for moving the knight that the player can only move the knight when it is his turn to move.

8. The notions of illocutionary force and different illocutionary acts involve really several quite different principles of distinction. First and most important, there is the point or purpose of the act (the difference, for example, between a statement and a question); second, the relative positions of S and H (the difference between a request and an order); third, the degree of commitment undertaken (the difference between a mere expression of intention and a promise); fourth, the difference in propositional content (the difference between predictions and reports); fifth, the difference in the way the proposition relates to the interest of S and H (the difference between boasts and laments, between warnings and predictions); sixth, the different possible expressed psychological states (the difference between a promise, which is an expression of intention, and a statement, which is an expression of belief); seventh, the different ways in which an utterance relates to the rest of the conversation (the difference between simply replying to what someone has said and objecting to what he has said). So we must not suppose, what the metaphor of "force" suggests, that the different illocutionary verbs mark off points on a single continuum. Rather, there are several different continua of 'illocutionary force', and the fact that the illocutionary verbs of English stop at certain points on these various continua and not at others is, in a sense, accidental. For example, we might have had an

Types of Illocutionary Act

		Request	Assert, state (that), affirm	Question[10]
Types of rule	Propositional content	Future act *A* of *H*.	Any proposition *p*.	Any proposition or propositional function.
	Preparatory	1. *H* is able to do *A*. *S* believes *H* is able to do *A* 2. It is not obvious to both *S* and *H* that *H* will do *A* in the normal course of events of his own accord.	1. *S* has evidence (reasons, etc.) for the truth of *p*. 2. It is not obvious to both *S* and *H* that *H* knows (does not need to be reminded of, etc.) *p*.	1. *S* does not know 'the answer', i.e., does not know if the proposition is true, or, in the case of the propositional function, does not know the information needed to complete the proposition truly (but see comment below). 2. It is not obvious to both *S* and *H* that *H* will provide the information at that time without being asked.
	Sincerity	*S* wants *H* to do *A*.	*S* believes *p*.	*S* wants this information.
	Essential	Counts as an attempt to get *H* to do *A*.	Counts as an undertaking to the effect that *p* represents an actual state of affairs.	Counts as an attempt to elicit this information from *H*.
	Comment:	*Order* and *command* have the additional preparatory rule that *S* must be in a position of authority over *H*. *Command* probably does not have the 'pragmatic' condition requiring non-obviousness. Furthermore in both, the authority relationship infects the essential condition because the utterance counts as an attempt to get *H* to do *A* *in virtue of the authority of S over H*.	Unlike *argue* these do not seem to be essentially tied to attempting to convince. Thus "I am simply stating that *p* and not attempting to convince you" is acceptable, but "I am arguing that *p* and not attempting to convince you" sounds inconsistent.	There are two kinds of questions, (*a*) real questions, (*b*) exam questions. In real questions *S* wants to know (find out) the answer; in exam questions, *S* wants to know if *H* knows.

illocutionary verb "rubrify", meaning to call something "red". Thus, "I hereby rubrify it" would just mean "It's red". Analogously, we happen to have an obsolete verb "macarize", meaning to call someone happy.[13]

Both because there are several different dimensions of illocutionary force, and because the same utterance act may be performed with a variety of different intentions, it is important to realize that one and the same utterance may constitute the performance of several different illocutionary acts. There may be several different non-synonymous illocutionary verbs that correctly characterize the utterance. For example suppose at a party a wife says "It's really quite late". That utterance may be at one level a

		Thank (for)	Advise	Warn
Types of rule	Propositional content	Past act A done by H.	Future act A of H.	Future event or state, etc., E.
	Preparatory	A benefits S and S believes A benefits S.	1. S has some reason to believe A will benefit H. 2. It is not obvious to both S and H that H will do A in the normal course of events.	1. H has reason to believe E will occur and is not in H's interest. 2. It is not obvious to both S and H that E will occur.
	Sincerity	S feels grateful or appreciative for A. ↓	S believes A will benefit H.	S believes E is not in H's best interest.
	Essential	Counts as an expression of gratitude of appreciation.	Counts as an undertaking to the effect that A is in H's best interest.	Counts as an undertaking to the effect that E is not in H's best interest.
	Comment:	Sincerity and essential rules overlap. Thanking is just expressing gratitude in a way that, e.g., promising is not just expressing an intention.	Contrary to what one might suppose advice is not a species of requesting. It is interesting to compare "advise" with "urge", "advocate" and "recommend". Advising you is not trying to get you to do something in the sense that requesting is. Advising is more like telling you what is best for you.	Warning is like advising, rather than requesting. It is not, I think, necessarily an attempt to get you to take evasive action. Notice that the above account is of categorical not hypothetical warnings. Most warnings are probably hypothetical: "If you do not do X then Y will occur."

		Greet	Congratulate
Types of rule	Propositional content	None.	Some event, act, etc., E related to H.
	Preparatory	S has just encountered (or been introduced to, etc.) H.	E is in H's interest and S believes E is in H's interest.
	Sincerity	None.	S is pleased at E. ↓
	Essential	Counts as courteous recognition of H by S.	Counts as an expression of pleasure at E.
	Comment:		"Congratulate" is similar to "thank" in that it is an expression of its sincerity condition.

statement of fact; to her interlocutor, who has just remarked on how early it was, it may be (and be intended as) an objection; to her husband it may be (and be intended as) a suggestion or even a request ("Let's go home") as well as a warning ("You'll feel rotten in the morning if we don't").

9. Some illocutionary verbs are definable in terms of the intended perlocutionary effect, some not. Thus requesting is, as a matter of its essential condition, an attempt to get a hearer to do something, but promising is not essentially tied to such effects on or responses from the hearer. If we could get an analysis of all (or even most) illocutionary acts in terms of perlocutionary effects, the prospects of analyzing illocutionary acts without reference to rules would be greatly increased. The reason for this is that language could then be regarded as just a conventional means for securing or attempting to secure natural responses or effects. The illocutionary act would then not essentially involve any rules at all. One could in theory perform the act in or out of a language, and to do it in a language would be to do with a conventional device what could be done without any conventional devices. Illocutionary acts would then be (optionally) conventional but not rule governed at all.

As is obvious from everything I have said, I think this reduction of the illocutionary to the perlocutionary and the consequent elimination of rules probably cannot be carried out. It is at this point that what might be called institutional theories of communication, like Austin's, mine, and I think Wittgenstein's, part company with what might be called naturalistic theories of meaning, such as, e.g., those which rely on a stimulus-response account of meaning.

NOTES

1. J. L. Austin, *How to Do Things with Words* (Oxford, 1962), especially lectures II, III, IV.
2. Cf. Ludwig Wittgenstein, *Philosophical Investigations* (New York, 1953), paras. 66, 67.
3. Alston in effect tries to analyze illocutionary acts using only brute notions (except the notion of a rule). As he points out, his analysis is unsuccessful. I suggest that it could not be successful without involving institutional notions. Cf. W. P. Alston, "Linguistic Acts," *American Philosophical Quarterly,* vol. 1, no. 2 (1964).
4. I contrast "serious" utterances with play acting, teaching a language, reciting poems, practicing pronunciation, etc., and I contrast "literal" with metaphorical, sarcastic, etc.
5. Cf. the discussion of predication in chapter 2.
6. For an interesting discussion of this condition, see Jerome Schneewind, "A Note on Promising," *Philosophical Studies,* vol. 17. no. 3 (April 1966), pp. 33–5.
7. As far as condition 1 is concerned, this is a bit misleading. Condition 1 is a general condition on any serious linguistic communication and is not peculiar to this or that dialect. Furthermore the use of the biconditional in this condition excludes ambiguous sentences. We have to assume that *T* is unambiguous.
8. Cf., e.g., J. Katz and P. Postal, *An Integrated Theory of Linguistic Descriptions* (Cambridge, Mass., 1964).
9. This law, incidentally, provides the solution to Moore's paradox: the paradox that I cannot assert both that *p* and that I do not believe *p,* even though the proposition that *p* is not inconsistent with the proposition that I do not believe *p.*
10. In the sense of "ask a question" not in the sense of "doubt".
11. As J. L. Austin himself points out, "Other Minds," *Proceedings of the Aristotelian Society,* supplementary vol. (1964); reprinted in J. L. Austin, *Philosophical Papers* (Oxford, 1961).
12. In this respect, Austin's classification of illocutionary acts into five categories seems somewhat ad hoc. *How to Do Things with Words,* pp. 150 ff.
13. I owe the former of these examples to Paul Grice, the latter to Peter Geach, "Ascriptivism," *Philosophical Review,* vol. 69 (1960), pp. 221–6.

10 A Taxonomy of Illocutionary Acts

JOHN R. SEARLE

I. INTRODUCTION

The primary purpose of this paper is to develop a reasoned classification of illocutionary acts into certain basic categories or types. It is to answer the question: How many kinds of illocutionary acts are there?

Since any such attempt to develop a taxonomy must take into account Austin's classification of illocutionary acts into his five basic categories of verdictive, expositive, exercitive, behabitive, and commissive, a second purpose of this paper is to assess Austin's classification to show in what respects it is adequate and in what respects inadequate. Furthermore, since basic semantic differences are likely to have syntactical consequences, a third purpose of this paper is to show how these different basic illocutionary types are realized in the syntax of a natural language such as English.

In what follows, I shall presuppose a familiarity with the general pattern of analysis of illocutionary acts offered in such works as *How to Do Things with Words* (Austin, 1962), *Speech Acts* (Searle, 1969), and "Austin on Locutionary and Illocutionary Acts" (Searle, 1968). In particular, I shall presuppose a distinction between the illocutionary force of an utterance and its propositional content as symbolized

$$F(p)$$

The aim of this paper then is to classify the different types of F.

II. DIFFERENT TYPES OF DIFFERENCES BETWEEN DIFFERENT TYPES OF ILLOCUTIONARY ACTS

Any taxonomical effort of this sort presupposes criteria for distinguishing one (kind of) illocutionary act from another. What are the criteria by which we can tell that of three actual utterances one is a report, one a prediction, and one a promise? In order to develop higher-order genera, we must first know how the species *promise, prediction, report*, etc., differ from one another. When one attempts to answer that question one discovers that there are several quite different principles of distinction; that is, there are different kinds of differences that enable us to say that the force of this utterance is different from the force of that utterance. For this reason the metaphor of force in the expression "illocutionary force" is misleading since it suggests that different illocutionary forces occupy different positions on a single continuum of force. What is actually the case is that there are several distinct criss-crossing continua. A related source of confusion is that we are inclined to confuse illocutionary verbs with types of illocutionary acts. We are inclined, for example, to think that where we have two non-synonymous illocutionary verbs they must necessarily mark two different kinds of illocutionary acts. In what follows, I shall try to keep a clear distinction between illocutionary verbs and illocutionary acts. Illocutions are a part of

John R. Searle, "A Taxonomy of Illocutionary Acts," from *Language, Mind, and Knowledge: Minnesota Studies in the Philosophy of Science*, Volume VII, ed. Keith Gunderson (University of Minnesota Press, 1975), pp. 344–369. © John R. Searle. Reprinted with permission of the author.

language as opposed to particular languages. Illocutionary verbs are always part of a particular language: French, German, English, or whatnot. Differences in illocutionary verbs are a good guide but by no means a sure guide to differences in illocutionary acts.

It seems to me there are (at least) twelve significant dimensions of variation in which illocutionary acts differ one from another and I shall—all too briskly—list them:

1. *Differences in the point (or purpose) of the (type of) act.* The point or purpose of an order can be specified by saying that it is an attempt to get the hearer to do something. The point or purpose of a description is that it is a representation (true or false, accurate or inaccurate) of how something is. The point or purpose of a promise is that it is an undertaking of an obligation by the speaker to do something. These differences correspond to the essential conditions in my analysis of illocutionary acts in chapter 3 of *Speech Acts* (Searle, 1969). Ultimately, I believe, essential conditions form the best basis for a taxonomy, as I shall attempt to show. It is important to notice that the terminology of "point" or "purpose" is not meant to imply, nor is it based on the view, that every illocutionary act has a definitionally associated perlocutionary intent. For many, perhaps most, of the most important illocutionary acts, there is no essential perlocutionary intent associated by definition with the corresponding verb, e.g. statements and promises are not by definition attempts to produce perlocutionary effects in hearers.

The point or purpose of a type of illocution I shall call its *illocutionary point.* Illocutionary point is part of but not the same as illocutionary force. Thus, e.g., the illocutionary point of requests is the same as that of commands: both are attempts to get hearers to do something. But the illocutionary forces are clearly different. In general, one can say that the notion of illocutionary force is the resultant of several elements of which illocutionary point is only one, though, I believe, the most important one.

2. *Differences in the direction of fit between words and the world.* Some illocutions have as part of their illocutionary point to get the words (more strictly, their propositional content) to match the world, others to get the world to match the words. Assertions are in the former category, promises and requests are in the latter. The best illustration of this distinction I know of is provided by Elizabeth Anscombe (1957). Suppose a man goes to the supermarket with a shopping list given him by his wife on which are written the words "beans, butter, bacon, and bread." Suppose as he goes around with his shopping cart selecting these items, he is followed by a detective who writes down everything he takes. As they emerge from the store both shopper and detective will have identical lists. But the function of the two lists will be quite different. In the case of the shopper's list, the purpose of the list is, so to speak, to get the world to match the words; the man is supposed to make his actions fit the list. In the case of the detective, the purpose of the list is to make the words match the world; the man is supposed to make the list fit the actions of the shopper. This can be further demonstrated by observing the role of "mistake" in the two cases. If the detective gets home and suddenly realizes that the man bought pork chops instead of bacon, he can simply erase the word "bacon" and write "pork chops." But if the shopper gets home and his wife points out he has bought pork chops when he should have bought bacon he cannot correct the mistake by erasing "bacon" from the list and writing "pork chops."

In these examples the list provides the propositional content of the illocution and the illocutionary force determines how that content is supposed to relate to the world. I propose to call this difference a difference in *direction of fit.* The detective's list has the *word-to-world* direction of fit (as do statements, descriptions, assertions, and explanations); the shopper's list has the *world-to-word* direction of fit (as do requests, commands, vows, promises). I represent the word-to-world direction of fit with a downward arrow thus ↓ and the world-to-word direction of fit with an upward arrow thus ↑. Direction of fit is always a consequence of illocutionary point. It would be very elegant if we could build our taxonomy entirely around this distinction in direction of fit, but though it will figure largely in our taxonomy, I am unable to make it the entire basis of the distinctions.

3. *Differences in expressed psychological*

states. A man who states, explains, asserts, or claims that *p expresses the belief that p;* a man who promises, vows, threatens, or pledges to do *A expresses an intention to do A;* a man who orders, commands, requests *H* to do *A expresses a desire (want, wish) that H do A;* a man who apologizes for doing *A expresses regret at having done A;* etc. In general, in the performance of any illocutionary act with a propositional content, the speaker expresses some attitude, state, etc., to that propositional content. Notice that this holds even if he is insincere, even if he does not have the belief, desire, intention, regret, or pleasure which he expresses, he nonetheless expresses a belief, desire, intention, regret, or pleasure in the performance of the speech act. This fact is marked linguistically by the fact that it is linguistically unacceptable (though not self-contradictory) to conjoin the explicit performative verb with the denial of the expressed psychological state. Thus one cannot say "I state that *p* but do not believe that *p*," "I promise that *p* but I do not intend that *p*," etc. Notice that this only holds in the first person performative use. One can say, "He stated that *p* but didn't really believe that *p*," "I promised that *p* but did not really intend to do it," etc. The psychological state expressed in the performance of the illocutionary act is the *sincerity condition* of the act, as analyzed in *Speech Acts,* chapter 3.

If one tries to do a classification of illocutionary acts based entirely on differently expressed psychological states (differences in the sincerity condition), one can get quite a long way. Thus, *belief* collects not only statements, assertions, remarks, and explanations, but also postulations, declarations, deductions, and arguments. *Intention* will collect promises, vows, threats, and pledges. *Desire* or *want* will collect requests, orders, commands, askings, prayers, pleadings, beggings, and entreaties. *Pleasure* doesn't collect quite so many—congratulations, felicitations, welcomes, and a few others.

In what follows, I shall symbolize the expressed psychological state with the capitalized initial letters of the corresponding verb, thus *B* for believe, *W* for want, *I* for intend, etc.

These three dimensions—illocutionary point, direction of fit, and sincerity condition—seem to me the most important, and I will build most

of my taxonomy around them, but there are several others that need remarking.

4. *Differences in the force or strength with which the illocutionary point is presented.* Both "I suggest we go to the movies" and "I insist that we go to the movies" have the same illocutionary point, but it is presented with different strengths. Analogously with "I solemnly swear that Bill stole the money" and "I guess Bill stole the money." Along the same dimension of illocutionary point or purpose there may be varying degrees of strength or commitment.

5. *Differences in the status or position of the speaker and hearer as these bear on the illocutionary force of the utterance.* If the general asks the private to clean up the room, that is in all likelihood a command or an order. If the private asks the general to clean up the room, that is likely to be a suggestion or proposal or request but not an order or command. This feature corresponds to one of the preparatory conditions in my analysis in Speech Acts, chapter 3.

6. *Differences in the way the utterance relates to the interests of the speaker and the hearer.* Consider, for example, the differences between boasts and laments, between congratulations and condolences. In these two pairs, one hears the difference as being between what is or is not in the interests of the speaker and hearer respectively. This feature is another type of preparatory condition according to the analysis in *Speech Acts.*

7. *Differences in relations to the rest of the discourse.* Some performative expressions serve to relate the utterance to the rest of the discourse (and also to the surrounding context). Consider, e.g., "I reply," "I deduce," "I conclude," and "I object." These expressions serve to relate utterances to other utterances and to the surrounding context. The features they mark seem mostly to involve utterances within the class of statements. In addition to simply stating a proposition, one may state it by way of objecting to what someone else has said, by way of replying to an earlier point, by way of deducing it from certain evidentiary premises, etc. "However," "moreover," and "therefore" also perform these discourse-relating functions.

8. *Differences in propositional content that are determined by illocutionary force indicating*

devices. The differences, for example, between a report and a prediction involve the fact that a prediction must be about the future whereas a report can be about the past or present. These differences correspond to differences in propositional content conditions as explained in *Speech Acts.*

9. *Differences between those acts that must always be speech acts, and those that can be, but need not be performed as speech acts.* For example, one may classify things by saying "I classify this as an *A* and this as a *B*." But, one need not say anything at all in order to be classifying; one may simply throw all the *A*s in the *A* box and all the *B*s in the *B* box. Similarly with estimate, diagnose, and conclude. I may make estimates, give diagnoses, and draw conclusions in saying "I estimate," "I diagnose," and "I conclude," but in order to estimate, diagnose, or conclude it is not necessary to say anything at all. I may simply stand before a building and estimate its height, silently diagnose you as a marginal schizophrenic, or conclude that the man sitting next to me is quite drunk. In these cases, no speech act, not even an internal speech act, is necessary.

10. *Differences between those acts that require extralinguistic institutions for their performance and those that do not.* There are a large number of illocutionary acts that require an extralinguistic institution and, generally, a special position by the speaker and the hearer within that institution in order for the act to be performed. Thus, in order to bless, excommunicate, christen, pronounce guilty, call the base runner out, bid three no-trumps, or declare war, it is not sufficient for any old speaker to say to any old hearer "I bless," "I excommunicate," etc. One must have a position within an extralinguistic institution. Austin sometimes talks as if he thought all illocutionary acts were like this, but plainly they are not. In order to make a statement that it is raining or promise to come and see you, I need only obey the rules of language. No extralinguistic institutions are required. This feature of certain speech acts, that they require extralinguistic institutions, needs to be distinguished from feature 5, the requirement of certain illocutionary acts that the speaker and possibly the hearer as well have a

certain status. Extralinguistic institutions often confer status in a way relevant to illocutionary force, but not all differences of status derive from institutions. Thus, an armed robber in virtue of his possession of a gun may *order* as opposed to, e.g., request, entreat, or implore victims to raise their hands. But his status here does not derive from a position within an institution but from his possession of a weapon.

11. *Differences between those acts where the corresponding illocutionary verb has a performative use and those where it does not.* Most illocutionary verbs have performative uses— e.g. "state," "promise," "order," "conclude." But one cannot perform acts of, e.g., boasting or threatening, by saying "I hereby boast," or "I hereby threaten." Not all illocutionary verbs are performative verbs.

12. *Differences in the style of performance of the illocutionary act.* Some illocutionary verbs serve to mark what we might call the special style in which an illocutionary act is performed. Thus, the difference between, for example, announcing and confiding need not involve any differences in illocutionary point or propositional content but only in the *style* of performance of the illocutionary act.

III. WEAKNESSES IN AUSTIN'S TAXONOMY

Austin advances his five categories very tentatively, more as a basis for discussion than as a set of established results: "I am not," he says, "putting any of this forward as in the very least definitive" (Austin, 1962, p. 151). I think they form an excellent basis for discussion but I also think that the taxonomy needs to be seriously revised because it contains several weaknesses. Here are Austin's five categories:

Verdictives. These "consist in the delivering of a finding, official or unofficial, upon evidence or reasons as to value or fact so far as these are distinguishable." Examples of verbs in this class are: acquit, hold, calculate, describe, analyze, estimate, date, rank, assess, and characterize.

Exercitives. One of these "is the giving of a decision in favor of or against a certain course of action or advocacy of it . . . ," "a decision that something is to be so, as distinct from a judgment that it is so." Some examples are: order, command, direct, plead, beg, recommend, entreat, and advise. Request is also an obvious example, but Austin does not list it. As well as the above, Austin also lists: appoint, dismiss, nominate, veto, declare closed, declare open, as well as announce, warn, proclaim, and give.

Commissives. "The whole point of a commissive," Austin tells us, "is to commit the speaker to a certain course of action." Some of the obvious examples are: promise, vow, pledge, covenant, contract, guarantee, embrace, and swear.

Expositives "are used in acts of exposition involving the expounding of views, the conducting of arguments, and the clarifying of usages and references." Austin gives many examples of these, among which are: affirm, deny, emphasize, illustrate, answer, report, accept, object to, concede, describe, class, identify, and call.

Behabitives. This class, with which Austin was very dissatisfied ("a shocker," he called it), "includes the notion of reaction to other people's behaviour and fortunes and of atti- tudes and expressions of attitudes to someone else's past conduct or imminent conduct."

Among the examples Austin lists are: apologize, thank, deplore, commiserate, congratulate, felicitate, welcome, applaud, criticize, bless, curse, toast, and drink. But also, curiously: dare, defy, protest, and challenge.

The first thing to notice about these lists is that they are not classifications of illocutionary acts but of English illocutionary verbs. Austin seems to assume that a classification of different verbs is *eo ipso* a classification of kinds of illocutionary acts, that any two nonsynonymous verbs must mark different illocutionary acts. But there is no reason to suppose that this is the case. As we shall see, some verbs, for example, mark the manner in which an illocutionary act is performed, e.g. "announce." One may announce orders, promises, and reports, but announcing is not on all fours with ordering, promising, and reporting. Announcing, to anticipate a bit, is not the name of a type of illocutionary act, but of the way in which some illocutionary act is performed. An announcement is never just an announcement. It must also be a statement, order, etc.

Even granting that the lists are of illocutionary verbs and not necessarily of different illocutionary acts, it seems to me, one can level the following criticisms against it.

1. First, a minor cavil, but one worth noting. Not all of the verbs listed are even illocutionary verbs. For example, "sympathize," "regard as," "mean to," "intend," and "shall." Take, "intend": it is clearly not performative. Saying, "I intend" is not intending; nor in the third person does it name an illocutionary act: "He intended . . ." does not report a speech act. Of course there is an illocutionary act of *expressing an intention,* but the illocutionary verb phrase is: "express an intention," not "intend." Intending is never a speech act; expressing an intention usually, but not always, is.

2. The most important weakness of the taxonomy is simply this. There is no clear or consistent principle or set of principles on the basis of which the taxonomy is constructed. Only in the case of Commissives has Austin clearly and unambiguously used illocutionary point as the basis of the definition of a category. Expositives, insofar as the characterization is clear, seem to be defined in terms of discourse relations (my feature 7). Exercitives seem to be at least partly defined in terms of the exercise of authority. Both considerations of status (my feature 5) as well as institutional considerations (my feature 10) are lurking in it. Behabitives do not seem to me at all well defined (as Austin, I am sure, would have agreed) but it seems to involve notions of what is good or bad for the speaker and hearer (my feature 6) as well as expressions of attitudes (my feature 3).

3. Because there is no clear principle of classification and because there is a persistent confusion between illocutionary acts and illocutionary verbs, there is a great deal of overlap from one category to another and a great deal of heterogeneity within some of the categories. The problem is not that there are borderline cases—any taxonomy that deals with the real world is likely to come up with borderline cases—nor is it merely that a few unusual cases will have the defining characteristics of more than one category; rather a very large number of verbs find themselves smack in the middle of two competing categories because the princi-

ples of classification are unsystematic. Consider, for example, the verb "describe," a very important verb in anybody's theory of speech acts. Austin lists it as both a verdictive and an expositive. Given his definitions, it is easy to see why: describing can be both the delivering of a finding and an act of exposition. But then any "act of exposition involving the expounding of views" could also in his rather special sense be "the delivering of a finding, official or unofficial, upon evidence or reasons." And indeed, a look at his list of expositives (pp. 161–162) is sufficient to show that most of his verbs fit his definition of verdictives as well as does "describe." Consider "affirm," "deny," "state," "class," "identify," "conclude," and "deduce." All of these are listed as expositives, but they could just as easily have been listed as verdictives. The few cases which are clearly not verdictives are cases where the meaning of the verb has purely to do with discourse relations, e.g., "begin by," "turn to," or where there is no question of evidence or reasons, e.g., "postulate," "neglect," "call," and "define." But then that is really not sufficient to warrant a separate category, especially since many of these—"begin by," "turn to," "neglect"—are not names of illocutionary acts at all.

4. Not only is there too much overlap from one category to the next, but within some of the categories there are quite distinct kinds of verbs. Thus Austin lists "dare," "defy," and "challenge" alongside "thank," "apologize," "deplore," and "welcome" as behabitives. But "dare," "defy," and "challenge" have to do with the hearer's subsequent actions, they belong with "order," "command," and "forbid" both on syntactical and semantic grounds, as I shall argue later. But when we look for the family that includes "order," "command," and "urge," we find these are listed as exercitives alongside "veto," "hire," and "demote." But these, again as I shall argue later, are in two quite distinct categories.

5. Related to these objections is the further difficulty that not all of the verbs listed within the classes really satisfy the definitions given, even if we take the definitions in the rather loose and suggestive manner that Austin clearly intends. Thus "nominate," "appoint," and "excommunicate" are not "giving of a decision in favour of or against a certain course of action," much less are they "advocating" it. Rather they are, as Austin himself might have said, *performances* of these actions, not *advocacies* of anything. That is, in the sense in which we might agree that ordering, commanding, and urging someone to do something are all cases of *advocating* that he do it, we cannot also agree that nominating or appointing is also advocating. When I appoint you chairman, I don't advocate that you be or become chairman; I *make* you chairman.

In sum, there are (at least) six related difficulties with Austin's taxonomy; in ascending order of importance: there is a persistent confusion between verbs and acts, not all the verbs are illocutionary verbs, there is too much overlap of the categories, too much heterogeneity within the categories, many of the verbs listed in the categories don't satisfy the definition given for the category, and, most important, there is no consistent principle of classification.

I don't believe I have fully substantiated all six of these charges and I will not attempt to do so within the confines of this paper, which has other aims. I believe, however, that my doubts about Austin's taxonomy will have greater clarity and force after I have presented an alternative. What I propose to do is take illocutionary point, and its corollaries, direction of fit and expressed sincerity conditions, as the basis for constructing a classification. In such a classification, other features—the role of authority, discourse relations, etc.—will fall into their appropriate places.

IV. ALTERNATIVE TAXONOMY

In this section, I shall present a list of what I regard as the basic categories of illocutionary acts. In so doing, I shall discuss briefly how my classification relates to Austin's.

Assertives. The point or purpose of the members of the assertive class is to commit the speaker (in varying degrees) to something's being the case, to the truth of the expressed proposition. All of the members of the assertive class are assessable on the dimension of assessment which includes *true* and *false*. Using Frege's assertion sign to mark the illocutionary point common to all the members of this class, and the symbols introduced above, we may symbolize this class as follows:

$\vdash \downarrow B(p)$.

The direction of fit is words to the world; the psychological state expressed is Belief (that p). It is important to emphasize that words such as "belief" and "commitment" are here intended to mark dimensions, they are so to speak determinables rather than determinates. Thus, there is a difference between *suggesting* that p or *putting it forward as a hypothesis* that p on the one hand and *insisting* that p or solemnly *swearing that p* on the other. The degree of belief and commitment may approach or even reach zero, but it is clear or will become clear that *hypothesizing that p* and *flatly stating that p* are in the same line of business in a way that neither is like requesting. Once we recognize the existence of *assertives* as a quite separate class, based on the notion of illocutionary point, then the existence of a large number of performative verbs that denote illocutions that seem to be assessable in the True-False dimension and yet are not just "statements" will be easily explicable in terms of the fact that they mark features of illocutionary force which are in addition to illocutionary point. Thus, for example, consider: "boast" and "complain." They both denote assertives with the added feature that they have something to do with the interest of the speaker (condition 6). "Conclude" and "deduce" are also assertives with the added feature that they mark certain relations between the assertive illocutionary act and the rest of the discourse or the context of utterance (condition 7). This class will contain most of Austin's expositives and many of his verdictives as well for the, by now I hope obvious, reason that they all have the same illocutionary point and differ only in other features of illocutionary force. The simplest test of an assertive is this: can you literally characterize it (inter alia) as true or false—though I hasten to add that this will give neither necessary nor sufficient conditions, as we shall see when we get to my fifth class.

These points about assertives will, I hope, be clearer when I discuss my second class, which, with some reluctance, I will call

Directives. The illocutionary point of these consists in the fact that they are attempts (of varying degrees, and hence, more precisely, they are determinates of the determinable which includes attempting) by the speaker to get the hearer to do something. They may be very modest "attempts" as when I invite you to do it or suggest that you do it, or they may be very fierce attempts as when I insist that you do it. Using the shriek mark for the illocutionary point indicating device for the members of this class generally, we have the following symbolism:

$! \uparrow W$ (H does A)

The direction of fit is world-to-words and the sincerity condition is want (or wish or desire). The propositional content is always that the hearer H does some future action A. Verbs denoting members of this class are *ask, order, command, request, beg, plead, pray, entreat*, and also *invite, permit*, and *advise*. I think also that it is clear that *dare, defy*, and *challenge* which Austin lists as behabitives are in this class. Many of Austin's exercitives are also in this class. Questions are a subclass of directives, since they are attempts by S to get H to answer, i.e., to perform a speech act.

Commissives. Austin's definition of commissives seems to me unexceptionable, and I will simply appropriate it as it stands with the cavil that several of the verbs he lists as commissive verbs do not belong in this class at all, such as "shall," "intend," "favor," and others. Commissives then are those illocutionary acts whose point is to committ the speaker (again in varying degrees) to some future course of action. Using "C" for the members of this class generally, we have the following symbolism:

$C \uparrow I$ (S does A)

The direction of fit is world-to-word and the sincerity condition is Intention. The propositional content is always that the speaker S does some future action A. Since the direction of fit is the same for commissives and directives, it would give us a more elegant taxonomy if we could show that they are really members of the same category. I am unable to do this because whereas the point of a promise is to commit the speaker to doing something (and not necessarily to try to get himself to do it) the point of a request is to try to get the hearer to do something (and not necessarily to commit or obligate him to do it). In order to assimilate the two categories, one would have to show that promises are really a species of requests to oneself (this has been suggested to me by Julian Boyd) or alternatively one would have to show that requests placed the hearer under an obligation (this has been suggested to me by William Alston and John Kearns). I have been unable to make either of these analyses work and am left with the inelegant solution of two separate categories with the same direction of fit.

A fourth category I shall call

Expressives. The illocutionary point of this class is to express the psychological state specified in the sincerity condition about a state of affairs specified in the propositional content. The paradigms of expressive verbs are "thank," "congratulate," "apologize," "condole," "deplore," and "welcome." Notice that in expressives there is no direction of fit. In performing an expressive, the speaker is neither trying to get the world to match the words nor the words to match the world; rather the truth of the expressed proposition is presupposed. Thus, for example, when I apologize for having stepped on your toe, it is not my purpose either to claim that your toe was stepped on nor to get it stepped on. This fact is neatly reflected in the syntax (of English) by the fact that the paradigm expressive verbs in their performative occurrence will not take *that* clauses but require a gerundive nominalization transformation (or some other nominal). One cannot say:

* I apologize that I stepped on your toe;

rather the correct English is,

I apologize for stepping on your toe.

Similarly, one cannot have:

* I congratulate you that you won the race

nor

* I thank you that you paid me the money.

One must have:

I congratulate you on winning the race (congratulations on winning the race)

I thank you for paying me the money (thanks for paying me the money).

These syntactical facts, I suggest, are consequences of the fact that there is no direction of fit in expressives. The truth of the proposition expressed in an expressive is presupposed. The symbolization therefore of this class must proceed as follows:

$$E \emptyset (P) (S/H + \text{property})$$

Where "E" indicates the illocutionary point common to all expressives "$\emptyset$" is the null symbol indicating no direction of fit, P is a variable ranging over the different possible psychological states expressed in the performance of the illocutionary acts in this class, and the propositional content ascribes some property (not necessarily an action) to either S or H. I can congratulate you not only on your winning the race, but also on your good looks. The property specified in the propositional content of an expressive must, however, be related to S or H. I cannot without some very special assumptions congratulate you on Newton's first law of motion.

It would be economical if we could include all illocutionary acts in these four classes, and would lend some further support to the general pattern of analysis adopted in *Speech Acts,* but it seems to me the taxonomy is still not complete. There is still left an important class of cases, where the state of affairs represented in the proposition expressed is realized or brought into existence by the illocutionary force–indicating device, cases where one brings a state of affairs into existence by declaring it to exist, cases where, so to speak, "saying makes it so." Examples of these cases are "I resign," "You're fired," "I excommunicate you," "I christen this ship the battleship Missouri," "I appoint you chairman," and "War is hereby declared." These cases were presented as paradigms in the very earliest discussions of performatives, but it seems to me they are still not adequately described in the literature and their relation to other kinds of illocutionary acts is usually misunderstood. Let us call this class

Declarations. It is the defining characteristic of this class that the successful performance of one of its members brings about the correspondence between the propositional content and reality, successful performance guarantees that the propositional concern corresponds to the world: if I successfully perform the act of appointing you chairman, then you are chairman; if I successfully perform the act of nominating you as candidate, then you are a candidate; if I successfully perform the act of declaring a state of war, then war is on; if I successfully perform the act of marrying you, then you are married.

The surface syntactical structure of many sentences used to perform declarations conceals this point from us because in them there is no surface syntactical distinction between propositional content and illocutionary force. Thus, "You're fired" and "I resign" do not seem to permit a distinction between illocutionary force and propositional content, but I think in fact that in their use to perform declarations their semantic structure is:

I declare: your employment is (hereby) terminated.
I declare: my position is (hereby) terminated.

Declarations bring about some alteration in the status or condition of the referred to object or objects solely in virtue of the fact that the declaration has been successfully performed. This feature of declarations distinguishes them from the other categories. In the history of the discussion of these topics since Austin's first introduction of his distinction between performatives and constatives, this feature of declarations has not been properly understood. The original distinction between constatives and performatives was supposed to be a distinction between utterances which are sayings (constatives, statements, assertions, etc.) and utterances which are doings (promises, bets, warnings, etc.). What I am calling declarations were included in the class of performatives. The main theme of Austin's mature work, *How to Do Things with Words,* is that this distinction collapses. Just as saying certain things constitutes getting married (a "performative") and saying certain things constitutes making a promise (another "performative"), so saying certain things constitutes making a statement (supposedly a "constative"). As Austin saw but as many

philosophers still fail to see, the parallel is exact. Making a statement is as much performing an illocutionary act as making a promise, a bet, a warning, or what have you. Any utterance will consist in performing one or more illocutionary acts.

The illocutionary force indicating device in the sentence operates on the propositional content to indicate among other things the direction of fit between the propositional content and reality. In the case of assertives, the direction of fit is words-to-world, in the case of directives and commissives, it is world-to-words; in the case of expressives there is no direction of fit carried by the illocutionary force because the existence of fit is presupposed. The utterance can't get off the ground unless there already is a fit. But now with the declarations we discover a very peculiar relation. The performance of a declaration brings about a fit by its very successful performance. How is such a thing possible?

Notice that all of the examples we have considered so far involve an extralinguistic institution, a system of constitutive rules in addition to the constitutive rules of language, in order that the declaration may be successfully performed. The mastery of those rules which constitute linguistic competence by the speaker and hearer is not in general sufficient for the performance of a declaration. In addition, there must exist an extralinguistic institution and the speaker and hearer must occupy special places within this institution. It is only given such institutions as the church, the law, private property, and the state and a special position of the speaker and hearer within these institutions that one can excommunicate, appoint, give and bequeath one's possessions, or declare war. There are two classes of exceptions to the principle that every declaration requires an extralinguistic institution. First there are supernatural declarations. When, e.g., God says "Let there be light" that is a declaration. Secondly there are declarations that concern language itself, as for example, when one says, "I define, abbreviate, name, call, or dub." Austin sometimes talks as if all performatives (and in the general theory, all illocutionary acts) required an extralinguistic institution, but this is plainly not the case. Declarations are a very special category of speech acts. We shall symbolize their structure as follows:

$$D \updownarrow \varnothing \, (p)$$

where D indicates the declarational illocutionary point; the direction of fit is both words-to-world and world-to-words because of the peculiar character of declarations; there is no sincerity condition, hence we have the null symbol in the sincerity condition slot; and we use the usual propositional variable "p."

The reason there has to be a relation of fit arrow here at all is that declarations do attempt to get language to match the world. But they do not attempt to do it either by describing an existing state of affairs (as do assertives) or by trying to get someone to bring about a future state of affairs (as do directives and commissives).

Some members of the class of declarations overlap with members of the class as assertives. This is because in certain institutional situations we not only ascertain the facts but we need an authority to lay down a decision as to what the facts are after the fact-finding procedure has been gone through. The argument must eventually come to an end and issue in a decision, and it is for this reason that we have judges and umpires. Both, the judge and the umpire, make factual claims; "you are out," "you are guilty." Such claims are clearly assessable in the dimension of word-world fit. Was he really tagged off base? Did he really commit the crime? They are assessable in the word-to-world dimension. But, at the same time, both have the force of declarations. If the umpire calls you out (and is upheld on appeal), then for baseball purposes you are out regardless of the facts in the case, and if the judge declares you guilty (and is upheld on appeal), then for legal purposes you are guilty. There is nothing mysterious about these cases. Institutions characteristically require illocutionary acts to be issued by authorities of various kinds which have the force of declarations. Some institutions require assertive claims to be issued with the force of declarations in order that the argument over the truth of the claim can come to an end somewhere and the next institutional steps which wait on the settling of the factual issue can proceed: the prisoner is released or sent to jail, the side is

retired, a touchdown is scored. The existence of this class we may dub "Assertive declarations." Unlike the other declarations, they share with assertives a sincerity condition. The judge, jury, and umpire can logically speaking lie, but the man who declares war or nominates you cannot lie in the performance of his illocutionary act. The symbolism for the class of assertive declarations, then, is this:

$$D_a \downarrow \updownarrow B(p)$$

where "D_a" indicates the illocutionary point of issuing an assertive with the force of a declaration, the first arrow indicates the assertive direction of fit, the second indicates the declarational direction of fit, the sincerity condition is belief, and the "p" represents the propositional content.

V. SOME SYNTACTICAL ASPECTS OF THE CLASSIFICATION

So far, I have been classifying illocutionary acts, and have used facts about verbs for evidence and illustration. In this section, I want to discuss explicitly some points about English syntax. If the distinctions marked in Section IV are of any real significance, they are likely to have various syntactical consequences, and I now propose to examine the deep structure of explicit performative sentences in each of the five categories; that is, I want to examine the syntactical structure of sentences containing the performative occurrence of appropriate illocutionary verbs for each of the five categories. Since all of the sentences we will be considering will contain a performative verb in the main clause, and a subordinate clause, I will abbreviate the usual tree structures in the following fashion: the sentence, e.g., "I predict John will hit Bill," has the deep structure shown in Figure 1. I will simply abbreviate this as: I predict + John will hit Bill. Parentheses will be used to mark optional elements or elements that are obligatory only for a restricted class of the verbs in question. Where there is a choice of one of two elements, I will put a stroke between the elements, e.g. I/you.

Assertives. The deep structure of such paradigm assertive sentences as "I state that it is raining" and "I predict he will come" is simply,

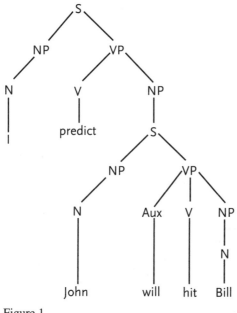

Figure 1

I verb (that) + S. This class, as a class, provides no further constraints; though particular verbs may provide further constraints on the lower node S. For example, "predict" requires that an Aux in the lower S must be future or, at any rate, cannot be past. Such assertive verbs as "describe," "call," "classify," and "identify" take a different syntactical structure, similar to many verbs of declaration, and I shall discuss them later.

Directives. Such sentences as "I order you to leave" and "I command you to stand at attention" have the following deep structure:

I verb you + you Fut Vol Verb (NP) (Adv).

"I order you to leave" is thus the surface structure realization of "I order you + you will leave" with equi NP deletion of the repeated "you." Notice that an additional syntactical argument for my including "dare," "defy," and "challenge" in my list of directive verbs and objecting to Austin's including them with "apologize," "thank," "congratulate," etc. is that they have the same syntactical form as do the paradigm directive verbs "order," "command," and "request." Similarly, "invite" and "advise" (in

one of its senses) have the directive syntax. "Permit" also has the syntax of directives, though giving permission is not, strictly speaking, trying to get someone to do something, rather it consists in removing antecedently existing restrictions on his doing it, and is therefore the illocutionary negation of a directive with a negative propositional content, its logical form is ~ !(~p).

Commissives. Such sentences as "I promise to pay you the money" and "I pledge allegiance to the flag" and "I vow to get revenge" have the deep structure

I verb (you) + I Fut Vol Verb (NP) (Adv).

Thus, "I promise to pay you the money" is the surface structure realization of "I promise you + I will pay you the money" with equi NP deletion of the repeated "I." We hear the difference in syntax between "I promise you to come on Wednesday" and "I order you to come on Wednesday" as being that "I" is the deep structure subject of "come" in the first and "you" is the deep structure subject of "come" in the second, as required by the verbs "promise" and "order" respectively. Notice that not all of the paradigm commissives have "you" as an indirect object of the performative verb. In the sentence "I pledge allegiance to the flag" the deep structure is not "I pledge to you flag + I will be allegiant." It is

I pledge + I will be allegiant to the flag.

Whereas there are purely syntactical arguments that such paradigm directive verbs as "order" and "command," as well as the imperative mood, require "you" as the deep structure subject of the lower node S, I do not know of any syntactical argument to show that commissives require "I" as the deep structure subject on their lower node S. Semantically, indeed, we must interpret such sentences as "I promise that Henry will be here on Wednesday" as meaning

I promise that *I will see to it* that Henry will be here next Wednesday,

insofar as we interpret the utterance as a genuine promise, but I know of no purely syntactical arguments to show that the deep structure of the former sentence contains the italicized elements in the latter.

Expressives. As I mentioned earlier, expressives characteristically require a gerundive transformation of the verb in the lower node S. We say:

I apologize for stepping on your toe.
I congratulate you on winning the race.
I thank you for giving me the money.

The deep structure of such sentences is:

I verb you + I/you VP ⇒ gerundive nom.

And, to repeat, the explanation of the obligatory gerundive is that there is no direction of fit. The forms that standardly admit of questions concerning direction of fit, *that* clauses and infinitives, are impermissible. Hence, the impossibility of

* I congratulate you that you won the race.
* I apologize to step on your toe.

However, not all of the permissible nominalization transformations are gerundive; the point is only that they must not produce *that* clauses or infinitive phrases, thus, we can have either

I apologize for behaving badly.

or

I apologize for my bad behavior.

but not,

* I apologize that I behaved badly.
* I apologize to behave badly.

Before considering declarations, I want now to resume discussion of those assertive verbs which have a different syntax from the paradigms above. I have said that the paradigm assertives have the syntactical form

I verb (that) + S.

But, if we consider such assertive verbs as "diagnose," "call," and "describe," as well as, "class," "classify," and "identify," we find that they do not fit this pattern at all. Consider "call," "describe," and "diagnose" in such sentences as

I call him a liar.
I diagnose his case as appendicitis.
I describe John as a Fascist.

In general the form of this is

I verb NP1 + NP1 be pred.

One cannot say

* I call that he is a liar.
* I diagnose that his case is appendicitis (perversely, some of my students find this form acceptable).
* I describe that John is a Fascist.

There, therefore, seems to be a very severe set of restrictions on an important class of assertive verbs which is not shared by the other paradigms. Would this justify us in concluding that these verbs were wrongly classed as assertives along with "state," "assert," "claim," and "predict" and that we need a separate class for them? It might be argued that the existence of these verbs substantiates Austin's claim that we require a separate class of verdictives distinct from expositives, but that would surely be a very curious conclusion to draw since Austin lists most of the verbs we mention above as expositives. He includes "describe," "class," "identify," and "call" as expositives and "diagnose" and "describe" as verdictives. A common syntax of many verdictives and expositives would hardly warrant the need for verdictives as a separate class. But leaving aside Austin's taxonomy, the question still arises, Do we require a separate semantic category to account for these syntactical facts? I think not. I think there is a much simpler explanation of the distribution of these verbs. Often, in assertive discourse, we focus our attention on some topic of discussion. The question is not just what is the propositional content we are asserting, but what do we say about the *object*(s) referred to in the propositional content: not just what do we state, claim, characterize, or assert, but how do we describe, call, diagnose, or identify *it*, some previously referred to topic of discussion. When, for example, there is a question of diagnosing or describing, it is always a question of diagnosing a person or his case, of describing a landscape or a party or a person, etc. These assertive illocutionary verbs give us a device for isolating topics from what is said about topics. But this very genuine syntactical difference does not mark a semantic difference big enough to justify the formation of a separate category. Notice in support of my argument here that the actual sentences in which the describing, diagnosing, etc., is done are seldom of the explicit performative type, but rather are usually in the standard indicative forms which are so characteristic of the assertive class.

Utterances of:

He is a liar.
He has appendicitis.
He is a Fascist.

are all characteristically *statements,* in the making of which we call, diagnose, and describe, as well as, accuse, identify, and characterize. I conclude then that there are typically two syntactical forms for assertive illocutionary verbs; one of which focusses on propositional content, the other on the object(s) referred to in the propositional content, but both of which are semantically assertives.

Declarations. I mention the syntactical form

I verb NP_1 + NP_1 be pred.

both to forestall an argument for erecting a separate semantic category for them and because many verbs of declaration have this form. Indeed, there appear to be several different syntactical forms for explicit performatives of declaration. I believe the following three cases are the most important.

1. I find you guilty as charged.
   I now pronounce you man and wife.
   I appoint you chairman.
2. War is hereby declared.
   I declare the meeting adjourned.
3. You're fired.
   I resign.
   I excommunicate you.

The deep syntactical structure of these three, respectively, is as follows:

1. I verb NP_1 + NP_1 be pred.

Thus, in our examples, we have

I find you + you be guilty as charged.
I pronounce you + you be man and wife.
I appoint you + you be chairman.
2. I declare + S.

Thus, in our examples we have

I/we (hereby) declare + a state of war exists.
I declare + the meeting be adjourned.

This form is the purest form of the declaration: the speaker in authority brings about a state of affairs specified in the propositional content by saying in effect, I declare the state of affairs to exist. Semantically, all declarations are of this character, though in class 1 the focusing on the topic produces an alteration in the syntax which is exactly the same syntax as we saw in such assertive verbs as "describe," "characterize," "call," and "diagnose," and in class 3 the syntax conceals the semantic structure even more.

3. The syntax of these is the most misleading. It is simply I verb (NP).

as in our examples,

I fire you.
I resign.
I excommunicate you.

The semantic structure of these, however, seems to me the same as class 2. "You're fired," if uttered as performance of the act of firing someone and not as a report means

I declare + your job is terminated.

Similarly, "I hereby resign" means

I hereby declare + my job is terminated.

"I excommunicate you" means

I declare + your membership in the church is terminated.

The explanation for the bemusingly simple syntactical structure of these sentences seems to me to be that we have some verbs which in their performative occurrence encapsulate both the declarative force and the propositional content.

VI. CONCLUSIONS

We are now in a position to draw certain general conclusions.

1. Many of the verbs we call illocutionary verbs are not markers of illocutionary point but of some other feature of the illocutionary act. Consider "insist" and "suggest." I can insist that

we go to the movies or I can suggest that we go to the movies; but I can also insist that the answer is found on p. 16 or I can suggest that it is found on p. 16. The first pair are directives, the second, assertives. Does this show that insisting and suggesting are different illocutionary acts altogether from assertives and directives, or perhaps that they are both assertives and directives? I think the answer to both questions is no. Both "insist" and "suggest" are used to mark the degree of intensity with which the illocutionary point is presented. They do not mark a separate illocutionary point at all. Similarly, "announce," "hint," and "confide" do not mark separate illocutionary points but rather the style or manner of performance of an illocutionary act. Paradoxical as it may sound, such verbs are illocutionary verbs, but not names of kinds of illocutionary acts. It is for this reason, among others, that we must carefully distinguish a taxonomy of illocutionary acts from one of illocutionary verbs.

2. In Section IV, I tried to classify illocutionary acts and, in Section V, I tried to explore some of the syntactical features of the verbs denoting member of each of the categories. But, I have not attempted to classify illocutionary verbs. If one did so, I believe the following would emerge.

(a) First, as just noted, some verbs do not mark illocutionary point at all, but some other feature, e.g., "insist," "suggest," "announce," "confide," "reply," "answer," interject," "remark," "ejaculate," and "interpose."

(b) Many verbs mark illocutionary point plus some other feature, e.g., "boast," "lament," "threaten," "criticize," "accuse," and "warn" all add the feature of goodness or badness to their primary illocutionary point.

(c) Some few verbs mark more than one illocutionary point, e.g., a *protest* involves both an expression of disapproval and a petition for change.

Promulgating a law has both a declarational status (the propositional content becomes law) and a directive status (the law is directive in intent). The verbs of assertive declaration fall into this class.

(d) Some few verbs can take more than one illocutionary point. Consider "warn" and "advise." Notice that both of these take either the directive syntax or the assertive syntax. Thus,

I warn you to stay away from   (directive)
    my wife!
I warn you that the bull is about   (assertive)
    to charge.
I advise you to leave.   (directive)
Passengers are hereby advised   (assertive)
    that the train will be late.

Correspondingly, it seems to me, that warning and advising may be either telling you *that* something is the case (with relevance to what is or is not in your interest) or telling you *to* do something about it (because it is or is not in your interest). They can be, but need not be, both at once.

3. The most important conclusion to be drawn from this discussion is this. There is not, as Wittgenstein (on one possible interpretation) and many others have claimed, an infinite or indefinite number of language games or uses of language. Rather, the illusion of limitless uses of language is engendered by an enormous unclarity about what constitutes the criteria for delimiting one language game or use of language from another. If we adopt illocutionary point as the basic notion on which to classify uses of language, then there are a rather limited number of basic things we do with language: we tell people how things are, we try to get them to do things, we commit ourselves to doing things, we express our feelings and attitudes, and we bring about changes through our utterances. Often, we do more than one of these at once in the same utterance.

11 Logic and Conversation

H. P. GRICE

It is a commonplace of philosophical logic that there are, or appear to be, divergences in meaning between, on the one hand, at least some of what I shall call the formal devices—~, $\wedge$, $\vee$, $\supset$, (x), $(\imath x)$, $(\exists x)$ (when these are given a standard two-valued interpretation)—and, on the other, what are taken to be their analogs or counterparts in natural language—such expressions as "not," "and," "or," "if," "all," "some" (or "at least one"), "the." Some logicians may at some time have wanted to claim that there are in fact no such divergences; but such claims, if made at all, have been somewhat rashly made, and those suspected of making them have been subjected to some pretty rough handling.

Those who concede that such divergences exist adhere, in the main, to one or the other of two rival groups, which for the purposes of this article I shall call the formalist and the informalist groups. An outline of a not uncharacteristic formalist position may be given as follows: Insofar as logicians are concerned with the formulation of very general patterns of valid inference, the formal devices possess a decisive advantage over their natural counterparts. For it will be possible to construct in terms of the formal devices a system of very general formulas, a considerable number of which can be regarded as, or are closely related to, patterns of inferences the expression of which involves some or all of the devices: Such a system may consist of a certain set of simple formulas that must be acceptable if the devices have the meaning that has been assigned to them, and an indefinite number of further formulas, many of them less obviously acceptable, each of which can be shown to be acceptable if the members of the original set are acceptable. We have, thus, a way of handling dubiously acceptable patterns of inference, and if, as is sometimes possible, we can apply a decision procedure, we have an even better way. Furthermore, from a philosophical point of view, the possession by the natural counterparts of those elements in their meaning, which they do not share with the corresponding formal devices, is to be regarded as an imperfection of natural languages; the elements in question are undesirable excrescences. For the presence of these elements has the result that the concepts within which they appear cannot be precisely/clearly defined, and that at least some statements involving them cannot, in some circumstances, be assigned a definite truth value; and the indefiniteness of these concepts is not only objectionable in itself but leaves open the way to metaphysics—we cannot be certain that none of these natural language expressions is metaphysically 'loaded'. For these reasons, the expressions, as used in natural speech, cannot be regarded as finally acceptable, and may

From *Syntax and Semantics*, volume 3, Peter Cole and Jerry L. Morgan, eds. (New York: Academic Press, 1975), pp. 41–58. Copyright © 1975 by H. Paul Grice. Reprinted by permission of the author.

turn out to be, finally, not fully intelligible. The proper course is to conceive and begin to construct an ideal language, incorporating the formal devices, the sentences of which will be clear, determinate in truth value, and certifiably free from metaphysical implications; the foundations of science will now be philosophically secure, since the statements of the scientist will be expressible (though not necessarily actually expressed) within this ideal language. (I do not wish to suggest that all formalists would accept the whole of this outline, but I think that all would accept at least some part of it.)

To this, an informalist might reply in the following vein. The philosophical demand for an ideal language rests on certain assumptions that should not be conceded; these are, that the primary yardstick by which to judge the adequacy of a language is its ability to serve the needs of science, that an expression cannot be guaranteed as fully intelligible unless an explication or analysis of its meaning has been provided, and that every explication or analysis must take the form of a precise definition that is the expression/assertion of a logical equivalence. Language serves many important purposes besides those of scientific inquiry; we can know perfectly well what an expression means (and so a fortiori that it is intelligible) without knowing its analysis, and the provision of an analysis may (and usually does) consist in the specification, as generalized as possible, of the conditions that count for or against the applicability of the expression being analyzed. Moreover, while it is no doubt true that the formal devices are especially amenable to systematic treatment by the logician, it remains the case that there are very many inferences and arguments, expressed in natural language and not in terms of these devices, that are nevertheless recognizably valid. So there must be a place for an unsimplified, and so more or less unsystematic, logic of the natural counterparts of these devices; this logic may be aided and guided by the simplified logic of the formal devices but cannot be supplanted by it; indeed, not only do the two logics differ, but sometimes they come into conflict; rules that hold for a formal device may not hold for its natural counterpart.

Now, on the general question of the place in philosophy of the reformation of natural language, I shall, in this article, have nothing to say. I shall confine myself to the dispute in its relation to the alleged divergences mentioned at the outset. I have, moreover, no intention of entering the fray on behalf of either contestant. I wish, rather, to maintain that the common assumption of the contestants that the divergences do in fact exist is (broadly speaking) a common mistake, and that the mistake arises from an inadequate attention to the nature and importance of the conditions governing conversation. I shall, therefore, proceed at once to inquire into the general conditions that, in one way or another, apply to conversation as such, irrespective of its subject matter.

IMPLICATURE

Suppose that A and B are talking about a mutual friend, C, who is now working in a bank. A asks B how C is getting on in his job, and B replies, "Oh quite well, I think; he likes his colleagues, and he hasn't been to prison yet." At this point, A might well inquire what B was implying, what he was suggesting, or even what he meant by saying that C had not yet been to prison. The answer might be any one of such things as that C is the sort of person likely to yield to the temptation provided by his occupation, that C's colleagues are really very unpleasant and treacherous people, and so forth. It might, of course, be quite unnecessary for A to make such an inquiry of B, the answer to it being, in the context, clear in advance. I think it is clear that whatever B implied, suggested, meant, etc., in this example, is distinct from what B said, which was simply that C had not been to prison yet. I wish to introduce, as terms of art, the verb "implicate" and the related nouns "implicature" (cf. implying) and "implicatum" (cf. what is implied). The point of this maneuver is to avoid having, on each occasion, to choose between this or that member of the family of verbs for which "*implicate*" is to do general duty. I shall, for the time being at least, have to assume to a considerable extent an intuitive understanding of the meaning of "say" in such contexts, and an ability to recognize particular verbs as members of the family with which "implicate" is associated. I can, however, make one or two remarks that may help to clarify the more problematic of these assumptions, namely, that connected with the meaning of the word "say."

In the sense in which I am using the word "say," I intend what someone has said to be closely related to the conventional meaning of the words (the sentence) he has uttered. Suppose someone to have uttered the sentence "He is in the grip of a vice." Given a knowledge of the English language, but no knowledge of the circumstances of the utterance, one would know something about what the speaker had said, on the assumption that he was speaking standard English, and speaking literally. One would know that he had said, about some particular male person or animal x, that at the time of the utterance (whatever that was), either (1) x was unable to rid himself of a certain kind of bad character trait or (2) some part of x's person was caught in a certain kind of tool or instrument (approximate account, of course). But for a full identification of what the speaker had said, one would need to know (a) the identity of x, (b) the time of utterance, and (c) the meaning, on the particular occasion of utterance, of the phrase "in the grip of a vice" [a decision between (1) and (2)]. This brief indication of my use of "say" leaves it open whether a man who says (today) "Harold Wilson is a great man" and another who says (also today) "The British Prime Minister is a great man" would, if each knew that the two singular terms had the same reference, have said the same thing. But whatever decision is made about this question, the apparatus that I am about to provide will be capable of accounting for any implicatures that might depend on the presence of one rather than another of these singular terms in the sentence uttered. Such implicatures would merely be related to different maxims.

In some cases the conventional meaning of the words used will determine what is implicated, besides helping to determine what is said. If I say (smugly), "He is an Englishman; he is, therefore, brave," I have certainly committed myself, by virtue of the meaning of my words, to its being the case that his being brave is a consequence of (follows from) his being an Englishman. But while I have said that he is an Eng-

lishman, and said that he is brave, I do not want to say that I have *said* (in the favored sense) that it follows from his being an Englishman that he is brave, though I have certainly indicated, and so implicated, that this is so. I do not want to say that my utterance of this sentence would be, *strictly speaking*, false should the consequence in question fail to hold. So *some* implicatures are conventional, unlike the one with which I introduced this discussion of implicature.

I wish to represent a certain subclass of non-conventional implicatures, which I shall call *conversational* implicatures, as being essentially connected with certain general features of discourse; so my next step is to try to say what these features are.

The following may provide a first approximation to a general principle. Our talk exchanges do not normally consist of a succession of disconnected remarks, and would not be rational if they did. They are characteristically, to some degree at least, cooperative efforts; and each participant recognizes in them, to some extent, a common purpose or set of purposes, or at least a mutually accepted direction. This purpose or direction may be fixed from the start (e.g., by an initial proposal of a question for discussion), or it may evolve during the exchange; it may be fairly definite, or it may be so indefinite as to leave very considerable latitude to the participants (as in a casual conversation). But at each stage, *some* possible conversational moves would be excluded as conversationally unsuitable. We might then formulate a rough general principle which participants will be expected (ceteris paribus) to observe, namely: Make your conversational contribution such as is required, at the stage at which it occurs, by the accepted purpose or direction of the talk exchange in which you are engaged. One might label this the *Cooperative Principle*.

On the assumption that some such general principle as this is acceptable, one may perhaps distinguish four categories under one or another of which will fall certain more specific maxims and submaxims, the following of which will, in general, yield results in accordance with the Cooperative Principle. Echoing Kant, I call these categories Quantity, Quality, Relation, and Manner. The category of *Quantity* relates to the quantity of information to be provided, and under it fall the following maxims: (1) Make your contribution as informative as is required (for the current purposes of the exchange). (2) Do not make your contribution more informative than is required. (The second maxim is disputable; it might be said that to be overinformative is not a transgression of the Cooperative Principle but merely a waste of time. However, it might be answered that such overinformativeness may be confusing in that it is liable to raise side issues; and there may also be an indirect effect, in that the hearers may be misled as a result of thinking that there is some particular *point* in the provision of the excess of information. However this may be, there is perhaps a different reason for doubt about the admission of this second maxim, namely, that its effect will be secured by a later maxim, which concerns relevance.)

Under the category of *quality* falls a super-maxim—"Try to make your contribution one that is true"—and two more specific maxims:

1. Do not say what you believe to be false.
2. Do not say that for which you lack adequate evidence.

Under the category of *Relation* I place a single maxim, namely, "Be relevant." Though the maxim itself is terse, its formulation conceals a number of problems that exercise me a good deal: questions about what different kinds and focuses of relevance there may be, how these shift in the course of a talk exchange, how to allow for the fact that subjects of conversation are legitimately changed, and so on. I find the treatment of such questions exceedingly difficult, and I hope to revert to them in a later work.

Finally, under the category of *Manner,* which I understand as relating not (like the previous categories) to what is said but, rather, to *how* what is said is to be said, I include the super-maxim—"Be perspicuous"—and various maxims such as:

1. Avoid obscurity of expression.
2. Avoid ambiguity.
3. Be brief (avoid unnecessary prolixity).
4. Be orderly.

And one might need others.

It is obvious that the observance of some of these maxims is a matter of less urgency than is the observance of others; a man who has expressed himself with undue prolixity would, in general, be open to milder comment than would a man who has said something he believes to be false. Indeed, it might be felt that the importance of at least the first maxim of Quality is such that it should not be included in a scheme of the kind I am constructing; other maxims come into operation only on the assumption that this maxim of Quality is satisfied. While this may be correct, so far as the generation of implicatures is concerned it seems to play a role not totally different from the other maxims, and it will be convenient, for the present at least, to treat it as a member of the list of maxims.

There are, of course, all sorts of other maxims (aesthetic, social, or moral in character), such as "Be polite," that are also normally observed by participants in talk exchanges, and these may also generate nonconventional implicatures. The conversational maxims, however, and the conversational implicatures connected with them, are specially connected (I hope) with the particular purposes that talk (and so, talk exchange) is adapted to serve and is primarily employed to serve. I have stated my maxims as if this purpose were a maximally effective exchange of information; this specification is, of course, too narrow, and the scheme needs to be generalized to allow for such general purposes as influencing or directing the actions of others.

As one of my avowed aims is to see talking as a special case or variety of purposive, indeed rational, behavior, it may be worth noting that the specific expectations or presumptions connected with at least some of the foregoing maxims have their analogues in the sphere of transactions that are not talk exchanges. I list briefly one such analogue for each conversational category.

1. *Quantity*. If you are assisting me to mend a car, I expect your contribution to be neither more nor less than is required; if, for example, at a particular stage I need four screws, I expect you to hand me four, rather than two or six.

2. *Quality*. I expect your contributions to be genuine and not spurious. If I need sugar as an

ingredient in the cake you are assisting me to make, I do not expect you to hand me salt; if I need a spoon, I do not expect a trick spoon made of rubber.

3. *Relation.* I expect a partner's contribution to be appropriate to immediate needs at each stage of the transaction; if I am mixing ingredients for a cake, I do not expect to be handed a good book, or even an oven cloth (though this might be an appropriate contribution at a later stage).

4. *Manner.* I expect a partner to make it clear what contribution he is making, and to execute his performance with reasonable dispatch.

These analogies are relevant to what I regard as a fundamental question about the Cooperative Principle and its attendant maxims, namely, what the basis is for the assumption which we seem to make, and on which (I hope) it will appear that a great range of implicatures depend, that talkers will in general (ceteris paribus and in the absence of indications to the contrary) proceed in the manner that these principles prescribe. A dull but, no doubt at a certain level, adequate answer is that it is just a well-recognized empirical fact that people *do* behave in these ways; they have learned to do so in childhood and not lost the habit of doing so; and, indeed, it would involve a good deal of effort to make a radical departure from the habit. It is much easier, for example, to tell the truth than to invent lies.

I am, however, enough of a rationalist to want to find a basis that underlies these facts, undeniable though they may be; I would like to be able to think of the standard type of conversational practice not merely as something that all or most do *in fact* follow but as something that it is *reasonable* for us to follow, that we *should not* abandon. For a time, I was attracted by the idea that observance of the Cooperative Principle and the maxims, in a talk exchange, could be thought of as a quasi-contractual matter, with parallels outside the realm of discourse. If you pass by when I am struggling with my stranded car, I no doubt have some degree of expectation that you will offer help, but once you join me in tinkering under the hood, my expectations become stronger and take more specific forms (in the absence of indications that you are merely an incompetent meddler); and talk exchanges seemed to me to exhibit, characteristically, certain features that jointly distinguish cooperative transactions:

1. The participants have some common immediate aim, like getting a car mended; their ultimate aims may, of course, be independent and even in conflict—each may want to get the car mended in order to drive off, leaving the other stranded. In characteristic talk exchanges, there is a common aim even if, as in an over-the-wall chat, it is a second-order one, namely, that each party should, for the time being, identify himself with the transitory conversational interests of the other.

2. The contributions of the participants should be dovetailed, mutually dependent.

3. There is some sort of understanding (which may be explicit but which is often tacit) that, other things being equal, the transaction should continue in appropriate style unless both parties are agreeable that it should terminate. You do not just shove off or start doing something else.

But while some such quasi-contractual basis as this may apply to some cases, there are too many types of exchange, like quarreling and letter writing, that it fails to fit comfortably. In any case, one feels that the talker who is irrelevant or obscure has primarily let down not his audience but himself. So I would like to be able to show that observance of the Cooperative Principle and maxims is reasonable (rational) along the following lines: that any one who cares about the goals that are central to conversation/communication (e.g., giving and receiving information, influencing and being influenced by others) must be expected to have an interest, given suitable circumstances, in participating in talk exchanges that will be profitable only on the assumption that they are conducted in general accordance with the Cooperative Principle and the maxims. Whether any such conclusion can be reached, I am uncertain; in any case, I am fairly sure that I cannot reach it until I am a good deal clearer about the nature of relevance and of the circumstances in which it is required.

It is now time to show the connection between the Cooperative Principle and maxims, on the one hand, and conversational implicature on the other.

A participant in a talk exchange may fail to fulfill a maxim in various ways, which include the following:

1. He may quietly and unostentatiously *violate* a maxim; if so, in some cases he will be liable to mislead.

2. He may *opt out* from the operation both of the maxim and of the Cooperative Principle; he may say, indicate, or allow it to become plain that he is unwilling to cooperate in the way the maxim requires. He may say, for example, "I cannot say more; my lips are sealed."

3. He may be faced by a *clash:* He may be unable, for example, to fulfill the first maxim of Quantity (Be as informative as is required) without violating the second maxim of Quality (Have adequate evidence for what you say).

4. He may *flout* a maxim; that is, he may *blatantly* fail to fulfill it. On the assumption that the speaker is able to fulfill the maxim and to do so without violating another maxim (because of a clash), is not opting out, and is not, in view of the blatancy of his performance, trying to mislead, the hearer is faced with a minor problem: How can his saying what he did say be reconciled with the supposition that he is observing the overall Cooperative Principle? This situation is one that characteristically gives rise to a conversational implicature; and when a conversational implicature is generated in this way, I shall say that a maxim is being *exploited.*

I am now in a position to characterize the notion of conversational implicature. A man who, by (in, when) saying (or making as if to say) that *p* has implicated that *q*, may be said to have conversationally implicated that *q,* provided that (1) he is to be presumed to be observing the conversational maxims, or at least the cooperative principle; (2) the supposition that he is aware that, or thinks that, *q* is required in order to make his saying or making as if to say *p* (or doing so in *those* terms) consistent with this presumption; and (3) the speaker thinks (and would expect the hearer to think that the speaker thinks) that it is within the competence of the hearer to work out, or grasp intuitively, that the supposition mentioned in (2) *is* required. Apply this to my initial example, to B's remark that C has not yet been to prison. In a suitable setting A might reason as follows: "(1) B has apparently violated the maxim 'Be relevant' and so may be regarded as having flouted one of the maxims conjoining perspicuity, yet I have no reason to suppose that he is opting out from the operation of the CP; (2) given the circumstances, I can regard his irrelevance as only apparent if, and only if, I suppose him to think that C is potentially dishonest; (3) B knows that I am capable of working out step (2). So B implicates that C is potentially dishonest."

The presence of a conversational implicature must be capable of being worked out; for even if it can in fact be intuitively grasped, unless the intuition is replaceable by an argument, the implicature (if present at all) will not count as a *conversational* implicature; it will be a *conventional* implicature. To work out that a particular conversational implicature is present, the hearer will rely on the following data: (1) the conventional meaning of the words used, together with the identity of any references that may be involved; (2) the Cooperative Principle and its maxims; (3) the context, linguistic or otherwise, of the utterance; (4) other items of background knowledge; and (5) the fact (or supposed fact) that all relevant items falling under the previous headings are available to both participants and both participants know or assume this to be the case. A general pattern for the working out of a conversational implicature might be given as follows: 'He has said that *p*; there is no reason to suppose that he is not observing the maxims, or at least the Cooperative Principle; he could not be doing this unless he thought that *q*; he knows (and knows that I know that he knows) that I can see that the supposition that he thinks that *q* is required; he has done nothing to stop me thinking that *q*; he intends me to think, or is at least willing to allow me to think, that *q*; and so he has implicated that *q*.'

EXAMPLES

I shall now offer a number of examples, which I shall divide into three groups.

Group A

Examples in which no maxim is violated, or at least in which it is not clear that any maxim is violated:

(1) A is standing by an obviously immobilized car and is approached by B, the following exchange takes place:

A: I am out of petrol.
B: There is a garage round the corner.

(Gloss: B would be infringing the maxim "Be relevant" unless he thinks, or thinks it possible, that the garage is open, and has petrol to sell; so he implicates that the garage is, or at least may be open, etc.) In this example, unlike the case of the remark "He hasn't been to prison yet," the unstated connection between B's remark and A's remark is so obvious that, even if one interprets the supermaxim of Manner, "Be perspicuous," as applying not only to the expression of what is said but also to the connection of what is said with adjacent remarks, there seems to be no case for regarding that supermaxim as infringed in this example.

(2) The next example is perhaps a little less clear in this respect:

A: Smith doesn't seem to have a girlfriend these days.
B: He has been paying a lot of visits to New York lately.

B implicates that Smith has, or may have, a girlfriend in New York. (A gloss is unnecessary in view of that given for the previous example.)

In both examples, the speaker implicates that which he must be assumed to believe in order to preserve the assumption that he is observing the maxim of relation.

Group B

An example in which a maxim is violated, but its violation is to be explained by the supposition of a clash with another maxim:

(3) A is planning with B an itinerary for a holiday in France. Both know that A wants to see his friend C, if to do so would not involve too great a prolongation of his journey:

A: Where does C live?
B: Somewhere in the South of France.

(Gloss: There is no reason to suppose that B is opting out; his answer is, as he well knows, less informative than is required to meet A's needs. This infringement of the first maxim of Quantity can be explained only by the supposition that B is aware that to be more informative would be to say something that infringed the maxim of Quality, "Don't say what you lack adequate evidence for," so B implicates that he does not know in which town C lives.)

Group C

Examples that involve exploitation, that is, a procedure by which a maxim is flouted for the purpose of getting in a conversational implicature by means of something of the nature of a figure of speech:

In these examples, though some maxim is violated at the level of what is said, the hearer is entitled to assume that that maxim, or at least the overall Cooperative Principle, is observed at the level of what is implicated.

(1a) A flouting of the first maxim of Quantity. A is writing a testimonial about a pupil who is a candidate for a philosophy job, and his letter reads as follows: "Dear Sir, Mr. X's command of English is excellent, and his attendance at tutorials has been regular. Yours, etc.' (Gloss: A cannot be opting out, since if he wished to be uncooperative, why write at all? He cannot be unable, through ignorance, to say more, since the man is his pupil; moreover, he knows that more information than this is wanted. He must, therefore, be wishing to impart information that he is reluctant to write down. This supposition is tenable only on the assumption that he thinks Mr. X is no good at philosophy. This, then, is what he is implicating.)

Extreme examples of a flouting of the first maxim of Quantity are provided by utterances of patent tautologies like "Women are women" and "War is war." I would wish to maintain that at the level of what is said, in my favored sense, such remarks are totally noninformative and so, at that level, cannot but infringe the first maxim of Quantity in any conversational context. They are, of course, informative at the level of what is implicated, and the hearer's identification of their informative content at this level is dependent on his ability to explain the speaker's selection of this *particular* patent tautology.

(1b) An infringement of the second maxim of Quantity, "Do not give more information than is required," on the assumption that the existence of such a maxim should be admitted. A wants to know whether *p*, and B volunteers not only the information that *p*, but information to the effect that it is certain that *p*, and that the evidence for its being the case that *p* is so-and-so and such-and-such.

B's volubility may be undesigned, and if it is so regarded by A it may raise in A's mind a doubt as to whether B is as certain as he says he is ('Methinks the lady doth protest too much'). But if it is thought of as designed, it would be an oblique way of conveying that it is to some degree controversial whether or not *p*. It is, however, arguable that such an implicature could be explained by reference to the maxim of Relation without invoking an alleged second maxim of Quantity.

(2a) Examples in which the first maxim of Quality is flouted.

(i) Irony: X, with whom A has been on close terms until now, has betrayed a secret of A's to a business rival. A and his audience both know this. A says "X is a fine friend." (Gloss: It is perfectly obvious to A and his audience that what A has said or has made as if to say is something he does not believe, and the audience knows that A knows that this is obvious to the audience. So, unless A's utterance is entirely pointless, A must be trying to get across some other proposition than the one he purports to be putting forward. This must be some obviously related proposition; the most obviously related proposition is the contradictory of the one he purports to be putting forward.)

(ii) Metaphor: Examples like "You are the cream in my coffee" characteristically involve categorial falsity, so the contradictory of what the speaker has made as if to say will, strictly speaking, be a truism; so it cannot be *that* that such a speaker is trying to get across. The most likely supposition is that the speaker is attributing to his audience some feature or features in respect of which the audience resembles (more or less fancifully) the mentioned substance.

It is possible to combine metaphor and irony by imposing on the hearer two stages of interpretation. I say "You are the cream in my coffee," intending the hearer to reach first the metaphor interpretant "You are my pride and joy" and then the irony interpretant "You are my bane."

(iii) Meiosis: Of a man known to have broken up all the furniture, one says "He was a little intoxicated."

(iv) Hyperbole: Every nice girl loves a sailor.

(2b) Examples in which the second maxim of Quality, "Do not say that for which you lack adequate evidence," is flouted are perhaps not easy to find, but the following seems to be a specimen. I say of X's wife, "She is probably deceiving him this evening." In a suitable context, or with a suitable gesture or tone of voice, it may be clear that I have no adequate reason for supposing this to be the case. My partner, to preserve the assumption that the conversational game is still being played, assumes that I am getting at some related proposition for the acceptance of which I *do* have a reasonable basis. The related proposition might well be that she is given to deceiving her husband, or possibly that she is the sort of person who would not stop short of such conduct.

(3) Examples in which an implicature is achieved by real, as distinct from apparent, violation of the maxim of Relation are perhaps rare, but the following seems to be a good candidate. At a genteel tea party, A says "Mrs. X is an old bag." There is a moment of appalled silence, and then B says "The weather has been quite delightful this summer, hasn't it?" B has blatantly refused to make what *he* says relevant to A's preceding remark. He thereby implicates that A's remark should not be discussed and, perhaps more specifically, that A has committed a social gaffe.

(4) Examples in which various maxims falling under the supermaxim "Be perspicuous" are flouted.

(i) Ambiguity. We must remember that we are

concerned only with ambiguity that is deliberate, and that the speaker intends or expects to be recognized by his hearer. The problem the hearer has to solve is why a speaker should, when still playing the conversational game, go out of his way to choose an ambiguous utterance. There are two types of cases:

(a) Examples in which there is no difference, or no striking difference, between two interpretations of an utterance with respect to straightforwardness; neither interpretation is notably more sophisticated, less standard, more recondite or more far-fetched than the other. We might consider Blake's lines: "Never seek to tell thy love, Love that never told can be." To avoid the complications introduced by the presence of the imperative mood, I shall consider the related sentence, "I sought to tell my love, love that never told can be." There may be a double ambiguity here. "My love" may refer to either a state of emotion or an object of emotion, and "love that never told can be" may mean either "Love that cannot be told" or "love that if told cannot continue to exist." Partly because of the sophistication of the poet and partly because of internal evidence (that the ambiguity is kept up), there seems to be no alternative to supposing that the ambiguities are deliberate and that the poet is conveying both what he would be saying if one interpretation were intended rather than the other, and vice versa; though no doubt the poet is not explicitly *saying* any one of these things but only conveying or suggesting them (cf. "Since she [nature] pricked thee out of women's pleasure, mine be thy love, and thy love's use their treasure.")

(b) Examples in which one interpretation is notably less straightforward than another. Take the complex example of the British General who captured the town of Sind and sent back the message *Peccavi*. The ambiguity involved ("I have Sind"/"I have sinned") is phonemic, not morphemic; and the expression actually used is unambiguous, but since it is in a language foreign to speaker and hearer, translation is called for, and the ambiguity resides in the standard translation into native English.

Whether or not the straightforward interpretant ("I have sinned") is being conveyed, it seems that the nonstraightforward must be.

There might be stylistic reasons for conveying by a sentence merely its nonstraightforward interpretant, but it would be pointless, and perhaps also stylistically objectionable, to go to the trouble of finding an expression that nonstraightforwardly conveys that p, thus imposing on an audience the effort involved in finding this interpretant, if this interpretant were otiose so far as communication was concerned. Whether the straightforward interpretant is also being conveyed seems to depend on whether such a supposition would conflict with other conversational requirements, for example, would it be relevant, would it be something the speaker could be supposed to accept, and so on. If such requirements are not satisfied, then the straightforward interpretant is not being conveyed. If they are, it is. If the author of *Peccavi* could naturally be supposed to think that he had committed some kind of transgression, for example, had disobeyed his orders in capturing Sind, and if reference to such a transgression would be relevant to the presumed interests of the audience, then he would have been conveying both interpretants; otherwise he would be conveying only the nonstraightforward one.

(ii) Obscurity. How do I exploit, for the purposes of communication, a deliberate and overt violation of the requirement that I should avoid obscurity? Obviously, if the Cooperative Principle is to operate, I must intend my partner to understand what I am saying despite the obscurity I import into my utterance. Suppose that A and B are having a conversation in the presence of a third party, for example, a child, then A might be deliberately obscure, though not too obscure, in the hope that B would understand and the third party not. Furthermore, if A expects B to see that A is being deliberately obscure, it seems reasonable to suppose that, in making his conversational contribution in this way, A is implicating that the contents of his communication should not be imparted to the third party.

(iii) Failure to be brief or succinct. Compare the remarks:

(a) Miss X sang "Home sweet home."
(b) Miss X produced a series of sounds that corresponded closely with the score of "Home sweet home."

Suppose that a reviewer has chosen to utter (b) rather than (a). (Gloss: Why has he selected that rigmarole in place of the concise and nearly synonymous "sang"? Presumably, to indicate some striking difference between Miss X's performance and those to which the word "singing" is usually applied. The most obvious supposition is that Miss X's performance suffered from some hideous defect. The reviewer knows that this supposition is what is likely to spring to mind, so that is what he is implicating.)

I have so far considered only cases of what I might call particularized conversational implicature—that is to say, cases in which an implicature is carried by saying that p on a particular occasion in virtue of special features of the context, cases in which there is no room for the idea that an implicature of this sort is *normally* carried by saying that *p*. But there are cases of generalized conversational implicature. Sometimes one can say that the use of a certain form of words in an utterance would normally (in the *absence* of special circumstances) carry such-and-such an implicature or type of implicature. Noncontroversial examples are perhaps hard to find, since it is all too easy to treat a generalized conversational implicature as if it were a conventional implicature. I offer an example that I hope may be fairly noncontroversial.

Anyone who uses a sentence of the form "X is meeting a woman this evening" would normally implicate that the person to be met was someone other than X's wife, mother, sister, or perhaps even close platonic friend. Similarly, if I were to say "X went into a house yesterday and found a tortoise inside the front door," my hearer would normally be surprised if some time later I revealed that the house was X's own. I could produce similar linguistic phenomena involving the expressions "*a garden,*" "*a car,*" "*a college,*" and so on. Sometimes, however, there would normally be no such implicature ("I have been sitting in a car all morning"), and sometimes a reverse implicature ("I broke a finger yesterday"). I am inclined to think that one would not lend a sympathetic ear to a philosopher who suggested that there are three senses of the form of expression "an X": one in which it means roughly "something that satisfies the conditions defining the word X,' another in

which it means approximately 'an X (in the first sense) that is only remotely related in a certain way to some person indicated by the context,' and yet another in which it means 'an X (in the first sense) that is closely related in a certain way to some person indicated by the context.' Would we not much prefer an account on the following lines (which, of course, may be incorrect in detail): When someone, by using the form of expression "an X," implicates that the X does not belong to or is not otherwise closely connected with some identifiable person, the implicature is present because the speaker has failed to be specific in a way in which he might have been expected to be specific, with the consequence that it is likely to be assumed that he is not in a position to be specific. This is a familiar implicature situation and is classifiable as a failure, for one reason or another, to fulfill the first maxim of Quantity. The only difficult question is why it should, in certain cases, be presumed, independently of information about particular contexts of utterance, that specification of the closeness or remoteness of the connection between a particular person or object and a further person who is mentioned or indicated by the utterance should be likely to be of interest. The answer must lie in the following region: Transactions between a person and other persons or things closely connected with him are liable to be very different as regards their concomitants and results from the same sort of transactions involving only remotely connected persons or things; the concomitants and results, for instance, of my finding a hole in *my* roof are likely to be very different from the concomitants and results of my finding a hole in someone else's roof. Information, like money, is often given without the giver's knowing to just what use the recipient will want to put it. If someone to whom a transaction is mentioned gives it further consideration, he is likely to find himself wanting the answers to further questions that the speaker may not be able to identify in advance; if the appropriate specification will be likely to enable the hearer to answer a considerable variety of such questions for himself, then there is a presumption that the speaker should include it in his remark; if not, then there is no such presumption.

Finally, we can now show that, conversational implicature being what it is, it must possess certain features.

1. Since, to assume the presence of a conversational implicature, we have to assume that at least the Cooperative Principle is being observed, and since it is possible to opt out of the observation of this principle, it follows that a generalized conversational implicature can be canceled in a particular case. It may be explicitly canceled, by the addition of a clause that states or implies that the speaker has opted out, or it may be contextually canceled, if the form of utterance that usually carries it is used in a context that makes it clear that the speaker IS opting out.

2. Insofar as the calculation that a particular conversational implicature is present requires, besides contextual and background information, only a knowledge of what has been said (or of the conventional commitment of the utterance), and insofar as the manner of expression plays no role in the calculation, it will not be possible to find another way of saying the same thing, which simply lacks the implicature in question, except where some special feature of the substituted version is itself relevant to the determination of an implicature (in virtue of one of the maxims of Manner). If we call this feature *nondetachability,* one may expect a generalized conversational implicature that is carried by a familiar, nonspecial locution to have a high degree of nondetachability.

3. To speak approximately, since the calculation of the presence of a conversational implicature presupposes an initial knowledge of the conventional force of the expression the utterance of which carries the implicature, a conversational implicatum will be a condition that is not included in the original specification of the expression's conventional force. Though it may not be impossible for what starts life, so to speak, as a conversational implicature to become conventionalized, to suppose that this is so in a given case would require special justification. So, initially at least, conversational implicata are not part of the meaning of the expressions to the employment of which they attach.

4. Since the truth of a conversational implicatum is not required by the truth of what is said (what is said may be true—what is implicated may be false), the implicature is not carried by what is said, but only by the saying of what is said, or by 'putting it that way.'

5. Since, to calculate a conversational implicature is to calculate what has to be supposed in order to preserve the supposition that the Cooperative Principle is being observed, and since there may be various possible specific explanations, a list of which may be open, the conversational implicatum in such cases will be a disjunction of such specific explanations; and if the list of these is open, the implicatum will have just the kind of indeterminacy that many actual implicata do in fact seem to possess.

12 Indirect Speech Acts

JOHN R. SEARLE

The simplest cases of meaning are those in which the speaker utters a sentence and means exactly and literally what he says. In such cases the speaker intends to produce a certain illocutionary effect in the hearer, and he intends to produce this effect by getting the hearer to recognize this intention to produce it, and he intends to get the hearer to recognize this intention in virtue of the hearer's knowledge of the rules that govern the utterance of the sentence. But notoriously, not all cases of meaning are this simple: In hints, insinuations, irony, and metaphor—to mention a few examples—the speaker's utterance meaning and the sentence meaning come apart in various ways. One important class of such cases is that in which the speaker utters a sentence, means what he says, but also means something more. For example, a speaker may utter the sentence "I want you to do it" by way of requesting the hearer to do something. The utterance is incidentally meant as a statement, but it is also meant primarily as a request, a request made by way of making a statement. In such cases a sentence that contains the illocutionary force indicators for one kind of illocutionary act can be uttered to perform, *in addition,* another type of illocutionary act. There are also cases in which the speaker may utter a sentence and mean what he says and also mean another illocution with a different propositional content. For example, a speaker may utter the sentence "Can you reach the salt?" and mean it not merely as a question but as a request to pass the salt.

In such cases it is important to emphasize that the utterance is meant as a request; that is, the speaker intends to produce in the hearer the knowledge that a request has been made to him, and he intends to produce this knowledge by means of getting the hearer to recognize his intention to produce it. Such cases, in which the utterance has two illocutionary forces, are to be sharply distinguished from the cases in which, for example, the speaker tells the hearer that he wants him to do something; and then the hearer does it because the speaker wants him to, though no request at all has been made, meant, or understood. The cases we will be discussing are indirect speech acts, cases in which one illocutionary act is performed indirectly by way of performing another.

The problem posed by indirect speech acts is the problem of how it is possible for the speaker to say one thing and mean that but also to mean something else. And since meaning consists in part in the intention to produce understanding in the hearer, a large part of that problem is that of how it is possible for the hearer to understand the indirect speech act when the sentence he hears and understands means something else.

From *Syntax and Semantics,* volume 3, Peter Cole and Jerry L. Morgan, eds. (New York: Academic Press, 1975), pp. 59–82. Copyright © by John R. Searle. Reprinted by permission of the author.

The problem is made more complicated by the fact that some sentences seem almost to be conventionally used as indirect requests. For a sentence like "Can you reach the salt?" or "I would appreciate it if you would get off my foot," it takes some ingenuity to imagine a situation in which their utterances would not be requests.

In *Speech Acts* I suggested that many such utterances could be explained by the fact that the sentences in question concern conditions of the felicitous performance of the speech acts they are used to perform indirectly—preparatory conditions, propositional content conditions, and sincerity conditions—and that their use to perform indirect speech acts consists in indicating the satisfaction of an essential condition by means of asserting or questioning one of the other conditions. Since that time a variety of explanations have been proposed, involving such things as the hypostatization of "conversational postulates" or alternative deep structures. The answer I originally suggested seems to me incomplete, and I want to develop it further here. The hypothesis I wish to defend is simply this: In indirect speech acts the speaker communicates to the hearer more than he actually says by way of relying on their mutually shared background information, both linguistic and nonlinguistic, together with the general powers of rationality and inference on the part of the hearer. To be more specific, the apparatus necessary to explain the indirect part of indirect speech acts includes a theory of speech acts, certain general principles of cooperative conversation (some of which have been discussed by Grice) and mutually shared factual background information of the speaker and the hearer, together with an ability on the part of the hearer to make inferences. It is not necessary to assume the existence of any conversational postulates (either as an addition to the theory of speech acts or as part of the theory of speech acts) nor any concealed imperative forces or other ambiguities. We will see, however, that in some cases, convention plays a most peculiar role.

Aside from its interest for a theory of meaning and speech acts, the problem of indirect speech acts is of philosophical importance for an additional reason. In ethics it has commonly been supposed that "good", "right", "ought", etc. somehow have an imperative or "action guiding" meaning. This view derives from the fact that sentences such as "You ought to do it" are often uttered by way of telling the hearer to do something. But from the fact that such sentences can be uttered as directives[1] it no more follows that "ought" has an imperative meaning than from the fact that "Can you reach the salt?" can be uttered as a request to pass the salt it follows that "can" has an imperative meaning. Many confusions in recent moral philosophy rest on a failure to understand the nature of such indirect speech acts. The topic has an additional interest for linguists because of its syntactical consequences, but I shall be concerned with these only incidentally.

A SAMPLE CASE

Let us begin by considering a typical case of the general phenomenon of indirection:

(1) Student X: *Let's go to the movies tonight.*
(2) Student Y: *I have to study for an exam.*

The utterance of (1) constitutes a proposal in virtue of its meaning, in particular because of the meaning of "Let's." In general, literal utterances of sentences of this form will constitute proposals, as in:

(3) Let's eat pizza tonight.

or:

(4) Let's go ice skating tonight.

The utterance of (2) in the context just given would normally constitute a rejection of the proposal, but not in virtue of its meaning. In virtue of its meaning it is simply a statement about Y. Statements of this form do not, in general, constitute rejections of proposals, even in cases in which they are made in response to a proposal. Thus, if Y had said:

(5) I have to eat popcorn tonight.

or:

(6) I have to tie my shoes.

in a normal context, neither of these utterances would have been a rejection of the proposal.

The question then arises, How does X know that the utterance is a rejection of the proposal? and that question is a part of the question, How is it possible for Y to intend or mean the utterance of (2) as a rejection of the proposal? In order to describe this case, let us introduce some terminology. Let us say that the *primary* illocutionary act performed in Y's utterance is the rejection of the *proposal* made by X, and that Y does that by way of performing a *secondary* illocutionary act of making a statement to the effect that he has to prepare for an exam. He performs the secondary illocutionary act by way of uttering a sentence the *literal* meaning of which is such that its literal utterance constitutes a performance of that illocutionary act. We may, therefore, further say that the secondary illocutionary act is literal; the primary illocutionary act is not literal. Let us assume that we know how X understands the literal secondary illocutionary act from the utterance of the sentence. The question is, How does he understand the nonliteral primary illocutionary act from understanding the literal secondary illocutionary act? And that question is part of the larger question, How is it possible for Y to mean the primary illocution when he only utters a sentence that means the secondary illocution, since to mean the primary illocution is (in large part) to intend to produce in X the relevant understanding?

A brief reconstruction of the steps necessary to derive the primary illocution from the literal illocution would go as follows. (In normal conversation, of course, no one would consciously go through the steps involved in this reasoning.)

Step 1. I have made a proposal to Y, and in response he has made a statement to the effect that he has to study for an exam (facts about the conversation).

Step 2. I assume that Y is cooperating in the conversation and that therefore his remark is intended to be relevant (principles of conversational cooperation).

Step 3. A relevant response must be one of acceptance, rejection, counterproposal, further discussion, etc. (theory of speech acts).

Step 4. But his literal utterance was not one of these, and so was not a relevant response (inference from steps 1 and 3).

Step 5. Therefore, he probably means more than he says. Assuming that his remark is relevant, his primary illocutionary point must differ from his literal one (inference from steps 2 and 4).[2] (This step is crucial. Unless a hearer has some inferential strategy for finding out when primary illocutionary points differ from literal illocutionary points, he has no way of understanding indirect illocutionary acts.)

Step 6. I know that studying for an exam normally takes a large amount of time relative to a single evening, and I know that going to the movies normally takes a large amount of time relative to a single evening (factual background information).

Step 7. Therefore, he probably cannot both go to the movies and study for an exam in one evening (inference from step 6).

Step 8. A preparatory condition on the acceptance of a proposal, or on any other commissive, is the ability to perform the act predicated in the propositional content condition (theory of speech acts).

Step 9. Therefore, I know that he has said something that has the consequence that he probably cannot consistently accept the proposal (inference from steps 1, 7, and 8).

Step 10. Therefore, his primary illocutionary point is probably to reject the proposal (inference from steps 5 and 9).

It may seem somewhat pedantic to set all of this out in 10 steps; but if anything, the example is still underdescribed—I have not, for example, discussed the role of the assumption of sincerity, or the ceteris paribus conditions that attach to various of the steps. Notice, also, that the conclusion is probabilistic. It is and ought to be. This is because the reply does not necessarily constitute a rejection of the proposal. Y might have gone on to say:

(7) I have to study for an exam, but let's go to the movies anyhow.
(8) I have to study for an exam, but I'll do it when we get home from the movies.

The inferential strategy is to establish, first, that the primary illocutionary point departs from the literal, and second, what the primary illocutionary point is.

The argument of this chapter will be that the theoretical apparatus used to explain this case will suffice to explain the general phenomenon of indirect illocutionary acts. That apparatus includes mutual background information, a theory of speech acts, and certain general principles of conversation. In particular, we explained this case without having to assume that sentence (2) is ambiguous or that it is "ambiguous in context" or that it is necessary to assume the existence of any "conversational postulates" in order to explain X's understanding the primary illocution of the utterance. The main difference between this case and the cases we will be discussing is that the latter all have a generality of *form* that is lacking in this example. I shall mark this generality by using bold type for the formal features in the surface structure of the sentences in question. In the field of indirect illocutionary acts, the area of directives is the most useful to study because ordinary conversational requirements of politeness normally make it awkward to issue flat imperative sentences (e.g., "Leave the room") or explicit performatives (e.g., "I order you to leave the room"), and we therefore seek to find indirect means to our illocutionary ends (e.g., "I wonder if you would mind leaving the room"). In directives, politeness is the chief motivation for indirectness.

SOME SENTENCES 'CONVENTIONALLY' USED IN THE PERFORMANCE OF INDIRECT DIRECTIVES

Let us begin, then, with a short list of some of the sentences that could quite standardly be used to make indirect requests and other directives such as orders. At a pretheoretical level these sentences naturally tend to group themselves into certain categories.[3]

Group 1

Sentences concerning H's ability to perform A

Can you reach the salt?
Can you pass the salt?
Could you be a little more quiet?
You could be a little more quiet.
You can go now (this may also be a permission = you may go now).
Are you able to reach the book on the top shelf?
Have you got change for a dollar?

Group 2

Sentences concerning S's wish or want that H will do A

I would like you to go now.
I want you to do this for me, Henry.
I would/should appreciate it if you would/ could do it for me.
I would/should be most grateful if you would/ could help us out.
I'd rather you didn't do that any more.
I'd be very much obliged if you would pay me the money back soon.
I hope you'll do it.
I wish you wouldn't do that.

Group 3

Sentences concerning H's doing A

Officers **will** henceforth wear ties at dinner.
Will you quit making that awful racket?
Would you kindly get off my foot?
Won't you stop making that noise soon?
Aren't you going to eat your cereal?

Group 4

Sentences concerning H's desire or willingness to do A

Would you be willing to write a letter of recommendation for me?
Do you want to hand me that hammer over there on the table?
Would you mind not making so much noise?
Would it be convenient for you to come on Wednesday?
Would it be too much (trouble) for you to pay me the money next Wednesday?

Group 5

Sentences concerning reasons for doing A

You ought to be more polite to your mother.
You should leave immediately.
Must you continue hammering that way?
Ought you to eat quite so much spaghetti?
Should you be wearing John's tie?
You had better go now.

Hadn't you better go now?

Why not stop here?

Why don't you try it just once?

Why don't you be quiet?

It would be better for you (for us all) if you would leave the room.

It wouldn't hurt if you left now.

It might help if you shut up.

It would be better if you gave me the money now.

It would be a good idea if you left town.

We'd all be better off if you'd just pipe down a bit.

This class also contains many examples that have no generality of form but obviously, in an appropriate context, would be uttered as indirect requests, e.g.,

> You're standing on my foot.
> I can't see the movie screen while you have that hat on.

Also in this class belong, possibly:

How many times have I told you (must I tell you) not to eat with your fingers?

I must have told you a dozen times not to eat with your mouth open.

If I have told you once I have told you a thousand times not to wear your hat in the house.

Group 6

Sentences embedding one of these elements inside another; also, sentences embedding an explicit directive illocutionary verb inside one of these contexts

Would you mind awfully if I asked you if you could write me a letter of recommendation?

Would it be too much if I suggested that you could possibly make a little less noise?

Might I ask you to take off your hat?

I hope you won't mind if I ask you if you could leave us alone.

I would appreciate it if you could make less noise.[4]

This is a very large class, since most of its members are constructed by permitting certain of the elements of the other classes.

SOME PUTATIVE FACTS

Let us begin by noting several salient facts about the sentences in question. Not everyone will agree that what follows are facts; indeed, most of the available explanations consist in denying one or more of these statements. Nonetheless, at an intuitive pretheoretical level each of the following would seem to be correct observations about the sentences in question, and I believe we should surrender these intuitions only in the face of very serious counterarguments. I will eventually argue that an explanation can be given that is consistent with all of these facts.

Fact 1: The sentences in question do not have an imperative force as part of their meaning. This point is sometimes denied by philosophers and linguists, but very powerful evidence for it is provided by the fact that it is possible without inconsistency to connect the literal utterance of one of these forms with the denial of any imperative intent, e.g.,

> I'd like you to do this for me, Bill, but I am not asking you to do it or requesting that you do it or ordering you to do it or telling you to do it.

> I'm just asking you, Bill: Why not eat beans? But in asking you that I want you to understand that I am not telling you to eat beans; I just want to know your reasons for thinking you ought not to.

Fact 2: The sentences in question are not ambiguous as between an imperative illocutionary force and a nonimperative illocutionary force. I think this is intuitively apparent, but in any case, an ordinary application of Occam's razor places the onus of proof on those who wish to claim that these sentences are ambiguous. One does not multiply meanings beyond necessity. Notice, also, that it is no help to say they are 'ambiguous in context,' for all that means is that one cannot always tell from what the sentence means what the speaker means by its utterance, and that is not sufficient to establish sentential ambiguity.

Fact 3: Notwithstanding facts 1 and 2, these are standardly, ordinarily, normally—indeed, I shall argue, conventionally—used to issue directives. There is a systematic relation between these and directive illocutions in a way that there is no systematic relation between "I have to study for an exam" and rejecting proposals. Additional evidence that they are standardly used to issue imperatives is that most of them take "please," either at the end of the sentence or preceding the verb, e.g.,

I want you to stop making that noise, please.
Could you please lend me a dollar?

When "please" is added to one of these sentences, it explicitly and literally marks the primary illocutionary point of the utterance as directive, even though the literal meaning of the rest of the sentence is not directive.

It is because of the combination of facts 1, 2, and 3 that there is a problem about these cases at all.

Fact 4: The sentences in question are not, in the ordinary sense, idioms.[5] An ordinary example of an idiom is "kicked the bucket" in "Jones kicked the bucket." The most powerful evidence I know that these sentences are not idioms is that in their use as indirect directives they admit of literal responses that presuppose that they are uttered literally. Thus, an utterance of "Why don't you be quiet, Henry?" admits as a response an utterance of "Well, Sally, there are several reasons for not being quiet. First, ..." Possible exceptions to this are occurrences of "would" and "could" in indirect speech acts, and I will discuss them later.

Further evidence that they are not idioms is that, whereas a word-for-word translation of "Jones kicked the bucket" into other languages will not produce a sentence meaning "Jones died," translations of the sentences in question will often, though by no means always, produce sentences with the same indirect illocutionary act potential of the English examples. Thus, e.g., "Pourriez-vous m'aider?" and "Können Sie mir helfen?" can be uttered as indirect requests in French or German. I will later discuss the problem of why some translate with equivalent indirect illocutionary force potential and some do not.

Fact 5: To say they are not idioms is not to say they are not idiomatic. All the examples given are idiomatic in current English, and—what is more puzzling—they are idiomatically used as requests. In general, nonidiomatic equivalents or synonyms would not have the same indirect illocutionary act potential. Thus, "Do you want to hand me the hammer over there on the table?" can be uttered as a request, but "Is it the case that you at present desire to hand me that hammer over there on the table?" has a formal and stilted character that in almost all contexts would eliminate it as a candidate for an indirect request. Furthermore, "Are you able to hand me that hammer?", though idiomatic, does not have the same indirect request potential as "Can you hand me that hammer?" That these sentences are idiomatic and are *idiomatically used as directives* is crucial to their role in indirect speech acts. I will say more about the relations of these facts later.

Fact 6: The sentences in question have literal utterances in which they are not also indirect requests. Thus, "Can you reach the salt?" can be uttered as a simple question about your abilities (say, by an orthopedist wishing to know the medical progress of your arm injury). "I want you to leave" can be uttered simply as a statement about one's wants, without any directive intent. At first sight, some of our examples might not appear to satisfy this condition, e.g.,

Why not stop here?
Why don't you be quiet?

But with a little imagination it is easy to construct situations in which utterances of these would be not directives but straightforward questions. Suppose someone had said "We ought not to stop here." Then "Why not stop here?" would be an appropriate question, without necessarily being also a suggestion. Similarly, if someone had just said "I certainly hate making all this racket," an utterance of "(Well, then) Why don't you be quiet?" would be an appropriate response, without also necessarily being a request to be quiet.

It is important to note that the intonation of these sentences when they are uttered as indirect requests often differs from their intonation when uttered with only their literal illocutionary force, and often the intonation pattern will be that characteristic of literal directives.

Fact 7: In cases where these sentences are uttered as requests, they still have their literal meaning and are uttered with and as having that literal meaning. I have seen it claimed that they have different meanings 'in context' when they are uttered as requests, but I believe that is obviously false. The man who says "I want you to do it" means literally that he wants you to do it. The point is that, as is always the case with indirection, he means not only what he says but something more as well. What is added in the indirect cases is not any additional or different *sentence* meaning, but additional *speaker* meaning. Evidence that these sentences keep their literal meanings when uttered as indirect requests is that responses that are appropriate to their literal utterances are appropriate to their indirect speech act utterances (as we noted in our discussion of fact 4), e.g.,

Can you pass the salt?
No, sorry, I can't, it's down there at the end of the table.
Yes, I can. (Here it is.)

Fact 8: It is a consequence of fact 7 that when one of these sentences is uttered with the primary illocutionary point of a directive, the literal illocutionary act is also performed. In every one of these cases, the speaker issues a directive *by way of* asking a question or making a statement. But the fact that his primary illocutionary intent is directive does not alter the fact that he is asking a question or making a statement. Additional evidence for fact 8 is that a subsequent report of the utterance can truly report the literal illocutionary act.

Thus, e.g., the utterance of "I want you to leave now, Bill" can be reported by an utterance of "He told me he wanted me to leave, so I left." Or, the utterance of "Can you reach the salt?" can be reported by an utterance of "He asked me whether I could reach the salt." Similarly, an utterance of "Could you do it for me, Henry; could you do it for me and Cynthia and the children?" can be reported by an utterance of "He asked me whether I could do it for him and Cynthia and the children."

This point is sometimes denied. I have seen it claimed that the literal illocutionary acts are always defective or are not 'conveyed' when the sentence is used to perform a nonliteral primary illocutionary act. As far as our examples are concerned, the literal illocutions are always conveyed and are sometimes, but not in general, defective. For example, an indirect speech act utterance of "Can you reach the salt?" may be defective in the sense that S may already know the answer. But even this form *need* not be defective. (Consider, e.g., "Can you give me change for a dollar?.") Even when the literal utterance is defective, the indirect speech act does not depend on its being defective.

AN EXPLANATION IN TERMS OF THE THEORY OF SPEECH ACTS

The difference between the example concerning the proposal to go to the movies and all of the other cases is that the other cases are systematic. What we need to do, then, is to describe an example in such a way as to show how the apparatus used on the first example will suffice for these other cases and also will explain the systematic character of the other cases.

I think the theory of speech acts will enable us to provide a simple explanation of how these sentences, which have one illocutionary force as part of their meaning, can be used to perform an act with a different illocutionary force. Each type of illocutionary act has a set of conditions that are necessary for the successful and felicitous performance of the act. To illustrate this, I will present the conditions on two types of acts within the two genuses, directive and commissive [*Speech Acts*].

A comparison of the list of felicity conditions on the directive class of illocutionary acts and our list of types of sentences used to perform indirect directives show that Groups 1–6 of types can be reduced to three types: those having to do with felicity conditions on the performance of a directive illocutionary act, those having to do with reasons for doing the act, and those embedding one element inside another one. Thus, since the ability of H to perform A (Group 1) is a preparatory condition, the desire of S that H perform A (Group 2) is the sincerity condition, and the predication of A of H (Group 3) is the propositional content condition, all of Groups 1–3 concern felicity conditions on directive illocutionary acts. Since wanting to do something is a reason par excellence for doing

	Directive (Request)	Commissive (Promise)
Preparatory condition	H is able to perform A.	S is able to perform A. H wants S to perform A.
Sincerity condition	S wants H to do A.	S intends to do A.
Propositional content condition	S predicates a future act A of H.	S predicates a future act A of S.
Essential condition	Counts as an attempt by S to get H to do A.	Counts as the undertaking by S of an obligation to do A.

it, Group 4 assimilates to Group 5, as both concern reasons for doing A. Group 6 is a special class only by courtesy, since its elements either are performative verbs or are already contained in the other two categories of felicity conditions and reasons.

Ignoring the embedding cases for the moment, if we look at our lists and our sets of conditions, the following generalizations naturally emerge.

Generalization 1: S can make an indirect request (or other directive) by either asking whether or stating that a preparatory condition concerning H's ability to do A obtains.

Generalization 2: S can make an indirect directive by either asking whether or stating that the propositional content condition obtains.

Generalization 3: S can make an indirect directive by stating that the sincerity condition obtains, but not by asking whether it obtains.

Generalization 4: S can make an indirect directive by either stating that or asking whether there are good or overriding reasons for doing A, except where the reason is that H wants or wishes, etc., to do A, in which case he can only ask whether H wants, wishes, etc., to do A.

It is the existence of these generalizations that accounts for the systematic character of the relation between the sentences in Groups 1–6 and the directive class of illocutionary acts. Notice that these are generalizations and not rules. The rules of speech acts (or some of them) are stated in the list of conditions presented earlier. That is, for example, it is a rule of the directive class of speech acts that the directive is defective if the hearer is unable to perform the act, but it is precisely not a rule of speech acts or of conversation that one can perform a directive by asking whether the preparatory condition obtains. The theoretical task is to show how that generalization will be a consequence of the rule, together with certain other information, namely, the factual background information and the general principles of conversation.

Our next task is to try to describe an example of an indirect request with at least the same degree of pedantry we used in our description of the rejection of a proposal. Let us take the simplest sort of case: At the dinner table, X says to Y, "Can you pass the salt?" by way of asking Y to pass the salt. Now, how does Y know that X is requesting him to pass the salt instead of just asking a question about his abilities to pass the salt? Notice that not everything will do as a request to pass the salt. Thus, if X had said "Salt is made of sodium chloride" or "Salt is mined in the Tatra mountains," without some special stage setting, it is very unlikely that Y would take either of these utterances as a request to pass the salt. Notice further that, in a normal conversational situation, Y does not have to go through any conscious process of inference to derive the conclusion that the utterance of "Can you pass the salt?" is a request to pass the salt. He simply hears it as a request. This fact is perhaps one of the main reasons why it is tempting to adopt the false conclusion that somehow these examples must have an imperative force as part of their meaning or that they are 'ambiguous in context,' or some such. What we need to do is offer an explanation that is consistent with all of facts 1–8 yet does not make the mistake of hypostatizing concealed imperative forces or conversational postulates. A bare-bones reconstruction of the steps necessary for Y to derive the conclusion from the utterance might go roughly as follows:

Step 1: X has asked me a question as to whether I have the ability to pass the salt (fact about the conversation).

Step 2. I assume that he is cooperating in the conversation and that therefore his utterance has some aim or point (principles of conversational cooperation).

Step 3. The conversational setting is not such as to indicate a theoretical interest in my salt-passing ability (factual background information).

Step 4. Furthermore, he probably already knows that the answer to the question is yes (factual background information). (This step facilitates the move to step 5, but is not essential.)

Step 5. Therefore, his utterance is probably not just a question. It probably has some ulterior illocutionary point (inference from steps 1, 2, 3, and 4). What can it be?

Step 6. A preparatory condition for any directive illocutionary act is the ability of H to perform the act predicated in the propositional content condition (theory of speech acts).

Step 7. Therefore, X has asked me a question the affirmative answer to which would entail that the preparatory condition for requesting me to pass the salt is satisfied (inference from steps 1 and 6).

Step 8: We are now at dinner and people normally use salt at dinner; they pass it back and forth, try to get others to pass it back and forth, etc. (background information).

Step 9: He has therefore alluded to the satisfaction of a preparatory condition for a request whose obedience conditions it is quite likely he wants me to bring about (inference from Steps 7 and 8).

Step 10: Therefore, in the absence of any other plausible illocutionary point, he is probably requesting me to pass him the salt (inference from steps 5 and 9).

The hypothesis being put forth in this chapter is that all the cases can be similarly analyzed. According to this analysis, the reason I can ask you to pass the salt by saying "Can you pass the salt?" but not by saying "Salt is made of sodium chloride" or "Salt is mined in the Tatra mountains" is that your ability to pass the salt is a preparatory condition for requesting you to pass the salt in a way that the other sentences are not related to requesting you to pass the salt. But obviously, that answer is not by itself sufficient, because not all questions about your abilities are requests. The hearer therefore needs some way of finding out when the utterance is just a question about his abilities and when it is a request made by way of asking a question about his abilities. It is at this point that the general principles of conversation (together with factual background information) come into play.

The two features that are crucial, or so I am suggesting, are, first, a strategy for establishing the existence of an ulterior illocutionary point beyond the illocutionary point contained in the meaning of the sentence, and second, a device for finding out what the ulterior illocutionary point is. The first is established by the principles of conversation operating on the information of the hearer and the speaker, and the second is derived from the theory of speech acts together with background information. The generalizations are to be explained by the fact that each of them records a strategy by means of which the hearer can find out how a primary illocutionary point differs from a secondary illocutionary point.

The chief motivation—though not the only motivation—for using these indirect forms is politeness. Notice that, in the example just given, the "Can you" form is polite in at least two respects. Firstly, X does not presume to know about Y's abilities, as he would if he issued an imperative sentence; and, secondly, the form gives—or at least appears to give—Y the option of refusing, since a yes-no question allows *no* as a possible answer. Hence, compliance can be made to appear a free act rather than obeying a command.[6]

SOME PROBLEMS

It is important to emphasize that I have by no means demonstrated the thesis being argued for in this chapter. I have so far only suggested a pattern of analysis that is consistent with the facts. Even supposing that this pattern of analysis could be shown to be successful in many more cases, there are still several problems that remain:

Problem 1

The biggest single problem with the foregoing analysis is this: If, as I have been arguing, the mechanisms by which indirect speech acts are meant and understood are perfectly general—having to do with the theory of speech acts, the principles of cooperative conversation, and shared background information—and not tied to any particular syntactical form, then why is it that some syntactical forms work better than others. Why can I ask you to do something by saying "Can you hand me that book on the top shelf?" but not, or not very easily, by saying "Is it the case that you at present have the ability to hand me that book on the top shelf?"

Even within such pairs as:

Do you want to do A?
Do you desire to do A?

and:

Can you do A?
Are you able to do A?

there is clearly a difference in indirect illocutionary act potential. Note, for example, that the first member of each pair takes "please" more readily than the second. Granting that none of these pairs are exact synonyms, and granting that all the sentences have some use as indirect requests, it is still essential to explain the differences in their indirect illocutionary act potential. How, in short, can it be the case that some sentences are not imperative idioms and yet function as forms for idiomatic requests?

The first part of the answer is this: The theory of speech acts and the principles of conversational cooperation do, indeed, provide a framework within which indirect illocutionary acts can be meant and understood. However, within this framework certain forms will tend to become conventionally established as the standard idiomatic forms for indirect speech acts. While keeping their literal meanings, they will acquire conventional uses as, e.g., polite forms for requests.

It is by now, I hope, uncontroversial that there is a distinction to be made between meaning and use, but what is less generally recognized is that there can be conventions of usage that are not meaning conventions. I am suggesting that "can you," "could you," "I want you to," and numerous other forms are conventional ways of making requests (and in that sense it is not incorrect to say they are idioms), but at the same time they do not have an imperative meaning (and in that sense it would be incorrect to say they are idioms). Politeness is the most prominent motivation for indirectness in requests, and certain forms naturally tend to become the conventionally polite ways of making indirect requests.

If this explanation is correct, it would go some way toward explaining why there are differences in the indirect speech forms from one language to another. The mechanisms are not peculiar to this language or that, but at the same time the standard forms from one language will not always maintain their indirect speech act potential when translated from one language to another. Thus, "Can you hand me that book?" will function as an indirect request in English, but its Czech translation, "Mužete mi podat tu Knížku?" will sound very odd if uttered as a request in Czech.

A second part of the answer is this: In order to be a plausible candidate for an utterance as an indirect speech act, a sentence has to be idiomatic to start with. It is very easy to imagine circumstances in which: "Are you able to reach that book on the top shelf?" could be uttered as a request. But it is much harder to imagine cases in which "Is it the case that you at present have the ability to reach that book on the top shelf?" could be similarly used. Why?

I think the explanation for this fact may derive from another maxim of conversation having to do with speaking idiomatically. In general, if one speaks unidiomatically, hearers assume that there must be a special reason for it, and in consequence, various assumptions of normal speech are suspended. Thus, if I say, archaically, "Knowest thou him who calleth himself Richard Nixon?," you are not likely to respond as you would to an utterance of "Do you know Richard Nixon?"

Besides the maxims proposed by Grice, there

seems to be an additional maxim of conversation that could be expressed as follows: "Speak idiomatically unless there is some special reason not to." For this reason, the normal conversational assumptions on which the possibility of indirect speech acts rests are in large part suspended in the nonidiomatic cases.

The answer, then, to problem 1 is in two parts. In order to be a plausible candidate at all for use as an indirect speech act, a sentence has to be idiomatic. But within the class of idiomatic sentences, some forms tend to become entrenched as conventional devices for indirect speech acts. In the case of directives, in which politeness is the chief motivation for the indirect forms, certain forms are conventionally used as polite requests. Which kinds of forms are selected will, in all likelihood, vary from one language to another.

Problem 2

Why is there an asymmetry between the sincerity condition and the others such that one can perform an indirect request only by asserting the satisfaction of a sincerity condition, not by querying it, whereas one can perform indirect directives by either asserting or querying the satisfaction of the propositional content and preparatory conditions?

Thus, an utterance of "I want you to do it" can be a request, but not an utterance of "Do I want you to do it?" The former can take "please," the latter cannot. A similar asymmetry occurs in the case of reasons: "Do you want to leave us alone?" can be a request, but not "You want to leave us alone."[7] Again, the former can take "please," the latter cannot. How is one to explain these facts?

I believe the answer is that it is odd, in normal circumstances, to ask other people about the existence of one's own elementary psychological states, and odd to assert the existence of other people's elementary psychological states when addressing them. Since normally you are never in as good a position as I am to assert what I want, believe, intend, and so on, and since I am normally not in as good a position as you to assert what you want, believe, intend, and so on, it is, in general, odd for me to ask you about my

states or tell you about yours. We shall see shortly that this asymmetry extends to the indirect performance of other kinds of speech acts.

Problem 3

Though this chapter is not intended as being about English syntactical forms, some of the sentences on our lists are of enough interest to deserve special comment. Even if it should turn out that these peculiar cases are really imperative idioms, like "how about . . .?," it would not alter the general lines of my argument; it would simply shift some examples out of the class of indirect speech acts into the class of imperative idioms.

One interesting form is 'why not plus verb,' as in "Why not stop here?" This form, unlike "Why don't you?," has many of the same syntactical constraints as imperative sentences. For example, it requires a voluntary verb. Thus, one cannot say "Why not resemble your grandmother?" unless one believes that one can resemble someone as a voluntary action, whereas one can say "Why not imitate your grandmother?" Furthermore, like imperative sentences, this form requires a reflexive when it takes a second-person direct object, e.g., "Why not wash yourself?" Do these facts prove that the 'Why not . . .?' (and the 'why . . .?') forms are imperative in meaning? I think they are not. On my account, the way an utterance of 'why not?' works is this: In asking "Why not stop here?" as a suggestion to stop here, S challenges H to provide reasons for not doing something on the tacit assumption that the absence of reasons for not doing something is itself a reason for doing it, and the suggestion to do it is therefore made indirectly in accordance with the generalization that alluding to a reason for doing something is a way of making an indirect directive to do it. This analysis is supported by several facts. First, as we have already seen, this form can have a literal utterance in which it is not uttered as a suggestion; second, one can respond to the suggestion with a response appropriate to the literal utterance, e.g., "Well, there are several reasons for not stopping here. First . . ." And third, one can report an utterance of one of these, without reporting any directive illocutionary forces, in the form "He asked me why we shouldn't stop there." And here the occurrence of the practical "should" or "ought" (not the theoretical "should" or "ought") is sufficient to account for the requirement of a voluntary verb.

Other troublesome examples are provided by occurrences of "would" and "could" in indirect speech acts. Consider, for example, utterances of "Would you pass me the salt?" and "Could you hand me that book?" It is not easy to analyze these forms and to describe exactly how they differ in meaning from "Will you pass me the salt?" and "Can you hand me that book?" Where, for example, are we to find the 'if' clause, which, we are sometimes told, is required by the so-called subjunctive use of these expressions? Suppose we treat the 'if' clause as "if I asked you to." Thus, "Would you pass me the salt?" is short for "Would you pass me the salt if I asked you to?"

There are at least two difficulties with this approach. First, it does not seem at all plausible for "could," since your abilities and possibilities are not contingent on what I ask you to do. But second, even for "would" it is unsatisfactory, since "Would you pass me the salt if I asked you to?" does not have the same indirect illocutionary act potential as the simple "Would you pass me the salt?" Clearly, both forms have uses as indirect directives, but, equally clearly, they are not equivalent. Furthermore, the cases in which "would" and "could" interrogative forms *do* have a nonindirect use seem to be quite different from the cases we have been considering, e.g., "Would you vote for a Democrat?" or "Could you marry a radical?" Notice, for example, that an appropriate response to an utterance of these might be, e.g., "Under what conditions?" or "It depends on the situation." But these would hardly be appropriate responses to an utterance of "Would you pass me the salt?" in the usual dinner table scene we have been envisaging.

"Could" seems to be analyzable in terms of "would" and possibility or ability. Thus, "Could you marry a radical" means something like "Would it be possible for you to marry a radical?" "Would", like "will," is traditionally analyzed either as expressing want or desire or as a future auxiliary.

The difficulty with these forms seems to be

an instance of the general difficulty about the nature of the subjunctive and does not necessarily indicate that there is any imperative meaning. If we are to assume that "would" and "could" have an imperative meaning, then it seems we will be forced to assume, also, that they have a commissive meaning as well, since utterances of "Could I be of assistance?" and "Would you like some more wine?" are both normally offers. I find this conclusion implausible because it involves an unnecessary proliferation of meanings. It violates Occam's razor regarding concepts. It is more economical to assume that "could" and "would" are univocal in "Could you pass the salt?," "Could I be of assistance?", "Would you stop making that noise?", and "Would you like some more wine?". However, a really satisfactory analysis of these forms awaits a satisfactory analysis of the subjunctive. The most plausible analysis of the indirect request forms is that the suppressed 'if' clause is the polite "if you please" or "if you will."

EXTENDING THE ANALYSIS

I want to conclude this chapter by showing that the general approach suggested in it will work for other types of indirection besides just directives. Obvious examples, often cited in the literature, are provided by the sincerity conditions. In general, one can perform any illocutionary act by asserting (though not by questioning) the satisfaction of the sincerity condition for that act. Thus, for example,

> I am sorry I did it. (an apology)
> I think/believe he is in the next room. (an assertion)
> I am so glad you won. (congratulations)
> I intend to try harder next time, coach. (a promise)
> I am grateful for your help. (thanks)

I believe, however, that the richest mine for examples other than directives is provided by commissives, and a study of the examples of sentences used to perform indirect commissives (especially offers and promises) shows very much the same patterns that we found in the study of directives. Consider the following sentences, any of which can be uttered to perform an indirect offer (or, in some cases, a promise).

(I) Sentences concerning the preparatory conditions:

(A) that S is able to perform the act:

Can I help you?
I can do that for you.
I could get it for you.
Could I be of assistance?

(B) that H wants S to perform the act:

Would you like some help?
Do you want me to go now, Sally?
Wouldn't you like me to bring some more next time I come?
Would you rather I came on Tuesday?

(II) Sentences concerning the sincerity condition:

I intend to do it for you.
I plan on repairing it for you next week.

(III) Sentences concerning the propositional content condition:

I will do it for you.
I am going to give it to you next time you stop by.
Shall I give you the money now?

(IV) Sentences concerning S's wish or willingness to do A:

I want to be of any help I can.
I'd be willing to do it (if you want me to).

(V) Sentences concerning (other) reasons for S's doing A:

I think I had better leave you alone.
Wouldn't it be better if I gave you some assistance?
You need my help, Cynthia.

Notice that the point made earlier about the elementary psychological states holds for these cases as well: One can perform an indirect illocutionary act by asserting, but not by querying, one's own psychological states; and one can perform an indirect illocutionary act by querying, but not by asserting, the presence of psychological states in one's hearer.

Thus, an utterance of "Do you want me to leave?" can be an offer to leave, but not "You want me to leave." (Though it can be, with the tag question "You want me to leave, don't you?") Similarly, "I want to help you out" can be uttered as an offer, but not "Do I want to help you out?"

The class of indirect commissives also includes a large number of hypothetical sentences:

If you wish any further information, just let me know.
If I can be of assistance, I would be most glad to help.
If you need any help, call me at the office.

In the hypothetical cases, the antecedent concerns either one of the preparatory conditions, or the presence of a reason for doing A, as in "If it would be better for me to come on Wednesday, just let me know." Note also that, as well as hypothetical sentences, there are iterated cases of indirection. Thus, e.g., "I think I ought to help you out" can be uttered as an indirect offer made by way of making an indirect assertion. These examples suggest the following further generalizations.

Generalization 5. S can make an indirect commissive by either asking whether or stating that the preparatory condition concerning his ability to do A obtains.

Generalization 6. S can make an indirect commissive by asking whether, though not by stating that, the preparatory condition concerning H's wish or want that S do A obtains.

Generalization 7. S can make an indirect commissive by stating that, and in some forms by asking whether, the propositional content condition obtains.

Generalization 8. S can make an indirect commissive by stating that, but not by asking whether, the sincerity condition obtains.

Generalization 9. S can make an indirect commissive by stating that or by asking whether there are good or overriding reasons for doing A, except where the reason is that S wants or desires to do A, in which case he can only state but not ask whether he wants to do A.

I would like to conclude by emphasizing that my approach does not fit any of the usual explanatory paradigms. The philosopher's paradigm has normally been to get a set of logically necessary and sufficient conditions for the phenomena to be explained; the linguist's paradigm has normally been to get a set of structural rules that will generate the phenomena to be explained. I am unable to convince myself that either of these paradigms is appropriate for the present problem. The problem seems to me somewhat like those problems in the epistemological analysis of perception in which one seeks to explain how a perceiver recognizes an object on the basis of imperfect sensory input. The question, "How do I know he has made a request when he only asked me a question about my abilities?" may be like the question, "How do I know it was a car when all I perceived was a flash going past me on the highway?" If so, the answer to our problem may be neither "I have a set of axioms from which it can be deduced that he made a request" nor "I have a set of syntactical rules that generate an imperative deep structure for the sentence he uttered."

ACKNOWLEDGMENTS

I am indebted for comments on earlier drafts of this study to Julian Boyd, Charles Fillmore, Dorothea Franck, Georgia Green, George Lakoff, Dagmar Searle, and Alan Walworth.

NOTES

1. The class of 'directive' illocutionary acts includes acts of ordering, commanding, requesting, pleading, begging, praying, entreating, instructing, forbidding, and others. See Searle (2) for an explanation of this notion.
2. For an explanation of the notion of 'illocutionary point' and its relation to illocutionary force, see Searle (2).
3. In what follows, I use the letters H, S, and A as abbreviations for "hearer," "speaker," and "act" or "action."
4. This form is also included in Group 2.
5. There are some idioms in this line of business, however, for example "How about" as used in proposals and requests: "How about going to the movies tonight?" "How about giving me some more beer?"
6. I am indebted to Dorothea Franck for discussion of this point.
7. This point does not hold for the etymologically prior sense of *want* in which it means 'need.'

REFERENCES

Searle, J. R. (1) *Speech Acts.* Cambridge University Press, New York and London: 1969.)
Searle, J. R. (2) A taxonomy of illocutionary acts. In K. Gunderson, ed., *Minnesota studies in the philosophy of language.* (University of Minnesota Press, Minneapolis: 1975).

13 Assertion

ROBERT STALNAKER

Let me begin with some truisms about assertions. First, assertions have content; an act of assertion is, among other things, the expression of a proposition—something that represents the world as being a certain way. Second, assertions are made in a context—a situation that includes a speaker with certain beliefs and intentions, and some people with their own beliefs and intentions to whom the assertion is addressed. Third, sometimes the content of the assertion is dependent on the context in which it is made, for example, on who is speaking or when the act of assertion takes place. Fourth, acts of assertion affect, and are intended to affect, the context, in particular the attitudes of the participants in the situation; how the assertion affects the context will depend on its content.

My aim in this paper is to sketch some theoretical concepts with which to develop these truisms, and to show how these concepts can be used to explain some linguistic phenomena. I want to suggest how content and context might be represented in a theory of speech, and how the interaction of content and context to which the above-mentioned truisms point might be described. I will not propose an analysis of assertion, but I will make some modest claims about the way assertions act on the contexts in which they are made, and the way contexts constrain the interpretation of assertions. In conclu-

sion, I will look briefly at an example of a phenomenon which I think these modest claims help to explain.

Three notions will play a central role in the theory I will sketch: the notion of a PROPOSITION, the notion of a PROPOSITIONAL CONCEPT, and the notion of SPEAKER PRESUPPOSITION. Each of these three notions will be defined or explained in terms of the notion of a POSSIBLE WORLD, or a possible state of the world, so one might think it important to begin with the question, what is a possible world? This is a good question, but I will not try to answer it here, and I am not sure that an abstract theory of speech should say very much in answer to it. In particular inquiries, deliberations, and conversations, alternative states of the subject matter in question are conceived in various different ways depending on the interests and attitudes of the participants in those activities. But one thing that is common to all such activities, and essential to them, is that the participants do seek to distinguish among alternative ways that things might be, or might have been. It may be that the best way to bring out the formal structure of such activities is to focus on what is done with a given relevant set of alternative states of the world, setting aside questions about the nature of the alternatives themselves. The decision to treat possible worlds, or possible situations, as PRIMITIVE ele-

Robert Stalnaker, "Assertion," *Syntax and Semantics*, ed. J. Kimball. Vol. 9, © 1978 Academic Press (New York), pp. 315–332. Reprinted with permission from Elsevier and the author.

ments in a theory of propositions and propositional attitudes does not require an ontological commitment to possible worlds as basic entities of the universe. Rather, it is a decision to theorize at a certain level of abstraction.[1]

The analysis of proposition in terms of possible worlds was first proposed in the context of intuitive semantics for modal logic.[2] The analysis is this: A proposition is a function from possible worlds into truth-values (true or false). More roughly and intuitively, a proposition is a rule for determining a truth-value as a function of the facts—of the way the world is. Or, a proposition is a way—any way—of picking out a set of possible states of affairs—all those for which the proposition takes the value true.

The intuitive motivation for this analysis is something like the following. A proposition—the content of an assertion or belief—is a representation of the world as being a certain way. But for any given representation of the world as being a certain way, there will be a set of all the possible states of the world which accord with the representation—which **are** that way. So any proposition determines a set of possible worlds. And, for any given set of possible worlds, to locate the actual world in that set is to represent the world as being a certain way. So every set of possible worlds determines a proposition. Furthermore, any two assertions or beliefs will represent the world as being the SAME way if and only if they are true in all the same possible worlds. If we assume, as seems reasonable, that representations which represent the world as being the same way have the same content (express the same proposition), then we can conclude that there is a one-one correspondence between sets of possible worlds and propositions. Given this correspondence, it seems reasonable to use sets of possible worlds, or (equivalently) functions from possible worlds into truth-values, to play the role of propositions in our theory. The analysis defines propositions in terms of their essential function—to represent the world.[3]

Supposing for convenience of exposition that there is just a small finite number of possible states of the world, we might represent a proposition by enumerating the truth-values that it has in the different possible worlds, as in the following matrix:

$$A \quad\quad i \quad\quad j \quad\quad k$$

T	F	T

i, j and k are the possible worlds—the different possible sets of facts that determine the truth-value of the proposition.

But there is also a second way that the facts enter into the determination of the truth-value of what is expressed in an utterance: It is a matter of fact that an utterance has the content that it has. What one says—the proposition he expresses—is itself something that might have been different if the facts had been different; and if one is mistaken about the truth-value of an utterance, this is sometimes to be explained as a misunderstanding of what was said rather than as a mistake about the truth-value of what was actually said. The difference between the two ways that truth-values depend on facts is exploited in the familiar riddle, *If you call a horse's tail a leg how many legs does a horse have?* The answer, of course, is four, since calling a tail a leg does not make it one, but one can see a different way to take the question.

Let me give a simple example: I said *You are a fool* to O'Leary. O'Leary is a fool, so what I said was true, although O'Leary does not think so. Now Daniels, who is no fool and who knows it, was standing nearby, and he thought I was talking to him. So both O'Leary and Daniels thought I said something false: O'Leary understood what I said, but disagrees with me about the facts; Daniels, on the other hand, agrees with me about the fact (he knows that O'Leary is a fool), but misunderstood what I said. Just to fill out the example, let me add that O'Leary believes falsely that Daniels is a fool. Now compare the possible worlds i, j and k. i is the world as it is, the world we are in; j is the world that O'Leary thinks we are in; and k is the world Daniels thinks we are in. If we ignore possible worlds other than i, j and k, we can use matrix A to represent the proposition I actually expressed. But the following TWO-DIMENSIONAL matrix also represents the second way that the truth-value of my utterance is a function of the facts:

B	i	j	k
i	T	F	T
j	T	F	T
k	F	T	F

The vertical axis represents possible worlds in their role as context—as what determines what is said. The horizontal axis represents possible worlds in their role as the arguments of the functions which are the propositions expressed. Thus the different horizontal lines represent WHAT IS SAID in the utterance in various different possible contexts. Notice that the horizontal line following i is the same as the one following j. This represents the fact that O'Leary and I agree about what was said. Notice also that the vertical column under i is the same as the one under k. This represents the fact that Daniels and I agree about the truth-values of both the proposition I in fact expressed and the one Daniels thought I expressed.

In a sense, I said something true at i and false at j and k, even though in none of these worlds did I express the proposition that is true in i and false in j and k. Although not expressed in any of the contexts, this proposition is represented in the matrix. I will call it the DIAGONAL PROPOSITION since it is the function from possible worlds into truth-values whose values are read along the diagonal of the matrix from upper left to lower right. In general, this is the proposition that is true at i for any i if and only if what is expressed in the utterance at i is true at i. I shall say more about diagonal propositions later.

I will call what a matrix like B represents a PROPOSITIONAL CONCEPT. A propositional concept is a function from possible worlds into propositions, or, equivalently, a function from an ordered pair of possible worlds into a truth-value. Each concrete utterance token can be associated with the propositional concept it determines, and, I will suggest below, some of the principles constraining the interpretation and evaluation of assertions are constraints on propositional concepts determined by assertive utterances rather than simply on the proposi-

tions expressed. This is my motivation for introducing propositional concepts, but one can study this kind of structure from an abstract point of view, independently of utterances or contexts of utterance. The abstract theory of what I am calling propositional concepts has received some attention from logicians recently under the name TWO-DIMENSIONAL MODAL LOGIC.[4] The theory focuses on the notion of a two-dimensional modal operator.

A two-dimensional modal operator is an operator which takes a propositional concept into a propositional concept. If o is such an operator, then the meaning of o will be a rule that gives you the propositional concept expressed by oP in terms of the one expressed by P, for any P. I will describe one such operator, and contrast it with more traditional extensional and intensional sentence operators.[5]

The dagger is an operator which takes the diagonal proposition and projects it onto the horizontal. If φ is the diagonal propositional determined by P, then $\dagger P$ expresses φ relative to all contexts. So if B is the propositional concept determined by my statement to O'Leary in the example above, the following matrix gives the propositional concept, $\dagger B$:

$\dagger B$	i	j	k
i	T	F	F
j	T	F	F
k	T	F	F

What $\dagger B$ says is roughly this: *What is said in S's utterance of* **You are a fool** *is true,* where the definite description, *What is said in S's utterance of* **You are a fool** may be a nonrigid designator—a description that refers to different propositions in different worlds. Notice that the dagger always yields a constant propositional concept as its value. That is, whatever the case with P, $\dagger P$ will always express the same proposition relative to every context. If P itself is already a constant propositional concept in this sense, then $\dagger P$ will express the same propositional concept as P.[6]

Compare this operator with a more familiar modal operator, propositional necessity. $\Box P$ expresses in any world the proposition that is true at that world if and only if the proposition expressed by P at that world is the necessary proposition—the one that is true in all possible worlds. Propositional necessity is a one-dimensional operator in the following sense: The proposition expressed by $\Box P$ at any point depends only on the proposition expressed by P at that point. To evaluate $\Box P$ on any horizontal line, one need look only at the values of P on that line. This distinction between one- and two-dimensional operators parallels, on the next level up, the distinction between extensional and intensional operators. Compare the extensional negation operator: to evaluate $\sim P$ at any point, one need look only at the value of P at that point. Extensional operators take points (truth-values) into points; one-dimensional operators take horizontal lines (propositions) into horizontal lines; two-dimensional operators take the whole matrix (the propositional concept) into another whole matrix. Each kind of operator is a generalization of the kind preceding it.[7]

Let me mention one complex operator, square-dagger, which says that the diagonal proposition is necessary. This can be understood as the A PRIORI TRUTH operator, observing the distinction emphasized in the work of Saul Kripke between a priori and necessary truth. An a priori truth is a statement that, while perhaps not expressing a necessary proposition, expresses a truth in every context. This will be the case if and only if the diagonal proposition is necessary, which is what the complex operator says. I will illustrate this with a version of one of Kripke's own examples (1971: 273–5). Suppose that in worlds i, j and k, a certain object, a metal bar, is one, two and three meters long, respectively, at a certain time t. Now suppose an appropriate authority fixes the reference of the expression *one meter* by making the following statement in each of the worlds i, j and k: *This bar is one meter long.* Matrix C below represents the propositional concept for this statement. Matrix $\Box\dagger C$ represents the propositional concept for the claim that this statement is a priori true:

C	i	j	k		$\Box\dagger C$	i	j	k
i	T	F	F		i	T	T	T
j	F	T	F		j	T	T	T
k	F	F	T		k	T	T	T

The proposition expressed by the authority is one that might have been false, although he couldn't have expressed a false proposition in that utterance.

I have said how propositions are to be understood, and what propositional concepts are. The third notion I need is the concept of speaker presupposition. This, I want to suggest, is the central concept needed to characterize speech contexts. Roughly speaking, the presuppositions of a speaker are the propositions whose truth he takes for granted as part of the background of the conversation. A proposition is presupposed if the speaker is disposed to act as if he assumes or believes that the proposition is true, and as if he assumes or believes that his audience assumes or believes that it is true as well. Presuppositions are what are taken by the speaker to be the COMMON GROUND of the participants in the conversation, what are treated as their COMMON KNOWLEDGE or MUTUAL KNOWLEDGE.[8] The propositions presupposed in the intended sense need not really be common or mutual knowledge; the speaker need not even believe them. He may presuppose any proposition that he finds it convenient to assume for the purpose of the conversation, provided he is prepared to assume that his audience will assume it along with him.

It is PROPOSITIONS that are presupposed—functions from possible worlds into truth-values. But the more fundamental way of representing the speaker's presuppositions is not as a set of propositions, but rather as a set of possible worlds, the possible worlds compatible with what is presupposed. This set, which I will call the CONTEXT SET, is the set of possible worlds recognized by the speaker to be the "live options" relevant to the conversation. A proposition is presupposed if and only if it is true in all of these possible worlds. The motivation for representing the speaker's presuppositions in terms of a set of possible worlds in this way is that this representation is appropriate to a description of the conversational process in terms of its essential purposes. To engage in conversation is, essentially, to distinguish among alternative possible ways that things may be. The purpose of expressing propositions is to make such distinctions. The presuppositions define the limits of the set of alternative possibilities among which speakers intend their expressions of propositions to distinguish.

Each participant in a conversation has his own context set, but it is part of the concept of presupposition that a speaker assumes that the members of his audience presuppose everything that he presupposes. We may define a NONDE-FECTIVE CONTEXT as one in which the presuppositions of the various participants in the conversation are all the same. A DEFECTIVE CONTEXT will have a kind of instability, and will tend to adjust to the equilibrium position of a nondefective context. Because hearers will interpret the purposes and content of what is said in terms of their own presuppositions, any unnoticed discrepancies between the presuppositions of speaker and addressees are likely to lead to a failure of communication. Since communication is the point of the enterprise, everyone will have a motive to try to keep the presuppositions the same. And because in the course of a conversation many clues are dropped about what is presupposed, participants will normally be able to tell that divergences exist if they do. So it is not unreasonable, I think, to assume that in the normal case contexts are nondefective, or at least close enough to being nondefective.

A context is CLOSE ENOUGH to being nondefective if the divergences do not affect the issues that actually arise in the course of the conversation. Suppose for example that you know that Jones won the election, believe mistakenly that I know it as well, and are prepared to take the truth of this proposition for granted if the occasion should arise, say by using it as a suppressed premise in an argument, or by using the description *the man who won the election* to refer to Jones. On my dispositional account of speaker presupposition, if you are prepared to use the proposition in this way, then you do presuppose that Jones won the election, even if you never

have the opportunity to display this disposition because the subject does not come up. Since I do not know that Jones won the election, I do NOT presuppose it, and so the context is defective. But the defect may be harmless.

It will not necessarily be harmless: If the news is of sufficiently urgent interest, your failure to raise the subject may count as a display of your disposition to take its truth for granted. There will not be exactly a failure of communication, but there will be a misperception of the situation if I infer from the fact that you do not tell me who won that you do not know either.

A conversation is a process taking place in an ever-changing context. Think of a state of a context at any given moment as defined by the presuppositions of the participants as represented by their context sets. In the normal, nondefective case, the context sets will all be the same, so for this case we can talk of the context set of the conversation. Now how does an assertion change the context? There are two ways, the second of which, I will suggest, should be an essential component of the analysis of assertion. I will mention the first just to set it apart from the second: The fact that a speaker is speaking, saying the words he is saying in the way he is saying them, is a fact that is usually accessible to everyone present. Such observed facts can be expected to change the presumed common background knowledge of the speaker and his audience in the same way that any obviously observable change in the physical surroundings of the conversation will change the presumed common knowledge. If a goat walked into the room, it would normally be presupposed, from that point, that there was a goat in the room. And the fact that this was presupposed might be exploited in the conversation, as when someone asks, *How did that thing get in here?* assuming that others will know what he is talking about. In the same way, when I speak, I presuppose that others know I am speaking, even if I do not assume that anyone knew I was going to speak before I did. This fact, too, can be exploited in the conversation, as when Daniels says *I am bald,* taking it for granted that his audience can figure out who is being said to be bald.

I mention this commonplace way that assertions change the context in order to make clear that the context on which an assertion has its ESSENTIAL effect is not defined by what is presupposed before the speaker begins to speak, but will include any information which the speaker assumes his audience can infer from the performance of the speech act.

Once the context is adjusted to accommodate the information that the particular utterance was produced, how does the CONTENT of an assertion alter the context? My suggestion is a very simple one: To make an assertion is to reduce the context set in a particular way, provided that there are no objections from the other participants in the conversation. The particular way in which the context set is reduced is that all of the possible situations incompatible with what is said are eliminated. To put it a slightly different way, the essential effect of an assertion is to change the presuppositions of the participants in the conversation by adding the content of what is asserted to what is presupposed. This effect is avoided only if the assertion is rejected.

I should emphasize that I do not propose this as a DEFINITION of assertion, but only as a claim about one effect which assertions have, and are intended to have—an effect that should be a component, or a consequence, of an adequate definition. There are several reasons why one cannot define assertion in terms of this effect alone. One reason is that other speech acts, like making suppositions, have and are intended to have the same effect. A second reason is that there may be various indirect, even nonlinguistic, means of accomplishing the same effect which I would not want to call assertions. A third reason is that the proposed essential effect makes reference to another speech act—the rejection of an assertion,[9] which presumably cannot be explained independently of assertion.

Our proposed effect is clearly not a sufficient condition for assertion. Is it even a necessary condition? It might be objected that a person who makes an assertion does not necessarily intend to get his audience to accept that what he asserts is true. The objector might argue as follows: Take one of your own examples, your statement to O'Leary that he is a fool. You knew in advance that O'Leary would not accept the assertion so according to your account, you knew in advance that your assertion would fail

to achieve its essential effect. That example should be anomalous if your account were correct, but it is not anomalous. Would it not be more plausible to characterize assertion as trying to get the audience to accept THAT THE SPEAKER ACCEPTS the content of the assertions?[10] But this Gricean twist is not required. My suggestion about the essential effect of assertion does not imply that speakers INTEND to succeed in getting the addressee to accept the content of the assertion, or that they believe they will, or even might succeed. A person may make an assertion knowing it will be rejected just as Congress may pass a law knowing it will be vetoed, a labor negotiator may make a proposal knowing it will be met by a counterproposal, or a poker player may place a bet knowing it will cause all the other players to fold. Such actions need not be pointless, since they all have secondary effects, and there is no reason why achieving the secondary effects cannot be the primary intention of the agent performing the action. The essential effects will still be relevant even when it is a foregone conclusion that the assertion, legislative act, proposal, or bet will be rejected, since one generally explains why the action has the secondary effects it has partly in terms of the fact that it would have had certain essential effects had it not been rejected.

One may think of a nondefective conversation as a game where the common context set is the playing field and the moves are either attempts to reduce the size of the set in certain ways or rejections of such moves by others. The participants have a common interest in reducing the size of the set, but their interests may diverge when it comes to the question of how it should be reduced. The overall point of the game will of course depend on what kind of conversation it is—for example, whether it is an exchange of information, an argument, or a briefing.

The game could be expanded by introducing other kinds of moves like making stipulations, temporary assumptions, or promise; asking question; and giving commands and permissions.[11] Each of these kinds of linguistic action is presumably performed against a background of presuppositions, and can be understood partly in terms of the effect that it has, or is intended to have, on the presuppositions, and on the subsequent behavior, of the other participants in the conversation.

This is a very abstract, and a very simple, sketch of what goes on when someone says something to someone else. But there is enough in it to motivate some principles that are useful for explaining regularities of linguistic usage. I will mention three such rules which illustrate the interaction of context and content. Given the framework of propositions, presupposition, and assertion, the principles are all pretty obvious, which is as it should be. They are not intended as empirical generalizations about how particular languages or idiosyncratic social practices work. Rather, they are proposed as principles that can be defended as essential conditions of rational communication, as principles to which any rational agent would conform if he were engaged in a practice that fits the kind of very abstract and schematic sketch of communication that I have given.[12]

I will list the three principles and then discuss them in turn.

1. A proposition asserted is always true in some but not all of the possible worlds in the context set.
2. Any assertive utterance should express a proposition, relative to each possible world in the context set, and that proposition should have a truth-value in each possible world in the context set.
3. The same proposition is expressed relative to each possible world in the context set.

The first principle says that a speaker should not assert what he presupposes to be true, or what he presupposes to be false. Given the meaning of presupposition and the essential effect ascribed to the act of assertion, this should be clear. To assert something incompatible with what is presupposed is self-defeating; one wants to reduce the context set, but not to eliminate it altogether. And to assert something which is already presupposed is to attempt to do something that is already done.

This rule, like the others, can be applied in several ways. If one could fix independently what was presupposed and what was said on a given occasion, then one could use the rule to

evaluate the speaker's action. If he failed to conform the rule, then he did something that, from the point of view of the conversation, was unreasonable, inefficient, disorderly, or uncooperative. But one can also use the rule, or the presumption that the speaker is conforming to the rule, as evidence of what was presupposed, or of what was said. Perhaps as more than just evidence. The rules may be taken to define partially what is presupposed and what is said in a context by constraining the relation between them. So, if a speaker says something that admits of two interpretations, one compatible with the context set and one not, then the context, through the principle, disambiguates. If the speaker says something that seems prima facie to be trivial, one may take it as a clue that the speaker's context set is larger than was realized—that the context was defective—or one may look for another interpretation of what he said. There are thus three ways to react to an apparent violation of the rule: First, one may conclude that the context is not as it seems. Second, one may conclude that the speaker didn't say (or didn't mean) what he seemed to say (or to mean). Third, one may conclude that the rule was indeed violated. Since there is usually a lot of flexibility in both the context and the interpretation of what is said, the third reaction will be an unusual one, although it will not be unusual to use the rule to explain why some utterance would have been deviant if it had occurred in a given context.

The second principle concerns truth-value gaps, and connects semantic presupposition with pragmatic speaker presupposition. The principle implies that if a sentence x semantically presupposes a proposition φ (in the sense that x expresses a truth or a falsehood only if φ is true), then φ is presupposed by the speaker in the sense of presupposition discussed above.

There are two different ways that a truth-value gap may arise: a sentence may fail to express a proposition at all in some possible situation, or it may succeed in expressing a proposition, but express one that is a PARTIAL function—one that is undefined for certain possible worlds. Both kinds of truth-value gap are excluded from the context set by this rule.

The rationale for this rule is as follows: The point of an assertion is to reduce the context set in a certain determinate way. But if the proposition is not true or false at some possible world, then it would be unclear whether that possible world is to be included in the reduced set or not. So the intentions of the speaker will be unclear.

Again this principle can be used in any of the three ways: to interpret what is said, as a clue to what is presupposed, or as a basis for evaluating the action of a speaker.

The third principle, which says that an utterance must express the SAME proposition relative to each possible world in the context set, is closely related in its motivation to a fundamental assumption of the logical atomists and the logical empiricist tradition. In Wittgenstein's terminology the assumption is this: Whether a proposition (read: sentence) has sense cannot depend on whether another proposition is true (cf. *Tractatus,* Proposition 2.0211). Meaning and truth must be sharply divided, according to this tradition, in order that one be able to use language to communicate in a determinate way. One must be able to tell what a statement says independently of any facts that might be relevant to determining its truth. Now it has always been clear that this kind of principle requires qualification, since it is a matter of fact that words mean what they mean. And the phenomena of context-dependence are evidence of other ways in which what is said is a function of what is true. The framework of presupposition and assertion at once provides a natural way to qualify this traditional assumption so as to make it compatible with the phenomena, and a clear explanation of why it must hold in the qualified version. To see why the principle must hold, look at the matrix for the propositional concept D. Suppose the context set consists of i, j and k, and the speaker's utterance determines D. What would he be asking his audience to do? Something

D	i	j	k
i	T	T	T
j	F	F	T
k	F	T	T

like this: If we are in the world i, leave the context set the same; if we are in world j, throw out worlds i and j, and if we are in world k, throw out just world i. But of course the audience does not know which of those worlds we are in, and if it did, the assertion would be pointless. So the statement, made in that context, expresses an intention that is essentially ambiguous. Notice that the problem is not that the speaker's utterance has failed to determine a unique proposition. Assuming that one of the worlds i, j or k is in fact the actual world, then that world will fix the proposition unambiguously. The problem is that since it is unknown which proposition it is that is expressed, the expression of it cannot do the job that it is supposed to do.[13]

As with the other principles, one may respond to apparent violations in different ways. One could take an apparent violation as evidence that the speaker's context set was smaller than it was thought to be, and eliminate possible worlds relative to which the utterance receives a divergent interpretation. Or, one could reinterpret the utterance so that it expresses the same proposition in each possible world. Consider an example: hearing a woman talking in the next room, I tell you, *That is either Zsa Zsa Gabor or Elizabeth Anscombe.* Assuming that both demonstrative pronouns and proper names are rigid designators—terms that refer to the same individual in all possible worlds—this sentence comes out expressing either a necessary truth or a necessary falsehood, depending on whether it is one of the two mentioned women or someone else who is in the next room. Let i be the world in which it is Miss Gabor, j the world in which it is Professor Anscombe, and k a world in which it is someone else, say Tricia Nixon Cox. Now if we try to bring the initial context set into conformity with the third principle by shrinking it, say by throwing out world k, we will bring it into conflict with the first principle by making the assertion trivial. But if we look at what is actually going on in the example, if we ask what possible states of affairs the speaker would be trying to exclude from the context set if he made that statement, we can work backward to the proposition expressed. A moment's reflection shows that what the speaker is saying is that the actual world is either i or j, and not k. What he means to communicate is that the diagonal proposition of the matrix *E* exhibited below, the proposition expressed by †*E*, is true.

E	*i*	*j*	*k*
i	T	T	T
j	T	T	T
k	F	F	F

†*E*	*i*	*j*	*k*
i	T	T	F
j	T	T	F
k	T	T	F

I suggest that a common way of bringing utterances into conformity with the third principle is to interpret them to express the diagonal proposition, or to perform on them the operation represented by the two-dimensional operator DAGGER. There are lots of examples. Consider: *Hesperus is identical with Phosphorus, it is now three o'clock, an ophthalmologist is an eye doctor.* In each case, to construct a context which conforms to the first principle, a context in which the proposition expressed is neither trivial nor assumed false, one must include possible worlds in which the sentence, interpreted in the standard way, expresses different propositions. But in any plausible context in which one of these sentences might reasonably be used, it is clear that the diagonal proposition is the one that the speaker means to communicate. The two-dimensional operator DAGGER may represent a common operation used to interpret, or reinterpret, assertions and other speech acts so as to bring them into conformity with the third principle constraining acts of assertion.

To conclude, let me show how this last suggestion can help to explain a puzzle concerning singular negative existential statements. The puzzle arises in the context of a causal or historical explanation theory of reference according to which proper names refer to their bearers, not in virtue of the fact that the bearer has certain properties expressed in the sense of the name, but rather in virtue of certain causal or historical connections between the referent and the speaker's use of the name.[14] According to this theory, the PROPOSITION expressed by a simple singular statement containing a proper name, like *O'Leary is a fool,* is the one that is true if and only if the individual who is in fact causally connected in the right way with the speaker's use of the name has the property expressed in the predicate. So the proposition is

determined as a function of the individual named rather than as a function of the name, or the sense of the name.

What does this theory say about statements like *O'Leary does not exist?* If the statement is true (which this one happens to be), then there is no individual appropriately related to the speaker's use of the name, and thus no proposition determined as a function of such an individual. So at least for TRUE negative existential statements, it seems that proper names must play a different role in the determination of the proposition expressed from the role they play in ordinary predicative statements.

Perhaps a negative existential statement says, simply, that there is no individual standing in the right causal relation to the speaker's use of the name.[15] This does seem to get the truth-conditions right for negative existential ASSERTIONS, but it clearly gets them wrong for some other kinds of singular negative existential constructions. Consider, for example, counterfactual suppositions, as in the antecedent of the conditional *If Aristotle hadn't existed, the history of philosophy would have been very different from the way it was.*[16] Clearly the proposition expressed in the antecedent of this conditional is not the proposition that our use of the name *Aristotle* is not appropriately connected with any individual. THAT proposition is compatible with Aristotle's existence. Furthermore, if Aristotle hadn't existed, then our uses of his name probably would not have existed either. The proper name seems to function in the antecedent of the counterfactual more like the way it functions in ordinary predicative statements: The proposition is determined as a function of the PERSON Aristotle; it is true in possible worlds where HE does not exist, and false in possible worlds where HE does exist.

So it seems that not only do proper names act differently in negative existential assertions than they do in singular predicative assertions, they also act differently in negative existential ASSERTIONS than they do in negative existential SUPPOSITIONS. What one asserts when he says *Aristotle does not exist* seems to be different from what one supposes when he says *Suppose Aristotle hadn't existed.*

Let us see how the pragmatic principle can account for these facts. Begin with the most straightforward semantic account of negative existential constructions: *Aristotle does not exist,* like *Aristotle was wise,* is a proposition about Aristotle. It is false in possible worlds whose domains contain the person WE call Aristotle and true in possible worlds whose domains do not contain that person. What if the name does not, in fact, refer? Suppose, for example, the statement is *Sherlock Holmes does not exist.* Then the proposition will be necessarily true, by the same rule, since the domain of no possible world contains the actual person we call Sherlock Holmes.[17] Now let us use this straightforward semantic account to construct a propositional concept for an utterance of *Sherlock Holmes does not exist.* Let the world *i* be the actual world. Let *j* be a world in which a famous detective named *Sherlock Holmes* lived in nineteenth-century London, and Sir Arthur Conan Doyle wrote a series of historical accounts of his cases. Let world *k* be a possible world in which Sir Arthur Conan Doyle was a famous detective named *Sherlock Holmes* who wrote a series of autobiographical accounts of his own cases under the pseudonym *Sir Arthur Conan Doyle.* These stipulations determine the following two-dimensional matrix for the utterance:

G	i	j	k
i	T	T	T
j	T	F	T
k	F	F	F

Now suppose *i, j* and *k* are a context set (say a person has heard these three rumors about the origin of the Sherlock Holmes stories and does not know which is true). As the matrix shows, the utterance violates the third principle, and so a reinterpretation is forced on it. Diagonalization, or the dagger operation, brings the utterance into line with the principle, and yields the intuitively right result:

	i	j	k
i	T	F	F
j	T	F	F
k	T	F	F

But now contrast the case of the counterfactual. To interpret the statement *If Aristotle hadn't existed, the history of philosophy would have been very different from the way it was,* we do not need to diagonalize, since in any possible context appropriate to THAT statement, it will be presupposed that Aristotle does exist. So the proposition supposed is the one obtained by the straightforward rule.[18] Again, this is intuitively the right result.

We have not escaped the conclusion that the content of the assertion *Aristotle did not exist* is different from the content of the supposition *suppose Aristotle hadn't existed.* But we have explained that consequence using a single SEMANTIC account of singular negative existential constructions—the account which is most natural, given the causal theory of names—together with independently motivated pragmatic principles.

The general strategy which this explanation illustrates is to use pragmatic theory—theory of conversational contexts—to take some of the weight of semantic and syntactic theory. Some other problems where I think this strategy and this theory will prove useful are the explanation of presupposition phenomena,[19] the explanation of the differences between subjunctive and indicative conditionals,[20] the analysis of definite descriptions, and the behaviour of deictic and anaphoric pronouns. My hope is that by recognizing the interaction of some relatively simple contextual factors with the rules for interpreting and evaluating utterances, one can defend simpler semantic and grammatical analyses and give more natural explanations of many linguistic phenomena.

ACKNOWLEDGMENT

The development of the ideas in this paper was stimulated by David Kaplan's lectures, some years ago, on the logic of demonstratives. The influence of Paul Grice's ideas about logic and conversation will also be evident. I have benefited from discussions of earlier versions of this paper with both of these philosophers and many others, including David Lewis, Zeno Vendler, and Edmund Gettier. I am indebted to the John Simon Guggenheim Memorial Foundation for research support.

NOTES

1. I argued in Stalnaker (1976) that one can take possible worlds seriously without accepting an implausible metaphysics.

2. The possible worlds analysis of propositions was suggested originally by Saul Kripke in the early 1960s.

3. I recognize that I am skating quickly over large problems here. In particular, the identity conditions which the analysis assigns to propositions have some extremely paradoxical consequences (such as that there is only one necessary proposition) which seem to make the analysis particularly unsuited for an account of the objects of propositional attitudes. I discuss some of these problems, inconclusively, in Stalnaker (1976).

4. The most general discussion of two-dimensional modal logic I know of is in Segerberg (1973). See also Aqvist (1973) and Kamp (1971). The earliest investigations of two-dimensional operators were, I believe, carried out in the context of tense logic by Frank Vlach and Hans Kamp at UCLA.

5. The tense logic analogue of the dagger operator was, according to David Lewis, invented by Frank Vlach and is discussed in his UCLA PhD dissertation (Vlach 1973). The notation is Lewis's. See Lewis (1973: 63–4n).

6. Another operator which has intuitive application is represented by Lewis as an upside-down dagger. What it does is to project the diagonal proposition onto the *vertical,* which, in effect, turns contingent truths into necessary truths and contingent falsehoods into necessary falsehoods. Hans Kamp (1971) proposed the temporal analogue of this operator as a representative of the sentence adverb *now. It is now true that A* said at time *t* expresses a proposition that is true at all times just in case *A* is true at *t*. The operator makes a difference when *now* is embedded in the context of other temporal modifiers. Using it, one can represent sentences like *Once, everyone now alive hadn't yet been born* without object language quantifiers over times. David Lewis and David Kaplan have suggested that this operator shows the semantic function of expressions like *actually* and *in fact,* as in *If I had more money than I in fact have, I would be happier.*

7. Although the dagger and the upside-down dagger are defined on propositional concepts, they can be generalized to any kind of two-dimensional intension. For example, they may be interpreted as operators on two-dimensional individual concepts, or on property concepts. Let *a* represent a definite description, say *the President of the United States,* and let *i, j* and *k* be three times, say 1967, 1971 and 1975. Matrix (i) below represents the two-dimensional intension of this definite description relative to these times. Matrix (ii) represents the rigid description, *the person who is in fact, or now, the President of the United States.* This is the two-dimensional intension of ⬇*a.* David Kaplan (Kaplan 1989) discusses this operator on singular terms and compares it with Keith Donnellan's account of the referential use of definite descriptions.

(i)

	i	*j*	*k*
i	LJ	RN	GF
j	LJ	RN	GF
k	LJ	RN	GF

(ii)

	i	*j*	*k*
i	LJ	LJ	LJ
j	RN	RN	RN
k	GF	GF	GF

8. I have discussed this concept of presupposition in two earlier papers, Stalnaker (1977) and "Pragmatic Presuppositions." Stephen Schiffer (Schiffer 1972: 30–42) and David Lewis (Lewis 1969: 52–60) have discussed concepts of mutual knowledge and common knowledge which resemble the notion of presupposition I have in mind. Paul Grice spoke, in the William James Lectures, of propositions having *common ground status* in a conversation (Grice 1989).

9. It should be made clear that to reject an assertion is not to assert or assent to the contradictory of the assertion, but only to refuse to accept the assertion. If an assertion is rejected, the context remains the same as it was. (More exactly, rejection of an assertion blocks the *second* kind of effect that assertions have on the context. The first kind of effect cannot be blocked or withdrawn.)

10. David Kaplan, in discussion, raised this objection.

11. David Lewis (1979) outlined a language game of commanding and permitting which would fit into this framework.

12. The influence of Grice's theory of conversation should be clear from my discussion of the application of these principles.

13. Clarification is needed to resolve an ambiguity. The third principle says that the proposition expressed in any possible world in the context set must coincide *within the context set* with the proposition expressed in any other possible world in the context set. So, for example, if the context set is {*i, j*}, then an utterance determining the propositional concept represented below will not violate the principle. Even though the proposition expressed in *i* diverges from the proposition expressed in *j,* the divergence is outside the context set. David Lewis pointed out the need for this clarification.

	i	j	k
i	T	F	T
j	T	F	F
k	F	T	T

14. The causal account of reference is defended, in general in Kripke (1972) and Donnellan (1971). Donnellan (1974) discusses the problem of singular negative existential statements in the context of this account of reference.

15. Donnellan's explanation of the *truth-conditions* for singular negative existential statements is roughly in accord with this suggestion, but he cautions that the rule he proposes "does not provide an *analysis* of such statements; it does not tell us what such statements mean, or what propositions they express. This means that in this case we are divorcing truth-conditions from meaning" (Donnellan 1974: 25). According to Donnellan, "no obvious way of representing propositions expressed by existential statements suggests itself" (ibid. 30).

16. Kripke, in talks on this subject, has made this point about counterfactuals with negative existential antecedents.

17. I believe this straightforward semantic account is the one that Kripke has defended in the talks mentioned in note 16.

18. It is interesting to note that if the conditional were in the indicative mood, the result would have been different. This is because an indicative conditional is appropriate only in a context where it is an open question whether the antecedent is true. So to say *If Aristotle didn't exist* is to suppose just what is asserted when one asserts *Aristotle didn't exist.*

19. This is discussed in Stalnaker (1977).

20. This is discussed in Stalnaker (1975).

REFERENCES

Aqvist, L. (1973). Modal logic with subjunctive conditionals and dispositional predicates, *Journal of Philosophical Logic* 2:1–76.

Donnellan, K. (1971). Proper names and identifying descriptions, in D. Davidson and G. Harman (eds.), *Semantics of Natural Language*, D. Reidel Publishing Co., Dordrecht, 356–79.

_____. (1974). Speaking of nothing, *Philosophical Review* 83: 3–31.

Grice, P. (1989). *Studies in the Way of Words*, Harvard University Press, Cambridge, Mass.

Kamp, H. (1971). Formal properties of "now", *Theoria* 37: 227–73.

Kaplan, D. (1989). Demonstratives, in J. Almog et al. (eds), *Themes from Kaplan*, Oxford University Press, Oxford, 481–563.

Kripke, S. (1972). *Naming and Necessity*, Harvard University Press, Cambridge, Mass.

Lewis, D. (1969). *Convention*, Harvard University Press, Cambridge, Mass.

_____. (1973). *Counterfactuals*, Harvard University Press, Cambridge, Mass.

_____. (1979). A problem about permission, in E. Saarinen et al. (eds.), *Essays in Honor of Jaakko Hintikka*, Reidel, Dordrecht, 163–75.

Schiffer, S. (1972). *Meaning*, Clarendon Press, Oxford.

Segerberg, K. (1973). Two-dimensional modal logic, *Journal of Philosophical Logic* 2:77–96.

Stalnaker, R. (1974). "Pragmatic presuppositions," in M. K. Munitz and Peter Unger, (eds.), *Semantics and Philosophy*, New York University Press, New York, 197–213.

_____. (1975). Indicative conditionals, *Philosophia* 5: 269–86.

_____. (1976). Possible worlds, *Nous* 10: 65–75.

_____. (1977). Presuppositions, *Journal of Philosophical Logic*, 447–57.

_____. (1981). Indexical Belief, *Synthese* 49: 129–51.

_____. (1984). *Inquiry*, Bradford Books, MIT Press, Cambridge, Mass.

_____. (1988). Belief Attribution and Context, in R. Grimm and D. Merrill, (eds.), *Contents of Thought* U. of Arizona Press, Tucson, 140–156.

Vlach, F. (1973). *"Now" and "Then". A formal study on the logic of tense anaphora*, PhD thesis, University of California, Los Angeles, Calif.

SUGGESTED FURTHER READING

Austin, J. L., *Philosophical Essays*, ed. J. O. Urmson and G. J. Warnock (London: Oxford University Press, 1970).

Austin, J. L., *How to Do Things with Words*, 2d ed., ed. J. O. Urmson and Marina Sbisa (Cambridge: Harvard University Press, 1975).

Bach, K., "Conversational Impliciture," *Mind and Language* 9 (1994): 124–162.

Bach, K., "The Myth of Conventional Implicature," *Linguistics and Philosophy* 22 (1999): 327–366.

Davis, Steven, "Perlocutions," *Linguistics and Philosophy* 3 (1979): 225–243.

Davis, Steven, ed., *Pragmatics: A Reader* (New York: Cambridge University Press, 1991).

Fotion, Nick, *John Searle* (Princeton: Princeton University Press, 2000).

Geach, Peter, "Assertion," *Philosophical Review* 74 (1965): 449–465.

Ginet, Carl, "Performativity," *Linguistics and Philosophy* 3 (1979): 245–265.

Grice, H. P., "Further Notes on Logic and Conversation," in *Syntax and Semantics: Pragmatics,* vol. 7, ed. Peter Cole (New York: Academic Press, 1978), pp. 113–127.

Harnish, Robert, ed., *Basic Topics in the Philosophy of Language* (Englewood Cliffs, N.J.: Prentice-Hall, 1994).

Holdcroft, David, *Words and Deeds* (London: Clarendon Press, 1978).

Kartunnen, Lauri and Stanley Peters, "Conventional Implicature," in *Syntax and Semantics*, vol. 11, ed. Choon-Kyu Oh and David A. Dinneen (New York: Academic Press, 1979), pp. 1–56.

Lewis, David, "Scorekeeping in a Language Game," *Journal of Philosophical Logic* 8 (1979): 339–359.

Martinich, A. P., "Conversational Maxims and Some Philosophical Problems," *Philosophical Quarterly* 30 (1980): 215–228.

Martinich, A. P., "A Pragmatic Solution to the Liar Paradox," *Philosophical Studies* 43 (1982): 63–67.

Martinich, A. P., *Communication and Reference* (Berlin and New York: Walter de Gruyter, 1984).

Martinich, A. P., "John Searle," in *Companion to Analytic Philosophy,* ed. A. P. Martinich and David Sosa (Oxford: Blackwell Publishers, 2001).

Searle, John, "Austin on Locutionary and Illocutionary Acts," *Philosophical Review* 77 (1968): 405–424.

Searle, John, *Speech Acts* (Cambridge: Cambridge University Press, 1969).

Searle, John, *Expression and Meaning* (Cambridge: Cambridge University Press, 1979).

Searle, John, *Intentionality* (Cambridge: Cambridge University Press, 1983).

Stalnaker, Robert, "Pragmatics," in *Semantics of Natural Language,* ed. Gilbert Harman and Donald Davidson (Dordrecht: D. Reidel, 1972), pp. 380–397.

Strawson, P. F. "Intention and Convention in Speech Acts," *Philosophical Review* 73 (1964): 439–460.

Vanderveken, Daniel, *Meaning and Speech Acts,* 2 vols. (Cambridge: Cambridge University Press, 1990).

Vendler, Zeno, *Res Cogitans* (Ithaca: Cornell University Press, 1972).

III | REFERENCE AND DESCRIPTIONS

There is a long philosophical tradition according to which the basic structure of language and the basic structure of reality are the same. The basic linguistic structure is supposed to be that of subjects and predicates while the basic ontological structure is supposed to be particulars and universals. Although these issues were treated in the main introduction of this book, a brief review is worthwhile.

Consider the sentence

Socrates is wise.

It can be divided into two parts: "Socrates" and "is wise." "Socrates" is the subject and "is wise" is the predicate. The function of "Socrates" and of subject expressions generally, according to this long tradition, is to refer to, pick out, or identify a particular object, in this case the man Socrates. Always, or at least typically, particular objects are individual things that have a position within space and time. So it makes sense to say that Socrates lived in Athens in the fifth century B.C. The function of "is wise" is to express or designate the property of being wise. Properties are things that particulars have and can share with other particulars. Thus, Socrates shares the property of being wise with Plato, Aristotle, and all the other wise human beings who ever lived. Because properties can be shared, they are sometimes called "universals." Thus there is an asymmetry between subjects and predicates. Socrates is one thing; he is not shared by other things; but being wise is shared by many particulars.

As it stands, our explanation of the functions of subjects and predicates is inadequate because it does not give any indication of the purpose of referring or predicating. What is their point? One can understand this only by understanding the function of subject/predicate sentences as a whole; their function is categorization. To categorize something physically is to group objects into different types or sorts. If one sorts coins, then one sorts all the pennies together, all the nickels together, all the dimes together, and so on. One might put each kind of coin into a box or container of some kind. Subject/predicate sentences have the function of mentally or conceptually categorizing things. Subject expressions denote individual objects, like individual coins, and locate them in the category expressed by the predicate, like the containers used for sorting coins. The function of "Socrates is wise," then, is to refer to Socrates for the purpose of categorizing him as having the property of being wise. If he fits into that category, then the statement is true. If he does not fit into that category, then the statement is false.

Of the two terms, 'subject' has exercised philosophers more. The reason is that philosophers have traditionally been concerned with whether anything that humans believe or say is true; and if anything is true then, it seems, language must somehow attach to the world.

Further, language attaches to the world through the relation of reference which holds between subjects and particulars. Although this claim appears to solve a problem, it actually creates many. One of the most basic is the Paradox of Reference and Existence:

(1) Everything referred to must exist.
(2) 'Hamlet' refers to Hamlet.
(3) Hamlet does not exist.

These three propositions are inconsistent because (1) and (2) entail

(3′) Hamlet exists.

which contradicts (3). Although most nonphilosophers would try to resolve the paradox by denying (1), most philosophers hold that (1) is true. They take this position because if it were possible to refer to things that did not exist, then reference could not guarantee that language attached to reality. Frege, Russell, and Strawson all agree that it is (2) that is false. The various explanations for why (2) is false are ingenious, if not always plausible.

According to Frege, (2) is false just because (1) and (3) are true. The reason that people think that (2) is true is that they confuse two kinds of meaning: sense (*Sinn*) and reference (*Bedeutung*). The sense of a word is the descriptive content that in effect gives a language user the wherewithal to pick out the referent. The *Sinn* or descriptive content for a proper name, like any meaningful word, has to be something that is shared by speaker and hearer. If a *Sinn* were not shared, communication would be impossible. (See the introduction for Section VIII, "The Nature of Language.") Frege recognizes that the primary way in which one person grasps a *Sinn* may differ from the primary way in which another person grasps it. For example, one person may grasp the *Sinn* of 'the morning star' as the brightest object in the morning sky, excluding the sun and moon, while another person may grasp the same *Sinn* as the last object, excluding the sun and moon, to disappear in the morning. Consequently, Frege holds that the *Sinn* of proper names is disjunctive. The *Sinn* of 'the morning star' being something like the *brightest star in the morning sky, excluding the sun and moon, or the last object, excluding the sun and moon, to disappear in the morning.* Other names, such as 'Plato' and 'Aristotle' will have even more elaborate *Sinne* because people primarily grasp those objects in many more ways than 'the morning star' is. For names associated with many descriptions, each disjunctive element may be given a weight, and the referent would be the object with the highest score of descriptive accuracy.

The distinction between *Sinn* and *Bedeutung* gives Frege a neat solution to the puzzle about identity statements when combined with one additional concept: The cognitive significance of a sentence is the combination of the sentence's *Sinn* and *Bedeutung*. The sentence

The morning star = the morning star

is trivial and uninformative because both the *Sinn* and *Bedeutung* of both terms flanking the '=' sign are identical. In contrast, the sentence,

The morning star = the evening star

is nontrivial and informative because, even though the *Bedeutung* of each term is the same, the *Sinn* of 'the morning star' is different from the *Sinn* of 'the evening star'. If we now add the concept of cognitive significance, that is, the combination of *Sinn* and *Bedeutung,* we can say that the difference between trivial identity statements and non-trivial ones is due to the difference in their cognitive significance.

The word translated as 'proposition' in "On Sense and Nominatum" is '*Gedanke*', which is translated as 'thought' in Frege's article, "The Thought," in Section I.

Let's now briefly consider how Russell would explain the falsity of (2). For him, 'Hamlet' does not refer (i.e., directly denote), because 'Hamlet', like all other ordinary proper names, whether of real or unreal objects, is a disguised or abbreviated description and not a genuine proper name. 'Hamlet' might be an abbreviation for 'The Danish prince who killed his uncle, who was married to widowed mother'. This description is not true of any object because (3) is true.

Although P. F. Strawson differs from Russell on many important matters, their views about ordinary proper names are similar insofar as Strawson thinks that proper names are "backed" by descriptions. In other respects, Strawson's account diverges from Russell's in important ways. For Strawson, it is people, not words or phrases, that primarily refer. (In his "Mr. Strawson on Referring," Russell in effect replied that talk about what a speaker does in using language has to do with psychology, not philosophy.) Also, since 'Hamlet' is a genuine proper name, a speaker may try to use it to refer, according to Strawson, but will fail to refer because (3) is true. Consequently, the speaker will fail to make a statement or express a proposition, and so there will be nothing to which a truth-value might be attached. In 1950, Strawson was not completely clear about this aspect of his theory, and so he expressed the point misleadingly by saying that when reference fails, "the question of whether [the speaker's] . . . statement was true or false simply *did not arise.*" Later he became clear that the failure to refer to something would result in no statement at all.

When "On Referring" was reprinted in *Essays in Conceptual Analysis* (ed. Antony Flew [1956]), Strawson added a few footnotes that qualified some of his positions. In the first one, he said that he regretted describing the use of definite descriptions in fiction as a "spurious" use, and added that he now preferred to call these uses 'secondary' ones. Later in the article, he expresses his wish to change the sentence, "Hence we can, using significant expressions, pretend to refer, in make-believe or in fiction, or mistakenly think we are referring when we are not referring to anything" to read as follows: "Hence we can, using significant expressions, refer in secondary ways, as in make-believe or in fiction, or mistakenly think we are referring to something in the primary way when we are not, in that way, referring to anything." These changes suggest that by 1956 Strawson started taking fictional uses more seriously than he had in 1950. However, there are two problems with his changes. First, given that he subscribes to the Axiom of Existence, what kind of existence should he think fictional objects have? Would he hold that it would be an existence that would correlate with the "secondary use" of language, that is, a secondary existence, like "subsistence," which would be intermediate between existence and nonexistence? If he did, then he would be subject to the Russellian objection that to say that fictional objects have a secondary existence is a pitiful or paltry evasion. Second, the phrase, 'secondary use,' remains somewhat pejorative, like a second-class citizen.

The problem in my opinion is the Axiom of Existence, which Frege, Russell, Strawson, and almost every other philosopher of language subscribes to. I think that axiom is straightforwardly false because so far as the use of language is concerned, referring to nonexistent objects is the same as referring to existent ones, and, as a linguistic act, no more difficult to do. In each case, the speaker uses some word or phrase either to introduce an object into discourse or to continue discussing an object already introduced. And since the introduction is linguistic, the presence of the object is not required. To see this clearly, it is helpful to give a brief and simplified rational reconstruction of how various objects get introduced into discourse during the course of language-learning and then to contrast that with how a language, already learned, introduces objects. When language-learning begins, the first things that parents talk to toddlers about and about which the toddler can talk are existent objects within the sensible environment of both. At the second stage, the speaker and hearer can talk about existent objects, previously experienced and talked about, that are not currently present. At the third stage, the speaker and hearer can talk about no longer existent objects that were once experienced by both the speaker and hearer. At the fourth stage, the speaker can talk about objects she has experienced that the hearer has not; and it does not matter whether these objects are existent now or not. At this stage, descriptive phrases are used to introduce objects (and also proper names). For example, a parent may say, "Great grandmother Helen would have loved to see you," to a child who has never seen the grandmother and never will. At the fifth stage, the speaker and hearer can talk about objects that never existed, and it does not matter whether they are objects that will someday exist ('your future grandchild') or never will exist ('Pegasus'). The speaker introduces such objects in exactly the same way that she did in the fourth stage, linguistically. To move from an earlier to a later stage requires only a little imagination, and it is not necessary to go through every intermediate stage to get to the fifth one.

It is no good for someone to object that sentences of the form, '*S* refers to *O* with name or description *D*', only make sense if there are values, that is, existent objects, for *O;* for that objection begs the question. The Axiom of Existence looses its point once an account is given of how reference can occur in the absence of an existent object. However, it may be helpful to add another element.

Reference, whether to real or fictional objects, must combine with predication to express propositions; and propositions are true or false. Consequently, if reference to fictional objects occurs, it must occur as part of a proposition, and hence there must be ways of evaluating such propositions as true or false. And there are. The sentence, 'Conan Doyle referred to Sherlock Holmes with the name "Sherlock Holmes"', would be true if in *The Adventures of Sherlock Holmes,* Arthur Conan Doyle wrote, "Sherlock Holmes lit his pipe." Some philosophical theories of fiction claim that every speech act about fiction should be understood as prefaced by a fiction-operator such as 'in fiction' or 'According to Conan Doyle in *The Adventures of Sherlock Holmes*'. I think these theories misrepresent the function of the phrases in question. Those phrases operate in the same way that 'According to the Magna Carta' or 'According to the Bill of Rights of the American Constitution', or 'According to *A Thousand Days*', namely, they indicate where one is to go for the evidence to evaluate the propositional content of the sentence.

So far as the understanding and evaluation of statements and other speech acts is concerned, there is no difference between some ancient history and fiction. In both cases, often the only evidence is the primary sources, texts. I am not espousing linguistic idealism. I am not claiming that there is nothing outside the text. I am not saying that what makes a proposition true in general is another text. If someone claims 'Caesar crossed the Rubicon', then what makes it true is the fact that Caesar crossed the Rubicon; but the best evidence for that fact are certain ancient manuscripts. Similarly, if the narrator of Albert Camus's *The Stranger* says, "Mother died today; or maybe yesterday. I really can't be sure," the best evidence of that is some text. I will not say what makes a fictional statement true; the issue is too difficult and not to the point. We assume that it is a fact that some statements in and about fiction are true, and construct a theory of reference consistent with that fact.

As a kind of intentional activity, talking only requires intentional objects. Sometimes the intentional object exists and sometimes it does not; sometimes the intentional object once existed and no longer does, and sometimes the object never did and never will.

Let's now return to the issue that began this discussion, Strawson's claim that talk about fiction is a "secondary" use of language. As my rational reconstruction indicated, talk about nonexistent objects, of which fictional objects are the salient kind, is secondary to talk about existent objects. But this is a point about language learning, not about the use of language learned. Once learned, talk about existent objects has no priority over talk about nonexistent objects. To think it does is to commit the genetic fallacy.

A distinction is sometimes drawn between real-world talk and fictional talk. In his stories about Sherlock Holmes, Conan Doyle used fictional, not real-world, talk to talk about Sherlock Holmes. (And I have already conceded that fictional talk in general is dependent on real life talk in general.) But when we, Conan Doyle's readers and critics, talk about Sherlock Holmes, we are not talking fictional talk. We are engaging in real-world talk to talk about a fictional object. And this real-world talk is logically dependent on Conan Doyle's fictional talk, because if he had not created the character in fiction, then we could not be talking about him now. So some real-world talk is logically dependent on fiction. In other words, some real-world talk is "secondary" to some fictional talk.

One last point on this topic. Fictional talk, talk about fiction, and real-world talk cannot be effectively segregated from each other. Real people, places, and things are talked about in fictional talk; this happens most conspicuously in historical fiction, but it also occurs in most fiction that would not be categorized as historical, such as any novel with a contemporary setting. Tom Wolfe wrote one novel about the real New York and one about the real Atlanta, Georgia; it contained many fictional characters, but some real people too. Since we have already seen that fictional characters exist in real-world talk, let's end by pointing out that real objects and fictional objects can be compared and contrasted in the same sentence: The presidential candidate in Jeremy Larner's *The Candidate* had much more integrity than Bill Clinton. Not only can we understand this sentence; we can know it is true.

I have been discussing the issue of how language attaches to the world by discussing the Paradox of Reference and Existence. Another aspect of this issue concerns the question of whether language attaches directly (immediately) to the world or whether it attaches indirectly (mediately). Russell says 'directly'; Frege and Strawson say 'indirectly'. One reason that Russell says 'directly' is that he wants to avoid skepticism. If the connection between the mental world of a human being and the nonmental world is indirect, then, Russell thinks, one can never be sure that what one is in fact referring to is the thing that one thinks one is referring to. A person may want to connect with reality at one point and unwittingly connect with it at a different point. Any mediating element, according to this view, has the potential of going awry or otherwise failing. (On the concept of intermediaries in philosophy, see Avrum Stroll, *Surfaces* [Minneapolis: University of Minnesota Press, 1988], pp. 152–159.) This is why Descartes thinks his 'cogito' avoids skepticism. Since nothing stands between a thinker and her thinking, a thinker cannot be mistaken about her existence as a thinker.

Similarly, Russell's distinction between the way proper names attach to reality, to wit, directly, and the way descriptions do when they do, to wit, indirectly, is grounded in a more basic epistemic distinction between knowledge by acquaintance, which is required for the use of genuine proper names, and knowledge by description, which is sufficient for the use of definite descriptions.

Although it is not immediately evident, even descriptions end up having words directly connected with their meanings. For example, the sentence, 'The king of France is wise' may be analyzed as 'There exists an object x such that x reigns malely over France and for all y if y reigns malely over France, then x is identical with y'. All the predicative or relational general words in this sentence ('reigns', 'malely', and 'is identical with') directly denote their meanings, namely, concepts or universals. Other words ('and' and 'if . . . , then') denote other general objects, truth-functions. (I assume 'France' is a logically proper name and am silent about quantifiers and variables, as Russell largely is.)

In contrast with Russell, proper names attach indirectly to reality according to Frege and Strawson. For Frege, *Sinn* mediates between the name and the referent, although he does hold that the mind is in direct contact with *Sinne*. For Strawson, as we said, proper names have to be "backed" by some descriptions that help the hearer pick out the object the speaker intends the hearer to pick out. When he says, "There are no logically proper names," he means that Russell is wrong to think that proper names denote their objects immediately and without the help of some descriptive content (Section I of "On Referring"). When he goes on to assert that "there are no descriptions (in this sense)," he means that *pace* Russell descriptions do not assert the existence of the things they are used to refer to; rather, the existence of the referent is presupposed.

Although Russell and Strawson are seemingly diametrically opposed, Keith Donnellan tries to effect an Hegelian-like synthesis of their views. They are both right and both wrong, and he has something better to offer that incorporates what is correct in his predecessors. For, according to Donnellan, there are two uses of descriptions, where Russell and Strawson saw only one. Russell focused on "the attributive use," while Strawson focused on "the referential use." Donnellan himself is particularly interested in the referential use, which is the same as or very close to the way proper names are used. Whether Donnellan is right depends crucially on the propriety of the distinction between attributive and referential uses.

Distinctions can be introduced in one or both of two different ways: by characterization and by examples. To characterize a distinction is to specify some property in virtue of which the distinction obtains. For example, there are two kinds of propositions: Atomic sentences are those of which no proper part is a sentence. Molecular sentences are all the others. In this example, the property of *having no proper part that is a sentence* is the characterizing property. Only one such property is needed and appropriate. If two properties were used, say, one to characterize atomic sentences and another to characterize molecular sentences, then there would be the risk of ending up with an improper distinction: There may be some things that have both properties or some with none. Sometimes a characterizing property can be broken into two parts. For example, suppose that our universe of discourse includes only human beings, and we define a bachelor as someone who is an unmarried, adult male. In this case, the one characterizing property of *being an unmarried, adult male* can be broken down into three parts (*being unmarried, being adult,* and *being male*). Nonetheless, the characterizing property is the one formed by the conjunction of the three simpler properties.

The other way of introducing a distinction is by examples. Here are two examples of atomic sentences:

Adam is happy,
Beth is rich.

Here are two examples of molecular sentences:

Adam is rich and Beth is happy;
It is not the case that Adam is rich.

One problem with introducing a distinction by examples is that the principle of the distinction is not made clear. So, even if a person develops a facility for recognizing the difference between things of kind K_1 and things of kind K_2, she may not know on what basis she is making the distinction. It is said that people who identify male and female chicks ("chicken-sexers") are virtually infallible but cannot explain how they do it: "It just looks like a female." Another problem, more serious, is that if a person does not know in virtue of what property a distinction is made, more than one property may be operating in making the division. In fact, I believe that Donnellan's distinction suffers in this way. Sometimes the examples that he gives turn on the difference between how many or what kind of beliefs the speaker and hearer have (e.g., the Smith's-murderer scenario and the martini-drinker scenario); and sometimes the examples turn on the desires of the speaker (e.g., the book on the table scenario). While Donnellan explicitly denies that the beliefs of the speaker are a crucial element of the distinction between attributive and referential uses (Section IV of his article), his denial is consistent with my point that sometimes the examples used to establish that there is such a distinction turns on the beliefs of the speaker and sometimes not.

Let's return to the general discussion of distinctions. Sometimes both the method of characterization and the method of examples is used in explaining a distinction, as in this case.

An atomic sentence is a sentence of which no proper part is a sentence, for example, 'Adam is happy' and 'Beth is rich'. A molecular sentence is any nonatomic sentence, for example, 'Adam is rich and Beth is happy'.

Immanuel Kant said that concepts without percepts are empty, and percepts without concepts are blind. Substitute 'characterization' for 'concept' and 'example' for 'percept' and you will see the sense in using both characterization and examples when drawing distinctions. Of course, using both does expose one to the possibility of incoherence; the examples and the characterization may not match. Suppose a prime number is defined as a whole number not divisible by any number without remainder other than by one and by itself, and four is given as the example of a prime number. It is obvious that the example does not fit the characterization. (*Exercise:* Give a different example in which we would be inclined to say that the characterization does not fit the examples.) The reason that the lack of fit between characterization and examples may go undetected in philosophy is that the distinctions (and hence the concepts used in characterizing the distinction) are often not understood clearly. To a large extent, philosophy consists of working toward clarifying basic concepts, and once the concepts become clear, a science is born.

Let's now consider what I take to be some defects in Donnellan's distinction between two uses of definite descriptions. His characterization is as follows: "A speaker who uses a definite description attributively in an assertion states something about whoever or whatever is the so-and-so. A speaker who uses a definite description referentially in a description, on the other hand, uses the description to enable his audience to pick out who or what he is talking about and states something about that person or thing" (Section III of his article). (Actually, this is only a partial characterization, since it applies only to assertions.) Now suppose that two men pass by. The one wearing a red shirt is quite attractive, the other quite unattractive. The speaker says, "The man in the red shirt (whoever he is) is quite attractive." The speaker is using the description 'The man in the red shirt referentially, according to Donnellan, since she intends that description to enable her audience to pick out whom or what she is talking about. However, the speaker is also using the description attributively, since she is talking about that person whoever he is, as the parenthetical phrase indicates. In fact, the function of the phrase 'whoever he is' is to indicate that the speaker has no elaborate knowledge of the object being referred to, and not to indicate a special use of a description. In order to save Donnellan's distinction, some philosophers say that some uses of definite descriptions are both referential and attributive, that is, that the distinction is not a proper one. But that is not Donnellan's view.

The fact that phrases of the form 'whoever x is' has the function of indicating relative absence of knowledge can also be used to show that Donnellan has not successfully associated the referring use of an expression with the way proper names are used. Suppose the winner of a lottery is "Stanislaus Martin" and that he is identified by that name even though he has not yet claimed his prize. Someone might say, "Stanislaus Martin, whoever he is, is the winner." This shows either that there is an attributive use of proper names, contrary to Donnellan's intentions, or that he has failed to characterize the referential use.

There are many other problems, I believe, with the way Donnellan draws his distinction. One is that he does not keep all the elements in his scenarios constant. For example, in the Smith's murderer scenario used to illustrate the referential use, the environment is the scene of the crime, the dramatis personae are only the speaker and the hearer. In the scenario used to illustrate the attributive use, the environment is a courtroom, the dramatis personae are the speaker, hearer, and the defendant. In the book on the table scenario used to illustrate the referential use, the speaker's motive is to have a book to read and the table need not be antique. In the corresponding scenario used to illustrate the attributive use, the speaker's motive is to remove an object that could damage the table, and it is necessary (for that example) that the table be antique. (Motives are not communicative intentions.) What Donnellan needed to show is that in the very same situation, the function of the description changes as the speaker's communicative intention, with respect to the description, changes; and this he did not do.

Two final points: In "Reference and Definite Descriptions," Donnellan did not make clear whether the attributive-referential distinction was supposed to be semantic or pragmatic. I believe that his later articles indicate that he wants it to be a pragmatic one. Some philosophers have argued that it is syntactic, but Donnellan has rejected this interpretation. The other point is that the sense of having an object "in mind" needed clarification. Donnellan's later work shows that he means that the speaker's use of a name is linked by a historical or causal chain to the intended referent. Donnellan's views about these chains are similar to those expressed by Saul Kripke in *Naming and Necessity,* part of which is Selection 20 in Section IV of this book.

14 On Sense and Nominatum

GOTTLOB FREGE

The idea of Sameness[1] challenges reflection. It raises questions which are not quite easily answered. Is Sameness a relation? A relation between objects? Or between names or signs of objects? I assumed the latter alternative in my *Begriffsschrift*. The reasons that speak in its favor are the following: "a=a" and "a = b" are sentences of obviously different cognitive significance: "a=a" is valid a priori and according to Kant is to be called analytic, whereas sentences of the form "a = b" often contain very valuable extensions of our knowledge and cannot always be justified in an a priori manner. The discovery that it is not a different and novel sun which rises every morning, but that it is the very same, certainly was one of the most consequential ones in astronomy. Even nowadays the recognition (identification) of a planetoid or a comet is not always a matter of self-evidence. If we wished to view identity as a relationship between the objects designated by the names "a' and "b" then "a = b" and "a = a" would not seem different if "a = b" is true. This would express a relation of a thing to itself, namely, a relation such that it holds between everything and itself but never between one thing and another. What one wishes to express with "a = b" seems to be that the signs or names 'a' and 'b' name the same thing; and in that case we would be dealing with those signs: a relation between them would be asserted. But this relation could hold only inasmuch as they name or designate something. The relation, as it were, is mediated through the connection of each sign with the same nominatum. This connection, however, is arbitrary. You cannot forbid the use of an arbitrarily produced process or object as a sign for something else. Hence, a sentence like "a = b" would no longer refer to a matter of fact but rather to our manner of designation; no genuine knowledge would be expressed by it. But this is just what we do want to express in many cases. If the sign 'a' differs from the sign 'b' only as an object (here by its shape) but not by its rôle as a sign, that is to say, not in the manner in which it designates anything, then the cognitive significance of "a = a" would be essentially the same as that of "a = b", if "a = b" is true. A difference could arise only if the difference of the signs corresponds to a difference in the way in which the designated objects are given. Let a, b, c be straight lines which connect the corners of a triangle with the

Translated by Herbert Feigl from the article "Ueber Sinn und Bedeutung," *Zeitschr. f. Philos. und Philos. Kritik,* 100 (1892). The terminology adopted is largely that used by R. Carnap in *Meaning and Necessity* (Chicago: University of Chicago Press, 1947). From *Readings in Philosophical Analysis*, Herbert Feigl and Wilfrid Sellars, eds. (New York: Appleton-Century-Crofts, 1949), pp. 85–102. Copyright © 1949 by Herbert Feigl and Wilfrid Sellars. Reprinted by permission of the estate of Herbert Feigl and by Wilfrid Sellars.

midpoints of the opposite sides. The point of intersection of a and b is then the same as that of b and c. Thus we have different designations of the same point and these names ('intersection of a and b', 'intersection of b and c') indicate also the manner in which these points are presented. Therefore the sentence expresses a genuine cognition.

Now it is plausible to connect with a sign (name, word combination, expression) not only the designated object, which may be called the nominatum of the sign, but also the sense (connotation, meaning) of the sign in which is contained the manner and context of presentation. Accordingly, in our examples the *nominata* of the expressions 'the point of intersection of a and b' and 'the point of intersection of b and c' would be the same—not their senses. The nominata of 'evening star' and 'morning star' are the same but not their senses.

From what has been said it is clear that I here understand by 'sign' or 'name' any expression which functions as a proper name, whose nominatum accordingly is a definite object (in the widest sense of this word). But no concept or relation is under consideration here. These matters are to be dealt with in another essay. The designation of a single object may consist of several words or various signs. For brevity's sake, any such designation will be considered as a proper name.

The sense of a proper name is grasped by everyone who knows the language or the totality of designations of which the proper name is a part;[2] this, however, illuminates the nominatum, if there is any, in a very one-sided fashion. A complete knowledge of the nominatum would require that we could tell immediately in the case of any given sense whether it belongs to the nominatum. This we shall never be able to do.

The regular connection between a sign, its sense and its nominatum is such that there corresponds a definite sense to the sign and to this sense there corresponds again a definite nominatum; whereas not one sign only belongs to one nominatum (object). In different languages, and even in one language, the same sense is represented by different expressions. It is true, there are exceptions to this rule. Certainly there

should be a definite sense to each expression in a complete configuration of signs, but the natural languages in many ways fall short of this requirement. We must be satisfied if the same word, at least in the same context, has the same sense. It can perhaps be granted that an expression has a sense if it is formed in a grammatically correct manner and stands for a proper name. But as to whether there is a denotation corresponding to the connotation is hereby not decided. The words 'the heavenly body which has the greatest distance from the earth' have a sense; but it is very doubtful as to whether they have a nominatum. The expression 'the series with the least convergence' has a sense; but it can be proved that it has no nominatum, since for any given convergent series, one can find another one that is less convergent. Therefore the grasping of a sense does not with certainty warrant a corresponding nominatum.

When words are used in the customary manner then what is talked about are their nominata. But it may happen that one wishes to speak about the words themselves or about their senses. The first case occurs when one quotes someone else's words in direct (ordinary) discourse. In this case one's own words immediately name (denote) the words of the other person and only the latter words have the usual nominata. We thus have signs of signs. In writing we make use of quotes enclosing the word-icons. A word-icon in quotes must therefore not be taken in the customary manner.

If we wish to speak of the sense of an expression 'A' we can do this simply through the locution 'the sense of the expression "A" '. In indirect (oblique) discourse we speak of the sense, e.g., of the words of someone else. From this it becomes clear that also in indirect discourse words do not have their customary nominata; they here name what customarily would be their sense. In order to formulate this succinctly we shall say: words in indirect discourse are used *indirectly,* or have *indirect* nominata. Thus we distinguish the *customary* from the *indirect* nominatum of a word; and similarly, its *customary* sense from its *indirect* sense. The indirect nominatum of a word is therefore its customary sense. Such exceptions must be kept in mind if one wishes correctly to comprehend the manner of connection between signs, senses, and nominata in any given case.

Both the nominatum and the sense of a sign must be distinguished from the associated image. If the nominatum of a sign is an object of sense perception, my image of the latter is an inner picture[3] arisen from memories of sense impressions and activities of mine, internal or external. Frequently this image is suffused with feelings; the definiteness of its various parts may vary and fluctuate. Even with the same person the same sense is not always accompanied by the same image. The image is subjective; the image of one person is not that of another. Hence, the various differences between the images connected with one and the same sense. A painter, a rider, a zoologist probably connect very different images with the name 'Bucephalus'. The image thereby differs essentially from the connotation of a sign, which latter may well be common property of many and is therefore not a part or mode of the single person's mind; for it cannot well be denied that mankind possesses a common treasure of thoughts which is transmitted from generation to generation.[4]

While, accordingly, there is no objection to speak without qualification of the sense in regard to images, we must, to be precise, add *whose* images they are and at what time they occur. One might say: just as words are connected with different images in two different persons, the same holds of the senses also. Yet this difference would consist merely in the manner of association. It does not prevent both from apprehending the same sense, but they cannot have the same image. *Si duo idem faciunt, non est idem.* When two persons imagine the same thing, each still has his own image. It is true, occasionally we can detect differences in the images or even in the sensations of different persons. But an accurate comparison is impossible because these images cannot be had together in one consciousness.

The nominatum of a proper name is the object itself which is designated thereby; the image which we may have along with it is quite subjective; the sense lies in between, not subjective as is the image, but not the object either. The following simile may help in elucidating these relationships. Someone observes the moon through a telescope. The moon is comparable with the nominatum; it is the object of the observation which is mediated through the real image projected by the object lens into the interior of the telescope, and through the retinal image of the observer. The first may be compared with the sense, the second with the presentation (or image in the psychological sense). The real image inside the telescope, however, is relative; it depends upon the standpoint, yet, it is objective in that it can serve several observers. Arrangements could be made such that several observers could utilize it. But every one of them would have only his own retinal image. Because of the different structures of the eyes not even geometrical congruence could be attained; a real coincidence would in any case be impossible. One could elaborate the simile by assuming that the retinal image of *A* could be made visible to *B;* or *A* could see his own retinal image in a mirror. In this manner one could possibly show how a presentation itself can be made into an object; but even so, it would never be to the (outside) observer what it is to the one who possesses the image. However, these lines of thought lead too far afield.

We can now recognize three levels of differences of words, expressions and complete sentences. The difference may concern at most the imagery, or else the sense but not the nominatum, or finally also the nominatum. In regard to the first level, we must note that, owing to the uncertain correlation of images with words, a difference may exist for one person that another does not discover. The difference of a translation from the original should properly not go beyond the first level. Among the differences possible in this connection we mention the shadings and colorings which poetry seeks to impart to the senses. These shadings and colorings are not objective. Every listener or reader has to add them in accordance with the hints of the poet or speaker. Surely, art would be impossible without some kinship among human imageries; but just how far the intentions of the poet are realized can never be exactly ascertained.

We shall henceforth no longer refer to the images and picturizations; they were discussed only lest the image evoked by a word be confused with its sense or its nominatum.

In order to facilitate brief and precise expression we may lay down the following formulations:

A proper name (word, sign, sign-compound, expression) expresses its sense, and designates or signifies its nominatum. We let a *sign express* its sense and *designate* its nominatum.

Perhaps the following objection, coming from idealistic or skeptical quarters, has been kept in abeyance for some time: "You have been speaking without hesitation of the moon as an object; but how do you know that the name 'the moon' has in fact a nominatum? How do you know that anything at all has a nominatum?" I reply that it is not our intention to speak of the image of the moon, nor would we be satisfied with the sense when we say 'the moon'; instead, we presuppose a nominatum here. We should miss the meaning altogether if we assumed that we had reference to images in the sentence "the moon is smaller than the earth." Were this intended we would use some such locution as 'my image of the moon'. Of course, we may be in error as regards that assumption, and such errors have occurred on occasion. However, the question whether we could possibly always be mistaken in this respect may here remain unanswered; it will suffice for the moment to refer to our intention in speaking and thinking in order to justify our reference to the nominatum of a sign; even if we have to make the proviso: if there is such a nominatum.

Thus far we have considered sense and nominatum only of such expressions, words, and signs which we called proper names. We are now going to inquire into the sense and the nominatum of a whole declarative sentence. Such a sentence contains a proposition.[5] Is this thought to be regarded as the sense or the nominatum of the sentence? Let us for the moment assume that the sentence has a nominatum! If we then substitute a word in it by another word with the same nominatum but a different sense, then this substitution cannot affect the nominatum of the sentence. But we realize that in such cases the proposition is changed; e.g., the proposition of the sentence "the morning star is a body illuminated by the sun" is different from

that of "the evening star is a body illuminated by the sun." Someone who did not know that the evening star is the same as the morning star could consider the one proposition true and the other false. The proposition can therefore not be the nominatum of the sentence; it will instead have to be regarded as its sense. But what about the nominatum? Can we even ask this question? A sentence as a whole has perhaps only sense and no nominatum? It may in any case be expected that there are such sentences, just as there are constituents of sentences which do have sense but no nominatum. Certainly, sentences containing proper names without nominata must be of this type. The sentence "Odysseus deeply asleep was disembarked at Ithaca" obviously has a sense. But since it is doubtful as to whether the name 'Odysseus' occurring in this sentence has a nominatum, so it is also doubtful that the whole sentence has one. However, it is certain that whoever seriously regards the sentence either as true or false also attributes to the name 'Odysseus' a nominatum, not only a sense; for it is obviously the nominatum of this name to which the predicate is either ascribed or denied. He who does not acknowledge the nominatum cannot ascribe or deny a predicate to it. It might be urged that the consideration of the nominatum of the name is going farther than is necessary; one could be satisfied with the sense, if one stayed with the proposition. If all that mattered were only the sense of the sentence (i.e., the proposition) then it would be unnecessary to be concerned with the nominata of the sentence-components, for only the sense of the components can be relevant for the sense of the sentence. The proposition remains the same, no matter whether or not the name 'Odysseus' has a nominatum. The fact that we are at all concerned about the nominatum of a sentence-component indicates that we generally acknowledge or postulate a nominatum for the sentence itself. The proposition loses in interest as soon as we recognize that one of its parts is lacking a nominatum. We may therefore be justified to ask for a nominatum of a sentence, in addition to its sense. But why do we wish that every proper name have not only a sense but also a nominatum? Why is the proposition alone not sufficient? We answer: because what matters to us is the truth-value. This, however, is not always the case. In listening to an epic, for example, we are fascinated by the euphony of the language and also by the sense of the sentences and by the images and emotions evoked. In turning to the question of truth we disregard the artistic appreciation and pursue scientific considerations. Whether the name 'Odysseus' has a nominatum is therefore immaterial to us as long as we accept the poem as a work of art.[6] Thus, it is the striving for truth which urges us to penetrate beyond the sense to the nominatum.

We have realized that we are to look for the nominatum of a sentence whenever the nominata of the sentence-components are the thing that matters; and that is the case whenever and only when we ask for the truth value.

Thus we find ourselves persuaded to accept the *truth-value* of a sentence as its nominatum. By the truth-value of a sentence I mean the circumstances of its being true or false. There are no other truth-values. For brevity's sake I shall call the one the True and the other the False. Every declarative sentence, in which what matters are the nominata of the words, is therefore to be considered as a proper name; and its nominatum, if there is any, is either the True or the False. These two objects are recognized, even if only tacitly, by everyone who at all makes judgments, holds anything as true, thus even by the skeptic. To designate truth-values as objects may thus far appear as a capricious idea or as a mere play on words, from which no important conclusion should be drawn. What I call an object can be discussed only in connection with the nature of concepts and relations. That I will reserve for another essay. But this might be clear even here: in every judgment[7]—no matter how obvious—a step is made from the level of propositions to the level of the nominata (the objective facts).

It may be tempting to regard the relation of a proposition to the True not as that of sense to nominatum but as that of the subject to the predicate. One could virtually say: "the proposition that 5 is a prime number is true." But on closer examination one notices that this does not say any more than is said in the simple sentence "5 is a prime number." The assertion of truth lies in both cases in the form of the sentences being asserted, and where this lacks its customary force, e.g., in the mouth of an actor on the stage, even the sentence "The proposition that 5 is a prime number is true" contains only a proposition, and the same proposition as "5 is a prime number." This makes clear that the relation of a proposition to the True must not be compared with the relation of subject and predicate. Subject and predicate (interpreted logically) are, after all, components of a proposition; they are on the same level as regards cognition. By joining subject and predicate, we always arrive only at a proposition; in this way we never move from a sense to a nominatum or from a proposition to its truth-value. We remain on the same level and never proceed from it to the next one. Just as the sun cannot be part of a proposition, so the truth-value, because it is not the sense, but an object, cannot be either.

If our conjecture (that the nominatum of a sentence is its truth-value) is correct, then the truth-value must remain unchanged if a sentence-component is replaced by an expression with the same nominatum but with a different sense. Indeed, Leibnitz declares: "*Eadem sunt, quae sibi mutuo substitui possunt, salva veritate.*" What else, except the truth-value, could be found, which quite generally belongs to every sentence and regarding which the nominata of the components are relevant and which would remain invariant for substitutions of the type indicated?

Now if the truth-value of a sentence is its nominatum, then all true sentences have the same nominatum, and likewise all false ones. This implies that all detail has been blurred in the nominatum of a sentence. What interests us can therefore never be merely the nominatum; but the proposition alone does not give knowledge; only the proposition together with its nominatum, i.e., its truth-value, does. Judging may be viewed as a movement from a proposition to its nominatum, i.e., its truth-value. Of course this is not intended as a definition. Judging is indeed something peculiar and unique. One might say that judging consists in the discerning of parts within the truth-value. This discernment occurs through recourse to the proposition. Every sense that belongs to a truth-value would correspond in its own manner to the analysis. I have, however, used the word 'part' in a particular manner here: I have transferred the relation of whole and part from the sentence to its nominatum. This I did by viewing the nominatum of a word as part of the nominatum of a sentence, when the word itself is part of the sentence. True enough, this way of putting things is objectionable since as regards the nominatum the whole and one part of it does not determine the other part; and also because the word 'part' in reference to bodies has a different customary usage. A special expression should be coined for what has been suggested above.

We shall now further examine the conjecture that the truth-value of a sentence is its nominatum. We have found that the truth-value of a sentence remains unaltered if an expression within the sentence is replaced by a synonymous one. But we have as yet not considered the case in which the expression-to-be-replaced is itself a sentence. If our view is correct, then the truth-value of a sentence, which contains another sentence as a part, must remain unaltered when we substitute for the part another of the same truth-value. Exceptions are to be expected if the whole or the part are either in direct or indirect discourse; for, as we have seen, in that case the nominata of the words are not the usual ones. A sentence in direct discourse nominates again a sentence but in indirect discourse it nominates a proposition.

Our attention is thus directed to subordinate sentences (i.e., dependent clauses). These present themselves of course as parts of a sentence-structure which from a logical point of view appears also as a sentence, and indeed as if it were a main clause. But here we face the question whether in the case of dependent clauses it also holds that their nominata are truth-values. We know already that this is not the case with sentences in indirect discourse. The grammarians view clauses as representatives of sentence-parts and divide them accordingly into subjective, relative, and adverbial clauses. This might suggest that the nominatum of a clause is not a truth-value but rather it is of similar nature as that of a noun or of an adjective or of an adverb; in short, of a sentence-part whose sense is not a proposition but only part thereof. Only a thorough investigation can provide clarity in this

matter. We shall herein not follow strictly along grammatical lines, but rather group together what is logically of comparable type. Let us first seek out such instances in which, as we just surmised, the sense of a clause is not a self-sufficient proposition.

Among the abstract clauses beginning with 'that' there is also the indirect discourse, of which we have seen that in it the words have their indirect (oblique) nominata which coincide with what are ordinarily their senses. In this case then the clause has as its nominatum a proposition, not a truth-value; its sense is not a proposition but it is the sense of the words "the proposition that . . .", which is only a part of the proposition corresponding to the total sentence-structure. This occurs in connection with 'to say', 'to hear', 'to opine', 'to be convinced', 'to infer', and similar words.[8] The situation is different, and rather complicated in connection with such words as 'to recognize', 'to know', 'to believe', a matter to be considered later.

One can see that in these cases the nominatum of the clause indeed consists in the proposition, because whether that proposition is true or false is immaterial for the truth of the whole sentence. Compare, e.g., the following two sentences: "Copernicus believed that the planetary orbits are circles" and "Copernicus believed that the appearance of the sun's motion is produced by the real motion of the earth." Here the one clause can be substituted for the other without affecting the truth. The sense of the principal sentence together with the clause is the single proposition; and the truth of the whole implies neither the truth nor the falsity of the clause. In cases of this type it is not permissible to replace in the clause one expression by another of the same nominatum. Such replacement may be made only by expressions of the same indirect nominatum, i.e., of the same customary sense. If one were to infer: the nominatum of a sentence is not its truth-value ("because then a sentence could always be replaced by another with the same truth-value"), he would prove too much; one could just as well maintain that the nominatum of the word 'morning star' is not Venus, for one cannot always substitute 'Venus' for "morning star". The only correct conclusion is that the nominatum of a sentence is *not always* its truth-value, and that 'morning star' does not always nominate the planet Venus; for this is indeed not the case when the word is used with its indirect nominatum. Such an exceptional case is before us in the clauses just considered, whose nominatum is a proposition.

When we say "it seems that . . ." then we mean to say "it seems to me that . . ." or "I opine that . . . ." This is the same case over again. Similarly with the expressions such as: 'to be glad', 'to regret', 'to approve', 'to disapprove', 'to hope', 'to fear'. When Wellington, toward the end of the battle of Belle-Alliance was glad that the Prussians were coming, the ground of his rejoicing was a conviction. Had he actually been deceived, he would not have been less glad, as long as his belief persisted; and before he arrived at the conclusion that the Prussians were coming he could not have been glad about it, even if in fact they were already approaching.

Just as a conviction or a belief may be the ground of a sentiment, so it can also be the ground of another conviction such as in inference. In the sentence "Columbus inferred from the roundness of the earth that he could, traveling westward, reach India" we have, as nominata of its parts two propositions: that the earth is round, and that Columbus traveling westward could reach India. What matters here is only that Columbus was convinced of the one as well as of the other and that the one conviction furnishes the ground for the other. It is irrelevant for the truth of our sentence whether the earth is really round and whether Columbus could have reached India in the manner he fancied. But it is not irrelevant whether for 'the earth' we substitute 'the planet accompanied by one satellite whose diameter is larger than one-fourth of its own diameter'. Here also we deal with the indirect nominata of the words.

Adverbial clauses of purpose with 'so that' likewise belong here; obviously the purpose is a proposition; therefore: indirect nominata of the words, expressed in subjunctive form.

The clause with 'that' after 'to command', 'to request', 'to forbid' would appear in imperative form in direct discourse. Imperatives have no nominata; they have only sense. It is true, commands or requests are not propositions, but they are of the same type as propositions. Therefore the words in the dependent clauses after 'to command', 'to request', etc. have indirect nominata. The nominatum of such a sentence is thus not a truth-value but a command, a request, and the like.

We meet a similar situation in the case of dependent questions in phrases like 'to doubt if', 'not to know what'. It is easy to see that the words, here too, have to be interpreted in terms of their indirect nominata. The dependent interrogatory clauses containing 'who', 'what', 'where', 'when', 'how', 'whereby', etc. often apparently approximate closely adverbial clauses in which the words have their ordinary nominata. These cases are linguistically distinguished through the mode of the verb. In the subjunctive we have a dependent question and the indirect nominata of the words, so that a proper name cannot generally be replaced by another of the same object.

In the instances thus far considered the words in the clause had indirect nominata; this made it intelligible that the nominatum of the clause itself is indirect, i.e., not a truth-value, but a proposition, a command, a request, a question. The clause could be taken as a noun; one might even say, as a proper name of that proposition, command, etc., in whose rôle it functions as the context of the sentence-structure.

We are now going to consider clauses of another type, in which the words do have their customary nominata although there does not appear a proposition as the sense or a truth-value as the nominatum. How this is possible will best be elucidated by examples.

"He who discovered the elliptical shape of the planetary orbits, died in misery."

If, in this example, the sense of the clause were a proposition, it would have to be expressible also in a principal sentence. But this cannot be done because the grammatical subject 'he who' has no independent sense. It merely mediates the relations to the second part of the sentence: 'died in misery'. Therefore the sense of the clause is not a complete proposition and its nominatum is not a truth-value, but Kepler. It might be objected that the sense of the whole does include a proposition as its part; namely, that there was someone who first recognized the elliptical shape of the planetary orbits; for if we accept the whole as true we cannot deny this part. Indubitably so; but only because otherwise the clause "he who discovered the elliptical shape, etc." would have no nominatum. Whenever something is asserted then the presupposition taken for granted is that the employed proper names, simple or compound, have nominata. Thus, if we assert "Kepler died in misery" it is presupposed that the name 'Kepler' designates something. However, the proposition that the name 'Kepler' designates something is, the foregoing notwithstanding, not contained in the sense of the sentence "Kepler died in misery." If that were the case the denial would not read "Kepler did not die in misery" but "Kepler did not die in misery, or the name 'Kepler' is without nominatum." That the name 'Kepler' designates something is rather the presupposition of the assertion "Kepler died in misery" as well as of its denial. Now, it is a defect of languages that expressions are possible within them, which, in their grammatical form, seemingly determined to designate an object, do not fulfill this condition in special cases; because this depends on the truth of the sentence. Thus it depends upon the truth of the sentence "there was someone who discovered the ellipticity of the orbits" whether the clause 'he who discovered the ellipticity of the orbits' really designates an object, or else merely evokes the appearance thereof, while indeed being without nominatum. Thus it may seem as if our clause, as part of its sense, contained the proposition that there existed someone who discovered the ellipticity of the orbits. If this were so, then the denial would have to read "he who first recognized the ellipticity of the orbits did not die in misery, or there was no one who discovered the ellipticity of the orbits." This, it is obvious, hinges upon an imperfection of language of which, by the way, even the symbolic language of analysis is not entirely free; there, also, sign compounds may occur which appear as if they designated something, but which at least hitherto are without nominatum, e.g., divergent infinite series. This can be avoided, e.g., through the special convention that the nominatum of divergent infinite series be the number 0. It is to be demanded that in a logically perfect language (logical symbolism) every expression constructed as a proper name in a grammatically correct manner out of already introduced

symbols, in fact designate an object; and that no symbol be introduced as a proper name without assurance that it have a nominatum. It is customary in logic texts to warn against the ambiguity of expressions as a source of fallacies. I deem it at least as appropriate to issue a warning against apparent proper names that have no nominata. The history of mathematics has many a tale to tell of errors which originated from this source. The demagogic misuse is close (perhaps closer) at hand as in the case of ambiguous expressions. 'The will of the people' may serve as an example in this regard; for it is easily established that there is no generally accepted nominatum of that expression. Thus it is obviously not without importance to remove once for all the source of these errors, at least as regards their occurrence in science. Then such objections as the one discussed above will become impossible, for then it will be seen that whether a proper name has a nominatum can never depend upon the truth of a proposition.

Our considerations may be extended from these subjective clauses to the logically related relative and adverbial clauses.

Relative clauses, too, are employed in the formation of compound proper names—even if, in contradistinction to subjective clauses, they are not sufficient by themselves for this purpose. These relative clauses may be regarded as equivalent to appositions. Instead of 'the square root of 4 which is smaller than 0' we can also say 'the negative square root of 4'. We have here a case in which out of a conceptual expression a compound proper name is formed, with the help of the definite article in the singular. This is at any rate permissible when one and only one object is comprised by the concept.[9] Conceptual expression can be formed in such a fashion that their characteristics are indicated through relative clauses as in our example through the clause 'which is smaller than 0'. Obviously, such relative clauses, just as the subjective clauses above, do not refer to a proposition as their sense nor to a truth-value as their nominatum. Their sense is only a part of a proposition, which in many cases, can be expressed by a simple apposition. As in the subjective clauses an independent subject is missing and it is therefore impossible to represent the sense of the clause in an independent principal sentence.

Places, dates and time-intervals are objects from a logical point of view; the linguistic symbol of a definite place, moment, or span of time must therefore be viewed as a proper name. Adverbial clauses of space or time can then be used in the formation of such proper names in a fashion analogous to the one we have just remarked in the case of subjective and relative clauses. Similarly, expressions for concepts which comprise places, etc., can be formed. Here too, it is to be remarked, the sense of the subordinate clauses cannot be rendered in a principal clause, because an essential constituent, namely the determination of place and time, is missing and only alluded to by a relative pronoun or a conjunction.[10]

In conditional clauses also, there is, just as we have realized in the case of subjective, relative, and adverbial clauses, a constituent with indeterminate indication corresponding to which there is a similar one in the concluding clause. In referring to one another the two clauses combine into a whole which expresses, as a rule, only one proposition. In the sentence "if a number is smaller than 1 and greater than 0, then its square is also smaller than 1 and greater than 0" this constituent in the conditional clause is 'a number' and in the concluding clause it is 'its'. Just through this indeterminacy the sense acquires the universal character which one expects of a law. But it is in this way also that it comes about that the conditional clause alone does not possess a complete proposition as its sense, and that together with the concluding clause it expresses a single proposition whose parts are no longer propositions. It is not generally the case that a hypothetical judgment correlates two judgments. Putting it in that (or a similar) manner would amount to using the word 'judgment' in the same sense that I have attributed to the word 'proposition'. In that case I would have to say: in a hypothetical proposition two propositions are related to each other. But this could be the case only if an indeterminately denoting constituent were absent;[11] but then universality would also be missing.

If a time point is to be indeterminately indicated in a conditional and a concluding clause, then this is not infrequently effected by *tempus praesens* of the verb, which in this case does not connote the present time. It is this grammatical form which takes the place of the indeterminately indicating constituent in the main and the dependent clause. "When the sun is at the Tropic of Cancer, the northern hemisphere has its longest day" is an example. Here, too, it is impossible to express the sense of the dependent clause in a main clause. For this sense is not a complete proposition; if we said: "the sun is at the Tropic of Cancer" we would be referring to the present time and thereby alter the sense. Similarly, the sense of the main clause is not a proposition either, only the whole consisting of main and dependent clause contains a proposition. Further, it may occur that several constituents common to conditional and concluding clause are indeterminately indicated.

It is obvious that subjective clauses containing 'who', 'what', and adverbial clauses with 'where', 'when' 'wherever' 'whenever' are frequently to be interpreted, inasmuch as their sense is concerned, as conditional sentences, e.g., "He who touches pitch soils himself."

Conditional clauses can also be replaced by relative clauses. The sense of the previously mentioned sentence can also be rendered by "the square of a number which is smaller than 1 and larger than 0, is smaller than 1 and larger than 0."

Quite different is the case in which the common constituent of main and dependent clause is represented by a proper name. In the sentence: "Napoleon who recognized the danger to his right flank, personally led his troops against the enemy's position" there are expressed two propositions:

(1) Napoleon recognized the danger to his right flank.
(2) Napoleon personally led his troops against the enemy's position.

When and where this happened can indeed be known only from the context, but is to be viewed as thereby determined. If we pronounce our whole sentence as an assertion we thereby assert simultaneously its two component sentences. If one of the components is false the whole is false. Here we have a case in which the dependent clause by itself has a sense in a complete proposition (if supplemented by temporal and spatial indications). The nominatum of such a clause is therefore a truth-value. We may therefore expect that we can replace it by a sentence of the same truth value without altering the truth of the whole. This is indeed the case; but it must be kept in mind that for a purely grammatical reason, its subject must be 'Napoleon'; because only then can the sentence be rendered in the form of a relative clause attached to 'Napoleon'. If the demand to render it in this form and if the conjunction with 'and' is admitted, then this limitation falls away.

Likewise, in dependent clauses with 'although' complete propositions are expressed. This conjunction really has no sense and does not affect the sense of the sentence; rather, it illuminates it in a peculiar fashion.[12] Without affecting the truth of the whole the implicate may be replaced by one of the same truth-value; but the illumination might then easily appear inappropriate, just as if one were to sing a song of sad content in a cheerful manner.

In these last instances the truth of the whole implied the truth of the component sentences. The situation is different if a conditional sentence expresses a complete proposition; namely, when in doing so it contains instead of a merely indicating constituent a proper name or something deemed equivalent to a proper name. In the sentence: "if the sun has already risen by now, the sky is heavily overcast," the tense is the present—therefore determinate. The place also is to be considered determinate. Here we can say that a relation is posited such that the case does not arise in which the antecedent sentence nominates the True and the consequent sentence nominates the False. Accordingly the given (whole) sentence is true if the sun has not as yet risen (no matter whether or not the sky be heavily overcast), and also if the sun has risen and the sky is heavily overcast. Since all that matters are only the truth-values, each of the component sentences can be replaced by another one of the same truth-value, without altering the truth-value of the whole sentence. In this case also, the illumination would usually seem inappropriate; the proposition could easily appear absurd; but this has nothing to do with the truth-value of the sentence. It must always be remembered that associated thoughts are evoked on the side; but these are not really expressed and must therefore not be taken account of; their truth-values cannot be relevant.[13]

We may hope we have considered the simple types of sentences. Let us now review what we have found out!

The sense of a subordinate clause is usually not a proposition but only part of one. Its nominatum is therefore not a truth-value. The reason for this is *either:* that the words in the subordinate clause have only indirect nominata, so that the nominatum, not the sense, of the clause is a proposition, *or,* that the clause, because of a contained indeterminately indicating constituent, is incomplete, such that only together with the principal clause does it express a proposition. However, there are also instances in which the sense of the dependent clause is a complete proposition, and in this case it can be replaced by another clause of the same truth-value without altering the truth-value of the whole, that is, inasmuch as there are no grammatical obstacles in the way.

In a survey of the various occurrent clauses one will readily encounter some which will not properly fit within any of the considered divisions. As far as I can see, the reason for that is that these clauses do not have quite so simple a sense. It seems that almost always we connect associated propositions with the main proposition which we express; these associated propositions, even if unexpressed, are associated with our words according to psychological laws also by the listener. And because they appear as associated automatically with our words (as in the case of the main proposition) we seem to wish, after all, to express such associated propositions along with the main propositions. The sense of the sentence thereby becomes richer and it may well happen that we may have more simple propositions than sentences. In some cases the sentence may be interpreted in this way, in others, it may be doubtful whether the associated proposition belongs to the sense of the sentence or whether it merely accompanies it.[14] One might find that in the sentence: "Napoleon, who recognized the danger to his right flank, personally led his troops against the enemy's position" there are not only the previously specified two propositions, but also the proposition that the recognition of the danger was the reason why he led his troops against the enemy. One may indeed wonder whether this proposition is merely lightly suggested or actually expressed. Consider the question whether our sentence would be false if Napoleon's resolution had been formed before the recognition of the danger. If our sentence were true even despite this, then the associated proposition should not be regarded as part of the sense of the sentence. In the alternative case the situation is rather complicated: we should then have more simple propositions than sentences. Now if we replace the sentence "Napoleon recognized the danger for his right flank" by another sentence of the same truth-value, e.g., by: "Napoleon was over forty-five years old" this would change not only our first but also our third proposition; and this might thereby change also the truth-value of the third proposition—namely, if his age was not the reason for his resolution to lead the troops against the enemy. Hence, it is clear that in such instances sentences of the same truth-value cannot always be substituted for one another. The sentence merely by virtue of its connection with another expresses something more than it would by itself alone.

Let us now consider cases in which this occurs regularly. In the sentence: "Bebel imagines that France's desire for vengeance could be assuaged by the restitution of Alsace-Lorraine" there are expressed two propositions which, however, do not correspond to the main and the dependent clause—namely:

(1) Bebel believes that France's desire for vengeance could be assuaged by the restitution of Alsace-Lorraine;
(2) France's desire for vengeance cannot be assuaged by the restitution of Alsace-Lorraine.

In the expression of the first proposition the words of the dependent clause have indirect nominata; while the same words, in the expression of the second proposition, have their usual nominata. Hence, we see that the dependent clause of our original sentence really is to be interpreted in a twofold way; i.e., with different nominata, one of which is a proposition and the other a truth-value. An analogous situation prevails with expressions like 'to know', 'to recognize', 'it is known'.

A condition clause and its related main clause express several propositions which, however, do not correspond one-to-one to the clauses. The sentence: "Since ice is specifically lighter than water, it floats on water" asserts:

(1) Ice is specifically lighter than water.
(2) If something is specifically lighter than water, it floats on water.
(3) Ice floats on water.

The third proposition, being implied by the first two, would perhaps not have to be mentioned expressly. However, neither the first and the third, nor the second and the third together would completely render the sense of our sentence. Thus we see that the dependent clause 'since ice is specifically lighter than water' expresses both our first proposition and part of the second. Hence, our clause cannot be replaced by another of the same truth-value; for thereby we are apt to alter our second proposition and could easily affect its truth-value.

A similar situation holds in the case of the sentence: "If iron were lighter than water it would float on water." Here we have the two propositions that iron is not lighter than water and that whatever is lighter than water floats on water. The clause again expresses the one proposition and part of the other. If we interpret the previously discussed sentence: "After Schleswig-Holstein was separated from Denmark, Prussia and Austria fell out with one another" as containing the proposition that Schleswig-Holstein once was separated from Denmark, then we have: firstly, the proposition, secondly, the proposition that, at a time more precisely determined by the dependent clause, Prussia and Austria fell out with one another. Here, too, the dependent clause expresses not only one proposition but also part of another. Therefore, it may not generally be replaced by another clause of the same truth-value.

It is difficult to exhaust all possibilities that present themselves in language; but I hope, in essence at least, to have disclosed the reasons why, in view of the invariance of the truth of a whole sentence, a clause cannot always be replaced by another of the same truth-value. These reasons are:

1. that the clause does not denote a truth-value in that it expresses only a part of a proposition;

2. that the clause, while it does denote a truth-value, is not restricted to this function in that its sense comprises, beside one proposition, also a part of another.

The first case holds

a. with the indirect nominata of the words;
b. if a part of the sentence indicates only indirectly without being a proper name.

In the second case the clause is to be interpreted in a twofold manner; namely, once with its usual nominatum; the other time with its indirect nominatum; or else, the sense of a part of the clause may simultaneously be a constituent of another proposition which, together with the sense expressed in the dependent clause, amounts to the total sense of the main and the dependent clause.

This makes it sufficiently plausible that instances in which a clause is not replaceable by another of the same truth-value do not disprove our view that the nominatum of a sentence is its truth-value and its sense a proposition.

Let us return to our point of departure now. When we discerned generally a difference in cognitive significance between "a = a" and "a = b" then this is now explained by the fact that for the cognitive significance of a sentence the sense (the proposition expressed) is no less relevant than its nominatum (the truth-value). If a = b, then the nominatum of 'a' and of 'b' is indeed the same and therefore also the truth-value of "a = b" is the same as that of "a = a". Nevertheless, the sense of 'b' may differ from the sense of 'a'; and therefore the proposition expressed by "a = b" may differ from the proposition expressed by "a = a"; in that case the two sentences do not have the same cognitive significance. Thus, if, as above, we mean by 'judgment' the transition from a proposition to its truth-value, then we can also say that the judgments differ from one another.

NOTES

1. I use this word in the sense of identity and understand "a = b" in the sense of "a is the same as b" or "a and b coincide".
2. In the case of genuinely proper names like 'Aristotle' opinions as regards their sense may diverge. As such may, e.g., be suggested: Plato's disciple and the teacher of Alexander the Great. Whoever accepts this sense will interpret the meaning of the statement "Aristotle was born in Stagira" differently from one who interpreted the sense of 'Aristotle' as the Stagirite teacher of Alexander the Great. As long as the nominatum remains the same, these fluctuations in sense are tolerable. But they should be avoided in the system of a demonstrative science and should not appear in a perfect language.
3. With the images we can align also the percepts in which the sense impressions and activities themselves take the place of those traces left in the mind. For our purposes the difference is unimportant, especially since besides sensations and activities recollections of such help in completing the intuitive presentation. 'Percept' may also be understood as the object, inasmuch as it is spatial or capable of sensory apprehension.
4. It is therefore inexpedient to designate fundamentally different things by the one word 'image' (or 'idea').
5. By 'proposition' I do not refer to the subjective activity of thinking but rather to its objective content which is capable of being the common property of many.
6. It would be desirable to have an expression for signs which have sense only. If we call them 'icons' then the words of an actor on stage would be icons; even the actor himself would be an icon.
7. A judgment is not merely the apprehension of a thought or proposition but the acknowledgment of its truth.
8. In "A lied, that he had seen B" the clause denotes a proposition of which it is said, firstly, that A asserted it as true, and, secondly, that A was convinced of its falsity.
9. According to our previous remarks such an expression should always be assured of a nominatum, e.g., through the special convention that the nomination be the number 0 if there is no object or more than one object denoted by the expression.
10. Regarding these sentences, however, several interpretations are easily conceivable. The sense of the sentence "after Schleswig-Holstein was torn away from Denmark, Prussia and Austria fell out with one another" could also be rendered by "after the separation of Schl.-H. from Denmark, Prussia and Austria fell out with one another." In this formulation it is sufficiently clear that we should not regard it as part of this sense that Schleswig-Holstein once was separated from Denmark; but rather that this is the necessary presupposition for the very existence of a nominatum of the expression 'after the separation of Schl.-H. from D.' Yet, our sentence could also be interpreted to the effect that Sch.-H. was once separated from D. This case will be considered later. In order to grasp the difference more clearly, let us identify ourselves with the mind of a Chinese who, with his trifling knowledge of European history, regards it as false that Schl.-H. was ever separated

from D. This Chinese would regard as neither true nor false the sentence as interpreted in the first manner. He would deny to it any nominatum because the dependent clause would be lacking a nominatum. The dependent clause would only apparently indicate a temporal determination. But if the Chinese interprets our sentence in the second manner, then he will find it expressing a proposition which he would consider false, in addition to a component which, for him, would be without nominatum.

11. Occasionally there is no explicit linguistic indication and the interpretation has to depend upon the total context.

12. Similarly in the cases of 'but', 'yet'.

13. The proposition of the sentence could also be formulated thus: "either the sun has not as yet risen or the sky is heavily overcast." This shows how to interpret this type of compound sentence.

14. This may be of importance in the question as to whether a given assertion be a lie, an oath, or a perjury.

15 On Denoting

BERTRAND RUSSELL

By a 'denoting phrase' I mean a phrase such as any one of the following: a man, some man, any man, every man, all men, the present King of England, the present King of France, the center of mass in the solar system at the first instant of the twentieth century, the revolution of the earth round the sun, the revolution of the sun round the earth. Thus a phrase is denoting solely in virtue of its *form*. We may distinguish three cases: (1) A phrase may be denoting, and yet not denote anything; e.g., 'the present King of France'. (2) A phrase may denote one definite object, e.g., 'the present King of England' denotes a certain man. (3) A phrase may denote ambiguously; e.g., 'a man' denotes not many men, but an ambiguous man. The interpretation of such phrases is a matter of considerable difficulty; indeed, it is very hard to frame any theory not susceptible of formal refutation. All the difficulties with which I am acquainted are met, so far as I can discover, by the theory which I am about to explain.

The subject of denoting is of very great importance, not only in logic and mathematics, but also in theory of knowledge. For example, we know that the center of mass of the solar system at a definite instant is some definite point, and we can affirm a number of propositions about it; but we have no immediate *acquaintance* with this point, which is only known to us by description. The distinction between *acquaintance* and *knowledge about* is the distinction between the things we have presentations of, and the things we only reach by denoting phrases. It often happens that we know that a certain phrase denotes unambiguously, although we have no acquaintance with what it denotes; this occurs in the above case of the center of mass. In perception we have acquaintance with the objects of perception, and in thought we have acquaintance with objects of a more abstract logical character; but we do not necessarily have acquaintance with the objects denoted by phrases composed of words with whose meanings we are acquainted. To take a very important instance: there seems no reason to believe that we are ever acquainted with other people's minds, seeing that these are not directly perceived; hence what we know about them is obtained through denoting. All thinking has to start from acquaintance, but it succeeds in thinking *about* many things with which we have no acquaintance.

The course of my argument will be as follows. I shall begin by stating the theory I intend to advocate;[1] I shall then discuss the theories of Frege and Meinong, showing why neither of them satisfies me; then I shall give the grounds in favor of my theory; and finally I shall briefly indicate the philosophical consequences of my theory.

My theory, briefly, is as follows. I take the notion of the *variable* as fundamental; I use

From *Mind* 14 (1905): 479–493. Reprinted by permission of Oxford University Press.

'$C(x)$' to mean a proposition[2] in which x is a constituent, where x, the variable, is essentially and wholly undetermined. Then we can consider the two notions '$C(x)$ is always true' and '$C(x)$ is sometimes true.'[3] Then *everything* and *nothing* and *something* (which are the most primitive of denoting phrases) are to be interpreted as follows:

C (everything) means '$C(x)$ is always true';
C (nothing) means '"$C(x)$ is false" is always true';
C (something) means 'It is false that "$C(x)$ is false" is always true'.[4]

Here the notion '$C(x)$ is always true' is taken as ultimate and indefinable, and the others are defined by means of it. *Everything, nothing,* and *something* are not assumed to have any meaning in isolation, but a meaning is assigned to *every* proposition in which they occur. This is the principle of the theory of denoting I wish to advocate: that denoting phrases never have any meaning in themselves, but that every proposition in whose verbal expression they occur has a meaning. The difficulties concerning denoting are, I believe, all the result of a wrong analysis of propositions whose verbal expressions contain denoting phrases. The proper analysis, if I am not mistaken, may be further set forth as follows.

Suppose now we wish to interpret the proposition, 'I met a man'. If this is true, I met some definite man; but that is not what I affirm. What I affirm is, according to the theory I advocate:

'"I met x, and x is human" is not always false'.

Generally, defining the class of men as the class of objects having the predicate *human,* we say that:

'C (a man)' means '"$C(x)$ and x is human" is not always false'.

This leaves 'a man', by itself, wholly destitute of meaning, but gives a meaning to every proposition in whose verbal expression 'a man' occurs.

Consider next the proposition 'all men are mortal'. This proposition[5] is really hypothetical and states that *if* anything is a man, it is mortal. That is, it states that if x is a man, x is mortal, whatever x may be. Hence, substituting 'x is human' for 'x is a man', we find:

'All men are mortal' means '"If x is human, x is mortal" is always true'.

This is what is expressed in symbolic logic by saying that 'all men are mortal' means '"x is human" implies "x is mortal" for all values of x'. More generally, we say:

'C (all men)' means '"If x is human, then $C(x)$ is true" is always true'.

Similarly

'C (no men)' means '"If x is human, then $C(x)$ is false" is always true'.
'C (some men)' will mean the same as 'C (a man)',[6] and
'C (a man)' means 'It is false that "$C(x)$ and x is human" is always false'.
'C (every man)' will mean the same as 'C (all men)'.

It remains to interpret phrases containing *the.* These are by far the most interesting and difficult of denoting phrases. Take as an example 'the father of Charles II was executed'. This asserts that there was an x who was the father of Charles II and was executed. Now, *the,* when it is strictly used, involves uniqueness; we do, it is true, speak of '*the son* of So-and-so' even when So-and-so has several sons, but it would be more correct to say '*a* son of So-and-so'. Thus for our purposes we take *the* as involving uniqueness. Thus when we say 'x was *the* father of Charles II' we not only assert that x had a certain relation to Charles II, but also that nothing else had this relation. The relation in question, without the assumption of uniqueness, and without any denoting phrases, is expressed by 'x begat Charles II'. To get an equivalent of 'x was the father of Charles II', we must add, 'If y is other than x, y did not beget Charles II', or what is equivalent, 'If y begat Charles II, y is identical with x'. Hence, 'x is the father of Charles II' becomes: 'x begat Charles II; and "if y begat Charles II, y is identical with x" is always true of y'.

Thus 'the father of Charles II was executed' becomes:

'It is not always false of x that x begat Charles II and that x was executed and that "if y begat Charles II, y is identical with x" is always true of y'.

This may seem a somewhat incredible interpretation; but I am not at present giving reasons, I am merely *stating* the theory.

To interpret 'C (the father of Charles II)', where C stands for any statement about him, we have only to substitute C (x) for 'x was executed' in the above. Observe that, according to the above interpretation C may be, 'C (the father of Charles II)' implies:

'It is not always false of x that "if y begat Charles II, y is identical with x" is always true of y',

which is what is expressed in common language by 'Charles II had one father and no more'. Consequently if this condition fails, *every* proposition of the form 'C (the father of Charles II)' is false. Thus e.g. every proposition of the form 'C (the present King of France)' is false. This is a great advantage in the present theory. I shall show later that it is not contrary to the law of contradiction, as might be at first supposed.

The above gives a reduction of all propositions in which denoting phrases occur to forms in which no such phrases occur. Why it is imperative to effect such a reduction, the subsequent discussion will endeavor to show.

The evidence for the above theory is derived from the difficulties which seem unavoidable if we regard denoting phrases as standing for genuine constituents of the propositions in whose verbal expressions they occur. Of the possible theories which admit such constituents the simplest is that of Meinong.[7] This theory regards any grammatically correct denoting phrase as standing for an *object*. Thus 'the present King of France', 'the round square', etc., are supposed to be genuine objects. It is admitted that such objects do not *subsist,* but nevertheless they are supposed to be objects. This is in itself a difficult view; but the chief objection is that such objects, admittedly, are apt to infringe the law of contradiction. It is contended, for example, that the existent present King of France exists, and also does not exist; that the round square is round, and also not round, etc. But this is intolerable; and if any theory can be found to avoid this result, it is surely to be preferred.

The above breach of the law of contradiction is avoided by Frege's theory. He distinguishes, in a denoting phrase, two elements, which we may call the *meaning* and the *denotation*.[8] Thus 'the center of mass of the solar system at the beginning of the twentieth century' is highly complex in *meaning,* but its *denotation* is a certain point, which is simple. The solar system, the twentieth century, etc., are constituents of the *meaning;* but the *denotation* has no constituents at all.[9] One advantage of this distinction is that it shows why it is often worthwhile to assert identity. If we say 'Scott is the author of *Waverley*', we assert an identity of denotation with a difference of meaning. I shall, however, not repeat the grounds in favor of this theory, as I have urged its claims elsewhere (loc. cit.), and am now concerned to dispute those claims.

One of the first difficulties that confronts us, when we adopt the view that denoting phrases *express* a meaning and *denote* a denotation,[10] concerns the cases in which the denotation appears to be absent. If we say 'the King of England is bald', that is, it would seem, not a statement about the complex *meaning* 'the King of England', but about the actual man denoted by the meaning. But now consider 'the King of France is bald'. By parity of form, this also ought to be about the denotation of the phrase 'the King of France'. But this phrase, though it has a *meaning* provided 'the King of England' has a meaning, has certainly no denotation, at least in any obvious sense. Hence one would suppose that 'the King of France is bald' ought to be nonsense; but it is not nonsense, since it is plainly false. Or again consider such a proposition as the following: 'If u is a class which has only one member, then that one member is a member of u', or, as we may state it, 'If u is a unit class, the u is a u'. This proposition ought to be *always* true, since the conclusion is true whenever the hypothesis is true. But 'the u' is a denoting phrase, and it is the denotation, not the meaning, that is said to be a u. Now if u is *not* a unit class, 'the u' seems to denote nothing; hence our proposition would seem to become nonsense as soon as u is not a unit class.

Now it is plain that such propositions do *not*

become nonsense merely because their hypotheses are false. The king in *The Tempest* might say, 'If Ferdinand is not drowned, Ferdinand is my only son'. Now 'my only son' is a denoting phrase, which, on the face of it, has a denotation when, and only when, I have exactly one son. But the above statement would nevertheless have remained true if Ferdinand had been in fact drowned. Thus we must either provide a denotation in cases in which it is at first sight absent, or we must abandon the view that the denotation is what is concerned in propositions which contain denotating phrases. The latter is the course that I advocate. The former course may be taken, as by Meinong, by admitting objects which do not subsist, and denying that they obey the law of contradiction; this, however, is to be avoided if possible. Another way of taking the same course (so far as our present alternative is concerned) is adopted by Frege, who provides by definition some purely conventional denotations for the cases in which otherwise there would be none. Thus 'the King of France', is to denote the null-class; 'the only son of Mr. So-and-so' (who has a fine family of ten), is to denote the class of all his sons; and so on. But this procedure, though it may not lead to actual logical error, is plainly artificial, and does not give an exact analysis of the matter. Thus if we allow that denoting phrases, in general, have the two sides of meaning and denotation, the cases where there seems to be no denotation cause difficulties both on the assumption that there really is a denotation and on the assumption that there really is none.

A logical theory may be tested by its capacity for dealing with puzzles, and it is a wholesome plan, in thinking about logic, to stock the mind with as many puzzles as possible, since these serve much the same purpose as is served by experiments in physical science. I shall therefore state three puzzles which a theory as to denoting ought to be able to solve; and I shall show later that my theory solves them.

(1) If *a* is identical with *b*, whatever is true of the one is true of the other, and either may be substituted for the other in any proposition without altering the truth or falsehood of that proposition. Now George IV wished to know whether Scott was the author of *Waverley;* and in fact Scott *was* the author of *Waverley.* Hence we may substitute *Scott* for *the author of 'Waverley',* and thereby prove that George IV wished to know whether Scott was Scott. Yet an interest in the law of identity can hardly be attributed to the first gentleman of Europe.

(2) By the law of excluded middle, either '*A* is *B*' or '*A* is not *B*' must be true. Hence either 'the present King of France is bald' or 'the present King of France is not bald' must be true. Yet if we enumerated the things that are bald, and then the things that are not bald, we should not find the present King of France in either list. Hegelians, who love a synthesis, will probably conclude that he wears a wig.

(3) Consider the proposition '*A* differs from *B*'. If this is true, there is a difference between *A* and *B*, which fact may be expressed in the form 'the difference between *A* and *B* subsists'. But if it is false that *A* differs from *B*, then there is no difference between *A* and *B*, which fact may be expresssed in the form 'the difference between *A* and *B* does not subsist'. But how can a non-entity be the subject of a proposition? 'I think, therefore I am' is no more evident than 'I am the subject of a proposition, therefore I am', provided 'I am' is taken to assert subsistence or being,[11] not existence. Hence, it would appear, it must always be self-contradictory to deny the being of anything; but we have seen, in connection with Meinong, that to admit being also sometimes leads to contradictions. Thus, if *A* and *B* do not differ, to suppose either that there is, or that there is not, such an object as 'the difference between *A* and *B*' seems equally impossible.

The relation of the meaning to the denotation involves certain rather curious difficulties, which seem in themselves sufficient to prove that the theory which leads to such difficulties must be wrong.

When we wish to speak about the *meaning* of a denoting phrase, as opposed to its *denotation,* the natural mode of doing so is by inverted commas. Thus we say:

The center of mass of the solar system is a point, not a denoting complex;
'The center of mass of the solar system' is a denoting complex, not a point.

Or again,

The first line of Gray's Elegy states a proposition.

'The first line of Gray's Elegy' does not state a proposition.

Thus taking any denoting phrase, say C, we wish to consider the relation between C and 'C', where the difference of the two is the kind exemplified in the above two instances.

We say, to begin with, that when C occurs it is the denotation that we are speaking about; but when 'C' occurs, it is the *meaning*. Now the relation of meaning and denotation is not merely linguistic through the phrase: there must be a logical relation involved, which we express by saying that the meaning denotes the denotation. But the difficulty which confronts us is that we cannot succeed in *both* preserving the connection of meaning and denotation *and* preventing them from being one and the same; also that the meaning cannot be got at except by means of denoting phrases. This happens as follows.

The one phrase C was to have both meaning and denotation. But if we speak of 'the meaning of C', that gives us the meaning (if any) of the denotation. 'The meaning of the first line of Gray's Elegy' is the same as 'The meaning of "The curfew tolls the knell of parting day",' and is not the same as 'The meaning of "the first line of Gray's Elegy".' Thus in order to get the meaning we want, we must speak not of 'the meaning of C', but of 'the meaning of "C",' which is the same as 'C' by itself. Similarly 'the denotation of C' does not mean the denotation we want, but means something which, if it denotes at all, denotes what is denoted by the denotation we want. For example, let 'C' be 'the denoting complex occurring in the second of the above instances'. Then C = 'the first line of Gray's Elegy', and the denotation of C = The curfew tolls the knell of parting day. But what we *meant* to have as the denotation was 'the first line of Gray's Elegy'. Thus we have failed to get what we wanted.

The difficulty in speaking of the meaning of a denoting complex may be stated thus: The moment we put the complex in a proposition, the proposition is about the denotation; and if we make a proposition in which the subject is 'the meaning of C', then the subject is the meaning (if

any) of the denotation, which was not intended. This leads us to say that, when we distinguish meaning and denotation, we must be dealing with the meaning: the meaning has denotation and is a complex, and there is not something other than the meaning, which can be called the complex, and be said to *have* both meaning and denotation. The right phrase, on the view in question, is that some meanings have denotations.

But this only makes our difficulty in speaking of meanings more evident. For suppose C is our complex; then we are to say that C is the meaning of the complex. Nevertheless, whenever C occurs without inverted commas, what is said is not true of the meaning, but only of the denotation, as when we say: The center of mass of the solar system is a point. Thus to speak of C itself, i.e., to make a proposition about the meaning, our subject must not be C, but something which denotes C. Thus 'C', which is what we use when we want to speak of the meaning, must be not the meaning, but something which denotes the meaning. And C must not be a constituent of this complex (as it is of 'the meaning of C'); for if C occurs in the complex, it will be its denotation, not its meaning, that will occur, and there is no backward road from denotations to meanings, because every object can be denoted by an infinite number of different denoting phrases.

Thus it would seem that 'C' and C are different entities, such that 'C' denotes C; but this cannot be an explanation, because the relation of 'C' to C remains wholly mysterious; and where are we to find the denoting complex 'C' which is to denote C? Moreover, when C occurs in a proposition, it is not only the denotation that occurs (as we shall see in the next paragraph); yet, on the view in question, C is only the denotation, the meaning being wholly relegated to 'C'. This is an inextricable tangle and seems to prove that the whole distinction of meaning and denotation has been wrongly conceived.

That the meaning is relevant when a denoting phrase occurs in a proposition is formally proved by the puzzle about the author of *Waverley*. The proposition 'Scott was the author of *Waverley*' has a property not possessed by 'Scott was Scott', namely the property that George IV wished to know whether it was true. Thus the two are not identical propositions;

hence the meaning of 'the author of *Waverley*' must be relevant as well as the denotation, if we adhere to the point of view to which this distinction belongs. Yet, as we have just seen, so long as we adhere to this point of view, we are compelled to hold that only the denotation can be relevant. Thus the point in question must be abandoned.

It remains to show how all the puzzles we have been considering are solved by the theory explained at the beginning of this article.

According to the view which I advocate, a denoting phrase is essentially *part* of a sentence, and does not, like most single words, have any significance on its own account. If I say 'Scott was a man', that is a statement of the form '*x* was a man', and it has 'Scott' for its subject. But if I say 'the author of *Waverley* was a man', that is not a statement of the form '*x* was a man', and does not have 'the author of *Waverley*' for its subject. Abbreviating the statement made at the beginning of this article, we may put, in place of 'the author of *Waverley* was a man', the following: 'One and only one entity wrote *Waverley*, and that one was a man'. (This is not so strictly what is meant as what was said earlier; but it is easier to follow.) And speaking generally, suppose we wish to say that the author of *Waverley* had the property φ, what we wish to say is equivalent to 'One and only one entity wrote *Waverley*, and that one had the property φ'.

The explanation of *denotation* is now as follows. Every proposition in which 'the author of *Waverley*' occurs being explained as above, the proposition 'Scott was the author of *Waverley*' (i.e., 'Scott was identical with the author of Waverley') becomes 'One and only one entity wrote *Waverley*, and Scott was identical with that one'; or, reverting to the wholly explicit form: 'It is not always false of *x* that *x* wrote *Waverley*, that it is always true of *y* that if *y* wrote *Waverley*, *y* is identical with *x*, and that Scott is identical with *x*'. Thus if '*C*' is a denoting phrase, it may happen that there is one entity *x* (there cannot be more than one) for which the proposition '*x* is identical with *C*' is true, this proposition being interpreted as above. We may then say that the entity *x* is the denotation of the phrase '*C*'. Thus Scott is the denotation of 'the author of *Waverley*'. The '*C*' in inverted commas will be merely

the phrase, not anything that can be called the meaning. The phrase per se has no meaning, because in any proposition in which it occurs the proposition, fully expressed, does not contain the phrase, which has been broken up.

The puzzle about George IV's curiosity is now seen to have a very simple solution. The proposition 'Scott was the author of *Waverley*', which was written out in its unabbreviated form in the preceding paragraph, does not contain any constituent 'the author of *Waverley*' for which we could substitute 'Scott'. This does not interfere with the truth of inferences resulting from making what is verbally the substitution of 'Scott' for 'the author of *Waverley*', so long as 'the author of *Waverley*' has what I call a *primary* occurrence in the proposition considered. The difference of primary and secondary occurrences of denoting phrases is as follows:

When we say: 'George IV wished to know whether so-and-so', or when we say 'So-and-so is surprising' or 'So-and-so is true', etc., the 'so-and-so' must be a proposition. Suppose now that 'so-and-so' contains a denoting phrase. We may either eliminate this denoting phrase from the subordinate proposition 'so-and-so', or from the whole proposition in which 'so-and-so' is a mere constituent. Different propositions result according to which we do. I have heard of a touchy owner of a yacht to whom a guest, on first seeing it, remarked, 'I thought your yacht was larger than it is'; and the owner replied, 'No, my yacht is not larger than it is'. What the guest meant was, 'The size that I thought your yacht was is greater than the size your yacht is'; the meaning attributed to him is, 'I thought the size of your yacht was greater than the size of your yacht'. To return to George IV and *Waverley*, when we say 'George IV wished to know whether Scott was the author of *Waverley*', we normally mean 'George IV wished to know whether one and only one man wrote Waverley and Scott was that man'; but we *may* also mean: 'One and only one man wrote *Waverley*, and George IV wished to know whether Scott was that man'. In the latter, 'the author of *Waverley*' has a *primary* occurrence; in the former, a *secondary*. The latter might be expressed by 'George IV wished to know, concerning the man who in fact wrote *Waverley*, whether he was Scott'. This would be true, for example, if George IV had seen Scott at a distance, and had asked 'Is that Scott?'. A *secondary* occurrence of a denoting phrase may be defined as one in which the phrase occurs in a proposition *p* which is a mere constituent of the proposition we are considering, and the substitution for the denoting phrase is to be effected in *p*, not in the whole proposition concerned. The ambiguity as between primary and secondary occurrences is hard to avoid in language; but it does no harm if we are on our guard against it. In symbolic logic it is of course easily avoided.

The distinction of primary and secondary occurrences also enables us to deal with the question whether the present King of France is bald or not bald, and generally with the logical status of denoting phrases that denote nothing. If '*C*' is a denoting phrase, say 'the term having the property *F*', then

'*C* has the property ϕ' means 'one and only one term has the property *F*, and that one has the property ϕ'.[12]

If now the property *F* belongs to no terms, or to several, it follows that '*C* has the property ϕ' is false for *all* values of ϕ. Thus 'the present King of France is bald' is certainly false; and 'the present King of France is not bald' is false if it means

'There is an entity which is now King of France and is not bald'.

but is true if it means

'It is false that there is an entity which is now King of France and is bald'.

That is, 'the King of France is not bald' is false if the occurrence of 'the King of France' is *primary,* and true if it is *secondary*. Thus all propositions in which 'the King of France' has a primary occurrence are false; the denials of such propositions are true, but in them 'the King of France' has a secondary occurrence. Thus we escape the conclusion that the King of France has a wig.

We can now see also how to deny that there is such an object as the difference between *A* and *B* in the case when *A* and *B* do not differ. If *A* and *B* do differ, there is one and only one entity

x such that '*x* is the difference between *A* and *B*' is a true proposition; if *A* and *B* do not differ, there is no such entity *x*. Thus according to the meaning of denotation lately explained, 'the difference between *A* and *B*' has a denotation when *A* and *B* differ, but not otherwise. This difference applies to true and false propositions generally. If '*a R b*' stands for '*a* has the relation *R* to *b*', then when *a R b* is true, there is such an entity as the relation *R* between *a* and *b;* when *a R b* is false, there is no such entity. Thus out of any proposition we can make a denoting phrase, which denotes an entity if the proposition is true, but does not denote an entity if the proposition is false. E.g., it is true (at least we will suppose so) that the earth revolves around the sun, and false that the sun revolves around the earth; hence 'the revolution of the earth round the sun' denotes an entity, while 'the revolution of the sun round the earth' does not denote an entity.[13]

The whole realm of non-entities, such as 'the round square', 'the even prime other than 2', 'Apollo', 'Hamlet', etc., can now be satisfactorily dealt with. All these are denoting phrases which do not denote anything. A proposition about Apollo means what we get by substituting what the classical dictionary tells us is meant by Apollo, say 'the sun-god'. All propositions in which Apollo occurs are to be interpreted by the above rules for denoting phrases. If 'Apollo' has a primary occurrence, the proposition containing the occurrence is false; if the occurrence is secondary, the proposition may be true. So again 'the round square is round' means 'there is one and only one entity *x* which is round and square, and that entity is round', which is a false proposition, not, as Meinong maintains, a true one. 'The most perfect Being has all perfections; existence is a perfection; therefore the most perfect Being exists' becomes:

'There is one and only one entity *x* which is most perfect; that one has all perfections; existence is a perfection; therefore that one exists'. As a proof, this fails for want of a proof of the premise 'there is one and only one entity *x* which is most perfect'.[14]

Mr. MacColl (*Mind,* N.S., No. 54, and again No. 55, page 401) regards individuals as of two sorts, real and unreal; hence he defines the null-class as the class consisting of all unreal individuals. This assumes that such phrases as 'the present King of France', which do not denote a real individual, do, nevertheless, denote an individual, but an unreal one. This is essentially Meinong's theory, which have seen reason to reject because it conflicts with the law of contradiction. With our theory of denoting, we are able to hold that there are no unreal individuals; so that the null-class is the class containing no members, not the class containing as members all unreal individuals.

It is important to observe the effect of our theory on the interpretation of definitions which proceed by means of denoting phrases. Most mathematical definitions are of this sort: for example '$m - n$ means the number which, added to n, gives m'. Thus $m - n$ is defined as meaning the same as a certain denoting phrase; but we agreed that denoting phrases have no meaning in isolation. Thus what the definition really ought to be is: 'Any proposition containing $m - n$ is to mean the proposition which results from substituting for "$m - n$" "the number which, added to n, gives m".' The resulting proposition is interpreted according to the rules already given for interpreting propositions whose verbal expression contains a denoting phrase. In the case where m and n are such that there is one and only one number x which, added to n, gives m, there is a number x which can be substituted for $m - n$ in any proposition containing $m - n$ without altering the truth or falsehood of the proposition. But in other cases, all propositions in which '$m - n$' has a primary occurrence are false.

The usefulness of *identity* is explained by the above theory. No one outside a logic-book ever wishes to say 'x is x', and yet assertions of identity are often made in such forms as 'Scott was the author of *Waverley*' or 'thou art the man'. The meaning of such propositions cannot be stated without the notion of identity, although they are not simply statements that Scott is identical with another term, the author of *Waverley,* or that thou art identical with another term, the man. The shortest statement of 'Scott is the author of *Waverley*' seems to be 'Scott wrote *Waverley;* and it is always true of y that if y wrote *Waverley*, y is identical with Scott'. It is in this way that identity enters into 'Scott is the

author of *Waverley*'; and it is owing to such uses that identity is worth affirming.

One interesting result of the above theory of denoting is this: when there is anything with which we do not have immediate acquaintance, but only definition by denoting phrases, then the propositions in which this thing is introduced by means of a denoting phrase do not really contain this thing as a constituent, but contain instead the constituents expressed by the several words of the denoting phrase. Thus in every proposition that we can apprehend (i.e. not only in those whose truth or falsehood we can judge of, but in all that we can think about), all the constituents are really entities with which we have immediate acquaintance. Now such things as matter (in the sense in which matter occurs in physics) and the minds of other people are known to us only by denoting phrases, i.e. we are not *acquainted* with them, but we know them as what has such and such properties. Hence, although we can form propositional functions $C(x)$ which must hold of such and such a material particle, or of So-and-so's mind, yet we are not acquainted with the propositions which affirm these things that we know must be true, because we cannot apprehend the actual entities concerned. What we know is 'So-and-so has a mind which has such and such properties', where A is the mind in question. In such a case, we know the properties of a thing without having acquaintance with the thing itself, and without, consequently, knowing any single proposition of which the thing itself is a constituent.

Of the many other consequences of the view I have been advocating, I will say nothing. I will only beg the reader not to make up his mind against the view—as he might be tempted to do, on account of its apparently excessive complication—until he has attempted to construct a theory of his own on the subject of denotation. This attempt, I believe, will convince him that, whatever the true theory may be, it cannot have such a simplicity as one might have expected beforehand.

NOTES

1. I have discussed this subject in *Principles of Mathematics,* Chap. V, and §476. The theory there advo-

cated is very nearly the same as Frege's, and is quite different from the theory to be advocated in what follows.

2. More exactly, a propositional function.

3. The second of these can be defined by means of the first, if we take it to mean, 'It is not true that "$C(x)$ is false" is always true'.

4. I shall sometimes use, instead of this complicated phrase, the phrase '$C(x)$ is not always false', or '$C(x)$ is sometimes true', supposed *defined* to mean the same as the complicated phrase.

5. As has been ably argued in Mr. Bradley's *Logic*, Book I, Chap. II.

6. Psychologically 'C (a man)' has a suggestion of *only one*, and 'C (some men)' has a suggestion of *more than one;* but we may neglect these suggestions in a preliminary sketch.

7. See *Untersuchungen zur Gegenstandstheorie und Psychologie* (Leipzig, 1904) the first three articles (by Meinong, Ameseder, and Mally respectively).

8. See his "Ueber Sinn und Bedeutung," *Zeitschrift für Phil. und Phil. Kritik,* 100. [Reprinted in this volume as "On Sense and Nominatum."]

9. Frege distinguishes the two elements of meaning and denotation everywhere, and not only in complex denoting phrases. Thus it is the *meanings* of the constituents of a denoting complex that enter into its *meaning,* not their *denotation.* In the proposition 'Mont Blanc is over 1,000 metres high', it is, according to him the *meaning* of 'Mont Blanc', not the actual mountain, that is a constituent of the *meaning* of the proposition.

10. In this theory, we shall say that the denoting phrase *expresses* a meaning; and we shall say both of the phrase and of the meaning that they *denote* a denotation. In the other theory, which I advocate, there is no *meaning,* and only sometimes a *denotation.*

11. I use these as synonyms.

12. This is the abbreviated, not the stricter, interpretation.

13. The propositions from which such suppositions are derived are not identical either with these entities or with the propositions that these entities have being.

14. The argument can be made to prove validly that all members of the class of most perfect Beings exist; it can also be proved formally that this class cannot have *more* than one member; but, taking the definition of perfection as possession of all positive predicates, it can be proved almost equally formally that the class does not have even one member.

16 Descriptions

BERTRAND RUSSELL

We dealt in the preceding chapter with the words *all* and *some;* in this chapter we shall consider the word *the* in the singular, and in the next chapter we shall consider the word *the* in the plural. It may be thought excessive to devote two chapters to one word, but to the philosophical mathematician it is a word of very great importance: like Browning's Grammarian with the enclitic δε, I would give the doctrine of this word if I were "dead from the waist down" and not merely in a prison.

We have already had occasion to mention "descriptive functions," i.e. such expressions as "the father of *x*" or "the sine of *x*." These are to be defined by first defining "descriptions."

A "description" may be of two sorts, definite and indefinite (or ambiguous). An indefinite description is a phrase of the form "a so-and-so," and a definite description is a phrase of the form "the so-and-so" (in the singular). Let us begin with the former.

"Who did you meet?" "I met a man." "That is a very indefinite description." We are therefore not departing from usage in our terminology. Our question is: What do I really assert when I assert "I met a man"? Let us assume, for the moment, that my assertion is true, and that in fact I met Jones. It is clear that what I assert is *not* "I met Jones." I may say "I met a man, but it

was not Jones"; in that case, though I lie, I do not contradict myself, as I should do if when I say I met a man I really mean that I met Jones. It is clear also that the person to whom I am speaking can understand what I say, even if he is a foreigner and has never heard of Jones.

But we may go further: not only Jones, but no actual man, enters into my statement. This becomes obvious when the statement is false, since then there is no more reason why Jones should be supposed to enter into the proposition than why anyone else should. Indeed the statement would remain significant, though it could not possibly be true, even if there were no man at all. "I met a unicorn" or "I met a sea-serpent" is a perfectly significant assertion, if we know what it would be to be a unicorn or a sea-serpent, i.e. what is the definition of these fabulous monsters. Thus it is only what we may call the *concept* that enters into the proposition. In the case of "unicorn," for example, there is only the concept: there is not also, somewhere among the shades, something unreal which may be called "a unicorn." Therefore, since it is significant (though false) to say "I met a unicorn," it is clear that this proposition, rightly analyzed, does not contain a constituent "a unicorn," though it does contain the concept "unicorn."

The question of "unreality," which con-

From *Introduction to Mathematical Philosophy* (London: George Allen and Unwin Ltd., 1919), pp. 167–180. Copyright © 1919 by George Allen & Unwin Publishers Ltd. Reprinted by permission of Taylor & Francis Books and The Bertrand Russell Peace Foundation.

fronts us at this point, is a very important one. Misled by grammar, the great majority of those logicians who have dealt with this question have dealt with it on mistaken lines. They have regarded grammatical form as a surer guide in analysis than, in fact, it is. And they have not known what differences in grammatical form are important. "I met Jones" and "I met a man" would count traditionally as propositions of the same form, but in actual fact they are of quite different forms: the first names an actual person, Jones; while the second involves a propositional function, and becomes, when made explicit: "The function 'I met x and x is human' is sometimes true." (It will be remembered that we adopted the convention of using "sometimes" as not implying more than once.) This proposition is obviously not of the form "I met x," which accounts for the existence of the proposition "I met a unicorn" in spite of the fact that there is no such thing as "a unicorn."

For want of the apparatus of propositional functions, many logicians have been driven to the conclusion that there are unreal objects. It is argued, e.g. by Meinong,[1] that we can speak about "the golden mountain," "the round square," and so on; we can make true propositions of which these are the subjects; hence they must have some kind of logical being, since otherwise the propositions in which they occur would be meaningless. In such theories, it seems to me, there is a failure of that feeling for reality which ought to be preserved even in the most abstract studies. Logic, I should maintain, must no more admit a unicorn than zoology can; for logic is concerned with the real world just as truly as zoology, though with its more abstract and general features. To say that unicorns have an existence in heraldry, or in literature, or in imagination, is a most pitiful and paltry evasion. What exists in heraldry is not an animal, made of flesh and blood, moving and breathing of its own initiative. What exists is a picture, or a description in words. Similarly, to maintain that Hamlet, for example, exists in his own world, namely, in the world of Shakespeare's imagination, just as truly as (say) Napoleon existed in the ordinary world, is to say something deliberately confusing, or else confused to a degree which is scarcely credible. There is only one

world, the "real" world: Shakespeare's imagination is part of it, and the thoughts that he had in writing Hamlet are real. So are the thoughts that we have in reading the play. But it is of the very essence of fiction that only the thoughts, feelings, etc., in Shakespeare and his readers are real, and that there is not, in addition to them, an objective Hamlet. When you have taken account of all the feelings roused by Napoleon in writers and readers of history, you have not touched the actual man; but in the case of Hamlet you have come to the end of him. If no one thought about Hamlet, there would be nothing left of him; if no one had thought about Napoleon, he would have soon seen to it that some one did. The sense of reality is vital in logic, and whoever juggles with it by pretending that Hamlet has another kind of reality is doing a disservice to thought. A robust sense of reality is very necessary in framing a correct analysis of propositions about unicorns, golden mountains, round squares, and other such pseudo-objects.

In obedience to the feeling of reality, we shall insist that, in the analysis of propositions, nothing "unreal" is to be admitted. But, after all, if there is nothing unreal, how, it may be asked, *could* we admit anything unreal? The reply is that, in dealing with propositions, we are dealing in the first instance with symbols, and if we attribute significance to groups of symbols which have no significance, we shall fall into the error of admitting unrealities, in the only sense in which this is possible, namely, as objects described. In the proposition "I met a unicorn," the whole four words together make a significant proposition, and the word "unicorn" by itself is significant, in just the same sense as the word "man." But the *two* words "a unicorn" do not form a subordinate group having a meaning of its own. Thus if we falsely attribute meaning to these two words, we find ourselves saddled with "a unicorn," and with the problem how there can be such a thing in a world where there are no unicorns. "A unicorn" is an indefinite description which describes nothing. It is not an indefinite description which describes something unreal. Such a proposition as "x is unreal" only has meaning when "x" is a description, definite or indefinite; in that case the proposition will be true if "x" is a description which describes nothing. But whether the description "*x*" describes something or describes nothing, it is in any case not a constituent of the proposition in which it occurs; like "a unicorn" just now, it is not a subordinate group having a meaning of its own. All this results from the fact that, when "*x*" is a description, "*x* is unreal" or "*x* does not exist" is not nonsense, but is always significant and sometimes true.

We may now proceed to define generally the meaning of propositions which contain ambiguous descriptions. Suppose we wish to make some statement about "a so-and-so," where "so-and-so's" are those objects that have a certain property ϕ, i.e. those objects *x* for which the propositional function ϕx is true. (E.g. if we take "a man" as our instance of "a so-and-so," ϕx will be "*x* is human.") Let us now wish to assert the property ψ of "a so-and-so," i.e. we wish to assert that "a so-and-so" has that property which *x* has when ψx is true. (E.g. in the case of "I met a man," ψx will be "I met *x*.") Now the proposition that "a so-and-so" has the property ψ is not a proposition of the form "ψx." If it were, "a so-and-so" would have to be identical with *x* for a suitable *x;* and although (in a sense) this may be true in some cases, it is certainly not true in such a case as "a unicorn." It is just this fact, that the statement that a so-and-so has the property ψ is not of the form ψx, which makes it possible for "a so-and-so" to be, in a certain clearly definable sense, "unreal." The definition is as follows:

The statement that "an object having the property ϕ has the property ψ"

means:

"The joint assertion of ϕx and ψx is not always false."

So far as logic goes, this is the same proposition as might be expressed by "some ϕ's are ψ's"; but rhetorically there is a difference, because in the one case there is a suggestion of singularity, and in the other case of plurality. This, however, is not the important point. The important point is that, when rightly analyzed, propositions verbally about "a so-and-so" are found to contain no constituent represented by this phrase. And that is why such propositions can be significant even when there is no such thing as a so-and-so.

The definition of *existence,* as applied to ambiguous descriptions, results from what was said at the end of the preceding chapter [chapter 15 of *Introduction to Mathematical Philosophy*]. We say that "men exist" or "a man exists" if the propositional function "*x* is human" is sometimes true; and generally "a so-and-so" exists if "*x* is so-and-so" is sometimes true. We may put this in other language. The proposition "Socrates is a man" is no doubt *equivalent* to "Socrates is human," but it is not the very same proposition. The *is* of "Socrates is human" expresses the relation of subject and predicate; the *is* of "Socrates is a man" expresses identity. It is a disgrace to the human race that it has chosen to employ the same word "is" for these two entirely different ideas—a disgrace which a symbolic logical language of course remedies. The identity in "Socrates is a man" is identity between an object named (accepting "Socrates" as a name, subject to qualifications explained later) and an object ambiguously described. An object ambiguously described will "exist" when at least one such proposition is true, i.e. when there is at least one true proposition of the form "*x* is a so-and-so," where "*x*" is a name. It is characteristic of ambiguous (as opposed to definite) descriptions that there may be any number of true propositions of the above form— Socrates is a man, Plato is a man, etc. Thus "a man exists" follows from Socrates, or Plato, or anyone else. With definite descriptions, on the other hand, the corresponding form of proposition, namely, "*x* is the so-and-so" (where "*x*" is a name), can only be true for one value of *x* at most. This brings us to the subject of definite descriptions, which are to be defined in a way analogous to that employed for ambiguous descriptions, but rather more complicated.

We come now to the main subject of the present chapter, namely, the definition of the word *the* (in the singular). One very important point about the definition of "a so-and-so" applies equally to "the so-and-so"; the definition to be sought is a definition of propositions in which this phrase occurs, not a definition of the phrase itself in isolation. In the case of "a so-and-so," this is fairly obvious: no one could suppose that "a man" was a definite object, which could be defined by itself. Socrates is a man, Plato is a man, Aristotle is a man, but we cannot infer that "a man" means the same as "Socrates" means and also the same as "Plato" means and also the same as "Aristotle" means, since these three names have different meanings. Nevertheless, when we have enumerated all the men in the world, there is nothing left of which we can say, "This is a man, and not only so, but it is *the* 'a man,' the quintessential entity that is just an indefinite man without being anybody in particular." It is of course quite clear that whatever there is in the world is definite: if it is a man it is one definite man and not any other. Thus there cannot be such an entity as "a man" to be found in the world, as opposed to specific men. And accordingly it is natural that we do not define "a man" itself, but only the propositions in which it occurs.

In the case of "the so-and-so" this is equally true, though at first sight less obvious. We may demonstrate that this must be the case, by a consideration of the difference between a *name* and a *definite description*. Take the proposition, "Scott is the author of *Waverley*." We have here a name, "Scott," and a description, "the author of *Waverley*," which are asserted to apply to the same person. The distinction between a name and all other symbols may be explained as follows:

A name is a simple symbol whose meaning is something that can only occur as subject, i.e. something of the kind that we defined as an "individual" or a "particular." And a "simple" symbol is one which has no parts that are symbols. Thus "Scott" is a simple symbol, because, though it has parts (namely, separate letters), these parts are not symbols. On the other hand, "the author of *Waverley*" is not a simple symbol, because the separate words that compose the phrase are parts which are symbols. If, as may be the case, whatever *seems* to be an "individual" is really capable of further analysis, we shall have to content ourselves with what may be called "relative individuals," which will be terms that, throughout the context in question, are never analyzed and never occur otherwise than as subjects. And in that case we shall have correspondingly to content ourselves with "rel-

ative names." From the standpoint of our present problem, namely, the definition of descriptions, this problem, whether these are absolute names or only relative names, may be ignored, since it concerns different stages in the hierarchy of "types," whereas we have to compare such couples as "Scott" and "the author of *Waverley*," which both apply to the same object, and do not raise the problem of types. We may, therefore, for the moment, treat names as capable of being absolute; nothing that we shall have to say will depend upon this assumption, but the wording may be a little shortened by it.

We have, then, two things to compare: (1) a *name*, which is a simple symbol, directly designating an individual which is its meaning, and having this meaning in its own right, independently of the meanings of all other words; (2) a *description*, which consists of several words, whose meanings are already fixed, and from which results whatever is to be taken as the "meaning" of the description.

A proposition containing a description is not identical with what that proposition becomes when a name is substituted, even if the name names the same object as the description describes. "Scott is the author of *Waverley*" is obviously a different proposition from "Scott is Scott": the first is a fact in literary history, the second a trivial truism. And if we put anyone other than Scott in place of "the author of *Waverley*," our proposition would become false, and would therefore certainly no longer be the same proposition. But, it may be said, our proposition is essentially of the same form as (say) "Scott is Sir Walter," in which two names are said to apply to the same person. The reply is that, if "Scott is Sir Walter" really means "the person named 'Scott' is the person named 'Sir Walter,'" then the names are being used as descriptions: i.e. the individual, instead of being named, is being described as the person having that name. This is a way in which names are frequently used in practice, and there will, as a rule, be nothing in the phraseology to show whether they are being used in this way or as names. When a name is used directly, merely to indicate what we are speaking about, it is no part of the *fact* asserted, or of the falsehood if our assertion happens to be false: it is merely part of the symbolism by which we express our thought. What we want to express is something which might (for example) be translated into a foreign language; it is something for which the actual words are a vehicle, but of which they are no part. On the other hand, when we make a proposition about "the person called 'Scott,'" the actual name "Scott" enters into what we are asserting, and not merely into the language used in making the assertion. Our proposition will now be a different one if we substitute "the person called 'Sir Walter.'" But so long as we are using names *as* names, whether we say "Scott" or whether we say "Sir Walter" is as irrelevant to what we are asserting as whether we speak English or French. Thus so long as names are used as names, "Scott is Sir Walter" is the same trivial proposition as "Scott is Scott." This completes the proof that "Scott is the author of *Waverley*" is not the same proposition as results from substituting a name for "the author of *Waverley*," no matter what name may be substituted.

When we use a variable, and speak of a propositional function, ϕx say, the process of applying general statements about x to particular cases will consist in substituting a name for the letter "x," assuming that ϕ is a function which has individuals for its arguments. Suppose, for example, that ϕx is "always true"; let it be, say, the "law of identity," $x=x$. Then we may substitute for "x" any name we choose, and we shall obtain a true proposition. Assuming for the moment that "Socrates," "Plato," and "Aristotle" are names (a very rash assumption), we can infer from the law of identity that Socrates is Socrates, Plato is Plato, and Aristotle is Aristotle. But we shall commit a fallacy if we attempt to infer, without further premises, that the author of *Waverley* is the author of *Waverley*. This results from what we have just proved, that, if we substitute a name for "the author of *Waverley*" in a proposition, the proposition we obtain is a different one. That is to say, applying the result to our present case: If "x" is a name, "$x=x$" is not the same proposition as "the author of *Waverley* is the author of *Waverley*," no matter what name "x" may be. Thus from the fact that all propositions of the form "$x=x$" are true we cannot infer, without more ado, that the author of *Waverley* is the author of *Waverley*. In fact, propositions of the form "the so-and-so is the so-and-so" are not always true: it is necessary that the so-and-so should *exist* (a term which will be explained shortly). It is false that the present King of France is the present King of France, or that the round square is the round square. When we substitute a description for a name, propositional functions which are "always true" may become false, if the description describes nothing. There is no mystery in this as soon as we realize (what was proved in the preceding paragraph) that when we substitute a description the result is not a value of the propositional function in question.

We are now in a position to define propositions in which a definite description occurs. The only thing that distinguishes "the so-and-so" from "a so-and-so" is the implication of uniqueness. We cannot speak of "*the* inhabitant of London," because inhabiting London is an attribute which is not unique. We cannot speak about "the present King of France," because there is none; but we can speak about "the present King of England." Thus propositions about "the so-and-so" always imply the corresponding propositions about "a so-and-so," with the addendum that there is not more than one so-and-so. Such a proposition as "Scott is the author of Waverley" could not be true if *Waverley* had never been written, or if several people had written it; and no more could any other proposition resulting from a propositional function x by the substitution of "the author of *Waverley*" for "x." We may say that "the author of *Waverley*" means "the value of x for which "x wrote *Waverley*' is true." Thus the proposition "the author of *Waverley* was Scotch," for example, involves:

(1) "x wrote *Waverley*" is not always false
(2) "if x and y wrote *Waverley*, x and y are identical" is always true
(3) "if x wrote *Waverley*, x was Scotch" is always true

These three propositions, translated into ordinary language, state:

(1) at least one person wrote *Waverley*
(2) at most one person wrote *Waverley*
(3) whoever wrote *Waverley* was Scotch

All these three are implied by "the author of *Waverley* was Scotch." Conversely, the three together (but no two of them) imply that the author of *Waverley* was Scotch. Hence the three together may be taken as defining what is meant by the proposition "the author of *Waverley* was Scotch."

We may somewhat simplify these three propositions. The first and second together are equivalent to: "There is a term c such that 'x wrote *Waverley*' is true when x is c and is false when x is not c." In other words, "There is a term c such that 'x wrote *Waverley*' is always equivalent to 'x is c.'" (Two propositions are "equivalent" when both are true or both are false.) We have here, to begin with, two functions of x, "x wrote *Waverley*" and "x is c," and we form a function of c by considering the equivalence of these two functions of x for all values of x; we then proceed to assert that the resulting function of c is "sometimes true," i.e. that it is true for at least one value of c. (It obviously cannot be true for more than one value of c.) These two conditions together are defined as giving the meaning of "the author of *Waverley* exists."

We may now define "the term satisfying the function ϕx exists." This is the general form of which the above is a particular case. "The author of *Waverley*" is "the term satisfying the function 'x wrote *Waverley*.'" And "the so-and-so" will always involve reference to some propositional function, namely, that which defines the property that makes a thing a so-and-so. Our definition is as follows:

"The term satisfying the function ϕx exists" means:
"There is a term c such that ϕx is always equivalent to 'x is c.'"

In order to define "the author of *Waverley* was Scotch," we have still to take account of the third of our three propositions, namely, "Whoever wrote *Waverley* was Scotch." This will be satisfied by merely adding that the c in question is to be Scotch. Thus "the author of *Waverley* was Scotch" is:

"There is a term c such that (1) 'x wrote *Waverley*' is always equivalent to 'x is c,' (2) c is Scotch."

And generally: "the term satisfying ϕx satisfies ψx" is defined as meaning:

"There is a term c such that (1) ϕx is always equivalent to 'x is c,' (2) ψx is true."

This is the definition of propositions in which descriptions occur.

It is possible to have much knowledge concerning a term described, i.e. to know many propositions concerning "the so-and-so," without actually knowing what the so-and-so is, i.e. without knowing any proposition of the form "x is the so-and-so," where "x" is a name. In a detective story propositions about "the man who did the deed" are accumulated, in the hope that ultimately they will suffice to demonstrate that it was A who did the deed. We may even go so far as to say that, in all such knowledge as can be expressed in words—with the exception of "this" and "that" and a few other words of which the meaning varies on different occasions—no names, in the strict sense, occur, but what seem like names are really descriptions. We may inquire significantly whether Homer existed, which we could not do if "Homer" were a name. The proposition "the so-and-so exists" is significant, whether true or false; but if a is the so-and-so (where "a" is a name), the words "a exists" are meaningless. It is only of descriptions—definite or indefinite—that existence can be significantly asserted; for, if "a" is a name, it *must* name something: what does not name anything is not a name, and therefore, if intended to be a name, is a symbol devoid of meaning, whereas a description, like "the present King of France," does not become incapable of occurring significantly merely on the ground that it describes nothing, the reason being that it is a *complex* symbol, of which the meaning is derived from that of its constituent symbols. And so, when we ask whether Homer existed, we are using the word "Homer" as an abbreviated description: we may replace it by (say) "the author of the *Iliad* and the *Odyssey*." The same considerations apply to almost all uses of what look like proper names.

When descriptions occur in propositions, it is necessary to distinguish what may be called "primary" and "secondary" occurrences. The abstract distinction is as follows. A description has a "primary" occurrence when the proposition in which it occurs results from substituting the description for "x" in some propositional function ϕx; a description has a "secondary" occurrence when the result of substituting the description for x in ϕx gives only *part* of the proposition concerned. An instance will make this clearer. Consider "the present King of France is bald." Here "the present King of France" has a primary occurrence, and the proposition is false. Every proposition in which a description which describes nothing has a primary occurrence is false. But now consider "the present King of France is not bald." This is ambiguous. If we are first to take "x is bald," then substitute "the present King of France" for "x," and then deny the result, the occurrence of "the present King of France" is secondary and our proposition is true; but if we are to take "x is not bald" and substitute "the present King of France" for "x," then "the present King of France" has a primary occurrence and the proposition is false. Confusion of primary and secondary occurrences is a ready source of fallacies where descriptions are concerned.

Descriptions occur in mathematics chiefly in the form of *descriptive functions,* i.e. "the term having the relation R to y," or "the R of y" as we may say, on the analogy of "the father of y" and similar phrases. To say "the father of y is rich," for example, is to say that the following propositional function of c: "'c is rich, and 'x begat y' is always equivalent to 'x is c,'" is "sometimes true," i.e. is true for at least one value of c. It obviously cannot be true for more than one value.

The theory of descriptions, briefly outlined in the present chapter, is of the utmost importance both in logic and in theory of knowledge. But for purposes of mathematics, the more philosophical parts of the theory are not essential, and have therefore been omitted in the above account, which has confined itself to the barest mathematical requisites.

REFERENCES

1. *Untersuchungen zur Gegenstandstheorie und Psychologie,* 1904.

17 On Referring

P. F. STRAWSON

We very commonly use expressions of certain kinds to mention or refer to some individual person or single object or particular event or place or process, in the course of doing what we should normally describe as making a statement about that person, object, place, event, or process. I shall call this way of using expressions the 'uniquely referring use'. The classes of expressions which are most commonly used in this way are: singular demonstrative pronouns ("this" and "that"); proper names e.g. "Venice," "Napoleon," "John"); singular personal and impersonal pronouns ("he," "she," "I," "you," "it"); and phrases beginning with the definite article followed by a noun, qualified or unqualified, in the singular (e.g. "the table," "the old man," "the king of France"). Any expression of any of these classes can occur as the subject of what would traditionally be regarded as a singular subject-predicate sentence; and would, so occurring, exemplify the use I wish to discuss.

I do not want to say that expressions belonging to these classes never have any other use than the one I want to discuss. On the contrary, it is obvious that they do. It is obvious that anyone who uttered the sentence, "The whale is a mammal," would be using the expression "the whale" in a way quite different from the way it would be used by anyone who had occasion seriously to utter the sentence, "The whale struck the ship." In the first sentence one is obviously *not* mentioning, and in the second sentence one obviously is mentioning, a particular whale. Again if I said, "Napoleon was the greatest French soldier," I should be using the word "Napoleon" to mention a certain individual, but I should not be using the phrase, "the greatest French soldier," to mention an individual, but to say something about an individual I had already mentioned. It would be natural to say that in using this sentence I was talking *about* Napoleon and that what I was *saying* about him was that he was the greatest French soldier. But of course I *could* use the expression, "the greatest French soldier," to mention an individual; for example, by saying: "The greatest French soldier died in exile." So it is obvious that at least some expressions belonging to the classes I mentioned *can* have uses other than the use I am anxious to discuss. Another thing I do not want to say is that in any given sentence there is never more than one expression used in the way I propose to discuss. On the contrary, it is obvious that there may be more than one. For example, it would be natural to say that, in seriously using the sentence, "The whale struck the ship," I was saying something about both a certain whale and a certain ship, that I was using each of the expressions "the whale" and "the ship" to mention a particular object; or, in other words, that I was using each of these expres-

From *Mind* 59 (1950): 320–344. Reprinted by permission of Oxford University Press.

sions in the uniquely referring way. In general, however, I shall confine my attention to cases where an expression used in this way occurs as the grammatical subject of a sentence.

I think it is true to say that Russell's theory of descriptions, which is concerned with the last of the four classes of expressions I mentioned above (i.e. with expressions of the form "the so-and-so"), is still widely accepted among logicians as giving a correct account of the use of such expressions in ordinary language. I want to show in the first place, that this theory, so regarded, embodies some fundamental mistakes.

What question or questions about phrases of the form "the so-and-so" was the theory of descriptions designed to answer? I think that at least one of the questions may be illustrated as follows. Suppose someone were now to utter the sentence, "The king of France is wise." No one would say that the sentence which had been uttered was meaningless. Everyone would agree that it was significant. But everyone knows that there is not at present a king of France. One of the questions the theory of descriptions was designed to answer was the question: How can such a sentence as "The king of France is wise" be significant even when there is nothing which answers to the description it contains, i.e., in this case, nothing which answers to the description "The king of France"? And one of the reasons why Russell thought it important to give a correct answer to this question was that he thought it important to show that another answer which might be given was wrong. The answer that he thought was wrong, and to which he was anxious to supply an alternative, might be exhibited as the conclusion of either of the following two fallacious arguments. Let us call the sentence "The king of France is wise" the sentence *S*. Then the first argument is as follows:

(1) The phrase, "the king of France," is the subject of the sentence *S*.

Therefore (2) if *S* is a significant sentence, *S* is a sentence *about* the king of France.

But (3) if there in no sense exists a king of France, the sentence is not about anything, and hence not about the king of France.

Therefore (4) since *S* is significant, there must in some sense (in some world) exist (or subsist) the king of France.

And the second argument is as follows:

(1) If *S* is significant, it is either true or false.

(2) *S* is true if the king of France is wise and false if the king of France is not wise.

(3) But the statement that the king of France is wise and the statement that the king of France is not wise are alike true only if there is (in some sense, in some world) something which is the king of France.

Hence (4) since S is significant, there follows the same conclusion as before.

These are fairly obviously bad arguments, and, as we should expect, Russell rejects them. The postulation of a world of strange entities, to which the king of France belongs, offends, he says, against "that feeling for reality which ought to be preserved even in the most abstract studies." The fact that Russell rejects these arguments is, however, less interesting than the extent to which, in rejecting their conclusion, he concedes the more important of their principles. Let me refer to the phrase, "the king of France," as the phrase D. Then I think Russell's reasons for rejecting these two arguments can be summarized as follows. The mistake arises, he says, from thinking that D, which is certainly the *grammatical* subject of S, is also the *logical* subject of S. But D is not the logical subject of S. In fact S, although grammatically it has a singular subject and a predicate, is not logically a subject-predicate sentence at all. The proposition it expresses is a complex kind of *existential* proposition, part of which might be described as a "uniquely existential" proposition. To exhibit the logical form of the proposition, we should rewrite the sentence in a logically appropriate grammatical form, in such a way that the deceptive similarity of S to a sentence expressing a subject-predicate proposition would disappear, and we should be safeguarded against arguments such as the bad ones I outlined above. Before recalling the details of Russell's analysis of S, let us notice what his answer, as I have so far given it, seems to imply. His answer seems to imply that in the case of a sentence which is similar to S in that (1) it is grammatically of the subject-predicate form and (2) its grammatical subject does not refer to anything, then the only alternative to its being meaningless is that it should not really (i.e. logically) be of the subject-predicate form at all, but of some quite different form. And this in its turn seems to imply that if there are any sentences which are genuinely of the subject-predicate form, then the very fact of their being significant, having a meaning, guarantees that there is something referred to by the logical (and grammatical) subject. Moreover, Russell's answer seems to imply that there are such sentences. For if it is true that one may be misled by the grammatical similarity of S to other sentences into thinking that it is logically of the subject-predicate form, then surely there must be other sentences grammatically similar to S, which *are* of the subject-predicate form. To show not only that Russell's answer seems to imply these conclusions, but that he accepted at least the first two of them, it is enough to consider what he says about a class of expressions which he calls "logically proper names" and contrasts with expressions, like D, which he calls "definite descriptions." Of logically proper names Russell says or implies the following things:

(1) That they and they alone can occur as subjects of sentences which are genuinely of the subject-predicate form.

(2) That an expression intended to be a logically proper name is *meaningless* unless there is some single object for which it stands: for the *meaning* of such an expression just is the individual object which the expression designates. To be a name at all, therefore, it *must* designate something.

It is easy to see that if anyone believes these two propositions, then the only way for him to save the significance of the sentence S is to deny that it is a logically subject-predicate sentence. Generally, we may say that Russell recognizes only two ways in which sentences which seem, from their grammatical structure, to be about some particular person or individual object or event, can be significant:

(1) The first is that their grammatical form should be misleading as to their logical form,

and that they should be analyzable, like S, as a special kind of existential sentence.

(2) The second is that their grammatical subject should be a logically proper name, of which the meaning is the individual thing it designates.

I think that Russell is unquestionably wrong in this, and that sentences which are significant, and which begin with an expression used in the uniquely referring way, fall into neither of these two classes. Expressions used in the uniquely referring way are never either logically proper names or descriptions, if what is meant by calling them "descriptions" is that they are to be analyzed in accordance with the model provided by Russell's theory of descriptions.

There are no logically proper names and there are no descriptions (in this sense).

Let us now consider the details of Russell's analysis. According to Russell, anyone who asserted S would be asserting that:

(1) There is a king of France
(2) There is not more than one king of France
(3) There is nothing which is king of France and is not wise

It is easy to see both how Russell arrived at this analysis, and how it enables him to answer the question with which we began, viz. the question: How can the sentence S be significant when there is no king of France? The way in which he arrived at the analysis was clearly by asking himself what would be the circumstances in which we would say that anyone who uttered the sentence S had made a true assertion. And it does seem pretty clear, and I have no wish to dispute, that the sentences (1)–(3) above do describe circumstances which are at least *necessary* conditions of anyone making a true assertion by uttering the sentence S. But, as I hope to show, to say this is not at all the same thing as to say that Russell has given a correct account of the use of the sentence S or even that he has given an account which, though incomplete, is correct as far as it goes; and is certainly not at all the same thing as to say that the model translation provided is a correct model for all (or for any) singular sentences beginning with a phrase of the form "the so-and-so."

It is also easy to see how this analysis enables Russell to answer the question of how the sentence S can be significant, even when there is no king of France. For, if this analysis is correct, anyone who utters the sentence S today would be jointly asserting three propositions, one of which (viz. that there is a king of France) would be false; and since the conjunction of three propositions, of which one is false, is itself false, the assertion as a whole would be significant, but false. So neither of the bad arguments for subsistent entities would apply to such an assertion.

II

As a step towards showing that Russell's solution of his problem is mistaken, and towards providing the correct solution, I want now to draw certain distinctions. For this purpose I shall, for the remainder of this section, refer to an expression which has a uniquely referring use as "an expression" for short; and to a sentence beginning with such an expression as "a sentence" for short. The distinctions I shall draw are rather rough and ready, and, no doubt, difficult cases could be produced which would call for their refinement. But I think they will serve my purpose. The distinctions are between:

(A1) a sentence
(A2) a use of a sentence
(A3) an utterance of a sentence

and, correspondingly, between:

(B1) an expression
(B2) a use of an expression
(B3) an utterance of an expression

Consider again the sentence, "The king of France is wise." It is easy to imagine that this sentence was uttered at various times from, say, the beginning of the seventeenth century onwards, during the reigns of each successive French monarch; and easy to imagine that it was also uttered during the subsequent periods in which France was not a monarchy. Notice that it was natural for me to speak of "the sentence" or "this sentence" being uttered at various times during this period; or, in other words, that it would be natural and correct to speak of *one and the* same sentence being uttered on all these various occasions. It is in the sense in which it would be correct to speak of one and the same sentence being uttered on all these various occa-sions that I want to use the expression (A1) "a sentence." There are, however, obvious differences between different *occasions of the use* of this sentence. For instance, if one man uttered it in the reign of Louis XIV and another man uttered it in the reign of Louis XV, it would be natural to say (to assume) that they were respectively talking about different people; and it might be held that the first man, in using the sentence, made a true assertion, while the second man, in using the same sentence, made a false assertion. If on the other hand two different men simultaneously uttered the sentence (e.g. if one wrote it and the other spoke it) during the reign of Louis XIV, it would be natural to say (assume) that they were both talking about the same person, and, in that case, in using the sentence, they *must* either both have made a true assertion or both have made a false assertion. And this illustrates what I mean by a *use* of a sentence. The two men who uttered the sentence, one in the reign of Louis XV and one in the reign of Louis XIV, each made a different use of the same sentence; whereas the two men who uttered the sentence simultaneously in the reign of Louis XIV, made the same use[1] of the same sentence. Obviously in the case of this sentence, and equally obviously in the case of many others, we cannot talk of *the sentence* being true or false, but only of its being used to make a true or false assertion or (if this is preferred) to express a true or a false proposition. And equally obviously we cannot talk of *the sentence* being *about* a particular person, for the same sentence may be used at different times to talk about quite different particular persons, but only of a *use* of the sentence to talk about a particular person. Finally it will make sufficiently clear what I mean by an utterance of a sentence if I say that the two men who simultaneously uttered the sentence in the reign of Louis XIV made two different utterances of the same sentence, though they made the same *use* of the sentence.

If we now consider not the whole sentence, "The king of France is wise," but that part of it which is the expression, "the king of France," it is obvious that we can make analogous, though not identical distinctions between (1) the expression, (2) a use of the expression, and (3) an utterance of the expression. The distinctions will not be identical; we obviously cannot correctly talk of the expression "the king of France" being used to express a true or false proposition, since in general only sentences can be used truly or falsely; and similarly it is only by using a sentence and not by using an expression alone, that you can talk about a particular person. Instead, we shall say in this case that you *use* the expression to *mention* or *refer to* a particular person in the course of using the sentence to talk about him. But obviously in this case, and a great many others, the *expression* (B1) cannot be said to mention, or refer to, anything, any more than the *sentence* can be said to be true or false. The same expression can have different mentioning-uses, as the same sentence can be used to make statements with different truth-values. 'Mentioning', or 'referring', is not something an expression does; it is something that someone can use an expression to do. Mentioning, or referring to, something is a characteristic of *a use* of an expression, just as 'being about' something, and truth-or-falsity, are characteristics of a *use* of a sentence.

A very different example may help to make these distinctions clearer. Consider another case of an expression which has a uniquely referring use, viz. the expression "I"; and consider the sentence, "I am hot." Countless people may use this same sentence; but it is logically impossible for two different people to make *the same use* of this sentence: or, if this is preferred, to use it to express the same proposition. The expression "I" may correctly be used by (and only by) any one of innumerable people to refer to himself. To say this is to say something about the expression "I": it is, in a sense, to give its meaning. This is the sort of thing that can be said about *expressions*. But it makes no sense to say of the *expression* "I" that it refers to a particular person. This is the sort of thing that can be said only of a particular use of the expression.

Let me use "type" as an abbreviation for "sentence or expression." Then I am not saying that there are sentences and expressions (types), *and* uses of them, *and* utterances of them, as there are ships *and* shoes *and* sealing-wax. I am saying that we cannot say *the same things* about types, uses of types, and utterances of types. And the fact is that we do talk about types;

and that confusion is apt to result from the failure to notice the differences between what we can say about these and what we can say only about the *uses* of types. We are apt to fancy we are talking about sentences and expressions when we are talking about the uses of sentences and expressions.

This is what Russell does. Generally, as against Russell, I shall say this. Meaning (in at least one important sense) is a function of the sentence or expression; mentioning and referring and truth or falsity, are functions of the use of the sentence or expression. To give the meaning of an expression (in the sense in which I am using the word) is to give *general directions* for its use to refer to or mention particular objects or persons; to give the meaning of a sentence is to give *general directions* for its use in making true or false assertions. It is not to talk about any particular occasion of the use of the sentence or expression. The meaning of an expression cannot be identified with the object it is used, on a particular occasion, to refer to. The meaning of a sentence cannot be identified with the assertion it is used, on a particular occasion, to make. For to talk about the meaning of an expression or sentence is not to talk about its use on a particular occasion, but about the rules, habits, conventions governing its correct use, on all occasions, to refer or to assert. So the question of whether a sentence or expression is *significant or not* has nothing whatever to do with the question of whether the sentence, *uttered on a particular occasion,* is, on that occasion, being used to make a true-or-false assertion or not, or of whether the expression is, on that occasion, being used to refer to, or mention, anything at all.

The source of Russell's mistake was that he thought that referring or mentioning, if it occurred at all, must be meaning. He did not distinguish (B1) from (B2); he confused expressions with their use in a particular context; and so confused meaning with mentioning, with referring. If I talk about my handkerchief, I can, perhaps, produce the object I am referring to out of my pocket. I cannot produce the meaning of the expression, "my handkerchief," out of my pocket. Because Russell confused meaning with mentioning, he thought that if there were any expressions having a uniquely referring use, which were what they seemed (i.e. logical subjects) and not something else in disguise, their meaning must *be* the particular object which they were used to refer to. Hence the troublesome mythology of the logically proper name. But if someone asks me the meaning of the expression "this"—once Russell's favorite candidate for this status—I do not hand him the object I have just used the expression to refer to, adding at the same time that the meaning of the word changes every time it is used. Nor do I hand him all the objects it ever has been, or might be, used to refer to. I explain and illustrate the conventions governing the use of the expression. This is giving the meaning of the expression. It *is* quite different from giving (in any sense of giving) the object to which it refers; for the expression itself does not refer to anything; though it can be used, on different occasion, to refer to innumerable things. Now as a matter of fact there is, in English, a sense of the word "mean" in which this word does approximate to "indicate, mention or refer to"; e.g. when somebody (unpleasantly) says, "I mean you"; or when I point and say, "That's the one I mean." But *the one I meant* is quite different from *the meaning of the expression* I used to talk of it. In this special sense of "mean," it is people who mean, not expressions. People use expressions to refer to particular things. But the meaning of an expression is not the set of things or the single thing it may correctly be used to refer to: the meaning is the set of rules, habits, conventions for its use in referring.

It is the same with sentences: even more obviously so. Everyone knows that the sentence, "The table is covered with books," is significant, and everyone knows what it means. But if I ask, "What object is that sentence about?" I am asking an absurd question—a question which cannot be asked about the sentence, but only about some use of the sentence: and in this case the sentence has not been used to talk about something, it has only been taken as an example. In knowing what it means, you are knowing how it could correctly be used to talk about things: so knowing the meaning has nothing to do with knowing about any particular use of the sentence to talk about anything. Similarly, if I ask: "Is the sentence true or false?" I am asking an absurd question, which becomes no less absurd if I add, "It must be one or the other since it is significant." The question is absurd, because the *sentence* is neither true nor false any more than it is *about* some object. Of course the fact that it is significant is the same as the fact that it *can* correctly be used to talk about something and that, in so using it, someone will be making a true or false assertion. And I will add that it will be used to make a true or false assertion *only* if the person using it *is* talking about something. If, when he utters it, he is not talking about anything, then his use is not a genuine one, but a spurious or pseudo-use: he is not making either a true or a false assertion, though he may think he is. And this points the way to the correct answer to the puzzle to which the theory of descriptions gives a fatally incorrect answer. The important point is that the question of whether the sentence is significant or not is quite independent of the question that can be raised about a particular use of it, viz. the question whether it is a genuine or a spurious use, whether it is being used to talk about something, or in make-believe, or as an example in philosophy. The question whether the sentence is significant or not is the question whether there exist such language habits, conventions or rules that the sentence logically could be used to talk about something; and is hence quite independent of the question whether it is being so used on a particular occasion.

III

Consider again the sentence, "The king of France is wise," and the true and false things Russell says about it.

There are at least two true things which Russell would say about the sentence:

(1) The first is that it is significant; that if anyone were now to utter it, he would be uttering a significant sentence.

(2) The second is that anyone now uttering the sentence would be making a true assertion only if there in fact at present existed one and only one king of France, and if he were wise.

What are the false things which Russell would say about the sentence? They are:

(1) That anyone now uttering it would be making a true assertion or a false assertion.

(2) That part of what he would be asserting would be that there at present existed one and only one king of France.

I have already given some reasons for thinking that these two statements are incorrect. Now suppose someone were in fact to say to you with a perfectly serious air: "The king of France is wise." Would you say, "That's untrue"? I think it is quite certain that you would not. But suppose he went on to ask you whether you thought that what he had just said was true, or was false; whether you agreed or disagreed with what he had just said. I think you would be inclined, with some hesitation, to say that you did not do either; that the question of whether his statement was true or false simply *did not arise,* because there was no such person as the king of France. You might, if he were obviously serious (had a dazed astray-in-the-centuries look), say something like: "I'm afraid you must be under a misapprehension. France is not a monarchy. There is no king of France." And this brings out the point that if a man seriously uttered the sentence, his uttering it would in some sense be *evidence* that he *believed* that there was a king of France. It would not be evidence for his believing this simply in the way in which a man's reaching for his raincoat is evidence for his believing that it is raining. But nor would it be evidence for his believing this in the way in which a man's saying, "It's raining," is evidence for his believing that it is raining. We might put it as follows. To say "The king of France is wise" is, in some sense of 'imply', to *imply* that there is a king of France. But this is a very special and odd sense of 'imply'. 'Implies' in this sense is certainly not equivalent to 'entails' (or 'logically implies'). And this comes out from the fact that when, in response to his statement, we say (as we should) "There is no king of France," we should certainly *not* say we were *contradicting* the statement that the king of France is wise. We are certainly not saying that it is false. We are, rather, giving a reason for saying that the question of whether it is true or false simply does not arise.

And this is where the distinction I drew ear-lier can help us. The sentence, "The king of France is wise," is certainly significant; but this does not mean that any particular use of it is true or false. We use it truly or falsely when we use it to talk about someone; when, in using the expression, "The king of France," we are in fact mentioning someone. The fact that the sentence and the expression, respectively, are significant just is the fact that the sentence *could* be used, in certain circumstances, to say something true or false, that the expression *could* be used, in certain circumstances, to mention a particular person; and to know their meaning is to know what sort of circumstances these are. So when we utter the sentence without in fact mentioning anybody by the use of the phrase, "The king of France," the sentence does not cease to be significant: We simply *fail* to say anything true or false because we simply fail to mention anybody by this particular use of that perfectly significant phrase. It is, if you like, a spurious use of the sentence, and a spurious use of the expression; though we may (or may not) mistakenly think it a genuine use.

And such spurious uses are very familiar. Sophisticated romancing, sophisticated fiction,[2] depend upon them. If I began, "The king of France is wise," and went on, "and he lives in a golden castle and has a hundred wives", and so on, a hearer would understand me perfectly well, without supposing *either* that I was talking about a particular person, *or* that I was making a false statement to the effect that there existed such a person as my words described. (It is worth adding that where the use of sentences and expressions is overtly fictional, the sense of the word "about" may change. As Moore said, it is perfectly natural and correct to say that some of the statements in *Pickwick Papers* are *about* Mr. Pickwick. But where the use of sentences and expressions is not overtly fictional, this use of "about" seems less correct; i.e. it would not *in general* be correct to say that a statement was about Mr. X or the so-and-so, unless there were such a person or thing. So it is where the romancing is in danger of being taken seriously that we might answer the question, "Who is he talking about?" with "He's not talking about anybody"; but, in saying this, we are not saying that what he is saying is either false or nonsense.)

Overtly fictional uses apart, however, I said just now that to use such an expression as "The king of France" at the beginning of a sentence was, in some sense of 'imply', to imply that there was a king of France. When a man uses such an expression, he does not *assert,* nor does what he says *entail,* a uniquely existential proposition. But one of the conventional functions of the definite article is to act as a *signal* that a unique reference is being made—a signal, not a disguised assertion. When we begin a sentence with "the such-and-such" the use of "the" shows, but does not state, that we are, or intended to be, referring to one particular individual of the species "such-and-such." *Which* particular individual is a matter to be determined from context, time, place, and any other features of the situation of utterance. Now, whenever a man uses any expression, the presumption is that he thinks he is using it correctly: so when he uses the expression, "the such-and-such," in a uniquely referring way, the presumption is that he thinks both that there is *some* individual of that species, and that the context of use will sufficiently determine which one he has in mind. To use the word "the" in this way is then to imply (in the relevant sense of 'imply') that the existential conditions described by Russell are fulfilled. But to use "the" in this way is not to *state* that those conditions are fulfilled. If I begin a sentence with an expression of the form, "the so-and-so," and then am prevented from saying more, I have made no statement of any kind; but I may have succeeded in mentioning someone or something.

The uniquely existential assertion supposed by Russell to be part of any assertion in which a uniquely referring use is made of an expression of the form "the so-and-so" is, he observes, a compound of two assertions. To say that there is a ϕ is to say something compatible with there being several ϕs; to say there is not more than one ϕ is to say something compatible with there being none. To say there is one ϕ and one only is to compound these two assertions. I have so far been concerned mostly with the alleged assertion of existence and less with the alleged assertion of uniqueness. An example which throws the emphasis on the latter will serve to bring out more clearly the sense of 'implied' in which a uniquely existential assertion is

implied, but not entailed, by the use of expressions in the uniquely referring way. Consider the sentence, "The table is covered with books." It is quite certain that in any normal use of this sentence, the expression "the table" would be used to make a unique reference, i.e. to refer to some one table. It is a quite strict use of the definite article, in the sense in which Russell talks on p. 30 of *Principia Mathematica,* of using the article "*strictly,* so as to imply uniqueness." On the same page Russell says that a phrase of the form "the so-and-so," used strictly, "will only have an application in the event of there being one so-and-so and no more." Now it is obviously quite false that the phrase "the table" in the sentence "the table is covered with books," used normally, will "only have an application in the event of there being one table and no more." It is indeed tautologically true that, in such a use, the phrase will have an application only in the event of there being one table and no more *which is being referred to,* and that it will be understood to have an application only in the event of there being one table and no more which it is understood as being used to refer to. To use the sentence is not to assert, but it is (in the special sense discussed) to imply, that there is only one thing which is *both* of the kind specified (i.e. a table) *and is being referred to* by the speaker. It is obviously not to assert this. To refer is not to say you are referring. To say there is *some table or other* to which you are referring is not the same as referring to a particular table. We should have no use for such phrases as "the individual I referred to" unless there were something which counted as referring. (It would make no sense to say you had pointed if there were nothing which counted as pointing.) So once more I draw the conclusion that referring to or mentioning a particular thing cannot be dissolved into any kind of assertion. To refer is not to assert, though you refer in order to go on to assert.

Let me now take an example of the uniquely referring use of an expression not of the form, "the so-and-so." Suppose I advance my hands, cautiously cupped, towards someone, saying, as I do so, "This is a fine red one." He, looking into my hands and seeing nothing there, may say: "What is? What are you talking about?" Or perhaps, "But there's nothing in your hands." Of course it would be absurd to say that, in saying "But you've got nothing in your hands," he was *denying* or *contradicting* what I said. So "this" is not a disguised description in Russell's sense. Nor is it a logically proper name. For one must know what the sentence means in order to react in that way to the utterance of it. It is precisely because the significance of the word "this" is independent of any particular reference it may be used to make, though not independent of the way it may be used to refer, that I can, as in this example, use it to *pretend* to be referring to something.

The general moral of all this is that communication is much less a matter of explicit or disguised assertion than logicians used to suppose. The particular application of this general moral in which I am interested is its application to the case of making a unique reference. It is a part of the significance of expressions of the kind I am discussing that they can be used, in an immense variety of contexts, to make unique references. It is no part of their significance to assert that they are being so used or that the conditions of their being so used are fulfilled. So the wholly important distinction we are required to draw is between

(1) using an expression to make a unique reference; and
(2) asserting that there is one and only one individual which has certain characteristics (e.g. is of a certain kind, or stands in a certain relation to the speaker, or both).

This is, in other words, the distinction between

(1) sentences containing an expression used to indicate or mention or refer to a particular person or thing; and
(2) uniquely existential sentences.

What Russell does is progressively to assimilate more and more sentences of class (1) to sentences of class (2), and consequently to involve himself in insuperable difficulties about logical subjects, and about values for individual variables generally: difficulties which have led him finally to the logically disastrous theory of names developed in the *Enquiry into Meaning*

and Truth and in *Human Knowledge*. That view of the meaning of logical-subject-expressions which provides the whole incentive to the Theory of Descriptions at the same time precludes the possibility of Russell's ever finding any satisfactory substitutes for those expressions which, beginning with substantival phrases, he progressively degrades from the status of logical subjects.[3] It is not simply, as is sometimes said, the fascination of the relation between a name and its bearer, that is the root of the trouble. Not even names come up to the impossible standard set. It is rather the combination of two more radical misconceptions: first, the failure to grasp the importance of the distinction (section II above) between what may be said of an expression and what may be said of a particular use of it; second, a failure to recognize the uniquely referring use of expressions for the harmless, necessary thing it is, distinct from, but complementary to, the predicative or ascriptive use of expressions. The expressions which can in fact occur as singular logical subjects are expressions of the class I listed at the outset (demonstratives, substantival phrases, proper names, pronouns): to say this is to say that these expressions, together with context (in the widest sense), are what one uses to make unique references. The point of the conventions governing the uses of such expressions is, along with the situation of utterance, to secure uniqueness of reference. But to do this, enough is enough. We do not, and we cannot, while referring, attain the point of complete explicitness at which the referring function is no longer performed. The actual unique reference made, if any, is a matter of the particular use in the particular context; the significance of the expression used is the set of rules or conventions which permit such references to be made. Hence we can, using significant expressions, pretend to refer, in make-believe or in fiction, or mistakenly think we are referring when we are not referring to anything.

This shows the need for distinguishing two kinds (among many others) of linguistic conventions or rules: rules for referring, and rules for attributing and ascribing; and for an investigation of the former. If we recognize this distinction of use for what it is, we are on the way to solving a number of ancient logical and metaphysical puzzles.

My last two sections are concerned, but only in the barest outline, with these questions.

IV

One of the main purposes for which we use language is the purpose of stating facts about things and persons and events. If we want to fulfill this purpose we must have some way of forestalling the question, "What (who, which one) are you talking about?" as well as the question, "What are you saying about it (him, her)?" The task of forestalling the first question is the referring (or identifying) task. The task of forestalling the second is the attributive (or descriptive or classificatory or ascriptive) task. In the conventional English sentence which is used to state, or to claim to state, a fact about an individual thing or person or event, the performance of these two tasks can be roughly and approximately assigned to separable expressions.[4] And in such a sentence, this assigning of expressions to their separate rôles corresponds to the conventional grammatical classification of subject and predicate. There is nothing sacrosanct about the employment of separable expressions for these two tasks. Other methods could be, and are, employed. There is, for instance, the method of uttering a single word or attributive phrase in the conspicuous presence of the object referred to; or that analogous method exemplified by, e.g., the painting of the words "unsafe for lorries" on a bridge, or the tying of a label reading "first prize" on a vegetable marrow. Or one can imagine an elaborate game in which one never used an expression in the uniquely referring way at all, but uttered only uniquely existential sentences, trying to enable the hearer to identify what was being talked of by means of an accumulation of relative clauses. (This description of the purposes of the game shows in what sense it would be a game: this is not the normal use we make of existential sentences.) Two points require emphasis. The first is that the necessity of performing these two tasks in order to state particular facts requires no tran-

scendental explanation: To call attention to it is partly to elucidate the meaning of the phrase, "stating a fact." The second is that even this elucidation is made in terms derivative from the grammar of the conventional singular sentence; that even the overtly functional, linguistic distinction between the identifying and attributive rôles that words may play in language is prompted by the fact that ordinary speech offers us separable expressions to which the different functions may be plausibly and approximately assigned. And this functional distinction has cast long philosophical shadows. The distinctions between particular and universal, between substance and quality, are such pseudo-material shadows, cast by the grammar of the conventional sentence, in which separable expressions play distinguishable roles.

To use a separate expression to perform the first of these tasks is to use an expression in the uniquely referring way. I want now to say something in general about the conventions of use for expressions used in this way, and to contrast them with conventions of ascriptive use. I then proceed to the brief illustration of these general remarks and to some further applications of them.

What in general is required for making a unique reference is, obviously, some device, or devices, for showing both *that* a unique reference is intended and *what* unique reference it is; some device requiring and enabling the hearer or reader to identify what is being talked about. In securing this result, the context of utterance is of an importance which it is almost impossible to exaggerate; and by "context" I mean, at least, the time, the place, the situation, the identity of the speaker, the subjects which form the immediate focus of interest, and the personal histories of both the speaker and those he is addressing. Besides context, there is, of course, convention—linguistic convention. But, except in the case of genuine proper names, of which I shall have more to say later, the fulfillment of more or less precisely stateable contextual conditions is *conventionally* (or, in a wide sense of the word, *logically*) required for the correct referring use of expressions in a sense in which this is not true of correct ascriptive uses. The requirement for the correct application of an expression in its ascriptive use to a certain thing is simply that the thing should be of a certain kind, have certain characteristics. The requirement for the correct application of an expression in its referring use to a certain thing is something over and above any requirement derived from such ascriptive meaning as the expression may have; it is, namely, the requirement that the thing should be in a certain relation to the speaker and to the context of utterance. Let me call this the contextual requirement. Thus, for example, in the limiting case of the word "I" the contextual requirement is that the thing should be identical with the speaker; but in the case of most expressions which have a referring use this requirement cannot be so precisely specified. A further, and perfectly general, difference between conventions for referring and conventions for describing is one we have already encountered, viz. that the fulfillment of the conditions for a correct ascriptive use of an expression is a part of what is stated by such a use; but the fulfillment of the conditions for a correct referring use of an expression is never part of what is stated, though it is (in the relevant sense of 'implied') implied by such a use.

Conventions for referring have been neglected or misinterpreted by logicians. The reasons for this neglect are not hard to see, though they are hard to state briefly. Two of them are, roughly: (1) the preoccupation of most logicians with definitions; (2) the preoccupation of some logicians with formal systems.

(1) A definition, in the most familiar sense, is a specification of the conditions of the correct ascriptive or classificatory use of an expression. Definitions take no account of contextual requirements. So that in so far as the search for the meaning or the search for the analysis of an expression is conceived as the search for a definition, the neglect or misinterpretation of conventions other than ascriptive is inevitable. Perhaps it would be better to say (for I do not wish to legislate about "meaning" or "analysis") that logicians have failed to notice that problems of use are wider than problems of analysis and meaning.

(2) The influence of the preoccupation with mathematics and formal logic is most clearly seen (to take no more recent examples) in the cases of Leibniz and Russell. The constructor of calculuses, not concerned or required to make factual statements, approaches applied logic with a prejudice. It is natural that he should assume that the types of convention with whose adequacy in one field he is familiar should be really adequate, if only one could see how, in a quite different field—that of statements of fact. Thus we have Leibniz striving desperately to make the uniqueness of unique references a matter of logic in the narrow sense, and Russell striving desperately to do the same thing, in a different way, both for the implication of uniqueness and for that of existence.

It should be clear that the distinction I am trying to draw is primarily one between different roles or parts that expressions may play in language, and not primarily one between different groups of expressions; for some expressions may appear in either role. Some of the kinds of words I shall speak of have predominantly, if not exclusively, a referring role. This is most obviously true of pronouns and ordinary proper names. Some can occur as wholes or parts of expressions which have a predominantly referring use, and as wholes or parts of expressions which have a predominantly ascriptive or classificatory use. The obvious cases are common nouns; or common nouns preceded by adjectives, including participial adjectives; or, less obviously, adjectives or participial adjectives alone. Expressions capable of having a referring use also differ from one another in at least the three following, not mutually independent, ways.

(1) They differ in the extent to which the reference they are used to make is dependent on the context of their utterance. Words like "I" and "it" stand at one end of this scale—the end of maximum dependence—and phrases like "the author of *Waverley*" and "the eighteenth king of France" at the other.

(2) They differ in the degree of 'descriptive meaning' they possess: by 'descriptive meaning' I intend 'conventional limitation, in application, to things of a certain general kind, or possessing certain general characteristics'. At one end of this scale stand the proper names we most commonly use in ordinary discourse;

men, dogs, and motor-bicycles may be called "Horace." The pure name has no descriptive meaning (except such as it may acquire *as a result of* some one of its uses as a name). A word like "he" has minimal descriptive meaning, but has some. Substantival phrases like "the round table" have the maximum descriptive meaning. An interesting intermediate position is occupied by 'impure' proper names like "The Round Table"—substantival phrases which have grown capital letters.

(3) Finally, they may be divided into the following two classes: (i) those of which the correct referring use is regulated by some *general* referring-cum-ascriptive conventions; (ii) those of which the correct referring use is regulated by no general conventions, either of the contextual or the ascriptive kind, but by conventions which are ad hoc for each particular use (though not for each particular utterance). To the first class belong both pronouns (which have the least descriptive meaning) and substantival phrases (which have the most). To the second class belong, roughly speaking, the most familiar kind of proper names. Ignorance of a man's name is not ignorance of the language. This is why we do not speak of the meaning of proper names. (But it won't do to say they are meaningless.) Again an intermediate position is occupied by such phrases as "The Old Pretender." Only an old pretender may be so referred to; but to know which old pretender is not to know a general, but an ad hoc, convention.

In the case of phrases of the form "the so-and-so" used referringly, the use of "the" together with the position of the phrase in the sentence (i.e. at the beginning, or following a transitive verb or preposition) acts as a signal *that* a unique reference is being made; and the following noun, or noun and adjective, together with the context of utterance, shows *what* unique reference is being made. In general the functional difference between common nouns and adjectives is that the former are naturally and commonly used referringly, while the latter are not commonly, or so naturally, used in this way, except as qualifying nouns; though they can be, and are, so used alone. And of course this functional difference is not independent of the descriptive force peculiar to each word. In general we should expect the descriptive force of nouns to be such that they are more efficient tools for the job of showing what unique reference is intended when such a reference is signalized; and we should also expect the descriptive force of the words we naturally and commonly use to make unique references to mirror our interest in the salient, relatively permanent and behavioral characteristics of things. These two expectations are not independent of one another; and, if we look at the differences between the commoner sort of common nouns and the commoner sort of adjectives, we find them both fulfilled. These are differences of the kind that Locke quaintly reports, when he speaks of our ideas of substances being *collections* of simple ideas; when he says that "powers make up a great part of our ideas of substances"; and when he goes on to contrast the identity of real and nominal essence in the case of simple ideas with their lack of identity and the shiftingness of the nominal essence in the case of substances. 'Substance' itself is the troublesome tribute Locke pays to his dim awareness of the difference in predominant linguistic function that lingered even when the noun had been expanded into a more or less indefinite string of adjectives. Russell repeats Locke's mistake with a difference when, admitting the inference from syntax to reality to the extent of feeling that he can get rid of this metaphysical unknown only if he can purify language of the referring function altogether, he draws up his programme for "abolishing particulars"; a programme, in fact, for abolishing the distinction of logical use which I am here at pains to emphasize.

The contextual requirement for the referring use of pronouns may be stated with the greatest precision in some cases (e.g. "I" and "you") and only with the greatest vagueness in others ("it" and "this"). I propose to say nothing further about pronouns, except to point to an additional symptom of the failure to recognize the uniquely referring use for what it is; the fact, namely, that certain logicians have actually sought to elucidate the nature of a variable by offering such *sentences* as "he is sick," "it is green," as examples of something in ordinary speech like a *sentential function*. Now of course it is true that the word "he" may be used on different occasions to refer to different people or different animals: so may the word "John" and the phrase "the cat." What deters such logicians from treating these two expressions as quasi-variables is, in the first case, the lingering superstition that a name is logically tied to a single individual, and, in the second case, the descriptive meaning of the word "cat." But "he," which has a wide range of applications and minimal descriptive force, only acquires a use as a referring word. It is this fact, together with the failure to accord to expressions, used referringly, the place in logic which belongs to them (the place held open for the mythical logically proper name), that accounts for the misleading attempt to elucidate the nature of the variable by reference to such words as "he," "she," "it."

Of ordinary proper names it is sometimes said that they are essentially words each of which is used to refer to just one individual. This is obviously false. Many ordinary personal names—names par excellence—are correctly used to refer to numbers of people. An ordinary personal name is, roughly, a word, used referringly, of which the use is *not* dictated by any descriptive meaning the word may have, and is *not* prescribed by any such general rule for use as a referring expression (or a part of a referring expression) as we find in the case of such words as "I," "this" and "the," but is governed by ad hoc conventions for each particular set of applications of the word to a given person. The important point is that the correctness of such applications does not follow from any *general* rule or convention for the use of the word as such. (The limit of absurdity and obvious circularity is reached in the attempt to treat names as disguised description in Russell's sense; for what is in the special sense implied, but not entailed, by my now referring to someone by name is simply the existence of someone, *now being referred to, who is conventionally referred to* by that name) Even this feature of names, however, is only a symptom of the purpose for which they are employed. At present our choice of names is partly arbitrary, partly dependent on legal and social observances. It would be perfectly possible to have a thorough-going *system* of names, based e.g. on dates of birth, or on a minute clas-

sification of physiological and anatomical differences. But the success of any such system would depend entirely on the convenience of the resulting name-allotments for the purpose of making unique references; and this would depend on the multiplicity of the classifications used and the degree to which they cut haphazardly across normal social groupings. Given a sufficient degree of both, the selectivity supplied by context would do the rest; just as is the case with our present naming habits. Had we such a system, we could use name-words descriptively (as we do at present, to a limited extent and in a different way, with some famous names) as well as referringly. But it is by criteria derived from consideration of the requirements of the referring task that we should assess the adequacy of any system of naming. From the naming point of view, no kind of classification would be better or worse than any other simply because of the kind of classification—natal or anatomical—that it was.

I have already mentioned the class of quasi-names, of substantival phrases which grow capital letters, and of which such phrases as "the Glorious Revolution," "the Great War," "the Annunciation," "the Round Table" are examples. While the descriptive meaning of the words which follow the definite article is still relevant to their referring role, the capital letters are a sign of that extralogical selectivity in their referring use, which is characteristic of pure names. Such phrases are found in print or in writing when one member of some class of events or things is of quite outstanding interest in a certain society. These phrases are embryonic names. A phrase may, for obvious reasons, pass into, and out of, this class (e.g. "the Great War").

V

I want to conclude by considering, all too briefly, three further problems about referring uses.

(a) *Indefinite references:* Not all referring uses of singular expressions forestall the question "What (who, which one) are you talking about?" There are some which either invite this question, or disclaim the intention or ability to answer it.

Examples are such sentence-beginnings as "A man told me that . . . ," "Someone told me that . . ." The orthodox (Russellian) doctrine is that such sentences are existential, but not uniquely existential. This seems wrong in several ways. It is ludicrous to suggest that part of what is asserted is that the class of men or persons is not empty. Certainly this is *implied* in the by now familiar sense of implication; but the implication is also as much an implication of the *uniqueness* of the particular object of reference as when I begin a sentence with such a phrase as "the table." The difference between the use of the definite and indefinite articles is, very roughly, as follows. We use "the" either when a previous reference has been made, and when "the" signalizes that the same reference is being made; or when, in the absence of a previous indefinite reference, the context (including the hearer's assumed knowledge) is expected to enable the hearer to tell *what* reference is being made. We use "a" either when these conditions are not fulfilled, or when, although a definite reference *could* be made, we wish to keep dark the identity of the individual to whom, or to which, we are referring. This is the *arch* use of such a phrase as "a certain person" or "someone"; where it could be expanded, not into "someone, but you wouldn't (or I don't) know who" but into "someone, but I'm not telling you who."

(b) *Identification statements:* By this label I intend statements like the following:

(i*a*) That is the man who swam the channel twice on one day.

(ii*a*) Napoleon was the man who ordered the execution of the Duc d'Enghien.

The puzzle about these statements is that their grammatical predicates do not seem to be used in a straightforwardly ascriptive way as are the grammatical predicates of the statements:

(i*b*) That man swam the channel twice in one day.

(ii*b*) Napoleon ordered the execution of the Duc d'Enghien.

But if, in order to avoid blurring the difference between (i*a*) and (i*b*) and (ii*a*) and (ii*b*), one says that the phrases which form the grammatical complements of (i*a*) and (ii*a*) are being used

referringly, one becomes puzzled about what is being said in these sentences. We seem then to be referring to the same person twice over and either saying nothing about him and thus making no statement, or identifying him with himself and thus producing a trivial identity.

The bogy of triviality can be dismissed. This only arises for those who think of the object referred to by the use of an expression as its meaning, and thus think of the subject and complement of these sentences as meaning the same because they could be used to refer to the same person.

I think the differences between sentences in the (*a*) group and sentences in the (*b*) group can best be understood by considering the differences between the circumstances in which you would say (i*a*) and the circumstances in which you would say (i*b*). You would say (i*a*) instead of (i*b*) if you knew or believed that your hearer knew or believed that *someone* had swum the channel twice in one day. You say (i*a*) when you take your hearer to be in the position of one who can ask: "Who swam the channel twice in one day?" (And in asking this, he is not saying that anyone did, though his asking it implies—in the relevant sense—that someone did.) Such sentences are like answers to such questions. They are better called 'identification-statements' than 'identities'. Sentence (i*a*) does not assert more or less than sentence (i*b*). It is just that you say (i*a*) to a man whom you take to know certain things that you take to be unknown to the man to whom you say (i*b*).

This is, in the barest essentials, the solution to Russell's puzzle about 'denoting phrases' joined by "is"; one of the puzzles which he claims for the theory of descriptions the merit of solving.

(3) *The logic of subjects and predicates:* Much of what I have said of the uniquely referring use of expressions can be extended, with suitable modifications, to the non-uniquely referring use of expressions; i.e. to some uses of expressions consisting of "the," "all the," "all," "some," "some of the," etc. followed by a noun, qualified or unqualified, in the *plural;* to some uses of "they," "them," "those," "these"; and to conjunctions of names. Expressions of the first kind have a special interest. Roughly speaking, orthodox modern criticism, inspired by mathe-

matical logic, of such traditional doctrines as that of the Square of Opposition and of some of the forms of the syllogism traditionally recognized as valid, rests on the familiar failure to recognize the special sense in which existential assertions may be implied by the referring use of expressions. The universal propositions of the fourfold schedule, it is said, must *either* be given a negatively existential interpretation (e.g. for A, "there are no Xs which are not Ys") or they must be interpreted as conjunctions of negatively and positively existential statements of, e.g., the form (for A) "there are no Xs which are not Ys, and there are Xs." The I and O forms are normally given a positively existential interpretation. It is then seen that, whichever of the above alternatives is selected, some of the traditional laws have to be abandoned. The dilemma, however, is a bogus one. If we interpret the propositions of the schedule as neither positively, nor negatively, nor positively *and* negatively, existential, but as sentences such that *the question of whether they are being used to make true or false assertions does not arise except when the existential condition is fulfilled for the subject term,* then all the traditional laws hold good together. And this interpretation is far closer to the most common uses of expressions beginning with "all" and "some" than is any Russellian alternative. For these expressions are most commonly used in the referring way. A literal-minded and childless man asked whether all his children are asleep will certainly not answer "Yes" on the ground that he has none; but nor will he answer "No" on this ground. Since he has no children, the question does not arise. To say this is not to say that I may not use the sentence, "All my children are asleep," with the intention of letting someone know that I have children, or of deceiving him into thinking that I have. Nor is it any weakening of my thesis to concede that singular phrases of the form "the so-and-so" may sometimes be used with a similar purpose. Neither Aristotelian nor Russellian rules give the exact logic of any expression of ordinary language; for ordinary language has no exact logic.

NOTES

1. This usage of "use" is, of course, different from (*a*) the current usage in which 'use' (of a particular word, phrase, sentence) = (roughly) 'rules for using' = (roughly) 'meaning'; and from (*b*) my own usage in the phrase 'uniquely referring use of expressions' in which 'use' = (roughly) 'way of using'.
2. The unsophisticated kind begins: "Once upon time there was . . ."
3. And this in spite of the danger-signal of that phrase, "*misleading* grammatical form."
4. I neglect relational sentences; for these require, not a modification in the principle of what I say, but a complication of the detail.

18 Mr. Strawson on Referring

BERTRAND RUSSELL

Mr. P. F. Strawson published in *Mind* of 1950 an article called "On Referring". This article is reprinted in *Essays in Conceptual Analysis,* selected and edited by Professor Antony Flew. The references that follow are to this reprint. The main purpose of the article is to refute my theory of descriptions. As I find that some philosophers whom I respect consider that it has achieved its purpose successfully, I have come to the conclusion that a polemical reply is called for. I may say, to begin with, that I am totally unable to see any validity whatever in any of Mr. Strawson's arguments. Whether this inability is due to senility on my part or to some other cause, I must leave readers to judge.

The gist of Mr. Strawson's argument consists in identifying two problems which I have regarded as quite distinct—namely, the problem of descriptions and the problem of egocentricity. I have dealt with both these problems at considerable length, but as I have considered them to be different problems, I have not dealt with the one when I was considering the other. This enables Mr. Strawson to pretend that I have overlooked the problem of egocentricity.

He is helped in this pretence by a careful selection of material. In the article in which I first set forth the theory of descriptions, I dealt specially with two examples: "The present King of France is bald" and "Scott is the author of

Waverley". The latter example does not suit Mr. Strawson, and he therefore entirely ignores it except for one quite perfunctory reference. As regards "the present King of France", he fastens upon the egocentric word "present" and does not seem able to grasp that, if for the word "present" I had substituted the words "in 1905", the whole of his argument would have collapsed.

Or perhaps not quite the whole for reasons which I had set forth before Mr. Strawson wrote. It is, however, not difficult to give other examples of the use of descriptive phrases from which egocentricity is wholly absent. I should like to see him apply his doctrine to such sentences as the following: "the square-root of minus one is half the square-root of minus four", or "the cube of three is the integer immediately preceding the second perfect number". There are no egocentric words in either of these two sentences, but the problem of interpreting the descriptive phrases is exactly the same as if there were.

There is not a word in Mr. Strawson's article to suggest that I ever considered egocentric words, still less, that the theory which he advocates in regard to them is the very one which I had set forth at great length and in considerable detail.[1] The gist of what he has to say about such words is the entirely correct statement that what

From *Mind* 66 (1957): 385–389. Copyright © 1957 by *Mind*. Reprinted with the permission of Blackwell Publishers.

they refer to depends upon when and where they are used. As to this, I need only quote one paragraph from *Human Knowledge* (p. 107):

'This' denotes whatever, at the moment when the word is used, occupies the centre of attention. With words which are not egocentric what is constant is something about the object indicated, but 'this' denotes a different object on each occasion of its use: what is constant is not the object denoted, but its relation to the particular use of the word. Whenever the word is used, the person using it is attending to something, and the word indicates this something. When a word is not egocentric, there is no need to distinguish between different occasions when it is used, but we must make this distinction with egocentric words, since what they indicate is something having a given relation to the particular use of the word.

I must refer also to the case that I discuss (pp. 101 ff.) in which I am walking with a friend on a dark night. We lose touch with each other and he calls, "Where are you?" and I reply "Here I am!" It is of the essence of a scientific account of the world to reduce to a minimum the egocentric element in an assertion, but success in this attempt is a matter of degree, and is never complete where empirical material is concerned. This is due to the fact that the meanings of all empirical words depend ultimately upon ostensive definitions, that ostensive definitions depend upon experience, and that experience is egocentric. We can, however, by means of egocentric words, *describe* something which is not egocentric; it is this that enables us to use a common language.

All this may be right or wrong, but, whichever it is, Mr. Strawson should not expound it as if it were a theory that he had invented, whereas, in fact, I had set it forth before he wrote, though perhaps he did not grasp the purport of what I said. I shall say no more about egocentricity since, for the reasons I have already given, I think Mr. Strawson completely mistaken in connecting it with the problem of descriptions.

I am at a loss to understand Mr. Strawson's position on the subject of names. When he is writing about me, he says: "There are no logically proper names and there are no descriptions (in this sense)" (p. 26). But when he is writing about Quine, in *Mind,* October, 1956, he takes a

quite different line. Quine has a theory that names are unnecessary and can always be replaced by descriptions. This theory shocks Mr. Strawson for reasons which, to me, remain obscure. However, I will leave the defence of Quine to Quine, who is quite capable of looking after himself. What is important for my purpose is to elucidate the meaning of the words "in this sense" which Mr. Strawson puts in brackets. So far I can discover from the context, what he objects to is the belief that there are words which are only significant because there is something that they mean, and if there were not this something, they would be empty noises, not words. For my part, I think that there must be such words if language is to have any relation to fact. The necessity for such words is made obvious by the process of ostensive definition. How do we know what is meant by such words as "red" and "blue"? We cannot know what these words mean unless we have seen red and seen blue. If there were no red and no blue in our experience, we might, perhaps, invent some elaborate description which we could substitute for the word "red" or for the word "blue". For example, if you were dealing with a blind man, you could hold a red-hot poker near enough for him to feel the heat, and you could tell him that red is what he would see if he could see—but of course for the word "see" you would have to substitute another elaborate description. Any description which the blind man could understand would have to be in terms of words expressing experiences which he had had. Unless fundamental words in the individual's vocabulary had this kind of direct relation to fact, language in general would have no such relation. I defy Mr. Strawson to give the usual meaning to the word "red" unless there is something which the word designates.

This brings me to a further point. "Red" is usually regarded as a predicate and as designating a universal. I prefer for purposes of philosophical analysis a language in which "red" is a subject, and, while I should not say that it is a positive error to call it a universal, I should say that calling it so invites confusion. This is connected with what Mr. Strawson calls my "logically disastrous theory of names" (p. 39). He does not deign to mention why he considers this theory "logically disastrous". I hope that on some future occasion he will enlighten me on this point.

This brings me to a fundamental divergence between myself and many philosophers with whom Mr. Strawson appears to be in general agreement. They are persuaded that common speech is good enough not only for daily life, but also for philosophy. I, on the contrary, am persuaded that common speech is full of vagueness and inaccuracy, and that any attempt to be precise and accurate requires modification of common speech both as regards vocabulary and as regards syntax. Everybody admits that physics and chemistry and medicine each require a language which is not that of everyday life. I fail to see why philosophy, alone, should be forbidden to make a similar approach towards precision and accuracy. Let us take, in illustration, one of the commonest words of everyday speech: namely, the word "day". The most august use of this word is in the first chapter of *Genesis* and in the Ten Commandments. The desire to keep holy the Sabbath "day" has led orthodox Jews to give a precision to the word "day" which it does not have in common speech: they have defined it as the period from one sunset to the next. Astronomers, with other reasons for seeking precision, have three sorts of day: the true solar day: the mean solar day; and the sidereal day. These have different uses: the true solar day is relevant if you are considering lighting-up time; the mean solar day is relevant if you are sentenced to fourteen days without the option; and the sidereal day is relevant if you are trying to estimate the influence of the tides in retarding the earth's rotation. All these four kinds of day—decalogical, true, mean, and sidereal—are more precise than the common use of the word "day". If astronomers were subject to the prohibition of precision which some recent philosophers apparently favour, the whole science of astronomy would be impossible.

For technical purposes, technical languages differing from those of daily life are indispensable. I feel that those who object to linguistic novelties, if they had lived a hundred and fifty years ago, would have stuck to feet and ounces, and would have maintained that centimetres and grams savour of the guillotine.

In philosophy, it is syntax, even more than vocabulary, that needs to be corrected. The subject-predicate logic to which we are accustomed depends for its convenience upon the fact that at the usual temperature of the earth there are approximately permanent "things". This would not be true at the temperature of the sun, and is only roughly true at the temperatures to which we are accustomed.

My theory of descriptions was never intended as an analysis of the state of mind of those who utter sentences containing descriptions. Mr. Strawson gives the name "S" to the sentence "The King of France is wise", and he says of me "The way in which he arrived at the analysis was clearly by asking himself what would be the circumstances in which we would say that anyone who uttered the sentence S had made a true assertion". This does not seem to me a correct account of what I was doing. Suppose (which God forbid) Mr. Strawson were so rash as to accuse his char-lady of thieving: she would reply indignantly, "I ain't never done no harm to no one". Assuming her a pattern of virtue, I should say that she was making a true assertion, although, according to the rules of syntax which Mr. Strawson would adopt in his own speech, what she said should have meant: "there was at least one moment when I was injuring the whole human race". Mr. Strawson would not have supposed that this was what she meant to assert, although he would not have used her words to express the same sentiment. Similarly, I was concerned to find a more accurate and analysed thought to replace the somewhat confused thoughts which most people at most times have in their heads.

Mr. Strawson objects to my saying that "the King of France is wise" is false if there is no King of France. He admits that the sentence is significant and not true, but not that it is false. This is a mere question of verbal convenience. He considers that the word "false" has an unalterable meaning which it would be sinful to regard as adjustable, though he prudently avoids telling us what this meaning is. For my part, I find it more convenient to define the word "false" so that every significant sentence is either true or false. This is a purely verbal question; and although I have no wish to claim the support of common usage, I do not think that he can claim it either. Suppose, for example, that in some country there was a law that no person could hold public office if he considered it false that the Ruler of the Universe is wise. I think an avowed atheist who took advantage of Mr. Strawson's doctrine to say that he did not hold this proposition false, would be regarded as a somewhat shifty character.

It is not only as to names and as to falsehood that Mr. Strawson shows his conviction that there is an unalterably right way of using words and that no change is to be tolerated however convenient it may be. He shows the same feeling as regards universal affirmatives—i.e. sentences of the form "All A is B". Traditionally, such sentences are supposed to imply that there are A's, but it is much more convenient in mathematical logic to drop this implication and to consider that "All A is B" is true if there are no A's. This is wholly and solely a question of convenience. For some purposes the one convention is more convenient, and for others, the other. We shall prefer the one convention or the other according to the purpose we have in view. I agree, however, with Mr. Strawson's statement (p. 52) that ordinary language has no exact logic.

Mr. Strawson, in spite of his very real logical competence, has a curious prejudice against logic. On page 43, he has a sudden dithyrambic outburst, to the effect that life is greater than logic, which he uses to give a quite false interpretation of my doctrines.

Leaving detail aside, I think we may sum up Mr. Strawson's argument and my reply to it as follows:

There are two problems, that of descriptions and that of egocentricity. Mr. Strawson thinks they are one and the same problem, but it is obvious from his discussion that he has not considered as many kinds of descriptive phrases as are relevant to the argument. Having confused the two problems, he asserts dogmatically that it is only the egocentric problem that needs to be solved, and he offers a solution of this problem which he seems to believe to be new, but which in fact was familiar before he wrote. He then thinks that he has offered an adequate theory of descriptions, and announces his supposed achievement with astonishing dogmatic certainty. Perhaps I am doing him an injustice, but I am unable to see in what respect this is the case.

NOTE

1. Cf. *Inquiry into Meaning and Truth,* chap. vii, and *Human Knowledge,* Part II, chap, iv.

19 Reference and Definite Descriptions

KEITH DONNELLAN

Definite descriptions, I shall argue, have two possible functions. They are used to refer to what a speaker wishes to talk about, but they are also used quite differently. Moreover, a definite description occurring in one and the same sentence may, on different occasions of its use, function in either way. The failure to deal with this duality of function obscures the genuine referring use of definite descriptions. The best-known theories of definite descriptions, those of Russell and Strawson, I shall suggest, are both guilty of this. Before discussing this distinction in use, I will mention some features of these theories to which it is especially relevant.

On Russell's view a definite description may denote an entity: "if '*C*' is a denoting phrase [as definite descriptions are by definition], it may happen that there is one entity x (there cannot be more than one) for which the proposition 'x is identical with *C*' is true. . . . We may then say that the entity x is the denotation of the phrase '*C*.'"[1] In using a definite description, then, a speaker may use an expression which denotes some entity, but this is the only relationship between that entity and the use of the definite description recognized by Russell. I shall argue, however, that there are two uses of definite descriptions. The definition of denotation given by Russell is applicable to both, but in one of these the definite description serves to do some-

thing more. I shall say that in this use the speaker uses the definite description to *refer* to something, and call this use the "referential use" of a definite description. Thus, if I am right, referring is not the same as denoting and the referential use of definite descriptions is not recognized on Russell's view.

Furthermore, on Russell's view the type of expression that comes closest to performing the function of the referential use of definite descriptions turns out, as one might suspect, to be a proper name (in "the narrow logical sense"). Many of the things said about proper names by Russell can, I think, be said about the referential use of definite descriptions without straining senses unduly. Thus the gulf Russell thought he saw between names and definite descriptions is narrower than he thought.

Strawson, on the other hand, certainly does recognize a referential use of definite definitions. But what I think he did not see is that a definite description may have a quite different role—may be used nonreferentially, even as it occurs in one and the same sentence. Strawson, it is true, points out nonreferential uses of definite descriptions,[2] but which use a definite description has seems to be for him a function of the kind of sentence in which it occurs; whereas, if I am right, there can be two possible uses of a definite description in the same sen-

From *Philosophical Review* 75 (1966): 281–304. Reprinted by permission of the publisher and the author.

tence. Thus, in "On Referring," he says, speaking of expressions used to refer, "Any expression of any of these classes [one being that of definite descriptions] can occur as the subject of what would traditionally be regarded as a singular subject-predicate sentence; and would, so occurring, exemplify the use I wish to discuss."[3] So the definite description in, say, the sentence "The Republican candidate for president in 1968 will be a conservative" presumably exemplifies the referential use. But if I am right, we could not say this of the sentence in isolation from some particular occasion on which it is used to state something; and then it might or might not turn out that the definite description has a referential use.

Strawson and Russell seem to me to make a common assumption here about the question of how definite descriptions function: that we can ask how a definite description functions in some sentence independently of a particular occasion upon which it is used. This assumption is not really rejected in Strawson's arguments against Russell. Although he can sum up his position by saying, "'Mentioning' or 'referring' is not something an expression does; it is something that someone can use an expression to do,"[4] he means by this to deny the radical view that a "genuine" referring expression *has* a referent, functions to refer, independent of the context of some use of the expression. The denial of this view, however, does not entail that definite descriptions cannot be identified as referring expressions in a sentence unless the sentence is being used. Just as we can speak of a function of a tool that is not at the moment performing its function, Strawson's view, I believe, allows us to speak of the referential function of a definite description in a sentence even when it is not being used. This, I hope to show, is a mistake.

A second assumption shared by Russell's and Strawson's account of definite descriptions is this. In many cases a person who uses a definite description can be said (in some sense) to presuppose or imply that something fits the description.[5] If I state that the king is on his throne, I presuppose or imply that there is a king. (At any rate, this would be a natural thing to say for anyone who doubted that there is a king.) Both Russell and Strawson assume that

where the presupposition or implication is false, the truth value of what the speaker says is affected. For Russell the statement made is false; for Strawson it has no truth value. Now if there are two uses of definite descriptions, it may be that the truth value is affected differently in each case by the falsity of the presupposition or implication. This is what I shall in fact argue. It will turn out, I believe, that one or the other of the two views, Russell's or Strawson's, may be correct about the nonreferential use of definite descriptions, but neither fits the referential use. This is not so surprising about Russell's view, since he did not recognize this use in any case, but it is surprising about Strawson's since the referential use is what he tries to explain and defend. Furthermore, on Strawson's account, the result of there being nothing which fits the description is a failure of reference.[6] This too, I believe, turns out not to be true about the referential use of definite descriptions.

II

There are some uses of definite descriptions which carry neither any hint of a referential use nor any presupposition or implication that something fits the description. In general, it seems, these are recognizable from the sentence frame in which the description occurs. These uses will not interest us, but it is necessary to point them out if only to set them aside.

An obvious example would be the sentence "The present King of France does not exist," used, say, to correct someone's mistaken impression that de Gaulle is the King of France.

A more interesting example is this. Suppose someone were to ask, "Is de Gaulle the King of France?" This is the natural form of words for a person to use who is in doubt as to whether de Gaulle is King or President of France. Given this background to the question, there seems to be no presupposition or implication that someone is the King of France. Nor is the person attempting to refer to someone by using the definite description. On the other hand, reverse the name and description in the question and the speaker probably would be thought to presuppose or imply this. "Is the King of France de Gaulle?" is the natural question for one to ask who wonders whether it is de Gaulle rather than someone else who occupies the throne of France.[7]

Many times, however, the use of a definite description does carry a presupposition or implication that something fits the description. If definite descriptions do have a referring role, it will be here. But it is a mistake, I think, to try, as I believe both Russell and Strawson do, to settle this matter without further ado. What is needed, I believe, is the distinction I will now discuss.

III

I will call the two uses of definite descriptions I have in mind the attributive use and the referential use. A speaker who uses a definite description attributively in an assertion states something about whoever or whatever is the so-and-so. A speaker who uses a definite description referentially in an assertion, on the other hand, uses the description to enable his audience to pick out whom or what he is talking about and states something about that person or thing. In the first case the definite description might be said to occur essentially, for the speaker wishes to assert something about whatever or whoever fits that description; but in the referential use the definite description is merely one tool for doing a certain job—calling attention to a person or thing—and in general any other device for doing the same job, another description or a name, would do as well. In the attributive use, the attribute of being the so-and-so is all important, while it is not in the referential use.

To illustrate this distinction, in the case of a single sentence, consider the sentence, "Smith's murderer is insane." Suppose first that we come upon poor Smith foully murdered. From the brutal manner of the killing and the fact that Smith was the most lovable person in the world, we might exclaim, "Smith's murderer is insane." I will assume, to make it a simpler case, that in a quite ordinary sense we do not know who murdered Smith (though this is not in the end essential to the case). This, I shall say, is an attributive use of the definite description.

The contrast with such a use of the sentence is one of those situations in which we expect and intend our audience to realize whom we have in mind when we speak of Smith's murderer and, most importantly, to know that it is this person about whom we are going to say something.

For example, suppose that Jones has been charged with Smith's murder and has been placed on trial. Imagine that there is a discussion of Jones's odd behavior at his trial. We might sum up our impression of his behavior by saying, "Smith's murderer is insane." If someone asks to whom we are referring, by using this description, the answer here is "Jones." This, I shall say, is a referential use of the definite description.

That these two uses of the definite description in the same sentence are really quite different can perhaps best be brought out by considering the consequences of the assumption that Smith had no murderer (for example, he in fact committed suicide). In both situations, in using the definite description "Smith's murderer," the speaker in some sense presupposes or implies that there is a murderer. But when we hypothesize that the presupposition or implication is false, there are different results for the two uses. In both cases we have used the predicate "is insane," but in the first case, if there is no murderer, there is no person of whom it could be correctly said that we attributed insanity to him. Such a person could be identified (correctly) only in case someone fitted the description used. But in the second case, where the definite description is simply a means of identifying the person we want to talk about, it is quite possible for the correct identification to be made even though no one fits the description we used.[8] We were speaking about Jones even though he is not in fact Smith's murderer and, in the circumstances imagined, it was his behavior we were commenting upon. Jones might, for example, accuse us of saying false things of him in calling him insane and it would be no defense, I should think, that our description, "the murderer of Smith," failed to fit him.

It is, moreover, perfectly possible for our audience to know to whom we refer, in the second situation, even though they do not share our presupposition. A person hearing our comment in the context imagined might know we are talking about Jones even though he does not think Jones guilty.

Generalizing from this case, we can say, I think, that there are two uses of sentences of the form, "The φ is ψ." In the first, if nothing is the φ then nothing has been said to be ψ. In the second, the fact that nothing is the φ does not have this consequence.

With suitable changes the same difference in use can be formulated for uses of language other than assertions. Suppose one is at a party and, seeing an interesting-looking person holding a martini glass, one asks, "Who is the man drinking a martini?" If it should turn out that there is only water in the glass, one has nevertheless asked a question about a particular person, a question that it is possible for someone to answer. Contrast this with the use of the same question by the chairman of the local Teetotalers Union. He has just been informed that a man is drinking a martini at their annual party. He responds by asking his informant, "Who is the man drinking a martini?" In asking the question the chairman does not have some particular person in mind about whom he asks the question; if no one is drinking a martini, if the information is wrong, no person can be singled out as the person about whom the question was asked. Unlike the first case, the attribute of being the man drinking a martini is all-important, because if it is the attribute of no one, the chairman's question has no straight-forward answer.

This illustrates also another difference between the referential and the attributive use of definite descriptions. In the one case we have asked a question about a particular person or thing even though nothing fits the description we used; in the other this is not so. But also in the one case our question can be answered; in the other it cannot be. In the referential use of a definite description we may succeed in picking out a person or thing to ask a question about even though he or it does not really fit the description; but in the attributive use if nothing fits the description, no straightforward answer to the question can be given.

This further difference is also illustrated by commands or orders containing definite descriptions. Consider the order, "Bring me the book on the table." If "the book on the table" is being used referentially, it is possible to fulfill the order even though there is no book on the table. If, for example, there is a book *beside* the table, though there is none *on* it, one might bring that book back and ask the issuer of the order whether this is "the book you meant." And it may be. But imagine we are told that someone has laid a book on our prize antique table, where nothing should be put. The order, "Bring me the book on the table" cannot now be obeyed unless there is a book that has been placed on the table. There is no possibility of bringing back a book which was never on the table and having it be the one that was meant, because there is no book that in that sense was "meant." In the one case the definite description was a device for getting the other person to pick the right book; if he is able to pick the right book even though it does not satisfy the description, one still succeeds in his purpose. In the other case, there is, antecedently, no "right book" except one which fits the description; the attribute of being the book on the table is essential. Not only is there no book about which an order was issued, if there is no book on the table, but the order itself cannot be obeyed. When a definite description is used attributively in a command or question and nothing fits the description, the command cannot be obeyed and the question cannot be answered. This suggests some analogous consequence for assertions containing definite descriptions used attributively. Perhaps the analogous result is that the assertion is neither true nor false: this is Strawson's view of what happens when the presupposition of the use of a definite description is false. But if so, Strawson's view works not for definite descriptions used referentially, but for the quite different use, which I have called the attributive use.

I have tried to bring out the two uses of definite descriptions by pointing out the different consequences of supposing that nothing fits the description used. There are still other differences. One is this: when a definite description is used referentially, not only is there in some sense a presupposition or implication that someone or something fits the description, as there is also in the attributive use, but there is a quite different presupposition; the speaker presupposes of some *particular* someone or something that he or it fits the description. In asking, for example,

"Who is the man drinking a martini?" where we mean to ask a question about that man over there, we are presupposing that that man over there is drinking a martini—not just that *someone* is a man drinking a martini. When we say, in a context where it is clear we are referring to Jones, "Smith's murderer is insane," we are presupposing that Jones is Smith's murderer. No such presupposition is present in the attributive use of definite descriptions. There is, of course, the presupposition that someone *or other* did the murder, but the speaker does not presuppose of someone in particular—Jones or Robinson, say—that he did it. What I mean by this second kind of presupposition that someone or something in particular fits the description—which is present in a referential use but not in an attributive use—can perhaps be seen more clearly by considering a member of the speaker's audience who believes that Smith was not murdered at all. Now in the case of the referential use of the description, "Smith's murderer," he could accuse the speaker of mistakenly presupposing both that someone or other is the murderer and that also Jones is the murderer, for even though he believes Jones not to have done the deed, he knows that the speaker was referring to Jones. But in the case of the attributive use, he can accuse the speaker of having only the first, less specific presupposition; he cannot pick out some person and claim that the speaker is presupposing that that person is Smith's murderer. Now the more particular presuppositions that we find present in referential uses are clearly not ones we can assign to a definite description in some particular sentence in isolation from a context of use. In order to know that a person presupposes that Jones is Smith's murderer in using the sentence "Smith's murderer is insane," we have to know that he is using the description referentially and also to whom he is referring. The sentence by itself does not tell us any of this.

IV

From the way in which I set up each of the previous examples it might be supposed that the important difference between the referential and the attributive use lies in the beliefs of the speaker. Does he believe of some particular person or thing that he or it fits the description used? In the Smith murder example, for instance, there was in the one case no belief as to who did the deed, whereas in the contrasting case it was believed that Jones did it. But this is, in fact, not an essential difference. It is possible for a definite description to be used attributively even though the speaker (and his audience) believes that a certain person or thing fits the description. And it is possible for a definite description to be used referentially where the speaker believes that nothing fits the description. It is true—and this is why, for simplicity, I set up the examples the way I did—that if a speaker does not believe that anything fits the description or does not believe that he is in a position to pick out what does fit the description, it is likely that he is not using it referentially. It is also true that if he and his audience would pick out some particular thing or person as fitting the description, then a use of the definite description is very likely referential. But these are only presumptions and not entailments.

To use the Smith murder case again, suppose that Jones is on trial for the murder and I and everyone else believe him guilty. Suppose that I comment that the murderer of Smith is insane, but instead of backing this up, as in the example previously used, by citing Jone's behavior in the dock, I go on to outline reasons for thinking that *anyone* who murdered poor Smith in that particularly horrible way must be insane. If now it turns out that Jones was not the murderer after all, but someone else was, I think I can claim to have been right if the true murderer is after all insane. Here, I think, I would be using the definite description attributively, even though I believe that a particular person fits the description.

It is also possible to think of cases in which the speaker does not believe that what he means to refer to by using the definite description fits the description, or to imagine cases in which the definite description is used referentially even though the speaker believes *nothing* fits the description. Admittedly, these cases may be parasitic on a more normal use; nevertheless, they are sufficient to show that such beliefs of the speaker are not decisive as to which use is made of a definite description.

Suppose the throne is occupied by a man I firmly believe to be not the king, but a usurper. Imagine also that his followers firmly believe that he is the king. Suppose I wish to see this man. I might say to his minions, "Is the king in his countinghouse?" I succeed in referring to the man I wish to refer to without myself believing that he fits the description. It is not even necessary, moreover, to suppose that his followers believe him to be the king. If they are cynical about the whole thing, know he is not the king, I may still succeed in referring to the man I wish to refer to. Similarly, neither I nor the people I speak to may suppose that *anyone* is the king and, finally, each party may know that the other does not so suppose and yet the reference may go through.

V

Both the attributive and the referential use of definite descriptions seem to carry a presupposition or implication that there is something which fits the description. But the reasons for the existence of the presupposition or implication are different in the two cases.

There is a presumption that a person who uses a definite description referentially believes that what he wishes to refer to fits the description. Because the purpose of using the description is to get the audience to pick out or think of the right thing or person, one would normally choose a description that he believes the thing or person fits. Normally a misdescription of that to which one wants to refer would mislead the audience. Hence, there is a presumption that the speaker believes *something* fits the description—namely, that to which he refers.

When a definite description is used attributively, however, there is not the same possibility of misdescription. In the example of "Smith's murderer" used attributively, there was not the possibility of misdescribing Jones or anyone else; we were not referring to Jones nor to anyone else by using the description. The presumption that the speaker believes *someone* is Smith's murderer does not arise here from a more specific presumption that he believes Jones or Robinson or someone else whom he can name or identify is Smith's murderer.

The presupposition or implication is borne by a definite description used attributively because if nothing fits the description the linguistic purpose of the speech act will be thwarted. That is, the speaker will not succeed in saying something true, if he makes an assertion; he will not succeed in asking a question that can be answered, if he has asked a question; he will not succeed in issuing an order that can be obeyed, if he has issued an order. If one states that Smith's murderer is insane, when Smith has no murderer, and uses the definite description nonreferentially, then one fails to say anything *true*. If one issues the order "Bring me Smith's murderer" under similar circumstances, the order cannot be obeyed; nothing would count as obeying it.

When the definite description is used referentially, on the other hand, the presupposition or implication stems simply from the fact that normally a person tries to describe correctly what he wants to refer to because normally this is the best way to get his audience to recognize what he is referring to. As we have seen, it is possible for the linguistic purpose of the speech act to be accomplished in such a case even though nothing fits the description; it is possible to say something true or to ask a question that gets answered or to issue a command that gets obeyed. For when the definite description is used referentially, one's audience may succeed in seeing to what one refers even though neither it nor anything else fits the description.

VI

The result of the last section shows something to be wrong with the theories of both Russell and Strawson; for though they give differing accounts of the implication or presupposition involved, each gives only one. Yet, as I have argued, the presupposition or implication is present for a quite different reason, depending upon whether the definite description is used attributively or referentially, and exactly what presuppositions or implications are involved is also different. Moreover, neither theory seems a correct characterization of the referential use. On Russell's there is a logical entailment: "The ϕ is ψ" entails "There exists one and only one φ." Whether or not this is so for the attributive use, it does not seem true of the referential use of the definite description. The "implication" that something is the φ, as I have argued, does not amount to an entailment; it is more like a presumption based on what is *usually* true of the use of a definite description to refer. In any case, of course, Russell's theory does not show—what is true of the referential use—that the implication that *something* is the φ comes from the more specific implication that *what is being referred to* is the φ. Hence, as a theory of definite descriptions, Russell's view seems to apply, if at all, to the attributive use only.

Russell's definition of denoting (a definite description denotes an entity if that entity fits the description uniquely) is clearly applicable to either use of definite descriptions. Thus whether or not a definite description is used referentially or attributively, it may have a denotation. Hence, denoting and referring, as I have explicated the latter notion, are distinct and Russell's view recognizes only the former. It seems to me, moreover, that this is a welcome result, that denoting and referring should not be confused. If one tried to maintain that they are the same notion, one result would be that a speaker might be referring to something without knowing it. If someone said, for example, in 1960 before he had any idea that Mr. Goldwater would be the Republican nominee in 1964, "The Republican candidate for president in 1964 will be a conservative," (perhaps on the basis of an analysis of the views of party leaders) the definite description here would *denote* Mr. Goldwater. But would we wish to say that the speaker had referred to, mentioned, or talked about Mr. Goldwater? I feel these terms would be out of place. Yet if we identify referring and denoting, it ought to be possible for it to turn out (after the Republican Convention) that the speaker had, unknown to himself, referred in 1960 to Mr. Goldwater. On my view, however, while the definite description used did *denote* Mr. Goldwater (using Russell's definition), the speaker used it *attributively* and did not *refer* to Mr. Goldwater.

Turning to Strawson's theory, it was supposed to demonstrate how definite descriptions are referential. But it goes too far in this direction. For there are nonreferential uses of definite descriptions also, even as they occur in one and the same sentence. I believe that Strawson's theory involves the following propositions:

1. If someone asserts that the φ is ψ he has not made a true or false statement if there is no φ.[9]
2. If there is no φ then the speaker has failed to refer to anything.[10]
3. The reason he has said nothing true or false is that he has failed to refer.

Each of these propositions is either false or, at best, applies to only one of the two uses of definite descriptions.

Proposition (1) is possibly true of the attributive use. In the example in which "Smith's murderer is insane" was said when Smith's body was first discovered, an attributive use of the definite description, there was no person to whom the speaker referred. If Smith had no murderer, nothing true was said. It is quite tempting to conclude, following Strawson, that nothing true or false was said. But where the definite description is used referentially, something true may well have been said. It is possible that something true was said of the person or thing referred to.[11]

Proposition (2) is, as we have seen, simply false. Where a definite description is used referentially it is perfectly possible to refer to something though nothing fits the description used.

The situation with proposition (3) is a bit more complicated. It ties together, on Strawson's view, the two strands given in (1) and (2). As an account of why, when the presupposition is false, nothing true or false has been stated, it clearly cannot work for the attributive use of definite descriptions, for the reason it supplies is that reference has failed. It does not then give the reason why, if indeed this is so, a speaker using a definite description attributively fails to say anything true or false if nothing fits the description. It does, however, raise a question about the referential use. Can reference fail when a definite description is used referentially?

I do not fail to refer merely because my audience does not correctly pick out what I am referring to. I can be referring to a particular man when I use the description "the man drinking a martini," even though the people to whom I speak fail to pick out the right person or any person at all. Nor, as we have stressed, do I fail to refer when nothing fits the description. But perhaps I fail to refer in some extreme circumstances, when there is nothing that *I* am willing to pick out as that to which I referred.

Suppose that I think I see at some distance a man walking and ask, "Is the man carrying a walking stick the professor of history?" We should perhaps distinguish four cases at this point. (a) There is a man carrying a walking stick; I have then referred to a person and asked a question about him that can be answered if my audience has the information. (b) The man over there is not carrying a walking stick, but an umbrella; I have still referred to someone and asked a question that can be answered, though if my audience sees that it is an umbrella and not a walking stick, they may also correct my apparently mistaken impression. (c) It is not a man at all, but a rock that looks like one; in this case, I think I still have referred to something, to the thing over there that happens to be a rock but that I took to be a man. But in this case it is not clear that my question can be answered correctly. This, I think, is not because I have failed to refer, but rather because, given the true nature of what I referred to, my question is not appropriate. A simple "No, that is not the professor of history" is at least a bit misleading if said by someone who realizes that I mistook a rock for a person. It may, therefore, be plausible to conclude that in such a case I have not asked a question to which there is a straightforwardly correct answer. But if this is true, it is not because nothing fits the description I used, but rather because what I referred to is a rock and my question has no correct answer when asked of a rock. (d) There is finally the case in which there is nothing at all where I thought there was a man with a walking stick; and perhaps here we have a genuine failure to refer at all, even though the description was used for the purpose of referring. There is no rock, nor anything else, to which I meant to refer; it was, perhaps, a trick of light that made me think there was a man there. I cannot say of anything, "That is what I was referring to, though I now see that it's not a man carrying a walking stick." This failure of refer-

ence, however, requires circumstances much more radical than the mere nonexistence of anything fitting the description used. It requires that there be nothing of which it can be said, "That is what he was referring to." Now perhaps also in such cases, if the speaker has asserted something, he fails to state anything true or false if there is nothing that can be identified as that to which he referred. But if so, the failure of reference and truth value does not come about merely because nothing fits the description he used. So (3) may be true of some cases of the referential use of definite descriptions; it may be true that a failure of reference results in a lack of truth value. But these cases are of a much more extreme sort than Strawson's theory implies.

I conclude, then, that neither Russell's nor Strawson's theory represents a correct account of the use of definite descriptions—Russell's because it ignores altogether the referential use, Strawson's because it fails to make the distinction between the referential and the attributive and mixes together truths about each (together with some things that are false).

VII

It does not seem possible to say categorically of a definite description in a particular sentence that it is a referring expression (of course, one could say this if he meant that it *might* be used to refer). In general, whether or not a definite description is used referentially or attributively is a function of the speaker's intentions in a particular case. "The murderer of Smith" may be used either way in the sentence "The murderer of Smith is insane." It does not appear plausible to account for this, either, as an ambiguity in the sentence. The grammatical structure of the sentence seems to me to be the same whether the description is used referentially or attributively: that is, it is not syntactically ambiguous. Nor does it seem at all attractive to suppose an ambiguity in the meaning of the words; it does not appear to be semantically ambiguous. (Perhaps we could say that the sentence is pragmatically ambiguous: the distinction between roles that the description plays is a function of the speaker's intentions.) These, of course, are intuitions; I do not have an argument for these conclusions. Nevertheless, the burden of proof is surely on the other side.

This, I think, means that the view, for example, that sentences can be divided up into predicates, logical operators, and referring expressions is not generally true. In the case of definite descriptions one cannot always assign the referential function in isolation from a particular occasion on which it is used.

There may be sentences in which a definite description can be used only attributively or only referentially. A sentence in which it seems that the definite description could be used only attributively would be "Point out the man who is drinking my martini." I am not so certain that any can be found in which the definite description can be used only referentially. Even if there are such sentences, it does not spoil the point that there are many sentences, apparently not ambiguous either syntactically or semantically, containing definite descriptions that can be used either way.

If it could be shown that the dual use of definite descriptions can be accounted for by the presence of an ambiguity, there is still a point to be made against the theories of Strawson and Russell. For neither, so far as I can see, has anything to say about the possibility of such an ambiguity and, in fact, neither seems compatible with such a possibility. Russell's does not recognize the possibility of the referring use, and Strawson's, as I have tried to show in the last section, combines elements from each use into one unitary account. Thus the view that there is an ambiguity in such sentences does not seem any more attractive to these positions.

VIII

Using a definite description referentially, a speaker may say something true even though the description correctly applies to nothing. The sense in which he may say something true is the sense in which he may say something true about someone or something. This sense is, I think, an interesting one that needs investigation. Isolating it is one of the byproducts of the distinction between the attributive and referential uses of definite descriptions.

For one thing, it raises questions about the notion of a statement. This is brought out by considering a passage in a paper by Leonard Linsky in which he rightly makes the point that one can refer to someone although the definite description used does not correctly describe the person:

. . . said of a spinster that "Her husband is kind to her" is neither true nor false. But a speaker might very well be referring to someone using these words, for he may think that someone is the husband of the lady (who in fact is a spinster). Still, the statement is neither true nor false, for it presupposes that the lady has a husband, which she has not. This last refutes Strawson's thesis that if the presupposition of existence is not satisfied, the speaker has failed to refer.[12]

There is much that is right in this passage. But because Linsky does not make the distinction between the referential and the attributive uses of definite descriptions, it does not represent a wholly adequate account of the situation. A perhaps minor point about this passage is that Linsky apparently thinks it sufficient to establish that the speaker in his example is referring to someone by using the definite description "her husband," that he *believe* that someone is her husband. This will only approximate the truth provided that the "someone" in the description of the belief means "someone in particular" and is not merely the existential quantifier, "there is someone or other." For in both the attributive and the referential use the belief that someone *or other* is the husband of the lady is very likely to be present. If, for example, the speaker has just met the lady and, noticing her cheerfulness and radiant good health, makes his remark from his conviction that these attributes are always the result of having good husbands, he would be using the definite description attributively. Since she has no husband, there is no one to pick out as the person to whom he was referring. Nevertheless, the speaker believed that *someone or other* was her husband. On the other hand, if the use of "her husband" was simply a way of referring to a man the speaker has just met whom he assumed to be the lady's husband, he would have referred to that man even though neither he nor anyone else fits the description. I think it is likely that in this passage Linsky did mean by "someone," in his description of the belief, "someone in particular." But even then, as we have seen, we have neither a sufficient nor a necessary condition for a referential use of the definite description. A definite description can be used attributively even when the speaker believes that some particular thing or person fits the description, and it can be used referentially in the absence of this belief.

My main point, here, however, has to do with Linsky's view that because the presupposition is not satisfied, the *statement* is neither true nor false. This seems to me possibly correct *if* the definite description is thought of as being used attributively (depending upon whether we go with Strawson or Russell). But when we consider it as used referentially, this categorical assertion is no longer clearly correct. For the man the speaker referred to may indeed be kind to the spinster; the speaker may have said something true about that man. Now the difficulty is in the notion of "the statement." Suppose that we know that the lady is a spinster, but nevertheless know that the man referred to by the speaker is kind to her. It seems to me that we shall, on the one hand, want to hold that the speaker said something true, but be reluctant to express this by "It is true that her husband is kind to her."

This shows, I think, a difficulty in speaking simply about "the statement" when definite descriptions are used referentially. For the speaker stated something, in this example, about a particular person, and his statement, we may suppose, was true. Nevertheless, we should not like to agree with his statement by using the sentence he used; we should not like to identify the true statement via the speaker's words. The reason for this is not so hard to find. If we say, in this example, "It is true that her husband is kind to her," *we* are now using the definite description either attributively or referentially. But we should not be subscribing to what the original speaker truly said if we use the description attributively, for it was only in its function as referring to a particular person that the definite description yields the possibility of saying something true (since the lady has no husband). Our reluctance, however, to endorse the original speaker's statement by using the definite description referentially to refer to the same

person stems from quite a different consideration. For if we too were laboring under the mistaken belief that this man was the lady's husband, we could agree with the original speaker using his exact words. (Moreover, it is possible, as we have seen, deliberately to use a definite description to refer to someone we believe not to fit the description.) Hence, our reluctance to use the original speaker's words does not arise from the fact that if we did we should not succeed in stating anything true or false. It rather stems from the fact that when a definite description is used referentially there is a presumption that the speaker believes that what he refers to fits the description. Since we, who know the lady to be a spinster, would not normally want to give the impression that we believe otherwise, we would not like to use the original speaker's way of referring to the man in question.

How then would we express agreement with the original speaker without involving ourselves in unwanted impressions about our beliefs? The answer shows another difference between the referential and attributive uses of definite descriptions and brings out an important point about genuine referring.

When a speaker says, "The ϕ is ψ," where "the ϕ" is used attributively, if there is no ϕ, we cannot correctly report the speaker as having said *of* this or that person or thing that it is ψ. But if the definite description is used referentially we can report the speaker as having attributed ψ to something. And *we* may refer to what the speaker referred to, using whatever description or name suits our purpose. Thus, if a speaker says, "Her husband is kind to her," referring to the man he was just talking to, and if that man is Jones, we may report him as having said *of Jones* that he is kind to her. If Jones is also the president of the college, we may report the speaker as having said *of the president of the college* that he is kind to her. And finally, if we are talking to Jones, we may say, referring to the original speaker, "He said of *you* that you are kind to her." It does not matter here whether or not the woman has a husband or whether, if she does, Jones is her husband. If the original speaker referred to Jones, he said of him that he is kind to her. Thus where the definite description is used referentially, but does not fit what was referred to, we can report what a speaker said and agree with him by using a description or name which does fit. In doing so we need not, it is important to note, choose a description or name which the original speaker would agree fits what he was referring to. That is, we can report the speaker in the above case to have said truly of Jones that he is kind to her even if the original speaker did not know that the man he was referring to is named Jones or even if he thinks he is not named Jones.

Returning to what Linsky said in the passage quoted, he claimed that, were someone to say "Her husband is kind to her," when she has no husband, *the statement* would be neither true nor false. As I have said, this is a likely view to hold if the definite description is being used attributively. But if it is being used referentially it is not clear what is meant by "the statement." If we think about what the speaker said about the person he referred to, then there is no reason to suppose he has not said something true or false about him, even though he is not the lady's husband. And Linsky's claim would be wrong. On the other hand, if we do not identify the statement in this way, what is the statement that the speaker made? To say that the statement he made was that her husband is kind to her lands us in difficulties. For we have to decide whether in using the definite description here in the identification of the statement, we are using it attributively or referentially. If the former, then we misrepresent the linguistic performance of the speaker; if the latter, then we are ourselves referring to someone and reporting the speaker to have said something of that person, in which case we are back to the possibility that he did say something true or false of that person.

I am thus drawn to the conclusion that when a speaker uses a definite description referentially he may have stated something true or false even if nothing fits the description, and that there is not a clear sense in which he has made a statement which is neither true nor false.

IX

I want to end by a brief examination of a picture of what a genuine referring expression is that

one might derive from Russell's views. I want to suggest that this picture is not so far wrong as one might suppose and that strange as this may seem, some of the things we have said about the referential use of definite descriptions are not foreign to this picture.

Genuine proper names, in Russell's sense, would refer to something without ascribing any properties to it. They would, one might say, refer to the thing itself, not simply the thing in so far as it falls under a certain description.[13] Now this would seem to Russell something a definite description could not do, for he assumed that if definite descriptions were capable of referring at all, they would refer to something only in so far as that thing satisfied the description. Not only have we seen this assumption to be false, however, but in the last section we saw something more. We saw that when a definite description is used referentially, a speaker can be reported as having said something *of* something. And in reporting what it was of which he said something we are not restricted to the description he used, or synonyms of it; we may ourselves refer to it using any descriptions, names, and so forth, that will do the job. Now this seems to give a sense in which we are concerned with the thing itself and not just the thing under a certain description, when we report the linguistic act of a speaker using a definite description referentially. That is, such a definite description comes closer to performing the function of Russell's proper names than certainly he supposed.

Secondly, Russell thought, I believe, that whenever we use descriptions, as opposed to proper names, we introduce an element of generality which ought to be absent if what we are doing is referring to some particular thing. This is clear from his analysis of sentences containing definite descriptions. One of the conclusions we are supposed to draw from that analysis is that such sentences express what are in reality completely general propositions: there is a ϕ and only one such and any ϕ is ψ. We might put this in a slightly different way. If there is anything which might be identified as reference here, it is reference in a very weak sense—namely, reference to *whatever* is the one and only one ϕ, if there is any such. Now this is something we might well say about the attributive use of definite descriptions, as should be evident from the previous discussion. But this lack of particularity is absent from the referential use of definite descriptions precisely because the description is here merely a device for getting one's audience to pick out or think of the thing to be spoken about, a device which may serve its function even if the description is incorrect. More importantly perhaps, in the referential use as opposed to the attributive, there is a *right* thing to be picked out by the audience and its being the right thing is not simply a function of its fitting the description.

ACKNOWLEDGMENTS

I should like to thank my colleagues, John Canfield, Sydney Shoemaker, and Timothy Smiley, who read an earlier draft and gave me helpful suggestions. I also had the benefit of the valuable and detailed comments of the referee for the paper, to whom I wish to express my gratitude.

NOTES

1. "On Denoting," reprinted in *Logic and Knowledge,* ed. Robert C. Marsh (London: 1956), p. 51.
2. "On Referring," reprinted in *Philosophy and Ordinary Language,* ed. Charles C. Caton (Urbana: 1963), pp. 162–163.
3. Ibid., p. 162.
4. Ibid., p. 170.
5. Here and elsewhere I use the disjunction "presuppose or imply" to avoid taking a stand that would side me with Russell or Strawson on the issue of what the relationship involved is. To take a stand here would be beside my main point as well as being misleading, since later on I shall argue that the presupposition or implication arises in a different way depending upon the use to which the definite description is put. This last also accounts for my use of the vagueness indicator, "in some sense."
6. In a footnote added to the original version of "On Referring" (op. cit., p. 181) Strawson seems to imply that where the presupposition is false, we still succeed in referring in a "secondary" way, which seems to mean "as we could be said to refer to fictional or make-believe things." But his view is still that we cannot refer in such a case in the "primary" way. This is, I believe, wrong. For a discussion of this modification of Strawson's view see Charles E. Caton, "Strawson on Referring," *Mind,* LXVIII (1959), 539–544.
7. This is an adaptation of an example (used for a somewhat different purpose) given by Leonard Lin-

sky in "Reference and Referents," in *Philosophy and Ordinary Language,* p. 80.
8. In "Reference and Referents" (pp. 74–75, 80), Linsky correctly points out that one does not fail to refer simply because the description used does not in fact fit anything (or fits more than one thing). Thus he pinpoints one of the difficulties in Strawson's view. Here, however, I use this fact about referring to make a distinction I believe he does not draw, between two uses of definite descriptions. I later discuss the second passage from Linsky's paper.
9. In "A Reply to Mr. Sellars," *Philosophical Review,* LXIII (1954), 216–231, Strawson admits that we do not always refuse to ascribe truth to what a person says when the definite description he uses fails to fit anything (or fits more than one thing). To cite one of his examples, a person who said, "The United States Chamber of Deputies contains representatives of two major parties," would be allowed to have said something true even though he had used the wrong title. Strawson thinks this does not constitute a genuine problem for his view. He thinks that what we do in such cases, "where the speaker's intended reference is pretty clear, is simply to amend his statement in accordance with his guessed intentions and assess the amended statement for truth or falsity; we are not awarding a truth value at all to the original statement" (p. 230).

The notion of an "amended statement," however, will not do. We may note, first of all, that the sort of case Strawson has in mind could arise only when a definite description is used referentially. For the "amendment" is made by seeing the speaker's intended reference. But this could happen only if the speaker had an intended reference, a particular person or thing in mind, independent of the description he used. The cases Strawson has in mind are presumably not cases of slips of the tongue or the like; presumably they are cases in which a definite description is used because the speaker believes, though he is mistaken, that he is describing correctly what he wants to refer to. We supposedly amend the statement by knowing to what he intends to refer. But what description is to be used in the amended statement? In the example, perhaps, we could use "the United States Congress." But this description might be one the speaker would not even accept as correctly describing what he wants to refer to, because he is misinformed about the correct title. Hence, this is not a case of deciding what the speaker meant to say as opposed to what he in fact said, for the speaker did not mean to say "the United States Congress." If this is so, then there is no bar to the "amended" statement containing any description that does correctly pick out what the speaker intended to refer to. It could be, e.g., "The lower house of the United States Congress." But this means that there is no one unique "amended" statement to be assessed for truth value. And, in fact, it should now be clear that the notion of the amended statement really plays no role anyway. For if we can

arrive at the amended statement only by first knowing to what the speaker intended to refer, we can
assess the truth of what he said simply by deciding
whether what he intended to refer to has the properties he ascribed to it.

10. As noted earlier (note 6), Strawson may allow that
one has possibly referred in a "secondary" way, but,
if I am right, the fact that there is no φ does not preclude one from having referred in the same way one
does if there is a φ.

11. For a further discussion of the notion of saying
something true *of* someone or something, see section
VIII.

12. "Reference and Referents," p. 80. It should be clear
that I agree with Linsky in holding that a speaker
may refer even though the "presupposition of existence" is not satisfied. And I agree in thinking this an
objection to Strawson's view. I think, however, that
this point, among others, can be used to define two
distinct uses of definite descriptions which, in turn,
yields a more general criticism of Strawson. So,
while I develop here a point of difference, which
grows out of the distinction I want to make, I find
myself in agreement with much of Linsky's article.

13. Cf. "The Philosophy of Logical Atomism," reprinted
in *Logic and Knowledge*, p. 200.

SUGGESTED FURTHER READING

Donnellan, Keith, "Putting Humpty Dumpty Together
Again," *Philosophical Review* 77 (1967): 203–215.

Donnellan, Keith, "Speaker Reference, Descriptions,
and Anaphora," in *Contemporary Perspectives in
the Philosophy of Language,* ed. Peter A. French,
Theodore E. Uehling, Jr., and Howard K. Wettstein
(Minneapolis: University of Minnesota Press,
1979), pp. 28–44.

Evans, Gareth, *Varieties of Reference* (Oxford: Oxford
University Press, 1982).

Geach, Peter, *Reference and Generality,* emended ed.
(Ithaca: Cornell University Press, 1965).

Kaplan, David, "What Is Russell's Theory of Descriptions?" in *Bertrand Russell,* ed. D. F. Pears (Garden
City, N.Y.: Anchor Books, 1972), pp. 227–244.

Kripke, Saul, "Speaker's Reference and Semantic Reference," in *Contemporary Perspectives in the Philosophy of Language,* ed. Peter French, Theodore
Uehling, Jr., and Howard Wettstein (Minneapolis:
University of Minnesota Press, 1977), pp. 6–27.

Linsky, Leonard, *Referring* (London: Routledge &
Kegan Paul, 1967).

MacKay, Alfred F., "Mr. Donnellan and Humpty Dumpty
on Referring," *Philosophical Review* 77 (1968):
197–202.

Martinich, A. P., "The Attributive Use of Proper Names,"
Analysis 37 (1979): 159–163.

Martinich, A. P., "Referring," *Philosophy and Phenomenological Research* 40 (1979): 157–172.

Martinich, A. P., *Communication and Reference* (Berlin
and New York: Walter de Gruyter, 1984), pp.
133–199.

Moore, A. W., ed., *Meaning and Reference* (New York:
Oxford University Press, 1993).

Neale, Stephen, *Descriptions* (Cambridge: MIT Press,
1990)

Ostertag, Gary, ed., *Definite Descriptions: A Reader*
(Cambridge: MIT Press, 1998).

Russell, Bertrand, "Denoting," in *Principles of Mathematics,* 2d ed. (New York: W. W. Norton & Company, Inc., 1937), pp. 53–65.

Searle, John R., *Expression and Meaning* (Cambridge:
Cambridge University Press, 1979), pp. 137–161.

Searle, John R., *Intentionality* (Cambridge: Cambridge
University Press, 1983), pp. 197–261.

Strawson, P. F., *Subject and Predicate in Logic and
Grammar* (London: Methuen & Company, 1974).

Stroll, Avrum, "On 'The,'" *Philosophy and Phenomenological Research* 16 (1955–56): 496–504.

Vendler, Zeno, "Singular Terms," in *Linguistics in Philosophy* (Ithaca: Cornell University Press, 1967),
pp. 33–69.

IV

NAMES AND DEMONSTRATIVES

John Stuart Mill categorizes names into connotative and nonconnotative ones. The word 'name' and 'noun' are related etymologically; so Mill's categorization is as much one of nouns as it is of names. For Mill, connotatative names include both common concrete nouns ('dog' and 'house') and adjectives ('white' and 'virtuous'). They denote objects (individual dogs, houses, white things, and virtuous things). Students often resist thinking of adjectives as names, but that is Mill's theory, and he is adopting a view that goes back at least as far as the Middle Ages. In addition to denoting objects, common nouns and adjectives also have a descriptive component that leads Mill to say that they connote or signify attributes. ('Attribute' is another name for property or quality.) Consider the expression, 'the woman wearing the green hat'. That phrase (we are assuming) denotes a certain woman. But it also describes her as a woman wearing a green hat, and that descriptive element is what Mill calls the 'connotative' aspect of an expression. Let's consider a simpler case. The word 'white' denotes all the things that are white and connotes the attribute of whiteness. It may seem paradoxical (and Plato struggled with this general issue), but 'white' does not name whiteness; and consequently the sentence, 'Whiteness is white' is false. The word 'whiteness' is a nonconnotative name. It denotes whiteness but connotes nothing. 'Whiteness' is an abstract name—it names something, namely, whiteness, without denoting the concrete object that is white. In general, all abstract nouns, nouns that denote individual abstract entities, are nonconnotatative.

So far, we have distinguished connotative from nonconnotative names, and have identified one kind of nonconnotative name, abstract names. We can now introduce one of the categories of names that we are particularly interested in: nonconnotative names of concrete objects. They are also called 'proper names', for example, the names 'Adam', 'Beth', and 'Carol'. They denote a singular spatio-temporal object without connoting anything.

This neat division of connotative and nonconnotative names, and the division of nonconnotative names into the abstract and the concrete ones, is complicated by the existence of a kind of name that denotes individuals (as proper names do) but is connotative (as proper names are not). They seem to be a hybrid of connotative and nonconotative elements. Mill sometimes calls them many-worded names and sometimes 'individual names.' His examples include 'the sun', 'the only son of John Stiles', 'the first emperor of Rome', and 'the author of the *Iliad*'.

Before 1905, Bertrand Russell accepted Mill's view that the so-called connotative names were names. But, as we saw in the preceding section, in "On Denoting" he came to reject it. Because of Mill's importance, Russell could not simply assert that they were not names; he had to argue for it. Calling them 'descriptions', possibly because he thought it would be easier to persuade people that descriptions are not names than to persuade them that individual names are not names, Russell asserted that proper names are simple, while descriptions are not. This view seems to be confirmed by a look at some typical names ('Adam', 'Beth', 'Carol') and some typical descriptions ('the best undergraduate student in Texas', 'a likely candidate for Congress', 'a soft bed'). Names, according to Russell, denote the things they name simply in virtue of their being the names of those things. They do not seem to describe the object they name. While some proper names like 'Baker' and 'Miller' started out as descriptions of the person who first had the name ('Adam the baker' and 'Bob the miller'), once that description became a proper name, it sloughed off its descriptive character and grew an initial capital letter. Adam Baker (the former 'Adam the baker') could change occupations without his name changing too. And Adam's great granddaughter Beth ('Beth Baker') could grow up to be a lawyer without anyone thinking that some ancestor of hers had been a baker.

The existence of names that have an obvious descriptive origin, such as 'Sitting Bull' and 'Song of Spring', does not change the fact that they denote individual people solely by being their names. The descriptiveness of 'Sitting Bull' and 'Song of Spring' is irrelevant to their functioning semantically as names. A person looking for Sitting Bull would not sensibly look for the person that most looked like a sitting bull. In contrast, descriptions (are used to) refer in virtue of their descriptive content. (Recall, however, that we saw in the preceding section that Keith Donnellan thinks that there is a way of referring with descriptions that does not essentially depend on their descriptive content.)

Russell thinks that the fact that proper names only denote and do not connote means that they are logically simple. Seemingly complex proper names, like 'Elizabeth Ann Metternich', are logically simple in the sense that the three parts are supposed to function as one in order to apply uniquely to some object. (Philosophers usually ignore the fact that few proper names are unique. There are many Sarah Smiths and Francisco Martinezes.) People do not find the denotation of 'Elizabeth Ann Metternich' by first identifying all the Metternichs, and then identifying all the Anns in that set, and then identifying the one Elizabeth in the set of Anns. Contrast 'Elizabeth Ann Metternich' with the phrase 'the small, female terrier'. In the right context, we know what object is being referred to by combining the meanings of 'small', 'female', and 'terrier'. In effect, we mentally identify the terriers, and then from these the female ones, and then from these the small one. One aid to thinking of the essential linguistic simplicity of proper names is to think of the complex ones as being fused or hyphenated: ElizabethAnnMetternich or Elizabeth-Ann-Metternich. No meaning would be lost in doing so. In contrast, if the component words of descriptions were fused, meaning would be lost: smallfemaleterrier. As one syllable, 'small' has no more meaning than 'so' in the word 'something'. The word 'butterfly' comes from the words 'butter' and 'fly', but once these latter words are fused, they do not retain their meaning. 'Butterfly' means a certain kind of flying insect, not something that is either butter or a fly. If the word was coined because someone associated butterflies with flying butter, that would be a mildly interesting fact about the word's origin, not a semantic fact about its meaning.) 'Cambridge' was named for a bridge on the River Cam, but it retained its name even though the original bridge no longer exists.

The upshot of the syntactic fact that proper names are simple and descriptions are not is that names directly denote objects, while descriptions denote objects in virtue of a mediating entity, their descriptive content. Also, the only thing that a proper name could mean, it seems, is the object it directly denotes since it connotes nothing. Descriptions could mean either (i) the objects they denote, (ii) their descriptive content, or (iii) nothing. It cannot be (i) because some descriptions are meaningful ('the round square') but denote nothing. It cannot be (ii) because descriptions ('a dog' or 'the dog that barks') do more than just describe; they indicate something about the number of objects that fit the descriptive content. So Russell opted for (iii), as explained in his theory of descriptions. Of course, although they mean nothing, they contribute to the meaning of a sentence.

One might object to Russell's view about proper names that 'Pegasus' and 'George Washington' are just as much proper names as anything even though Pegasus never existed and Washington no longer does. Russell's reply is first to concede that 'Pegasus', 'George Washington', and proper names of existing objects should all be treated the same, and second to deny that any of these ordinary proper names are genuine or logically proper names. According to Russell, they are in fact disguised or abbreviated descriptions. 'Pegasus' is an abbreviation for something like 'the flying horse that landed on Mt. Helicon', and 'George Washington' is an abbreviation for something like 'the first president of the United States'. So, paradoxically, Russell's attempt to prove that proper names are not definite descriptions was not an attempt to prove that words like 'Cade Himmel' belong to a different logical category from 'the youngest grandchild of John Edward Martinich'. Rather, for some time Russell maintained that the genuine or logically proper names are demonstratives and other indexical words, such as 'this', 'that', 'I', 'here', and 'now'. (Russell later came to hold that not even these were proper names since 'this', for example, is an abbreviation for the description, 'the object being pointed to at the present time'.)

The best alternative to Russell's theory of proper names was John Searle's revision of Frege's view. Each proper name has a set of descriptions, almost always a disjunctive set and often indeterminate, in virtue of which a speaker or hearer knows what object the name names. Saul Kripke explains Searle's 'description theory' of names in preparation for trying to refute it.

According to Kripke, Russell was right to think that proper names do not have descriptive content, *Sinne,* to use Frege's term, but wrong to think that ordinary names are not logically proper names. For his positive view, Kripke argued that proper names denote the object that they are causally connected to by their initial or 'baptismal' use. Hilary Putnam in the same spirit argued that the meaning of common nouns for natural kinds, for example, 'water' and 'gold', are the objects they denote and not the objects that might be determined by a concept or anything else 'in the head,' of the ordinary user of the words. Ordinary speakers determine which objects are paradigmatic denotations for words, and then specialists, that is, scientists, determine the extension of those words, based upon their knowledge of the nature of paradigms; thus water is anything that is H_2O, and nothing else. A counterintuitive consequence of Putnam's view is that prior to the discovery of water in the eighteenth century, no one knew the meaning of 'water'.

Gareth Evans in "The Causal Theory of Names" criticizes aspects of both the description theory and the causal theory of names before presenting his own view, which preserves what he takes to be the underlying intuitions of those superseded theories. Evans distinguishes two kinds of description theories: one a theory about what a speaker denotes by a name and one a theory about what a name itself denotes. Both are defective. It is important to note that both the description theory and the causal theory answer the question, 'Given that reference occurs, what determines what object is referred to?' This question presupposes that there is an answer to the question, 'Under what conditions does reference occur?' that is not answered by the causal theory. According to Evans, an adequate answer to the latter theory involves an intentional account of names.

Searle's article, "Proper Names and Intentionality," is a brilliant defense of his views against criticisms such as Kripke's. Since his defense is sometimes stated in the technical terms of his complete treatment of these matters in *Intentionality,* some brief remarks about three of these terms will be helpful. First, his idea of "intentional content" is best explained by example. The intentional content of Beth's belief that it is raining is the proposition that it is raining and the intentional content of Carol's desire to eat a piece of pie is the proposition that Carol is eating a piece of pie. The intentional content should not be confused with the object toward which the intentional state is directed. For example, the object of Carol's desire is the pie itself, not a proposition. Second, an intentional state often requires other intentional states; thus, the intention to become president of the United States is only possible if accompanied by the belief that the United States is a republic, that its leader is a president, that its leader is elected at fixed intervals, and so on. Searle calls this complex of intentional states the "Network." Third, in addition to the Network, which is intentional and representational, there are nonrepresentational abilities and ways of doing things that Searle calls the "Background."

Demonstratives seem to be like proper names, and unlike descriptions, in that they do not seem to describe the objects they denote. And Bertrand Russell, as we have seen, came to think that demonstratives were the only kind of words that were logically proper names, as opposed to ordinary proper names. However, demonstratives or indexicals seem to differ from proper names in that they pick out different objects in different contexts. For example, the referent of the word 'I' varies as the speaker varies. In "Dthat," David Kaplan explores some of the consequences of construing demonstratives as contributing a conceptual (descriptive) element to the proposition it expresses. He also nicely summarizes some of the main issues related to reference, names, and the nature of propositions.

David Kaplan's "On the Logic of Demonstratives" gives a formal treatment of the semantics of demonstrative words, as suggested by his comment in "Dthat," that is, he extends first-order predicate logic with identity to include demonstratives. In "On the Logic of Demonstratives," Kaplan drives a wedge between the concepts of logical truth and necessity by pointing out that any statement of 'I am here now' is logically true but not necessarily true. (A problem case is 'I am not here now' on a telephone answering machine.) The *content* of the statement 'I am here now', said by Kaplan on 20 April 1973, has a different *content* from 'I am here now', said by Martinich on 28 December 2006. The content is a function from possible worlds to extensions.

There is another element of the intuitive sense of meaning that needs to be considered. The meaning of 'I am here now' is the same no matter who says it. Kaplan calls this intuitive sense of meaning 'character'. The character of a word or phrase in a context determines the content of what is said, that is, the character of a word is the function that assigns to each context a content. Kaplan presented a more extended treatment of demonstratives in "Demonstratives," and further thoughts about them in

"Afterthoughts," both in *Themes from Kaplan*, edited by Joseph Almog, John Perry, and Howard Wettstein (New York: Oxford University Press, 1989).

John Perry's article, "The Problem of the Essential Indexical," is transitional. It discusses one demonstrative, namely, 'I', and also the topic of the next section of this book, propositional attitudes. He considers sentences in which the use of 'I' is essential to the determination of the belief that the speaker has. The belief reported by the sentence 'I am making a mess' is not the same as the belief reported by 'Jane Jones is making a mess' even if Jane Jones is making both statements. For example, Jones knows 'I am making a mess' is true, if she sees baking flour leaking out of her own shopping cart and recognizes it as her own. But she will not know that 'Jane Jones is making a mess' is true if she does not know her own name (perhaps due to amnesia). Alternatively, in different circumstances, Jones may know that 'Jane Jones is making a mess' is true, if she hears that sentence broadcast over a public address system without knowing that 'I am making a mess' (if, again, for some reason she does not know her own name).

Perry argues that a necessary condition for explaining the oddity of these situations is to distinguish between the belief state that a person is in and the objects denoted by that belief state. For physicalists, the belief state can be identified with a brain state. Suppose Adam, Beth, and Carol, in three different supermarkets, are each leaking flour from the bag of flour in their shopping carts. Each one is in the same type of belief state, namely, a belief state that relates each of them to their own leaking. That is, each belief state is indexical. However, each shopper's belief is related to a different object. Adam's trail of flour is not identical with Beth's or Carol's, and Beth's is not identical with Carol's. Each one believes something different.

Perry shows that the standard accounts of *de dicto* and *de re* beliefs will not solve the problem of correctly accounting for beliefs that essentially involve indexicals. And, while he does not pretend to offer a theory of such beliefs, he insists that, "no philosophy of belief can be plausible that does not take account of" the distinction between belief states and beliefs.

20 Of Names

JOHN STUART MILL

I. NAMES ARE NAMES OF THINGS, NOT OF OUR IDEAS

"A name," says Hobbes, "is a word taken at pleasure to serve for a mark which may raise in our mind a thought like to some thought we had before, and which, being pronounced to others, may be to them a sign of what thought the speaker had before in his mind." This simple definition of a name as a word (or set of words) serving the double purpose of a mark to recall to ourselves the likeness of a former thought and a sign to make it known to others appears unexceptionable. Names, indeed, do much more than this, but whatever else they do grows out of and is the result of this, as will appear in its proper place. . . .

III. GENERAL AND SINGULAR NAMES

All names are names of something, real or imaginary, but all things have not names appropriated to them individually. For some individual objects we require and, consequently, have separate distinguishing names; there is a name for every person and for every remarkable place. Other objects of which we have not occasion to speak so frequently we do not designate by names of their own; but when the necessity arises for naming them, we do so by putting together several words, each of which, by itself, might be and is used for an indefinite number of

other objects, as when I say, "this stone": "this" and "stone" being, each of them, names that may be used of many other objects besides the particular one meant, though the only object of which they can both be used at the given moment, consistently with their signification, may be the one of which I wish to speak.

Were this the sole purpose for which names that are common to more things than one could be employed, if they only served, by mutually limiting each other, to afford a designation for such individual objects as have no names of their own, they could only be ranked among contrivances for economising the use of language. But it is evident that this is not their sole function. It is by their means that we are enabled to assert *general* propositions, to affirm or deny any predicate of an indefinite number of things at once. The distinction, therefore, between *general* names and *individual* or *singular* names is fundamental, and may be considered as the first grand division of names.

A general name is, familiarly defined, a name which is capable of being truly affirmed, in the same sense, of each of an indefinite number of things. An individual or singular name is a name which is only capable of being truly affirmed, in the same sense, of one thing.

Thus, *man* is capable of being truly affirmed of John, George, Mary, and other persons without assignable limit, and it is affirmed of all of them in the same sense, for the word "man"

From *System of Logic*, Book I, Chapter 2, Section 5.

expresses certain qualities, and when we predicate it of those persons, we assert that they all possess those qualities. But *John* is only capable of being truly affirmed of one single person, at least in the same sense. For, though there are many persons who bear that name, it is not conferred upon them to indicate any qualities or any thing which belongs to them in common, and cannot be said to be affirmed of them in any *sense* at all, consequently not in the same sense. "The king who succeeded William the Conqueror" is also an individual name. For that there cannot be more than one person of whom it can be truly affirmed is implied in the meaning of the words. Even *"the* king," when the occasion or the context defines the individual of whom it is to be understood, may justly be regarded as an individual name. . . .

It is necessary to distinguish *general* from *collective* names. A general name is one which can be predicated of *each* individual of a multitude; a collective name cannot be predicated of each separately, but only of all taken together. "The seventy-sixth regiment of foot in the British army," which is a collective name, is not a general but an individual name, for though it can be predicated of a multitude of individual soldiers taken jointly, it cannot be predicated of them severally. We may say, "Jones is a soldier, and Thompson is a soldier, and Smith is a soldier," but we cannot say, "Jones is the seventy-sixth regiment, and Thompson is the seventy-sixth regiment, and Smith is the seventy-sixth regiment." We can only say, "Jones, and Thompson, and Smith, and Brown, and so forth (enumerating all the soldiers) are the seventy-sixth regiment."

"The seventy-sixth regiment" is a collective name, but not a general one; "a regiment" is both a collective and a general name—general with respect to all individual regiments of each of which separately it can be affirmed, collective with respect to the individual soldiers of whom any regiment is composed.

IV. CONCRETE AND ABSTRACT

The second general division of names is into *concrete* and *abstract*. A concrete name is a name which stands for a thing; an abstract name is a name which stands for an attribute of a thing. Thus *John, the sea, this table* are names of things. *White,* also, is a name of a thing, or rather of things. Whiteness, again, is the name of a quality or attribute of those things. Man is a name of many things; humanity is a name of an attribute of those things. *Old* is a name of things; *old age* is a name of one of their attributes. . . . By *abstract,* then, I shall always, in logic proper, mean the opposite of *concrete;* by an abstract name, the name of an attribute; by a concrete name, the name of an object.

Do abstract names belong to the class of general or to that of singular names? Some of them are certainly general. I mean those which are names not of one single and definite attribute but of a class of attributes. Such is the word *color,* which is a name common to whiteness, redness, etc. Such is even the word *whiteness,* in respect of the different shades of whiteness to which it is applied in common; the word *magnitude,* in respect of the various degrees of magnitude and the various dimensions of space; the word *weight,* in respect of the various degrees of weight. Such also is the word *attribute* itself, the common name of all particular attributes. But when only one attribute, neither variable in degree nor in kind, is designated by the name—as visibleness, tangibleness, equality, squareness, milk-whiteness—then the name can hardly be considered general; for though it denotes an attribute of many different objects, the attribute itself is always conceived as one, not many. To avoid needless logomachies, the best course would probably be to consider these names as neither general nor individual, and to place them in a class apart.

It may be objected to our definition of an abstract name that not only the names which we have called abstract, but adjectives which we have placed in the concrete class, are names of attributes; that *white,* for example, is as much the name of the color as *whiteness* is. But (as before remarked) a word ought to be considered as the name of that which we intend to be understood by it when we put it to its principal use, that is, when we employ it in predication. When we say "snow is white," "milk is white," "linen is white," we do not mean it to be understood that snow or linen or milk is a color. We mean that they are things having the color. The reverse is the case with the word *whiteness;* what we affirm to *be* whiteness is not snow but the color of snow. Whiteness, therefore, is the name of the color exclusively, white is a name of all things whatever having the color, a name, not of the quality whiteness, but of every white object. It is true, this name was given to all those various objects on account of the quality, and we may therefore say, without impropriety, that the quality forms part of its signification; but a name can only be said to stand for, or to be a name of, the things of which it can be predicated. We shall presently see that all names which can be said to have any signification, all names by applying which to an individual we give any information respecting that individual, may be said to *imply* an attribute of some sort, but they are not names of the attribute; it has its own proper abstract name.

V. CONNOTATIVE AND NON-CONNOTATIVE

This leads to the consideration of a third great division of names, into *connotative* and *non-connotative,* the latter sometimes, but improperly, called *absolute.* This is one of the most important distinctions which we shall have occasion to point out and one of those which go deepest into the nature of language.

A non-connotative term is one which signifies a subject only, or an attribute only. A connotative term is one which denotes a subject and implies an attribute. By a subject is here meant anything which possesses attributes. Thus John, or London, or England are names which signify a subject only. Whiteness, length, virtue, signify an attribute only. None of these names, therefore, are connotative. But *white, long, virtuous,* are connotative. The word *white* denotes all white things, as snow, paper, the foam of the sea, etc., and implies, or in the language of the schoolmen, *connotes,* the attribute *whiteness.* The word *white* is not predicated of the attribute, but of the subjects, snow, etc.; but when we predicate it of them, we convey the meaning that the attribute whiteness belongs to them. The same may be said of the other words above cited. Virtuous, for example, is the name of a

class which includes Socrates, Howard, the Man of Ross, and an undefinable number of other individuals, past, present, and to come. These individuals, collectively and severally, can alone be said with propriety to be denoted by the word; of them alone can it properly be said to be a name. But it is a name applied to all of them in consequence of an attribute which they are supposed to possess in common, the attribute which has received the name of virtue. It is applied to all beings that are considered to possess this attribute, and to none which are not so considered.

All concrete general names are connotative. The word *man,* for example, denotes Peter, Jane, John, and an indefinite number of other individuals of whom, taken as a class, it is the name. But it is applied to them because they possess, and to signify that they possess, certain attributes. These seem to be corporeity, animal life, rationality, and a certain external form which, for distinction, we call the human. Every existing thing which possessed all these attributes would be called a man; and anything which possessed none of them, or only one, or two, or even three of them without the fourth, would not be so called. For example, if in the interior of Africa there were to be discovered a race of animals possessing reason equal to that of human beings but with the form of an elephant, they would not be called men. Swift's Houyhnhnms would not be so called. Or if such newly-discovered beings possessed the form of man without any vestige of reason, it is probable that some other name than that of man would be found for them. How it happens that there can be any doubt about the matter will appear hereafter. The word *man,* therefore, signifies all these attributes and all subjects which possess these attributes. But it can be predicated only of the subjects. What we call men are the subjects, the individual Stiles and Nokes, not the qualities by which their humanity is constituted. The name, therefore, is said to signify the subjects *directly,* the attributes *indirectly;* it *denotes* the subjects, and implies, or involves, or indicates, or, as we shall say henceforth, *connotes,* the attributes. It is a connotative name.

Connotative names have hence been also called *denominative,* because the subject which they denote is denominated by, or receives a name from, the attribute which they connote. Snow and other objects receive the name white because they possess the attribute which is called whiteness; Peter, James, and others receive the name man because they possess the attributes which are considered to constitute humanity. The attribute, or attributes, may, therefore, be said to denominate those objects or to give them a common name.

It has been seen that all concrete general names are connotative. Even abstract names, though the names only of attributes, may, in some instances, be justly considered as connotative; for attributes themselves may have attributes ascribed to them, and a word which denotes attributes may connote an attribute of those attributes. Of this description, for example, is such a word as *fault,* equivalent to *bad* or *hurtful quality.* This word is a name common to many attributes and connotes hurtfulness, an attribute of those various attributes. When, for example, we say that slowness in a horse is a fault, we do not mean that the slow movement, the actual change of place of the slow horse, is a bad thing, but that the property or peculiarity of the horse, from which it derives that name, the quality of being a slow mover, is an undesirable peculiarity.

In regard to those concrete names which are not general but individual, a distinction must be made.

Proper names are not connotative; they denote the individuals who are called by them, but they do not indicate or imply any attributes as belonging to those individuals. When we name a child by the name Paul or a dog by the name Caesar, these names are simply marks used to enable those individuals to be made subjects of discourse. It may be said, indeed, that we must have had some reason for giving them those names rather than any others, and this is true, but the name, once given, is independent of the reason. A man may have been named John because that was the name of his father; a town may have been named Dart-mouth because it is situated at the mouth of the Dart. But it is no part of the signification of the word John that the father of the person so called bore the same name, nor even of the word Dart-mouth to be

situated at the mouth of the Dart. If sand should choke up the mouth of the river or an earthquake change its course and remove it to a distance from the town, the name of the town would not necessarily be changed. That fact, therefore, can form no part of the signification of the word; for otherwise, when the fact confessedly ceased to be true, no one would any longer think of applying the name. Proper names are attached to the objects themselves and are not dependent on the continuance of any attribute of the object.

But there is another kind of names, which, although they are individual names—that is, predicable only of one object—are really connotative. For, though we may give to an individual a name utterly unmeaning, unmeaningful which we call a proper name—a word which answers the purpose of showing what thing it is we are talking about, but not of telling anything about it; yet a name peculiar to an individual is not necessarily of this description. It may be significant of some attribute or some union of attributes which, being possessed by no object but one, determines the name exclusively to that individual. "The sun" is a name of this description; "God," when used by a monotheist, is another. These, however, are scarcely examples of what we are now attempting to illustrate, being, in strictness of language, general, not individual names, for, however they may be *in fact* predicable only of one object, there is nothing in the meaning of the words themselves which implies this; and, accordingly, when we are imagining and not affirming, we may speak of many suns; and the majority of mankind have believed, and still believe, that there are many gods. But it is easy to produce words which are real instances of connotative individual names. It may be part of the meaning of the connotative name itself, that there can exist but one individual possessing the attribute which it connotes, as, for instance, "the *only* son of John Stiles"; "the *first* emperor of Rome." Or the attribute connoted may be a connection with some determinate event, and the connection may be of such a kind as only one individual could have, or may, at least, be such as only one individual actually had, and this may be implied in the form of the expression. "The father of Socrates" is an example of the one kind (since Socrates could not have had two fathers), "the author of the Iliad," "the murderer of Henri Quatre," of the second. For, though it is conceivable that more persons than one might have participated in the authorship of the Iliad or in the murder of Henri Quatre, the employment of the article *the* implies that, in fact, this was not the case. What is here done by the word *the* is done in other cases by the context; thus, "Caesar's army" is an individual name if it appears from the context that the army meant is that which Caesar commanded in a particular battle. The still more general expressions, "the Roman army," or "the Christian army," may be individualized in a similar manner. Another case of frequent occurrence has already been noticed; it is the following: The name, being a many-worded one, may consist, in the first place, of a *general* name, capable therefore, in itself, of being affirmed of more things than one, but which is, in the second place, so limited by other words joined with it that the entire expression can only be predicated of one object, consistently with the meaning of the general term. This is exemplified in such an instance as the following: "the present prime minister of England." "Prime Minister of England" is a general name; the attributes which it connotes may be possessed by an indefinite number of persons, in succession, however, not simultaneously, since the meaning of the name itself imports (among other things) that there can be only one such person at a time. This being the case, and the application of the name being afterward limited, by the article and the word *present,* to such individuals as possess the attributes at one indivisible point of time, it becomes applicable only to one individual. And, as this appears from the meaning of the name without any extrinsic proof, it is strictly an individual name.

From the preceding observations it will easily be collected that whenever the names given to objects convey any information—that is, whenever they have properly any meaning—the meaning resides not in what they *denote* but in what they *connote.* The only names of objects which connote nothing are *proper* names, and these have, strictly speaking, no signification.

As a proper name is said to be the name of the one individual which it is predicated of, so (as well from the importance of adhering to anal-

ogy as for the other reasons formerly assigned) a connotative name ought to be considered a name of all the various individuals which it is predicable of, or, in other words, *denotes,* and not of what it connotes. But by learning what things it is a name of, we do not learn the meaning of the name; for to the same thing we may, with equal propriety, apply many names, not equivalent in meaning. Thus I call a certain man by the name Sophroniscus; I call him by another name, the father of Socrates. Both these are names of the same individual, but their meaning is altogether different. They are applied to that individual for two different purposes: the one merely to distinguish him from other persons who are spoken of; the other to indicate a fact relating to him, the fact that Socrates was his son. I further apply to him these other expressions: a man, a Greek, an Athenian, a sculptor, an old man, an honest man, a brave man. All these are, or may be, names of Sophroniscus, not, indeed, of him alone, but of him and each of an indefinite number of other human beings. Each of these names is applied to Sophroniscus for a different reason, and by each whoever understands its meaning is apprised of a distinct fact or number of facts concerning him, but those who knew nothing about the names except that they were applicable to Sophroniscus would be altogether ignorant of their meaning. It is even possible that I might know every single individual of whom a given name could be with truth affirmed and yet could not be said to know the meaning of the name. A child knows who are its brothers and sisters long before it has any definite conception of the nature of the facts which are involved in the signification of those words. . . . Since, however, the introduction of a new technical language as the vehicle of speculations on subjects belonging to the domain of daily discussion is extremely difficult to effect and would not be free from inconvenience even if effected, the problem for the philosopher, and one of the most difficult which he has to resolve, is, in retaining the existing phraseology, how best to alleviate its imperfections. This can only be accomplished by giving to every general concrete name which there is frequent occasion to predicate a definite and fixed connotation in order that it may be known what attributes, when we call an object by that name, we really mean to predicate of the object. And the question of most nicety is how to give this fixed connotation to a name with the least possible change in the objects which the name is habitually employed to denote, with the least possible disarrangement, either by adding or subtraction, of the group of objects which, in however, imperfect a manner, it serves to circumscribe and hold together, and with the least vitiation of the truth of any propositions which are commonly received as true.

This desirable purpose of giving a fixed connotation where it is wanting is the end aimed at whenever any one attempts to give a definition of a general name already in use, every definition of a connotative name being an attempt either merely to declare, or to declare and analyze, the connotation of the name. And the fact that no questions which have arisen in the moral sciences have been subjects of keener controversy than the definitions of almost all the leading expressions is a proof how great an extent the evil to which we have adverted has attained.

21 Naming and Necessity

SAUL KRIPKE

LECTURE I

. . . The first topic in the pair of topics is naming. By a name here I will mean a proper name, i.e., the name of a person, a city, a country, etc. It is well known that modern logicians also are very interested in definite descriptions: phrases of the form "the x such that ϕx," such as "the man who corrupted Hadleyburg." Now, if one and only one man ever corrupted Hadleyburg, then that man is the referent, in the logician's sense, of that description. We will use the term 'name' so that it does *not* include definite descriptions of that sort, but only those things which in ordinary language would be called 'proper names'. If we want a common term to cover names and descriptions, we may use the term 'designator'.

It is a point, made by Donnellan,[1] that under certain circumstances a particular speaker may use a definite description to refer, not to the proper referent, in the sense that I've just defined it, of that description, but to something else which he wants to single out and which he thinks is the proper referent of the description, but which in fact isn't. So you may say, "The man over there with the champagne in his glass is happy," though he actually only has water in his glass. Now, even though there is no champagne in his glass, and there may be another man in the room who does have champagne in his glass, the speaker *intended* to refer, or maybe, in some sense of 'refer', *did* refer, to the man he thought had the champagne in his glass. Nevertheless, I'm just going to use the term 'referent of the description' to mean the object uniquely satisfying the conditions in the definite description. This is the sense in which it's been used in the logical tradition. So, if you have a description of the form "the x such that ϕx," and there is exactly one x such that ϕx, that is the referent of the description. . . .

Many people have said that the theory of Frege and Russell is false, but, in my opinion, they have abandoned its letter while retaining its spirit, namely, they have used the notion of a cluster concept. Well, what is this? The obvious problem for Frege and Russell, the one which comes immediately to mind, is already mentioned by Frege himself. He said,

In the case of genuinely proper names like "Aristotle" opinions as regards their sense may diverge. As such may, e.g., be suggested: Plato's disciple and the teacher of Alexander the Great. Whoever accepts this sense will interpret the meaning of the statement "Aristotle was born in Stagira," differently from one who interpreted the sense of "Aristotle" as the Stagirite teacher of Alexander the Great. As long as the

From *Naming and Necessity* (Cambridge: Harvard University Press, 1980). Reprinted by permission of the publishers and the author from *Naming and Necessity* by Saul A. Kripke, Cambridge, Mass., Harvard University Press. Copyright © 1972, 1980 by Saul A. Kripke. Also by permission of Basil Blackwell Ltd.

nominatum remains the same, these fluctuations in sense are tolerable. But they should be avoided in the system of a demonstrative science and should not appear in a perfect language.[2]

So, according to Frege, there is some sort of looseness or weakness in our language. Some people may give one sense to the name "Aristotle," others may give another. But of course it is not only that; even a single speaker when asked "What description are you willing to substitute for the name?" may be quite at a loss. In fact, he may know many things about him; but any particular thing that he knows he may feel clearly expresses a contingent property of the object. If "Aristotle" meant *the man who taught Alexander the Great,* then saying "Aristotle was a teacher of Alexander the Great" would be a mere tautology. But surely it isn't; it expresses the fact that Aristotle taught Alexander the Great, something we could discover to be false. So, *being the teacher of Alexander the Great* cannot be part of [the sense of] the name.

The most common way out of this difficulty is to say "really it is not a weakness in ordinary language that we can't substitute a *particular* description for the name; that's all right. What we really associate with the name is a *family* of descriptions." A good example of this is in *Philosophical Investigations,* where the idea of family resemblances is introduced and with great power.

Consider this example. If one says "Moses did not exist," this may mean various things. It may mean: the Israelites did not have a *single* leader when they withdrew from Egypt—or: their leader was not called Moses—or: there cannot have been anyone who accomplished all that the Bible relates of Moses— . . . But when I make a statement about Moses,— am I always ready to substitute some *one* of those descriptions for "Moses"? I shall perhaps say: by "Moses" I understand the man who did what the Bible relates of Moses, or at any rate, a good deal of it. But how much? Have I decided how much must be proved false for me to give up my proposition as false? Has the name "Moses" got a fixed and unequivocal use for me in all possible cases?[3]

According to this view, and a *locus classicus* of it is Searle's article on proper names,[4] the referent of a name is determined not by a single description but by some cluster or family. Whatever in some sense satisfies enough or most of the family is the referent of the name. I shall return to this view later. It may seem, as an analysis of ordinary language, quite a bit more plausible than that of Frege and Russell. It may seem to keep all the virtues and remove the defects of this theory.

Let me say (and this will introduce us to another new topic before I really consider this theory of naming) that there are two ways in which the cluster concept theory, or even the theory which requires a single description, can be viewed. One way of regarding it says that the cluster or the single description actually gives the meaning of the name; and when someone says "Walter Scott," he means *the man such that such and such and such and such.*

Now another view might be that even though the description in some sense doesn't give the *meaning* of the name, it is what *determines its reference* and although the phrase "Walter Scott" isn't *synonymous* with "the man such that such and such and such and such," or even maybe with the family (if something can be synonymous with a family), the family or the single description is what is used to determine to whom someone is referring when he says "Walter Scott." Of course, if when we hear his beliefs about Walter Scott we find that they are actually much more nearly true of Salvador Dali, then according to this theory the reference of this name is going to be Mr. Dali, not Scott. There are writers, I think, who explicitly deny that names have meaning at all even more strongly than I would but still use this picture of how the referent of the name gets determined. A good case in point is Paul Ziff, who says, very emphatically, that names don't have meaning at all, [that] they are not a part of language in some sense. But still, when he talks about how we determine what the reference of the name was, then he gives this picture. Unfortunately I don't have the passage in question with me, but this is what he says.[5]

The difference between using this theory as a theory of meaning and using it as a theory of reference will come out a little more clearly later on. But some of the attractiveness of the theory is lost if it isn't supposed to give the meaning of the name; for some of the solutions of problems that I've just mentioned will not be right, or at least won't clearly be right, if the description doesn't give the meaning of the name. For example, if someone said "Aristotle does not exist" *means* "there is no man doing such and such," or in the example from Wittgenstein, "Moses does not exist," *means* "no man did such and such," that might depend (and in fact, I think, does depend) on taking the theory in question as a theory of the meaning of the name "Moses," not just as a theory of its reference. Well, I don't know. Perhaps all that is immediate now is the other way around: if "Moses" means the same as "the man who did such and such" then to say that Moses did not exist is to say that the man who did such and such did not exist, that is, that no one person did such and such. If, on the other hand, "Moses" is not synonymous with any description, then even if its reference is in some sense determined by a description, statements containing the name cannot in general be *analyzed* by replacing the name by a description, though they may be materially equivalent to statements containing a description. So the analysis of singular existence statements mentioned above will have to be given up, unless it is established by some special argument, independent of a general theory of the meaning of names; and the same applies to identity statements. In any case, I think it's false that "Moses exists" means that at all. So we won't have to see if such a special argument can be drawn up.[6]

Before I go any further into this problem, I want to talk about another distinction which will be important in the methodology of these talks. Philosophers have talked (and, of course, there has been considerable controversy in recent years over the meaningfulness of these notions) [about] various categories of truth, which are called 'a priori', 'analytic', 'necessary'—and sometimes even 'certain' is thrown into this batch. The terms are often used as if *whether* there are things answering to these concepts is an interesting question, but we might as well regard them all as meaning the same thing. Now, everyone remembers Kant (a bit) as making a distinction between 'a priori' and 'analytic'. So maybe this distinction is still made. In

contemporary discussion very few people, if any, distinguish between the concepts of statements being a priori and their being necessary. At any rate I shall *not* use the terms 'a priori' and 'necessary' interchangeably here.

Consider what the traditional characterizations of such terms as 'a priori' and 'necessary' are. First the notion of a prioricity is a concept of epistemology. I guess the traditional characterization from Kant goes something like: a priori truths are those which can be known independently of any experience. This introduces another problem before we get off the ground, because there's another modality in the characterization of 'a priori', namely, it is supposed to be something which *can* be known independently of any experience. That means that in some sense it's *possible* (whether we do or do not in fact know it independently of any experience) to know this independently of any experience. And possible for whom? For God? For the Martians? Or just for people with minds like ours? To make this all clear might [involve] a host of problems all of its own about what sort of possibility is in question here. It might be best therefore, instead of using the phrase 'a priori truth', to the extent that one uses it at all, to stick to the question of whether a particular person or knower knows something a priori or believes it true on the basis of a priori evidence.

I won't go further too much into the problems that might arise with the notion of a prioricity here. I will say that some philosophers somehow change the modality in this characterization from *can* to *must*. They think that if something belongs to the realm of a priori knowledge, it couldn't possibly be known empirically. This is just a mistake. Something may belong in the realm of such statements that *can* be known a priori but still may be known by particular people on the basis of experience. To give a really common sense example: anyone who has worked with a computing machine knows that the computing machine may give an answer to whether such and such a number is prime. No one has calculated or proved that the number is prime; but the machine has given the answer: this number is prime. We, then, if we believe that the number is prime, believe it on the basis of our knowledge of the laws of physics, the construction of the machine, and so on. We therefore do not believe this on the basis of purely a priori evidence. We believe it (if anything is a posteriori at all) on the basis of a posteriori evidence. Nevertheless, maybe this could be known a priori by someone who made the requisite calculations. So '*can* be known a priori' doesn't mean '*must* be known a priori'.

The second concept which is in question is that of necessity. Sometimes this is used in an epistemological way and might then just mean a priori. And of course, sometimes it is used in a physical way when people distinguish between physical and logical necessity. But what I am concerned with here is a notion which is not a notion of epistemology but of metaphysics, in some (I hope) nonpejorative sense. We ask whether something might have been true, or might have been false. Well, if something is false, it's obviously not necessarily true. If it is true, might it have been otherwise? Is it possible that, in this respect, the world should have been different from the way it is? If the answer is "no," then this fact about the world is a necessary one. If the answer is "yes," then this fact about the world is a contingent one. This in and of itself has nothing to do with anyone's knowledge of anything. It's certainly a philosophical thesis, and not a matter of obvious definitional equivalence, either that everything a priori is necessary or that everything necessary is a priori. Both concepts may be vague. That may be another problem. But at any rate they are dealing with two different domains, two different areas, the epistemological and the metaphysical. Consider, say, Fermat's last theorem—or the Goldbach conjecture. The Goldbach conjecture says that an even number greater than 2 must be the sum of two prime numbers. If this is true, it is presumably necessary, and, if it is false, presumably necessarily false. We are taking the classical view of mathematics here and assume that in mathematical reality it is either true or false.

If the Goldbach conjecture is false, then there is an even number, *n,* greater than 2, such that for no primes p_1 and p_2, both $< n$, does $n = p_1 + p_2$. This fact about *n,* if true, is verifiable by direct computation, and thus is necessary if the results of arithmetical computations are neces-

sary. On the other hand, if the conjecture is true, then every even number exceeding 2 is the sum of two primes. Could it then be the case that, although in fact every such even number is the sum of two primes, there might have been such an even number which was not the sum of two primes? What would that mean? Such a number would have to be one of 4, 6, 8, 10, . . . ; and, by hypothesis, since we are assuming Goldbach's conjecture to be true, each of these can be shown, again by direct computation, to be the sum of two primes. Goldbach's conjecture, then, cannot be contingently true or false; whatever truth-value it has belongs to it by necessity.

But what we can say, of course, is that right now, as far as we know, the question can come out either way. So, in the absence of a mathematical proof deciding this question, none of us has any a priori knowledge about this question in either direction. We don't know whether Goldbach's conjecture is true or false. So right now we certainly don't know anything a priori about it. . . .

Let's use some terms quasi-technically. Let's call something a 'rigid designator' if in every possible world it designates the same object, a 'nonrigid' or 'accidental designator' if that is not the case. Of course we don't require that the objects exist in all possible worlds. Certainly Nixon might not have existed if his parents had not gotten married, in the normal course of things. When we think of a property as essential to an object we usually mean that it is true of that object in any case where it would have existed. A rigid designator of a necessary existent can be called 'strongly rigid.'

One of the intuitive theses I will maintain in these talks is that *names* are rigid designators. Certainly they seem to satisfy the intuitive test mentioned above: although someone other than the U.S. President in 1970 might have been the U.S. President in 1970 (e.g., Humphrey might have), no one other than Nixon might have been Nixon. In the same way, a designator rigidly designates a certain object if it designates that object wherever the object exists; if, in addition, the object is a necessary existent, the designator can be called 'strongly rigid.' For example, "the President of the U.S. in 1970" designates a certain man, Nixon; but someone else (e.g.,

Humphrey) might have been the President in 1970, and Nixon might not have; so this designator is not rigid.

In these lectures, I will argue, intuitively, that proper names are rigid designators, for although the man (Nixon) might not have been the President, it is not the case that he might not have been Nixon (though he might not have been *called* "Nixon"). Those who have argued that to make sense of the notion of rigid designator, we must antecedently make sense of "criteria of transworld identity" have precisely reversed the cart and the horse; it is *because* we can refer (rigidly) to Nixon, and stipulate that we are speaking of what might have happened to *him* (under certain circumstances), that "transworld identifications" are unproblematic in such cases.[7]

The tendency to demand purely qualitative descriptions of counterfactual situations has many sources. One, perhaps, is the confusion of the epistemological and the metaphysical, between a prioricity and necessity. If someone identifies necessity with a prioricity, and thinks that objects are named by means of uniquely identifying properties, he may think that it is the properties used to identify the object which, being known about it a priori, must be used to identify it in all possible worlds, to find out which object is Nixon. As against this, I repeat: (1) Generally, things aren't 'found out' about a counterfactual situation, they are stipulated; (2) possible worlds need not be given purely qualitatively, as if we were looking at them through a telescope. And we will see shortly that the properties an object has in every counterfactual world have nothing to do with properties used to identify it in the actual world. . . .

LECTURE II

Last time we ended up talking about a theory of naming which is given by a number of theses:

(1) To every name or designating expression "*X*," there corresponds a cluster of properties, namely the family of those properties φ such that A believes "φ*X*."

(2) One of the properties, or some conjointly, are believed by *A* to pick out some individual uniquely.

(3) If most, or a weighted most, of the φ's are satisfied by one unique object *y*, then *y* is the referent of "*X*."

(4) If the vote yields no unique object, "*X*" does not refer.

(5) The statement, "If *X* exists, then *X* has most of the φ's" is known a priori by the speaker.

(6) The statement, "If *X* exists, then *X* has most of the φ's" expresses a necessary truth (in the idiolect of the speaker).

(C) For any successful theory, the account must not be circular. The properties which are used in the vote must not themselves involve the notion of reference in such a way that it is ultimately impossible to eliminate.

(C) is not a thesis but a condition on the satisfaction of the other theses. In other words, theses (1)–(6) cannot be satisfied in a way which leads to a circle, in a way which does not lead to any independent determination of reference. The example I gave last time of a blatantly circular attempt to satisfy these conditions was a theory of names mentioned by William Kneale. I was a little surprised at the statement of the theory when I was reading what I had copied down, so I looked it up again. I looked it up in the book to see if I'd copied it down accurately. Kneale *did* use the past tense. He said that though it is not trifling to be told that Socrates was the greatest philosopher of ancient Greece, it is trifling to be told that Socrates was called "Socrates." Therefore, he concludes, the name "Socrates" must simply mean "the individual called 'Socrates'." Russell, as I've said, in some places gives a similar analysis. Anyway, as stated using the past tense, the condition wouldn't be circular, because one certainly could decide to use the term "Socrates" to refer to whoever was called "Socrates" by the Greeks. But, of course, in that sense it's not at all trifling to be told that Socrates was called "Socrates." If this is any kind of fact, it might be false. Perhaps we know that *we* call him "Socrates"; that hardly shows that the Greeks did so. In fact, of course, they may have pronounced the name differently. It may be, in the case of this particular name, that transliteration from the Greek is so good that the English version is not pronounced *very* differently from the Greek. But that won't be so in the general case. Certainly it is not trifling to be told that Isaiah was called "Isaiah." In fact, it is false to be told that Isaiah was called "Isaiah"; the prophet wouldn't have recognized this name at all. And of course the Greeks didn't call their country anything like "Greece." Suppose we amend the thesis so that it reads: it's trifling to be told that Socrates is called "Socrates" by us, or at least, by me, the speaker. Then in some sense this is fairly trifling. I don't think it is necessary or analytic. In the same way, it is trifling to be told that horses are called "horses," without this leading to the conclusion that the word "horse" simply *means* "the animal called a 'horse'." As a theory of the reference of the name "Socrates" it will lead immediately to a vicious circle. If one was determining the referent of a name like 'Glunk' to himself and made the following decision, "I shall use the term 'Glunk' to refer to the man that I call 'Glunk'," this would get one nowhere. One had better have some independent determination of the referent of "Glunk." This is a good example of a blatantly circular determination. Actually sentences like "Socrates is called 'Socrates'" are very interesting and one can spend, strange as it may seem, hours talking about their analysis. I actually did, once, do that. I won't do that, however, on this occasion. (See how high the seas of language can rise. And at the lowest points too.) Anyway this is a useful example of a violation of the noncircularity condition. The theory will satisfy all of these statements, perhaps, but it satisfies them only because there is some independent way of determining the reference independently of the particular condition: being the man called "Socrates."

I have already talked about, in the last lecture, thesis (6). Theses (5) and (6), by the way, have converses. What I said for thesis (5) is that the statement that if X exists, X has most of the φ's, is a priori true for the speaker. It will also be true under the given theory that certain converses of this statement hold true also a priori for the speaker, namely: if any unique thing has most of the properties φ in the properly weighted sense, it is X. Similarly a certain converse to this will be *necessarily* true, namely: if anything has most of the properties φ in the properly

weighted sense, it is X. So really one can say that it is both a priori and necessary that something is X if and only if it uniquely has most of the properties φ. This really comes from the previous theses (1)–(4), I suppose. And (5) and (6) really just say that a sufficiently reflective speaker grasps this theory of proper names. Knowing this, he therefore sees that (5) and (6) are true. The objections to theses (5) and (6) will *not* be that some speakers are unaware of this theory and therefore don't know these things.

What I talked about in the last lecture is thesis (6). It's been observed by many philosophers that, if the cluster of properties associated with a proper name is taken in a very narrow sense, so that only one property is given any weight at all, let's say one definite description to pick out the referent—for example, Aristotle was the philosopher who taught Alexander the Great— then certain things will seem to turn out to be necessary truths which are not necessary truths—in this case, for example, that Aristotle taught Alexander the Great. But as Searle said, it is not a necessary truth but a contingent one that Aristotle ever went into pedagogy. Therefore, he concludes that one must drop the original paradigm of a single description and turn to that of a cluster of descriptions.

To summarize some things that I argued last time, this is not the correct answer (whatever it may be) to this problem about necessity. For Searle goes on to say,

Suppose we agree to drop "Aristotle" and use, say, "the teacher of Alexander," then it is a necessary truth that the man referred to is Alexander's teacher—but it is a contingent fact that Aristotle ever went into pedagogy, though I am suggesting that it is a necessary fact that Aristotle has the logical sum, inclusive disjunction, of properties commonly attributed to him. . . .[8]

This is what is not so. It just is not, in any intuitive sense of necessity, a necessary truth that Aristotle had the properties commonly attributed to him. There is a certain theory, perhaps popular in some views of the philosophy of history, which might both be deterministic and yet at the same time assign a great role to the individual in history. Perhaps Carlyle would associate with the meaning of the name of a great man his achievements. According to such a view it will be necessary, once a certain individual is born, that he is destined to perform various great tasks and so it will be part of the very nature of Aristotle that he should have produced ideas which had a great influence on the western world. Whatever the merits of such a view may be as a view of history or the nature of great men, it does not seem that it should be trivially true on the basis of a theory of proper names. It would seem that it's a contingent fact that Aristotle ever did *any* of the things commonly attributed to him today, *any* of these great achievements that we so much admire. . . .

To clear up one thing which some people have asked me: When I say that a designator is rigid, and designates the same thing in all possible worlds, I mean that, as used in *our* language, it stands for that thing, when *we* talk about counterfactual situations. I don't mean, of course, that there mightn't be counterfactual situations in which in the other possible worlds people actually spoke a different language. One doesn't say that "two plus two equals four" is contingent because people might have spoken a language in which "two plus two equals four" meant that seven is even. Similarly, when we speak of a counterfactual situation, we speak of it in English, even if it is part of the description of that counterfactual situation that we were all speaking German in that counterfactual situation. We say, "suppose we had all been speaking German" or "suppose we had been using English in a nonstandard way." Then we are describing a possible world or counterfactual situation in which people, including ourselves, did speak in a certain way different from the way we speak. But still, in describing that world, we use *English* with *our* meanings and *our* references. It is in this sense that I speak of a rigid designator as having the same reference in all possible worlds. I also don't mean to imply that the thing designated exists in all possible worlds, just that the name refers rigidly to that thing. If you say "suppose Hitler had never been born" then "Hitler" refers here, still rigidly, to something that would not exist in the counterfactual situation described.

Given these remarks, this means we must cross off thesis (6) as incorrect. The other theses

have nothing to do with necessity and can survive. In particular thesis (5) has nothing to do with necessity and it can survive. If I use the name "Hesperus" to refer to a certain planetary body when seen in a certain celestial position in the evening, it will not therefore be a necessary truth that Hesperus is ever seen in the evening. That depends on various contingent facts about people being there to see and things like that. So even if I should say to myself that I will use "Hesperus" to name the heavenly body I see in the evening in yonder position of the sky, it will not be necessary that Hesperus was ever seen in the evening. But it may be a priori in that this is how I have determined the referent. If I have determined that Hesperus is the thing that I saw in the evening over there, then I will know, just from making that determination of the referent, that if there is any Hesperus at all it's the thing I saw in the evening. This at least survives as far as the arguments we have given up to now go.

How about a theory where thesis (6) is eliminated? Theses (2), (3), and (4) turn out to have a large class of counterinstances. Even when theses (2)–(4) are true, thesis (5) is usually false; the truth of theses (3) and (4) is an empirical "accident', which the speaker hardly knows a priori. That is to say, other principles really determine the speaker's reference, and the fact that the referent coincides with that determined by (2)–(4) is an "accident', which we were in no position to know a priori. Only in a rare class of cases, usually initial baptisms, are all of (2)–(5) true.

What picture of naming do these Theses [(1)–(5)] give you? The picture is this. I want to name an object. I think of some way of describing it uniquely and then I go through, so to speak, a sort of mental ceremony: By "Cicero" I shall mean the man who denounced Catiline; and that's what the reference of "Cicero" will be. I will use "Cicero" to designate rigidly the man who (in fact) denounced Catiline, so I can speak of possible worlds in which he did not. But still my intentions are given by first, giving some condition which uniquely determines an object, then using a certain word as a name for the object determined by this condition. Now there may be some cases in which we actually do this. Maybe, if you want to stretch and call it description, when you say: I shall call that heavenly body over there "Hesperus."[9] That is really a case where the theses not only are true but really even give a correct picture of how the reference is determined. Another case, if you want to call this a name, might be when the police in London use the name "Jack" or "Jack the Ripper" to refer to the man, whoever he is, who committed all these murders, or most of them. Then they are giving the reference of the name by a description.[10] But in many or most cases, I think the theses are false. So let's look at them.[11]

Thesis (1), as I say, is a definition. Thesis (2) says that one of the properties believed by A of the object, or some conjointly, are believed to pick out some individual uniquely. A sort of example people have in mind is just what I said: I shall use the term "Cicero" to denote the man who denounced Catiline (or first denounced him in public, to make it unique). This picks out an object uniquely in this particular reference. Even some writers such as Ziff in *Semantic Analysis,* who don't believe that names have meaning in any sense, think that this is a good picture of the way reference can be determined.

Let's see if thesis (2) is true. It seems, in some a priori way, that it's got to be true, because if you don't think that the properties you have in mind pick out anyone uniquely—let's say they're all satisfied by two people—then how can you say which one of them you're talking about? There seem to be no grounds for saying you're talking about the one rather than about the other. Usually the properties in question are supposed to be some famous deeds of the person in question. For example, Cicero was the man who denounced Catiline. The average person, according to this, when he refers to Cicero, is saying something like "the man who denounced Catiline" and thus has picked out a certain man uniquely. It is a tribute to the education of philosophers that they have held this thesis for such a long time. In fact, most people, when they think of Cicero, just think of a *famous Roman orator,* without any pretension to think either that there was only one famous Roman orator or that one must know something else about Cicero to have a referent for the name. Consider Richard Feynman, to whom many of us are able to refer. He is a leading con-

temporary theoretical physicist. Everyone *here* (I'm sure!) can state the contents of one of Feynman's theories so as to differentiate him from Gell-Mann. However, the man in the street, not possessing these abilities, may still use the name "Feynman." When asked he will say: well he's a physicist or something. He may not think that this picks out anyone uniquely. I still think he uses the name "Feynman" as a name for Feynman.

But let's look at some of the cases where we do have a description to pick out someone uniquely. Let's say, for example, that we know that Cicero was the man who first denounced Catiline. Well, that's good. That really picks someone out uniquely. However, there is a problem, because this description contains another name, namely "Catiline." We must be sure that we satisfy the conditions in such a way as to avoid violating the noncircularity condition here. In particular, we must not say that Catiline was the man denounced by Cicero. If we do this, we will really not be picking out anything uniquely, we will simply be picking out a pair of objects A and B, such that A denounced B. We do not think that this was the only pair where such denunciations ever occurred; so we had better add some other conditions in order to satisfy the uniqueness condition.

If we say Einstein was the man who discovered the theory of relativity, that certainly picks out someone uniquely. One can be sure, as I said, that everyone *here* can make a compact and independent statement of this theory and so pick out Einstein uniquely; but many people actually don't know enough about this stuff, so when asked what the theory of relativity is, they will say: "Einstein's theory," and thus be led into the most straightforward sort of vicious circle.

So thesis (2), in a straightforward way, fails to be satisfied when we say Feynman is a famous physicist without attributing anything else to Feynman. In another way it may not be satisfied in the proper way even when it is satisfied: If we say Einstein was "the man who discovered relativity theory," that does pick someone out uniquely; but it may not pick him out in such a way as to satisfy the noncircularity condition, because the theory of relativity may in turn be picked out as "Einstein's theory." So thesis (2) seems to be false. . . .

Let's go on to thesis (3): If most of the φ's, suitably weighted, are satisfied by a unique object γ, then γ is the referent of the name for the speaker. Now, since we have already established that Thesis (2) is wrong, why should any of the rest work? . . . Suppose most of the φ's are in fact satisfied by a unique object. Is that object necessarily the referent of "X" for A? Let's suppose someone says that Gödel is the man who proved the incompleteness of arithmetic, and this man is suitably well educated and is even able to give an independent account of the incompleteness theorem. He doesn't just say, "Well, that's Gödel's theorem," or whatever. He actually states a certain theorem, which he attributes to Gödel as the discoverer. Is it the case, then, that if most of the φ's are satisfied by a unique object γ, then γ is the referent of the name "X" for A? Let's take a simple case. In the case of Gödel that's practically the only thing many people have heard about him—that he discovered the incompleteness of arithmetic. Does it follow that whoever discovered the incompleteness of arithmetic is the referent of "Gödel"?

Imagine the following blatantly fictional situation. (I hope Professor Gödel is not present.) Suppose that Gödel was not in fact the author of this theorem. A man named "Schmidt," whose body was found in Vienna under mysterious circumstances many years ago, actually did the work in question. His friend Gödel somehow got hold of the manuscript and it was thereafter attributed to Gödel. On the view in question, then, when our ordinary man uses the name "Gödel," he really means to refer to Schmidt, because Schmidt is the unique person satisfying the description, "the man who discovered the incompleteness of arithmetic." Of course you might try changing it to "the man who *published* the discovery of the incompleteness of arithmetic." By changing the story a little further one can make even this formulation false. Anyway, most people might not even know whether the thing was published or got around by word of mouth. Let's stick to "the man who discovered the incompleteness of arithmetic." So, since the man who discovered the incompleteness of

arithmetic is in fact Schmidt, we, when we talk about "Gödel," are in fact always referring to Schmidt. But it seems to me that we are not. We simply are not. One reply, which I will discuss later, might be: You should say instead, "the man to whom the incompleteness of arithmetic is commonly attributed," or something like that. Let's see what we can do with that later.

But it may seem to many of you that this is a very odd example, or that such a situation occurs rarely. This also is a tribute to the education of philosophers. Very often we use a name on the basis of considerable misinformation. The case of mathematics used in the fictive example is a good case in point. What do we know about Peano? What many people in this room may 'know' about Peano is that he was the discoverer of certain axioms which characterize the sequence of natural numbers, the so-called "Peano axioms." Probably some people can even state them. I have been told that these axioms were not first discovered by Peano but by Dedekind. Peano was of course not a dishonest man. I am told that his footnotes include a credit to Dedekind. Somehow the footnote has been ignored. So on the theory in question the term "Peano," as we use it, really refers to— now that you've heard it you see that you were really all the time talking about—Dedekind. But you were not. Such illustrations could be multiplied indefinitely.

Even worse misconceptions, of course, occur to the layman. In a previous example I supposed people to identify Einstein by reference to his work on relativity. Actually, I often used to hear that Einstein's most famous achievement was the invention of the atomic bomb. So when we refer to Einstein, we refer to the inventor of the atomic bomb. But this is not so. Columbus was the first man to realize that the earth was round. He was also the first European to land in the western hemisphere. Probably none of these things are true, and therefore, when people use the term "Columbus" they really refer to some Greek if they use the roundness of the earth, or to some Norseman, perhaps, if they use the "discovery of America." But they don't. So it does not seem that if most of the φ's are satisfied by a unique object γ, then γ is the referent of the name. This seems simply to be false.[12]

Thesis (4): If the vote yields no unique object the name does not refer. Really this case has been covered before—has been covered in my previous examples. First, the vote may not yield a *unique* object, as in the case of Cicero or Feynman. Secondly, suppose it yields *no* object, that nothing satisfies most, or even any, substantial number, of the φ's. Does that mean the name doesn't refer? No: in the same way that you may have false beliefs about a person which may actually be true of someone else, so you may have false beliefs which are true of absolutely no one. And these may constitute the totality of your beliefs. Suppose, to vary the example about Gödel, no one had discovered the incompleteness of arithmetic—perhaps the proof simply materialized by a random scattering of atoms on a piece of paper—the man Gödel being lucky enough to have been present when this improbable event occurred. Further, suppose arithmetic is in fact complete. One wouldn't really expect a random scattering of atoms to produce a correct proof. A subtle error, unknown through the decades, has still been unnoticed—or perhaps not actually unnoticed, but the friends of Gödel. . . . So even if the conditions are not satisfied by a unique object the name may still refer. I gave you the case of Jonah last week. Biblical scholars, as I said, think that Jonah really existed. It isn't because they think that someone ever was swallowed by a big fish or even went to Nineveh to preach. These conditions may be true of no one whatsoever and yet the name "Jonah" really has a referent. In the case above of Einstein's invention of the bomb, possibly no one really deserves to be called the "inventor" of the device.

Thesis 5 says that the statement "If X exists, then X has most of the φ's," is a priori true for A. Notice that even in a case where (3) and (4) *happen* to be true, a typical speaker hardly knows a priori that they are, as required by the theory. I *think* that my belief about Gödel is in fact correct and that the "Schmidt" story is just a fantasy. But the belief hardly constitutes a priori knowledge. . . .

Someone, let's say, a baby, is born; his parents call him by a certain name. They talk about him to their friends. Other people meet him. Through various sorts of talk the name is spread from link to link as if by a chain. A speaker who is on the far end of this chain, who has heard about, say Richard Feynman, in the marketplace or elsewhere, may be referring to Richard Feynman even though he can't remember from whom he first heard of Feynman or from whom he ever heard of Feynman. He knows that Feynman is a famous physicist. A certain passage of communication reaching ultimately to the man himself does reach the speaker. He then is referring to Feynman even though he can't identify him uniquely. He doesn't know what a Feynman diagram is, he doesn't know what the Feynman theory of pair production and annihilation is. Not only that: he'd have trouble distinguishing between Gell-Mann and Feynman. So he doesn't have to know these things, but, instead, a chain of communication going back to Feynman himself has been established, by virtue of his membership in a community which passed the name on from link to link, not by a ceremony that he makes in private in his study: "By 'Feynman' I shall mean the man who did such and such and such and such." . . . On our view, it is not how the speaker thinks he got the reference, but the actual chain of communication, which is relevant.

I think I said the other time that philosophical theories are in danger of being false, and so I wasn't going to present an alternative theory. Have I just done so? Well, in a way; but my characterization has been far less specific than a real set of necessary and sufficient conditions for reference would be. Obviously the name is passed on from link to link. But of course not every sort of causal chain reaching from me to a certain man will do for me to make a reference. There may be a causal chain from our use of the term "Santa Claus" to a certain historical saint, but still the children, when they use this, by this time probably do not refer to that saint. So other conditions must be satisfied in order to make this into a really rigorous theory of reference. I don't know that I'm going to do this because, first, I'm sort of too lazy at the moment; secondly, rather than giving a set of necessary and sufficient conditions which will work for a term like reference, I want to present just a *better picture* than the picture presented by the received views.

Haven't I been very unfair to the description theory? Here I have stated it very precisely—more precisely, perhaps, than it has been stated by any of its advocates. So then it's easy to refute. Maybe if I tried to state mine with sufficient precision in the form of six or seven or eight theses, it would also turn out that when you examine the theses one by one, they will all be false. That might even be so, but the difference is this. What I think the examples I've given show is not simply that there's some technical error here or some mistake there, but that the whole picture given by this theory of how reference is determined seems to be wrong from the fundamentals. It seems to be wrong to think that we give ourselves some properties which somehow qualitatively uniquely pick out an object and determine our reference in that manner. What I am trying to present is a better picture—a picture which, if more details were to be filled in, might be refined so as to give more exact conditions for reference to take place.

One might never reach a set of necessary and sufficient conditions. I don't know, I'm always sympathetic to Bishop Butler's 'Everything is what it is and not another thing'—in the non-trivial sense that philosophical analyses of some concept like reference, in completely different terms which make no mention of reference, are very apt to fail. Of course in any particular case when one is given an analysis one has to look at it and see whether it is true or false. One can't just cite this maxim to oneself and then turn the page. But more cautiously, I want to present a better picture without giving a set of necessary and sufficient conditions for reference. Such conditions would be very complicated, but what is true is that it's in virtue of our connection with other speakers in the community, going back to the referent himself, that we refer to a certain man.

There may be some cases where the description picture is true, where some man really gives a name by going into the privacy of his room and saying that the referent is to be the unique thing with certain identifying properties. "Jack the Ripper" was a possible example which I gave. Another was "Hesperus." Yet another case which can be forced into this description is that of meeting someone and being told his name.

Except for a belief in the description theory, in its importance in other cases, one probably wouldn't think that that was a case of giving oneself a description, i.e., "the guy I'm just meeting now." But one can put it in these terms if one wishes, and if one has never heard the name in any other way. Of course, if you're introduced to a man and told, "That's Einstein," you've heard of him before, it may be wrong, and so on. But maybe in some cases such a paradigm works—especially for the man who first gives someone or something a name. Or he points to a star and says, "That is to be Alpha Centauri." So he can really make himself this ceremony: "By 'Alpha Centauri' I shall mean the star right over there with such and such coordinates." But in general this picture fails. In general our reference depends not just on what we think ourselves, but on other people in the community, the history of how the name reached one, and things like that. It is by following such a history that one gets to the reference. . . .

A rough statement of a theory might be the following: An initial "baptism" takes place. Here the object may be named by ostension, or the reference of the name may be fixed by a description.[13] When the name is "passed from link to link," the receiver of the name must, I think, intend when he learns it to use it with the same reference as the man from whom he heard it. If I hear the name "Napoleon" and decide it would be a nice name for my pet aardvark, I do not satisfy this condition.[14] (Perhaps it is some such failure to keep the reference fixed which accounts for the divergence of present uses of "Santa Claus" from the alleged original use.)

Notice that the preceding outline hardly *eliminates* the notion of reference; on the contrary, it takes the notion of intending to use the same reference as a given. There is also an appeal to an initial baptism which is explained in terms either of fixing a reference by a description, or ostension (if ostension is not to be subsumed under the other category).[15] (Perhaps there are other possibilities for initial baptisms.) Further, the George Smith case casts some doubt as to the sufficiency of the conditions. Even if the teacher does refer to his neighbor, is it clear that he has passed on his reference to the pupils?

Why shouldn't their belief be about any other man named "George Smith"? If he says that Newton was hit by an apple, somehow his task of transmitting a reference is easier, since he has communicated a common misconception about Newton.

To repeat, I may not have presented a theory, but I do think that I have presented a better picture than that given by description theorists.

I think the next topic I shall want to talk about is that of statements of identity. Are these necessary or contingent? The matter has been in some dispute in recent philosophy. First, everyone agrees that descriptions can be used to make contingent identity statements. If it is true that the man who invented bifocals was the first Postmaster General of the United States—that these were one and the same—it's contingently true. That is, it might have been the case that one man invented bifocals and another was the first Postmaster General of the United States. So certainly when you make identity statements using descriptions—when you say "the x such that φx and the x such that ψx are one and the same"—that can be a contingent fact. But philosophers have been interested also in the question of identity statements between names. When we say "Hesperus is Phosphorus" or "Cicero is Tully," is what we are saying necessary or contingent? Further, they've been interested in another type of identity statement, which comes from scientific theory. We identify, for example, light with electromagnetic radiation between certain limits of wavelengths, or with a stream of photons. We identify heat with the motion of molecules; sound with a certain sort of wave disturbance in the air; and so on. Concerning such statements the following thesis is commonly held. First, that these are obviously contingent identities: we've found out that light is a stream of photons, but of course it might not have been a stream of photons. Heat is in fact the motion of molecules; we found that out, but heat might not have been the motion of molecules. Secondly, many philosophers feel damned lucky that these examples are around. Now, why? These philosophers, whose views are expounded in a vast literature, hold to a thesis called "the identity thesis" with respect to some psychological concepts. They think, say, that pain is just a certain material state of the brain or of the body, or what have you—say the stimulation of C-fibers. (It doesn't matter what.) Some people have then objected, "Well, look, there's perhaps a correlation between pain and these states of the body; but this must just be a contingent *correlation* between two different things, because it was an empirical discovery that this correlation ever held. Therefore, by 'pain' we must mean something different from this state of the body or brain; and, therefore, they must be two different things."

Then it's said, "Ah, but you see, this is wrong! Everyone knows that there can be contingent identities." First, as in the bifocals and Postmaster General case, which I have mentioned before. Second, in the case, believed closer to the present paradigm, of theoretical identifications, such as light and a stream of photons, or water and a certain compound of hydrogen and oxygen. These are all contingent identities. They might have been false. It's no surprise, therefore, that it can be true as a matter of contingent fact and not of any necessity that feeling pain, or seeing red, is just a certain state of the human body. Such psychophysical identifications can be contingent facts just as the other identities are contingent facts. And of course there are widespread motivations—ideological, or just not wanting to have the 'nomological dangler' of mysterious connections not accounted for by the laws of physics, one to one correlations between two different kinds of thing, material states, and things of an entirely different kind, which lead people to want to believe this thesis.

I guess the main thing I'll talk about first is identity statements between names. . . .

Let's suppose we refer to the same heavenly body twice, as "Hesperus" and "Phosphorus." We say: Hesperus is that star over there in the evening; Phosphorus is that star over there in the morning. Actually, Hesperus is Phosphorus. Are there really circumstances under which Hesperus wouldn't have been Phosphorus? Supposing that Hesperus is Phosphorus, let's try to describe a possible situation in which it would not have been. Well, it's easy. Someone goes by and he calls two *different* stars "Hesperus" and "Phosphorus." It may even be under the same conditions as prevailed when we introduced the names "Hesperus" and "Phosphorus." But are those circumstances in which Hesperus is not Phosphorus or would not have been Phosphorus? It seems to me that they are not.

Now, of course I'm committed to saying that they're not, by saying that such terms as "Hesperus" and "Phosphorus," when used as names, are rigid designators. They refer in every possible world to the planet Venus. Therefore, in that possible world too, the planet Venus is the planet Venus and it doesn't matter what any other person has said in this other possible world. How should we describe this situation? He can't have pointed to Venus twice, and in the one case called it "Hesperus" and in the other "Phosphorus," as we did. If he did so, then "Hesperus is Phosphorus" would have been true in that situation too. He pointed maybe neither time to the planet Venus—at least one time he didn't point to the planet Venus, let's say when he pointed to the body he called "Phosphorus." Then in that case we can certainly say that the name "Phosphorus" might not have referred to Phosphorus. We can even say that in the very position when viewed in the morning that we found Phosphorus, it might have been the case that Phosphorus was not there—that something else was there, and that even, under certain circumstances it would have been *called* "Phosphorus." But that still is not a case in which Phosphorus was not Hesperus. There might be a possible world in which, a possible counterfactual situation in which, "Hesperus" and "Phosphorus" weren't names of the things they in fact are names of. Someone, if he did determine their reference by identifying descriptions, might even have used the very identifying descriptions we used. But still that's not a case in which Hesperus wasn't Phosphorus. For there couldn't have been such a case, given that Hesperus is Phosphorus.

Now this seems very strange because in advance, we are inclined to say, the answer to the question whether Hesperus is Phosphorus might have turned out either way. So aren't there really two possible worlds—one in which Hesperus was Phosphorus, the other in which Hesperus wasn't Phosphorus—in advance of our discovering that these were the same? First, there's one sense in which things might turn out either way, in which it's clear that that doesn't

imply that the way it finally turns out isn't necessary. For example, the four color theorem might turn out to be true and might turn out to be false. It might turn out either way. It still doesn't mean that the way it turns out is not necessary. Obviously, the 'might' here is purely 'epistemic'—it merely expresses our present state of ignorance, or uncertainty.

But it seems that in the Hesperus-Phosphorus case, something even stronger is true. The evidence I have before I know that Hesperus is Phosphorus is that I see a certain star or a certain heavenly body in the evening and call it "Hesperus," and in the morning and call it "Phosphorus." I know these things. There certainly is a possible world in which a man should have seen a certain star at a certain position in the evening and called it "Hesperus" and a certain star in the morning and called it "Phosphorus"; and should have concluded—should have found out by empirical investigation—that he names two different stars, or two different heavenly bodies. At least one of these stars or heavenly bodies was not Phosphorus, otherwise it couldn't have come out that way. But that's true. And so it's true that given the evidence that someone has antecedent to his empirical investigation, he can be placed in a sense in exactly the same situation, that is a qualitatively identical epistemic situation, and call two heavenly bodies "Hesperus" and "Phosphorus," without their being identical. So in that sense we can say that it might have turned out either way. Not that it might have turned out either way as to Hesperus's being Phosphorus. Though for all we knew in advance, Hesperus wasn't Phosphorus, that couldn't have turned out any other way, in a sense. But being put in a situation where we have exactly the same evidence, qualitatively speaking, it could have turned out that Hesperus was not Phosphorus; that is, in a counterfactual world in which "Hesperus" and "Phosphorus" were not used in the way that we use them, as names of this planet, but as names of some other objects, one could have had qualitatively identical evidence and concluded that "Hesperus" and "Phosphorus" named two different objects.[16] But we, using the names as we do right now, can say in advance, that if Hesperus and Phosphorus are one and the same, then in no other possible world can they be different. We use "Hesperus" as the name of a certain body and "Phosphorus" as the name of a certain body. We use them as names of those bodies in all possible worlds. If, in fact, they are the *same* body, then in any other possible world we have to use them as a name of that object. And so in any other possible world it will be true that Hesperus is Phosphorus. So two things are true: first, that we do not know a priori that Hesperus is Phosphorus, and are in no position to find out the answer except empirically. Second, this is so because we could have evidence qualitatively indistinguishable from the evidence we have and determine the reference of the two names by the positions of two planets in the sky, without the planets being the same.

Of course, it is only a contingent truth (not true in every other possible world) that the star seen over there in the evening is the star seen over there in the morning, because there are possible worlds in which Phosphorus was not visible in the morning. But that contingent truth shouldn't be identified with the statement that Hesperus is Phosphorus. It could only be so identified if you thought that it was a necessary truth that Hesperus is visible over there in the evening or that Phosphorus is visible over there in the morning. But neither of those are necessary truths even if that's the way we pick out the planet. These are the contingent marks by which we identify a certain planet and give it a name.

NOTES

1. Keith Donnellan, "Reference and Definite Descriptions," *Philosophical Review* 75 (1966), pp. 281–304, [reprinted in this volume]. See also Leonard Linsky, "Reference and Referents," in *Philosophy and Ordinary Language*, ed. Caton (University of Illinois Press, Urbana: 1963.) Donnellan's distinction seems applicable to names as well as to descriptions. Two men glimpse someone at a distance and think they recognize him as Jones. 'What is Jones doing?' 'Raking the leaves'. If the distant leaf-raker is actually Smith, then in some sense they are *referring* to Smith, even though they both use "Jones" *as a name of* Jones. In the text, I speak of the 'referent' of a name to mean the thing named by the name— e.g., Jones, not Smith—even though a speaker may sometimes properly be said to use the name to refer to someone else. Perhaps it would have been less misleading to use a technical term, such as 'denote' rather than 'refer'. My use of 'refer' is such as to sat-

isfy the schema, "The referent of '*X*' is *X*," where "*X*" is replaceable by any name or description. I am tentatively inclined to believe, in opposition to Donnellan, that his remarks about reference have little to do with semantics or truth-conditions, though they may be relevant to a theory of speech acts. Space limitations do not permit me to explain what I mean by this, much less defend the view, except for a brief remark: Call the referent of a name or description in my sense the 'semantic referent'; for a name, this is the thing named, for a description, the thing uniquely satisfying the description.

Then the speaker may *refer* to something other than the semantic referent if he has appropriate false beliefs. I think this is what happens in the naming (Smith-Jones) cases and also in the Donnellan 'champagne' case; the one requires no theory that names are ambiguous, and the other requires no modification of Russell's theory of descriptions.

2. Gottlob Frege, "On Sense and Nominatum," translated by Herbert Feigl in *Readings in Philosophical Analysis,* ed. Herbert Feigl and Wilfrid Sellars (Appleton Century Crofts: 1949), p. 86. [Reprinted in this volume.]

3. Ludwig Wittgenstein, *Philosophical Investigations,* trans. G. E. M. Anscombe (MacMillan: 1953), §79.

4. John R. Searle, "Proper Names," *Mind* 67 (1958), 166–73.

5. Ziff's most detailed statement of his version of the cluster-of-descriptions theory of the reference of names is in "About God," reprinted in *Philosophical Turnings* (Cornell University Press, Ithaca, and Oxford University Press, London: 1966) pp. 94–96. A briefer statement is in his *Semantic Analysis,* (Cornell University Press, Ithaca: 1960) pp. 102–105 (esp. pp. 103–104). The latter passage suggests that names of things with which we are acquainted should be treated somewhat differently (using ostension and baptism) from names of historical figures, where the reference is determined by (a cluster of) associated descriptions. On p. 93 of *Semantic Analysis* Ziff states that "simple strong generalization(s) about proper names" are impossible; "one can only say what is so for the most part. . . ." Nevertheless Ziff clearly states that a cluster-of-descriptions theory is a reasonable such rough statement, at least for historical figures. For Ziff's view that proper names ordinarily are not words of the language and ordinarily do not have meaning, see pp. 85–89 and 93–94 of *Semantic Analysis.*

6. Those determinists who deny the importance of the individual in history may well argue that had Moses never existed, someone else would have arisen to achieve all that he did. Their claim cannot be refuted by appealing to a correct philosophical theory of the meaning of 'Moses exists'.

7. Of course I don't imply that language contains a name for every object. Demonstratives can be used as rigid designators, and free variables can be used as rigid designators of unspecified objects. Of course when we specify a counterfactual situation, we do

not describe the whole possible world, but only the portion which interests us.

8. Searle, "Proper Names," in Caton, op. cit., p. 160.

9. An even better case of determining the reference of a name by description, as opposed to ostension, is the discovery of the planet Neptune. Neptune was hypothesized as the planet which caused such and such discrepancies in the orbits of certain other planets. If Leverrier indeed gave the name "Neptune" to the planet before it was ever seen, then he fixed the reference of "Neptune" by means of the description just mentioned. At that time he was unable to see the planet even through a telescope. At this stage, an a priori material equivalence held between the statements "Neptune exists" and "some one planet perturbing the orbit of such and such other planets exists in such and such a position," and also such statements as "if such and such perturbations are caused by a planet, they are caused by Neptune" had the status of a priori truths. Nevertheless, they were not *necessary* truths, since "Neptune" was introduced as a name rigidly designating a certain planet. Leverrier could well have believed that if Neptune had been knocked off its course one million years earlier, it would have caused no such perturbations and even that some other object might have caused the perturbations in its place.

10. Following Donnellan's remarks on definite descriptions, we should add that in some cases, an object may be identified, and the reference of a name fixed, using a description which may turn out to be false of its object. The case where the reference of "Phosphorus" is determined as the "morning star," which later turns out not to be a star, is an obvious example. In such cases, the description which fixes the reference clearly is in no sense known a priori to hold of the object, though a more cautious substitute may be. If such a more cautious substitute is available, it is really the substitute which fixes the reference in the sense intended in the text.

11. Some of the theses are sloppily stated in respect of fussy matters like use of quotation marks and related details. (For example, theses (5) and (6), as stated, presuppose that the speaker's language is English.) Since the purport of the theses is clear, and they are false anyway, I have not bothered to set these things straight.

12. The cluster-of-descriptions theory of naming would make "Peano discovered the axioms for number theory" express a trivial truth, not a misconception, and similarly for other misconceptions about the history of science. Some who have conceded such cases to me have argued that there are *other* uses of the same proper names satisfying the cluster theory. For example, it is argued, if we say, "Gödel proved the incompleteness of arithmetic," we are, of course, referring to Gödel, not to Schmidt. But, if we say, "Gödel relied on a diagonal argument in this step of the proof," don't we here, perhaps, refer to *whoever proved the theorem?* Similarly, if someone asks, "What did Aristotle (or Shakespeare) have in mind here?", isn't he talking about the author of the pas-

sage in question, whoever he is? By analogy to Donnellan's usage for descriptions, this might be called an "attributive" use of proper names. If this is so, then assuming the Gödel-Schmidt story, the sentence "Gödel proved the incompleteness theorem" is false, but 'Gödel used a diagonal argument in the proof' is (at least in some contexts) true, and the reference of the name 'Gödel' is ambiguous. Since some counterexamples remain, the cluster-of-descriptions theory would still, in general, be false, which was my main point in the text; but it would be applicable in a wider class of cases than I thought. I think, however, that no such ambiguity need be postulated. It is, perhaps, true that sometimes when someone uses the name "Gödel," his main interest is in whoever proved the theorem, and *perhaps,* in some sense, he 'refers' to him. I do not think that this case is different from the case of Smith and Jones. If I mistake Jones for Smith, I may *refer* (in an appropriate sense) to Jones when I say that Smith is raking the leaves; nevertheless I do not use "Smith" ambiguously, as a name sometimes of Smith and sometimes of Jones, but univocally as a name of Smith. Similarly, if I erroneously think that Aristotle wrote such-and-such passage, I may perhaps sometimes use "Aristotle" to *refer* to the actual author of the passage, even though there is no ambiguity in my use of the name. In both cases, I will withdraw my original statement, and my original use of the name, if apprised of the facts. Recall that, in these lectures, 'referent' is used in the technical sense of the thing named by a name (or uniquely satisfying a description), and there should be no confusion.

13. A good example of a baptism whose reference was fixed by means of a description was that of naming Neptune in n. 9. The case of a baptism by ostension can perhaps be subsumed under the description concept also. Thus the primary applicability of the description theory is to cases of initial baptism. Descriptions are also used to fix a reference in cases of designation which are similar to naming except that the terms introduced are not usually called 'names'. The terms "one meter," "100 degrees Centigrade," have already been given as examples, and other examples will be given later in these lectures. Two things should be emphasized concerning the case of introducing a name via a description in an initial baptism. First, the description used is not synonymous with the name it introduces but rather fixes its reference. Here we differ from the usual description theorists. Second, most cases of initial baptism are far from those which originally inspired the description theory. Usually a baptizer is acquainted in some sense with the object he names and is able to name it ostensively. Now the inspiration of the description theory lay in the fact that we can often use names of famous figures of the past who are long dead and with whom no living person is acquainted; and it is precisely these cases which, on our view, cannot be correctly explained by a description theory.

14. I can transmit the name of the aardvark to other peo-

ple. For each of these people, as for me, there will be a certain sort of causal or historical connection between my use of the name and the Emperor of the French, but not one of the required type.

15. Once we realize that the description used to fix the reference of a name is not synonymous with it, then the description theory can be regarded as presupposing the notion of naming or reference. The requirement I made that the description used not itself involve the notion of reference in a circular way is something else and is crucial if the description theory is to have any value at all. The reason is that the description theorist supposes that each speaker essentially uses the description he gives in an initial act of naming to determine his reference. Clearly, if he introduces the name "Cicero" by the determination, "By 'Cicero' I shall refer to the man I call 'Cicero'," he has by this ceremony determined no reference at all. Not all description theorists thought that they were eliminating the notion of reference altogether. Perhaps some realized that some notion of ostension, or primitive reference, is required to back it up. Certainly Russell did.

16. There is a more elaborate discussion of this point in the third lecture, where its relation to a certain sort of counterpart theory is also mentioned.

22 Meaning and Reference

HILARY PUTNAM

Unclear as it is, the traditional doctrine that the notion "meaning" possesses the extension/intension ambiguity has certain typical consequences. The doctrine that the meaning of a term is a concept carried the implication that meanings are mental entities. Frege, however, rebelled against this "psychologism." Feeling that meanings are *public* property—that the *same* meaning can be "grasped" by more than one person and by persons at different times—he identified concepts (and hence "intensions" or meanings) with abstract entities rather than mental entities. However, "grasping" these abstract entities was still an individual psychological act. None of these philosophers doubted that understanding a word (knowing its intension) was just a matter of being in a certain psychological state (somewhat in the way in which knowing how to factor numbers in one's head is just a matter of being in a certain very complex psychological state).

Secondly, the timeworn example of the two terms 'creature with a kidney' and 'creature with a heart' does show that two terms can have the same extension and yet differ in intension. But it was taken to be obvious that the reverse is impossible: two terms cannot differ in extension and have the same intension. Interestingly, no argument for this impossibility was ever offered. Probably it reflects the tradition of the ancient and medieval philosophers, who assumed that the concept corresponding to a term was just a conjunction of predicates, and hence that the concept corresponding to a term must *always* provide a necessary and sufficient condition for falling into the extension of the term. For philosophers like Carnap, who accepted the verifiability theory of meaning, the concept corresponding to a term provided (in the ideal case, where the term had "complete meaning") a *criterion* for belonging to the extension (not just in the sense of "necessary and sufficient condition," but in the strong sense of *way of recognizing* whether a given thing falls into the extension or not). So theory of meaning came to rest on two unchallenged assumptions:

(1) That knowing the meaning of a term is just a matter of being in a certain psychological state (in the sense of "psychological state," in which states of memory and belief are "psychological states"; no one thought that knowing the meaning of a word was a continuous state of consciousness, of course).

From *Journal of Philosophy* 70 (1973): 699–711. Copyright © 1973 by *Journal of Philosophy*. Reprinted by permission of the author and *Journal of Philosophy*. Presented in an APA symposium on Reference, December 28, 1973. A very much expanded version of this paper appeared under the title "The Meaning of "Meaning'" in *Language, Mind, and Knowledge*, Keith Gunderson, ed. (Minneapolis: University of Minnesota Press, 1975), pp. 131–193.

(2) That the meaning of a term determines its extension (in the sense that sameness of intension entails sameness of extension).

I shall argue that these two assumptions are not jointly satisfied by *any* notion, let alone any notion of meaning. The traditional concept of meaning is a concept which rests on a false theory.

ARE MEANINGS IN THE HEAD?

For the purpose of the following science-fiction examples, we shall suppose that somewhere there is a planet we shall call Twin Earth. Twin Earth is very much like Earth: in fact, people on Twin Earth even speak *English*. In fact, apart from the differences we shall specify in our science-fiction examples, the reader may suppose that Twin Earth is *exactly* like Earth. He may even suppose that he has a Doppelgänger— an identical copy—on Twin Earth, if he wishes, although my stories will not depend on this.

Although some of the people on Twin Earth (say, those who call themselves "Americans" and those who call themselves "Canadians" and those who call themselves "Englishmen," etc.) speak English, there are, not surprisingly, a few tiny differences between the dialects of English spoken on Twin Earth and standard English.

One of the peculiarities of Twin Earth is that the liquid called "water" is not H_2O but a different liquid whose chemical formula is very long and complicated. I shall abbreviate this chemical formula simply as XYZ. I shall suppose that XYZ is indistinguishable from water at normal temperatures and pressures. Also, I shall suppose that the oceans and lakes and seas of Twin Earth contain XYZ and not water, that it rains XYZ on Twin Earth and not water, etc.

If a space ship from Earth ever visits Twin Earth, then the supposition at first will be that "water" has the same meaning on Earth and on Twin Earth. This supposition will be corrected when it is discovered that "water" on Twin Earth is XYZ, and the Earthian space ship will report somewhat as follows.

"On Twin Earth the word 'water' means XYZ."

Symmetrically, if a space ship from Twin Earth ever visits Earth, then the supposition at

first will be that the word 'water' has the same meaning on Twin Earth and on Earth. This supposition will be corrected when it is discovered that "water" on Earth is H_2O, and the Twin Earthian space ship will report:

"On Earth the word 'water' means H_2O."

Note that there is no problem about the extension of the term 'water': the word simply has two different meanings (as we say); in the sense in which it is used on Twin Earth, the sense of water$_{TE}$, what *we* call "water" simply isn't water, while in the sense in which it is used on Earth, the sense of water$_E$, what the Twin Earthians call "water" simple isn't water. The extension of 'water' in the sense of water$_E$ is the set of all wholes consisting of H_2O molecules, or something like that; the extension of water in the sense of water$_{TE}$ is the set of all wholes consisting of XYZ molecules, or something like that.

Now let us roll the time back to about 1750. The typical Earthian speaker of English did not know that water consisted of hydrogen and oxygen, and the typical Twin-Earthian speaker of English did not know that "water" consisted of XYZ. Let Oscar$_1$ be such a typical Earthian English speaker, and let Oscar$_2$ be his counterpart on Twin Earth. You may suppose that there is no belief that Oscar$_1$ had about water that Oscar$_2$ did not have about "water." If you like, you may even suppose that Oscar$_1$ and Oscar$_2$ were exact duplicates in appearance, feelings, thoughts, interior monologue, etc. Yet the extension of the term "water" was just as much H_2O on Earth in 1750 as in 1950; and the extension of the term 'water' was just as much XYZ on Twin Earth in 1750 as in 1950. Oscar$_1$ and Oscar$_2$ understood the term 'water' differently in 1750 *although they were in the same psychological state,* and although, given the state of science at the time, it would have taken their scientific communities about fifty years to discover that they understood the term 'water' differently. Thus the extension of the term 'water' (and, in fact, its "meaning" in the intuitive preanalytical usage of that term) is *not* a function of the psychological state of the speaker by itself.[1]

But, it might be objected, why should we accept it that the term 'water' had the same extension in 1750 and in 1950 (on both Earths)? Suppose I point to a glass of water and say "this liquid is called water." My "ostensive definition" of water had the following empirical presupposition: that the body of liquid I am pointing to bears a certain sameness relation (say, *x is the same liquid as y,* or *x is the same$_L$ as y*) to most of the stuff I and other speakers in my linguistic community have on other occasions called "water." If this presupposition is false because, say, I am—unknown to me—pointing to a glass of gin and not a glass of water, then I do not intend my ostensive definition to be accepted. Thus the ostensive definition conveys what might be called a "defeasible" necessary and sufficient condition: the necessary and sufficient condition for being water is bearing the relation *same$_L$* to the stuff in the glass; but this is the necessary and sufficient condition only if the empirical presupposition is satisfied. If it is not satisfied, then one of a series of, so to speak, "fallback" conditions becomes activated.

The key point is that the relation *same$_L$* is a *theoretical* relation: whether something is or is not the same liquid as *this* may take an indeterminate amount of scientific investigation to determine. Thus, the fact that an English speaker in 1750 might have called XYZ "water," whereas he or his successors would not have called XYZ water in 1800 or 1850 does not mean that the "meaning" of 'water' changed for the average speaker in the interval. In 1750 or in 1850 or in 1950 one might have pointed to, say, the liquid in Lake Michigan as an example of "water." What changed was that in 1750 we would have mistakenly thought that XYZ bore the relation *same$_L$* to the liquid in Lake Michigan, whereas in 1800 or 1850 we would have known that it did not.

Let us now modify our science-fiction story. I shall suppose that molybdenum pots and pans *can't* be distinguished from aluminum pots and pans save by an expert. (This could be true for all I know, and, *a fortiori,* it could be true for all I know by virtue of "knowing the meaning" of the words *aluminum* and *molybdenum.*) We will now suppose that molybdenum is as common on Twin Earth as aluminum is on Earth, and that aluminum is as rare on Twin Earth as molybdenum is on Earth. In particular, we shall assume

that "aluminum" pots and pans are made of molybdenum on Twin Earth. Finally, we shall assume that the words 'aluminum' and 'molybdenum' are *switched* on Twin Earth: 'aluminum' is the name of *molybdenum,* and 'molybdenum' is the name of *aluminum.* If a space ship from Earth visited Twin Earth, the visitors from Earth probably would not suspect that the "aluminum" pots and pans on Twin Earth were not made of aluminum, especially when the Twin Earthians *said* they were. But there is one important difference between the two cases. An Earthian metallurgist could tell very easily that "aluminum" was molybdenum, and a Twin Earthian metallurgist could tell equally easily that aluminum was "molybdenum." (The shudder quotes in the preceding sentence indicate Twin Earthian usages.) Whereas in 1750 no one on either Earth or Twin Earth could have distinguished water from "water," the confusion of aluminum with "aluminum" involves only a part of the linguistic communities involved.

This example makes the same point as the preceding example. If Oscar$_1$ and Oscar$_2$ are standard speakers of Earthian English and Twin Earthian English, respectively, and neither is chemically or metallurgically sophisticated, then there may be no difference at all in their psychological states when the use the world 'aluminum'; nevertheless, we have to say that 'aluminum' has the extension *aluminum* in the idiolect of Oscar$_1$ and the extension molybdenum in the idiolect of Oscar$_2$. (Also we have to say that Oscar$_1$ and Oscar$_2$ mean different things by 'aluminum'; that 'aluminum' has a different meaning on Earth than it does on Twin Earth, etc.) Again we see that the psychological state of the speaker does *not* determine the extension (*or* the "meaning," speaking preanalytically) of the word.

Before discussing this example further, let me introduce a *non*-science-fiction example. Suppose you are like me and cannot tell an elm from a beech tree. We will say that the extension of 'elm' in my idiolect is the same as the extension of 'elm' in anyone else's, viz., the set of all elm trees, and that the set of all beech trees is the extension of 'beech' in *both* of our idiolects. Thus 'elm' in my idiolect has a different extension from 'beech' in your idiolect (as it should).

Is it really credible that this difference in extension is brought about by some difference in our *concepts?* My *concept* of an elm tree is exactly the same as my concept of a beech tree (I blush to confess). If someone heroically attempts to maintain that the difference between the extension of 'elm' and the extension of 'beech' in *my* idiolect is explained by a difference in my psychological state, then we can always refute him by constructing a "Twin Earth" example—just let the worlds 'elm' and 'beech' be switched on Twin Earth (the way 'aluminum' and 'molybdenum' were in the previous example). Moreover, suppose I have a Doppelgänger on Twin Earth who is molecule for molecule "identical" with me. If you are a dualist, then also suppose my Doppelgänger thinks the same verbalized thoughts I do, has the same sense data, the same dispositions, etc. It is absurd to think *his* psychological state is one bit different from mine: yet he 'means' *beech* when he says "elm," and I "mean" *elm* when I say "elm." Cut the pie any way you like, "meanings" just ain't in the *head!*

A SOCIOLINGUISTIC HYPOTHESIS

The last two examples depend upon a fact about language that seems, surprisingly, never to have been pointed out: that there is *division of linguistic labor.* We could hardly use such words as 'elm' and 'aluminum' if no one possessed a way of recognizing elm trees and aluminum metal; but not everyone to whom the distinction is important has to be able to make the distinction. Let us shift the example; consider *gold.* Gold is important for many reasons: it is a precious metal; it is a monetary metal; it has symbolic value (it is important to most people that the "gold" wedding ring they wear *really* consist of gold and not just *look* gold); etc. Consider our community as a "factory": in this "factory" some people have the "job" of *wearing gold wedding rings;* other people have the "job" of selling gold wedding rings; still other people have the job of *telling whether or not something is really gold.* It is not at all necessary or efficient that every one who wears a gold ring (or a gold cufflink, etc.), or discusses the "gold standard," etc., engage in buying and selling gold. Nor is it necessary or efficient that every one

who buys and sells gold be able to tell whether or not something is really gold in a society where this form of dishonesty is uncommon (selling fake gold) and in which one can easily consult an expert in case of doubt. And it is *certainly* not necessary or efficient that every one who has occasion to buy or wear gold be able to tell with any reliability whether or not something is really gold.

The foregoing facts are just examples of mundane division of labor (in a wide sense). But they engender a division of linguistic labor: every one to whom gold is important for any reason has to *acquire* the word 'gold'; but he does not have to acquire the *method of recognizing* whether something is or is not gold. He can rely on a special subclass of speakers. The features that are generally thought to be present in connection with a general name—necessary and sufficient conditions for membership in the extension, ways of recognizing whether something is in the extension, etc.—are all present in the linguistic community *considered as a collective body;* but that collective body divides the "labor" of knowing and employing these various parts of the "meaning" of 'gold'.

This division of linguistic labor rests upon and presupposes the division of *non*linguistic labor, of course. If only the people who know how to tell whether some metal is really gold or not have any reason to have the word 'gold' in their vocabulary, then the word 'gold' will be as the word 'water' was in 1750 with respect to that subclass of speakers, and the other speakers just won't acquire it at all. And some words do not exhibit any division of linguistic labor: 'chair', for example. But with the increase of division of labor in the society and the rise of science, more and more words begin to exhibit this kind of division of labor. 'Water', for example, did not exhibit it at all before the rise of chemistry. Today it is obviously necessary for every speaker to be able to recognize water (reliably under normal conditions), and probably most adult speakers even know the necessary and sufficient condition "water is H_2O," but only a few adult speakers could distinguish water from liquids that superficially resembled water. In case of doubt, other speakers would rely on the judgment of these "expert" speakers.

Thus the way of recognizing possessed by these "expert" speakers is also, through them, possessed by the collective linguistic body, even though it is not possessed by each individual member of the body, and in this way the most *recherché* fact about water may become part of the *social* meaning of the word although unknown to almost all speakers who acquire the word.

It seems to me that this phenomenon of division of linguistic labor is one that it will be very important for sociolinguistics to investigate. In connection with it, I should like to propose the following hypothesis:

HYPOTHESIS OF THE UNIVERSALITY OF THE DIVISION OF LINGUISTIC LABOR: Every linguistic community exemplifies the sort of division of linguistic labor just described; that is, it possesses at least some terms whose associated "criteria" are known only to a subset of the speakers who acquire the terms, and whose use by the other speakers depends upon a structured cooperation between them and the speakers in the relevant subsets.

It is easy to see how this phenomenon accounts for some of the examples given above of the failure of the assumptions (1 and 2). When a term is subject to the division of linguistic labor, the "average" speaker who acquires it does not acquire anything that fixes its extension. In particular, his individual psychological state *certainly* does not fix its extension; it is only the sociolinguistic state of the collective linguistic body to which the speaker belongs that fixes the extension.

We may summarize this discussion by pointing out that there are two sorts of tools in the world: there are tools like a hammer or a screwdriver which can be used by one person; and there are tools like a steamship which require the cooperative activity of a number of persons to use. Words have been thought of too much on the model of the first sort of tool.

INDEXICALITY AND RIGIDITY

The first of our science-fiction examples— 'water' on Earth and on Twin Earth in 1750— does not involve division of linguistic labor, or at least does not involve it in the same way the

examples of 'aluminum' and 'elm' do. There were not (in our story, anyway) any "experts" on water on Earth in 1750, nor any experts on "water" on Twin Earth. The example *does* involve things which are of fundamental importance to the theory of reference and also to the theory of necessary truth, which we shall now discuss.

Let W_1 and W_2 be two possible worlds in which I exist and in which this glass exists and in which I am giving a meaning explanation by pointing to this glass and saying "This is water." Let us suppose that in W_1 the glass is full of H_2O and in W_2 the glass is full of XYZ. We shall also suppose that W_1 is the *actual* world, and that XYZ is the stuff typically called "water" in the world W_2 (so that the relation between English speakers in W_1 and English speakers in W_2 is exactly the same as the relation between English speakers on Earth and English speakers on Twin Earth). Then there are two theories one might have concerning the meaning of 'water':

(1) One might hold that 'water' was *world-relative* but *constant* in meaning (i.e., the word has a constant relative meaning). On this theory, 'water' means the same in W_1 and W_2; it's just that water is H_2O in W_1, and water is XYZ in W_2.

(2) One might hold that water is H_2O in all worlds (the stuff called "water" in W_2 isn't water), but 'water' doesn't have the same meaning in W_1 and W_2.

If what was said before about the Twin Earth case was correct, then (2) is clearly the correct theory. When I say "*this* (liquid) is water," the "this" is, so to speak, a *de re* "this"—i.e., the force of my explanation is that "water" is whatever bears a certain equivalence relation (the relation we called "*same$_L$*" above) to the piece of liquid referred to as "this" *in the actual world*.

We might symbolize the difference between the two theories as a "scope" difference in the following way. On theory (1), the following is true:

(1') (For every world W) (for every x in W) (x is water $\equiv x$ bears *same$_L$* to the entity referred to as "this" in W)

while on theory (2):

(2′) (For every world W) (For every x in W) (x is water ≡ x bears $same_L$ to the entity referred to as "this" *in the actual world W_1*)

I call this a "scope" difference because in (1′) 'the entity referred to as "this"' is within the scope of 'For every world W'—as the qualifying phrase 'in W' makes explicit—whereas in (2′) 'the entity referred to as "this"' means "the entity referred to as 'this' *in the actual world*," and has thus a reference *independent* of the bound variable 'W'.

Kripke calls a designator "rigid" (in a given sentence) if (in that sentence) it refers to the same individual in every possible world in which the designator designates. If we extend this notion of rigidity to substance names, then we may express Kripke's theory and mine by saying that the term 'water' is *rigid*.

The rigidity of the term "water' follows from the fact that when I give the "ostensive definition": "*this* (liquid) is water," I intend (2′) and not (1′).

We may also say, following Kripke, that when I give the ostensive definition "*this* (liquid) is water," the demonstrative 'this' is *rigid*.

What Kripke was the first to observe is that this theory of the meaning (or "use," or whatever) of the word 'water' (and other natural-kind terms as well) has startling consequences for the theory of necessary truth.

To explain this, let me introduce the notion of a *cross-world relation*. A two-term relation R will be called *cross-world* when it is understood in such a way that its extension is a set of ordered pairs of individuals *not all in the same possible world*. For example, it is easy to understand the relation *same height as* as a cross-world relation: just understand it so that, e.g., if x is an individual in a world W_1 who is 5 feet tall (in W_1) and y is an individual in W_2 who is 5 feet tall (in W_2), then the ordered pair x,y belongs to the extension of *same height as*. (Since an individual may have different heights in different possible worlds in which that same individual exists, strictly speaking, it is not the ordered pair x,y that constitutes an element of the extension of *same height as*, but rather the ordered pair x-in-world-W_1, y-in-world-W_2.)

Similarly, we can understand the relation $same_L$ (same liquid as) as a cross-world relation by understanding it so that a liquid in world W_1 which has the same important physical properties (in W_1) that a liquid in W_2 possesses (in W_2) bears $same_L$ to the latter liquid.

Then the theory we have been presenting may be summarized by saying that an entity x, in an arbitrary possible world, is *water* if and only if it bears the relation $same_L$ (construed as a cross-world relation) to the stuff we call "water" in the actual world.

Suppose, now, that I have not yet discovered what the important physical properties of water are (in the actual world)—i.e., I don't yet know that water is H_2O. I may have ways of *recognizing* water that are successful (of course, I may make a small number of mistakes that I won't be able to detect until a later stage in our scientific development), but not know the microstructure of water. If I agree that a liquid with the superficial properties of "water" but a different microstructure *isn't really water*, then my ways of recognizing water cannot be regarded as an analytical specification of what *it is to be* water. Rather, the operational definition, like the ostensive one, is simply a way of pointing out a standard—pointing out the stuff *in the actual world* such that, for x to be water, in *any* world, is for x to bear the relation $same_L$ to the *normal* members of the class of *local* entities that satisfy the operational definition. "Water" on Twin Earth is not water, even if it satisfies the operational definition, because it doesn't bear $same_L$ to the *local* stuff that satisfies the operational definition, and local stuff that satisfies the operational definition but has a microstructure different from the rest of the local stuff that satisfies the operational definition isn't water either, because it doesn't bear $same_L$ to the *normal* examples of the local "water."

Suppose, now, that I discover the microstructure of water—that water is H_2O. At this point I will be able to say that the stuff on Twin Earth that I earlier *mistook* for water isn't really water. In the same way, if you describe, not another planet in the actual universe, but another possible universe in which there is stuff with the chemical formula XYZ which passes the "operational test" for *water*, we shall have to say that

that stuff isn't water but merely XYZ. You will not have described a possible world in which "water is XYZ," but merely a possible world in which there are lakes of XYZ, people drink XYZ (and not water), or whatever. In fact, once we have discovered the nature of water, nothing counts as a possible world in which water doesn't have that nature. Once we have discovered that water (in the actual world) is H_2O, *nothing counts as a possible world in which water isn't H_2O.*

On the other hand, we can perfectly well imagine having experiences that would convince us (and that would make it rational to believe that) water *isn't* H_2O. In that sense, it is conceivable that water isn't H_2O. It is conceivable but it isn't possible! Conceivability is no proof of possibility.

Kripke refers to statements that are rationally unrevisable (assuming there are such) as *epistemically necessary*. Statements that are true in all possible worlds he refers to simply as necessary (or sometimes as "metaphysically necessary"). In this terminology, the point just made can be restated as: a statement can be (metaphysically) necessary and epistemically contingent. Human intuition has no privileged access to metaphysical necessity.

In this paper, our interest is in theory of meaning, however, and not in theory of necessary truth. Words like 'now', 'this', 'here' have long been recognized to be *indexical*, or *token-reflexive*—i.e., to have an extension which varies from context to context or token to token. For these words, no one has ever suggested the traditional theory that "intension determines extension." To take our Twin Earth example: if I have a Doppelgänger on Twin Earth, then when I think "I have a headache," *he* thinks "I have a headache." But the extension of the particular token of 'I' in his verbalized thought is himself (or his unit class, to be precise), while the extension of the token of 'I' in *my* verbalized thought is *me* (or my unit class, to be precise). So the same word, 'I', has two different extensions in two different idiolets; but it does not follow that the concept I have of myself is in any way different from the concept my Doppelgänger has of himself.

Now then, we have maintained that indexicality extends beyond the *obviously* indexical words and morphemes (e.g., the tenses of verbs). Our theory can be summarized as saying that words like 'water' have an unnoticed indexical component: "water" is stuff that bears a certain similarity relation to the water *around here*. Water at another time or in another place or even in another possible world has to bear the relation *same*$_L$ to *our* "water" *in order to be water.* Thus the theory that (1) words have "intensions," which are something like concepts associated with the words by speakers; and (2) intension determines extension—cannot be true of natural-kind words like 'water' for the same reason it cannot be true of obviously indexical words like 'I'.

The theory that natural-kind words like 'water' are indexical leaves it open, however, whether to say that 'water' in the Twin Earth dialect of English has the same *meaning* as 'water' in the Earth dialect and a different extension—which is what we normally say about 'I' in different idiolects—thereby giving up the doctrine that "meaning (intension) determines extension," or to say, as we have chosen to do, that difference in extension is *ipso facto* a difference in meaning for natural-kind words, thereby giving up the doctrine that meanings are concepts, or, indeed, mental entities of *any* kind.[2]

It should be clear, however, that Kripke's doctrine that natural-kind words are rigid designators and our doctrine that they are indexical are but two ways of making the same point.

We have now seen that the extension of a term is not fixed by a concept that the individual speaker has in his head, and this is true both because extension is, in general, determined *socially*—there is division of linguistic labor as much as of "real" labor—and because extension is, in part, determined *indexically*. The extension of our terms depends upon the actual nature of the particular things that serve as paradigms, and this actual nature is not, in general, fully known to the speaker. Traditional semantic theory leaves out two contributions to the determination of reference—the contribution of society and the contribution of the real world; a better semantic theory must encompass both.

NOTES

1. See note 2 and the corresponding text.
2. Our reasons for rejecting the first option—to say that 'water' has the same meaning on Earth and on Twin Earth, while giving up the doctrine that meaning determines reference—are presented in "The Meaning of 'Meaning'." They may be illustrated thus: Suppose 'water' has the same meaning on Earth and on Twin Earth. Now, let the word 'water' become phonemically different on Twin Earth—say, it becomes 'quaxel'. Presumably, this is not a change in meaning per se, on any view. So 'water' and 'quaxel' have the same meaning (although they refer to different liquids). But this is highly counterintuitive. Why not say, then, that 'elm' in my idiolect has the same meaning as 'beech' in your idiolect, although they refer to different trees?

23

The Causal Theory of Names

GARETH EVANS

I

1. In a paper which provides the starting point of this enquiry Saul Kripke opposes what he calls the description theory of names and makes a counterproposal of what I shall call the causal theory.[1] To be clear about what is at stake and what should be the outcome in the debate he initiated seems to me important for our understanding of talk and thought about the world in general as well as for our understanding of the functioning of proper names. I am anxious therefore that we identify the profound bases and likely generalizations of the opposing positions and do not content ourselves with counterexamples.

I should say that Kripke deliberately held back from presenting his ideas as a theory. I shall have to tighten them up, and I may suggest perhaps unintended directions of generalization; therefore his paper should be checked before the causal theory I consider is attributed to him.

There are two related but distinguishable questions concerning proper names. The first is about what the name denotes upon a particular occasion of its use when this is understood as being partly determinative of what the speaker strictly and literally said. I shall use the faintly barbarous coinage: *what the speaker denotes* (upon an occasion) for this notion. The second

is about *what the name denotes;* we want to know what conditions have to be satisfied by an expression and an item for the first to be the, or a, name of the second. There is an entirely parallel pair of questions concerning general terms. In both cases it is ambiguity which prevents an easy answer of the first in terms of the second; to denote X it is not sufficient merely to utter something which is X's name.

Consequently there are two description theories, not distinguished by Kripke.[2] The description theory of speaker's denotation holds that a name "N.N." denotes X upon a particular occasion of its use by a speaker S just in case X is uniquely that which satisfies all or most of the descriptions ϕ such that S would assent to "N.N. is ϕ" (or "*That* N.N. is ϕ"). Crudely: the cluster of information S has associated with the name determines its denotation upon a particular occasion by *fit*. If the speaker has no individuating information he will denote nothing.

The description theory of what a name denotes holds that, associated with each name as used by a group of speakers who believe and intend that they are using the name with the same denotation, is a description or set of descriptions cullable from their beliefs which an item has to satisfy to be the bearer of the name. This description is used to explain the role of the name in existential, identity and

From *Aristotelian Society: Supplementary Volume 47* (1973): 187–208. Reprinted by courtesy of the Editor of the Aristotelian Society. Copyright © 1973 The Aristotelian Society.

opaque contexts. The theory is by no means committed to the thesis that every user of the name must be in possession of the description; just as Kripke is not committed to holding that every user of the expression "one meter" knows about the meter rod in Paris by saying that its reference is fixed by the description "Length of stick S in Paris." Indeed if the description is arrived at in the manner of Strawson[3]—averaging out the different beliefs of different speakers—it is most unlikely that the description will figure in every user's name-associated cluster.

The direct attack in Kripke's paper passes this latter theory by; most conspicuously the charge that the description theory ignores the social character of naming. I shall not discuss it explicitly either, though it will surface from time to time and the extent to which it is right should be clear by the end of the paper.

Kripke's direct attacks are unquestionably against the first description theory. He argues:

(a) An ordinary man in the street can denote the physicist Feynman by using the name "Feynman" and say something true or false of him even though there is no description uniquely true of the physicist which he can fashion. (The conditions aren't necessary.)

(b) A person who associated with the name "Gödel" merely the description "prover of the incompleteness of arithmetic" would nonetheless be denoting Gödel and saying something false of him in uttering "Gödel proved the incompleteness of arithmetic" even if an unknown Viennese by the name of Schmidt had in fact constructed the proof which Gödel had subsequently broadcast as his own. (If it is agreed that the speaker does not denote Schmidt the conditions aren't sufficient; if it is also agreed that he denotes Gödel, again they are not necessary.)

The strong thesis (that the description theorist's conditions are sufficient) is outrageous. What the speaker denotes in the sense we are concerned with is connected with saying in that strict sense which logicians so rightly prize, and the theory's deliverances of strict truth conditions are quite unacceptable. They would have the consequence, for example, that if I was previously innocent of knowledge or belief regarding Mr. Y, and X is wrongly introduced to me as

Mr. Y, then I must speak the truth in uttering "Mr. Y is here" since X satisfies the overwhelming majority of descriptions I would associate with the name and X is there. I have grave doubts as to whether anyone has ever seriously held this thesis.

It is the weaker thesis—that some descriptive identification is necessary for a speaker to denote something—that it is important to understand. Strictly, Kripke's examples do not show it to be false since he nowhere provides a convincing reason for not taking into account speakers' possession of descriptions like "man bearing such-and-such a name"; but I too think it is false. It can be seen as the fusion of two thoughts. First: that in order to be saying something by uttering an expression one must utter the sentence with certain intentions; this is felt to require, in the case of sentences containing names, that one be aiming at something with one's use of the name. Secondly—and this is where the underpinning from a certain Philosophy of Mind becomes apparent—to have an intention or belief concerning some item (which one is not in a position to demonstratively identify) one must be in possession of a description uniquely true of it. Both strands deserve at least momentary scrutiny.

We are prone to pass too quickly from the observation that neither parrots nor the wind *say* things to the conclusion that to say that *p* requires that one must intend to say that *p* and therefore, so to speak, be able to identify *p* independently of one's sentence. But the most we are entitled to conclude is that to say something one must intend to say something by uttering one's sentence (one normally will intend to say what it says). The application of the stricter requirement would lead us to relegate too much of our discourse to the status of mere mouthing. We constantly use general terms of whose satisfaction conditions we have but the dimmest idea. "Microbiologist," "chlorine" (the stuff in swimming pools), "nicotine" (the stuff in cigarettes); these (and countless other words) we cannot define nor offer remarks which would distinguish their meaning from that of closely related words. It is wrong to say that we say nothing by uttering sentences containing these expressions, even if we recoil from the strong thesis, from saying that what we do say is determined by those hazy ideas and half-identifications we would offer if pressed.

The Philosophy of Mind is curiously popular but rarely made perfectly explicit.[4] It is held by anyone who holds that S believes that a is F if and only if

$$\exists\phi[(S \text{ believes } \exists x(\phi x \& (\forall y)(\phi y \to x = y) \& \text{F}x)) \& \phi a \& (\forall y)(\phi y \to y = a)]$$

Obvious alterations would accommodate the other psychological attitudes. The range of the property quantifier must be restricted to exclude such properties as "being identical with a" otherwise the criterion is trivial.[5] The situation in which a thinking planning or wanting human has some item which is the object of his thought, plan or desire is represented as a species of essentially the same situation as that which holds when there is no object and the thought, plan or desire is, as we might say, purely general. There are thoughts, such as the thought that there are 11-fingered men, for whose expression general terms of the language suffice. The idea is that when the psychological state involves an object, a general term believed to be uniquely instantiated and in fact uniquely instantiated by the item which is the object of the state will figure in its specification. This idea may be coupled with a concession that there are certain privileged objects to which one may be more directly related; indeed such a concession appears to be needed if the theory is to be able to allow what appears an evident possibility: object-directed thoughts in a perfectly symmetrical or cyclical universe.

This idea about the nature of object-directed psychological attitudes obviously owes much to the feeling that there must be something we can say about what is believed or wanted even when there is no appropriate object actually to be found in the world. But it can also be seen as deriving support from a principle of charity: so attribute objects to beliefs that true belief is maximized. (I do not think this is an acceptable principle; the acceptable principle enjoins minimizing the attribution of *inexplicable* error and therefore cannot be operated without a theory of the causation of belief for the creatures under investigation.)

We cannot deal comprehensively with this Philosophy of Mind here. My objections to it are essentially those of Wittgenstein. For an item to be the object of some psychological attitude of yours may be simply for you to be placed in a context which relates you to that thing. What makes it one rather than the other of a pair of identical twins that you are in love with? Certainly not some specification blue printed in your mind; it may be no more than this: it was one of them and not the other that you have met. The theorist may gesture to the description "the one I have met" but can give no explanation for the impossibility of its being outweighed by other descriptions which may have been acquired as a result of error and which may in fact happen to fit the other, unmet, twin. If God had looked into your mind, he would not have seen there with whom you were in love, and of whom you were thinking.

With that I propose to begin considering the causal theory.

2. The causal theory as stated by Kripke goes something like this. A speaker, using a name "NN" on a particular occasion will denote some item x if there is a causal chain of *reference-preserving* links leading back from his use on that occasion ultimately to the item x itself being involved in a name-acquiring transaction such as an explicit dubbing or the more gradual process whereby nick names stick. I mention the notion of a reference-preserving link to incorporate a condition that Kripke lays down; a speaker S's transmission of a name "NN" to a speaker S' constitutes a reference-preserving link only if S intends to be using the name with the same denotation as he from whom he in his turn learned the name.

Let us begin by considering the theory in answer to our question about speaker's denotation (i.e., at the level of the individual speaker). In particular, let us consider the thesis that it is *sufficient* for someone to denote x on a particular occasion with the name that this use of the name on that occasion be a causal consequence of his exposure to other speakers using the expression to denote x.

An example which might favorably dispose one towards the theory is this. A group of people are having a conversation in a pub, about a certain Louis of whom *S* has never heard before. *S* becomes interested and asks: "What did Louis do then?" There seems to be no question but that *S* denotes a particular man and asks about him. Or on some subsequent occasion *S* may use the name to offer some new thought to one of the participants: "Louis was quite right to do that." Again he clearly denotes whoever was the subject of conversation in the pub. This is difficult to reconcile with the description theory since the scraps of information which he picked up during the conversation might involve some distortion and fit someone else much better. Of course he has the description "the man they were talking about" but the theory has no explanation for the impossibility of its being outweighed.

The causal theory can secure the right answer in such a case but I think deeper reflection will reveal that it too involves a refusal to recognize the insight about contextual determination I mentioned earlier. For the theory has the following consequence: that at any future time, no matter how remote or forgotten the conversation, no matter how alien the subject matter and confused the speaker, S will denote one particular Frenchman—perhaps Louis XIII—so long as there is a causal connection between his use at that time and the long distant conversation.

It is important in testing your intuitions against the theory that you imagine the predicate changed—so that he says something like "Louis was a basketball player" which was not heard in the conversation and which arises as the result of some confusion. This is to prevent the operation of what I call the "mouthpiece syndrome" by which we attach sense and reference to a man's remarks only because we hear someone else speaking through him; as we might with a messenger, carrying a message about matters of which he was entirely ignorant.

Now there is no knock-down argument to show this consequence unacceptable; with pliant enough intuitions you can swallow anything in philosophy. But notice how little *point* there is in saying that he denotes one French King rather than any other, or any other person named by the name. There is now nothing that the speaker is prepared to say or do which relates him differentially to that one King. This is why it is so outrageous to say that he believes that

Louis XIII is a basketball player. The notion of saying has simply been severed from all the connections that made it of interest. Certainly we did not think we were letting ourselves in for this when we took the point about the conversation in the pub. What has gone wrong?[6]

The causal theory again ignores the importance of surrounding context, and regards the capacity to denote something as a magic trick which has somehow been passed on, and once passed on cannot be lost. We should rather say: in virtue of the context in which the man found himself the man's dispositions were bent towards one particular man—Louis XIII—whose states and doings alone he would count as serving to verify remarks made in that context using the name. And of course that context can persist, for the conversation can itself be adverted to subsequently. But it can also disappear so that the speaker is simply not sensitive to the outcome of any investigations regarding the truth of what he is said to have said. And at this point saying becomes detached, and uninteresting.

(It is worth observing how ambivalent Kripke is on the relation between denoting and believing; when the connection favors him he uses it; we are reminded for example that the ordinary man has a false belief about Gödel and not a true belief about Schmidt. But it is obvious that the results of the 'who are they believing about?' criterion are bound to come dramatically apart from the results of the 'who is the original bearer of the name?' criterion, if for no other reason than that the former must be constructed to give results in cases where there is no name and where the latter cannot apply. When this happens we are sternly reminded that "X refers" and "X says" are being used in *technical* senses.[7] But there are limits. One could regard the aim of this paper to restore the connection which must exist between strict truth conditions and the beliefs and interests of the users of the sentences if the technical notion of strict truth conditions is to be of interest to us.)

Reflection upon the conversation in the pub appeared to provide one reason for being favorably disposed towards the causal theory. There is another connected reason we ought to examine briefly. It might appear that the causal theory provides the basis for a general nonintentional answer to the problem of ambiguity. The problem is clear enough: What conditions have to be satisfied for a speaker to have said that *p* when he utters a sentence which may appropriately be used to say that *q* and that *r* and that *s* in addition? Two obvious alternative answers are (a) the extent to which it is reasonable for his audience to conclude that he was saying that *p,* and (b) his intending to say that *p.*

Neither is without its difficulties. We can therefore imagine someone hoping for a natural extension of the causal theory to general terms which would enable him to explain for example how a child who did not have determinative intentions because of the technical nature of the subject matter may still say something determinate using a sentence which is in fact ambiguous.

I touch upon this to ensure that we are keeping the range of relevant considerations to be brought to bear upon the debate as wide as it must be. But I think little general advantage can accrue to the causal theory from thus broadening the considerations. The reason is that it simply fails to have the generality of the other two theories; it has no obvious application, for example, to syntactic ambiguity or to ambiguity produced by attempts to refer with nonunique descriptions, or pronouns. It seems inconceivable that the general theory of disambiguation required for such cases would be inadequate to deal with the phenomenon of shared names and would require ad hoc supplementation from the causal theory.

I want to stress how, precisely because the causal theory ignores the way context can be determinative of what gets *said,* it has quite unacceptable consequences. Suppose for example on a T.V. quiz program I am asked to name a capital city and I say "Kingston is the capital of Jamaica"; I should want to say that I had said something strictly and literally true even though it turns out that the man from whom I had picked up this scrap of information was actually referring to Kingston-upon-Thames and making a racist observation.

It may begin to appear that what gets said is going to be determined by what name is used, what items bear the name, and general principles of contextual disambiguation. The causal

origin of the speaker's familiarity with the name, save in certain specialized "mouthpiece cases," does not seem to have a critical role to play.

This impression may be strengthened by the observation that a causal connection between my use of the name and use by others (whether or nor leading back ultimately to the item itself) is simply not necessary for me to use the name to say something. Amongst the Wagera Indians, for example, "newly born children receive the names of deceased members of their family according to fixed rules . . . the first born takes on the name of the paternal grandfather, the second that of the father's eldest brother, the third that of the maternal grandfather."[8] In these and other situations (names for streets in U.S. cities etc.,) a knowledgeable speaker may excogitate a name and use it to denote some item which bears it without any causal connection whatever with the use by others of that name.

These points might be conceded by Kripke while maintaining the general position that the denotation of a name in a community is still to be found by tracing a causal chain of reference preserving links back to some item. It is to this theory that I now turn.

3. Suppose a parallel theory were offered to explain the sense of general terms (not just terms for natural kinds). One would reply as follows: "There aren't two fundamentally different mechanisms involved in a word's having a meaning: one bringing it about that a word acquires a meaning, and the other—a causal mechanism—which operates to ensure that its meaning is preserved. The former processes are operative all the time; whatever explains how a word gets its meaning also explains how it preserves it, if preserved it is. Indeed such a theory could not account for the phenomenon of a word's changing its meaning. It is perfectly possible for this to happen without anyone's intending to initiate a new practice with the word; the causal chain would then lead back too far."

Change of meaning would be decisive against such a theory of the meaning of general terms. Change of denotation is similarly decisive against the causal theory of names. Not only are changes of denotation imaginable, but it appears that they actually occur. We learn from Isaac Taylor's book: *Names and their History,* 1898:

In the case of 'Madagascar' a hearsay report of Malay or Arab sailors misunderstood by Marco Polo . . . has had the effect of transferring a corrupt form of the name of a portion of the African mainland to the great African Island.

A simple imaginary case would be this: Two babies are born, and their mothers bestow names upon them. A nurse inadvertently switches them and the error is never discovered. It will henceforth undeniably be the case that the man universally known as "Jack" is so called because a woman dubbed some other baby with the name.

It is clear that the causal theory unamended is not adequate. It looks as though, once again, the intentions of the speakers to use the name to refer to something must be allowed to count in determination of what it denotes.

But it is not enough to say that and leave matters there. We must at least sketch a theory which will enable "Madagascar" to be the name of the island yet which will not have the consequence that "Gödel" would become a name of Schmidt in the situation envisaged by Kripke nor "Goliath" a name of the Philistine killed by David. (Biblical scholars now suggest that David did not kill Goliath, and that the attribution of the slaying to Elhannan the Bethlehemite in 2 *Samuel* 21 xix is correct. David is thought to have killed a Philistine but not Goliath)[9]. For although this has never been explicitly argued I would agree that even if the 'information' connected with the name in possession of an entire community was merely that "Goliath was the Philistine David slew" this would still not mean that "Goliath" referred in that community to that man, and therefore that the sentence expressed a truth. And if we simultaneously thought that the name *would* denote the Philistine slain by Elhannan then both the necessity and sufficiency of the conditions suggested by the description theory of the denotation of a name are rejected. This is the case Kripke should have argued but didn't.

4. Before going on to sketch such a theory in the second part of this paper let me survey the posi-

tion arrived at and use it to make a summary statement of the position I wish to adopt.

We can see the undifferentiated description theory as the expression of two thoughts.

(a) the denotation of a name is determined by what speakers intend to refer to by using the name

(b) the object a speaker intends to refer to by his use of a name is that which satisfies or fits the majority of descriptions which make up the cluster of information which the speaker has associated with the name.

We have seen great difficulties with (a) when this is interpreted as a thesis at the micro level. But consideration of the phenomenon of a name's getting a denotation, or changing it, suggests that there being a community of speakers using the name with such and such as the intended referent is likely to be a crucial constituent in these processes. With names, as with other expressions in the language, what they signify depends upon what we use them to signify—a truth whose recognition is compatible with denying the collapse of saying into meaning at the level of the individual speaker.

It is in (b) that the real weakness lies: the bad old Philosophy of Mind which we momentarily uncovered. Not so much in the idea that the intended referent is determined in a more or less complicated way by the associated information, but the specific form the determination was supposed to take: *fit.* There is something absurd in supposing that the intended referent of some perfectly ordinary use of a name by a speaker could be some item utterly isolated (causally) from the user's community and culture simply in virtue of the fact that it fits better than anything else the cluster of descriptions he associates with the name. I would agree with Kripke in thinking that the absurdity resides in the absence of any causal relation between the item concerned and the speaker. But it seems to me that he has mislocated the causal relation; the important causal relation lies between that item's states and doings and the speaker's body of information—not between the item's being dubbed with a name and the speaker's contemporary use of it.

Philosophers have come increasingly to realize that major concepts in epistemology and the philosophy of mind have causality embedded within them. Seeing and knowing are both good examples.

The absurdity in supposing that the denotation of our contemporary use of the name "Aristotle" could be some unknown (*n.b.*) item whose doings are causally isolated from our body of information is strictly parallel to the absurdity in supposing that one might be seeing something one has no causal contact with solely upon the ground that there is a splendid match between object and visual impression.

There probably is some *degree of fit* requirement in the case of seeing which means that after some amount of distortion or fancy we can no longer maintain that the causally operative item was still being seen. And I think it is likely that there is a parallel requirement for referring. We learn for example from E. K. Chambers' *Arthur of Britain* that Arthur had a son Anir "whom legend has perhaps confused with his burial place." If Kripke's notion of reference fixing is such that those who said Anir was a burial place of Arthur might be denoting a person, it seems that it has little to commend it, and is certainly not justified by the criticisms he makes against the description theory. But the existence or nature of this 'degree of fit' requirement will not be something I shall be concerned with here.

We must allow then that the denotation of a name in the community will depend in a complicated way upon what those who use the term intend to refer to, but we will so understand 'intended referent' that typically a *necessary* (but not sufficient) condition for *x*'s being the intended referent of *S*'s use of a name is that *x* should be the source of causal origin of the body of information that *S* has associated with the name.

II

5. The aim I have set myself, then, is modest; it is not to present a complete theory of the denotation of names. Without presenting a general theory to solve the problem of ambiguity I cannot present a theory of speaker's denotation, although I will make remarks which prejudice that issue. I propose merely to sketch an account of what makes an expression into a name for something that will allow names to change their denotations.

The enterprise is more modest yet for I propose to help myself to an undefined notion of speaker's reference by borrowing from the theory of communication. But a word of explanation.

A speaker may have succeeded in *getting it across* or in *communicating* that *p* even though he uses a sentence which may not appropriately be used to say that *p*. Presumably this success consists in his audience's having formed a belief about him. This need not be the belief that the speaker intended to say in the strict sense that *p*, since the speaker may succeed in getting something across despite using a sentence which he is known to know cannot appropriately be used to say that *p*. The speaker will have referred to *a*, in the sense I am helping myself to, only if he has succeeded in getting it across that *Fa* (for some substitution *F*). Further stringent conditions are required. Clearly this notion is quite different from the notion of denotation which I have been using, tied as denotation is to saying in the strict sense. One may refer to *x* by using a description that *x* does not satisfy; one may not thus denote *x*.

Now a speaker may know or believe that there is such-and-such an item in the world and intend to refer to it. And this is where the suggestion made earlier must be brought to bear, for *that* item is not (in general) the satisfier of the body of information the possession by the speaker of which makes it true that he knows of the existence of the item; it is rather that item which is causally responsible for the speaker's possession of that body of information, or dominantly responsible if there is more than one. (The point is of course not specific to this intention, or to intention as opposed to other psychological attitudes.) Let us then, very briefly, explore these two ideas: source and dominance.

Usually our knowledge or belief about particular items is derived from information-gathering transactions, involving a causal interaction with some item or other, conducted ourselves, or is derived, maybe through a long chain, from the transactions of others. Perception of the item is the main but by no means the only way an item can impress itself on us; for example, a man can be the source of things we discover by rifling through his suitcase or by reading his works.

A causal relation is of course not sufficient; but we may borrow from the theory of knowledge and say something like this. X is the source of the belief S expresses by uttering "Fa" if there was an episode which caused S's belief in which X and S were causally related in a type of situation apt for producing knowledge that something F-s ($\exists x(Fx)$)—a type of situation in which the belief that something F-s would be caused by something's F-ing. That it is a way of producing knowledge does not mean that it cannot go wrong; that is why X, by smoking French cigarettes can be the source of the belief S expresses by "a smokes Greek cigarettes."

Of course some of our information about the world is not so based; we may deduce that there is a tallest man in the world and deduce that he is over six feet tall. No man is the source of this information; a name introduced in relation to it might function very much as the unamended description theory suggested.

Legend and fancy can create new characters, or add bodies of sourceless material to other dossiers; restrictions on the causal relation would prevent the inventors of the legends turning out to be the sources of the beliefs their legends gave rise to. Someone other than the ϕ can be the source of the belief S expresses by "a is the ϕ"; Kripke's Gödel, by claiming the proof, was the source of the belief people manifested by saying "Gödel proved the incompleteness of arithmetic," not Schmidt.

Misidentification can bring it about that the item which is the source of the information is different from the item about which the information is believed. I may form the belief about the wife of some colleague that she has nice legs upon the basis of seeing someone else—but the girl I saw is the source.

Consequently a cluster or dossier of information can be dominantly of[10] an item though it contains elements whose source is different. And we surely want to allow that persistent misidentification can bring it about that a cluster is dominantly of some item other than that it was dominantly of originally.

Suppose I get to know a man slightly. Suppose then a suitably primed identical twin takes over his position, and I get to know him fairly well, not noticing the switch. Immediately after the switch my dossier will still be dominantly of the original man, and I falsely believe, as I would acknowledge if it was pointed out, that *he* is in the room. Then I would pass through a period in which neither was dominant; I had not misidentified one as the other, an asymmetrical relation, but rather confused them. Finally the twin could take over the dominant position; I would not have false beliefs about who is in the room, but false beliefs about, e.g., when I first met the man in the room. These differences seem to reside entirely in the differences in the believer's reactions to the various discoveries, and dominance is meant to capture those differences.

Dominance is not simply a function of *amount* of information (if that is even intelligible). In the case of persons, for example, each man's life presents a skeleton and the dominant source may be the man who contributed to covering most of it rather than the man who contributed most of the covering. Detail in a particular area can be outweighed by spread. Also the believer's reasons for being interested in the item at all will weigh.

Consider another example. If it turns out that an impersonator had taken over Napoleon's role from 1814 onwards (post-Elba) the cluster of the typical historian would still be dominantly of the man responsible for the earlier exploits (α in diagram 1) and we would say that they had false beliefs about who fought at Waterloo. If however the switch had occurred much earlier, it being an unknown army officer being impersonated, then their information would be dominantly of the later man (β in diagram 2). They did not have false beliefs about who was the general at Waterloo, but rather false beliefs about that general's early career.

I think we can say that *in general* a speaker intends to refer to the item that is the dominant source of his associated body of information. It is important to see that this will not change from occasion to occasion depending upon subject matter. Some have proposed[11] that if in case 1 the historian says "Napoleon fought skillfully at Waterloo" it is the imposter β who is the

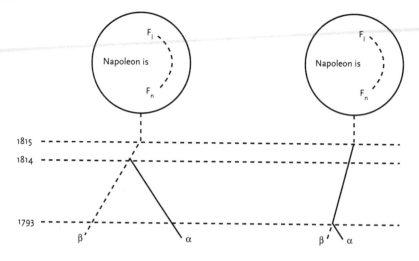

intended referent, while if he had said in the next breath ". . . unlike his performance in the Senate" it would be α. This seems a mistake; not only was what the man said false, what he intended to say was false too, as he would be the first to agree; it wasn't Napoleon who fought skilfully at Waterloo.

With this background then we may offer the following tentative definition: "NN" is a name of x if there is a community C—

1. in which it is common knowledge that members of C have in their repertoire the procedure of using "NN" to refer to x (with the intention of referring to x);

2. the success in reference in any particular case being intended to rely on common knowledge between speaker and hearer that "NN" has been used to refer to x by members of C and not upon common knowledge of the satisfaction by x of some predicate embedded in "NN"[12]

(In order to keep the definition simple no attempt is made to cover the sense in which an unused institutionally approved name is a name.)

This distinction (between use-because-(we know)-we-use-it and use upon other bases) is just what is needed to distinguish dead from live metaphors; it seems to me the only basis on which to distinguish the referential functioning of names, which may grammatically be descriptions, from that of descriptions.[13]

The definition does not have the consequence that the description "the man we call 'NN' " is a name, for *its* success as a referential device does not rely upon common knowledge that *it* is or has been used to refer to x.

Intentions alone don't bring it about that a name gets a denotation; without the intentions being manifest there cannot be the common knowledge required for the practice.

Our conditions are more stringent than Kripke's since for him an expression becomes a name just so long as someone has dubbed something with it and thereby caused it to be in common usage. This seems little short of magical. Suppose one of a group of villagers dubbed a little girl on holiday in the vicinity "Goldilocks" and the name caught on. However suppose that there were two identical twins the villagers totally failed to distinguish. I should deny that "Goldilocks" is the name of either—even if by some miracle each villager used the name consistently but in no sense did they fall into two coherent subcommunities. (The name might denote the girl first dubbed if for some peculiar reason the villagers were deferential to the introducer of the name—of this more below.)

Consider the following case. An urn is discovered in the Dead Sea containing documents in which are found fascinating mathematical proofs. Inscribed at the bottom is the name "Ibn Khan" which is quite naturally taken to be the name of the constructor of the proofs. Consequently it passes into common usage amongst mathematicians concerned with that branch of mathematics. "Khan conjectured here that . . ." and the like. However suppose the name was the name of the scribe who had transcribed the proofs much later; a small "*id scripsit*" had been obliterated.

Here is a perfect case where there is a coherent community using the name with the mathematician as the intended referent and a consequence of the definition would be that "Ibn Khan" would be one of his names. Also, "Malachai" would have been the name of the author of the Biblical work of the same name despite that its use was based upon a misapprehension ("Malachai" means my messenger).[14]

Speakers within such traditions use names under the misapprehension that their use is in conformity with the use of other speakers referring to the relevant item. The names would probably be withdrawn when that misapprehension is revealed, or start a rather different life as "our" names for the items (cf., "Deutero Isaiah" etc.) One might be impressed by this, and regard it as a reason for denying that those within these traditions spoke the literal truth in using the names. It is very easy to add a codicil to the definition which would have this effect.

Actually it is not a very good reason for denying that speakers within such traditions are speaking the literal truth.[15] But I do not want to insist upon any decision upon this point. This is because one can be concessive and allow the definition to be amended without giving up anything of importance. First: the definition with its codicil will still allow many names to change their denotation. Secondly: it obviously fails to follow from the fact that, in our example, the community of mathematicians were not denoting the mathematician [but] that they were denoting the scribe and were engaged in strictly speaking massive falsehood of him.

Let me elaborate the first of these points.

There is a fairly standard way in which people get their names. If we use a name of a man we expect that it originated in the standard manner and this expectation may condition our use of it. But consider names for people which are obviously nicknames, or names for places or pieces of music. Since there is no standard way in which these names are bestowed subsequent users will not in general use the name under any view as to its origin, and therefore when there is a divergence between the item involved in the name's origin and the speakers' intended referent there will be no *mis*apprehension, no latent motive for withdrawing the name, and thus no bar to the name's acquiring a new denotation even by the amended definition. So long as they have no reason to believe that the name has dragged any information with it, speakers will treat the revelation that the name had once been used to refer to something different with the same sort of indifference as that with which they greet the information that "meat" once meant groceries in general.

We can easily tell the story in case 2 of our Napoleon diagram so that α was the original bearer of the name "Napoleon" and it was transferred to the counterfeit because of the similarity of their appearances and therefore without the intention on anyone's part to initiate a new practice. Though this is not such a clear case I should probably say that historians have used the name "Napoleon" to refer to β. They might perhaps abandon it, but that of course fails to show that they were all along denoting α. Nor does the fact that someone in the know might come along and say "Napoleon was a fish salesman and was never at Waterloo" show anything. The relevant question is: "Does this contradict the assertion that was made when the historians said "Napoleon was at Waterloo?" To give an affirmative answer to this question requires the prior determination that they have all along been denoting α.

We need one further and major complication. Although standardly we use expressions with the intention of conforming with the general use made of them by the community, sometimes we use them with the *overriding* intention to conform to the use made of them by some other person or persons. In that case I shall say that we use the expression *deferentially* (with respect to that other person or group of persons). This is true of some general terms too: "viol," "minuet" would be examples.

I should say, for example, that the man in the conversation in the pub used "Louis" deferentially. This is not just a matter of his ignorance; he could, indeed, have an opinion as to who this Louis is (the man he met earlier perhaps) but still use the expression deferentially. There is an important gap between

> intending to refer to the φ and believing that α = the φ

and

> intending to refer to *a*

for even when he has an opinion as to who they are talking about I should say that it was the man they were talking about, and not the man he met earlier, that he intended to refer to.

Archaeologists might find a tomb in the desert and claim falsely that it is the burial place of some little known character in the Bible. They could discover a great deal about the man in the tomb so that he and not the character in the Bible was the dominant source of their information. But, given the nature and point of their enterprise, the archaeologists are using the name deferentially to the authors of the Bible. I should say, then, that they denote that man, and say false things about him. Notice that in such a case there is some point to this characterization.

The case is in fact no different with any situation in which a name is used with the overriding intention of referring to something satisfying such and such a description. Kripke gives the example of "Jack the Ripper." Again, after the arrest of a man *a* not in fact responsible for the crimes, *a* can be the dominant source of speakers' information but the intended referent could well be the murderer and not *a*. Again this will be productive of a whole lot of falsehood.

We do not use all names deferentially, least of all deferentially to the person from whom we picked them up. For example the mathematicians did not use the name "Ibn Khan" with the *overriding* intention of referring to whoever bore that name or was referred to by some other person or community.

We must thus be careful to distinguish two reasons for something that would count as "withdrawing sentences containing the name":

(a) the item's not bearing the name "NN" ("Ibn Khan," "Malachai"), and

(b) the item's not being NN (the biblical archaeologists).

I shall end with an example that enables me to draw these threads together and summarize where my position differs from the causal theory.

A youth *A* leaves a small village in the Scottish highlands to seek his fortune having acquired the nickname "Turnip" (the reason for choosing a nickname is I hope clear). Fifty or so years later a man *B* comes to the village and lives as a hermit over the hill. The three or four villagers surviving from the time of the youth's departure believe falsely that this is the long-departed villager returned. Consequently they use the name "Turnip" among themselves and it gets into wider circulation among the younger villagers who have no idea how it originated. I am assuming that the older villagers, if the facts were pointed out would say: "It isn't Turnip after all" rather than "It appears after all that Turnip did not come from this village." In that case I should say that they use the name to refer to *A,* and in fact, denoting him, say false things about him (even by uttering "Here is Turnip coming to get his coffee again.")

But they may die off, leaving a homogeneous community using the name to refer to the man over the hill. I should say the way is clear to its becoming his name. The story is not much affected if the older villagers pass on some information whose source is *A* by saying such things as "Turnip was quite a one for the girls," for the younger villagers' clusters would still be dominantly of the man over the hill. But it is an important feature of my account that the information that the older villagers gave the younger villagers could be so rich, coherent and important to them that *A* could be the dominant source of their information, so that they too would acknowledge "That man over the hill isn't Turnip after all."

A final possibility would be if they used the name deferentially towards the older villagers, for some reason, with the consequence that no matter who was dominant they denote whoever the elders denote.

CONCLUSION

6. Espousers of both theories could reasonably claim to be vindicated by the position we have arrived at. We have secured for the description

theorist much that he wanted. We have seen for at least the most fundamental case of the use of names (nondeferentially used names) the idea that their denotation is fixed in a more or less complicated way by the associated bodies of information that one could cull from the users of the name turns out not to be so wide of the mark. But of course that the fix is by causal origin and not by fit crucially affects the impact this idea has upon the statement of the truth conditions of existential or opaque sentences containing names. The theorist can also point to the idea of dominance as securing what he was trying, admittedly crudely, to secure with his talk of the "majority of" the descriptions, and to the 'degree of fit requirement' as blocking consequences he found objectionable.

The causal theorist can also look with satisfaction upon the result, incorporating as it does his insight about the importance of causality into a central position. Further, the logical doctrines he was concerned to establish, for example the noncontingency of identity statements made with the use of names, are not controverted. Information is individuated by source; if *a* is the source of a body of information nothing else could have been. Consequently nothing else could have been *that a*.

The only theorists who gain no comfort are those who, ignoring Kripke's explicit remarks to the contrary,[16] supposed that the causal theory could provide them with a totally *nonintentional* answer to the problem posed by names. But I am not distressed by their distress.

Our ideas also point forwards; for it seems that they, or some close relative, must be used in explaining the functioning of at least some demonstratives. Such an expression as "That mountaineer" in "That mountaineer is coming to town tonight" may advert to a body of information presumed in common possession, perhaps through the newspapers, which fixes its denotation. No one can be that mountaineer unless he is the source of that information no matter how perfectly he fits it, and of course someone can be *that* mountaineer and fail to fit

quite a bit of it. It is in such generality that defense of our ideas must lie.

But with these hints I must leave the subject.

REFERENCES

1. S. A. Kripke, "Naming and Necessity," in Davidson and Harman, eds. *Semantics of Natural Languages*, pp. 253–355. [Reprinted in this volume.]
2. This can be seen in the way the list of theses defining the Description Theory alternate between those mentioning a speaker and those that don't, culminating in the uneasy idea of an idiolect of one. The description theorists of course do not themselves distinguish them clearly either, and many espouse both.
3. P. F. Strawson, *Individuals* (Methuen), p. 191.
4. For example see J. R. Searle, *Speech Acts*, p. 87; E. Gellner, "Ethics and Logic," *Proceedings of the Aristotelian Society* (1954–5), B. Russell *Problems of Philosophy*, p. 29. E. Sosa criticizes it in "Quantifiers, Belief, and Sellars," in Davis, Hockney, and Wilson, eds., *Philosophical Logic*, p. 69.
5. I owe this observation to G. Harman.
6. Kripke expresses doubts about the sufficiency of the conditions for this sort of reason [see p. 282, this volume].
7. Id. [p. 285, this volume].
8. E. Delhaise, "Les Wagera," *Monogr. Ethnogr.* 1909.
9. Robinson, *History of Israel*, p. 187.
10. The term is D. Kaplan's, see "Quantifying In" [reprinted in this volume], in Davidson and Hintikka, eds., *Words and Objections:* I think there are clear similarities between my notion of a dominant source and notions he is there sketching. However I want nothing to do with vividness. I borrow the term "dossier" from H. P. Grice's paper "Vacuous Names" in the same volume.
11. K. S. Donnellan, "Proper Names and Identifying Descriptions" in Davidson and Harman, eds., p. 371.
12. For the notion of "common knowledge" see D. K. Lewis, *Convention* and the slightly different notion in S. Schiffer, *Meaning* (Oxford, Oxford University Press: 1972). For the notion of "a procedure in the repertoire" see H. P. Grice "Utterer's Meaning, Sentence Meaning, Word Meaning," *Foundations of Language* (1968). Clearly the whole enterprise owes to Grice but no commitment is here made to any specific version of the theory of communication.
13. And if Schiffer is right much more as well—see *Meaning*, chapter V.
14. See Otto Eissfeldt, *The Old Testament*, p. 441.
15. John McDowell has persuaded me of this, as of much else. He detests my conclusions.
16. Kripke [p. 282, this volume].

24

Proper Names and Intentionality

JOHN R. SEARLE

I. THE NATURE OF THE PROBLEM

The problem of proper names ought to be easy, and at one level I think it is: we need to make repeated references to the same object, even when the object is not present, and so we give the object a name. Henceforward this name is used to refer to that object. However, puzzles arise when we reflect on the following sorts of considerations: objects are not given to us prior to our system of representation; what counts as one object or the same object is a function of how we divide up the world. The world does not come to us already divided up into objects; we have to divide it; and how we divide it is up to our system of representation, and in that sense is up to us, even though the system is biologically, culturally, and linguistically shaped. Furthermore, in order that someone can give a name to a certain object or know that a name is the name of that object, he has to have some *other* representation of that object independently of just having the name.

For the purposes of this study we need to explain how the use of proper names fits in with our general account of Intentionality. Both definite descriptions and indexicals serve to express at least a certain chunk of Intentional content. The expression may not by itself be sufficient to identify the object referred to, but in cases where the reference succeeds there is enough other Intentional content available to the speaker to nail down the reference. This thesis holds even for "referential" uses of definite descriptions, where the Intentional content that is actually expressed in the utterance may not even be true of the object referred to.[1] But what about proper names? They obviously lack an explicit Intentional content, but do they serve to focus the speaker's and hearer's Intentionality in some way; or do they simply refer to objects without any intervening Intentional content? On my account the answer is obvious. Since linguistic reference is always dependent on or is a form of mental reference and since mental reference is always in virtue of Intentional content including Background and Network,[2] proper names must in some way depend on Intentional content, and it is now time to make that way—or those ways—fully explicit.

The problem of proper names used to be put in the form, "Do proper names have sense?", and in contemporary philosophy there are supposed to be two competing answers to that question: an affirmative answer given by the "descriptivist" theory, according to which a name refers by being associated with a description or perhaps a cluster of descriptions, and a negative answer given by the "causal" theory according to which a name refers because of a "causal chain" connecting the utterance of the name to the bearer of the name or at least to the naming ceremony in which the bearer of the name got the name. I believe that neither side should be satisfied with these labels. The causal theory would be better described as the external causal chain of communication theory,[3] and the descriptivist theory would be better described as the Intentionalist or internalist theory, for reasons which will emerge in this discussion.

Labels apart, it is important to get clear at the start about what exactly is at issue between these two theories. Almost without exception, the accounts I have seen of the descriptivist theory are more or less crude distortions of it, and I want to make explicit four of the most common misconceptions of the issues in order to set them aside so that we can get at the real issues.

First, the issue is most emphatically not about whether proper names must be exhaustively analyzed in completely general terms. I do not know of any descriptivist theorist who has ever maintained that view, though Frege sometimes talks as if he might be sympathetic to it. In any case it has never been my view, nor, I believe, has it ever been the view of Strawson or Russell.

Second, as far as I am concerned the issue is not really about analyzing proper names in *words* at all. In my earlier writings on this subject[4] I pointed out that in some cases the only "identifying description" a speaker might have that he associates with the name is simply the ability to recognize the object.

Third, some authors[5] think that the descriptivist holds that proper names are associated with a 'dossier' in the speaker's mind and that the issue is between this dossier conception and the conception of the use of a proper name as analogous to pointing. But that again is a misconception of descriptivism. On the descriptivist account, pointing is precisely an example that fits his thesis, since pointing succeeds only in virtue of the intentions of the pointer.

Fourth, Kripke claims that on the descriptivist picture "some man really gives a name by going into the privacy of his own room and saying that the referent is to be the unique thing with certain identifying properties."[6] But that is

not the view any descriptivist known to me ever espoused and it is not surprising that Kripke gives no source for this strange view.

But if these four accounts misrepresent descriptivism and the issues between descriptivist and causal theories, what exactly are these views and the issues between them? The issue is simply this: Do proper names refer by setting *internal* conditions of satisfaction in a way that is consistent with the general account of Intentionality that I have been providing, or do proper names refer in virtue of some *external* causal relation? Let us try to state this issue a little more precisely. The descriptivist is committed to the view that in order to account for how a proper name refers to an object we need to show how the object *satisfies* or *fits* the "descriptive" Intentional content that is associated with the name in the minds of speakers; some of this Intentionality will normally be expressed or at least be expressible in words. The causal theorist is committed to the view that no such Intentionalist analysis will ever do the job and that in order to account for the relation of successful reference between the utterance of a name and the object referred to we need to show some sort of external causal connection between the utterance of a name and the object. Both theories are attempts to answer the question, "How in the utterance of a name does the speaker succeed in referring to an object?" The answer given by the descriptivist is that the speaker refers to the object because and only because the object satisfies the Intentional content associated with the name. The causal theorist answers that the speaker refers to an object because and only because there is a causal chain of communication connecting the speaker's utterance with the object or at least with the baptism of the object—an important qualification we will come to later.

II. THE CAUSAL THEORY

There are different versions of the causal theory and I shall not try to discuss all of them. The most influential have been those of Kripke and Donnellan, and I shall confine most of my discussion to their views. They are not identical, but I will call attention to the differences between them only when necessary to avoid confusion.

I begin with Kripke's version.

A rough statement of a theory might be the following. An initial baptism takes place. Here the object may be named by ostension, or the reference of the name may be fixed by a description. When the name is "passed from link to link", the receiver of the name must, I think, intend when he hears it to use it with the same reference as the man from whom he heard it.[7]

There are several things to notice about this passage. First, the account of the introduction of the name in the baptism is entirely descriptivist. The baptism either gives us an Intentional content in verbal form, a definite description (Kripke gives the example of the introduction of the name "Neptune" for a then as yet unperceived planet), or it gives the Intentional content of a perception when an object is named ostensively. In the perceptual case, there is indeed a causal connection, but as it is Intentional causation, internal to the perceptual content, it is useless to the causal theorist in his effort to give an external causal account of the relation of name to object. Of course, in such cases there will also be an external causal account in terms of the impact of the object on the nervous system, but the external causal phenomena will not by themselves give an ostensive definition of the name. To get the ostensive definition the perceiver has to perceive the object, and that involves more than the physical impact of the object on his nervous system. So it is an odd feature of Kripke's version of the causal theory that the external causal chain does not actually reach up to the object, it only reaches to the baptism of the object, to the name introduction ceremony, and from that point on what fixes the reference is an Intentional content which may or may not also have an external causal connection to the object. Many, perhaps most, philosophers think of the causal theory of names as asserting a causal connection between the referring use of names and the object they name, but in Kripke's case at least that isn't really true. An interesting point and one we will come back to later.

Some authors, e.g. Devitt,[8] are disappointed with this aspect of Kripke's account and want to reserve the notion of genuinely "designational" names to those that are causally connected to the object itself. But this seems quite arbitrary. There is nothing to prevent us from introducing a name by description and using it to refer, even as a "rigid designator"; and in any case, there are lots of proper names of abstract entities, e.g., numerals are names of numbers, and abstract entities are incapable of initiating physical causal chains.

A second feature to notice about Kripke's account is that the causal chain isn't, so to speak, *pure*. In addition to causation and baptism, an extra Intentionalistic element is allowed to creep in: each speaker must intend to refer to the same object as the person from whom he learned the name. So this does give us some Intentional content associated with each use of a name 'N' in the causal chain, viz., "N is the object referred to by the person from whom I got the name." Now this is an odd requirement for the following reason: if everybody in the chain actually had this restricted intention, and if the Intentional content were in fact satisfied, i.e., if each speaker really did succeed in referring to the same object, then it would follow trivially that the reference would go right back to the target of the initial baptism and the talk about causation would be redundant. But that is presumably not Kripke's idea, since that would have no explanatory power and would in fact be circular. We would explain successful reference in virtue of a chain of successful references. Kripke's idea is clearly this: you will account for how the Intentional content is satisfied, that is, how the reference is successful, in terms of external causation plus the intention that it should be successful. So Kripke sets three conditions to account for how each token utterance refers to the initial target: initial baptism, causal chain, restricted Intentional content. And the account is still external in this sense: though each link in the chain of communication is perceived by both speaker and hearer, "It is not how the speaker thinks he got the reference but the actual chain of communication which is relevant."[9]

Before criticizing Kripke's account let us turn to Donnellan's.

The main idea is that when a speaker uses a name intending to refer to an individual and predicate something of it, successful reference will occur when there is an individual that enters into the historically correct explanation of who [sic] it is that the speaker intended to predicate something of. That individual will then be the referent and the statement made will be true or false depending on whether it has the property designated by the predicate.[10]

The passage has two key elements: (a) "historically correct explanation of" (b) "who it is that the speaker intended to predicate something of." To help us with (a) Donellan introduces the idea of an "omniscient observer of history." The omniscient observer will see whom or what we meant even if we can't give any Intentional content that fits whom or what we meant. But then in what did our satisfying (b) consist? What fact about *us* makes it the case that when we said, for example, "Socrates is snub nosed", it was *Socrates* that we "intended to predicate something of"? Evidently, on Donnellan's account, no fact about us at all—except for the causal chain connecting our utterance to Socrates. But, then, what is the nature of this chain; what does the omniscient observer look for and why? Rorty assures us that the causal theory needs only "ordinary physical causation," the banging of object against object, as it were. I think Donnellan's observer is going to have to look for Intentional causation and Intentional content. I will come back to this point.

Kripke insists, and I take it that Donnellan would agree, that the causal theory is not intended as a complete theory but rather as a "picture" of how proper names work. Still, we want to know if it is an accurate picture, and one way to proceed is to try to get counterexamples, examples of names that don't work according to the picture. Does the causal theory (or picture) as stated, for example, by Kripke give us sufficient conditions of successful reference using proper names? The answer, I think, is clearly no. There are numerous counterexamples in the literature, but perhaps the most graphic is from Gareth Evans.[11] "Madagascar" was originally the name of a part of Africa. Marco Polo, though he presumably satisfied Kripke's condition of intending to use the name with the same reference as "the man from whom he heard it," nonetheless referred to an island off the coast of Africa, and that island is now what we mean by

"Madagascar". So, the use of the name "Madagascar" satisfies a causal condition that connects it with the African mainland, but that is not sufficient to enable it to refer to the African mainland. The question we need to come back to is how and why does it refer to Madagascar instead of the African mainland, given that the causal chain goes to the mainland?

If a Kripkean causal chain picture does not give us a sufficient condition does it at least give us a necessary condition? Here again the answer seems to me clearly no. In general it is a good idea to use examples that have been presented against one as examples that actually work in one's favor, so let us consider the following from Kaplan.[12] He writes that the description theory couldn't be right because, for example, it says in the *Concise Biographical Dictionary* (Concise Publications: Walla Walla, Washington) that "Rameses VIII" is "One of a number of ancient pharaohs about whom nothing is known." But surely we can refer to him even though we do not satisfy the description theory for using his name. Actually what the example shows is that a great deal is known about Rameses VIII, and indeed he is a rather ideal case even for the most naive version of the description theory since we seem to have a perfect identifying description. Rameses VIII is the pharaoh named "Rameses" who ruled Egypt after a pharaoh named "Rameses VII."[13] That is, imagine, as I suppose is the case, that we have at least some knowledge of the history of ancient Egypt, including the knowledge that pharaohs with the same name are numbered sequentially. Suppose for the sake of argument that we know quite a bit about Rameses VII and Rameses IX. We could then use, without any hesitation, the name "Rameses VIII" to refer to the Rameses who came between Rameses VII and Rameses IX, even though the various causal chains stretching back from us to ancient Egypt miss Rameses VIII. What we have in this case is an example of the Network in operation; in this case, it is that part of the Network containing knowledge about the past.

In general one can say that the whole Network of Intentionality is nailed down causally, *via* Intentional causation, to the real world at various points, but it would be a serious mistake to suppose that the Network must nail down, by any kind of causation, at every single point that reference is made using a proper name.[14] I believe the reason that causal theorists make this mistake is that they overdraw the analogy between reference and perception, an analogy that is made explicitly by Donnellan.[15] Perception does nail down to the world in this way at every point, because every perceptual experience has the causal self-referentiality of Intentional content that we have discussed earlier. But proper names do not carry that kind of causation, even of Intentional causation. It is possible to satisfy the conditions for successfully using a proper name even though there is no causal connection, either Intentional or external, between the utterance of the name and the object referred to. Indeed, this will be the use for any system of names where one can identify the bearer of the name from the position of the name in the system. I can, for example, refer to M Street in Washington simply because I know that there is in that city an alphabetical sequence of street names, "A", "B", "C", etc. I needn't have any causal connection with M Street in order to do that.[16] And the point is even clearer if we consider names of abstract entities: if I count up to 387, the numeral names the number without any causal chain connecting me and any alleged baptismal ceremony of that number.

There are plenty of acknowledged counterexamples to the claim that the causal theory gives us either necessary or sufficient conditions for the use of a proper name to refer to its bearer. Why are the authors of these theories not impressed by these examples? There is, by the way, an odd asymmetry in the role of counterexamples in these discussions: alleged counterexamples to the descriptivist theory are generally regarded as disastrous for the theory; counterexamples to the causal theory are cheerfully accepted as if they did not matter. The reason why the causal theorists are not impressed, I suspect, is that they feel that, as Kripke says explicitly, the causal theory offers a more adequate *picture* of how names work even if it cannot account for every case. After all, the counterexamples may just be odd and marginal cases and what we really want to know is what is central and essential to the operation of the institu-

tion of proper names. Furthermore, the counterexamples are not really very important to us theoretically unless they are backed by some independently motivated theory, some account of why they are counterexamples. I am in sympathy with both of these impulses and I believe we should look for the essential character of the institution and not be too impressed by odd examples, and I believe the counterexamples are only interesting if backed by a theory that explains them. Indeed, I would like to see counterexamples to both the causal and descriptivist theory treated with these same attitudes. The difficulty is that counterexamples I have presented do seem to raise serious difficulties for the causal theory (or picture) and they are backed by a theory of Intentionality. In the Madagascar case the Intentionality that attaches to the name shifts the reference from the terminus of the causal chain to the object that satisfies the associated Intentional content, and in the case of locating names in systems of names the position of a name as an element in the Network gives sufficient Intentionality to secure reference for the name without any causal chain.

Let us then turn to the more important question: Does the causal theory or picture give the essential character of the institution of proper names? I think the answer is clearly no. To see this, imagine a primitive hunter-gatherer community with a language containing proper names. (And it is not at all implausible to imagine a language used by a primitive community; as far as we know it was in such communities that human languages evolved in the first place.) Imagine that everybody in the tribe knows everybody else and that newborn members of the tribe are baptized at ceremonies attended by the entire tribe. Imagine, furthermore, that as the children grow up they learn the names of people as well as the local names of mountains, lakes, streets, houses, etc., by ostension. Suppose also that there is a strict taboo in this tribe against speaking of the dead, so that no one's name is ever mentioned after his death. Now the point of the fantasy is simply this: As I have described it, this tribe has an institution of proper names used for reference in exactly the same way that our names are used for reference, but *there is not a single use of a name in the tribe that satisfies the causal chain of communication theory.* As I have described it there is not a single chain of communication of the sort favored by Kripke, Donnellan, and others. Every use of the name in this tribe as I described it satisfies the descriptivist claim that there is an Intentional content associating the name with the object. In this case we are to suppose that the people are taught the names by ostension and that they learn to recognize their fellow tribe members, mountains, houses, etc. The teaching sets up an Intentional content which the object satisfies.[17]

It seems to me that the causal theorist might make the following reply: The spirit of the causal theory is kept in this example, because though there is no chain of *communication* there is nonetheless a *causal* connection between the acquisition of the name and the object named because the object is presented ostensively. The answer to that is twofold. First, the kind of causal connection that teaches the use of the name is straightforward Intentional causation; it is not externalist at all. That is, the kind of causal connection that is set up in these cases is a descriptivist causal connection. When I say "Baxter", I mean the man I am able to *recognize as* Baxter or the man to whom I was *introduced as* Baxter, or the man whom I *saw* baptized as Baxter, and in each of these cases the causal element implied by the italicized term is Intentional causation. In every case the causal condition is part of the Intentional content associated with the name. And notice that what counts is not the fact that I give a *verbal* description, but that there is an Intentional content.

If the causal theory is to be an alternative to the descriptivist theory, the causation in question must not be descriptivist, it must not be internal, otherwise the causal theory is just a variant of the descriptivist theory. It just amounts to the claim that descriptivism includes some, e.g., perceptual, elements in the Intentional content associated with the use of the name. But, secondly, we needn't even suppose that all of the names in the community are introduced by ostension. As Kripke concedes, there may be names in the community that are introduced purely by description. Suppose that the astronomers and meteorologists of the commu-

nity are able to predict storms and astronomical events in the future and that they attach proper names to these future events and phenomena. These names are taught to all the members of the community purely by description and there isn't any question of the events causing the names because the events are in the future. Now here it seems to me is a community that satisfies all of the conditions essential for having proper names and having the institution of proper names that function to refer in the way that our proper names function to refer, but there is not a single use of a proper name that satisfies the story, picture, or theory of the causal theorists.

If we so easily describe an example of an entire community that satisfies the conditions for using proper names but does not satisfy the conditions laid down by the causal theory, how are we to account for the fact that the theory has seemed so plausible to so many philosophers? What are we to make of this dispute? Notice that in neither Donnellan nor in Kripke was the causal theory presented as the result of some independently motivated account of the use of names, rather it was presented as a briefly sketched alternative to the descriptivist theory. The main thrust of both arguments was in attempting to refute descriptivism, and if we are to understand what is going on in this dispute we must now turn to that theory.

III. THE DESCRIPTIVIST ACCOUNT OF PROPER NAMES

You will not understand the descriptivist theories unless you understand the views they were originally opposed to. At the time I wrote "Proper names"[18] in 1955 there were three standard views of names in the philosophical literature: Mill's view that names have no connotation at all but simply a denotation, Frege's view that the meaning of a name is given by a single associated definite description, and what might be called the standard logic textbook view that the meaning of a name "*N*" is simply "called N". Now the first and third of these views seem to be obviously inadequate. If the problem of a theory of proper names is to answer the question, "In virtue of what does the speaker in the utterance of a name succeed in referring to a particular object?", then Mill's account is simply a refusal to answer the question; it simply says that the name refers to the object, and that's that. But the third answer is also defective. As I wrote in *Speech Acts,*

the description, "The man called X" will not do, or at any rate will not do by itself, as a satisfaction of the principle of identification. For if you ask me, "Whom do you mean by X?" and I answer, "The man called X", even if it were true that there is only one man who is called X, I am simply saying that he is the man whom other people refer to by the name "X". But if they refer to him by the name "X" then they must also be prepared to substitute an identifying description for "X" and if they in turn substitute "the man called X", the question is only carried a stage further and cannot go on indefinitely without circularity or infinite regress. My reference to an individual may be parasitic on someone else's but this parasitism cannot be carried on indefinitely if there is to be any reference at all.

For this reason it is no answer at all to the question of what if anything is the sense of a proper name "X" to say its sense or part of its sense is "called X". One might as well say that part of the meaning of "horse" is "called a horse". It is really quite amazing how often this mistake is made.[19]

Perhaps equally amazing is that Kripke makes this same point,[20] even using the same example of "horse" as if it were an objection or difficulty for the description theory, when in fact it was one of the fundamental theses of the theory, at least in its recent formulations. Notice, however, that the above passage does not imply that one cannot refer to an object by a name "N" when the only identifying description one has of the object is "called "N"", rather it says that this by itself cannot be a complete account of how proper names refer, for such identifying descriptions are dependent on there being some other identifying descriptions of a completely different sort. The polemical aim of the passage was to attack the standard logic textbook view, not for giving a false account of how reference is secured but for giving an account which is incomplete and lacking in explanatory power. Often, in fact, one does make what I called parasitic references using a proper name: often the only identifying description one associates with a name "N" is simply the "object called N in my community or by my interlocutors". In such a case, my use of the name is parasitic on other speakers' use of the name in the sense that my reference, using a name to which I can attach only the Intentional content "called N", is successful only if there are now or have been other people who use or have used the name "N" and attach a semantic or Intentional content of a completely different sort. (And remember, "identifying description" does not imply "in words", it simply means: Intentional content, including Network and Background, sufficient to identify the object, and that content may or may not be in words.) Thus, for example, if all I know about Plotinus is that I have heard other people talk about somebody using the name "Plotinus", I can still refer to Plotinus using "Plotinus", but my ability to do that is parasitic on other speakers.

Frege's account, then, is the most promising, and it was that account I sought to develop. Its chief merit is that Frege sees that with proper names, as with any term capable of referring, there must be some Intentional content in virtue of which it refers. Its chief demerits are that he seems to have thought that semantic content was always in words, specifically definite descriptions, and that the description gave a definition or sense of the name. One additional virtue of the Fregean account, and the account I tried to develop, is that they enable us to answer certain puzzling questions concerning the occurrence of proper names in identity statements, in existential statements, and in intensional-with-an-s statements about Intentional states, and, as far as I can see, no causal theorist to date has given a satisfactory answer to these questions.

Now in the light of this brief sketch of the motivations for the descriptivist theory let us have another look at the causal theory. From the point of view of the descriptivist theory, what the causal analysis amounts to is the following: *the "causal chain of communication" is simply a characterization of the parasitic cases seen from an external point of view.* Let me try to make this clear. Kripke says that at each link in the chain of communication the speaker must have the intention, "when I utter "N" I mean to refer to the same object as the person from whom I got the name

'*N*' ". The descriptivist says that one sort of identifying description that one can attach to a name "*N*" is "the person referred to by others in my linguistic community as '*N*' ". Both sides agree that this is not enough by itself: Kripke insists that the chain must terminate in an initial baptism; the descriptivist allows for a variety of ways in which it can terminate, of which an initial baptism is one. Where is the difference? As far as the issue between descriptivism and the causal theory is concerned there is no difference: Kripke's theory is just a variant form of descriptivism. But what about the causal chain? Doesn't the causal theory require an external causal chain that guarantees successful reference? *The external causal chain plays no explanatory role whatever in either Kripke's or Donnellan's account,* as I will explain shortly. The only chain that matters is a transfer of Intentional content from one use of an expression to the next; in every case reference is secured in virtue of descriptivist Intentional content in the mind of the speaker who uses the expression. This will become clearer when we turn to the alleged counterexamples, but you can see it already in Kripke's characterization: Suppose that there is an initial baptism of a mountain with the name '*N*' and then a chain with ten links, each of a person who utters '*N*' intending to use it to refer to whatever the person he got it from used it. Assuming there is no intervening Intentionality, no other beliefs, etc., about *N,* this by itself is sufficient to guarantee that each person refers to the initial target of the baptism solely in virtue of the fact that there is one and only one object that satisfies or fits his or her Intentional content. After the speaker who made the initial baptism, subsequent Intentional contents are parasitic on the prior ones for achieving reference. Of course there will be an external causal characterization of the chain, and an omniscient observer could observe Mr. One talking to Mrs. Two and so on down to Mr. Ten, and he could describe a sequence of events without mentioning any Intentionality, without any mention of descriptive content. But the sequence of features characterized by the external observer are not what secures reference. Reference, for Kripke, is secured entirely by descriptive content.

The way to test which feature is doing the work, descriptive content or causal chain, is to vary one while holding the other constant and see what happens. Suppose that Miss Seven decides to use the name not to refer to the same thing as the person from whom she got it but to refer to her pet poodle instead. Externally described, the chain of communication can be exactly the same: the name "*N*" goes from One to Ten, but the shift in Intentional content means that Seven, Eight, Nine, and Ten are referring to a poodle and not a mountain, solely because the poodle and not the mountain satisfies their identifying description (this is much like the Madagascar example). Or, conversely, imagine that the chain is one of constant descriptive content, each parasitic on the prior speaker back to the initial baptism, but vary the external causal story in any way you like and this still will not affect the reference. Now which is doing the work, Intentionality or "ordinary physical causation"?

In response to the suggestion that the descriptivist can easily accommodate their account, Kripke, Donnellan, and Devitt all insist that on the descriptivist view the speaker would have to remember from whom he got the name. But this seems to me plainly false. I can (and do), for example, make parasitic references using the name "Plotinus" in the manner I considered above without remembering from whom I got the name. I just intend to refer to the same person as the person (whoever that may be) from whom I got the name, in accordance with Kripke's version of descriptivism.

But why does it matter? What difference does it make whether the chain is described by way of Intentional content or external physical causation? Because the issue, to repeat, is whether reference succeeds in virtue of the fact that the object referred to fits or satisfies some associated description or whether reference is achieved by virtue of some facts about the world quite independently of how those facts are represented in the mind: some condition which the utterance of the expression meets which is independent of the contents of any associated description. Kripke and Donnellan claim to be arguing against the conception of reference by way of associated Intentional content and in favor of external causal conditions. I am arguing that to the extent that their account works, it works because it is descriptivist; the external causal chain plays no explanatory role. And I am not saying that their account can be forced into the descriptivist mould, but that when closely scrutinized the very account they offer is descriptivist on its face. We should not be surprised that they have so little to say about causation. It plays no role in their accounts. To see this further let us turn to Donnellan.

Suppose someone says 'Socrates was snub-nosed', and we ask to whom he is referring. The central idea is that this calls for a historical explanation; we search not for an individual who might best fit the speaker's descriptions of the individual to whom he takes himself to be referring . . . but rather for an individual *historically related* to his use of the name 'Socrates' on this occasion. It might be that an omniscient observer of history would see an individual related to an author of dialogues, that one of the central charaters of these dialogues was *modelled* upon that individual, that these dialogues have been handed down and that the speaker has read translations of them, that the speaker's now predicating snub-nosedness of something is *explained* by his having read these translations. . . . 'What individual, if any, would the speaker describe in this way, even perhaps mistakenly?' (my italics).[21]

This passage seems to me to give a very reasonable account—the question it leaves us is: What is the omniscient observer supposed to look for and why? What considerations does he make in deciding "what individual, if any, would the speaker describe in this way"? Since there are an indefinite number of "historical relations" there must be some principle for selecting those that are relevant. What is it? I think that the answer is implicit in the passage. We are to take two sets of Intentional contents as decisive. First, the author of the dialogues *modelled* one of the central characters on an actual individual, that is, the author had a representation of the individual in question and intended the name "Socrates" in the dialogue to refer to him. Second, the speaker, having read the dialogues, intended his use of "Socrates" to refer to the same person that the author of the dialogues referred to. The speaker in his turn will pick up a lot of extra descriptions from the

dialogues and these may or may not be true of the man he is referring to.

Now, if we ask the man, "Whom do you mean by 'Socrates'?", he might give us some of these descriptions, and, as Donnellan points out, these descriptions might not be true of the man referred to as "Socrates" by the author of the dialogues but true of someone else, say the author himself. Suppose the man says, 'By "Socrates" I mean the man who invented the method of dialogue", and suppose the author of the dialogues invented it himself and modestly attributed it to Socrates. Now if we then say, "All the same the man was really referring to the person referred to by the author as 'Socrates' and not to the man who *in fact* invented the dialogue method," we are committed to the view that the speaker's Intentional content, "I am referring to the same man as the author of the dialogues referred to," takes precedence over his content, "I am referring to the inventor of the dialogue method." When he gave us the latter answer, he gave it to us on the assumption that one and the same man satisfied both. If they come apart, that is, if each Intentional content is satisfied by a different person, it is up to the speaker which one takes precedence. The speaker expressed a fragment of his Network of Intentional contents. If that fragment doesn't fit the object which satisfies the rest of the Network, the omniscient observer will, quite reasonably, suppose that the rest of the Network takes precedence. He is referring to the historical Socrates even if he gave a false description, but that supposition is a supposition about how the man's Intentional content determines reference. Thus on both Kripke's and Donnellan's accounts the conditions of successful reference are descriptivist right down to the ground.

IV. DIFFERENCES BETWEEN THE TWO ACCOUNTS

Though both the "descriptivist" and the "causal" theories are at bottom descriptivist, there are still several important differences between them.

1. According to the causal theory the transfer of Intentionality in the chain of communication is really the essence of the institution of proper names. According to the descriptivist it is just an incidental feature. It is not the essential or defin-

ing trait of the institution at all. And the purpose of the parable of the hunter-gatherer community was to make just this point: the tribe has the institution of proper names to refer, but there are no chains of communication, no parasitic references. Another way to make the same point is to see that though parasitic reference is always possible for proper names this sort of parasitism is also possible for any word at all that expresses an Intentional content, including general terms. Consider, for example, the words "structuralism" and "structuralist". For a long time I had only the haziest of ideas what these words meant. I knew that structuralism was some kind of fashionable theory, but that was about the limit of my knowledge. Still, given my Network and Background, I could use the word "structuralism" in a parasitic way; I could, for example, ask, "Are there still a lot of structuralists in France?", or, "Is Pierre a structuralist?" And notice that this parasitism is not restricted to natural kind terms of the sort Putnam talks about. It wasn't a case of identifying passing structuralists ostensively by their surface appearance and hoping that one day scientific investigation would reveal their true nature. As far as this difference between the descriptivist and causal theory is concerned, the argument would appear to favor the descriptivist claim that chains of communication are not the essential feature of the institution of proper names, though both sides would agree that they do in fact commonly occur.

2. The descriptivist finds it very implausible to suppose that in the chains of communication, when they do occur, the only Intentionality which secures reference is that each speaker intends to refer to the same object as the previous speaker. In real life a whole lot of information gets transferred in the chain of communication and some of this information will be relevant to securing reference. For example, the *type* of thing named by the name—whether it is a mountain or a man or a moose or whatever—is generally associated with the name even in the parasitic cases; and if the speaker is wildly mistaken about this we are disinclined to say that he really succeeded in referring. Suppose, for example, that he hears a discussion about Socrates's philosophy of mathematics and he confusedly supposes that "Socrates" is the name of an odd number. Suppose he says "I think Socrates is not a prime but is divisible by 17." He satisfies Kripke's version of the causal theory, but he is not successful in referring to Socrates. Furthermore, where the initial target of the baptism is not identical with the object that satisfies the associated nonparasitic content we don't always construe the reference as going to the initial target. In the Madagascar case, each speaker we suppose intended to refer to the same object as the previous speaker, but Marco Polo introduced some new Intentional content that took precedence over the chain of communication. He identified an island and not a portion of the African continent.

It is a little-noticed but absurd consequence of Kripke's view that it sets no constraints at all on what the name might turn out to refer to. Thus, for example, it might turn out that by "Aristotle" I am referring to a bar stool in Joe's Pizza Place in Hoboken in 1957 if that is what the causal chain happened to lead to. I want to say: by "Aristotle" I couldn't be referring to a bar stool, because that is not what I mean by "Aristotle". And Kripke's remarks about essentialism are not enough to block this result for they are all *de re* necessities attaching to objects themselves but not attaching any restrictive Intentional content to the use of the name. Thus, even if it is a *de re* metaphysical necessity that the actual man had a certain mother and father, that tells us nothing at all about how the name refers to that man and not to a bar stool.

3. In general the descriptivist is inclined to prefer the first-order Intentional content and see the parasitic cases as less important; the causal theorist emphasizes the parasitic identifying description. The germ of truth in the causal theory seems to me this: For names of objects where we are not directly acquainted with the object we will often tend to give precedence to the parasitic Intentional content. For example, for names of remote historical figures, e.g., Napoleon or Socrates, or famous people, e.g., Nixon, given a conflict between the first-order Intentional content and the parasitic we will usually prefer the latter. Why? Because the chain of parasitic Intentionality will get us back to the original target of the baptism and that we

are usually, though not always, inclined to think is what matters. In this respect, proper names differ from general terms. Since the point of having proper names is just to refer to objects, not to describe them, it often doesn't really matter to us much what descriptive content is used to identify the object as long as it identifies the right object, where the "right object" is just the one that other people use the name to refer to.

V. ALLEGED COUNTEREXAMPLES TO DESCRIPTIVISM

With this discussion in mind let us turn to the counterexamples. The counterexamples I have seen to the descriptivist theory fail in general because the authors look only at what the agent might *say* and not at the *total Intentional content* he has in his head, and also because they neglect the role of the Network and the Background. Each counterexample is designed to show that a speaker will refer to an object in the utterance of a name even though the associated definite description is not satisfied by that object or is satisfied by something else or by nothing. I will show that in each case reference is achieved only because the object satisfies the Intentional content in the mind of the speaker.

Example 1: The Gödel/Schmidt Case (Kripke)

The only thing Jones knows or thinks he knows about Kurt Gödel is that he is the author of the famous incompleteness proof. But suppose, in fact, that the proof was written by another man, Schmidt. Now when we ask Jones for an identifying description of "Gödel" he says, "the author of the proof of the incompleteness of arithmetic". But in fact when Jones uses "Gödel" he is referring to Gödel and not to the man who satisfies his description.

It is obvious from what I have said that the correct account of this case is that Jones has quite a bit more Intentional content than just the description he gives. At the very least he has "the man called 'Gödel' in my linguistic community or at least by those from whom I got the name". The reason he doesn't give this as an answer when asked for an identifying descrip-

tion is that he assumes that something more than this is wanted. This much Intentionality is already possessed by whoever asked him for the identifying description.

It is characteristic of these discussions that the authors too seldom give us the sentences in which we are supposed to imagine the same occurring, but if we consider actual sentences, this example could go in either direction. Suppose Jones says, "On line 17 of his proof, Gödel makes what seems to me to be a fallacious inference", and suppose we ask him who he means by "Gödel". He responds, "I mean the author of the famous incompleteness theorem", and we, then, say, "Well, in fact, Gödel did not prove that theorem, it was originally proven by Schmidt". Now what does Jones say? It seems to me that he might well say that by "Gödel" he just means the author of the incompleteness proof regardless of what he is, in fact, called. Kripke concedes that there could be such uses. They involve what I have called secondary aspect uses of proper names.[22] But Jones needn't say that. He might say, "I was referring to the man whom I have heard called 'Kurt Gödel', regardless of whether or not he proved the incompleteness of arithmetic". On the other hand suppose Jones says, "Kurt Gödel lived in Princeton". In this case, it seems to me much more likely that if he finds that Gödel does not satisfy the nonparasitic definite description that he attached to the name he would simply fall back on the parasitic Intentional content that he attaches to the name. But in either case it is the speaker's Intentional content that determines reference. It is not enough to look just at what a speaker says in response to a particular question, one has to look at his total Intentional content, as well as Background capacities associated with a name and at what he would say if informed that different parts of that content were satisfied by different objects. There seems to me nothing in this example that need bother the descriptivist.

Example 2: Thales the Well Digger (Donnellan)[23]

Suppose that all that a certain speaker knows or thinks he knows about Thales is that he is the Greek philosopher who said that all is water.

But suppose there never was a Greek philosopher who said such a thing. Suppose that Aristotle and Herodotus were referring to a well digger who said, "I wish all were water so I wouldn't have to dig these damned wells". In such a case, according to Donnellan, when the speaker uses the name "Thales" he is referring to that well digger. Furthermore, suppose there was a hermit who never had any dealings with anyone, who actually held that all was water. Still, when we say "Thales" we are plainly not referring to that hermit.

There are really two aspects to this argument: one about the hermit, the other about the well digger. On the surface, the well digger case is formally similar to the Gödel/Schmidt case. The speaker always has his parasitic Intentional content to fall back on if his associated description is satisfied by some object that doesn't fit the rest of his Intentional content. However, this case also raises the separate issue of how the Network of the speaker's beliefs will set some further constraints on the chain of parasitic Intentionality. Suppose that Herodotus had heard a frog at the bottom of a well making croaking noises that sounded like the Greek for "all is water"; suppose further that this frog is a family pet named "Thales", and that this incident is the origin of the view that somebody held that all is water. When I use the name "Thales", taking myself to be referring to a Greek philosopher, am I referring to that frog? I think not. Similar doubts could be raised about the well digger: I can think of sentences where I would be inclined to say that I was referring to the well digger and other sentences in which I would be inclined to say that I failed to refer to anyone because there was no such person as Thales the philosopher. But in the cases in which I am referring to a well digger I do so because the well digger satisfies enough of my descriptive content; in particular, he satisfies the content, "The person referred to as 'Thales' by the people from whom I got this use of the name", that is, he satisfies the parasitic Intentional content of the sort we mentioned before. In the case of the hermit, the reason we feel no inclination at all to say we are referring to him with the name "Thales" is that he does not satisfy the condition of fitting into the relevant Network of Intentionality. When we say "Thales is the Greek philosopher who held that all is water", we don't just mean *anybody* who held that all is water, we mean that person who was known to other Greek philosophers as arguing that all is water, who was referred to in his time or subsequently by some Greek variant or predecessor of the expression we now pronounce as "Thales", whose works and ideas have come down to us posthumously through the writings of other authors, and so on. Now, to repeat, in all these cases there will be an external causal account of how we got that information, but what secures reference is not the external causal chain, but the sequence of the transfer of Intentional contents. The reason we are not tempted to allow the hermit to qualify as Thales is that he simply does not fit into the Network and the Background. This example is somewhat analogous to the example of the humanoid who invented bifocals eighty billion years before Benjamin Franklin was ever alive. When he said Franklin invented bifocals, we meant: relative to our Network and Background.

Example 3: The Two Patches (Donnellan)[24]

Suppose a man sees two identical colored patches on a screen, one above the other. Suppose he names the top one "*A*" and the bottom one "*B*". The only identifying description he can give for *A* is "the one on top". But suppose that, unknown to him, we have given him inverting lenses so that the one he thinks is on top is really on the bottom and vice versa. In such a case the identifying description he can give is actually false of the object referred to, yet his reference to *A* is nonetheless successful.

I will deal with this example rather swiftly. *A* is the one he actually sees right *there*. It is the one causing *this* visual experience. You couldn't ask for a better 'identifying description' than that. Expressions like "the one on top" are strictly for public consumption, and though one can imagine cases in which they would take precedence over the Intentional presentation, in most cases the presentational content either in perception or in memory is sufficient to pick out *A*. But suppose that he forgets that he saw it. Suppose he even forgets that he thought it was on top. He just remembers that the name named a patch. Can't he still use the name to refer to the patch? Of course. There is no reason why a parasitic Intentional content might not depend on one's own earlier Intentional contents. Now A is just identified as "the one I was previously able to identify as '*A*'", a limiting case, perhaps, but nonetheless a possible one.

Example 4: The Twin Earth (Putnam et al.)[25]

The correct account of how a name secures reference for us here on earth cannot be that it does it by way of an associated descriptive content, because if there were a twin earth our names would still refer to objects on our earth and not to objects on twin earth, even though any description of an object on earth would equally well fit its Doppelgänger on twin earth. In order to account for how reference thus succeeds unambiguously on earth we have to recognize the role of external causal links between utterances and objects.

I have already answered this sort of objection in Chapter 2 [of *Intentionality*] concerning perception and in Chapter 8 concerning indexical expressions. For the case of proper names it suffices to say that the causal self-referentiality of all perceptual forms of Intentionality, the self-referentiality of indexical forms of Intentionality, and in general the way we are indexically related to our own Intentional contents, including the Network and Background, is sufficient to block any possible twin earth ambiguities. We can see this even in the parasitic cases. When, for example, I say that the only description I associate with "Plotinus" is "called Plotinus", I don't mean just any object ever called "Plotinus" by someone. I mean, inter alia, rather the *person* that *I* have heard and read referred to as Plotinus. The fact that a Doppelgänger on twin earth could also be called "Plotinus" is as irrelevant as the fact that somebody might have (and no doubt somebody has) named his dog "Plotinus", or that many other people have been called "Plotinus".

VI. MODAL ARGUMENTS

This book is about Intentionality and not about modality, and I have therefore avoided the

modal issues up to this point. However, some philosophers think that Kripke's modal arguments are decisive against any version of descriptivism, so I will therefore digress at least briefly to consider them.

Frege had argued that the definite description that a speaker associated with a proper name provided the "sense", in his technical meaning of that word, of the proper name for that speaker. I argued against Frege that the associated definite description couldn't provide a sense or definition of the proper name because that would have as consequence that, for example, it was an analytic necessity that Aristotle was the most famous teacher of Alexander, if a speaker associated the definite description, "the most famous teacher of Alexander the Great", as the sense of the proper name "Aristotle". I argued that the associated cluster of Intentional contents that speakers associate with a proper name is related to the name by some much weaker relation than definition, and that this approach would preserve the virtues of Frege's account while avoiding its absurd consequences. Kripke begins his criticism of my account by distinguishing descriptivism construed as a theory of reference from descriptivism construed as a theory of meaning, and by claiming that if descriptivism is construed only as a theory of reference, a theory of how reference with proper names is secured, then it is unable to provide a Fregean solution to the puzzles concerning proper names in identity statements, existential statements, and statements concerning propositional attitudes. He doesn't say anything in support of this latter claim, and in any case it seems to me plainly false. I try to show that proper names don't have definitions in the usual sense but that reference is secured by an associated Intentional content. Thus, in Kripke's terms I am providing a theory of reference but not a theory of meaning. However, the distinction is not as sharp as he suggests, for the following reason: the Intentional content associated with a proper name can figure as part of the *propositional content* of a statement made by a speaker using that name, even though the speaker's associated Intentional content is not part of the *definition* of the name. And that is why one can provide a descriptivist theory of how proper names secure reference (and hence give a theory of reference and not a theory of meaning for proper names) while at the same time showing that the methods by which proper names secure reference explain how the meaning of utterances made using those names contains descriptive content (and hence give an account of names which has consequences for the meanings of propositions containing those names). For example, on the descriptivist account a speaker can believe that Hesperus shines near the horizon while not believing that Phosphorus shines near the horizon, even though Hesperus and Phosphorus are identical. A speaker can consistently believe this if he associates independent Intentional contents with each name, even though in neither case does the Intentional content provide a definition of the name. The cluster theory, so-called, is able to account for such puzzles while at the same time advancing the theory as an account of how reference is secured and not as an account of meaning in the strict and narrow Fregean sense.

Indeed the account I am providing suggests the direction for a solution to Kripke's "puzzle about belief".[26] Here is the puzzle: Suppose a bilingual speaker, not knowing that "Londres" and "London" name the same city, sincerely asserts in French "Londres est jolie" and yet also sincerely asserts in English "London is not pretty". Does he or does he not believe that London is pretty? The first step in solving the puzzle is to note that because the speaker associates different Intentional contents with "Londres" and "London" the contribution that each word makes to the proposition in the man's head is different and therefore he believes two propositions which, though they cannot both be true (because they refer to the same object and attribute inconsistent properties to it), are not contradictories. The case is analogous to the Hesperus-Phosphorus example.[27]

The main modal argument used against my account is the rigid designator argument. In its crudest versions the argument goes as follows:

(1) Proper names are rigid designators.
(2) Definite descriptions are not rigid designators; and, by parity of reasoning, Intentional contents are not rigid designators.

Therefore:

(3) Proper names are not equivalent in meaning or sense or functioning to definite descriptions or Intentional contents of any sort.

Even if we grant the first premise for the sake of the discussion, it seems to me the argument fails for two reasons. First, some definite descriptions are indeed rigid designators. Indeed, any definite description that expresses identity conditions for the object, that is, any description which specifies features which determine the identity of the object will be a rigid designator. Any description expressing properties necessary and sufficient for, for example, being identical with Aristotle, will be a rigid designator. Indeed, it was this feature that I was trying to get at in my earliest discussion of proper names when I said the question of the rule for using a name must be connected to the question of the *identity* of the object.[28] But second, and more important for this discussion, any definite description at all can be treated as a rigid designator by indexing it to the actual world. I can, by simple fiat, decide to use the expression "The inventor of bifocals" in such a way that it refers to the actual person who invented bifocals and continues to refer to that very person in any possible world, even in a possible world in which he did not invent bifocals.[29] Such a use of the definite description will always take wide scope or will be in a sense scopeless in the way that is characteristic of proper names. Since any definite description whatever can be made into a rigid designator, it does not show that the functioning of proper names differs from the function of definite descriptions to show that proper names are always (or almost always) rigid designators and definite descriptions are in general not rigid designators.

VII. HOW DO PROPER NAMES WORK?

I said at the beginning that the answer to this question ought to be fairly easy, and I think it is provided that we keep certain principles in mind. The facts we seek to explain are: Names are used to refer to objects. In general, the contribution that a name makes to the truth conditions of statements is simply that it is used to refer to an object. But there are some statements where the contribution of the name is not, or is not solely, that it is used to refer to an object: in identity statements, in existential statements, and in statements about Intentional states. Furthermore, a name is used to refer to the same object in different possible worlds where it has different properties from those it has in the actual world.

The principles we need to keep in mind when we explain these facts are:

1. In order that a name should ever come to be used to refer to an object in the first place there must be some independent representation of the object. This may be by way of perception, memory, definite description, etc., but there must be enough Intentional content to identify which object the name is attached to.

2. Once the connection between name and object has been set up, speakers who have mastered the Background practice of using names may make use of the fact that the connection between name and object has been set up, without knowing anything more about the object. Provided they don't have any Intentional content wildly inconsistent with the facts about the object, their only Intentional content might be that they are using the name to refer to what others are using it to refer to, but such cases are parasitic on the nonparasitic forms of identification of the object.

3. All reference is in virtue of Intentional content (broadly construed), whether the reference is by way of names, descriptions, indexicals, tags, labels, pictures, or whatever. The object is referred to only if it fits or satisfies some condition or set of conditions expressed by or associated with the device that is used to refer to it. In the limiting case these conditions may be simple Background capacities for recognition, as, for example, in the case we considered in Chapter 2 where the only Intentional content that a man had associated with the name was simply his capacity to recognize the bearer, or they may be parasitic Intentional contents of the sort described in principle 2. Principles 1 and 2 are simply applications of principle 3.

4. What counts as an object and hence as a possible target for naming and referring is always determined relative to a system of representation. Given that we have a system rich enough to individuate objects (e.g., rich enough to count one horse, a second horse, a third horse . . .), and to identify and reidentify objects (e.g., rich enough to determine what must be the case if that is to be the *same horse* as the one we saw yesterday), we can then attach names to objects in such a way as to preserve the attachment of the same names to the same objects, even in counterfactual situations where the Intentional content associated with the name is no longer satisfied by the object. Principles 1, 2, and 3 only have application in a representational system which satisfies principle 4.

I believe these principles explain the facts we mentioned above. The whole purpose of having the institution of proper names is to enable us to refer to objects, but since there will be some Intentional content associated with a name, this Intentional content can figure as part of the propositional content of a statement made using a name in identity statements, in existential statements, and in statements about Intentional states, even though the normal and primary function is not to express Intentional content but just to refer to objects, and even though the associated Intentional content is not part of the definition of the name. And the explanation of the fact that names can be introduced by and used with an Intentional content which is not a rigid designator, and still the name can be used as a rigid designator, is simply that we have a notion of the identity of an object which is separable from those particular Intentional contents which are used to identify the object. Thus, for example, we have a notion of *the same man* which is independent of such descriptions as the author of the *Odyssey*. We can then use the name "Homer" to refer to the man who was the actual author of the *Odyssey* even in possible worlds where Homer did not write the *Odyssey*.

Part of the appearance that there is something especially problematic about these rather simple explanations is that there is a family of different sorts of cases in which these principles operate. First, the central cases. The most important and extensive use of names for each of us is of people, places, etc., with which we are in daily, or at least frequent, personal contact. Baptism apart, one originally learns these names from other people, but, once learned, the name is associated with such a rich collection of Intentional contents in the Network that one does not depend on other people to determine which object one is referring to. Think, for example, of the names of your close friends and family members, of the town where you live or the streets in your neighborhood. Here there is no question of any chain of communication. Examples of such names for me would be "Berkeley, California" or "Alan Code".

Second, there are names which have prominent uses, where the uses are not based on acquaintance with the object. The Intentional content associated with these names is for the most part derived from other people, but it is rich enough to qualify as *knowledge about* the object. Examples for me would be such names as "Japan" or "Charles de Gaulle". In such cases, the Intentional content is rich enough so that it sets very strong constraints on the sort of things that could be referred to by my uses of the names. For example, regardless of the chain of communication, it couldn't turn out that by "de Gaulle" I am referring to a Florentine tapestry, or by "Japan" I am referring to a butterfly.

Third, there are uses of names where one is almost totally dependent on other people's prior usage to secure reference. It is these cases that I have described as parasitic, for in these cases the speaker does not have enough Intentional content to qualify as knowledge about the object. The object may not even be generally referred to by the name that he has acquired for it. For me such a name would be "Plotinus". Even in these cases the limited Intentional content places some constraints on the type of object named. In my use, Plotinus couldn't have turned out to be a prime number.

NOTES

1. See John R. Searle, "Referential and Attributive," in *Expression and Meaning* (Cambridge: Cambridge University Press, 1979), pp. 137–61.
2. In what follows in this chapter I will use "Intentional content" broadly so as to include relevant elements of the Network and Background.
3. Keith Donnellan recognizes the inappropriateness of the label for his views. Cf. "Speaking of Nothing," *The Philosophical Review*, 83 (January 1974), pp. 3–32; reprinted in S. P. Schwartz, ed., *Naming,*

Necessity and Natural Kinds (Ithaca and London: Cornell University Press, 1977), pp. 216–44.
4. In, e.g., *Speech Arts* (Cambridge: Cambridge University Press, 1969), p. 90.
5. The term, I believe, was first used by H. P. Grice in "Vacuous Names," in Davidson and Hintikka, eds., *Words and Objections* (Dordrecht: Reidel, 1969), pp. 118–45.
6. Saul Kripke, "Naming and Necessity," in G. Harman and D. Davidson, eds., *Semantics of Natural Language* (Dordrecht: Reidel, 1972), p. 300.
7. Kripke, op. cit. p. 302.
8. M. Devitt, *Designation* (Chicago: University of Chicago Press, 1981), esp. chapter 2, pp. 25–64.
9. Kripke, op. cit., p. 300.
10. Donnellan, op. cit., p. 229.
11. Gareth Evans, "The Causal Theory of Names," *Proceedings of the Aristotelian Society,* suppl. vol. 47, pp. 187–208; reprinted in Schwartz, ed., op. cit., pp. 192–215. [Reprinted in this volume.]
12. David Kaplan, "Bob and Carol and Ted and Alice," in K. J. Hintikka et al., eds., *Approaches to Natural Language* (Dordrecht and Boston: Reidel, 1973), pp. 490–518.
13. For reasons we will shortly investigate, this description is parasitic on other speakers, but it is nonetheless sufficient to identify about whom we are talking.
14. I am indebted to Jim Stone for discussion of this point.
15. In Schwartz, ed., op. cit., p. 232.
16. Evans, op. cit., gives several examples of this sort.
17. It does not, of course, set up a definition, for reasons I gave in "Proper Names," *Mind,* 67 (1958), pp. 166–73.
18. Op. cit.
19. Op. cit., pp. 170–171.
20. Kripke, op. cit., pp. 283–84.
21. Donnellan, op. cit., pp. 229–30.
22. "Referential and Attributive," in *Expression and Meaning,* p. 148.
23. Keither Donnellan, "Proper Names and Identifying Descriptions," *Synthese,* 21 (1970), pp. 335–58.
24. Ibid., pp. 347ff.
25. Hilary Putnam, "The Meaning of 'Meaning'," in *Philosophical Papers,* vol. 2, *Mind, Language and Reality* (Cambridge: Cambridge University Press, 1975), pp. 215–71.
26. Saul Kripke, "A Puzzle about Belief," in A. Margalit, ed., *Meaning and Use* (Dordrecht: Reidel, 1976), pp. 239–83. [Reprinted in this volume.]
27. Kripke considers the approach I suggest but rejects it on what I believe are inadequate grounds. He thinks that the same puzzle could arise if the speaker associated the same "identifying properties" with each name without knowing that they were the same. The speaker thinks, for example, in English "London is in England", and in French "Londres est en Angleterre", without knowing that England is Angleterre. But once again if we look at the total Intentional content we suppose is in the man's head in order to imagine him saying "Londres est jolie"

and simultaneously "London is not pretty", we must suppose that he has different Intentional contents associated with "London" and "Londres". At the very least we must suppose that he thinks they are two *different cities* and that, by itself, has all sorts of ramifications in his network: e.g., he thinks "is identical with Londres" to be false of the town he refers to as "London", while true of that town he refers to as "Londres"; he thinks London and Londres have different locations on the surface of the earth, different inhabitants, etc. The moral as usual is: to resolve the puzzle don't just look at the sentences he utters, look at the total Intentional content in the man's head.

28. In *Mind* (1958), op. cit.

29. A similar point is made by D. Kaplan with his notion of "Dthat" ("Dthat," in P. Cole, ed., *Syntax and Semantics,* vol. 9 (New York: 1978) [reprinted in this volume], and by A. Plantinga with his notion of an "Alpha transform," in "The Boethian Compromise," *American Philosophical Quarterly,* 15, (April 1978), pp. 129–38.

25 Dthat

DAVID KAPLAN

Donnellan, in "Reference and Definite Descriptions" says, "Using a definite description referentially a speaker may say something true even though the description correctly applies to nothing."[1] His example—taken from Linsky[2]—has someone saying of a spinster:

Her husband is kind to her

after having had Mr. Jones—actually the spinster's brother—misintroduced as the spinster's husband. And—to fill it out—having noticed Jones' solicitous attention to his sister. The speaker used the nondenoting description "Her husband" to refer to Mr. Jones. And so, what he said was true.

There are a lot of entities associated with the utterance of "Her husband is kind to her" which are commonly said to have been said: tokens, types, sentences, propositions, statements, etc. The something-true-said, Donnellan calls a *statement*.

On the other hand, "If . . . the speaker has just met the lady and, noticing her cheerfulness and radiant good health, made his remark from his conviction that these attributes are always the result of having good husbands, he would be using the definite description attributively."[3]

After pointing out that "in general, whether or not a definite description is used referentially or attributively is a function of the speaker's intentions in a particular case,"[4] he mentions that according to Russell's theory of descriptions, the use of *the* ϕ might be thought of as involving reference "in a very weak sense . . . to *whatever* is the one and only one ϕ, if there is any such."[5] Donnellan then concludes:

Now this is something we might well say about the attributive use of definite descriptions. . . . But this lack of particularity is absent from the referential use of definite descriptions precisely because the description is here merely a device for getting one's audience

Do not partake in this article before reading the following Warning: This paper was prepared for and read at the 1970 Stanford Workshop on Grammar and Semantics. Peter Cole has persuaded me—against my better judgement—that it has aged long enough to be digestible. The paper has not been revised other than to remove the subtitle comment "[Stream of Consciousness Draft: Errors, confusions, and disorganizations are not to be taken seriously]." That injunction must still be strictly obeyed. Some parts of this ramble are straightened out in the excessive refinements of "Bob and Carol and Ted and Alice" (which appeared in the proceedings for which this was destined). A more direct presentation of the resulting theory along with some of its applications is to be found in my *Demonstratives*. An intermediate progress report occurs in "On the Logic of Demonstratives." "DTHAT" is pronounced as a single syllable.
From *Syntax and Semantics*, volume 9, Peter Cole, ed. (New York: Academic Press, 1978), pp. 221–253.

to pick out or think of the thing to be spoken about, a device which may serve its function even if the description is incorrect. More importantly perhaps, in the referential use as opposed to the attributive, there is a right thing to be picked out by the audience, and its being the right thing is not simply a function of its fitting the description.[6]

Donnellan develops his theory by adducing a series of quite plausible examples to help him answer certain theoretical questions, e.g., are there sentences in which the contained definite description can only be used referentially (or only attributively)? Can reference fail when a definite description is used referentially?, etc.

In my own reading and rereading of Donnellan's article I always find it both fascinating and maddening. Fascinating, because the fundamental distinction so clearly reflects an accurate insight into language use, and maddening, because: first, the examples seem to me to alternate between at least two clearly discriminable concepts of *referential use;* second, the notion of *having someone in mind* is not analyzed but used; and third, the connections with the developed body of knowledge concerning intensional logics—their syntax and semantics—are not explicitly made, so we cannot immediately see what Donnellan and intensional logic have to offer each other, if anything.

As one of the body developers, I find this last snub especially inexcusable. This is not a divergent perception for those of my ilk. Hintikka remarks (plaintively?), "The only thing I miss in Donnellan's excellent paper is a clear realization that the distinction he is talking about is only operative in contexts governed by propositional attitudes or other modal terms."[7]

Hintikka's remark is at first surprising, since none of Donnellan's examples seem to have this form. But the remark falls into place when we recognize that Donnellan is concerned essentially with a given speaker who is *asserting* something, *asking* something, or *commanding* something. And thus if we pull back and focus our attention on the sentence *describing* the speech act:

John asserted that Mary's husband is kind to her "the intentional operator appears."

Probably Hintikka wanted to argue that the sentence:

Her husband is kind to her

is not itself ambiguous in the way that, say:

Every boy kissed a girl

is. The fact that an ambiguous sentence is produced by embedding ϕ in some sentential context (for example, an intensional or temporal operator) should not be construed to indicate an ambiguity in ϕ. For were it so, (almost?) all sentences would be ambiguous.

Donnellan's distinction is a contribution to the redevelopment of an old and commonsensical theory about language which—at least in the philosophical literature—has rather been in a decline during the ascendency of semantics over epistemology of the 1930s, '40s, and '50s. The commonsense theory is one that Russell wrestled with in *The Principles of Mathematics*[8] but seemed to reject in "On Denoting."[9] This theory asserts roughly that the correct analysis of a typical speech act, for example,

John is tall

distinguishes *who* is being talked about, i.e. the individual under consideration—here, John—from *how* he is being characterized—here, as tall.

Russell's analysis of the proposition expressed by

John is tall

provides it with two components: the property expressed by the predicate is tall, and the individual John. That's right, John himself, right there, trapped in a proposition.

During the Golden Age of Pure Semantics we were developing a nice homogeneous theory, with language, meanings, and entities of the world each properly segregated and related one to another in rather smooth and comfortable ways. This development probably came to its peak in Carnap's *Meaning and Necessity.*[10] Each *designator* has both an intension and an extension. Sentences have truth-values as extensions and propositions as intensions, predicates have classes as extensions and properties as intensions, terms have individuals as extensions and *individual concepts* as intensions, and so on. The intension of a compound is a function of the intensions of the parts and similarly the extension (except when intensional operators appear). There is great beauty and power in this theory.

But there remained some nagging doubts: proper names, demonstratives, and quantification into intensional contexts.

Proper names may be a practical convenience in our mundane transactions, but they are a theoretician's nightmare. They are like bicycles. Everyone easily learns to ride, but no one can correctly explain how he does it. Completely new theories have been proposed within the last few years, in spite of the fact that the subject has received intense attention throughout this century, and in some portions of Tibet people have had proper names for even longer than that.

The main difficulty has to do, I believe, with the special intimate relationship between a proper name and its bearer. Russell said that in contrast with a common noun, like "unicorn," a proper name *means* what it names. And if it names nothing, it means nothing. In the case of "unicorn" we have a meaning, perhaps better a *descriptive meaning,* which we make use of in looking for such things. But in the case of the name "Moravcsik" there is just Moravcsik. There is no basis on which to ask whether Moravcsik exists. Such a question is—for Russell—meaningless. But people persist in asking this question. Maybe not this very question, but analogous ones like:

Does Santa Claus exist?

There were other apparent difficulties in Russell's theory. The astronomical discovery that Hesperus was identical with Phosphorus became a triviality. The sentence expressing it expressed the same proposition as "Hesperus is identical with Hesperus." Furthermore, although the bearer of a given proper name is the be-all and end-all of the name's semantic relata, almost every proper name has dozens of bearers.

And then there are the unforgivable distortions of the minimal descriptive content of proper names. We all know of butchers named "Baker" and dogs named "Sir Walter." The ultimate in such perversity occurs in titles of the top administrative officers at UCLA. We have four vice-chancellors at UCLA, one of whom has the title "The Vice-Chancellor."

All in all, proper names are a mess and if it weren't for the problem of how to get the kids to come in for dinner, I'd be inclined to just junk them.

At any rate, the attempt during the Golden Age was to whip proper names into line. In fact into the line of common nouns. People do ask:

Does Santa Claus exist?

So that must mean something like:

Does a unicorn exist?

They do ask:

Is Hesperus identical with Phosphorus?

So that must mean something like:

Are bachelors identical with college graduates?

Thus was waged a war of attrition against proper names. Many were unmasked as disguised descriptions, e.g. "Aristotle" means *the student of Plato and teacher of Alexander who. . . .*—not an unreasonable proposal.

However, some of these exposés did seem a bit oppressive, e.g. Russell's suggestion that:

Scott is Sir Walter

really means:

The person named "Scott" is the person named "Sir Walter"

followed by his nonchalant remark: "This is a way in which names are frequently used in practice, and there will, as a rule, be nothing in the phraseology to show whether they are being used in this way or as names."[11] But at least they isolated the few real troublemakers—who turned out not to be our good old proper names at all but a handful of determined outside demonstratives: "this," "that," etc.

In summary, the technique was first to expose a proper name as a disguised description (sometimes on tenuous and unreliable evidence) and then ruthlessly to eliminate it.

We thus reduce the exciting uncertainties of:

Socrates is a man

to the banality of:

All men are mortal

The demonstratives were still there, but they were so gross they could be ignored.

Lately, under the pressure of the new interest in singular propositions generated by intensional logic, the verities of the Golden Age are breaking down. Once logicians became interested in formalizing a logic of necessity, belief, knowledge, assertion, etc., traditional syntactical ways quickly led to formulas like

John asserted that x is a spy

with free 'x' and then with 'x' bound to an anterior operator. Under what circumstances does a given individual, taken as value of 'x', satisfy this formula? Answer: If the appropriate singular proposition was the content of John's assertive utterance.

It seems that in at least certain speech acts, what I am trying to express can't quite be put into words. It is that proposition of Russell's with John trapped in it.

The property of being tall is exactly expressed by "is tall," and the concept of the unique spy who is shorter than all other spies is exactly expressed by "the shortest spy"; but no expression exactly expresses John. An expression may express a concept or property that, in reality, only John satisfies. There are many such distinct concepts; none of which is John himself.

I would like to distinguish between the kind of propositions which were considered by Aristotle (*all S is P, some S is not P*, etc.) and the kind of proposition considered by the early Russell. I call the former *general propositions* and the latter *singular propositions*. Suppose, just for definiteness, that we fix attention on sentences of simple subject-predicate form. The following are examples:

(1) A spy is suspicious.
(2) Every spy is suspicious.
(3) The spy is suspicious.
(4) John is suspicious.

Now let us think of the proposition associated with each sentence as having two components. Corresponding to the predicate we have the property of being suspicious; and corresponding to the subject we have either what Russell

in 1903 called a *denoting concept* or an individual. Let us take the proposition to be the ordered couple of these two components.

Again, to fix ideas, let us provide a possible-world style of interpretation for these notions. We think of each total or complete possible state of affairs as a possible world. The possible worlds are each continuants through time and may in fact overlap at certain times. For example, a possible world may agree with the actual world up to the time at which some individual made a particular decision; the possible world may then represent an outcome of a decision other than the one actually taken. (In science fiction, such cases are called *alternate time lines*.)

Within this framework we can attempt to represent a number of the semantic notions in question. We might represent the property of *being suspicious* by that function P which assigns to each possible world w and each time t the set of all those individuals of w which, in w, are suspicious at t. We might represent the denoting concepts expressed by the denoting phrases 'A spy', 'Every spy', and 'The spy' as, say, the ordered couples: $<$'A',$S>$, $<$'Every',$S>$, $<$'The', $S>$ where S is the property (represented as above) of *being a spy*.[12] The fact that the logical words 'A', 'Every', and 'The' are just carried along reflects our treatment of them as *syncategorematic*, i.e. as having no independent meaning but as indicators of how to combine the meaning-bearing parts (here "spy" and the predicate) in determining the meaning of the whole. For (1), (2), and (3) the corresponding propositions are now represented by:

(5) $<<$'A',$S>P>$
(6) $<<$'Every',$S>P>$
(7) $<<$'The',$S>P>$

It should be clear that each of (5)–(7) will determine a function which assigns to each possible world w and time t a truth value. And in fact the truth value so assigned to any w and t will be exactly the truth value in w at t of the corresponding sentence. For example: (6) determines that function which assigns truth to a given w and t if and only if every member of $S(w,t)$ is a member of $P(w,t)$. Notice that the function so determined by (6) also correctly assigns to each w and t the truth value in w at t of (2). (For the purpose of (7), let us take * to be a "truth value" which is assigned to w and t when $S(w,t)$ contains other than a single member.)

The proposition corresponding to (4) would be:

(8) $<$John,$P>$

not $<$'John',$P>$ mind you, but $<$John,$P>$. And (8) will determine that function F which assigns Truth to w and t if and only if John is a member of $P(w,t)$. If John is an individual of w at the time t (i.e. John exists in w and is alive at t) but is not a member of $P(w,t)$, then $F(w,t)$ is falsehood; and if John is not an individual of w at the time t, then $F(w,t)$ is *.

This brief excursion into possible-world semantics is only to fix ideas in a simple way within that framework (I will later make further use of the framework) and is not put forward as an ideal (in any sense: generalizability, elegance, etc.) representation of the semantic notions of property, proposition, denoting concept, etc. My main motivation is to present a representation which will clearly distinguish singular and general propositions.

It would, of course, have been possible to supply a representation of the proposition expressed by (4) which is, in a sense, formally equivalent to (8) and which blurs the distinction I wish to emphasize. I do it now lest anyone think that the possibility is a relevant refutation of my later remarks. Let us clearly depart from Russell by associating a denoting concept:

(9) $<$'Proper Name',$J>$

where J is what we might call *John's essence,* the property of *being John,* namely, that function which assigns to each possible world w and time t the set {John} if John is an individual of w and is alive in w at t and the empty set otherwise. The analogue to (8) is now

(10) $<<$'Proper Name',$J> P>$

It will be noted that we have now treated the proper name "John" rather like the definite description "The John," in which the proper name plays the role of a common noun. Accordingly the function from possible worlds and times to truth values which is determined by (10) is identical with that determined by:

(11) $<<$'The',$J> P>$

There are certainly other representations of these propositions which ally various subgroups. In fact, once any formal structure is established, the production of isomorphic structures satisfying specified "internal" conditions is largely a matter of logical ingenuity of the "pure" kind.[13]

To return to the point, I have represented propositions in a way which emphasizes the singular-general distinction, because I want to revive a view of language alternate to that of the Golden Age. The view of the Golden Age is, I believe, undoubtedly correct for a large portion of language behavior, in particular, communication by means of general propositions. But the alternate view accounts for a portion of language behavior not accommodated by the view of the Golden Age.

The alternate view is: *that some or all of the denoting phrases used in an utterance should not be considered part of the content of what is said but should rather be thought of as contextual factors which help us interpret the actual physical utterance as having a certain content.* The most typical of such contextual factors is the fact that the speaker's utterance is to be taken as an utterance of some specific language, say, English. When I utter "yes," which means *yes* in English and *no* in Knoh, you must know I am speaking Knoh to know I have said *no.* It is no *part* of what I have said that I am speaking Knoh, though Knoh being a complete tongue, I could add that by uttering "I am speaking English." Such an utterance is of doubtful utility in itself; but, fortunately, there are other means by which this fact can be ascertained by my auditor, e.g. by my general physical appearance, or, if I am not a native Knoh, by my pointing to Knoh on a celestial globe. A homelier example has a haberdasher utter to a banker, "I am out of checks." Whether the utterance takes place in the store or at the bank will help the banker determine what the haberdasher has said. In either case it is no *part* of what was said that the haberdasher used "checks" to mean bank checks rather than suits with a checkered pattern. Of course the haberdasher could go on, if he desired, to so comment on his past performance, but that would be to say something else. Still closer to home is my wife's utterance: "It's up to you to punish Jordan for what happened today." It is by means of various subtle contextual clues that I understand her to be charging me to administer discipline to our son and not to be calling on me to act where the United Nations has failed. Again, should I exhibit momentary confusion she might, by a comment, a gesture, or simply some more discourse on the relevant naughtiness, assist me in properly decoding her first utterance so that I could understand what she was, in fact, saying. There are other ways—more controversial than the intentional resolution of the reference of a proper name among the many persons so dubbed—in which contextual factors determine the content of an utterance containing a proper name; but I am reserving all but the most blatantly obvious remarks for later.

Now let us narrow our attention to utterances containing *singular denoting phrases* (i.e. denoting phrases which purport to stand for a unique individual, such as "the spy," "John", "$\sqrt{2}$," etc.).[14]

How can contextual factors determine that part of the content of an utterance which corresponds to a singular denoting phrase? Two ways have already been mentioned: by determining what language is being spoken and by determining which of the many persons so dubbed a proper name stands for. But the most striking way in which such contextual factors enter is in connection with *demonstratives:* "this," "this spy," "that book," etc. In at least some typical uses of these phrases, it is required that the utterance be accompanied by a *demonstration*—paradigmatically, a pointing—which indicates the object for which the phrase stands.[15] I will speak of a *demonstrative use* of a singular denoting phrase when the speaker intends that the object for which the phrase stands be designated by an associated demonstration.[16]

Now we can add another example of a subject-predicate sentence to those of (1)–(4):

(12) He [the speaker points at John] is suspicious.

I am adopting the convention of enclosing a description of the relevant demonstration in square brackets immediately following each denoting phrase which is used demonstratively.[17]

What shall we take as the proposition corresponding to (12) (which I also call the *content* of the *utterance* (12))? In line with our program of studying contextual factors which are not part of what is said but whose role is rather to help us interpret the utterance as *having* a certain content, we shall take the component of the proposition which corresponds to the demonstrative to be the individual demonstrated. Thus the varying *forms* which such a demonstration can take are not reflected in the content of the utterance (i.e. the proposition). The demonstration "gives us" the element of the proposition corresponding to the demonstrative. But *how* the demonstration gives that individual to us is here treated as irrelevant to the content of the utterance; just as the different *ways* by which I might have come to understand which Jordan was relevant to my wife's utterance, or the different *ways* by which one might come to understand that a speaker is speaking Knoh rather than English, do not alter the content of those utterances. Thus, for example, the utterances (in English):

(13) He [the speaker points at John, as John stands on the demonstration platform nude, clean shaven, and bathed in light] is suspicious.
(14) He [the speaker points at John, as John lurks in shadows wearing a trenchcoat, bearded, with his hat pulled down over his face] is suspicious.

are taken, along with other refinements of (12), as expressing the same proposition, namely:

(15) <John, *P*>.

It should immediately be apparent that we are in store for some delightful anomalies. Erroneous beliefs may lead a speaker to put on a demonstration which does not demonstrate what he thinks it does, with the result that he will be under a misapprehension as to *what* he has said. Utterances of identity sentences containing one or more demonstratives may express necessary propositions, though neither the speaker nor his auditors are aware of it. In fact, we get extreme cases in which linguistic competence is simply insufficient to completely determine the content of what is said. Of course this was already established by the case of the Knoh-English translation problem, but the situation is more dramatic using the demonstratives.

The present treatment is not inevitable. An alternative is to incorporate the demonstration in the proposition. We would argue as follows: Frege's *sense and denotation* distinction[18] can be extended to all kinds of indicative devices. In each case we have the object indicated (the "denotation") and the manner of indication (the "sense"). It is interesting to note that (at least in Feigl's translation) Frege wrote of "the sense (connotation, meaning) of the sign in which is contained the *manner and context* of presentation of the denotation of the sign."[19] I think it reasonable to interpret Frege as saying that the sense of a sign is what is grasped by the linguistically competent auditor, and it seems natural to generalize and say that it is the "sense" of the demonstration that is grasped by the competent auditor of utterances containing demonstratives. Thus we see how the drawn-out English utterance:

(16) That [the speaker points at Phosphorus in early morning] is the same planet as that [the speaker points at Hesperus in the early evening].

could be both informative and true.

Let us call the preceding a *Fregean treatment of demonstratives.* It is worth developing (which means primarily working on the ontology (metaphysics?) of demonstrations and the semantics of demonstration descriptions) but, I believe, will ultimately be unsatisfactory. For now I'll just outline some of the reasons. The demonstrative use of demonstratives plays an important role in language learning, in general, in the learning and use of proper names, in our misty use of *de re* modalities, in our better grounded use of what Quine calls the *relational* senses of epistemic verbs (i.e. the senses of

those intensional verbs that permit quantification in).[20] And, in general, I believe that we can sharpen our epistemological insights in a number of areas by taking account of what I call the demonstrative use of expression. Such uses are far more widespread than one imagined.

I earlier called the Fregean treatment of demonstratives "unsatisfactory." I would be more cautious in saying that it was wrong. (Though I do think an empirical argument from linguistic behavior could be developed to show that it is wrong. I take Donnellan's study of the phenomenology of what he calls referential use to be an excellent start in that direction.) What I am confident of is that if we force all phenomena that suggest a special *demonstrative* use of language, along with what I regard as a corresponding feature—a special *singular* form of proposition—into the Fregean mold of linguistic elements with a sense and a denotation, the sense being the element which appears in the proposition (thus leaving us with only general propositions), then important insights will be lost. I don't deny that on a phenomenon-by-phenomenon basis we can (in some sense) keep stretching Frege's brilliant insights to cover. With a little ingenuity I think we *can* do that. But we shouldn't.

Now let me offer a slightly different and somewhat a priori justification for studying the phenomena of demonstrative uses of expressions and singular propositions. I leave aside the question whether we have correctly analyzed any actual linguistic behavior, whether concerned with the so-called demonstrative *phrases* or otherwise.

Having explained so clearly and precisely what such a use of language would amount to, in terms of a possible-world semantics, I can simply resolve to so use the word "that" in the future. At a minimum I could introduce the *new* word "dthat" for the demonstrative use of "that." Couldn't I? I can, and I will. In fact, I do.

I like this intentional (i.e. stipulative) way of looking at the use of "dthat" because I believe that in many cases where there are competing Fregean and demonstrative analyses of some utterances or class of utterances the matter can be resolved simply by the intentions of the speaker (appropriately conveyed to the auditor?). Thus in the case of proper names (to which I will return below) I might simply resolve to use them demonstratively (i.e. as demonstrating the individual whom they are a name of in the nomenclature of an earlier paper[21]) on certain occasions and in a Fregean way[22] on other occasions. Of course one who did not have a clear understanding of the alternatives might have difficulty in characterizing his own use, but once we have explored each choice there is nothing to prevent us from choosing either, "unnatural" though the choice may be.

It should probably be noted that despite the accessibility of the semantics of "dthat" our *grasp* of the singular propositions so expressed is, in John Perry's apt phrase, a bit of *knowledge by description* as compared with our rather more direct acquaintance with the general propositions expressed by nondemonstrative utterances.

Armed with "dthat" we can now explore and possibly even extend the frontiers of demonstrations.

When we considered the Fregean analysis of demonstrations, we attempted to establish parallels between demonstrations and descriptions.[23] Insofar as this aspect of the Fregean program is successful, it suggests the possibility of a demonstrative analysis of descriptions. *If pointing can be taken as a form of describing, why not take describing as a form of pointing?* Note that our demonstrative analysis of demonstrations need not, indeed should not, deny or even ignore the fact that demonstrations have both a sense and a demonstratum. It is just that according to the demonstrative analysis the sense of the demonstration does not appear in the proposition. Instead the sense is used only to fix the demonstratum which itself appears directly in the proposition. I propose now to do the same for descriptions. Instead of taking the sense of the description as subject of the proposition, we use the sense only to fix the denotation which we then take directly as subject component of the proposition. I now take the utterance of the description as a demonstration and describe it with the usual quotation devices, thus:

(17) Dthat ["the spy"] is suspicious.

For fixity of ideas, let us suppose, what is surely false, that in fact, actuality, and reality

there is one and only one spy, and John is he. We might express this so:

(18) "the spy" denotes John.[24]

In the light of (18), (17) expresses:

(19) <John, *P*>

(also known as '(8)' and '(15)').

Recollecting and collecting we have:

(3) The spy is suspicious.
(4) John is suspicious.
(7) <<'The',*S*> *P*>
(12) He [the speaker points at John] is suspicious.

or as we might now write (12):

(20) Dhe [the speaker points at John] is suspicious.[25]

Earlier we said that an utterance of (3) expresses (7), and only an utterance of (12) [i.e. (20)] or possibly (4) expresses (19). I have already suggested that an utterance of (4) may sometimes be taken in a Fregean way to express something like (7), and now I want to point out that for want of "dthat" some speakers may be driven to utter (3) when they intend what is expressed by (17).

If an utterance of (3) may indeed sometimes express (19), then Donnellan was essentially correct in describing his referential and attributive uses of definite descriptions as a "duality of function." And it might even be correct to describe this duality as an *ambiguity* in the sentence type (3). I should note right here that my demonstrative use is not quite Donnellan's referential use—a deviation that I will expatiate on below—but it is close enough for present purposes.

The ambiguity in question here is of a rather special kind. For under no circumstances could the choice of disambiguation for an utterance of (3) affect the truth-value. Still there are two distinct propositions involved, and even two distinct functions from possible worlds and times to truth-values, determined by the two propositions.

Before continuing with the ambiguity in (3), it would be well to interject some remarks on sentence types and sentence tokens (of which utterances are one kind) especially as they relate to demonstratives.

Sentence types vary considerably in the degree to which they contain implicit and explicit references to features of the context of utterance. The references I have in mind here are those that affect the truth-value of the sentence type on a particular occasion of utterance. At one extreme stand what Quine (in *Word and Object*) called *eternal sentences:* those in which the feature linguists call tense does not really reflect a perspective from some point in time, which contain no *indexicals* such as "now," "here," "I," etc., and whose component names and definite descriptions are not understood to require contextual determination as did the "Jordan" of our earlier example. Quine describes such sentences as "those whose truth value stays fixed through time and from speaker to speaker."[26] But I prefer my own vaguer formulation: *those sentences which do not express a perspective from within space-time.* Quine and I would both count "In 1970 American women exceed American men in wealth" as eternal; he would (presumably) also count "The UCLA football team always has, does, and will continue to outclass the Stanford football team" as eternal. I would not.

Truth values are awarded directly to eternal sentences without any relativization to time, place, etc.[27] But for the fugitive sentence no stable truth value can be awarded. Let us consider first tensed sentences, e.g.:

(21) American men will come to exceed American women in intelligence.

Without disputing the facts, if (21) were true at one time, it would fail to be true at some later time. (Since one doesn't come to exceed what one already exceeds.)

Now let's dredge up the possible worlds. We associated with (21) a function which assigns to each possible world and time a truth value. Such a function seems to represent, for reasons which have been much discussed, at least part of the meaning of (21) or part of what we grasp when we understand (21).[28] There is another kind of "content" associated with a fugitive sentence like (21), namely, the content of a particular utterance of (21). In a sense, any particular utterance (token) of a fugitive sentence (type) is an *eternalization* of the fugitive sentence. The

relativization to time is fixed by the time of utterance. We can associate with each utterance of a fugitive sentence the same kind of function from possible worlds to truth values that we associate directly with eternal sentences.

Before becoming completely lost in a vague nomenclature, let me make some stipulations. I will call the function which assigns to a time and a possible world the truth value of a given fugitive sentence (type) at that time in that world the *meaning* of the given sentence. The meaning of a sentence is what a person who is linguistically competent grasps, it is common to all utterances of the sentence, and it is one of the components which goes into determining the *content* of any particular utterance of the sentence. The *content* of an utterance is that function which assigns to each possible world the truth value which the utterance would take if it were evaluated with respect to that world. There is some unfortunate slack in the preceding characterizations, which I will try to reduce.[29]

Let ϕ be a fugitive sentence like (21); let $\bar{\phi}$ be the meaning of ϕ, let W be the set of possible worlds; let T be the set of times (I assume that all possible worlds have the same temporal structure and, in fact, the very same times, i.e. a given time in one world has a unique counterpart in all others); let U be the set of possible utterances; for $u \varepsilon U$ let $S(u)$ be the sentence uttered in u; let $T(u)$ be the time of u (when only $S(u)$ and $T(u)$ are relevant; we might identify u with $<S(u), T(u)>$ and let $\bar{u}$ be the content of u. The relation between the meaning of a sentence (whose only fugitive aspect is its temporality) and the content of one of its possible utterances can now be concisely expressed as follows:

(22) $\Lambda u\varepsilon U\Lambda w\varepsilon W(\bar{u}(w) = \overline{S(u)}\,(T(u),w))$

or, identifying u with $<S(u),T(u)>$:

(23) $\Lambda w\varepsilon W\Lambda t\varepsilon T\,(<\overline{\phi},t>(w) = \bar{\phi}(t,w))$

To put it another way, an utterance of ϕ fixes a time, and the content of the utterance takes account of the truth value of ϕ in all possible worlds but *only at that time.*

From (22) and (23) it would appear that the notions of meaning and content are interdefinable. Therefore, since we already have begun developing the theory of meaning for fugitive sentences (see especially the work of Montague),[30] why devote any special attention to the theory of content? Is it not simply a subtheory of a definitional extension of the theory of meaning? I think not. But the reasons go beyond simple examples like (21) and take us, hopefully, back to the main track of this paper. It is worth looking more deeply into the structure of utterances than a *simple* definition of that notion within the theory of meaning would suggest. (I stress *simple* because I have not yet really investigated sophisticated definitions.)

First we have problems about the counterfactual status of possible utterances: Are utterances *in* worlds, are they assumed to occur in worlds in which their content is being evaluated, or are they extraworldly, with their content evaluated independent of their occurrence? Consider the infamous 'I am here now', or perhaps more simply:

(24) An utterance is occurring.

Is the meaning of (24) to assign to a time and world the truth-value which an utterance of (24) *would* take *were* it to occur in that world at that time? Or does it assign simply the truth value of (24) in that world at that time? Presumably the latter. But this is to assume that utterances come complete, with the value of all their contextually determined features filled in (otherwise the utterance alone—without being set in a world—would not have a content). I do not want to make this assumption since I am particularly interested in the way in which a demonstration, for example, picks out its demonstratum.

And now we are back to the ambiguity in (3). I would like to count my *verbal* demonstration, as in (17), as part of the sentence type. Then it seems that an utterance of such a sentence either must include a world, or else, what is more plausible, must be in a world. I guess what I want to say, what I should have said, is that an utterance has to occur *somewhere,* in some world, and the world in which it occurs is a crucial factor in determining what the content is. This really says something about how (I think) I want to treat (possible) demonstrations. I want the same (possible) demonstrations (e.g. ["the spy"]) to determine different demonstrata in different worlds (or possibly even at different times in the same world). Now I see why I was so taken with the Fregean treatment of demonstrations. We should be able to represent demonstrations as something like functions from worlds, times, etc., to demonstrata. Thus, *just like the meaning of a definite description!* The difference lies in how the content of a particular utterance is computed.

I realize that the foregoing is mildly inconsistent, but let us push on. Let u be an utterance of (17) in w at t, and let u' be an utterance of (3) in w at t. Let's not worry, for now, about the possibility of a clash of utterances. If we look at the content of u and the content of u' we will see that they differ—though they will always agree in w. The content of u is like what I earlier called a singular proposition (except that I should have fixed the time), whereas the content of u' is like what I earlier called a general proposition. For the content of u to assign truth to a given world w', the individual who must be suspicious in w' at t is not the denotation of "the spy" in w' at t, but rather the denotation of "the spy" in w at t. The *relevant individual* is determined in the world in which the utterance takes place, and then that same individual is checked for suspicion in all other worlds, whereas for the content of u', we determine a (possibly) new relevant individual in each world.[31]

What is especially interesting is that these two contents must agree in the world w, the world in which the utterance took place.

Now note that the verbal form of (3) might have been adopted by one who lacked "dthat" to express what is expressed by (17). We seem to have here a kind of *de dicto–de re* ambiguity in the verbal form of (3) and without benefit of any intensional operator. No question of an utterer's intentions has been brought into play. *There is no question of an analysis in terms of scope, since there is no operator.* The two sentence types (3) and (17) are such that when uttered in the same context they have different contents but always the same truth value where uttered. Donnellan vindicated! (Contrary to my own earlier expectations.)

I am beginning to suspect that I bungled things even worse than I thought in talking about meanings, contents, etc. The meaning of a sentence type should probably be a function from utterances to *contents* rather than from something like utterances to truth values. If this correction were made, then we could properly say that (13) and (17) differ in meaning.

It would also give a more satisfactory analysis of a sentence type like:

(25) Dthat ['the morning star'] is identical with dthat ['the evening star'].

Although (25) expresses a true content on some possible occasions of use and a false content on others, it is not simply contingent, since on all possible occasions its content is either necessary or impossible. (I am assuming that distinct individuals don't merge.) Even one who grasped the meaning of (25) would not of course know its truth value simply on witnessing an utterance. Thus we answer the question how an utterance of an identity sentence can be informative though *necessary!*

Another example on the question of necessity. Suppose I now utter:

(26) I am more than thirty-six years old.

What I have said is true. Is it necessary? This may be arguable. (*Could* I be younger than I am at this very same time?) But the fact that the sentence, if uttered at an earlier time or by another person, could express something false is certainly irrelevant. The point is: simply to look at the spectrum of *truth-values* of different utterances of (25) and (26) and not at the spectrum of *contents* of different utterances of (25) and (26) is to miss something interesting and important.

I earlier said that my demonstrative use is not quite Donnellan's referential use, and I want now to return to that point. When a speaker uses an expression demonstratively he *usually* has in mind—so to speak—an intended demonstratum, and the demonstration is thus *teleological.* Donnellan and I disagree on how to bring the intended demonstratum into the picture. To put it crudely, Donnellan believes that for most purposes we should take the demonstratum to be the intended demonstratum. I believe that these are different notions that may well involve different objects.

From my point of view the situation is interesting precisely because we have a case here in which a person can fail to say what he intended to say, and the failure is not a linguistic error (such as using the wrong word) but a factual one. It seems to me that such a situation can arise only in the demonstrative mode.

Suppose that without turning and looking I point to the place on my wall which has long been occupied by a picture of Rudolf Carnap and I say:

(27) Dthat [I point as above] is a picture of one of the greatest philosophers of the twentieth century.

But unbeknownst to me, someone has replaced my picture of Carnap with one of Spiro Agnew. I think it would simply be wrong to argue an "ambiguity" in the demonstration, so great that it can be bent to my intended demonstratum. I have said of a picture of Spiro Agnew that it pictures one of the greatest philosophers of the twentieth century. And my speech and demonstration suggest no other natural interpretation to the linguistically competent public observer.

Still, it would be perhaps equally wrong not to pursue the notion of the intended demonstratum. Let me give three reasons for that pursuit:

1. The notion is epistemologically interesting in itself.

2. It may well happen—as Donnellan has pointed out—that we succeed in communicating what we intended to say in spite of our failure to say it. (E.g. the mischievous fellow who switched pictures on me would understand full well what I was intending to say.)

3. There are situations where the demonstration is sufficiently ill-structured in itself so that we would regularly take account of the intended demonstratum as, *within limits,* a legitimate disambiguating or vagueness-removing device.

I have two kinds of examples for this third point. First, there are the cases of vague demonstrations by a casual wave of the hand. I suppose that ordinarily we would allow that a demonstration had been successful if the intended object were *roughly* where the speaker pointed. That is, we would not bring out surveying equipment to help determine the content of the speaker's assertion; much more relevant is what he intended to point at. Second, whenever I point at something, from the surveyor's point of view I point at many things. When I point at my son (and say "I love dthat"), I may also be pointing at a book he is holding, his jacket, a button on his jacket, his skin, his heart, and his dog standing behind him—from the surveyor's point of view. *My point is that if I intended to point at my son and it is true that I love him, then what I said is true.* And the fact that I do not love his jacket does not make it equally false. There are, of course, limits to what can be accomplished by intentions (even the best of them). No matter how hard I intend Carnap's picture, in the earlier described case, I do not think it reasonable to call the content of my utterance true.

Another example where I would simply distinguish the content asserted and the content intended is in the use of "I."[32] A person might utter:

(28) I am a general.

intending—that is "having in mind"—de Gaulle, and being under the delusion that he himself was de Gaulle. But the linguistic constraints on the possible demonstrata of "I" will not allow anyone other than de Gaulle to so demonstrate de Gaulle, no matter how hard they try.

All this familiarity with demonstratives has led me to believe that I was mistaken in "Quantifying In" in thinking that the most fundamental cases of what I might now describe as a person having a propositional attitude (believing, asserting, etc.) toward a singular proposition required that the person be *en rapport* with the subject of the proposition. It is now clear that I can assert *of* the first child to be born in the twenty-first century that *he* will be bald, simply by assertively uttering,

(29) Dthat ['the first child to be born in the twenty-first century'] will be bald.

I do not now see exactly how the requirement of being *en rapport* with the subject of a singular proposition fits in. Are there two kinds of singular propositions? Or are there just two different ways to know them?

EXCITING FUTURE EPISODES

1. Making sense out of the foregoing.
2. Showing how nicely (3) and (17) illustrate an early point about the possibility of incorpo-

rating contextual factors (here, a demonstration) as part of the content of the utterance. Another example compares uses of 'the person at whom I am pointing' as demonstration and as subject.

3. Justifying calling (17) a *de re* form by showing how it can be used to explicate the notion of modality de re without depending on scope.

4. Extending the demonstrative notion to *in*definite descriptions to see if it is possible to so explicate the ± specific idea. (It isn't.)

5. Improving (by starting all over) the analysis of the relation between Montague's treatment of indexicals and my treatment of demonstratives.

6. Showing how the treatment of proper names in the Kripke-Kaplan-Donnellan way (if there is such) is akin (?) to demonstratives.

7. Discussing the role of common noun phrases in connection with demonstratives, as in:

(30) Dthat coat [the speaker points at a boy wearing a coat] is dirty.

8. Quine's contention that the content of any utterance can also be expressed by an eternal sentence. Is it true?

9. Much more to say about the phenomenology of intending to demonstrate *x,* and also about the truth-conditions of '*y* intends to demonstrate *x*'.

10. Demonstratives, dubbings, definitions, and other forms of language learning. Common nouns: what they mean and how we learn it. This section will include such pontifications as the following:

It is a mistake to believe that normal communication takes place through the encoding and decoding of general propositions, by means of our grasp of *meanings*. It is a more serious mistake, because more pernicious, to believe that other aspects of communication can be accounted for by a vague reference to "contextual features" of the utterance. Indeed, we first learn the meanings of almost all parts of our language by means quite different from those of the formal definitions studied in metamathematics; and the means used for first teaching the meanings of words, rather than withering away, are regularly and perhaps even essentially employed thereafter in all forms of communication.

ACKNOWLEDGMENTS

This work was supported by the National Science Foundation.

NOTES

1. Keith S. Donnellan, "Reference and Definite Descriptions," *The Philosophical Review*, 75 (1966): 298. [Reprinted in this volume.]
2. Leonard Linsky, "Reference and Referents," in *Philosophy and Ordinary Language*, ed. C. Caton (Urbana: 1963).
3. Donnellan, "Reference and Definite Descriptions," p. 299.
4. Ibid., p. 297.
5. Ibid., p. 303.
6. Ibid.
7. Jaakko Hintikka, "Individual, Possible Worlds, and Epistemic Logic," *Noûs*, 1 (1967): 47.
8. Bertrand Russell, *The Principles of Mathematics* (Cambridge, England: 1903).
9. Bertrand Russell, "On Denoting," *Mind*, 14 (1905): 479–93.
10. Rudolf Carnap, *Meaning and Necessity* (Chicago: 1947).
11. Bertrand Russell, *Introduction to Mathematical Philosophy* (London: 1920), p. 174.
12. Both "denoting concept' and "denoting phrase' are Russell's terms used in Russell's way.
13. An example is the possibility of producing set theoretical representations of the system of natural numbers which make all even numbers alike in certain set theoretical features (distinct from such numerical features as divisibility by two) and all odd numbers alike in other set theoretical features, or which provide simple and elegant definitions (i.e. representations) of certain basic numerical operations and relations such as *less than* or *plus*, etc.
14. It is not too easy to single out such phrases without the help of some theory about logical form or some semantical theory. I suppose what I am after is what linguists call syntactical criteria. But I have had difficulty in finding one which will not let in phrases like "a spy." Another difficulty is concerned with phrases like "John's brother" which seem to vary in their uniqueness suppositions. "John's brother is the man in dark glasses" carries, for me, the supposition that John has just one brother; whereas "The man in dark glasses is John's brother" does not. In fact the latter seems the most natural formulation when suppositions about the number of John's brothers are completely absent, since both "The man in dark glasses is one of John's brothers" and "The man in dark glasses is a brother of John" suppose, for me, that John has more than one brother.
15. The question whether all uses of demonstratives are accompanied by demonstrations depends on a number of factors, some empirical, some stipulative, and some in the twilight zone of theoretical ingenuity. The stipulative question is whether we use 'demonstrative' to describe certain phrases which might also be described by enumeration or some such syntactical device, e.g. all phrases beginning with either "this" or "that" and followed by a common noun phrase; or whether we use 'demonstrative' to describe a certain characteristic use of such phrases. In the latter case it may be stipulatively true that an utterance containing a demonstrative must be accompanied by a demonstration. In the former case, the question turns both on how people in fact speak and on how clever our theoretician is in producing *recherché* demonstrations to account for apparent counterexamples.
16. This formulation probably needs sharpening. Don't take it as a definition.
17. It should not be supposed that my practice indicates any confidence as to the nature and structure of what I call *demonstrations* or the proper form for a *demonstration-description* to take. Indeed, these are difficult and important questions which arise repeatedly in what follows.
18. Gottlob Frege, "Ueber Sinn und Bedeutung," *Zeitschrift Fur Philosophie und Philosophische Kritik*. Translated (by Feigl) in *Readings in Philosophical Analysis*, eds. H. Feigl and W. Sellars (New York: 1949). [Reprinted in this volume.] Also translated (by Black) in *Translations from the Writings of Gottlob Frege*, eds. P. Geach and M. Black (Oxford: 1966).
19. Ibid., emphasis added.
20. W. V. Quine, "Quantifiers and Propositional Attitudes," *Journal of Philosophy*, 53 (1955): 177–87. [Reprinted in this volume.]
21. David Kaplan, "Quantifying In," *Synthese*, 19 (1968): 178–214. [Reprinted in this volume.] I will attempt later to press the case that this use of proper names, which involves no waving of hands or fixing of glance, may be assimilated to the more traditional forms of demonstrative use.
22. "In the case of genuinely proper names like 'Aristotle' opinions as regards their sense may diverge. As such may, e.g., be suggested: Plato's disciple and the teacher of Alexander the Great. Whoever accepts this sense will interpret the meaning of the statement 'Aristotle was born in Stagira' differently from one who interpreted the sense of 'Aristotle' as the Stagirite teacher of Alexander the Great" (from Feigl's translation of Frege's "Ueber Sinn und Bedeutung").
23. A third kind of indicative device is the picture. Consideration of pictures, which to me lie somewhere between pointing and describing, may help drive home the parallels—in terms of the distinction between the object indicated and the manner of indication—between description, depiction, and demonstration.
24. That all utterances are in English is a general and implicit assumption except where it is explicitly called into question.
25. "Dhe" is really a combination of the demonstrative with a common noun phrase. It stands for "dthat male." More on such combinations later.

26. W. V. Quine, *Word and Object* (Cambridge, Mass.: 1960), p. 193.

27. There are, of course, two hidden relativizations involved even for eternal sentences. One is to a *language,* i.e. an association of meanings with words. The Knoh-English example was meant to dramatize this relativization. The other is to a possible world. There is always the implicit reference to the actual world when we use just the expression 'true'. If the analogy between moments of time and possible worlds holds—as some philosophers think—then maybe we should begin our classification of sentences not with explicitly dated eternal sentences like "in 1970 . . ." but with 'perfect' sentences like "In the possible world Charlie in 1970 . . .".

28. Rather than talking directly to these functions, I should really talk of entities like <<'The',*S*>*P*> and only derivatively of the functions.

29. This is aside from the inadequacy mentioned in the previous note, which continues to bother me.

30. The most relevant works are "Pragmatics" (1968) and "Pragmatics and Intensional Logic" (1970), both reprinted in Richard Montague, *Formal Philosophy* (New Haven, 1974).

31. I am still bothered by the notion of an utterance at t in w, where there is no utterance at t in w.

32. "I" is, of course, a demonstrative; as opposed, e.g. to "the person who is uttering this utterance," which contains only the demonstrative 'this utterance'. Let us compare utterances of:

    (i) I am exhausted
    (ii) The person who is uttering this utterance is exhausted

    both uttered by s on the same occasion (!): To find the truth value of the content of (ii) in w' we must first locate the same utterance in w' (if it exists there at all) and see who, if anyone, is uttering it. Since s could well be exhausted silently in w', the two contents are not the same.

26 On the Logic of Demonstratives

DAVID KAPLAN

In this paper, I propose to outline briefly a few results of my investigations into the theory of demonstratives: words and phrases whose *in*tension is determined by the contexts of their use. Familiar examples of demonstratives are the nouns 'I', 'you', 'here', 'now', 'that', and the adjectives 'actual' and 'present'. It is, of course, clear that the *ex*tension of 'I' is determined by the context—if you and I both say 'I' we refer to different persons. But I would now claim that the intension is also so determined. The intension of an 'eternal' term (like 'the Queen of England in 1973') has generally been taken to be represented by a function which assigns to each possible world the Queen of England in 1973 of that world. Such functions would have been called *individual concepts* by Carnap. It has been thought by some—myself among others—that by analogy, the intension of 'I' could be represented by a function from speakers to individuals (in fact, the identity function). And, similarly, that the intensions of 'here' and 'now' would be represented by (identity) functions on places and times. The role of contextual factors in determining the extension (with respect to such factors) of a demonstrative was thought of as analogous to that of a possible world in determining the extension of 'the Queen of England in 1973' (with respect to that possible world). Thus an enlarged view of an intension was derived. The intension of an expression was to be represented by a function from certain factors to the extension of an expression (with respect to those factors). Originally such factors were simply possible worlds, but as it was noticed that the so-called tense operators exhibited a structure highly analogous to that of the modal operators, the factors with respect to which extension was to be determined were enlarged to include moments of time. When it was noticed that contextual factors were required to determine the extension of sentences containing demonstratives, a still more general notion was developed and called an 'index'. The extension of an expression was to be determined with respect to an index. The intension of an expression was that function which assigned to every index the extension at that index. Here is a typical passage.

The above example supplies us with a statement whose truth-value is not constant but varies as a function of $i \in I$. This situation is easily appreciated in the context of time-dependent statements; that is, in the case where I represents the instants of time. Obviously the same statement can be true at one moment and false at another. For more general situations one must not think of the $i \in I$ as anything as simple as instants of time or even possible worlds. In general we will have

$$i = (w, t, p, a, \ldots)$$

David Kaplan, "On the Logic of Demonstratives," *Journal of Philosophical Logic* 8 (1) © 1978, pp. 81–98, Kluwer Academic Publishers, with kind permission from Springer Science and Business Media and the author.

where the index *i* has many *coordinates:* for example, *w* is a *world, t* is a *time, p = (x, y, z)* is a (3-dimensional) *position* in the world, *a* is an *agent,* etc. All these coordinates can be varied, possibly independently, and thus affect the truth-values of statements which have indirect reference to these coordinates. (From the Advice of a prominent logician.)

A sentence φ was taken to be logically true if true at every index (in every 'structure'), and □ φ was taken to be true at a given index (in a given structure) just in case φ was true at every index (in that structure). (Or possibly, just in case φ was true at every index *which differed from the given index only in possible world coordinate.*) Thus the familiar principle of modal generalization: if ⊨ φ, then ⊨ □ φ, is validated.

This view, in its treatment of demonstratives, now seems to me to have been technically wrong (though perhaps correctable by minor modification) and, more importantly, conceptually misguided.

Consider the sentence

(1) I am here now.

It is obvious that for many choices of index—i.e. for many quadruples ⟨w, x, p, t⟩ where *w* is a possible world, *x* is a person, *p* is a place, and *t* is a time—(1) will be false. In fact, (1) is true only with respect to those indices ⟨w, x, p, t⟩ which are such that in the world *w, x* is located at *p* at the time *t*. Thus (1) fares about on a par with

(2) David Kaplan is in Los Angeles on 21 April 1973.

(2) is contingent, and so is (1).

But here we have missed something essential to our understanding of demonstratives. Intuitively, (1) is deeply, and in some sense universally, true. One need only understand the meaning of (1) to know that it cannot be uttered falsely. No such guarantees apply to (2). A *Logic of Demonstratives* which does not reflect this intuitive difference between (1) and (2) has bypassed something essential to the logic of demonstratives.

Here is a proposed correction. Let the class of indices be narrowed to include only the *proper* ones—namely, those ⟨w, x, p, t⟩ such that in the

world *w, x is* located at *p* at the time *t.* Such a move may have been intended originally since improper indices are like impossible worlds; no such contexts *could* exist and thus there is no interest in evaluating the extensions of expressions with respect to them. Our reform has the consequence that (1) comes out, correctly, to be logically true. Now consider

(3) □ I am here now.

Since the contained sentence (namely (1)) is true at every proper index, (3) also is true at every proper index and thus also is logically true. (As would be expected by the aforementioned principle of modal generalization.)

But (3) should not be *logically* true, since it is false. It is certainly *not* necessary that I be here now. But for several contingencies I would be working in my garden now, or even writing this in a location outside of Los Angeles.

Perhaps enough has now been said to indicate that there are difficulties in the attempt to assimilate the role of a *context* in a logic of demonstratives to that of a *possible world* in the familiar modal logics or a *moment of time* in the familiar tense logics.

I believe that the source of the difficulty lies in a conceptual confusion between two kinds of meaning. Ramifying Frege's distinction between sense and denotation, I would add two varieties of sense: content and character. The content of an expression is always taken *with respect to* a given context of use. Thus when I say

(4) I was insulted yesterday

a specific content—*what I said*—is expressed. Your utterance of the same sentence, or mine on another day, would not express the same content. What is important to note is that it is not just the truth-value that may change; what is said is itself different. Speaking today, my utterance of (4) will have a content roughly equivalent to that which

(5) David Kaplan is insulted on 20 April 1973

would have spoken by you or anyone at any time. Since (5) contains no demonstratives, its content is the same with respect to all contexts. This content is what Carnap called an 'intension' and what, I believe, has been often referred to as a 'proposition'. So my theory is that different contexts for (4) produce not just different truth-values, but different propositions.

Turning now to character, I call that component of the sense of an expression which determines how the content is determined by the context the 'character' of an expression. Just as contents (or intensions) can be represented by functions from possible worlds to extensions, so characters can be represented by functions from contexts to contents. The character of 'I' would then be represented by *the function (or rule, if you prefer) which assigns to each context that content which is represented by the constant function from possible words to the agent of the context.* The latter function has been called an 'individual concept'. Note that the character of 'I' is represented by a function from contexts to individual *concepts,* not from contexts to individuals. It was the idea that a function from contexts to individuals could represent the intension of 'I' which led to the difficulties discussed earlier.

Now what is it that a competent speaker of English knows about the world 'I'? Is it the content with respect to some particular occasion of use? No. It is the character of 'I': the rule italicized above. Competent speakers recognize that the proper use of 'I' is—loosely speaking—to refer to the speaker. Thus, that component of sense which I call 'character' is best identified with what might naturally be called 'meaning'.

To return, for a moment, to (1). The character (meaning) of (1) determines each of the following:

(a) In different contexts, an utterance of (1) expresses different contents (propositions).

(b) In most (if not all) contexts, an utterance of (1) expresses a contingent proposition.

(c) In all contexts, an utterance of (1) expresses a true proposition (i.e. a proposition which is true at the world of the context).

On the basis of (c), we might claim that (1) is analytic (i.e. it is true solely in virtue of its meaning). Although as we see from (b), (1) rarely or never expresses a necessary proposition. This separation of analyticity and necessity is made possible—even, I hope, plausible—by distinguishing the kinds of entities of which

'is analytic' and 'is necessary' are properly predicated: characters (meanings) are analytic; contents (propositions) are necessary.

The distinction between character and content was unlikely to be noticed before demonstratives came under consideration, because demonstrative-free expressions have a constant character, that is, they express the same content in every context. Thus, character becomes an uninteresting complication in the theory.

Though I have spoken above of contexts of utterance, my primary theoretical notion of *content with respect to a context* does not require that the agent of the context utter the expression in question. I believe that there are good reasons for taking this more general notion as fundamental.

I believe that my distinction between character and content can be used to throw light on Kripke's distinction between the *a-priori* and the necessary. Although my distinction lies more purely within logic and semantics, and Kripke's distinction is of a more general epistemic metaphysical character,[1] both seem to me to be of the same *structure.* (I leave this remark in a rather cryptic state.)

The distinction between content and character and the related analysis of demonstratives have certainly been foreshadowed in the literature (though they are original-with-me, in the sense that I did not consciously extract them from prior sources). But to my knowledge they have not previously been cultivated to meet the standards for logical and semantical theories which currently prevail. In particular, Strawson's distinction between the significance (meaningfulness) of a sentence and the statement (proposition) which is expressed in a given use is clearly related.[2] Strawson recognizes that such sentences as 'The *present* King of France is *now* bald' may express different propositions in different utterances, and he identifies the meaningfulness of the sentence with its potential for expressing a true or false proposition in some possible utterance. Though he does not explicitly discuss *the* meaning of the sentence, it is clear that he would not identify such a meaning with any of the propositions expressed by particular utterances. Unfortunately Strawson seems to regard the fact that sentences containing demonstratives can be used to express different propositions as immunizing such sentences against treatment by 'the logician'.

In order to convince myself that it is possible to carry out a consistent analysis of the semantics of demonstratives along the above lines, I have attempted to carry through the program for a version of first-order predicate logic. The result is the following Logic of Demonstratives.

If my views are correct, the introduction of demonstratives into intensional logics will require more extensive reformulation than was thought to be the case.

THE LOGIC OF DEMONSTRATIVES

The *Language* LD is based on first-order predicate logic with identity and descriptions. We deviate slightly from standard formulations in using two sorts of variables, one sort for positions and a second sort for individuals other than positions (hereafter called simply 'individuals').

Primitive Symbols for Two Sorted Predicate Logic

0. Punctuation: (,)
1. (i)   An infinite set of individual variables: $\mathcal{V}_i$
   (ii) An infinite set of position variables: $\mathcal{V}_p$
2. (i)   An infinite number of m-n-place predicates, for all natural numbers m, n
   (ii) The 1-0-place predicate: Exist
   (iii) The 1-1-place predicate: Located
3. (i)   An infinite number of m-n-place i-functors (functors which form terms denoting individuals)
   (ii) An infinite number of m-n-place p-functors (functors which form terms denoting positions)
4. Sentential Connectives: $\land, \lor, \neg, \rightarrow, \leftrightarrow$
5. Quantifiers: $\forall, \exists$
6. Definite Description Operator: the
7. Identity: $=$

Primitive Symbols for Modal and Tense Logic

8. Modal Operators: $\Box, \Diamond$
9. Tense Operators: F (it will be the case that)
                     P (it has been the case that)
                     G (one day ago, it was the case that)

Primitive Symbols for the Logic of Demonstratives

10. Three one-place sentential operators:
    N (it is now the case that)
    A (it is actually the case that)
    Y (yesterday, it was the case that)
11. A one-place functor: dthat
12. An individual constant (0-0-place i-functor): I
13. A position constant (0-0-place p-functor): Here

The *well-formed expressions* are of three kinds: formulas, position terms (p-terms), and individual terms (i-terms).

1. (i)   If $\alpha \in \mathcal{V}_i$, then α is an i-term.
   (ii) If $\alpha \in \mathcal{V}_p$, then α is a p-term.
2. If π is an m-n-place predicate, $\alpha_1 \ldots \alpha_m$ are i-terms, and $\beta_1 \ldots \beta_n$ are p-terms, then $\pi\alpha_1 \ldots \alpha_m\beta_1 \ldots \beta_n$ is a formula.
3. (i)   If η is an m-n-place i-functor, $\alpha_1 \ldots \alpha_m$, $\beta_1 \ldots \beta_n$ as in 2, then $\eta\alpha_1 \ldots \alpha_m\beta_1 \ldots \beta_n$ is an i-term.
   (ii) If η is an m-n-place p-functor, $\alpha_1 \ldots \alpha_m$, $\beta_1 \ldots \beta_n$ as in 2, then $\eta\alpha_1 \ldots \alpha_m\beta_1 \ldots \beta_n$ is a p-term.
4. If ϕ, ψ are formulas, then $(\phi \land \psi)$, $(\phi \lor \psi)$, $\neg\phi$, $(\phi \rightarrow \psi)$, $(\phi \leftrightarrow \psi)$ are formulas.
5. If ϕ is a formula and $\alpha \in \mathcal{V}_i \cup \mathcal{V}_p$, then $\forall\alpha\phi$, $\exists\alpha\phi$ are formulas.
6. If ϕ is a formula, then
   (i)   if $\alpha \in \mathcal{V}_i$, then   the $\alpha \phi$ is an i-term.
   (ii) if $\alpha \in \mathcal{V}_p$, then   the $\alpha \phi$ is a p-term.
7. If both α, β are either i-terms or p-terms, then $\alpha = \beta$ is a formula.
8. If ϕ is a formula, then $\Box\phi, \Diamond\phi$ are formulas.
9. If ϕ is a formula, then $F\phi, P\phi, G\phi$ are formulas.
10. If ϕ is a formula, then $N\phi, A\phi, Y\phi$ are formulas.
11. (i)   If α is an i-term, then dthat α is an i-term.
    (ii) If α is a p-term, then   dthat α is a p-term.

Semantics for LD

Definition. $\mathfrak{A}$ *is an LD Structure iff there are* $\mathcal{C} \mathcal{W} \mathcal{U} \mathcal{P} \mathcal{T} \mathcal{I}$ *such that*
1. $\mathfrak{A} = \langle \mathcal{C} \mathcal{W} \mathcal{U} \mathcal{P} \mathcal{T} \mathcal{I} \rangle$.
2. $\mathcal{C}$ is a non-empty set (the set of *contexts*, see 10 below).

3. If $c \in \mathcal{C}$, then (i) $c_A \in \mathcal{U}$ (the *agent* of c).
   (ii) $c_T \in \mathcal{T}$ (the *time* of c).
   (iii) $c_p \in \mathcal{P}$ (the *position* of c).
   (iv) $c_w \in \mathcal{W}$ (the *world* of c).
4. $\mathcal{W}$ is a non-empty set (the set of *worlds*).
5. $\mathcal{U}$ is a non-empty set (the set of all *individuals,* see 9 below).
6. $\mathcal{P}$ is a non-empty set (the set of *positions;* common to all worlds).
7. $\mathcal{T}$ is the set of integers (thought of as the *times;* common to all worlds).
8. $\mathcal{I}$ is a function which assigns to each predicate and functor an appropriate *intension* as follows:
   (i) if π is an *m-n*-place predicate, $\mathcal{I}_\pi$ is a function such that for each $t \in \mathcal{T}$ and $w \in \mathcal{W}$, $\mathcal{I}_\pi(tw) \subseteq (\mathcal{U}^m \times \mathcal{P}^n)$.
   (ii) If η is an *m-n*-place *i*-functor, $\mathcal{I}_\eta$ is a function such that that for each $t \in \mathcal{T}$ and $w \in \mathcal{W}$, $\mathcal{I}_\eta(tw) \in (\mathcal{U} \cup \{\dagger\})^{(\mathcal{U}^m \times \mathcal{P}^n)}$.
   (Note: $\dagger$ is a completely alien entity, in neither $\mathcal{U}$ nor $\mathcal{P}$, which represents an 'undefined' value of the function. In a normal set theory we can take $\dagger$ to be $\{\mathcal{U}, \mathcal{P}\}$.)
   (iii) If η is an *m-n*-place *p*-functor, $\mathcal{I}_\eta$ is a function such that for each $t \in \mathcal{T}$, and $w \in \mathcal{W}$, $\mathcal{I}_\eta(tw) \in (\mathcal{P} \cup \{\dagger\})^{(\mathcal{U}^m \times \mathcal{P}^n)}$.
9. $i \in \mathcal{U}$ iff $\exists t \in \mathcal{T} \, \exists w \in \mathcal{W} \, \langle i \rangle \in \mathcal{I}_{Exists}(tw)$.
10. If $c \in \mathcal{C}$, then $\langle c_A c_p \rangle \in \mathcal{I}_{Located}(c_T c_w)$.
11. If $\langle i\, p \rangle \in \mathcal{I}_{Located}(tw)$, then $\langle i \rangle \in \mathcal{I}_{Exists}(tw)$.

Truth and Denotation in a Context

We write: $\models^{\mathfrak{A}}_{cftw} \phi$ for ϕ when taken in the context c (under the assignment f and in the structure $\mathfrak{A}$) *is true with respect to* the time t and the world w.

We write: $|\alpha|^{\mathfrak{A}}_{cftw}$ for *the denotation of* α taken in the context c (under the assignment f and in the structure $\mathfrak{A}$) *with respect to* the time t and the world w.

In general we will omit the superscript '$\mathfrak{A}$', and we will assume that the structure $\mathfrak{A}$ is $\langle \mathcal{C} \mathcal{W} \mathcal{U} \mathcal{P} \mathcal{T} \mathcal{I} \rangle$

Definition. f is an assignment (with respect to $\langle \mathcal{C} \mathcal{W} \mathcal{U} \mathcal{P} \mathcal{T} \mathcal{I} \rangle$) iff

$\exists f_1 f_2 (f_1 \in \mathcal{U}^{\mathcal{V}_i} \, \& \, f_2 \in \mathcal{P}^{\mathcal{V}_p} \, \& \, f = f_1 \cup f_2)$.

Definition. $f^\alpha_x = (f \sim \{\langle \alpha f(\alpha) \rangle\}) \cup \{\langle \alpha x \rangle\}$ (i.e. the assignment which is just like f except that it assigns x to α).

For the following recursive definitions, assume that $c \in \mathcal{C}$, f is an assignment, $t \in \mathcal{T}$, and $w \in \mathcal{W}$.

1. If α is a variable, $|\alpha|_{cftw} = f(\alpha)$.
2. $\models_{cftw} \pi \alpha_1 \ldots \alpha_m \beta_1 \ldots \beta_n$ iff
   $\langle |\alpha_1|_{cftw} \ldots |\beta_n|_{cftw} \rangle \in \mathcal{I}_\pi(tw)$.
3. If η is neither I nor Here (see 12, 13 below), then $|\eta \alpha_1 \ldots \alpha_m \beta_1 \ldots \beta_n|_{cftw}$
$$= \begin{cases} \mathcal{I}_\eta(tw)(\langle |\alpha_1|_{cftw} \ldots |\beta_n|_{cftw} \rangle), \text{ if none of } \\ |\alpha_j|_{cftw} |\beta_k|_{cftw} \text{ are } \dagger \\ \dagger, \text{ otherwise.} \end{cases}$$
4. (i) $\models_{cftw} (\phi \wedge \psi)$ iff $\models_{cftw} \phi$ & $\models_{cftw} \psi$.
   (ii) $\models_{cftw} \neg \phi$ iff $\sim \models_{cftw} \phi$.
   etc.
5. (i) If $\alpha \in \mathcal{V}_i$, then $\models_{cftw} \forall \alpha \phi$ iff $\forall_i \in \mathcal{U}$ $\models_{cf^\alpha_i tw} \phi$.
   (ii) If $\alpha \in \mathcal{V}_p$, then $\models_{cftw} \forall \alpha \phi$ iff $\forall_p \in \mathcal{P}|$ $\models_{cf^\alpha_p tw} \phi$.
   Similarly for $\exists \alpha \phi$.
6. (i) If $\alpha \in \mathcal{V}_i$, then $|\text{the } \alpha \, \phi|_{cftw}$
$$= \begin{cases} \text{the unique } i \in \mathcal{U} \text{ such that } \models_{cf^\alpha_i tw} \phi, \\ \text{if there is such.} \\ \dagger, \text{ otherwise.} \end{cases}$$
   (ii) Similarly for $\alpha \in \mathcal{V}_p$.
7. $\models_{cftw} \alpha = \beta$ iff $|\alpha|_{cftw} = |\beta|_{cftw}$.
8. (i) $\models_{cftw} \Box \phi$ iff $\forall w' \in \mathcal{W}$ $\models_{cftw'} \phi$.
   (ii) $\models_{cftw} \Diamond \phi$ iff $\exists w' \in \mathcal{W}$ $\models_{cftw'} \phi$.
9. (i) $\models_{cftw} F\phi$ iff $\exists t' \in \mathcal{T}$ such that $t' > t$ and $\models_{cft'w} \phi$.
   (ii) $\models_{cftw} P\phi$ iff $\exists t' \in \mathcal{T}$ such that $t' < t$ and $\models_{cft'w} \phi$.
   (iii) $\models_{cftw} G\phi$ iff $\models_{cf(t-1)w} \phi$.
10. (i) $\models_{cftw} N\phi$ iff $\models_{cfc_Tw} \phi$.
    (ii) $\models_{cftw} A\phi$ iff $\models_{cftw} \phi$.
    (iii) $\models_{cftw} Y\phi$ iff $\models_{cf(c_T-1)w} \phi$.
11. $|\text{dthat } \alpha|_{cftw} = |\alpha|_{cfc_Tc_w}$
12. $|I|_{cftw} = c_A$.
13. $|\text{Here}|_{cftw} = c_P$.

Remark 1. Expressions containing demonstratives will, in general, express different concepts in different contexts. We call the concept expressed in a given context the *Content* of the expression in that context. The Content of a sentence in a context is, roughly, the proposition the sentence would express if uttered in that context.

This description is not quite accurate on two counts. First, it is important to distinguish an *utterance* from a *sentence-in-a-context*. The former notion is from the theory of speech acts, the latter from semantics. Utterances take time, and utterances of distinct sentences cannot be simultaneous (i.e. in the same context). But in order to develop a logic of demonstratives it seems most natural to be able to evaluate several premises and a conclusion all in the same context. Thus, the notion of ϕ being true in c and $\mathfrak{A}$ does not require an utterance of ϕ. In particular, c_A need not be uttering ϕ in c_W at c_T. Second, the truth of a proposition is not usually thought of as dependent on a time as well as a possible world. The time is thought of as fixed by the context. If ϕ is a sentence, the more usual notion of the proposition expressed by ϕ-in-c is what is here called the Content of $N\phi$ in c.

Where Γ is either a term or a formula, we write: $\{\Gamma\}_{cf}^{\mathfrak{A}}$ for the Content of Γ in the context c (under the assignment f and in the structure $\mathfrak{A}$).

Definition.
(i) If ϕ is a formula, $\{\phi\}_{cf}$ = that function which assigns to each $t \in \mathcal{T}$ and $w \in \mathcal{W}$, Truth if $\vDash_{cftw}^{\mathfrak{A}} \phi$, and Falsehood otherwise.
(ii) If α is a term, $\{\alpha\}_{cf}$ = that function which assigns to each $t \in \mathcal{T}$ and $w \in \mathcal{W}$, $|\alpha|_{cftw}^{\mathfrak{A}}$

Remark 2. $\vDash_{cftw}^{\mathfrak{A}} \phi$ iff $\{\phi\}_{cf}^{\mathfrak{A}}(tw)$ = Truth. Roughly speaking, the sentence ϕ taken in the context c is *true with respect to t and w* iff the proposition expressed by ϕ-in-the-context-c would be true at the time t if w were the actual world. In the formal development of pages 360 and 361 was smoother to ignore the conceptual break marked by the notion of *Content in a context* and to directly define *truth in a context with respect to a possible time and world*. The important conceptual role of the notion of Content is partially indicated by the following two definitions.

Definition. ϕ is *true in the context c* (in the structure $\mathfrak{A}$) iff for every assignment f, $\{\phi\}_{cf}^{\mathfrak{A}}(c_T, c_W)$ = Truth.

Definition. ϕ is *valid in LD* ($\vDash \phi$) iff for every LD structure $\mathfrak{A}$, and every context c of $\mathfrak{A}$, ϕ is true in c (in $\mathfrak{A}$).

Remark 3. $\vDash (\alpha = \text{dthat } \alpha)$, $\vDash$ N (Located I, Here), $\vDash$ Exist I, $\sim \vDash \Box (\alpha = \text{dthat } \alpha)$, $\sim \vDash$

$\Box$N(Located I, Here), $\sim \vDash \Box$ (Exist I). In the converse direction we have the usual results in view of the fact that $\vDash(\Box\phi \to \phi)$.

Definition. If $\alpha_1 \ldots \alpha_n$ are all the free variables of ϕ in alphabetical order, then *the closure of ϕ* = AN$\forall \alpha_1 \ldots \alpha_n \phi$.

Definition. ϕ *is closed* iff ϕ is equivalent to its closure (in the sense of *Remark 12*, below).

Remark 4. If ϕ is closed, then ϕ is true in c (and $\mathfrak{A}$) iff for every assignment f, time t, and world w $\vDash_{cftw}^{\mathfrak{A}} \phi$.

Definition. Where Γ is either a term or a formula, *the Content of Γ in the context c (in the structure $\mathfrak{A}$) is stable* iff for every assignment f, $\{\Gamma\}_{cf}^{\mathfrak{A}}$ is a constant function (i.e. $\{\Gamma\}_{cf}^{\mathfrak{A}}(tw)$ = $\{\Gamma\}_{cf}^{\mathfrak{A}}(t'w')$, for all t, t', w, w' in $\mathfrak{A}$).

Remark 5. Where ϕ is a formula, α is a term, and β is a variable, each of the following has a stable Content in every context (in every structure): $AN\phi$, dthat α, β, I, Here.

If we were to extend the notion of Content to apply to operators, we would see that all demonstratives have a stable Content in every context. The same is true of the familiar logical constants, although it does not hold for the modal and tense operators (not, at least, according to the foregoing development).

Remark 6. That aspect of the meaning of an expression which determines what its Content will be in each context, we call the *Character* of the expression. Although a lack of knowledge about the context (or perhaps about the structure) may cause one to mistake the Content of a given utterance, the Character of each well formed expression is determined by rules of the language (such as 1–13, page 361) which are presumably known to all competent speakers. Our notation '$\{\phi\}_{cf}^{\mathfrak{A}}$' for the Content of an expression gives a natural notation for the Character of an expression, namely '$\{\phi\}$'.

Definition. Where Γ is either a term or a formula, the *Character of Γ* is that function which assigns to each structure $\mathfrak{A}$, assignment f, and context c of $\mathfrak{A}$, $\{\Gamma\}_{cf}^{\mathfrak{A}}$

Definition. Where Γ is either a term or a formula, *the Character of Γ is stable* iff for every structure $\mathfrak{A}$, and assignment f the Character of Γ (under f in $\mathfrak{A}$) is a constant function (i.e. $\{\Gamma\}_{cf}^{\mathfrak{A}} = \{\Gamma\}_{c'f}^{\mathfrak{A}}$ for all c, c' in $\mathfrak{A}$).

Remark 7. A formula or term has a stable Character iff it has the same Content in every context (for each, $\mathfrak{A}, f$).

Remark 8. A formula or term has a stable Character iff it contains no essential occurrence of a demonstrative.

Remark 9. The logic of demonstratives determines a sub-logic of those formulas of LD which contain no demonstratives. These formulas (and their equivalents which contain inessential occurrences of demonstratives) are exactly the formulas with a stable Character. The logic of demonstratives brings a new perspective even to formulas such as these. The sub-logic of LD which concerns only formulas of stable Character is not identical with traditional logic. Even for such formulas, the familiar Principle of Necessitation: if $\models \phi$, then $\models \Box \phi$, fails. And so does its tense logic counterpart: if $\models \phi$, then $\models (\neg P \neg \phi \wedge \neg F \neg \phi \wedge \phi)$. From the perspective of LD, validity is truth in every possible *context*. For traditional logic, validity is truth in every possible *circumstance*. Each possible context determines a possible circumstance, but it is not the case that each possible circumstance is part of a possible context. In particular, the fact that each possible context has an agent implies that any possible circumstance in which no individuals exist will not form a part of any possible context. Within LD, a possible context is represented by $\langle \mathfrak{A}, c \rangle$ and a possible circumstance by $\langle \mathfrak{A}, t, w \rangle$. To any $\langle \mathfrak{A}, c \rangle$, there corresponds $\langle \mathfrak{A}, c_T, c_W \rangle$. But it is not the case that to every $\langle \mathfrak{A}, t, w \rangle$ there exists a context c of $\mathfrak{A}$ such that $t = c_T$ and $w = c_W$. The result is that in LD such sentences as $\exists x$ Exist x and $\exists x \exists p$ Located x, p are valid, although they would not be so regarded in traditional logic. At least not in the neo-traditional logic that countenances empty worlds. Using the semantical developments of pages 360 and 361, we can define this traditional sense of validity (for formulas which do not contain demonstratives) as follows. First note that by *Remark 7*, if ϕ has a stable Character

$$\models_{cftw}^{\mathfrak{A}} \phi \text{ iff } \models_{c'ftw}^{\mathfrak{A}} \phi.$$

Thus for such formulas we can define,

ϕ *is true at tw (in $\mathfrak{A}$)* iff for every assignment f and every context c

$$\models_{cftw}^{\mathfrak{A}} \phi.$$

The neo-traditional sense of validity is now definable as follows: $\models_T \phi$ if for all structures $\mathfrak{A}$, times t, and worlds w, ϕ is true at tw (in $\mathfrak{A}$).

(Properly speaking, what I have called the neo-traditional sense of validity is the notion of validity now common for a quantified S5 modal tense logic with individual variables ranging over possible individuals and a predicate of existence.) Adding the subscript 'LD' for explicitness, we can now state some results.

(i) If ϕ contains no demonstratives, if $\models_T \phi$, then $\models_{LD} \phi$.

(ii) $\models_{LD} \exists x$ Exist x, but $\sim \models_T \exists x$ Exist x.

Of course $\Box \exists x$ Exist x is not valid even in LD. Nor are its counterparts, $\neg F \neg \exists x$ Exist x and $\neg P \neg \exists x$ Exist x.

This suggests that we can transcend the context-oriented perspective of LD by generalizing over times and worlds so as to capture those possible circumstances $\langle \mathfrak{A}, t, w \rangle$ which do not correspond to any possible contexts $\langle \mathfrak{A}, c \rangle$. We have the following result:

(iii) If ϕ contains no demonstratives
$\models_T \phi$ iff $\models_{LD} \Box (\neg P \neg \phi \wedge \neg F \neg \phi \wedge \phi)$.

Although our definition of the neo-traditional sense of validity was motivated by consideration of demonstrative-free formulas, we could apply it also to formulas containing essential occurrences of demonstratives. To do so would nullify the most interesting features of the logic of demonstratives. But it raises the question: can we express our new sense of validity in terms of the neo-traditional sense? This can be done:

(iv) $\models_{LD} \phi$ iff $\models_T \text{AN}\phi$.

Remark 10. Rigid designators (in the sense of Kripke) are terms with a stable Content. Since Kripke does not discuss demonstratives, his examples all have, in addition, a stable Character (by *Remark 8*). Kripke claims that for proper names α, β it may happen that $\alpha = \beta$, though not *a-priori*, is nevertheless necessary. This, in spite of the fact that the names α, β may be introduced by means of descriptions α', β' for which $\alpha' = \beta'$ is not necessary. An analogous situation holds in LD. Let α', β' be definite descriptions (without free variables) such that $\alpha' = \beta'$ is not *a-priori,* and consider the rigid terms dthat α' and dthat β' which are formed from them. We know that $\vDash$ (dthat α' = dthatβ' $\leftrightarrow$ α' = β'). Thus, if $\alpha' = \beta'$ is not *a-priori,* neither is dthatα' = dthat β'. But, since $\vDash$[dthat α' = dthatβ' $\rightarrow$ $\Box$(dthatα' = dthatβ')], it may happen that dthatα' = dthatβ' is necessary. The converse situation can also be illustrated in LD. Since (α' = dthatα') is valid (see *Remark 3*), it is surely capable of being known *a-priori.* But if α' lacks a stable Content (in some context c), $\Box$ (α' = dthatα') will be false.

Remark 11. Our *o-o*-place *i*-functors are not proper names, in the sense of Kripke, since they do not have a stable Content. But they can easily be converted by means of the stabilizing influence of dthat. Even dthat α lacks a stable Character. The process by which such expressions are converted into expressions with a stable Character is 'dubbing'—a form of definition in which context may play an essential role. The means to deal with such context-indexed definitions is not available in our object language.

There would, of course, be no difficulty in supplementing our language with a syntactically distinctive set of *o-o*-place *i*-functors whose semantics requires them to have both a stable Character and a stable Content in every context. Variables already behave this way; what is wanted is a class of constants that behave, in these respects, like variables.

The difficulty comes in expressing the definition. My thought is that when a name, like 'Bozo', is introduced by someone saying, in some context c^*, 'Let's call the Governor, "Bozo"', we have a context-indexed definition of the form: $A = {}_{c^*}\alpha$, where A is a new constant (here, 'Bozo') and α is some term whose denotation depends on context (here, 'the Governor'). The intention of such a dubbing is, presumably, to induce the semantical clause: for all c, $\{A\}^{\mathfrak{A}}_{cf} = \{\alpha\}^{\mathfrak{A}}_{c^*f}$. Such a clause gives A a stable Character. The context indexing is required by the fact that the Content of α (the 'definiens') may vary from context to context. Thus the

same semantical clause is not induced by taking either $A = \alpha$ or even $A = $ dthat α as an axiom.

I think it likely that such definitions play a practically (and perhaps theoretically) indispensable role in the growth of language, allowing us to introduce a vast stock of names on the basis of a meagre stock of demonstratives and some ingenuity in the staging of demonstrations.

Perhaps such introductions should not be called 'definitions' at all, since they essentially enrich the expressive power of the language. What a nameless man may express by 'I am hungry' may be inexpressible in remote contexts. But once he says 'Let's call me "Bozo"' his Content is accessible, to us all.

Remark 12. The strongest form of logical equivalence between two formulas ϕ and ϕ' is sameness of Character, $\{\phi\} = \{\phi'\}$. This form of synonymy is expressible in terms of validity:

$$\{\phi\} = \{\phi'\} \text{ iff } \vDash\Box[\neg P\neg(\phi\leftrightarrow\phi') \wedge \neg F\neg(\phi\leftrightarrow\phi') \wedge (\phi\leftrightarrow\phi')].$$

[Using *Remark 9* (iii) and dropping the condition, which was stated only to express the intended range of applicability of $\vDash_T$, we have: $\{\phi\} = \{\phi'\}$ if $\vDash_T (\phi\leftrightarrow\phi')$.] Since definitions of the usual kind (as opposed to dubbings) are intended to introduce a short expression as a mere abbreviation of a longer one, the Character of the defined sign should be the same as the Character of the definiens. Thus, with LD, definitional axioms must take the form indicated above.

Remark 13. If β is a variable of the same sort as the term α but is not free in α, then $\{$dthat $\alpha\}$ = $\{$the β $AN(\beta = \alpha)\}$. Thus for every formula ϕ, there can be constructed a formula ϕ' such that ϕ' contains no occurrence of dthat and $\{\phi\} = \{\phi'\}$.

Remark 14. Y (yesterday) and G (one day ago) superficially resemble one another in view of the fact that $\vDash (Y\phi \leftrightarrow G\phi)$. But the former is a demonstrative whereas the latter is an iterative temporal operator. 'One day ago it was the case that one day ago it was the case that John yawned' means that John yawned the day before yesterday. But 'Yesterday it was the case that yesterday it was the case that John yawned' is only a stutter.

POSSIBLE REFINEMENTS

(1) The primitive predicates and functors of first-order predicate logic are all taken to be extensional. Alternatives are possible.

(2) Many conditions might be added on $\mathscr{P}$; many alternatives might be chosen for $\mathscr{T}$. If the elements of $\mathscr{T}$ do not have a natural relation to play the role of $<$, such a relation must be added to the structure.

(3) When K is a set of LD formulas, $K \vDash \phi$ is easily defined in any of the usual ways.

(4) Aspects of the contexts other than c_A, c_P, c_T, and c_W would be used if new demonstratives (e.g. pointings, 'You', etc.) were added to the language. (Note that the subscripts A, P, T, W are external parameters. They may be thought of as functions applying to contexts, with c_A being the value of A for the context c.)

(5) Special continuity conditions through time might be added for the predicate Exists.

(6) If individuals lacking positions are admitted as agents of contexts, 3(iii) of page 361 should be weakened to $c_p \in \mathscr{P} \cup \{\dagger\}$. It would no longer be the case that $\vDash$ Located I, Here. If individuals also lacking temporal location (disembodied minds?) are admitted as agents of contexts, a similar weakening is required of 3(ii). In any case it would still be true that $\vDash$ Exist I.

ACKNOWLEDGMENTS

This paper was originally composed in two parts. The formal "Logic of Demonstratives" was first presented at the Irvine Summer Institute on the Philosophy of Language in 1971. It was expanded in 1973. The initial discursive material was written on 20 April 1973, as part of a research proposal. This paper was intended as a companion piece to and progress report on the material in "Dthat." D. Kaplan, "Dthat" in Peter Cole (ed.), *Syntax and Semantics, 9, Pragmatics* (Academic Press: New York, 1978), 221–43. Also reprinted in P. French *et al.* (eds), *Contemporary Perspectives in the Philosophy of Language* (Minneapolis: University of Minnesota Press, 1979), pp. 383–400. A more extensive presentation occurs in my manuscript "Demonstratives," in J. Almog. J. Perry, and H. Wettstein (eds.), *Themes from Kaplan* (Oxford University Press, 1989). This work was supported by the National Science Foundation.

NOTES

1. S. Kripke, "Naming and Necessity," in Donald Davidson and Gilbert Harman (eds.), *Semantics of Natural Language* (Dordrecht: Reidel, 1972), 253–355; Addenda, pp. 763–9.
2. P. Strawson, *Introduction to Logical Theory* (New York: John Wiley & Sons, 1952).

The Problem of the Essential Indexical

JOHN PERRY

I once followed a trail of sugar on a supermarket floor, pushing my cart down the aisle on one side of a tall counter and back the aisle on the other, seeking the shopper with the torn sack to tell him he was making a mess. With each trip around the counter, the trail became thicker. But I seemed unable to catch up. Finally it dawned on me. I was the shopper I was trying to catch.

 I believed at the outset that the shopper with a torn sack was making a mess. And I was right. But I didn't believe that I was making a mess. That seems to be something I came to believe. And when I came to believe that, I stopped following the trail around the counter, and rearranged the torn sack in my cart. My change in beliefs seems to explain my change in behavior. My aim in this paper is to make a key point about the characterization of this change, and of beliefs in general.

At first characterizing the change seems easy. My beliefs changed, didn't they, in that I came to have a new one, namely, *that I am making a mess?* But things are not so simple.

The reason they are not is the importance of the word "I" in my expression of what I came to believe. When we replace it with other designations of me, we no longer have an explanation of my behavior and so, it seems, no longer an attribution of the same belief. It seems to be an *essential* indexical. But without such a replacement, all we have to identify the belief is the

sentence "I am making a mess". But that sentence by itself doesn't seem to identify the crucial belief, for if someone else had said it, they would have expressed a different belief, a false one.

I argue that the essential indexical poses a problem for various otherwise plausible accounts of belief. I first argue that it is a problem for the view that belief is a relation between subjects and propositions conceived as bearers of truth and falsity. The problem is not solved merely by replacing or supplementing this with a notion of *de re* belief. Nor is it solved by moving to a notion of a proposition which, rather than true or false absolutely, is only true or false at an index or in a context (at a time, for a speaker, say). Its solution requires us to make a sharp distinction between objects of belief and belief states, and to realize that the connection between them is not so intimate as might have been supposed.[1]

LOCATING BELIEFS

I want to introduce two more examples. In the first a professor, who desires to attend the department meeting on time, and believes correctly that it begins at noon, sits motionless in his office at that time. Suddenly he begins to move. What explains his action? A change in belief. He believed all along that the department

From *Noûs* 13 (1979): 3–20. Copyright © 1979 by *Noûs*. Reprinted with the permission of Blackwell Publishers.

meeting starts at noon; he came to believe, as he would have put it, that it starts *now.*

The author of the book, *Hiker's Guide to the Desolation Wilderness,* stands in the wilderness beside Gilmore Lake, looking at the Mt. Tallac trail as it leaves the lake and climbs the mountain. He desires to leave the wilderness. He believes that the best way out from Gilmore Lake is to follow the Mt. Tallac trail up the mountain to Cathedral Peaks trail, on to the Floating Island trail, emerging at Spring Creek Tract Road. But he does not move. He is lost. He isn't sure whether he is standing beside Gilmore Lake, looking at Mt. Tallac, or beside Clyde Lake looking at Jack's peak, or beside Eagle Lake looking at one of the Maggie peaks. Then he begins to move along the Mt. Tallac trail. If asked, he would have explained the crucial change in his beliefs this way: "I came to believe that *this* is the Mt. Tallac trail and *that* is Gilmore Lake."

In these three cases the subjects in explaining their actions, would use indexicals to characterize certain beliefs they came to have. These indexicals are essential, in that replacement of them by other terms destroys the force of the explanation, or at least requires certain assumptions to be made to preserve it.

Suppose I had said, in the manner of de Gaulle, "I came to believe that John Perry is making a mess." I would no longer have explained why I stopped and looked in my own cart. To explain that I would have to add, "and I believe that I am John Perry," bringing in the indexical again. After all, suppose I had really given my explanation in the manner of de Gaulle, and said "I came to believe that de Gaulle is making a mess." That wouldn't have explained my stopping at all. But it really would have explained it every bit as much as "I came to believe John Perry is making a mess". For if I added "and I believe that I am de Gaulle" the explanations would be on par. The only reason "I came to believe John Perry is making a mess" seems to explain my action is our natural assumption that I did believe I was John Perry and didn't believe I was de Gaulle. So replacing the indexical 'I' with another term designating the same person really does, as claimed, destroy the explanation.

Similarly, our professor, as he sets off down the hall, might say "I believe the meeting starts at noon", rather than "I believe the meeting starts now". In accepting the former as an explanation, we would be assuming he believes it is *now* noon. If he believed it was now 5 p.m., he wouldn't have explained his departure by citing his belief that the meeting starts at noon, unless he was a member of a department with very long meetings. After all, he believed that the meeting started at noon all along, so that belief can hardly explain a change in his behavior. Basically similar remarks apply to the lost author.

I shall use the term "locating beliefs" to refer to one's beliefs about where one is, when it is, and who one is. Such beliefs seem essentially indexical. Imagine two lost campers who trust the same guidebook but disagree about where they are. If we were to try to characterize the beliefs of these campers without the use of indexicals, it would seem impossible to bring out this disagreement. If, for example, we characterized their beliefs by the set of "eternal sentences," drawn from the guidebook they would mark "true", there is no reason to suppose that the sets would differ. They could mark all of the same sentences "true", and still disagree in their locating beliefs. It seems that there has to be some indexical element in the characterization of their beliefs to bring out this disagreement. But as we shall see there is no room for this indexical element in the traditional way of looking at belief, and even when its necessity is recognized, it is not easy to see how to fit it in.

THE DOCTRINE OF PROPOSITIONS

I shall first consider how the problem appears to a traditional way of thinking of belief. The doctrines I describe were held by Frege, but I shall put them in a way that does not incorporate his terminology or the details of his view.[2] This traditional way, which I call the "doctrine of propositions", has three main tenets. The first is that belief is a relation between a subject and an object, the latter being denoted, in a canonical belief report, by a that-clause. So "Carter believes that Atlanta is the capital of Georgia" reports that a certain relation, *believing,* obtains between Carter and a certain object—at least in a suitably wide sense of object—*that Atlanta is the capital of Georgia.* These objects are called *propositions.*

The second and the third tenets concern such objects. The second is that they have a truth-value in an absolute sense, as opposed to merely being true for a person or at a time. The third has to do with how we individuate them. It is necessary, for *that S* and *that S′* to be the same, that they have the same truth-value. But it is not sufficient, for *that the sea is salty* and *that milk is white* are not the same proposition. It is necessary that they have the same truth condition, in the sense that they attribute to the same objects the same relation. But this also is not sufficient, for *that Atlanta is the capital of Georgia* and *that Atlanta is the capital of the largest state east of the Mississippi* are not the same proposition. Carter, it seems, might believe the first but not the second. Propositions must not only have the same truth-value, and concern the same objects and relations, but also involve the same concepts. For Frege, this meant that if *that S = that S′,* S and S′ must have the same sense. Others might eschew senses in favor of properties and relations, others take concepts to be just words, so that sameness of propositions is just sameness of sentences. What these approaches have in common is the insistence that propositions must be individuated in a more "fine-grained" way than is provided by truth-value or the notion truth conditions employed above.

THE PROBLEM

It's clear that the essential indexical is a problem for the doctrine of propositions. What answer can it give to the question, "What did I come to believe when I straightened up the sugar?" The sentence "I am making a mess" doesn't identify a proposition. For this sentence is not true or false absolutely, but only as said by one person or another; had another shopper said it when I did, he would have been wrong. So the sentence by which I identify what I came to believe doesn't identify, by itself, a proposition. There is a *missing conceptual ingredient:* a sense for which I am the reference, or a complex of properties I alone have, or a singular term

that refers to no one but me. To identify the proposition I came to believe, the advocate of the doctrine of propositions must identify this missing conceptual ingredient.

An advocate of the doctrine of propositions, his attention drawn to indexicals, might take this attitude towards them: they are communicative shortcuts. Just before I straightened up the sack I must have come to believe some propositions with the structure α *is making a mess,* where α is some concept which I alone "fit" (to pick a phrase neutral among the different notions of a concept). When I say "I believe I am making a mess," my hearers know that I believe some such proposition of this form; which one in particular is not important for the purposes at hand.

If this is correct, we should be able to identify the proposition I came to believe, even if doing so isn't necessary for ordinary communicative purposes. But then the doctrine of propositions is in trouble, for any candidate will fall prey to the problems mentioned above. If *that α is making a mess* is what I came to believe, then "I came to believe that A is making a mess", where A expressed α, should be an even better explanation than the original, where I used "I" as a communicative shortcut. But, as we saw, any such explanation will be defective, working only on the assumption that I believed that I was α.

To this it might be replied that though there may be no replacement for "I" that generally preserves explanatory force, all that needs to be claimed is that there is such a replacement on each occasion. The picture is this. On each occasion that I use "I", there is some concept I have in mind that fits me uniquely, and which is the missing conceptual ingredient in the proposition that remains incompletely identified when I characterize my beliefs. The concept I use to think of myself isn't necessarily the same each time I do so, and of course I must use a different one than others do, since it must fit me and not them. Because there is no general way of replacing the "I" with a term that gets at the missing ingredient, the challenge to do so in response to a particular example is temporarily embarassing. But the doctrine of propositions doesn't require a general answer.

This strategy doesn't work for two reasons. First, even if I was thinking of myself as, say, the only bearded philosopher in a Safeway store west of the Mississippi, the fact that I came to believe that the only such philosopher was making a mess explains my action only on the assumption that I believed that I was the only such philosopher, which brings in the indexical again. Second, in order to provide me with an appropriate proposition as the object of belief, the missing conceptual ingredient will have to fit me. Suppose I was thinking of myself in the way described, but that I wasn't bearded and wasn't in a Safeway store—I had forgotten that I had shaved and gone to the A & P instead. Then the proposition supplied by this strategy would be false, while what I came to believe, *that I was making a mess,* was true.

This strategy assumes that whenever I have a belief I would characterize by using a sentence with an indexical *d,*

I believe that . . . d . . .

that there is some conceptual ingredient *c,* such that it is also true that,

I believe that *d* is *c*

and that, on this second point, I am right. But there is no reason to believe this would always be so. Each time I say "I believe it is *now* time to rake the leaves," I need not have some concept that uniquely fits the time at which I speak.

From the point of view of the doctrine of propositions, belief reports such as "I believe that I am making a mess" are deficient, for there is a missing conceptual ingredient. From the point of view of locating beliefs, there is something lacking in the propositions offered by the doctrine, a missing indexical ingredient.

The problem of the essential indexical reveals that something is badly wrong with the traditional doctrine of propositions. But the traditional doctrine has its competitors anyway, in response to philosophical pressures from other directions. Perhaps attention to these alternative or supplementary models of belief will provide a solution to our problem.

DE RE BELIEF

One development in the philosophy of belief seems quite promising in this respect. It involves qualifying the third tenet of the doctrine of propositions, to allow a sort of proposition individuated by an object or sequence of objects, and a part of a proposition of the earlier sort. The motivation for this qualification or supplementation comes from belief reports, which give rise to the same problem, that of the missing conceptual ingredient, as does the problem of the essential indexical.

The third tenet of the doctrine of propositions is motivated by the failure of substitutivity of co-referential terms within the that-clause following "believes". But there seems to be a sort of belief report, or a way of understanding some belief reports, that allows such substitution, and such successful substitution becomes a problem for a theory designed to explain its failure. For suppose Patrick believes that, as he would put it, the dean is wise. Patrick doesn't know Frank, much less know that he lives next to the dean, and yet I might in certain circumstances say "Patrick believes Frank's neighbor is wise." Or I might say "There is someone whom Patrick believes to be wise," and later on identify that someone as "Frank's neighbor." The legitimacy of this cannot be understood on the unqualified doctrine of propositions; I seem to have gone from one proposition, *that the dean of the school is wise,* to another, *that Frank's neighbor is wise;* but the fact that Patrick believes the first seems to be no reason he should believe the second. And the quantification into the belief report seems to make no sense at all on the doctrine of propositions, for the report doesn't relate Patrick to an individual known variously as "the dean" and "Frank's neighbor", but only with a concept expressed by the first of these terms.

The problem here is just that of a missing conceptual ingredient. It looked in the original report as if Patrick was being said to stand in the relation of belief to a certain proposition, a part of which was a conceptual ingredient expressed by the words "the dean". But if I am permitted to exchange those words for others, "Frank's neighbor", which are not conceptually equivalent, then apparently the initial part of the proposition he was credited with belief in was not the conceptual ingredient identified by "the dean" after all. So what proposition was it

Patrick was originally credited with belief in? And "There is someone such that Patrick believes that he is wise" seems to credit Patrick with belief in a proposition, without telling us which one. For after the "believes" we have only "he is wise", where the "he" doesn't give us an appropriate conceptual ingredient, but functions as a variable ranging over individuals.

We do seem in some circumstances to allow such substitutivity, and make ready sense of quantification into belief reports. So the doctrine of propositions must be qualified. We can look upon this sort of belief as involving a relation to a new sort of proposition, consisting of an object or sequence of objects and a conceptual ingredient, a part of a proposition of the original kind, or what we might call an "open proposition". This sort of belief and this kind of proposition we call "*de re*", the sort of belief and the sort of proposition that fits the original doctrine, "*de dicto*". Taken this way we analyze "Patrick believes that the dean of the school is wise", as reporting a relation between Patrick and a proposition consisting of a certain person variously describable as "the dean" and "Frank's neighbor" and something, *that x is wise,* which would yield a proposition with the addition of an appropriate conceptual ingredient. Since the dean himself, and not just a concept expressed by the words "the dean" is involved, substitution holds and quantification makes sense.

Here, as in the case of the essential indexical, we were faced with a missing conceptual ingredient. Perhaps, then, this modification of the third tenet will solve the earlier problem as well. But it won't. Even if we suppose—as I think we should—that when I said "I believe that I am making a mess" I was reporting a *de re* belief, our problem will remain.

One problem emerges when we look at accounts that have been offered of the conditions under which a person has a *de re* belief. The most influential treatments of *de re* belief have tried to explain it in terms of *de dicto* belief or something like it. Some terminological regimentation is helpful here. Let us couch reports of *de re* belief in the terms "*X* believes of *a* that he is so and so", reserving the simpler "*X* believes that *a* is so-and-so" for *de dicto* belief. The simplest account of *de re* belief in terms of de dicto belief is this:

X believes of *y* that he is so and so

just in case

There is a concept α such that α fits *y* and *X* believes that α is so and so.

Now it is clear that if this is our analysis of *de re* belief, the problem of the essential indexical is still with us. For we are faced with the same problem we had before. I can believe that I am making a mess, even if there is no concept α such that I alone fit α and I believe that α is making a mess. Since I don't have any *de dicto* belief of the sort, on this account I don't have a *de re* belief of the right sort either. So, even allowing *de re* belief, we still don't have an account of the belief I acquired.

Now this simple account of *de re* belief has not won many adherents, because it is commonly held that *de re* belief is a more interesting notion than it allows. This proposal trivializes it. Suppose Nixon is the next President. Since I believe that the next president will be the next President I would on this proposal, believe of Nixon that he is the next president, even though I am thoroughly convinced that Nixon will not be the next President.[3]

To get a more interesting or useful notion of *de re* belief, philosophers have suggested that there are limitations on the conceptual ingredient involved in the *de dicto* belief which yields the *de re* belief. Kaplan, for example, requires not only that there be some α such that I believe that α will be the next President and that α denotes Nixon, for me to believe of Nixon that he will be the next President, but also that α be a *vivid name of Nixon for me* ([9:225 ff.]). Hintikka requires that α denote the same individual in every possible world compatible with what I believe ([7: 40 ff.]). Each of these philosophers explains these notions in such a way that in the circumstances imagined, I would not believe of Nixon that he is the next President.

However well these proposals deal with other phenomena connected with *de re* belief, they cannot help with the problem of the essential indexical. They tighten the requirements laid down by the original proposal, but those were apparently already too restrictive. If in order to believe that I am making a mess I need not have any conceptual ingredient α that fits me, *a fortiori* I am not required to have one that is a vivid name of myself for me, or one that picks out the same individual in every possible world compatible with what I believe.

Perhaps this simply shows that the approach of explaining *de re* belief in terms of *de dicto* belief is incorrect. I think it does show that. But even so, the problem remains. Suppose we do not insist on an account of *de re* belief in terms of *de dicto* belief, but merely suppose that whenever we ascribe a belief, and cannot find a suitable complete proposition to serve as the object because of a missing conceptual ingredient, we are dealing with *de re* belief. Then we will ascribe a *de re* belief to me in the supermarket, I believed *of* John Perry that he was making a mess. But it won't be my having such a *de re* belief that explains my action.

Suppose there were mirrors at either end of the counter so that as I pushed my cart down the aisle in pursuit I saw myself in the mirror. I take what I see to be the reflection of the messy shopper going up the aisle on the other side, not realizing that what I am really seeing is a reflection of a reflection of myself. I point and say, truly, "I believe that he is making a mess." In trying to find a suitable proposition for me to believe, we would be faced with the same sorts of problems we had with my earlier report, in which I used "I" instead of "he". We would not be able to eliminate an indexical element in the term referring to me. So here we have *de re* belief; I believe of John Perry that he is making of a mess. But then that I believe of John Perry that he is making a mess doesn't explain my stopping; in the imagined circumstances I would accelerate, as would the shopper I was trying to catch. But then, even granting that when I say "I believe that I am making a mess" I attribute to myself a certain *de re* belief, the belief of John Perry that he is making a mess, our problem remains.

If we look at it with the notion of a locating belief in mind, the failure of the introduction of *de re* belief to solve our problems is not surprising. *De re* propositions remain non-indexical. Propositions individuated in part by objects remain as insensitive to what is essential in locating beliefs as those individuated wholly by concepts. Saying that I believed of John Perry that he was making a mess leaves out the crucial change, that I came to think of the messy shopper not merely as the shopper with the torn sack, or the man in the mirror, but as *me*.

RELATIVIZED PROPOSITIONS

It seems that to deal with essential indexicality we must somehow incorporate the indexical element into what is believed, the object of belief. If we do so, we come up against the second tenet of the doctrine of propositions, that such objects are true or false absolutely. But the tools for abandoning this tenet have been provided in recent treatments of the semantics of modality, tense, and indexicality. So this seems a promising direction.

In possible worlds semantics for necessity and possibility we have the notion of truth at a world. In a way this doesn't involve a new notion of a proposition and in a way it does. When Frege insisted that his "thoughts" were true or false absolutely, he didn't mean that they had the same truth-value in all possible worlds. Had he used a possible worlds framework, he would have had their truth-values vary from world to world, and simply insisted on a determinate truth-value in each world and in particular in the actual world. In a way, then, taking propositions to be functions from possible worlds to truth-values is just a way of looking at the old notion of a proposition.

Still, this way of looking at it invites generalization, that takes us away from the old notion. From a technical point of view, the essential idea is that a proposition is or is represented by a function from an index to a truth-value; when we get away from modality, this same technical idea may be useful, though something other than possible worlds are taken as indices. To deal with temporal operators, we can use the notion of truth at a time. Here the indices will be times, and our propositions will be functions from times to truth-values. For example, *that Elizabeth is Queen of England* is a proposition true in 1960 but not in 1940. Hence "At sometime or other Elizabeth is Queen of England" is true, simpliciter. (See[10] and [13], especially "Pragmatics".)

Now consider "I am making a mess". Rather than thinking of this as partially identifying an absolutely true proposition, with the "I" showing the place of the missing conceptual ingredient, why not think of it as completely identifying a new-fangled proposition, that is true or false only *at a person?* More precisely, it is one that is true or false at a time and a person, since though true when I said it, it has since occasionally been false.

If we ignore possibility and necessity, it seems that regarding propositions as functions to truth-values from indices which are pairs of persons and times will do the trick, and that so doing will allow us to exploit relations between elements within the indices to formulate rules which bring out differences between indexicals. "I am tired now" is true at the pair consisting of the person *a* and the time *t* if and only if *a* is tired at *t,* while "You will be tired" is true at the same index if and only if the addressee of *a* at *t* is tired at some time later than *t.*

Does this way of looking at the matter solve the problem of the essential indexical? I say "I believe that I am making a mess". On our amended doctrine of propositions, this ascribes a relation between me and *that I am making a mess,* which is a function from indices to truth values. The belief report seems to completely specify the relativized proposition involved; there is no missing conceptual ingredient. So the problem must be solved.

But it isn't. I believed that a certain proposition, *that I am making a mess* was true—true for me. So belief that this proposition was true for me then doesn't differentiate me from the other shopper, and can't be what explains my stopping and searching my cart for the torn sack. Once we have adopted these new-fangled propositions, which are only true at times for persons, we have to admit also that we believe them as true for persons at times, and not absolutely. And then our problem returns.

Clearly an important distinction must be made. All believing is done by persons at times, or so we may suppose. But the time of belief and the person doing the believing cannot be generally identified with the person and time relative to which the proposition believed is held true. You now believe that *that I am making a mess* was true for me, then, but you certainly don't believe it is true for you now, unless you are reading this in a supermarket. Let us call *you* and *now* the context of belief, and *me* and *then* the context of evaluation. The context of belief may be the same as the context of evaluation, but need not be.

Now the mere fact that I believed that proposition *that I making a mess* to be true for someone at some time did not explain my stopping the cart. You believe so now, and doubtless have no more desire to mess up supermarkets than I did. But you are not bending over to straighten up a sack of sugar.

The fact that I believed this proposition true for Perry at the time he was in the supermarket does not explain my behavior either. For so did the other shopper. And you also now believe this proposition was true for Perry at the time he was in the supermarket.

The important difference seems to be that for me the context of belief was just the context of evaluation, but for the other shopper it wasn't and for you it isn't. But this doesn't do the trick either.

Consider our tardy professor. He is doing research on indexicals, and has written on the board "My meeting starts now". He believes that the proposition expressed by this sentence is true at noon for him. He has believed so for hours, and at noon the context of belief comes to be the context of evaluation. These facts give us no reason to expect him to move.

Or suppose I think to myself that the person making the mess should say so. Turning my attention to the proposition, I certainly believe *that I am making a mess* is true for the person who ought to be saying it (or the person in the mirror, or the person at the end of the trail of sugar) at that time. The context of evaluation is just the context of belief. But there is no reason to suppose I would stop my cart.

One supposes that in these cases the problem is that the context of belief is not believed to be the context of evaluation. But formulating the required belief will simply bring up the problem of the essential indexical again. Clearly and correctly we want the tardy professor, when he finally sees he must be off to the meeting, to be ready to say "I believe that the time at which it is true *that the meeting starts now* is now." On the present proposal, we analyze the belief he thereby ascribes to himself as belief in the proposition *that the time at which it is true that the meeting starts now is now.* But he certainly can believe at noon, that this whole proposition is true at noon, without being ready to say "It's starting now" and leave. We do not yet have a solution to the problem of the essential indexical.

LIMITED ACCESSIBILITY

One may take all that has been said so far as an argument for the existence of a special class of propositions, propositions of limited accessibility. For what have we really shown? All attempts to find a formula of the form "A is making a mess", with which any of us at any time could express what I believed, have failed. But one might argue that we can hardly suppose that there wasn't anything that I believed; surely I believed just that proposition which I expressed, on that occasion, with the words "I am making a mess". That we cannot find a sentence that always expresses this proposition when said by anyone does not show that it does not exist. Rather it should lead us to the conclusion that there is a class of propositions which can only be expressed in special circumstances. In particular, only I could express the proposition I expressed when I said "I am making a mess." Others can see, perhaps by analogy with their own case, that there is a proposition that I express, but it is in a sense inaccessible to them.

Similarly, at noon on the day of the meeting, we could all express the proposition the tardy professor expressed with the words "The meeting starts now". But once that time has past, the proposition becomes inaccessible. We can still identify it, as the proposition which was expressed by those words at that time. But we cannot express it with those words any longer, for with each passing moment they express a different proposition. And we can find no other words to express it.

The advocate of such a stock of propositions of limited accessibility may not need to bring in special propositions accessible only at certain places. For it is plausible to suppose that other indexicals can be eliminated in favor of "I" and "now". Perhaps "That is Gilmore Lake" just comes to "What I see now in front of me is Gilmore Lake". But elimination of either "I" or "now" in favor of the other seems impossible.

Such a theory of propositions of limited accessibility seems acceptable, even attractive, to some philosophers.[4] It's acceptability or attractiveness will depend on other parts of one's metaphysics; if one finds plausible reasons elsewhere for believing in a universe that has, in addition to our common world, myriads of private perspectives, the idea of propositions of limited accessability will fit right in.[5] I have no knock-down argument against such propositions, or the metaphysical schemes that find room for them. But I believe only in a common actual world. And I do not think the phenomenon of essential indexicality forces me to abandon this view.

THE OBVIOUS SOLUTION?

Let's return to the device of the true-false exam. Suppose the lost author had been given such an exam before and after he figured out where he was. Would we expect any differences in his answers? Not so long as the statements contained no indexicals. "Mt. Tallac is higher than either of the Maggie Peaks" would have been marked the same way before and after, the same way he would have marked it at home in Berkeley. His mark on that sentence would tell us nothing about where he thought he was. But if the exam were to contain such sentences as "That is Gilmore Lake in front of me" we would expect a dramatic change, from "False" or "Unsure" to "True".

Imagine such an exam given to various lost campers in different parts of the Wilderness. We could classify the campers by their answers, and such a classification would be valuable for prediction and explanation. Of all the campers who marked "This is Gilmore Lake" with "True", we would say they believed that they were at Gilmore Lake. And we should expect them to act accordingly; if they possessed the standard guidebook, and wished to leave the Wilderness, we might expect what is, given one way of looking at it, the same behavior: taking the path up the mountain above the shallow end of the lake before them.

Now consider all the good-hearted people who have ever been in a supermarket, noticed sugar on the floor, and been ready to say "I am making a mess." They all have something important in common, something that leads us to expect their next action to be that of looking into their grocery carts in search of the torn sack. Or consider all the responsible professors who have ever uttered "The department meeting is starting now." They too have something important in common; they are in a state which will lead those just down the hall to go to the meeting, those across campus to curse and feel guilty, those on leave to smile.

What the members within these various groups have in common is not what they believe. There is no *de dicto* proposition that all the campers or shoppers or professors believe. And there is no person whom all the shoppers believe to be making a mess, no lake all the campers believe to be Gilmore Lake, and no time at which all the professors believe their meetings to be starting.

We are clearly classifying the shoppers, campers, and professors into groups corresponding to what we have been calling "relativized propositions"—abstract objects corresponding to sentences containing indexicals. But what members of each group have in common, which makes the groups significant, is not belief that a certain relativized proposition is true. Such belief, as we saw, is belief that such a proposition is true at some context of evaluation. Now all of the shoppers believe that *that I am making a mess* is true at some context of evaluation or other, but so does everyone else who has ever given it a moment's thought. And similar remarks apply to the campers and the professors.

If believing the same relativized proposition isn't what the members of each of the groups have in common with one another, why is it being used as a principle of classification? I propose we look at things in this way. The shoppers, for example, are all in a certain belief state, a state which, given normal desires and other belief states they can be expected to be in, will lead each of them to examine his cart. But, although they are all in the same belief state (not

the same *total* belief state, of course), they do not all have the same belief (believe the same thing, have the relation of belief to the same object).

We use sentences with indexicals or relativized propositions to individuate belief states, for the purposes of classifying believers in ways useful for explanation and prediction. That is, belief states individuated in this way enter into our common sense theory about human behavior and more sophisticated theories emerging from it. We expect all good-hearted people in that state which leads them to say "I am making a mess" to examine their grocery carts, no matter what belief they have in virtue of being in that state. That we individuate belief states in this way doubtless has something to do with the fact that one criterion for being in the states we postulate, at least for articulate sincere adults, is being disposed to utter the indexical sentence in question. A good philosophy of mind should explain this in detail; my aim is merely to get clear about what it is that needs explaining.

The proposal, then, is that there is not an identity, or even an isomorphic correspondence, but only a systematic relationship between the belief states one is in and what one thereby believes. The opposite assumption, that belief states should be classified by propositions believed, seems to be built right into traditional philosophies of belief. Given this assumption, whenever we have believers in the same belief state, we must expect to find a proposition they all believe, and differences in belief state lead us to expect a difference in proposition believed. The bulk of this paper consisted in following such leads to nowhere (or to propositions of limited accessibility).

Consider a believer whose belief states are characterized by a structure of sentences with indexicals or relativized propositions (those marked "true" in a very comprehensive exam, if we are dealing with an articulate sincere adult). This structure, together with the context of belief—the time and identity of the speaker— will yield a structure of *de re* propositions. The sequence of objects will consist of the values which the indexicals take in the context. The open propositions will be those yielded by the relativized proposition when shorn of its indexical elements. These are what the person believes, in virtue of being in the states he is in, when and where he is in them.[6]

This latter structure is important, and classifications of believers by *what* they believe is appropriate for many purposes. For example, usually, when a believer moves from context to context, his belief states adjust to preserve beliefs held. As time passes, I go from the state corresponding to "The meeting will begin" to the one corresponding to "The meeting is beginning" and finally to "The meeting has begun". All along I believe of noon that it is when the meeting begins. But I believe it in different ways. And to these different ways of believing the same thing, different actions are appropriate: preparation, movement, apology. Of course if the change of context is not noted, the adjustment of belief states will not occur, and a wholesale change from believing truly to believing falsely may occur. This is what happened to Rip Van Winkle. He awakes in the same belief states he fell asleep in twenty years earlier, unadjusted to the dramatic change in context, and so with a whole new set of beliefs, such as that he is a young man, mostly false.

We have here a metaphysically benign form of limited accessibility. Anyone at any time can have access to any proposition. But not in any way. Anyone can believe of John Perry that he is making a mess. And anyone can be in the belief state classified by the sentence "I am making a mess". But only I can have that belief by being in that state.

There is room in this scheme for *de dicto* propositions, for the characterization of one's belief states may include sentences without any indexical element. If there are any, they could appear on the exam. For this part of the structure, the hypothesis of perfect correspondence would be correct.

A more radical proposal would do away with objects of belief entirely. We would think of belief as a system of relations of various degrees between persons and other objects. Rather than saying I believed in the *de re* proposition consisting of me and the open proposition, *x is making a mess,* we would say that I stand in the relation, believing to be making a mess, to myself. There are many ways to stand in this relation to myself, that is, a variety of belief states I might

be in. And these would be classified by sentences with indexicals. On this view *de dicto* belief, already demoted from its central place in the philosophy of belief, might be seen as merely an illusion, engendered by the implicit nature of much indexicality.

To say that belief states must be distinguished from objects of belief, cannot be individuated in terms of them, and are what is crucial for the explanation of action, is not to give a full fledged account of belief, or even a sketchy one. Similarly, to say that we must distinguish the object seen from the state of the seeing subject, and that the latter is crucial for the explanation of action guided by vision, is not to offer a full fledged account of vision. But just as the arguments from illusion and perceptual relativity teach us that no philosophy of perception can be plausible that is not cognizant of this last distinction, the problem of the essential indexical should teach us that no philosophy of belief can be plausible that does not take account of the first.

ACKNOWLEDGMENTS

Versions of this paper were read at philosophy department colloquia at U.C.L.A., Claremont Graduate School, and Stanford, to the Washington State University at Bellingham Philosophy Conference, and to the Meeting of Alberta Philosophy Department. I am indebted to philosophers participating in these colloquia for many helpful criticisms and comments. I owe a special debt to Michael Bratman, and Dagfinn Føllesdal, for detailed comments on the penultimate version. Most of the ideas in this paper were developed while I held a fellowship from the Guggenheim Foundation and was on sabbatical leave from Stanford University, and I thank both for their support.

NOTES

1. In thinking about the problem of the essential indexical, I have been greatly helped by the writings of Hector-Neri Castañeda on indexicality and related topics. Castañeda focused attention on these problems, and made many of the points made here, in [1], [2] and [3]. More recently his views on these matters have been developed as a part of his comprehensive system of generalized phenomenalism. See particularly [4] and [5]. Having benefited so much from Castañeda's collection of "protophilosophical data", I regret that differences of approach and limitations of competence and space have prevented me from incorporating a discussion of his theory into this essay. I hope to make good this omission at some future time.

2. See [11] for a critique of Frege's views on index-icality.

3. For the classic discussion of these problems, see [12].

4. Frege seems to accept something like it, as necessary for dealing with "I", in [6].

5. See [5] especially section II.

6. This two-tiered structure of belief states and propositions believed will remind the reader familiar with David Kaplan's [8] of his system of characters and contents. This is no accident, for my approach to the problem of the essential indexical was formed by using the distinction as found in earlier versions of Kaplan's work to try to find a solution to the problem as articulated by Castañeda. Kaplan's treatment of indexicality was by and large shaped by considerations other than the problem of the essential indexical. So, while any plausibility one finds in what I say about that problem should be transmitted to the general outlines of his system, at least, by providing an epistemological motivation for something like the character/content distinction, any implausibility one finds will not necessarily be so transmitted. Nor should one take any details one manages to find in this essay as a guide to the details of Kaplan's system.

REFERENCES

[1] Hector-Neri Castañeda, "'He': A Study in the Logic of Self-consciousness," *Ratio* 8(1966): 130–57.

[2] ———."Indicators and Quasi-indicators," *American Philosophical Quarterly* 4(1967): 85–100.

[3] ———."On the Logic of Attributions of Self Knowl-edge to Others," *The Journal of Philosophy* 65(1968): 439–56.

[4] ———."On the Philosophical Foundations of the Theory of Communication: Reference," *Midwestern Studies in Philosophy* 2(1977): 165–86.

[5] ———."Perception, Belief, and the Structure of Physical Objects and Consciousness," *Synthese* 35(1977): 285–351.

[6] Gotlobb Frege, "The Thought: A Logical Inquiry," translated by A. M. and Marcelle Quinton, *Mind* 65(1956): 289–311; reprinted in P. F. Strawson (ed.), *Philosophical Logic* (Oxford: Oxford University Press, 1967): 17–38.

[7] Jaakko Hintikka, "Individuals, Possible Worlds, and Epistemic Logic," *Noûs* 1(1967): 33–62.

[8] David Kaplan, *Demonstratives* (Mimeographed, UCLA, 1977).

[9] ———."Quantifying In," in Donald Davidson and Jaakko Hintikka (eds.) *Words and Objections* (Dordrecht: Reidel, 1969): 206–42. [Reprinted in this volume.]

[10] Richard Montague, "Pragmatics," in Richmond H. Thomason (ed.), *Formal Philosophy: Selected Papers of Richard Montague* (New Haven: Yale University Press, 1974): 95–118.

[11] John Perry, "Frege on Demonstratives," *Philosophical Review* 86(1977): 474–97.

[12] Williard van Orman Quine, "Quantifiers and Propositional Attitudes," reprinted in *Ways of Paradox* (New York: Random House, 1966): 183–94. [Reprinted in this volume.]

[13] Dana Scott, "Advice on Modal Logic," in Karel Lambert (ed.), *Philosophical Problems in Logic* (Dordrecht: Reidel, 1970): 143–73.

SUGGESTED FURTHER READING

Altham, J. E. J., "The Causal Theory of Names," *The Aristotelian Society Supplementary Volume* 47 (1973): 209–225.

Bilgrami, Akeel, "Realism without Internalism: A Critique of Searle on Intentionality," *Journal of Philosophy* 86 (1989): 57–72.

Donnellan, Keith, "Proper Names and Identifying Descriptions," in *Semantics of Natural Languages,* ed. Donald Davidson and Gilbert Harman (New York: Humanities Press, Inc., 1972), pp. 356–379.

Donnellan, Keith, "Speaking of Nothing," *The Philosophical Review* 83 (1974): 3–32.

Donnellan, Keith, "Speaker Reference, Descriptions and Anaphora," in *Syntax and Semantics,* vol. 9, ed. Peter Cole (New York: Academic Press, 1978), pp. 47–68.

Donnellan, Keith, "The Contingent A Priori and Rigid Designators," in *Contemporary Perspectives in the Philosophy of Language,* ed. Peter French, Theodore Uehling, Jr., and Howard Wettstein (Minneapolis: University of Minnesota Press, 1979), pp. 45–60.

Devitt, Michael, *Designation* (New York: Columbia University Press, 1980).

Evans, Gareth, *The Varieties of Reference* (Oxford: Clarendon Press, 1982).

Kaplan, David, "The Logic of Demonstratives," in *Contemporary Perspectives in the Philosophy of Language,* ed. Peter A. French, Theodore Uehling, Jr., and Howard Wettstein (Minneapolis: University of Minnesota Press, 1979), pp. 401–410.

Kaplan, David, "Afterthoughts," in *Themes from Kaplan,* ed. J. Almond, J. Perry, and H. Wettstein (New York: Oxford University Press, 1989), pp. 565–614.

Kaplan, David, "Demonstratives," in *Themes from Kaplan,* ed. J. Almond, J. Perry, and H. Wettstein (Oxford: Oxford University Press, 1989), pp. 481–563.

Kraut, Richard, "Indiscernibility and Ontology," *Synthese* 44 (1980): 113–135.

Linsky, Leonard, *Names and Descriptions* (Chicago: University of Chicago Press, 1977).

Marcus, Ruth Barcan, *Modalities: Philosophical Essay Pages* (New York: Oxford University Press, 1993).

McCulloch, Gregory, *The Game of the Name* (Oxford: Clarendon Press, 1989).

Mill, John Stuart, *A System of Logic,* Book I, chapters 1 and 2.

Perry, John, "Frege on Demonstratives," *Philosophical Review* 86 (1977): 474–497.

Perry, John, *The Problem of the Essential Indexical and Other Essays* (New York: Oxford University Press, 1993).

Putnam, Hilary, "Is Semantics Possible?" in *Language, Belief, and Metaphysics,* ed. H. E. Kiefer and M. K. Munitz (Albany: State University of New York Press, 1970), pp. 50–63.

Russell, Bertrand, "The Philosophy of Logical Atomism," in *Logic and Knowledge,* ed. Robert C. Marsh (London: George Allen and Unwin, 1956), pp. 177–281.

Yourgrau, Palle, ed., *Demonstratives* (New York: Oxford University Press, 1990).

V PROPOSITIONAL ATTITUDES

Almost everyone, before they investigate the problem carefully, will agree that most sentences or statements refer to the situation they describe. "The cat is on the mat" seems to refer to the situation or state of affairs in which a cat is on a mat. It is natural to think that the sentence would refer to such a situation even if it occurs in a longer sentence. For example, the sentence "It is raining and the cat is on the mat" seems to refer in part to the situation in which a cat is on the mat.

So, why shouldn't "The cat is on the mat" refer to the very same situation in sentences like, "John believed that the cat is on the mat" and "Mary sees the cat is on the mat"? The issue is complicated because there are situations in which people are reluctant to draw the consequences one would expect them to draw when a sentence follows a phrase like "believes" or "sees." For consider this sequence of propositions:

John believes that the cat is on the mat.
The cat is Tabby.
John believes that Tabby is on the mat.

Suppose that the first two propositions are true. Further suppose that John does not know that "Tabby" is the name of the cat or that Tabby is the cat. Then he would very likely deny that Tabby is on the mat if he were asked about the matter. And this is good evidence that he does not believe that Tabby is on the mat. If this is correct, then it seems that the first two propositions may be true and the third false. This is good, though not decisive, evidence that the first two propositions do not entail the third, and one plausible explanation for why the entailment does not hold is that in the first sentence "the cat is on the mat" refers to something other than the situation of a cat being on the mat. More particularly, "the cat" in "the cat is on the mat" does not refer to Tabby the cat even though the cat is Tabby.

The same kind of argument could be constructed for a great number of verbs such as "think," "know," "doubt," "see," and "hear," which Bertrand Russell called "propositional attitude verbs" because they seem to express some attitude that a person might take with respect to a proposition. Thus, the proposition that the cat is on the mat might be thought, known, or doubted. (Although it is not obvious that one sees or hears propositions, verbs like "see" and "hear" are included by extension because they seem to have the same logic as the others.)

W. V. Quine in "Quantifiers and Propositional Attitudes" explores the differences between sentences like "Ralph believes that someone is a spy" and "There is someone whom Ralph believes is a spy." The latter sentence seems to entail that a person exists who is the object of Ralph's belief. The former does not: it might be true even if Ralph is benighted and there is no one who exists that he believes to be a spy.

Donald Davidson in "Saying That" is concerned with another problem involving "that" clauses: what do they mean or refer to? It is natural to think that "Jocasta" in the sentence "Oedipus does not believe that Jocasta is his mother" refers to Jocasta. This becomes dubious, however, once one considers the apparent consequences of that view. For example, since Jocasta is his mother, "Jocasta" and "his mother" refer to the same person and hence "Jocasta" should be replaceable in "Oedipus does not believe that Jocasta is his mother." But, if the replacement is made, the result is the sentence "Oedipus does not believe that his mother is his mother." And this sentence seems false.

Davidson's solution to this problem is to treat the word "that" in "that"-clauses in the same way it is treated in a sentence like "That is a dog," namely, as a demonstrative pronoun. What "that" in "that"-clauses demonstrates or points out is the clause or sentence immediately following it. That is, the clause or sentence following the word "that" in "that"-clauses should be understood as displayed, not used. Thus, "Oedipus does not believe that Jocasta is his mother" should be construed as "Oedipus does not believe that:

Jocasta is his mother."

David Kaplan's "Quantifying In" develops the problems raised by both Quine and Davidson. After explicating Quine's and Frege's views, Kaplan gives a kind of Fregean treatment of "that"-clauses. "Jocasta" does not have its normal reference to Jocasta; but it need not be construed as referring to its normal sense either. Rather, "Jocasta" can be held tentatively to refer to itself, namely, the name "Jocasta." Kaplan also draws valuable distinctions between the descriptive content of a name, its genetic content (i.e., the origin of the name) and introduces the notion of a vivid name.

Jon Barwise and John Perry in "Semantic Innocence and Uncompromising Situations" sketch a semantic theory that is motivated or inspired by the belief that the clauses that complete expressions like "John believes that" or "Mary sees that" refer to the very same things that they do when they occur alone. That is, they refer to situations, which are complexes of objects and properties. "The cat is on the mat" refers to the complex of a cat, a mat, and the relation of being on something. They call this "pre-Fregean semantic innocence," because they think that Frege corrupted philosophers by his argument to establish that the reference of a sentence or statement is its truth-value. Their own view is summarized in these two paragraphs:

Our approach is to treat the sentence as embedded and the semantics as innocent, and to deny that the problems that Frege and others have seen with this approach amount to much of anything.

For example, we take a statement of the form *X sees S* to embed a statement *S,* and to be true just in case *X* sees a scene (a specific kind of situation) that belongs to some type in the interpretation of *S.* We take *X believes that S,* in its most central and ordinary uses, to say that *X* has a certain complex relational property built of the objects and properties that are constituents of the proposition that *S.* In both cases, the parts of the embedded statement have their usual interpretations in the whole. What can be wrong with this innocent approach?

Jon Barwise and John Perry reject or at least have serious reservations about the line of reasoning that was described at the beginning of this section. Contrary to the standard view, they hold that "John sees the cat on the mat" and "Tabby is the cat on the mat" at least sometimes entail "John sees Tabby on the mat." If the entailment does not seem to hold, it is only because one is confusing what a speaker says by uttering the sentence with what the speaker sometimes conversationally implies. In certain situations, to say "John sees that Tabby is on the mat" conversationally implies that John knows that the cat's name is "Tabby" or that John would assent to the question, "Is Tabby on the mat?" But not in all situations. Suppose that Tabby is owned by Adam and Beth, both of whom are concerned that Tabby be watched at all times; that they ask John, who has never seen or heard of Tabby before, to watch the cat ("John, please watch the cat"). Since they never mention Tabby's name to him, he does not know it. If sometime later Adam asks Beth whether John is watching the cat, Beth may truly, precisely and nonmisleadingly say, "John sees that Tabby is on the mat" without implying or leading Adam to think that John could answer affirmatively to the question, "Is Tabby on the mat?"

Analogous explanations could be given for other situations like these in which substitution of co-referential expressions appear to break down in the so-called opaque contexts of verbs like "believe," "think," "see," and "hear."

Barwise and Perry would agree with most of this, I believe. Their one reservation is that substitution does break down when a singular term is used attributively rather than referentially, as Donnellan describes the distinction in "Reference and Definite Descriptions." Nonetheless, one should question whether this is a proper distinction or whether it does not also arise from confusing the reference achieved through the use of singular terms with conversationally implied reference. (See my *Communication and Reference,* pp. 169–179.)

Most philosophers accept Church's argument or something like it. Church's argument uses the following four statements:

(5) Sir Walter Scott is the author of *Waverley.*
(6) Sir Walter Scott is the man who wrote the twenty-nine *Waverley* novels altogether.
(7) The number, such that Sir Walter Scott is the man that wrote that many *Waverley* novels altogether, is twenty-nine.
(8) The number of counties in Utah is twenty-nine.

Church claims that since each statement clearly has the same reference as the next, (5) has the same reference as (8); and since (5) and (8) have nothing in common except their truth-value, if reference is preserved when one statement refers to the same thing as another, the reference of a statement must be its truth-value.

In order to make their own view plausible, it is important for Barwise and Perry to explain why Church's argument is not cogent. They accomplish this with great insight. Roughly, their general claim is that Church's argument takes two incompatible views or perspectives of reference. According to the first perspective, all that is important in referring is the object that eventually gets picked out by an expression, no matter how complex the expression is and no matter what descriptive words are used in order to help pick it out. From this perspective, it is not important whether Cicero is picked out by "the Roman orator" or "the statesman that condemned Catiline." Thus, statements (5)–(8) all have the same logical form: a=b. And each can be rendered in effect as follows:

(5′) Scott is Scott.
(6′) Scott is Scott.
(7′) 29 is 29.
(8′) 29 is 29.

The number twenty-nine of course is not mentioned in (5′) because it is not designated in any way in (5). But it is not mentioned in (6′) either because its designation in (6) is not relevant to the ultimate reference of the terms flanking the "is" of identity. What is identified in (5) is Scott with Scott; and the same holds for (6). The fact that "twenty-nine" occurs in (6) is not significant since its occurence is subordinate to and not essential to the ultimate reference to Scott. In (7) and (8), the situation is reversed. Scott is not mentioned in (8′) because he is not designated in any way in (8). And he is not mentioned in (7′) either because his designation is not relevant to the ultimate reference of the terms flanking the "is" of identity. What is identified in (7) is the number twenty-nine with the number twenty-nine. The name "Sir Walter Scott" occurs in (7) only in a subordinate clause and is not essential to the reference to the number at issue. But, seen from this perspective, the inference from (6′) to (7′) and hence from (6) to (7) is invalid.

The second way of looking at reference is to count those concepts and references that are intermediate to the ultimate reference as significant to the form of the statement. From this perspective, it is important how one refers to an object, just as it is important to ordinary people whether they are referred to as "that lovable darling" or "that S.O.B." Roughly, from this second perspective, the meaning of the sentence is important to the way it refers. From this perspective, the inference from (6) to (7) is acceptable because they mean roughly the same thing. But from this same perspective, the inference from (5) to (6) is illicit because they do not have the same meaning, as is the inference from (7) to (8) for the same reason. It is only by conflating the two different perspectives on referring that Church's argument looks plausible.

Barwise and Perry think that Donnellan's distinction between the attributive and referential uses of definite descriptions captures these two perspectives of "reference" in a very broad sense. My own view is that both perspectives ought to be part of a complete theory of reference and that Donnellan in effect strips the referential use of all descriptive content but keeps it in the attributive use.

In addition to its other merits, Barwise and Perry's article is important because it promises to formalize certain informal claims made by J. L. Austin and criticizes certain formal treatments of Frege, Quine, and Davidson.

Saul Kripke in "A Puzzle about Belief" gives a very clear statement of the problems that have worried philosophers about the logic of sentences that report explicit beliefs. The basic problem is that if the meaning of a proper name is the object it denotes, as Kripke and Putnam maintain, how is it possible for a person to know the meaning of two proper names ('London' and 'Londres'), the meaning to be the very same object (London), and for the speaker not to know that the meaning of the one name ('London') is identical with the meaning of the other name ('Londres'). Perhaps the beginning of an answer would go along these lines. Although the meaning of a name is the object it denotes, every object is presented to the person from a certain perspective (or as imagined in some way); the perspective is not relevant to the meaning of the name (because it is merely the way an individual represents it); and the same meaning of a word can be represented in more than one way without the person knowing that he or she is doing so.

In "Semantics for Belief," Robert Stalnaker considers the conflict between three widely held propositions: (i) necessarily equivalent objects of belief are identical; (ii) certain specific sentences, like "Two plus two equals four" and "The cube root of sixty-four is four," are necessarily equivalent; and (iii) it is possible to believe one of the sentences and not to believe the other. Stalnaker thinks that (ii) is false and uses the two-dimensional semantics that he explained in "Assertion" (Section II) to develop his view. The key proposition is this: "Under certain conditions, the content of an assertion is not the proposition determined by the ordinary semantical rules, but instead the diagonal proposition of the propositional concept determined."

28 Quantifiers and Propositional Attitudes

W. V. QUINE

I

The incorrectness of rendering 'Ctesias is hunting unicorns' in the fashion:

$(\exists x)$ (x is a unicorn $\cdot$ Ctesias is hunting x)

is conveniently attested by the nonexistence of unicorns, but is not due simply to that zoological lacuna. It would be equally incorrect to render "Ernest is hunting lions" as:

(1) $(\exists x)$ (x is a lion $\cdot$ Ernest is hunting x),

where Ernest is a sportsman in Africa. The force of (1) is rather that there is some individual lion (or several) which Ernest is hunting; stray circus property, for example. The contrast recurs in "I want a sloop." The version:

(2) $(\exists x)$ (x is a sloop $\cdot$ I want x)

is suitable insofar only as there may be said to be a certain sloop that I want. If what I seek is mere relief from slooplessness, then (2) gives the wrong idea.

The contrast is that between what may be called the *relational* sense of lion-hunting or sloop-wanting, viz., (1)–(2), and the likelier or *notional* sense. Appreciation of the difference is evinced in Latin and Romance languages by a distinction of mood in subordinate clauses; thus "*Procuro un perro que habla*" has the relational sense:

$(\exists x)$ (x is a dog $\cdot$ x talks $\cdot$ I seek x)

as against the notional "*Procuro un perro que hable*":

I strive that $(\exists x)$ (x is a dog $\cdot$ x talks $\cdot$ I find x).

Pending considerations to the contrary in later pages, we may represent the contrast strikingly in terms of permutations of components. Thus (1) and (2) may be expanded (with some violence to both logic and grammar) as follows:

(3) $(\exists x)$ (x is a lion $\cdot$ Ernest strives that Ernest finds x),
(4) $(\exists x)$ (x is a sloop $\cdot$ I wish that I have x),

whereas "Ernest is hunting lions" and "I want a sloop" in their notional senses may be rendered rather thus:

(5) Ernest strives that $(\exists x)$ (x is a lion $\cdot$ Ernest finds x),
(6) I wish that $(\exists x)$ (x is a sloop $\cdot$ I have x).

The contrasting versions (3)–(6) have been wrought by so paraphrasing "hunt" and "want" as to uncover the locutions "strive that" and "wish that," expressive of what Russell has called propositional attitudes. Now of all exam-

From *Journal of Philosophy* 53 (1956): 177–187. Copyright © 1956 by *Journal of Philosophy*. Reprinted by permission of the publisher. It is reprinted here minus fifteen lines.

ples of *propositional attitudes*, the first and foremost is *belief*; and, true to form, this example can be used to point up the contrast between relational and notional senses still better than (3)–(6) do. Consider the relational and notional senses of believing in spies:

(7) $(\exists x)$ (Ralph believes that x is a spy),
(8) Ralph believes that $(\exists x)$ (x is a spy).

Both may perhaps be ambiguously phrased as "Ralph believes that someone is a spy," but they may be unambiguously phrased respectively as "There is someone whom Ralph believes to be a spy" and "Ralph believes there are spies." The difference is vast; indeed, if Ralph is like most of us, (8) is true and (7) false.

In moving over to propositional attitudes, as we did in (3)–(6), we gain not only the graphic structural contrast between (3)–(4) and (5)–(6) but also a certain generality. For we can now multiply examples of striving and wishing, unrelated to hunting and wanting. Thus we get the relational and notional senses of wishing for a president:

(9) $(\exists x)$ (Witold wishes that x is president),
(10) Witold wishes that $(\exists x)$ (x is president).

According to (9), Witold has his candidate; according to (10) he merely wishes the appropriate form of government were in force. Also we open other propositional attitudes to similar consideration—as witness (7)–(8).

However, the suggested formulations of the relational senses—viz., (3), (4), (7), and (9)—all involve quantifying into a propositional-attitude idiom from outside. This is a dubious business, as may be seen from the following example.

There is a certain man in a brown hat whom Ralph has glimpsed several times under questionable circumstances on which we need not enter here; suffice it to say that Ralph suspects he is a spy. Also there is a gray-haired man, vaguely known to Ralph as rather a pillar of the community, whom Ralph is not aware of having seen except once at the beach. Now Ralph does not know it, but the men are one and the same. Can we say of this *man* (Bernard J. Ortcutt, to give him a name) that Ralph believes him to be a spy? If so, we find ourselves accepting a conjunction of the type:

(11) w sincerely denies '. . .' · w believes that . . .

as true, with one and the same sentence in both blanks. For, Ralph is ready enough to say, in all sincerity, "Bernard J. Ortcutt is no spy." If, on the other hand, with a view to disallowing situations of the type (11), we rule simultaneously that

(12) Ralph believes that the man in the brown hat is a spy,
(13) Ralph does not believe that the man seen at the beach is a spy,

then we cease to affirm any relationship between Ralph and any man at all. Both of the component "that"-clauses are indeed about the man Ortcutt; but the "that" must be viewed in (12) and (13) as sealing those clauses off, thereby rendering (12) and (13) compatible because not, as wholes, about Ortcutt at all. It then becomes improper to quantify as in (7); "believes that" becomes, in a word, referentially opaque.[1]

No question arises over (8); it exhibits only a quantification *within* the "believes that" context, not a quantification *into* it. What goes by the board, when we rule (12) and (13) both true, is just (7). Yet we are scarcely prepared to sacrifice the relational construction "There is someone whom Ralph believes to be a spy," which (7) as against (8) was supposed to reproduce.

The obvious next move is to try to make the best of our dilemma by distinguishing two senses of belief: *belief*$_1$, which disallows (11), and *belief*$_2$, which tolerates (11) but makes sense of (7). For belief$_1$, accordingly, we sustain (12)–(13) and ban (7) as nonsense. For belief$_2$, on the other hand, we sustain (7); and for *this* sense of belief we must reject (13) and acquiesce in the conclusion that Ralph believes$_2$ that the man at the beach is a spy even though he *also* believes$_2$ (and believes$_1$) that the man at the beach is not a spy.

II

But there is a more suggestive treatment. Beginning with a single sense of belief, viz., belief$_1$ above, let us think of this at first as a relation between the believer and a certain *intension*, named by the "that"-clause. Intentions are creatures of darkness, and I shall rejoice with the reader when they are exorcised, but first I want to make certain points with the help of them. Now intensions named thus by "that"-clauses, without free variables, I shall speak of more specifically as intensions of degree 0, or propositions. In addition I shall (for the moment) recognize intensions of degree 1, or attributes. These are to be named by prefixing a variable to a sentence in which it occurs free; thus $z(z$ is a spy) is spyhood. Similarly we may specify intensions of higher degrees by prefixing multiple variables.

Now just as we have recognized a dyadic relation of belief between a believer and a proposition, thus:

(14) Ralph believes that Ortcutt is a spy,

so we may recognize also a triadic relation of belief among a believer, an object, and an attribute, thus:

(15) Ralph believes $z(z$ is a spy) of Ortcutt.

For reasons which will appear, this is to be viewed not as dyadic belief between Ralph and the proposition *that* Ortcutt has $z(z$ is a spy), but rather as an irreducibly triadic relation among the three things Ralph, $z(z$ is a spy), and Ortcutt. Similarly there is tetradic belief:

(16) Tom believes $yz(y$ denounced $z)$ of Cicero and Catiline,

and so on.

Now we can clap on a hard and fast rule against quantifying into propositional-attitude idioms; but we give it the form now of a rule against quantifying into names of intensions. Thus, though (7) as it stands becomes unallowable, we can meet the needs which prompted (7) by quantifying rather into the triadic belief construction, thus:

(17) $(\exists x)$ (Ralph believes $z(z$ is a spy) of x).

Here then, in place of (7), is our new way of saying that there is someone whom Ralph believes to be a spy.

Belief$_1$ was belief so construed that a proposition might be believed when an object was specified in it in one way, and yet not believed when the same object was specified in another way; witness (12)–(13). Hereafter we can adhere uniformly to this narrow sense of belief, both for the dyadic case and for triadic and higher; in each case the term which names the intension (whether proposition or attribute or intension of higher degree) is to be looked on as referentially opaque.

The situation (11) is thus excluded. At the same time the effect of belief$_2$ can be gained, simply by ascending from dyadic to triadic belief as in (15). For (15) does relate the men Ralph and Ortcutt precisely as belief$_2$ was intended to do. (15) does remain true of Ortcutt under any designation; and hence the legitimacy of (17). Similarly, whereas from:

Tom believes that Cicero denounced Catiline

we cannot conclude:

Tom believes that Tully denounced Catiline,

on the other hand we can conclude from:

Tom believes $y(y$ denounced Catiline) of Cicero

that

Tom believes $y(y$ denounced Catiline) of Tully,

and also that

(18) $(\exists x)$(Tom believes $y(y$ denounced Catiline) of x).

From (16), similarly, we may infer that

(19) $(\exists w)(\exists x)$(Tom believes $zy(y$ denounced $z)$ of w and x).

Such quantifications as:

$(\exists x)$ (Tom believes that x denounced Catiline),
$(\exists x)$ (Tom believes $y(y$ denounced $x)$ of Cicero)

still count as nonsense, along with (7); but such legitimate purposes as these might have served are served by (17)–(19) and the like. Our names of intensions, and these only, are what count as referentially opaque.

Let us sum up our findings concerning the seven numbered statements about Ralph. (7) is now counted as nonsense, (8) as true, (12)–(13) as true, (14) as false, and (15) and (17) as true. Another that is true is:

(20) Ralph believes that the man seen at the beach is not a spy,

which of course must not be confused with (13).

The kind of exportation which leads from (14) to (15) should doubtless be viewed in general as implicative. Under the terms of our illustrative story, (14) happens to be false; but (20) is true, and it leads by exportation to:

> (21) Ralph believes $z(z$ is not a spy) of the man seen at the beach.

The man at the beach, hence Ortcutt, does not receive reference in (20), because of referential opacity; but he does in (21), so we may conclude from (21) that

> (22) Ralph believes $z(z$ is not a spy) of Ortcutt.

Thus (15) and (22) both count as true. This is not, however, to charge Ralph with contradictory beliefs. Such a charge might reasonably be read into:

> (23) Ralph believes $z(z$ is a spy $\cdot$ z is not a spy) of Ortcutt,

but this merely goes to show that it is undesirable to look upon (15) and (22) as implying (23).

It hardly needs be said that the barbarous usage illustrated in (15)–(19) and (21)–(23) is not urged as a practical reform. It is put forward by way of straightening out a theoretical difficulty, which, summed up, was as follows: Belief contexts are referentially opaque; therefore it is prima facie meaningless to quantify into them; how then to provide for those indispensable relational statements of belief, like "There is someone whom Ralph believes to be a spy"?

Let it not be supposed that the theory which we have been examining is just a matter of allowing unbridled quantification into belief contexts after all, with a legalistic change of notation. On the contrary, the crucial choice recurs at each point: quantify if you will, but pay the price of accepting near-contraries like (15) and (22) at each point at which you choose to quantify. In other words: distinguish as you please between referential and non-referential positions, but keep track, so as to treat each kind appropriately. The notation of intensions, of degree one and higher, is in effect a device for inking in a boundary between referential and nonreferential occurrences of terms.

III

Striving and wishing, like believing, are propositional attitudes and referentially opaque. (3) and (4) are objectionable in the same way as (7), and our recent treatment of belief can be repeated for these propositional attitudes. Thus, just as (7) gave way to (17), so (3) and (4) give way to:

> (24) $(\exists x)$ (x is a lion $\cdot$ Ernest strives z(Ernest finds z) of x),
> (25) $(\exists x)$ (x is a sloop $\cdot$ I wish z(I have z) of x),

a certain breach of idiom being allowed for the sake of analogy in the case of "strives."

These examples came from a study of hunting and wanting. Observing in (3)–(4) the quantification into opaque contexts, then, we might have retreated to (1)–(2) and forborne to paraphrase them into terms of striving and wishing. For (1)–(2) were quite straightforward renderings of lion-hunting and sloop-wanting in their relational senses; it was only the notional senses that really needed the breakdown into terms of striving and wishing, (5)–(6).

Actually, though, it would be myopic to leave the relational senses of lion-hunting and sloop-wanting at the unanalyzed stage (1)–(2). For, whether or not we choose to put these over into terms of wishing and striving, there are other relational cases of wishing and striving which require our consideration anyway—as witness (9). The untenable formulations (3)–(4) may indeed be either corrected as (24)–(25) or condensed back into (1)–(2); on the other hand we have no choice but to correct the untenable (9) on the pattern of (24)–(25), viz., as:

> $(\exists x)$ (Witold wishes y(y is president) of x).

The untenable versions (3)–(4) and (9) all had to do with wishing and striving in the relational sense. We see in contrast that (5)–(6) and (10), on the notional side of wishing and striving, are innocent of any illicit quantification into opaque contexts from outside. But now notice that exactly the same trouble begins also on the notional side, as soon as we try to say not just that Ernest hunts lions and I want to sloop, but that *someone* hunts lions or wants a sloop. This move carries us, ostensibly, from (5)–(6) to:

(26) $(\exists w)$ (w strives that $(\exists x)$ (x is a lion · w finds x)),

(27) $(\exists w)$ (w wishes that $(\exists x)$ (x is a sloop · w has x)),

and these do quantify unallowably into opaque contexts.

We know how, with help of the attribute apparatus, to put (26)–(27) in order; the pattern, indeed, is substantially before us in (24)–(25). Admissible versions are:

$(\exists w)$ (w strives $y(\exists x)$ (x is a lion · y finds x) of w),

$(\exists w)$ (w wishes $y(\exists x)$ (x is a sloop · y has x) of w),

or briefly:

(28) $(\exists w)$ (w strives $y(y$ finds a lion) of w),

(29) $(\exists w)$ (w wishes $y(y$ has a sloop) of w).

Such quantification of the subject of the propositional attitude can of course occur in belief as well; and, if the subject is mentioned in the belief itself, the above pattern is the one to use. Thus "Someone believes he is Napoleon" must be rendered:

$(\exists w)$ (w believes $y(y = $ Napoleon) of w).

For concreteness I have been discussing belief primarily, and two other propositional attitudes secondarily: striving and wishing. The treatment is, we see, closely parallel for the three; and it will pretty evidently carry over to other propositional attitudes as well—e.g., hope, fear, surprise. In all cases my concern is, of course, with a special technical aspect of the propositional attitudes: the problem of quantifying in.

IV

There are good reasons for being discontent with an analysis that leaves us with propositions, attributes, and the rest of the intensions. Intensions are less economical than extensions (truth values, classes, relations), in that they are more narrowly individuated. The principle of their individuation, moreover, is obscure.

Commonly logical equivalence is adopted as the principle of individuation of intensions. More explicitly: if S and S' are any two sentences with n ($\geqq 0$) free variables, the same in each, then the respective intensions which we name by putting the n variables (or "that," if $n = 0$) before S and S' shall be one and the same intension if and only if S and S' are logically equivalent. But the relevant concept of logical equivalence raises serious questions in turn.[2] The intensions are at best a pretty obscure lot.

Yet it is evident enough that we cannot, in the foregoing treatment of propositional attitudes, drop the intensions in favor of the corresponding extensions. Thus, to take a trivial example, consider "w is hunting unicorns." On the analogy of (28), it becomes:

w strives $y(y$ finds a unicorn) of w.

Correspondingly for the hunting of griffins. Hence, if anyone w is to hunt unicorns without hunting griffins, the attributes

$y(y$ finds a unicorn),

$y(y$ finds a griffin)

must be distinct. But the corresponding classes are identical, being empty. So it is indeed the attributes, and not the classes, that were needed in our formulation. The same moral could be drawn, though less briefly, without appeal to empty cases.

But there is a way of dodging the intensions which merits serious consideration. Instead of speaking of intensions we can speak of sentences, naming these by quotation. Instead of:

w believes that . . .

we may say:

w believes-true '. . .'.

Instead of:

(30) w believes $y(\ldots y \ldots)$ of x

we may say:

(31) w believes '. . . y . . .' satisfied by x.

The words "believes satisfied by" here, like "believes of" before, would be viewed as an irreducibly triadic predicate. A similar shift can be made in the case of the other propositional attitudes, of course, and in the tetradic and higher cases.

This semantic reformulation is not, of course, intended to suggest that the subject of the propositional attitude speaks the language of the quotation, or any language. We may treat a mouse's fear of a cat as his fearing true a certain English sentence. This is unnatural without being therefore wrong. It is a little like describing a prehistoric ocean current as clockwise.

How, where, and on what grounds to draw a boundary between those who believe or wish or strive that *p,* and those who do not quite believe or wish or strive that *p,* is undeniably a vague and obscure affair. However, if anyone does approve of speaking of belief of a proposition at all and of speaking of a proposition in turn as meant by a sentence, then certainly he cannot object to our semantical reformulation "w believes-true *S*" on any special grounds of obscurity; for "w believes-true *S*" is explicitly definable in *his* terms as "w believes the proposition meant by *S*." Similarly for the semantical reformulation (31) of (30); similarly for the tetradic and higher cases; and similarly for wishing, striving, and other propositional attitudes.

Our semantical versions do involve a relativity to language, however, which must be made explicit. When we say that *w* believes-true *S,* we need to be able to say what language the sentence *S* is thought of as belonging to; not because *w* needs to understand *S,* but because *S* might by coincidence exist (as a linguistic form) with very different meanings in two languages.[3] Strictly, therefore, we should think of the dyadic "believes-true *S*" as expanded to a triadic "w believes-true *S* in *L*"; and correspondingly for (31) and its suite.

As noted two paragraphs back, the semantical form of expression:

(32) *w* believes-true '. . .' in *L*

can be explained in intensional terms, for persons who favor them, as:

(33) *w* believes the proposition meant by '. . .'
        in *L,*

thus leaving no cause for protest on the score of relative clarity. Protest may still be heard, however, on a different score: (32) and (33), though equivalent to each other, are not strictly equivalent to the "w believes that . . ." which is our real concern. For, it is argued, in order to infer (33) we need not only the information about *w* which "w believes that . . ." provides, but also some extraneous information about the language *L.*

Church[4] brings the point out by appeal to translations, substantially as follows. The respective statements:

> *w* believes that there are unicorns,
> *w* believes the proposition meant by "There are unicorns" in English

go into German as:

(34) *w glaubt, dass es Einhörne gibt,*

(35) *w glaubt diejenige Aussage, die* "There are unicorns" *auf Englisch bedeutet,*

and clearly (34) does not provide enough information to enable a German ignorant of English to infer (35).

The same reasoning can be used to show that "There are unicorns" is not strictly or analytically equivalent to:

> "There are unicorns" is true in English.

Nor, indeed, was Tarski's truth paradigm intended to assert analytic equivalence. Similarly, then, for (32) in relation to "w believes that . . ."; a systematic agreement in truth value can be claimed, and no more. This limitation will prove of little moment to persons who share my skepticism about analyticity.

What I find more disturbing about the semantical versions, such as (32), is the need of dragging in the language concept at all. What is a language? What degree of fixity is supposed? When do we have one language and not two? The propositional attitudes are dim affairs to begin with, and it is a pity to have to add obscurity to obscurity by bringing in language variables too. Only let it not be supposed that any clarity is gained by restituting the intensions.

NOTES

1. See *From a Logical Point of View* (Cambridge, Mass.: Harvard University Press: 1953, 2d ed., 1961), pp. 142–159; also "Three grades of modal involvement," Essay 13 of *Ways of Paradox* (New York: Random House, 1966).
2. See my "Two dogmas of empiricism," in *From a Logical Point of View,* op. cit.; also "Carnap and logical truth," Essay 10 in *Ways of Paradox,* op. cit.
3. This point is made by Church, "On Carnap's analysis of statements of assertion and belief," *Analysis,* 10 (1950), 97–99.
4. Ibid., with an acknowledgment to Langford.

29 On Saying That

DONALD DAVIDSON

"I wish I had said that," said Oscar Wilde in applauding one of Whistler's witticisms. Whistler, who took a dim view of Wilde's originality, retorted, "You will, Oscar; you will." The function of this tale (from Holbrook Jackson's *The Eighteen-Nineties*) is to remind us that an expression like "Whistler said that" may on occasion serve as a grammatically complete sentence. Here we have, I suggest, the key to a correct analysis of indirect discourse, an analysis that opens a lead to an analysis of psychological sentences generally (sentences about propositional attitudes, so-called), and even, though this looks beyond anything to be discussed in the present paper, a clue to what distinguishes psychological concepts from others.

But let us begin with sentences usually deemed more representative of *oratio obliqua,* for example "Galileo said that the earth moves" or "Scott said that Venus is an inferior planet." One trouble with such sentence is that we do not know their logical form. And to admit this is to admit that, whatever else we may know about them, we do not know the first thing. If we accept surface grammar as guide to logical form, we will see "Galileo said that the earth moves" as containing the sentence "the earth moves," and this sentence in turn as consisting of the singular term 'the earth', and a predicate, 'moves'. But if 'the earth' is, in this context, a singular term, it can be replaced, so far as the truth or falsity of the containing sentence is concerned, by any other singular term that refers to the same thing.

The notorious apparent invalidity of this rule can only be apparent, for the rule no more than spells out what is involved in the idea of a (logically) singular term. Only two lines of explanation, then, are open: we are wrong about the logical form, or we are wrong about the reference of the singular term.

What seems anomalous behavior on the part of what seem singular terms dramatizes the problem of giving an orderly account of indirect discourse, but the problem is more pervasive. For what touches singular terms touches what they touch, and that is everything: quantifiers, variables, predicates, connectives. Singular terms refer, or pretend to refer, to the entities over which the variables of quantification range, and it is these entities of which the predicates are or are not true. So it should not surprise us that if we can make trouble for the sentence "Scott said that Venus is an inferior planet" by substituting "the Evening Star" for "Venus," we can equally make trouble by substituting "is identical with Venus or with Mercury" for the coextensive "is an inferior planet." The difficulties with indirect discourse cannot be solved simply by abolishing singular terms.

From *Synthese* 19 (1968–69): 130–146. Copyright © 1968 by D. Reidel Publishing Company, Dordrecht, Holland. Reprinted by permission of the publisher.

What should we ask of an adequate account of the logical form of a sentence? Above all, I would say, such an account must lead us to see the semantic character of the sentence—its truth or falsity—as owed to how it is composed, by a finite number of applications of some of a finite number of devices that suffice for the language as a whole, out of elements drawn from a finite stock (the vocabulary) that suffices for the language as a whole. To see a sentence in this light is to see it in the light of a theory for its language, a theory that gives the form of every sentence in that language. A way to provide such a theory is by recursively characterizing a truth-predicate, along the lines suggested by Tarski, that satisfies this criterion: the theory entails, for each sentence s (when described in a standardized way), that the truth-predicate holds of s if and only if_____.—Here the blank is to be filled by a sentence in the metalanguage that is true if and only if s is true in the object language.[1] If we accept Tarski's further requirement that no undefined semantical notions be used in characterizing a truth-predicate, then no theory can satisfy the criterion except by describing every sentence in terms of a semantically significant structure.

A satisfactory theory of meaning for a language must, then, give an explicit account of the truth-conditions of every sentence, and this can be done by giving a theory that satisfies Tarski's criteria; nothing less should count as showing how the meaning of every sentence depends on its structure.[2] Two closely linked considerations support the idea that the structure with which a sentence is endowed by a theory of truth in Tarski's style deserves to be called the logical form of the sentence. By giving such a theory, we demonstrate in a persuasive way that the language, though it consists in an indefinitely large number of sentences, can be comprehended by a creature with finite powers. A theory of truth may be said to supply an effective explanation of the semantic role of each significant expression in any of its appearances. Armed with the theory, we can always answer the question, "What are these familiar words doing here?" by saying how they contribute to the truth-conditions of the sentence. (This is not to assign a 'meaning', much less a reference, to every significant expression.)

The study of the logical form of sentences is often seen in the light of another interest, that of expediting inference. From this point of view, to give the logical form of a sentence is to catalogue the features relevant to its place on the logical scene, the features that determine what sentences it is a logical consequence of, and what sentences it has as logical consequences. A canonical notation graphically encodes the relevant information, making theory of inference simple, and practice mechanical where possible.

Obviously the two approaches to logical form cannot yield wholly independent results, for logical consequence is defined in terms of truth. To say a second sentence is a logical consequence of a first is to say, roughly, that the second is true if the first is no matter how the nonlogical constants are interpreted. Since what we count as a logical constant can vary independently of the set of truths, it is clear that the two versions of logical form, though related, need not be identical. The relation, in brief, seems this. Any theory of truth that satisfies Tarski's criteria must take account of all truth-affecting iterative devices in the language. In the familiar languages for which we know how to define truth the basic iterative devices are reducible to the sentential connectives, the apparatus of quantification, and the description operator if it is primitive. Where one sentence is a logical consequence of another on the basis of quantificational structure alone, a theory of truth will therefore entail that if the first sentence is true, the second is. There is no point, then, in not including the expressions that determine quantificational structure among the logical constants, for when we have characterized truth, on which any account of logical consequence depends, we have already committed ourselves to all that calling such expressions logical constants could commit us. Adding to this list of logical constants will increase the inventory of logical truths and consequence-relations beyond anything a truth definition demands, and will therefore yield richer versions of logical form. For the purposes of the present paper, however, we can cleave to the most austere interpretations of logical consequence and logical form, those that are forced on us when we give a theory of truth.

We are now in a position to explain our aporia over indirect discourse: what happens is that the relation between truth and consequence just sketched appears to break down. In a sentence like "Galileo said that the earth moves" the eye and mind perceive familiar structure in the words "the earth moves." And structure there must be if we are to have a theory of truth at all, for an infinite number of sentences (all sentences in the indicative, apart from some trouble over tense) yield sense when plugged into the slot in "Galileo said that _____." So if we are to give conditions of truth for all the sentences so generated, we cannot do it sentence by sentence, but only by discovering an articulate structure that permits us to treat each sentence as composed of a finite number of devices that make a stated contribution to its truth conditions. As soon as we assign familiar structure, however, we must allow the consequences of that assignment to flow, and these, as we know, are in the case of indirect discourse consequences we refuse to buy. In a way, the case is even stranger than that. Not only do familiar consequences fail to flow from what looks to be familiar structure, but our common sense of language feels little assurance in any inferences based on the words that follow the 'said that' of indirect discourse (there are exceptions).

So the paradox is this: on the one hand, intuition suggests, and theory demands, that we discover semantically significant structure in the 'content-sentences' of indirect discourse (as I shall call sentences following "said that"). On the other hand, the failure of consequence-relations invites us to treat contained sentences as semantically inert. Yet logical form and consequence relations cannot be divorced in this way.

One proposal at this point is to view the words that succeed the "said that" as operating within concealed quotation marks, their sole function being to help refer to a sentence, and their semantic inertness explained by the usual account of quotation. One drawback of this proposal is that no usual account of quotation is acceptable, even by the minimal standards we have set for an account of logical form. For according to most stories, quotations are singular terms without significant semantic structure, and since there must be an infinite number of different quotations, no language that contains them can have a recursively defined truth-

predicate. This may be taken to show that the received accounts of quotation must be mistaken—I think it does. But then we can hardly pretend that we have solved the problem of indirect discourse by appeal to quotation.[3]

Perhaps it is not hard to invent a theory of quotation that will serve: the following theory is all but explicit in Quine. Simply view quotations as abbreviations for what you get if you follow these instructions: to the right of the first letter that has opening quotation-marks on its left write right-hand quotation marks, then the sign for concatenation, and then left-hand quotation marks, in that order; do this after each letter (treating punctuation signs as letters) until you reach the terminating right-hand quotation marks. What you now have is a complex singular term that gives what Tarski calls a structural description of an expression. There is a modest addition to vocabulary: names of letters and of punctuation signs, and the sign for concatenation. There is a corresponding addition to ontology: letters and punctuation signs. And finally, if we carry out the application to sentences in indirect discourse, there will be the logical consequences that the new structure dictates. For two examples, each of the following will be entailed by "Galileo said that the earth moves":

$(\exists x)$ (Galileo said that "the ea"⌢x⌢"th moves")

and (with the premise "r=the 18th letter in the alphabet"):

Galileo said that "the ea"⌢the 18th letter in the alphabet⌢"th moves"

(I have clung to abbreviations as far as possible.) These inferences are not meant in themselves as criticism of the theory of quotation; they merely illuminate it.

Quine discusses the quotational approach to indirect discourse in *Word and Object,*[4] and abandons it for what seems, to me, a wrong reason. Not that there is not a good reason; but to appreciate *it* is to be next door to a solution, as I shall try to show.

Let us follow Quine through the steps that lead him to reject the quotational approach. The version of the theory he considers is not the one once proposed by Carnap to the effect that "said that" is a two-place predicate true of ordered pairs of people and sentences.[5] The trouble with this idea is not that it forces us to assimilate indirect discourse to direct, for it does not. The "said that" of indirect discourse, like the "said" of direct, may relate persons and sentences, but be a different relation; the former, unlike the latter, may be true of a person, and a sentence he never spoke in a language he never knew. The trouble lies rather in the chance that the same sentence may have different meanings in different languages—not too long a chance either if we count ideolects as languages.

Not that it is impossible to find words (as written or sounded) which express quite different ideas in different languages. For example, "Empedokles liebt" do fairly well as a German or an English sentence, in one case saying what Empedokles loved and in the other telling us what he did from the top of Etna. We can scoff at the notion that if we analyze "Galileo said that the earth moves" as asserting a relation between Galileo and the sentence "The earth moves" we must assume Galileo spoke English, but we cannot afford to scoff at the assumption that on this analysis the words of the content-sentence are to be understood as an English sentence.[6]

Calling the relativity to English an assumption may be misleading; perhaps the reference to English is explicit, as follows. A long-winded version of our favorite sentence might be "Galileo spoke a sentence that meant in his language what 'The earth moves' means in English." Since in this version it takes everything save "Galileo" and "The earth moves" to do the work of "said that," we must count the reference to English as explicit in the "said that." To see how odd this is, however, it is only necessary to reflect that the English words "said that," with their built-in reference to English, would no longer translate (by even the roughest extensional standards) the French "dit que."

We can shift the difficulty over translation away from the "said that" or "dit que" by taking these expressions as three-place predicates relating a speaker, a sentence, and a language, the reference to a language to be supplied either by our (in practice nearly infallible) knowledge of the language to which the quoted material is to be taken as belonging, or by a demonstrative reference to the language of the entire sentence.

Each of these suggestions has its own appeal, but neither leads to an analysis that will pass the translation test. To take the demonstrative proposal, translation into French will carry "said that" into "dit que," the demonstrative reference will automatically, and hence perhaps still within the bounds of strict translation, shift from English to French. But when we translate the final singular term, which names an English sentence, we produce a palpably false result.

These exercises help bring out important features of the quotational approach. But now it is time to remark that there would be an anomaly in a position, like the one under consideration, that abjured reference to propositions in favor of reference to languages. For languages (as Quine remarks in a similar context in *Word and Object*) are at least as badly individuated, and for much the same reasons, as propositions. Indeed, an obvious proposal linking them is this: languages are identical when identical sentences express identical propositions. We see, then, that quotational theories of indirect discourse, those we have discussed anyway, cannot claim an advantage over theories that frankly introduce intensional entities from the start; so let us briefly consider theories of the latter sort.

It might be thought, and perhaps often is, that if we are willing to welcome intensional entities without stint—properties, propositions, individual concepts, and whatever else—then no further difficulties stand in the way of giving an account of the logical form of sentences in *oratio obliqua*. This is not so. Neither the languages Frege suggests as models for natural languages nor the languages described by Church are amenable to theory in the sense of a truth-definition meeting Tarski's standards.[7] What stands in the way in Frege's case is that every referring expression has an infinite number of entities it may refer to, depending on the context, and there is no rule that gives the reference in more complex contexts on the basis of the reference in simpler ones. In Church's languages, there is an infinite number of primitive expressions; this directly blocks the possibility of recursively characterizing a truth-predicate satisfying Tarski's requirements.

Things might be patched up by following a leading idea of Carnap's *Meaning and Neces-*

sity and limiting the semantic levels to two: extensions and (first-level) intensions.[8] An attractive strategy might then be to turn Frege, thus simplified, upside down by letting each singular term refer to its sense or intension, and providing a reality function (similar to Church's delta function) to map intensions onto extensions. Under such treatment our sample sentence would emerge like this: "The reality of Galileo said that the earth moves." Here we must suppose that "the earth" names an individual concept which the function referred to by "moves" maps onto the proposition that the earth moves; the function referred to by "said that" in turn maps Galileo and the proposition that the earth moves onto a truth value. Finally, the name, "Galileo" refers to an individual concept which is mapped, by the function referred to by "the reality of" onto Galileo. With ingenuity, this theory can accommodate quantifiers that bind variables both inside and outside contexts created by verbs like "said" and "believes." There is no special problem about defining truth for such a language: everything is on the up and up, purely extensional save in ontology. This seems to be a theory that might do all we have asked. Apart from nominalistic qualms, why not accept it?

My reasons against this course are essentially Quine's. Finding right words of my own to communicate another's saying is a problem in translation (216–217). The words I use in the particular case may be viewed as products of my total theory (however vague and subject to correction) of what the originating speaker means by anything he says: such a theory is indistinguishable from a characterization of a truth-predicate, with his language as object language and mine as metalanguage. The crucial point is that within limits there is no choosing between alternative theories which differ in assigning clearly nonsynonymous sentences of mine as translations of his same utterance. This is Quine's thesis of the indeterminacy of translation (218–221).[9] An example will help bring out the fact that the thesis applies not only to translation between speakers of conspicuously different languages, but also to cases nearer home.

Let someone say (and now discourse is direct), "There's a hippopotamus in the refrigerator"; am I necessarily right in reporting him as having said that there is a hippopotamus in the refrigerator? Perhaps; but under questioning he goes on, "It's roundish, has a wrinkled skin, does not mind being touched. It has a pleasant taste, at least the juice, and it costs a dime. I squeeze two or three for breakfast." After some finite amount of such talk we slip over the line where it is plausible or even possible to say correctly that he said there was a hippopotamus in the refrigerator, for it becomes clear he means something else by at least some of his words than I do. The simplest hypothesis so far is that my word "hippopotamus" no longer translates his word "hippopotamus"; my word "orange" might do better. But in any case, long before we reach the point where homophonic translation must be abandoned, charity invites departures. Hesitation over whether to translate a saying of another by one or another of various nonsynonymous sentences of mine does not necessarily reflect a lack of information: it is just that beyond a point there is no deciding, even in principle, between the view that the Other has used words as we do but has more or less weird beliefs, and the view that we have translated him wrong. Torn between the need to make sense of a speaker's words and the need to make sense of the pattern of his beliefs, the best we can do is choose a theory of translation that maximizes agreement. Surely there is no future in supposing that in earnestly uttering the words "There's a hippopotamus in the refrigerator" the Other has disagreed with us about what can be in the refrigerator if we also must then find ourselves disagreeing with him about the size, shape, color, manufacturer, horsepower, and wheelbase of hippopotami.

None of this shows there is no such thing as correct reporting, through indirect discourse, what another said. All that the indeterminacy shows is that if there is one way of getting it right there are other ways that differ substantially in that nonsynonymous sentences are used after "said that." And this is enough to justify our feeling that there is something bogus about the sharpness questions of meaning must in principle have if meanings are entities.

The lesson was implicit in a discussion started some years ago by Benson Mates. Mates claimed that the sentence "Nobody doubts that whoever believes that the seventh consulate of Marius lasted less than a fortnight believes that the seventh consulate of Marius lasted less than a fortnight" is true and yet might well become false if the last word were replaced by the (supposed synonymous) words "period of fourteen days," and that this could happen no matter what standards of synonymy we adopt short of the question-begging "substitutable everywhere *salva veritate.*"[10] Church and Sellars responded by saying the difficulty could be resolved by firmly distinguishing between substitutions based on the speaker's use of language and substitutions colored by the use attributed to others.[11] But this is a solution only if we think there is some way of telling, in what another says, what is owed to the meanings he gives his words and what to his beliefs about the world. According to Quine, this is a distinction not there to be drawn.

The detour has been lengthy; I return now to Quine's discussion of the quotational approach in *Word and Object.* As reported above, Quine rejects relativization to a language on the grounds that the principle of the individuation of languages is obscure, and the issue when languages are identical irrelevant to indirect discourse (214). He now suggests that instead of interpreting the content-sentence of indirect discourse as occurring in a language, we interpret it as voiced by a speaker at a time. The speaker and time relative to which the content-sentence needs understanding is, of course, the speaker of that sentence, who is thereby indirectly attributing a saying to another. So now "Galileo said that the earth moves" comes to mean something like "Galileo spoke a sentence that in his mouth meant what 'The earth moves' now means in mine." Quine makes no objection to this proposal because he thinks he has something simpler and at least as good in reserve. But in my opinion the present proposal deserves more serious consideration, for I think it is nearly right, while Quine's preferred alternatives are seriously defective.

The first of these alternatives is Scheffler's inscriptional theory.[12] Scheffler suggests that sentences in indirect discourse relate a speaker and an utterance: the role of the content-

sentence is to help convey what sort of utterance it was. What we get this way is, "Galileo spoke a that-the-earth-moves utterance." The predicate "*x* is-a-that-the-earth-moves-utterance" has, so far as theory of truth and of inference are concerned, the form of an unstructured one-place predicate. Quine does not put the matter quite this way, and he may resist my appropriation of the terms 'logical form' and 'structure' for purposes that exclude application to Scheffler's predicate. Quine calls the predicate "compound" and describes it as composed of an operator and a sentence (214, 215). These are matters of terminology; the substance, about which there may be no disagreement, is that on Scheffler's theory sentences in *oratio obliqua* have no logical relations that depend on structure in the predicate, and a truth-predicate that applies to all such sentences cannot be characterized in Tarski's style. The reason is plain: there is an infinite number of predicates with the syntax "*x* is-a-_____-utterance" each of which is, in the eyes of semantic theory, unrelated to the rest.

Quine has seized one horn of the dilemma. Since attributing semantic structure to content-sentences in indirect discourse apparently forces us to endorse logical relations we do not want, Quine gives up the structure. The result is that another desideratum of theory is neglected, that truth be defined.

Consistent with his policy of renouncing structure that supports no inferences worth their keep, Quine contemplates one further step; he says, ". . . a final alternative that I find as appealing as any is simply to dispense with the objects of the propositional attitudes" (216). Where Scheffler still saw "said that" as a two-place predicate relating speakers and utterances, though welding content-sentences into one-piece one-place predicates true of utterances, Quine now envisions content-sentence and "said that" welded directly to form the one-place predicate "*x* said-that-the-earth-moves," true of persons. Of course some inferences inherent in Scheffler's scheme now fall away: we can no longer infer "Galileo said something" from our sample sentence, nor can we infer from it and "Someone denied that the earth moves" the sentence "Someone denied what Galileo said." Yet as Quine reminds us, inferences like these may fail on Scheffler's analysis too when the analysis is extended along the obvious line to belief and other propositional attitudes, since needed utterances may fail to materialize (215). The advantages of Scheffler's theory over Quine's "final alternative" are therefore few and uncertain; this is why Quine concludes that the view that invites the fewest inferences is "as appealing as any."

This way of eliminating unwanted inferences unfortunately abolishes most of the structure needed by the theory of truth. So it is worth returning for another look at the earlier proposal to analyze indirect discourse in terms of a predicate relating an originating speaker, a sentence, and the present speaker of the sentence in indirect discourse. For that proposal did not cut off any of the simple entailments we have been discussing, and it alone of recent suggestions promised, when coupled with a workable theory of quotation, to yield to standard semantic methods. But there is a subtle flaw.

We tried to bring out the flavor of the analysis to which we have returned by rewording our favorite sentence as "Galileo uttered a sentence that meant in his mouth what 'The earth moves' means now in mine." We should not think ill of this verbose version of "Galileo said that the earth moves" because of apparent reference to a meaning ("what 'The earth moves' means"); this expression is not treated as a singular term in the theory. We are indeed asked to make sense of a judgment of synonymy between utterances, but not as the foundation of a theory of language, merely as an unanalyzed part of the content of the familiar idiom of indirect discourse. The idea that underlies our awkward paraphrase is that of *samesaying*: when I say that Galileo said that the earth moves, I represent Galileo and myself as samesayers.

And now the flaw is this. If I merely *say* we are samesayers, Galileo and I, I have yet to *make* us so; and how am I to do this? Obviously, by saying what he said; not by using his words (necessarily), but by using words the same in import here and now as his then and there. Yet this is just what, on the theory, I cannot do. For the theory brings the content-sentence into the act sealed in quotation marks, and on any standard theory of quotation, this means the content-sentence is

mentioned and not used. In uttering the words "The earth moves" I do not, according to this account, say anything remotely like what Galileo is claimed to have said; I do not, in fact, say anything. My words in the frame provided by "Galileo said that ____" merely help refer to a sentence. There will be no missing the point if we expand quotation in the style we recently considered. Any intimation that Galileo and I are samesayers vanishes in this version:

Galileo said that 'T'⌒'h'⌒'e'⌒''⌒'e'⌒'a'⌒'r'⌒'t'⌒'h'⌒''⌒'m'⌒'o'⌒'v'⌒'e'⌒'s'

We seem to have been taken in by a notational accident, a way of referring to expressions that when abbreviated produces framed pictures of the very words referred to. The difficulty is odd; let's see if we can circumvent it. Imagine an altered case. Galileo utters his words "Eppur si muove," I utter my words, "The earth moves." There is no problem yet in recognizing that we are samesayers; an utterance of mine matches an utterance of his in purport. I am not now using my words to help refer to a sentence; I speak for myself, and my words refer in their usual way to the earth and to its movement. If Galileo's utterance "Eppur si muove" made us samesayers, then some utterance or other of Galileo's made us samesayers. The form "($\exists x$) (Galileo's utterance x and my utterance y make us samesayers)" is thus a way of attributing any saying I please to Galileo provided I find a way of replacing 'y' by a word or phrase that refers to an appropriate utterance of mine. And surely there is a way I can do this: I need only produce the required utterance and replace 'y' by a reference to it. Here goes:

The earth moves.
($\exists x$) (Galileo's utterance x and my last utterance make us samesayers).

Definitional abbreviation is all that is needed to bring this little skit down to:

The earth moves.
Galileo said that.

Here the "that" is a demonstrative singular term referring to an utterance (not a sentence).

This form has a small drawback in that it

leaves the hearer up in the air about the purpose served by saying "The earth moves" until the act has been performed. As if, say, I were first to tell a story and then add, "That's how it was once upon a time." There's some fun to be had this way, and in any case no amount of telling what the illocutionary force of our utterances is is going to insure that they have that force. But in the present case nothing stands in the way of reversing the order of things, thus:

Galileo said that.
The earth moves.

Perhaps it is now safe to allow a tiny orthographic change, a change without semantic significance, but suggesting to the eye the relation of introducer and introduced: we may suppress the stop after "that" and the consequent capitalization:

Galileo said that the earth moves.

Perhaps it should come as no surprise to learn that the form of psychological sentences in English apparently evolved through about the stages our ruminations have just carried us. According to the *Oxford English Dictionary,*

The use of *that* is generally held to have arisen out of the demonstrative pronoun pointing to the clause which it introduces. Cf. (1) He once lived here: we all know *that;* (2) *That* (now *this*) we all know: he once lived here; (3) We all know *that* (or *this*): he once lived here; (4) We all know *that* he once lived here . . . [13]

The proposal then is this: sentences in indirect discourse, as it happens, wear their logical form on their sleeves (except for one small point). They consist of an expression referring to a speaker, the two-place predicate "said," and a demonstrative referring to an utterance. Period. What follows gives the content of the subject's saying, but has no logical or semantic connection with the original attribution of a saying. This last point is no doubt the novel one, and upon it everything depends: from a semantic point of view the content-sentence in indirect discourse is not contained in the sentence whose truth counts.

We would do better, in coping with this subject, to talk of inscriptions and utterances and speech acts, and avoid reference to sentences.[14]

For what an utterance of "Galileo said that" does is announce a further utterance. Like any utterance, this first may be serious or silly, assertive or playful; but if it is true, it must be followed by an utterance synonymous with some other. The second utterance, the introduced act, may also be true or false, done in the mode of assertion or of play. But if it is as announced, it must serve at least the purpose of conveying the content of what someone said. The role of the introducing utterance is not unfamiliar: we do the same with words like "This is a joke," "This is an order," "He commanded that," "Now hear this." Such expressions might be called performatives, for they are used to usher in performances on the part of the speaker. A certain interesting reflexive effect sets in when performatives occur in the first-person present tense, for then the speaker utters words which if true are made so exclusively by the content and mode of the performance that follows, and the mode of this performance may well be in part determined by that same performative introduction. Here is an example that will also provide the occasion for a final comment on indirect discourse.

"Jones asserted that Entebbe is equatorial" would, if we parallel the analysis of indirect discourse, come to mean something like, 'An utterance of Jones' in the assertive mode had the content of this utterance of mine. Entebbe is equatorial.' The analysis does not founder because the modes of utterance of the two speakers may differ; all that the truth of the performative requires is that my second utterance, in whatever mode (assertive or not) match in content an assertive utterance of Jones. Whether such an asymmetry is appropriate in indirect discourse depends on how much of assertion we read into saying. Now suppose I try: "I assert that Entebbe is equatorial." Of course by saying this I may not assert anything; mood of words cannot guarantee mode of utterance. But if my utterance of the performative is true, then I do say something in the assertive mode that has the content of my second utterance—I do, that is, assert that Entebbe is equatorial. If I do assert it, an element in my success is no doubt my utterance of the performative, which announces an assertion; thus performatives tend to be self-fulfilling. Perhaps it is this feature of performatives that has misled some philosophers into thinking that performatives, or their utterances, are neither true nor false.

On the analysis of indirect discourse just proposed, standard problems seem to find a just solution. The appearance of failure of the laws of extensional substitution is explained as due to our mistaking what are really two sentences for one: we make substitutions in one sentence, but it is the other (the utterance of) which changes in truth. Since an utterance of "Galileo said that" and any utterance following it are semantically independent, there is no reason to predict, on grounds of form alone, any *particular* effect on the truth of the first from a change in the second. On the other hand, if the second utterance had been different in any way at all, the first utterance *might* have had a different truth value, for the reference of the "that" would have changed.

The paradox, that sentences (utterances) in *oratio obliqua* do not have the logical consequences they should if truth is to be defined, is resolved. What follows the verb "said" has only the structure of a singular term, usually the demonstrative "that." Assuming the "that" refers, we can infer that Galileo said something from "Galileo said that"; but this is welcome. The familiar words coming in the train of the performative of indirect discourse do, on my account, have structure, but it is familiar structure and poses no problem for theory of truth not there before indirect discourse was the theme.

Since Frege, philosophers have become hardened to the idea that content-sentences in talk about propositional attitudes may strangely refer to such entities as intensions, propositions, sentences, utterances and inscriptions. What is strange is not the entities, which are all right in their place (if they have one), but the notion that ordinary words for planets, people, tables and hippopotami in indirect discourse may give up these pedestrian references for the exotica. If we could recover our pre-Fregean semantic innocence, I think it would seem to us plainly incredible that the words "The earth moves," uttered after the words "Galileo said that," mean anything different, or refer to anything else,

than is their wont when they come in other environments. No doubt their role in *oratio obliqua* is in some sense special; but that is another story. Language is the instrument it is because the same expression, with semantic features (meaning) unchanged, can serve countless purposes. I have tried to show how our understanding of indirect discourse does not strain this basic insight.

ACKNOWLEDGMENTS

I am indebted to W. V. Quine and John Wallace for suggestions and criticisms. My research was in part supported by the National Science Foundation.

REFERENCES

1. Alfred Tarski, "The Concept of Truth in Formalized Languages," in *Logic, Semantics, Metamathematics* (Oxford: 1956), pp. 152–278. The criterion is roughly Tarski's Convention T that defines the concept of a truth-predicate.
2. The view that a characterization of a truth-predicate meeting Tarski's criteria is the core of a theory of meaning is defended in my "Truth and Meaning," [reprinted in this volume] *Synthese* 17 (1967) 304–323.
3. For documentation and details see my "Theories of Meaning and Learnable Languages," in *Logic, Methodology and Philosophy of Science, Proceedings of the 1964 International Congress,* ed. Yehoshua Bar-Hillel (Amsterdam: 1965), pp. 388–390.
4. *Word and Object* (Cambridge, Mass.: 1960) chapter VI. Hereafter numerals in parentheses refer to pages of this book.
5. R. Carnap, *The Logical Syntax of Language* (London: 1937), p. 248. The same was in effect proposed by P. T. Geach, *Mental Acts* (London: 1957).
6. The point is due to A. Church, "On Carnap's Analysis of Statements of Assertion and Belief," *Analysis* 10 (1950) 97–99.
7. G. Frege, "On Sense and Reference," [reprinted in this volume] in *Philosophical Writings,* ed. P. Geach and M. Black (Oxford: 1952) and A. Church, "A Formulation of the Logic of Sense and Denotation," in *Structure, Method, and Meaning: Essays in Honor of H. M. Sheffer* ed. Henle, Kallen and Langer (New York: 1951).
8. R. Carnap, *Meaning and Necessity* (Chicago: 1947). The idea of an essentially Fregean approach limited to two semantic levels has also been suggested by Michael Dummett (in an unpublished manuscript). Neither of these proposals is in detail entirely satisfactory in the light of present concerns, for neither leads to a language for which a truth-predicate can be characterized.

9. My assimilation of a translation manual to a theory of truth is not in Quine. For more on this, see the article in reference 2.

10. B. Mates, "Synonymity," in *Meaning and Interpretation* (Berkeley: 1950), pp. 201–226. The example is Church's.

11. A. Church, "Intensional Isomorphism and Identity of Belief," *Philosophical Studies* 5 (1954) 65–73; W. Sellars, "Putnam on Synonymity and Belief," *Analysis* 15 (1955) 117–20.

12. I. Scheffler, "An Inscriptional Approach to Indirect Quotation," *Analysis* 14 (1954) 83–90.

13. J. A. H. Murray et al., eds., *The Oxford English Dictionary* (Oxford: 1933) vol. XI, p. 253. Cf. C. T. Onions, *An Advanced English Syntax* (New York: 1929), pp. 154–156. I first learned that "that" in such contexts evolved from an explicit demonstrative in J. Hintikka, *Knowledge and Belief* (Ithaca: 1962), p. 13. Hintikka remarks that a similar development has taken place in German and Finnish. I owe the reference to the *O.E.D.* to Eric Stiezel.

14. I assume that a theory of truth for a language containing demonstratives must strictly apply to utterances and not to sentences, or will treat truth as a relation between sentences, speakers, and times. The point is discussed in "Truth and Meaning," (see ref. 2) [pp. 106–107, this volume].

30 Quantifying In[1]

DAVID KAPLAN

I

Expressions are used in a variety of ways. Two radically different ways in which the expression "nine" can occur are illustrated by the paradigms:

(1) Nine is greater than five,
(2) Canines are larger than felines.

Let us call the kind of occurrence illustrated in (1) a *vulgar* occurrence, and that in (2) an *accidental* occurrence (or, following Quine, an orthographic accident). For present purposes we need not try to define either of these notions; but presumably there are no serious logical or semantical problems connected with occurrences of either kind. The first denotes, is open to substitution and existential generalization, and contributes to the meaning of the sentence which contains it. To the second, all such concerns are inappropriate.

There are other occurrences of the word "nine," illustrated in

(3) "Nine is greater than five" is a truth of arithmetic,
(4) It is necessary that nine is greater than five,
(5) Hegel believed that nine is greater than five.

These diverge from the paradigm of vulgar occurrence (they fail the substitution test, the existential generalization test, and probably oth-

ers as well), but they are not, at least to the untutored mind, clearly orthographic accidents either: for in them, the meaning of "nine" seems, somehow, relevant. Let us call them *intermediate occurrences* and their contexts *intermediate contexts.*

These intermediate occurrences have come in for considerable discussion lately. Two kinds of analyses which have been proposed can be conveniently characterized as: (a) assimilating the intermediate occurrences to the accidental occurrences, and (b) assimilating the intermediate occurrences to the vulgar occurrences.

The former view, that the intermediate occurrences are to be thought of like accidental ones, I identify with Quine. Such a charge is slightly inaccurate; I make it chiefly for the sake of dramatic impact. My evidence, carefully selected, is that he has proposed in a few places that quotation contexts, as in (3), be thought of as single words and that "believes that nine is greater than five" be thought of as a simple predicate. And that after introducing a dichotomous classification of occurrences of names into those which he terms 'purely referential' (our vulgar—his criterion is substitutivity) and those which he terms 'nonreferential' (our intermediate and accidental) he writes, "We are not unaccustomed to passing over occurrences that somehow 'do not count'—'mary' in 'summary', 'can' in 'canary'; and we can allow similarly for

From *Synthese* 19 (1968–69): 178–214. David Kaplan, "Quantifying In," *Synthese* 19. Copyright © 1968 by D. Reidel Publishing Company, Dordrecht, Holland. Reprinted by permission of the publisher.

all non-referential occurrences of terms, once we know what to look out for." Further, his very terminology: "opaque" for a context in which names occur nonreferentially, seems to suggest an indissoluble whole, unarticulated by semantically relevant components.[2] But be that as it may, I shall put forward this analysis—the assimilation of intermediate occurrence to accidental ones—primarily in order to contrast its defeatist character with the sanguine view of Frege (and his followers) that we can assimilate the intermediate occurrences to vulgar ones.

II

The view that the occurrences of "nine" in (3), (4), and (5) are accidental may be elaborated, as Quine has done, by contrasting (3), (4), and (5) with:

(6) Nine is such that the result of writing it followed by 'is greater than five' is a theorem of Arithmetic,

(7) Nine is such that necessarily it is greater than five,

(8) Nine is such that Hegel believed it to be greater than five,

in which we put, or attempt to put, "nine" into purely referential position. Quine would still term the occurrences of "five" as nonreferential; thus, the "necessarily it is greater than five" in (7) might be thought of as an atomic predicate expressing some property of the number of baseball positions (assuming (7) to be true). And similarly for (6) and (8). I am not trying to say how we would "ordinarily" understand (6)–(8). I merely use these forms, in which the occurrence of "nine" does not stand within the so-called opaque construction, as a kind of canonical form to express what must be carefully explained, namely that here we attribute a property to a certain number, and that the correctness of this attribution is independent of the manner in which we refer to the number. Thus (6), (7), and (8) are to be understood in such a way that the result of replacing the occurrence of "nine" by any other expression denoting that number would not affect the truth value of the sentence. This includes replacement by a variable, thus validating existential generalization. In these respects (6)–(8) do indeed resemble (1).

But (3)–(5), which are to be understood in the natural way, are such that the result of substituting "the number of planets" for the occurrences of "nine" would lead from truth to falsehood (didn't Hegel "prove" that the number of planets=5?). Thus, for Quine, these contexts are opaque, and the result of replacing the occurrences of "nine" by the variable "x" and prefixing "$\exists x$" would lead from truth to formulas of, at best, questionable import. In fact, Quine deems such quantification into an opaque context flatly "improper."[3] In these respects (3)–(5) resemble (2). Although the impropriety of substituting or quantifying on the occurrence of "nine" in (2) is gross compared with that involved in applying the corresponding operations to (3)–(5), the view I am here characterizing would make this difference a matter of degree rather than of kind.

I will not expatiate on the contrast between (3)–(5) and (6)–(8), since Quine and others have made familiarity with this contrast a part of the conventional wisdom of our philosophical times. But note that (6)–(8) are not introduced as defined forms whose nonlogical apparatus is simply that of (3)–(5), in the way in which

Exactly one thing is greater than five

can be defined in terms of the non-logical apparatus of (1). Instead (6)–(8) are introduced as new primitive forms.

Earlier I said that (3)–(5) should be understood in the natural way, whereas careful explanation was required for (6)–(8). But will careful explanation suffice? Will anything suffice? What we have done, or rather what we have sketched, is this: a certain skeletal language structure has been given, here using fragments of English, so of course an English reading is at once available, and then certain logical transformations have been pronounced valid. Predicate logic was conducted in this way before Gödel and Tarski, and modal logic was so conducted before Carnap and others began to supply semantical foundations. The earlier method, especially as applied to modal logic (we might call it the run-it-up-the-axiom-list-and-see-if-anyone-deduces-a-contradiction method), seems to me to have been stimulated more by a compulsive permutations-and-combinations mentality than by the true philosophical temperament.

Thus, it just is not enough to describe the form (6) and say that the predicate expresses a property of numbers so that both Leibniz' law, and existential generalization apply. What property of numbers is this? It makes no sense to talk of the result of writing a number. We can write numerals and various other names of numbers but such talk as (6), in the absence of a theory of standard names, is surely based on confusion of mention and use.[4] One is tempted to make the same remark about (7), but in this case an alternative explanation is possible in a metaphysical tradition connected with so-called "Aristotelian essentialism." It is claimed that among the properties of a thing, e.g. being greater than 5, and numbering the planets, some hold of it necessarily, others only contingently. Quine has ably expounded the inevitability of this view of (7).[5]

In contrast to (6) and (7), we can put a strong prima facie case for the sensicalness of (8) by way of illustrative examples which indicate important uses of the form exemplified in (8) as compared with that of the form exemplified in (5). Russell mentions, in a slightly different context, the man who remarked to an acquaintance "I thought that your yacht was longer than it is." The correct rendering here is clearly in the style of (8), viz:

The length of your yacht is such that I thought that your yacht was longer than that.

not in the style of (5);

I thought that your yacht was longer than the length of your yacht.

In "Quantifiers and Propositional Attitudes," Quine supports the use of (8) as against (5) by an ingenious use of existential quantification. He contrasts:

(9) Ralph believes that someone is a spy,

in which the quantifier occurs within the opaque construction, as does the term in (5), with:

(10) Someone is such that Ralph believes that he is a spy,

which is an existential generalization of a formula of the form (8). After pointing out that (9) may be rephrased as:

Ralph believes that there are spies,

Quine remarks, "The difference is vast; indeed, if Ralph is like most of us, [(9)] is true and [(10)] is false." In this connection recall that according to Quine's theory of referential opacity, (10) can not be obtained by existential generalization directly from a formula of the form (5) say,

Ralph believes that Ortcutt is a spy,

since the occurrence of the term to be generalized on is here assimilated to that of the orthographic accident and thus is not immediately open to such a move.

Let me sum up what I have called Quine's elaboration of the view that intermediate occurrences are to be assimilated to accidental ones. For those cases in which it is desired to make connections between what occurs within the opaque construction and what occurs without, a special new primitive form is introduced, parallel to the original, but containing one (or more than one) of the crucial terms in a purely referential position. Quine refers to the new form as expressing the *relational* sense of belief. The possibility of introducing such forms always exists and the style of their introduction seems uniform, but since they are primitive each such introduction must be supplied with an ad hoc justification (to the effect that the predicate or operator being introduced makes sense).

III

Let me turn now to the Fregean view that assimilates intermediate occurrences to vulgar ones. The brilliant simplicity of Frege's leading idea in the treatment of intermediate occurrences has often been obscured by a failure to separate that idea from various turgid details involved in carrying the program through in particular interesting cases. But theory must be served.

Frege's main idea, as I understand it, was just this. There are no *real* intermediate occurrences; the appearance of intermediacy created by apparent failures of substitutivity and the like is due to confusion about what is denoted by the given occurrence. Frege here calls our attention to an implicit assumption made in testing for substitutivity and the like. Namely, that a denoting expression must *always* have its usual denotation, and, a fortiori, that two expressions must have the same denotation in a given context if they usually (i.e. in most contexts) have the same denotation.

But we are all familiar with many counterexamples to the assumption that a name always has its usual denotation. Consider:

(11) Although F.D.R. ran for office many times, F.D.R. ran on television only once.

The natural analysis of (11) involves pointing out that the name "F.D.R." is ambiguous, and that in the second clause it denotes a television show rather than a man. Substitutions or any other logical operations based on the assumption that the name has here its usual denotation are pointless and demonstrate nothing. But transformations based on a *correct* analysis of the name's denotation *in this context* will reveal the occurrence to be vulgar. I call this the natural analysis, but it is of course possible for a fanatical mono-denotationalist to insist that his transformations have shown the context:

. . . ran on television only once

to be opaque, and so to conclude that the second occurrence of "F.D.R." in (11) is not purely referential. This view may be expressed moderately, resulting only in an insistence that (11) is improper unless the second clause is rewritten as:

the television show named "F.D.R." ran on television only once.

Often when there is a serious possibility of confusion, we conform to the practice (even if not the theory) of the fanatical mono-denotationalist and do introduce a new word, add a subscript, or put the original in bold face, italics, or quotation marks. It is often good practice to continue to so mark the different uses of an expression, even when there is little possibility of confusion. Discovering and marking such ambiguities plays a considerable and useful role in philosophy (some, not I, would say it is the essence of philosophy), and much of what has proved most engaging and at the same time most fruitless in logical theory might have been avoided had the first 25 years of this century not seen a lapse from Frege's standards of mention and use. It would be unwary of us to suppose that we have now caught all such ambiguities. Thus, we should not leap to conclusions of opacity.

I indicated in the case of the fanatical mono-denotationalist how it is possible to trade a finding of opacity for one of ambiguity. Frege attempts his assimilation of intermediate occurrences to vulgar ones by indicating (some would say, postulating) ambiguities where others have seen only opacity. It is not denied that the ambiguities involved in the Fregean analysis are far more subtle than that noted in (11), but on his analysis the difference is seen as a matter of degree rather than of kind.

Frege referred to intermediate occurrences as *ungerade* (indirect, oblique). And the terminology is a natural one, for on his conception such an occurrence does not refer directly to its usual denotation but only, at best, indirectly by way of some intermediate *entity* such as a sense or an expression. I will return to this subject later. For now just notice that occurrences which Quine would call purely referential, Frege might call standardly referential; and those in contexts Quine would call referentially opaque, Frege might call nonstandardly referential, but in either case for Frege the occurrences are fully referential. So we require no special nonextensional logic, no restrictions on Leibniz' law, on existential generalization, etc., except those attendant upon consideration of a language containing ambiguous expressions. And even these can be avoided if we follow the practice of the fanatical mono-denotationalist and require linguistic reform so that distinct uses of expressions are marked by some distinction in the expressions themselves. This feature of a development of Frege's doctrine has been especially emphasized by Church.[6]

This then is Frege's treatment of intermediate contexts—obliquity indicates ambiguity. This doctrine accounts in a very natural way for the well-known logical peculiarities of intermediate contexts, such as the failure of substitutivity, existential generalization, etc.

IV

The difficulties in Frege's treatment appear in attempting to work out the details—details of the sort: exactly what *does* "nine" denote in (3)–(5)?

Frege's treatment of oblique contexts is often described as one according to which expressions in such contexts denote their ordinary sense or meaning or intension (I here use these terms interchangeably). But this is a bad way of putting the matter for three reasons. (1) It is, I believe, historically inaccurate. It ignores Frege's remarks about quotation marks (see below) and other special contexts. (2) It conflates two separate principles: (a) expressions in oblique contexts don't have their ordinary denotation (which is true), and (b) expressions in oblique contexts denote their ordinary sense (which is not, in general, true). And (3) in focussing attention too rapidly on the special and separate problems of intensional logic, we lose sight of the beauty and power of Frege's general method of treating oblique contexts. We may thus lose the motivation that that general theory might provide for an attack on the problems of the special theory. My own view is that Frege's explanation, by way of ambiguity, of what appears to be the logically deviant behavior of terms in intermediate contexts is so theoretically satisfying that if we have not yet discovered or satisfactorily grasped the peculiar intermediate objects in question, then we should simply continue looking.

There is, however, a method which may assist in the search. Look for something denoted by a compound, say, a sentence, in the oblique context. (In ordinary contexts sentences are taken to denote their own truth values and to be intersubstitutable on that basis.) And then using the fundamental principle: the denotation of the compound is a function of the denotation of the parts, look for something denoted by the parts. It was the use of this principle which, I believe, led to Carnap's discovery of individual concepts,[7] and also led Frege to the view that quotation marks produce an oblique context within which each component expression denotes itself[8] (it is clear in quotation contexts what the whole compound denotes).

Frege's view of quotation contexts would allow for quantification into such contexts, but of course we would have to quantify over expressions (since it is expressions that are denoted in such contexts), and we would have to make some provision to distinguish when a given symbol in such a context is being used as

a variable and when it is being used as a constant, i.e. to denote itself. This might be done by taking some distinctive class of symbols to serve as variables.

Let us symbolize Frege's understanding of quotation marks by using forward and backward capital F's. (Typographical limitations have forced elimination of the center horizontal bar of the capital F's.) Then, using Greek letters for variables ranging over expressions we can express such truths as:

(12) $\exists \alpha [\ulcorner \alpha$ is greater than five$\urcorner$ is a truth of arithmetic].[9]

Such is Frege's treatment of quotation marks: it seems to me more interesting and certainly much more fruitful (for the development of any theory in which quotation contexts are at all common) than the usual orthographic accident treatment according to which the quotation marks seal off the context, which is treated as a single indissoluble word. And it is well known that for serious theoretical purposes, quotation marks (under the conventional treatment) are of little use.

The ontological status of meanings or senses is less well settled than that of expressions. But we can again illustrate the principle involved in searching for the intermediate entities, and perhaps even engender an illusion of understanding, by introducing some symbolic devices. First, in analogy to the conventional use of quotation marks, I introduce meaning marks. Their use is illustrated in the following:

(13) The meaning of "brother" = ^{m}male sibling^{m}.

Now we can adapt the idea used in producing (12) to meaning marks, so as to produce a Fregean interpretation of them. The context produced by the meaning marks will then not be thought of as referentially opaque but rather such that each expression in such a context will denote its own meaning. Quantification in is permitted, but restricted of course to quantification over meanings. Following the earlier pattern, let us symbolize the new meaning marks with forward and backward capital M's. Using italic letters for variables ranging over meanings, we can express such truths as:

(14) $\exists a \exists b[^{\text{M}}a$ kicked $b^{\text{M}} = {}^{\text{M}}b$ was kicked by $a^{\text{M}}]$

I leave to the reader the problem of making sense of (12)–(14).

This comparison of meaning marks with quotation marks also allows me to make another point relevant to Quine's "Quantifiers and Propositional Attitudes." In his section IV, Quine suggests that by a harmless shift in idiom we can replace talk of meanings by talk of expressions, thus achieving ontological security. I agree, but the parallel can be exploited in either direction: as suggested by the introduction of meaning marks, we might also try to replace talk of expressions by talk of meanings, thus achieving ontological insight. These structural parallels are most helpful in constructing a logic of intensions.[10]

V

We have finished comparing the treatments of (3)–(5) with respect to the two main analyses of intermediate occurrences: assimilation to orthographic accident versus assimilation to vulgar occurrence. The forms involved in (6)–(8) were introduced in connection with what I called Quine's elaboration of the first line. Now what can be done in this direction following Frege's line? The purpose of the new forms in (6)–(8) is to get an expression out from an accidental position to a vulgar one; or, in Quine's terminology, to move a term from an opaque context to a purely referential position. There should be no problem here on Frege's theory, because what is opaque for Quine is already fully referential for Frege. Thus the term is in a fully referential position in the first place. But this will not quite satisfy the demands of (6)–(8), because the term in question does not denote the right thing.

At this point it will be useful to reformulate (3)–(8) [or at least (4), (5), (7), and (8)] so as to make explicit what the objects of belief and necessity are. In so doing we take a step along Frege's path, for the nonsubstitutability of one true sentence for another in such contexts would indicate to Frege an ambiguity in both of them: the sentences lack their usual denotation, a truth value, and instead denote some other entity. Before saying what, note that the necessity symbol will stand for a property—of something or other—and the belief symbol will stand for a two-place relation—between a person and something or other. (This in contrast to treating the necessity symbol simply as a 1-place referentially opaque sentential connective and similarly for belief.) Quine takes the step in Frege's direction in the article under discussion and favors it in the sister article "Three Grades of Modal Involvement." So I take it here. Now what shall the sentences denote? For my present purposes it will suffice to take the ontologically secure position and let them denote expressions, in particular, themselves.[11] Making this explicit, we rewrite (4) and (5) as:

(15) **N** "nine is greater than five"
(16) Hegel **B** "nine is greater than five"

On the usual reading of quotation marks, (15) and (16) still basically formulate the non-Fregean view, with the referential opacity now charged against the quotes. Keeping in mind that the shift to (7) and (8) was for the purpose of moving "nine" to a purely referential position, we can rewrite (7) and (8) as:

(17) **Nec** ("x is greater than five," nine)

(which may be read: 'x is greater than 5' is necessarily true of nine), and

(18) Hegel **Bel** ("x is greater than five," nine).

Here the symbol for necessity becomes a two-place predicate and that for belief a three-place predicate. "x is greater than five" stands for a compound predicate, with the bold face letter "x" used only as a *place holder* to indicate subject position. The opacity of quotation marks deny such place holders a referential position in any **Nec** or **Bel** context. 'Nec' and 'Bel' are intended to express Quine's relational sense of necessity and belief.[12]

Frege would reformulate (15) and (16) as:

(19) **N** ⌜nine is greater than five⌝.
(20) Hegel B ⌜nine is greater than five⌝.

Notice that we can use the same predicates as in (15) and (16) since

⌜nine is greater than five⌝ = "nine is greater than five"

just as

$$(3 \times 10^2) + (6 \times 10^1) + (8 \times 10^0) = 368.$$

It should now be clear that although the occurrences of "nine" in (19) and (20) are fully referential, (19) and (20) won't do for the purposes of (17) and (18), because the occurrences of "nine" in (17) and (18) refer to quite a different entity. Combining (17) with:

(21) Nine numbers the planets,

we derive:

(22) $\exists y[y$ numbers the planets & **Nec** ("**x** is greater than five," $y)]$.

But (19) and (21) seem to yield only:

$\exists y[y$ numbers the planets & **N** ⌜nine is greater than five⌝],

in which the quantifier binds nothing in the necessity context, or:

$\exists \alpha$ [α numbers the planets & **N** ⌜α is greater than five⌝],

which is false because the planets are not numbered by an expression (recall our conventions about Greek variables).

Thus the Fregean formulations appear to lack the kind of recurrence of a variable both within and without the necessity context that is characteristic of quantified modal logic and that appears in (22). But this difficulty can be considerably mitigated by taking note of the fact that though the number nine and the expression 'nine' are distinct entities, there is an important relationship between them. The second denotes the first. We can follow Church[6] by introducing a denotation predicate, 'Δ', into our language, and so restore, at least in an *indirect* way (recall Frege's indirect reference by way of intermediate entities) the connection between occurrences of an expression within and without the modal context, as in:

(23) $\exists y$ [y numbers the planets &$\exists \alpha(\Delta(\alpha,y)$& **N** ⌜$\alpha$ is greater than five⌝)].

I propose (23), or some variant, as Frege's version of (22); and

(24) $\exists \Delta$ [$\Delta(\alpha,$ nine) &**N** ⌜α is greater than five⌝),

or some variant, as Frege's version of (17). (We shall return later to the variants.) (23) and (24) may not be as exciting as (22) and (17), but neither do they commit us to essentialism. It may well be that (24), and its variants, supply all the connection between occurrences of expressions within and without modal contexts as can sensibly be allowed.

When I summed up Quine's elaboration of the orthographic accident theory of intermediate occurrences I emphasized the fact that to move an expression in an opaque construction to referential position, a new *primitive* predicate (such as '**Nec**' and '**Bel**' of (17) and (18)) had to be introduced and supplied with an interpretation. In contrast, the same effect is achieved by Frege's method using only the original predicates plus logical signs, including 'Δ', and of course the ontological decomposition involved in the use of the Frege quotes.

Turning now to belief I propose:

(25) $\exists \alpha[\Delta(\alpha,$ nine) & Hegel **B** ⌜α is greater than five⌝],

or some variant, as Frege's version of Quine's (18).

VI

If we accept (25) as the interpretation of Quine's (18), we can justify a crucial form of inference he seems to consider valid and explain certain seemingly paradoxical results which he accepts.

Quine recites the following story.

There is a certain man in a brown hat whom Ralph has glimpsed several times under questionable circumstances on which we need not enter here; suffice it to say that Ralph suspects he is a spy. Also there is a gray-haired man, vaguely known to Ralph as rather a pillar of the community, whom Ralph is not aware of having seen except once at the beach. Now Ralph does not know it, but the men are one and the same.

Quine then poses the question, "Can we say of this *man* (Bernard J. Ortcutt, to give him a name) that Ralph believes him to be a spy?" The critical facts of the story are summarized in what we would write as:

(26) Ralph **B** "the man in the brown hat is a spy,"

(27) Ralph **B** "the man seen at the beach is not a spy,"

(28) the man in the brown hat = the man seen at the beach = Ortcutt.

Quine answers his own query by deriving what we would write as:

(29) Ralph **Bel** ("x is a spy," the man in the brown hat)

from (26). He says of this move, "The kind of exportation which leads from [(26)] to [(29)] should doubtless be viewed in general as implicative."[13] Now our versions of (26) and (29) are:

(30) Ralph **B** $\ulcorner$the man in the brown hat is a spy$\urcorner$,

(31) $\exists\alpha[\Delta(\alpha,$ $\ulcorner$the man in the brown hat) & Ralph **B** $\ulcorner\alpha$ is a spy$\urcorner$].

And (31) certainly is implied by (30) and the nearly analytic truth:

Δ("the man in the brown hat," the man in the brown hat).[14]

We thus justify exportation.

In discussing a seeming paradox Quine notes that exportation will also lead from (27) to:

Ralph **Bel** ("x is not a spy," the man seen at the beach)

and hence, by (28), to:

(32) Ralph **Bel** ("x is not a spy," Ortcutt).

Whereas (29) and (28) yield:

(33) Ralph **Bel** ("x is a spy," Ortcutt).

Thus, asserts Quine,

[(32)] and [(33)] both count as true. This is not, however, to charge Ralph with contradictory beliefs. Such a charge might reasonably be read into:

[(34)] Ralph **Bel** ("x is a spy and x is not a spy," Ortcutt),]

but this merely goes to show that it is undesirable to look upon [(32)] and [(33)] as implying [(34)].

At first blush it may appear that avoidance of that undesirable course [looking upon (32) and

(33) as implying (34)] calls for the most intense kind of concentration and focus of interest. In fact one may be pessimistically inclined to take the easy way out and simply dispose of (32), (33), (34) and any other assertions involving **Bel** as nonsense. But, as Quine says, "How then to provide for those indispensable relational statements of belief, like 'There is someone whom Ralph believes to be a spy'.?"

Fortunately our versions of Bel again conform to Quine's intuitions. (32),(33) and (34) go over respectively into:

(35) $\exists\alpha[\Delta(\alpha,$ Ortcutt) & Ralph **B** $\ulcorner\alpha$ is not a spy$\urcorner$],

(36) $\exists\alpha[\Delta(\alpha,$ Ortcutt) & Ralph **B** $\ulcorner\alpha$ is a spy$\urcorner$],

(37) $\exists\alpha[\Delta(\alpha,$ Ortcutt) & Ralph **B** $\ulcorner\alpha$ is a spy and α is not a spy$\urcorner$]

which clearly verify Quine's claims, even in the presence of the suppressed premise:

$\forall\alpha\forall\beta[$Ralph **B** $\ulcorner\alpha$ is a spy$\urcorner$ & Ralph **B** $\ulcorner\beta$ is not a spy$\urcorner$ $\rightarrow$ Ralph **B** $\ulcorner\alpha$ is a spy and β is not a spy$\urcorner$]

VII

So far so good. But further exploration with our version of **Bel** suggests that the rule of exportation fails to mesh with the intuitive ideas that originally led Quine to the introduction of **Bel**. And I believe that our version will also allow us to see more clearly exactly what problems lay before us if we are to supply a notion answering to these motivating intuitions. As I hope later developments will show, there are a number of different kinds of counter-cases which could be posed. I will only develop one at this point.

Suppose that the situation is as stated in (9). We would now express (9) as:

(38) Ralph **B** "$\exists y$ y is a spy."

Believing that spies differ widely in height, Ralph believes that one among them is shortest. Thus,

(39) Ralph **B** "the shortest spy is a spy."

Supposing that there is in fact one shortest spy, by exportation (39) yields:

(40) Ralph **Bel** ("x is a spy," the shortest spy)

which, under the same supposition, by existential generalization yields:

(41) $\exists y$ Ralph **Bel** ("**x** is a spy," y).

And (41) currently expresses (10). But (10) was originally intended to express a fact which would interest the F.B.I. (recall Quine's comment that if Ralph is like most of us, (10) is false), and we would not expect the interest of that organization to be piqued by Ralph's conviction that no two spies share a size.

Two details of this case can be slightly improved. First, the near analyticity of Ralph's crucial belief, as expressed in (39), can be eliminated by taking advantage of Ralph's belief that all members of the C.P.U.S.A. (none of which are known to him) are spies. Second, we can weaken the assumption of Ralph's special ideas about spy sizes by using only the well-known fact that two persons can not be born at exactly the same time at exactly the same place (where the place of birth is an interior point of the infant's body). Given any four spatial points a, b, c, d not in a plane, we can use the relations: t_1 is earlier than t_2, and p_1 is closer to $a(b, c, d)$ than p_2 is, to order all space time points. We can then form such names as "the least spy" with the meaning: ^{m}that spy whose spatio-temporal location at birth precedes that of all other spies^m.

Details aside, the point is that exportation, as represented in our current version of **Bel**, conflicts with the intention that there be a 'vast' difference between (9) and (10). Still, I am convinced that we are on the right track. That track, roughly speaking, is this: instead of trying to introduce a new primitive relation like Quine's **Bel,** we focus on trying to define it (or something as close to it as we can sensibly come, remember modal logic) using just the dyadic **B** plus other logical and semi-logical apparatus such as quantifiers, Δ, etc. and also possibly other seemingly more fundamental epistemological notions.

Some years ago I thought that this task was hopeless and took basically the same attitude toward such quantified belief contexts as Quine takes toward quantified modal logic.[15] At that earlier time I used to argue with my colleague, Montgomery Furth, who shares my attitude toward Frege's theory, about the meaningfulness of such quantifications in as in (10). (This was after noticing the difficulty, indicated above, in our current analysis.[16]) Furth suggested that a solution might lie in somehow picking out certain kinds of names as being required for the exportation. But this just seemed essentialism all over again and we gave up. Although still uncertain that (10) makes sense, I think I can show that it comes to something like what Furth had in mind. Indeed, the analogies between the relational senses of belief and necessity are so strong that I have often wondered why Quine's scepticism with regard to **Nec** did not extend to **Bel**.

There is even an inadequacy in our proposed analysis, (24), of **Nec** parallel to that displayed for our proposed analysis, (25), of **Bel.** Although our analysis of **Nec** avoids essentialism, it also avoids rejecting:

(42) **Nec** ("**x** = the number of planets," nine),

which comes out true on the understanding:

(43) $\exists \alpha (\Delta(\alpha, \text{nine}) \ \& \ \mathbf{N} \ulcorner \alpha = \text{the number of planets}\urcorner)$

in view of the facts that

$\mathbf{N} \ulcorner$the number of planets = the number of planets$\urcorner$

and

Δ("the number of planets," nine).

In a sense, we have not avoided essentialism but only inessentialism, since so many of nine's properties become essential. Small consolation to know of our essential rationality if each blunder and error is equally ingrained.

The parallel inadequacies of our versions of **Nec** and **Bel** are now apparent. Our analyses credit nine with an excess of essence and put Ralph *en rapport* with an excess of individuals.

VIII

What is wanted is "a frankly inequalitarian attitude toward various ways of specifying the number [nine]".[17] This suggests to me that we should restrict our attention to a smaller class of names; names which are so intimately connected with what they name that they could not but name it. I shall say that such a name *necessarily denotes* its object, and I shall use "Δ_N" to symbolize this more discriminating form of denotation.

Such a relation is available; based on the notion of a *standard name*. A standard name is one whose denotation is fixed on logical, or perhaps I should say linguistic, grounds alone. Numerals and quotation names are prominent among the standard names.[18] Such names do, in the appropriate sense, necessarily denote their denotations.

Russell and some others who have attempted to treat proper names of persons as standard names have emphasized the purely referential function of such names and their apparent lack of descriptive content. But consideration of the place value system of arabic numerals and our conventions for the construction of quotation names of expressions should convince us that what is at stake is not pure reference in the absence of any descriptive structure, but rather reference freed of *empirical* vicissitudes. Numbers and expressions, like every other kind of entity, can be named by names which are such that empirical investigation is required to determine their denotations. "The number of planets" and "9" happen to denote the same number. The former might, under other circumstances or at some other time, denote a different number, but so long as we hold constant our conventions of language, "9" will denote the same number under all possible circumstances. To wonder what number is named by the German "die Zahl der Planeten" may betray astronomical ignorance, but to wonder what number is named by the German "Neun" can indicate only linguistic incompetence.[19]

$\Delta_N(\alpha, x)$ cannot be analyzed in terms of the analyticity of some sentence of the form

$$\Delta(\text{---}, \ldots);$$

since:

$\Delta(\text{"the number of planets," the number of planets})$

is analytic, but "the number of planets" is not a standard name of the number of planets (viz: nine), and

$\Delta(\text{"9," the number of planets})$

is not analytic, although "9" is a standard name of that number. We have in Δ_N a relation that holds between the standard name and the number itself, independent of any particular way of specifying the number. Thus there is a certain intimacy between "9" and 9, lacking between "the number of planets" and the number of planets, which allows "9" to go proxy for 9 in assertions of necessity.

There is a sense in which the finite ordinals (which we can take the entities here under discussion to be) find their essence in their ordering. Thus, names which reflect this ordering in an a priori way, as by making true statements of order analytic, capture all that is essential to these numbers. And our careless attitude toward any intrinsic features of these numbers (e.g. whether zero is a set, and if so whether it has any members) suggests that such names may have captured all there is to these numbers.[20] I am less interested in urging an explanation of the special intimacy between "nine" and nine, than in noting the fact. The phenomenon is widespread, extending to expressions, pure sets of finite rank, and others of their ilk. I would require any adequate explanation to generalize so as to handle all such cases, and I should hope that such an explanation would also support the limitations which I suggest below on the kinds of entities eligible for standard names.[21]

The foregoing considerations suggest simple variants for our current Fregean versions of (17) and (42). We replace (24) with:

$\exists\alpha(\Delta_N(\alpha, \text{nine})\&N \ulcorner\alpha$ is greater than five$\urcorner$

as our analysis of (17), and we replace (43) with:

$\exists\alpha(\Delta_N(\alpha, \text{nine})\&N \ulcorner\alpha$ = the number of planets$\urcorner)$

as our analysis of (42). According to the reformed analyses, (17) and (42) come out respectively as true and false, which accords much better with our intuitions and may even satisfy the essentialist.[22] All, it is hoped, without a lapse into irreducible (though questionable) metaphysical assumptions.

There are, however, limitations on the resort to standard names. Only abstract objects can have standard names, since only they (and not all of them) lack that element of contingency which makes the rest of us liable to failures of existence. Thus, Quine can have no standard name, for he might not be. And then what shall his standard name name? Quine's singleton, {Quine}, though abstract, is clearly no better off.

Numerals are reliable; they always pick out the same number. But to suppose a standard name for Quine would presuppose a solution to the more puzzling problem of what features to take into account in determining that an individual of one possible world is 'the same person' as that of another. Often when the worlds have a common part, as when we consider alternative futures to the present, the individual(s) can be traced back to the common part by the usual continuity conditions and there compared. But for individuals not extant during an overlap such techniques are unavailing. It seems that such radically disjoint worlds are sometimes contemplated by modal logicians. I am not here passing final judgment but only remarking the relevance of a second difference between Quine and Nine: namely, that he presents a very real problem of transworld identification while it does not.

Thus the device of using standard names, which accounts nicely for my own intuitions regarding the essential properties of numbers, appears to break down when set to discriminating essential properties of persons. I am consoled by the fact that my own intuitions do not assign essential properties to persons in any broad metaphysical sense, which is not to say that quantified modal logic can have no interesting interpretation when trans-world identifications are made from the point of view of a frankly special interest.

IX

All this on **Nec** was aimed toward analogy with **Bel** and a charge of inconsistent scepticism against Quine. We have patched our first version of **Nec** with a more discriminating sense of denotation. The same trick would work for **Bel**, if Ralph would confine his cogitations to numbers and expressions. If not, we must seek some other form of special intimacy between name and object which allows the former to go proxy for the latter in Ralph's cognitive state.

I believe that the fundamental difficulty with our first version of **Bel** is that Δ gave us a relation between name and object in which Ralph played no significant role. Supposing all speakers of English to have available approximately the same stock of names (i.e. singular terms), this puts us all *en rapport* with the same persons. But the interesting relational sense of belief, and the one which I suppose Quine to have been getting at with (10), is one which provides Ralph with access to some but not all persons of whom he can frame names. What we are after this time is a three-place relation between Ralph, a name (which I here use in the broad sense of singular term) α, and a person x. For this purpose I will introduce two special notions: that of a name α being *of x* for Ralph, and that of a name being *vivid*, both of which I will compare with the notion of a name *denoting x*.

Let us begin by distinguishing the *descriptive content* of a name from the *genetic character* of the name as used by Ralph. The first goes to user-independent features of the name, the second to features of a particular user's acquisition of certain beliefs involving the name. It is perhaps easiest to make the distinction in terms not of names but of pictures, with consideration limited to pictures which show a single person. Those features of a picture, in virtue of which we say it resembles or is a likeness of a particular person, comprise the picture's descriptive content. The genetic character of a picture is determined by the causal chain of events leading to its production. In the case of photographs and portraits we say that the picture is *of* the person who was photographed or who sat for the portrait. The same relation presumably holds between a perception and the perceived object.[23] This relation between picture and person clearly depends entirely on the genetic character of the picture. Without attempting a definition, we can say that for a picture to be *of* a person, the person must serve significantly in the causal chain leading to the picture's production and also serve as object for the picture. The second clause is to prevent all of an artist's paintings from being *of* the artist. I will shortly say a bit more about how I understand this relation, which I designate with the italicized '*of*'.

The "user-independence" of the descriptive

content of a picture lies in the fact that "identical" pictures, such as two prints made from a single negative, will resemble all the same persons. In this sense, the descriptive content of a picture is a function of what we might call the picture-type rather than the picture-token. The "user-dependent" nature of the genetic character of a picture lies in the fact that "identical" paintings can be such that they are *of* different persons (e.g. twins sitting separately for portraits). Thus the genetic character of a picture is a function only of the picture-token. In order to accommodate genesis, I use 'picture' throughout in the sense of 'picture-token'.

Armed with *resemblance* and *of*-ness, let me recite just a few of the familiar facts of portraiture. First, not all pictures *of* a person resemble that person. Of two recent pictures taken of me, one resembles Steve Allen and the other resembles nothing on earth. Secondly, not all pictures which resemble a person are *of* that person. It is obvious that a picture *of* one twin will, if it resembles the twin it is *of,* also resemble the other twin. What is more interesting is that a picture which resembles a person may not be *of* any person at all. My camera may have had a hallucination due to light leaks in its perceptual system. Similarly, if I have drawn my conception of how the typical man will look in one million years, even if a man looking like that now exists, my picture is not *of* him (unless he sat as a model or played some other such role). Thirdly, a picture may be *of* more than one person, as when, by the split mirror technique, we obtain a composite photograph showing one man's head on another man's body. Indeed, in summary, a single picture may be *of* no one, one person, or many persons, while resembling no one, one person, or many persons, with any degree of overlap between those whom it is *of* and those whom it resembles. Of course, if photographs did not frequently, indeed usually, resemble their subjects, they could not serve many of the purposes for which we use them. Still, on occasion, things can and do go awry, and a bad photograph of one is yet a photograph *of* one.

I turn now to cases in which the causal chain from object to picture is relatively indirect. If one or several witnesses describe the criminal to a police artist who then constructs a picture, I shall say that it is a picture *of* the criminal, even when after such a genesis the resulting picture has quite ceased to resemble the criminal. Similarly, had a photograph of Julius Caesar been xeroxed, and the xerox copy televised to a monastery, where it was copied by a monk, and so was reproduced down through the ages, I would call the resulting copy, no matter how distorted, no matter who, if anyone, it resembled, a picture of Julius Caesar.[24]

A police artist's reconstruction of Santa Claus, based on a careful reading of the poem *The Night Before Christmas,* is not a picture *of* anyone no matter how many people make themselves up so that it exactly resembles them, and no matter whether the artist regards the poem as fact or fiction. Even if in combining facial features of known statistical frequencies the artist correctly judges that the resulting picture will resemble someone or other, that person has no special causal efficacy in the production of the picture and so it still will not be a picture *of* anyone. And if the story of Medusa originated in imagination or hallucination (as opposed to misperception or misapprehension), then a rendering based on that legend is *of* no one, notwithstanding the existence of any past, present, or future snake-haired women.

In addition to the link with reality provided by the relation of resemblance the descriptive content of a picture determines its *vividness.* A faded picture showing the back of a man wearing a cloak and lurking in shadow will lack vividness. A clear picture, head on, full length, life size, showing fingerprints, etc. would be counted highly vivid. What is counted as vivid may to some extent depend on special interests. To the clothier, nude portraits may be lacking in detail, while to the foot fetishist a picture showing only the left big toe may leap from the canvas. Though special interests may thus weight detail, I would expect that increase in detail always increases vividness. It should be clear that there are no necessary connections between how vivid a picture is and whether it is *of* anyone or whether it resembles anyone.

Returning now to names, it is their descriptive content that determines what if anything they denote. Thus, denotation is the analogue for names to resemblance for pictures. The genetic character of a name in a given person's usage will account for how he *acquired* the name, that is how he heard of such a thing and, if he believes that such a thing exists, how he came to believe it. It is the genetic character of the name that determines what if anything it is a name *of*. (I here use the same nomenclature, '*of*', for names as for pictures.) The user-dependence of this notion is required by the fact that Ralph and Fred may each have acquired the name "John Smith," but in such a way that for Ralph it is a name *of* one John Smith while for Fred it is a name *of* another John Smith.

I would suppose that students of rhetoric realize that most of the lines of argument traditionally classified as 'informal fallacies' (*ad hominem, ad vericundiam*, etc.) are commonly considered relevant or even determinative by reasonable men.[25] Cases such as that of the two John Smiths, which emphasize the importance of genetic features in language use, indicate limitations that must be placed on the traditional dichotomy between *what* we believe (assert, desire, etc.) and *how* we came to believe it.

Let us attempt to apply these considerations to the case of proper names. Proper names denote each of the usually many persons so dubbed. Ralph may acquire a proper name in a number of different ways. He may have attended a dubbing with the subject present. I reconstruct such dubbings as consisting of a stipulative association of the name with a perception *of* the subject. Thus, the name becomes a name *of* the subject, and as it passes from Ralph to others retains this feature in the manner of the picture *of* Julius Caesar. We may of course dub on the basis of a hallucination, in which case the name is a name *of* nothing, though it will still denote each actual person, if any, that may be so dubbed. Dubbings sometimes take place with the subject absent, in which case some other name (usually a description) stands in for the perception, and the stipulatively introduced proper name takes its genetic character from the stand-in name. If the latter only denotes the subject (and is not a name *of* the subject for the user in question), the proper name can do no better. This having a name *of* x, I shall later take to be essential to

having a belief about x, and I am unwilling to adopt any theory of proper names which permits me to perform a dubbing in absentia, as by solemnly declaring "I hereby dub the first child to be born in the twenty-second century 'Newman 1'," and thus grant myself standing to have beliefs about that as yet unborn child. Another presumably more common way to acquire a proper name is in casual conversation or reading, e.g. from the headline, "Mayor Indicted; B. J. Ortcutt sought by F.B.I.". In such cases we retrace the causal sequence from Ralph back through his immediate source to its immediate source and so on. An especially difficult case of this sort arises when someone other than Ortcutt, say Wyman, is introduced to Ralph as Ortcutt. Suppose that the introduction took place with intent to deceive and that Fred, who made the introduction, acquired the name "Ortcutt" as a name *of* Ortcutt. Clearly we should count "Ortcutt" as a name *of* Wyman for Ralph, but also, through Fred, as a name *of* Ortcutt. The situation is analogous to the composite photograph made by the split mirror technique. But here the much greater vividness of the perceptual half of the equation may outweigh the dim reflection of Ortcutt.

I leave to the reader the useful exercise of constructing cases of names (not necessarily proper) which are analogues to each of the cited cases of pictures.

The notion of a vivid name is intended to go to the purely internal aspects of individuation. Consider typical cases in which we would be likely to say that Ralph knows x or is acquainted with x. Then look only at the conglomeration of images, names, and partial descriptions which Ralph employs to bring x before his mind. Such a conglomeration, when suitably arranged and regimented, is what I call a vivid name. As with pictures, there are degrees of vividness and the whole notion is to some degree relative to special interests. The crucial feature of this notion is that it depends only on Ralph's current mental state, and ignores all links whether by resemblance or genesis with the actual world. If the name is such, that on the assumption that there exists some individual x whom it both denotes and resembles we should say that Ralph knows x or is acquainted with x, then the name is vivid.

The vivid names "represent" those persons who fill major roles in that *inner story* which consists of all those sentences which Ralph believes. I have placed "represent' here in scare-quotes to warn that there may not actually exist anything which is so "represented." Ralph may enjoy an inner story totally out of contact with reality, but this is not to deny it a cast of robust and clearly delineated characters. Life is often less plausible than art. Of course a vivid name should make an existence *claim.* If Ralph does not believe that there is a Santa Claus, I would not call any Santa Claus name vivid, no matter how lively it is in other respects.

There are certain features which may contribute strongly to vividness but which I feel we should not accept as absolute requirements. It is certainly too much to require that a vivid name must provide Ralph with a means of recognizing its purported object under all circumstances, for we do not follow the careers of even those we know best that closely. There are always gaps. We sometimes even fail to recognize ourselves in early photographs or recent descriptions, simply because of gaps in our self-concept.[26] It also seems to me too much to require that Ralph believes himself to have at some time perceived the purported object of a vivid name since a scholar may be better acquainted with Julius Caesar than with his own neighbor. Some have also suggested that the appropriate kind of name must provide Ralph with the means of locating its purported object. But parents and police are frequently unable to locate persons well known to them. Also, a vivid biography of a peasant somewhere in Asia, may involve none but the vaguest spatio-temporal references.

One might understand the assertion, "Ralph has an opinion as to who Ortcutt is" as a claim that Ralph can place Ortcutt among the leading characters of his inner story, thus that Ralph believes some sentence of the form $\ulcorner\alpha = \text{Ortcutt}\urcorner$ with α vivid. This, I believe, is the view of Hintikka. Hintikka institutionalizes the sense of 'represents' with usual quotes by allowing existential generalization on the leading character or inner individual "represented" by a vivid name. Although his symbolism allows him to distinguish between those inner individuals which are

actual and those which are not, a central role is assigned to something close to what I call a vivid name.[27] In emphasizing this conceptual separation of vividness, which makes a name a *candidate* for exportation, from those features depending on genesis and resemblence, which determine what actual person, if anyone, the name really represents (without quotes), Hintikka (if I have him right) and I are in agreement.

It is a familiar fact of philosophy that no idea, description, or image can insure itself against non-natural causes. The most vivid of names may have had its origin in imagination or hallucination. Thus, to freely allow exportation a name must not only be vivid but must also be a name *of* someone, and indeed a name *of* the person it denotes. This last is an accuracy requirement which no doubt is rarely satisfied by the most vivid names we use. Our most vivid names can be roughly characterized as those elaborate descriptions containing all we believe about a single person. Such names will almost certainly contain inaccuracies which will prevent them from actually denoting anyone. Also such names are often not *of* a single person but result from conflation of information about several persons (as in Fred's prevaricating introduction of Wyman to Ralph).

One proposal for handling such difficulties would be to apply the method of best fit to our most vivid names, i.e. to seek the individual who comes closest to satisfying the two conditions: that the name denotes him and is *of* him. But it seems that this technique would distort the account of conflations, never allowing us to say that there are two persons whom Ralph believes to be one. There is an alternate method which I favor. Starting with one of our most vivid names, form the largest core, all of which is *of* the same person and which denotes that person. A vivid name resulting from conflation may contain more than one such core name. The question is whether such a core, remaining after excision of inaccuracy, is yet vivid. If so, I will say that the core name *represents* the person whom it both denotes and is of to Ralph.

Our task was to characterize a relation between Ralph, a name, and a person, which could replace Δ in a variant analysis of **Bel.** For this I will use the above notion of representation. To repeat, I will say α *represents x to* Ralph (symbolized: "$R(α, x,$ Ralph)") if and only if (i) α denotes x, (ii) α is a name *of x* for Ralph, and (iii) α is (sufficiently) vivid. Our final version of (33) is the following variant of (36):

(44) $∃α[R(α,$ Ortcutt, Ralph) & Ralph **B** ⌜α is a spy⌝].

X

Part of our aim was to restrict the range of persons with whom Ralph is *en rapport* (in the sense of **Bel**). This was done by means of clauses (ii) and (iii). Clause (ii) excludes all future persons such as Newman 1[28] and indeed any person past, present, or future who has not left his mark on Ralph. The addition of clause (iii) excludes any person who has not left a vivid mark on Ralph.

The crucial exportation step for the case of the shortest spy is now blocked, because in spite of Ralph's correct belief that such a person exists, "the shortest spy" is not, for Ralph, a name *of* him.[29]

Clause (iii) takes account of the desire to allow Ralph beliefs *about* (again in the sense of **Bel**) only those persons he 'has in mind', where the mere acquisition of, say, a proper name *of x* would not suffice to put x in mind. Furthermore, if we were to drop clause (iii), and allow any name which both denotes x and is a name *of x* to represent x to Holmes, then after Holmes observed the victim, "the murderer" would represent the murderer to him. And thus we would have:

$∃y∃α[R(α, y,$ Holmes)&Holmes **B**⌜α = the murderer⌝],

which is our present analysis of:

$∃y$ Holmes **Bel** ("x = the murderer," y),

which is, roughly, Quine's translation of:

There is someone whom Holmes believes to be the murderer.

But this last should presage an arrest and not the mere certification of homicide. Clause (iii) is intended to block such cases. At some point in his investigation, the slow accretion of evidence, all "pointing in a certain direction" may just push Holmes' description over the appropriate vividness threshold so that we *would* say that there is now someone whom Holmes believes to be the murderer.

Clause (iii) could also be used to block exportation of "the shortest spy." But that would not eliminate the need for clause (ii) which is still needed to insure that we export to the right individual.

Although I believe that all three clauses are required to block all the anomalies of exportation, I am less interested in a definitive analysis of that particular inference than I am in separating and elucidating certain notions which may be useful in epistemological discussions. According to my analysis, Ralph must have quite a solid conception of x before we can say that Ralph believes x to be a spy. By weakening the accuracy requirements on the notion of representation we obtain in general new relational senses of belief.[30] Any such notion, based on a clearly specified variant of (36), may be worthy of investigation.

XI

A vivid name is a little bit like a standard name, but not much. It can't guarantee existence to its purported object, and although it has a kind of inner reliability by way of Ralph's use of such names to order his inner world, a crucial condition of reliability—the determinateness of standard identities—fails. A standard identity is an identity sentence in which both terms are standard names. It is corollary to the reliability of standard names, that standard identities are either true under all circumstances or false under all circumstances. But not so for identities involving vivid names. We can easily form two vivid names, one describing Bertrand Russell as logician, and another describing Russell as social critic, which are such that the identity sentence simply can not be decided on internal evidence. In the case of the morning star and the evening star, we can even form names which allow us to locate the purported objects (if we are willing to wait for the propitious moment) without the identity sentence being determinate. Of course Ralph may believe the negation of the identity sentence for all distinct pairs of vivid names, but such beliefs may simply be wrong. And the names can remain vivid even after such inaccurate nonidentities are excised. It may happen that Ralph comes to change his beliefs so that where he once believed a nonidentity between vivid names, he now believes an identity. And at some intermediate stage of wonder he believes neither the identity nor the nonidentity. Such Monte Cristo cases may be rare in reality (though rife in fiction),[31] but they are nevertheless clearly possible. They could be ruled out only by demanding an unreasonably high standard of vividness, to wit: no gaps, or else by adding an artificial and ad hoc requirement that all vivid names contain certain format items, e.g. exact place and date of birth. Either course would put us out of *rapport* with most of our closest friends. Thus, two vivid names can represent the same person to Ralph although Ralph does not believe the identity sentence. He may simply wonder, or he may disbelieve the identity sentence and so believe of one person that he is two. Similarly two vivid names can represent different persons to Ralph although Ralph does not believe the non-identity sentence. Again, Ralph may either suspend judgment or disbelieve the non-identity and so believe of two persons that they are one. Since this last situation is perhaps more plausible than the others, it is important to see that theoretically the cases are on a par. In fact, a case where Ralph has so conflated two persons and is then disabused by his friend Fred, becomes a case of believing one person to be two simply by assuming that Ralph was right in the first place and that Fred lied.

Quine acknowledges that Ralph can believe of one person that he is two on Quine's own understanding of **Bel,** when he remarks, as mentioned in VI above, that

(32) Ralph **Bel** ("**x** is not a spy," Ortcutt),

and

(33) Ralph **Bel** ("**x** is a spy," Ortcutt),

do not express an inconsistency on Ralph's part and do not imply (34). The background story justifying (32) and (33) involves Ralph twice spotting Ortcutt but under circumstances so dif-

ferent that Ralph was unaware that he was seeing the same man again. Indeed he believed he was not seeing the same man again, since on the one occasion he thought, "There goes a spy," and on the other, "Here is no spy." My point is that though one may quibble about whether each or either of the names of Ortcutt were vivid in the particular cases as described by Quine,[32] and so question whether in those cases exportation should have been permitted, no plausible characterization of appropriate conditions for vividness can prevent analogous cases from arising.

Cases of the foregoing kind, which agree with Quine's intuitions, argue an inadequacy in his regimentation of language. For in the same sense in which (32) and (33) do not express an inconsistency on Ralph's part, neither should (33) and

(45) ~Ralph **Bel** ("**x** is a spy," Ortcutt)

express an inconsistency on ours. Indeed it seems natural to claim that (45) is a consequence of (32). But the temptation to look upon (33) and (45) as contradictory is extremely difficult to resist. The problem is that since Quine's **Bel** suppresses mention of the specific name being exported, he can not distinguish between

(46) $\exists\alpha[\ulcorner R(\alpha, \text{Ortcutt}, \text{Ralph}) \& \sim \text{Ralph } B \ulcorner\alpha$ is a spy$\urcorner]$

and

(47) $\sim\exists\alpha[R(\alpha, \text{Ortcutt}, \text{Ralph}) \& \text{Ralph } B \ulcorner\alpha$ is a spy$\urcorner]$

If (45) is read as (46), there is no inconsistency with (32); in fact, on this interpretation (45) is a consequence of (32) (at least on the assumption that Ralph does not have contradictory beliefs). But if (45) is read as (47) (Quine's intention, I suppose), it is inconsistent with (33) and independent of (32).

So long as Ralph can believe of one person that he is two, as in Quine's story, we should be loath to make either (46) or (47) inexpressible.[33] If (33) is read as (44), we certainly must retain some way of expressing (47) since it expresses the negation of (33). Is it important to retain expression of (46)? In Quine's story, something stronger than (46) holds, namely (32), which we now read as:

(48) $\exists\alpha[\mathbf{R}(\alpha,\ \text{Ortcutt, Ralph})\&\text{Ralph}\ \mathbf{B}\ \ulcorner\alpha\ \text{is not a spy}\urcorner]$

But we can continue the story to a later time at which Ralph's suspicions regarding even the man at the beach have begun to grow. Not that Ralph now proclaims that respected citizen to be a spy, but Ralph now suspends judgment as to the man's spyhood. At this time (48) is false, and (46) is true. If we are to have the means to express such suspensions of judgment, something like (46) is required.

I have gone to some trouble here to indicate the source of the notational inadequacy in the possibility of a single person bearing distinct exportable names not believed to name the same thing, and also to argue in favor of maintaining the possibility of such names. I have done this because logicians working in this field have for the most part been in accord with Quine in adopting the simpler language form. In my view the consequence of adopting such a form is either to exclude natural interpretations by setting an impossibly high standard for vividness, and thus for exportation, or else to make such partial expressions of suspended judgment as (46) inexpressible.

XII

When earlier I argued for Frege's method—seek the intermediate entity—it was on the grounds that a clarified view of the problem was worth at least a momentary ontological risk. But now it appears that to give adequate expression to the epistemological situation requires explicit quantificational certification of the status of such entities. I am undismayed and even would urge that the conservative course so far followed of taking expressions as the intermediate entities is clearly inadequate to the task. Many of our beliefs have the form: "The color of her hair is_____," or "The song he was singing went _____," where the blanks are filled with images, sensory impressions, or what have you, but certainly not words. If we cannot even *say* it with words but have to paint it or sing it, we certainly cannot believe it with words.

My picture theory of meaning played heavily on the analogy between names and pictures. I believe that the whole theory of sense and denotation can be extended to apply to pictures as well as words. (How can an identity "sentence" with the components filled by pictures be both true and informative?) If we explicitly include such visual images among names, we gain a new perspective on the claim that we can definitively settle the question of whether Bernard J. Ortcutt is such that Ralph believes him to be a spy by confronting Ralph with Ortcutt and asking "Is he a spy?" Ralph's response will depend on recognition, a comparison of current images with stored ones. And stored images are simply one more form of description, worth perhaps a thousand words, but thoroughly comparable to words. Thus Ralph's answer in such a situation is simply one more piece in the whole jigsaw of his cognitive structure. He might answer "yes" for some confrontations (compare—"yes" for some names), "no" for others, and withhold judgment for still others.

The suggested extension of the intermediate entities poses an interesting problem for the ontologist. Must we posit a realm of special mental entities as values for the variables used in analyzing the relational sense of belief, or will a variant on the trick of taking sentences as the objects of belief also account for beliefs involving visual images, odors, sounds, etc.?[34]

XIII

There are, I believe, two rather different problem areas connected with the analysis of intermediate contexts. The first problem area, which lies squarely within what is usually called the philosophy of language, involves chiefly the more fundamental nonrelational interpretation of intermediate contexts. It calls for an explanation of the seemingly logically deviant behavior of expressions in such contexts and perhaps also for a more exact statement of just what inferences, if any, are valid for such contexts. Here I feel that Frege's method outlines a generally acceptable solution. I especially appreciate the fact that for Frege intermediate contexts are not seen as exceptions to a powerful and heretofore general logical theory but rather are seen as fully accessible to that theory with the noted anomalies explained as due to a misreading of "initial conditions" leading to an inappropriate application of the laws. This accounting for seemingly aberrant phenomena in terms of the correct application of a familiar theory is explanation at its most satisfying. By contrast, the view I have associated with Quine—that intermediate contexts are referentially inarticulate—contents itself with a huge and unobvious class of "exceptions to the rules." This is shabby explanation, if explanation at all.

The second problem area specifically concerns the relational interpretation of intermediate contexts. Here I have tried to show how Frege's method, though it may provide a basis for unifying the relational and nonrelational interpretation of a given intermediate context and though it immediately provides for some form of quantification in, does not by itself necessarily provide the most interesting (and perhaps indispensible) relational interpretation. Further analysis, often specific to the context in question, may be required in order to produce an appropriately discriminating form of Δ which will yield results in conformity with our intuitive demands. Indeed, such an investigation may well lead far beyond the philosophy of language proper into metaphysics and epistemology. I know of no earlier source than "Quantifiers and Propositional Attitudes" in which relational uses of intermediate contexts are so clearly identified throughout an area of concern more urgent than modal logic. In that article Quine early expressed his remarkable insights into the pervasiveness of the relational forms and the need for a special analysis of their structure. And in fact following Quine's outlook and attempting to refine the conditions for valid applications of exportation, one might well arrive at the same metaphysical and epistemological insights as those obtained in attempting to refine Δ. What is important is that we should achieve some form of analysis of these contexts without recourse to the very idioms we are attempting to analyze.

The problem of interpreting the most interesting form of quantification in, appears in various guises: as the problem of making transworld identifications, as the problem of finding favored names, and as the problem of distinguishing 'essential' from 'accidental' properties. The present paper suggests two polar techniques for finding favored names. It is curious and somehow satisfying that they so neatly divide the objects between them, the one applying only to objects capable of being perceived (or at least of initiating causal chains), the other applying only to purely abstract objects. I am well aware of obscurities and difficulties in my formulations of the two central notions—that of a standard name and that of a name being *of* an object for a particular user. Yet both seem to me promising and worthy of further investigation.

ACKNOWLEDGMENTS

The first half of my reflections was read to the Harvard Philosophy Colloquium in January 1966. Its writing was aided by conversations with Montgomery Furth. The present ending has been influenced by a number of different persons, most significantly by Saul Kripke and Charles Chastain. But they should not be held to blame for it. Furth, who also read the penultimate version, is responsible for any remaining deficiencies aside from section IX about which he is skeptical. My research has been partially supported by N.S.F. Grant GP-7706.

NOTES

1. This paper is intended as a commentary on Quine's "Quantifiers and Propositional Attitudes." Quine's article was first published in 1956 and I have been thinking about it ever since. Quine has not been idle while I have been thinking, but his subsequent writings do not seem to have repudiated any part of "Quantifiers and Propositional Attitudes" [reprinted in this volume] which remains, to my mind, the best brief introduction to the field.

2. The quotation is from *Word and Object*, p. 144, wherein the inspiration for 'opaque' is explicitly given. The assimilation of intermediate occurrences to accidental ones might fairly be said to represent a *tendency* on Quine's part. The further evidence of *Word and Object* belies any simplistic characterization of Quine's attitudes toward intermediate occurrences.

3. In "Three Grades of Modal Involvement," p. 172 and other places. An intriguing suggestion for notational efficiency at no loss (or gain) to Quine's theory is to take advantage of the fact that occurrences of variables within opaque contexts which are bindable from without are prohibited, and use the vacated forms as "a way of indicating, selectively and changeably, just what positions in the contained sentence are to shine through as referential on any particular occasion" (*Word and Object*, p. 199). We

interpret, "Hegel believed that x is greater than five" with bindable "x," as "x is such that Hegel believed it to be greater than five" which is modeled on (8). Similarly, "Hegel believed that x is greater than y" is now read as, "x and y are such that Hegel believed the former to be greater than the latter." (8) itself could be rendered as, "$\exists x[x =$ nine & Hegel believed that x is greater than five]," and still not be a logical consequence of (5).

4. The reader will recognize that I have incorporated, without reference, many themes upon which Quine has harped, and that I have not attempted to make my agreement with him explicit at each point at which it occurs. Suffice it to say that the agreements far outweigh the disagreements, and that in both the areas of agreement and of disagreement I have benefited greatly from his writings.

5. See especially the end of "Three Grades of Modal Involvement." I am informed by scholarly sources that Aristotelian essentialism has its origin in "Two Dogmas of Empiricism." It reappears significantly in "Reply to Professor Marcus," where essential properties of numbers are discussed, and in *Word and Object*, p. 199, where essential properties of persons are discussed. I will later argue that the two cases are unlike.

6. In "A Formulation of the Logic of Sense and Denotation."

7. See *Meaning and Necessity*, section 9, for the discovery of the explicandum, and section 40 for the discovery of the explicans.

8. See "On Sense and Nominatum," pp. 58, 59 [see p. 200, this volume] in *Translations from the Philosophical Writings of Gottlob Frege*.

9. The acute reader will have discerned a certain similarity in function, though not in foundation, between the Frege quotes and another familiar quotation device.

10. These parallels are exhibited at some length in my dissertation, *Foundations of Intensional Logic*.

11. A drawback to this position is that the resulting *correct* applications of Leibniz' Law are rather unexciting. More interesting intermediate entities can be obtained by taking what Carnap, in *Meaning and Necessity* calls 'intensions'. Two expressions have the same intension, in this sense, if they are logically equivalent. Other interesting senses of 'intension' might be obtained by weakening the notion of logical equivalence to logical equivalence within sentential logic, intuitionistic logic, etc. Church suggests alternatives which might be understood along these lines.

12. I have approximately followed the notational devices used by Quine in "Quantifiers and Propositional Attitudes." Neither of us recommend the notation for practical purposes, even with the theory as is. An alternative notation is suggested in note 3 above.

13. Also, see *Word and Object*, p. 211, for an implicit use of exportation.

14. The "nearly" of "nearly analytic" is accounted for by a small scruple regarding the logic of singular terms. If a language L containing the name '$\iota y F y$' is extended to a metalanguage L' containing the predicate "Δ" for denotation-in-L and also containing the logical particles, including quotes, in their usual meaning, then I regard

$$[\exists x\, x = \iota y F y \rightarrow \Delta('\iota y F y',\iota y F y)]$$

as fully analytic in L'. My reasons for thinking so depend, in part, on my treatment of quotation names as standard names, for which see section VIII. I am being careful, because Quine suggests disagreement in an impatient footnote to "Notes on the Theory of Reference" (I am grateful to Furth, who recalled the footnote.) I do not know whether our disagreement, if a fact, is over quotation or elsewhere. The whole question of analyticity is less than crucial to my line of argument.

15. For a recent expression see *Word and Object,* section 41.

16. The same difficulty was noticed, independently, by John Wallace and reported in a private communication.

17. Quoted from the end of Quine's "Reply to Professor Marcus." I fully agree with Quine's characterization of the case, though not with the misinterpretation of Church's review of "Notes on Existence and Necessity" from which Quine's characterization springs.

18. See the discussion of what Carnap calls *L-determinate individual expressions in Meaning and Necessity*, section 18, and also Tarski's discussion of what he calls *structural descriptive names* in "The Concept of Truth in Formalized Languages," section 1.

19. The latter wonder is not to be confused with an ontological anxiety concerning the nature of nine, which is more appropriately expressed by dropping the word "number" in the wonder description.

20. Benacerraf so concludes in "What Numbers Could Not Be."

21. The present discussion of standard names is based on that in the more technical environment of my dissertation, pp. 55–57.

22. Given this understanding of **Nec,** it is interesting to note that on certain natural assumptions '$\Delta_N(\alpha, y)$' is itself expressed by '$\mathbf{Nec}(\ulcorner \alpha = \mathbf{x} \urcorner, y)$'.

23. Note that an attempt to identify the object perceived in terms of resemblance with the perception rather than in terms of the causal chain leading to the perception would seriously distort an account of misperception.

24. The corresponding principle for determining who it is that a given proper name, as it is used by some speaker, names, was first brought to my attention by Saul Kripke. Kripke's examples incorporated both the indirect path from person named to person naming and also the possible distortions of associated descriptions.

The existence of a relatively large number of persons with the same proper name gives urgency to this problem even in mundane settings. In theoretical discussions it is usually claimed that such difficulties are settled by "context." I have recently found at least vague recognition of the use of genetic factors to account for the connection between name and named in such diverse sources as Henry Leonard: "Probably for most of us there is little more than a vaguely felt willingness to mean . . . whatever the first assigners of the name intended by it." (*An Introduction to Principles of Right Reason,* section 30.2), and P. F. Strawson: "[T]he identifying description . . . may include a reference to another's reference to that particular . . . So one reference may borrow the credentials . . . from another; and that from another." (*Individuals,* footnote 1, p. 182). Though in neither case are genetic and descriptive features clearly distinguished.

Kripke's insights and those of Charles Chastain, who has especially emphasized the role of *knowledge* in order to establish the desired connection between name and named, are in large part responsible for the heavy emphasis I place on genetic factors.

25. Although it is useful for scholarly purposes to have a catalogue of such "fallacies" (such as that provided in Carney and Scheer, *Fundamentals of Logic*), the value of such discussions in improving the practical reasoning of rational beings seems to me somewhat dubious. A sensitive discussion of a related form of argument occurs in Angell, *Reasoning and Logic, especially* pp. 422–423.

26. Such failures may also be due to self-deception, an inaccurate self-concept, but then the purported object does not exist at all.

27. Insofar as I understand Hintikka's "Individuals, Possible Worlds, and Epistemic Logic," the domain of values of the bound variables fluctuates with the placement of the bound occurrences of the variables. If, in a quantifier's matrix, the occurrences of the variable bound to the quantifier fall only within uniterated epistemological contexts, then the variables range over possible(?) individuals "represented" by vivid names. If, on the other hand, no occurrences of the variable fall within epistemological (or other opaque) contexts, then the variables range over the usual actual individuals. And if the variable occurs both within and without an epistemological context, then the values of the variables are inner individuals which are also actual. Thus if Ralph believes in Santa Claus, and σ is Ralph's vivid Santa Claus description, Hintikka would treat "$\ulcorner$Ralph believes that σ = Santa Claus$\urcorner$," as true and as implying "$\exists x$ Ralph believes that x = Santa Claus," but would treat "$\exists x[x$ = Santa Claus & Ralph believes that x = Santa Claus]" and presumably "$\exists x[\exists y \; y = x$& Ralph believes that x = Santa Claus]" as false, and not as consequences of "$\ulcorner \sigma$ = Santa Claus & Ralph believes that σ = Santa Claus$\urcorner$."

28. I disregard precognition explained by a reverse causal chain.

29. We might say in such cases that the name *specifies* its denotation, in the sense in which a set of specifications, though not generated by the object specified, is written with the intention that there is or will be an object so described.

30. One such weakened notion of representation is that expressed by "Ralph **Bel** ($\ulcorner \alpha = x, y \urcorner$)," analyzed as in (44) using our current **R**, which here, in contrast to the situation for Δ_N (see reference 22 above), is not equivalent to "**R**(α, y, Ralph)." Still this new notion of representation, when used in place of our current R in an analysis of the form of (44), leads to the same relational sense of belief.

31. Note especially the "secret identity" genre of children's literature containing Superman, Batman, etc.

32. At least one author, Hintikka, has seemed unwilling to allow Ralph a belief *about* Ortcutt merely on the basis of Ralph's few glimpses of Ortcutt skulking around the missile base. See his "Individuals, Possible Worlds, and Epistemic Logic," footnote 13.

33. Another way out is to accept the fact that two names may represent the same person to Ralph though Ralph believes the nonidentity, but to put an ad hoc restriction on exportation. For example to analyze (33) as: "$\exists \alpha[\mathbf{R}(\alpha$, Ortcutt, Ralph) & Ralph **B** $\ulcorner \alpha$ is a spy$\urcorner$]& $\sim\exists\alpha[\mathbf{R}(\alpha$, Ortcutt, Ralph) & $\sim$Ralph **B** $\ulcorner \alpha$ is a spy$\urcorner$]." This prevents exportation where contradiction threatens. But again much that we would like to say is inexpressible in Quine's nomenclature.

34. It should be noted that in Church's "On Carnap's Analysis of Statements of Assertion and Belief" serious objections are raised to even the first step.

BIBLIOGRAPHY

R. B. Angell, *Reasoning and Logic* (New York: 1963).

P. Benacerraf, "What Numbers Could Not Be," *Philosophical Review,* 74 (1965) 47–73.

R. Carnap, *Meaning and Necessity* (Chicago: 1947) 2d ed., 1956.

D. Carney and K. Scheer, *Fundamentals of Logic* (New York: 1964).

A. Church, "A Formulation of the Logic of Sense and Denotation," in *Structure, Method, and Meaning,* ed. by P. Henle, M. Kallen, and S. K. Langer (New York: 1951).

A. Church, "On Carnap's Analysis of Statements of Assertion and Belief," *Analysis* 10 (1949–50) 97–99.

A. Church, Review of Quine's "Notes on Existence and Necessity," *Journal of Symbolic Logic,* 8 (1943) 45–47.

G. Frege, "On Sense and Reference," originally published in *Zeitschrift fur Philosophie und philosophische Kritik,* 100 (1892) 25–50; translated in *Translations from the Philosophical Writings of Gottlob Frege,* ed. by P. Geach and M. Black (Oxford: 1960).

K. J. Hintikka, "Individuals, Possible Worlds, and Epistemic Logic," *Nôus,* 1 (1967) 33–62.

D. Kaplan, *Foundations of Intensional Logic* (Dissertation), University Microfilms, (Ann Arbor: 1964).

H. S. Leonard, *An Introduction to Principles of Right Reason* (New York: 1957).

W. V. Quine, "Notes on Existence and Necessity," *The Journal of Philosophy,* 40 (1943) 113–127.

W. V. Quine, "Two Dogmas of Empiricism," *Philosophical Review,* 60 (1951) 20–43; reprinted in [15].

W. V. Quine, "Notes on the Theory of Reference", in *From a Logical Point of View.*

W. V. Quine, *From a Logical Point of View* (Cambridge, Mass: 1953), 2nd ed., 1961.

W. V. Quine, "Three Grades of Modal Involvement," in *Proceedings of the XIth International Congress of Philosophy, Brussels, 1953,* vol. 14, pp. 65–81, Amsterdam; reprinted in *The Ways of Paradox and Other Essays.*

W. V. Quine, "Quantifiers and Propositional Attitudes," *The Journal of Philosophy,* 53 (1956) 177–187; reprinted (minus 15 lines) in *The Ways of Paradox and Other Essays* [and in this volume].

W. V. Quine, *Word and Object* (New York: 1960). W. V. Quine, "Reply to Professor Marcus," *Synthese,* 13 (1961) 323–330; reprinted in *The Ways of Paradox and Other Essays.*

W. V. Quine, *The Ways of Paradox and Other Essays* (New York: 1966).

P. F. Strawson, *Individuals* (London: 1959).

A. Tarski, "The Concept of Truth in Formalized Languages," originally published in Polish in *Prace Towarzystwa Naukowego Warszawskiego,* Wydzial III, no. 34 (1933); translated in A. Tarski, *Logic, Semantics, Metamathematics* (Oxford: 1956) pp. 152–278.

31

Semantic Innocence and Uncompromising Situations

JON BARWISE AND JOHN PERRY

Since Frege, philosophers have become hardened to the idea that content sentences in talk about propositional attitudes may strangely refer to such entities as intensions, propositions, sentences, utterances and inscriptions . . . *If we could but recover our pre-Fregean semantic innocence*, I think it would be plainly incredible that the words "the earth moves," uttered after the words "Galileo said that," mean anything different, or refer to anything else, than is their wont when they come in other environments.

Donald Davidson, "On Saying That"[1]

I. SITUATIONS COMPROMISED

The present authors have managed to recover their pre-Fregean semantic innocence by rediscovering an old idea, that statements stand for situations, complexes of objects and properties in the world. The idea is found in various forms in Russell, Wittgenstein, and Austin, and more recently in Gustav Bergmann and other midwestern realists, but it has had little appeal for those whose philosophy of language is guided by the traditional model of formal semantics.

Situations were compromised by Frege's supposition that the reference of a sentence must be a truth-value. This approach left no room for situations, and major figures such as Church, Quine, and Davidson have followed Frege in this regard. Carnap tried to take propo-

sitions as the designata of sentences in his early *Introduction to Semantics,* and his propositions were something like states of affairs or situations. But Church, in his review of this book, gave a formal proof that this could not work.[2] This argument used ideas from Frege to show that the reference of a sentence must be a truth-value, granted principles to which Carnap was committed.

We have developed a model-theoretic conception of semantics which takes situations seriously. We were forced to do this to give an innocent account of the semantics of perception and belief, respectively. Having developed situation semantics, we remembered the old proof that it was impossible. Reexamining Church's argument from this new perspective shows that it conflates two quite different ways of looking at the relation between statements and situations.

In this paper we sketch (quite briefly) enough of our conception of situations and their types to allow us to share our reexamination. A fuller development of situation semantics will appear in due course.

II. TYPES OF SITUATIONS

The basic picture we wish to promote goes like this. The world, at least the common-sense

From *The Foundations of Analytic Philosophy,* vol. 6 of *Midwest Studies in Philosophy,* Peter French, Theodore E. Uehling, Jr., and Howard K. Wettstein, eds. (Minneapolis: University of Minnesota Press, 1981), pp. 387–403. Reprinted by permission of the authors.

world that human language reflects, consists not just of objects and sets of objects, nor of objects, properties, and relations, but of objects having properties and standing in relations to one another. There are parts of the world, clearly recognized (although not precisely individuated) in common sense and human language, that we call situations.

We are certain that situations are part of the world because we see them (as when we see Hoover Tower casting a shadow on Stanford), because we find ourselves in situations (our being late with this paper puts us in an embarrassing one), and because we find we have always believed them (as we have frequently believed that Columbus discovered America). States of affairs are situations, events and episodes are situations in time, scenes are visually perceived situations, changes are sequences of situations, and facts are situations enriched (or polluted) by language.

Situations have properties of two sorts, internal and external. The cat's walking on the piano distressed Henry. Its doing so is what we call an external property of the event. The event consists of a certain cat performing a certain activity on a certain piano; these are its internal properties.

Simple indicative statements classify situations according to their internal properties, by stating that the actual situation is a certain *type* of situation. To represent the internal properties or type of a situation we use partial functions that take sequences of relations and objects as arguments and 1 or 0 as values. The type of situation that distressed Henry is one in which

$$s(\text{on, the cat, the piano}) = 1$$

The type of situation s' in which the cat is not walking on the piano but is where he belongs, on the mat, satisfies

$$s'(\text{on, the cat, the piano}) = 0$$
$$s'(\text{on, the cat, the mat}) = 1.$$

Belief in the world is belief in a largest situation; its type we call the world type.

We take properties and relations seriously; they are neither meanings nor sets of individuals nor sets of sequences of individuals. The domain A of individuals and the domain R of relations are parallel products of conceptual activity, that of individuation. They are equally abstract but equally the most concrete items we deal with in perception and in language. Individuation provides the articulation of the world necessary for language to get a hold on it.

Actual situations are part of the actual world. The conceptual activity that individuates the world lets us classify the situations according to their types. However, once we have some of the facts, we realize that they might have been otherwise, that there are situation types that are not realized by actual situations. These unrealized situation types are involved in many of our hopes, fears, intentions, and beliefs. Much of our mental life and hence the language we use to describe that mental life involves such unrealized situation types.

III. INTERPRETATION AND EVALUATION

How does language get a hold on the world? It does so at the most rudimentary level by having simple indicative statements describe types of situations, and a sentence's meaning is what suits it for this task. But meaning is a notoriously slippery and complex notion, conflating many distinct aspects of the use of language. Just as the number 100 is the sum of many different columns of smaller numbers, so are there many ways one might try to break down meaning into smaller components. Certain ways of doing this are rather well entrenched in philosophy: Frege's reference versus sense, Carnap's extension versus intension. More recently David Kaplan has advocated a three-level system of character, intension (or content), and extension.[3] Our own attempt also has three levels: *linguistic meaning, interpretation, and evaluation.*

About linguistic meaning we shall have little to say here, except by way of examples indicating how it gives rise to interpretation, but must be kept distinct from it. This we have learned from Kaplan's work on indexicality. (It is also an important insight of Austin's, and Austin's work in general is valuable for the situation-oriented philosopher.)[4] Kaplan superimposes his top layer, character, on a possible-worlds semantics. Character and intension or content he sees as aspects of Frege's notion of sense. We believe the bottom two layers of this structure are in need of drastic reorganization, and that the top can benefit from awareness of the situations below. Our middle layer is *not* Frege's sense, for our interpretations are complexes of objects and properties, not denizens of a Fregean third realm, and not procedures or functions from possible worlds to extensions that have been used by recent philosophers of language to interpret Frege's senses. Objects and properties are found at Frege's level of reference. But Frege's notion of reference reflects his view that a realm of sense is available to provide needed specificity for embedded statements. We think this is quite misguided; hence our middle level is at best a drastic reworking of reference.

There is much that can be explored at the levels of interpretation and evaluation that seems to be largely insulated from other complexities of linguistic meaning. We do this by following two methodological principles. Our first principle is that, at the level of interpretation, indicative statements stand for, describe, or *designate* (as we will officially say) types of situations.

Our second principle is a version of compositionality, the claim that the meaning of a statement is a function of the meanings of its parts. Stated so vaguely, it could hardly be false.

Frege used this principle in his theory at both levels: the reference of a complex expression is a function of the references of its parts and similarly for sense. Our second methodological principle is the principle of modest and flexible compositionality: be compositional at the level of interpretation, but be modest in our goals, and not overly rigid. Modestly, bite off as little as possible from "meaning" so as to make the interpretations of a whole functions of the interpretation of its parts. Flexibly, realize that there may be more than one way to make a whole out of parts.

There are deliberate ambiguities in these principles. When we said that statements are to designate situation types, we used the plural to mask a complication. Namely, a single statement does not designate a single situation type, but a set of situation types. For example, "Someone is asleep" does not describe a single situation type, that of some particular individual

being asleep; rather, it describes the type of situation in which *someone* is asleep. That is, it will designate the set of types of situations in which someone is asleep.

Similarly "Jackie or Molly has fleas" designates the set of types of situations in which either Jackie or Molly or both have fleas. We shall call a set of situation types a *proposition* so that statements designate propositions.

Another ambiguity in the first principle is that between statement and sentence, and here our first principle begins to interact with our second. The sentence "I am a Nebraskan" has a linguistic meaning that is independent of which English speaker uses it, or when (within bounds of time where the individual words do not take on different meanings or the whole becomes idiomatic). However, it expresses different propositions (types of situations) depending on who says it. Said by the first author, the resulting statement designates a set of unrealized types of situations. As said by the second, the resulting statement is different and contains the actual world type among those it designates.

In our emphasis on statements and types of situations we follow J. L. Austin in his famous paper "Truth." However, Austin tried to have his "descriptive conventions" take one straight from sentences to situation types, a move which conflates two steps that need to be kept separate. (Here Austin failed to implement the insight mentioned above; Kaplan's system does.) The way that utterances of "I am a Nebraskan" give rise to different statements is an important part of linguistic meaning, but one that gets in the way of having sentences designate situation types. Hence our emphasis on statements.[5]

A sentence is a sentence of some language, and part of what the language provides is the linguistic meaning of the sentence. In a particular use, the linguistic meaning provides interpretations of the parts and the whole. The interpretation of the whole is to be the set of situation types designated by the statement. (This is an oversimplification; as we shall see. The interpretation of the parts underdetermines the interpretation of the whole.) In general, the statement will have one interpretation that is independent of the way things really are in the world: that is, an interpretation determined by the statement, the set A of objects, and the set R of relations, but independent of the structure of the world as it happens to be. This must be the case since we can interpret statements that turn out to be false or that have to do with situations that are inaccessible to us.

Let us now turn to our second methodological principle—modest and flexible compositionality. First, let us look at a trivial application. The interpretation of "Jackie barks" is to be a proposition, the set of situation types s in which Jackie barks, i.e.,

$\{s \mid s(\text{is barking}, \text{Jackie}) = 1\}.$

It is also to be a function of the interpretation of the parts of the statement, so "Jackie" must supply the object Jackie and "barks" the property of barking. That is, the simplest choice of interpretations compatible with our principles is to interpret "Jackie" as Jackie and "barks" as the property of barking. At the level of interpretation, then, we find objects as the interpretations of names, variables, and other noncomplex terms, properties and relations as the interpretation of simple predicates, and propositions (i.e., sets of situation types) as the interpretation of statements.

There is a tendency in twentieth-century philosophy of language to conflate properties with meanings; this must be avoided. When the first author says "Mollie is this color," pointing to a rug of a certain color, and the second author says "Jackie is this color," pointing to a book, they use exactly the same verb phrase with the same meaning. But if the colors of the rug and the book are different, the predicates stand for quite different properties in the two statements.

To carry the analysis of interpretation one step further, let us find out what the interpretation of a complex predicate, or verb phrase, like "loves Mary" is. At first there is a problem. We interpret "loves" by a two-place relation l and "Mary" by Mary, and need to get out of the two some property—the property of loving Mary. Do we need to assume that this is a primitive or can we construct it out of what we have on hand?

To show how to construct it, we start from our first principle. For any a in A, we want the statement that a loves Mary to be interpreted as the set of situation types s in which a loves Mary,

$s(l, \text{a}, \text{Mary}) = 1$. Call this proposition, this set of situation types, p(a). The function from any a in A to p(a) has two important properties: (1) it can be defined solely in terms of the interpretations l of "loves" and Mary of "Mary," and (2) from this function and any $a \in A$ we can construct the proposition that a loves Mary, namely, p(a). These are just the properties we require of an interpretation of "loves Mary."

Thus, we define P to be the set of all propositions obtainable from A and R, and we call any function from A into P a *complex property*. They are our analogue of Russell's propositional functions. Any primitive property p can be identified with a complex property p*—the property of having p—by defining p*(x) to be the proposition that x has p,

$p^*(x) = \{s \in \mathbf{S} \mid s(p,x) = 1\}.$

So, in general, the interpretation of a verb phrase is a complex property.

A moment's thought will convince the reader that the conjunction of two statements Φ and ψ should be interpreted by intersection of their respective interpretations. If we use $[\![\Phi]\!]$ to denote the interpretation of Φ, then $[\![\Phi \text{ and } \psi]\!] = [\![\Phi]\!] \cap [\![\psi]\!]$. Similarly, $[\![\Phi \text{ or } \psi]\!] = [\![\rho]\!] \cup [\![\psi]\!]$. What about negation?

Austin, in "Truth," laments the confusion between falsity and negation, and with this we must agree. In the situation we are aware of here in our study, it is not true that Jackie is barking. Jackie is not present to our senses; she is just not part of this situation. Thus, while the proposition that Jackie is barking does not contain the type of the situation we are aware of, neither does the proposition that Jackie is *not* barking. Knowing Jackie, she probably is barking at home. Thus, the statement that Jackie is not barking is interpreted as the set of types s such that s (is barking, Jackie) = 0, whereas the statement "It is false that Jackie is barking" can be interpreted as $\{s \mid s(\text{is barking}, \text{Jackie}) \neq 1\}$. Only this last proposition contains the situation we are aware of. Since situation types are partial world types, they never take on more than one value 0 or 1, but being partial, they may take on neither. This does not mean that we have a "three-valued logic." A statement is either true or it is not.

Situation semantics is much more flexible than more traditional approaches in ways that should please the linguist or philosopher of language who has not let traditional logic get too firm a hold on his thought processes. The proposal we are making leads to a rethinking of much of traditional logic. Certain classically simple concepts like negation and material implication are seen as conflations of several notions, brought about by working with only a single situation—the world.

In speaking of flexible compositionality, however, we had in mind another and absolutely central aspect of our theory. Recall that our system has three levels: meaning, interpretation, and evaluation. The idea behind the third category is this. Often by taking a look at the world or at some part of the world (or even at some pertinent situation type that does not fit the world) an expression can be fitted with a "value-laden interpretation"—an interpretation that depends on how the situation type arranges things. This value-laden interpretation is an alternative contribution that the expression can make to the interpretation of the statement of which it forms a part.

Some obvious sorts of evaluation consist in (1) determining whether a given type of situation is in a given proposition; (2) determining the extension of a property in a given situation; (3) determining the properties an individual has in a given situation. We think that certain traditional semantical categories, such as Frege's *bedeutung* or the more modern notion of extension, are sort of a jumble between interpretation and evaluation, provoked by the central role of evaluation in understanding language. Thus propositions have been taken to be truth-values, properties conflated with extensions, and in Montague's work individuals have almost been identified with sets of properties.

Sensitivity to the differences between value-free and value-laden interpretations of statements is dulled by the logical tradition that ignored situations. For unembedded sentences in simple situations, value-laden and value-free interpretations will not be so different, and in particular their truth-values will agree, so long as the salient situation type belongs to a part of the world.

But the distinction is hard to ignore when sentences are embedded in perception and belief contexts. Thus everyone can feel the two readings of

Sally saw a dog with fleas jump in the pool.

or

Sally thinks the dean's secretary is a dean.

One who fails to see the alternative interpretations when the statements are unembedded is forced to find an alternative source for the ambiguity of the embedding statements. The appeal is naturally to scope, and this way of looking at things is so engrained as to be confused with the phenomena itself. We see the ambiguity as simply a matter of the interpretation of the embedded sentence, not a matter of scope.

Applied to definite descriptions, the value-free, value-laden distinction is simply Donnellan's distinction between attributive and referential uses.[6] Russell's theory of definite descriptions focused on their value-free or attributive use, Frege's and Strawson's on their value-laden use. Donnellan saw that these should not be alternative theories, but alternative uses accounted for by a single theory. Donnellan was unsure what sort of ambiguity he was drawing attention to; some philosophers have thought he was simply calling attention to the potential ambiguity, due to scope, when sentences containing definite descriptions were embedded. We think that Donnellan put his finger on a straightforward semantic ambiguity, and that the attributive-referential distinction is one manifestation of a ubiquitous and important phenomenon of value loading.

IV. INNOCENT SEMANTICS

One can find two reasons in Frege for giving up innocence. The first is that substitution of co-referential expressions within statements embedded in certain linguistic contexts does not preserve truth of the whole embedding statement. Such contexts are now often called, following Quine, "referentially opaque." Propositional attitudes are widely believed to be referentially opaque. We believe that by and large they are not. In any case, there should be general agreement that *some* are not. One such context is nonepistemic perception:

(1) Sally sees Mollie run.

Another is ordinary belief:

Sally believes that my dog is running.

Some arguments for referential opacity seem to be based on ignoring the difference between value-laden and value-free interpretation. One might argue, for example, that non-epistemic perception is opaque, citing the falsity of

(1)′ Sally sees the dog with the red collar run.

But (1)′ is only false if the description is used attributively; that is, if the type of scene Sally is said to see has the property of having a red collar as a constituent. But so used, the substitution of "the dog with the red collar" for "Mollie" does not preserve interpretation. On the other hand, if the description is value-loaded (using a type of a larger portion of the world than Sally sees to do the loading), (1)′ is true if (1) is, given that Mollie is the dog in question.

Some arguments for referential opacity seem based on a confusion between conversational implicatures and semantic entailments. Thus we think that "Smith believes Cicero was an orator" does not imply, but at most suggests, that Smith would check "Cicero was an orator" true. The suggestion is clearly cancelable: "Smith believes that Cicero was an orator, but only knows to call him 'Tully'."[7]

In any case, it seems clear to us that there are transparent sentence-embedding propositional attitudes. But Frege's second reason for giving up innocence was a set of considerations that convinced him that any such contexts would be equivalent to "It is true that . . ."

In "Sense and Reference" he asks what the reference of an entire declarative sentence should be, when it is "concerned with the reference of its words." He concludes that it is the truth-value. A key point in favor of this is that the truth-value of an expression remains unchanged when a part of the sentence is replaced by an expression having the same reference. "What else but the truth-value could be found," asks Frege, "that belongs quite generally to every sentence if the reference of its

components is relevant, and remains unchanged by substitutions of the kind in question?"[8]

An innocent semantics takes the reference of the statement—that aspect of signification that depends on the reference of its parts—to be just that which contributes to the reference of the wholes in which it is embedded. If we take the reference of the sentence to be its truth value, an innocent semantics is hopeless, as Frege sees:

If now the truth value of a sentence is its reference, then on the one hand all true sentences have the same reference and so, on the other hand, do all false sentences. From this we can see that in the reference of a sentence all that is specific is obliterated.[9]

Given that Mollie is running and Richard lying, this would leave an innocent semantics committed to the equivalence of

(1) Sally sees Mollie run
(2) Sally sees Richard lie

or

(3) Sally believes that Mollie is running
(4) Sally believes that Richard is lying.

A semantics that could not grant these pairs different truth values would be quite hopeless.

The tradition has come to grips with Frege's loss of innocence in two ways: (i) for plausibly opaque propositional attitudes, treat the sentences as embedded and the semantics as guilty; (ii) for undeniably transparent propositional attitudes, treat the embedding of the sentence as illusory, adopting an analysis that removed the seemingly transparent position out of its spot in the embedded sentence. The semantics for that portion of the sentence left embedded will again be noninnocent.

Our approach is to treat the sentence as embedded and the semantics as innocent, and to deny that the problems that Frege and others have seen with this approach amount to much of anything.

For example, we take a statement of the form *X sees S* to embed a statement S, and to be true just in case X sees a scene (a specific kind of situation) that belongs to some type in the interpretation of S. We take *X believes that S,* in its most central and ordinary uses, to say that X has a certain complex relational property built of the objects and properties that are constituents of the proposition that S. In both cases, the parts of the embedded statement have their usual interpretations in the whole. What can be wrong with this innocent approach?

V. THE FREGE–CHURCH SLINGSHOT

Frege's own arguments against innocence do not seem very impressive. To his question, "What else but the truth value could be found, that belongs quite generally to every sentence if the reference of its components is relevant, and remains unchanged by substitutions . . . ?" we answer, "The situations designated." In the situation, all that is specific is not lost.

Again, Frege says that "the reference of a sentence may always be sought, whenever the reference of its components is involved, and this is the case when and only when we are inquiring after the truth-value." This seems to imply that we are only interested in the reference of the components of a sentence when we are inquiring about its truth value; but this is not so. If I am told "Smith believes his neighbor is a fool," I might be quite interested in the reference of "his neighbor," without caring at all about the truth of the embedded sentence.

There is, however, a very influential argument, virtually a priori, suggested no doubt by Frege's remarks, laid down explicitly by Church in his review of Carnap, and deployed in various forms with formal rigor and ruthless vigor by Quine, Davidson, and others, which seems to rule out the very possibility of a nontrivial situation semantics. The argument is so small, seldom encompassing more than half a page, and employs such a minimum of ammunition—a theory of descriptions and a popular notion of logical equivalence—that we dub it *the slingshot.* As developed by Church, the conclusion is that all sentences with the same truth-value must designate the same thing. As developed by Quine, we are put in the dilemma of either accepting "extensionality," which means seeing no distinction between (1) and (2) or (3) and (4), or losing our innocence and accepting opacity. Davidson used the slingshot to rule out straighforward innocent semantics, and then applied

incredible resources of ingenuity to recover lost innocence in roundabout ways.

Church gives a form of the slingshot in the opening sections of his *Introduction to Mathematical Logic,* to motivate taking truth values as the key notion in developing logic. This version of the argument is especially interesting because, being for a reader who does not already know logic, Church cannot fall back on an appeal to any accepted notion of logical equivalence. This makes it eminently suited for reexamination, to see just where it goes wrong. Church considers these sentences:

(5) Sir Walter Scott is the author of *Waverley.*

(6) Sir Walter Scott is the man who wrote the twenty-nine *Waverley* novels altogether.

(7) The number, such that Sir Walter Scott is the man that wrote that many *Waverley* novels altogether, is twenty-nine.

(8) The number of counties in Utah is twenty-nine.

Church argues that as we go from each sentence to the next, what the sentences denote is the same. But the first and last seem to have nothing of importance in common except their truth value; he says, "Elaboration of examples of this kind leads us quickly to the conclusion, as at least plausible, that all true sentences have the same denotation."[10]

Sentence (6) results from (5) by replacement of one description by another, where both descriptions describe the same person, Scott. Sentence (8) results from (7) by a similar move, with the descriptions describing the same number, twenty-nine. The step from (6) to (7), however, is of a different sort. Church says that (6), though perhaps not synonymous with (7), "is at least so nearly so as to ensure having the same denotation."[11]

The argument is like an ambiguous figure or an Escher drawing. If you are aware of situations, you have to keep shifting perspective to let the argument trick you. From one perspective the first and last steps are fine but the middle step is all wrong. From a second perspective the middle step is reasonably good but the first and last steps are completely unfounded.

Intuitively, situations are complexes of

objects and relations (under which we shall from now on subsume properties). Given this conception, the role of the parts of the sentence is to identify objects and relations out of which the complex is constructed. Let us hold this in mind, and go through the steps of the argument from both perspectives.

To get from (5) to (6), we need to suppose that the great difference between "the author of *Waverley*" and "the man who wrote the twenty-nine *Waverley* novels altogether" makes absolutely no difference to the situations described by the two sentences, that is, that the contribution these two descriptions make to the situation is just to identify Scott. Thus, the first perspective is the one where all four definite descriptions are interpreted by the objects they happen to describe, Scott in two cases, the number twenty-nine in the other two.

But from this perspective, the step from (6) to (7) does not work at all. Recall we are attempting to show that all four sentences must designate the same situations. But from our current perspective, (6) designates a situation whose only constituent object is Scott, whereas, (7) designates one whose only constituent object is the number twenty-nine.

Now let us focus on the step from (6) to (7). If we attempt to see these sentences as designating the same situation, then it must be that of Scott's having written exactly twenty-nine *Waverley* novels altogether. To see them as designating this situation, however, we must pay close attention to the properties involved in the definite descriptions. This is not unreasonable. If you take situations seriously, it is quite natural to distinguish two ways in which descriptions might contribute to the sentence. The need is for the materials to build a situation, a complex of objects and properties, and why should the description not contribute the individual described or the properties involved in the description of the situation?

Thus, the second perspective, which is suggested anyway if we take situations seriously, is the one where "the author of *Waverley*" is not interpreted simply as Scott, but contributes the complex of objects and properties it mentions to the situations the sentence describes. But this perspective is absolutely fatal to the step from (5) to (6) or from (7) to (8). The descriptions of Scott, and those of twenty-nine even more so, contribute radically different objects and properties to the overall situation. Sentence (7) designates twenty-nine's being the number of *Waverley* novels Scott wrote, but sentence (8) designates twenty-nine's being the number of counties in Utah: distinct situations if ever there were distinct situations.

So we see that from the first perspective, the one Frege would have us take, where in the reference of the description all that is specific is obliterated, the first and last steps of the argument are fine but the middle is wrong. From the second perspective, more in line with Russell's theory of descriptions, the middle step comes off better but the first and the last steps are wrong. Under neither reading are we compelled to accept the argument.

The connection between the slingshot and Russell's theory of descriptions was, in effect, commented on by Gödel in his essay "Russell's Mathematical Logic," for he used a sort of reverse slingshot to motivate Russell's theory:

But different true sentences may indicate different true things. Therefore, this view about sentences makes it necessary either to drop the above mentioned principle (of compositionality) . . . or to deny that a descriptive phrase denotes the object described. Russell did the latter by taking the viewpoint that a descriptive phrase denotes nothing at all but only has meaning in context, . . .[12]

Gödel goes on to say that he cannot help feeling that the puzzling conclusion of the slingshot "has only been evaded by Russell's theory of descriptions and that there is something behind it which is not yet completely understood."[13]

We believe that "something" was gotten at by Donnellan, with the referential and attributive distinction, and that this version of the slingshot, and every version of it, simply turns on shifts from value-free to value-laden interpretations. We value load the definite descriptions for the first step, take them as value-free for the next, and then load them again to finish the argument.

Church speaks of the intimate relation between (6) and (7) but, as he is introducing logical ideas at this point, does not exploit the fact that they are logically equivalent in the traditional sense: true in just the same models. From one perspective they are both identity statements (*Scott is Scott, twenty-nine is twenty-nine,* respectively). From the other they are contingent, but nevertheless true in just the same models. For the philosopher who has learned the traditional notion of logical equivalence, it is easy to be impressed by this. It might seem that logically equivalent statements must stand for the same thing; they must, after all, be equivalent in their *logical* powers or they would not be called that. But this line of thought would use the idea that all true sentences stand for the same thing as a premise for an argument where it is also the conclusion. If sentences designate truth values, then, of course, sentences that have the same truth value under all assignments to the nonlogical constants will be equivalent in what they designate. But if statements designate something else, they might be equivalent in truth value in virtue of logical structure, while being nonequivalent in what they designate. On our theory, "logical equivalence" is a misnomer for the relation between statements true in the same models; such statements need not have the same subject matter, in the sense of objects and properties designated by their parts, at all. As soon as such "logically equivalent" statements differing in subject matter are embedded in other statements, the differences in their logical powers become evident. The standard notion of logical equivalence plays an important role in the uses of the slingshot to which we now turn.

VI. QUINE AND THE SLINGSHOT

Quine uses various forms of the slingshot throughout his writings. One of the most explicit of these uses comes in his discussion of what he calls the extensionality principle: statements occur within other statements either truth functionally or opaquely, which forces one to give up semantic innocence.[14] When we suppose that (1) and (3) might be true, and (2) and (4) false, but still maintain that the parts of the embedded sentences make their usual contributions to the wholes, we are violating the extensionality principle.

Quine does not say that such violation is impossible, only that it is "not easy." Suppose S and S' are true and that F is a referentially transparent sentence-embedding context. Quine wants to argue that if F(S) is true, so is F(S'), and conversely. First note that

(A)
$\{x \mid S \ \& \ x = \varnothing\} = \{x \mid S' \ \& \ x = \varnothing\} = \{\varnothing\}$
(B)
S is logically equivalent to $[\{\varnothing\} = \{x \mid S \ \& \ x = \varnothing\}]$
S' is logically equivalent to $[\{\varnothing\} = \{x \mid S' \ \& \ x = \varnothing\}]$

From F(S) we obtain $F([\{\varnothing\} = \{x \mid S \& x = \varnothing\}])$ by substitution of logical equivalents, then we obtain $F([\{\varnothing\} = \{x \mid S' \& x = \varnothing\}])$ by (A) and the referential transparency of F, and then F(S') by another substitution of logical equivalents. If S and S' are both false, trade $\varnothing$ for $\{\phi\}$. Thus, if F is referentially transparent, it will treat sentences that just happen to have the same truth-values alike.

Quine finds in this argument "compelling" grounds for the principle of extentionality, a principle he was to come to advocate for the whole of science.[15] And yet he quite explicitly observes that for it to work we must suppose not only that the embedding context is transparent but that logical equivalents are interchangable in it. The argument simply takes us from the premise that transparent contexts do not discriminate among "logically equivalent" statements to the conclusion that they do not discriminate among statements that happen to be equivalent in truth value.

All the versions of the slingshot turn on the fact that logically equivalent statements can differ in subject matter, i.e., in what individuals and relations their parts designate.

Let us call a context that is transparent and in which logical equivalents are interchangeable *unconcerned* (about subject matter). Those that are transparent but in which logical equivalents are not interchangeable we shall call *concerned*. There seem to be a number of clearly concerned contexts. The most compelling is perception:

(9) Fred sees Betty enter.

(10) Fred sees Betty enter and (Sally smoke or Sally not smoke).

The statements embedded in (9) and (10) are logically equivalent. "Fred sees" seems clearly a transparent context. And yet we cannot go from (9) to (10). If we did, we should have to admit that Fred either saw Sally smoke or saw Sally not smoke, even though, as we may suppose, Fred has never laid eyes on Sally. The admission would be forced by the principles:

If Fred sees P and Q, then Fred sees Q

If Fred sees P or Q, then Fred sees P or Fred sees Q.

One could of course deny one of these principles to save the principle of extensionality, or one could deny that perception statements such as (9) and (10) are transparent. But we see no motive for either move. Quine seems to convey the attitude that unconcerned contexts are in the natural order of things, but, to be fair, does not say that there are no concerned contexts. His argument has to do with his statement operator "nec," and he carefully stipulates that logical equivalents are interchangeable within it without change of truth value. Other writers are not always so careful.

VII. DAVIDSON AND THE SLINGSHOT

The term "slingshot" was originally suggested to us by Donald Davidson's use of this compact piece of philosophical artillery in his wars against some of the giants of our industry. It is an essential part of his criticisms of Reichenbach on events and of Austin on truth, for example. The biggest giant Davidson takes on is Frege, however, for Davidson has consistently resisted the idea that statements embedded in propositional attitudes retain specificity by referring to Fregean senses. For this resistance, and for his recognition of situations, particularly in the analysis of action statements, he should be applauded. Unfortunately, Davidson was blocked from the most straightforward implementation of these insights by his devotion to the slingshot, a weapon constructed of Frege's own materials. To vary the pun, although Davidson resisted original *sinn,* he succumbed to original *bedeutung.*

To see how the slingshot corrupts Davidson, let us briefly look at his criticisms of Reichen-

bach. In *Elements of Symbolic Logic* Reichenbach developed a formal symbolic logic in which he quantified over situations, events, and facts. For Reichenbach the terms "fact" and "event" were synonymous, and events "have the physical existence of things, and not the fictitious existence of situations."[16] Thus his events and facts are analogous to our situations, his situations to our situation types.

Reichenbach sees a close relation between statements like (11) and (12):

(11) Scott wrote *Waverley*
(12) The event of Scott writing *Waverley* took place.

He refers to such statements as alternative ways of "splitting" a situation: "thing splitting" and "event splitting." The close relation is that a certain situation "corresponds" to (11) which is referred to by the description in (12). Reichenbach does not think that there is any singular term, manifest or hidden, in (11) that refers to the situation; only the statement as a whole has this relation to it; the transformation from (11) to (12) is "holistic."

Davidson finds much of value in Reichenbach's theory.[17] He acknowledges and emphasizes the importance of recognizing situations in resolving a number of problems about the logic of action statements. But he has to reject the leading component of Reichenbach's idea: he does not think (11) can correspond to the situation referred to by the description in (12) unless (11) also contains a (hidden) argument place for events. At this point, we think, Davidson purchases philosophical insight at the cost of syntactic plausibility.

The villain here is the slingshot. It convinces Davidson that Reichenbach's proposal is "radically defective," in leading inevitably to the conclusion that there is only one big event. The deployment of the slingshot depends on the principle,

If S and S′ are logically equivalent, then, for every event e, e consists in the fact that S if and only if e consists in the fact that S′.

This is just the assumption that "e consists in the fact that" provides an unconcerned context. Here Davidson is being less cautious than

Quine was, perhaps more awed by the phrase "logical equivalence." There is no reason at all to suppose this operator would be unconcerned, as should now be pretty clear. The natural development of the idea of a statement corresponding to an event or class of events will have that event or class of events determined by the objects and properties the parts of the statement designate. And logically equivalent statements can have parts that designate very different sets of objects and relations. Reichenbach would have no reason to accept the principle.

Logical equivalence as an unargued-for criterion for statement codesignation plays a key role in another important paper of Davidson's. In "Truth and Meaning" he considers the possibility of a semantical system something like ours.[18] Our level of interpretation is an aspect of meaning that is assigned to statements in a (modest and flexible) way as a function of the interpretations of the parts. Such a system, Davidson argues, must conclude that all true sentences have the same meaning, and so, too, all of the false ones. This version of the slingshot takes up very little room:

> But now suppose that 'R' and 'S' abbreviate any two sentences alike in truth value. Then the following four sentences have the same reference:
>
> (1) R
> (2) $\hat{x}(x = x.R) = \hat{x}(x = x)$
> (3) $\hat{x}(x = x.S) = \hat{x}(x = x)$
> (4) S
>
> For (1) and (2) are logically equivalent, as are (3) and (4), whereas (3) differs from (2) only in containing the singular term '$\hat{x}(x = x.S)$' where (2) contains '$x(x = x.R)$' and these refer to the same thing if S and R are alike in truth value.[19]

This difficulty for such a theory of meaning looms when we make two assumptions Davidson describes as reasonable:

> that logically equivalent singular terms have the same reference; and that a singular term does not change its reference if a contained singular term is replaced by another with the same reference.[20]

Davidson notes that the argument is essentially Frege's, cites Church, and says that "the argu-

ment does not depend on any particular identification of the entities to which sentences are supposed to refer."

Although we do not speak this way, in assigning interpretations to whole statements, we might be said to be treating them as singular terms. Let us look at Davidson's two principles, then, from the perspective of someone who treats statements as singular terms referring to situations. The first principle would be totally unacceptable, for it is really simply the rejection of this very idea. This is not surprising, since it was the rejection of the whole idea by Frege that led to the use of "logical equivalence" that the statement of the principle exploits. In spite of what Davidson says, it is hard to imagine any among those who have decided that statements designate at all who would accept this principle, except those who had decided they designate truth values. The second principle is ambiguous, depending on whether complex singular terms are given a value-free or value-laden interpretation. Taken the first way, and assuming the first principle, the first step in the argument works but not the second. Taken the second way, the first step fails.

VIII. FINAL REMARKS

In many contexts embedded statements seem to contribute something more specific than their truth-values to the embedding statement. Frege's choice of the truth-value as that which belongs to the statement in virtue of the references of its parts precluded taking this appearance at face value. His approach was to look to another aspect of meaning for the specificity provided by the embedded statement. Others who are skeptical of meaning beyond reference, like Quine, have been led to doubt the very intelligibility of such statement-embedding contexts. A third approach is to recognize that statements do contribute something to the larger wholes in which they are found, something that turns on the designations of their parts, but to deny that when this occurs they are truly embedded. Quine takes this attitude too at times, and Davidson's article from which our opening quotation was taken adopts a radical version of this approach. Perhaps a combination of the first and third attitudes is something like philosophical orthodoxy. Frege's approach is taken toward certain cases ("de dicto"): the statement is embedded, but what it provides does not turn on the reference of its parts. The third attitude is taken toward other cases ("de re"): the parts of the contained statement do provide their designations to the whole, but the statements are not really embedded, they only seem to be at the level of superficial syntax.

An alternative is to question Frege's original decision. Here we think the slingshot has had a real and unfortunate influence. Perhaps its most important use was the first, Church's in his review of Carnap's *Introduction to Semantics*. Church used principles internal to Carnap's system to show that it must have truth-values as the designations of sentences, rather than the situation-like propositions Carnap had intended. Church's argument turned on the principle that "L-equivalent" sentences have the same designation and on the assumption that substitution of two quite different singular terms designating the null class preserved the designation of the sentence in which they occur ('Λ' and '$(\lambda x)(x = x \& \sim \ldots)$', where ' $\ldots$ ' is some true but not L-true sentence). His argument seems decisive against Carnap's system as it stands. One possible response would have been to rethink Carnap's principles about designation and his conception of propositions, to see if the slingshot could be avoided. But both Church and Carnap went in another direction and assumed that what is specific is not to be found in the reference of the sentence. Awesomely formal deployments of the slingshot seem to put this beyond question. One can see the whole development of possible-worlds semantics, and much else in the philosophy of language of the past thirty years, as an outgrowth of this response to Church's deployment of the slingshot against Carnap.

We like to view situation semantics and possible-worlds semantics as two lines meeting in a single point, that point being where there is only one world and one situation. We believe a more workable semantics for natural language can be developed along the line we are proposing and that many of the valuable insights of the possible worlds approach can be incorporated into it. It may turn out, however, that the seman-tic facts will not fit such a narrow-minded view, and that we will have to look at the complex plane determined by the two lines. If so, we leave it to the reader to decide which line is the real axis and which is the imaginary.

NOTES

1. Donald Davidson, "On Saying That," reprinted in *The Logic of Grammar,* ed. Donald Davidson and Gilbert Harman (Encino, Calif.: 1975), p. 152. Originally published in *Synthese* 19 (1968–69). Our italics. [Reprinted in this volume.]
2. Rudolf Carnap, *Introduction to Semantics* (Cambridge: 1942); Alonzo Church, "Carnap's *Introduction to Semantics,*" *Philosophical Review* 52 (1943):298–305.
3. David Kaplan, "Dthat" [reprinted in this volume] and "On the Logic of Demonstratives," in *Contemporary Perspectives in the Philosophy of Language,* ed. Peter A. French, Theodore E. Uehling, Jr., and Howard K. Wettstein (Minneapolis: 1979), pp. 383–412.
4. J. L. Austin, *Philosophical Papers* (Oxford: 1961). See particularly "Truth" and "Unfair to Facts."
5. We try to use "sentence" and "statement" properly, except when discussing the views of others where it seems inappropriate.
6. Keith Donnellan, "Reference and Definite Descriptions," *Philosophical Review* 75 (1966): 281–304 [reprinted in this volume]; "Putting Humpty Dumpty Together Again," *Philosophical Review* 77 (1968):203–15. Ruth Marcus remarks in passing in "Modalities and Intensional Languages," *Synthese* 14 (1962), that descriptions can function as proper names, i.e., "purely referentially"; she takes their normal use to be more like the attributive; see page 283.
7. See J. O. Urmson, "Criteria of Intentionality," in *Logic and Philosophy for Linguists* ed. J. M. E. Moravcsik (The Hague: 1974), pp. 226–37. See also Jon Barwise, "Scenes and Other Situations," unpublished paper, Stanford University, and John Perry, "Belief and Acceptance," *Midwest Studies in Philosophy* 5 (1980):533–42 and "The Problem of the Essential Indexical," *Noûs* 13 (1979):3–21.
8. Gottlob Frege, "On Sense and Reference" [reprinted in this volume] in *Translations from the Philosophical Writings of Gottlob Frege,* ed. and trans. Peter Geach and Max Black (Oxford: 1960) p. 64.
9. Ibid., 65.
10. Alonzo Church, *Introduction to Mathematical Logic* (Princeton: 1956), p. 25.
11. Ibid.
12. Kurt Gödel, "Russell's Mathematical Logic," reprinted in *Philosophy of Mathematics,* ed. Paul Benacerraf and Hilary Putnam (Englewood Cliffs, N.J.: 1966), pp. 214–15.
13. Ibid.

14. W. V. Quine, "Three Grades of Modal Involvement," in *Ways of Paradox,* revised and enlarged edition (Cambridge: 1976), pp. 163–64.

15. W. V. Quine, "The Scope and Language of Science," in *Ways of Paradox,* p. 242.

16. Hans Reichenbach, *Elements of Symbolic Logic* (New York: 1966), p. 272. Relevant sections are reprinted in *The Logic of Grammar,* ed. Davidson and Harman.

17. Donald Davidson, "The Logical Form of Action Sentences," in *The Logic of Grammar,* pp. 235–46. This essay was originally published in *The Logic of Decision and Action,* ed. Nicholas Rescher (Pittsburgh: 1967).

18. Donald Davidson, "Truth and Meaning" [reprinted in this volume] in *Philosophical Logic,* ed. J. W. Davis et al. (Dordrecht: 1969) pp. 1–20. This essay was originally published in *Synthese* 17 (1967).

19. Ibid., p. 3 [p. 99, this volume].

20. Ibid., pp. 2–3 [p. 99, this volume].

32 A Puzzle about Belief

SAUL KRIPKE

In this paper I will present a puzzle about names and belief. A moral or two will be drawn about some other arguments that have occasionally been advanced in this area, but my main thesis is a simple one: that the puzzle *is* a puzzle. And, as a corollary, that any account of belief must ultimately come to grips with it. Any speculation as to solutions can be deferred.

The first section of the paper gives the theoretical background in previous discussion, and in my own earlier work, that led me to consider the puzzle. The background is by no means necessary to *state* the puzzle: as a philosophical puzzle, it stands on its own, and I think its fundamental interest for the problem of belief goes beyond the background that engendered it. As I indicate in the third section, the problem really goes beyond beliefs expressed using names, to a far wider class of beliefs. Nevertheless, I think that the background illuminates the genesis of the puzzle, and it will enable me to draw one moral in the concluding section.

The second section states some general principles which underlie our general practice of reporting beliefs. These principles are stated in much more detail than is needed to comprehend the puzzle; and there are variant formulations of the principles that would do as well. Neither this section nor the first is necessary for an intuitive grasp of the central problem, discussed in the

third section, though they may help with fine points of the discussion. The reader who wishes rapid access to the central problem could skim the first two sections lightly on a first reading.

In one sense the problem may strike some as no puzzle at all. For, in the situation to be envisaged, all the relevant facts can be described in *one* terminology without difficulty. But, in *another* terminology, the situation seems to be impossible to describe in a consistent way. This will become clearer later.

I. PRELIMINARIES: SUBSTITUTIVITY

In other writings,[1] I developed a view of proper names closer in many ways to the old Millian paradigm of naming than to the Fregean tradition which probably was dominant until recently. According to Mill, a proper name is, so to speak, *simply* a name. It *simply* refers to its bearer, and has no other linguistic function. In particular, unlike a definite description, a name does not describe its bearer as possessing any special identifying properties.

The opposing Fregean view holds that to each proper name, a speaker of the language associates some property (or conjunction of properties) which determines its referent as the unique thing fulfilling the associated property (or properties). This property(ies) constitutes the 'sense' of the name. Presumably, if '. . .' is a proper name, the associated properties are those that the speaker would supply, if asked, "Who is '. . .'?" If he would answer '. . . is the man who _____," the properties filling the second blank are those that determine the reference of the name for the given speaker and constitute its "sense". Of course, given the name of a famous historical figure, individuals may give different, and equally correct, answers to the "Who is . . . ?" question. Some may identify Aristotle as the philosopher who taught Alexander the Great, others as the Stagirite philosopher who studied with Plato. For these two speakers, the sense of "Aristotle" will differ: in particular, speakers of the second kind, but not of the first kind, will regard "Aristotle, if he existed, was born in Stagira" as analytic.[2] Frege (and Russell)[3] concluded that, strictly speaking, different speakers of English (or German!) ordinarily use a name such as "Aristotle' in different senses (though with the same reference). Differences in properties associated with such names, strictly speaking, yield different idiolects.[4]

Some later theorists in the Frege-Russellian tradition have found this consequence unattractive. So they have tried to modify the view by 'clustering' the sense of the name (e.g., Aristotle is the thing having the following long list of properties, or at any rate most of them), or, better for the present purpose, socializing it (what determines the reference of 'Aristotle' is some roughly specified set of *community-wide* beliefs about Aristotle).

One way to point up the contrast between the strict Millian view and Fregean views involves—if we permit ourselves this jargon— the notion of propositional content. If a strict Millian view is correct, and the linguistic function of a proper name is completely exhausted by the fact that it names its bearer, it would appear that proper names of the same thing are everywhere interchangeable not only *salva veritate* but even *salva significatione:* the proposition expressed by a sentence should remain the same no matter what name of the object it uses. Of course this will not be true if the names are 'mentioned' rather than 'used': "'Cicero' has six letters" differs from "'Tully' has six letters" in truth-value, let alone in content. (The exam-

ple, of course, is Quine's.) Let us confine ourselves at this stage to *simple* sentences involving no connectives or other sources of intensionality. If Mill is completely right, not only should "Cicero was lazy" have the same *truth-value* as "Tully was lazy," but the two sentences should express the same *proposition,* have the same content. Similarly "Cicero admired Tully," "Tully admired Cicero," "Cicero admired Cicero," and "Tully admired Tully," should be four ways of saying the same thing.[5]

If such a consequence of Mill's view is accepted, it would seem to have further consequences regarding "intensional' contexts. Whether a sentence expresses a necessary truth or a contingent one depends only on the proposition expressed and not on the words used to express it. So any simple sentence should retain its 'modal value' (necessary, impossible, contingently true, or contingently false) when 'Cicero' is replaced by 'Tully' in one or more places, since such a replacement leaves the content of the sentence unaltered. Of course this implies that coreferential names are substitutable in modal contexts *salva veritate:* "It is necessary (possible) that Cicero . . ." and "It is necessary (possible) that Tully . . ." must have the same truth value no matter how the dots are filled by a simple sentence.

The situation would seem to be similar with respect to contexts involving knowledge, belief, and epistemic modalities. Whether a given subject believes something is presumably true or false of such a subject no matter how that belief is expressed; so if proper name substitution does not change the content of a sentence expressing a belief, coreferential proper names should be interchangeable *salva veritate* in belief contexts. Similar reasoning would hold for epistemic contexts ("Jones knows that . . .") and contexts of epistemic necessity ("Jones knows a priori that . . .") and the like.

All this, of course, would contrast strongly with the case of definite descriptions. It is well known that substitution of coreferential descriptions in simple sentences (without operators), on any reasonable conception of 'content', *can* alter the content of such a sentence. In particular, the modal value of a sentence is not invariant under changes of coreferential descriptions:

"The smallest prime is even" expresses a necessary truth, but "Jones's favorite number is even" expresses a contingent one, even if Jones's favorite number happens to be the smallest prime. It follows that coreferential descriptions are *not* interchangeable *salva veritate* in modal contexts: "It is necessary that the smallest prime is even" is true while "It is necessary that Jones's favorite number is even" is false.

Of course there is a '*de re*' or 'large scope' reading under which the second sentence is true. Such a reading would be expressed more accurately by "Jones's favorite number is such that it is necessarily even" or, in rough Russellian transcription, as "One and only one number is admired by Jones above all others, and any such number is necessarily even (has the property of necessary evenness)." Such a *de re* reading, if it makes sense at all, by definition must be subject to a principle of substitution *salva veritate,* since necessary evenness is a property of the *number,* independently of how it is designated; in this respect there can be no contrast between names and descriptions. The contrast, according to the Millian view, must come in the *de dicto* or "small scope" reading, which is the *only* reading, for belief contexts as well as modal contexts, that will concern us in this paper. If we wish, we can emphasize that this is our reading in various ways. Say, "It is necessary that: Cicero was bald" or, more explicitly, "The following proposition is necessarily true: Cicero was bald," or even, in Carnap's 'formal' mode of speech,[6] "'Cicero was bald' expresses a necessary truth." Now the Millian asserts that all these formulations retain their truth value when 'Cicero' is replaced by 'Tully', even though 'Jones's favorite Latin author' and 'the man who denounced Catiline' would *not* similarly be interchangeable in these contexts even if they are codesignative.

Similarly for belief contexts. Here too *de re beliefs*—as in "Jones believes, *of* Cicero (or: *of* his favorite Latin author), that he was bald" do *not* concern us in this paper. Such contexts, if they make sense, are by definition subject to a substitutivity principle for both names and descriptions. Rather we are concerned with the *de dicto* locution expressed explicitly in such formulations as, "Jones believes that: Cicero was bald" (or: "Jones believes that: the man who denounced Catiline was bald"). The material after the colon expresses the *content* of Jones's belief. Other, more explicit, formulations are: "Jones believes the proposition—that—Cicero—was—bald," or even in the 'formal' mode, "The sentence 'Cicero was bald' gives the content of a belief of Jones." In all such contexts, the strict Millian seems to be committed to saying that codesignative names, but not codesignative descriptions, are interchangeable *salva veritate.*[7]

Now it has been widely assumed that these apparent consequences of the Millian view are plainly false. First, it seemed that sentences can alter their *modal* values by replacing a name by a codesignative one. "Hesperus is Hesperus" (or, more cautiously: "If Hesperus exists, Hesperus is Hesperus") expresses a necessary truth, while "Hesperus is Phosphorus" (or: "If Hesperus exists, Hesperus is Phosphorus") expresses an empirical discovery and hence, it has been widely assumed, a contingent truth. (It might have turned out, and hence might have been, otherwise.)

It has seemed even more obvious that codesignative proper names are not interchangeable in belief contexts and epistemic contexts. Tom, a normal speaker of the language, may sincerely assent to "Tully denounced Catiline," but not to "Cicero denounced Catiline." He may even deny the latter. And his denial is compatible with his status as a normal English speaker who satisfies normal criteria for using both 'Cicero' and 'Tully' as names for the famed Roman (without knowing that 'Cicero' and 'Tully' name the same person). Given this, it seems obvious that Tom believes that: Tully denounced Catiline, but that he does not believe (lacks the belief) that: Cicero denounced Catiline.[8] So it seems clear that codesignative proper names are not interchangeable in belief contexts. It also seems clear that there must be two distinct propositions or contents expressed by 'Cicero denounced Catiline' and 'Tully denounced Catiline'. How else can Tom believe one and deny the other? And the difference in propositions thus expressed can only come from a difference in *sense* between 'Tully' and 'Cicero'. Such a conclusion agrees with a Fregean theory and seems to be incompatible with a purely Millian view.[9]

In the previous work mentioned above, I rejected one of these arguments against Mill, the modal argument. 'Hesperus is Phosphorus', I maintained, expresses just as necessary a truth as 'Hesperus is Hesperus'; there are no counterfactual situations in which Hesperus and Phosphorus would have been different. Admittedly, the truth of 'Hesperus is Phosphorus' was not known a priori, and may even have been widely disbelieved before appropriate empirical evidence came in. But these epistemic questions should be separated, I have argued, from the metaphysical question of the necessity of 'Hesperus is Phosphorus'. And it is a consequence of my conception of names as 'rigid designators' that codesignative proper names are interchangeable *salva veritate* in all contexts of (metaphysical) necessity and possibility; further, that replacement of a proper name by a codesignative name leaves the modal value of any sentence unchanged.

But although my position confirmed the Millian account of names in modal contexts, it equally appears at first blush to imply a *non-Millian* account of epistemic and belief contexts (and other contexts of propositional attitude). For I presupposed a sharp contrast between epistemic and metaphysical possibility: before appropriate empirical discoveries were made, men might well have failed to know that Hesperus was Phosphorus, or even to believe it, even though they of course knew and believed that Hesperus was Hesperus. Does not this support a Fregean position that 'Hesperus' and 'Phosphorus' have different 'modes of presentation' that determine their references? What else can account for the fact that, before astronomers identified the two heavenly bodies, a sentence using 'Hesperus' could express a common belief, while the same context involving 'Phosphorus' did not? In the case of 'Hesperus' and 'Phosphorus', it is pretty clear what the different 'modes of presentation' would be: one mode determines a heavenly body by its typical position and appearance, in the appropriate season, in the evening; the other determines the same body by its position and appearance, in the appropriate season, in the morning. So it appears that even though, according to my view, proper names would be *modally* rigid—would have the same reference when we use them to speak of counterfactual situations as they do when used to describe the actual world—they would have a kind of Fregean 'sense' according to how that rigid reference is fixed. And the divergences of 'sense' (in this sense of 'sense') would lead to failures of interchangeability of codesignative names in contexts of propositional attitude, though not in modal contexts. Such a theory would agree with Mill regarding modal contexts but with Frege regarding belief contexts. The theory would not be *purely* Millian.[10]

After further thought, however, the Fregean conclusion appears less obvious. Just as people are said to have been unaware at one time of the fact that Hesperus is Phosphorus, so a normal speaker of English apparently may not know that Cicero is Tully, or that Holland is the Netherlands. For he may sincerely assent to 'Cicero was lazy', while dissenting from 'Tully was lazy', or he may sincerely assent to 'Holland is a beautiful country', while dissenting from 'The Netherlands is a beautiful country'. In the case of 'Hesperus' and 'Phosphorus', it seemed plausible to account for the parallel situation by supposing that 'Hesperus' and 'Phosphorus' fixed their (rigid) references to a single object in two conventionally different ways, one as the 'evening star' and one as the 'morning star'. But what corresponding *conventional* 'senses', even taking 'senses' to be 'modes of fixing the reference rigidly', can plausibly be supposed to exist for 'Cicero' and 'Tully' (or 'Holland' and 'the Netherlands')? Are not these just two names (in English) for the same man? Is there any special *conventional, community-wide* 'connotation' in the one lacking in the other?[11] I am unaware of any.[12]

Such considerations might seem to push us toward the extreme Frege-Russellian view that the senses of proper names vary, strictly speaking, from speaker to speaker, and that there is no community-wide sense but only a community-wide reference.[13] According to such a view, the sense a given speaker attributes to such a name as 'Cicero' depends on which assertions beginning with 'Cicero' he accepts and which of these he regards as *defining*, for him, the name (as opposed to those he regards as mere factual beliefs 'about Cicero'). Similarly, for 'Tully'. For example, someone may define 'Cicero' as 'the Roman orator whose speech was Greek to Cassius', and 'Tully' as 'the Roman orator who denounced Catiline'. Then such a speaker may well fail to accept 'Cicero is Tully' if he is unaware that a single orator satisfied both descriptions (if Shakespeare and history are both to be believed). He may well, in his ignorance, affirm 'Cicero was bald' while rejecting 'Tully was bald', and the like. Is this not what actually occurs whenever someone's expressed beliefs fail to be indifferent to interchange of 'Tully' and 'Cicero'? Must not the source of such a failure lie in two distinct associated descriptions, or modes of determining the reference, of the two names? If a speaker does, as luck would have it, attach the same identifying properties both to 'Cicero' and to 'Tully', he *will*, it would seem, use 'Cicero' and 'Tully' interchangeably. All this appears at first blush to be powerful support for the view of Frege and Russell that in general names are peculiar to idiolects, with 'senses' depending on the associated 'identifying descriptions'.

Note that, according to the view we are now entertaining, one *cannot* say, "Some people are unaware that Cicero is Tully." For, according to this view, there is no single proposition denoted by the 'that' clause, that the community of normal English speakers expresses by 'Cicero is Tully'. Some—for example, those who define both 'Cicero' and 'Tully' as 'the author of *De Fato*'—use it to express a trivial self-identity. Others use it to express the proposition that the man who satisfied one description (say, that he denounced Catiline) is one and the same as the man who satisfied another (say, that his speech was Greek to Cassius). There is no single fact, 'that Cicero is Tully', known by some but not all members of the community.

If I were to assert, "Many are unaware that Cicero is Tully," *I* would use 'that Cicero is Tully' to denote the proposition that *I* understand by these words. If this, for example, is a trivial self-identity, I would assert falsely, and irrelevantly, that there is widespread ignorance in the community of a certain self-identity.[14] I

can, of course, say, "Some English speakers use both 'Cicero' and 'Tully' with the usual referent (the famed Roman) yet do not assent to 'Cicero is Tully'"

This aspect of the Frege-Russellian view can, as before, be combined with a concession that names are rigid designators and that hence the description used to fix the reference of a name is not synonymous with it. But there are considerable difficulties. There is the obvious intuitive unpalatability of the notion that we use such proper names as 'Cicero', 'Venice', 'Venus' (the planet) with differing 'senses' and for this reason do not 'strictly speaking' speak a single language. There are the many well-known and weighty objections to any description or cluster-of-descriptions theory of names. And is it definitely so clear that failure of interchangeability in belief contexts implies some difference of sense? After all, there is a considerable philosophical literature arguing that even word pairs that are straightforward synonyms if any pairs are—"doctor" and "physician," to give one example—are not interchangeable *salva veritate* in belief contexts, at least if the belief operators are iterated.[15]

A minor problem with this presentation of the argument for Frege and Russell will emerge in the next section: if Frege and Russell are right, it is not easy to state the very argument from belief contexts that appears to support them.

But the clearest objection, which shows that the others should be given their proper weight, is this: the view under consideration does not in fact account for the phenomena it seeks to explain. As I have said elsewhere,[16] individuals who "define 'Cicero'" by such phrases as "the Catiline denouncer," "the author of *De Fato*," etc., are relatively rare: their prevalence in the philosophical literature is the product of the excessive classical learning of some philosophers. Common men who clearly use 'Cicero' as a name for Cicero may be able to give no better answer to "Who was Cicero?" than "a famous Roman orator," and they probably would say the same (if anything!) for 'Tully'. (Actually, most people probably have never heard the name 'Tully'.) Similarly, many people who have heard of both Feynman and Gell-

Mann, would identify each as 'a leading contemporary theoretical physicist'. Such people do not assign 'senses' of the usual type to the names that uniquely identify the referent (even though they use the names with a determinate reference). But to the extent that the *indefinite* descriptions attached or associated can be called 'senses', the 'senses' assigned to 'Cicero' and 'Tully', or to 'Feynman' and 'Gell-Mann', are *identical*.[17] Yet clearly speakers of this type can ask, "Were Cicero and Tully one Roman orator, or two different ones?" or "Are Feynman and Gell-Mann two different physicists, or one?" without knowing the answer to either question by inspecting 'senses' alone. Some such speaker might even conjecture, or be under the vague false impression, that, as he would say, 'Cicero was bald but Tully was not'. The premise of the argument we are considering for the classic position of Frege and Russell—that whenever two codesignative names fail to be interchangeable in the expression of a speaker's beliefs, failure of interchangeability arises from a difference in the 'defining' descriptions the speaker associates with these names—is, therefore, false. The case illustrated by 'Cicero' and 'Tully' is, in fact, quite usual and ordinary. So the apparent failure of codesignative names to be everywhere interchangeable in belief contexts, is not to be explained by differences in the 'senses' of these names.

Since the extreme view of Frege and Russell does not in fact explain the apparent failure of the interchangeability of names in belief contexts, there seems to be no further reason—for present purposes—not to give the other overwhelming prima facie considerations against the Frege-Russell view their full weight. Names of famous cities, countries, persons, and planets are the common currency of our common language, not terms used homonymously in our separate idiolects.[18] The apparent failure of codesignative names to be interchangeable in belief contexts remains a mystery, but the mystery no longer seems so clearly to argue for a Fregean view as against a Millian one. Neither differing public senses nor differing private senses peculiar to each speaker account for the phenomena to be explained. So the apparent existence of such phenomena no longer gives a prima facie argument for such differing senses.

One final remark to close this section. I have referred before to my own earlier views in "Naming and Necessity." I said above that these views, inasmuch as they make proper names rigid and transparent[19] in modal contexts, favor Mill, but that the concession that proper names are not transparent in belief contexts appears to favor Frege. On a closer examination, however, the extent to which these opacity phenomena really support Frege against Mill becomes much more doubtful. And there are important theoretical reasons for viewing the "Naming and Necessity" approach in a Millian light. In that work I argued that ordinarily the real determinant of the reference of names of a former historical figure is a chain of communication, in which the reference of the name is passed from link to link. Now the legitimacy of such a chain accords much more with Millian views than with alternatives. For the view supposes that a learner acquires a name from the community by determining to use it with the same reference as does the community. We regard such a learner as using "Cicero is bald" to express the same thing the community expresses, regardless of variations in the properties different learners associate with 'Cicero', as long as he determines that he will use the name with the referent current in the community. That a name can be transmitted in this way accords nicely with a Millian picture, according to which only the reference, not more specific properties associated with the name, is relevant to the semantics of sentences containing it. It has been suggested that the chain of communication, which on the present picture determines the reference, might thereby itself be called a 'sense'. Perhaps so—if we wish[20]—but we should not thereby forget that the legitimacy of such a chain suggests that it is just preservation of reference, as Mill thought, that we regard as necessary for correct language learning.[21] (This contrasts with such terms as 'renate' and 'cordate', where more than learning the correct extension is needed.) Also, as suggested above, the doctrine of rigidity in modal contexts is dissonant, though not necessarily inconsistent, with a view that invokes anti-Millian considerations to explain propositional attitude contexts.

The spirit of my earlier views, then, suggests that a Millian line should be maintained as far as is feasible.

II. PRELIMINARIES: SOME GENERAL PRINCIPLES

Where are we now? We seem to be in something of a quandary. On the one hand, we concluded that the failure of 'Cicero' and 'Tully' to be interchangeable *salva veritate* in contexts of propositional attitude was by no means explicable in terms of different 'senses' of the two names. On the other hand, let us not forget the initial argument against Mill: if reference is *all there is* to naming, what semantic difference can there be between 'Cicero' and 'Tully'? And if there is no semantic difference, do not 'Cicero was bald' and 'Tully was bald' express exactly the same proposition? How, then, can anyone believe that Cicero was bald, yet doubt or disbelieve that Tully was?

Let us take stock. Why do we think that anyone can believe that Cicero was bald, but fail to believe that Tully was? Or believe, without any logical inconsistency, that Yale is a fine university, but that Old Eli is an inferior one? Well, a normal English speaker, Jones, can sincerely assent to 'Cicero was bald' but not to 'Tully was bald'. And this even though Jones uses 'Cicero' and 'Tully' in standard ways—he uses 'Cicero' in this assertion as a name for the Roman, not, say, for his dog, or for a German spy.

Let us make explicit the *disquotational principle* presupposed here, connecting sincere assent and belief. It can be stated as follows, where '*p*' is to be replaced, inside and outside all quotation marks, by any appropriate standard English sentence: "*If a normal English speaker, on reflection, sincerely assents to 'p', then he believes that p.*" The sentence replacing '*p*' is to lack indexical or pronominal devices or ambiguities, that would ruin the intuitive sense of the principle (e.g., if he assents to "You are wonderful," he need not believe that you—the reader—are wonderful).[22] When we suppose that we are dealing with a normal speaker of English, we mean that he uses all words in the sentence in a standard way, combines them according to the appropriate syntax, etc.: in short, he uses the sentence to mean what a normal speaker should mean by it. The 'words' of the sentence may include proper names, where these are part of the common discourse of the community, so that we can speak of using them in a standard way. For example, if the sentence is "London is pretty," then the speaker should satisfy normal criteria for using 'London' as a name of London, and for using 'is pretty' to attribute an appropriate degree of pulchritude. The qualification "on reflection" guards against the possibility that a speaker may, through careless inattention to the meaning of his words or other momentary conceptual or linguistic confusion, assert something he does not really mean, or assent to a sentence in linguistic error. "Sincerely" is meant to exclude mendacity, acting, irony, and the like. I fear that even with all this it is possible that some astute reader—such, after all, is the way of philosophy—may discover a qualification I have overlooked, without which the asserted principle is subject to counterexample. I doubt, however, that any such modification will affect any of the uses of the principle to be considered below. Taken in its obvious intent, after all, the principle appears to be a self-evident truth. (A similar principle holds for sincere affirmation or assertion in place of assent.)

There is also a strengthened 'biconditional' form of the disquotational principle, where once again any appropriate English sentence may replace '*p*' throughout: *A normal English speaker who is not reticent will be disposed to sincere reflective assent to 'p' if and only if he believes that p.*[23] The biconditional form strengthens the simple one by adding that failure to assent indicates lack of belief, as assent indicates belief. The qualification about reticence is meant to take account of the fact that a speaker may fail to avow his beliefs because of shyness, a desire for secrecy, to avoid offense, etc. (An alternative formulation would give the speaker a sign to indicate lack of belief—not necessarily disbelief—in the assertion propounded, in addition to his sign of assent.)

Maybe again the formulation needs further tightening, but the intent is clear.

Usually below the simple disquotational principle will be sufficient for our purposes, but once we will also invoke the strengthened form. The simple form can often be used as a test for disbelief, provided the subject is a speaker with the modicum of logicality needed so that, at least after appropriate reflection, he does not hold simultaneously beliefs that are straightforward contradictions of each other—of the forms 'p' and '$\sim p$'.[24] (Nothing in such a requirement prevents him from holding simultaneous beliefs that jointly *entail* a contradiction.) In this case (where 'p' may be replaced by any appropriate English sentence), the speaker's assent to the negation of 'p' indicates not only his disbelief that p but also his failure to believe that p, using only the simple (unstrengthened) disquotational principle.

So far our principle applies only to speakers of English. It allows us to infer, from Peter's sincere reflective assent to "God exists," that he believes that God exists. But of course we ordinarily allow ourselves to draw conclusions, stated in English, about the beliefs of speakers of any language: we infer that Pierre believes that God exists from his sincere reflective assent to "*Dieu existe.*" There are several ways to do this, given conventional translations of French into English. We choose the following route. We have stated the disquotational principle in English, for English sentences; an analogous principle, stated in French (German, etc.) will be assumed to hold for French (German, etc.) sentences. Finally, we assume the *principle of translation: if a sentence of one language expresses a truth in that language, then any translation of it into any other language also expresses a truth (in that other language).* Some of our ordinary practice of translation may violate this principle; this happens when the translator's aim is not to preserve the content of the sentence, but to serve—in some other sense—the same purposes in the home language as the original utterance served in the foreign language.[25] But if the translation of a sentence is to mean the same as the sentence translated, preservation of truth-value is a minimal condition that must be observed.

Granted the disquotational principle ex-pressed in each language, reasoning starting from Pierre's assent to '*Dieu existe*' continues thus. First, on the basis of his utterance and the French disquotational principle we infer (in French):

> Pierre croit que Dieu existe.

From this we deduce,[26] using the principle of translation:

> Pierre believes that God exists.

In this way we can apply the disquotational technique to all languages.

Even if I apply the disquotational technique to English alone, there is a sense in which I can be regarded as tacitly invoking a principle of translation. For presumably I apply it to speakers of the language other than myself. As Quine has pointed out, to regard others as speaking the same language as I is in a sense tacitly to assume a *homophonic* translation of their language into my own. So when I infer from Peter's sincere assent to or affirmation of "God exists" that he believes that God exists, it is arguable that, strictly speaking, I combine the disquotational principle (for Peter's idiolect) with the principle of (homophonic) translation (of Peter's idiolect into mine). But for most purposes, we can formulate the disquotational principle for a single language, English, tacitly supposed to be the common language of English speakers. Only when the possibility of individual differences of dialect is relevant need we view the matter more elaborately.

Let us return from these abstractions to our main theme. Since a normal speaker—normal even in his use of 'Cicero' and 'Tully' as names—can give sincere and reflective assent to "Cicero was bald" and simultaneously to "Tully was not bald," the disquotational principle implies that he believes that Cicero was bald and believes that Tully was not bald. Since it seems that he need not have contradictory beliefs (even if he is a brilliant logician, he need not be able to deduce that at least one of his beliefs must be in error), and since a substitutivity principle for coreferential proper names in belief contexts would imply that he does have contradictory beliefs, it would seem that such a substitutivity principle must be incorrect.

Indeed, the argument appears to be a reductio ad absurdum of the substitutivity principle in question.

The relation of this argument against substitutivity to the classical position of Russell and Frege is a curious one. As we have seen, the argument can be used to give prima facie support for the Frege-Russell view, and I think many philosophers have regarded it as such support. But in fact this very argument, which has been used to support Frege and Russell, cannot be stated in a straightforward fashion if Frege and Russell are right. For suppose Jones asserts, "Cicero was bald, but Tully was not." If Frege and Russell are right, I cannot deduce, using the disquotational principle:

(1) Jones believes that Cicero was bald but Tully was not,

since, in general, Jones and I will not, strictly speaking, share a common idiolect unless we assign the same "senses' to all names. Nor can I combine disquotation and translation to the appropriate effect, since homophonic translation of Jones's sentence into mine will in general be incorrect for the same reason. Since in fact I make no special distinction in sense between 'Cicero' and 'Tully'—to me, and probably to you as well, these are interchangeable names for the same man—and since according to Frege and Russell, Jones's very affirmation of (1) shows that for him there is some distinction of sense, Jones must therefore, on Frege-Russellian views, use one of these names differently from me, and homophonic translation is illegitimate. Hence, if Frege and Russell are right, we *cannot* use this example in the usual straightforward way to conclude that proper names are not substitutable in belief contexts—even though the example, and the ensuing negative verdict on substitutivity, has often been thought to support Frege and Russell!

Even according to the Frege-Russellian view, however, *Jones* can conclude, using the disquotational principle, and expressing his conclusion in his own idiolect:

(2) I believe that Cicero was bald but Tully was not.

I cannot endorse this conclusion in Jones's own words, since I do not share Jones's idiolect. I *can* of course conclude, "(2) expresses a truth in Jones's idiolect." I can also, if I find out the two 'senses' Jones assigns to 'Cicero' and 'Tully,' introduce two names 'X' and 'Y' into my own language with these same two senses ('Cicero' and 'Tully' have already been preempted) and conclude:

(3) Jones believes that X was bald and Y was not.

All this is enough so that we can still conclude, on the Frege-Russellian view, that codesignative names are not interchangeable in belief contexts. Indeed this can be shown more simply on this view, since codesignative descriptions plainly are not interchangeable in these contexts and for Frege and Russell names, being essentially abbreviated descriptions, cannot differ in this respect. Nevertheless, the simple argument, apparently free of such special Frege-Russellian doctrinal premises (and often used to support these premises), in fact cannot go through if Frege and Russell are right.

However, if, *pace* Frege and Russell, widely used names are common currency of our language, then there no longer is any problem for the simple argument, using the disquotational principle, to (2). So, it appears, on pain of convicting Jones of inconsistent beliefs—surely an unjust verdict—we must not hold a substitutivity principle for names in belief contexts. If we used the *strengthened* disquotational principle, we could invoke Jones's presumed lack of any tendency to assent to 'Tully was bald' to conclude that he does not believe (lacks the belief) that Tully was bald. Now the refutation of the substitutivity principle is even stronger, for when applied to the conclusion that Jones believes that Cicero was bald but does not believe that Tully was bald, it would lead to a straightout contradiction. The contradiction would no longer be in Jones's beliefs but in our own.

This reasoning, I think, has been widely accepted as proof that codesignative proper names are not interchangeable in belief contexts. Usually the reasoning is left tacit, and it may well be thought that I have made heavy weather of an obvious conclusion. I wish, however, to question the reasoning. I shall do so without challenging any particular step of the argument. Rather I shall present—and this will form the core of the present paper—an argument for a paradox about names in belief contexts that invokes *no* principle of substitutivity. Instead it will be based on the principles—apparently so obvious that their use in these arguments is ordinarily tacit—of disquotation and translation.

Usually the argument will involve more than one language, so that the principle of translation and our conventional manual of translation must be invoked. We will also give an example, however, to show that a form of the paradox may result within English alone, so that the only principle invoked is that of disquotation (or, perhaps, disquotation plus *homophonic* translation). It will intuitively be fairly clear, in these cases, that the situation of the subject is "essentially the same' as that of Jones with respect to 'Cicero' and 'Tully'. Moreover, the paradoxical conclusions about the subject will parallel those drawn about Jones on the basis of the substitutivity principle, and the arguments will parallel those regarding Jones. Only in these cases, no special substitutivity principle is invoked.

The usual use of Jones's case as a counterexample to the substitutivity principle is thus, I think, somewhat analogous to the following sort of procedure. Someone wishes to give a reductio ad absurdum argument against a hypothesis in topology. He does succeed in refuting this hypothesis, but his derivation of an absurdity from the hypothesis makes essential use of the unrestricted comprehension schema in set theory, which he regards as self-evident. (In particular, the class of all classes not members of themselves plays a key role in his argument.) Once we know that the unrestricted comprehension schema and the Russell class lead to contradiction by themselves, it is clear that it was an error to blame the earlier contradiction on the topological hypothesis.

The situation would have been the same if, after deducing a contradiction from the topological hypothesis plus the 'obvious' unrestricted comprehension schema, it was found that a similar contradiction followed if we replaced the topological hypothesis by an apparently 'obvious' premise. In both cases it would be clear

that, even though we may still not be confident of any specific flaw in the argument against the topological hypothesis, blaming the contradiction on that hypothesis is illegitimate: rather we are in a 'paradoxical' area where it is unclear *what* has gone wrong.[27]

It is my suggestion, then, that the situation with respect to the interchangeability of codesignative names is similar. True, such a principle, when combined with our normal disquotational judgments of belief, leads to straightforward absurdities. But we will see that the 'same' absurdities can be derived by replacing the interchangeability principle by our normal practices of translation and disquotation, or even by disquotation alone.

The particular principle stated here gives just one particular way of 'formalizing' our normal inferences from explicit affirmation or assent to belief; other ways of doing it are possible. It is undeniable that we *do* infer, from a normal Englishman's sincere affirmation of 'God exists' or 'London is pretty', that he believes, respectively, that God exists or that London is pretty; and that we would make the same inferences from a Frenchman's affirmation of *'Dieu existe'* or *'Londres est jolie'*. Any principles that would justify such inferences are sufficient for the next section. It will be clear that the particular principles stated in the present section are sufficient, but in the next section the problem will be presented informally in terms of our inferences from foreign or domestic assertion to belief.

III. THE PUZZLE

Here, finally(!), is the puzzle. Suppose Pierre is a normal French speaker who lives in France and speaks not a word of English or of any other language except French. Of course he has heard of that famous distant city, London (which he of course calls *'Londres'*) though he himself has never left France. On the basis of what he has heard of London, he is inclined to think that it is pretty. So he says, in French, *"Londres est jolie."*

On the basis of his sincere French utterance, we will conclude:

(4) Pierre believes that London is pretty.

I am supposing that Pierre satisfies all criteria for being a normal French speaker, in particular, that he satisfies whatever criteria we usually use to judge that a Frenchman (correctly) uses 'est jolie' to attribute pulchritude and uses 'Londres'—standardly—as a name of London.

Later, Pierre, through fortunate or unfortunate vicissitudes, moves to England, in fact to London itself, though to an unattractive part of the city with fairly uneducated inhabitants. He, like most of his neighbors, rarely ever leaves this part of the city. None of his neighbors know any French, so he must learn English by 'direct method', without using any translation of English into French: by talking and mixing with the people he eventually begins to pick up English. In particular, everyone speaks of the city, 'London', where they all live. Let us suppose for the moment—though we will see below that this is not crucial—that the local population are so uneducated that they know few of the facts that Pierre heard about London in France. Pierre learns from them everything they know about London, but there is little overlap with what he heard before. He learns, of course—speaking English—to call the city he lives in 'London'. Pierre's surroundings are, as I said, unattractive, and he is unimpressed with most of the rest of what he happens to see. So he is inclined to assent to the English sentence:

(5) London is not pretty.

He has *no* inclination to assent to:

(6) London is pretty.

Of course he does not for a moment withdraw his assent from the French sentence, *"Londres est jolie",*; he merely takes it for granted that the ugly city in which he is now stuck is distinct from the enchanting city he heard about in France. But he has no inclination to change his mind for a moment about the city he stills calls *'Londres'.*

This, then, is the puzzle. If we consider Pierre's past background as a French speaker, his entire linguistic behavior, on the same basis as we would draw such a conclusion about many of his countrymen, supports the conclusion (4) above that he believes that London is pretty. On the other hand, after Pierre lived in

London for some time, he did not differ from his neighbors—his French background aside—either in his knowledge of English or in his command of the relevant facts of local geography. His English vocabulary differs little from that of his neighbors. He, like them, rarely ventures from the dismal quarter of the city in which they all live. He, like them, knows that the city he lives in is called 'London' and knows a few other facts. Now Pierre's neighbors would surely be said to use 'London' as a name for London and to speak English. Since, as an English speaker, he does not differ at all from them, we should say the same of him. But then, on the basis of his sincere assent to (5), we should conclude:

(7) Pierre believes that London is not pretty.

How can we describe this situation? It seems undeniable that Pierre *once* believed that London is pretty—at least before he learned English. For at that time, he differed not at all from countless numbers of his countrymen, and we would have exactly the same grounds to say of him as of any of them that he believes that London is pretty: if any Frenchman who was both ignorant of English and never visited London believed that London is pretty, Pierre did. Nor does it have any plausibility to suppose, because of his later situation *after* he learns English, that Pierre should *retroactively* be judged *never* to have believed that London is pretty. To allow such ex post facto legislation would, as long as the future is uncertain, endanger our attributions of belief to *all* monolingual Frenchmen. We would be forced to say that Marie, a monolingual who firmly and sincerely asserts, *"Londres est jolie,"* may or may not believe that London is pretty depending on the *later* vicissitudes of her career (if later she learns English and . . . , . . .). No: Pierre, like Marie, believed that London is pretty when he was monolingual.

Should we say that Pierre, now that he lives in London and speaks English, no longer believes that London is pretty? Well, unquestionably Pierre *once* believed that London is pretty. So we would be forced to say that Pierre has *changed his mind, has given up his previous belief.* But has he really done so? Pierre is very set in his ways. He reiterates, with vigor, every assertion he has ever made in French. He says he has not changed his mind about anything, has *not* given up any belief. Can we say he is wrong about this? If we did not have the story of his living in London and his English utterances, on the basis of his normal command of French we would be *forced* to conclude that he *still* believes that London is pretty. And it does seem that this is correct. Pierre has neither changed his mind nor given up any belief he had in France.

Similar difficulties beset any attempt to deny him his new belief. His French past aside, he is just like his friends in London. Anyone else, growing up in London with the same knowledge and beliefs that he expresses in England, we would undoubtedly judge to believe that London is not pretty. Can Pierre's French past nullify such a judgment? Can we say that Pierre, because of his French past, does not believe that (5)? Suppose an electric shock wiped out all his memories of the French language, what he learned in France, and his French past. He would then be *exactly* like his neighbors in London. He would have the *same* knowledge, beliefs, and linguistic capacities. We then presumably would be forced to say that Pierre believes that London is ugly if we say it of his neighbors. But surely no shock that *destroys* part of Pierre's memories and knowledge can *give* him a new belief. If Pierre believes (5) *after* the shock, he believed it before, despite his French language and background.

If we would deny Pierre, in his bilingual stage, his belief that London is pretty *and* his belief that London is not pretty, we combine the difficulties of both previous options. We still would be forced to judge that Pierre once believed that London is pretty but does no longer, in spite of Pierre's own sincere denial that he has lost any belief. We also must worry whether Pierre would *gain* the belief that London is not pretty if he totally forgot his French past. The option does not seem very satisfactory.

So now it seems that we must respect both Pierre's French utterances and their English counterparts. So we must say that Pierre has contradictory beliefs, that he believes that London is pretty *and* he believes that London is not

pretty. But there seem to be insuperable difficulties with this alternative as well. We may suppose that Pierre, in spite of the unfortunate situation in which he now finds himself, is a leading philosopher and logician. He would *never* let contradictory beliefs pass. And surely anyone, leading logician or no, is in principle in a position to notice and correct contradictory beliefs if he has them. Precisely for this reason, we regard individuals who contradict themselves as subject to greater censure than those who merely have false beliefs. But it is clear that Pierre, as long as he is unaware that the cities he calls 'London' and '*Londres*' are one and the same, is in no position to see, by logic alone, that at least one of his beliefs must be false. He lacks information, not logical acumen. He cannot be convicted of inconsistency: to do so is incorrect.

We can shed more light on this if we change the case. Suppose that, in France, Pierre, instead of affirming "*Londres est jolie,*" had affirmed, more cautiously, "*Si New York est jolie, Londres est jolie aussi,*" so that he believed that *if* New York is pretty, so is London. Later Pierre moves to London, learns English as before, and says (in English) "London is *not* pretty." So he now believes, further, that London is not pretty. Now from the two premises, both of which appear to be among his beliefs (a) If New York is pretty, London is, and (b) London is not pretty, Pierre should be able to deduce by *modus tollens* that New York is not pretty. But no matter how great Pierre's logical acumen may be, *he cannot in fact make any such deduction, as long as he supposes that 'Londres' and 'London' may name two different cities.* If he *did* draw such a conclusion, he would be guilty of a fallacy.

Intuitively, he may well suspect that New York is pretty, and just this suspicion may lead him to suppose that '*Londres*' and 'London' probably name distinct cities. Yet, if we follow our normal practice of reporting the beliefs of French and English speakers, *Pierre has available to him (among his beliefs) both the premises of a modus tollens argument that New York is not pretty.*

Again, we may emphasize Pierre's *lack* of belief instead of his belief. Pierre, as I said, has no disposition to assent to (6). Let us concentrate on this, ignoring his disposition to assent to (5). In fact, if we wish we may change the case: suppose Pierre's neighbors think that since they rarely venture outside their own ugly section, they have no right to any opinion as to the pulchritude of the whole city. Suppose Pierre shares their attitude. Then, judging by his failure to respond affirmatively to "London is pretty," we may judge, from Pierre's behavior as an *English* speaker, that he lacks the belief that London is pretty: never mind whether he disbelieves it, as before, or whether, as in the modified story, he insists that he has no firm opinion on the matter.

Now (using the *strengthened* disquotational principle), we can derive a contradiction, not merely in Pierre's judgments, but in our own. For on the basis of his behavior as an English speaker, we concluded that he does *not* believe that London is pretty (that is, that it is not the case that he believes that London is pretty). But on the basis of his behavior as a *French* speaker, we must conclude that he *does* believe that London is pretty. This is a contradiction.[28]

We have examined four possibilities for characterizing Pierre while he is in London: (a) that at that time we no longer respect his French utterance (*'Londres est jolie'*), that is that we no longer ascribe to him the corresponding belief; (b) that we do not respect his English utterance (or lack of utterance); (c) that we respect neither; (d) that we respect both. Each possibility seems to lead us to say something either plainly false or even downright contradictory. Yet the possibilities appear to be logically exhaustive. This, then, is the paradox.

I have no firm belief as to how to solve it. But beware of one source of confusion. It is no solution in itself to observe that some *other* terminology, which evades the question whether Pierre believes that London is pretty, may be sufficient to state all the relevant facts. I am fully aware that complete and straightforward descriptions of the situation are possible and that in this sense there is no paradox. Pierre is disposed to sincere assent to *'Londres est jolie'* but not to 'London is pretty'. He uses French normally, English normally. Both with *'Londres'* and 'London' he associates properties sufficient to determine that famous city, but he does not realize that they determine a single city. (And his uses of *'Londres'* and 'London' are historically [causally] connected with the same single city, though he is unaware of that.) We may even give a rough statement of his beliefs. He believes that the city he calls *'Londres'* is pretty, that the city he calls 'London' is not. No doubt other straightforward descriptions are possible. No doubt some of these are, in a certain sense, *complete* descriptions of the situation.

But none of this answers the original question. Does Pierre, or does he not, believe that London is pretty? I know of no answer to *this* question that seems satisfactory. It is no answer to protest that, in some *other* terminology, one can state 'all the relevant facts'.

To reiterate, this is the puzzle: Does Pierre, or does he not, believe that London is pretty? It is clear that our normal criteria for the attribution of belief lead, when applied to *this* question, to paradoxes and contradictions. One set of principles adequate to many ordinary attributions of belief, but which leads to paradox in the present case, was stated in Section II; and other formulations are possible. As in the case of the logical paradoxes, the present puzzle presents us with a problem for customarily accepted principles and a challenge to formulate an acceptable set of principles that does not lead to paradox, is intuitively sound, and supports the inferences we usually make. Such a challenge cannot be met simply by a description of Pierre's situation that evades the question whether he believes that London is pretty.

One aspect of the presentation may misleadingly suggest the applicability of Frege-Russellian ideas that each speaker associates his own description or properties to each name. For as I just set up the case Pierre learned one set of facts about the so-called *'Londres'* when he was in France, and *another* set of facts about 'London' in England. Thus it may appear that 'what's really going on' is that Pierre believes that *the city* satisfying *one* set of properties *is* pretty, while he believes that *the city* satisfying *another* set of properties is not pretty.

As we just emphasized, the phrase 'what's really going on' is a danger signal in discussions of the present paradox. The conditions stated may—let us concede for the moment—describe 'what's really going on'. But they do not resolve the problem with which we began, that of the behavior of names in belief contexts: Does Pierre, or does he not, believe that London (not the city satisfying such-and-such description, but *London*) is pretty? No answer has yet been given.

Nevertheless, these considerations may appear to indicate that descriptions, or associated properties, are highly relevant somehow to an ultimate solution, since at this stage it appears that the entire puzzle arises from the fact that Pierre originally associated different identifying properties with 'London' and '*Londres*'. Such a reaction may have some force even in the face of the now fairly well known arguments against 'identifying descriptions' as in any way 'defining', or even 'fixing the reference' of names. But in fact the special features of the case, as I set it out, are misleading. The puzzle can arise even if Pierre associates exactly the same identifying properties with both names.

First, the considerations mentioned above in connection with 'Cicero' and 'Tully' establish this fact. For example, Pierre may well learn, in France, 'Platon' as the name of a major Greek philosopher, and later, in England, learns 'Plato' with the same identification. Then the same puzzle can arise: Pierre may have believed, when he was in France and was monolingual in French, that Plato was bald (he would have said, "*Platon était chauve*"), and later conjecture, in English, "Plato was not bald," thus indicating that he believes or suspects that Plato was *not* bald. He need only suppose that, in spite of the similarity of their names, the man he calls '*Platon*' and the man he calls '*Plato*' were two distinct major Greek philosophers. In principle, the same thing could happen with 'London' and '*Londres*'.

Of course, most of us learn a *definite* description about London, say 'the largest city in England'. Can the puzzle still arise? It is noteworthy that the puzzle can still arise even if Pierre associates to '*Londres*' and to 'London' *exactly* the same *uniquely identifying* properties. How can this be? Well, suppose that Pierre believes that London is the largest city in (and capital of) England, that it contains Buckingham Palace,

the residence of the Queen of England, and he believes (correctly) that these properties, conjointly, uniquely identify the city. (In this case, it is best to suppose that he has never seen London, or even England, so that he uses *only* these properties to identify the city. Nevertheless, he has learned English by 'direct method'.) These uniquely identifying properties he comes to associate with "London" after he learned English, and he expresses the appropriate beliefs about 'London' in English. Earlier, when he spoke nothing but French, however, he associated *exactly* the same uniquely identifying properties with '*Londres*'. He believed that '*Londres*', as he called it, could be uniquely identified as the capital of England, that it contained Buckingham Palace, that the Queen of England lived there, etc. Of course he expressed these beliefs, like most monolingual Frenchmen, in French. In particular, he used '*Angleterre*' for England, '*le Palais de Buckingham*' (pronounced '*Bookeengam*'!) for Buckingham Palace, and '*la Reine d'Angleterre*' for the Queen of England. But if any Frenchman who speaks no English can ever be said to associate *exactly* the properties of being the capital of England, etc., with the name '*Londres*', Pierre in his monolingual period did so.

When Pierre becomes a bilingual, *must* he conclude that 'London' and '*Londres*' name the same city, because he defined each by the same uniquely identifying properties?

Surprisingly, no! Suppose Pierre had affirmed '*Londres est jolie*'. If Pierre has any reason—even just a 'feeling in his bones', or perhaps exposure to a photograph of a miserable area which he was told (in English) was part of 'London'—to maintain 'London is not pretty', he need not contradict himself. He need only conclude that 'England' and '*Angleterre*' name two different countries, that "Buckingham Palace' and '*le Palais de Buckingham*' (recall the pronunciation!) name two different palaces, and so on. Then he can maintain *both* views without contradiction, and regard *both* properties as uniquely identifying.

The fact is that the paradox reproduces itself on the level of the 'uniquely identifying properties' that description theorists have regarded as 'defining' proper names (and a fortiori, as fixing their references). Nothing is more reasonable than to suppose that if two names, A and B, and a single set of properties, S, are such that a certain speaker believes that the referent of A uniquely satisfies all of S and that the referent of B also uniquely satisfies all of S, then that speaker is committed to the belief that A and B have the same reference. In fact, the identity of the referents of A and B is an easy *logical consequence* of the speaker's beliefs.

From this fact description theorists concluded that names can be regarded as synonymous, and hence interchangeable *salva veritate* even in belief contexts, provided that they are 'defined' by the same uniquely identifying properties.

We have already seen that there is a difficulty in that the set S of properties need not in fact be uniquely identifying. But in the present paradoxical situation there is a surprising difficulty even if the supposition of the description theorist (that the speaker believes that S is uniquely fulfilled) in fact holds. For, as we have seen above, Pierre is in no position to draw ordinary logical consequences from the conjoint set of what, when we consider him separately as a speaker of English and as a speaker of French, we would call his beliefs. He cannot infer a contradiction from his separate beliefs that London is pretty and that London is not pretty. Nor, in the modified situation above, would Pierre make a normal *modus tollens* inference from his beliefs that London is not pretty and that London is pretty if New York is. Similarly here, if we pay attention only to Pierre's behavior as a French speaker (and at least in his monolingual days he was no different from any other Frenchmen), Pierre satisfies all the normal criteria for believing that *'Londres'* has a referent uniquely satisfying the properties of being the largest city in England, containing Buckingham Palace, and the like. (If Pierre did not hold such beliefs, no Frenchman *ever* did.) Similarly, on the basis of his (later) beliefs expressed in English, Pierre also believes that the referent of 'London' uniquely satisfies these same properties. But Pierre cannot combine the two beliefs into a single set of beliefs from which he can draw the normal conclusion that 'London' and *'Londres'* must have the same referent. (Here the trouble

comes not from 'London' and *'Londres'* but from 'England' and *'Angleterre'* and the rest.) Indeed, if he *did* draw what would appear to be the normal conclusion in this case and any of the other cases, Pierre would in fact be guilty of a logical fallacy.

Of course the description theorist could hope to eliminate the problem by 'defining' *'Angleterre'*, 'England', and so on by appropriate descriptions also. Since in principle the problem may rear its head at the next 'level' and at each subsequent level, the description theorist would have to believe that an 'ultimate' level can eventually be reached where the defining properties are 'pure' properties not involving proper names (or natural kind terms or related terms, see below!). I know of no convincing reason to suppose that such a level can be reached in any plausible way, or that the properties can continue to be uniquely identifying if one attempts to eliminate all names and related devices.[29] Such speculation aside, the fact remains that Pierre, judged by the *ordinary* criteria for such judgments, *did* learn both *'Londres'* and 'London' by *exactly* the same set of identifying properties; yet the puzzle remains even in this case.

Well, then, is there any way out of the puzzle? Aside from the principles of disquotation and translation, only our normal practice of translation of French into English has been used. Since the principles of disquotation and translation seem self-evident, we may be tempted to blame the trouble on the translation of *'Londres est jolie'* as 'London is pretty', and ultimately, then, on the translation of *'Londres'* as 'London.'[30] Should we, perhaps, permit ourselves to conclude that *'Londres'* should not, 'strictly speaking' be translated as 'London'? Such an expedient is, of course, desperate: the translation in question is a standard one, learned by students together with other standard translations of French into English. Indeed, *'Londres'* is, in effect, introduced into French as the French version of 'London'.

Since our backs, however, are against the wall, let us consider this desperate and implausible expedient a bit further. If *'Londres'* is *not* a correct French version of the English 'London', under what circumstances can proper names be translated from one language to another?

Classical description theories suggest the answer: translation, strictly speaking, is between idiolects; a name in one idiolect can be translated into another when (and only when) the speakers of the two idiolects associate the same uniquely identifying properties with the two names. We have seen that any such proposed restriction, not only fails blatantly to fit our normal practices of translation and indirect discourse reportage, but does not even appear to block the paradox.[31]

So we still want a suitable restriction. Let us drop the references to idiolects and return to 'Londres' and 'London' as names in French and English, respectively—the languages of two communities. If 'Londres' is not a correct French translation of 'London', could any other version do better? Suppose I introduced another word into French, with the stipulation that *it* should always be used to translate 'London'. Would not the same problem arise for this word as well? The only feasible solution in this direction is the most drastic: decree that no sentence containing a name can be translated except by a sentence containing the phonetically identical name. Thus when Pierre asserts 'Londres est jolie', we English speakers can at best conclude, if anything: Pierre believes that *Londres* is pretty. Such a conclusion is, of course, not expressed in English, but in a word salad of English and French; on the view now being entertained, we cannot state Pierre's belief in *English* at all.[32] Similarly, we would have to say: Pierre believes that *Angleterre* is a monarchy, Pierre believes that *Platon* wrote dialogues, and the like.[33]

This 'solution' appears at first to be effective against the paradox, but it is drastic. What is it about sentences containing names that makes them—a substantial class—intrinsically untranslatable, express beliefs that cannot be reported in any other language? At best, to report them in the other language, one is forced to use a word salad in which names from the one language are imported into the other. Such a supposition is both contrary to our normal practice of translation and very implausible on its face.

Implausible though it is, there is at least this much excuse for the 'solution' at this point. Our normal practice with respect to some famous people and especially for geographical localities is to have different names for them in dif-

ferent languages, so that in translating sentences we translate the names. But for a large number of names, especially names of people, this is not so: the person's name is used in the sentences of all languages. At least the restriction in question merely urges us to mend our ways by doing *always* what we presently do *sometimes*.

But the really drastic character of the proposed restriction comes out when we see how far it may have to extend. In "Naming and Necessity" I suggested that there are important analogies between proper names and natural kind terms, and it seems to me that the present puzzle is one instance where the analogy will hold. Putnam, who has proposed views on natural kinds similar to my own in many respects, stressed this extension of the puzzle in his comments at the conference. Not that the puzzle extends to all translations from English to French. At the moment, at least, it seems to me that Pierre, if he learns English and French separately, without learning any translation manual between them, must conclude, if he reflects enough, that 'doctor' and '*médecin*', and '*heureux*' and 'happy', are synonymous, or at any rate, coextensive;[34] any potential paradox of the present kind for these word pairs is thus blocked. But what about '*lapin*' and 'rabbit', or 'beech' and '*hêtre*'? We may suppose that Pierre is himself neither a zoologist nor a botanist. He has learned each language in its own country and the examples he has been shown to illustrate '*les lapins*' and 'rabbits', 'beeches' and '*les hêtre*' are distinct. It thus seems to be possible for him to suppose that '*lapin*' and 'rabbit', or 'beech' and '*hêtre*', denote distinct but superficially similar kinds or species, even though the differences may be indiscernible to the untrained eye. (This is especially plausible if, as Putnam supposes, an English speaker—for example, Putnam himself—who is not a botanist may use 'beech' and 'elm' with their normal (distinct) meanings, even though he cannot himself distinguish the two trees.[35] Pierre may quite plausibly be supposed to wonder whether the trees which in France he called '*les hêtres*' were beeches or elms, even though as a speaker of French he satisfies all usual criteria for using '*les hêtres*' normally. If beeches and elms will not serve, better pairs of ringers exist that cannot be told apart except by an expert.) Once Pierre is in such a situation, paradoxes analogous to the one about London obviously can arise for rabbits and beeches. Pierre could affirm a French statement with *'lapin',* but deny its English translation with 'rabbit'. As above, we are hard-pressed to say what Pierre *believes.* We were considering a 'strict and philosophical' reform of translation procedures which proposed that foreign proper names should always be appropriated rather than translated. Now it seems that we will be forced to do the same with all words for natural kinds. (For example, on price of paradox, one must not translate *'lapin'* as "rabbit'!) No longer can the extended proposal be defended, even weakly, as 'merely' universalizing what we already do sometimes. It is surely too drastic a change to retain any credibility.[36]

There is yet another consideration that makes the proposed restriction more implausible: even this restriction does not really block the paradox. Even if we confine ourselves to a single language, say English, and to phonetically identical tokens of a single name, we can still generate the puzzle. Peter (as we may as well say now) may learn the name 'Paderewski' with an identification of the person named as a famous pianist. Naturally, having learned this, Peter will assent to "Paderewski had musical talent," and *we* can infer—using 'Paderewski', as we usually do, to name the Polish musician and statesman:

(8) Peter believes that Paderewski had musical talent.

Only the disquotational principle is necessary for our inference; no translation is required. Later, in a different circle, Peter learns of someone called 'Paderewski' who was a Polish nationalist leader and prime minister. Peter is skeptical of the musical abilities of politicians. He concludes that probably two people, approximate contemporaries no doubt, were both named 'Paderewski'. Using 'Paderewski' as a name for the *statesman,* Peter assents to, "Paderewski had no musical talent." Should we infer, by the disquotational principle,

(9) Peter believes that Paderewski had no musical talent.

or should we not? If Peter had not had the past history of learning the name 'Paderewski' in another way, we certainly would judge him to be using 'Paderewski' in a normal way, with the normal reference, and we would infer (9) by the disquotational principle. The situation is parallel to the problem with Pierre and London. Here, however, no restriction that names should not be translated, but should be phonetically repeated in the translation, can help us. Only a single language and a single name are involved. If any notion of translation is involved in this example, it is homophonic translation. Only the disquotational principle is used explicitly.[37] (On the other hand, the original 'two languages' case had the advantage that it would apply even if we spoke languages in which all names must denote uniquely and unambiguously.) The restriction that names must not be translated is thus ineffective, as well as implausible and drastic.

I close this section with some remarks on the relation of the present puzzle to Quine's doctrine of the 'indeterminacy of translation', with its attendant repudiation of intentional idioms of 'propositional attitude' such as belief and even indirect quotation. To a sympathizer with these doctrines the present puzzle may well seem to be just more grist for a familiar mill. The situation of the puzzle seems to lead to a breakdown of our normal practices of attributing belief and even of indirect quotation. No obvious paradox arises if we describe the same situation in terms of Pierre's sincere assent to various sentences, together with the conditions under which he has learned the name in question. Such a description, although it does not yet conform to Quine's strict behavioristic standards, fits in well with his view that in some sense direct quotation is a more 'objective' idiom than the propositional attitudes. Even those who, like the present writer, do not find Quine's negative attitude to the attitudes completely attractive must surely acknowledge this.

But although sympathizers with Quine's view can use the present examples to support it, the differences between these examples and the considerations Quine adduces for his own skepticism about belief and translation should not escape us. Here we make no use of hypothetical exotic systems of translation differing radically from the usual one, translating *'lapin',* say, as 'rabbit stage' or 'undetached part of a rabbit'. The problem arises entirely within our usual and customary system of translation of French into English; in one case, the puzzle arose even within English alone, using at most 'homophonic' translation. Nor is the problem that many different interpretations or translations fit our usual criteria, that, in Davidson's phrase,[38] there is more than one 'way of getting it right'. The trouble here is not that many views as to Pierre's beliefs get it right, but that they all definitely get it *wrong*. A straightforward application of the principles of translation and disquotation to all Pierre's utterances, French and English, yields the result that Pierre holds inconsistent beliefs, that logic alone should teach him that one of his beliefs is false. Intuitively, this is plainly incorrect. If we refuse to apply the principles to his French utterances at all, we would conclude that Pierre never believed that London is pretty, even though, before his unpredictable move, he was like any other monolingual Frenchman. This is absurd. If we refuse to ascribe the belief in London's pulchritude only after Pierre's move to England, we get the counterintuitive result that Pierre has changed his mind, and so on. But we have surveyed the possibilities above: the point was not that they are 'equally good', but that all are *obviously wrong*. If the puzzle is to be used as an argument for a Quinean position, it is an argument of a fundamentally different kind from those given before. And even Quine, if he wishes to incorporate the notion of belief even into a 'second level' of canonical notation,[39] must regard the puzzle as a real problem.

The alleged indeterminacy of translation and indirect quotation causes relatively little trouble for such a scheme for belief; the embarrassment it presents to such a scheme is, after all, one of riches. But the present puzzle indicates that the usual principles we use to ascribe beliefs are apt, in certain cases, to lead to contradiction, or at least, patent falsehoods. So it presents a problem for any project, Quinean or other, that wishes to deal with the 'logic' of belief on any level.[40]

IV. CONCLUSION

What morals can be drawn? The primary moral—quite independent of any of the discussion of the first two sections—is that the puzzle *is* a puzzle. As any theory of truth must deal with the Liar Paradox, so any theory of belief and names must deal with this puzzle.

But our theoretical starting point in the first two sections concerned proper names and belief. Let us return to Jones, who assents to "Cicero was bald" and to "Tully was not bald." Philosophers, using the disquotational principle, have concluded that Jones believes that Cicero was bald but that Tully was not. Hence, they have concluded, since Jones does not have contradictory beliefs, belief contexts are not 'Shakespearean' in Geach's sense: codesignative proper names are not interchangeable in these contexts *salva veritate*.[41]

I think the puzzle about Pierre shows that the simple conclusion was unwarranted. Jones's situation strikingly resembles Pierre's. A proposal that 'Cicero' and 'Tully' *are* interchangeable amounts roughly to a homophonic 'translation' of English into itself in which 'Cicero' is mapped into 'Tully' and vice versa, while the rest is left fixed. Such a 'translation' can, indeed, be used to obtain a paradox. But should the problem be blamed on this step? Ordinarily we would suppose without question that sentences in French with *'Londres'* should be translated into English with 'London'. Yet the same paradox results when we apply this translation too. We have seen that the problem can even arise with a single name in a single language, and that it arises with natural kind terms in two languages (or one: see below).

Intuitively, Jones's assent to both 'Cicero was bald' and 'Tully was not bald' arises from sources of just the same kind as Pierre's assent to both *'Londres est jolie'* and 'London is not pretty'.

It is wrong to blame unpalatable conclusions about Jones on substitutivity. The reason does not lie in any specific fallacy in the argument but rather in the nature of the realm being entered. Jones's case is just like Pierre's: both are in an area where our normal practices of attributing belief, based on the principles of disquotation and translation or on similar principles, are questionable.

It should be noted in this connection that the principles of disquotation and translation can lead to 'proofs' as well as 'disproofs' of substitutivity in belief contexts. In Hebrew there are two names for Germany, transliteratable roughly as '*Ashkenaz*' and '*Germaniah*'—the first of these may be somewhat archaic. When Hebrew sentences are translated into English, both become 'Germany'. Plainly a normal Hebrew speaker analogous to Jones might assent to a Hebrew sentence involving '*Ashkenaz*' while dissenting from its counterpart with '*Germaniah*'. So far there is an argument *against* substitutivity. But there is also an argument *for* substitutivity, based on the principle of translation. Translate a Hebrew sentence involving '*Ashkenaz*' into English, so that '*Ashkenaz*' goes into 'Germany'. Then retranslate the result into Hebrew, this time translating 'Germany' as '*Germaniah*'. By the principle of translation, both translations preserve truth-value. So: the truth-value of any sentence of Hebrew involving '*Ashkenaz*' remains the same when '*Ashkenaz*' is replaced by '*Germaniah*'—a 'proof' of substitutivity! A similar 'proof' can be provided wherever there are two names in one language, and a normal practice of translating both indifferently into a single name of another language.[42] (If we combine the 'proof' and 'disproof' of substitutivity in this paragraph, we could get yet another paradox analogous to Pierre's: our Hebrew speaker both believes, and disbelieves, that Germany is pretty. Yet no amount of pure logic or semantic introspection suffices for him to discover his error.)

Another consideration, regarding natural kinds: previously we pointed out that a bilingual may learn '*lapin*' and 'rabbit' normally in each respective language yet wonder whether they are one species or two, and that this fact can be used to generate a paradox analogous to Pierre's. Similarly, a speaker of *English* alone may learn 'furze' and 'gorse' normally (separately), yet wonder whether these are the same, or resembling kinds. (What about "rabbit" and 'hare'?) It would be easy for such a speaker to assent to an assertion formulated with 'furze' but withhold assent from the corresponding assertion involving 'gorse'. The situation is quite analogous to that of Jones with respect to 'Cicero' and 'Tully'. Yet 'furze' and 'gorse', and other pairs of terms for the same natural kind, are normally thought of as *synonyms*.

The point is *not*, of course, that codesignative proper names *are* interchangeable in belief contexts *salva veritate*, or that they *are* interchangeable in simple contexts even *salva significatione*. The point is that the absurdities that disquotation plus substitutivity would generate are exactly paralleled by absurdities generated by disquotation plus translation, or even 'disquotation alone' (or: disquotation plus homophonic translation). Also, though our naive practice may lead to 'disproofs' of substitutivity in certain cases, it can also lead to 'proofs' of substitutivity in some of these same cases, as we saw two paragraphs back. When we enter into the area exemplified by Jones and Pierre, we enter into an area where our normal practices of interpretation and attribution of belief are subjected to the greatest possible strain, perhaps to the point of breakdown. So is the notion of the *content* of someone's assertion, the *proposition* it expresses. In the present state of our knowledge, I think it would be foolish to draw any conclusion, positive or negative, about substitutivity.[43]

Of course nothing in these considerations prevents us from observing that Jones can sincerely assert both "Cicero is bald" and "Tully is not bald," even though he is a normal speaker of English and uses 'Cicero' and 'Tully' in normal ways, and with the normal referent. Pierre and the other paradoxical cases can be described similarly. (For those interested in one of my own doctrines, we can still say that there was a time when men were in no epistemic position to assent to 'Hesperus is Phosphorus' for want of empirical information, but it nevertheless expressed a necessary truth.)[44] But it is no surprise that quoted contexts fail to satisfy a substitutivity principle within the quotation marks. And, in our *present* state of clarity about the problem, we are in no position to apply a disquotation principle to these cases, nor to judge when two such sentences do, or do not, express the same 'proposition'.

Nothing in the discussion impugns the conventional judgment that belief contexts are 'referentially opaque', if 'referential opacity' is construed so that failure of coreferential *definite descriptions* to be interchangeable *salva veritate* is sufficient for referential opacity. No doubt Jones can believe that the number of planets is even, without believing that the square of three is even, if he is under a misapprehension about the astronomical, but not the arithmetical facts. The question at hand was whether belief contexts were 'Shakespearean', not whether they were 'referentially transparent'. (Modal contexts, in my opinion, are 'Shakespearean' but 'referentially opaque'.)[45]

Even were we inclined to rule that belief contexts are not Shakespearean, it would be implausible at present to use the phenomenon to support a Frege-Russellian theory that names have descriptive 'senses' through 'uniquely identifying properties'. There are the well-known arguments against description theories, independent of the present discussion; there is the implausibility of the view that difference in names is difference in idiolect; and finally, there are the arguments of the present paper that differences of associated properties do not explain the problems in any case. Given these considerations, and the cloud our paradox places over the notion of 'content' in this area, the relation of substitutivity to the dispute between Millian and Fregean conclusions is not very clear.

We repeat our conclusions: philosophers have often, basing themselves on Jones's and similar cases, supposed that it goes virtually without saying that belief contexts are not 'Shakespearean'. I think that at present, such a definite conclusion is unwarranted. Rather Jones's case, like Pierre's, lies in an area where our normal apparatus for the ascription of belief is placed under the greatest strain and may even break down. There is even less warrant at the present time, in the absence of a better understanding of the paradoxes of this paper, for the use of alleged failures of substitutivity in belief contexts to draw any significant theoretical conclusion about proper names. Hard cases make bad law.[46]

NOTES

1. "Naming and Necessity," in *The Semantics of Natural Languages,* D. Davidson and G. Harman (eds.), Dordrecht, Reidel, 1971, pp. 253–355 and 763–769.(Also forthcoming as a separate monograph, pub. Basil Blackwell.) "Identity and Necessity" in *Identity and Individuation,* M. Munitz (ed.), New York, New York University Press, 1971, pp. 135–164. Acquaintance with these papers is not a prerequisite for understanding the central puzzle of the present paper, but is helpful for understanding the theoretical background.

2. Frege gives essentially this example as the second footnote of "On Sense and Reference" [Reprinted in this volume as "On Sense and Nominatum."]. For the "Who is . . . ?" to be applicable one must be careful to elicit from one's informant properties that he regards as defining the name and determining the referent, not mere well-known facts about the referent. (Of course this distinction may well seem fictitious, but it is central to the original Frege-Russell theory.)

3. For convenience Russells' terminology is assimilated to Frege's. Actually, regarding genuine or 'logically proper' names, Russell is a strict Millian: 'logically proper names' *simply* refer (to immediate objects of acquaintance). But, according to Russell, what are ordinarily called 'names' are not genuine, logically proper names, but disguised definite descriptions. Since Russell also regards definite descriptions as in turn disguised notation, he does not associate any 'senses' with descriptions, since they are not genuine singular terms. When all disguised notation is eliminated, the only singular terms remaining are logically proper names, for which no notion of 'sense' is required. When we speak of Russell as assigning 'senses' to names, we mean ordinary names and for convenience we ignore his view that the descriptions abbreviating them ultimately disappear on analysis.

On the other hand, the explicit doctrine that names are abbreviated definite descriptions is due to Russell. Michael Dummett, in his recent *Frege* (London, Duckworth, and New York, Harper and Row, 1973, pp. 110–111) denies that Frege held a description theory of senses. Although as far as I know Frege indeed makes no explicit statement to that effect, his examples of names conform to the doctrine, as Dummett acknowledges. Especially his 'Aristotle' example is revealing. He defines 'Aristotle' just as Russell would; it seems clear that in the case of a famous historical figure, the 'name' is indeed to be given by answering, in a uniquely specifying way, the 'who is' question. Dummett himself characterizes a sense as a "criterion . . . such that the referent of the name, if any, is whatever object satisfies that criterion." Since presumably the satisfaction of the criterion must be unique (so a unique referent is determined), doesn't this amount to defining names by unique satisfaction of properties, i.e., by descriptions? *Perhaps* the point is that the property in question need not be expressible by a usual predicate of English, as might be plausible if the referent is one of the speaker's acquaintances rather than a historical figure. But I doubt that even Russell, father of the explicitly formulated description theory, ever meant to require that the description must always be expressible in (unsupplemented) English.

In any event, the philosophical community has generally understood Fregean senses in terms of descriptions, and we deal with it under this usual understanding. For present purposes this is more important than detailed historical issues. Dummett acknowledges (p. 111) that few substantive points are affected by his (allegedly) broader interpretation of Frege; and it would not seem to be relevant to the problems of the present paper.

4. See Frege's footnote in "On Sense and Reference" mentioned in note 2 above and especially his discussion of 'Dr. Gustav Lauben' in *"Der Gedanke"* (in the recent Geach-Stoothoff translation, "Thoughts," *Logical Investigations,* Oxford, Blackwell, 1977, pp. 11–12).

5. Russell, as a Millian with respect to genuine names, accepts this argument with respect to 'logically proper names'. For example—taking for the moment 'Cicero' and 'Tully' as 'logically proper names', Russell would hold that if I judge that Cicero admired Tully, I am related to Cicero, Tully, and the admiration relation in a certain way: since Cicero *is* Tully, I am related in exactly the same way to Tully, Cicero, and admiration; therefore I judge that Tully admired Cicero. Again, if Cicero *did* admire Tully, then according to Russell a single fact corresponds to all of 'Cicero admired Tully', 'Cicero admired Cicero', etc. Its constituent (in addition to admiration) is the man Cicero, taken, so to speak, twice.

Russell thought that 'Cicero admired Tully' and 'Tully admired Cicero' are in fact obviously not interchangeable. For him, this was one argument that 'Cicero' and 'Tully' are *not* genuine names, and that the Roman orator is no constituent of propositions (or 'facts', or 'judgments') corresponding to sentences containing the name.

6. Given the arguments of Church and others, I do not believe that the formal mode of speech is synonymous with other formulations. But it can be used as a rough way to convey the idea of scope.

7. It may well be argued that the Millian view implies that proper names are *scopeless* and that for them the *de dicto-de re* distinction vanishes. This view has considerable plausibility (my own views on rigidity will imply something like this for *modal* contexts), but it need not be argued here either way: *de re* uses are simply not treated in the present paper.

Christopher Peacocke ("Proper Names, Reference, and Rigid Designation," in *Meaning, Reference, and Necessity,* S. Blackburn (ed.), Cambridge, Cambridge University Press, 1975; see Section I), uses what amounts to the equivalence of the *de dicto-de re* constructions in *all* contexts (or, put alternatively, the lack of such a distinction) to characterize the notion of rigid designation. I agree that for *modal* contexts, this is (roughly) equivalent to my own notion, also that for proper names Peacocke's equivalence holds for temporal contexts. (This is roughly equivalent to the 'temporal rigidity' of names.) I also agree that it is very plausible to extend the principle to all contexts. But, as Peacocke recognizes, this appears to imply a substitutivity principle for codesignative proper names in belief contexts, which is widely assumed to be false. Peacocke proposed to use Davidson's theory of intensional contexts to block this conclusion (the material in the 'that' clause is a separate sentence). I myself cannot accept Davidson's theory; but even if it were true, Peacocke in effect acknowledges that it does not really dispose of the difficulty (p. 127, first paragraph). (Incidentally, if Davidson's theory does block any inference to the transparency of belief contexts with respect to names, why does Peacocke assume without argument that it does not do so for modal contexts, which have a similar grammatical structure?) The problems are thus those of the present paper; until they are resolved I prefer at present to keep to my earlier more cautious formulation.

Incidentally, Peacocke hints a recognition that the received platitude—that codesignative names are not interchangeable in belief contexts—may not be so clear as is generally supposed.

8. The example comes from Quine, *Word and Object,* Cambridge, Mass., MIT Press, 1960, p. 145. Quine's conclusion that 'believes that' construed *de dicto* is opaque has widely been taken for granted. In the formulation in the text I have used the colon to emphasize that I am speaking of belief *de dicto*. Since, as I have said, belief *de dicto* will be our *only* concern in this paper, in the future the colon will usually be suppressed, and all "believes that" contexts should be read *de dicto* unless the contrary is indicated explicitly.

9. In many writings Peter Geach has advocated a view that is non-Millian (he would say 'non-Lockean') in that to each name a sortal predicate is attached by definition ('Geach', for example, by *definition* names a man). On the other hand, the theory is not completely Fregean either, since Geach denies that any definite description that would identify the referent of the name among things of the same sort is analytically tied to the name. (See, for example, his *Reference and Generality,* Ithaca, Cornell University Press, 1962, pp. 43–45.) As far as the present issues are concerned, Geach's view can fairly be assimilated to *Mill*'s rather than to Frege's. For such ordinary names as 'Cicero' and 'Tully' will have both the same reference and the same (Geachian) sense (namely, that they are names of a man). It would thus seem that they ought to be interchangeable everywhere. (In *Reference and Generality,* Geach appears not to accept this conclusion, but the prima facie argument for the conclusion will be the same as on a purely Millian view.)

10. In an unpublished paper, Diana Ackerman urges the problem of substitutivity failures against the Millian view and, hence, against my own views. I believe that others may have done so as well. (I have the impression that the paper has undergone considerable revision, and I have not seen recent versions.) I agree that this problem is a considerable difficulty

for the Millian view, and for the Millian *spirit* of my own views in "Naming and Necessity." (See the discussion of this in the text of the present paper.) On the other hand I would emphasize that there need be no *contradiction* in maintaining that names are *modally* rigid, and satisfy a substitutivity principle for modal contexts, while denying the substitutivity principle for belief contexts. The entire apparatus elaborated in "Naming and Necessity" of the distinction between epistemic and metaphysical necessity, and of giving a meaning and fixing a reference, was meant to show, among other things, that a Millian substitutivity doctrine for modal contexts can be maintained even if such a doctrine for epistemic contexts is rejected. "Naming and Necessity" never asserted a substitutivity principle for epistemic contexts.

It is even consistent to suppose that differing modes of (rigidly) fixing the reference is responsible for the substitutivity failures, thus adopting a position intermediate between Frege and Mill, on the lines indicated in the text of the present paper. "Naming and Necessity" may even perhaps be taken as suggesting, for some contexts where a conventional description rigidly fixes the reference ('Hesperus-Phosphorus'), that the mode of reference fixing is relevant to epistemic questions. I knew when I wrote "Naming and Necessity" that substitutivity issues in epistemic contexts were really very delicate, due to the problems of the present paper, but I thought it best not to muddy the waters further. (See notes 43–44.)

After this paper was completed, I saw Alvin Plantinga's paper "The Boethian Compromise," *The American Philosophical Quarterly* 15 (April, 1978): 129–138. Plantinga adopts a view intermediate between Mill and Frege, and cites substitutivity failures as a principal argument for his position. He also refers to a forthcoming paper by Ackerman. I have not seen this paper, but it probably is a descendant of the paper referred to above.

11. Here I use 'connotation' so as to imply that the associated properties have an a priori tie to the name, at least as rigid reference fixers, and therefore must be true of the referent (if it exists). There is another sense of 'connotation', as in 'The Holy Roman Empire', where the connotation need not be assumed or even believed to be true of the referent. In some sense akin to this, classicists and others with some classical learning may attach certain distinct 'connotations' to 'Cicero' and 'Tully'. Similarly, 'the Netherlands' may suggest low altitude to a thoughtful ear. Such 'connotations' can hardly be thought of as community-wide; many use the names unaware of such suggestions. Even a speaker aware of the suggestion of the name may not regard the suggested properties as true of the object; cf. 'The Holy Roman Empire'. A 'connotation' of this type neither gives a meaning nor fixes a reference.

12. Some might attempt to find a difference in 'sense' between 'Cicero' and 'Tully' on the grounds that

"Cicero is called 'Cicero'" is trivial, but "Tully is called 'Cicero'" may not be. Kneale, and in one place (probably at least implicitly) Church, have argued in this vein. (For Kneale, see "Naming and Necessity," p. 283.) So, it may be argued, being called 'Cicero', is part of the sense of the name 'Cicero,' but not part of that of 'Tully.' I have discussed some issues related to this in "Naming and Necessity," pp. 283–286. (See also the discussions of circularity conditions elsewhere in "Naming and Necessity.") Much more could be said about and against this kind of argument; perhaps I will sometime do so elsewhere. Let me mention very briefly the following parallel situation (which may be best understood by reference to the discussion in "Naming and Necessity"). Anyone who understands the meaning of "is called' and of quotation in English (and that 'alienists' is meaningful and grammatically appropriate) knows that "alienists are called 'alienists'" expresses a truth in English, even if he has no idea what 'alienists' means. He need *not* know that 'psychiatrists are called 'alienists'" expresses a truth. None of this goes to show that 'alienists' and 'psychiatrists' are not synonymous, or that 'alienists' has *being called 'alienists'* as part of its meaning when 'psychiatrists' does not. Similarly for 'Cicero' and 'Tully'. There is no more reason to suppose that being so-called is part of the meaning of a name than of any other word.

13. A view follows Frege and Russell on this issue even if it allows each speaker to associate a cluster of descriptions with each name, provided that it holds that the cluster varies from speaker to speaker and that variations in the cluster are variations in idiolect. Searle's view thus is Frege-Russellian when he writes in the concluding paragraph of "Proper Names" (*Mind* 67 [1958]: 166–173), "'Tully = Cicero' would, I suggest, be analytic for most people; the same descriptive presuppositions are associated with each name. But of course if the descriptive presuppositions were different it might be used to make a synthetic statement."

14. Though here I use the jargon of propositions, the point is fairly insensitive to differences in theoretical standpoints. For example, on Davidson's analysis, I would be asserting (roughly) that many are unaware-of-the-content-of the following *utterance* of mine: Cicero is Tully. This would be subject to the same problem.

15. Benson Mates, "Synonymity," *University of California Publications in Philosophy* 25 (1950): 201–226; reprinted in *Semantics and the Philosophy of Language,* L. Linsky (ed.), University of Illinois Press, 1952. (There was a good deal of subsequent discussion. In Mates's original paper the point is made almost parenthetically.) Actually, I think that Mates's problem has relatively little force against the argument we are considering for the Fregean position. Mates's puzzle in no way militates against some such principle as: if one word is synonymous with another, then a sufficiently reflective speaker

subject to no linguistic inadequacies or conceptual confusions who sincerely assents to a simple sentence containing the one will also (sincerely) assent to the corresponding sentence with the other in its place.

It is surely a crucial part of the present 'Fregean' argument that codesignative names may have distinct 'senses', that a speaker may assent to a simple sentence containing one and deny the corresponding sentence containing the other, even though he is *guilty of no conceptual or linguistic confusion, and of no lapse in logical consistency*. In the case of *two straightforward synonyms, this is not so.*

I myself think that Mates's argument is of considerable interest, but that the issues are confusing and delicate and that, if the argument works, it probably leads to a paradox or puzzle rather than to a definite conclusion. (See also notes 23, 28, and 46.)

16. "Naming and Necessity," pp. 291 (bottom)-293.

17. Recall also note 12.

18. Some philosophers stress that names are not *words* of a language, or that names are not *translated* from one language to another. (The phrase 'common currency of our common language' was meant to be neutral with respect to any such alleged issue.) Someone may use 'Mao Tse-Tung', for example, in English, though he knows not one word of Chinese. It seems hard to deny, however, that *"Deutschland," "Allemagne,"* and "Germany," are the German, French, and English names of a single country, and that one translates a French sentence using *"Londres"* by an English sentence using "London." Learning these facts is part of learning German, French, and English.

It would appear that *some* names, especially names of countries, other famous localities, and some famous people *are* thought of as part of a language (whether they are called 'words' or not is of little importance). Many other names are not thought of as part of a language, especially if the referent is not famous (so the notation used is confined to a limited circle), or if the same name is used by speakers of all languages. As far as I can see, it makes little or no *semantic* difference whether a particular name is thought of as part of a language or not. Mathematical notation such as '<' is also ordinarily not thought of as part of English, or any other language, though it is used in combination with English words in sentences of mathematical treatises written in English. (A French mathematician can use the notation though he knows not one word of English.) 'Is less than', on the other hand, *is* English. Does this difference have any semantic significance?

I will speak in most of the text as if the names I deal with are part of English, French, etc. But it matters little for what I say whether they are thought of as parts of the language or as adjuncts to it. And one need not say that a name such as *'Londres'* is 'translated' (if such a terminology suggested that names have 'senses,' I too would find it objectionable), as long as one acknowledges that *sentences* containing it are properly translated into English using 'London'.

19. By saying that names are transparent in a context, I mean that codesignative names are interchangeable there. This is a deviation for brevity from the usual terminology, according to which the *context* is transparent. (I use the usual terminology in the paper also.)

20. But we must use the term 'sense' here in the sense of 'that which fixes the reference', not 'that which gives the meaning', otherwise we shall run afoul of the rigidity of proper names. If the source of a chain for a certain name is in fact a given object, we use the name to designate that object even when speaking of counterfactual situations in which some *other* object originated the chain.

21. The point is that, according to the doctrine of "Naming and Necessity," when proper names are transmitted from link to link, even though the beliefs about the referent associated with the name change radically, the change is not to be considered a linguistic change, in the way it was a linguistic change when 'villain' changed its meaning from 'rustic' to 'wicked man'. As long as the reference of a name remains the same, the associated beliefs about the object may undergo a large number of changes without these changes constituting a change in the language.

If Geach is right, an appropriate sortal must be passed on also. But see footnote 58 of "Naming and Necessity."

22. Similar appropriate restrictions are assumed below for the strengthened disquotational principle and for the principle of translation. Ambiguities need not be excluded if it is tacitly assumed that the sentence is to be understood in one way in all its occurrences. (For the principle of translation it is similarly assumed that the translator matches the *intended* interpretation of the sentence.) I do not work out the restrictions on indexicals in detail, since the intent is clear.

Clearly, the disquotational principle applies only to *de dicto*, not *de re*, attributions of belief. If someone sincerely assents to the near triviality "The tallest foreign spy is a spy," it follows that he believes that: the tallest foreign spy is a spy. It is well known that it does *not* follow that he believes, *of* the tallest foreign spy, that he is a spy. In the latter case, but not in the former, it would be his patriotic duty to make contact with the authorities.

23. What if a speaker assents to a sentence, but fails to assent to a synonymous assertion? Say, he assents to "Jones is a doctor," but not to "Jones is a physician." Such a speaker either does not understand one of the sentences normally, or he should be able to correct himself "on reflection." As long as he confusedly assents to 'Jones is a doctor' but not to 'Jones is a physician', we *cannot* straightforwardly apply disquotational principles to conclude that he does or does not believe that Jones is a doctor, because his assent is not "reflective."

Similarly, if someone asserts, "Jones is a doctor but not a physician," he should be able to recognize his inconsistency without further information. We have formulated the disquotational principles so they need not lead us to attribute belief as long as we have grounds to suspect conceptual or linguistic confusion, as in the cases just mentioned.

Note that if someone says, "Cicero was bald but Tully was not," there need be *no* grounds to suppose that he is under *any* linguistic or conceptual confusion.

24. This should not be confused with the question whether the speaker simultaneously believes *of* a given object, both that it has a certain property and that it does not have it. Our discussion concerns *de dicto* (notional) belief, not *de re* belief.

I have been shown a passage in Aristotle that appears to suggest that *no one* can really believe both of two explicit contradictories. If we wish to use the *simple* disquotational principle as a test for disbelief, it suffices that this be true of *some* individuals, after reflection, who are simultaneously aware of both beliefs, and have sufficient logical acumen and respect for logic. Such individuals, if they have contradictory beliefs, will be shaken in one or both beliefs after they note the contradiction. For such individuals, sincere reflective assent to the negation of a sentence implies disbelief in the proposition it expresses, so the test in the text applies.

25. For example, in translating a historical report into another language, such as, "Patrick Henry said, 'Give me liberty or give me death!'" the translator may well translate the quoted material attributed to Henry. He translates a presumed truth into a falsehood, since Henry spoke English; but probably his reader is aware of this and is more interested in the content of Henry's utterance than in its exact words. Especially in translating fiction, where truth is irrelevant, this procedure is appropriate. But some objectors to Church's 'translation argument' have allowed themselves to be misled by the practice.

26. To state the argument precisely, we need in addition a form of the Tarskian disquotation principle for truth: For each (French or English) replacement for '*p*', infer " '*p*' is true" from "*p*," and conversely. (Note that " '*p*' is true" becomes an English sentence even if '*p*' is replaced by a French sentence.) In the text we leave the application of the Tarskian disquotational principle tacit.

27. I gather that Burali-Forti originally thought he had 'proved' that the ordinals are not linearly ordered, reasoning in a manner similar to our topologist. Someone who heard the present paper delivered told me that König made a similar error.

28. It is not possible, in this case, as it is in the case of the man who assents to "Jones is a doctor" but not to "Jones is a physician," to refuse to apply the disquotational principle on the grounds that the subject must lack proper command of the language or be subject to some linguistic or conceptual confusion. As long as Pierre is unaware that 'London' and '*Lon-*

dres' are codesignative, he need not lack appropriate linguistic knowledge, nor need he be subject to any linguistic or conceptual confusion, when he affirms '*Londres est jolie*' but denies 'London is pretty'.

29. The 'elimination' would be most plausible if we believed, according to a Russellian epistemology, that all my language, when written in unabbreviated notation, refers to constituents with which I am 'acquainted' in Russell's sense. Then no one speaks a language intelligible to anyone else; indeed, no one speaks the same language twice. Few today will accept this.

A basic consideration should be stressed here. Moderate Fregeans attempt to combine a roughly Fregean view with the view that names are part of our common language, and that our conventional practices of interlinguistic translation and interpretation are correct. The problems of the present paper indicate that it is very difficult to obtain a requisite socialized notion of sense that will enable such a program to succeed. Extreme Fregeans (such as Frege and Russell) believe that in general names are peculiar to idiolects. They therefore would accept no general rule translating '*Londres*' as 'London', nor even translating one person's use of 'London' into another's. However, if they follow Frege in regarding senses as "objective', they must believe that in principle it makes sense to speak of two people using two names in their respective idiolects with the same sense, and that there must be (necessary and) sufficient conditions for this to be the case. If these conditions for sameness of sense are satisfied, translation of one name into the other is legitimate, otherwise not. The present considerations (and the extension of these below to natural kind and related terms), however, indicate that the notion of sameness of sense, if it is to be explicated in terms of sameness of identifying properties and if these properties are themselves expressed in the languages of the two respective idiolects, presents interpretation problems of the same type presented by the names themselves. Unless the Fregean can give a method for identifying sameness of sense that is free of such problems, he *has no sufficient conditions for sameness of sense, nor for translation to be legitimate.* He would therefore be forced to maintain, contrary to Frege's intent, that not only in practice do few people use proper names with the same sense but that *it is in principle meaningless to compare senses.* A view that the identifying properties used to define senses should always be expressible in a Russellian language of 'logically proper names' would be one solution to this difficulty but involves a doubtful philosophy of language and epistemology.

30. If any reader finds the term 'translation' objectionable with respect to names, let him be reminded that all I mean is that French sentences containing '*Londres*' are uniformly translated into English with 'London'.

31. The paradox would be blocked if we required that they define the names by the same properties

expressed in the same words. There is nothing in the motivation of the classical description theories that would justify this extra clause. In the present case of French and English, such a restriction would amount to a decree that neither *'Londres'*, nor any other conceivable French name, could be translated as 'London'. I deal with this view immediately below.

32. Word salads of two languages (like ungrammatical 'semisentences' of a single language) need not be unintelligible, though they are makeshifts with no fixed syntax. "If God did not exist," Voltaire said, *"il faudrait l'inventer."* The meaning is clear.

33. Had we said, "Pierre believes that the country he calls *'Angleterre'* is a monarchy," the sentence would be English, since the French word would be mentioned but not used. But for this very reason we would not have captured the sense of the French original.

34. Under the influence of Quine's *Word and Object,* some may argue that such conclusions are not inevitable: perhaps he will translate *'médecin'* as 'doctor stage', or "undetached part of a doctor'! If a Quinean skeptic makes an empirical prediction that such reactions from bilinguals as a matter of fact can occur, I doubt that he will be proved correct. (I don't know what Quine would think. But see *Word and Object,* p. 74, first paragraph.) On the other hand, if the translation of *'médecin'* as 'doctor' rather than 'doctor part' in this situation *is,* empirically speaking, inevitable, then even the advocate of Quine's thesis will have to admit that there is something special about one particular translation. The issue not crucial to our present concerns, so I leave it with these sketchy remarks. But see also note 36.

35. Putnam gives the example of elms and beeches in "The Meaning of 'Meaning'" (in *Language, Mind, and Knowledge,* Minnesota Studies in the Philosophy of Science 7; also reprinted in Putnam's *Collected Papers*). See also Putnam's discussion of other examples on pp. 139–143; also my own remarks on 'fool's gold', tigers, etc., in "Naming and Necessity," pp. 316–323.

36. It is unclear to me how far this can go. Suppose Pierre hears English spoken only in England, French in France, and learns both by direct method. (Suppose also, that no one else in each country speaks the language of the other.) Must he be sure that "hot' and *'chaud'* are coextensive? In practice he certainly would. But suppose somehow his experience is consistent with the following bizarre—and of course, false!—hypothesis: England and France differ atmospherically so that human bodies are affected very differently by their interaction with the surrounding atmosphere. (This would be more plausible if France were on another planet.) In particular, within reasonable limits, things that feel cold in one of the countries feel hot in the other, and vice versa. Things don't change their *temperature* when moved from England to France, they just *feel* different because of their effects on human physiology. Then *'chaud',* in French, would be true of the things that

are called 'cold' in English! (Of course the present discussion is, for space, terribly compressed. See also the discussion of 'heat' in "Naming and Necessity." We are simply creating, for the physical property 'heat', a situation analogous to the situation for natural kinds in the text.)

If Pierre's experiences were arranged somehow so as to be consistent with the bizarre hypothesis, and he somehow came to believe it, he might simultaneously assent to *'C'est chaud'* and 'This is cold' without contradiction, even though he speaks French and English normally in each country separately.

This case needs much more development to see if it can be set up in detail, but I cannot consider it further here. Was I right in assuming in the text that the difficulty could not arise for *'mémecin'* and 'doctor'?

37. One might argue that Peter and we do speak different dialects, since in Peter's idiolect 'Paderewski' is used ambiguously as a name for a musician and a statesman (even though these are in fact the same), while in our language it is used unambiguously for a musician-statesman. The problem then would be whether Peter's dialect can be translated homophonically into our own. Before he hears of 'Paderewski-the-statesman', it would appear that the answer is affirmative for his (then unambiguous) use of 'Paderewski', since he did not differ from anyone who happens to have heard of Paderewski's musical achievements but not of his statesmanship. Similarly for his later use of 'Paderewski', if we ignore his earlier use. The problem is like Pierre's, and is essentially the same whether we describe it in terms of whether Peter satisfies the condition for the disquotational principle to be applicable, or whether homophonic translation of his dialect into our own is legitimate.

38. D. Davidson, "On Saying That," in *Words and Objections,* D. Davidson and J. Hintikka (eds.), Dordrecht, Reidel, 1969, p. 166.

39. In *Word and Object,* p. 221, Quine advocates a second level of canonical notation, "to dissolve verbal perplexities or facilitate logical deductions," admitting the propositional attitudes, even though he thinks them "baseless" idioms that should be excluded from a notation "limning the true and ultimate structure of reality."

40. In one respect the considerations mentioned above on natural kinds show that Quine's translation apparatus is insufficiently skeptical. Quine is sure that the native's *sentence* "Gavagai!" should be translated "Lo, a rabbit!" provided that its affirmative and negative stimulus meanings for the native match those of the English sentence for the Englishman; skepticism sets in only when the linguist proposes to translate the *general term* 'gavagai' as 'rabbit' rather than 'rabbit stage', 'rabbit part', and the like. But there is another possibility that is independent of (and less bizarre than) such skeptical alternatives. In the geographical area inhabited by the natives, there may be a species indistinguishable to the nonzoologist from

rabbits but forming a distinct species. Then the 'stimulus meanings', in Quine's sense, of 'Lo, a rabbit!' and 'Gavagai!' may well be identical (to nonzoologists), especially if the ocular irradiations in question do not include a specification of the geographical locality. ('Gavagais' produce the same ocular irradiation patterns as rabbits.) Yet 'Gavagai!' and 'Lo, a rabbit!' are hardly synonymous; on typical occasions they will have opposite truth-values.

I believe that the considerations about names, let alone natural kinds, emphasized in "Naming and Necessity" go against any simple attempt to base interpretation solely on maximizing agreement with the affirmations attributed to the native, matching of stimulus meanings, etc. The 'Principle of Charity' on which such methodologies are based was first enunciated by Neil Wilson in the special case of proper names as a formulation of the cluster-of-descriptions theory. The argument of "Naming and Necessity" is thus directed against the simple 'Principle of Charity' for that case.

41. Geach introduced the term 'Shakespearean' after the line, "a rose/By any other name, would smell as sweet."

Quine seems to define 'referentially transparent' contexts so as to imply that coreferential names and definite descriptions must be interchangeable *salva veritate*. Geach stresses that a context may be 'Shakespearean' but not 'referentially transparent' in this sense.

42. Generally such cases may be slightly less watertight than the 'London'-'*Londres*' case. '*Londres*' just is the French version of 'London', while one cannot quite say that the same relation holds between '*Ashkenaz*' and '*Germaniah*'. Nevertheless:

(a) Our standard practice in such cases is to translate both names of the first language into the single name of the second.

(b) Often no nuances of 'meaning' are discernible differentiating such names as '*Ashkenaz*' and '*Germaniah*', such that we would not say either that Hebrew would have been impoverished had it lacked one of them (or that English is impoverished because it has only one name for Germany), any more than a language is impoverished if it has only one word corresponding to 'doctor' and 'physician'. Given this, it seems hard to condemn our practice of translating both names as 'Germany' as 'loose'; in fact, it would seem that Hebrew just has two names for the same country where English gets by with one.

(c) any inclinations to avoid problems by declaring, say, the translation of '*Ashkenaz*' as 'Germany' to be loose should be considerably tempered by the discussion of analogous problems in the text.

43. In spite of this official view, perhaps I will be more assertive elsewhere.

In the case of 'Hesperus' and 'Phosphorus' (in contrast to 'Cicero' and 'Tully'), where there is a case for the existence of conventional community-wide 'senses' differentiating the two—at least, two distinct modes of 'fixing the reference of two rigid designators'—it is more plausible to suppose that the two names are definitely not interchangeable in belief contexts. According to such a supposition, a belief that Hesperus is a planet is a belief that a certain heavenly body, rigidly picked out as seen in the evening in the appropriate season, is a planet; and similarly for Phosphorus. One may argue that translation problems like Pierre's will be blocked in this case, that '*Vesper*' must be translated as 'Hesperus', not as 'Phosphorus'. As against this, however, two things:

(a) We should remember that sameness of properties used to fix the reference does *not* appear to guarantee in general that paradoxes will not arise. So one may be reluctant to adopt a solution in terms of reference-fixing properties for this case if it does not get to the heart of the general problem.

(b) The main issue seems to me here to be—how essential is a particular mode of fixing the reference to a correct learning of the name? If a parent, aware of the familiar identity, takes a child into the fields in the morning and says (pointing to the morning star) "That is called 'Hesperus'," has the parent mistaught the language? (A parent who says, "Creatures with kidneys are called 'cordates'," definitely has mistaught the language, even though the statement is extensionally correct.) To the extent that it is *not* crucial for correct language learning that a particular mode of fixing the reference be used, to that extent there is no 'mode of presentation' differentiating the 'content' of a belief about 'Hesperus' from one about 'Phosphorus'. I am doubtful that the original method of fixing the reference *must* be preserved in transmission of the name.

If the mode of reference fixing *is* crucial, it can be maintained that otherwise identical beliefs expressed with 'Hesperus' and with 'Phosphorus' have definite differences of 'content', at least in an epistemic sense. The conventional ruling against substitutivity could thus be maintained without qualms for some cases, though not as obviously for others, such as 'Cicero' and 'Tully'. But it is unclear to me whether even 'Hesperus' and 'Phosphorus' do have such conventional 'modes of presentation'. I need not take a definite stand, and the verdict may be different for different particular pairs of names. For a brief related discussion, see "Naming and Necessity," p. 331, first paragraph.

44. However, some earlier formulations expressed disquotationally such as "It was once unknown that Hesperus is Phosphorus" are questionable in the light of the present paper (but see the previous note for this case). I was aware of this question by the time "Naming and Necessity" was written, but I did not wish to muddy the waters further than necessary at that time. I regarded the distinction between epistemic and metaphysical necessity as valid in any case and adequate for the distinctions I wished to make. The considerations in this paper are relevant to the earlier discussion of the 'contingent a priori' as well; perhaps I will discuss this elsewhere.

45. According to Russell, definite descriptions are not genuine singular terms. He thus would have regarded any concept of 'referential opacity' that includes definite descriptions as profoundly misleading. He also maintained a substitutivity principle for 'logically proper names' in belief and other attitudinal contexts, so that for him belief contexts were as 'transparent', in any philosophically decent sense, as truth-functional contexts.

Independently of Russell's views, there is much to be said for the opinion that the question whether a context is 'Shakespearean' is more important philosophically—even for many purposes for which Quine invokes his own concept—than whether it is 'referentially opaque'.

46. I will make some brief remarks about the relation of Benson Mates's problem (see note 15) to the present one. Mates argued that such a sentence as (*) 'Some doubt that all who believe that doctors are happy believe that physicians are happy', may be true, even though 'doctors' and 'physicians' are synonymous, and even though it would have been false had 'physicians' been replaced in it by a second occurrence of 'doctors'. Church countered that (*) could not be true, since its translation into a language with only one word for doctors (which would translate both 'doctors' and 'physicians') would be false. If *both* Mates's and Church's intuitions were correct, we might get a paradox analogous to Pierre's.

Applying the principles of translation and disquotation to Mates's puzzle, however, involves many more complications than our present problem. First, if someone assents to 'Doctors are happy', but refuses assent to 'Physicians are happy', prima facie disquotation does not apply to him since he is under a linguistic or conceptual confusion. (See note 23.) So there are as yet no grounds, merely because this happened, to doubt that all who believe that doctors are happy believe that physicians are happy.

Now suppose someone assents to 'Not all who believe that doctors are happy believe that physicians are happy.' What is the source of his assent? If it is failure to realize that 'doctors' and 'physicians' are synonymous (this was the situation Mates originally envisaged), then he is under a linguistic or conceptual confusion, so disquotation does not clearly apply. Hence we have no reason to conclude from this case that (*) is true. Alternatively, he may realize that 'doctors' and 'physicians' are synonymous; but he applies disquotation to a man who assents to 'Doctors are happy' but not to 'Physicians are happy', ignoring the caution of the previous paragraph. Here he is not under a simple linguistic confusion (such as failure to realize that 'doctors' and 'physicians' are synonymous), but he appears to be under a deep conceptual confusion (misapplication of the disquotational principle). Perhaps, it may be argued, he misunderstands the 'logic of belief'. Does his conceptual confusion mean that we cannot straightforwardly apply disquotation to his utterance, and that therefore we cannot conclude from

his behavior that (*) is true? I think that, although the issues are delicate, and I am not at present completely sure what answers to give, there is a case for an affirmative answer. (Compare the more extreme case of someone who is so confused that he thinks that someone's *dissent* from 'Doctors are happy' implies that he believes that doctors are happy. If someone's utterance, 'Many believe that doctors are happy', is based on such a misapplication of disquotation, surely we in turn should not apply disquotation to it. The utterer, at least in this context, does not really know what 'belief' means.)

I do *not* believe the discussion above ends the matter. Perhaps I can discuss Mates's problem at greater length elsewhere. Mates's problem is perplexing, and its relation to the present puzzle is interesting. But it should be clear from the preceding that Mates's argument involves issues even more delicate than those that arise with respect to Pierre. First, Mates's problem involves delicate issues regarding iteration of belief contexts, whereas the puzzle about Pierre involves the application of disquotation only to affirmations of (or assents to) *simple* sentences. More important, Mates's problem would not arise in a world where no one ever was under a linguistic or a conceptual confusion, no one ever thought anyone else was under such a confusion, no one ever thought anyone ever thought anyone was under such a confusion, and so on. It is important, both for the puzzle about Pierre and for the Fregean argument that 'Cicero' and 'Tully' differ in 'sense', that they would still arise in such a world. They are entirely free of the delicate problem of applying disquotation to utterances directly or indirectly based on the existence of linguistic confusion. See notes 15 and 28, and the discussion in the text of Pierre's logical consistency.

Another problem discussed in the literature to which the present considerations may be relevant is that of 'self-consciousness', or the peculiarity of 'I'. Discussions of this problem have emphasized that 'I', even when Mary Smith uses it, is not interchangeable with 'Mary Smith', nor with any other conventional singular term designating Mary Smith. If she is 'not aware that she is Mary Smith', she may assent to a sentence with 'I', but dissent from the corresponding sentence with 'Mary Smith'. It is quite possible that any attempt to clear up the logic of all this will involve itself in the problem of the present paper. (For this purpose, the present discussion might be extended to demonstratives and indexicals.)

The writing of this paper had partial support from a grant from the National Science Foundation, a John Simon Guggenheim Foundation Fellowship, a Visiting Fellowship at All Souls College, Oxford, and a sabbatical leave from Princeton University. Various people at the Jerusalem Encounter and elsewhere, who will not be enumerated, influenced the paper through discussion.

33   Semantics for Belief

ROBERT STALNAKER

When we attribute a belief by saying something of the form *x believes that P,* we say that a certain relation, expressed by *believes,* holds between *x* and an object of belief—something denoted by the sentential complement, *that P.* There are lots of theories about what these objects of belief are: some say they are structured complexes made up of senses or concepts; others argue that they are sentences themselves, or sets of sentences; they have been held to be *sui generis* primitive objects—unanalyzed propositions. Perhaps they are sets of possible worlds, or possible and impossible worlds, or sets of situations or partial worlds. A defense of any such account of the object of belief should be motivated by a general theoretical account of the nature of the belief relation—one that can contribute both to a philosophical explanation of intentionality and to empirical accounts of cognitive states and processes. It must also be able to contribute to an explanation of the semantic facts about belief attribution. There is some tension between these two requirements for an adequate account of the object of belief. The facts about belief attributions suggest that the objects of belief should be individuated very finely: for almost any two distinct sentential clauses, *that P* and *that Q,* one can find a context where it seems plausible to say that some-

one believes that *P,* but disbelieves that *Q.* Such facts tend to push one to take the objects of belief to be sentences, or close copies of sentences. But any theoretical account that tries to explain belief and other cognitive states as capacities and dispositions to interact with the extra-linguistic world will tend to motivate a more coarse-grained conception of content. Whatever the details of such an account, belief will relate a believer, not to a sentence, but to the information that a sentence conveys; it may be difficult to come up with a conception of information or informational content that distinguishes sentences that the facts of belief attribution seem to distinguish.

The account of the object of belief that I want to defend faces this tension in a particular acute form. Theoretical considerations, I have argued, motivate a coarse-grained conception of informational content, a conception that individuates contents in terms of their truth-conditions.[1] Such a conception of content is appropriate both to solve philosophical problems about the nature of intentionality and to give an adequate characterization of the capacities that a science of cognitive processes seeks to explain. But the assumption that sentential clauses in belief attributions refer to coarse-grained informational contents—contents that are identical if they are

Robert Stalnaker, "Semantics for Belief" from *Philosophical Topics* (15) © 1987 The Board of Trustees of the University of Arkansas. Used with the permission of the author and the University of Arkansas Press, www.uspress.com.

necessarily equivalent—seems to have consequences that are obviously false. It is obvious that anyone who is less than deductively omniscient will fail to believe everything necessarily equivalent to what he believes.

We need three assumptions to get a particular case of this kind of conflict: first, we need to assume the general account of objects of belief that says that necessarily equivalent objects of belief are identical. Second, we need to assume that some specific sentences *P* and *Q* are necessarily equivalent. Third, we need the intuitive judgment that it is possible to believe that *P* while disbelieving that *Q*. The most common response is to take the examples to refute the general account. The main burden of this response is to give and motivate some alternative theoretical account. A second more heroic response is to reject the intuitive judgments about beliefs, arguing that we don't really believe what we seem to believe. The main burden of this response is to explain away the appearances. My strategy will be different from both of these. I will question the second assumption, that sentences that appear to be necessarily equivalent really are, in the relevant context, equivalent. There is, I will suggest, more complexity and flexibility—and more context-dependence—in the relationship between sentences or sentential complements and the propositions they express or denote. Sentences necessarily equivalent in one context may be only contingently equivalent in another.

The task of defending the coarse-grained conception of informational content is a large one; in this paper I will concentrate on only a small part of it. I will adopt, as a working hypothesis, the hypothesis that objects of belief are individuated by their truth-conditions, as represented in the possible worlds framework, taking for granted the theoretical considerations that motivate this conception of content. Thoughts or propositions, I will hypothesize, are functions from possible worlds into truth-values. My task will be to sketch a general strategy, and some particular devices, for reconciling this conception of content with the phenomena concerning belief attribution.

The examples I will focus on will be examples of necessary and impossible propositions,

since this is where the apparent divergence between theory and fact becomes most dramatic. That is, I will focus on examples of statements of the form *x believes that P* or *x wonders whether P* that are problematic in the following way: on the one hand, straightforward and well-motivated semantical rules imply that the complement, *that P,* denotes a necessary truth or a necessary falsehood; on the other hand, the complement seems intuitively to denote a possible object of belief or doubt. Given our working hypothesis, necessary truths and falsehoods are not possible non-trivial objects of belief or doubt, so there is a prima facie conflict in such an example. My strategy for discovering a resolution of the conflict will be this: first, ignoring the semantical rules for a moment, try to characterize a context for the belief statement and a *contingent* possible worlds proposition defined on that context that seems intuitively to be what the statement says that the believer believes. If one can do this, it is plausible to conclude (given our working hypothesis) that that proposition is the one denoted by the sentential complement. Now comes the second and the harder part of the problem: to find a systematic way of connecting the proposition that the belief statement seems to be saying the agent believes with the semantical rules for the sentential complement that seems to be expressing that proposition; that is, to find a systematic explanation for the fact that the complement denotes, in that context, that proposition.

For example, suppose we begin with the statement *O'Leary believes that Hesperus is Mars.* Our semantical theory tells us that the proposition *that Hesperus is Mars* is necessarily false—true in no possible world. Yet clearly we can easily imagine a story in which the belief attribution seems intuitively to be true. The first task, according to the strategy I will follow, is to try to tell such a story in the language of the possible worlds framework. To do this, we ask, is there a way the world might be such that to believe that Hesperus is Mars is to believe that the world is that way? If so, then we can characterize a contingent proposition—the one that would be true if and only if the world were the way O'Leary thinks it is—that seems to be the content of O'Leary's belief. Then we can go on to attack the second, harder question: how is it possible for the expression *that Hesperus is Mars* to denote the contingent proposition that our intuitive inquiry tells us it must denote? If we can show how to provide answers to these two kinds of questions—answers that generalize to cover all the standard problematic examples—then, I think, we will have reconciled our working hypothesis with the phenomena concerning attributions of belief.

The same strategy can be applied to a simpler but parallel problem. Consider, not belief attributions, but simple assertions; not *O'Leary believes that Hesperus is Mars,* but O'Leary's assertion, *Hesperus is Mars.* The problem, in the case of this example at least, is essentially the same: given our hypothesis, there is a conflict between the theoretical conclusion that the assertion expresses a necessary falsehood and the intuitive judgment that the assertion conveys a coherent, if incorrect, piece of information. To resolve the conflict, we need to answer two questions corresponding to the two questions asked about the belief example: first, what contingent proposition seems to represent the information conveyed? Second, how can that sentence convey that information?

I will look first at the assertion question, which I have discussed in more detail elsewhere,[2] since it is easier, and it should help answer the question about belief. It should help because it is natural to assume that the information O'Leary conveys when he says *Hesperus is Mars* is the same as the information that is the belief content reported in the statement *O'Leary believes that Hesperus is Mars.* And it is also natural to assume that the explanation of how that assertion can convey that information will correspond to an explanation of how the belief attribution can attribute that belief. But the parallel is not perfect; there are some additional problematic features of belief contexts, and a solution to the assertion problem will take us only part of the way toward a solution to the problem about belief.

To help characterize assertions and their contexts, I will need to introduce and explain a piece of descriptive apparatus: the notion of a *propositional concept.* I will first define this notion in the abstract; second, I will say how I

want to apply this notion to the description of assertions in context; third, I will contrast the notion of propositional concept with a different semantical notion with which it has been sometimes confused. This contrasting notion is formally somewhat similar, but plays a quite different role in the explanation of linguistic phenomena.

A propositional concept is a function from possible worlds into propositions. Since, on our working hypothesis, propositions are themselves functions from a domain of possible worlds, a propositional concept may be thought of as a two-dimensional proposition. If, for purposes of exposition, we assume a small finite number of possible worlds, we can represent propositions by simply enumerating the truth-values for the different possible worlds. For example, if i, j and k are the relevant possible worlds, the following represents a proposition:

	i	j	k
	T	F	T

To represent a propositional concept in an analogous way, just write a line of truth-values like this for each possible world as follows:

	i	j	k
i	T	F	T
j	F	T	T
k	F	T	F

Each horizontal line represents the value of the propositional concept for the argument written to the left of that line.

To see how propositional concepts are applied to the description of assertions in context, recall two simple and, I hope, uncontroversial facts. First, acts of assertion (and all other speech acts) are performed in a context in which certain information is taken for granted as the presumed common background against which the speech act is interpreted. Second, among the items of information taken for granted or presupposed in this way by the speaker will be the proposition that the act of assertion itself is taking place. Now we can represent the presumed background information as a set of possible worlds—the possible worlds compatible with the background information. This set of alternative possibilities is the set of possible situations between which the speaker intends to distinguish with his speech acts.

In terms of this representation of the presumed background information, the second of the uncontroversial facts mentioned above comes to something like this: in every possible world that is compatible with the background information, the assertion in question is taking place. When O'Leary says *the cat is on the mat,* he is speaking not only in the actual world but also in all the other possible worlds compatible with the beliefs, presumptions, and presuppositions of those who believe, presume, or presuppose that O'Leary is speaking. In particular, he is speaking in all those possible worlds compatible with the background presuppositions that O'Leary himself is making as he speaks.

Given these facts, it follows that when someone makes an assertion, his words determine not only a proposition, but a propositional concept, relative to the possible worlds compatible with the speaker's presumed background information. We can describe various features of the speech situation, and state various constraints on the relation between assertions and their contexts, in terms of the properties of the propositional concept determined in this way. For example, some propositional concepts will be constant relative to the context, and others will not. If the point of an assertion is to convey the information contained in the proposition expressed, then it is clear that an appropriate assertion will determine a constant propositional concept.

Now let me contrast propositional concepts with a different two-dimensional semantical object: what David Kaplan, in his work on demonstratives, has called *character.*[3] Characters are like propositional concepts in that they are functions from something into content, where content is, or determines, a function from possible worlds into truth-values. Thus character, like propositional concept, suggests a two-stage process of semantic evaluation. But the arguments of Kaplan's character functions are (or may be) different from the arguments of propositional concepts, and they play a different role in semantic description and explanation.

In Kaplan's theory of demonstratives, a *context* is represented by an index—an n-tuple that specifies all the features of the situation in which a discourse takes place on which the content of the expression of some specific pragmatic language might depend. For example, if the language contains tenses, the content of some sentences will depend on time of utterance, and so one element of the index must be a time; if the language contains first and second person pronouns, the content of some sentences will depend on who is speaking, and to whom, so the index must have places specifying a speaker and an addressee. The semantical rules for such a language will assign to the sentences a function from indices into propositions; these functions are the characters of the sentences to which they are assigned. So, for example, the character of *I love you* might be a function taking an index, $\langle a, b, t \rangle$ into the proposition that is true (in a given possible world) if and only if a loves b at time t in that world.

So a character is a kind of meaning: it is associated by the semantic theory of a specific language with expression *types*. Sentences have the content they have, in a given context, *because* they have the character they have. In contrast, a propositional concept is not a kind of meaning, and is not associated with expression types of a language by the semantic theory for that language. Propositional concepts are determined by particular utterance *tokens* and their contexts. The same sentence type, with the same meaning, used in different contexts may determine different propositional concepts. And utterances don't have the content they have *because* they determine a certain propositional concept. This gets things backwards. Rather, an utterance determines a certain propositional concept because it has the content it has in the various possible worlds in which that particular concrete utterance token exists.

Not only is a propositional concept not a meaning, it is not even a function of the meaning of the sentence whose utterance determines it. To determine the relevant propositional concept, one needs to know, not only what the sentence used in fact means—what it means in the actual world—but also what it means in the various alternative possible worlds in which the utterance takes place. Since meaning may vary from world to world, an eternal sentence (a sentence that, in Kaplan's terminology, has constant character) may determine a variable propositional concept, and may determine different propositional concepts on different occasions of use.

So, despite some superficial similarities, character and propositional concept are quite different notions. They belong to different theories—theories that are applied at different stages in the explanation of speech. And they are not competing notions: neither can do the job that the other was designed to do.

Now with the notion of a propositional concept at hand to help us describe the situation, let us apply the strategy outlined above to the assertion problem. Consider O'Leary's assertion, *Hesperus is Mars*. If we approach the question "What is O'Leary saying?" not by asking about the semantical rules for the sentence O'Leary is using, but instead by asking what the world would be like if what O'Leary seems intuitively to be saying were true, then an answer is not hard to find. There are possible worlds that resemble the actual world with respect to the way the heavens appear to the untrained eye, but in which the solar system is quite differently arranged. The solar system in these worlds has the same planets as our world has, and they have the same names. But in these counterfactual worlds, Mars appears in the evening at the very place where Venus in fact appears, and it has quite the same appearance as Venus in fact has (at least to the untrained eye). Ancient astronomers in these worlds called this planet that appears in the evening (not of course knowing that it was a planet) by a name from which descends the name *Hesperus*—a name used by the modern English speakers of these counterfactual worlds to refer to that planet.

Now a man like O'Leary, who has the superficial knowledge of the solar system that most of us have, and who is inclined sometimes to misremember what he has read or heard, might well believe that a world of the kind I have described is the actual world. If he did believe this, he might express his belief by saying "Hesperus is Mars." And if he did say this, I think we would all conclude that he was saying that the world was something like the world I have described.

Call the actual world *i* and some representative from the class of counterfactual worlds I have described *j*. The conclusion I am claiming we all should reach is that the content of O'Leary's assertion seems to be the contingent proposition that is false at *i* and true at *j*.

Now let us look at the semantical rules for the sentence *Hesperus is Mars*. Both *Hesperus* and *Mars* are proper names. Suppose Kripke has convinced us all that proper names are rigid designators—singular terms that refer to the same individual relative to all possible worlds. Assume also that *is* expresses identity in this context. From these assumptions, together with the assumption that Hesperus is, in fact, distinct from Mars, it follows that the content of O'Leary's assertion is the proposition that is necessarily false—false even at *j*, the possible world that is the way O'Leary seems to be saying that the world is. So the result of applying otherwise well-motivated semantical rules conflicts with our holistic intuitive judgment.

To resolve the conflict, let us look not just at the proposition determined, but at the whole propositional concept: ask not just what does *Hesperus is Mars* say (according to the semantical rules)—what is its truth-value at various alternative possible worlds—but also what *would* it say if it were said in various alternative possible worlds. If we consider just the two possible worlds I have labeled *i* and *j*, the propositional concept is this one:

	i	*j*
i	F	F
j	T	T

In *j*, "Hesperus" rigidly designates Mars, and so the sentence *Hesperus is Mars* expresses (according to the semantical rules we are assuming) the necessary truth.

Note that while neither of the horizontal propositions that make up this propositional concept is the contingent proposition that O'Leary seems to be expressing, there is a proposition determined by the propositional concept that is the intuitively right one: this is the *diagonal proposition*—the one that for each possible world is true if and only if the horizontal proposition expressed in that world is true at that world. This suggests the following hypothesis: *Under certain conditions, the content of an assertion is not the proposition determined by the ordinary semantical rules, but instead the diagonal proposition of the propositional concept determined.* To make this hypothesis precise, we need only spell out the conditions under which the operation is to be performed. I have tried to go some way toward doing this in Chapter 4 [not reprinted here]. The general strategy is a Gricean one.[4] There are various independently motivated pragmatic maxims governing discourse. When a speaker seems to be violating one of these in a blatant way, a cooperative conversational strategy may require that the addressee reinterpret what is said in a way that makes it conform to the maxims. One way to reinterpret—a way that is appropriate to the violation of a particular pragmatic maxim— is to diagonalize: to take the assertion to express the diagonal proposition of the propositional concept determined by the utterance and its context. This operation yields intuitively plausible results, and it helps to reconcile semantical rules that work well in most contexts with apparently recalcitrant phenomena.

I want to turn now from the assertion problem to the problem about belief. The main problem concerns the way beliefs are attributed to others: that is, it concerns the relationship between the sentential complement used by a speaker to attribute a belief to someone and the proposition that the subject of the attribution is said to believe. But let us look first at belief from the believer's point of view. Propositional concepts can help us to understand the relationship between the content of a belief and the way that a believer might represent his belief to himself. Imagine O'Leary not asserting anything about the solar system, but just thinking about it. He might be out on a clear evening, looking up at that so-called star he has seen so often, thinking to himself, *that's Mars.* The content of that

thought is obviously something like the contingently false proposition described above. A hypothesis similar to the one sketched above for the assertion example will explain how that mental event—that act of thought—can have that content.[5]

Finally, let us look at belief attribution: statements of the form *x believes that P.* There is an additional problem that arises here, a problem that prevents us from simply generalizing, in a mechanical way, the explanation of the problematic assertions to an explanation of problematic attributions of belief. The problem arises from the following difference between the assertion case and the belief attribution case: in the case of assertion, the speaker—the person who chooses the words to be uttered—is the same person as the one whose attitudes the words are chosen to express. We have only one point of view to contend with—that of the speaker. But in the belief case, the speaker's point of view will normally be different from that of the subject to whom the attitude is attributed. The subject's language, if any, may be different from the speaker's; the background information against which the speaker's utterance is to be evaluated may be very different from the information that might be exploited by the subject whose belief is described in the utterance. So the means available to the subject for putting his belief into words might be very different from the means available to the speaker.

This contrast between the points of view of speaker and subject affects the possibility of the diagonalization explanation in belief attribution cases because it makes it difficult to construct an appropriate propositional concept, and difficult to generalize about when a sentential complement should be interpreted by a diagonal proposition. In the assertion case, it is relatively clear how a sentence determines a propositional concept, relative to the possible worlds compatible with the presuppositions of the speaker. It is clear because of the fact that it will be presupposed by the speaker (that is, it will be true in all possible worlds compatible with the speaker's context) that the utterance event is taking place. But to extend the kind of explanation I am proposing to the belief attribution case, we need to define a propositional concept not just for the possible words compatible with the presuppositions of the speaker, but also for the possible worlds that are, or might be, compatible with the beliefs of the subject of the attribution.[6] When the beliefs of the subject are very different from the presuppositions of the speaker, it is not always obvious how this is to be done.

Consider the example with which we began: *O'Leary believes that Hesperus is Mars.* Suppose this is said by Daniels to me. Of course Daniels and I both know that Hesperus is Venus, and not Mars. There are no possible worlds compatible with the background presuppositions of *our* conversation in which the solar system is arranged so that Mars appears where Venus in fact appears in the evening. And O'Leary—the subject—is not participating in our conversation, and does not know about it. We cannot ask what proposition the complement of Daniels' statement about O'Leary expresses in each of the possible worlds compatible with O'Leary's beliefs. We cannot ask this since that statement does not exist in all of those possible worlds. Nevertheless, if required to extend the propositional concept, to define it for those possible worlds, it is intuitively pretty clear, at least for this example, how we should do it. We ask something like the following question: If Daniels were to utter the sounds he is uttering in a possible world compatible with O'Leary's beliefs, what would the content of those sounds be? If the solar system were arranged so that Mars appears in the evening where Venus in fact does, then Daniels and I, as well as O'Leary, would use the name *Hesperus* to refer to Mars. And so, according to the semantical rules in that world, Daniels' sentential complement, *that Hesperus is Mars,* expresses a necessary truth. If we extend the propositional concept in this way, defining it for the situations that might, for all Daniels and I are presupposing, be compatible with O'Leary's beliefs, then the diagonal of that propositional concept will be the proposition that seems, intuitively, to be the one O'Leary is said to believe.

What if O'Leary speaks some language other than English? That will make no difference to the explanation, so long as he has some acquaintance with Venus as it appears in the evening, either through having seen it or through having acquired some name that denotes Venus because Venus appears where it does in the evening. The propositional concept we construct is the one not for the sentence as O'Leary would use or understand it, but for the sentence as the speaker and addressee would use and understand it if they were in the possible worlds relative to which the propositional concept is being defined. Because *our* name *Hesperus* would denote Mars if the solar system had been differently arranged in a certain way, *we* can use the clause *that Hesperus is Mars* to refer to the proposition that the solar system is differently arranged in that way.

O'Leary's belief about Hesperus and Mars is a belief about the solar system, and not a belief about the English language. But the diagonalization explanation will also work for cases where the belief in question is a linguistic belief, expressed in the material mode. Consider this example, adapted from an argument of Alonzo Church and discussed by Tyler Burge[7]: *Alfred believes that a fortnight is a period of ten days.* It is intuitively clear that if what this statement says is true, then in possible worlds compatible with Alfred's beliefs, *fortnight,* in English, means *period of ten days.* The proposition Alfred is said to believe, it seems plausible to suppose, is the one that is true in possible worlds with that rule of English, and false in others. That proposition is the diagonal of the appropriate propositional concept.

Church, in his discussion of a related example, notes the failure of a translation test.[8] Whatever the example sentence says, it is clear that its translation into German cannot say the same thing. German has no word for *fortnight,* so the German translation of that word would have to be the same as the translation of the phrase *period of fourteen days.* Church, as I understand him, uses this failure to argue for the conclusion that the example sentence does not succeed in saying what it seems to be saying. It ought, Church suggests, to be reformulated in explicitly metalinguistic terms. But we can explain the failure of the translation test without drawing this conclusion. According to the kind of account I am suggesting, belief attributions are, in cases requiring diagonalization, highly context-dependent. Translation into another language will alter the possible contexts of use for a sentence, and may do so in ways that affect the possible interpretations of the sentence. In the example sentence, it is essential to the context of use that the language being spoken be English, and this is why translation into German yields a sentence that cannot be used to say what the English sentence says.

Of course we do not always diagonalize, and where we do not, we can use language and concepts not available to the subject to attribute belief. If Alfred believes that Bernard will be gone for fourteen days, we can truly say *Alfred believes that Bernard will be gone for a fortnight,* whatever Alfred's beliefs about the word *fortnight.* We can also, in *de re* or relational belief attributions, use referring expressions not available to the subject. So, for example, if O'Leary and I can see that there is one and only one man in the room wearing a faded denim leisure suit, and if that man is in fact van Fraassen, and if Daniels believes that van Fraassen is a spy, then I can truly say to O'Leary, *Daniels believes that the man in the faded denim leisure suit is a spy,* even if Daniels is not present, and does not know that van Fraassen even owns a faded denim leisure suit.

The situation gets slightly more complicated with examples that are *de re* belief attributions but that also require diagonalization. Consider the following examples borrowed and adapted from a paper by Bas van Fraassen.[9] *Daniels believes that the man in the faded denim leisure suit is Kaplan* (said by me to O'Leary in circumstances like those described above), and *Daniels believes that I am Kaplan* (said by van Fraassen). What would the world be like if the belief that these statements seem to attribute to Daniels were true? (I assume that both statements attribute the same belief to him.) It would be a world in which Daniels' use of the name *Kaplan*—the particular use that in fact refers to David Kaplan, Professor of Philosophy at UCLA and author of a monumental but still unpublished manuscript on demonstratives—referred instead to Bas van Fraassen. That is, it would be a possible world in which the correct historical explanation of Daniels' use of the name *Kaplan* (in cases where *in fact* it refers to

David Kaplan) involves, in the relevant way, van Fraassen instead of Kaplan. We will get the proposition that is true in just those possible worlds if we diagonalize the propositional *function* concept for the predicate *being Kaplan,* and then predicate the result of van Fraassen. In this way, we can apply the diagonalization strategy to *de re* or relational belief attributions as well as to *de dicto* or notional attributions.

It is interesting to compare these last two examples with examples obtained by reversing subject and predicate in the complements. *Daniels believes that Kaplan is the man in the faded denim leisure suit,* and *Daniels believes that Kaplan is* I. Despite the symmetry of identity, these sentences seem clearly to say something different from the ones they were derived from. I think the first would normally be appropriate only if Daniels were present, and true only if he were aware of someone wearing the outfit described. I am not sure what the second sentence would be trying to say.

The procedure I am proposing for extending propositional concepts so that the diagonalization strategy can be applied to problematic belief attributions takes examples case by case. It is not, as yet, very satisfactory if we are looking for a systematic way to explain why the complements of belief attributions denote the propositions that they seem to denote. But if, using this procedure, we can find a possible worlds proposition that is a plausible candidate to be the object of belief being attributed in the various problematic examples, then we will at least have a good way of answering the first of the questions that our working hypothesis suggested that we ask. That is, if we can do this, we will be able to reconcile the hypothesis with the phenomena by finding possible worlds propositions for the recalcitrant examples. And it will not be completely mysterious how these propositions can be expressed by the sentences that seem to express them.

ACKNOWLEDGMENTS

An earlier version of this paper was written while I was a National Endowment of the Humanities Fellow at the Center for Advanced Study in the Behavioral Sciences in Stanford. I am grateful to both institutions for support.

NOTES

1. In Stalnaker (1984).
2. "Assertion," reprinted in this volume.
3. Kaplan (1989).
4. See e.g. Grice (1989).
5. In "Indexical Belief," I consider in more detail some now familiar problems concerning belief from the believer's point of view, applying the diagonalization strategy to them.
6. The possible worlds compatible with what the speaker presupposed define the basic context for the interpretation of the speaker's speech act. In the case of a belief attribution, the possible worlds that may, for all the speaker presupposes, be compatible with what the subject of the attribution believes define what I have called the *derived context*. This is the context relative to which the sentential complement is interpreted. In "Belief Attribution and Context," I argue that some of the same pragmatic maxims that constrain the relation between speech acts and basic contexts will constrain the relation between content attribution clauses and derived contexts.
7. Burge (1978).
8. Church (1954).
9. See van Fraassen (1979). This is a descendant of an unpublished paper that suggested these examples.

REFERENCES

Burge, T. (1978). Belief and synonymy, *Journal of Philosophy* 75: 119–38.
Church, A. (1954). Intensional isomorphism and identity of belief, *Philosophical Studies* 5: 65–73.
Grice, P. (1989). *Studies in the Way of Words,* Harvard University Press, Cambridge, Mass.
Kaplan, D. (1989). Demonstratives, in J. Almog el al. (eds). *Themes from Kaplan,* Oxford University Press, Oxford, 481–563.
Stalnaker, R. (1984). *Inquiry,* Bradford Books, MIT Press, Cambridge, Mass.
———. (1988). Belief attribution and context, in R. Grimm and D. Merrill (eds.), *Contents of Thought,* U. of Arizona Press, Tucson, 1988, 140–156.
Van Frassen, B. C. (1979). Propositional attitudes in weak pragmatics, *Studia Logica* 38: 365–74.

SUGGESTED FURTHER READING

Austin, David F., *What Is the Meaning of "This"? A Puzzle about Demonstrative Belief* (Ithaca: Cornell University Press, 1990).
Barwise, Jon, "Scenes and Other Situations," *Journal of Philosophy* 78 (1981): 369–397.
Barwise, Jon and John Perry, *Situations and Attitudes* (Cambridge: MIT Press, 1983).
Carnap, Rudolf, *Meaning and Necessity,* 2d ed. (Chicago: University of Chicago Press, 1956).
Church, Alonzo, "On Carnap's Analysis of Statements of Assertion and Belief," *Analysis* 10 (1950): 97–99.
Crimmins, Mark, *Talk about Belief* (Cambridge: MIT Press, 1992).
Crimmins, Mark, "Hesperus and Phosporus: Sense, Pretense, and Reference," *Philosophical Review* (1998): 1–48.
Crimmins, Mark and John Perry, "The Prince and the Phone Booth: Reporting Puzzling Beliefs," *Journal of Philosophy* 86 (1989): 685–711.
Hintikka, Jaakko, *Knowledge and Belief* (Ithaca: Cornell University Press, 1962).
Hintikka, Jaakko, "Semantics for Propositional Attitudes," in *Philosophical Logic,* ed. J. W. Davis et al. (Dordrecht: D. Reidel, 1969), pp. 21–45.
Loar, Brian, *Mind and Meaning* (Cambridge: Cambridge University Press, 1981).

Marcus, Ruth Barcan, "A Proposed Solution to a Puzzle about Belief," in *Midwest Studies in Philosophy,* vol. 6, ed. Peter A. French, Theodore E. Uehling, Jr., and Howard K. Wettstein (Minneapolis: University of Minnesota Press, 1981), pp. 501–510.
Marcus, Ruth Barcan, "Rationality and Believing the Impossible," *Journal of Philosophy* 80 (1983): 321–329.
Partee, Barbara, "Belief-Sentences and the Limits of Semantics," in *Processes, Beliefs and Questions,* ed. Stanley Peters and Esa Saarinen (Dordrecht: D. Reidel, 1982), pp. 88–106.
Quine, W. V., "Reference and Modality," in *From a Logical Point of View,* 2d ed. (New York: Harper & Row, 1961), pp. 139–159.
Richard, Mark, *Propositional Attitudes: An Essay on Thoughts and How We Ascribe Them* (New York: Cambridge University Press, 1990).
Salmon, Nathan and Scott Soames, *Propositions and Attitudes* (New York: Oxford University Press, 1988).
Sosa, David, "The Import of the Puzzle about Belief," *Philosophical Review* 105 (1996): 373–402.
Stroll, Avrum, "Proper Names, Names, and Fictive Objects," *Journal of Philosophy* 95 (1998): 522–534.
Van Fraassen, Bas. "Propositional Attitudes in Weak Pragmatics," *Studia Logica* 38 (1979): 365–374.

VI METAPHOR AND PRETENSE

Any adequate theory of language or language use must be able to account for not just the wide variety of literal utterances but also those used as figures of speech and in fiction. Of the figures of speech, metaphor is the most salient. Philosophers of language have puzzled about how to handle metaphor and other figures of speeches for a long time. A more recent worry is how to handle various aspects of fictional language. In recent years, many philosophers have thought of fiction as a mode of pretense. Two articles in this section deal with metaphor and two with pretense. A standard definition of metaphor is "a figure of speech in which a word or phrase denoting one kind of object or idea is used in place of another in order to suggest similarity between them." According to one view, metaphors always involve comparisons between two things. One version of this, the simile theory, is that metaphors are abbreviations of similes. Thus, the metaphor, "My lover is a treasure," is an abbreviation of "My lover is like a treasure." One objection to this is that metaphors are always or typically false, if taken literally, and similes are always or typically true. A variation on the simile theory is the semantic interaction theory, according to which two semantic components, one intended literally and one intended nonliterally, interact with each other. One objection to this view is that the keyword, "interaction," is metaphorical and thus fails to state literally and precisely how metaphors work. Another objection is that there are metaphors that contain no literal component in the sense intended by the interaction theorist. For example, referring to two arrogant people who came to an agreement, someone might say, "Prima donnas embraced."

As explained in an earlier section, there are two basic approaches to meaning: a semantic approach and a pragmatic approach. Donald Davidson's article, "What Metaphors Mean," is a semantic treatment of metaphor that is consistent with his general theory of meaning presented in "Truth and Meaning." Much of Davidson's article is valuable for the criticisms it makes of traditional views, both the simile theory and Max Black's interaction theory.

A. P. Martinich in "A Theory of Metaphor" explains metaphor within Grice's pragmatic theory of conversation and Searle's theory of speech acts. Metaphors are similar to indirect speech acts in that both are conversationally implied due to the nonfulfillment of conversational maxims. They are unlike indirect speech acts insofar as the speaker only "makes as if to say" what would normally be said by the words he or she utters. Martinich no longer holds exactly the views expressed in his article. Without abandoning a pragmatic approach, he agrees with Davidson that "understanding a metaphor is as much a creative endeavor as making a metaphor, and as little guided by rules." An audience interprets what a speaker means by trying to incorporate an understanding of the speaker's beliefs and behavior (linguistic and nonlinguistic) in the simplest, most plausible, least disruptive way. In other words, the audience attempts to achieve a cognitive equilibrium when confronted with any situation.

Fiction has sometimes been described as pretending, and recently the concept of pretending has been applied to a wide array of philosophical problems. "Fictionalism," as it is often called, has been used in aesthetics, meta-ethics, and the philosophy of mathematics. Several philosophers think that the concept of pretending or linguistically "doing as if" is also fruitful for solving several different problems in the philosophy of language. To put this in another way, several philosophers treat the sentences that give rise to the problems as playing a role in a pretense. In the selections by Mark Crimmins and Frederick Kroon, pretending is held to be operating in the use of negative existential statements, identity statements, sentences expressing psychological attitudes, and proper names of both fiction and reality.

In "Hesperus and Phosphorus: Sense, Pretense, and Reference," Mark Crimmins suggests that philosophers take seriously a certain phenomenological experience. In line with a comment by Russell, Crimmins claims that when he asserts identities between, say, Hesperus and Phosphorus or between some child and the adult that child becomes, he claims that he experiences the object of the identity as two objects. This is part of the phenomenology of asserting identity. (The experience of twoness is not part of my phenomenology.) Crimmins's more important point is that a speaker's use of proper names of fictional characters, for example, in the sentence "Ann is as clever as Holmes and more modest than Watson," involves him in "a shallow pretense: a shared, conspiratorial make-believe that we can refer with the names 'Holmes' and 'Watson'." The speaker is making as if to refer to Holmes and Watson but cannot really be referring to them, because they don't exist. He claims that "to understand me, you have to see that I intend my utterance to be *as if* a statement comparing Ann to two other people, and *only as if* that."

While Crimmins uses fictionalism to advance the case for the causal or direct reference theory, Frederick Kroon uses it to advance the case for neo-descriptivism. According to the latter theory, the meaning of a proper name is "given by (a cluster of) egocentric properties in terms of broadly causal relationships between a speaker and his environment," as Kroon says. Kroon accepts Crimmins's claims about the phenomenology of the experience of the use of names, but he criticizes Crimmins for not saying enough about the content of modes of presentation and for not giving the right meaning to the expressions "is identical with" and "exists."

As impressive as the work of Crimmins and Kroon is, I think that it rests on sand because Kendall Walton, from whom they take the concept of pretending, has not given a theoretically adequate account of pretending.

The cogency of Crimmins's views depends on the clarity of the concept of pretending. He relies on Kendall Walton's explication of pretending in *Mimesis as Make-Believe* (Harvard University Press, 1990). There is reason to be dubious about the theoretical value of this concept of pretending. Pretending is usually explicated as making-believe. *The Oxford English Dictionary* gives two definitions for "make believe": (i) "to cause people to believe," and (ii) "to pretend to do something; to simulate a belief *that*" ("make" IV.52.e). Definition (i) is inconsistent with pretense theory. According to that theory, fiction is precisely not the causing of people to believe what appears to be said. If it is a fiction that a clock is striking thirteen, as it does in *1984*, the text is not causing people to believe that the clock is striking thirteen. The whole point of pretense theory is to neutralize the normal belief inducing function of statements. The second clause of (ii) "to simulate a belief *that*" seems to fit pretense theory. It is plausible that to pretend to be trapped in a box, as a mime might, involves simulating a belief that one is trapped in a box. A person trapped in a box may assume bodily positions similar to those assumed by the mime. Nonetheless, definition (ii) is no help to the pretense theory because the analysis of "to simulate a belief *that*" is as obscure as making-believe is. Simulating a belief is another way of pretending, as the beginning of (ii) indicates. But since making-believe is supposed to explicate pretending, pretending cannot be used to explicate making-believe. The main entry for "pretending" in the *Oxford English Dictionary* is not any more helpful. Many of the definitions are too general ("to intend") or clearly irrelevant to fiction ("to purpose, design, plan"). The relevant ones are uninformative: "make pretence; to make believe" (item 15). The mutual explication of pretending as making-believe and making-believe as pretending indicates that the definitions are circular and hence uninformative.

One might argue that these dictionary definitions are irrelevant to the intelligibility of pretending as making-believe because the concept that is used in pretense theory is the one that Kendall Walton explicated in *Mimesis as Make-Believe* and his explication amounts to something approaching a precise definition of pretending. For Walton, fiction as make-believe is to be analyzed as a special form of imaginative activity, specifically "exercises of the imagination involving *props*" (Walton 1990: 12). What Walton says about imagining is unhelpful. For him, imagining can be done with or without images, deliberately or spontaneously, occurrently or nonoccurrently, solitarily or collectively, with or without "props" (Walton 1990: 13–19). Because all of these pairs of properties are either contradictories or virtually so, we are no closer to understanding what imagining is than we were before we were given this information. Walton adds that imagining is also not entertaining or believing a proposition. It cannot be entertaining a proposition because entertaining a proposition is always occurrent but imagining is not (Walton 1990: 19). (He does not say whether all entertaining a proposition is imagining a proposition.)

Imagining, according to Walton, cannot be believing because imaginings are never true. (It is not obvious that this is true. If someone says, "I imagine that Sandra Day O'Connor retired when she did in part in order to ensure that a Republican justice would replace her," what the speaker imagines may well be true.) Although it is true that imagining is not believing, it is not so obvious that believing does not involve imagining. When a person reads a historical narrative, the reader often imagines the events described. This is not to say that the reader has an image for each event. Believing a historical statement would seem to be preceded by or to presuppose understanding the statement, and this understanding seems to include imagining or thinking of it. It is hardly possible to understand that Napoleon attacked with three divisions without imagining or thinking of the proposition that he attacked with three divisions. If proponents of pretense theory would object that believing requires understanding but not imagining, then they need to explain what the difference is. However, it seems to me that trying to distinguish between understanding and imagining a proposition is irrelevant, because understanding historical works and fictional works involves the same cognitive processes whatever they are. The relevant difference concerns the different connections that fiction and history have to truth or evidence (cf. Walton 1990: 77).

The primary aim of history, but not fiction, is to express truths about the past, based on certain kinds of evidence. (The author of a history or fiction may have a different personal aim. The author of a work of historical fiction may have as his primary aim the expression of historical truth; a historian may have as his aim the telling of a good story.)

Both Crimmins and Kroon are happy to settle for "shallow pretense," because they recognize that full-blown imaginative engagement is not operating in the uses of the expressions they are discussing, but I do not think that a weak commitment to a defective concept can provide an adequate foundation for a theory.

I believe that the key concept for explaining fiction is not that of pretending but that of suspending a maxim, as explained in the introduction ("Speech Acts") to Section II. Fiction, roughly, is telling a story with the maxim of quality suspended. This kind of storytelling creates institutional facts, which include fictional objects as components. Referring to fictional characters is referring to institutional objects.

34 What Metaphors Mean

DONALD DAVIDSON

Metaphor is the dreamwork of language and, like all dreamwork, its interpretation reflects as much on the interpreter as on the originator. The interpretation of dreams requires collaboration between a dreamer and a waker, even if they be the same person; and the act of interpretation is itself a work of the imagination. So too understanding a metaphor is as much a creative endeavor as making a metaphor, and as little guided by rules.

These remarks do not, except in matters of degree, distinguish metaphor from more routine linguistic transactions: all communication by speech assumes the interplay of inventive construction and inventive construal. What metaphor adds to the ordinary is an achievement that uses no semantic resources beyond the resources on which the ordinary depends. There are no instructions for devising metaphors; there is no manual for determining what a metaphor "means" or "says"; there is no test for metaphor that does not call for taste.[1] A metaphor implies a kind and degree of artistic success; there are no unsuccessful metaphors, just as there are no unfunny jokes. There are tasteless metaphors, but these are turns that nevertheless have brought something off, even if it were not worth bringing off or could have been brought off better.

This paper is concerned with what metaphors mean, and its thesis is that metaphors mean what the words, in their most literal interpretation, mean, and nothing more. Since this thesis flies in the face of contemporary views with which I am familiar, much of what I have to say is critical. But I think the picture of metaphor that emerges when error and confusion are cleared away makes metaphor a more, not a less, interesting phenomenon.

The central mistake against which I shall be inveighing is the idea that a metaphor has, in addition to its literal sense or meaning, another sense or meaning. This idea is common to many who have written about metaphor: it is found in the works of literary critics like Richards, Empson, and Winters; philosophers from Aristotle to Max Black; psychologists from Freud and earlier, to Skinner and later; and linguists from Plato to Uriel Weinreich and George Lakoff. The idea takes many forms, from the relatively simple in Aristotle to the relatively complex in Black. The idea appears in writings which maintain that a literal paraphrase of a metaphor can be produced, but it is also shared by those who hold that typically no literal paraphrase can be found. Some stress the special insight metaphor can inspire and make much of the fact that ordinary language, in its usual functioning, yields no such insight. Yet this view too sees metaphor as a form of communication alongside ordinary communication; it conveys truths or falsehoods about the world much as plainer language does, though the message may be considered more exotic, profound, or cunningly garbed.

The concept of metaphor as primarily a vehicle for conveying ideas, even if unusual ones, seems to me as wrong as the parent idea that a metaphor has a special meaning. I agree with the view that metaphors cannot be paraphrased, but I think this is not because metaphors say something too novel for literal expression but because there is nothing there to paraphrase. Paraphrase, whether possible or not, is appropriate to what is *said:* we try, in paraphrase, to say it another way. But if I am right, a metaphor doesn't say anything beyond its literal meaning (nor does its maker say anything, in using the metaphor, beyond the literal). This is not, of course, to deny that a metaphor has a point, nor that that point can be brought out by using further words.

In the past those who have denied that metaphor has a cognitive content in addition to the literal have often been out to show that metaphor is confusing, merely emotive, unsuited to serious, scientific, or philosophic discourse. My views should not be associated with this tradition. Metaphor is a legitimate device not only in literature but in science, philosophy, and the law: it is effective in praise and abuse, prayer and promotion, description and prescription. For the most part I don't disagree with Max Black, Paul Henle, Nelson Goodman, Monroe Beardsley, and the rest in their accounts of what metaphor accomplishes, except that I think it accomplishes more and that what is additional is different in kind.

My disagreement is with the explanation of how metaphor works its wonders. To anticipate: I depend on the distinction between what words mean and what they are used to do. I think metaphor belongs exclusively to the domain of use. It is something brought off by the imaginative employment of words and sentences and depends entirely on the ordinary meanings of those words and hence on the ordinary meanings of the sentences they comprise.

It is no help in explaining how words work in metaphor to posit metaphorical or figurative meanings, or special kinds of poetic or meta-phorical truth. These ideas don't explain metaphor, metaphor explains them. Once we understand a metaphor we can call what we grasp the "metaphorical truth" and (up to a point) say what the "metaphorical meaning" is. But simply to lodge this meaning in the metaphor is like explaining why a pill puts you to sleep by saying it has a dormative power. Literal meaning and literal truth-conditions can be assigned to words and sentences apart from particular contexts of use. This is why adverting to them has genuine explanatory power.

I shall try to establish my negative views about what metaphors mean and introduce my limited positive claims by examining some false theories of the nature of metaphor.

A metaphor makes us attend to some likeness, often a novel or surprising likeness, between two or more things. This trite and true observation leads, or seems to lead, to a conclusion concerning the meaning of metaphors. Consider ordinary likeness or similarity: two roses are similar because they share the property of being a rose; two infants are similar by virtue of their infanthood. Or, more simply, roses are similar because each is a rose, infants, because each is an infant.

Suppose someone says "Tolstoy was once an infant." How is the infant Tolstoy like other infants? The answer comes pat: by virtue of exhibiting the property of infanthood, that is, leaving out some of the wind, by virtue of being an infant. If we tire of the phrase "by virtue of," we can, it seems, be plainer still by saying the infant Tolstoy shares with other infants the fact that the predicate "is an infant" applies to him; given the word "infant," we have no trouble saying exactly how the infant Tolstoy resembles other infants. We could do it without the word "infant"; all we need is other words that mean the same. The end result is the same. Ordinary similarity depends on groupings established by the ordinary meanings of words. Such similarity is natural and unsurprising to the extent that familiar ways of grouping objects are tied to usual meanings of usual words.

A famous critic said that Tolstoy was "a great moralizing infant." The Tolstoy referred to here is obviously not the infant Tolstoy but Tolstoy the adult writer; this is metaphor. Now in what sense is Tolstoy the writer similar to an infant? What we are to do, perhaps, is think of the class of objects which includes all ordinary infants and, in addition, the adult Tolstoy and then ask ourselves what special, surprising property the members of this class have in common. The appealing thought is that given patience we could come as close as need be to specifying the appropriate property. In any case, we could do the job perfectly if we found words that meant exactly what the metaphorical "infant" means. The important point, from my perspective, is not whether we can find the perfect other words but the assumption that there is something to be attempted, a metaphorical meaning to be matched. So far I have been doing no more than crudely sketching how the concept of meaning may have crept into the analysis of metaphor, and the answer I have suggested is that since what we think of as garden variety similarity goes with what we think of as garden variety meanings, it is natural to posit unusual or metaphorical meanings to help explain the similarities metaphor promotes.

The idea, then, is that in metaphor certain words take on new, or what are often called "extended," meanings. When we read, for example, that "the Spirit of God moved upon the face of the waters," we are to regard the word "face" as having an extended meaning (I disregard further metaphor in the passage). The extension applies, as it happens, to what philosophers call the extension of the word, that is, the class of entities to which it refers. Here the word "face" applies to ordinary faces, and to waters in addition.

This account cannot, at any rate, be complete, for if in these contexts the words "face" and "infant" apply correctly to waters and to the adult Tolstoy, then waters really do have faces and Tolstoy literally was an infant, and all sense of metaphor evaporates. If we are to think of words in metaphors as directly going about their business of applying to what they properly do apply to, there is no difference between metaphor and the introduction of a new term into our vocabulary: to make a metaphor is to murder it.

What has been left out is any appeal to the original meaning of the word. Whether or not metaphor depends on new or extended mean-

ings, it certainly depends in some way on the original meanings; an adequate account of metaphor must allow that the primary or original meanings of words remain active in their metaphorical setting.

Perhaps, then, we can explain metaphor as a kind of ambiguity: in the context of a metaphor, certain words have either a new or an original meaning, and the force of the metaphor depends on our uncertainty as we waver between the two meanings. Thus when Melville writes that "Christ was a chronometer," the effect of metaphor is produced by our taking "chronometer" first in its ordinary sense and then in some extraordinary or metaphorical sense.

It is hard to see how this theory can be correct. For the ambiguity in the word, if there is any, is due to the fact that in ordinary contexts it means one thing and in the metaphorical context it means something else; but in the metaphorical context we do not necessarily hesitate over its meaning. When we do hesitate, it is usually to decide which of a number of metaphorical interpretations we shall accept; we are seldom in doubt that what we have is a metaphor. At any rate, the effectiveness of the metaphor easily outlasts the end of uncertainty over the interpretation of the metaphorical passage. Metaphor cannot, therefore, owe its effect to ambiguity of this sort.[2]

Another brand of ambiguity may appear to offer a better suggestion. Sometimes a word will, in a single context, bear two meanings where we are meant to remember and to use both. Or, if we think of wordhood as implying sameness of meaning, then we may describe the situation as one in which what appears as a single word is in fact two. When Shakespeare's Cressida is welcomed bawdily into the Grecian camp, Nestor says, "Our general doth salute you with a kiss." Here we are to take "general" two ways: once as applying to Agamemnon, who is the general; and once, since she is kissing everyone, as applying to no one in particular, but everyone in general. We really have a conjunction of two sentences: our general, Agamemnon, salutes you with a kiss; and everyone in general is saluting you with a kiss.

This is a legitimate device, a pun, but it is not the same device as metaphor. For in metaphor there is no essential need of reiteration; whatever meanings we assign the words, they keep through every correct reading of the passage.

A plausible modification of the last suggestion would be to consider the key word (or words) in a metaphor as having two different kinds of meaning at once, a literal and a figurative meaning. Imagine the literal meaning as latent, something that we are aware of, that can work on us without working in the context, while the figurative meaning carries the direct load. And finally, there must be a rule which connects the two meanings, for otherwise the explanation lapses into a form of the ambiguity theory. The rule, at least for many typical cases of metaphor, says that in its metaphorical role the word applies to everything that it applies to in its literal role, and then some.[3]

This theory may seem complex, but it is strikingly similar to what Frege proposed to account for the behavior of referring terms in modal sentences and sentences about propositional attitudes like belief and desire. According to Frege, each referring term has two (or more) meanings, one which fixes its reference in ordinary contexts and another which fixes its reference in the special contexts created by modal operators or psychological verbs. The rule connecting the two meanings may be put like this: the meaning of the word in the special contexts makes the reference in those contexts to be identical with the meaning in ordinary contexts.

Here is the whole picture, putting Frege together with a Fregean view of metaphor: we are to think of a word as having, in addition to its mundane field of application or reference, two special or supermundane fields of application, one for metaphor and the other for modal contexts and the like. In both cases the original meaning remains to do its work by virtue of a rule which relates the various meanings.

Having stressed the possible analogy between metaphorical meaning and the Fregean meanings for oblique contexts, I turn to an imposing difficulty in maintaining the analogy. You are entertaining a visitor from Saturn by trying to teach him how to use the word "floor." You go through the familiar dodges, leading him from floor to floor, pointing and stamping and repeating the word. You prompt him to make experiments, tapping objects tentatively with his tentacle while rewarding his right and wrong tries. You want him to come out knowing not only that these particular objects or surfaces are floors but also how to tell a floor when one is in sight or touch. The skit you are putting on doesn't *tell* him what he needs to know, but with luck it helps him to learn it.

Should we call this process learning something about the world or learning something about language? An odd question, since what is learned is that a bit of language refers to a bit of the world. Still, it is easy to distiguish between the business of learning the meaning of a word and using the word once the meaning is learned. Comparing these two activities, it is natural to say that the first concerns learning something about language, while the second is typically learning something about the world. If your Saturnian has learned how to use the word "floor," you may try telling him something new, that *here* is a floor. If he has mastered the word trick, you have told him something about the world.

Your friend from Saturn now transports you through space to his home sphere, and looking back remotely at earth you say to him, nodding at the earth, "floor." Perhaps he will think this is still part of the lesson and assume that the word "floor" applies properly to the earth, at least as seen from Saturn. But what if you thought he already knew the meaning of "floor," and you were remembering how Dante, from a similar place in the heavens, saw the inhabited earth as "the small round floor that makes us passionate"? Your purpose was metaphor, not drill in the use of language. What difference would it make to your friend which way he took it? With the theory of metaphor under consideration, very little difference, for according to that theory a word has a new meaning in a metaphorical context; the occasion of the metaphor would, therefore, be the occasion for learning the new meaning. We should agree that in some ways it makes relatively little difference whether, in a given context, we think a word is being used metaphorically or in a previously unknown, but literal way. Empson, in *Some Versions of Pastoral*, quotes these lines from Donne: "As our blood labours to beget / Spirits, as like souls as it can, . . . /

So must pure lover's soules descend. . . ." The modern reader is almost certain, Empson points out, to take the word "spirits" in this passage metaphorically, as applying only by extension to something spiritual. But for Donne there was no metaphor. He writes in his *Sermons,* "The spirits . . . are the thin and active part of the blood, and are a kind of middle nature, between soul and body." Learning this does not matter much; Empson is right when he says, "It is curious how the change in the word [that is, in what we think it means] leaves the poetry unaffected."[4]

The change may be, in some cases at least, hard to appreciate, but unless there is a change, most of what is thought to be interesting about metaphor is lost. I have been making the point by contrasting learning a new use for an old word with using a word already understood; in one case, I said, our attention is directed to language, in the other, to what language is about. Metaphor, I suggested, belongs in the second category. This can also be seen by considering dead metaphors. Once upon a time, I suppose, rivers and bottles did not, as they do now, literally have mouths. Thinking of present usage, it doesn't matter whether we take the word "mouth" to be ambiguous because it applies to entrances to rivers and openings of bottles as well as to animal apertures, or we think there is a single wide field of application that embraces both. What does matter is that when "mouth" applied only metaphorically to bottles, the application made the hearer *notice* a likeness between animal and bottle openings. (Consider Homer's reference to wounds as mouths.) Once one has the present use of the word, with literal application to bottles, there is nothing left to notice. There is no similarity to seek because it consists simply in being referred to by the same word.

Novelty is not the issue. In its context a word once taken for a metaphor remains a metaphor on the hundredth hearing, while a word may easily be appreciated in a new literal role on a first encounter. What we call the element of novelty or surprise in a metaphor is a built-in aesthetic feature we can experience again and again, like the surprise in Haydn's Symphony no. 94, or a familiar deceptive cadence.

If metaphor involved a second meaning, as ambiguity does, we might expect to be able to specify the special meaning of a word in a metaphorical setting by waiting until the metaphor dies. The figurative meaning of the living metaphor should be immortalized in the literal meaning of the dead. But although some philosophers have suggested this idea, it seems plainly wrong. "He was burned up" is genuinely ambiguous (since it may be true in one sense and false in another), but although the slangish idiom is no doubt the corpse of a metaphor, "He was burned up" now suggests no more than that he was very angry. When the metaphor was active, we would have pictured fire in the eyes or smoke coming out of the ears.

We can learn much about what metaphors mean by comparing them with similes, for a simile tells us, in part, what a metaphor merely nudges us into noting. Suppose Goneril had said, thinking of Lear, "Old fools are like babes again"; then she would have used the words to assert a similarity between old fools and babes. What she did say, of course, was "Old fools are babes again," thus using the words to intimate what the simile declared. Thinking along these lines may inspire another theory of the figurative or special meaning of metaphors: the figurative meaning of a metaphor is the literal meaning of the corresponding simile. Thus "Christ was a chronometer" in its figurative sense is synonymous with "Christ was like a chronometer," and the metaphorical meaning once locked up in "He was burned up" is released in "He was like someone who was burned up" (or perhaps "He was like burned up").

There is, to be sure, the difficulty of identifying the simile that corresponds to a given metaphor. Virginia Woolf said that a highbrow is "a man or woman of thoroughbred intelligence who rides his mind at a gallop across country in pursuit of an idea." What simile corresponds? Something like this, perhaps: "A highbrow is a man or woman whose intelligence is like a thoroughbred horse and who persists in thinking about an idea like a rider galloping across country in pursuit of . . . well, something."

The view that the special meaning of a metaphor is identical with the literal meaning of a corresponding simile (however "corresponding" is spelled out) should not be confused with the common theory that a metaphor is an elliptical simile.[5] This theory makes no distinction in meaning between a metaphor and some related simile and does not provide any ground for speaking of figurative, metaphorical, or special meanings. It is a theory that wins hands down so far as simplicity is concerned, but it also seems too simple to work. For if we make the literal meaning of the metaphor to be the literal meaning of a matching simile, we deny access to what we originally took to be the literal meaning of the metaphor, and we agreed almost from the start that *this* meaning was essential to the working of the metaphor, whatever else might have to be brought in the way of a nonliteral meaning.

Both the elliptical simile theory of metaphor and its more sophisticated variant, which equates the figurative meaning of the metaphor with the literal meaning of a simile, share a fatal defect. They make the hidden meaning of the metaphor all too obvious and accessible. In each case the hidden meaning is to be found simply by looking to the literal meaning of what is usually a painfully trivial simile. This is like that—Tolstoy like an infant, the earth like a floor. It is trivial because everything is like everything, and in endless ways. Metaphors are often very difficult to interpret and, so it is said, impossible to paraphrase. But with this theory, interpretation and paraphrase typically are ready to the hand of the most callow.

These simile theories have been found acceptable, I think, only because they have been confused with a quite different theory. Consider this remark by Max Black:

When Schopenhauer called a geometrical proof a mousetrap, he was, according to such a view, *saying* (though not explicitly): "A geometrical proof is *like a mousetrap*, since both offer a delusive reward, entice their victims by degrees, lead to disagreeable surprise, etc." This is a view of metaphor as a condensed or elliptical *simile*.[6]

Here I discern two confusions. First, if metaphors are elliptical similes, they say *explicitly* what similes say, for ellipsis is a form of abbreviation, not of paraphrase or indirection. But, and this is the more important matter, Black's statement of what the metaphor says goes far

beyond anything given by the corresponding simile. The simile simply says a geometrical proof is like a mousetrap. It no more *tells* us what similarities we are to notice than the metaphor does. Black mentions three similarities, and of course we could go on adding to the list forever. But is this list, when revised and supplemented in the right way, supposed to give the *literal* meaning of the simile? Surely not, since the simile declared no more than the similarity. If the list is supposed to provide the figurative meaning of the simile, then we learn nothing about metaphor from the comparison with simile—only that both have the same figurative meaning. Nelson Goodman does indeed claim that "the difference between simile and metaphor is negligible," and he continues, "Whether the locution be 'is like' or 'is,' the figure *likens* picture to person by picking out a certain common feature. . . ."[7] Goodman is considering the difference between saying a picture is sad and saying it is like a sad person. It is clearly true that both sayings liken picture to person, but it seems to me a mistake to claim that either way of talking "picks out" a common feature. The simile says there is a likeness and leaves it to us to pick out some common feature or features; the metaphor does not explicitly assert a likeness, but if we accept it as a metaphor, we are again led to seek common features (not necessarily the same features the associated simile suggests; but that is another matter).

Just because a simile wears a declaration of similitude on its sleeve, it is, I think, far less plausible than in the case of metaphor to maintain that there is a hidden second meaning. In the case of simile, we note what it literally says, that two things resemble one another; we then regard the objects and consider what similarity would, in the context, be to the point. Having decided, we might then say the author of the simile intended us—that is, meant us—to notice that similarity. But having appreciated the difference between what the words meant and what the author accomplished by using those words, we should feel little temptation to explain what has happened by endowing the words themselves with a second, or figurative, meaning. The point of the concept of linguistic meaning is to explain what can be done with words. But the supposed figurative meaning of a simile explains nothing; it is not a feature of the word that the word has prior to and independent of the context of use, and it rests upon no linguistic customs except those that govern ordinary meaning.

What words do do with their literal meaning in simile must be possible for them to do in metaphor. A metaphor directs attention to the same sorts of similarity, if not the same similarities, as the corresponding simile. But then the unexpected or subtle parallels and analogies it is the business of metaphor to promote need not depend, for their promotion, on more than the literal meanings of words.

Metaphor and simile are merely two among endless devices that serve to alert us to aspects of the world by inviting us to make comparisons. I quote a few stanzas of T. S. Eliot's "The Hippopotamus":

> The broad-backed hippopotamus
> Rests on his belly in the mud;
> Although he seems so firm to us
> He is merely flesh and blood.
>
> Flesh and blood is weak and frail,
> Susceptible to nervous shock;
> While the True Church can never fail
> For it is based upon a rock.
>
> The hippo's feeble steps may err
> In compassing material ends,
> While the True Church need never stir
> To gather in its dividends.
>
> The 'potamus can never reach
> The mango on the mango-tree;
> But fruits of pomegranate and peach
> Refresh the Church from over sea.

Here we are neither told that the Church resembles a hippopotamus (as in simile) nor bullied into making this comparison (as in metaphor), but there can be no doubt the words are being used to direct our attention to similarities between the two. Nor should there be much inclination, in this case, to posit figurative meanings, for in what words or sentences would we lodge them? The hippopotamus really does rest on his belly in the mud; the True Church, the poem says literally, never can fail. The poem

does, of course, intimate much that goes beyond the literal meanings of the words. But intimation is not meaning.

The argument so far has led to the conclusion that as much of metaphor as can be explained in terms of meaning may, and indeed must, be explained by appeal to the literal meanings of words. A consequence is that the sentences in which metaphors occur are true or false in a normal, literal way, for if the words in them don't have special meanings, sentences don't have special truth. This is not to deny that there is such a thing as metaphorical truth, only to deny it of sentences. Metaphor does lead us to notice what might not otherwise be noticed, and there is no reason, I suppose, not to say these visions, thoughts, and feelings inspired by the metaphor, are true or false.

If a sentence used metaphorically is true or false in the ordinary sense, then it is clear that it is usually false. The most obvious semantic difference between simile and metaphor is that all similes are true and most metaphors are false. The earth is like a floor, the Assyrian did come down like a wolf on the fold, because everything is like everything. But turn these sentences into metaphors, and you turn them false; the earth is like a floor, but it is not a floor; Tolstoy, grown up, was like an infant, but he wasn't one. We use a simile ordinarily only when we know the corresponding metaphor to be false. We say Mr. S. is like a pig because we know he isn't one. If we had used a metaphor and said he was a pig, this would not be because we changed our mind about the facts but because we chose to get the idea across a different way.

What matters is not actual falsehood but that the sentence be taken to be false. Notice what happens when a sentence we use as a metaphor, believing it false, comes to be thought true because of a change in what is believed about the world. When it was reported that Hemingway's plane had been sighted, wrecked, in Africa, the New York *Mirror* ran a headline saying, "Hemingway Lost in Africa," the word "lost" being used to suggest he was dead. When it turned out he was alive, the *Mirror* left the headline to be taken literally. Or consider this case: a woman sees herself in a beautiful dress and says, "What a dream of a dress!"—and then wakes up. The point of the metaphor is that the dress is like a dress one would dream of and therefore isn't a dream-dress. Henle provides a good example from *Anthony and Cleopatra* (2.2):

> The barge she sat in, like a burnish'd throne
> Burn'd on the water

Here simile and metaphor interact strangely, but the metaphor would vanish if a literal conflagration were imagined. In much the same way the usual effect of a simile can be sabotaged by taking the comparison too earnestly. Woody Allen writes, "The trial, which took place over the following weeks, was like a circus, although there was some difficulty getting the elephants into the courtroom."[8]

Generally it is only when a sentence is taken to be false that we accept it as a metaphor and start to hunt out the hidden implication. It is probably for this reason that most metaphorical sentences are *patently* false, just as all similes are trivially true. Absurdity or contradiction in a metaphorical sentence guarantees we won't believe it and invites us, under proper circumstances, to take the sentence metaphorically.

Patent falsity is the usual case with metaphor, but on occasion patent truth will do as well. "Business is business" is too obvious in its literal meaning to be taken as having been uttered to convey information, so we look for another use; Ted Cohen reminds us, in the same connection, that no man is an island.[9] The point is the same. The ordinary meaning in the context of use is odd enough to prompt us to disregard the question of literal truth.

Now let me raise a somewhat Platonic issue by comparing the making of a metaphor with telling a lie. The comparison is apt because lying, like making a metaphor, concerns not the meaning of words but their use. It is sometimes said that telling a lie entails saying what is false; but this is wrong. Telling a lie requires not that what you say be false but that you think it false. Since we usually believe true sentences and disbelieve false, most lies are falsehoods; but in any particular case this is an accident. The parallel between making a metaphor and telling a lie is emphasized by the fact that the same sentence can be used, with meaning unchanged, for either purpose. So a woman who believed in witches but did not think her neighbor a witch might say, "She's a witch," meaning it metaphorically; the same woman, still believing the same of witches and her neighbor but intending to deceive, might use the same words to very different effect. Since sentence and meaning are the same in both cases, it is sometimes hard to prove which intention lay behind the saying of it; thus a man who says "Lattimore's a Communist" and means to lie can always try to beg off by pleading a metaphor.

What makes the difference between a lie and a metaphor is not a difference in the words used or what they mean (in any strict sense of meaning) but in how the words are used. Using a sentence to tell a lie and using it to make a metaphor are, of course, totally different uses, so different that they do not interfere with one another, as say, acting and lying do. In lying, one must make an assertion so as to represent oneself as believing what one does not; in acting, assertion is excluded. Metaphor is careless to the difference. It can be an insult, and so be an assertion, to say to a man "You are a pig." But no metaphor was involved when (let us suppose) Odysseus addressed the same words to his companions in Circe's palace; a story, to be sure, and so no assertion—but the word, for once, was used literally of men.

No theory of metaphorical meaning or metaphorical truth can help explain how metaphor works. Metaphor runs on the same familiar linguistic tracks that the plainest sentences do; this we saw from considering simile. What distinguishes metaphor is not meaning but use—in this it is like assertion, hinting, lying, promising, or criticizing. And the special use to which we put language in metaphor is not—cannot be—to "say something" special, no matter how indirectly. For a metaphor *says* only what shows on its face—usually a patent falsehood or an absurd truth. And this plain truth or falsehood needs no paraphrase—it is given in the literal meaning of the words.

What are we to make, then, of the endless energy that has been, and is being, spent on methods and devices for drawing out the content of a metaphor? The psychologists Robert Verbrugge and Nancy McCarrell tell us that:

Many metaphors draw attention to common systems of relationships or common transformations, in which the identity of the participants is secondary. For example, consider the sentences: *A car is like an animal, Tree trunks are straws for thirsty leaves and branches.* The first sentence directs attention to systems of relationships among energy consumption, respiration, self-induced motion, sensory systems, and, possibly, a homunculus. In the second sentence, the resemblance is a more constrained type of transformation: suction of fluid through a vertically oriented cylindrical space from a source of fluid to a destination.[10]

Verbrugge and McCarrell don't believe there is any sharp line between the literal and metaphorical uses of words; they think many words have a "fuzzy" meaning that gets fixed, if fixed at all, by a context. But surely this fuzziness, however it is illustrated and explained, cannot erase the line between what a sentence literally means (given its context) and what it "draws our attention to" (given its literal meaning as fixed by the context). The passage I have quoted is not employing such a distinction: what it says the sample sentences direct our attention to are facts expressed by paraphrases of the sentences. Verbrugge and McCarrell simply want to insist that a correct paraphrase may emphasize "systems of relationships" rather than resemblances between objects.

According to Black's interaction theory, a metaphor makes us apply a "system of commonplaces" associated with the metaphorical word to the subject of the metaphor: in "Man is a wolf" we apply commonplace attributes (stereotypes) of the wolf to man. The metaphor, Black says, thus "selects, emphasizes, suppresses, and organizes features of the principal subject by implying statements about it that normally apply to the subsidiary subject."[11] If paraphrase fails, according to Black, it is not because the metaphor does not have a special cognitive content, but because the paraphrase "will not have the same power to inform and enlighten as the original. . . . One of the points I most wish to stress is that the loss in such cases is a loss in cognitive content; the relevant weak-

ness of the literal paraphrase is not that it may be tiresomely prolix or boringly explicit; it fails to be a translation because it fails to give the insight that the metaphor did."[12]

How can this be right? If a metaphor has a special cognitive content, why should it be so difficult or impossible to set it out? If, as Owen Barfield claims, a metaphor "says one thing and means another," why should it be that when we try to get explicit about what it means, the effect is so much weaker—"put it that way," Barfield says, "and nearly all the tarning, and with it half the poetry, is lost."[13] Why does Black think a literal paraphrase "inevitably says too much—and with the wrong emphasis"? Why inevitably? Can't we, if we are clever enough, come as close as we please?

For that matter, how is it that a simile gets along without a special intermediate meaning? In general, critics do not suggest that a simile says one thing and means another—they do not suppose it *means* anything but what lies on the surface of the words. It may make us think deep thoughts, just as a metaphor does; how come, then, no one appeals to the "special cognitive content" of the simile? And remember Eliot's hippopotamus; there there was neither simile nor metaphor, but what seemed to get done was just like what gets done by similes and metaphors. Does anyone suggest that the *words* in Eliot's poem have special meanings?

Finally, if words in metaphor bear a coded meaning, how can this meaning differ from the meaning those same words bear in the case where the metaphor *dies*—that is, when it comes to be part of the language? Why doesn't "He was burned up" as now used and meant mean *exactly* what the fresh metaphor once meant? Yet all that the dead metaphor means is that he was very angry—a notion not very difficult to make explicit.

There is, then, a tension in the usual view of metaphor. For on the one hand, the usual view wants to hold that a metaphor does something no plain prose can possibly do and, on the other hand, it wants to explain what a metaphor does by appealing to a cognitive content—just the sort of thing plain prose is designed to express. As long as we are in this frame of mind, we must harbor the suspicion that it *can* be done, at least up to a point.

There is a simple way out of the impasse. We must give up the idea that a metaphor carries a message, that it has a content or meaning (except, of course, its literal meaning). The various theories we have been considering mistake their goal. Where they think they provide a method for deciphering an encoded content, they actually tell us (or try to tell us) something about the *effects* metaphors have on us. The common error is to fasten on the contents of the thoughts a metaphor provokes and to read these contents into the metaphor itself. No doubt metaphors often make us notice aspects of things we did not notice before; no doubt they bring surprising analogies and similarities to our attention; they do provide a kind of lens or lattice, as Black says, through which we view the relevant phenomena. The issue does not lie here but in the question of how the metaphor is related to what it makes us see.

It may be remarked with justice that the claim that a metaphor provokes or invites a certain view of its subject rather than saying it straight out is a commonplace; so it is. Thus Aristotle says metaphor leads to a "perception of resemblances." Black, following Richards, says a metaphor "evokes" a certain response: "a suitable hearer will be led by a metaphor to construct a . . . system."[14] This view is neatly summed up by what Heraclitus said of the Delphic oracle: "It does not say and it does not hide, it intimates."[15]

I have no quarrel with these descriptions of the effects of metaphor, only with the associated views as to *how* metaphor is supposed to produce them. What I deny is that metaphor does its work by having a special meaning, a specific cognitive content. I do not think, as Richards does, that metaphor produces its result by having a meaning which results from the interaction of two ideas; it is wrong, in my view, to say, with Owen Barfield, that a metaphor "says one thing and means another"; or with Black that a metaphor asserts or implies certain complex things by dint of a special meaning and *thus* accomplishes its job of yielding an "insight." A metaphor does its work through other interme-

diaries—to suppose it can be effective only by conveying a coded message is like thinking a joke or a dream makes some statement which a clever interpreter can restate in plain prose. Joke or dream or metaphor can, like a picture or a bump on the head, make us appreciate some fact—but not by standing for, or expressing, the fact.

If this is right, what we attempt in "paraphrasing" a metaphor cannot be to give its meaning, for that lies on the surface; rather we attempt to evoke what the metaphor brings to our attention. I can imagine someone granting this and shrugging it off as no more than an insistence on restraint in using the word "meaning." This would be wrong. The central error about metaphor is most easily attacked when it takes the form of a theory of metaphorical meaning, but behind that theory, and statable independently, is the thesis that associated with a metaphor is a cognitive content that its author wishes to convey and that the interpreter must grasp if he is to get the message. This theory is false, whether or not we call the purported cognitive content a meaning.

It should make us suspect the theory that it is so hard to decide, even in the case of the simplest metaphors, exactly what the content is supposed to be. The reason it is often so hard to decide is, I think, that we imagine there is a content to be captured when all the while we are in fact focusing on what the metaphor makes us notice. If what the metaphor makes us notice were finite in scope and propositional in nature, this would not in itself make trouble; we would simply project the content the metaphor brought to mind onto the metaphor. But in fact there is no limit to what a metaphor calls to our attention, and much of what we are caused to notice is not propositional in character. When we try to say what a metaphor "means," we soon realize there is no end to what we want to mention.[16] If someone draws his finger along a coastline on a map, or mentions the beauty and deftness of a line in a Picasso etching, how many things are drawn to your attention? You might list a great many, but you could not finish since the idea of finishing would have no clear application. How many facts or propositions are conveyed by a photograph? None, an infinity, or one great unstatable fact? Bad question. A picture is not worth a thousand words, or any other number. Words are the wrong currency to exchange for a picture.

It's not only that we can't provide an exhaustive catalogue of what has been attended to when we are led to see something in a new light; the difficulty is more fundamental. What we notice or see is not, in general, propositional in character. Of course it *may* be, and when it is, it usually may be stated in fairly plain words. But if I show you Wittgenstein's duck-rabbit, and I say, "It's a duck," then with luck you see it as a duck; if I say, "It's a rabbit," you see it as a rabbit. But no proposition expresses what I have led you to see. Perhaps you have come to realize that the drawing can be seen as a duck or as a rabbit. But one could come to know this without ever seeing the drawing as a duck or as a rabbit. Seeing as is not seeing that. Metaphor makes us see one thing as another by making some literal statement that inspires or prompts the insight. Since in most cases what the metaphor prompts or inspires is not entirely, or even at all, recognition of some truth or fact, the attempt to give literal expression to the content of the metaphor is simply misguided.

The theorist who tries to explain a metaphor by appealing to a hidden message, like the critic who attempts to state the message, is then fundamentally confused. No such explanation or statement can be forthcoming because no such message exists.

Not, of course, that interpretation and elucidation of a metaphor are not in order. Many of us need help if we are to see what the author of a metaphor wanted us to see and what a more sensitive or educated reader grasps. The legitimate function of so-called paraphrase is to make the lazy or ignorant reader have a vision like that of the skilled critic. The critic is, so to speak, in benign competition with the metaphor-maker. The critic tries to make his own art easier or more transparent in some respects than the original, but at the same time he tries to reproduce in others some of the effects the original had on him. In doing this the critic also, and perhaps by the best method at his command, calls attention to

the beauty or aptness, the hidden power, of the metaphor itself.

NOTES

1. I think Max Black is wrong when he says, "The rules of our language determine that some expressions must count as metaphors." He allows, however, that what a metaphor "means" depends on much more: the speaker's intention, tone of voice, verbal setting, etc. "Metaphor," in his *Models and Metaphors* (Ithaca, N.Y.: 1962), p. 29.
2. Nelson Goodman says metaphor and ambiguity differ chiefly "in that the several uses of a merely ambiguous term are coeval and independent" while in metaphor "a term with an extension established by habit is applied elsewhere under the influence of that habit"; he suggests that as our sense of the history of the "two uses" in metaphor fades, the metaphorical word becomes merely ambiguous (*Languages of Art* [Indianapolis, Ind.: 1968]. p. 71). In fact in many cases of ambiguity, one use springs from the other (as Goodman says) and so cannot be coeval. But the basic error, which Goodman shares with others, is the idea that two "uses" are involved in metaphor in anything like the way they are in ambiguity.
3. The theory described is essentially that of Paul Henle. "Metaphor," in *Language, Thought and Culture*, ed. Henle (Ann Arbor, Mich: 1958).
4. William Empson, *Some Versions of Pastoral* (London: 1935), p. 133.
5. J. Middleton Murray says a metaphor is a "compressed simile," *Countries of the Mind,* 2d ser. (Oxford: 1931), p. 3. Max Black attributes a similar view to Alexander Bain, *English Composition and Rhetoric*, enl. ed. (London: 1887).
6. Black, p. 35.
7. Goodman, pp. 77–78.
8. Woody Allen, *New Yorker,* 21 November 1977, p. 59.
9. Ted Cohen, "Figurative Speech and Figurative Acts," *Journal of Philosophy* 72 (1975): 671. Since the negation of a metaphor seems always to be a potential metaphor, there may be as many platitudes among the potential metaphors as there are absurds.
10. Robert R. Verbrugge and Nancy S. McCarrell, "Metaphoric Comprehension: Studies in Reminding and Resembling," *Cognitive Psychology* 9 (1977): 499.
11. Black, pp. 44–45.
12. Ibid., p. 46.
13. Owen Barfield, "Poetic Diction and Legal Fiction," in *The Importance of Language,* ed. Max Black (Englewood Cliffs, N.J. 1962), p. 55.
15. I use Hannah Arendt's attractive translation of "σημαίνει": it clearly should not be rendered as "mean" in this context.
16. Stanley Cavell mentions the fact that most attempts

at paraphrase end with "and so on" and refers to Empson's remark that metaphors are "pregnant" (*Must We Mean What We Say?* [New York: 1969], p. 79). But Cavell doesn't explain the endlessness of paraphrase as I do, as can be learned from the fact that he thinks it distinguishes metaphor from some ("but perhaps not all") literal discourse. I hold that the endless character of what we call the paraphrase of a metaphor springs from the fact that it attempts to spell out what the metaphor makes us notice, and to this there is no clear end. I would say the same for any use of language.

35   A Theory for Metaphor

A. P. MARTINICH

Much recent work on the concept of a metaphor, though interesting, lacks one feature essential to an adequate theory of metaphor, namely, its placement within a more general theory of language or language use. The reason metaphor needs to be placed within a more general theory is that metaphor itself is a logically derivative phenomenon—derivative, in particular, from some aspect of language use. In this article, I will place metaphor within H. P. Grice's theory of conversation. By extending Grice's theory to account for metaphor, I am holding in effect that metaphor is pragmatically and not semantically based. Although there is a sense in which the sentence used metaphorically has a metaphorical meaning, this meaning is itself a consequence of the mechanisms that give rise to the metaphor and are not what makes the metaphor possible. In Grice's terminology, the metaphorical meaning of an utterance is an instance of utterance occasion meaning and not (applied) timeless utterance meaning.

I. PRELIMINARY THEORETICAL DISTINCTIONS

Grice distinguishes a number of different elements within the total content of what a speaker signifies.[1] The first division he makes is into what the speaker says (or makes-as-if-to-say) and what he implies. Both of these elements come into play in the explanation of metaphor. Let's begin with the former notion. There are various senses of the word "say." A parrot can say, "Polly wants a cracker" and yet not mean anything by what he says. We are not interested in this sense of "say." An actor, rehearsing his lines for a play can say "All the world's a stage" and mean those words to have their normal meaning without meaning that all the world's a stage. We are not interested in this sense of "say" either. The sense of "say" in which we are interested involves more than simply uttering words and intending them to be perceived as having a meaning. In order to count as an instance of saying something, the words uttered must be used to refer to something or predicate something and have some force, directly or indirectly. A citizen, discussing a proposed governmental budget, might utter the sentence, "There will be $100 billion deficit this year," and thereby *say that* there will be a $100 billion deficit. We can correctly report the citizen to be *saying that* such and such, while we cannot correctly report the parrot or the actor as saying anything in our sense, because neither the parrot nor the actor uses the utterance to communicate anything. Because of the legitimacy of using the "say that" locution in indirect speech to report what a speaker says, let's use the portmanteau expression "saying-that" to express this sense of "say." This sense of "say" is closely tied to the

From *Journal of Literary Semantics* 13 (1984): 35–56. Reprinted by permission of Julius Groos Verlag.

words actually uttered and their ordinary meanings; but more, it includes all the references and predications that result from that utterance and whatever force, direct or indirect, it might have.

Connected with saying-that is the notion of making-as-if-to-say. This notion is more difficult to characterize than saying-that. But it is easily illustrated. A disgruntled worker in a financially depressed, politically repressive country utters the sentence, "This is a *fine* country" sarcastically. The worker does not say-that his is a fine country. He intends to communicate by implication that his is *not* a fine country by flouting the maxim of quality. What he does is to make-as-if-to-say that his is a fine country.

One of the most difficult and important issues for a theory of metaphor to get right concerns the question of whether a person who utters a sentence metaphorically says-that anything or only makes-as-if to say something. On the one hand, it is correct to hold that a speaker who utters a sentence metaphorically, for example, "My love is a red rose," is not asserting that his love is a red rose. For, if he were, then he would be saying something false, and, surely, a person who utters a metaphor typically is not speaking falsely, *pace* Plato. A person who speaks metaphorically aims at the truth. To hold that a person who speaks metaphorically is speaking falsely is a kind of philistinism. These considerations incline one to say that a person who speaks metaphorically does not say-that anything but only makes-as-if-to-say something. On the other hand, a metaphor can contain its literal reference or its literal predication (though not both). Suppose the parents of an ebullient young woman are disturbed by her reckless social life. Her Dutch uncle might say to them, "I will clip the wings of the butterfly" and refer to himself while also speaking metaphorically. Or he might say, "That butterfly will be home by 10:00 P.M." and predicate being home by 10:00 P.M. It is also important to recognize that some metaphorical utterances have their literal illocutionary forces. The Dutch uncle might say, "I promise that I will clip that butterfly's wings" and thereby make a promise. Since a metaphorical utterance can have its literal illocutionary force, and its literal reference or predication, one is inclined to think that a person who speaks

metaphorically is saying what would normally be said by a sentence. I think the truth lies in between these two extreme positions. A person who speaks metaphorically does succeed in performing some of the subacts that together constitute a complete act of saying-that, namely, reference, predication, and illocutionary force. However, a person who speaks metaphorically does not say-that what he would normally be taken to have said-that if he were speaking literally; further, he does not represent himself as saying-that such and such but only makes-as-if to say it by flouting a maxim of quality.

It is very important to distinguish what a speaker says (or makes-as-if-to-say) from what he communicates in some other way. Merrie Bergmann has conflated these elements and has consequently come up with a defective theory of metaphor. She holds that metaphors are typically used successfully to make true assertions.[2] The falsity of her view is evidenced by typical metaphors: Mary is a butterfly; the Middle East is a time bomb. If someone were actually asserting these sentences, he would be asserting respectively that Mary is a butterfly and that the Middle East is a time bomb. Both assertions are patently false. What is not false is what a speaker might be implying by uttering the sentences in question metaphorically. Bergmann holds that what the speaker communicates by such utterances are assertions; but she is mistaken. For what a person asserts must be explicit and determined by the rules governing the use of the words uttered; but what a person, speaking metaphorically, means by the sentence in question is not explicit in the utterance, but implicit, and is not governed by the rules for the use of those words. What the speaker communicates, he communicates by some kind of implication. This notion of implication returns us to Grice's second main element of what a speaker signifies.

Grice distinguishes two different kinds of implication: conventional and nonconventional. These terms are a bit misleading and I prefer to call them "linguistic" and "nonlinguistic" implication, respectively. What a speaker says linguistically implies what it does in virtue of the meanings of the words used. Thus, saying that *even Bill likes Mary* linguistically implies *people other than Bill like Mary* in virtue of the meaning of the word "even," just as "John loves Mary and Mary is happy" entails "John loves Mary" in virtue of the meaning of "and." Linguistic implication is not crucial to the understanding of metaphor and is mentioned only to distinguish it from nonlinguistic implication. There are several types of nonlinguistic implication, of which the most important is conversational implication, and it is this type that is crucial to the understanding of metaphor.

Saying-that p conversationally implies that q just in case (a), a speaker has said (or made-as-if-to-say) that $p;$ (b), the speaker is observing the conversational maxims or, at least, the cooperative principle; and (c), the satisfaction of conditions (a) and (b) jointly make it highly plausible that the speaker means that q. The crucial element in this notion of conversational implication is that of a conversational maxim. Grice has pointed out that conversation is regulated by certain global conventions, which he calls conversational maxims and which he divides into four categories: quantity, quality, relation, and manner. The maxims of quantity are "Make your contribution as informative as is necessary" and "Do not make your contribution more informative than is necessary." The maxims of quality are, "Do not say what is false" and "Do not say that for which you lack sufficient evidence." The maxim of relation is, "Be relevant." The maxims of manner are "Be clear," "Avoid ambiguity," "Be brief," and "Be orderly." I should also mention that an important feature of a conversational implication is that, in order to understand what has been implicated, the audience must draw an inference, and the audience must go through a characteristic and more or less complex pattern of reasoning in order to calculate what implication has been made. For example, suppose Professor Wisdom is supposed to write a letter of recommendation for his student Nullset. Wisdom writes "Nullset is a very well groomed young man, who has beautiful handwriting." If Wisdom says nothing more than this, then he does not say, but conversationally implies, that Nullset is not a very good candidate. For the addressee reasons: Wisdom has said that Nullset is well-groomed, etc.; he is observing the cooperative principle; and,

by the maxim of quantity, he would be making a stronger claim about Nullset's philosophical ability if he were able to. Since he has not made a stronger claim, he must be unable to, and that implies that he thinks that Nullset is not a very good philosopher.

II. FLOUTING THE MAXIM OF QUALITY

Conversational maxims regulate our discourse and usually are observed by interlocutors—usually, but not always. Grice distinguishes four different ways in which a maxim might be contravened and thereby go unfulfilled. First, a speaker might violate a maxim; that is, he might quietly and unostentatiously contravene a maxim. Liars contravene a maxim of quality of course; but it is important to recognize that not all violations are sinister. Any honest mistake violates a maxim of quality. Moreover, a good teacher often says what is false in order to help his students learn more easily, because the literal and unadulterated truth about something is often too difficult or even impossible for them to understand. Second, a speaker might opt out of a maxim. A person who is asked for the details of a private meeting might say, "I'm sorry; I cannot say. That information is privileged," thereby opting out of a maxim of quantity. A person who is asked to explain Einstein's theory of relativity briefly might reply, "There is no brief explanation," thereby opting out of a maxim of manner. Third, a speaker might flout a maxim. Our disgruntled laborer who said, "This is a fine country," provided an example of flouting a maxim of quality. Grice claims there is also a fourth way of not fulfilling a maxim: by being faced with a clash of maxims. However, a moment's reflection should reveal that this alleged fourth way is not a genuine way of not fulfilling a maxim but a reason for not doing so. A person might violate or opt out of or flout a maxim if he is faced with a clash of maxims; but the clash itself is not a way of contravening them. A person who is required to speak both truly and briefly about a complicated subject may be faced with a clash and may either violate one of the maxims, opt out of one, or what is least likely in this case, flout one. Of the three remaining ways of contravening a maxim, flouting is the one most relevant to the analysis of metaphor.

If we accept Grice's formulation of the maxims of quality, then a central thesis about metaphors can be stated simply and in nontechnical language:[3] Every metaphor either is (or is thought to be) literally false or is supposed to be false. This disjunction reflects a genuine division of two types of metaphor. I shall call metaphors that are literally false *standard* metaphors; and those that are supposed to be false *nonstandard* metaphors. By "supposed," I do not mean that the metaphor is intended to be false but that the metaphor is *treated as if* or *entertained as if* it were false in order to consider the consequences, as when, in a reductio ad absurdum argument, the proposition to be proved is *supposed* to be false in order to show that the consequences of such a supposition are absurd. Most of this article will be devoted to standard cases of metaphor because the nonstandard cases are derivative, rare, and merely an unavoidable complication to the theory. Until further notice, then, by "metaphor" I will mean "standard metaphor."

Every metaphorical proposition is false. Every metaphor flouts the first maxim of quality. This is not to say or imply that the point of a metaphor (what the speaker intends to communicate) is false. On the contrary, the point of a metaphor is typically true. Further, the point of a metaphor is conversationally implied in virtue of the fact that the speaker *flouts* the first maxim of quality. This is not to say or imply that any metaphorical proposition is a lie. Indeed, no metaphor *can* be a lie. It can be inapt or inept, imaginative or dull, cheery or morbid, or any number of other things. But no metaphor is a lie. The reason is that every lie, by definition, must be unostentatious; it violates the first maxim of quality. A metaphor, in contrast, flouts the maxim. A hearer relies on the open and ostentatious falsity of the utterance as one important clue that the speaker is speaking metaphorically.

III. ANALYSIS OF A METAPHOR

Let's now see how the foregoing applies to the analysis of a particular metaphor. Suppose someone writes the sentence, "My love is a red rose," in the context of a poem, singing the praises of his lover. The audience reads the sentence and tries to interpret it. If the audience takes the poet to be saying-that his love is a red rose, then the audience must take the poet to be uttering a patent falsehood and not fulfilling the maxim of quality, "Do not say that which is false." But the audience knows that the poet cannot be intending to utter a patent falsehood, because a falsehood would make sense in the context only if it were disguised and the audience is justified in believing that the poet is observing the conversational maxims. Consequently, the audience infers that the poet is not saying-that his love is a red rose, but only making-as-if-to-say that she is. Once the audience has determined that the speaker is only making-as-if-to-say something, it is then able to begin calculating the actual content of what the speaker has signified. Since the poet is signifying by implication, he must believe that the audience is able to work out the implication. For this reason, the features of the rose that are exploited will be those that the audience is as likely to know as the poet. They will be held mutually or, as we might say, commonly. Max Black saw this point, more or less clearly, and made it part of his theory of metaphor. He calls such features "related commonplaces."[4] Typically, metaphors do exploit "related commonplaces." (Jones is a dog [gorilla]; my love is a red rose [a doll]). Yet, it is also true that some metaphors do not trade on commonplaces, such as "The fog came in on tiny cat's feet." Such metaphors are, however, exceptional, the work of poets or poetic spirits. Such metaphors force the audience to explore the concepts introduced by the metaphor in order to come up with terms that, working in conjunction with the metaphor, will yield the meaning the poet intends, the metaphorical truth. Nonetheless, even in such "creative" metaphors it must be possible for the audience to determine which properties of the metaphorical term the speaker is thinking of and which the speaker thinks that the audience will think that the speaker thinks the audience will think of. And these features we call salient.[5] What features these will be cannot be specified in advance of extensive knowledge of the context: who the speakers are, what their mutual beliefs are; what has been said earlier in the conversation, etc.

Not all salient properties are meant by the speaker; there are too many of them. Thus the set of salient properties must be further reduced. There are two further principles that limit the properties the speaker intends to be operative in the metaphor. One concerns a conversational requirement. Since the speaker has flouted a maxim of quality, he is exploiting that maxim and thereby conversationally implying something. The pattern of inference involved in calculating what the speaker conversationally implies typically involves the maxim of relation: be relevant. In order to interpret what the poet means, it is necessary to understand his utterance as relevant to the context. The poet is comparing his lover to a rose and hence, given that his comparison is apt, only those salient properties will be considered that are relevant to the poet's attitude toward his love.

The other principle that limits the salient properties is this: the properties intended are only those that contribute to a true conclusion. One plausible statement of the salient features of a rose, relevant to the context of utterance and leading to a true conclusion, is that a red rose is beautiful, or sweet smelling, or highly valued. Putting the poet's sentence and the statement of salience together and drawing an obvious inference, we construct the following argument:

My love is a red rose.
A red rose is beautiful, or sweet smelling, or highly valued . . . .
Therefore, my love is beautiful, or sweet smelling or highly valued . . . .

There are at least four things to notice about this argument as it relates generally to the analysis of metaphors. First, the conclusion is presumably true. People who use metaphors aim at the truth, even in those cases in which they fall wide or short of the mark. The premise expressing the salient features of the rose, the major premise, is also true and typically such premises will be true, though not always. Some metaphors can trade on false but commonly held beliefs or false beliefs mutually held by speaker and audience, even when they alone hold the false beliefs; other metaphors can trade on myths or folklore that the community knows to be false. Take for example the folklore that elephants have infallible memories. Someone might exploit this folkloric belief and say, "Jones has the memory of an elephant" without believing that elephants have prodigious memories.[6] Also notice that the argument about the rose is valid, and typically such arguments will be valid although again they may not, and need not always be. There is no reason why a good metaphor cannot trade on some subtle or not so subtle fallacious pattern of reasoning. Consider the metaphor, "Mary is a block of ice." As John Searle has argued, there is no similarity between Mary, in the sense in which she is cold, and a block of ice, in the sense in which it is cold. Thus, the comparison theory of metaphor is false because it holds that all metaphors trade on similarity and not just most of them. Nonetheless, the sentence "Mary is a block of ice" can be used successfully as a metaphor. The explanation, I think, is that the metaphor trades on an equivocation on "cold":

Mary is a block of ice.
Blocks of ice are cold.
Therefore, Mary is cold.

"Cold" is equivocal; it means "low in temperature" in the major premise and "unresponsive" in the conclusion.

The second thing to notice about the argument we are considering is that the first premise has its literal meaning. If "My love is a red rose" did not have its literal meaning, then it would not play its proper role in the argument. If, in the first premise, "red rose" did not mean what it normally does, then the first premise jointly with the second premise would not entail the conclusion and the point of the metaphor would not be conveyed. Moreover, if "red rose" did not have its normal meaning, then there would be no way for the audience to determine what form the second premise of the argument should take. Donald Davidson has argued at length that sentences used metaphorically retain their literal meaning.[7] Davidson also holds that sentences used metaphorically say what they literally mean. He does not, however, commit himself on the more difficult issue of whether a speaker who utters a metaphor says anything. I have argued that such a speaker does not say-that s completely, but does perform some acts that count as parts of saying-that.

Third, notice that the second or major premise expressing the salient features of the rose ends with an ellipsis. Peter Geach distinguishes between two kinds of pronouns: pronouns of laziness and others. We can make an analogous distinction for types of ellipses: dots of laziness and others. Dots of laziness are a kind of abbreviation. They mark a context that could be filled out if it were desired or necessary, as in the sentence, "The fifty states of the United States are Alabama, Alaska, Arkansas, . . ." The other kind of dots indicate a context that cannot be completed, as in "The natural numbers are 1, 2, 3, . . ." All sentences of natural languages are finite in length and there are an infinite number of natural numbers, so no sentence can specify them all. The dots at the end of the major premise are not dots of laziness. There is no way to fill out the sentence completely and determinately. What a person means by an utterance is not always, if ever, wholly determinate. Usually, the border of what a speaker means is penumbral. Also, since a speaker and his audience are likely to differ about how many features of a rose should be included in the major premise and people will differ about which proposed features are actual features of roses, it is to the communicative advantage of both speaker and audience to leave the major premise disjunctively indeterminate. This kind of indeterminacy does not constitute a defect in our analysis of metaphor. Just the opposite. Most metaphors, and, more generally, most cases of conversational implication, exhibit just this kind of indeterminateness and for the reasons given here. Grice thinks that conversational implications generally should be formulated as open disjunctions of propositions and this seems to me to be largely correct. The disjunctive sentences are clearly inclusive disjunctions; so it is possible—indeed, it is intended—that more than one of the disjuncts are true; yet, should one turn out to be false or should the audience either dispute the truth of one of the disjuncts or not take one as partially constituting the premise, the truth of the premise is still safeguarded by the other disjuncts. The view that the supplied premise (or premises) is

an open disjunction also helps us pinpoint one objectionable feature of the comparison view of metaphor. According to the comparison view, the meaning of every metaphor can be rendered by some literal paraphrase. Further, it implies, if it does not say, that the literal paraphrase is a determinate and precise sentence. It is this part of the theory that is objectionable. Metaphors are typically vague and indeterminate. This is not a defect. This indeterminateness is one of the more intriguing features of metaphors; it is what encourages the audience to play with and explore the concepts involved—to look for relationships between things not previously countenanced.[8]

Fourth, the argument about the metaphor involving the red rose can be used to answer a criticism against the interaction view of metaphor. That criticism briefly is that the key term employed in that view is metaphorical and, hence, defective as an analysis. What literal sense, to put the objection interrogatively, can be given to the notion that the terms of a metaphor interact?[9] Our theory supplies an answer: notice first that understanding a metaphor requires that the audience must supply one or more premises that will work in conjunction with the metaphor that will (seem to) entail the conclusion, that is, the proposition that expresses the point of the metaphor. Further, and more important, such an argument will often be a syllogism, and what will allow the two premises to work jointly is the metaphor term, which occurs as the middle term of the syllogism. Middle terms are those that mediate the two other terms of the syllogism or, we might say, interact with both premises. There is, perhaps, a stronger sense of interaction to be noted; it concerns the principle of selecting the missing premise. In formulating the missing premise, the audience must take into account the following constraints: whatever term is selected, it must be relevant to the topic, salient, and contribute to yielding a true conclusion.

IV. METAPHOR AND OTHER FIGURES OF SPEECH

Metaphor is a figure of speech, and it may be instructive to compare it with three other figures of speech. One crucial mark of a metaphor, I have claimed, is that it would be false if it were asserted. However, a speaker who uses a metaphor does not assert it but, by flouting the second maxim of quality, only makes-as-if-to-say what the metaphor expresses. The correct treatment of hyperbole is strictly analogous to metaphor. Hyperboles, like metaphors, are cases of flouting the second maxim of quality. A person who speaks hyperbolically, that is, who consciously and intentionally exaggerates what he knows to be the truth and intends his audience to recognize this, does not say-that but only makes-as-if-to-say.

Hyperbole should be contrasted with simple overstatement, by which a person who unconsciously or unintentionally expresses a proposition that is stronger than the evidence warrants. The same proposition can be overstatement in one person's mouth and hyperbole in another's. A person who states "Every American who wants to be successful can be" without realizing that circumstances of nature and society prevent some people from achieving their full potential has simply overstated the truth. However, a person who both realizes the truth and intends that his audience will understand it may express the same proposition and thereby speak hyperbolically for effect. Hyperbole is a rhetorical device; overstatement is a mistake. Hyperbole differs from metaphor in that the expressed hyperbolic proposition always entails the proposition that should have been expressed and does not require any additional premises as metaphors do. If someone says, "Jones has never been late to anything in his life," he probably means, "Jones is almost never late for anything" and the former entails the latter.

There is a curious asymmetry between metaphor and hyperbole on the one hand, and meiosis on the other, in two ways. First, meiosis unlike hyperbole and metaphor, does not contravene a maxim of quality but a maxim of quantity: contribute as much to the conversation as is required. Meiosis contributes too little. While an hyperbolic proposition entails what ought to be said, meiosis is entailed by what ought to be said. Second, because the proposition the speaker expresses is not false, there is no need to interpret it as not being said-that.

Finally, consider irony. Ironical utterances, like metaphors and hyperboles, appear to contravene a maxim of quality. The contravention is, however, only apparent and not genuine. A person who speaks ironically is not saying what is obviously false; if he were, he would be conveying something that is explicitly contradictory. For example, if the disgruntled worker who uttered the sentence, "This is a *fine* country," and meant that his country is not a fine country, were saying that his is a fine country, then he would be contradicting himself. Ironical utterances, like metaphors and hyperboles, constitute cases of making-as-if-to-say; the speaker means just the opposite of what he makes-as-if-to-say.

V. NONSTANDARD METAPHORS

I have now concluded my treatment of standard metaphors, that is, those metaphorical propositions which would be false if asserted and which, by flouting the second maxim of quality, are cases of making-as-if-to-say. (Thus, "metaphor" no longer means "standard metaphor.") I need now to discuss the nature of nonstandard metaphors, that is, metaphorical propositions, which, if asserted, would be literally true. The first thing to say about such metaphors is that they are rare. The second thing is that they must be treated, because they are genuine cases of metaphor. The third thing is that treatment is more complicated than that of standard metaphors. It is difficult to think of good examples of nonstandard metaphors. Here is the best that I have been able to come up with. Suppose Princess Grace of Monaco is speaking with an American friend about her daughter Caroline. She might say, "Caroline is our princess." Here we have a case of a nonstandard metaphor. Since Caroline is a princess by virtue of her birth to a princely family, Grace's utterance, if asserted, would be literally true. Grace means it, however, metaphorically. The metaphor operates in the following way. When Grace utters "Caroline is our princess," the American must interpret what Grace means. The American reasons that, if Grace means (or means only) that Caroline is the daughter of a prince, then her utterance is defective because it flouts the first maxim of quantity since it is mutually obvious to Grace and the American that Caroline is the daughter of a prince. Consequently, the American reasons that, since Grace is not (simply) stating the obvious, she must be implying something. Since the assumption that the proposition expressed is (simply) true would make it defective, the audience supposes that the proposition is false in order to test the consequences. If Grace intends the American to suppose the proposition is false, then the second maxim of quality is being flouted in that way. Hence, Grace must mean her utterance to be construed metaphorically. Using a folkloric belief as the major premise, the American constructs the following syllogism:

> Caroline is a princess.
> Princesses are beautiful or admired or well-loved or slightly spoiled or . . .
> Therefore, Caroline is beautiful or admired or well-loved or slightly spoiled or . . .

What unites the standard and nonstandard cases of metaphor are the role that falsity plays in generating the metaphor and the characteristic form of conversational implication, leaning on either true or folkloric or mythic or communal beliefs.

A less clear-cut case of a nonstandard metaphor is provided by Julia Driver's poem, "The Prostitute," which begins

> I am stripped,
> an old screw.

Taking "stripped" literally to mean "deprived of clothes" and "screw" as "woman who engages in sexual intercourse," we can suppose the sentence is literally true but in this sense plays little or no part in its metaphorical interpretation. The metaphorical interpretation depends upon another interpretation of the meaning of the sentence. In addition to the meaning already cited, the sentence can mean, "I am an old metal fastener with a defective spiral ridge running around me." In this latter sense, it is patently false of the speaker, flouts the first maxim of quality, and invites a standard metaphorical interpretation. This example is interesting, however, because the first and second sense of the sentence are not independent. The two senses of "screw" in the poem are etymologically related.

The reading of the sentence, "I am stripped, an old screw," that is literally true invites, at least by association, the reading of the sentence that is patently false and metaphorical. (Much more could be said about the metaphor; for example, a stripped metal fastener is virtually useless as is an old prostitute.)

I have claimed that nonstandard metaphors are genuine metaphors but rare and derivative on standard ones. My view is importantly different from the view that the comparatively rare metaphors that are or would be literally true if asserted are not importantly different from the statistically more numerous cases of metaphors that are or would be literally false if asserted. This latter view is defective for two reasons, one positive and one negative. Positively, this view cannot adequately explain how speakers can expect their audience to understand that a metaphor is being broached. On my view, an audience knows that a standard metaphor is being broached largely by the patent falsity of the metaphorical proposition. And if a metaphorical proposition does not appear to be patently false, then there must be some other mechanism that eventually leads the audience to suppose that the literally true proposition must be supposed to be false in order to understand what the speaker means. On my view this other mechanism is the flouting of some conversational maxim—it might be any of the maxims other than the first maxim of quality—that forces the audience to suppose that the utterance is patently false and hence to be interpreted as a standard metaphor would be.

Negatively, the view that some literally true metaphors are merely statistically rare and not conceptually derivative has led some theorists mistakenly to classify as metaphors utterances that are not metaphors. I shall use some of Ted Cohen's work as an example. Cohen gives three examples of allegedly true metaphors: "No man is an island"; "Jesus was a carpenter"; and "Moscow is a cold city."[10] Each of these sentences must be given a different treatment.

As for "No man is an island," my view is that it is not a metaphor at all. It is true and not false that no man is an island. This is not to imply that Donne's line is not a figure of speech. It is. "No man is an island" is trivially true, and for that reason it is a case of meiosis. One might wonder how such a trivial truth could be so poetically powerful? The answer is that it is powerful in the richness of its associations, conveyed by conversational implication. In saying, "No man is an island," Donne is saying something trivial. The reader must, consequently, muse about the relevance of a triviality; he reasons, presumably, in a way analogous to a case of metaphor:

No man is an island.

Every island is separated from every other thing of its own kind, does not depend upon any other thing of its own kind for its existence or well-being, and is not diminished by the destruction of any other of its own kind; . . .

Therefore, no man is separated from every other thing of its own kind, does not depend upon any other thing of its own kind for its existence or well-being, and is not diminished by the destruction of any other of its own kind; . . .

This argument is invalid; yet not the less effective as poetry for all that. In short, while what Donne has said is trivial, what he has linguistically communicated via conversational implication is not at all trivial, but, on the contrary, profound.

Concerning "Jesus was a carpenter," a speaker who says this speaks truly. Perhaps, however— and this seems to be Cohen's point—the speaker might well mean more than he says. He might mean that Jesus fashions valuable things out of unfashioned worthless things. If this statement of what the speaker additionally means seems itself metaphorical, it can be paraphrased in ways to eliminate those elements: Jesus causes things that have no value in themselves to become things that do have value in themselves. What is important to notice is that we have specified what the speaker means by specifying that the speaker *means what he says and means more than what he says.* And this specification does not commit us to holding that "Jesus is a carpenter" is a metaphor. For, to appeal to the classic formula, "to utter a metaphor is to say one thing and to mean something else" (i.e., something inconsistent with what you say.) In the case under consideration, the speaker does not mean something inconsistent with what he said,

merely something additional, just as anyone conversationally implying something means something additional to what he says.

Finally, "Moscow is a cold city" is not a metaphor; it is ambiguous, perhaps, a pun. It has two literal readings: "Moscow is a city that often has low temperatures" and "Moscow is not a cordial city." "Cold," in the latter sentence, is a dead metaphor; but dead metaphors are not metaphors.

VI. GENERALIZING THE THEORY

In Section II, I said that if we accept Grice's formulation of the maxim of quality, then every metaphor is (or is thought to be) literally false or is supposed to be false. However, Grice's formulation of the maxim of quality is not correct. The principal problem with it is that it is too narrow. As Grice formulates them, "Do not say that which is false" and "Do not say that for which you lack evidence," the maxims apply only to speech acts that have truth-values, for example, statements and assertions. Many speech acts do not have a truth-value, for example, questions, promises, and requests. All of this is important for our theory because many metaphors are embedded in utterances that would not have a truth-value if uttered literally, for example, the Dutch uncle's utterance, "I promise I will clip that butterfly's wings." So, such simple cases cannot be explained in our original formulation about standard and nonstandard metaphors. However, the problem is easily corrected by replacing Grice's too narrow maxims of quality with a sufficiently broad one and generalizing our initial formulation to accord with the broader maxim of quality.

In another article, I have argued that Grice's maxims of quality should be replaced by this one: do not participate in a speech act unless you satisfy all the conditions required for its successful and nondefective performance.[11] This maxim is obviously broad enough to cover the entire spectrum of speech acts. The question now is, What was the intuition behind the distinction between standard and nonstandard metaphors? We can get at it if we consider the following sentences that might be uttered in the Dutch uncle situation.

I state that Mary will have her wings clipped.

I promise that Mary will have her wings clipped.

I ask whether Mary will have her wings clipped.

I insist that Mary will have her wings clipped.

In each case, the same proposition is involved: that Mary will have her wings clipped. Yet, in each case the force of the utterance would be different if the sentence were uttered literally. Searle would say that each utterance involves the same propositional content and each attempted speech act would be defective for the same reason if the relevant sentence were uttered literally. In each case, what Searle calls "the propositional content condition" would be flouted. These are cases of standard metaphors. That is, a standard metaphor is one in which the propositional content condition is flouted. Nonstandard metaphors are those in which the propositional content is supposed to be flouted. This formulation of the distinction between standard and nonstandard metaphors is unavoidably stated in technical terms in order to describe the phenomenon of metaphor correctly and with the required generality.

VII. A COMPARISON WITH SEARLE'S THEORY OF METAPHOR

There are some important similarities between my theory of metaphor and that of John Searle. The spirit is the same. Both are pragmatic theories that exploit features of Grice's theory of linguistic communication. We also differ in several significant respects. My theory is logically stronger than Searle's in three important ways. First, Searle claims that the stimulus to treat a sentence as being uttered metaphorically is the result of "falsehood, semantic nonsense, violations of the rules of speech acts, or violations of conversational principles of communication."[12] My view is stronger in that I claim that all standard metaphors flout one maxim, the maxim of quality and all nonstandard metaphors must be supposed to contravene it. Second, Searle does not make clear whether, when a speaker utters a sentence s metaphorically, he is saying-that s or only making-as-if-to-say it. I have argued for the latter view, while also explaining how a

speaker communicates some parts of what he says. Third, I have specified that the premises that are added to the metaphor, in order to infer what the point of the metaphor is, are constrained by three principles: they must involve features or properties that are salient to the metaphorical term; they must fulfill the maxim of relation by being relevant to the topic of the conversation; and they must help form a premise that ends to yield a true conclusion.

There is one respect in which Searle's theory has a superficial appearance of being stronger than mine. In contrast with my principles of salience and relevance and truth-producing premises, Searle specifies nine supposed principles for computing the features relevant to the metaphor. Yet, on reflection, these nine principles turn out to be vacuous. Searle intends his nine principles to constitute at least a partial answer to the question, How is it possible for the hearer who hears the utterance "S is P" to know that the speaker means "S is R".[13] I want to show that Searle's nine principles fail to answer this question in any part, because the principles are so weak as to permit any possible feature or property of a thing to be a value of R.

Any feature or property will either be true of an object or false of it; and Searle allows any feature or property whether true or false of an object to play a role in the interpretation of a metaphor. This is objectionable because it fails to limit the possible features or properties of an object to those that are relevant to a metaphorical interpretation of a sentence. A theory of metaphor must provide principles that specify which features or properties might be relevant to a metaphor in order to allow the audience to know which features or properties the speaker means to imply by the metaphor. We can see this argument against Searle's principles more clearly by considering what he says about the metaphorical applicability of all those features or properties that are true of an object and then all those features or properties that are false of an object. According to Principle 1, a feature or property could be true of the object by definition; according to Principle 2, a feature or property could be contingently true of an object. Since every feature that is true of an object is either necessarily true, that is, true by definition, or contingently true, Searle has in no way restricted the actual features of an object to those that might play a role in a metaphor.

What about features that are not true of an object? Again, Searle allows such a latitude that no feature is excluded from possibly playing a role in a metaphor. Citing Principles 3 and 4 is sufficient to show this. Principle 3 allows features that are often said of or believed to be true of an object; Principle 4 allows features that a thing does not have as well as those that are not even like any feature it has. In short, Searle's theory suffers from being too weak for failing to explain when a feature or property might play a role in a metaphor and when it would not.

VIII. REPLY TO OBJECTIONS TO A PRAGMATIC THEORY OF METAPHOR

The theory of metaphor I have been advancing is blatantly pragmatic. Since some distinguished theorists have claimed that metaphor is a semantic phenomenon, their claims should be discussed, if only briefly. Max Black is perhaps the most distinguished philosophical proponent of this view. He says that in a metaphor, the focal or metaphorical term "obtains a new meaning, which is not quite its meaning in literal uses, not quite the meaning which any literal substitute would have."[14] This is in line with his general view that metaphor is a semantic phenomenon: "'metaphor' must be classified as a term belonging to 'semantics' and not to 'syntax.'"[15] When Black expressed this view, there was no well-developed pragmatic theory such as Searle's revision of Austin's theory of speech acts and Grice's theory of linguistic communication; so it is not surprising that Black opts for a semantic theory against a syntactic theory and does not consider the possibility of a pragmatic theory. And it is not surprising that his arguments on behalf of a semantic treatment are not very telling against a pragmatic theory. He holds that "The chairman plowed though the discussion" and "The poor are the negroes of Europe" (attributed to Chamfort) are "unmistakeably *instances* of metaphor."[16] They are such only in context. We can imagine a crazed chairman driving a plow through a meeting of his committee; in which

case the first sentence, if asserted, would be literally true. And we can imagine a slightly different history of Europe, in which the statement made by "The poor are the negroes of Europe" would be literally true and not a metaphor. The upshot is that whether a sentence is used literally or metaphorically depends on the context of its use; and is, I maintain, a fit subject for a pragmatic theory.

Recently, L. Jonathan Cohen has also urged that metaphor be given a semantic treatment.[17] Since Peter Lamarque has acutely criticized Cohen's views, it is not necessary for me to provide an extended response.[18] Lamarque correctly notes several respects in which metaphors do not parallel genuine illocutionary acts, and this is sufficient to undermine Cohen's case. There is just one issue about which I disagree with Lamarque. He holds that Tom's ironical utterance of

(5) That was a brilliant thing to do.

can be correctly reported by

(7) Tom said that that was a brilliant thing to do.

And he holds that Tom's metaphorical utterance of

(9) The rats have driven me out of the house.

can be correctly reported as

(10) Tom said that the rats have driven him out of his house.

I have already explained why I think sentences (7) and (10) do not correctly report Tom's actions. Ironical and metaphorical utterances are not cases of *saying-that* something, but of *making-as-if-to-say* something. This objection to Lamarque does not diminish the force of his criticisms of Cohen's views. So, the objections of-Black and Cohen do not seem to stand in the way of the kind of pragmatic theory I have presented.

NOTES

1. H. P. Grice, "Logic and Conversation," in *Syntax and Semantics*, vol. 3, ed. Peter Cole and Jerry L. Morgan (New York: Academic Press, 1975), pp. 44–45.

2. Cf. Merrie Bergmann, "Metaphorical Assertions," *The Philosophical Review* 91 (1982), 225–245.

3. Bergmann in "Metaphorical Assertions," p. 234, confuses what is conversationally implied by a metaphor, the point of the metaphor, with what a speaker asserts by a metaphor. What a speaker asserts must be closely tied to the conventional meaning of the words he utters, but what Bergmann calls the metaphorical assertion is either loosely tied or not tied at all to the conventional meaning.

4. Max Black, "Metaphor," in *Models and Metaphors* (Ithaca: Cornell University Press, 1954), p. 41; see also Max Black, "More about Metaphor," in *Metaphor and Thought,* ed. Andrew Ortony (New York: Cambridge University Press, 1979), pp. 28–29.

5. For more about salience, see Andrew Ortony, "Beyond Literal Similarity," *Psychological Review* 86 (1976), 161–180, and "The Role of Similarity in Similes and Metaphors," in *Metaphor and Thought,* ed. Andrew Ortony (New York: Cambridge University Press, 1979), pp. 186–201; and Merrie Bergmann, "Metaphorical Assertions," 234–239.

6. See also John Searle, "Metaphor," in his *Expression and Meaning* (Cambridge: Cambridge University Press, 1979), pp. 88–90.

7. See his "What Metaphors Mean," *Critical Inquiry* 5 (1978), 31–47; John Searle, in "Metaphor," p. 77, and Ted Cohen, in "Figurative Speech and Figurative Acts," *The Journal of Philosophy* 72 (1975), 670, hold the same view.

8. I think that my treatment of the role played by open disjunctive propositions is the theoretical counterpart of Black's "implicative complex"; see "More about Metaphor," p. 28.

9. Searle hints at this criticism; see his "Metaphor," p. 92.

10. "Figurative Speech and Figurative Acts," p. 671.

11. A. P. Martinich, "Conversational Maxims and Some Philosophical Problems," *Philosophical Quarterly* 30 (1980), 215–228.

12. Searle, "Metaphor," p. 105.

13. Ibid., p. 103.

14. Black, "Metaphor," p. 39.

15. Ibid.

16. Ibid., p. 26.

17. L. Jonathan Cohen, "The Semantics of Metaphor," in Ortony, *Metaphor and Thought,* p. 65.

18. Peter Lamarque, "Metaphor and Reported Speech: In Defence of a Pragmatic Theory," *Journal of Literary Semantics* 11 (1982), 14–18.

36 Hesperus and Phosphorus: Sense, Pretense, and Reference

MARK CRIMMINS

In "On Sense and Reference," surrounding his discussion of how we describe what people say and think, identity is Frege's first stop and his last. We will follow Frege's plan here, but we will stop also in the land of make-believe.

Identity challenges reflection, says Frege. By *identity* Frege intends whatever it is we attribute when we say, for instance, that Hesperus is *the same thing* as Phosphorus. It can seem odd, he says, to think of identity as a relation between *things;* for what interest could attach to a thing's being *itself?* It is odd, too, to think of identity as the relation that holds between different *names* of a thing, for then the statement that Hesperus *is* Phosphorus would be held to concern neither Hesperus nor Phosphorus, but only the name 'Hesperus' and the name 'Phosphorus' (and this would alienate the identity statement from such apparent kin as the statement that Hesperus is the same *size* as Phosphorus). Frege's resolution of the dilemma is well known: intermediate between a name and the thing named is a *mode of presentation* of the thing; the name expresses *that* way of thinking about the thing. A true identity statement like 'Hesperus is Phosphorus' is not *trivial* because the entity that in the statement is said to be identical to itself is conceived differently under the two names: the names 'Hesperus' and 'Phosphorus' express different modes of presentation of a single object.

Russell, too, finds his reflection challenged by identity. In "The Philosophy of Logical Atomism" he writes:

> Identity is a rather puzzling thing at first sight. When you say 'Scott is the author of *Waverly*', you are half-tempted to think there are two people, one of whom is Scott and the other the author of *Waverly,* and they happen to be the same. That is obviously absurd, but that is the sort of way one is always tempted to deal with identity.[1]

Russell instead deals with identity by holding that nontrivial, true identity statements like 'Hesperus is Phosphorus' do not attribute relations at all. Rather, they assert complex claims about what *sorts* of things exist: for instance, 'Hesperus is Phosphorus' might assert that there exists a thing that is both the first star visible in the evening sky (in one season) and the last star visible in the morning sky (in another season).

I want to underline, however, Russell's phenomenological confession: *when we say* 'Scott is the author of *Waverly*', we are half-tempted to see what we are doing as stating of *two things* (Scott and the author of *Waverly*), that these two things 'happen to be the same'. Russell is right about the semantic phenomenology. At least, it is like that for me, too, and even more strongly in other cases (Hesperus and Phosphorus, Superman and Clark, the child and the adult). I

Mark Crimmins, "Hesperus and Phosphorus: Sense, Pretense, and Reference," *The Philosophical Review*, 107 (1998) pp. 1–47. © Cornell University. Reprinted by permission of the publisher and the author.

agree, as well, that it would be absurd to think that we seriously mean to be claiming of *two* things that they are the same thing. This peculiar feeling of talking about two things cannot reveal what we are seriously doing. But before we dismiss this peculiar feeling, perhaps we should consider whether it is clear that in making a serious identity statement, everything we do is done seriously.

1. MAKE-BELIEVE AND TRUTH

Statements (and more generally uses of sentences) that rely on make-believe can be used to express genuine claims, and can be candidates for genuine truth and falsehood. Let me support this with an example in which the role of make-believe is more blatant.

Suppose that I am trying to describe to you Ann's cleverness and modesty, and that I cannot find words to express neatly and perspicuously just the traits I want to characterize. I might compare her to some of our mutual acquaintances. I might, that is, say:

(1) Ann is as clever as X and more modest than Y.

But let us suppose that none of our mutual acquaintances will do. The traits I have in mind, however, are related in a relatively direct way to traits that Conan Doyle portrays his characters as having. So I might say:

(2) The degree of cleverness and the degree of modesty that actually are such that in the Sherlock Holmes stories there is portrayed mere being a person named 'Holmes' with that degree of cleverness and there being a person named 'Watson' with that degree of modesty, are such that Ann's degree of cleverness is comparable to the former, and her degree of modesty is greater than the latter.

While perspicuous, that takes a long time to say, it is not easy to follow, and one needs considerable conceptual sophistication to formulate or to understand it. What I actually say, of course, is:

(3) Ann is as clever as Holmes and more modest than Watson.

In saying this I am not really comparing Ann to two other people. But it is important to see that I am *making as if* to do exactly that. My use of the sentence (3) is framed from within a shallow pretense: a shared, conspiratorial make-believe that we can refer with the names 'Holmes' and 'Watson' to people who are as described in Conan Doyle's stories. It is this pretense that explains my choice of these words in this particular arrangement. Sentence (3) is a sentence for comparing a person to two other people, and, viewed from inside the context of our shallow pretense, the sentence indeed expresses a comparison of Ann to two other people. Certainly, the kind of 'making as if' this exemplifies is not the sort of pretense that draws us into imaginative play; that is why I call it a shallow pretense. But it is nonetheless a form of pretense: to understand me, you have to see that I intend my utterance to be *as if* a statement comparing Ann to two other people, and *only as if* that. You have, that is, to distinguish what's so from what's pretend-so.

The point of pretending, shallowly, with you that I am saying something about three people is that, in so doing, I genuinely say what I would have said in the laborious (2). The crucial distinction is between the sort of claim I make as if to express (I make as if to express a claim about three people), and the sort of claim I genuinely, seriously express (I genuinely express a claim about just one person, namely Ann). I speak within the pretense, pretendedly about the world as we pretend it to be. But I also speak *through* the pretense, about the world as it really is. Somehow, the context of pretending allows me to generate with a pretend assertion of one sort of claim a genuine, serious assertion of a different sort of claim.

But how does this work? What is the connection between what goes on within the pretense and what is really, seriously going on?

Answering that question satisfactorily means confronting a web of issues about the nature of assertion and content. But until we have made a bit of headway in our main tack (we are headed, I remind you, to a consideration of statements about what people think and say), the relevant subtleties are likely to seem more subtle than relevant.

Let's focus on the question of the truth condition of my utterance—that is, on the question what the world really must be like if my utterance is in fact to be a true utterance.[2] The answer I favor will require elaboration, but it is straightforward: the utterance is really true just in case it is true within the pretense. In elaborating this, I will borrow heavily from Kendall Walton's work on make-believe.[3]

If we make believe as I am inviting us to with statement (3), then we are making believe that with 'Holmes' and 'Watson' I can refer to persons with certain levels of cleverness and modesty. So *within the pretense,* what it takes for (3) to be true is that Ann's cleverness approximate Holmes's and that her modesty exceed Watson's. Thus, for the statement to be correctly attributed truth within the pretense (for it to be *fictionally true*), what must *really* be the case is that Ann's cleverness and modesty compare suitably to what is attributed to the characters of Conan Doyle's stories. That is to say, (2) specifies the condition of the fictional truth of (3). And this condition, I propose, is also the genuine truth condition of (3), the condition that must be met if my utterance is to be seriously true.

To lay this out a bit more systematically, I need to develop a distinction between two ways in which propositions can come to be fictionally true: propositions can be *expressly make-believe,* or their being fictionally true can be *generated from reality.*[4] If we expressly make believe that a certain hill is Mount Olympus and that you and I are the gods, then those propositions are directly *forced* to be fictionally true; they are in a sense stipulative, foundational truths of the make-believe. But consider the proposition that a god soon will tumble down the mountain. In our context, this proposition might well be fictionally true, because you or I might well soon tumble; so, if you say 'a god soon will tumble down the mountain', you might turn out to have spoken fictionally truly. In this case, whether it is fictionally true that a god will tumble depends not only on what we are expressly making believe, but also on whether one of us in fact will soon tumble down the hill. Understanding our make-believe involves not only grasping what facts are expressly made-believe to obtain, but also grasping how further pretend-facts are generated from anticipated or unanticipated real facts. As Walton puts it, the *principles of generation* governing our make-believe determine how real facts and fictionally true propositions generate further fictionally true propositions. In this example, we might naturally and spontaneously adopt principles of generation according to which actual tumbles down the hill generate fictional truths about tumbles down the mountain. The important point here is that the fictional truth of some claims depends not only on the imposed parameters of the make-believe (which include the claims that are expressly made-believe and the principles of generation), but also on real-world facts that are in no sense constitutive of the make-believe. I think that statement (3) is such a claim, and that it is made precisely to express a serious commitment to the real world's being such as to make the statement fictionally true.

Here, then, is what I take to be going on in (3):

- There is a transient context of make-believe, in which certain propositions are expressly made-believe; for instance: that there are two persons to whom we can refer with the names 'Holmes' and 'Watson', that the former was a brilliant detective, and that the latter was his faithful sidekick.
- The fictional truth of certain other propositions is generated from reality. That is to say, these propositions are fictionally true in consequence of various real-world facts and of the parameters of the make-believe. Among the fictionally true propositions, depending on whether Ann indeed is sufficiently clever and modest, might be the proposition that Ann is as clever as the detective we can refer to as 'Holmes' and more modest than the physician we can refer to as 'Watson'.[5]
- It is fictionally true that I have expressed a proposition with my utterance of (3)—more particularly, it is fictionally true that there are people to whom we can refer as 'Holmes' and as 'Watson' such that I have asserted the proposition that Ann is as clever as the former and more modest than the latter. Note that since there really are no

such people, there really is no such proposition; however, since it is fictionally true that there are such people, it is fictionally true that there is such a proposition.

- Given the parameters of the make-believe, for it to be fictionally true that the proposition I have expressed with (3) is true, is for (2) to be true. In short, (2) expresses the fictional-truth condition of my utterance.
- For my utterance to be genuinely, seriously true it is necessary and sufficient that it be fictionally true. Thus, (2) expresses the truth condition of my utterance.[6]

This account of (3) involves a postulation of *semantic pretense,* This puts it in league with quite a few other semantic accounts, including, for example, certain theories of metaphor and of talk apparently about numbers. Accounts that postulate semantic pretense break in two the semantic explanation of a statement. First, we explain the semantic properties (such as the logical form, truth conditions, and modal content) of the sort of statement the speaker makes *as if* to make, and second, we explain how the facts about the pretense fix the genuine semantic properties of the serious statement.

The point of postulating semantic pretense is to answer the question, what is a sentence like that doing in a speech act like this? We start with strong opinions about the serious semantic properties of the speech act and strong opinions about the semantic properties for which the sentence is really suited, but these opinions clash: the **sentence doesn't seem suited** to expressing what it actually is used to express.

Part of postulating semantic pretense is to claim that the apparent structure of a sentence is misleading as to the claims made in uses of it. But we do not simply claim this; we explain the use of *that* sentence by its being structurally suited to perform a certain task *within a pretense,* and we explain how its performance of that task suits it for use in genuinely expressing what it otherwise has no business expressing. The aim is to provide satisfying accounts both of what we say and of how we can manage to say it *like that.*

Semantic pretense might find use in a language for any number of reasons. A key one is to let us express using ready, tidy linguistic resources claims that, perspicuously stated, would require cumbersome formulations or unfamiliar terminology.

Semantic pretense involves a special path from the semantic properties of words to the semantic properties of utterances. In that sense it is a kind of figure of speech, and I expect that some philosophers would prefer to say that in such cases the notions of genuine *saying* and of utterance *truth* are out of place. These philosophers would hold that statement (3) could be *true* only if the names 'Holmes' and 'Watson' really referred. But, for one thing, ordinary intuitions about truth and saying are on my side: I have *said that* Ann is very clever and modest, and, supposing she is, my utterance is true. Moreover, the behavior of the sentence (3) when embedded in larger sentences (for instance, in a denial or as the antecedent of a conditional) shows that we linguistically treat this use of the sentence as a genuinely expressive use. Certainly there is a legitimate notion of a statement's *perspicuously* portraying a state of affairs, on which (3) does not perspicuously portray the state of affairs that I take it actually to portray. But it would be unfortunate to assume that every genuine linguistic portrayal of a state of affairs must be a perspicuous portrayal. Obviously, one can opt for a narrow concept of utterance truth by staunchly refusing to admit truth of all but perspicuous sayings. The only complaint against that concept of utterance truth is its irrelevance. The narrow concept of utterance truth does not in general capture the kind of utterance correctness that we normally use 'true' to mark, and it does not track the features of utterances that are central in their status as assertions, denials, and so on. I will adopt here the ordinary concept of utterance truth that allows imperspicuous sayings such as (3) to be true, and I hope that what follows will constitute a partial defense of the utility of this concept.

2. BACK TO HESPERUS AND PHOSPHORUS

Let's assume for now that Frege is correct in taking the names 'Hesperus' and 'Phosphorus' to somehow signal distinct ways of thinking of

Venus. I am not asking you to assume that there are abstract entities suited to being called modes of presentation, nor to assume that ways of thinking have any particular connection to descriptions or features of the object thought about, nor that those who share a mode of presentation are in any intuitive sense cognitively similar, nor that a way of thinking is what a competent user of a name grasps. Indeed, all I ask you to assume with me is that we in fact use the names to effect *some* way of classifying actual and possible thoughts about Venus, some as 'Hesperus thoughts', and others as 'Phosphorus thoughts'. The classification may be obscure, artificial, vague, and certainly it may vary from context to context, but I will assume that in fact we do make such a classification. I hope that this is uncontroversial. I will speak of Hesperus and Phosphorus thoughts as involving 'the Hesperus-mode (of presentation)' and 'the Phosphorus-mode', which unfortunately gives the impression that modes of presentation are assumed to be constituents of thoughts, but I want to be understood simply as meaning that the thoughts are on one side or the other of the distinction that we in fact use the names to signal. Given this, it is trivially true that the thoughts we classify as 'Hesperus thoughts' all involve exactly the same mode of presentation—but of course it is open to us (and indeed it is plausible) to hold that this single mode of presentation encompasses very different cases. After placing more cards on the table, I will return briefly to questions about how classifications of thoughts by modes of presentation might be explained. But in this paper I am primarily concerned not with what distinctions we make among thoughts when we distinguish by ways of thinking, but rather with how the language that we use to report those distinctions manages to do that.

I am going to explore the idea that our talk about what people say or think often involves semantic pretense. As a way of sneaking up on that idea I propose first simply to plant a pretense in order to examine its fruit.

Let's make believe that Hesperus and Phosphorus are two things, that thinking of a thing using the Hesperus-mode constitutes thinking of one of them, and that thinking of a thing using the Phosphorus-mode constitutes thinking of the other. Thus, we are making believe different things about the thoughts we in fact classify as 'Hesperus thoughts' and as 'Phosphorus thoughts.' This make-believe is best described by giving its principles of generation:

> (4) It is fictionally true that there are two things to which we can refer as 'Hesperus' and 'Phosphorus'; when and only when a thought involves the Hesperus-mode, it is fictionally true that the thought concerns the one thing, and when and only when a thought involves the Phosphorus-mode, it is fictionally true that the thought concerns the other thing.

Real facts about people thinking of Venus in the two different ways make it fictionally true that they are thinking of two different things. Thoughts are correctly classified within the pretense as being 'about Hesperus' just when they in fact involve the Hesperus-mode, and they are correctly classified as 'about Phosphorus' just when they in fact involve the Phosphorus-mode. In a sense, we are pretending-apart Venus, by pretending of two kinds of thoughts about it that they are thoughts about different things.

This leaves a great deal open: which features of Venus are we to make believe that the pretended two things possess—just how are we to pretend-apart all that we believe about Venus? Suppose for the moment that, apart from what I have already laid down, I don't say; suppose that I leave our make-believe in this extremely fragmentary state. Remember, I am not suggesting guidelines for imaginative play here, but only establishing a shallow pretense for semantic purposes; we are instituting a manner of speaking, not painting a fantasy world. As I will clarify, we should think of the pretense as a license for representing distinctions about modes of presentation *as* distinctions among the objects presented.

Having imposed the shallow pretense, I want to show how to exploit it as a tool in saying things. I want to show that there are various claims about the real person Hammurabi that our pretense makes much easier to state, since, given what we are now making believe, we can simply report how Hammurabi is related to the *things* Hesperus and Phosphorus.

Let's start with:

(5) Hesperus is visible in the evening, and Hammurabi correctly attributed this feature to it.

There is a strong intuition about the semantic *structure* of this statement that might be expressed as follows: Hammurabi is said here to attribute a certain *feature* to a certain *thing;* his way of thinking of the thing is not brought into play. This is what the sentence *feels like*, semantically; it does not feel as though there are modes of presentation mentioned explicitly, nor even brought in by ellipsis or by tacit proviso. In the tradition of philosophical semantics, this would be deemed a paradigmatically *de re* belief sentence: designed for relating Hammurabi to Hesperus without entailing anything special about how he thinks of the thing. I call statements of that kind *notionally open*—they classify the agent's thought by reference only, and leave open the question how the agent thinks of the thing.

Accordingly, in the context of our makebelieve, let's regard (5) as entirely notionally open: as expressing a claim simply about how Hammurabi is related to a particular object, namely the one we call 'Hesperus', without mention of modes of presentation. But remember that, given what we are pretending, it is fictionally true that someone has a belief about the thing we call 'Hesperus' exactly when they *really* have a belief involving the Hesperus-mode. So this statement is fictionally true just in case Hammurabi in reality had a belief attributing evening visibility to a thing, in which belief he employed the Hesperus-mode. I will adopt a semi-formal notation that lets me express such claims without horrible awkwardness. Where m_H is the mode of presentation in question, the fictional truth turns on the claim diagrammed in (6):

(6) Hammurabi believed: $[m_H]$ is visible in the evening.

This bracket notation is a cognitive twist on the sort of concatenated use-and-mention quotation used in:

(7) Chip says that we are 'politically correct'.

In (6), we are using the bracket notation in a formula that, in describing a belief, partly describes what is allegedly believed to be so, and also describes the agent's alleged way of thinking of the subject matter of the belief. The formula (6) portrays a state of affairs that obtains just in case Hammurabi had a belief ascribing evening visibility, and this belief involved the mode of presentation m_H in the 'subject-position'. (It does not entail that Hammurabi's belief is *about* the mode of presentation.) At the cost of a more complex notation, this state of affairs can be diagrammed more perspicuously.[7]

$$m_H$$
$$\downarrow$$

(8) Hammurabi's belief: $\langle\langle$evening-visible, ???$\rangle\rangle$

The point I want to dwell on is that (6), which is the (nonfictional) condition for the fictional truth of (5), is what we might call 'Fregean' or *de dicto*, or, to choose a term with less baggage, *notionally loaded*—it characterizes Hammurabi's belief by mode of presentation. This shows that by situating ourselves within a shallow pretense, we can exploit a sentence that is *intrinsically* notionally open to characterize beliefs in a notionally loaded way, at least in the sense that the condition of the statement's *fictional* truth is a notionally loaded condition. But I ask you to treat the utterance not merely as a pretend-statement, but also as a genuine, serious statement—one that, like our earlier example about Holmes and Watson, has as its genuine truth condition the condition of its fictional truth. Voilà: a notionally open sentence determines a notionally loaded truth condition. (More revealingly, a notionally open *truth condition* within the pretense generates a notionally loaded serious truth condition.)

This strategy pays off too in:

(9) Hesperus, but not Phosphorus, was thought by Hammurabi to be visible in the evening.

Supposing that the statement, viewed from within the pretense, is notionally open (and once again that is how the sentence structurally *feels*),[8] it is fictionally true just in case Hammurabi attributed evening visibility to a thing under the Hesperus-mode, but not under the

Phosphorus-mode. The condition of fictional truth, then, and hence the genuine truth condition, is the proposition given in (10):

(10) Hammurabi believed: $[m_H]$ is visible in the evening, but Hammurabi did not believe: $[m_P]$ is visible in the evening.

Once again, our simple make-believe bends an intrinsically notionally open sentence to notionally loaded purposes.

Many philosophers have followed Frege in holding that sentences like

(11) Hammurabi believed that Hesperus was brighter than Phosphorus

are, in virtue of the semantic conventions of our language, equipped for ascribing modes of presentation—they are intrinsically notionally loaded sentences. Others have insisted that, despite appearances, such sentences express claims that are entirely notionally open. Now, our make-believe has set up a middle ground. Suppose we consider (11) to be intrinsically notionally open, and suppose I use it within our pretense, in order to make a serious statement. Then, just as before, the pretend-statement is notionally open, but the requirement for its fictional truth—and hence its serious truth condition—is notionally loaded. The statement is genuinely true just in case Hammurabi believed of a thing thought of under the Hesperus-mode that it was brighter than a thing thought of under the Phosphorus-mode—that is, just in case:

(12) Hammurabi believed: $[m_H]$ is brighter than $[m_P]$.

3. THE PRETENSE ACCOUNT

Maybe the manner in which our stipulated make-believe has enabled these notionally loaded claims is revealing of how ordinary notionally loaded attitude talk really works. Maybe, that is to say, attitude-ascribing sentences really are intrinsically notionally open, and yet standard utterances of them have notionally loaded truth conditions, owing to our standard use of something relevantly like the pretense I have suggested. This is the 'pretense account' that I want to pursue. There will be

obstacles. We need, for one thing, to address the issue of what *modal contents* are expressed by attitude reports (as contrasted with their truth conditions); and we need to confront a variety of other interesting issues and examples.

But the obstacle that must first be addressed is stark implausibility. For one thing, the pretense account about attitude reports may seem theoretically far-fetched—attitude reports, after all, form a large, important, and relentlessly scrutinized class of serious statements, and the pretense account has at the very least not often struck theorists as an obvious line of explanation. To be sure, there are many partly related ideas in the literature: Quine deems attitude reporting a 'dramatic idiom', several philosophers treat the talk as describing unreal notional or belief 'worlds' or 'theories', and cognitive simulation theorists have suggested that reporting another's attitudes is really a matter of voicing the attitudes one takes on in simulating the other. Nonetheless, nothing very like the present hypothesis has gained currency.[9]

More importantly, it would surprise and confuse an ordinary speaker to suggest that in discussing Hammurabi's beliefs about Venus, she herself is pretending that Hesperus and Phosphorus are two things rather than one. She might insist that she knows how to pretend that, and that she is quite sure that that is not what she is doing. Normally, we use notionally loaded attitude talk without engaging in the kind of imaginative exercise that would be instigated by the instructions 'Let's pretend that Hesperus and Phosphorus are two things'.

But the pretense account does not require this kind of imaginative pretense. I have said that all it requires is a *shallow* (limited, provisional) pretense that really amounts to the institution of a manner of speaking. Let me clarify what I think the pretense account should be committed to. According to the pretense account, in distinguishing thoughts by mode of presentation we talk as if we are distinguishing among the things thought about—we use our linguistic tools that are designed for specifying and distinguishing among the things thought about. In particular, when we are distinguishing among multiple modes of presentation of a single thing, we standardly talk as if we are referring to different things (for example, Hesperus and Phosphorus). It seems to me that this much should be granted plausibility by every ordinary speaker. According to the pretense account, the way this sort of talk accomplishes the task is illuminated by an account in terms of principles of generation. This requires there being a distinction between what is *as-if-so* and what is really so. What is as-if-so needn't be what we are licensed to imagine (as in more familiar cases of pretense); for the correctness of the pretense account, it need only be that what is as-if-so governs what is correct to say when we are speaking as if we are referring to different things. If we do quite standardly talk as if we are linguistically manipulating things when really we are manipulating modes of presentation, and if the pretense account gives a plausible story about how thing-language manages to do this work, then it matters not at all that we do not ordinarily think of ourselves as pretending that Hesperus and Phosphorus are two things.

So the objection from ordinary-speaker-bafflement can be met by distinguishing, in the class of pretendings, shallow speaking-as-if from imaginative play. Nothing depends on whether the word 'pretense' is appropriate to speaking-as-if. The important commitments of the pretense account are that in ordinary notionally loaded talk there is a distinction between what is as-if-so and what is so, and that the principles of generation proposed by the account are correct.

That the pretense account has not emerged as a contender among theorists (which anyway is not a great objection) can be explained by too much focus on the compositional model on which what a sentence is used to say is built up largely from the meanings of its components. The mechanism of semantic pretense (which surely is sufficiently systematic as not to raise special worries about how finite minds can grasp it) allows dramatic shifts from component-meanings to serious statement-content.

Thus, we should be careful not to overstate the degree of immediate implausibility we face here. There are also several considerations boosting the pretense account's plausibility. Principally, the account manages to answer nicely to key truth-conditional and phenomeno-logical intuitions, as might best be seen in contrast with the Russellian and Fregean accounts of attitude statements.

Synthesizing Russellianism and Fregeanism

The Russellian account[10] has it that all attitude reports are notionally open. To say that Hammurabi believes that Hesperus brighter is than Phosphorus is not to require anything whatever of the modes of presentation Hammurabi employs in the attributed belief. He simply must believe of the *thing* Hesperus (and how he thinks of that thing is irrelevant), that it is brighter than the *thing* Phosphorus (and, again, how he thinks of that thing is irrelevant). Famously, this has implausible consequences: if Hammurabi believes that Hesperus is brighter than Phosphorus, then he necessarily also believes that Phosphorus is brighter than Hesperus (and, even, that Hesperus is brighter than Hesperus). This has led to the stigmatization of Russellianism as a view that sacrifices all truth-conditional plausibility to the dubious idol Logical Purity. But attention to the bizarre inferences licensed by Russellianism obscures a deep source of plausibility for the account. When I say 'Hammurabi believes that Hesperus is brighter than Phosphorus', it *feels like* I am simply talking about Hammurabi, believing, Hesperus, brightness, and Phosphorus—it feels like I am simply portraying a state of affairs in which an individual (Hammurabi) believes that a thing (Hesperus) is brighter than a thing (Phosphorus). Davidson expresses a related point when he writes that if we could regain our pre-Fregean semantic innocence, we would find it incredible to think that names in that-clauses stand for anything different from what they stand for in other contexts.[11] That is surely right, but even more is true: when we focus on the phenomenology of attitude reporting, keeping at arm's length the truth-conditional intuitions informed by worries about substitutivity, it can seem that Russellianism *has to be right*, for what it feels like semantically is that there are no references to modes of presentation, utterances, syntactic structures, or the like. Russellianism is truth-conditionally absurd, but it is the phenomenologically natural semantics for attitude sentences; we have to be led *away* from it by the substitution puzzles.

Frege is led by those puzzles to postulate an interesting—to my mind *too* interesting—hypothesis about our language: in the context of attitude sentences, he proposes, names stand for modes of presentation rather than for their bearers. The effect of this device is that I use the names in (11) to refer *not* to Hesperus and Phosphorus, but to the Hesperus-mode and the Phosphorus-mode. Putting aside qualms about whether modes of presentation really are things to be referred to, I believe that Frege provides an apparatus that issues in rather plausible judgments about the truth conditions and logical properties of a wide class of attitude reports. We do use attitude sentences to ascribe modes of presentation, and Frege's proposed device would explain this neatly, were it not for a major problem. As Davidson remarks, it seems frankly incredible that our language actually employs such a device: when we use names in attitude ascriptions, it feels like we are using them *as names*, and not as names of modes of presentation. Fregeanism accommodates notionally loaded truth conditions, but it is phenomenologically absurd.

The pretense account we are exploring, it seems to me, keeps the good bits of both Russellianism and Fregeanism, while avoiding their worst problems.

According to the pretense account, there really are notionally loaded uses of attitude ascriptions. In using an attitude ascription to attribute a mode of presentation, the speaker adopts a pretense that allows her to talk about thoughts involving that mode of presentation as if she were talking about thoughts *about* a distinctive object. So she uses language that is designed for talking about objects rather than about modes of presentation.

On this account, it is no surprise that the phenomenology of using names in attitude sentences (just like the use of 'Holmes' in (3)) is that of using names to refer to things, since, within the pretense, this is exactly what the speaker is doing. Indeed, within the pretense, this is *all* that she is doing. The logical form of the pretend claim is entirely Russellian: the

agent's belief is classified simply by what things it is about, and modes of presentation do not come into it. In one phenomenological respect the pretense account even has the advantage over Russellianism. Russellianism captures the feeling that the names 'Hesperus' and 'Phosphorus', in (11), are simply used to refer. But, and this is related to Russell's observation about identity, even when one knows that Hesperus *is* Phosphorus, in using (11) one feels as though one is referring to different things with those names. The phenomenology of (11) is precisely that of expressing a state of affairs relating Hammurabi to *two* things. It feels like we are distinguishing *Hesperus*, and Hammurabi's attitudes about *it*, from *Phosphorus*, and Hammurabi's attitudes about *it*. Sober-minded philosophers with robust senses of reality notice this, realize that it cannot be taken seriously, and decide, too hastily, that it cannot be taken *at all*.

The pretense account allows essentially Fregean truth conditions for attitude ascriptions, and so it garners the plausibility that comes with that. But there is no need for the Fregean rule that names take on special sorts of referents in such contexts. As regards names, the pretense account gets by with the straightforward principle that they are devices for talking about their bearers. We reconcile these intuitions: that some attitude reports are notionally loaded, that the names in them function as names normally do, that the names are in some sense not treated as names of the same thing, and that the sentence wears its logical form on its sleeve—there is no tacit or explicit component of the sentence that stands for a mode of presentation.

De Re/De Dicto Unmarked

Another merit of the account is that it allows a de re/de dicto distinction that is not syntactically marked. Most theorists who have expressed a view on the matter believe that many attitude reports are notionally open, and of course it is compatible with the pretense account that sometimes attitude ascriptions are used independently of any pretense and that they are in these cases notionally open. For reasons that I will not pursue here, I am not convinced that there are any ordinary notionally open reports.[12] However, even if I were convinced that there are lots of them, I would remain unconvinced that the distinction between notionally open and notionally loaded reports is syntactically marked. For I very much doubt that a report in which names 'take wide scope' with respect to the attitude verb must be notionally open. Consider again:

(9) Hesperus, but not Phosphorus, was thought by Hammurabi to be visible in the evening.

Here, the names take wide scope (meaning roughly that they are not logically contained in the attitude verb phrase), and yet the overwhelmingly natural interpretation of this statement is the notionally loaded one. The idea that wide scope forces notional openness, it seems to me, comes from assuming that the question whether a statement is notionally loaded must be settled by the logical form of the sentence being used. But the pretense account shows that this assumption is dispensable.

Empty Names No Worry

The pretense account accounts particularly smoothly for the function of nonreferring names in attitude reports such as:

(13) Elijah believes that Santa is overworked.

Just as we talk as if there are distinctive objects corresponding to the Hesperus and Phosphorus concepts, we talk as if there is a distinctive object corresponding to the Santa-mode. Hence, the statement's truth requires that Elijah have an overwork-attributing belief involving that mode of presentation. We will see below how this dovetails with a nice account, due to Walton and Gareth Evans, of statements about existence and nonexistence.

Birds of a Feather

The pretense account suggests a tight connection between notionally loaded propositional attitude reports and certain other statements.[13] Consider first:

(14) Hammurabi was fond of Hesperus but not of Phosphorus.

If we employ the pretense account exactly as before, then for this statement to be true is for

Hammurabi in reality to direct fondness toward a thing thought of under the Hesperus-mode but not under the Phosphorus-mode. Evidently, objectual attitudes like fondness, fearing, and remembering present no new challenge to the pretense account. Consider also:

(15) It was Hesperus, not Phosphorus, that Hammurabi often saw in the evening sky.
(16) Hammurabi saw Hesperus more often than he saw Phosphorus.
(17) Hammurabi's way was lit more often by Hesperus than by Phosphorus.

Each of these sentences can be used naturally by a speaker aware of the identity, in each case the speaker would naturally take the truth of her utterance *not* to allow switching the names, and yet in each case it seems very awkward to hold that there are special opaque senses (for example, of 'lit by') or that names are functioning other than as names of their bearers. It seems prima facie plausible that what is at work in these cases is at least approximately what is at work in notionally loaded attitude reports. And, independently, it seems prima facie very plausible that in these cases we are making as if to refer to different things with the names 'Hesperus' and 'Phosphorus'. This in itself is support for the pretense account: it groups like with like.

Here is how I would explain these statements. In these cases our make-believe about the modes of presentation helps to generate further fictional truths about the pretended two objects. To square our make-believe with the fact that sightings of Venus in different situations are connected with the Hesperus-mode and the Phosphorus-mode, we make believe that, in certain situations, it is Hesperus and not Phosphorus that is seen (indeed, it is Hesperus and not Phosphorus that is *there*), and in others vice versa. Our make-believe does not, of course, resolve all the questions one might have as to just how this is a coherent fiction. But for the purposes of the statements in question, it need not do so, so long as it is clear what to count, within the make-believe, as manifestations of Hesperus versus Phosphorus. And this is pretty clear: we count evening manifestations of Venus as manifestations of Hesperus, and morning manifestations as manifestations of Phosphorus. Thus, for instance, the truth condition of

(16)—that is, the real-world requirement for its fictional truth—is perhaps that Hammurabi saw Venus in the evening more often than he saw it in the morning.

Suppose that Hammurabi wakens abruptly and is wrong about what time it is (and confused about what season it is). It might be correct (the pretense account predicts) to report, "Hammurabi believes that Hesperus is in the sky; but he is wrong—really it's Phosphorus". This indeed seems a natural thing to say, and the pretense account shows how it is entirely compatible with holding that Hammurabi's belief is *really* true (its falsity being merely fictional).

No doubt, special features of the Hesperus/Phosphorus example account for there being a natural way to pretend-apart manifestations of Hesperus and of Phosphorus. There is no similarly natural way to pretend-apart manifestations of Cicero and of Tully (except in the sense of pretending-apart cases of *hearing about* Cicero and cases of *hearing about* Tully, as well, of course, as *believing about* Cicero versus Tully). Where such pretendings-apart are natural, the present account would predict, statements analogous to (15), (16), and (17) will be available.

The Usual Case

One respect in which the Hesperus/Phosphorus example is exceptional is that in it, distinctions about modes of presentation are undeniably live issues. Few deny that in the case of 'Hammurabi believed that Hesperus is brighter than Phosphorus', the speaker is at some communicative level or other distinguishing among (what might be called) modes of presentation. This is exceptional. In most ordinary attitude reports, modes of presentation seem to be the farthest things from our minds. If I say,

(18) Buchanan thinks that Gingrich is a communist

it is not nearly so obviously natural to regard me as talking about modes of presentation.

It would be compatible with the pretense account to hold that the statement (18) is notionally open (for the account is an account only of notionally loaded statements). However, I am convinced that the statement is in fact notionally

loaded. If (18) were notionally open, then for its truth it would suffice that Buchanan recalled once seeing a man adrift in a pro-communist parade (who in fact was Gingrich, though Buchanan did not recognize him), and took him to be a communist. But surely that in fact does not suffice for the truth of my statement. For my statement to be true, Buchanan must attribute communism to Gingrich thinking of him, as we might put it, relevantly normally. Given the thin understanding of a mode of presentation that we have been employing, we can as well say that Buchanan must employ the relevantly normal mode of presentation of Gingrich (it is unimportant whether that strikes you as just the right characterization of how Buchanan must think of Gingrich so long as you grant that the report is notionally loaded).

On the face of it, these two observations are in tension. Intuitively, modes of presentation are far from our minds in the statement, and yet what is claimed is notionally loaded. But there is a synthesis: the possibility of other modes of presentation of Gingrich is *truth-conditionally ignored* in the statement.

There are at least two senses in which a possibility might be said to be ignored in a statement. First, it might be *presuppositionally ignored*—it might be presupposed that the possibility is not actual; but this surely is not necessary here—nothing requires presupposing that Buchanan really has no irrelevant mode of presentation. The crucial sense in which a possibility can be ignored is that it can be truth-conditionally ignored—it can be tacitly settled that the possibility is not to be regarded as relevant to the truth of the statement. In a statement of

(19) There is milk in the refrigerator

the possibility that there is a dried drip of milk on the shelf might be ignored—it might be tacitly settled that this is not to be *counted* a case of there being milk in the refrigerator despite its really *being* a case of there being milk in the refrigerator. I believe that this is aptly regarded as a form of pretense, since it is a (tacit) determination not to count as a P what really is a P (the proper explanation of such cases[14] will advert to principles of generation). Returning to our example, in context it is clear that only thoughts involving the relevantly normal mode of presentation *are to be counted thoughts about Gingrich.* More precisely, we are engaging in a make-believe with the following principle of generation:

> (20) Thoughts involving the relevantly normal mode of presentation of Gingrich (and only those) generate fictional truths that one is thinking *about Gingrich.*

The parallel with the pretense operative in the Hesperus/Phosphorus case is this: in both cases thoughts involving a certain mode of presentation (and only such thoughts) generate fictional truths that the thoughts concern a distinctive object. In the Hesperus/Phosphorus case, this requires pretending Venus apart into two *merely* fictional objects; in the case of Gingrich, no pretending-apart is required—Gingrich himself can serve within the pretense as the needed distinctive object. By ignoring other modes of presentation in this way, our talk simply of beliefs *about Gingrich* acquires notionally loaded truth conditions. Like the pretense about milk in (19), the pretense about thoughts about Gingrich normally doesn't draw notice until truth-conditional intuitions are canvassed. This resolves the observed tension and brings the usual case under the wing of the pretense account.

It is absolutely essential to the plausibility of this application of the pretense account that we keep in mind the shallow nature of the claimed pretense. The claim is simply that we use one categorization of thoughts (being about Gingrich) to effect a different categorization (involving the normal mode of presentation of Gingrich). We talk as if we are discussing any thoughts about Gingrich whatsoever in order really to discuss only thoughts that involve the normal mode of presentation of him. The proposed principle of generation embodies that idea.

If a pretense really plays this role in (18), then surely a similar pretense operates in just about every ordinary attitude report, for the puzzling tension we observed about that statement is rather the rule than the exception: modes of presentation are not often on our minds in attitude reporting, but it is usually counterintuitive to view reports as notionally open. In the unexceptional cases, some mode of presentation of the entity has an obvious claim to relevance; so it is plausible that, as in the Gingrich case, we quite standardly truth-conditionally ignore all but the obviously relevant mode of presentation of an entity.[15] In the exceptional cases, such as the Hesperus/Phosphorus case and many others familiar in the philosophical literature, it is still more plausible to postulate pretenses involving modes of presentation, for modes of presentation are quite plausibly "in the air" in such statements, and the pretense account offers an account (which I hope by now has begun to seem reasonably plausible) of how they enter into the truth conditions of the statements.

Beginning at Home

If the pretense account is correct, then it seems that speaking about modes of presentation as if we were speaking about the objects presented is something that we do spontaneously and naturally. But why should that be? Let me distinguish this question from an easier one. It is not surprising to find that our natural ways of thinking about the thoughts of others involve pretense in one form or another. It is certainly plausible—and recent work in philosophy and cognitive psychology has only made it more so—that we often make sense of others by figuring out how to see things their way. So it would come as no surprise that attitude reporting involves pretense in some way. But the pretense account postulates a specific sort of pretense that is not a matter of pretending to be someone else, or to be in their shoes. Why should it be natural to make as if one is distinguishing among objects when one is really distinguishing modes of presentation?

There may be a deep explanation of the naturalness of this pretense based on features of normal first-person access to one's attitudes. Consider how absurd it would be for Hammurabi, in thought, to self-ascribe attitudes in a way that makes the attributed modes of presentation explicit:

> (21) I believe that Hesperus, thought of under my Hesperus-mode, is brighter than Phosphorus, thought of under my Phosphorus-mode.
>
> (22) When I see Hesperus tonight, I will imagine holding Hesperus, thought of under my Hesperus-mode, in my hand.

The absurdity here is something beyond the mere awkwardness and terminological unfamiliarity of the third-person case. It has to do with the fact that the modes of presentation explicitly self-attributed in these cases are *already there*, in that they are *employed* in the ascriptions to represent the individuals that the attitudes are about. Normally, when one has reason to consider a self-ascription of an attitude about a thing, in the context of ascription one thinks of the thing using the very mode of presentation that one has reason to ascribe to oneself.[16] Thus, in the first-person case, the strategy of distinguishing among modes of presentation as if among objects presented is an utterly natural and elegant cognitive shorthand.

A similar consideration extends to the third-person case to whatever extent it is typical that when we represent to ourselves *which thing* another's attitude is about, we represent it *using* the very mode of presentation we ascribe to the other. Perhaps that indeed is typical, but the question may be controversial. But even if it is not typical, the familiarity of the pretense strategy from the first-person case might make it thoroughly natural in the third-person case as well (especially if third-person ascription in some way involves simulated or proxy first-person ascription). It is important to see, in any case, that the pretense hypothesis is not obviated by a simulation account of third-person ascription, since it is needed even for understanding first-person ascriptions.

4. MODES OF PRESENTATION

The pretense account employs the notion of a mode of presentation, and nothing could be more important in assessing the account than determining the prospects for satisfying explanations of what modes of presentation are, and of the access to them that speakers and hearers rely on in producing and understanding attitude reports.

I have little novel to say about these matters here.[17] The use to which modes of presentation are put in the pretense account does require that modes of presentation group together actual and possible cases of thinking about (or thinking as if about) a thing. It is not required that they be natural kinds of mental representation, nor that they be stably associated with natural language expressions, nor that to engage in discourse *about* them one need to *grasp* them.

For a given mode of presentation, it might be that knowing what it is (knowing what it is to employ it) is prior to one's capacity to participate in the kind of pretense that the pretense account describes. But, however natural that seems, it is not necessary. I am attracted to the view that our fundamental access to certain modes of presentation comes from our capacities to participate in pretenses of just this kind. In such cases, we in the first instance have the capacity to understand what it takes to be, fictionally, thinking *about* this or that object, and only derivatively on this do we have any conception of the modes of presentation—of the requirements for its being fictionally true that someone is thinking of these objects.[18]

5. MODAL CONTENT AND INNOCENCE

So far we have explored a proposal restricted to the question of truth conditions; we have not decided what the pretense account should say about the modal contents expressed by attitude reports.

In addition to having truth conditions, I will assume, utterances of sentences can express modal contents. My chief assumption about modal content is this: the modal content of an utterance answers the question, what must a possible situation be like for it to be accurately portrayed by this (actual) utterance?[19] In many semantic theories, utterances of sentences are said to express propositions, or portray states of affairs; these semantic values (according to many such theories) determine the modal content of the utterance.

So conceived, the modal content of an utterance and the utterance's truth condition have to agree about the utterance's truth *value* (they have to 'agree at the actual world'), but the truth condition of an utterance need not be equivalent to its modal content. For instance, an utterance of the sentence:

(23) This utterance does not exist

has an impossible truth condition (it cannot occur truly) but a contingently false modal content (the utterance correctly describes just those possible situations in which it does not exist). An utterance's truth condition and its modal content are the answers to different questions. The truth condition answers the question, what must be so if this is to be a true utterance? The modal content answers the question, what must a possible situation be like for it to be accurately described by this (actual) utterance? The answers to these questions can come apart, sometimes dramatically. Indeed, shared truth *value* is the only necessary link.[20] A semantic account of truth conditions, then, seriously underdetermines an account of modal content.

Now, it is open to us in developing the pretense account simply to identify the modal contents of attitude ascriptions with their truth conditions. However, this would be a mistake. To see why, let's return to the idea of semantic innocence—the idea that a name in an attitude report stands for just its ordinary referent.

The pretense account as we have developed it thus far seems two-faced about semantic innocence. The account entails that a name in an ascription behaves completely innocently *within* the pretense; we pretend to relate the agent simply to the bearer of the name. But even if the name names a real thing, the ascription's truth condition is not a proposition that contains the thing as a constituent. This may appear to be a problematic loss of semantic innocence. Consider the argument from (24) and (25) to (26):

(24) Hammurabi believed that Hesperus is visible in the evening.
(25) Hesperus is a planet.
(26) So, there is a real thing such that Hammurabi had a belief attributing evening visibility to it.

Surely this is a valid argument. One might worry that if the pretense account were true, the inference would be invalid, since the truth condition of (24) would be a proposition not about Hesperus but about a mode of presentation—

(27) Hammurabi believed: [m_H] is visible in the evening

—which has no *logical* connection to the thing Hesperus itself.

A first response to this worry is to observe that on the pretense account there indeed is an

entailment here: so long as the premises are true, so is the conclusion. This is because the mode of presentation that our make-believe concerns is always a mode of presentation of the name's bearer, if it has one.[21] Thus, if (24) is true, then Hammurabi's belief is about what our use of the name 'Hesperus' names, if anything. If (25) is true, then our use of the name 'Hesperus' really does name something, and so the conclusion (26) must be true.

But demonstrating a truth-conditional entailment may not be enough. There is an intuition that not only is there a truth-conditional entailment, there is also an entailment in modal content: the modal contents of the premises necessitate the modal content of the conclusion. Any possible situation correctly described by the premises is correctly described by the conclusion as well. There is a natural line of reasoning that might lead one to doubt the entailment in modal content. I will reject this line, but it will be useful to sketch it. The line starts with an argument that the modal content of (24) does not *by itself* entail that of (26), because the argument from just (24) to (26) is relevantly like the clearly invalid argument from (28) to (29):

(28) Elijah believes that Santa is overworked.
(29) So, there is a real thing such that Elijah has a belief attributing overwork to it.

So *if* there is an entailment in modal content from (24) and (25) to (26), the line goes, the premise (25) is indispensable. But if the modal content of (24) does not entail the modal content of (26) by itself, then it is absurd to suppose that it might do so when conjoined with the information *that Venus is a planet* (which is the modal content of (25)). For if (24) does not by itself entail (26), then it does not entail that Hammurabi has a belief about Venus. The modal content of (25) could be relevant to the entailment only if the modal content of (24) were itself about Venus; but if it were, surely premise (25) would not be required for the entailment. So, while there is a logical entailment, one might well doubt that there is an entailment in modal content.[22]

But I cannot accept this line of reasoning. If there is not an entailment in modal content from (24) on its own to (26), it must be that there are possible situations in which Hammurabi believes that Hesperus is visible in the evening, but in which Hammurabi's belief is not about Venus. But how could that be? Might a belief correctly so described be about a different thing? Then we face the unattractive prospect that Hammurabi might believe, and believe *truly*, that Hesperus is visible in the evening, in a situation in which Hesperus is not visible in the evening. It seems hardly more palatable to admit a situation in which Hammurabi believes that Hesperus is visible in the evening, but in which his belief is about nothing whatever. This constitutes a strong case for the claim that in any situation in which Hammurabi believes that Hesperus is visible in the evening, his belief is about Venus—and so a strong case for the entailment in modal content from (24) on its own to (26).

Fortunately, the pretense account can admit an entailment in modal content. Because of the gap between truth condition and modal content, and because the Hesperus-mode actually presents Venus, it is consistent with the pretense account that (24) expresses a modal content true of just those possible worlds in which Hammurabi attributes evening-visibility *to Venus* using the Hesperus-mode (for if so, modal content and truth condition would agree as to truth value). Of course, it is one thing for a view to be coherent and another for it to be defensible.

One way to defend it would be to hold that the Hesperus-mode denotes Venus essentially, so that it follows from Hammurabi's having a belief employing it that the belief is about Venus. But I will set this possibility aside, since a far less contentious motivation is available.

We need to answer the question, what possible situations are truly described by the utterance of (24)? If this question is capable of an answer, it must be possible to view the utterance not simply as determining a real-world condition for its actual fictional truth, but also as determining a condition that must be met by a possible world if the utterance is to be fictionally true in relation to that world. But what can it mean for an utterance to be fictionally true in relation to another really possible world? I suggest that we need the notion of genuine possibilities generating fictional possibilities. This

notion is needed anyway, since even ordinary pretenses like our gods on the hill game extend modally. It is fictionally true that I *might* have pushed a god and made him fall, and this fact about fictional possibility is generated by the real possibility that I should have pushed you and made you fall. Just as real-world facts about the Hesperus-mode make it fictionally true that there are facts 'about Hesperus,' so certain genuine possibilities make it fictionally true that there are certain sorts of possibilities 'for Hesperus.' The attitude report correctly describes just those possible worlds that generate fictional possibilities that, fictionally, are described truly by the utterance.

The key question regarding semantic innocence, we can now see, is: which real possibilities generate fictional possibilities in which there are attitudes 'about Hesperus' and 'about Phosphorus'? The argument from (24) to (26) fails to exhibit an entailment in modal content if we answer this question in a particular way: by deciding that *all* possibilities in which there are attitudes involving the Hesperus-mode generate fictional possibilities involving attitudes 'about Hesperus.' If this is the right answer, then the possible worlds (if there are any) in which Hammurabi uses the Hesperus-mode to think not about Venus but about Mercury generate fictional possibilities in which Hammurabi is thinking 'about Hesperus.' But this clearly cannot be the right answer. Instead, the contours of our pretense seem normally to be such that only possibilities about attitudes that both involve the Hesperus-mode *and are about Venus* generate fictional possibilities concerning attitudes 'about Hesperus.'[23] Plausibly, this is a reflection within the pretense of the rigidity of names.[24]

If this is right, then (24) gives a true description only of possible situations in which Hammurabi's belief is about Venus, and so there is an entailment from that statement to (26). There is no similar entailment from (28) to (29) because the principles of generation that generate fictional thoughts (and fictionally possible thoughts) 'about Santa' are not similarly tied to any real individual. Indeed, plausibly *no* genuine possibilities in which the Santa-mode succeeds in denoting generate fictionally possible cases of thinking 'about Santa' (another reflection within the pretense of the rigidity of names).

These considerations suggest a general semantic account of attitude reports. The modal contents of attitude reports (typically) concern the real objects, if any, that the ascribed attitude allegedly concerns, as well as the required modes of presentation. For instance, we can express the modal content of 'Hammurabi believes that Hesperus is brighter than Phosphorus' as follows:

(30) Hammurabi believed: Venus[m_H] is brighter than Venus [m_P].

That is, Hammurabi believed that Venus (thought of under the Hesperus-mode) is brighter than Venus (thought of under the Phosphorus-mode). This seems to me just the right account of modal content. It is not an unfamiliar account: Stephen Schiffer's 'hidden indexical theory,' John Perry's and my 'unarticulated constituents' account, Mark Richard's 'Russellian Annotated Matrix' account, and François Recanati's 'quasi-singular proposition' account offer roughly the same story.[25] The key problem for this semantic account has been that despite its plausible verdicts concerning which statements are true about which possible situations, the various developments of it have seemed ad hoc and false to the phenomenology of ordinary speech. The pretense account offers a deep and phenomenologically plausible explanation for the semantics. Perhaps surprisingly, what grounds the semantics is not any technical riff from philosophical logic, but an understanding of indirectly serious discourse that has been made possible by Walton's work in aesthetics.

6. EXISTENCE AND IDENTITY

Now the promised return to identity. To set the stage, I will make two observations: one about a curious pattern in our talk about identity, the other about a prima facie difficulty for the pretense account of attitude reporting.

Here, like it or not, is how we (and not only unjustly rebuked undergraduate metaphysicians!) talk about identity:

(31) When *two things* are identical, the one thing has the same properties as *the other thing*.

As for the prima facie problem for the pretense account, consider:

(32) Galileo knew that Hesperus is Phosphorus.

According to the pretense account, it is fictionally true that the names 'Hesperus' and 'Phosphorus' name two objects, and so the speaker here fictionally claims that Galileo knew of *two* things that they are numerically identical. But no two things are identical, and so surely the statement is fictionally false, *whatever* Galileo believed. This would be a devastating problem for the pretense account, since surely (32) is relevantly like the other attitude reports we have considered, and in fact it is true.

In addressing these issues, I will draw on an account due to Walton and Evans of statements attributing existence and nonexistence. The details of their presentations differ, but both hold that in saying

(33) Santa does not exist

one is pretending (or at least alluding to a pretense) that one can refer to a thing with a certain kind of use of the name 'Santa', in order to *disavow* such uses; one's statement is true just in case such uses do not refer. One very attractive feature of these accounts, as Walton and Evans emphasize, is that they capture the semantic phenomenology of such uses of empty names: they *feel* just like ordinary uses of referring names. This is respected by taking the use of the name, within the pretense, to *be* an ordinary use of a referring name.

Walton suggests, somewhat tentatively, that in talking about what does and does not exist we might be engaging in a pretense to the effect that 'exists' expresses a discriminating property—a property that not everything has. This makes marvelous sense of a lot of puzzling talk about existence:

(34) I've discovered that there are some things which don't really exist but which I had been duped into thinking exist. Among them are Santa, the tooth fairy, and Barney.

This talk makes perfect sense if we view it as framed within a pretense that there is a thing for every mode of presentation, except that some of these things do not have a certain property—one that we can refer to (within the pretense) as 'existence'. The things of which it is fictionally true that they have this property are exactly *everything*—everything in reality, that is. We pretend that there are more things than just those, but that everything else doesn't have this property. More precisely, while it is fictionally true of all modes of presentation that they denote things, it is fictionally true that a mode of presentation denotes a thing *that has the property expressed by 'exists'* just when that mode of presentation actually denotes a thing. When the speaker says 'There are some things that do not exist', I would say, she is relying both on the genuine universal property of existence (which informs 'There are') and the pretended discriminating property (which informs 'do not exist'). Within the pretense, this might be described as the distinction between *being* and *really existing*. Of course, no such ontological distinction is seriously employed by the account, nor does the account attribute such an ontological distinction to us—our talk really concerns only real things and real modes of presentation.

The considerations about modal content in the previous section may suggest a contribution to this account. So far, I have sketched only an account of the truth conditions of statements about existence, as contrasted with their modal content. Evans does not discuss the modal content of these statements. Walton suggests that in a nonexistence statement "what one asserts is simply that to attempt to refer in a certain way is to fail."[26] But this is problematic. Consider: it does not seem that possible worlds in which the Santa-mode denotes someone normally are correctly described as worlds in which Santa exists. And it does not seem right that possible worlds in which Venus does not exist but in which the Hesperus-mode denotes something other than Venus are normally correctly described as worlds in which Hesperus exists. Further, it does seem right to describe a world in which Venus exists as one in which Hesperus exists, even if no attempts to refer happen in it or in any nearby worlds. Probably these observations do not constitute a knock-down argument. But it seems to me that our attention is misdirected if, in assessing whether a statement like (33) correctly describes a possible situation, we focus on (potential) attempted acts of reference *in that*

situation. It seems to me that the critical question must be what an attempted reference *from here* picks out *there*. More precisely, we need to ask which real possibilities make it fictionally true that there are possibilities in which 'Santa exists'. I believe that the following ideas are defensible: normally, (a) no possible world makes it fictionally true that there is a possible world in which 'Santa exists' (so that (33) normally expresses a necessary content despite having a contingent truth condition), and (b) all and only possible worlds in which Venus exists make it fictionally true that there are possible worlds in which 'Hesperus exists'.[27] It seems to me that this suggestion has the merit of construing the modal content of existence claims as ontological rather than meta-representational: they are really about what things there are, and not about our referential access to things.

In the case of identity, the observation about our odd identity-talk and the difficulty for the pretense account about (32) cry out for a parallel explanation. In talking about identity we standardly talk as if we think that things can be identical to *other* things. We talk as if identity, which in fact is as celibate as a relation can be, is promiscuous. More precisely, we pretend that with certain of our linguistic devices that normally express identity, we can express a relation that can hold between distinct objects. It is fictionally true that this relation holds between two objects when these fictional objects result from pretending-apart a single object (as in the case of Hesperus and Phosphorus).[28] In our pretense, for instance, Hesperus and Phosphorus are *two* objects that fictionally bear to each other the pretended promiscuous identity-relation: the one thing is, fictionally, the 'same as' the other thing.

One pay-off for the pretense account about attitude ascription is that statements like (32) are accommodated neatly. Within the pretense, the speaker of (32) is claiming that Galileo knew of two things that they bear the promiscuous identity-relation to each other. And it is fictionally true that the two things named by 'Hesperus' and 'Phosphorus' *do* bear that relation to each other. The real-world requirement for the fictional truth of (32) is the (true) claim (35):

(35) Galileo knowledgeably believed: $[m_H]$ is $[m_P]$.

(This proposition entails that the two modes of presentation in fact co-denote.) And, using our general apparatus, we see that the serious modal content of the statement is equivalent to:

(36) Galileo knowledgeably believed: Venus [m_H] is Venus [m_P].

What of identity claims themselves?

Frege's account, remember, allows even informative and true identity claims simply to attribute the relation of strict identity between the referents of referring expressions. The *distinction* between the two sides of the equation that explains the substantial nature of the statements is simply the difference in the modes of presentation tied to the terms. This seems to me a satisfying explanation both of the truth conditions of these claims and of their substantiality. Frege did not address the question of modal content, but I believe that there is also a satisfying account of modal content open to him, namely Kripke's: identity claims (at least those in which the singular terms are referring devices and indeed refer) have necessary or impossible contents, depending on whether they are in fact true. That Frege's account of truth conditions coheres with Kripke's account of modal content is another manifestation of the gap between truth conditions and modal content.

I am happy to allow that Frege's explanation of identity statements is often exactly right. But it does not offer a fully satisfying explanation of certain identity statements, in particular, those of which Russell's phenomenological confession rings most true: it feels as though we are saying of one thing that it is the same thing as *another thing*. In these cases, the pretense account offers a promising alternative picture. Consider, as framed within our running pretense, the statement:

(37) Hesperus is Phosphorus.

Suppose that for this statement to be true is for it to be fictionally true. For it to be fictionally true is for it to be fictionally true that the two objects denoted by these names stand in the pretended promiscuous identity relation. For that to be fictionally true is for it (really) to be the case that the object denoted by the Hesperus-mode is the very object denoted by the Phosphorus-

mode. Thus, the truth conditions offered by the pretense account are entirely Fregean. (Actually, that is only half true, since identity statements with nonreferring singular terms are deemed by the Fregean account not to possess truth values, whereas sometimes they are deemed *false* on the pretense account.[29] This offers accurate predictions; consider: 'He is Santa Claus'.) Furthermore, the Kripkean account of modal content open to Frege is open as well to the pretense account. The extra apparatus of the pretense account retains approximately Fregean truth conditions and Kripkean modal content, but it supplies a satisfying explanation of Russell's phenomenological observation—one, moreover, that coheres with an enhanced understanding of how we ascribe modes of presentation in reporting thought and talk.

7. APPENDIX

We will run through a number of examples and issues to exercise the pretense account.

7.1 Speakers Mistaken about Identities

Here is a potential problem. Suppose the speaker of

(11) Hammurabi believed that Hesperus was brighter than Phosphorus

herself believes that the two names name different objects. Surely, one might object, she is not *making believe* that the names name different objects, and yet the report means just what it means in our mouths—so the pretense account does not seem to apply correctly.[30]

Recall our distinction between what is expressly made-believe and what is fictionally true. Fictional truths that are not themselves expressly made-believe are generated from what is made-believe with help from reality. In the statement

(3) Ann is as clever as Holmes and more modest than Watson

we do not *make believe* that Ann really is so related to individuals bearing those names. Whether this statement is fictionally true depends on Ann's actual cleverness and modesty. It may in fact be fictionally true, and we may believe that it is fictionally true, but even if so it is not something we are expressly making believe to be true, since it could be fictionally false consistently with everything we are making believe. While it may be only in odd cases that someone is mistaken about what she is expressly making believe, it is quite common to be mistaken about what is fictionally true; we might well be mistaken about whether (3) is fictionally true.

The pretense account requires that for each of the two modes of presentation ascribed in (11), real facts about attitudes involving that mode of presentation generate fictional truths (fictionally) about a distinctive object. It is not entailed by this that the speaker must make believe that there are two objects, for she might assume that the two required objects are supplied by reality. Recall that we took the speaker of

(18) Buchanan thinks that Gingrich is a communist

to be making believe of a certain mode of presentation that it is *the way* to think of Gingrich. For the same reasons, it is plausible to take the speaker of (11) to be making believe, of the two modes of presentation, that each is the only way to think of the thing thus thought of. Since the modes of presentation in fact denote just one object, in fact her make-believe generates a certain *merely* fictional truth—a claim that is fictionally true and not really true—namely, the claim that the modes of presentation denote two objects. The speaker of (11) knows that it is *fictionally true* that the modes of presentation denote two objects. But since she is unaware that Hesperus is Phosphorus, she thinks that the *reason* that it is fictionally true that there are two objects so denoted is that it is *true* that there are two objects so denoted. She thinks something is genuinely true (and only derivatively fictionally true) when really it is merely fictionally true. She rightly assumes that it is correct to talk as if there are two objects, but she is mistaken about why it is correct to talk that way. The response to the objection, then, is that, true, the claim that there are two objects rather than one is not something she is making believe; nonetheless,

this is something that is fictionally true for her, and that is all that is entailed by the pretense account. This is a case of *resolute fictional truth*, in which a believed proposition counts as fictionally true even if the belief is false.[31]

7.2 Intentional Identity

Consider Geach's example of what he calls *intentional identity*.[32]

(38) Hob thinks a witch has blighted Bob's mare, and Nob wonders whether she killed Cob's sow.

Let us assume that the speaker and hearers do not believe in witches, and assume that no person has harmed the mare and sow.

This sentence might admit of importantly different readings. Perhaps on one reading (which is promoted if one inserts 'in addition' after 'Nob'), it is asserted that Hob believes the claim that exactly one witch blighted Bob's mare, Nob is said to believe that too, and to wonder whether it is true that there is just one witch who blighted Bob's mare, who also killed Cob's sow. Let us call this the in-addition reading. It can be explained by taking there to be a tacit claim that Nob too believes that a witch has blighted Bob's mare, and by taking 'she' to be, in Geach's terminology, a pronoun of laziness for the description 'the witch who has blighted Bob's mare' (and the description can be treated in Russell's way, with narrow scope):

(39) Hob thinks that just one witch has blighted Bob's mare, Nob thinks that just one witch has blighted Bob's mare, and Nob wonders whether there is someone who is the one witch who has blighted Bob's mare and who killed Cob's sow.

There is also a reading that involves something more aptly called intentional identity (and it is this reading that Geach has in mind). This reading is promoted if one replaces 'a witch' with 'a certain witch', and replaces 'she' with 'that witch'. It is difficult to explain this reading without portraying the statement as entailing that *there is* a witch. For now let us yield to this difficulty, and paraphrase the reading in question as:

(40) A certain witch is such that Hob thinks that she blighted has Bob's mare, and Nob wonders whether she killed Cob's sow.

This reading tends to be dismissed by the sober; after all, it is stipulated that the speaker does not believe in witches. But that may be to take the statement too seriously. In a pretense in which a mode of presentation generates fictional facts about a distinctive object, it might well be that attitudes involving a certain mode of presentation make it fictionally true that there are attitudes about a certain witch (a witch who fictionally does not 'exist', supposing the mode of presentation fails to refer). Let us call such a mode of presentation a 'witch-generating' one. On the pretense account, the statement is fictionally true just if it is fictionally true that there is a witch, about whom Hob and Nob have such-and-such beliefs. Hence, the real-world requirement for fictional truth, and also the truth condition of the serious statement, would be this:

(41) There is a witch-generating mode of presentation m such that Hob believes: [m] has blighted Bob's mare, and Nob wonders whether: [m] killed Cob's sow.[33]

Let us call this the fictional-object reading of (38). Notice that it does not require that Nob share Hob's belief. This is appropriate, for (as Geach points out) statement (38) might be correctly used in the following sort of case: the community is agreed that there is a witch that has been damaging livestock; Hob says 'That witch has blighted Bob's mare' and Nob says (elsewhere at the same time) 'That witch may have killed Cob's sow'.

It is possible, too, that there is a reading that combines the in-addition reading with the fictional-object reading, in the obvious way (adjust (41) by requiring Nob to have the same belief that Hob is said to have).

A related phenomenon also is nicely described by Geach:[34]

Although I see no reason to doubt that:

(42) The witch who blighted Bob's mare killed Cob's sow is analyzable as:
(43) Just one witch blighted Bob's mare and she killed Cob's sow

it seems doubtful whether these two are mutually replaceable *salva veritate* in a context like "Nob wonders whether". If we prefix 'Nob wonders whether' to (42), the result seems to be analyzable, not as:

(44) Nob wonders whether (the following is the case): just one witch blighted Bob's mare and she killed Cob's sow

but rather in some such way as this:

(45) Nob assumes that just one witch blighted Bob's mare, and Nob wonders whether she (that same witch) killed Cob's sow.[35]

The pretense account might offer an explanation as follows. The use in

(46) Nob wonders whether the witch who blighted Bob's mare killed Cob's sow

of the description 'the witch who blighted Bob's mare' is, pretendedly, a wide-scoped description—a specification of *the thing* Nob's wonder is said to be about—which means that really it serves to specify the mode of presentation that Nob's wonder is said to involve. This allows, correctly, that (46) need not imply that Nob really assumes that there is such a witch (the ascribed wonder seems consistent with serious doubts on that issue). It explains, too, why it is admissible to add 'of course, that witch doesn't exist'. And it explains why Geach's strategy of paraphrase will not work for:

(47) Nob wonders whether the witch who blighted Bob's mare exists.

Another very perplexing puzzle about intentional identity is due to Walter Edelberg.[36] On natural readings, neither of (48) and (49) entails the other:

(48) Arsky thinks someone murdered Smith, and Barsky thinks he murdered Jones.
(49) Barsky thinks someone murdered Jones, and Arsky thinks he murdered Smith.

Now, the in-addition readings of these statements do not entail one another. So we are home free if the in-addition readings are in question. But the most puzzling version of this case defeats those readings. Suppose the circumstances known to the speaker and hearer are as follows: No one really has murdered or even has wounded Smith or Jones, but both have suffered serious wounds. Barsky and Arsky are aware of these wounds. Barsky has no suspects, but he believes that just one person wounded both men, and he believes that Jones, but not Smith, has died from his wounds. Arsky has no suspects, he does not believe that just one person wounded both men, and he believes that Smith, but not Jones, has died from his wounds. In these circumstances, Edelberg holds, there are natural readings on which (48) seems true and (49) seems false.

I am not sure he is right about this; our ability to interpret these statements in the described circumstances may involve some non-trivial charitable creative reinterpretation. But let's assume that there are the needed readings, and explore what they might be. The circumstances block in-addition readings, because Barsky does not believe that Smith has been murdered and Arsky does not believe that Jones has been murdered. Fictional-object readings may be possible, however. Here is a try at expressing such readings:

(50) The one Arsky thinks murdered Smith, Barsky thinks murdered Jones.
(51) The one Barsky thinks murdered Jones, Arsky thinks murdered Smith.

Now, these seem to me on the right track: to whatever extent (48) and (49) have the readings that Edelberg needs, so do (50) and (51). One apparent difficulty with these readings is that these sentences seem to entail that Arsky and Barsky have particular suspects in the attacks. But really all that is required by the fictional-object treatment is that they have modes of presentation of the attackers (as in the circumstances plausibly they do) that fictionally generate objects of thought (as again is plausible). If you can get yourself in the frame of mind wherein (50) sounds true of the described situation, ask yourself: *who* is it that Arsky thinks murdered Smith and that Barsky thinks murdered Jones? I think the answer will be: *Smith's attacker.* Plausibly, then, it is fictionally true that there is an object denotable as 'Smith's attacker', who makes (50) true. Now ask yourself, in that same frame of mind, but now focus-

ing on the false-seeming (51), who is it that Barsky thinks murdered Jones (and that Arsky doesn't think murdered Smith)? I think the answer will be: *Jones's attacker.* What plausibly is going on, then, is this: fictionally there are two individuals, denotable as 'Smith's attacker' and 'Jones's attacker'; it is fictionally true that Barsky believes both that these individuals are identical and that since Jones's attacker murdered Jones, so did Smith's attacker; nonetheless, when we say 'the one whom Barsky thinks murdered Jones', it is fictionally Jones's attacker rather than Smith's attacker that is denoted—perhaps because, while he thinks that Smith's attacker is guilty of the same murder, it is only guilt by association ('identity'!) with the primary suspect (Jones's attacker).

7.3 Embedded Ascriptions

Consider:

(52) Sarah believes that Ray suspects that Laurie is pregnant.

Applying the pretense account, we face a new issue: what does it take for it to be fictionally true that a given object of thought (in this case, Laurie) is being ascribed by one person (Sarah) as the object of another person's (Ray's) attitudes? The pretense account has it that for Ray's suspicion fictionally to be about Laurie, it must involve a certain mode of presentation, call it m_L. For Sarah's belief fictionally to attribute to Ray a suspicion about Laurie, then, should require Sarah really to have a belief whose truth requires Ray to think of Laurie using m_L.

Now, here we face a rather abstruse complication. For the truth of Sarah's belief to turn on a fact about m_L (namely the question whether Ray has a suspicion involving it) does not rule out that she has a very odd, irrelevant way of thinking about m_L itself—perhaps one she would be likely to acquire only in a philosophy class devoted to the alleged Fregean hierarchy problems. But surely that possibility *is* ruled out by (52)—the statement, then, is *second-order notionally loaded;* it entails that Sarah has a certain kind of grasp on the way she takes Ray to think of Laurie. To capture this, it is plausible to hold that Sarah counts fictionally as ascribing an attitude *about Laurie* just if she really has the proper grasp on the mode of presentation required for an attitude fictionally to be about Laurie. The truth condition of (52) might be represented in this way:

(53) Sarah believes: $[m_R]$ suspects: $[[m_{mL}]]$ is pregnant.

The double brackets, I stipulate (and it really is an additional stipulation about the notation), indicate that the mode of presentation specified within is, according to this proposition, Sarah's second-order mode of presentation—that is, her mode of presentation of the mode of presentation of Laurie that she attributes to Ray. This likely seems complicated, but in my view the 'output' is just what we should hope for: (52) is treated as a notionally loaded ascription of a notionally loaded ascription of an attitude.[37]

7.4 Anaphora and *De Se* Reports

Consider:

(54) When Fred came in, Doris doubted that he was Fred.

This notionally loaded ascription seems to present the following difficulty for the pretense account: If the account applies to it, then in the statement it must be fictionally true that the uses of 'he' and of 'Fred' in the complement clause refer to two objects. However, the use of 'he' is anaphoric on the earlier use of 'Fred', so surely it is not fictionally true that the use of 'he' refers to anything but what the use of 'Fred' refers to.

The analogous example (55) is if anything even more troublesome:

(55) Sometimes, when I see an important philosopher, I don't realize that she *is* that philosopher [or: that she is *she*].

The pretense account would predict that by the time we get to the complement clause, it is fictionally true that 'she' and 'that philosopher' (or the second 'she') refer to two things (and no doubt that these things are 'identical'). But *each* of these two expressions seems to be anaphoric on 'an important philosopher'.

One response is that while anaphora requires co-reference, co-reference in the context of the sort of pretense we are exploring is just a bit lib-

eral: expressions co-refer only when they refer to things that are identical, but remember that it can be fictionally true that *two* things are identical. The response, then, is that the anaphoric connections in these examples are consistent with its being fictionally true that the expressions in the complement clauses refer to two things. In each case, that is, it is clear that the speaker is pretending that there are two 'numerically identical' things, and it is clear to which of them the various names and pronominal phrases refer.[38]

A different response to the problem about (54) would be to treat some of the pronominal phrases here as 'lazy for' descriptions (such as 'the person who came in'). In spelling out this response, there is a decision to be made about the scope of these descriptions. If they take narrow scope with respect to the attitude verbs (if they are descriptions that the agents allegedly would use), then, for instance, the claim made in (54) is just the claim that would be made in (58):

(58) When Fred came in, Doris doubted that the person who came in was Fred.

But this does not require what should be required, that Doris be said to have a doubt that a certain *person* is Fred. If the descriptions take wide scope (if they are descriptions that the speakers are using to describe things), then the pretense account enters into the response more centrally: in statement (54), that is to say, it would be fictionally true that the speaker's tacit use of 'the person who came in' denotes a thing thinkable only in a certain way. Statement (54) would express, within the pretense, what is expressed in (59):

(59) When Fred came in, the person who came in was such that Doris doubted that he was Fred.

Similar considerations apply to '*de se*' cases. Suppose that Lingens has amnesia and is lost in a library,[39] and that you are reading on a computer screen a report of his progress. The report presents evidence that the lost man is, unbeknownst to himself, Lingens. You say:

(60) That man doesn't think that he is Lingens.
(61) I think that he is Lingens.

The explanation of (60) is that you are pretending-apart Lingens into two people, and (pretendedly) claiming that the man doesn't believe that these two people ('he' and Lingens) are identical. For that man fictionally to have a belief about the first of these two people, the belief must involve a certain mode of presentation (call it m_1), which is such that the man thinks of someone that way when he thinks of them first-personally. For him fictionally to have a belief about the second person, his belief must involve a certain mode of presentation (call it m_2) which requires thinking of Lingens as being called 'Lingens'. In (61), similarly, the speaker is pretending-apart 'he' and Lingens, and (pretendedly) claiming that he believes that the two are identical. The two fictional individuals again correspond to two ascribed modes of presentation m_3 (corresponding to 'he') and m_4 (corresponding to 'Lingens').

Plausibly, m_2 and m_4 are the same mode of presentation. What about m_1 and m_3? Using m_1 requires of Lingens that he think of himself first-personally, while using m_3 requires of you that you think of Lingens as 'that man in the report.' Now, this is not obviously incompatible with m_1 and m_3 being the same mode of presentation. Remember that we are not assuming that modes of presentation reflect cognitive similarities between the agents who employ them; here we are taking them to be simply whatever classification of thoughts we in fact make in notionally loaded attitude reports. For the pretense account, the question of the identity of m_1 and m_3 amounts to the question of the fictional identity of the individuals ('he' and 'he') that the reports fictionally concern. Is it fictional that you have claimed of just one person both that you believe him to be Lingens and that Lingens does not? I am not sure, but suppose that you send an electronic message to Lingens's terminal in the library:

(62) Unlike you, I think that you are Lingens.

Here, surely, the pretense account sees a single fictional individual being used to ascribe a first-personal belief to Lingens and a 'that man in the report' belief to you. We might say that an interpersonally heterogeneous mode of presentation is ascribed. This is perfectly coherent, and thus

we have seen how (60), (61), and (62) can all be true.

Exercise for the reader: explore the consequences for this account of (62) of your receiving the error message, 'User cannot send message to own terminal'.

ACKNOWLEDGMENTS

This paper has benefited from very generous help. Thanks to participants in my seminar at the University of Michigan and to audiences at MIT, Wayne State University, New York University, and Stanford. I am particularly grateful to Kent Bach, David Braun, Alex Byrne, Ray Elugardo, Avrom Faderman, Graeme Forbes, Ned Hall, David Hills, Jim Joyce, Michael McKinsey, Joe Moore, Larry Powers, François Recanati, Ian Rumfitt, Stephen Schiffer, Laura Schroeter, Dan Sperber, Loretta Torrago, Ken Walton, Steve Yablo, Ed Zalta, and the editors of the *Philosophical Review*.

NOTES

1. *The Philosophy of Logical Atomism* (La Salle, Illinois: Open Court, 1985), 115.
2. Speaking of *the* truth condition of an utterance is in general dangerous, since one needs to decide to hold fixed certain features of the utterance in order to ask what *more* is needed if it is to be a true utterance. To see this, notice that what's wrong with the following view is not *falsity*: every utterance has the same truth condition: that the utterance be a true one. It is only when certain aspects of the utterance are held fixed (perhaps including its syntax and some 'lexical' features of the constituent expressions, contextual facts and speaker intentions), that a more specific truth condition can be isolated. But for the moment let's go with the flow.
3. *Mimesis as Make-Believe* (Cambridge: Harvard University Press, 1990), and "Metaphor and Prop Oriented Make-Believe," *European Journal of Philosophy* 1 (1993): 39–56.
4. Walton's distinction between directly and indirectly generated (or primary and implied), fictionally true propositions seems to cross-cut this one. See *Mimesis as Make-Believe*, 140–44.
5. Why mention these metalinguistic propositions rather than, say, 'the proposition that Ann is as clever as Holmes and more modest than Watson'? Since 'Holmes' and 'Watson' do not really refer to anything, I do not assume that there is any such proposition. Indeed I think that there is no such proposition, and so that there is no such proposition that can be even fictionally true. In explaining *what* is fictionally so, I want to identify propositions that are fictionally true, and so of course I restrict myself to all the propositions that there are.
6. It is compatible with this account that there is a 'fictionally operator' governing the statement, but I

don't see any point in postulating hidden syntax in this sort of case. I prefer to see this statement as employing a trope, akin to metaphor, characterized by a distinctive path connecting utterances to their truth conditions.

It perhaps is preferable to view this case not as involving a pretend (and also serious) *assertion*, but as involving two pretend (and also serious) *predications*—namely, of 'is as clever as Holmes' and of 'is more modest than Watson'. We then would inquire after the (fictional and serious) conditions of applicability, analogously to how we have sought truth conditions. There is no reason to restrict this sort of analysis to entire speech acts, nor even to utterances of whole sentences.

7. See my *Talk about Beliefs,* chapter 4. The need for complexity in a perspicuous notation is an important motivation for semantic pretense.

8. The reader may feel, too, that this sentence would naturally be used in making a notionally loaded claim. I agree, and what I hope to make clear is just how this sentence can do that. But the first step is to notice how the intuition about what the sentence can be used to *claim* conflicts with an intuition about how it is semantically structured. I will show how to reconcile these intuitions.

9. See W. V. O. Quine, *Word and Object* (Cambridge: MIT, 1960), esp. 219; Daniel Dennett, "Beyond Belief," in *The Intentional Stance* (Cambridge: MIT, 1987); François Recanati, "Domains of Discourse," *Linguistics and Philosophy* 19 (1996): 445–75; Walter Edelberg, "Intentional Identity and the Attitudes," *Linguistics and Philosophy* 15 (1992): 561–96, and "A Perspectivalist Semantics for the Attitudes," *Noûs* 29 (1995): 316–42; Robert Gordon, "Folk Psychology as Simulation," *Mind and Language* 1 (1986): 158–71; Alan Leslie, "Some Implications of Pretense for Mechanisms Underlying the Child's Theory of Mind," in *Developing Theories of Mind,* ed. J. Astington, P. Harris, and D. Olson (Cambridge: Cambridge University Press, 1988), 19–46. See also Fred Landman, *Towards a Theory of Information* (Dordrecht: Foris, 1986).

10. See for instance Nathan Salmon, *Frege's Puzzle* (Cambridge: MIT, 1986), and Scott Soames, "Direct Reference, Propositional Attitudes and Semantic Content," *Philosophical Topics* 15 (1987): 44–87.

11. "On Saying That," in *Inquiries into Truth and Interpretation* (New York: Oxford University Press, 1984).

12. See my "Notional Specificity," *Mind and Language* 10 (1995): 464–77.

13. There recently has been a flurry of interest in apparent failures of substitution in other than the 'classic' propositional attitude contexts. See for instance Anne Bezuidenhout, "Pragmatics and Singular Reference," *Mind and Language* 11 (1996): 133–59; Jennifer Saul, "Substitution and Simple Sentences," *Analysis* (1997): 102–8; Graeme Forbes, "How Much Substitutivity?" *Analysis* 57 (1997): 109–13.

14. Such cases are enormously common. See John

Searle, "Literal Meaning," in *Expression and Meaning* (Cambridge: Cambridge University Press, 1979).

15. Given our thin conception of mode of presentation, remember, there is no distinction between specifying a single mode of presentation and specifying a type or class of modes of presentation. Considerations like those supporting the notional loadedness of the Gingrich case seem to me to support taking most ordinary reports to be notionally loaded as regards not only particulars (like Gingrich) but also universals (like being a communist), but I ignore this in the present discussion.

16. For an abnormal case in which this is not so, see my "I Falsely Believe That P," *Analysis* 52 (1992): 191.

17. For useful recent work on these questions, see Jennifer Saul, "The Pragmatics of Attitude Ascription," forthcoming. See also my *Talk about Beliefs* (Cambridge: MIT, 1992), especially chapter 5, and "Notional Specificity."

18. This is connected to certain suggestions Evans makes in his discussion of existence statements in *Varieties of Reference* (New York: Oxford University Press, 1982). Relevant also is one way in which, according to Walton, metaphors can be *essential;* see "Metaphor and Prop Oriented Make-Believe."

19. A conception of content built around this assumption is familiar from Kripke's *Naming and Necessity* (Cambridge: Harvard University Press, 1981). The theoretical centrality of such a notion of content (but not its semantic reality) is questioned by Michael Dummett in appendix 3 of *The Interpretation of Frege's Philosophy* (Cambridge: Harvard University Press, 1981), and by Evans in "Reference and Contingency," in *Collected Papers* (New York: Oxford University Press, 1985).

20. Given any two true sentences *p* and *q*, whatever their truth conditions and modal contents, we can construct (using the 'Actually' operator of philosophical logic) a sentence whose truth condition is necessarily equivalent to that of *p* and yet whose modal content is necessarily equivalent to that of *q*, namely, 'Actually *p*, and if actually *q* then *q*'. And for any two false sentences *p* and *q*, the same feature is possessed by 'Actually *p*, or if not actually *q* then *q*'.

21. This needs to be unpacked carefully if names are individuated in the ordinary way, such that different things can have the same name. We must understand the use of the name in the ascription as borrowing from one of one's personal traditions of univocally using the name to refer (one has different 'Aristotle' traditions for what one at least suspects might be different Aristotles). The mode of presentation in question must concern not just any bearer of the name, but what the name in fact names within that tradition. The source of this constraint will become clear later in the present section.

22. I should note the possibility of considering both premises to be framed from within the pretense. We can interpret (25) as meaning 'Hesperus is *really* a planet' in analogy to 'Hesperus (really) exists'. As will be clearer after our discussion of existence and

identity, this might give (25) the truth condition that the Hesperus-mode denotes a planet. If (25) is given this interpretation, there can be an entailment in modal content even if the modal content expressed by (24) has nothing essential to do with Venus.

23. If 'the Hesperus-mode' owes its nature to the contours of this pretense, then it seems to follow that it is necessary that thoughts involving it concern Venus.

24. Certain examples suggest that this principle of generation is defeasible: 'Had Hesperus not been Phosphorus, I would have believed that Hesperus was not Phosphorus'. Related examples are considered by Michael Dummett in *Frege: Philosophy of Language* (Cambridge: Harvard University Press, 1973), 113; Landman in *Towards a Theory of Information*; and Bezuidenhout in "Pragmatics and Singular Reference."

25. Schiffer, "Naming and Knowing," in *Midwest Studies in Philosophy 2*, ed. P. French, T. Uehling, and H. Wettstein (Minneapolis: University of Minnesota Press, 1977); Crimmins and Perry, "The Prince and the Phone Booth," *Journal of Philosophy* 86 (1989): 685–711; Crimmins, *Talk about Beliefs;* Richard, *Propositional Attitudes* (Cambridge: Cambridge University Press, 1990); Recanati, *Direct Reference* (Oxford: Blackwell, 1993).

26. *Mimesis as Make-Believe*, 426. He also considers the possibility that one seriously asserts that it is fictionally true that one speaks truly in making the statement.

27. However, as noted earlier, such constraints may be defeasible, offering resources to explain such sentences as 'Had Santa existed, I would have gotten more toys' and 'Had Hesperus not been Phosphorus . . .'.

28. We might allow that there are other ways for it to become fictionally true that this relation holds, to allow, for instance, for the fictional truth of 'Zeus is Jupiter'.

29. This too is only approximately true, depending on how the contours of the pretended promiscuous 'identity' relation are to be spelled out. In particular, we might well allow 'Santa is Santa' and 'Zeus is Jupiter' to be counted true—in the pretense, 'identity' extends to 'things that don't exist'.

30. Steve Yablo first called such examples to my attention.

31. In a reenactment of Waterloo, one might believe that it is in fact Napoleon's sword in one's hand, and yet the fictional truth of this claim would not depend on its truth.

32. "Intentional Identity" and "The Perils of Pauline," in *Logic Matters* (Berkeley: University of California Press, 1972). In thinking about intentional identity I

have profited from Edelberg's "A New Puzzle about Intentional Identity," *Journal of Philosophical Logic* 15 (1986): 1–25; "Intentional Identity and the Attitudes," and "A Perspectivalist Semantics for the Attitudes"; as well as Michael McKinsey's "Mental Anaphora," *Synthese* 66 (1986): 159–75.

33. This need not entail, as we would put it colloquially, that Nob assumes that the witch exists; it does plausibly entail that he does not assume that she does not exist. This seems right: we can unproblematically append to (38) 'but is unsure whether she even exists'.

34. "Intentional Identity," 151 (sentence labels altered).

35. As Geach notes, the example is not completely compelling. A better case (McKinsey's) is: Nob wishes that he caught the fish that got away (where the speaker doubts there really is such a fish).

36. "A New Puzzle about Intentional Identity."

37. I continue to find persuasive the argument in *Talk about Beliefs* (193–94) for the claim that modes of presentation of modes of presentation are ascribed in embedded reports. The hierarchy has no end, but this is not a *problem:* thought is nowhere bare.

38. A possible reason for discomfort with this response is that it seems to predict that (56) would be an apt surrogate for (54), when really it is at best awkward:

(56) ? When Fred came in, Doris doubted that he was the same person as Fred.

In contrast, (57) does seem an apt surrogate:

(57) When someone who in fact was Fred came in, Doris doubted that he was the same person as Fred.

This is prima facie evidence that the response is not on the right track, since if (56) did involve the predicted sort of pretense, as (57) clearly does, surely it would be no more awkward than (57).

On the other hand, perhaps (56) is not really so very awkward, and perhaps the awkwardness it has can be explained consistently with taking it to be semantically equivalent to (54). For instance, it might be that the crucial difference between (54) and (56) is a garden-path phenomenon—that it owes to a cognitive effect of the increased 'parsing distance' between 'he' and 'Fred'. The hearer discovers that she must, so to speak, pretend-apart Fred only when she encounters the second occurrence of 'Fred'. In (56), perhaps, this realization is more surprising, since it comes only after the hearer has been lulled into being unprepared for it. So it seems that this response can be defended.

39. See John Perry, "The Problem of the Essential Indexical," in *The Problem of the Essential Indexical* (New York: Oxford University Press, 1993).

37 Descriptivism, Pretense, and the Frege-Russell Problems

FREDERICK KROON

1. THEORIES OF REFERENCE AND THE FREGE-RUSSELL PROBLEMS

Contrary to frequent declarations that descriptivism as a theory of how names refer is dead and gone, such a descriptivism is, to all appearances, alive and well. Or rather, a descendent of that doctrine is alive and well. This new version—neo-descriptivism, for short—is supposedly immune from the usual arguments against descriptivism, in large part because it avoids classical descriptivism's emphasis on salient, first-come-to-mind properties and holds instead that a name's reference-fixing content is typically given by (a cluster of) egocentric properties specified in terms of broadly causal relationships between a speaker and his environment: properties like *being the actual individual called 'Aristotle' referred to by my informants' use of the name, being the actual individual called 'George Bush' whom I have seen/heard described as the U.S. President who started the second Gulf War,* and so on.[1] (The addition of the rigidifier 'actually' is to make name-occurrences rigid; the rigidity of (most) names is not in contention.) What these neo-descriptivists claim is that the usual modal, semantical, and epistemological arguments against classical descriptivism don't get much of a foothold against this new version, especially if we don't insist (as we shouldn't) that

speakers be able to state these properties on demand. It is enough that these are properties implicit in the semantic judgments of speakers. Recent attacks notwithstanding, such a neo-descriptivism has struck many philosophers as a credible and worthy successor to classical descriptivism.[2]

It almost goes without saying that part of the conventional descriptivist wisdom accepted by these neo-descriptivists is that their theory is able to solve the problems that motivated the rise of descriptivism at the start of the twentieth century: the problems of why true identity statements can be informative, how to analyze singular negative existentials, and why co-referring names can't always be interchanged *salva veritate* in propositional attitude reports (the Frege-Russell problems, for short).[3] *Almost* without saying: for what led these neo-descriptivists to their version of descriptivism was not, by and large, the desire to solve these familiar problems but to get the account of reference determination right in the face of the Kripke-Donnellan arguments against classical descriptivism. Still, once we have a credible descriptivist account of the reference-fixing content of name uses, it seems that little stands in the way of directly using that account to solve the other problems, in particular the informativeness and negative existential problems. (Puzzles about belief are much

F. Kroon, "Descriptivism, Pretense, and the Frege-Russell Problems," *The Philosophical Review*, 113 (2004), pp. 1–30. © Cornell University. Reprinted by permission of the publisher and the author.

less straightforward, as Russell already pointed out.)

Such a (strong) neo-descriptivism about content can be contrasted with a weak form of neo-descriptivism according to which reference is fixed in the manner described by strong neo-descriptivism but where it is not assumed that reference-fixing descriptions yield semantic content.[4] Until further notice, it is the strong form of the theory I will have in mind. (Strong) neo-descriptivists think that their theory can do what Frege and Russell wanted descriptivism to do, without running into the problems that face descriptivism's supposed nemesis—the New Theory of Reference, often touted as the new orthodoxy in philosophical semantics following the "death" of descriptivism. For the New Theory's commitment to a Millian or direct reference theory of names means that it can't explain in semantic terms just how true identities can be informative, or how true negative existentials can have any content, let alone a true content.[5] If, as Millianism holds, the semantic content of a name is just its referent, there just aren't enough contents to explain content in these cases. The neo-descriptivist has no such "not enough contents to explain content" problem.

I think that there is much to be said for the neo-descriptivist program, but I also think defenders of neo-descriptivism need to do rather more than they have done so far where the Frege-Russell problems are concerned. The locutions that give rise to Frege-Russell problems—"Frege-Russell locutions"—have certain features that reflect a kind of remarkable underlying phenomenology and should make us suspicious of any simple-minded application of neo-descriptivist ideas to these problems. By contrast, a number of New Theorists have drawn attention to these features in an attempt to argue that the New Theory is in fact well placed to solve the problems, despite the apparent lack of promise afforded by its semantic framework. The tool they offer in support is the idea of semantic pretense.

In this paper I shall argue for another way of understanding these features. After showing why we need to take them seriously, I argue that the appeal to semantic pretense by New Theorists won't work. Among other things, it makes a mystery of the modal properties of Frege-Russell locutions. Focusing on the informativeness and negative existential problems, I then argue for a wholly different way of understanding the relevance of pretense to the Frege-Russell problems. It turns out that, on this alternative model, neo-descriptivism has much to gain from an appeal to pretense.

2. THE PHENOMENOLOGY OF FREGE-RUSSELL LOCUTIONS

Consider again the Frege-Russell problems: the negative existential problem, the informativeness problem, and the various problems about belief and other propositional attitude reports. As Mark Crimmins pointed out in an important paper some years ago (1998), one remarkable feature of all the locutions implicated in these problems is their Janus-faced character. On the one hand, most of us think that the contribution made by the names involved in these locutions to what the locutions are used to communicate is in many cases not exhausted by the objects denoted by the names. Thus, 'Hamlet doesn't exist' is (used to say something) true without 'Hamlet' denoting anyone; 'Hesperus is identical to Phosphorus' is true and informative even though there is only one object denoted by the two names 'Hesperus' and 'Phosphorus'; 'Hammurabi believed that only Hesperus, and not Phosphorus as well, was visible in the evening' is true despite there being only one object denoted by these names. On the other hand, we can also detect an intuitive sense in which the truth of the communicated content seems to depend on the disposition of various objects of reference alone. Intuitively, it is because of Hamlet's not existing that 'Hamlet doesn't exist' is true; it is because of Hesperus and Phosphorus bearing the relation of identity to each other (something they needn't have done) that 'Hesperus is in fact identical to Phosphorus' is true; it is because of the distinct beliefs Hammurabi had about these two celestial bodies—identical bodies, as it turns out—that 'Hammurabi believed that only Hesperus, and not Phosphorus as well, was visible in the evening' is true. Putting things this way is a natural way of registering our sense of what's going on.

This sense is, of course, most familiar in the case of negative existentials, where it has often been used to support the doctrine that there are genuine fictional objects. But Russell realized it was rather more general. This is how he puts the point in the case of identity statements:

When you say 'Scott is the author of Waverley', you are half-tempted to think there are two people, one of whom is Scott and the other the author of Waverley, and that they happen to be the same. That is obviously absurd, but that is the sort of way one is always tempted to deal with identity. (1985,115)

Russell is surely right on both counts: we are half tempted to think of identity this way, even though the intuitive thought that there are two things we are identifying is absurd. But, absurd or not, this intuitive underlying "phenomenology" is not easily disposed of. There is a remarkable robustness about the phenomenology: it erupts into our linguistic practices, not just in our sense of what is going on, and not in a way that we can easily suppress. And, as Crimmins emphasizes, a phenomenology of this absurdly profligate yet robust kind infects all the Frege-Russell locutions.

Consider negative existentials again. One might expect the unchallenged assertion of a negative existential 'N doesn't exist' to be a conversation-stopper, since the name N is somehow declared to be empty, to have no application. But this is simply not the case. What typically happens after an utterance of a negative existential is further, often even busier, conversation, seemingly about the very object declared to be non-existent. This is scarcely surprising, for negative existentials often leave open too many possibilities, and so cry out for explanation or clarification ('What do you mean, Miranda doesn't exist. Is she a fictional character, perhaps, or one of Anne's imaginary friends, or . . . ?'). Consider, for example, the way *Time Magazine* answered Canadian Prime Minister Mulroney's puzzled question "Who is Murphy Brown?" after Dan Quayle's notorious attack on Murphy Brown's morals:

(1) Murphy Brown does not exist. She is a much-loved TV character played by Candice Bergen. Murphy is a blonde media anchor-goddess and wiseguy and now a defiantly unmarried madonna. (*Time International,* June 1, 1992)

Or consider informative identities again, say:

(2) Hesperus is in fact identical to Phosphorus.

Competent speakers of English treat such a sentence as trivially equivalent to the following (apparently) plural identity sentence:

(3) Hesperus and Phosphorus are in fact identical.

Philosophers and linguists commonly think of the plural in such a case as a bogus plural, a syntactic product of the fact that we have a conjunction of two referring expressions. But that view is not reflected in the behavior of ordinary speakers. Even knowledgeable speakers are just as likely to phrase a statement like (3) in terms of a more blatant plural, for example,

(4) Those two famous celestial bodies of Babylonian astronomy, Hesperus and Phosphorus, are in fact identical.

Competent users of English simply do not see the second one as deviant, even if philosophers do.

Or consider belief reports again. We don't simply say:

(5) Hammurabi believed that only Hesperus, and not Phosphorus as well, was visible in the evening.

Knowledgeable speakers are just as likely to phrase this report in terms of a plural *de re* construction, for example,

(6) Of those two famous celestial bodies of Babylonian astronomy, Hesperus and Phosphorus, the first was believed by Hammurabi to be visible in the evening but not the second.

Here the attribution of plurality is no longer confined within a *de dicto* report, but seems to be made to the very objects the belief is about.[6]

3. SEMANTIC PRETENSE

The question, then, is how to account for the phenomenology, given its remarkable robustness. But if it is indeed implausible to suppose that the phenomenology involves some kind of mistake on the part of speakers, aren't we then committed to taking the phenomenology seriously? And doesn't that in turn entail that we should adopt a realistic construal of the phenomenology, accepting that there really are objects that don't exist (perhaps Meinongian objects of some kind, as in Zalta 1988), and even objects that are distinct, yet in the relevant sense identical (the "guises" of Casteñeda 1989, say)? And shouldn't we then say that it is the disposition of these objects that makes the various statements (1)–(6) true?

Mark Crimmins (1998) thinks that we can take the phenomenology seriously, yet steer a middle road between such a realistic construal of the phenomenology and a standard error theory. As a supporter of the New Theory of Reference, he believes that the very profligacy of the phenomenology can be turned to its advantage. Roughly speaking, even if the New Theory doesn't admit "enough contents to explain content," in Frege-Russell locutions speakers seem to talk *as if* there are contents aplenty, and this doing-as-if might be enough to generate a reasonable replacement proposition. More precisely, the view is that such locutions involve a kind of semantic pretense, a doing-as-if the world is a certain rather profligate way, in order to make a serious true-or-false claim about the world, with facts about what makes something true in the pretense fixing the genuine semantic properties of the serious claim.

The idea, which owes much to Ken Walton's make-believe account of fiction (1990), is broadly this. Suppose we have in place the notion of a game of make-believe: roughly, a stretch of imaginative activity, involving one or more actors, subject to rules that determine what is to be imagined as part of the game. In Walton's influential development of this idea, children as well as adults play such games on the basis of props that mandate that they imagine certain things. Thus, a children's game may require its participants to imagine that a certain oddly shaped stump is a bear, that actions done to the stump are acts against the bear, and so on. Another sort of game, indulged in by children as well as adults, involves reading or listening to a

story, a game that requires its participants to imagine that certain events really happened (that there really was a famous detective called 'Holmes' who lived on Baker Street, for example). In Walton's terminology, a sentence, proposition, or utterance is *fictional* or *fictionally true* (true in the game of make-believe) when the conventions pertaining to props of the relevant kind *require* participants in the game to imagine its being true.[7] Principles that tell us what kinds of circumstances make a certain kind of proposition or sentence (-utterance) fictionally true are called 'principles of generation'.

Walton emphasizes the role of the imagination, but that suggests a degree and quality of involvement that may not be necessary to our participation in forms of make-believe. To use a phrase used earlier, it is often enough to "do-as-if" the world is a certain way, where that may involve forms of linguistic and cognitive activity that fall well short of full imaginative involvement. As to why speakers would engage in such less committed forms of pretense, one kind of reason deserves special mention. The following example suggests that doing so sometimes provides a natural and efficient way in which a speaker can make a serious assertion about the world. Consider Johnny's mother as she watches Johnny put a bungy cord around the stump and pull on it. Johnny's action makes it fictional that Johnny has lassoed a bear, a fictional truth that is likely to engage Johnny's imagination to a significant degree. But it is not what interests his mother as she impatiently tells him that "that's the second lasso you have broken on the bear this afternoon." What would make that utterance fictionally true is the obtaining of a certain real world truth condition: Johnny's breaking a second bungy cord on the stump. Her utterance shows her transient involvement in Johnny's game, an involvement that shows that she is "doing-as-if" the bungy cord is a lasso but not necessarily a strongly, imaginative involvement in that game. Her purpose in this case is not primarily to *pretend* to assert something through her involvement in the game, but to *genuinely* assert something about the real world, namely that Johnny has broken a second bungy cord on the stump. She thereby indulges in what Crimmins calls a piece of semantic pretense, saying something that is, as she thinks, fictionally true in order to assert that the world is a certain way—the way that makes her utterance fictionally true.

Following Mark Richard (2000), let's call this phenomenon 'piggy backing'. More precisely, to piggy back is to make an utterance u within a pretense in which u has a real world truth condition c, thereby asserting a proposition that is in fact true if c obtains. (For reasons that will become clear later, Crimmins thinks that we can't in general assume that what is asserted is simply that c obtains.) In Crimmins's application of this idea to the case of propositional attitude reports, an utterance of a sentence of the form 'Hammurabi believed that Hesperus was F and Phosphorus was G' is embedded in the pretense that there are two objects, one named 'Hesperus', the other 'Phosphorus', and that thinking of a thing using the 'Hesperus' mode of presentation constitutes thinking of one of them, and that thinking of a thing using the 'Phosphorus' mode of presentation constitutes thinking of the other. The pretense thus employs principles of generation along the lines of:

P1 If (and only if) someone has a thought, belief, etc., involving the Hesperus-mode (alternatively, the Phosphorus-mode), then it is fictionally true that they have a thought, belief, etc. about the object named 'Hesperus' (alternatively, the object named 'Phosphorus').

Now consider my utterance of 'Hammurabi believed that only Hesperus, and not Phosphorus as well, was visible in the evening'. Given my little transient game of make-believe, it is thus fictionally true that I have said that Hammurabi believed of the object named 'Hesperus' that it was visible in the evening, while disbelieving of the object named 'Phosphorus' that it was visible in the evening. But in this kind of case my interest is clearly not in the content of the pretense itself but in what it says about Hammurabi's real belief state. According to Crimmins, we engage in this kind of pretense in order to piggy back: what I am trying to assert with my utterance (*really* assert) is a claim in fact true if the real world truth condition of my utterance

holds, and hence (by P1) a claim in fact true if Hammurabi believed under the Hesperus-mode, while disbelieving under the Phosphorus-mode, that the object presented by the mode was visible in the evening.

It is far from obvious, however, how this kind of account might be extended to deal with a report like 'Sally knows that Hesperus and Phosphorus are in fact identical', for in the pretense the sentence 'Hesperus and Phosphorus are in fact identical' seems to say something strictly impossible. Crimmins's answer is that when we speak of identity, we speak as if it is a relation that can hold between distinct objects. He suggests that such talk therefore involves an additional bit of pretense, namely that "with certain of our linguistic devices that normally express identity, we can express a relation which can hold between distinct objects" (1998, 35), where it is fictionally true that this promiscuous relation holds between two objects when these objects result from pretending-apart a single object, using two different modes of presentation. In particular, we have:

P2 If (and only if) the Hesperus- and Phosphorus-modes are modes that present the same thing, then it is fictionally true that the (distinct) objects named 'Hesperus' and 'Phosphorus' are identical.

It follows that, through my piggy backing on the pretense and relying on P2 (and an obvious embedding principle for propositional attitude reports), my utterance of '(Sally knows that) Hesperus and Phosphorus are in fact identical' is used to assert a claim that is in fact true just in case (Sally knows that) the Hesperus- and Phosphorus-modes are modes of the same thing.

So that is how semantic pretense allows us to accommodate the profligate object-involving phenomenology of propositional attitude reports as well as of plural-sounding identity claims. Crimmins himself thinks that where attitude reports are concerned, such an account vindicates important New Theory intuitions, since at one level it vindicates the idea that such reports can be seen as semantically innocent, with neo-Russellian logical syntax, even if at another level it suggests that we can't escape something like Fregean truth conditions.

That leaves us with just one other case, the case of negative existentials. This case had already been given a pretense treatment by Walton (1990); here I'll simply present Crimmins's version of Walton's view. Again appealing to modes of presentation, Crimmins thinks that in uttering something like 'Hamlet doesn't exist', the speaker pretends that all modes of presentation, including the Hamlet-mode, present something, and that, in addition, 'exists' is a predicate that partitions the domain of discourse into two sets, the things that exist and those that don't. The principle of generation for 'exists' then yields:

P3 If (and only if) the Hamlet-mode presents an individual, then it is fictionally true that the object named 'Hamlet' exists.

By piggy backing, it follows that an utterance of '(Sally knows that) Hamlet doesn't exist' is used to assert a claim in fact true just in case (Sally knows that) the Hamlet-mode doesn't present anything.

4. SOME PROBLEMS

So there we have it: a unified explanation of how Frege-Russell locutions can be used to assert something genuinely true, one that accepts the apparent logico-semantic properties of these locutions and to that extent takes the accompanying phenomenology seriously, without, however, accepting a realistic construal of the phenomenology.

But despite its considerable elegance and power, this explanation faces some thorny problems. First of all, note the relatively underdetermined nature of Crimmins's understanding of modes of presentation. He says little more than that the Hesperus-mode is whatever allows us to classify together certain thoughts about Venus as Hesperus-thoughts (likewise for the Phosphorus-mode), adding that any such classification "may be obscure, artificial, vague, and ... vary from context to context" (1998, 8–9).[8] That is about all we are told about modes of presentation, and this silence contributes to the following problem. What we might call the 'modal' problem concerns the troubling issue of the modal content of what speakers assert

through using Frege-Russell locutions. In order to know the proposition asserted with an utterance of a Frege-Russell locution, we must know what *possible* situations are described by this utterance, not just what actual situation is described. Piggy backing, however, yields only the actual truth condition of a fictionally true Frege-Russell locution, in a way that seems to resist extrapolation to other possible worlds. Take an utterance of 'Hamlet doesn't exist' or 'Hesperus exists'. Given our rather robust modal intuitions about such cases, it seems that the propositions asserted by means of such utterances can't simply be propositions about modes of presentation. After all, there surely are worlds where the Hamlet-mode does present something, but of which it is false to say that Hamlet exists (according to Kripkean orthodoxy, Hamlet *couldn't* have existed). Similarly, Hesperus could surely have existed without presenting via the Hesperus-mode.

Preferring to leave the idea of a mode open enough to allow for this conception of modes, Crimmins deals with this modal issue in a surprisingly indirect way. He argues that what is asserted with such an utterance is true at a world w just when w is so as to make the utterance *fictionally* true at w, and then relies on intuitions about when this is so:

[W]e need to ask which real possibilities make it fictionally true that there are possibilities in which "[Hamlet] exists". I believe the following ideas are defensible: normally, (a) no possible world makes it fictionally true that there is a possible world in which "[Hamlet] exists" ..., and (b) all and only possible worlds in which Venus exists make it fictionally true that there are possible worlds in which "Hesperus exists". (1998, 34–35) [page 513 above]

But as a strategy for discerning modal content, this seems almost completely ad hoc. Nothing is said about what might possibly ground such intuitions, and yet something is sorely needed, given that ordinary, unproblematic facts about the fiction are not enough to bear the explanatory burden, while facts about modes turn out not to be enough either.

The modal problem raises questions about the very basis of the semantic pretense approach. The second problem for the approach, which might be termed the 'meaning' problem, relates to the semantic pretense treatment of negative existentials and identity statements in particular. For the semantic pretense approach to work, 'exists' and 'is identical with' must be taken to be special fictional predicates, whose meanings differ from the meanings they have in other contexts. But it seems best to accept such ambiguities only as a last resort. If we agree, with Crimmins (1998, 33ff.), that there is a perfectly common meaning of 'exists' on which it is a predicate true of anything whatsoever, and a perfectly common meaning of 'is identical to' on which it is a predicate that applies to anything and itself (nothing else), why not use these meanings to solve the problems rather than invent meanings that are suggested only by the desire to solve these problems in semantic pretense terms? Gareth Evans (1982, chap. 10), endorsing the view in Kripke (1973) that 'exists' is universal, has even argued that we should regard the universality of 'exists' as a *constraint* on an adequate analysis of negative existentials. Even if this is too strong, we might well insist that we should treat 'exists' this way if at all possible.

Worse, in certain cases the usual and fictional meanings must both be present if we are to avoid trouble. Consider again:

(4) Those two famous celestial bodies of Babylonian astronomy, Hesperus and Phosphorus, are in fact identical.

Given the usual understanding of numerical quantifiers in terms of identity, (4) seems to require the predicate of identity to be used in two different senses, else we have a contradiction of the form 'There exists x and y such that $x \neq y$ & $x = h$ & $y = p$ & ... & $x = y$'.[9] But, contradiction or not, the idea that two different meanings are involved surely can't be right, since there are familiar ways of rephrasing the claim that suggest that, all along, only one meaning was intended:

(7) Remember those two famous celestial bodies of Babylonian astronomy, Hesperus and Phosphorus? Well, it turns out they aren't really two: they are identical.

So the doctrine of semantic pretense faces some severe problems.[10] But if it fails, what

remains? How else are we to make sense of the object-involving phenomenology of Frege-Russell locutions? Not, I think, by rejecting the phenomenology or embracing its commitments in realist fashion. In the next section, I argue for a quite different way of understanding the role of pretense in at least the cases of negative existentials and identity statements. (The case of prepositional attitude reports involves other complexities, and I have nothing further to say about them in this paper.) The final section returns us to the debate between New Theorists and neo-descriptivists.

5. PRETENSE REVISITED

To see how pretense can help us understand the role of the object-involving phenomenology of existential and identity statements without running into the problems that face Crimmins's account, consider the class of what we might loosely call 'quasi-contradictions' and 'quasi-truisms': sentences, often quite mundane, whose form is explicitly contradictory or truistic and that use this feature to convey something that may well be both true and nontrivial.[11] As an example, think of an apparent contradiction like

(8) That woman is not a woman,

or an apparent truism like

(9) That woman is a woman,

and think of the assertive utterance of such a sentence in a situation in which a speaker wants to say that his demonstration does (not) pick out a woman. For example, imagine (8) or (9) uttered while the speaker's audience is watching a play in which a certain person plays the part of a woman, in order to say that the person playing the part is (not) a woman (both claims are in effect present in a famous scene in the movie *Shakespeare in Love*).[12] Or imagine it uttered by a speaker in the face of his audience's suspicion that a certain person in their view is a woman, in order to say that this person is (not) a woman.

Assuming that the logical form of (8) or (9) is 'That$_{\text{dem}}$ F is (not) F', it is clear that what a speaker conveys in this way is not what such a sentence literally expresses: a contradiction or truism of some kind.[13] But neither does he simply convey some kind of Gricean implicature explicable in terms of Gricean mechanisms but not amounting to something that the speaker can rightfully be said to *assert* with his utterance. Confronted by an assertive utterance of (8) or (9), it seems entirely appropriate for the audience to report, "The speaker asserted that that woman is (not) a woman," where what the speaker is said to have asserted is a noncontradictory, nontrivial proposition stating, roughly, that some demonstrated individual is (not) a woman. That is the kind of account I shall assume in what follows.[14]

But how, in more precise terms, should we understand this asserted content and the way in which the audience works out this content? It would, I think, be a mistake simply to invoke something like Donnellan's referential/attributive distinction. That distinction is simply too crude to allow us to understand the full communicative purpose of such statements. This criticism can already be made of some of Donnellan's own examples. Both Donnellan (1966) and Kripke (1973) (citing Donnellan) give the example of referential uses of descriptions that are believed by the speaker and even his audience to misdescribe the intended referent (say, use of the expression 'the king' to talk about some usurper). But to call these 'referential' uses underdescribes the communicative situation. There is a striking sense in which the speaker does as if the description correctly describes the intended referent, and that he achieves his communicative purpose partly through knowing that his audience knows that he is doing as if the description is apt.[15] Unlike standard cases of the referential/attributive distinction, correction of the speaker would simply be misplaced.

Correction of the speaker would obviously also be misplaced in the case of (8) or (9). Indeed, the statement itself is the corrective. The extent to which the distinction fails to yield an adequate view of the communicative situation in (8) and (9) is further underlined by the following consideration. Suppose you have been talking to me about "that woman" (the one you claim is standing at the bus stop across the road from us). If, after peering into the rain, I begin to realize that you are confused by the light and the drifting rain, and that there is no object for your demonstrative to pick out (no person, no waving branch, etc.), I might challenge your references to "that woman" by insisting:

(10) Wait, that woman is not a woman. She is really just a figment of your imagination—there is nothing there.

Here there is no object for me to have in mind. No referential interpretation is possible (not even one involving a queer entity—a "figment of the imagination"—that you have temporarily confused with a woman.)[16] It seems that this kind of case involves a pure "doing-as-if" I am correctly describing someone, without there being any object for me to describe. All I can be doing in such a case is simply doing as if, or pretending that, your (and now my) demonstrative reference is apt in order to assert that such demonstrative reference is entirely inapt when understood from outside of this pretense.

With that in mind, here is the suggestion about how in general to interpret (8) (and similarly (9)). A speaker's utterance of such a sentence shows him to be opportunistically engaged in pretense. The speaker pretends that his demonstrative reference is apt, typically by pretending, about a certain salient individual, that this individual is a woman, and at other times by pretending that there is a demonstratively salient individual who is a woman (as in (10)). (The salience is a function of features that, in the context, make it appropriate to describe an individual as a woman.) Focusing on the typical case for now, note that the speaker may indulge in such pretense for any of a number of reasons. Perhaps, for example, the best way to identify a particular individual is by playing along with the author's mistaken view that the individual in question is a woman. Or perhaps the speaker and his audience are watching a certain individual playing a female role in a play, where pretending that they are thereby watching a woman is something they are supposed to do because of the game of make-believe they are playing.

Whatever the reason for the pretense, the interpretative tension generated by the speaker's utterance of 'that woman is not a woman' now tells his audience that he is only *pretending* that his means of securing reference with 'that woman' singles out a woman. Understood apart from this pretense, his means of securing reference is therefore best construed as the determiner of semantic reference for a *weakened* complex demonstrative, say, 'that person' or even 'that object'. (How much weaker will depend on context and/or the speaker's intentions. I'll use 'that individual', which can be understood in either of these two ways.) The speaker pretends that this reference determiner successfully picks out an individual who is a woman, thus justifying his use, *inside* the pretense, of the stronger complex demonstrative 'that woman'. What the speaker then asserts is that, construed from *outside* of the pretense, this determiner does not single out an individual who is a woman. Now in the typical situation of utterance, both the speaker and audience know that there really is a demonstratively salient individual present. In such a case, therefore, the speaker succeeds in asserting that, outside of the pretense, his reference determiner singles out an individual who is *not* a woman. (In addition, of course, he thereby asserts *of* the individual referred to on the basis of this determiner that this individual is not a woman.)[17]

In short, (part of) what the speaker asserts with a typical utterance of the quasi-contradictory (8) is something like the following internally negated claim:

(8₁) Outside of the pretense that the underlying reference determiner (for the tacitly understood demonstrative 'that individual') secures reference to an individual who is a woman, it secures reference to an individual who is *not* a woman.

Similarly, (part of) what the speaker asserts with a typical utterance of the quasi-truistic (9) is something like the following claim:

(9) Outside of the pretense that the underlying reference determiner (for 'that individual') secures reference to an individual who is a woman, it secures reference to an individual who is indeed a woman.

Now of course, the *form* in which (8₁) and (9) articulate this asserted content is clumsy, but that is because each is really only a schema. For the moment, I want to give the content in a neutral way, one that offends neither a neo-descriptivist nor a New Theorist. For neo-

descriptivists, what determines the reference, at any world, of the speaker's tacit use of 'that individual' in the actual world is presumably something like the property *being the actual individual of whom I am demonstratively aware*. In that case, (8₁) and (9) can be given particularly simple formulations: 'Outside of the pretense that the actual unique individual of whom I am demonstratively aware is a woman, this individual is (not) a woman'. New Theorists, who presumably have a preference for something like a causal theory of demonstrative reference, will prefer a different formulation.

The gloss I put on (8) and (9) harbors a suggestion about how to interpret the profligate phenomenology of informative identity statements and negative existentials. Instead of Crimmins's idea that in uttering such statements a speaker pretends that different modes of presentation (for example, the Hesperus- and Phosphorus-modes) present different objects, or that a particular mode (for example, the Hamlet-mode) presents an object, suppose we take the speaker to pretend that the *reference determiners* underlying his use of distinct names like 'Hesperus' and 'Phosphorus' secure reference to distinct objects, or that the *reference determiner* underlying his use of a name like 'Hamlet' secures reference to a particular object. (And, of course, not just the reference determiners for the speaker's use of these names; the pretense involves the thought that other people, differently situated, are also able to secure reference to these objects.) As before, there is no need to suppose that the pretense in question is of a deeply imaginative kind. While this will no doubt be so in certain cases, in other cases, it may be rooted in little more than the desire to "do-as-if" a certain way of seeing the world is correct simply in order to raise questions about that way. Whatever the initial reasons for the pretense, what interests me, as it does Crimmins, is how entering into pretense gives speakers a way of talking about the real world.

The emphasis on reference determination gives a rather different picture from the semantic pretense picture of why it is fictionally true that there are two objects, Hesperus and Phosphorus, or why it is fictionally true that there is such a person as Hamlet. It also gives a very different picture of what speakers manage to assert with their utterance of sentences like (1)–(4). Take a plural-sounding identity like (4):

(4) Those two famous celestial bodies of Babylonian astronomy, Hesperus and Phosphorus, are in fact identical.

Assuming, contrary to Crimmins, that 'is identical to' stands for the usual strict relation of identity, we have in place the thought that this attribution involves a contradiction inside a pretense.[18] That scenario is reminiscent of the interpretative tension that led to the interpretative gloss we were able to place on (8). As before, it is the speaker's use of the device of a blatant contradiction (this time, that distinct things are identical) that now allows his audience to understand that he is claiming the world to be different, in relevant respects, from the way his pretense depicts it to be.

It is easy to see what these relevant respects are. When distinct things are declared identical, the predicate is the relational one of identity, which holds pairwise only between an entity and itself: a single object. By analogy with (8), therefore, (part of) what the speaker asserts with (4) is something like:

(4) Outside the scope of the pretense that the underlying reference determiners for my use of 'Hesperus' and 'Phosphorus' secure reference to *two* celestial bodies (thereby warranting talk, inside of the pretense, of 'those *two* famous, etc, celestial bodies Hesperus and Phosphorus'), these reference determiners secure reference to an object X and an object Y related by identity; hence secure reference to a single object only.

Like (8_I) and (9), (4) is clumsy, but that is once again an artifact of a desire to remain neutral for now. (4) is a schema that ought to commend itself to both New Theorists and neo-descriptivists. Neo-descriptivists will interpret it as a claim to the effect that certain properties— say, *being the actual celestial body of my acquaintance called 'Hesperus' that, on the basis of my acquaintance, I take to be the brightest such body in the evening sky and being the actual celestial body of my acquaintance called 'Phosphorus' that, on the basis of my*

acquaintance, I take to be the brightest such body in the morning sky—rigidly apply to a single object once these properties are construed from outside of the pretense that they identify two objects. Allusions to pretense aside, this is just the kind of reading we can expect neo-descriptivists to favor. New Theorists will presumably appeal to a causal-historical theory of some kind. Assuming they agree that speakers have sufficient cognitive grasp on the means of reference determination (a point I return to below), they will prefer to tell the story in terms of the way in which the speaker pretends that his tokenings of the names 'Hesperus' and 'Phosphorus' have their causal-historical origin in distinct objects. The speaker's utterance of (4) then allows him to assert that, outside of this pretense, these tokenings have their origin in a single object.

Turn finally to the case of singular negative existentials, in some ways the most interesting and difficult of the Frege-Russell locutions. I claim that in their case it is the systematic interaction of negation, pretense, and the meaning of 'exists', again on the model of (8), that enables speakers to assert appropriate propositions. Recall the way in which someone who utters (8) as part of (10) succeeds in asserting that there is not even a demonstratively salient *individual* present. It seems that in this case what is asserted with an utterance of (8) is not the internally negated (8_I) but the weaker externally negated (8_E):

(8_E) Outside of the pretense that the underlying reference determiner (for the demonstrative 'that individual') secures reference to an individual who is a woman, it is *not* the case that it secures reference to an individual who is a woman,

where the speaker's intention to rule out interpretation (8_I) as an account of what he is saying may become evident only when he adds: "She is really just a figment of the imagination—there is nothing there."

So context may have a complex hand in determining the intended reading of (8) in such a case: the audience may need to do some disentangling. But how would a speaker mount an effective, *unambiguous* challenge to the thought that there is a woman to be demonstrated in the first place, a challenge not in need of disentangling in this way? Well, suppose we agree with Kripke and Evans that 'exists' stands for a universal property, one possessed by everything there is even if most things don't possess it essentially.[19] Now consider the statement:

(11) That woman doesn't exist.

Given that existence is universal, this is trivially equivalent to 'That woman who exists doesn't exist'. (Since 'who exists' is redundant, it is naturally elided.) Earlier I suggested that an utterance of 'That woman is not a woman' concerns the fate of the reference determiner for an appropriately weakened version of 'that [individual who is a] woman', namely 'that individual'. By analogy, (11) concerns the fate of the reference determiner for an appropriately weakened version of 'that woman [who exists]', namely 'that woman', hypothetically stripped of its association with existence. By parity with (8), it might now be thought that an utterance of 'That woman who exists doesn't exist' could be used to assert either the internally negated claim

(11_I) Outside of the pretense that the underlying reference determiner (for the demonstrative 'that woman') secures reference to a woman who exists, it secures reference to a woman who *doesn't* exist

or the weaker externally negated claim

(11_E) Outside of the pretense that the underlying reference determiner (for the demonstrative 'that woman') secures reference to a woman who exists, it is *not* the case that it secures reference to a woman who exists.

But since everything exists, the first reading (11_I) is simply not available. Hence we are left with (11_E) as the only reading, or, more simply (eliding the redundant 'who exists'),

(11) Outside of the pretense that the underlying reference determiner (for the demonstrative 'that woman') secures reference to a woman, it is *not* the case that it secures reference to a woman.[20]

Once again, (11) is only a schema. Neo-descriptivists will presumably take (11) to say

something like 'Outside of the pretense that there is a unique actual demonstratively salient individual who is a woman, there is no such individual'—apart from the appeal to pretense, surely the kind of reading we would have expected from neo-descriptivists (and the kind of reading most of us would, pre-analytically, have assigned to (11)). Such a descriptivist reading of the pretense mechanism also secures a natural way of saying that there is not even a demonstratively salient *person* or *object,* let alone a woman: instead of saying, "That *woman* doesn't exist," for example, a speaker might say, "That *person* doesn't exist" in order to assert that, outside of the pretense that there is an actual person of which he is demonstratively aware, there is no such person.

What, finally, about negative existentials involving names rather than demonstratives, say 'Hamlet doesn't exist' or 'Vulcan doesn't exist'? They can be accorded the same kind of treatment. Like (11), negative existentials featuring names have the logical form of ordinary negated subject-predicate statements that have the existence of their bearers as a presupposition. In this sense they are no different from ordinary subject-predicate statements like 'George Bush doesn't lie'. Thus consider:

(12) Hamlet doesn't exist.

Take this to have the force of 'the individual who is Hamlet, and who exists, doesn't exist', an explicit case of a quasi-contradiction. (Similarly, 'Hamlet does exist' can be taken as a quasi-truism.) In uttering this sentence a speaker adopts the pretense that the reference determiner underlying his use of the name 'Hamlet' secures reference to some individual, and hence an individual who exists, and uses the resulting interpretative tension to assert that

(12) Outside of the pretense that the underlying reference determiner (for my use of 'Hamlet') secures reference to an individual, it fails to secure reference to any individual.

Neo-descriptivists will once again offer their own interpretation of such a schema. They will presumably take (12) to say something like 'Outside of the pretense that there is a unique actual individual called 'Hamlet' whom I have seen or heard described as a Danish prince intent on avenging the death of his father, etc., there is no such individual'. An utterance of 'Vulcan doesn't really exist' will be deemed to assert something like 'Outside of the pretense that there is a unique actual planet responsible in thus-and-so a way for such-and-such perturbations in the orbit of Mercury, there is no such object'. And so on. Pretense aside, these are just the kinds of readings we would in any case have expected from neo-descriptivists, at least assuming normal knowledge on the part of speakers.[21] Causal-historical theorists would no doubt want to tell the story in a different way, say in terms of causal-historical chains that are pretended to be whole but are in fact broken. Pretense aside, this is in fact close to the story in Donnellan (1974).

6. BACK TO DESCRIPTIVISM

Because of the role played by pragmatic considerations in this account of identity statements and negative existentials (specifically, the emphasis placed on the way speakers exploit the literal, semantic content of predicates like 'exist' in order to assert what is not semantically expressed), I'll call it the 'pragmatic pretense' account of such statements, to contrast with Crimmins's semantic pretense account. The preceding section assumed a kind of neutrality between the ways neo-descriptivists and New Theorists might interpret pragmatic pretense. In this final section, I argue that while each interpretation is capable of solving the modal problem facing Crimmins's appeal to semantic pretense (the problem of how to account for the *necessity* of statements like (4) and (12)), there is nonetheless reason to prefer a neo-descriptivist version.

To see why each interpretation is capable of solving the modal problem, take the neo-descriptivist interpretation first, and consider the question whether the neo-descriptivist version of (4)—say, '[Outside of the pretense] the actual brightest celestial body in the evening sky = the actual brightest celestial body in the morning sky'—is true or false when evaluated at worlds other than the actual world @. Since the role of a rigidifier like 'actually' is to shift truth evaluation and reference at a world w back to the actual world (Davies and Humberstone

1980), the answer depends solely on what the terms refer to at @. That way we get the welcome result that (4) is used to say something that is not just true but *necessarily* true, since every world containing Venus is a world where the actual brightest celestial body in the morning sky (Venus) is the actual brightest celestial body in the evening sky (Venus again).

Similarly, (12) is necessarily true: because there is no actual individual called 'Hamlet' whom we are acquainted with on the basis of reading *Hamlet*, there is no possible world containing this individual. The neo-descriptivist's interpretation of the pragmatic pretense account thus yields a clear sense in which 'Hamlet doesn't exist' is used to assert something that is necessary rather than contingent.

But of course there is also a sense in which (4) and even (12) say something that is contingent rather than necessary: Hesperus mightn't have been Phosphorus (distinct celestial bodies might have been the brightest bodies in the evening and morning sky), and Hamlet might have existed (the Hamlet story might have been recorded history). To its credit, Crimmins's appeal to modes of presentation is able to capture such a sense, but so, as it turns out, can the neo-descriptivist interpretation of pragmatic pretense. It is true that '[Outside of the pretense] the actual brightest celestial body in the morning sky = the actual brightest celestial body in the evening sky' holds at the actual world @ and at all worlds considered as counterfactual alternatives to @. But suppose we change our perspective, and instead consider worlds under the supposition that they are actual, rather than worlds considered as counterfactual alternatives to the actual world @. This is an utterly natural perspective for any pretense theorist, for the pretense treatment of sentences like (4) and (12) highlights the way speakers and listeners contemplating such sentences routinely do *as if* some other world is the actual world. It is now easy to see why (4) appears contingent. There clearly are worlds w, now considered as actual, such that in w the unique actual object that appears as the brightest celestial body in the evening sky is *not* the same as the unique actual object that appears in w as the brightest celestial body in the morning sky ("actual" from the point of view of w). Indeed, in uttering (4) the speaker pretends that the actual world is just such a world w. And the same can be said about (12). There are worlds w such that w contains an actual person called 'Hamlet' whom we are acquainted with on the basis of reading *Hamlet* ("actual" from the point of view of w). In uttering (12) the speaker pretends that the actual world is just such a world w.

This is a familiar result, of course, taken from the annals of two-dimensional modal semantics. It suggests that how (4) and (12) divide the class of possibilities is subject to two construals, yielding a sense in which (4) and (12) count as necessary and another sense in which they count as contingent.[22] But it is important to note that such an appeal to two-dimensionalism doesn't help only neo-descriptivism. It helps *any* account that classifies names as rigid designators, no matter how reference is seen as determined and no matter how semantic content is understood. Thus, consider a weak neo-descriptivist view according to which appropriate descriptions fix the reference of the uses of names (thereby ensuring their rigidity) but don't provide their content. Even if such a theory doesn't depict these descriptions as themselves rigidified, occurrences of such descriptions in (4) and (12) should be understood as rigidified if (4) and (12) are to capture their modal behavior. As before, this yields a solution to the modal problem (more generally, it means we can apply the two-dimensional modal framework to show how (4) and (12) are in one sense necessary, in another sense contingent).

Exactly the same type of appeal also shows how the New Theorists' interpretation of pragmatic pretense can solve the modal problem. New Theorists think that names are (*de jure*) rigid designators, and so must think that, if schemas (4) and (12) are to tell the full modal story, descriptions of the broad form 'the object standing at the origin of the relevant causal chains underlying the current use of N' should again be read as rigidified. In that case, New Theorists too can count (4) and (12) as necessary (and, in another sense, contingent)—an especially welcome result in the case of (12), since the New Theory's commitment to Millianism, combined with the view that fictional names are empty, makes it hard for New Theo-

rists to identify any other suitable sense in which (12) is used to say something true, let alone something that is *necessarily* true.[23]

So the pragmatic pretense account provides New Theorists as well as neo-descriptivists (both strong and weak) with a means of solving Crimmins's modal problem. Despite this, I think the account favors a version of neo-descriptivism. My argument is a simple variant of a certain familiar argument for neo-descriptivism. Earlier I said that on the pragmatic pretense account even New Theorists should agree that speakers are in implicit cognitive possession of the means of reference determination for the names they use, where these reference determiners are now taken as causal-historical chains. The reason is this: Apart from the fact that attributing such a grasp results in some welcome unification (it allows us to interpret the descriptive *informativeness* of what a speaker asserts with an identity or negative existential—a feature granted even by New Theorists—in terms of the informativeness of a story about the fate of certain causal-historical chains),[24] the role that the pragmatic pretense account assigns to pretense in such statements *requires* us to attribute such a grasp. After all, the account claims that speakers assertively uttering such a statement focus on a contrast they see as significant: they pretend that their reference determiners secure reference to *two* things, or to *some*thing, before asserting that in reality—that is, apart from the pretense—they secure reference to one thing, or to nothing. But that requires speakers to have a robust conception of that contrast: robust enough to explain how they are able to view the pretend-scenario as coherent, while knowing what it takes for the real world—the world as it is apart from the pretense—to be different in relevant respects from the world of the pretense. If the facts that determine reference are genuinely beyond a speaker's ken, no such robust conception seems possible.

The rest of the argument will be familiar.[25] A causal-historical theory that assigns a central role to speakers' implicit knowledge of relevant causal-historical chains looks indistinguishable from a version of descriptivism on which reference determination is a function of the fact that speakers implicitly conceive of the reference of the names they use in terms of such underlying chains. Why not, in that case, opt for some such version of descriptivism? That would unify cases susceptible to a causal-historical treatment of reference with cases ("descriptive" names) not susceptible to such treatment. The resulting "causal theory made self-conscious" (as Brian Loar once put it) is precisely the kind of descriptivist theory of reference determination for ordinary names preferred by contemporary neo-descriptivists.

Let me emphasize the limits of this argument. There is nothing in what I have said that argues directly for interpreting pragmatic pretense in terms of a neo-descriptivist theory of semantic *content* for names. Both the preceding argument and the solution to the modal problem are already available to a weak neo-descriptivism about reference determination that resists understanding the notion of semantic content in neo-descriptivist terms (perhaps even preferring a Millian account). So we are left with a relatively modest conclusion: whatever the merits of neo-descriptivism as a theory of semantic *content*, from the point of view of interpreting the idea of pragmatic pretense there is much to be said for at least a neo-descriptivist theory of *reference determination*. Still, this conclusion is far from inconsequential, given that this paper began with the problem of neo-descriptivism's apparent inability to deal with the phenomenology of Frege-Russell locutions. If I am right in thinking that the phenomenology of identity statements and negative existentials is plausibly understood in terms of pragmatic pretense rather than semantic pretense, it thus turns out that neo-descriptivism has a great deal to gain from acknowledging the role that pretense plays in our understanding of such locutions.

ACKNOWLEDGEMENTS

This paper was written while I was a Fellow in the Philosophy Programme of the Research School of Social Sciences at the Australian National University. I am grateful to the School and the Programme for their support. Thanks also to audiences at the University of New England, Monash University, the University of Sydney, the Australian National University, and Victoria University of Wellington for numerous useful comments. I owe special thanks to an anonymous referee for this journal, and to David Braddon-Mitchell, Martin Davies, Richard L. Epstein, Frank Jackson, Jonathan McKeown-Green, and Daniel Stoljar. An early version of this paper appeared in a University of Auckland festschrift in honor of Krister Segerberg.

NOTES

1. See, for example, Searle 1983, Lewis 1984, 1994, Kroon 1987, and Jackson 1998a, 1998b. (Although I am assuming that these theorists take the reference-fixing properties associated with the use of a name as specifying something akin to the semantic *content* of that use, some would prefer to say that their theory does away with the notion of semantic content as ordinarily understood; cf. Jackson 1998b.)

2. See Soames 2004 for an extended attack on such a causal-descriptivist account of reference. There are, of course, other descriptivist successors to classical descriptivism, for example, the pure metalinguistic description theory of Jerry Katz (1994, 2001), according to which a name N has a meaning (*the bearer of N*) that doesn't determine reference. Such a theory is very different in kind from the kind of neo-descriptivism considered here, even though it proposes solutions to some of the same problems.

3. See Frege 1952 and Russell 1905. 'Frege-Russell problems' is a slight misnomer, since, unlike Russell, Frege did not discuss the problem of singular existential statements. (Frege 1979, 60, suggests that he would have construed them as misleadingly formulated metalinguistic statements.)

4. Weak neo-descriptivism is thus what some call a descriptive theory of 'intentionality' rather than 'content'. Cf. Stanley 1997, 568. As Stanley points out, Kripke's modal argument is ineffective against such a descriptivism even if the descriptions invoked are nonrigid.

5. On the theory of direct reference, see, for example, Almog, Perry, and Wettstein 1989, Salmon 1986, Recanati 1993, and Soames 2002. Salmon prefers the label 'theory of direct reference' for the negative theory that proper names, demonstratives, and other noncompound indexicals do not have descriptive semantic content, using 'Millianism' for the positive view that the semantic content of such a term is its referent. I shall use the more common positive reading for both terms.

6. The robustness of such attributions of plurality is reinforced by examples that are quantified in form. Thus, forgetting names and even positions of the planets, I may say, "There are two celestial bodies marked in that early map of the heavens we saw that have turned out to be identical—but I have quite forgotten which celestial bodies." I may then add: "And Hammurabi believed one of them, but not the other, to be visible in the evening." Both the theory in Crimmins 1998 and the theory developed in this paper seem to have the resources to handle such quantified locutions.

7. Like many New Theory sympathizers, Walton and Crimmins think that sentences containing fictional

names do not express propositions, so that it is strictly impossible to imagine the truth of the proposition expressed by a sentence like 'Hamlet is a Danish prince'. What can be imagined is that there *is* a proposition expressed by our utterances of 'Hamlet is a Danish prince'. Kripke's influential John Locke Lectures (1973) contain an early defense of such a view.

8. In Crimmins 1992 such modes are said to be instanced by what Crimmins calls 'notions'—particular representations of objects that form part of thoughts. Crimmins 1998 is far less forthcoming, at one point even suggesting that "our access to certain modes of presentation comes from our capacities to participate in pretenses of just this kind" (26). [See page 509.]

9. Cf. Richard 2000, 218ff., which clearly takes the idea that an identity statement might involve an implicit or explicit contradiction to be (only slightly) less tolerable than the idea that we might be using '=' with two meanings.

10. See also Stanley 2001. Stanley takes much of what he says as an attack on "hermeneutic fictionalism" in general (roughly speaking, any pretense account of some seemingly serious bit of discourse), although I doubt that his specific criticisms affect the sort of pretense view developed below.

11. Earlier versions of part of the argument in this section occur in Kroon 2000 and 2001.

12. The movie contains an exchange about the real sex of the person playing the part of Juliet in the first performance of *Romeo and Juliet*—as it turns out, Lady Viola, Shakespeare's lover. With Queen Elizabeth I secretly in attendance, the Queen's Master of the Revels enters the theatre and loudly charges: "That woman [pointing to Lady Viola] is a woman," whereupon the Queen rises from her seat and calmly retorts that he is mistaken. Imagine she used the actual words: 'That woman is not a woman'.

13. The contradiction or truism need not be at the level of semantic content. If, for example, the semantic contribution of F in 'That F is G' is at the level of character rather than content (Borg 2000), it follows that there is no possible context of utterance at which a sentence like (8) expresses a true content: contradiction enough for my purposes. Note that a speaker doesn't avoid the contradiction by including the qualifier 'really', as in 'That woman is not *really* a woman'. All the evidence suggests that 'really' in such cases is simply a pragmatic device used to highlight the fact that how matters stand may conflict with expectations or appearances. Since its chosen way of specifying how matters stand is in this case contradictory, its use doesn't by itself harbor a way of explaining away the contradiction.

14. Such an assertion-attributing account also applies to broadly metaphorical uses of language (indeed, quasi-contradictions and quasi-truisms could be construed as a kind of metaphor). Thus, Mary might say, "The President is a pain," thereby asserting, and not just implicating, something that is not semantically expressed. What she asserts is that *the President is behaving in an annoying manner,* an assertion-

attributing construal confirmed by the way we say, "Mary said/asserted that the President is a pain." (Cf. Soames 2002, 210ff., which cites such cases to support a certain account of the propositions asserted through attitude ascriptions.)

15. What makes the citation of such cases in Kripke 1973 somewhat surprising is that Kripke's lectures are, in part, a sophisticated attempt to show the relevance of pretense to talk of fiction. But we often use fictional descriptions in order to say something serious about real people who feature in our fictions, for example, 'The famous bear-hunter has finally returned for dinner'. Such cases, which rely on a form of pretense, seem continuous with the cases of deliberate misdescription given by Donnellan and Kripke.

16. Since (10) is supposed to be true in the absence of any demonstrated object, this provides further reason for taking the logical form of (8) at face value, and not, for example, construing it as a sentence whose underlying logical form contextually supplied fillers (say, 'That *person over there whose appearance made us think it was a* woman is not a woman', or even 'That *so-called* woman is not a woman'; cf. Borg 2000, n. 22). As for the thought that (10) might be made true by the literal presence of a "figment of the imagination" (a demonstratively salient figment, no less), this strikes me as barely credible. A "figment of the imagination" doesn't seem to be a *kind* of thing at all. Talk of "figments of the imagination" is best seen as metaphorical talk, allowing a speaker to signal what he sees as the role played by a person's imagination when the person actually believes that the world is as the speaker merely pretends it to be. In the spirit of Walton 1990, and contrary to Kripke 1973 and Salmon 1998, it seems to me that predicates like 'is a failed posit', 'is an imaginary friend', and even 'is a fictional character' should be understood in a similar pretense fashion.

17. We derive this (second) content simply by adopting the non-pretense perspective on the speaker's words in (8). Accepting a direct reference theory of content, New Theorists will understand this second content in an object-involving way. Not so those who subscribe to a neo-descriptivist account of content, since they don't acknowledge a second layer of content above the reference-fixing content.

18. The contradiction is blatant in the case of (4), and especially (7), but in my view is also implicitly present in the simple forms (2) and (3). Speakers and their audience realize that beneath the surface of such locutions is the ever-present possibility of trivially equivalent plural formulations.

19. Kripke 1973; Evans 1982, chap. 10. See also Chakrabarti 1997. Nakhnikian and Salmon (1957) provide an early defense of the view that 'exists' has a use as a universal predicate, and there are signs of such a view in Russell's and even Frege's work (Frege 1979 holds that 'exists' so understood is merely a *grammatical* predicate). For present purposes, we can take 'exists' to stand for existence at some time or other, although it is not hard to incorporate the tensed use of 'exists' (as in 'Homer did

exist, but Holmes didn't') into the account I defend. For a very different account of the use of 'exists' as a tensed predicate, see Salmon 1998.

20. Note that the qualifier 'really', present in the alternative formulation 'That woman does not *really* exist', plays no role in this derivation of (11), just as it played no role in the derivation of (8_I) and (8_E). As before (note 13 above), I take 'really' to have a purely pragmatic, contrast-emphasizing role, a contrast that often barely needs emphasis (which is why the word is readily omitted). Compare this to Evans 1982, chap. 10, which assigns a pivotal but problematic *semantic* role to 'really'. Because Evans's account entails that 'Really A(t)' is true only if t genuinely refers, it rules out the evident equivalence of 'That woman doesn't really exist' and 'Really [in reality], that woman doesn't exist', and fails to explain the use of 'really' in closely related locutions like (10).

21. Because of the role assigned to pretense, the fact that an audience may have radically different knowledge from the speaker is only a limited barrier to communication on the present account. Thus, consider a knowledgeable speaker's utterance of 'Hamlet doesn't exist'. Given that the audience knows that it is part of the speaker's pretense that people can be acquainted with the person called 'Hamlet' in radically different ways, the audience knows that the speaker's utterance indirectly discredits a whole range of ways of trying to secure reference to such a person (cf. Walton 1990, 425ff.), including the method of deferring to other users of the name. Consequently, someone who only knows that "Hamlet is the person called 'Hamlet' I have heard others talk about under that name," and who then hears the speaker's words but is told nothing else (not even that 'Hamlet' is a fictional name), thereby still learns that—in his words—"Hamlet doesn't exist." Such a case is difficult for many other (partly) descriptive accounts of negative existentials, including the theory in Salmon 1998.

22. In the current jargon, it all depends on whether the focus is on secondary/C-intensions or on primary/A-intensions. See Jackson 1998a, 2004, and Chalmers 1996, 2004 (the latter describes Chalmers's distinctive epistemic interpretation of two-dimensional semantics). Stalnaker (2001, 2004) urges a contrasting "metasemantic" interpretation of the two-dimensional framework, one based on a causal-historical view of reference.

23. New Theorists like Salmon (1998) and Soames (2002, 89–95) maintain the necessity of (12) in the context of an account that lets fictional names like 'Hamlet' stand for abstract fictional objects. But such an account is of no use to the many Millians who think that true singular negative existentials feature genuinely empty names, not names for special objects. Perhaps the most promising alternative is Braun's (1993) view that negative existentials containing empty names semantically express true "unfilled" propositions—prepositional structures that lack constituents corresponding to empty terms,

and hence are true, and indeed *necessarily* true, to the extent that they involve the negation of certain unfilled and hence non-true propositions. But such a view also faces serious problems. Among other things, it is forced to count positive statements like 'Hamlet is a fictional character' and 'Vulcan is a failed posit' as non-true, even though these are surely no less true than negative statements like 'Hamlet/Vulcan doesn't exist', and in a sense even serve to explain the truth of the latter (cf. also Reimer 2001). Braun's way of making sense of the (necessary) truth of a negative existential like (12) therefore fails to make sense of the truth of certain statements to which the negative existential is explanatorily linked.

24. Note that a speaker's grasp of such a story leaves room for the informational role of distinctive, salient beliefs like 'Aristotle was a famous Greek philosopher'. For although the Donnellan-Kripke arguments against classical descriptivism show that this belief plays no direct reference-determining role for the name 'Aristotle', causal-historical theorists and neo-descriptivists alike think that the *causal history* of such a belief (as the firmly held, but fallible, product of processes of information acquisition) is relevant to reference determination—a belief's causal history may be necessary for disambiguating the reference of a speaker's use of a name, say.

25. Cf. especially Lewis 1984, 1994, and Jackson 1998a, 1998b. Critics include Devitt and Sterelny (1999, 61).

BIBLIOGRAPHY

Almog, Joseph, John Perry, and Howard Wettstein, eds. 1989. *Themes from Kaplan.* Oxford: Oxford University Press.

Borg, Emma. 2000. Complex Demonstratives. *Philosophical Studies* 97:229–49.

Braun, David. 1993. Empty Names. *Noûs* 27:449–69.

Casteñeda, Hector-Neri. 1989. *Thinking, Language, and Experience.* Minneapolis: University of Minnesota Press.

Chakrabarti, Arindam. 1997. *Denying Existence.* Boston: Kluwer.

Chalmers, David. 1996. *The Conscious Mind.* Oxford: Oxford University Press.

———. 2004. Epistemic Two-Dimensional Semantics. *Philosophical Studies* 118:153–226.

Crimmins, Mark. 1992. *Talk about Beliefs.* Cambridge: MIT Press.

———. 1998. Hesperus and Phosphorus: Sense, Pretense, and Reference. *Philosophical Review* 107: 1–47.

Davies, Martin, and Lloyd Humberstone. 1980. Two Notions of Necessity. *Philosophical Studies* 38:1–30.

Devitt, Michael, and Kim Sterelny. 1999. *Language and Reality.* 2nd ed. Cambridge: MIT Press.

Donnellan, Keith. 1966. Reference and Description. *Philosophical Review* 75:281–304.

———. 1974. Speaking of Nothing. *Philosophical Review* 83:3–31.

Evans, Gareth. 1982. *The Varieties of Reference.* Oxford: Oxford University Press.

Frege, Gottlob. 1952. On Sense and Reference. In *Translations from the Philosophical Writings of Gottlob Frege,* trans. Peter Geach and Max Black, 56–78. Oxford: Basil Blackwell.

———. 1979. Dialogue with Pünjer on Existence. In *Posthumous Writings,* ed. Hans Hermes, Friedrich Kambartel, and Friedrich Kaulbach, 53–67. Oxford: Basil Blackwell.

Jackson, Frank. 1998a. *From Metaphysics to Ethics.* Oxford: Oxford University Press.

———. 1998b. Reference and Description Revisited. In *Philosophical Perspectives,* vol.12, ed. James Tomberlin, 201–18. Atascadero, Calif.: Ridgeview.

———. 2004. Why We Need A-Intensions. *Philosophical Studies* 118:257–77.

Katz, Jerrold. 1994. Names without Bearers. *Philosophical Review* 103:1–39.

———. 2001. The End of Millianism: Multiple Bearers, Improper Names, and Compositional Meaning. *Journal of Philosophy* 98:137–66.

Kripke, Saul. 1973. Reference and Existence. John Locke Lectures (unpublished). Oxford: Oxford University Press.

———. 1980. *Naming and Necessity.* Cambridge: Harvard University Press.

Kroon, Frederick. 1987. Causal Descriptivism. *Australasian Journal of Philosophy* 65:1–17.

———. 2000. 'Disavowal through Commitment' Theories of Negative Existentials. In *Empty Names, Fiction and the Puzzles of Existence,* ed. Anthony Everett and Thomas Hofweber, 95–116. Stanford: CSLI Publications.

———. 2001. Fictionalism and the Informativeness of Identity. *Philosophical Studies* 106:197–225.

Lewis, David. 1984. Putnam's Paradox. *Australasian Journal of Philosophy* 62:221–37.

———. 1994. David Lewis: Reduction of Mind. In *A Companion to the Philosophy of Mind,* ed. Samuel Guttenplan, 412–31. Oxford: Blackwell.

Nakhnikian, George, and Wesley Salmon. 1957. 'Exists' as a Predicate. *Philosophical Review* 66:535–42.

Recanati, François. 1993. *Direct Reference: From Language to Thought.* Oxford: Blackwell.

Reimer, Marga. 2001. The Problem of Empty Names. *Australasian Journal of Philosophy* 79:491–506.

Richard, Mark. 2000. Semantic Pretense. In *Empty Names, Fiction and the Puzzles of Existence,* ed. Anthony Everett and Thomas Hofweber, 205–32. Stanford: CSLI Publications.

Russell, Bertrand. 1905. On Denoting. *Mind* 14:479–93.

———. 1956. The Philosophy of Logical Atomism. In *Logic and Knowledge,* ed. Robert C. Marsh, 241–54. London: Macmillan.

Salmon, Nathan. 1986. *Frege's Puzzle.* Cambridge: MIT Press.

———. 1998. Nonexistence. *Noûs* 32:277–319.

Searle, John. 1983. *Intentionality.* Cambridge: Cambridge University Press.

Soames, Scott. 2002. *Beyond Rigidity: The Unfinished Semantic Agenda of Naming and Necessity.* New York: Oxford University Press.

———. 2004. Reference and Description. In *The Oxford Handbook of Contemporary Analytic Philosophy,* ed. Frank Jackson and Michael Smith. Oxford: Oxford University Press.

Stalnaker, Robert. 2001. On Considering a Possible World as Actual. *Proceedings of the Aristotelian Society,* supp. vol. 75:141–56.

———. 2004. Assertion Revisited: On the Interpretation of Two-Dimensional Modal Semantics. *Philosophical Studies* 118:299–322.

Stanley, Jason. 1997. Names and Rigid Designation. In *A Companion to the Philosophy of Language,* ed. Bob Hale and Crispin Wright, 555–85. Oxford: Blackwell.

———. 2001. Hermeneutic Fictionalism. In *Midwest Studies,* vol. 25: *Figurative Language,* ed. Peter French and Howard Wettstein, 36–71. Oxford: Blackwell.

Walton, Kendall. 1990. *Mimesis as Make-Believe.* Cambridge: Harvard University Press.

Zalta, Edward. 1988. *Intensional Logic and the Metaphysics of Intentionality.* Cambridge: MIT Press.

SUGGESTED FURTHER READING

Beardsley, Monroe, "Metaphor," in *The Encyclopedia of Philosophy,* vol. 5, pp. 284–289.

Black, Max, "Metaphor," in *Models and Metaphor* (Ithaca: Cornell University Press, 1954), pp. 41–60.

Cooper, David E., *Metaphor* (Oxford: Blackwell, 1986).

Fogelin, Robert, *Figuratively Speaking* (New Haven: Yale University Press, 1988).

Johnson, Mark, ed., *Philosophical Perspectives on Metaphor* (Minneapolis: University of Minneapolis Press, 1981).

Kittay, Eva, *Metaphor: Its Cognitive Force and Linguistic Structure* (Oxford: Clarendon Press, 1987).

Lakoff, George and Mark Johnson, *Metaphors We Live By* (Chicago: University of Chicago Press, 1980).

Martinich, A. P., "A Theory of Fiction," *Philosophy and Literature* 25 (2001): 96–112.

Ortony, Andrew, ed., *Metaphor and Thought,* 2d ed. (Cambridge: Cambridge University Press, 1993).

Sacks, Sheldon, ed., *On Metaphor* (Chicago: University of Chicago Press, 1981).

Salmon, Nathan, "Nonexistence," *Nous* 32 (1998): 277–319.

Schiffer, Stephen, "Language-Created Language-Independent Entities," *Philosophical Topics* 24 (1996): 149–167.

Searle, John R., "Metaphor," in *Expression and Meaning* (New York: Cambridge University Press, 1979), pp. 76–116.

Thomasson, Amie, "Fictional Characters and Literary Practices," *British Journal of Aesthetics* 43 (2003): 138–157.

Thomasson, Amie, "Speaking of Fictional Characters," *Dialectica* 57 (2003): 205–223.

Walton, K. L., *Mimesis as Make-Believe: On the Foundations of the Representational Arts* (Cambridge: Harvard University Press, 1990).

VII INTERPRETATION AND TRANSLATION

There are two sides to communication: the meaning conveyed by the utterer or speaker and the understanding achieved by the audience. While the studies of meaning and interpretation have proceeded *pari passu* within the continental tradition, the study of meaning has predominated within the Anglo-American one. However, a substantial amount of work has been done on linguistic understanding during the past thirty years. Most of this work has been presented under the rubric of theories of interpretation or translation. This should initially appear strange, because there seems to be a more or less sharp difference between linguistic understanding, interpretation, and translation. Understanding seems to be restricted to what the speaker clearly says and perhaps conversationally implies. Interpretation seems to presuppose knowledge of what the speaker clearly means in order to explain (i) those aspects of the speaker's meaning that are difficult or dubious, (ii) what implications the speaker's meaning has beyond those that she intended to convey, and (iii) what place the speaker's utterances (no matter what genre it may belong to) have within a larger cultural context. (The sense in which interpretations give a meaning is that of meaning as significance, as explained in the introduction to Section I, "Truth and Meaning.") If the audience does not respond in any appropriate way to the speaker's utterance, "Please close the door," it makes sense for the speaker to follow up with "Do you understand what I'm saying to you?" but not with "Can you interpret what I am saying?" Understanding, not interpretation, is the required activity. If a student proceeds to write in this manner, "When T. S. Eliot says 'April is the cruelest month', he means that April is the cruelest month," or "When Hamlet says 'To be or not to be, that is the question,' he means that the question is to be or not to be," the student is failing to do what is required.

Nonetheless, linguistic understanding and interpretation are similar in that both can be reported in the same language as the utterances they take as their source material. A sentence of English can be understood or interpreted in English. In contrast, translation requires a second language. To replace 'Jones is a bachelor' with 'Jones is an unmarried, adult, male' is to give a paraphrase, not a translation. (Davidson holds that translation involves three languages. His point is illustrated by this sentence: 'Piove' in Italian means 'Es regnet' in German.) Further, translation is like linguistic under-

541

standing insofar as translation is supposed to preserve the meaning of the original utterance, while it is unlike interpretation, which aims at going beyond the meaning of the utterance.

Given these intuitive differences between linguistic understanding, interpretation, and translation, why do W. V. Quine, Donald Davidson, and others seem to use them interchangeably? The reason is that they believe that there is no principled difference among these supposedly three activities. The activities of understanding, interpreting, or translating an utterance involve (theoretically) forming a set of sentences in one's own language that accounts for the behavior of the speaker. This set, for Quine, includes sentences about much more than the speaker's verbal behavior; it includes sentences about the speaker's physical condition and nonverbal behavior and about the speaker's environment and previous experience. For Davidson, this set also includes sentences about the speaker's beliefs. (Although the interpretation or translation itself may not mention all of the elements just specified, they are necessary for constructing the interpretation or translation.) For Quine and Davidson, the fact that the words 'understanding', 'interpretation', and 'translation' are conventionally used in different circumstances is not relevant to the fact that the cognitive activity is the same in each case. In other words, the difference between 'understanding' and 'interpretation' is a matter of usage, not meaning. 'Understanding' is appropriately used when the author's meaning is relatively straightforward and undisputed; 'interpretation' is appropriately used when that meaning is not. 'Translation' is appropriately used when various linguistic features of the relevant idiolects (phonology, syntax, semantics) almost never overlap.

To see that linguistic understanding and interpretation are fundamentally the same, consider some lines from a moderately difficult poem, Andrew Marvell's "An Horatian Ode on Cromwell's Return from Ireland":

And now the Irish are ashamed
To see themselves in one year tamed:
. . . .
They can affirm his praises best,
And have, though overcome, confessed
How good he is, how just,
And fit for highest trust.

On one understanding or interpretation, Marvell means that the Irish ought to be ashamed that they were defeated so quickly and that they do admit that Cromwell is a good, just, and trustworthy person. On another understanding or interpretation, Marvell, being ironic, means that Cromwell ought to be ashamed of his victory over the Irish and they have every right to think he is not good, just, or trustworthy. If one wonders how the second understanding is plausible, the interpreter can point out that Cromwell mercilessly had women and other noncombatants slaughtered at Drogheda and Wexford. If, in the light of these facts, one now wonders how the first understanding can plausibly be asserted, the interpreter may claim that the Irish themselves had slaughtered Protestants at Ulster and that Cromwell was good and just because he was God's instrument in meting out justice on the Irish. The reason that either 'understanding' or 'interpretation' can be used about these lines is that almost every aspect of the author's meaning is difficult or dubious. What is important is that to justify either statement of Marvell's meaning is to show that linguistic understanding is tied together with judgments about nonlinguistic matters, just as interpretations obviously are. The example of a poem is not essential. The same point could be illustrated with innumerable prose texts, both fictional and nonfictional.

Concerning translation, the claim has often been made that every translation is an interpretation. The converse, that every interpretation is a translation, follows from the fact that each person has her own idiolect. Quine and Davidson do not think that human beings strictly speak the same language. Idiolects lack sufficient similarity to make them instances of any one thing that would constitute an entity in its own right. English, French, German, and Chinese are simply clusters of idiolects. A so-called natural language is constituted roughly by the facts that the idiolects of a community of people overlap to a very great degree. Understanding or interpreting what someone says in effect involves correlating some utterance of the speaker's idiolect with some utterance of one's own, just as translation does. Thus, understanding, interpretation, and translation are the same thing.

The locus classicus for Quine's views about interpretation is "Translation and Meaning" in *Word and Object*. His project is to discover the nature of meaning, but his perspective is radically different from typical work in that area. He considers what it would be like for a person to come to understand a language with which he had no previous acquaintance, direct or indirect. In other words, he considers how an adult would learn a completely new language. In such a situation, the linguist, like an infant, must initially rely upon sensory stimulation. Suppose the native speaker utters, "Gavagai" as the linguist notices a rabbit run by. The linguist may plausibly guess that "Gavagai" means "Rabbit" or "There's a rabbit." Suppose that other situations give further credence to this guess. The linguist can check this translation by himself saying "Gavagai" in the presence of a rabbit and checking the native's reaction. In simple terms, the native's reaction can be either positive or negative. Of course, what kind of behavior counts in this regard is also a matter of guesswork or hypothesis. If the native's response is positive, the acceptability of the translation becomes firmer. If it is negative, the linguist has to entertain other hypotheses about either (a) the meaning of 'Gavagai', or (b) the situation—was it really a rabbit?—or (c) the native's sensations or truthfulness. At no point is the linguist only assigning a so-called meaning to an utterance; he is always also making judgments about other aspects of the situation. These judgments form a massively interconnecting network. Originally, Quine maintained that it was only the entire network, and no individual sentence, that makes sense. More recently, he has moderated his thesis by claiming that only large sets of sentences make sense. This is a brief explanation of what Quine means by holism.

Let's return to the linguist's translation of "Gavagai" as "Rabbit." If someone would be equally likely to respond positively to "Gavagai" as to "Rabbit" in some situation, then those utterances have the same "affirmative stimulus meaning." If the person would be equally likely to respond negatively to each of those words, then the utterances would have the same "negative stimulus meaning." The ordered pair of an utterance's affirmative and negative stimulus meaning is its stimulus meaning. Pairs of utterances that have the same affirmative and negative stimulus meaning are stimulus synonymous. This is the only sense of "synonymy" that Quine thinks is legitimate. (See "Two Dogmas of Empiricism" in Section I.) A sentence that has only affirmative stimulus meaning, for example, 'A black horse is black', is stimulus analytic. A sentence that has only negative stimulus meaning, for example, 'A black horse is not black', is stimulus contradictory.

The foregoing gives a very simplified picture of the linguist's learning. For example, nothing has been said about the effects of collateral information. The native may say "Gavagai" not because he sees a rabbit but because he hears one of his friends say it or because he sees a kind of fly that infests rabbits and thus leads him to believe that rabbits are present.

The basic sentences are observation sentences in the sense of being tied to what the speaker and hearer perceive; they are also occasion sentences in the sense that the speaker's inclination to utter or assent to the sentence depends on what the observational environment is from occasion to occasion. "Gavagai" may be uttered on the occasions of a rabbit's being present and not otherwise.

It it necessary also to explain how nonobservation and nonoccasion ("standing") sentences can be learned. Quine's short answer is that they are learned by analogies; and the analogies depend upon isolating recurring sounds (perhaps 'gav' and 'gai') and recurring patterns (what may eventually be identified as subject/predicate, adjective/noun, verb/adverb patterns). These analogies require segmenting utterances into smaller parts, which grammar calls variously words and morphemes.

"Gavagai" and "Rabbit" have been referred to as utterances; Quine considers them, more specifically, to be sentences. Only sentences that are tied to the kind of sensory stimulus conditions described here can be synonymous (or contradictory if their affirmative and negative stimulus meanings are the opposite of each other). 'Rabbit' used as a sentence has the same stimulus meaning as 'There's a rabbit' and not the same meaning as 'rabbit' used as a word. Sentences are primary; "words are learned only by abstraction from their roles in learned sentences" (*Word and Object,* p. 51). Individual words or phrases do not have any determinate meaning. 'Gavagai', construed as a sentence, has the same stimulus meaning no matter whether it, construed as a word, is properly applied to rabbits, undetached rabbit parts, or brief temporal segments of rabbits, even though 'rabbit', 'undetached rabbit part', and 'rabbit-stage' intuitively have different meanings.

The basic sentences of a language as Quine conceives it are tied to conditions of sensory stimulations. Individual words are not. They are identified by their recurrence as parts of sentences. The linguist forms hypotheses about how to segment longer utterances into shorter ones. If we take an infant learning English as an example, exposure to numerous occurrences of utterances like 'Giveittomama', 'Giveittodaddy', 'Kissmama', 'Kissdaddy' will lead the child to hypothesize that 'give', 'it', 'to', 'mama', 'daddy', and 'kiss' have different and predictable occurrences. These constitute "analytical hypotheses." Quine is not saying that the infant will do this explicitly or reflectively; he is engaging in rational reconstruction. He is saying that this is a good way to explain the learning of the child; and the adult linguist does seem to follow this procedure explicitly and reflectively. Quine would probably agree with Davidson's remark that these are "claims about what must be said to give a satisfactory description of the competence" of the speaker.

Because there is no one set of analytical hypotheses that fits the behavior of a speaker better than a different set of analytical hypotheses, there is no one set of hypotheses that can be said to give the correct meaning of the words of the language. This is what Quine means by the indeterminacy of translation: there is no fact of the matter about what a speaker means.

John Searle in "Indeterminacy, Empiricism, and the First Person" gives both a clear statement and powerful critique of Quine's views. He argues that Quine's mistake is to ignore the speaker's point of view. The speaker knows what he means by an utterance, knows, say, that by the word 'rabbit' he means a certain animal and not an undetached part or temporal stage of it. And a theory of meaning that denies this is mistaken.

In "Belief and the Basis of Meaning," Davidson shows that an audience does not merely attribute a meaning to an utterance when she interprets it but also attributes a belief to the speaker. For example, if someone says, "Es schneit" and the audience interprets this as meaning 'It is snowing', she must also (in normal cases) hold that the speaker believes that snow is white. In fact, the interpreter also attributes intentions to the speaker and makes various judgments about the situation within which the utterance is made. Davidson says, "My claim is only that making detailed sense of a person's intentions and beliefs cannot be independent of making sense of his utterances." Attributions of meanings to sentences and beliefs and intentions to speakers mutually affect each other.

In "A Nice Derangement of Epitaphs," Davidson argues that the fact that interpreters need to adapt their understanding of what a speaker's sentence means in the light of what the speaker plausibly believes, in addition to his or her prior beliefs about what the uttered words mean, threatens the distinction between what the speaker means and what his words mean. In other words, the literal meaning of a sentence is typically not its "conventional or established" meaning. What is needed for correct interpretation to occur is not acceptance of a conventional ("prior") understanding of the speaker's words, but an understanding of what the speaker means by the words on that occasion (the "passing theory"). In other words, interpretation is theoretically ad hoc. The ad hoc theory that is used to interpret a particular utterance does not need to rely on some shared understanding of a language either. For example, an interpreter can understand what Mrs. Malaprop says by uttering, "That's a nice derangement of epitaphs," even though the interpreter does not share with the speaker the meaning of 'derangement' or 'epitaphs'. Davidson concludes with the stunning claim: "there is no such thing as a language, not if a language is anything like what many philosophers and linguists have supposed."

38 Translation and Meaning

W. V. QUINE

§7. FIRST STEPS OF RADICAL TRANSLATION[1]

We have been reflecting in a general way on how surface irritations generate, through language, one's knowledge of the world. One is taught so to associate words with words and other stimulations that there emerges something recognizable as talk of things, and not to be distinguished from truth about the world. The voluminous and intricately structured talk that comes out bears little evident correspondence to the past and present barrage of non-verbal stimulation; yet it is to such stimulation that we must look for whatever empirical content there may be. In this chapter we shall consider how much of language can be made sense of in terms of its stimulus conditions, and what scope this leaves for empirically unconditioned variation in one's conceptual scheme.

A first uncritical way of picturing this scope for empirically unconditioned variation is as follows: two men could be just alike in all their dispositions to verbal behavior under all possible sensory stimulations, and yet the meanings or ideas expressed in their identically triggered and identically sounded utterances could diverge radically, for the two men, in a wide range of cases. To put the matter thus invites, however, the charge of meaninglessness: one may protest that a distinction of meaning unre-flected in the totality of dispositions to verbal behavior is a distinction without a difference.

Sense can be made of the point by recasting it as follows: the infinite totality of sentences of any given speaker's language can be so permuted, or mapped onto itself, that (*a*) the totality of the speaker's dispositions to verbal behavior remains invariant, and yet (*b*) the mapping is no mere correlation of sentences with *equivalent* sentences, in any plausible sense of equivalence however loose. Sentences without number can diverge drastically from their respective correlates, yet the divergences can systematically so offset one another that the overall pattern of associations of sentences with one another and with non-verbal stimulation is preserved. The firmer the direct links of a sentence with non-verbal stimulation, of course, the less that sentence can diverge from its correlate under any such mapping.

The same point can be put less abstractly and more realistically by switching to translation. The thesis is then this: manuals for translating one language into another can be set up in divergent ways, all compatible with the totality of speech dispositions, yet incompatible with one another. In countless places they will diverge in giving, as their respective translations of a sentence of the one language, sentences of the other language which stand to each other in no plau-

Willard Van Orman Quine, *Word and Object*, pp. 26–79. © 1960, MIT Press, Cambridge, MA.
Reprinted by permission of the publisher and the author.

sible sort of equivalence however loose. The firmer the direct links of a sentence with non-verbal stimulation, of course, the less drastically its translations can diverge from one another from manual to manual. It is in this last form, as a principle of indeterminacy of translation, that I shall try to make the point plausible in the course of this chapter. But the chapter will run longer than it would if various of the concepts and considerations ancillary to this theme did not seem worthy of treatment also on their own account.

We are concerned here with language as the complex of present dispositions to verbal behavior, in which speakers of the same language have perforce come to resemble one another; not with the processes of acquisition, whose variations from individual to individual it is to the interests of communication to efface. The sentence 'That man shoots well', said while pointing to an unarmed man, has as present stimulation the glimpse of the marksman's familiar face. The contributory past stimulation includes past observations of the man's shooting, as well as remote episodes that trained the speaker in the use of the words. The past stimulation is thus commonly reckoned in part to the acquisition of language and in part to the acquisition of collateral information; however, this subsidiary dichotomy can await some indication of what it is good for and what general clues there are for it in observable verbal behavior. (cf. §§9, 12, 14) Meanwhile what is before us is the going concern of verbal behavior and its currently observable correlations with stimulation. Reckon a man's current language by his current dispositions to respond verbally to current stimulation, and you automatically refer all past stimulation to the learning phase. Not but that even this way of drawing a boundary between language in acquisition and language in use has its fluctuations, inasmuch as we can consult our convenience in what bound we set to the length of stimulations counted as current. This bound, a working standard of what to count as specious present, I call the *modulus* of stimulation.

The recovery of a man's current language from his currently observed responses is the task of the linguist who, unaided by an interpreter, is out to penetrate and translate a language hitherto unknown. All the objective data he has to go on are the forces that he sees impinging on the native's surfaces and the observable behavior, vocal and otherwise, of the native. Such data evince native "meanings" only of the most objectively empirical or stimulus-linked variety. And yet the linguist apparently ends up with native "meanings" in some quite unrestricted sense; purported translations, anyway, of all possible native sentences.

Translation between kindred languages, e.g., Frisian and English, is aided by resemblance of cognate word forms. Translation between unrelated languages, e.g., Hungarian and English, may be aided by traditional equations that have evolved in step with a shared culture. What is relevant rather to our purposes is *radical* translation, i.e., translation of the language of a hitherto untouched people. The task is one that is not in practice undertaken in its extreme form, since a chain of interpreters of a sort can be recruited of marginal persons across the darkest archipelago. But the problem is the more nearly approximated the poorer the hints available from interpreters; thus attention to techniques of utterly radical translation has not been wanting.[2] I shall imagine that all help of interpreters is excluded. Incidentally I shall here ignore phonematic analysis, early though it would come in our field linguist's enterprise; for it does not affect the philosophical point I want to make.

The utterances first and most surely translated in such a case are ones keyed to present events that are conspicuous to the linguist and his informant. A rabbit scurries by, the native says 'Gavagai', and the linguist notes down the sentence 'Rabbit' (or 'Lo, a rabbit') as tentative translation, subject to testing in further cases. The linguist will at first refrain from putting words into his informant's mouth, if only for lack of words to put. When he can, though, the linguist has to supply native sentences for his informant's approval, despite the risk of slanting the data by suggestion. Otherwise he can do little with native terms that have references in common. For, suppose the native language includes sentences S_1, S_2, and S_3, really translatable respectively as 'Animal', 'White', and 'Rabbit'. Stimulus situations always differ, whether relevantly or not; and, just because volunteered responses come singly, the classes of situations under which the native happens to have volunteered S_1, S_2, and S_3 are of course mutually exclusive, despite the hidden actual meanings of the words. How then is the linguist to perceive that the native would have been willing to assent to S_1 in all the situations where he happened to volunteer S_3, and in some but perhaps not all of the situations where he happened to volunteer S_2? Only by taking the initiative and querying combinations of native sentences and stimulus situations so as to narrow down his guesses to his eventual satisfaction.

So we have the linguist asking 'Gavagai?' in each of various stimulatory situations, and noting each time whether the native assents, dissents, or neither. But how is he to recognize native assent and dissent when he sees or hears them? Gestures are not to be taken at face value; the Turks' are nearly the reverse of our own. What he must do is guess from observation and then see how well his guesses work. Thus suppose that in asking 'Gavagai?' and the like, in the conspicuous presence of rabbits and the like, he has elicited the responses 'Evet' and 'Yok' often enough to surmise that they may correspond to 'Yes' and 'No', but has no notion which is which. Then he tries the experiment of echoing the native's own volunteered pronouncements. If thereby he pretty regularly elicits 'Evet' rather than 'Yok', he is encouraged to take 'Evet' as 'Yes'. Also he tries responding with 'Evet' and 'Yok' to the native's remarks; the one that is the more serene in its effect is the better candidate for 'Yes'. However inconclusive these methods, they generate a working hypothesis. If extraordinary difficulties attend all his subsequent steps, the linguist may decide to discard that hypothesis and guess again.[3]

Let us then suppose the linguist has settled on what to treat as native signs of assent and dissent. He is thereupon in a position to accumulate inductive evidence for translating 'Gavagai' as the sentence 'Rabbit'. The general law for which he is assembling instances is roughly that the native will assent to 'Gavagai?' under just those stimulations under which we, if asked, would assent to 'Rabbit?'; and correspondingly for dissent.

But we can do somewhat more justice to what the linguist is after in such a case if, instead of speaking merely of stimulations under which the native will assent or dissent to the queried sentence, we speak in a more causal vein of stimulations that will *prompt* the native to assent or dissent to the queried sentence. For suppose the queried sentence were one rather to the effect that someone is away tracking a giraffe. All day long the native will assent to it whenever asked, under all manner of irrelevant attendant stimulations; and on another day he will dissent from it under the same irrelevant stimulations. It is important to know that in the case of 'Gavagai?' the rabbit-presenting stimulations actually prompt the assent, and that the others actually prompt the dissent.

In practice the linguist will usually settle these questions of causality, however tentatively, by intuitive judgment based on details of the native's behavior: his scanning movements, his sudden look of recognition, and the like. Also there are more formal considerations which, under favorable circumstances, can assure him of the prompting relation. If, just after the native has been asked S and has assented or dissented, the linguist springs stimulation σ on him, asks S again, and gets the opposite verdict, then he may conclude that σ did the prompting.

Note that to prompt, in our sense, is not to elicit. What elicits the native's 'Evet' or 'Yok' is a combination: the prompting stimulation plus the ensuing query 'Gavagai?'

§8. STIMULATION AND STIMULUS MEANING

It is important to think of what prompts the native's assent to 'Gavagai?' as stimulations and not rabbits. Stimulation can remain the same though the rabbit be supplanted by a counterfeit. Conversely, stimulation can vary in its power to prompt assent to 'Gavagai' because of variations in angle, lighting, and color contrast, though the rabbit remain the same. In experimentally equating the uses of 'Gavagai' and 'Rabbit' it is stimulations that must be made to match, not animals.

A visual stimulation is perhaps best identified, for present purposes, with the pattern of chromatic irradiation of the eye. To look deep into the subject's head would be inappropriate even if feasible, for we want to keep clear of his idiosyncratic neural routings or private history of habit formation. We are after his socially inculcated linguistic usage, hence his responses to conditions normally subject to social assessment. Ocular irradiation *is* inter-subjectively checked to some degree by society and linguist alike, by making allowances for the speaker's orientation and the relative disposition of objects.

In taking the visual stimulations as irradiation patterns we invest them with a fineness of detail beyond anything that our linguist can be called upon to check for. But this is all right. He can reasonably conjecture that the native would be prompted to assent to 'Gavagai' by the microscopically same irradiations that would prompt him, the linguist, to assent to 'Rabbit', even though this conjecture rests wholly on samples where the irradiations concerned can at best be hazarded merely to be pretty much alike.

It is not, however, adequate to think of the visual stimulations as momentary static irradiation patterns. To do so would obstruct examples which, unlike 'Rabbit', affirm movement. And it would make trouble even with examples like 'Rabbit', on another account: too much depends on what immediately precedes and follows a momentary irradiation. A momentary leporiform image flashed by some artifice in the midst of an otherwise rabbitless sequence might not prompt assent to 'Rabbit' even though the same image would have done so if ensconced in a more favorable sequence. The difficulty would thus arise that far from hoping to match the irradiation patterns favorable to 'Gavagai' with those favorable to 'Rabbit', we could not even say unequivocally of an irradiation pattern, of itself and without regard to those just before and after, that it is favorable to 'Rabbit' or that it is not.[4] Better, therefore, to take as the relevant stimulations not momentary irradiation patterns, but evolving irradiation patterns of all durations up to some convenient limit or *modulus*. Furthermore we may think of the ideal experimental situation as one in which the desired ocular exposure concerned is preceded and followed by a blindfold.

In general the ocular irradiation patterns are best conceived in their spatial entirety. For there are examples such as 'Fine weather' which, unlike 'Rabbit', are not keyed to any readily segregated fragments of the scene. Also there are all those rabbit-free patterns that are wanted as prompting dissent from 'Rabbit'. And as for the patterns wanted as prompting assent to 'Rabbit', whole scenes will still serve better than selected portions might; for the difference between center and periphery, which is such an important determinant of visual attention, is then automatically allowed for. Total ocular irradiation patterns that differ in centering differ also in limits, and so are simply different patterns. One that shows the rabbit too peripherally simply will not be one that prompts assent to 'Gavagai' or 'Rabbit'.

Certain sentences of the type of 'Gavagai' are the sentences with which our jungle linguist must begin, and for these we now have before us the makings of a crude concept of empirical meaning. For meaning, supposedly, is what a sentence shares with its translation; and translation at the present stage turns solely on correlations with non-verbal stimulation.

Let us make this concept of meaning more explicit and give it a neutrally technical name. We may begin by defining the *affirmative stimulus meaning* of a sentence such as 'Gavagai', for a given speaker, as the class of all the stimulations (hence evolving ocular irradiation patterns between properly timed blindfoldings) that would prompt his assent. More explicitly, in view of the end of §7, a stimulation σ belongs to the affirmative stimulus meaning of a sentence S for a given speaker if and only if there is a stimulation σ' such that if the speaker were given σ', then were asked S, then were given σ, and then were asked S again, he would dissent the first time and assent the second. We may define the *negative* stimulus meaning similarly with 'assent' and 'dissent' interchanged, and then define the *stimulus meaning* as the ordered pair of the two. We could refine the notion of stimulus meaning by distinguishing degrees of doubtfulness of assent and dissent, say by reaction time; but for the sake of fluent exposition let us forbear. The imagined equating of 'Gavagai' and 'Rabbit' can now be stated thus: they have the same stimulus meaning.

A stimulus meaning is the stimulus meaning of a sentence for a speaker at a date; for we must allow our speaker to change his ways. Also it varies with the modulus, or maximum duration recognized for stimulations. For, by increasing the modulus we supplement the stimulus meaning with some stimulations that were too long to count before. Fully ticketed, therefore, a stimulus meaning is the stimulus meaning *modulo n* seconds of sentence S for speaker a at time t.

The stimulations to be gathered into the stimulus meaning of a sentence have for vividness been thought of thus far as visual, unlike the queries that follow them. Actually, of course, we should bring the other senses in on a par with vision, identifying stimulations not with just ocular irradiation patterns but with these and the various barrages of other senses, separately and in all synchronous combinations. Perhaps we can pass over the detail of this.

The affirmative and negative stimulus meanings of a sentence (for a given speaker at a given time) are mutually exclusive. Granted, our subject might be prompted once by a given stimulation σ to assent to S, and later, by a recurrence of σ, to dissent from S; but then we would simply conclude that his meaning for S had changed. We would then reckon σ to his affirmative stimulus meaning of S as of the one date and to his negative stimulus meaning of S as of the other date.

Yet the affirmative and negative stimulus meanings do not determine each other; for many stimulations may be expected to belong to neither. In general, therefore, comparison of whole stimulus meanings can be a better basis for translations than comparison merely of affirmative stimulus meanings.

What now of that strong conditional, the 'would' in our definition of stimulus meaning? Its use here is no worse than its use when we explain 'x is soluble in water' as meaning that x would dissolve if it were in water. What the strong conditional defines is a disposition, in this case a disposition to assent to or dissent from S when variously stimulated. The disposition may be presumed to be some subtle structural condition, like an allergy and like solubility; like an allergy, more particularly, in not being understood. The ontological status of dispositions, or the philosophical status of talk of dispositions, is a matter which I defer to §46 [not included here]; but meanwhile we are familiar enough in a general way with how one

sets about guessing, from judicious tests and samples and observed uniformities, whether there is a disposition of a specified sort.

The stimulus meaning of a sentence for a subject sums up his disposition to assent to or dissent from the sentence in response to present stimulation. The stimulation is what activates the disposition, as opposed to what instills it (even though the stimulation chance to contribute somehow to the instilling of some further disposition).

Yet a stimulation must be conceived for these purposes not as a dated particular event but as a universal, a repeatable event form. We are to say not that two like stimulations have occurred, but that the same stimulation has recurred. Such an attitude is implied the moment we speak of sameness of stimulus meaning for two speakers. We could indeed overrule this consideration, if we liked, by readjusting our terminology. But there would be no point, for there remains elsewhere a compelling reason for taking the stimulations as universals; viz., the strong conditional in the definition of stimulus meaning. For, consider again the affirmative stimulus meaning of a sentence S: the class Σ of all those stimulations that *would* prompt assent to S. If the stimulations were taken as events rather than event forms, then Σ would have to be a class of events which largely did not and will not happen, but which would prompt assent to S if they were to happen. Whenever Σ contained one realized or unrealized particular stimulatory event σ, it would have to contain all other unrealized duplicates of σ; and how many are there of *these*? Certainly it is hopeless nonsense to talk thus of unrealized particulars and try to assemble them into classes. Unrealized entities have to be construed as universals.

We were impressed in §3 [not included here] with the interdependence of sentences. We may well have begun then to wonder whether meanings even of whole sentences (let alone shorter expressions) could reasonably be talked of at all, except relative to the other sentences of an inclusive theory. Such relativity would be awkward, since, conversely, the individual component sentences offer the only way into the theory. Now the notion of stimulus meaning partially resolves the predicament. It isolates a sort of net empirical import of each of various single sentences without regard to the containing theory, even though without loss of what the sentence owes to that containing theory. It is a device, as far as it goes, for exploring the fabric of interlocking sentences, a sentence at a time.

Between the notion of stimulus meaning and Carnap's remarks on empirical semantics[5] there are connections and differences worth noting. He suggests exploring the meaning of a term by asking the subject whether he would apply it under various imaginary circumstances, to be described to him. That approach has the virtue of preserving contrasts between such terms as 'goblin' and 'unicorn' despite the non-existence of contrasting instances in the world. Stimulus meaning has the same virtue, since there are stimulation patterns that would prompt assent to 'Unicorn?' and not to 'Goblin?'. Carnap's approach presupposes some decision as to what descriptions of imaginary circumstances are admissible; e.g., 'unicorn' would be not wanted in descriptions used in probing the meaning of 'unicorn'. He hints of appropriate restrictions for the purpose, mentioning "size, shape, color"; and my notion of stimulus meaning itself amounts to a firmer definition in that same direction. There remains a significant contrast in the uses the two of us make of subjunctive conditionals: I limit them to my investigator's considered judgment of what the informant would do if stimulated; Carnap has his investigator putting such conditionals to the judgment of the informant. Certainly my investigator would in practice ask the same questions as Carnap's investigator, as a quick way of estimating stimulus meanings, if language for such questions happened to be available. But stimulus meaning can be explored also at the first stages of radical translation, where Carnap's type of questionnaire is unavailable. On this score it is important, as we shall see in §12, that my theory has to do primarily with sentences of a sort and not, like Carnap's, with terms.

§9. OCCASION SENTENCES; INTRUSIVE INFORMATION

Occasion sentences, as against *standing* sentences, are sentences such as 'Gavagai', 'Red',

'It hurts', 'His face is dirty', which command assent or dissent only if queried after an appropriate prompting stimulation. Verdicts to standing sentences *can* be prompted too: stimulation implemented by an interferometer once prompted Michelson and Morley to dissent from the standing sentence 'There is ether drift', and a speaker's assent can be prompted yearly to 'The crocuses are out', daily to 'The *Times* has come'. But these standing sentences contrast with occasion sentences in that the subject may repeat his old assent or dissent unprompted by current stimulation when we ask him again on later occasions, whereas an occasion sentence commands assent or dissent only as prompted all over again by current stimulation. Standing sentences grade off toward occasion sentences as the interval between possible repromptings diminishes; and the occasion sentence is the extreme case where that interval is less than the modulus. Like the stimulus meanings themselves, the distinction between standing sentences and occasion sentences is relative to the modulus; an occasion sentence modulo n seconds can be a standing sentence modulo $n - 1$.

The stimulations belonging to neither the affirmative nor the negative stimulus meaning of an occasion sentence are just those that would inhibit a verdict on the queried sentence, whether through indecisiveness (as in the case of a poor glimpse) or through shocking the subject out of his wits. On the other hand the stimulations belonging to neither the affirmative nor the negative stimulus meaning of a standing sentence are of two sorts: besides the inhibitory ones there are the *irrelevant* ones, which neither prompt nor inhibit. Querying the sentence on the heels of such a stimulation would elicit a verdict, but always the one that the query would have elicited without the attendant stimulation; never a change of verdict.

The stimulus meaning is a full cross-section of the subject's evolving dispositions to assent to or dissent from a sentence, if the sentence is an occasion sentence; less so if it is a standing sentence. Standing sentences can differ among themselves in "meaning," by any intuitive account,[6] as freely as occasion sentences; but, the less susceptible they are to prompted assent and dissent, the fewer clues are present in stimulus meaning. The notion of stimulus meaning is thus most important for occasion sentences, and we shall limit our attention for a while to them.

Even for such favored occasion sentences as 'Gavagai' and 'Rabbit', actually, sameness of stimulus meaning has its shortcomings as a synonymy relation. The difficulty is that an informant's assent to or dissent from 'Gavagai?' can depend excessively on prior collateral information as a supplement to the present prompting stimulus. He may assent on the occasion of nothing better than an ill-glimpsed movement in the grass, because of his earlier observation, unknown to the linguist, of rabbits near the spot. Since the linguist would not on his own information be prompted by that same poor glimpse to assent to 'Rabbit?', we have here a discrepancy between the present stimulus meaning of 'Gavagai' for the informant and that of 'Rabbit' for the linguist.

More persistent discrepancies of the same type can be imagined, affecting not one native but all, and not once but regularly. There may be a local rabbit-fly,[7] unknown to the linguist, and recognizable some way off by its long wings and erratic movements; and seeing such a fly in the neighborhood of an ill-glimpsed animal could help a native to recognize the latter as a rabbit. Ocular irradiations combining poor glimpses of rabbits with good ones of rabbit-flies would belong to the stimulus meaning of 'Gavagai' for natives generally, and not to that of 'Rabbit' for the linguist.

And, to be less fanciful, there are all those stimulations that incorporate verbal hints from native kibitzers. Thus suppose that the stimulation on the heels of which the informant is asked 'Gavagai?' is a composite stimulation presenting a bystander pointing to an ill-glimpsed object and saying 'Gavagai'. This composite stimulation will probably turn out to belong to the affirmative stimulus meaning of 'Gavagai' for the informant, and not to the stimulus meaning of 'Rabbit' for most English speakers, on whom the force of the bystander's verbal intervention would be lost. Such cases would not fool our linguist, but they do count against defining synonymy as sameness of stimulus

meaning. For we must remember that every sufficiently brief stimulation pattern, though it be one that never gets actualized or that the linguist would never use, still by definition belongs to the stimulus meaning of 'Gavagai' for a man at a given time if it is one that *would* prompt his assent at that time.

Intuitively the ideal would be to accord to the affirmative meaning of 'Gavagai' just those stimulations that would prompt assent to 'Gavagai?' on the strength purely of an understanding of 'Gavagai', unaided by collateral information: unaided by recent observation of rabbits near the spot, unaided by knowledge of the nature and habits of the rabbit-fly, unaided by conversance with the kibitzer's language. On the face of it there is a difficulty in excluding this third aid, considering our continuing dependence on the subject's understanding of 'Gavagai'. But also the trouble is more widespread. It is precisely that we have made no general experimental sense of a distinction between what goes into a native's learning to apply an expression and what goes into his learning supplementary matters about the objects concerned. True, the linguist can press such a distinction part way; he can filter out such idiosyncratic bits of collateral matter as the informant's recent observation of rabbits near the spot, by varying his times and his informants and so isolating a more stable and more social stimulus meaning as common denominator. But any socially shared information, such as that about the rabbit-fly or the ability to understand a bystander's remark, will continue to affect even that common denominator. There is no evident criterion whereby to strip such effects away and leave just the meaning of 'Gavagai' properly so-called—whatever meaning properly so-called may be.

Thus, to depict the difficulty in more general terms, suppose it said that a particular class Σ comprises just those stimulations each of which suffices to prompt assent to a sentence S outright, without benefit of collateral information. Suppose it said that the stimulations comprised in a further class Σ', likewise sufficient to prompt assent to S, owe their efficacy rather to certain widely disseminated collateral information, C. Now couldn't we just as well have said, instead, that on acquiring C, men have found it convenient implicitly to change the very "meaning" of S, so that the members of Σ' now suffice outright like members of Σ? I suggest that we may say either; even historical clairvoyance would reveal no distinction, though it reveal all stages in the acquisition of C, since meaning can evolve *pari passu*. The distinction is illusory: as mistaken as the notion that we can determine separately what to talk about and what to say about it. It is simply a question whether to call the transitivity shortcuts changes of meaning or condensations of proof; and in fact an unreal question. What we objectively have is just an evolving adjustment to nature, reflected in an evolving set of dispositions to be prompted by stimulations to assent to or dissent from sentences. These dispositions may be conceded to be impure in the sense of including worldly knowledge, but they contain it in a solution which there is no precipitating.

Incidentally, note that stimulus meanings as defined in §8 can even suffer some discrepancies that are intuitively attributable neither to differences of meaning nor to differences of collateral information. Thus take shocked silence. To begin with, if the speaker is already stunned at time t, all stimulus meanings for him at t will be empty. This outcome of the definition of stimulus meaning is unnatural but harmless, since we can ignore stimulus meanings for stunned persons. But in the case of a speaker alert at t there are stimulations that *would* stun him at t and so *would* preclude any assent to or dissent from the ensuing 'Gavagai?'. These, by definition, belong to neither the affirmative nor the negative stimulus meaning of 'Gavagai' for him at t. Now where a discrepancy in stimulus meanings will ensue is where a stimulation is such as would stun one speaker and not another; for it could belong say to the negative stimulus meaning of 'Gavagai' or 'Rabbit' for the latter speaker and to neither the affirmative nor the negative stimulus meaning for the former speaker. This again is a discrepancy that would not puzzle the linguist, but that exists under our definition. Also there are interferences of less drastic sorts. The native may dissent from 'Gavagai' in plain sight of the rabbit's ears, because the rabbit is in no position for shooting;[8] he has misjudged the linguist's motive for asking 'Gavagai?'.

We have now seen that stimulus meaning as defined falls short in various ways of one's intuitive demands on "meaning" as undefined, and that sameness of stimulus meaning is too strict a relation to expect between a native occasion sentence and its translation—even in so benign a case as 'Gavagai' and 'Rabbit'. Yet stimulus meaning, by whatever name, may be properly looked upon still as the objective reality that the linguist has to probe when he undertakes radical translation. For the stimulus meaning of an occasion sentence is by definition the native's total battery of present dispositions to be prompted to assent to or to dissent from the sentence; and these dispositions are just what the linguist has to sample and estimate. We do best to revise not the notion of stimulus meaning, but only what we represent the linguist as doing with stimulus meanings. The fact is that he translates not by identity of stimulus meanings, but by significant approximation of stimulus meanings.

If he translates 'Gavagai' as 'Rabbit' despite the discrepancies in stimulus meaning imagined above, he does so because the stimulus meanings seem to coincide to an overwhelming degree and the discrepancies, so far as he finds them, seem best explained away or dismissed as effects of unidentified interferences. Some discrepancies he may sift out, as lately suggested, by varying his times and informants. Some, involving poor glimpses or shock or verbal intrusions, he would not even bother to bring to fulfillment by a querying of the sentence. Some, such as those involving the rabbit-fly, he will dismiss as effects of unidentified interferences if he does not encounter them often. In taking this last rather high line, clearly he is much influenced by his natural expectation that any people in rabbit country would have *some* brief expression that could in the long run be best translated simply as 'Rabbit'. He conjectures that the now-unexplained discrepancies between 'Gavagai' and 'Rabbit' are ones that may eventually be reconciled with his translation, after he has somehow got deep enough into the native language to ask sophisticated questions.

In practice, of course, the natural expectation that the natives will have a brief expression for 'Rabbit' counts overwhelmingly. The linguist hears 'Gavagai' once, in a situation where a rabbit seems to be the object of concern. He will then try 'Gavagai' for assent or dissent in a couple of situations designed perhaps to eliminate 'White' and 'Animal' as alternative translations, and will forthwith settle upon 'Rabbit' as translation without further experiment—though always in readiness to discover through some unsought experience that a revision is in order. I made the linguist preternaturally circumspect, and maximized his bad luck in respect of discrepant observations, in order to consider what theoretical bearing a native's collateral information can have upon the linguist's in fact wholly facile opening translation.

§10. OBSERVATION SENTENCES

Some stimulus meanings are less susceptible than others to the influences of intrusive information. There is on this score a significant contrast between 'Red' and 'Rabbit' even when 'Red' is taken on a par with 'Rabbit' as announcing not a passing sense datum but an enduring objective trait of the physical object. True, there are extreme cases where we may be persuaded, by collateral information about odd lighting and juxtaposition, that something is really red that did not seem so or vice versa; but, despite such cases, there is less scope for collateral information in deciding whether a glimpsed thing is red than in deciding whether it is a rabbit. In the case of 'Red', therefore, sameness of stimulus meaning comes unusually close to what one intuitively expects of synonymy.

Color words are notoriously ill matched between remote languages, because of differences in customary grouping of shades. But this is no present problem; it means merely that there may well be no native occasion sentence, at least no reasonably simple one, with approximately the stimulus meaning of 'Red'. Again, even if there is one, there may still be a kind of trouble in equating it to 'Red', just because of the vagueness of color boundaries in both languages. But this again is no problem of collateral information; it is a difficulty that would remain even if a distinction between meaning and collateral information were successfully drawn. It can be coped with by a rough matching of statistical scatterings. The penumbra of vagueness of 'Red' consists of stimulations in

respect of which the stimulus meanings of 'Red' tend to vary from speaker to speaker and from occasion to occasion; correspondingly for the penumbra of vagueness of the native sentence; and then 'Red' is a good translation to the extent that it resembles the native sentence umbra for umbra and penumbra for penumbra.

In terms of direct behavioral evidence, how do those fluctuations of stimulus meaning that are attributable to a penumbra of vagueness differ from those fluctuations of stimulus meaning (e.g. of 'Gavagai') that are laid to variations of collateral information from occasion to occasion? Partly in that the penumbral fluctuations increase rather smoothly as the stimulations grade off, while the fluctuations laid to collateral information are more irregular, suggesting intrusion of extraneous factors. But mainly in that each individual's assent or dissent tends to be marked by doubt and hesitation when the prompting stimulation belongs to the penumbra. If we were to complicate the notion of stimulus meaning to the extent of weighting each stimulation inversely according to reaction time (cf. §8), then discrepancies in stimulus meaning from speaker to speaker would tend to count for little where due to vagueness, and for more where not.

If 'Red' is somewhat less susceptible than 'Rabbit' to the influences of intrusive information, there are other sentences that are vastly more so. An example is 'Bachelor'. An informant's assent to it is prompted genuinely enough by the sight of a face, yet it draws mainly on stored information and none on the prompting stimulation except as needed for recognizing the bachelor friend concerned. As one says in the uncritical jargon of meaning, the trouble with 'Bachelor' is that its meaning transcends the looks of the prompting faces and concerns matters that can be known only through other channels. 'Rabbit' is a little this way, as witness papier-mâché counterfeits; 'Bachelor' much more so. The stimulus meaning of 'Bachelor' cannot be treated as its "meaning" by any stretch of the imagination, unless perhaps accompanied by a stretch of the modulus.

A mark of the intrusion of collateral information, except when the information is generally shared as in the examples of the kibitzer and the rabbit-fly (§9), was discrepancy in stimulus meaning from speaker to speaker of the same language. In a case like 'Bachelor', therefore, we may expect the discrepancies to be overwhelming; and indeed they are. For any two speakers whose social contacts are not virtually identical, the stimulus meanings of 'Bachelor' will diverge far more than those of 'Rabbit'.

The less susceptible the stimulus meaning of an occasion sentence is to the influences of collateral information, the less absurdity there is in thinking of the stimulus meaning of the sentence as the meaning of the sentence. Occasion sentences whose stimulus meanings vary none under the influence of collateral information may naturally be called *observation sentences*, and their stimulus meanings may without fear of contradiction be said to do full justice to their meanings. These are the occasion sentences that wear their meanings on their sleeves. Or, better, we may speak of degrees of observationality; for even the stimulus meaning of 'Red' can, we noted, be made to fluctuate a little from occasion to occasion by collateral information on lighting conditions. What we have is a gradation of observationality from one extreme, at 'Red' or above, to the other extreme at 'Bachelor' or below.

In the foregoing paragraph we have wallowed most unfastidiously in the conceptual slough of meaning and collateral information. But now it is interesting to note that what we have dredged out, a notion of degree of observationality, is not beyond cleaning up and rendering respectable. For, in behavioral terms, an occasion sentence may be said to be the more observational the more nearly its stimulus meanings for different speakers tend to coincide. Granted, this definition fails to give demerit marks for the effects of generally shared information, such as that about the rabbit-fly. But, as argued in §9, I suspect that no systematic experimental sense is to be made of a distinction between usage due to meaning and usage due to generally shared collateral information.

The notion of observationality is relative to the modulus of stimulation. This is not to be wondered at, since the notion of stimulus meaning was relative to the modulus (cf. §8), and so is the very distinction between habit formation and habit formed (cf. §7). Observationality increases with the modulus, in the following way.

A typical case of discrepancy between the stimulus meanings of 'Gavagai', for two natives, is the case where one native and not the other has lately seen rabbits near the spot that they are now viewing. An ill-glimpsed movement would now prompt the one native and not the other to assent to 'Gavagai?'. But if we make the modulus long enough to include as part of the one native's present stimulation his recent observation of rabbits near the spot, then what had been a discrepancy between stimulus meanings is a mere difference of stimulations: the one stimulation is such as would prompt either native to assent, and the other neither. Increase the modulus sufficiently to take in extended periods of learning about friends and you even increase the observationality of 'Bachelor'. But let us forget moduli again for a while, thus keeping our variables down.

We have defined observationality for occasion sentences somewhat vaguely, as degree of constancy of stimulus meaning from speaker to speaker. It would not do to use this definition generally among standing sentences, since the stimulus meaning of a standing sentence can show fair constancy from speaker to speaker for the wrong reason: mere sparseness of member stimulations. Among standing sentences that are well over toward the occasion end (cf. §9), however, the notion of observationality works quite as well as among occasion sentences, and is significant in the same way; viz., the higher the observationality, the better we can get on with translation by stimulus meaning. We could hope, e.g., to translate 'The tide is out' by a rough matching of stimulus meanings; not so 'There is a famous novelist on board'.

Viewing the graded notion of observationality as the primary one, we may still speak of sentences simply as observation sentences when they are high in observationality. In a narrow sense, just 'Red' would qualify; in a wider sense, also 'Rabbit' and 'The tide is out'. It is for observation sentences in some such sense that the notion of stimulus meaning constitutes a reasonable notion of meaning.

To philosophers 'observation sentence' suggests the datum sentences of science. On this score our version is not amiss; for the observation sentences as we have identified them are just the occasion sentences on which there is pretty sure to be firm agreement on the part of well-placed observers. Thus they are just the sentences on which a scientist will tend to fall back when pressed by doubting colleagues. Moreover, the philosophical doctrine of infallibility of observation sentences is sustained under our version. For there is scope for error and dispute only insofar as the connections with experience whereby sentences are appraised are multifarious and indirect, mediated through time by theory in conflicting ways; there is none insofar as verdicts to a sentence are directly keyed to present stimulation. (This immunity to error is, however, like observationality itself, for us a matter of degree.) Our version of observation sentences departs from a philosophical tradition in allowing the sentences to be about ordinary things instead of requiring them to report sense data, but this departure has not lacked proponents.[9]

In estimating the stimulus meaning of a sentence for a speaker at a given time, the linguist is helped by varying the time and speaker. In choosing a translation, he is helped by comparing native speakers and so eliminating idiosyncrasies of stimulus meaning. Still the notion of stimulus meaning itself, as defined, depends on no multiplicity of speakers. Now the notion of observationality, in contrast, is social. The behavioral definition offered for it above turns on similarities of stimulus meanings over the community.

What makes an occasion sentence low on observationality is, by definition, wide intersubjective variability of stimulus meaning. Language as a socially inculcated set of dispositions is substantially uniform over the community, but it is uniform in different ways for different sentences. If a sentence is one that (like 'Red' and 'Rabbit') is inculcated mostly by something like direct ostension, the uniformity will lie at the surface and there will be little variation in stimulus meaning; the sentence will be highly observational. If it is one that (like 'Bachelor') is inculcated through connections with other sentences, linking up thus indirectly with past stimulations of other sorts than those that serve directly to prompt present assent to the sentence, then its stimulus meaning will vary with the speakers' pasts, and the sentence will count

as very unobservational. The stimulus meaning of a very unobservational occasion sentence for a speaker is a product of two factors, a fairly standard set of sentence-to-sentence connections and a random personal history; hence the largely random character of the stimulus meaning from speaker to speaker.

Now this random character has the effect not only that the stimulus meaning of the sentence for one speaker will differ from the stimulus meaning of *that* sentence for other speakers. It will differ from the stimulus meaning also of any other discoverable sentence for other speakers, in the same language or any other. Granted, a great complex English sentence can be imagined whose stimulus meaning for one man matches, by sheer exhaustion of cases, another man's stimulus meaning of 'Bachelor'; but such a sentence would never be spotted, because nobody's stimulus meaning of 'Bachelor' would ever be suitably inventoried to begin with.

For, consider again how it was with 'Gavagai'. Here the stimulations belonging to the affirmative stimulus meaning share a distinctive trait that is salient, to us as well as to the native: the containing of rabbit glimpses. The trait is salient enough so that the linguist generalizes on it from samples: he expects the next glimpse of a rabbit to prompt assent to 'Gavagai' as past ones have. His generalization is repeatedly borne out, and he concludes with his conjecture that the native's whole stimulus meaning of 'Gavagai'—never experimentally exhausted, of course—will tend to match ours of 'Rabbit'. Now a similar effort with a non-observational native occasion sentence, of the type of our 'Bachelor', would have bogged down in its early stages. Sample stimulations belonging to the affirmative stimulus meaning of such a sentence, for the given native, would show no tempting common traits by which to conjecture further cases, or none but such as fail to hold up on further tries.

§11. INTRASUBJECTIVE SYNONYMY OF OCCASION SENTENCES

Stimulus meaning remains defined without regard to observationality. But when applied to non-observational sentences like 'Bachelor' it bears little resemblance to what might reasonably be called meaning. Translation of 'Soltero' as 'Bachelor' manifestly cannot be predicated on identity of stimulus meanings between speakers; nor can synonymy of 'Bachelor' and 'Unmarried man'.

But curiously enough the stimulus meanings of 'Bachelor' and 'Unmarried man' are, despite all this, identical for any one speaker.[10] An individual would at any one time be prompted by the same stimulations to assent to 'Bachelor' and 'Unmarried man'; and similarly for dissent. *Stimulus synonymy*, or sameness of stimulus meaning, is as good a standard of synonymy for non-observational occasion sentences as for observation sentences as long as we stick to one speaker. For each speaker, 'Bachelor' and 'Unmarried man' are stimulus-synonymous without having the same meaning in any acceptably defined sense of 'meaning' (for stimulus meaning is, in the case of 'Bachelor', nothing of the kind). Very well; here is a case where we may welcome the synonymy and let the meaning go.

The one-speaker restriction presents no obstacle to saying that 'Bachelor' and 'Unmarried man' are stimulus-synonymous for the whole community, in the sense of being thus for each member. A practical extension even to the two-language case is not far to seek if a bilingual speaker is at hand. 'Bachelor' and 'Soltero' will be stimulus-synonymous for him. Taking him as a sample, we may treat 'Bachelor' and 'Soltero' as synonymous for the translation purposes of the two whole linguistic communities that he represents. Whether he is a good enough sample would be checked by observing the fluency of his communication in both communities and by comparing other bilinguals.

Section 10 left the linguist unable to guess the trend of the stimulus meaning of a non-observational occasion sentence from sample cases. We now see a way, though costly, in which he can still accomplish radical translation of such sentences. He can settle down and learn the native language directly as an infant might.[11] Having thus become bilingual, he can translate the non-observational occasion sentences by introspected stimulus synonymy.

This step has the notable effect of initiating clear recognition of native falsehoods. As long as the linguist does no more than correlate the native's observation sentences with his own by stimulus meaning, he cannot discount any of the native's verdicts as false—unless *ad hoc*, most restrainedly, to simplify his correlations. But once he becomes bilingual and so transcends the observation sentences, he can bicker with the native as a brother.

Even short of going bilingual there is no difficulty in comparing two non-observational native sentences to see if they are intrasubjectively stimulus-synonymous for the native. The linguist can do this without having intuitively conjectured the trend of stimulus meaning of either sentence. He need merely query the sentences in parallel under random stimulations until he either hits a stimulation that prompts assent or dissent to one sentence and not to the other, or else is satisfied at last that he is not going to. A visiting Martian who never learns under what circumstances to apply 'Bachelor', or 'Unmarried man' either, can still find out by the above method that 'Bachelor' for one English speaker does not have the same stimulus meaning as 'Bachelor' for a different English speaker and that it has the same as 'Unmarried man' for the same speaker. He can, anyway, apart from one difficulty: there is no evident reason why it should occur to him thus blindly to try comparing 'Unmarried man' with 'Bachelor'. This difficulty makes the intrasubjective stimulus synonymy of non-observational occasion sentences less readily accessible to an alien linguist than the stimulus synonymy of observation sentences such as 'Gavagai' and 'Rabbit'. Still the linguist can examine for intrasubjective stimulus synonymy any pair of native occasion sentences that it occurs to him to wonder about; and we shall see in §15 how indirect considerations can even suggest such pairs for examination.

Between the stimulus meaning of any sentence for one man and the stimulus meaning of the same or any other sentence for another man there are almost bound to be countless discrepancies in point of verbally contaminated stimulations, as long as one man understands a language that the other does not. The argument is that of the kibitzer case in §9. The translating linguist had for this reason to discount verbally contaminated discrepancies. But intrasubjective comparisons are free of this trouble. Intrasubjectively we can even compare the occasion sentences 'Yes', 'Uh huh', and 'Quite' for stimulus synonymy, though the stimulations that enter into the stimulus meanings of these sentences are purely verbal in their relevant portions. A further advantage of the intrasubjective situation appears in the case of stimulations that would at a given time shock one speaker and not another into silence (cf. §9); for clearly these will constitute no discrepancies intrasubjectively. Altogether the equating of stimulus meanings works out far better intrasubjectively than between subjects: it goes beyond observation sentences, it absorbs shock, and it better accommodates verbal stimulations.

Verbal stimulations can plague even the intrasubjective comparisons when they are stimulations of "second intention"—i.e., when besides consisting of words they are about words. Second-intention examples are the bane of theoretical linguistics, also apart from synonymy studies. Thus take the linguist engaged in distinguishing between those sequences of sounds or phonemes that can occur in English speech and those that cannot: all his excluded forms can return to confound him in second-intention English, as between quotation marks. Now some second-intention stimulations that could prompt a subject to assent to one of the queries 'Bachelor?' and 'Unmarried man?' to the exclusion of the other are as follows: a stimulation presenting the spelling of 'bachelor'; a stimulation presenting the words 'rhymes with 'harried man''; a stimulation presenting a glimpse of a bachelor friend together with a plea to redefine 'bachelor'. It is not easy to find a behavioral criterion of second intention whereby to screen such cases, especially the last.

Leaving that problem unsolved, we have still to note another and more humdrum restriction that needs to be observed in equating sentences by stimulus meanings: we should stick to short sentences. Otherwise subjects' mere incapacity to digest long questions can, under our definitions, issue in difference of stimulus meanings between long and short sentences which we should prefer to find synonymous. A stimulation may prompt assent to the short sentence and not to the long one just because of the opacity of the long one; yet we should then like to

say not that the subject has shown the meaning of the long sentence to be different, but merely that he has failed to encompass it. Still a concept of synonymy initially significant only for short sentences can be extended to long sentences by analogy, e.g. as follows. By a *construction*, linguistically speaking, let us understand any fixed way of building a composite expression from arbitrary components of appropriate sort, one or more at a time. (What is fixed may include certain additive words, as well as the way of arranging the unfixed components.) Now two sentence-forming constructions may be so related that whenever applied to the same components they yield mutually synonymous results, as long as the results are short enough to be compared for synonymy. In this event it is natural, by extension, to count also as mutually synonymous any results of applying those constructions to identical components however long. But to simplify ensuing considerations let us continue to reason without reference to this refinement where we can.

Our success with 'Bachelor' and 'Unmarried man' has been sufficient, despite the impasse at second intention, to tempt us to overestimate how well intrasubjective stimulus synonymy withstands collateral information. By way of corrective, consider the Himalayan explorer who has learned to apply 'Everest' to a distant mountain seen from Tibet and 'Gaurisanker' to one seen from Nepal. As occasion sentences these words have mutually exclusive stimulus meanings for him until his explorations reveal, to the surprise of all concerned, that the peaks are identical. His discovery is painfully empirical, not lexicographic; nevertheless the stimulus meanings of 'Everest' and 'Gaurisanker' coincide for him thenceforward.[12]

Or again consider the occasion sentences 'Indian nickel' and 'Buffalo nickel'. These have distinct stimulus meanings for a boy for his first minute or two of passive acquaintance with these coins, and when he gets to turning them over, the stimulus meanings tend to fuse.

Do they fully fuse? The question whether 'Indian nickel' and 'Buffalo nickel' have the same stimulus meaning for a given subject is the question whether any sequence of ocular irradiations or other stimulation (within the modulus), realized or not, *would* now prompt the subject to assent to or dissent from 'Indian nickel' and not 'Buffalo nickel' or vice versa. Among such stimulations are those that present, to all appearances, a coin whose obverse is like that of an Indian nickel but whose reverse bears some device other than the buffalo. Such stimulations can with a little felony even be realized. After a modulus-long examination of such a hybrid coin, a novice might conclude with surprise that there are after all two kinds of Indian nickel, while an expert, sure of his numismatics, might conclude that the coin must be fraudulent. For the expert, 'Indian nickel' and 'Buffalo nickel' are stimulus-synonymous; for the novice not.

The novice does believe and continues to believe, as the expert does, that all Indian nickels are buffalo nickels and vice versa; for the novice has not been and will not be actually subjected to the surprising stimulation described. But the mere fact that there is such a stimulation pattern and that the novice *would* now thus respond to it (whether we know it or not) is what, by definition, makes the stimulus meanings of 'Indian nickel' and 'Buffalo nickel' differ for the novice even as of now.

To keep our example pertinent we must abstract from what may be called the conniving mode of speech: the mode in which we knowingly speak of Olivier as Macbeth, of a statue of a horse as a horse, of a false nickel as a nickel. Even the expert would in practice speak of the prepared coin as "that Indian nickel with the whoozis on the back," adding that it was phony. Here we have a broader usage of 'nickel', under which nobody would seriously maintain even that all Indian nickels are in point of fact buffalo nickels and vice versa; whereas our purpose in the example is to examine two supposedly coextensive terms for sameness of stimulus meaning. In the example, therefore, read 'Indian nickel' and 'buffalo nickel' as 'real Indian nickel', 'real buffalo nickel'.

From the example we see that two terms can in fact be coextensive, or true of the same things, without being intrasubjectively stimulus-synonymous as occasion sentences. They can be believed coextensive without being, even for the believer, stimulus-synonymous as occasion sentences; witness 'Indian nickel' and 'Buffalo

nickel' for the novice. But when as in the expert's case the belief is so firm that no pattern of stimulation (within the modulus) would suffice to dislodge it, they are stimulus-synonymous as occasion sentences.

So it is apparent that intrasubjective stimulus synonymy remains open to criticism, from intuitive preconceptions, for relating occasion sentences whose stimulus meanings coincide on account of collateral information. Now there is still a way of cutting out the effects of idiosyncratic information: we can hold out for virtual constancy over the community. In this social sense of stimulus synonymy, 'Indian nickel' and 'Buffalo nickel' would cease to count as stimulus-synonymous, because of such speakers as our novice; whereas 'Bachelor' and 'Unmarried man' might still rate as stimulus-synonymous even socially, as being intrasubjectively stimulus-synonymous for nearly everybody. There is still no screen against the effects of collateral information common to the community; but, as urged in §9 earlier, I think that at that point the ideal becomes illusory.

§12. SYNONYMY OF TERMS

In starting our consideration of meaning with sentences we have hewn the line of §§3 and 4 [not included here], where it was stressed that words are learned only by abstraction from their roles in learned sentences. But there are one-word sentences, such as 'Red' and 'Rabbit'. Insofar as the concept of stimulus meaning may be said to constitute in some strained sense a meaning concept for these, it would seem to constitute a meaning concept for general terms like 'red' and 'rabbit'. This, however, is a mistake. Stimulus synonymy of the occasion sentences 'Gavagai' and 'Rabbit' does not even guarantee that 'gavagai' and 'rabbit' are coextensive terms, terms true of the same things.

For, consider 'gavagai'. Who knows but what the objects to which this term applies are not rabbits after all, but mere stages, or brief temporal segments, of rabbits? In either event the stimulus situations that prompt assent to 'Gavagai' would be the same as for 'Rabbit'. Or perhaps the objects to which 'gavagai' applies are all and sundry undetached parts of rabbits;

again the stimulus meaning would register no difference. When from the sameness of stimulus meanings of 'Gavagai' and 'Rabbit' the linguist leaps to the conclusion that a gavagai is a whole enduring rabbit, he is just taking for granted that the native is enough like us to have a brief general term for rabbits and no brief general term for rabbit stages or parts.

A further alternative likewise compatible with the same old stimulus meaning is to take 'gavagai' as a singular term naming the fusion, in Goodman's sense, of all rabbits: that single though discontinuous portion of the spatiotemporal world that consists of rabbits. Thus even the distinction between general and singular terms is independent of stimulus meaning. The same point can be seen by considering, conversely, the singular term 'Bernard J. Ortcutt': it differs none in stimulus meaning from a general term true of each of the good dean's temporal segments, and none from a general term true of each of his spatial parts. And a still further alternative in the case of 'gavagai' is to take it as a singular term naming a recurring universal, rabbithood. The distinction between concrete and abstract object, as well as that between general and singular term, is independent of stimulus meaning.

Commonly we can translate something (e.g. 'for the sake of') into a given language though nothing in that language corresponds to certain of the component syllables. Just so the occasion sentence 'Gavagai' is translatable as saying that a rabbit is there, even if no part of 'Gavagai' nor anything at all in the native language quite corresponds to the term 'rabbit'. Synonymy of 'Gavagai' and 'Rabbit' as sentences turns on considerations of prompted assent; not so synonymy of them as terms. We are right to write 'Rabbit', instead of 'rabbit', as a signal that we are considering it in relation to what is synonymous with it as a sentence and not in relation to what is synonymous with it as a term.

Does it seem that the imagined indecision between rabbits, stages of rabbits, integral parts of rabbits, the rabbit fusion, and rabbithood must be due merely to some special fault in our formulation of stimulus meaning, and that it should be resoluble by a little supplementary pointing and questioning? Consider, then, how. Point to a rabbit and you have pointed to a stage of a rabbit, to an integral part of a rabbit, to the rabbit fusion, and to where rabbithood is manifested. Point to an integral part of a rabbit and you have pointed again to the remaining four sorts of things; and so on around. Nothing not distinguished in stimulus meaning itself is to be distinguished by pointing, unless the pointing is accompanied by questions of identity and diversity: 'Is this the same gavagai as that?', 'Do we have here one gavagai or two?'. Such questioning requires of the linguist a command of the native language far beyond anything that we have as yet seen how to account for. We cannot even say what native locutions to count as analogues of terms as we know them, much less equate them with ours term for term, except as we have also decided what native devices to view as doing in their devious ways the work of our own various auxiliaries to objective reference: our articles and pronouns, our singular and plural, our copula, our identity predicate.[13] The whole apparatus is interdependent, and the very notion of term is as provincial to our culture as are those associated devices. The native may achieve the same net effects through linguistic structures so different that any eventual construing of our devices in the native language and vice versa can prove unnatural and largely arbitrary. (cf. §15.) Yet the net effects, the occasion sentences and not the terms, can match up in point of stimulus meanings as well as ever for all that. Occasion sentences and stimulus meaning are general coin; terms and reference are local to our conceptual scheme.[14]

It will perhaps be countered that there is no essential difficulty in spotting judgments of identity on the part of the jungle native, or even of a speechless animal. This is true enough for qualitative identity, better called resemblance. In an organism's susceptibility to the conditioning of responses we have plentiful criteria for his standards of resemblance of stimulations. But what is relevant to the preceding reflections is numerical identity. Two pointings may be pointings to a numerically identical rabbit, to numerically distinct rabbit parts, and to numerically distinct rabbit stages; the inscrutability lies not in resemblance, but in the anatomy of sentences. We could equate a native expression with any of the disparate English terms 'rabbit', 'rabbit stage', 'undetached rabbit part', etc., and still, by compensatorily juggling the translation of numerical identity and associated particles, preserve conformity to stimulus meanings of occasion sentences.[15]

Intrasubjective stimulus synonymy, for all its advantages over the two-speaker case, is similarly powerless to equate terms. Our Martian can find as he did that 'Bachelor' and 'Unmarried man' are synonymous occasion sentences for the English speaker, but still either *term* to the exclusion of the other might, so far as he knows, apply not to men but to their stages or parts or even to a scattered concrete totality or an abstract attribute.

We saw that coextensiveness of terms, or even believed coextensiveness, is not sufficient for their stimulus synonymy as occasion sentences. We now see also that it is not necessary. Where other languages than our own are involved, coextensiveness of terms is not a manifestly clearer notion than synonymy or translation itself; it is no clearer than the considerations, whatever they are, that make for contextual translation of the identity predicate, the copula, and related particles.

Yet surely the main interest of the synonymy of 'Bachelor' and 'Unmarried man' as occasion sentences was the line it seemed to give on the synonymy of 'bachelor' and 'unmarried man' as terms. Now within English the situation is not beyond saving. To get synonymy of terms from synonymy of the corresponding occasion sentences we need only add a condition that will screen out such pairs as 'bachelor' and 'part of a bachelor'; and this we can do by requiring that the subject be prepared to assent to the standing sentence 'All *F*s are *G*s and vice versa', thinking of '*F*' and '*G*' as the terms in question. The definition becomes this: '*F*' and '*G*' are stimulus-synonymous as terms for a speaker at *t* if and only if as occasion sentences they have the same stimulus meaning for him at *t* and he would assent to 'All *F*s are *G*s and vice versa' if asked at *t*. But we can simplify this definition, by strengthening the latter part to make it assure the former part. Instead of just saying he would assent to 'All *F*s are *G*s and vice versa' as things stand at *t*, we can say he would still assent to it, if to anything, following any stimulation that might be imposed at *t*. (The 'if to anything' accommodates shock.) This strengthened condi-

tion assures that '*F*' and '*G*' will also agree in stimulus meaning as occasion sentences; for, if each stimulation would leave the subject prepared to assent to 'All *F*s are *G*s and vice versa' if to anything, then none would prompt him to assent to or dissent from one of '*F*' and '*G*' and not the other.[16]

For reasons evident in §14, I call a sentence *stimulus-analytic* for a subject if he would assent to it, or nothing, after every stimulation (within the modulus). Our condition of stimulus synonymy of '*F*' and '*G*' as general terms then reduces to stimulus analyticity of 'All *F*s are *G*s and vice versa'. This condition has its parallel for singular terms, represented by '*a*' and '*b*'; viz., stimulus analyticity of '*a* = *b*'. But note that our formulations apply only to English and to languages whose translations of 'all', 'are', and '=' are somehow settled in advance. This limitation is to be expected in notions relating to terms.

Our simplification of the definition of term synonymy extends it to all terms, regardless of whether their objects are such that we could reasonably use the terms as occasion sentences. We must not conclude, from seeming appropriateness of the definition as applied to terms like 'rabbit', 'bachelor', and 'buffalo nickel', that it is as appropriate to the wider domain. However, let us leave that question and think further about the narrower domain.

Our version of synonymy makes the terms 'Indian nickel' and 'buffalo nickel' synonymous for the expert of §11, and not for the novice. It is open to criticism, from intuitive preconceptions, for its equating of terms whose coextensiveness the subject has learned by exploration and experiment and not merely by encompassing their "meanings." Such, then, is the concept of stimulus synonymy of terms that comes out of stimulus synonymy of occasion sentences for individual speakers. We can still socialize the concept and so cut out the effects of idiosyncratic information, as we did for occasion sentences: we can count just those terms as socially stimulus-synonymous that come out stimulus-synonymous for each individual speaker almost without exception. Socially, 'bachelor' and 'unmarried man' remain stimulus-synonymous while 'Indian nickel' and 'buffalo nickel' do not.

We welcome this consequence of socializing our concept of stimulus synonymy because our intuitive semantics[17] rates 'bachelor' and 'unmarried man' as synonymous, and probably 'Indian nickel' and 'buffalo nickel' not. But now what can have been the cause of those intuitive ratings themselves? Not, I think, any close analogue, however unconscious, of our present construction: not an implicit sociological guess that under extraordinary stimulation most people would hold 'bachelor' and 'unmarried man' coextensive while many would let 'Indian nickel' and 'buffalo nickel' diverge. A likelier place to seek the cause is in the difference between how we whose mother tongue is English learn 'bachelor' and how we learn 'Indian nickel'. We learn 'bachelor' by learning appropriate associations of words with words, and 'Indian nickel' by learning directly to associate the term with sample objects.[18] It is the difference, so central to Russell's philosophy, between description and acquaintance. It is kept before us in synchronic behavior as a difference between the non-observational occasion sentences, with their random variation in stimulus meaning from speaker to speaker, and observation sentences with their socially uniform stimulus meanings. (Cf. §10.) One looks to 'unmarried man' as semantically anchoring 'bachelor' because there is no socially constant stimulus meaning to govern the use of the word; sever its tie with 'unmarried man' and you leave it no very evident social determination, hence no utility in communication.

'Brother', in its synonymy with 'male sibling', is essentially like 'bachelor' in its synonymy with 'unmarried man'. We learn 'brother' (in its accurate adult use) only by verbal connections with sentences about childbirth, and 'sibling' by verbal connections with 'brother' and 'sister'. The occasion sentences 'Brother' and 'Sibling' are non-observational: their stimulus meanings vary over society in as random a fashion as that of 'Bachelor', and it is only the few verbal links that give the terms the fixity needed in communication.

Many terms of systematic theoretical science are of a third sort. They are like 'bachelor' and 'brother' in having no socially constant stimulus meanings to govern their use; indeed such a term is commonly useless in the role of occasion sentence, so that there is no question of stimulus meaning. Yet they are unlike 'bachelor' and 'brother' in having a more complex network of verbal connections, so that no one tie seems crucial to communication. Thus it is that in theoretical science, unless as recast by semantics enthusiasts, distinctions between synonymies and "factual" equivalences are seldom sensed or claimed. Even the identity historically introduced into mechanics by defining 'momentum' as 'mass times velocity' takes its place in the network of connections on a par with the rest; if a physicist subsequently so revises mechanics that momentum fails to be proportional to velocity, the change will probably be seen as a change of theory and not peculiarly of meaning.[19] Synonymy intuitions do not emerge here, just because the terms are linked to the rest of language in more ways than words like 'bachelor' are.[20]

§13. TRANSLATING LOGICAL CONNECTIVES

In §§7 through 11 we accounted for radical translation of occasion sentences, by approximate identification of stimulus meanings. Now there is also a decidedly different domain that lends itself directly to radical translation: that of *truth functions* such as negation, logical conjunction, and alternation. For this purpose the sentences put to the native for assent or dissent may be occasion sentences and standing sentences indifferently. Those that are occasion sentences will have to be accompanied by a prompting stimulation, if assent or dissent is to be elicited; the standing sentences, on the other hand, can be put without props. Now by reference to assent and dissent we can state semantic criteria for truth functions; i.e., criteria for determining whether a given native idiom is to be construed as expressing the truth function in question. The semantic criterion of negation is that it turns any short sentence to which one will assent into a sentence from which one will dissent, and vice versa. That of conjunction is that it produces compounds to which (so long as the component sentences are short) one is prepared to assent always and only when one is prepared to assent to each component. That of alternation is similar with assent changed twice to dissent.

The point about short components is merely, as in §11, that when they are long the subject may get mixed up. Identification of a native idiom as negation, or conjunction, or alternation, is not to be ruled out in view of a subject's deviation from our semantic criteria when the deviation is due merely to confusion. No limit is imposed on the lengths of the component sentences to which negation, conjunction, or alternation may be applied; it is just that the test cases for first spotting such constructions in a strange language are cases with short components.

When we find that a native construction fulfills one or another of these three semantic criteria, we can ask no more toward an understanding of it. Incidentally we can then translate the idiom into English as 'not', 'and', or 'or' as the case may be, but only subject to sundry humdrum provisos; for it is well known that these three English words do not represent negation, conjunction, and alternation exactly and unambiguously.

Any construction for compounding sentences from sentences is counted in logic as expressing a truth function if it fulfills this condition: the compound has a unique truth value (truth or falsity) for each assignment of truth values to the components. Semantic criteria can obviously be stated for all truth functions along the lines already followed for negation, conjunction, and alternation.

This approach ill accords with a doctrine of "prelogical mentality." To take the extreme case, let us suppose that certain natives are said to accept as true certain sentences translatable in the form 'p and not p'. Now this claim is absurd under our semantic criteria. And, not to be dogmatic about them, what criteria might one prefer? Wanton translation can make natives sound as queer as one pleases. Better translation imposes our logic upon them, and would beg the question of prelogicality if there were a question to beg.[21]

Consider, for that matter, the Spaniard with his 'No hay nada'. Lovers of paradox may represent him as flouting the law of double negation. Soberer translators may reckon 'no' and 'nada', in this context, as halves of one negative.

That fair translation preserves logical laws is implicit in practice even where, to speak paradoxically, no foreign language is involved. Thus when to our querying of an English sentence an English speaker answers 'Yes and no', we

assume that the queried sentence is meant differently in the affirmation and negation; this rather than that he would be so silly as to affirm and deny the same thing. Again, when someone espouses a logic whose laws are ostensibly contrary to our own, we are ready to speculate that he is just giving some familiar old vocables ('and', 'or', 'not', 'all', etc.) new meanings. This talk of meaning is intuitive, uncritical, and undefined, but it is a piece with translation; what it registers is our reluctance under such circumstances to "translate" the speaker's English into our English by the normal tacit method of homophonic translation.

Or consider the familiar remark that even the most audacious system-builder is bound by the law of contradiction. How is he really bound? If he were to accept contradiction, he would so readjust his logical laws as to insure distinctions of some sort; for the classical laws yield all sentences as consequences of any contradiction. But then we would proceed to reconstrue his heroically novel logic as a non-contradictory logic, perhaps even as familiar logic, in perverse notation.

The maxim of translation underlying all this is that assertions startlingly false on the face of them are likely to turn on hidden differences of language. This maxim is strong enough in all of us to swerve us even from the homophonic method that is so fundamental to the very acquisition and use of one's mother tongue.

The common sense behind the maxim is that one's interlocutor's silliness, beyond a certain point, is less likely than bad translation—or, in the domestic case, linguistic divergence.[22] Another account of the matter, as it touches logical laws in the domestic case, is as follows. The logical particles 'and', 'all', etc. are learned only from sentential contexts. Dropping a logical law means a devastatingly widespread unfixing of truth values of contexts of the particles concerned, leaving no fixity to rely on in using those particles. In short, their meanings are gone; new ones may be supplied. What prompts a sense of meaning-involvement here is thus at bottom the same as in the case of 'bachelor' and 'unmarried man' (§12).

Let us now resume our reflections on logic under radical translation. We have settled a people's logical laws completely, so far as the truth-functional part of logic goes, once we have fixed our translations by the above semantic criteria. Truths of this part of logic are called *tautologies*: the truth-functional compounds that are true by truth-functional structure alone. There is a familiar tabular routine for determining, for sentences in which the truth functions are however immoderately iterated and superimposed, just what assignments of truth values to the ultimate component sentences will make the whole compound true; and the tautologies are the compounds that come out true under all assignments.

But the truth functions and tautologies are only the simplest of the logical functions and logical truths. Can we perhaps do better? The logical functions that most naturally next suggest themselves are the categoricals, traditionally designated A, E, I, and O, and commonly construed in English by the constructions 'all are' ('All rabbits are timid'), 'none are', 'some are', 'some are not'. A semantic criterion for A perhaps suggests itself as follows: the compound commands assent (from a given speaker) if and only if the affirmative stimulus meaning (for him) of the first component is a subclass of the affirmative stimulus meaning of the second component and the negative stimulus meanings are conversely related. How to vary this for E, I, and O is obvious enough, except that the whole idea is wrong in view of §12. Thus take A. All Indian nickels are buffalo nickels, and even are believed by the novice to be buffalo nickels, but still the affirmative stimulus meaning of 'Indian nickel', for our novice anyway, has stimulus patterns in it that are not in the affirmative stimulus meaning of 'Buffalo nickel'. On this score the suggested semantic criterion is at odds with 'All Fs are Gs' in that it goes beyond extension. And it has a yet more serious failing of the opposite kind; for, whereas rabbit stages are not rabbits, we saw that in point of stimulus meaning there is no distinction.

The difficulty is fundamental. The categoricals depend for their truth on the objects, however external and however inferential, of which the component terms are true; and what those objects are is not uniquely determined by stimulus meanings. Indeed the categoricals, like plural endings and identity, are part of our own special apparatus of objective reference, whereas

stimulus meaning is, to repeat §12, common coin. Of what we think of as logic, the truth-functional part is the only part the recognition of which, in a foreign language, we seem to be able to pin down to behavioral criteria.

The condition that was seen to be inadequate as a semantic condition for the A copula does still determine a copula. Let me write 'pars' for this copula. Its usage is to be such that a compound of the form ' . . . pars . . .', formed of two occasion sentences S_1 and S_2 in that order, is a standing sentence and is to command assent of just the speakers for whom the affirmative stimulus meaning of S_1 is a subclass of that of S_2 and conversely for the negative. Thus, if we think of S_1 and S_2 as general terms—a detail of translation left open by stimulus meaning—then 'F pars G' says approximately that every F is part of the fusion of the Gs; and if we think of S_1 and S_2 as singular terms, 'a pars b' says approximately that a is part of b. The theory of the part relation, called mereology by Leséniewski and the calculus of individuals by Goodman and Leonard,[23] is thus more amenable to radical semantic criteria than is the logic of the syllogism. But we must give full weight to the word 'approximately', twice used just now; the correspondence is rather poor, because, as remarked two paragraphs back, our semantic criterion makes demands beyond extension.

§14. SYNONYMOUS AND ANALYTIC SENTENCES

By its etymology, 'synonymous' applies to names. Though in use the term is intended simply to impute sameness of meaning, an effect of its etymology is seen in a tendency to invoke some other word, 'equivalent' or 'equipollent', for cases where both of the compared expressions are (unlike 'bachelor') verbally complex. My use of 'synonymous' is not thus restricted; I intend the word to carry the full generality of 'same in meaning', whatever that is. Indeed I have made no essential use of a distinction between word and phrase. Even the first object of translation, say 'Gavagai', may or may not in the end be parsed as a string of several words, depending on one's eventual choice of analytical hypotheses (§§15, 16).

Taking this minor liberalization hereafter for granted, we still must distinguish between a broad and a narrow type of synonymy, or sameness of meaning, as applied to sentences. The broad one may be formulated in intuitive terms thus: the two sentences command assent concomitantly and dissent concomitantly, and this concomitance is due strictly to word usage rather than to how things happen in the world. One usually hears the matter described in terms rather of truth values than of assent and dissent; but I warp it over to the latter terms in order to maximize chances of making sense of the relation on the basis of verbal behavior.

For some purposes a narrower sort of synonymy of sentences is wanted, such as what Carnap calls intensional isomorphism, involving certain part-by-part correspondences of the sentences concerned. But such variant versions can be defined on the basis of the broader one. Synonymy of parts is defined by appeal to analogy of roles in synonymous wholes; then synonymy in the narrower sense is defined for the wholes by appeal to synonymy of homologous parts. So let us concentrate on the broader and more basic notion of sentence synonymy.

By talking in terms of assent and dissent here instead of in terms of truth values we introduce this difficulty: assent and dissent can be influenced by confusion due to a sentence's length and complexity. But this difficulty can be accommodated in the way sketched in §11. Also it would be automatically taken care of under the program, just now mentioned, of deriving a relation of synonymy of sentence fragments and thence constructing a reformed synonymy relation for wholes. Let us pass over these points, for there is a more basic problem.

When the sentences are occasion sentences, the envisaged notion of synonymy is pretty well realized in intrasubjective stimulus synonymy, especially as socialized. For we can argue that only verbal habit can plausibly account for concomitant variation of two occasion sentences, in point of assent and dissent, over the whole gamut of possible stimulations. There are still the unscreened effects of community-wide collateral information, but there is no evident reason not to count such information simply as a determinant of the verbal habit (§9). When the sentences are standing sentences which, like 'The *Times* has come', closely resemble occasion sentences in the variability of assent and dissent, stimulus synonymy still does pretty well.

But the less variable the standing sentences are in point of assent and dissent, the sparser their stimulus meanings will be and hence the more poorly stimulus synonymy will approximate to synonymy of the envisaged sort. For, however sparse its stimulus meaning, a sentence retains its connections with other sentences and plays its distinctive part in theories. The sparseness of its stimulus meaning is no sparseness of meaning intuitively speaking, but has the effect that stimulus meaning fails to do the sentence much justice.

By lengthening the modulus of stimulation we can enrich the stimulus meanings and so tighten the relation of stimulus synonymy; for, the longer the stimulations, the better their chance of influencing assent and dissent. However, matters get out of hand when the modulus is excessive. Thus consider stimulus synonymy modulo a month. To say that two sentences are now so related is to say that any and every pattern of month-long stimulation, if begun now and terminated next month with a querying of the two sentences, would elicit the same verdict on both. The trouble is that there is no telling what to expect under fairly fantastic stimulation sequences of such duration. The subject might revise his theories in unforeseeable ways that would be claimed to change meanings of words. There is no reason to expect the concomitances of sentences under such circumstances to reflect present sameness of meaning in any intuitively plausible sense. Lengthening the modulus enriches stimulus meanings and tightens stimulus synonymy only as it diminishes scrutability of stimulus synonyms.

Stimulus synonymy, on an optimum modulus, is an approximation to what philosophers loosely call sameness of confirming experiences and of disconfirming experiences. It is an approximation to what it might mean "to speak of two statements as standing in the same germaneness-relation to the same particular experiences."[24] Where standing sentences are of highly unoccasional type, the inadequacy of stimulus synonymy to synonymy intuitively so-called is shared by the vaguer formulations just now noted. And it is shared by the proposal of Perkins and Singer, viz., that we compare sentences for synonymy by putting them to our informant for verification and seeing whether he proceeds similarly in both cases.[25] The trouble lies in the interconnections of sentences. If the business of a sentence can be exhausted by an account of the experiences that would confirm or disconfirm it as an isolated sentence in its own right, then the sentence is substantially an occasion sentence. The significant trait of other sentences is that experience is relevant to them largely in indirect ways, through the mediation of associated sentences. Alternatives emerge: experiences call for changing a theory, but do not indicate just where and how. Any of various systematic changes can accommodate the recalcitrant datum, and all the sentences affected by any of those possible alternative readjustments would evidently have to count as disconfirmed by that datum indiscriminately or not at all. Yet the sentences can be quite unlike with respect to content, intuitively speaking, or role in the containing theory.

Grice and Strawson try (*loc. cit.*) to meet this difficulty by defining S_1 and S_2 as synonymous when, for every assumption as to the truth values of other sentences, the same experiences confirm (and disconfirm) S_1 on that assumption as confirm (and disconfirm) S_2 on that assumption. Now instead of 'every assumption as to the truth values of other sentences' we can as well say simply 'every sentence S'; for S can be the logical conjunction of those "other sentences" in question or their negations. So S_1 and S_2 are defined to be synonymous when, for every S, the same experiences confirm (and disconfirm) S_1 on the hypothesis S as confirm (and disconfirm) S_2 on S. The notion of confirmatory and disconfirmatory experiences had a behavioral approximation in our notion of stimulus meaning; but can we relativize it thus to a hypothesis S? I think we can; for confirmation or disconfirmation of S_1 on S is presumably confirmation or disconfirmation of the conditional sentence consisting of S as antecedent and S_1 as consequent. Then the proposed definition of synonymy becomes: S_1 and S_2 are synonymous if for every S the conditional compound of S and S_1 and that of S and S_2

are stimulus-synonymous. But now it is apparent that the definition fails to provide a tighter relation between S_1 and S_2 than stimulus synonymy. For, if S_1 and S_2 are stimulus-synonymous then *a fortiori* the conditionals are too.

A variant suggestion would be to define S_1 and S_2 as synonymous when, for every S, the logical conjunction of S and S_1 and that of S and S_2 are stimulus-synonymous. But this is yet more readily seen not to provide a tighter relation.

If either of these ventures had succeeded, the synonymy yielded would still have been strictly intralinguistic; for the auxiliary S, belonging to one language, gets joined to both S_1 and S_2. But the language would not have to be our own. For, by §13, conjunction is translatable; and so is the conditional, if we take it in the material sense 'Not (p and not q)'.

The general relation of intrasubjective sentence synonymy thus unsuccessfully sought is interdefinable with another elusive notion of intuitive philosophical semantics: that of an *analytic* sentence. Here the intuitive notion is that the sentence is true purely by meaning and independently of collateral information: thus 'No bachelor is married', 'Pigs are pigs', and, by some accounts, '$2 + 2 = 4$'.[26] The interdefinitions run thus: sentences are synonymous if and only if their biconditional (formed by joining them with 'if and only if') is analytic, and a sentence is analytic if and only if synonymous with self-conditionals ('If p then p').

As synonymy of sentences is related to analyticity, so stimulus synonymy of sentences is related to stimulus analyticity (§12).

Philosophical tradition hints of three nested categories of firm truths: the analytic, the *a priori*, and the necessary. Whether the first exhausts the second, and the second the third, are traditional matters of disagreement, though none of the three has traditionally been defined in terms of detectable features of verbal behavior. Pressed nowadays for such a clarification, some who are content to take the three as identical have responded in this vein: the analytic sentences are those that we are prepared to affirm come what may. This comes to naught unless we independently circumscribe the 'what may'. Thus one may object that we would not adhere to 'No bachelor is married' if we found a married bachelor; and how are we to disallow his example without appealing to the very notion of analyticity we are trying to define? One way is to take 'come what may' as 'come what stimulation (§8) may'; and this gives virtually the definition (§12) of stimulus analyticity.[27]

We improved stimulus synonymy a bit by socializing it. We can do the same for analyticity, calling socially stimulus-analytic just the sentences that are stimulus-analytic for almost everybody. But analyticity in even this improved sense will apply as well to 'There have been black dogs' as to '2 + 2 = 4' and 'No bachelor is married'. Let us face it: our socialized stimulus synonymy and stimulus analyticity are still not behavioristic reconstructions of intuitive semantics, but only a behavioristic ersatz.

At the end of §12 we speculated on what makes for the intuition of synonymy of terms. Similar considerations apply to intuitions of sentence synonymy and analyticity. Such an intuition figures in the case of analyticity despite the technical sound of the word; sentences like 'No unmarried man is married', 'No bachelor is married', and '2 + 2 = 4' have a feel that everyone appreciates. Moreover the notion of "assent come what may" gives no fair hint of the intuition involved. One's reaction to denials of sentences typically felt as analytic has more in it of one's reaction to ungrasped foreign sentences.[28] Where the sentence concerned is a law of logic, something of the ground of this reaction was discerned in §13: dropping a logical law disrupts a pattern on which the communicative use of a logical particle heavily depends. Much the same applies to '2 + 2 = 4', and even to 'The parts of the parts of a thing are parts of the thing'. The key words here have countless further contexts to anchor their usage, but somehow we feel that if our interlocutor will not agree with us on these platitudes, there is no depending on him in most of the further contexts containing the terms in question.

Examples like 'No bachelor is married' rate as analytic both directly on the vague count just now conjectured and by virtue of coming from logical truths by synonymy substitution.

If the mechanism of analyticity intuitions is substantially as I have vaguely suggested, they will in general tend to set in where bewilderment sets in as to what the man who denies the sentence can be talking about. This effect can be gradual and also cumulative.[29] The intuitions are blameless in their way, but it would be a mistake to look to them for a sweeping epistemological dichotomy between analytic truths as by-products of language and synthetic truths as reports on the world. I suspect that the notion of such a dichotomy only encourages confused impressions of how language relates to the world.[30] Stimulus analyticity, our strictly vegetarian imitation, is of course not here in question.

§15. ANALYTICAL HYPOTHESES

We have had our linguist observing native utterances and their circumstances passively, to begin with, and then selectively querying native sentences for assent and dissent under varying circumstances. Let us sum up the possible yield of such methods. (1) Observation sentences can be translated. There is uncertainty, but the situation is the normal inductive one. (2) Truth functions can be translated. (3) Stimulus-analytic sentences can be recognized. So can the sentences of the opposite type, the "stimulus-contradictory" sentences, which command irreversible dissent. (4) Questions of intrasubjective stimulus synonymy of native occasion sentences even of non-observational kind can be settled if raised, but the sentences cannot be translated.

And how does the linguist pass these bounds? In broad outline as follows. He segments heard utterances into conveniently short recurrent parts, and thus compiles a list of native "words." Various of these he hypothetically equates to English words and phrases, in such a way as to conform to (1)–(4). Such are his *analytical hypotheses*, as I call them. Their conformity to (1)–(4) is ideally as follows. The sentence translations derivable from the analytical hypotheses are to include those already established under (1); they are to fit the prior translation of truth functions, as of (2); they are to carry sentences that are stimulus-analytic or stimulus-contradictory, according to (3), into English sentences that are likewise stimulus-analytic or stimulus-contradictory; and they are to carry sentence pairs that are stimulus-synonymous, according to (4), into English sentences that are likewise stimulus-synonymous.

The analytical hypotheses are begun, however tentatively, long before the work of (1)–(4) is finished, and they help guide the choice of examples for investigation under (1)–(4). This point is essential to (4), since without indirect hints through analytical hypotheses there is virtually no telling what pairs of non-observational sentences to try for intrasubjective stimulus synonymy.

Our recipe is overschematic. If the analytical hypotheses give some English platitude as translation of some native standing sentence, there would be encouragement in finding that the latter also commands general and unreflective assent among natives, even if neither is quite stimulus-analytic. Degrees of approximation to stimulus analyticity, as well as degrees of observationality, would be allowed for in a truer account. And anyway the analytical hypotheses are not strictly required to conform to (1)–(4) with respect to quite every example; the neater the analytical hypotheses, the more tolerance.

Tolerance is bound to have been exercised if a native sentence, believed by the whole community with a firmness that no stimulus pattern of reasonable duration would suffice to shake, is translated as 'All rabbits are men reincarnate'. To translate a stimulus-analytic native sentence thus into an English sentence that is not stimulus-analytic is to invoke translator's license. I think this account gives such a translation quite the proper air: that of a bold departure, to be adopted only if its avoidance would seem to call for much more complicated analytical hypotheses. For certainly, the more absurd or exotic the beliefs imputed to a people, the more suspicious we are entitled to be of the translations; the myth of the prelogical people marks only the extreme.[31] For translation theory, banal messages are the breath of life.

It may occur to the reader to try to derive from stimulus analyticity a finer analyticity concept by screening out sentences such as the native one about reincarnation, using this criterion: through indirect considerations they get translated into sentences of another language that are not stimulus-analytic. However, this criterion is illusory because of its relativity to analytical hypotheses, which, as stressed in succeeding pages, are not determinate functions of linguistic behavior.

Let us now get back to the analytical hypotheses for a more leisurely consideration of their form and content. They are not in general held to equational form. There is no need to insist that the native word be equated outright to any one English word or phrase. Certain contexts may be specified in which the word is to be translated one way and others in which the word is to be translated in another way. The equational form may be overlaid with supplementary semantical instructions *ad libitum*. Since there is no general positional correspondence between the words and phrases of one language and their translations in another, some analytical hypotheses will be needed also to explain syntactical constructions. These are usually described with help of auxiliary terms for various classes of native words and phrases. Taken together, the analytical hypotheses and auxiliary definitions constitute the linguist's jungle-to-English dictionary and grammar. The form they are given is immaterial because their purpose is not translation of words or constructions but translation of coherent discourse; single words and constructions come up for attention only as means to that end.

Nevertheless there is reason to draw particular attention to the simple form of analytical hypothesis which equates a native word or construction to a hypothetical English equivalent. For hypotheses need thinking up, and the typical case of thinking up is the case where the linguist apprehends a parallelism in function between some component fragment of a translated whole native sentence and some component word of the translation of the sentence. Only in some such way can we account for anyone's ever thinking to translate a native locution radically into English as a plural ending, or as the identity predicate '=', or as a categorical copula, or as any other part of our domestic apparatus of objective reference. It is only by such outright projection of prior linguistic habits that the linguist can find general terms in the native language at all, or, having found them, match them with his own; stimulus meanings never suffice to determine even what words are terms, if any, much less what terms are coextensive.

The method of analytical hypotheses is a way of catapulting oneself into the jungle language by the momentum of the home language. It is a way of grafting exotic shoots on to the old familiar bush until only the exotic meets the eye. From the point of view of a theory of translational meaning the most notable thing about the analytical hypotheses is that they exceed anything implicit in any native's dispositions to speech behavior. By bringing out analogies between sentences that have yielded to translation and others they extend the working limits of translation beyond where independent evidence can exist.

Not that (1)–(4) themselves cover all available evidence. For remember that we stated those only with reference to a linguist whose gathering of data proceeded by querying native sentences for assent and dissent under varying circumstances. A linguist can broaden his base, as remarked in §11, by becoming bilingual. Point (1) is thereupon extended to this: (1′) All occasion sentences can be translated. Point (4) drops as superfluous. But even our bilingual, when he brings off translations not allowed for under (1′)–(3), must do so by essentially the method of analytical hypotheses, however unconscious. Thus suppose, unrealistically to begin with, that in learning the native language he had been able to simulate the infantile situation to the extent of keeping his past knowledge of languages out of account. Then, when as a bilingual he finally turns to his project of a jungle-to-English manual, he will have to project analytical hypotheses much as if his English personality were the linguist and his jungle personality the informant; the differences are just that he can introspect his experiments instead of staging them, that he has his notable inside track on non-observational occasion sentences, and that he will tend to feel his analytical hypotheses as obvious analogies when he is aware of them at all. Now of course the truth is that he would not have strictly simulated the infantile situation in learning the native language, but would have helped himself with analytical hypotheses all along the way; thus the elements of the situation would in practice be pretty inextricably scrambled. What with this circumstance and the fugitive nature of introspective method, we have been better off theo-

rizing about meaning from the more primitive paradigm: that of the linguist who deals observably with the native informant as live collaborator rather than first ingesting him.

Whatever the details of its expository devices of word translation and syntactical paradigm, the linguist's finished jungle-to-English manual has as its net yield an infinite *semantic correlation* of sentences: the implicit specification of an English sentence, or various roughly interchangeable English sentences, for every one of the infinitely many possible jungle sentences. Most of the semantic correlation is supported only by analytical hypotheses, in their extension beyond the zone where independent evidence for translation is possible. That those unverifiable translations proceed without mishap must not be taken as pragmatic evidence of good lexicography, for mishap is impossible.

Thus let us recall §12, where we saw that stimulus meaning was incapable of deciding among 'rabbit', 'rabbit stage', and various other terms as translations of 'gavagai'. If by analytical hypothesis we take 'are the same' as translation of some construction in the jungle language, we may proceed on that basis to question our informant about sameness of gavagais from occasion to occasion and so conclude that gavagais are rabbits and not stages. But if instead we take 'are stages of the same animal' as translation of that jungle construction, we will conclude from the same subsequent questioning of our informant that gavagais are rabbit stages. Both analytical hypotheses may be presumed possible. Both could doubtless be accommodated by compensatory variations in analytical hypotheses concerning other locutions, so as to conform equally to all independently discoverable translations of whole sentences and indeed all speech dispositions of all speakers concerned. And yet countless native sentences admitting no independent check, not falling under (1′)–(3), may be expected to receive radically unlike and incompatible English renderings under the two systems.

There is an obstacle to offering an actual example of two such rival systems of analytical hypotheses. Known languages are known through unique systems of analytical hypotheses established in tradition or painfully arrived at by unique skilled linguists. To devise a con-

trasting system would require an entire dupli-
cate enterprise of translation, unaided even by
the usual hints from interpreters. Yet one has
only to reflect on the nature of possible data and
methods to appreciate the indeterminacy. Sentences translatable outright, translatable by
independent evidence of stimulatory occasions,
are sparse and must woefully under-determine
the analytical hypotheses on which the translation of all further sentences depends. To project
such hypotheses beyond the independently
translatable sentences at all is in effect to impute
our sense of linguistic analogy unverifiably to
the native mind. Nor would the dictates even of
our own sense of analogy tend to any intrinsic
uniqueness; using what first comes to mind
engenders an air of determinacy though freedom reign. There can be no doubt that rival systems of analytical hypotheses can fit the totality
of speech behavior to perfection, and can fit the
totality of dispositions to speech behavior as
well, and still specify mutually incompatible
translations of countless sentences insuscepti-
ble of independent control.

§16. ON FAILURE TO PERCEIVE THE INDETERMINACY

Thus the analytical hypotheses, and the grand
synthetic one that they add up to, are only in an
incomplete sense hypotheses. Contrast the case
of translation of the occasion sentence 'Gavagai' by similarity of stimulus meaning. This is a
genuine hypothesis from sample observations,
though possibly wrong. 'Gavagai' and 'There's
a rabbit' have stimulus meanings for the two
speakers, and these are roughly the same or significantly different, whether we guess right or
not. On the other hand no such sense is made of
the typical analytical hypothesis. The point is
not that we cannot be sure whether the analytical hypothesis is right, but that there is not even,
as there was in the case of 'Gavagai', an objective matter to be right or wrong about.

There are at least seven causes of failure to
appreciate this point. One is that analytical
hypotheses are confirmed in the field. Now this
simply means that supplementary cases of the
sorts summed up under (1)–(4) or (1')–(3) of §15
are gathered after the analytical hypotheses have
been framed. The unverifiable consequences

I mean are translations not covered by (1)–(4)
or even (1')–(3). They can be defended only
through the analytical hypotheses, now and
forever.

Another of the causes of failure to appreciate
the point is confusion of it with the more superficial reflection that uniqueness of grammatical
systematization is not to be expected. Obviously the grammatical theories can differ in
word segmentations, in parts of speech, in constructions, and perforce then in dictionaries of
translation, and still have identical net outputs
in the way of whole sentences and even of English sentence translations. But I am talking of
difference in net output.

A third cause of failure to appreciate the point
is confusion of it with the platitude that uniqueness of translation is absurd. The indeterminacy
that I mean is more radical. It is that rival systems of analytical hypotheses can conform to all
speech dispositions within each of the languages concerned and yet dictate, in countless
cases, utterly disparate translations; not mere
mutual paraphrases, but translations each of
which would be excluded by the other system of
translation. Two such translations might even be
patently contrary in truth value, provided there
is no stimulation that would encourage assent to
either.

A fourth and major cause of failure to appreciate the point is a stubborn feeling that a true
bilingual surely is in a position to make uniquely
right correlations of sentences generally between his languages. This feeling is fostered by
an uncritical mentalistic theory of ideas: each
sentence and its admissible translations express
an identical idea in the bilingual's mind. The
feeling can also survive rejection of the ideas:
one can protest still that the sentence and its
translations all correspond to some identical
even though unknown neural condition in the
bilingual. Now let us grant that; it is only to say
that the bilingual has his own private semantic
correlation—in effect his private implicit system
of analytical hypotheses—and that it is somehow in his nerves. My point remains; for my
point is then that another bilingual could have a
semantic correlation incompatible with the first
bilingual's without deviating from the first bilingual in his speech dispositions within either language, except in his dispositions to translate.

A fifth cause is that linguists adhere to implicit supplementary canons that help to limit their choice of analytical hypotheses. For example, if a question were to arise over equating a short native locution to 'rabbit' and a long one to 'rabbit part' or vice versa (§12), they would favor the former course, arguing that the more conspicuously segregated wholes are likelier to bear the simpler terms. Such an implicit canon is all very well, unless mistaken for a substantive law of speech behavior.

A sixth cause is that a few early analytical hypotheses carry the linguist so far. Once he has hypotheses covering identity, the copula, and associated particles, he can translate terms by stimulus synonymy of sentences. A few further hypotheses can create a medium in which to challenge native statements and elicit argument, or even to ask about intuitive synonymy. Abundant new structural data are then forthcoming, and one fails to note the free prior decisions to which these data owe their significance.

A seventh cause is that in framing his analytical hypotheses the linguist is subject to practical constraints. For he is not, in his finitude, free to assign English sentences to the infinitude of jungle ones in just any way whatever that will fit his supporting evidence; he has to assign them in some way that is manageably systematic with respect to a manageably limited set of repeatable speech segments. Once he has cut the segments, begun his analytical hypotheses, and devised an auxiliary apparatus of word classes for his formulations, his freedom of subsequent choice is narrowed further still.

The linguist's working segmentation does yet more than narrow the possibilities of analytical hypotheses. It even contributes to setting, for him or the rest of us, the ends of translation. For a premium is put on structural parallels: on correspondence between the parts of the native sentence, as segmented, and the parts of the English translation. Other things being equal, the more literal translation is seen as more literally a translation.[32] A tendency to literal translation is assured anyway, since the purpose of segmentation is to make long translations constructible from short correspondences; but one goes farther and makes of this tendency an objective— and an objective that even varies in detail with the practical segmentation adopted.

Complete radical translation goes on, and analytical hypotheses are indispensable. Nor are they capricious; we have seen in outline how they are supported. May we not then say that in those very ways of thinking up and supporting the analytical hypotheses a sense *is* after all given to sameness of meaning of the expressions which those hypotheses equate? No. We could claim this only if no two conflicting sets of analytical hypotheses could be tied for first place on all theoretically accessible evidence. The indefinability of synonymy by reference to the methodology of analytical hypotheses is formally the same as the indefinability of truth by reference to scientific method. Also the consequences are parallel. Just as we may meaningfully speak of the truth of a sentence only within the terms of some theory or conceptual scheme, so on the whole we may meaningfully speak of interlinguistic synonymy only within the terms of some particular system of analytical hypotheses.

May we conclude that translational synonymy at its worst is no worse off than truth in physics? To be thus reassured is to misjudge the parallel. In being able to speak of the truth of a sentence only within a more inclusive theory, one is not much hampered; for one is always working within some comfortably inclusive theory, however tentative. Truth is even overtly relative to language, in that e.g. the form of words 'Brutus killed Caesar' could by coincidence have unrelated uses in two languages; yet this again little hampers one's talk of truth, for one works within some language. In short, the parameters of truth stay conveniently fixed most of the time. Not so the analytical hypotheses that constitute the parameter of translation. We are always ready to wonder about the meaning of a foreigner's remark without reference to any one set of analytical hypotheses, indeed even in the absence of any; yet two sets of analytical hypotheses equally compatible with all linguistic behavior can give contrary answers, unless the remark is of one of the limited sorts that can be translated without recourse to analytical hypotheses.

Something of the true situation verges on visibility when the sentences concerned are extremely theoretical. Thus who would undertake to translate 'Neutrinos lack mass' into the jungle language? If anyone does, we may expect him to coin words or distort the usage of old ones. We may expect him to plead in extenuation that the natives lack the requisite concepts; also that they know too little physics. And he is right, except for the hint of there being some free-floating, linguistically neutral meaning which we capture, in 'Neutrinos lack mass', and the native cannot.

Containment in the Low German continuum facilitated translation of Frisian into English (§7), and containment in a continuum of cultural evolution facilitated translation of Hungarian into English. In facilitating translation these continuities encourage an illusion of subject matter: an illusion that our so readily intertranslatable sentences are diverse verbal embodiments of some intercultural proposition or meaning, when they are better seen as the merest variants of one and the same intracultural verbalism. The discontinuity of radical translation tries our meanings: really sets them over against their verbal embodiments, or, more typically, finds nothing there.

Observation sentences peel nicely; their meanings, stimulus meanings, emerge absolute and free of residual verbal taint. Similarly for occasion sentences more generally, since the linguist can go native. Theoretical sentences such as 'Neutrinos lack mass', or the law of entropy, or the constancy of the speed of light are at the other extreme. It is of such sentences above all that Wittgenstein's dictum holds true: "Understanding a sentence means understanding a language."[33] Such sentences, and countless ones that lie intermediate between the two extremes, lack linguistically neutral meaning.

There is no telling how much of one's success with analytical hypotheses is due to real kinship of outlook on the part of the natives and ourselves, and how much of it is due to linguistic ingenuity or lucky coincidence. I am not sure that it even makes sense to ask. We may alternately wonder at the inscrutability of the native mind and wonder at how very much like us the native is, where in the one case we have merely muffed the best translation and in the other case we have done a more thorough job of reading our own provincial modes into the native's speech.

Thus consider, in contrast, a simple instance where cultural difference does objectively manifest itself in language without intervention of analytical hypotheses. Certain islanders are said to speak of pelicans as their half-brothers.[34] One is not of course put off by this obvious shorthand translation of a native word as 'half-brother' rather than in some such more inclusive fashion as 'half-brother or totem associate'. There remains an objective cultural difference apart from that, and it is linguistically reflected as follows: the islanders have a short occasion sentence that commands an islander's assent indiscriminately on presentation of any of his half-brothers or any pelican, and presumably no comparably short one for the case of half-brothers exclusively, whereas English is oppositely endowed. Such contrasts, between peoples' basic or short-sentence partitionings of stimulations, are genuine cultural contrasts objectively describable by reference to stimulus meanings.[35] Where cultural contrasts begin to be threatened with meaninglessness is rather where they depend on analytical hypotheses.

One frequently hears it urged[36] that deep differences of language carry with them ultimate differences in the way one thinks, or looks upon the world. I would urge that what is most generally involved is indeterminacy of correlation. There is less basis of comparison—less sense in saying what is good translation and what is bad—the farther we get away from sentences with visibly direct conditioning to non-verbal stimuli and the farther we get off home ground.

Our advantage with a compatriot is that with little deviation the automatic or homophonic (§13) hypothesis of translation fills the bill. If we were perverse and ingenious, we could scorn that hypothesis and devise other analytical hypotheses that would attribute unimagined views to our compatriot, while conforming to all his dispositions to verbal response to all possible stimulations. Thinking in terms of radical translation of exotic languages has helped make factors vivid, but the main lesson to be derived concerns the empirical slack in our own beliefs. For our own views could be revised into those attributed to the compatriot in the impractical joke imagined; no conflicts with experience could ever supervene, except such as would attend our present sensible views as well. To the same degree that the radical translation of sentences is under-determined by the totality of dispositions to verbal behavior, our own theories and beliefs in general are under-determined by the totality of possible sensory evidence time without end.

It may be protested that when two theories agree thus in point of all possible sensory determinants, they are in an important sense not two but one. Certainly such theories are, as wholes, empirically equivalent. If something is affirmed in the one theory and denied in the other, one may argue that the particular form of words affirmed and denied is itself unlike in meaning in the two cases but that the containing theories as wholes have the same net meaning still. Similarly one may protest that two systems of analytical hypotheses are, as wholes, equivalent so long as no verbal behavior makes any difference between them; and, if they offer seemingly discrepant English translations, one may again argue that the apparent conflict is a conflict only of parts seen out of context. Now this account is fair enough, apart from its glibness on the topic of meaning; and it helps to make the principle of indeterminacy of translation less surprising. When two systems of analytical hypotheses fit the totality of verbal dispositions to perfection and yet conflict in their translations of certain sentences, the conflict is precisely a conflict of parts seen without the wholes. The principle of indeterminacy of translation requires notice just because translation proceeds little by little and sentences are thought of as conveying meanings severally. That it requires notice is plainly illustrated by the almost universal belief that the objective references of terms in radically different languages can be objectively compared.

The indeterminacy of translation has been less generally appreciated than its somewhat protean domestic analogue. In mentalistic philosophy there is the familiar predicament of private worlds. In speculative neurology there is the circumstance that different neural hookups can account for identical verbal behavior. In language learning there is the multiplicity of individual histories capable of issuing in identical verbal behavior. Still one is ready to say of the domestic situation in all positivistic reasonableness that if two speakers match in all dispositions to verbal behavior, there is no sense in imagining semantic differences between them. It is ironic that the interlinguistic case is less noticed, for it is just here that the semantic indeterminacy makes clear empirical sense.

NOTES

1. An interim draft of Chapter II was published, with omissions, as "Meaning and Translation." Half of that essay survives verbatim here, comprising a scattered third of this chapter.
2. See Pike.
3. See Firth, *Elements of Social Organization*, p. 23, on the analogous matter of identifying a gesture of greeting.
4. This difficulty was raised by Davidson.
5. *Meaning and Necessity,* 2d ed., Suppl. D. See also Chisholm, *Perceiving,* pp. 175 ff., and his references.
6. Twice I have been started to find my use of 'intuitive' misconstrued as alluding to some special and mysterious avenue of knowledge. By an intuitive account I mean one in which terms are used in habitual ways, without reflecting on how they might be defined or what presuppositions they might conceal.
7. Here I am indebted to Davidson.
8. Here I am indebted to Raymond Firth.
9. For remarks on this matter and references, see von Mises, *Positivism,* pp. 91–95, 379. To the main theme of this paragraph I sense harmony in Strawson, *Individuals,* p. 212: "If any facts deserve . . . to be called . . . atomic facts, it is the facts stated by those propositions which demonstratively indicate the incidence of a general feature." For the propositions alluded to seem, in the light of adjacent text, to correspond pretty well to what I have called occasion sentences.
10. It can be argued that this much-used example of synonymy has certain imperfections having to do with ages, divorce, and bachelors of arts. Another example much used in philosophy, 'brother' and 'male sibling', may be held to bog down under certain church usages. An example that is perhaps unassailable is 'mother's father' and 'maternal grandfather' (poetic connotations not being here in point), or 'widower' and 'man who lost his wife' (Jakobson). However, with this much by way of caveat against quibbling, perhaps we can keep to our conventional example and overlook its divagations.
11. See Chapter III for reflections on the infant's learning of our own language [not reprinted here].
12. I am indebted to Davidson for this point and to Schrödinger, *What Is Life?* for the example. I am told that the example is wrong geographically.
13. Strawson is making this point when he writes that "feature-placing sentences do not introduce particulars into our discourse" ("Particular and General," p. 244).
14. Russell conceived of what he called "object words" as in effect occasion sentences (*Inquiry,* Ch. IV), but,

like Carnap (see end of §8), he failed to note the present point: that the use of a word as an occasion sentence, however determinate, does not fix the extension of the word as a term.

15. On this theme see further §§15 and 16.

16. Incoherent behavior is possible, but there is a limit to the bizarreness of exceptions worth allowing for in these behavioral formulations.

17. See note 5.

18. To be precise about the example, we learn 'nickel' and 'Indian' in direct association with sample objects or likenesses, and then 'Indian nickel' is self-explanatory once we see one.

19. See the last section of my "Carnap and Logical Truth."

20. Putnam in "The Analytic and the Synthetic" has offered an illuminating account of the synonymy intuition in terms of a contrast between terms that connote clusters of traits and terms that do not. My account fits with his and perhaps adds to the explanation. His cases of clustering correspond to my observational terms such as 'Indian nickel' and theoretical terms such as 'momentum', as against 'bachelor'.

21. Malinowski, pp. 68 ff., spared his islanders the imputation of prelogicality by so varying his translations of terms, from occurrence to occurrence, as to sidestep contradiction. Leach, p. 130, protested; but no clear criterion emerged. It is understandable that the further alternative of blaming the translation of conjunctions, copulas, or other logical particles is nowhere considered; for any considerable complexity on the part of the English correlates of such words would of course present the working translator with forbidding practical difficulties. Eventually Levy-Bruhl, pp. 130 f., gave up his original doctrine of prelogical mentality; but the considerations that operated are not easy to relate to the present ones.

22. Cf. Wilson's principle of charity: "We select as designatum that individual which will make the largest possible number of . . . statements true" (Wilson, "Substances without Subtrata").

23. See Goodman, *Structure of Appearance,* pp. 42 ff., and further references therein.

24. Grice and Strawson, p. 156.

25. See Perkins and Singer. It is significant that their examples are occasion sentences.

26. There is a small confusion that I should like to take this opportunity to resolve, though it lies aside from the main course of the present reflections. Those who talk confidently of analyticity have been known to disagree on the analyticity of the truths of arithmetic, but are about unanimous on that of the truths of logic. We who are less clear on the notion of analyticity may therefore seize upon the generally conceded analyticity of the truths of logic as a partial extensional clarification of analyticity; but to do this is not to embrace the analyticity of the truths of logic as an antecedently intelligible doctrine. I have been misunderstood on this score by Gewirth, p. 406 n., and others. Contrast my "Truth by Convention." Not that all criticisms of my remarks on truths of logic turn on this misunderstanding. Pap's criticism in *Semantics*

and Necessary Truth, p. 237 n., is another matter, and was answered anticipatorily in my "Carnap and Logical Truth," end of IX (to which he had no access). Strawson's criticism in "Propositions, Concepts, and Logical Truths" is another still, and an interesting one, which I cannot claim to have answered anywhere. Speaking of "Truth by Convention," I would remark that my much-cited definition of logical truth therein was meant only as an improved exposition of a long-current idea. So I was not taken aback at Bar-Hillel's finding the idea in Bolzano; I was, though, at recently uncovering an anticipation of my specific exposition, in Ajdukiewicz.

27. I am indebted to Davidson for the concept of stimulus analyticity, as well as for this observation concerning it. Mates also may be said to have taken a step in somewhat this direction, in his proposal of contrary-to-fact questionnaires ("Analytic Sentences," p. 532).

28. Cf. Grice and Strawson, pp. 150 f.

29. Apostel and his associates have explored this matter experimentally by asking subjects to classify chosen sentences, with and without the guidance of prior headings. Their findings suggest a gradualism of intuitive analyticity. For earlier experimentation on synonymy intuitions, see Naess. On gradualism, see also Goodman, "On Likeness of Meaning," and White, "The Analytic and the Synthetic."

30. The notion, reminiscent of Kant, is often uncritically assumed in modern epistemological writing. Sometimes it has been given a semblance of foundation in terms of "semantical rules" or "meaning postulates" (Carnap, *Meaning and Necessity,* especially 2d ed.), but these devices only assume the notion in a disguised form. (See my "Two Dogmas of Empiricism" and "Carnap and Logical truth.") The notion has long had its doubters; Duhem's views in 1906, pp. 303, 328, 347 f., are scarcely congenial to it, and idealists have expressly scouted it. (See Gewirth, p. 399, for references.) My misgivings over the notion came out in a limited way in "Truth by Convention" (1936), and figured increasingly in my lectures at Harvard. Tarski and I long argued the point with Carnap there in 1939–40. Soon White was pursuing the matter with Goodman and me in triangular correspondence. Essays questioning the distinction issued from a number of pens, sometimes independently of the Harvard discussions; for instance Reid, 1943. Carnap and White mentioned my position in their 1950 papers, but my published allusions to it were slight (1940, p. 55; 1943, p. 120; 1944, Intro.; 1947, pp. 44 f.) until in 1950 I was invited to address the American Philosophical Association on the issue, and so wrote "Two Dogmas." The ensuing controversy has run to many articles and several books. Besides items mentioned in notes of this section and §12, see particularly Pasch (Part I), White (*Toward Reunion in Philosophy,* pp. 133–63), and Bennett. The title of "Two Dogmas," by the way, has proved unfortunate in its unintended but very real suggestion that there is no empiricism without the dogmas in question; cf. e.g. Hofstadter, pp. 410, 413.

31. See §13 on this myth and the principle of charity.
32. Hence Lewis's concept of analytic meaning, and Carnap's of intensional isomorphism.
33. *Blue and Brown Books,* p. 5. Perhaps the doctrine of indeterminacy of translation will have little air of paradox for readers familiar with Wittgenstein's latter-day remarks on meaning.
34. The example is from Lienhardt, p. 97. His discussion of it accords somewhat with mine.
35. A striking example is the comparison of color words in Lenneberg and Roberts, pp. 23–30.
36. Thus Cassirer, D. D. Lee, Sapir (Ch. X), Whorf. See further Bedau's review.

BIBLIOGRAPHY

Ajdukiewicz, Kazimierz. "Sprache und Sinn." *Erkenntnis* 4 (1934), pp. 100–138.

Apostel, L., W. Mays, A. Morf, and J. Piaget. *Les liaisons analytiques et synthétiques dans les comporements du sujet.* Paris: Presses Universitaires, 1957

Bar-Hillel, Yehoshua. "Bolzano's definition of analytic propositions." *Theoria* 16 (1950), pp. 91–117.

Bedau, H. A. Review of Whorf. *Philosophy of Science* 24 (1957). pp. 289–293.

Bennett, Jonathan. "Analytic-synthetic." *Proceedings of the Aristotelian Society* 59 (1959), pp. 163–188.

Carnap, Rudolf. *Der logische Aufbau der Welt.* Berlin, 1928.

———. *Meaning and Necessity.* Chicago: University, 1947. 2nd ed., with supplements, 1956.

Cassirer, Ernst. *Language and Myth.* New York: Harper, 1946.

Chisholm, R. M. *Perceiving: A Philosophical Study.* Ithaca: Cornell, 1957.

Duhem, Pierre. *La théorie physique: Son objet et sa structure.* Paris, 1906.

Evans-Pritchard, E. E. (ed.). *The Institutions of Primitive Society.* Oxford: Blackwell, 1954.

Firth, Raymond. *Elements of Social Organization.* London: Watts, 1951.

Gewirth, Alan. "The distinction between analytic and synthetic truths." *Journal of Philosophy* 50 (1953), pp. 397–426.

Goodman, Nelson. "On likeness of meaning." *Analysis* 10 (1949), pp. 1–7. Reprinted with revisions in Linsky.

———. *The Structure of Appearance.* Cambridge, Mass.: Harvard, 1951.

Grice, H. P., and P. F. Strawon. "In defense of a dogma." *Philosophical Review* 65 (1956), pp. 141–158.

Hofstader, Albert. "The myth of the whole: an examination of Quine's view of knowledge." *Journal of Philosophy* 51 (1954), pp. 397–417.

Hook, Sidney (ed.). *John Dewey: Philosopher of Science and Freedom.* New York: Dial, 1950.

Lee, Dorothy D. "Conceptual implications of an Indian language." *Philosophy of Science* 5(1938), pp. 89–102.

Lee, O. H. (ed.) *Philosopical Essays for A. N. Whitehead.* New York: Longmans. 1936.

Lenneberg, E. H., and J. M. Roberts. "The language of experience." *International Journal of American Linguitics,* suppl., 1956.

Lévy-Bruhl, Lucien. *Les Carnets.* Paris: Presses Universitaires, 1949.

Lewis, C. I. "The modes of meaning." *Philosophy and Phenomenological Research* 4 (1944), pp. 236–249. Reprinted in Linsky.

Lienhardt, Godfrey. "Modes of thought." In Evans-Pritchard, pp. 95–107.

Linsky, Leonard (ed.). *Semantics and the Philosophy of Language.* Urbana: University of Illinois, 1952.

Malinowski, Bronisław. *Coral Gardens and Their Magic,* vol. 2. New York: American, 1935.

Mates, Benson. "Synonymity." *University of California Publications in Philosophy* 25 (1950), pp. 201–226. Reprinted in Linsky.

Mises, Richard von. *Positivism: A Study in Human Understanding.* Cambridge, Mass.: Harvard, 1951.

Naess, Arne. *Interpretation and Preciseness.* Oslo: Dybwad, 1953.

Pap, Arthur. *Semantics and Necessary Truth.* New Haven: Yale, 1958.

Pasch, Alan. *Experience and the* Analytic. Chicago: University, 1959.

Perkins, Moreland, and Irving Singer. "Analyticity." *Journal of Philosophy* 48 (1951), pp. 485–497.

Pike, Kenneth. *Phonemics: A Technique for Reducing Languages to Writing.* Ann Arbor: University of Michigan, 1947.

Putnam. Hilary. "The analytic and the synthetic." *Minnesota Studies in the Philosophy of Science* 3, Minneapolis, Minn., University, 1962.

Quine, W. V. "Truth by convention." In O. H. Lee, pp. 90–124.

———. "Carnap and logical truth." Mimeographed. Written early in 1954 at the request of P. A. Schilpp for a volume he had been planning. Published in Italian in *Rivista di filosofia* 48 (1957), pp. 3–29. Portions also published under the title "Logical truth," in Hook, *American Philosophers at Work,* New York, Criterion, 1956.

Russell, B. *An Inquiry into Meaning and Truth.* New York: Norton, 1941.

Sapir, Edward. *Language.* New York, 1921.

Strawson, P. F. "Particular and Individual," *Proceedings of the Aristotelian Society* 54 (1954), pp. 233–260.

———. "Propositions, concepts, and logical truths." *Philosophical Quarterly* 7 (1957), pp. 15–25.

———. *Individuals.* London: Methuen, 1959.

White, Morton. "The analytic and the synthetic: An untenable dualism." In Hook, *John Dewey,* pp. 316–330.

———. *Toward Reunion in Philosophy.* Cambridge, Mas.: Harvard, 1956.

Wilson, N. L. "Substances without substrata." *Review of Metaphysics* 12 (1959), pp. 521–539.

Wittgenstein, Ludwig. *The Blue and Brown Books.* Oxford: Blackwell, 1958.

Whorf, B. L. *Language, Thought and Reality: Selected Writings of Benjamin Lee Whorf.* (J. B. Carroll, ed.) M.I.T.: Technology Press and New York: Wiley. 1956.

39 Belief and the Basis of Meaning

DONALD DAVIDSON

Meaning and belief play interlocking and complementary roles in the interpretation of speech. By emphasizing the connection between our grounds for attributing beliefs to speakers, and our grounds for assigning meanings to their utterances, I hope to explain some problematic features both of belief and of meaning.

We interpret a bit of linguistic behavior when we say what a speaker's words mean on an occasion of use. The task may be seen as one of redescription. We know that the words 'Es schneit' have been uttered on a particular occasion and we want to redescribe this uttering as an act of saying that it is snowing.[1] What do we need to know if we are to be in a position to redescribe speech in this way, that is, to interpret the utterances of a speaker? Since a competent interpreter can interpret any of a potential infinity of utterances (or so we may as well say), we cannot specify what he knows by listing cases. He knows, for example, that in uttering 'Es schneit' under certain conditions and with a certain intent, Karl has said that it is snowing; but there are endless further cases. What we must do then is state a finite theory from which particular interpretations follow. The theory may be used to describe an aspect of the interpreter's competence at understanding what is said. We may, if we please, also maintain that there is a mechanism in the interpreter that corresponds to the theory. If this means only that there is some mechanism or other that performs that task, it is hard to see how the claim can fail to be true.

Theory of interpretation is the business jointly of the linguist, psychologist, and philosopher. Its subject matter is the behavior of a speaker or speakers, and it tells what certain of their utterances mean. Finally, the theory can be used to describe what every interpreter knows, namely a specifiable infinite subset of the truths of the theory. In what follows, I shall say a little, and assume a lot, about the form a theory of interpretation can take. But I want to focus on the question how we can tell that any such theory is true.

One answer comes pat. The theory is true if its empirical implications are true; we can test the theory by sampling its implications for truth. In the present case, this means noticing whether or not typical interpretations a theory yields for the utterances of a speaker are correct. We agreed that any competent interpreter knows whether the relevant implications are true; so any competent interpreter can test a theory in this way. This does not mean, of course, that finding a true theory is trivial; it does mean that given a theory, testing it may require nothing arcane.

The original question, however, is how we know that a particular interpretation is correct, and our pat answer is not addressed to this ques-

From *Synthese* 27 (1974): 309–323. Copyright © 1974 by Kluwer Academic Publishers. Reprinted with the permission of Kluwer Academic Publishers.

tion. An utterance can no doubt be interpreted by a correct theory, but if the problem is to determine when an interpretation is correct, it is no help to support the theory that yields it by giving samples of correct interpretations. There is an apparent impasse; we need the theory before we can recognize evidence on its behalf.

The problem is salient because uninterpreted utterances seem the appropriate evidential base for a theory of meaning. If an acceptable theory could be supported by such evidence, that would constitute conceptual progress, for the theory would be specifically semantical in nature, while the evidence would be described in nonsemantical terms. An attempt to build on even more elementary evidence, say behavioristic evidence, could only make the task of theory construction harder, though it might make it more satisfying. In any case, we can without embarrassment undertake the lesser enterprise.

A central source of trouble is the way beliefs and meanings conspire to account for utterances. A speaker who holds a sentence to be true on an occasion does so in part because of what he means, or would mean, by an utterance of that sentence, and in part because of what he believes. If all we have to go on is the fact of honest utterance, we cannot infer the belief without knowing the meaning, and have no chance of inferring the meaning without the belief.

Various strategies for breaking into this circle suggest themselves. One is to find evidence for what words mean that is independent of belief. It would have to be independent of intentions, desires, regrets, wishes, approvals, and conventions too, for all of these have a belief component. Perhaps there are some who think it would be possible to establish the correctness of a theory of interpretation without knowing, or establishing, a great deal about beliefs, but it is not easy to imagine how it could be done.

Far more plausible is the idea of deriving a theory of interpretation from detailed information about the intentions, desires, and beliefs of speakers (or interpreters, or both). This I take to be the strategy of those who undertake to define or explain linguistic meaning on the basis of nonlinguistic intentions, uses, purposes, functions, and the like: the traditions are those of

Mead and Dewey, of Wittgenstein and Grice. This strategy will not meet the present need either, I think.

There can be nothing wrong, of course, with the methodological maxim that when baffling problems about meanings, reference, synonymy, and so on arise, we should remember that these concepts, like those of word, sentence, and language themselves, abstract away from the social transactions and setting which give them what content they have. Everyday linguistic and semantic concepts are part of an intuitive theory for organizing more primitive data, so only confusion can result from treating these concepts and their supposed objects as if they had a life of their own. But this observation cannot answer the question how we know when an interpretation of an utterance is correct. If our ordinary concepts suggest a confused theory, we should look for a better theory, not give up theorizing.

There can be no objection either to detailing the complicated and important relations between what a speaker's words mean and his nonlinguistic intentions and beliefs. I have my doubts about the possibility of *defining* linguistic meaning in terms of nonlinguistic intentions and beliefs, but those doubts, if not the sources of those doubts, are irrelevant to the present theme.

The present theme is the nature of the evidence for the adequacy of a theory of interpretation. The evidence must be describable in nonsemantic, nonlinguistic terms if it is to respond to the question we have set; it must also be evidence we can imagine the virgin investigator having without his already being in possession of the theory it is supposed to be evidence for. This is where I spy trouble. There is a principled, and not merely a practical, obstacle to verifying the existence of detailed, general and abstract beliefs and intentions, while being unable to tell what a speaker's words mean. We sense well enough the absurdity in trying to learn without asking him whether someone believes there is a largest prime, or whether he intends, by making certain noises, to get someone to stop smoking by that person's recognition that the noises were made with that intention. The absurdity lies not in the fact that it would be very hard to find out these things without language, but in the fact that we have no good idea how to set about authenticating the existence of such attitudes when communication is not possible.

This point is not happily stated by saying that our sophisticated beliefs and intentions and thoughts are like silent utterances. My claim is only that making detailed sense of a person's intentions and beliefs cannot be independent of making sense of his utterances. If this is so, then an inventory of a speaker's sophisticated beliefs and intentions cannot be the evidence for the truth of a theory for interpreting his speech behavior.

Since we cannot hope to interpret linguistic activity without knowing what a speaker believes, and cannot found a theory of what he means on a prior discovery of his beliefs and intentions, I conclude that in interpreting utterances from scratch—in *radical* interpretation—we must somehow deliver simultaneously a theory of belief and a theory of meaning. How is this possible?

In order to make the problem sharp and simple enough for a relatively brief discussion, let me make a change in the description of the evidential base for a theory of interpretation. Instead of utterances of expressions, I want to consider a certain attitude toward expressions, an attitude that may or may not be evinced in actual utterances. The attitude is that of holding true, relativized to time. We may as well suppose we have available all that could be known of such attitudes, past, present, and future. Finally, I want to imagine that we can describe the external circumstances under which the attitudes hold or fail to hold. Typical of the sort of evidence available then would be the following: a speaker holds "Es schneit' true when and only when it is snowing. I hope it will be granted that it is plausible to say we can tell when a speaker holds a sentence to be true without knowing what he means by the sentence, or what beliefs he holds about its unknown subject matter, or what detailed intentions do or might prompt him to utter it. It is often argued that we must assume that most of a speaker's utterances are of sentences he holds true: if this is right, the independent availability of the evidential base is

assured. But weaker assumptions will do, since even the compulsive liar and the perennial kidder may be found out.

The problem, then, is this: we suppose we know what sentences a speaker holds true, and when, and we want to know what he means and believes. Perhaps we could crack the case if we knew enough about his beliefs and intentions, but there is no chance of this without prior access to a theory of interpretation. Given the interpretations, we could read off beliefs from the evidential base, but this assumes what we want to know.

I am struck by the analogy with a well-known problem in decision theory. Suppose an agent is indifferent between getting $5.00, and a gamble that offers him $11.00 if a coin comes up heads, and $0.00 if it comes up tails. We might explain (i.e., "interpret') his indifference by supposing that money has a diminishing marginal utility for him: $5.00 is midway on his subjective value scale between $0.00 and $11.00. We arrive at this by assuming the gamble is worth the sum of the values of the possible outcomes as tempered by their likelihoods. In this case, we assume that heads and tails are equally likely. Unfortunately there is an equally plausible alternative explanation: since $5.00 obviously isn't midway in utility between $0.00 and $11.00, the agent must believe tails are more likely to come up than heads; if he thought heads and tails equally probable, he would certainly prefer the gamble, which would then be equal to a straight offer of $5.50.

The point is obvious. Choices between gambles are the result of two psychological factors, the relative values the chooser places on the outcomes, and the probability he assigns to those outcomes, conditional on his choice. Given the agent's beliefs (his subjective probabilities) it's easy to compute his relative values from his choices; given his values, we can infer his beliefs. But given only his choices, how can we work out both his beliefs and his values?

The problem is much like the problem of interpretation. The solution in the case of decision theory is neat and satisfying; nothing as good is available in the theory of meaning. Still, one can, I think, see the possibility of applying an analogous strategy. Simplified a bit, Frank

Ramsey's proposal for coping with the problem of decision theory is this.[2] Suppose that there are two alternatives, getting $11.00 and getting $0.00, and that there is an event E such that the agent is indifferent between the following two gambles: Gamble One—if E happens the agent receives $11.00; if E fails to happen he gets $0.00. Gamble Two—if E happens he gets $0.00; if E fails to happen he gets $11.00. The agent's indifference between the gambles shows that he must judge that E is as likely to happen as not. For if he thought E more likely to occur than not, he would prefer the first gamble which promises him $11.00 if E occurs, and if he thought E more likely not to occur than to occur he would prefer the second gamble which pairs E's non-occurrence with $11.00. This solves, for decision theory, the problem of how to separate out subjective probability from subjective utility, for once an event like E is discovered, it is possible to scale other values, and then to determine the subjective probabilities of all events.

In this version of decision theory, the evidential base is preferences between alternatives, some of them wagers; preference here corresponds to the attitude of holding true in the case of interpretation, as I put that problem. Actual choices in decision theory correspond to actual utterances in interpretation. The explanation of a particular preference involves the assignment of a comparative ranking of values and an evaluation of probabilities. Support for the explanation doesn't come from a new kind of insight into the attitudes and beliefs of the agent, but from more observations of preferences of the very sort to be explained. In brief, to explain (i.e., interpret) a particular choice or preference, we observe *other* choices or preferences; these will support a theory on the basis of which the original choice or preference can be explained. Attributions of subjective values and probabilities are part of the theoretical structure, and are convenient ways of summarizing facts about the structure of basic preferences; there is no way to test for them independently. Broadly stated, my theme is that we should think of meanings and beliefs as interrelated constructs of a single theory just as we already view subjective values and probabilities as interrelated constructs of decision theory.

One way of representing some of the explanatory facts about choice behavior elicited by a theory of decision is to assign numbers to measure, say, the subjective values of outcomes to a particular agent. So we might assign the numbers 0, 1, and 2 as measures of the values to someone of receiving $0.00, $5.00, and $11.00 respectively. To the unwary this could suggest that for that agent $11.00 was worth twice as much as $5.00. Only by studying the underlying theory would the truth emerge that the assignment of numbers to measure utilities was unique up to a linear transformation, but not beyond. The numbers 2, 4, and 6 would have done as well in recording the facts, but 6 is not twice 4. The theory makes sense of comparisons of differences, but not of comparisons of absolute magnitudes. When we represent the facts of preference, utility, and subjective probability by assigning numbers, only some of the properties of numbers are used to capture the empirically justified pattern. Other properties of the numbers used may therefore be chosen arbitrarily, like the zero point and the unit in measuring utility or temperature.

The same facts may be represented by quite different assignments of numbers. In the interpretation of speech, introducing such supposed entities as propositions to be meanings of sentences or objects of belief may mislead us into thinking the evidence justifies, or should justify, a kind of uniqueness that it does not. In the case of decision theory, we can establish exactly which properties of numbers are relevant to the measurement of utility and which to the measurement of probability. Propositions being much vaguer than numbers, it is not clear to what extent they are overdesigned for their job.

There is not just an analogy between decision theory and interpretation theory, there is a connection. Seen from the side of decision theory, there is what Ward Edwards once dubbed the "presentation problem' for empirical applications of decision theory. To learn the preferences of an agent, particularly among complex gambles, it is obviously necessary to describe the options in words. But how can the experimenter know what those words mean to the subject? The problem is not merely theoretical: it is well known that two descriptions of what the experimenter takes to be the same option may elicit quite different responses from a subject. We are up against a problem we discussed a moment ago in connection with interpretation: it is not reasonable to suppose we can interpret verbal behavior without fine-grained information about beliefs and intentions, nor is it reasonable to imagine we can justify the attribution of preferences among complex options unless we can interpret speech behavior. A radical theory of decision must include a theory of interpretation and cannot presuppose it.

Seen from the side of a theory of interpretation, there is the obvious difficulty in telling when a person accepts a sentence as true. Decision theory, and the commonsense ideas that stand behind it, help make a case for the view that beliefs are best understood in their role of rationalizing choices or preferences. Here we are considering only one special kind of belief, the belief that a sentence is true. Yet even in this case, it would be better if we could go behind the belief to a preference which might show itself in choice. I have no detailed proposal to make at the moment how this might, or should, be done. A first important step has been made by Richard Jeffrey.[3] He eliminates some troublesome confusions in Ramsey's theory by reducing the rather murky ontology of the theory, which dealt with events, options, and propositions to an ontology of propositions only. Preferences between propositions holding true then becomes the evidential base, so that the revised theory allows us to talk of degrees of belief in the truth of propositions, and the relative strength of desires that propositions be true. As Jeffrey points out, for the purposes of his theory, the objects of these various attitudes could as well be taken to be sentences. If this change is made, we can unify the subject matter of decision theory and theory of interpretation. Jeffrey assumes, of course, the sentences are understood by agent and theory builders in the same way. But the two theories may be united by giving up this assumption. The theory for which we should ultimately strive is one that takes as evidential base preferences between sentences— preferences that one sentence rather than another be true. The theory would then explain individual preferences of this sort by attributing

beliefs and values to the agent, and meanings to his words.[4]

In this paper I shall not speculate further on the chances for an integrated theory of decision and interpretation; so I return to the problem of interpreting utterances on the basis of information about when, and under what external circumstances, the sentences they exemplify are held true. The central ideas in what I have said so far may be summarized: behavioral or dispositional facts that can be described in ways that do not assume interpretations, but on which a theory of interpretation can be based, will necessarily be a vector of meaning and belief. One result is that to interpret a particular utterance it is necessary to construct a comprehensive theory for the interpretation of a potential infinity of utterances. The evidence for the interpretation of a particular utterance will therefore have to be evidence for the interpretation of all utterances of a speaker or community. Finally, if entities like meanings, propositions, and objects of belief have a legitimate place in explaining speech behavior, it is only because they can be shown to play a useful role in the construction of an adequate theory. There is no reason to believe in advance that these entities will be any help, and so it cannot be an independent goal of a theory or analysis to identify the meanings of expressions or the objects of belief.

The appreciation of these ideas, which we owe largely to Quine, represents one of the few real breakthroughs in the study of language. I have put things in my own way, but I think that the differences between us are more matters of emphasis than of substance. Much that Quine has written understandably concentrates on undermining misplaced confidence in the usefulness or intelligibility of concepts like those of analyticity, synonymy, and meaning. I have tried to accentuate the positive. Quine, like the rest of us, wants to provide a theory of interpretation. His animadversions on meanings are designed to discourage false starts; but the arguments in support of the strictures provide foundations for an acceptable theory.

I have accepted what I think is essentially Quine's picture of the problem of interpretation, and the strategy for its solution that I want to propose will obviously owe a great deal to him.

There also will be some differences. One difference concerns the form the theory should take. Quine would have us produce a translation manual (a function, recursively given) that yields a sentence in the language of the interpreter for each sentence of the speaker (or more than one sentence in the case of ambiguity). To interpret a particular utterance one would give the translating sentence and specify the translation manual. In addition, it would be necessary to know exactly what information was preserved by a translation manual that met the empirical constraints: what was invariant, so to speak, from one acceptable translation manual to another.

I suggest making the theory explicitly semantical in character, in fact, that the theory should take the form of a theory of truth in Tarski's style.[5] In Tarski's style, but with modifications to meet present problems. For one thing, we are after a *theory* of truth where Tarski is interested in an explicit definition. This is a modification I will not discuss now: it mainly concerns the question how rich an ontology is available in the language in which the theory is given. Secondly, in order to accommodate the presence of demonstrative elements in natural language it is necessary to relativize the theory of truth to times and speakers (and possibly to some other things). The third modification is more serious and comes to the heart of the business under discussion. Tarski's Convention T demands of a theory of truth that it put conditions on some predicate, say 'is true', such that all sentences of a certain form are entailed by it. These are just those sentences with the familiar form: ' "Snow is white" is true if and only if snow is white'. For the formalized languages that Tarski talks about, T-sentences (as we may call these theorems) are known by their syntax, and this remains true even if the object language and metalanguage are different languages and even if for quotation marks we substitute something more manageable. But in radical interpretation a syntactical test of the truth of T-sentences would be worthless, since such a test would presuppose the understanding of the object language one hopes to gain. The reason is simple: the syntactical test is merely meant to formalize the relation of synonymy or translation, and this relation is taken as unproblematic in Tarski's

work on truth. Our outlook inverts Tarski's: we want to achieve an understanding of meaning or translation by assuming a prior grasp of the concept of truth. What we require, therefore, is a way of judging the acceptability of T-sentences that is not syntactical, and makes no use of the concepts of translation, meaning, or synonymy, but is such that acceptable T-sentences will in fact yield interpretations.

A theory of truth will be materially adequate, that is, will correctly determine the extension of the truth predicate, provided it entails, for each sentence s of the object language, a theorem of the form 's is true if and only if p' where 's' is replaced by a description of s and 'p' is replaced by a sentence that is true if and only if s is. For purposes of interpretation, however, truth in a T-sentence is not enough. A theory of truth will yield interpretations only if its T-sentences state truth conditions in terms that may be treated as 'giving the meaning' of object language sentences. Our problem is to find constraints on a theory strong enough to guarantee that it can be used for interpretation.

There are constraints of a formal nature that flow from the demand that the theory be finitely axiomatized, and that it satisfy Convention T (as appropriately modified).[6] If the metalanguage is taken to contain ordinary quantification theory, it is difficult, if not impossible, to discover anything other than standard quantificational structures in the object language. This does not mean that anything whatever can be read into the object language simply by assuming it to be in the metalanguage; for example, the presence of modal operators in the metalanguage does not necessarily lead to a theory of truth for a modal object language.

A satisfactory theory cannot depart much, it seems, from standard quantificational structures or their usual semantics. We must expect the theory to rely on something very like Tarski's sort of recursive characterization of satisfaction, and to describe sentences of the object language in terms of familiar patterns created by quantification and cross-reference, predication, truth-functional connections, and so on. The relation between these semantically tractable patterns and the surface grammar of sentences may, of course, be very complicated.

The result of applying the formal constraints is, then, to fit the object language as a whole to the procrustean bed of quantification theory. Although this can no doubt be done in many ways if any, it is unlikely that the differences between acceptable theories will, in matters of logical form, be great. The identification of the semantic features of a sentence will then be essentially invariant: correct theories will agree on the whole about the quantificational structure to be assigned to a given sentence.

Questions of logical form being settled, the logical constants of quantification theory (including identity) will have been perforce discovered in the object language (well concealed, probably, beneath the surface). There remain the further primitive expressions to be interpreted. The main problem is to find a systematic way of matching predicates of the metalanguage to the primitive predicates of the object language so as to produce acceptable T-sentences. If the metalanguage predicates translate the object language predicates, things will obviously come out right; if they have the same extensions, this might be enough. But it would be foreign to our program to use these concepts in stating the constraints: the constraints must deal only with sentences and truth. Still, it is easy to see how T-sentences for sentences with indexical features sharply limit the choice of interpreting predicates; for example the T-sentence for 'Das ist weiss' must have something like this form: 'For all speakers of German x and all times t "Das ist weiss" is true spoken by x at t if and only if the object demonstrated by x at t is white'. There may, as Quine has pointed out in his discussions of ontological relativity, remain room for alternative ontologies, and so for alternative systems for interpreting the predicates of the object language. I believe the range of acceptable theories of truth can be reduced to the point where all acceptable theories will yield T-sentences that we can treat as giving correct interpretations, by application of further reasonable and non-question-begging constraints. But the details must be reserved for another occasion.

Much more, obviously, must be said about the empirical constraints on the theory—the conditions under which a T-sentence may be accepted as correct. We have agreed that the evidential base for the theory will consist of facts about the circumstances under which speakers hold sentences of their language to be true. Such evidence, I have urged, is neutral as between meaning and belief and assumes neither. It now needs to be shown that such data can provide a test for the acceptability of T-sentences.

I propose that we take the fact that speakers of a language hold a sentence to be true (under observed circumstances) as prima-facie evidence that the sentence is true under those circumstances. For example, positive instances of 'Speakers (of German) hold "Es schneit" true when, and only when, it is snowing' should be taken to confirm not only the generalization, but also the T-sentence, '"Es schneit" is true (in German) for a speaker x at time t if and only if it is snowing at t (and near x)'.

Not all the evidence can be expected to point the same way. There will be differences from speaker to speaker, and from time to time for the same speaker, with respect to the circumstances under which a sentence is held true. The general policy, however, is to choose truth-conditions that do as well as possible in making speakers hold sentences true when (according to the theory and the theory builder's view of the facts) those sentences are true. That is the general policy, to be modified in a host of obvious ways. Speakers can be allowed to differ more often and more radically with respect to some sentences than others, and there is no reason not to take into account the observed or inferred individual differences that may be thought to have caused anomalies (as seen by the theory).[7]

Building the theory cannot be a matter of deciding on an appropriate T-sentence for one sentence of the object language at a time; a pattern must be built up that preserves the formal constraints discussed above while suiting the evidence as well as may be. And of course the fact that a theory does not make speakers universal holders of truths is not an inadequacy of the theory; the aim is not the absurd one of making disagreement and error disappear. The point is rather that widespread agreement is the only possible background against which disputes and mistakes can be interpreted. Making sense of the utterances and behavior of others, even their most aberrant behavior, requires us to find a great deal of reason and truth in them. To see too much unreason on the part of others is simply to undermine our ability to understand what it is they are so unreasonable about. If the vast amount of agreement on plain matters that is assumed in communication escapes notice, it's because the shared truths are too many and too dull to bear mentioning. What we want to talk about is what's new, surprising, or disputed.

A theory for interpreting the utterances of a single speaker, based on nothing but his attitudes toward sentences, would, we may be sure, have many equally eligible rivals, for differences in interpretation could be offset by appropriate differences in the beliefs attributed. Given a community of speakers with apparently the same linguistic repertoire, however, the theorist will strive for a single theory of interpretation: this will greatly narrow his practical choice of preliminary theories for each individual speaker. (In a prolonged dialogue, one starts perforce with a socially applicable theory, and refines it as evidence peculiar to the other speaker accumulates.)

What makes a social theory of interpretation possible is that we can construct a plurality of private belief structures: belief is built to take up the slack between sentences held true by individuals and sentences true (or false) by public standards. What is private about belief is not that it is accessible to only one person, but that it may be idiosyncratic. Attributions of belief are as publicly verifiable as interpretations, being based on the same evidence: if we can understand what a person says, we can know what he believes.

If interpretation is approached in the style I have been discussing, it is not likely that only one theory will be found satisfactory. The resulting indeterminacy of interpretation is the semantic counterpart of Quine's indeterminacy of translation. On my approach, the degree of indeterminacy will, I think, be less than Quine contemplates: this is partly because I advocate adoption of the principle of charity on an across-the-board basis, and partly because the uniqueness of quantificational structure is apparently assured if Convention T is satisfied. But in any case the question of indeterminacy is

not central to the concerns of this paper. Indeterminacy of meaning or translation does not represent a failure to capture significant distinctions; it marks the fact that certain apparent distinctions are not significant. If there is indeterminacy, it is because when all the evidence is in, alternative ways of stating the facts remain open. An analogy from decision theory has already been noted: if the numbers 1, 2, and 3 capture the meaningful relations in subjective value between three alternatives, then the numbers -17, -2, and $+13$ do as well. Indeterminacy of this kind cannot be of genuine concern.

What is important is that if meaning and belief are interlocked as I have suggested, then the idea that each belief has a definite object, and the idea that each word and sentence has a definite meaning, cannot be invoked in describing the goal of a successful theory. For even if, contrary to what may reasonably be expected, there were no indeterminacy at all, entities such as meanings and objects of belief would be of no independent interest. We could, of course, invent such entities with a clear conscience if we were sure there were no permissible variant theories. But if we knew this, we would know how to state our theories without mention of the objects.

Theories of belief and meaning may require no exotic objects, but they do use concepts which set such theories apart from the physical and other nonpsychological sciences: concepts like those of meaning and belief are, in a fundamental way, not reducible to physical, neurological, or even behavioristic concepts. This irreducibility is not due, however, to the indeterminacy of meaning or translation, for if I am right, indeterminacy is important only for calling attention to how the interpretation of speech must go hand in hand with the interpretation of action generally, and so with the attribution of desires and beliefs. It is rather the methods we must invoke in constructing theories of belief and meaning that ensure the irreducibility of the concepts essential to those theories. Each interpretation and attribution of attitude is a move within a holistic theory, a theory necessarily governed by concern for consistency and general coherence with the truth, and it is this that sets these theories forever apart from those that describe mindless objects, or describe objects as mindless.[8]

NOTES

1. I use the expression 'says that' in the present context in such a way that a speaker says (on a particular occasion) that it is snowing if and only if he utters words that (on that occasion) mean that it is snowing. So a speaker may say that it is snowing without *his* meaning, or asserting, that it is snowing.

2. F. P. Ramsey, "Truth and Probability."

3. R. Jeffrey, *The Logic of Decision.*

4. For progress in developing such a theory, see my "Toward a Unified Theory of Meaning and Action."

5. A. Tarski, "The Concept of Truth in Formalized Languages."

6. See Essays 5 ["In Defence of Convention T"] and 9 ["Radical Interpretation"].

7. For more on such modifications, see Essay 11 ["Thought and Talk"], and particularly D. Lewis, "Radical Interpretation."

8. See Essay 11 of *Essays on Actions and Events.*

40 A Nice Derangement of Epitaphs

DONALD DAVIDSON

Goodman Ace wrote radio sitcoms. According to Mark Singer, Ace often talked the way he wrote:

Rather than take for granite that Ace talks straight, a listener must be on guard for an occasional entre nous and me . . . or a long face no see. In a roustabout way, he will maneuver until he selects the ideal phrase for the situation, hitting the nail right on the thumb. The careful conversationalist might try to mix it up with him in a baffle of wits. In quest of this pinochle of success, I have often wrecked my brain for a clowning achievement, but Ace's chickens always come home to roast. From time to time, Ace will, in a jerksome way, monotonize the conversation with witticisms too humorous to mention. It's high noon someone beat him at his own game, but I have never done it; cross my eyes and hope to die, he always wins thumbs down.[1]

I quote at length because philosophers have tended to neglect or play down the sort of language-use this passage illustrates. For example, Jonathan Bennett writes,

I doubt if I have ever been present when a speaker did something like shouting "Water!" as a warning of fire, knowing what "Water!" means and knowing that his hearers also knew, but thinking that they would expect him to give to "Water!" the normal meaning of "Fire!"[2];

Bennett adds that, "Although such things could happen, they seldom do." I think such things happen all the time; in fact, if the conditions are generalized in a natural way, the phenomenon is ubiquitous.

Singer's examples are special in several ways. A malapropism does not have to be amusing or surprising. It does not have to be based on a cliché, and of course it does not have to be intentional. There need be no play on words, no hint of deliberate pun. We may smile at someone who says, "Lead the way and we'll precede," or, with Archie Bunker, "We need a few laughs to break up the monogamy," because he has said something that, given the usual meanings of the words, is ridiculous or fun. But the humor is adventitious.

Ace's malaprops generally make some sort of sense when the words are taken in the standard way, as in "Familiarity breeds attempt," or "We're all cremated equal," but this is not essential ("the pinochle of success"). What is interesting is the fact that in all these cases the hearer has no trouble understanding the speaker in the way the speaker intends.

It is easy enough to explain this feat on the hearer's part: the hearer realizes that the "standard" interpretation cannot be the intended interpretation; through ignorance, inadvertence, or design the speaker has used a word similar in sound to the word that would have "correctly" expressed his meaning. The absurdity or inap-

From *Philosophical Grounds of Rationality*, ed. Richard Grandy and Richard Warner (Oxford: Clarendon Press, 1986), pp. 157–174. Copyright © 1985 by Donald Davidson. Reprinted with permission of Donald Davidson.

propriateness of what the speaker would have meant had his words been taken in the "standard" way alerts the hearer to trickery or error; the similarity in sound tips him off to the right interpretation. Of course there are many other ways the hearer might catch on; similarity of sound is not essential to the malaprop. Nor for that matter does the general case require that the speaker use a real word: most of "The Jabberwock" is intelligible on first hearing.

It seems unimportant, so far as understanding is concerned, who makes a mistake, or whether there is one. When I first read Singer's piece on Goodman Ace, I thought that the word 'malaprop', though the name of Sheridan's character, was not a common noun that could be used in place of 'malapropism'. It turned out to be my mistake. Not that it mattered: I knew what Singer meant, even though I was in error about the word; I would have taken his meaning in the same way if he had been in error instead of me. We could both have been wrong and things would have gone as smoothly.

This talk of error or mistake is not mysterious or open to philosophical suspicions. I was wrong about what a good dictionary would say, or what would be found by polling a pod of experts whose taste or training I trust. But error or mistake of this kind, with its associated notion of correct usage, is not philosophically interesting. We want a deeper notion of what words, when spoken in context, mean; and like the shallow notion of correct usage, we want the deep concept to distinguish between what a speaker, on a given occasion, means, and what his words mean. The widespread existence of malapropisms and their kin threatens the distinction, since here the intended meaning seems to take over from the standard meaning.

I take for granted, however, that nothing should be allowed to obliterate or even blur the distinction between speaker's meaning and literal meaning. In order to preserve the distinction we must, I shall argue, modify certain commonly accepted views about what it is to 'know a language', or about what a natural language is. In particular, we must pry apart what is literal in language from what is conventional or established.

Here is a preliminary stab at characterizing what I have been calling literal meaning. The term is too incrusted with philosophical and other extras to do much work, so let me call what I am interested in *first meaning*. The concept applies to words and sentences as uttered by a particular speaker on a particular occasion. But if the occasion, the speaker, and the audience are 'normal' or 'standard' (in a sense not to be further explained here), then the first meaning of an utterance will be what should be found by consulting a dictionary based on actual usage (such as Webster's Third). Roughly speaking, first meaning comes first in the order of interpretation. We have no chance of explaining the image in the following lines, for example, unless we know what 'foison' meant in Shakespeare's day:

> Speak of the spring and foison of the year,
> The one doth shadow of your beauty show,
> The other as your bounty doth appear . . .[3]

Little here is to be taken literally, but unless we know the literal, or first, meaning of the words we do not grasp and cannot explain the image.

But 'the order of interpretation' is not at all clear. For there are cases where we may first guess at the image and so puzzle out the first meaning. This might happen with the word 'tires' in the same sonnet:

> On Helen's cheek all art of beauty set,
> And you in Grecian tires are painted new.

And of course it often happens that we can descry the literal meaning of a word or phrase by first appreciating what the speaker was getting at.

A better way to distinguish first meaning is through the intentions of the speaker. The intentions with which an act is performed are usually unambiguously ordered by the relation of means to ends (where this relation may or may not be causal). Thus the poet wants (let us say) to praise the beauty and generosity of his patron. He does this by using images that say the person addressed takes on every good aspect to be found in nature or in man or woman. This he does in turn by using the word 'tire' to mean 'attire' and the word 'foison' to mean 'harvest'. The order established here by 'by' can be reversed by using the phrase 'in order to'. In the 'in order to' sequence, first meaning is the first meaning referred to. ('With the intention of' with 'ing' added to the verb does as well.)

Suppose Diogenes utters the words, "I would have you stand from between me and the sun' (or their Greek equivalent) with the intention of uttering words that will be interpreted by Alexander as true if and only if Diogenes would have him stand from between Diogenes and the sun, and this with the intention of asking Alexander to move from between him and the sun, and this with the intention of getting Alexander to move from between him and the sun, and this with the intention of leaving a good anecdote to posterity. Of course these are not the only intentions involved; there will also be the Gricean intentions to achieve certain of these ends through Alexander's recognition of some of the intentions involved. Diogenes' intention to be interpreted in a certain way requires such a self-referring intention, as does his intention to ask Alexander to move. In general, the first intention in the sequence to require this feature specifies the first meaning.

Because a speaker necessarily intends first meaning to be grasped by his audience, and it is grasped if communication succeeds, we lose nothing in the investigation of first meaning if we concentrate on the knowledge or ability a hearer must have if he is to interpret a speaker. What the speaker knows must correspond to something the interpreter knows if the speaker is to be understood, since if the speaker is understood he has been interpreted as he intended to be interpreted. The abilities of the speaker that go beyond what is required of an interpreter—invention and motor control—do not concern me here.

Nothing said so far limits first meaning to language; what has been characterized is (roughly) Grice's nonnatural meaning, which applies to any sign or signal with an intended interpretation. What should be added if we want to restrict first meaning to linguistic meaning? The usual answer would, I think, be that in the case of language the hearer shares a complex system or theory with the speaker, a system which makes possible the articulation of logical relations between utterances, and explains the ability to interpret novel utterances in an organized way.

This answer has been suggested, in one form or another, by many philosophers and linguists, and I assume it must in some sense be right. The difficulty lies in getting clear about what this sense is. The particular difficulty with which I am concerned in this paper (for there are plenty of others) can be brought out by stating three plausible principles concerning first meaning in language: we may label them by saying they require that first meaning be systematic, shared, and prepared.

(1) *First meaning is systematic.* A competent speaker or interpreter is able to interpret utterances, his own or those of others, on the basis of the semantic properties of the parts, or words, in the utterance, and the structure of the utterance. For this to be possible, there must be systematic relations between the meanings of utterances.

(2) *First meanings are shared.* For speaker and interpreter to communicate successfully and regularly, they must share a method of interpretation of the sort described in (1).

(3) *First meanings are governed by learned conventions or regularities.* The systematic knowledge or competence of the speaker or interpreter is learned in advance of occasions of interpretation and is conventional in character.

Probably no one doubts that there are difficulties with these conditions. Ambiguity is an example: often the 'same' word has more than one semantic role, and so the interpretation of utterances in which it occurs is not uniquely fixed by the features of the interpreter's competence so far mentioned. Yet, though the verbal and other features of the context of utterance often determine a correct interpretation, it is not easy or perhaps even possible to specify clear rules for disambiguation. There are many more questions about what is required of the competent interpreter. It does not seem plausible that there is a strict rule fixing the occasions on which we should attach significance to the order in which conjoined sentences appear in a conjunction: the difference between 'They got married and had a child' and 'They had a child and got married'. Interpreters certainly can make these distinctions. But part of the burden of this paper is that much that they can do ought not to count as part of their basic *linguistic* competence. The contrast in what is meant or implied by the use of 'but' instead of 'and' seems to me another matter, since no amount of common sense unaccompanied by linguistic lore would enable an interpreter to figure it out.

Paul Grice has done more than anyone else to bring these problems to our attention and to help sort them out. In particular, he has shown why it is essential to distinguish between the literal meaning (perhaps what I am calling first meaning) of words and what is often implied (or implicated) by someone who uses those words. He has explored the general principles behind our ability to figure out such implicatures, and these principles must, of course, be known to speakers who expect to be taken up on them. Whether knowledge of these principles ought to be included in the description of linguistic competence may not have to be settled: on the one hand they are things a clever person could often figure out without previous training or exposure and they are things we could get along without. On the other hand they represent a kind of skill we expect of an interpreter and without which communication would be greatly impoverished.

I dip into these matters only to distinguish them from the problem raised by malapropisms and the like. The problems touched on in the last two paragraphs all concern the ability to interpret words and constructions of the kind covered by our conditions (1)–(3); the questions have been what is required for such interpretation, and to what extent various competencies should be considered linguistic. Malapropisms introduce expressions not covered by prior learning, or familiar expressions which cannot be interpreted by any of the abilities so far discussed. Malapropisms fall into a different category, one that may include such things as our ability to perceive a well-formed sentence when the actual utterance was incomplete or grammatically garbled, our ability to interpret words we have never heard before, to correct slips of the tongue, or to cope with new idiolects. These phenomena threaten standard descriptions of

linguistic competence (including descriptions for which I am responsible).

How should we understand or modify (1)–(3) to accommodate malapropisms? Principle (1) requires a competent interpreter to be prepared to interpret utterances of sentences he or she has never heard uttered before. This is possible because the interpreter can learn the semantic role of each of a finite number of words or phrases and can learn the semantic consequences of a finite number of modes of composition. This is enough to account for the ability to interpret utterances of novel sentences. And since the modes of composition can be iterated, there is no clear upper limit to the number of sentence utterances of which can be interpreted. The interpreter thus has a system for interpreting what he hears or says. You might think of this system as a machine which, when fed an arbitrary utterance (and certain parameters provided by the circumstances of the utterance), produces an interpretation. One model for such a machine is a theory of truth, more or less along the lines of a Tarski Truth definition. It provides a recursive characterization of the truth-conditions of all possible utterances of the speaker, and it does this through an analysis of utterances in terms of sentences made up from the finite vocabulary and the finite stock of modes of composition. I have frequently argued that command of such a theory would suffice for interpretation.[4] Here however there is no reason to be concerned with the details of the theory that can adequately model the ability of an interpreter. All that matters in the present discussion is that the theory has a finite base and is recursive, and these are features on which most philosophers and linguists agree.

To say that an explicit theory for interpreting a speaker is a model of the interpreter's linguistic competence is not to suggest that the interpreter knows any such theory. It is possible, of course, that most interpreters could be brought to acknowledge that they know some of the axioms of a theory of truth; for example, that a conjunction is true if and only if each of the conjuncts is true. And perhaps they also know theorems of the form 'An utterance of the sentence "There is life on Mars" is true and only if there is life on Mars at the time of the utterance'. On the other hand, no one now has explicit knowledge of a fully satisfactory theory for interpreting the speakers of any natural language.

In any case, claims about what would constitute a satisfactory theory are not, as I said, claims about the propositional knowledge of an interpreter, nor are they claims about the details of the inner workings of some part of the brain. They are rather claims about what must be said to give a satisfactory description of the competence of the interpreter. *We* cannot describe what an interpreter can do except by appeal to a recursive theory of a certain sort. It does not add anything to this thesis to say that if the theory does correctly describe the competence of an interpreter, some mechanism in the interpreter must correspond to the theory.

Principle (2) says that for communication to succeed, a systematic method of interpretation must be shared. (I shall henceforth assume there is no harm in calling such a method a theory, as if the interpreter were using the theory we use to describe his competence.) The sharing comes to this: the interpreter uses his theory to understand the speaker; the speaker uses the same (or an equivalent) theory to guide his speech. For the speaker, it is a theory about how the interpreter will interpret him. Obviously this principle does not demand that speaker and interpreter speak the same language. It is an enormous convenience that many people speak in similar ways, and therefore can be interpreted in more or less the same way. But in principle communication does not demand that any two people speak the same language. What must be shared is the interpreter's and the speaker's understanding of the speaker's words.

For reasons that will emerge, I do not think that principles (1) and (2) are incompatible with the existence of malapropisms; it is only when they are combined with principle (3) that there is trouble. Before discussing principle (3) directly, however, I want to introduce an apparent diversion.

The perplexing issue that I want to discuss can be separated off from some related matters by considering a distinction made by Keith Donnellan, and something he said in its defense. Donnellan famously distinguished between two uses of definite descriptions. The *referential* use is illustrated as follows: Jones says 'Smith's murderer is insane', meaning that a certain man, whom he (Jones) takes to have murdered Smith, is insane. Donnellan says that even if the man that Jones believes to have murdered Smith did not murder Smith, Jones has referred to the man he had in mind; and if that man is insane, Jones has said something true. The same sentence may be used *attributively* by someone who wants to assert that the murderer of Smith, whoever he may be, is insane. In this case, the speaker does not say something true if no one murdered Smith, nor has the speaker referred to anyone.

In reply, Alfred MacKay objected that Donnellan shared Humpty Dumpty's theory of meaning: '"When *I* use a word," Humpty Dumpty said, ". . . it means just what I choose it to mean."' In the conversation that went before, he had used the word 'glory' to mean 'a nice knock-down argument'. Donnellan, in answer, explains that intentions are connected with expectations and that you cannot intend to accomplish something by a certain means unless you believe or expect that the means will, or at least could, lead to the desired outcome. A speaker cannot, therefore, intend to mean something by what he says unless he believes his audience will interpret his words as he intends (the Gricean circle). Donnellan says,

If I were to end this reply to MacKay with the sentence 'There's glory for you' I would be guilty of arrogance and, no doubt, of overestimating the strength of what I have said, but given the background I do not think I could be accused of saying something unintelligible. I would be understood, and would I not have meant by 'glory' 'a nice knockdown argument'?[5]

I like this reply, and I accept Donnellan's original distinction between two uses of descriptions (there are many more than two). But apparently I disagree with *some* view of Donnellan's, because unlike him I see almost no connection between the answer to MacKay's objection and the remarks on reference. The reason is this. MacKay says you cannot change what words mean (and so their reference if that is relevant) merely by intending to; the answer is that this is true, but you can change the meaning provided you believe (and perhaps are justified in believing) that the interpreter has adequate clues for the new interpretation. You may deliberately provide those clues, as Donnellan did for his final 'There's glory for you'.

The trouble is that Donnellan's original distinction had nothing to do with words changing their meaning or reference. If, in the referential use, Jones refers to someone who did not murder Smith by using the description 'Smith's murderer', the reference is none the less achieved by way of the normal meanings of the words. The words therefore must have their usual reference. All that is needed, if we are to accept this way of describing the situation, is a firm sense of the difference between what *words* mean or refer to and what *speakers* mean or refer to. Jones may have referred to someone else by using words that referred to Smith's murderer; this is something he may have done in ignorance or deliberately. Similarly for Donnellan's claim that Jones has said something true when he says 'Smith's murderer is insane', provided the man he believes (erroneously) to have murdered Smith is insane. Jones has said something true by using a sentence that is false. This is done intentionally all the time, for example in irony or metaphor. A coherent theory could not allow that under the circumstances Jones' sentence was true; nor would Jones think so if he knew the facts. Jones' belief about who murdered Smith cannot change the truth of the sentence he uses (and for the same reason cannot change the reference of the words in the sentence).

Humpty Dumpty is out of it. He cannot mean what he says he means because he knows that 'There's glory for you' cannot be interpreted by Alice as meaning 'There's a nice knockdown argument for you'. We know he knows this because Alice says 'I don't know what you mean by "glory"', and Humpty Dumpty retorts, 'Of course you don't—til I tell you'. It is Mrs. Malaprop and Donnellan who interest me; Mrs. Malaprop because she gets away with it without even trying or knowing, and Donnellan because he gets away with it on purpose.

Here is what I mean by 'getting away with it': the interpreter comes to the occasion of utterance armed with a theory that tells him (or so he believes) what an arbitrary utterance of the speaker means. The speaker then says something with the intention that it will be interpreted in a certain way, and the expectation that it will be so interpreted. In fact this way is not provided for by the interpreter's theory. But the speaker is nevertheless understood; the interpreter adjusts his theory so that it yields the speaker's intended interpretation. The speaker has 'gotten away with it'. The speaker may or may not (Donnellan, Mrs. Malaprop) know that he has got away with anything; the interpreter may or may not know that the speaker intended to get away with anything. What is common to the cases is that the speaker expects to be, and is, interpreted as the speaker intended although the interpreter did not have a correct theory in advance.

We do not need bizarre anecdotes or wonderlands to make the point. We all get away with it all the time; understanding the speech of others depends on it. Take proper names. In small, isolated groups everyone may know the names everyone else knows, and so have ready in advance of a speech encounter a theory that will, without correction, cope with the names to be employed. But even this semantic paradise will be destroyed by each new nickname, visitor, or birth. If a taboo bans a name, a speaker's theory is wrong until he learns of this fact; similarly if an outrigger canoe is christened.

There is not, so far as I can see, any theory of names that gets around the problem. If some definite description gives the meaning of a name, an interpreter still must somehow add to his theory the fact that the name new to him is to be matched with the appropriate description. If understanding a name is to give some weight to an adequate number of descriptions true of the object named, it is even more evident that adding a name to one's way of interpreting a speaker depends on no rule clearly stated in advance. The various theories that discover an essential demonstrative element in names do provide at least a partial rule for adding new names. But the addition is still an addition to the method of interpretation—what we may think of as the interpreter's view of the current language of the speaker. Finding a demonstrative element in names, or for that matter in mass nouns or words for natural kinds, does not reduce these words to pure demonstratives; that is why a new word in any of these categories requires a change in the interpreter's theory, and therefore a change in our description of his understanding of the speaker.

Mrs. Malaprop and Donnellan make the case general. There is no word or construction that cannot be converted to a new use by an ingenious or ignorant speaker. And such conversion, while easier to explain because it involves mere substitution, is not the only kind. Sheer invention is equally possible, and we can be as good at interpreting it (say in Joyce or Lewis Carroll) as we are at interpreting the errors or twists of substitution. From the point of view of an ultimate explanation of how new concepts are acquired, learning to interpret a word that expresses a concept we do not already have is a far deeper and more interesting phenomenon than explaining the ability to use a word new to us for an old concept. But both require a change in one's way of interpreting the speech of another, or in speaking to someone who has the use of the word.

The contrast between acquiring a new concept or meaning along with a new word and merely acquiring a new word for an old concept would be salient if I were concerned with the infinitely difficult problem of how a first language is learned. By comparison, my problem is simple. I want to know how people who already have a language (whatever exactly that means) manage to apply their skill or knowledge to actual cases of interpretation. All the things I assume an interpreter knows or can do depend on his having a mature set of concepts, and being at home with the business of linguistic communication. My problem is to describe what is involved in the idea of 'having a language' or of being at home with the business of linguistic communication.

Here is a highly simplified and idealized proposal about what goes on. An interpreter has, at any moment of a speech transaction, what I persist in calling a theory. (I call it a theory, as remarked before, only because a description of the interpreter's competence requires a recursive account.) I assume that the interpreter's theory has been adjusted to the evidence so far available to him: knowledge of the character, dress, role, sex of the speaker, and whatever else has been gained by observing the speaker's behavior, linguistic or otherwise. As the speaker speaks his piece the interpreter alters his theory, entering hypotheses about new names, altering the interpretation of familiar predicates, and revising past interpretations of particular utterances in the light of new evidence.

Some of what goes on may be described as improving the method of interpretation as the evidential base enlarges. But much is not like that. When Donnellan ends his reply to MacKay by saying "There's glory for you," not only he, but his words, are correctly interpreted as meaning 'There's a nice knockdown argument for you'. That's how he intends us to interpret his words, and we know this, since we have, and he knows we have, and we know he knows we have (etc.), the background needed to provide the interpretation. But up to a certain point (before MacKay came on the scene) this interpretation of an earlier utterance by Donnellan of the same words would have been wrong. To put this differently: the theory we actually use to interpret an utterance is geared to the occasion. We may decide later we could have done better by the occasion, but this does not mean (necessarily) that we now have a better theory for the next occasion. The reason for this is, as we have seen, perfectly obvious: a speaker may provide us with information relevant to interpreting an utterance in the course of making the utterance.

Let us look at the process from the speaker's side. The speaker wants to be understood, so he intends to speak in such a way that he will be interpreted in a certain way. In order to judge how he will be interpreted, he forms, or uses, a picture of the interpreter's readiness to interpret along certain lines. Central to this picture is what the speaker believes is the starting theory of interpretation the interpreter has for him. The speaker does not necessarily speak in such a way as to prompt the interpreter to apply this prior theory; he may deliberately dispose the interpreter to modify his prior theory. But the speaker's view of the interpreter's prior theory is not irrelevant to what he says, nor to what he means by his words; it is an important part of what he has to go on if he wants to be understood.

I have distinguished what I have been calling the *prior theory* from what I shall henceforth call the *passing theory*. For the hearer, the prior theory expresses how he is prepared in advance to interpret an utterance of the speaker, while the passing theory is how he *does* interpret the utterance. For the speaker, the prior theory is what he *believes* the interpreter's prior theory to be, while his passing theory is the theory he *intends* the interpreter to use.

I am now in a position to state a problem that arises if we accept the distinction between the prior and the passing theory and also accept the account of linguistic competence given by principles (1)–(2). According to that account, each interpreter (and this includes speakers, since speakers must be interpreters) comes to a successful linguistic exchange prepared with a 'theory' which constitutes his basic linguistic competence, and which he shares with those with whom he communicates. Because each party has such a shared theory and knows that others share his theory, and knows that others know he knows (etc.), some would say that the knowledge or abilities that constitute the theory may be called conventions.

I think that the distinction between the prior and the passing theory, if taken seriously, undermines this commonly accepted account of linguistic competence and communication. Here is why. What must be shared for communication to succeed is the passing theory. For the passing theory is the one the interpreter actually uses to interpret an utterance, and it is the theory the speaker intends the interpreter to use. Only if these coincide is understanding complete. (Of course, there are degrees of success in communication; much may be right although something is wrong. This matter of degree is irrelevant to my argument.)

The passing theory is where, accident aside, agreement is greatest. As speaker and interpreter talk, their prior theories become more alike; so do their passing theories. The asymptote of agreement and understanding is when passing theories coincide. But the passing theory cannot in general correspond to an interpreter's linguistic competence. Not only does it have its changing list of proper names and gerrymandered vocabulary, but it includes every successful—i.e., correctly interpreted—use of any other word or phrase, no matter how far out of the ordinary. Every deviation from ordinary usage, as long as it is agreed on for the moment (knowingly deviant, or not, on one, or both, sides), is in the passing theory as a feature of what the words mean on that occasion. Such meanings, transient though they may be, are literal; they are what I have called first meanings. A passing theory is not a theory of what anyone (except perhaps a philosopher) would call an actual natural language. 'Mastery' of such a language would be useless, since knowing a passing theory is only knowing how to interpret a particular utterance on a particular occasion. Nor could such a language, if we want to call it that, be said to have been learned, or to be governed by conventions. Of course things previously learned were essential to arriving at the passing theory, but what was learned could not have been the passing theory.

Why should a passing theory be called a theory at all? For the sort of theory we have in mind is, in its formal structure, suited to be the theory for an entire language, even though its expected field of application is vanishingly small. The answer is that when a word or phrase temporarily or locally takes over the role of some other word or phrase (as treated in a prior theory, perhaps), the entire burden of that role, with all its implications for logical relations to other words, phrases, and sentences, must be carried along by the passing theory. Someone who grasps the fact that Mrs. Malaprop means 'epithet' when she says 'epitaph' must give 'epithet' all the powers 'epitaph' has for many other people. Only a full recursive theory can do justice to these powers. These remarks do not depend on supposing Mrs. Malaprop will always make this 'mistake'; once is enough to summon up a passing theory assigning a new role to 'epitaph'.

An interpreter's prior theory has a better chance of describing what we might think of as a natural language, particularly a prior theory brought to a first conversation. The less we know about the speaker, assuming we know he belongs to our language community, the more nearly our prior theory will simply be the theory we expect someone who hears our unguarded speech to use. If we ask for a cup of coffee, direct a taxi driver, or order a crate of lemons, we may know so little about our intended interpreter that we can do no better than to assume that he will interpret our speech along what we take to be standard lines. But all this is relative. In fact we always have the interpreter in mind; there is no such thing as how we expect, in the abstract, to be interpreted. We inhibit our higher vocabulary, or encourage it, depending on the most general considerations, and we cannot fail to have premonitions as to which of the proper names we know are apt to be correctly understood.

In any case, my point is this: most of the time prior theories will not be shared, and there is no reason why they should be. Certainly it is not a condition of successful communication that prior theories be shared: consider the malaprop from ignorance. Mrs. Malaprop's theory, prior and passing, is that 'A nice derangement of epitaphs' means a nice arrangement of epithets. An interpreter who, as we say, knows English, but does not know the verbal habits of Mrs. Malaprop, has a prior theory according to which 'A nice derangement of epitaphs' means a nice derangement of epitaphs; but his passing theory agrees with that of Mrs. Malaprop if he understands her words.

It is quite clear that in general the prior theory is neither shared by speaker and interpreter nor is it what we would normally call a language. For the prior theory has in it all the features special to the idiolect of the speaker that the interpreter is in a position to take into account before the utterance begins. One way to appreciate the difference between the prior theory and our ordinary idea of a person's language is to reflect on the fact that an interpreter must be expected to have quite different prior theories for different speakers—not as different, usually, as his passing theories; but these are matters that depend on how well the interpreter knows his speaker.

Neither the prior nor the passing theory describes what we would call the language a person knows, and neither theory characterizes a speaker's or interpreter's linguistic competence. Is there any theory that would do better?

Perhaps it will be said that what is essential to the mastery of a language is not knowledge of any particular vocabulary, or even detailed grammar, much less knowledge of what any speaker is apt to succeed in making his words

and sentences mean. What is essential is a basic framework of categories and rules, a sense of the way English (or any) grammars may be constructed, plus a skeleton list of interpreted words for fitting into the basic framework. If I put all this vaguely, it is only because I want to consider a large number of actual or possible proposals in one fell swoop; for I think they all fail to resolve our problem. They fail for the same reasons the more complete and specific prior theories fail: none of them satisfies the demand for a description of an ability that speaker and interpreter share and that is adequate to interpretation.

First, any general framework, whether conceived as a grammar for English, or a rule for accepting grammars, or a basic grammar plus rules for modifying or extending it—any such general framework, by virtue of the features that make it general, will by itself be insufficient for interpreting particular utterances. The general framework or theory, whatever it is, may be a key ingredient in what is needed for interpretation, but it can't be all that is needed since it fails to provide the interpretation of particular words and sentences as uttered by a particular speaker. In this respect it is like a prior theory, only worse because it is less complete.

Second, the framework theory must be expected to be different for different speakers. The more general and abstract it is, the more difference there can be without it mattering to communication. The theoretical possibility of such divergence is obvious; but once one tries to imagine a framework rich enough to serve its purpose, it is clear that such differences must also be actual. It is impossible to give examples, of course, until it is decided what to count in the framework: a sufficiently explicit framework could be discredited by a single malapropism. There is some evidence of a more impressive sort that internal grammars do differ among speakers of 'the same language'. James McCawley reports that recent work by Haber shows

that there is appreciable variation as to what rules of plural formation different speakers have, the variation being manifested in such things as the handling of novel words that an investigator has presented his subjects with, in the context of a task that will force them to use the word in the plural.... Haber suggests that her subjects, rather than having a uniformly applicable process of plural formation, each have a "core" system, which covers a wide range of cases, but not necessarily everything, plus strategies . . . for handling cases that are not covered by the "core" system . . . . Haber's data suggest that speakers of what are to the minutest details "the same dialect" often have acquired grammars that differ in far more respects than their speech differs in.[6]

I have been trying to throw doubt on how clear the idea of 'speaking the same dialect' is, but here we may assume that it at least implies the frequent sharing of passing theories.

Bringing in grammars, theories, or frameworks more general than, and prior to, prior theories just emphasizes the problem I originally presented in terms of the contrast between prior theories and passing theories. Stated more broadly now, the problem is this: what interpreter and speaker share, to the extent that communication succeeds, is not learned and so is not a language governed by rules or conventions known to speaker and interpreter in advance; but what the speaker and interpreter know in advance is not (necessarily) shared, and so is not a language governed by shared rules or conventions. What is shared is, as before, the passing theory; what is given in advance is the prior theory, or anything on which it may in turn be based.

What I have been leaving out of account up to now is what Haber calls a 'strategy', which is a nice word for the mysterious process by which a speaker or hearer uses what he knows in advance plus present data to produce a passing theory. What two people need, if they are to understand one another through speech, is the ability to converge on passing theories from utterance to utterance. Their starting points, however far back we want to take them, will usually be very different—as different as the ways in which they acquired their linguistic skills. So also, then, will the strategies and stratagems that bring about convergence differ.

Perhaps we can give content to the idea of two people 'having the same language' by saying that they tend to converge on passing theories; degree or relative frequency of convergence would then be a measure of similarity of language. What use can we find, however, for the concept of a language? We could hold that

any theory on which a speaker and interpreter converge is a language; but then there would be a new language for every unexpected turn in the conversation, and languages could not be learned and no one would want to master most of them.

We just made a sort of sense of the idea of two people 'having the same language', though we could not explain what a language is. It is easy to see that the idea of 'knowing' a language will be in the same trouble, as will the project of characterizing the abilities or capacities a person must have if he commands a language. But we might try to say in what a person's ability to interpret or speak to another person consists: it is the ability that permits him to construct a correct, that is, convergent, passing theory for speech transactions with that person. Again, the concept allows of degrees of application.

This characterization of linguistic ability is so nearly circular that it cannot be wrong: it comes to saying that the ability to communicate by speech consists in the ability to make oneself understood, and to understand. It is only when we look at the structure of this ability that we realize how far we have drifted from standard ideas of language mastery. For we have discovered no learnable common core of consistent behavior, no shared grammar or rules, no portable interpreting machine set to grind out the meaning of an arbitrary utterance. We may say that linguistic ability is the ability to converge on a passing theory from time to time— this is what I have suggested, and I have no better proposal. But if we do say this, then we should realize that we have abandoned not only the ordinary notion of a language, but we have erased the boundary between knowing a language and knowing our way around in the world generally. For there are no rules for arriving at passing theories, no rules in any strict sense, as opposed to rough maxims and methodological generalities. A passing theory really is like a theory at least in this, that it is derived by wit, luck, and wisdom from a private vocabulary and grammar, knowledge of the ways people get their point across, and rules of thumb for figuring out what deviations from the dictionary are most likely. There is no more chance of regularizing, or teaching, this process than there is of regularizing or teaching the process of creating new theories to cope with new data in any field—for that is what this process involves.

The problem we have been grappling with depends on the assumption that communication by speech requires that speaker and interpreter have learned or somehow acquired a common method or theory of interpretation—as being able to operate on the basis of shared conventions, rules, or regularities. The problem arose when we realized that no method or theory fills this bill. The solution to the problem is clear. In linguistic communication nothing corresponds to a linguistic competence as often described: that is, as summarized by principles (1)–(3). The solution is to give up the principles. Principles (1) and (2) survive when understood in rather unusual ways, but principle (3) cannot stand, and it is unclear what can take its place. I conclude that there is no such thing as a language, not if a language is anything like what many philosophers and linguists have supposed. There is therefore no such thing to be learned, mastered, or born with. We must give up the idea of a clearly defined shared structure which language-users acquire and then apply to cases. And we should try again to say how convention in any important sense is involved in language; or, as I think, we should give up the attempt to illuminate how we communicate by appeal to conventions.

NOTES

1. *The New Yorker,* 4 April 1977, p. 56.
2. Jonathan Bennett, *Linguistic Behavior,* Cambridge, 1976, p. 186.
3. Shakespeare, Sonnet 53.
4. See the essays on radical interpretation in my *Inquiries into Truth and Interpretation,* Oxford, 1984.
5. Keith Donnellan, "Putting Humpty Dumpty Together Again," *The Philosophical Review,* 77 (1968), p. 213. Alfred MacKay's article, "Mr. Donnellan and Humpty Dumpty on Referring" appeared in the same issue of *The Philosophical Review,* pp. 197–202.
6. James McCawley, "Some Ideas Not to Live By," *Die Neuern Sprachen,* 75 (1976), p. 157. These results are disputed by those who believe the relevant underlying rules and structures are prewired. My point obviously does not depend on the example, or the level at which deviations are empirically possible.

41 Indeterminacy, Empiricism, and the First Person

JOHN R. SEARLE

The aim of this article is to assess the significance of W. V. Quine's indeterminacy thesis. If Quine is right, the thesis has vast ramifications for the philosophy of language and mind; if he is wrong, we ought to be able to say exactly how and why.

I

Let us begin by stating the behaviorist assumptions from which Quine originally proceeds. For the sake of developing an empirical theory of meaning, he confines his analysis to correlations between external stimuli and dispositions to verbal behavior. In thus limiting the analysis, he does not claim to capture all the intuitions we have about the pretheoretical notion, but rather the "objective reality"[1] that is left over if we strip away the confusions and incoherencies in the pretheoretical "meaning." The point of the "behavioristic ersatz" is to give us a scientific, empirical account of the objective reality of meaning. On this view, the objective reality is simply a matter of being disposed to produce utterances in response to external stimuli. The stimuli are defined entirely in terms of patterns of stimulations of the nerve endings, and the responses entirely in terms of sounds and sound patterns that the speaker is disposed to emit. But we are not supposed to think that between the stimulus and the verbal response there are any mental entities. We are not supposed to think that there is any consciousness, intentionality, thoughts, or any internal "meanings" connecting the stimuli to the noises. There is just the pattern of stimulus and the pattern of learned response. There will, of course, be neurophysiological mechanisms mediating the input and the output, but the details of their structure do not matter to a theory of meaning, since any mechanism whatever that systematically associated stimulus and response would do the job as well. For example, any computer or piece of machinery that could emit the right sounds in response to the right stimuli would have "mastered" a language as well as any other speaker, because that is all there is to the mastery of a language. Quine, I take it, does not deny the existence of inner mental states and processes; he just thinks they are useless and irrelevant to developing an empirical theory of language.

Such a view is linguistic behaviorism with a vengeance. It has often been criticized and, in my view, often refuted, for example, by Noam Chomsky in his review of B. F. Skinner.[2] On one construal, my Chinese room argument can also be interpreted as a refutation.[3] One way to refute this version of extreme linguistic behaviorism (let us call it "behaviorism" for short) would be to offer a reductio ad absurdum of its

From *Journal of Philosophy* 84 (1987): 123–146. Copyright © 1987 by *Journal of Philosophy*. Reprinted with the permission of the author and the publisher.

basic premises; and, indeed, it seems to me that Quine has offered us one such famous reductio (ch. 2). If behaviorism were true, then certain distinctions known independently to be valid would be lost. For example, we all know that, when a speaker utters an expression, there is a distinction between his meaning rabbit and his meaning rabbit stage or undetached rabbit part. But, if we actually applied the assumptions of behaviorism to interpreting the language of an alien tribe, we would find there was no way of making these distinctions as plain facts of the matter about the language used by the native speakers. Suppose, for example, the natives shouted "Gavagai!" whenever a rabbit ran past, and suppose we tried to translate this into our English as "There's a rabbit!" or simply, "Rabbit!" The stimulus—which, remember, is defined entirely in terms of stimulations of nerve endings—is equally appropriate for translating "Gavagai!" as "There's a stage in the life history of a rabbit!" or "There's an undetached part of a rabbit!" The same pattern of stimulation of the photoreceptor cells does duty for all three translations. So, if all there were to meaning were patterns of stimulus and response, then it would be impossible to discriminate meanings, which are in fact discriminable. That is the reductio ad absurdum.

It is crucial to this argument to see that, even if we got more patterns of stimulus and response for our tribe, that still would not enable us to make the discriminations we need to make. Suppose we learned their expression for "is the same as' and tried to use it to enable us to tell whether they meant rabbit or rabbit stage or undetached rabbit part. We could get the rabbit to run past again, and if they said "Same gavagai," we would have at least pretty good evidence that they did not mean, for example, rabbit stage by 'gavagai'. But this would be no help to us at all, because exactly the same sorts of doubt that we had about 'gavagai' in the first place would now apply to the expression for 'is the same as'. As far as matching stimuli and responses is concerned, we could equally well translate it as 'is a part of' or 'belongs with'. The conclusion we are forced to is this: assuming linguistic behaviorism, there will be endlessly different and inconsistent translations, all

of which can be made consistent with all actual and possible evidence concerning the totality of the speech dispositions of the native speakers. As far as the behavioral evidence is concerned, there is nothing to choose between one translation and another even though the two are inconsistent.[4]

On Quine's view, the unit of analysis for empirically testing translations is not words or individual expressions but whole sentences. The only direct empirical checks we have on translations are for those sentences which are associated directly with stimulus conditions, the "observation sentences." On this view, 'Gavagai!', 'Rabbit!', 'Rabbit stage!', 'Undetached rabbit part!' all have the same determinate stimulus meaning; they have "stimulus synonymy," since the same stimulus conditions would prompt assent to or dissent from them. The indeterminacy arises when we attempt to form "analytical hypotheses" that state the meanings of particular words or other elements of the sentence. The indeterminacy that attaches to the elements of observation sentences is at least constrained by the stimulus conditions that prompt assent to or dissent from those sentences. The determinate stimulus meaning that attaches to observation sentences should at least seem puzzling to us, however, since sentences that have the same stimulus meaning do not in any ordinary sense of 'meaning' have the same meaning. By any reasonable standard of objective reality, it is a matter of objective reality that "There's a rabbit" and "There's an undetached rabbit part" just do not mean the same things. The significance of this point for the over-all theory will emerge later.

Now, why exactly is Quine's argument a reductio ad absurdum of extreme linguistic behaviorism? There are two positions which are inconsistent:

1. The thesis of behaviorism: The objective reality of meaning consists entirely of correlations between external stimuli and dispositions to verbal behavior.[5]

2. In a given case of speech behavior, there can be a plain fact of the matter about whether a native speaker meant, e.g., rabbit, as opposed to rabbit stage, or unde-

tached rabbit part, by the utterance of an expression.

If alternative and inconsistent translation schemes can all be made consistent with the same patterns of stimulus and response, then there cannot be any fact of the matter about which is right, because, according to (1), there isn't anything else to be right about. But this is inconsistent with (2); so if we accept (2), (1) must be false.

I think it is clear which of (1) or (2) we have to give up. Quine has simply refuted extreme linguistic behaviorism. But why am I so confident about that? Why not give up (2)? The answer is the obvious one: if behaviorism were correct, it would have to be correct for us as speakers of English as well as for speakers of Gavagai-talk. And we know from our own case that we do mean by 'rabbit' something different from 'rabbit stage' or 'undetached rabbit part'. If any English-speaking neighbor, having read Quine, decides that he can't tell whether by "'rabbit' I mean rabbit, undetached rabbit part, or rabbit stage, then so much the worse for him. When I saw a rabbit recently, as I did in fact, and I called it a rabbit, I meant rabbit. In all discussions in the philosophy of language and the philosophy of mind, it is absolutely essential at some point to remind oneself of the first-person case. No one, for example, can convince us by argument, however ingenious, that pains do not exist if in fact we have them, and similar considerations apply to Quine's example. If somebody has a theory according to which there isn't any difference between my meaning rabbit and my meaning rabbit part, then I know that his theory is simply mistaken; and the only interest his theory can have for me is in trying to discover where he went wrong. I want to emphasize this point, since it is often regarded as somehow against the rules in these discussions to raise the first-person case.

In a different philosophical environment from the one we live in, this might well be the end of the discussion. Linguistic behaviorism was tried and refuted by Quine using reductio ad absurdum arguments. But, interestingly, he does not regard it as having been refuted. He wants to hold behaviorism, together with the conclusion

that, where analytical hypotheses about meaning are concerned, there simply are no facts of the matter, together with a revised version of (2), the thesis that we can in fact make valid distinctions between different translations. And some authors, such as Donald Davidson[6] and John Wallace,[7] who reject behaviorism, nonetheless accept a version of the indeterminacy thesis. Davidson, in fact, considers and rejects my appeal to the first-person case. Why does the thesis of the indeterminacy of translation continue to be accepted? And what larger issues are raised by the dispute? I now turn to these questions.

II

We need to consider three theses:

A. The indeterminacy of translation
B. The inscrutability of reference
C. The relativity of ontology

In this section, I will first explain the relations between (A) and (B), and then try to say more about the character of the thesis Quine is advancing. In the next section, I will try to show that (C) is best construed as an unsuccessful maneuver to rescue the theory from the apparently absurd consequences of (A) and (B).

The thesis of the indeterminacy of translation is that, where questions of translation and, therefore, of meaning are concerned, there is no such thing as getting it right or wrong. This is not because of an epistemic gulf between evidence and conclusion, but because there is no fact of the matter to be right or wrong about.

From (A), so stated, (B) follows immediately. For if there is no fact of the matter about whether or not a speaker *meant* rabbit as opposed to rabbit stage, then equally, there is no fact of the matter about whether or not he is *referring* to a rabbit or a rabbit stage. In Fregean terminology, indeterminacy of sense entails inscrutability of reference.

Now, if we were to construe (A) as just the claim that there are no psychological facts of the matter about meanings in addition to facts about correlations of stimulus and response, then it would seem puzzling that we didn't derive that conclusion immediately from extreme linguistic behaviorism. It would seem puzzling that there is so much heavy going about 'gavagai', etc. But thesis (A) is stronger than just the thesis of behaviorism; that is, it is stronger than the claim that there isn't any meaning in addition to correlations of stimulus and response. It says further that there is an indefinite number of equally valid but inconsistent ways of correlating stimulus and verbal response in the vocabulary of an alien language with that of our language. The thesis that there are no objectively real meanings in addition to dispositions to verbal behavior was already assumed at the beginning of the discussion. Quine rejected any appeal to meanings, in any psychological sense, from the start. That was never at issue. What was at issue was the possibility of empirically motivated correct translations from one language to another, *given behaviorism;* the issue was whether or not there is an empirically motivated notion of sameness of meaning left over after we have adopted extreme linguistic behaviorism.

We will see the importance of this consideration when we see why several criticisms that are made of Quine miss the mark. Chomsky, for example, has repeatedly claimed that Quine's thesis of indeterminacy is simply the familiar underdetermination of hypothesis by empirical evidence.[8] Because any empirical hypothesis makes a claim that goes beyond the evidence, there will always be inconsistent hypotheses that are consistent with any actual or possible evidence. But underdetermination, so construed, does not entail that there is "no fact of the matter." Now Quine's response to Chomsky's objection seems at first sight puzzling. He grants that indeterminacy is underdetermination, but claims that it is underdetermination at one remove and, therefore, that there is no fact of the matter. He claims that, even if we have established all the facts about physics, semantics is still indeterminate. He writes:

Then when I say there is no fact of the matter, as regards, say, the two rival manuals of translation, what I mean is that both manuals are compatible with all the same distributions of states and relations over elementary particles. In a word, they are physically equivalent.[9]

But this answer seems inadequate to Chomsky and at one time seemed inadequate to me,

because underdetermination at one remove is still just underdetermination. It wouldn't be sufficient to show that there is no fact of the matter. The objection to Quine that Chomsky makes (and that I used to make) is simply this: for any given higher-level "emergent" or "supervenient" property, there will be (at least) two levels of underdetermination. There will be a level of the underdetermination of the underlying physical theory, but there will also be a theory at the higher level, for example, at the level of psychology; and information at the level of microphysics is, by itself, not sufficient to determine the level of psychology. As Chomsky once put it, if you fix the physics, the psychology is still open; but equally, if you fix the psychology, the physics is still open. For example, the theory of all the dispositions of physical particles that go to make up my body, by itself, would leave open the question of whether or not I am in pain. The thesis that I am in pain is underdetermined at one remove. Now why is it supposed to be any different with meaning? Of course, there are two levels of underdetermination, but in both cases there are facts of the matter—in one case, facts of psychology, and in the other case, facts of physics. I now believe that this answer misses Quine's point altogether because it fails to see that he is assuming from the start that there is no psychologically real level of meaning beyond simple physical dispositions to respond to verbal stimuli. To repeat, Quine assumes from the very start the nonexistence of (objectively real) meanings in any psychological sense. If you assume that they are so much as possible, his argument fails. But now it begins to look as though the real issue is not about indeterminacy at all; it is about extreme linguistic behaviorism.

Many philosophers assume that Quine's discussion is sufficient to refute any sort of mentalistic or intentionalistic theory of meaning. But what our discussion of Chomsky's objections suggests is that this misconstrues the nature of the discussion altogether. It is only *assuming* the nonexistence of intentionalistic meanings that the argument for indeterminacy succeeds at all. Once that assumption is abandoned, that is, once we stop begging the question against mentalism, it seems to me that Chomsky's objection is completely valid. Where meanings psychologically construed are concerned, there is the familiar underdetermination of hypothesis by evidence, and that underdetermination is in addition to the underdetermination at the level of physical particles or brute physical behavior. So what? These are familiar points about any psychological theory. There is nothing special about meaning and nothing to show that where meaning is concerned there is no fact of the matter.

To deepen our understanding of these points, we must now turn to the thesis of the relativity of ontology.

III

Quine recognizes that the proofs of the indeterminacy of translation and of the inscrutability of reference seem to be leading to absurd consequences. He writes:

We seem to be maneuvering ourselves into the absurd position that there is no difference on any terms, interlinguistic or intralinguistic, objective or subjective, between referring to rabbits and referring to rabbit parts or stages; or between referring to formulas and referring to their Gödel numbers. Surely this is absurd, for it would imply that there is no difference between the rabbit and each of its parts or stages, and no difference between a formula and its Gödel number. Reference would seem now to become nonsense not just in radical translation but at home.[10]

The indeterminacy thesis seems to have the absurd consequence that indeterminacy and inscrutability apply to the first-person case, to oneself: "If it is to make sense to say even of oneself that one is referring to rabbits and formulas and not to rabbit stages and Gödel numbers, then it should make sense equally to say it of someone else."[11]

Quine recognizes something that many of his critics have missed, and that is the real absurdity of the indeterminacy argument once you follow out its logical consequences: followed to its conclusion, the argument has nothing essentially to do with translating from one language to another or even understanding another speaker of one's own language. If the argument is valid, then it must have the result that there isn't any difference *for me* between *meaning* rabbit or rabbit stage, and that has the further result that there isn't any difference for me

between *referring* to a rabbit and referring to a rabbit stage, and there isn't any difference for me between something's *being* a rabbit and its *being* a rabbit stage. And all of this is a consequence of the behaviorist assumption that there isn't any meaning beyond behaviorist meaning. Once we concede that as far as behaviorist "stimulus meaning" is concerned, 'There's a rabbit' and 'There's a rabbit stage' are "stimulus synonymous," then the rest follows, because on the behaviorist hypothesis there isn't any other kind of objectively real meaning or synonymy. I think, with Quine, that these consequences are absurd on their face, but if there is any doubt about their absurdity, recall that the whole argument about 'Gavagai' was understood by me (or you) only because we know the difference for our own case between meaning rabbit, rabbit stage, rabbit part, etc.

I said in the last section that the thesis of indeterminacy is the thesis that there cannot be empirically well-motivated translations of the words of one language into those of another, given behaviorism. But if this thesis is correct, then there cannot even be "correct" translations from a language into itself. By observing my idiolect of English, I can't tell whether by 'rabbit' I mean rabbit stage, rabbit part, or whatnot. Quine need not have considered Gavagai speakers. He could have simply observed in his own case that there was no "empirical" difference between his meaning one thing or the other and, therefore, that there was no real difference at all. And that result, as he correctly sees, is absurd. *If the indeterminacy thesis were really true, we would not even be able to understand its formulation; for when we were told there was no "fact of the matter" about the correctness of the translation between rabbit and rabbit stage, we would not have been able to hear any (objectively real) difference between the two English expressions to start with.*

Here is Quine's picture: I am a machine capable of receiving "nerve hits" and capable of emitting sounds. I am disposed to emit certain sounds in response to certain nerve hits; and, objectively speaking, that is all there is to meaning. Now the stimulus meaning of "There's a rabbit stage" is the same as that of "There's a rabbit," since the sounds are caused by the same nerve hits. It isn't just that Quine has a technical notion of "stimulus meaning" which he wants to add to our commonsense notion of meaning. No, he thinks that, as far as objective reality is concerned, stimulus meaning is all the meaning there is. And it is his notion of stimulus meaning which generates the absurdity.

The resolution of this "quandary," according to Quine, lies in perceiving the *relativity* of reference and ontology. "Reference is nonsense except relative to a coordinate system",[12] and the coordinate system is provided by a background language. The question for me of whether I am referring to a rabbit by 'rabbit' is answered by simply taking the English background language for granted, by "acquiescing in our mother tongue and taking its words at face value" (49). Just as in physics it makes sense to speak of the position and velocity of an object only relative to a coordinate system, so analogously it makes sense to talk of the reference of an expression only relative to some background language. Indeed, where translation from another language is concerned, reference is doubly relative: relative first to the selection of a background language into which to translate the target language, and relative second to the arbitrary selection of a translation manual for translating words of the target into the background.

Now, does this answer remove the apparent absurdity? I do not see how it does; indeed I shall argue that it simply repeats the problem without solving it.

I believe that with the thesis of relativity we have reached the crux of the indeterminacy argument. For this issue we can forget all about 'gavagai' and radical translation; they were merely picturesque illustrations of the consequences of behaviorism. The crucial thesis can be exemplified as follows:

There is no empirical difference between the claim that I meant rabbit by 'rabbit' and the claim that I meant, e.g., rabbit stage by 'rabbit'.

This is a consequence of the original thesis of *Word and Object,* and it is now admitted to be absurd. So to get out of the absurdity we substitute a revised relativity thesis:

Relative to one arbitrarily selected translation scheme we can truly say that I meant rabbit, relative to another scheme, equally arbitrary, that I meant, e.g.,

rabbit stage, *and there is no empirical difference between the two schemes.*

But the revised thesis is just as absurd as— and indeed expresses the same absurdity as— the first. And this should not surprise us, because the original absurdity arose in a discourse that already was relativized; it arose relative to my idiolect of English. The absurdity is that, if I assume my idiolect is a fixed set of dispositions to verbal behavior, then any translation of one word into itself or another of my idiolect is absolutely arbitrary and without empirical content. There is no way for me to tell whether by 'rabbit' I mean rabbit, rabbit stage, rabbit part, etc. This applies even to simple disquotation: there is no way even to justify the claim that by 'rabbit' I mean rabbit. Now, it does not meet this difficulty to say that we can fix meaning and reference by making an arbitrary selection of a translation manual. The arbitrariness of the selection of the translation manual is precisely the problem, since it is a reflection of the arbitrariness of the selection from among the original range of alternative analytical hypotheses. Quine's thesis of relativity does not remove the absurdity; it simply restates it.

When Quine advises us to acquiesce in our mother tongue and take words at their face value, we have to remind ourselves that, on his account, our mother tongue consists entirely of a set of dispositions to verbal behavior in response to sensory stimuli, and, so construed, the empirical face value of 'rabbit' and that of 'rabbit stage' are indistinguishable. We really cannot have it both ways. We cannot, on the one hand, insist on a rigorous behaviorism that implies that there is no fact of the matter and then, when we get in trouble, appeal to a naive notion of a mother tongue or home language with words having a face value in excess of their empirical behavioral content. If we are serious about our behaviorism, the mother tongue is the mother of indeterminacy, and the face value is counterfeit if it suggests that there are empirical differences when in fact there are none.

But what about the analogy with physics? Will that rescue us from the absurdity? One of the peculiar features of this entire discussion is the speed with which breathtaking conclusions are drawn on the basis of a few sketchy remarks and underdescribed examples. To try to get at least a little bit clearer about what is going on, let us try to state this particular issue a little more carefully. To begin, I want to state some more of the commonsense, pre-Quinean intuitions that lead me, and to a certain extent Quine himself, to think that the theses of indeterminacy and inscrutability lead or threaten to lead to absurd results. To make it intuitively easier, let us consider the case of translation from one language to another, though it is important to remember that any difficulty we find with translation from one language to another we will also find with the case of one language alone. Let us suppose that, as I am out driving with two French friends, Henri and Pierre, a rabbit suddenly crosses in front of the car, and I declare, "There's a rabbit." Let us suppose further that Henri and Pierre do not know the meaning of the English 'rabbit', so each tries to translate it in a way that is consistent with my dispositions to verbal behavior. Henri, we may suppose, concludes that 'rabbit' means *stade de lapin*. Pierre, on the basis of the same evidence, decides it means *parti non-détachée d'un lapin*. Now according to our pre-Quinean intuitions, the problem for both Henri and Pierre is quite simple: they both got it wrong. It is just a plain fact about me that when I said "rabbit," I did not mean *stade de lapin* or partie *non-détachée d'un lapin*. Those are just bad translations. Of course, when I say that, I am making certain assumptions about the meanings of these expressions in French and, therefore, about the meanings that Henri and Pierre attach to these expressions. And these assumptions, like any other empirical assumptions, are subject to the usual underdetermination of hypotheses by evidence. Assuming that I got the assumptions right, Henri and Pierre are just mistaken. But even assuming that I got my assumptions wrong, if they are wrong in a certain specific way, then Henri and Pierre are just right. That is, if, for example, Henri means by *stade de lapin* what I mean by *lapin,* then he understands me perfectly; he simply has an eccentric way of expressing this understanding. The important thing to notice is that, in either case, whether they are right about my original meaning or I am right in thinking that they are wrong, there is a plain fact of the matter to be right or wrong about.[13]

These are some of the commonsense intuitions that we need to answer. Does the analogy with the relativity of motion get us out of this quandary? Let's take the idea seriously and try it out. Suppose that in the car during our rabbit conversation Henri expresses the view that we are going 60 miles an hour, while Pierre on the other hand insists we are going only 5 miles an hour. Later it turns out that Pierre was observing a large truck we were passing and was estimating our speed relative to it, while Henri was talking about our speed relative to the road surface. Once these relativities are identified there is no longer even the appearance of paradox or disagreement. Pierre and Henri are both right. But are they analogously both right about the translation of 'rabbit' once the coordinate systems have been identified? Is it a case of moving at different semantic speeds relative to different linguistic coordinate systems? It seems to me that these absurdities are just as absurd when relativized.

On Quine's view, I am right relative to English in thinking that I meant rabbit, Pierre is right relative to French in thinking that I meant *partie non-détachée d'un lapin,* and Henri is also right relative to French in thinking that I meant *stade de lapin—even though Henri and Pierre are inconsistent with each other, and both are inconsistent with the translation I would give.* And it is not an answer to this point to maintain that the appearance of inconsistency derives from the fact that we each have different translation manuals, because the problem we are trying to deal with is that we know independently that both of their translation manuals are just plain wrong. It was the apparent wrongness of the translation manuals that we were trying to account for. To put the point more generally; the aim of the analogy with physics was to show how we could remove the apparent paradoxes and absurdities by showing that they were just as apparent but as unreal as in the physics case. We see that there is no absurdity in supposing that we can be going both 5 and 60 miles an hour at the same time, once we see that our speed is relative to different coordinate systems. But the analogy between physics and meaning fails. Even after we have relativized meaning, we are still left with the same absurdities we had before.

Why does the analogy break down? In physics the position and motion of a body consist entirely in its relations to some coordinate system; but there is more to meaning than just the relations that a word has to the language of which it is a part; otherwise the question of translation could never arise in the first place. We can't detach the specific motion or position of an object from a reference to a specific coordinate system and translate it into another system in the way we can detach a specific meaning from a specific linguistic system and find an expression that has that very meaning in another linguistic system. Of course, a word means what it does only relative[14] to a language of which it is a part, but the very relativity of the *possession* of meaning presupposes the nonrelativity of the *meaning* possessed. This has no analogue in the relativity of physical position and motion.

Someone might object that I seem to be assuming the very "myth of the museum" that Quine is challenging, the view that there exists a class of mental entities called "meanings." But my point is neutral between the various theories of meaning. Let meaning be a matter of ideas in the head a la Hume, dispositions to behavior a la Quine, uses of words a la Wittgenstein, or intentional capacities a la me. It doesn't matter for this point. Whatever meaning is, we need to distinguish the true thesis that a word has the particular meaning it has only relative to a language from the false thesis that the meaning itself is relative to a language. Indeed, we are now in a position to state the argument in a way that is independent of any particular theory of meaning: grant me that there is a distinction between meaningful and meaningless phonetic sequences (words). Thus, in English, 'rabbit' is meaningful, 'flurg' is meaningless. Such remarks are always made relative to a language. Perhaps in some other language 'flurg' is meaningful and 'rabbit' is meaningless. But if 'rabbit' is meaningful in English and 'flurg' is meaningless, there must be some feature that 'rabbit' has in English which 'flurg' lacks. Let's call that feature its *meaning,* and the class of such features of words we can call *meanings.* Now, from the fact that 'rabbit' has the particular feature it has relative to English, it does not follow that

the feature, its meaning, can exist only relative to English. Indeed, the question whether 'rabbit' has a translation into another language is precisely the question whether in the other language there is an expression with that very feature. The analogy between relativity in physics and semantics breaks down because there are no features of position and motion except relations to coordinate systems. And Quine's argument is a reductio ad absurdum because it shows that the totality of dispositions to speech behavior is unable to account for distinctions concerning the feature, meaning, which we know independently to exist, the distinction between the meaning of 'rabbit' and that of 'rabbit stage', for example. You cannot avoid the reductio by calling attention to the fact that 'rabbit' has the feature, its meaning, only relative to English, because the reductio is about the feature itself, and the feature itself is not relative to English.

My aim so far has not been to refute extreme linguistic behaviorism, but to show:

> First, the thesis of the indeterminacy of translation is just as well (indeed, I think better) construed as a reductio ad absurdum of the premises from which it was derived as it is construed as a surprising result from established premises.

> Second, the theory of the relativity of ontology does not succeed in answering the apparent absurdities that the thesis of indeterminacy and inscrutability leads us into.

What about refuting linguistic behaviorism on its own terms? There have been so many refutations of behaviorism in its various forms that it seems otiose to repeat any of them here. But it is worth pointing out that Quine's argument has the form of standard and traditional refutations of behaviorism. We know from our own case, from the first-person case, that behaviorism is wrong, because we know that our own mental phenomena are not equivalent to dispositions to behavior. Having the pain is one thing, being disposed to exhibit pain behavior is another. Pain behavior is insufficient to account for pain, because one might exhibit the behavior and not have the pain, and one might have the pain and not exhibit it. Analogously, on Quine's argument, dispositions to verbal behavior are not sufficient to account for meanings, because one might exhibit behavior appropriate for a certain meaning, but that still might not be what one meant.

If someone has a new theory of the foundations of mathematics and from his new axioms he can derive that $2 + 2 = 5$, what are we to say? Do we say that he has made an important new discovery? Or do we say, rather, that he has disproved his axioms by a reductio ad absurdum? I find it hard to imagine a more powerful reductio ad absurdum argument against behaviorism than Quine's indeterminacy argument, because it denies the existence of distinctions that we know from our own case are valid.

IV

I have tried to show how the doctrines of indeterminacy and inscrutability depend on the special assumptions of behaviorism and that, consequently, the results can equally be taken as a refutation of that view. But now an interesting question arises. Why do philosophers who have no commitment to behaviorism accept these views? I will consider Donald Davidson, because he accepts the doctrine of indeterminacy while explicitly denying behaviorism. Davidson takes the frankly intentionalistic notion of "holding a sentence true" (i.e., believing that it is true) as the basis on which to build a theory of meaning. What then is the area of agreement between him and Quine which generates the indeterminacy? And what does he have to say about the "quandary" that Quine faces? How does he deal with the first-person case? Davidson answers the first question this way:

The crucial point on which I am with Quine might be put: all the evidence for or against a theory of truth (interpretation, translation) comes in the form of facts about what events or situations in the world cause, or would cause, speakers to assent to, or dissent from, each sentence in the speakers' repertoire.[15]

That is, as long as the unit of analysis is a whole sentence and as long as what causes the speaker's response is an objective state of affairs in the world—whether the response is assent and dissent, as in Quine, or holding a sentence true, as in Davidson—Davidson agrees with Quine about the indeterminacy thesis. (There are some differences about the extent of its application.)

But how exactly does the argument work for Davidson? How does Davidson, who rejects behaviorism, get the result that reference is inscrutable? I believe a close look at the texts suggests that he does accept a modified version of Quine's conception of an empirical theory of language. Though he accepts an intentionalistic psychology, he insists that semantic facts about the meanings of utterances must be equally accessible to all the participants in the speech situation, and thus for him the first-person case has no special status.

Quine grants us an apparatus of stimuli and dispositions to verbal response. Davidson grants us conditions in the world (corresponding to Quine's stimuli), utterances, and the psychological attitude of "holding true," directed at sentences. But, since the unit of empirical test is still the sentence, as opposed to parts of the sentence, and since different schemes of interpreting sentences in terms of parts of sentences can be made consistent with the same facts about which sentences a speaker holds true and under what conditions the speaker holds those sentences true, Davidson claims we still get inscrutability. The basic idea is that there will be different ways of matching up objects with words, any number of which could equally well figure in a truth theory that explained why a speaker held a sentence true.

The puzzle about Davidson is that, if you set out the argument as a series of steps, it doesn't follow that there is inscrutability *unless* you add an extra premise concerning the nature of an empirical theory of language. Here are the steps:

1. The unit of empirical analysis in radical interpretation is the sentence (as opposed to subsentential elements).
2. The only empirical evidence for radical interpretation is the fact that speakers "hold true" certain sentences in certain situations.
3. There are alternative ways of matching words with objects which are inconsis-

tent, but any number of which could equally well explain why a speaker held a sentence true.

But these three do not entail any inscrutability or indeterminacy about what the speaker actually meant and what he is referring to. For that you need an extra premise. What is it? I believe that it amounts to the following:

4. All semantic facts must be publicly available to both speaker and hearer. If the interpreter cannot make a distinction on the basis of *public,* empirical evidence, then there is no distinction to be made.

Here is one of his examples: if everything has a shadow, then in a circumstance in which a speaker holds true the sentence 'Wilt is tall', we can take 'Wilt' to refer to Wilt and 'is tall' to refer to tall things, or we can with equal empirical justification take 'Wilt' to refer to the shadow of Wilt and 'is tall' to refer to the shadows of tall things. The first theory tells us that 'Wilt is tall' is true iff Wilt is tall. The second theory tells us that 'Wilt is tall' is true iff the shadow of Wilt is the shadow of a tall thing.

Davidson summarizes the argument thus:

The argument for the inscrutability of reference has two steps. In the first step we recognize the empirical equivalence of alternative reference schemes. In the second step we show that, although an interpreter of the schemer can distinguish between the schemer's schemes, the existence of alternative schemes for interpreting the schemer prevents the interpreter from uniquely identifying the reference of the schemer's predicates, in particular his predicate 'refers' (whether or not indexed or relativized). *What an interpreter cannot on empirical grounds decide about the reference of a schemer's words* cannot be an empirical feature of those words. So those words do not, even when chosen from among arbitrary alternatives, uniquely determine a reference scheme.[16]

In order to understand this argument it is crucial to see that it rests on the special assumption I mentioned about the nature of an empirical account of language and about the public character of semantics. From the mere fact that alternative reference schemes are consistent with all the *public* empirical data it simply doesn't follow by itself that there is any indeter-

minacy or inscrutability. Indeed, this is simply the familiar undetermination thesis all over again: different hypotheses will account equally for the speaker's "hold true" attitudes, but, all the same, one of the hypotheses may be right about exactly what he meant by his words while another hypothesis may be wrong. In order to get the result of inscrutability, an additional premise is needed: since language is a public matter, all the facts about meaning must be public facts. Meaning is an "empirical" matter, and what is empirical about language must be equally accessible to all interpreters. Only given this assumption, this special conception of what constitutes the "empirical" and "public" character of language, can the argument be made to go through.

In order to deepen our understanding of what is going on here, let us contrast the commonsense account of the speech situation with Davidson's account. On the commonsense account, when I make the assertion, "Wilt is tall," by 'Wilt' I refer to Wilt, and by 'is tall' I mean: is tall. When I say "Wilt," I make no reference explicitly or implicitly to shadows, and, similarly, when I say "is tall," I make no reference to shadows. Now these are just plain facts about me. They are not theoretical hypotheses designed to account for my behavior or my "hold true" attitudes. On the contrary, any such theory has to start with facts such as these. But, on Davidson's view, there is no empirical basis for attributing these different intentional states to me. Since all the empirical facts we are allowed to use are facts about what sentences I hold true and under what (publicly observable) conditions, there is no way to make the distinctions that our commonsense intuitions insist on. As with behaviorism, different and inconsistent interpretations at the subsentence level, at the level of words and phrases, will all be consistent with all the facts about what sentences I hold true under what conditions. But now it begins to look as if Davidson's version of inscrutability might also be a reductio ad absurdum of his premises, just as Quine's account was a reductio ad absurdum of behaviorism.

Before we draw any such conclusion, let us first see how Davidson deals with the obvious objection that is suggested by the commonsense account: since we do know in our *own* use of language that we are referring to Wilt, for example, and not to Wilt's shadow, and since what we seek in understanding another person is precisely what we already have in our own case, namely (more or less) determinate senses with determinate references, why should anyone else's references and senses be any less determinate than our own? Of course, in any given case I might get it wrong. I might suppose someone was referring to Wilt when really it was the shadow he was talking about. But that is the usual underdetermination of hypotheses about other minds from publicly available evidence. It does not show any form of inscrutability. What, in short, does Davidson say about the "quandary" that Quine faces, the first-person case?

Perhaps someone (not Quine) will be tempted to say, "But at least the speaker knows what he is referring to." One should stand firm against this thought. The semantic features of language are public features. What no one can in the nature of the case figure out from the totality of the relevant evidence cannot be a part of meaning. And since every speaker must, in some dim sense at least, know this, *he cannot even intend to use his words with a unique reference for he knows that there is no way for his words to convey the reference to another.*[17]

Quine tries to avoid the quandary by an appeal to relativity, but on Davidson's view there really isn't any quandary in the first place. Semantic features are public features, and since the public features are subject to the indeterminacy, *there is no such thing as unique reference.* Furthermore, "in some dim sense" I must know this; so *I can't even intend to refer to rabbits as opposed to rabbit parts, and I can't intend to refer to Wilt as opposed to Wilt's shadow.*[18]

Now, I believe this is a very strange view to hold, and I propose to examine it a bit further. First of all, let us grant that, for "public" languages such as French and English, there is at least one clear sense in which semantic features are, indeed, public features. I take it all that means is that different people can understand the same expressions in the same way in French and English. Furthermore, let us grant, at least for the sake of argument, that the public features

are subject to underdetermination in at least this sense: I could give different but inconsistent interpretations of someone's words, all of which would be consistent with all of the actual and possible evidence I had about which sentences he held true. Now what follows? In our discussion of Quine's view we saw that indeterminacy, as opposed to underdetermination, is a consequence only if we deny mentalism from the start; it is not a consequence of underdetermination by itself. But, similarly, on Davidson's view the indeterminacy follows only if we assume from the start that different semantic facts must necessarily produce different "publicly observable" consequences. Only given this assumption can we derive the conclusion that speaker's meaning and reference are indeterminate and inscrutable. But, I submit, we know quite independently that this conclusion is false, and, therefore, the premises from which it is derived cannot all be true. How do we know the conclusion is false? We know it because in our own case we know that we mean, e.g., Wilt as opposed to Wilt's shadow, rabbit as opposed to rabbit stage. When I seek to understand another speaker, I seek to acquire in his case what I already have for my own case. Now, in my own case, when I understand myself, I know a great deal more than just under what external conditions I hold what sentences true. To put it crudely: in addition, I know what I mean. Furthermore, if another person understands me fully, he will know what I mean, and this goes far beyond just knowing under what conditions I hold what sentences true. So, if his understanding me requires much more than just knowing what sentences I hold true under what conditions, then my understanding him requires much more than knowing what sentences he holds true under what conditions. Just knowing his "hold true" attitudes will never be enough for me fully to understand him. Why should it be? It would not be enough for me to understand me; and since, to repeat, what I need to acquire in his case is what I already have in my own case, I will need more than just these attitudes.

But what about Davidson's claim that what an interpreter cannot figure out from the totality of the relevant evidence cannot be part of meaning? Well, it all depends on what we are allowed to count as "figuring out from the totality of the relevant evidence." On the commonsense account, I do figure out from the relevant "evidence" that by 'Wilt' you mean Wilt and not Wilt's shadow, and the "evidence" is quite conclusive. How does it work? In real life I understand the speech of another not only within a Network of shared assumptions, but more importantly against a Background of nonrepresentational mental capacities—ways of being and behaving in the world which are both culturally and biologically shaped and which are so basic to our whole mode of existence that it is hard even to become aware of them (see my *Intentionality*, ch. 5). Now, given the Background, it will, in general, be quite out of the question that, when you say in English, "Wilt is tall" or "There goes a rabbit," you could with equal justification be taken to be talking about Wilt's shadow or rabbit stages. We get that surprising result only if we forget about real life and imagine that we are trying to understand the speech of another by constructing a "theory," using as "evidence" only his "hold true" attitudes directed toward sentences or his dispositions to make noises under stimulus conditions. Language is indeed a public matter, and, in general, we can tell what a person means if we know what he says and under what conditions he says it. But this certainty derives not from the supposition that the claim about what he means must be just a summary of the (publicly available) evidence; it is rather the same sort of certainty we have about what a man's intentions are from watching what he is doing. In both cases we know what is going on because we know how to interpret the "evidence." And in both cases the claims we make go beyond being mere summaries of the evidence, in a way that any claim about "other minds" goes beyond being a summary of the "public" evidence. But the fact that the interpretation of the speech of another is subject to the same sort of underdetermination[19] as any other claim about other minds does not show either that there is any indeterminacy or that we cannot, in general, figure out exactly what other people mean from what they say.

I conclude that our reaction to Davidson's version should be the same as our reaction to Quine's: in each case the conclusion of the argument is best construed as a reductio ad absurdum of the premises. Davidson's view is in a way more extreme than Quine's because he holds a view which is, I believe, literally incredible. Plugging in the first-person example to what he literally says, Davidson holds that what no external observer can decide from external evidence cannot be part of what I mean. Since such observers can't decide between inconsistent interpretations, and since I must, in some dim sense at least, know this, I cannot even intend to use 'rabbit' to mean rabbit as opposed to rabbit stage or undetached rabbit part, for I know there is no way for my words to convey this reference to another. This does not seem to me even remotely plausible. I know exactly which I mean, and though someone might get it wrong about me, just as I might get it wrong about him, the difficulty is the usual "other-minds problem" applied to semantics.

V

In any discussion like this there are bound to be issues much deeper than those which surface in the actual arguments of the philosophers involved. I believe that the deepest issue between me on the one hand and Davidson and Quine on the other concerns the nature of an empirical theory of language.

Both Quine and Davidson adopt the thought experiment of "radical translation" as a model for building an account of meaning. In radical translation an interpreter or translator tries to understand speakers of a language of which he has no prior knowledge whatever. On Davidson's view, "all understanding of the speech of another involves radical interpretation."[20] But the model of an unknown foreign language enables us to make more precise what sorts of assumptions and evidence we need to interpret someone else's speech.

Notice that the model of radical translation already invites us, indeed forces us, to adopt a third-person point of view. The question now becomes, How would *we* know the meaning of the utterances of some *other* person? And the immediate difficulty with that way of posing the question is that it invites confusion between the epistemic and the semantic; it invites confusion between the question, *How* do you know? and the question, *What* is it that you know *when* you know? But the linguistically relevant facts must be the same in the questions, What is it for me to understand another person when he says "It's raining"? and What is it for me to understand myself when I say "It's raining"? since, to repeat, what I have when I understand him is exactly what he has when he understands me. But then I already understand me; so anything I can learn from studying his case I could learn from studying my case.

Still, the thought experiment of radical translation can be very useful in semantic theory because it focuses the question of how we communicate meaning from one speaker to another. The difficulty is that both Quine and Davidson set further constraints on the task of radical translation than those which any field linguist would in fact employ. I have twice watched the linguist Kenneth L. Pike[21] perform the "monolingual demonstration" where he begins to construct a translation of a totally alien language into English. And it seems quite clear to any observer of Pike that he does not confine his conception of translation to that described by Davidson and Quine. For example, Pike does not confine his investigation to matching verbal behavior and sensory stimuli in the manner of Quine, nor does he confine it to "hold true" attitudes in the manner of Davidson. Rather, he tries to figure out what is going on in the mind of the native speaker, even at the level of particular words. And he can do this because he presupposes that he shares with the speaker of the exotic language a substantial amount of Network and Background (see n.12).

Now granted that the thought experiment of radical interpretation is useful in understanding the notion of communication, why shouldn't the problem of radical interpretation be posed in commonsense mentalistic terms? Why should we place on it the further behavioristic or "empirical" constraints that Quine and Davidson so obviously do? Quine's writings contain scattered remarks of the following sort: "Our talk of external things, our very notion of things, is just a conceptual apparatus that helps us to foresee and control the triggering of our sensory receptors in the light of previous triggering of

our sensory receptors. The triggering, first and last, is all we have to go on."[22]

Such a remark has the air of discovery, but I believe it simply expresses a preference for adopting a certain level of description. Suppose one substituted for the phrase "triggering of our sensory receptors" in this paragraph, the phrase "the movement of molecules." One could then argue that the movement of molecules, first and last, is all we have to go on. Both the "movement of molecules" version and the "sensory receptors" version are equally true and equally arbitrary. In a different philosophical tradition, one might also say that all we have to go on, first and last, is the thrownness (*Geworfenheit*) and the foundedness (*Befindlichkeit*) of Dasein in the lifeworld (*Lebenswelt*). Such remarks are characteristic of philosophy, but it is important to see that what looks like a discovery can equally be interpreted as simply the expression of preference for a certain level of description over others. The three choices I gave are all equally interpretable as equally true. How do we choose among them? I believe that all three—sensory receptors, molecules, and Dasein—are insufficient levels of description for getting at certain fundamental questions of semantics. Why? Because the level of semantics that we need to analyze also involves a level of intentionality. Semantics includes the level at which we express beliefs and desires in our intentional utterances, at which we mean things by sentences and mean quite specific things by certain words inside of sentences. Indeed, I believe that the intentionalistic level is already implicit in the quotation from Quine when he uses the expressions 'foresee' and 'control'. These convey intentionalistic notions, and, on Quine's own version of referential opacity, they create referentially opaque contexts. No one, with the possible exception of a few neurophysiologists working in laboratories, tries to foresee and control anything at the level of sensory receptors. Even if we wanted to, we simply don't know enough about this level. Why then in Quine do we get this round declaration that all we have to go on is the stimulation of the sensory receptors? I think it rests on a resolute rejection of mentalism in linguistic analysis, with a consequent insistence on having a third-person point of view. Once you grant that a fundamental unit of analysis is intentionality, then it seems you are forced to accept the first-person point of view as in some sense epistemically different from the point of view of the third-person observer. It is part of the persistent objectivizing tendency of philosophy and science since the seventeenth century that we regard the third-person objective point of view as preferable to, as somehow more "empirical" than, the first-person, "subjective" point of view. What looks then like a simple declaration of scientific fact—that language is a matter of stimulations of nerve endings—turns out on examination to be the expression of a metaphysical preference and, I believe, a preference that is unwarranted by the facts. The crucial fact in question is that performing speech acts—and meaning things by utterances—goes on at a level of intrinsic first-person intentionality. Quine's behaviorism is motivated by a deep antimentalistic metaphysics which makes the behaviorist analysis seem the only analysis that is scientifically respectable.

A similar though more subtle form of rejection of the first-person point of view emerges in Davidson's writings in a number of places. Davidson tacitly supposes that what is empirical must be equally and publicly accessible to any competent observer. But why should it be? It is, for example, a plain empirical fact that I now have a pain, but that fact is not equally accessible to any observer. In Davidson, the crucial claims in the passages I quoted are where he says, 'What an interpreter cannot on empirical grounds decide about the reference of a schemer's words cannot be an empirical feature of those words'; and prior to that where he claims, "What no one can in the nature of the case figure out from the totality of the relevant evidence cannot be a part of meaning." Both of these have an air of truism, but in actual usage they express a metaphysical preference for the third-person point of view, a preference which is assumed and not argued for; because, as in Quine's case, it seems part of the very notion of an empirical theory of language, an obvious consequence of the fact that language is a public phenomenon. What Davidson says looks like a tautology: What can't be decided empirically isn't empirical. But the way he uses this is not as a tautology. What he means is: What can't be conclusively settled on third-person objective

tests cannot be an actual feature of language as far as semantics is concerned. On one use "empirical" means: subject to objective third-person tests. On the other use it means: actual or factual. There are then two different senses of "empirical"; and the argument against the first-person case succeeds only if we assume, falsely, that what isn't conclusively testable by third-person means isn't actual. On the other hand, once we grant that there is a distinction between the public evidence available about what a person means and the claim that he means such and such—that is, once we grant that the familiar underdetermination of evidence about other minds applies to semantic interpretation—there is no argument left for inscrutability.

The rival view that is implicit in my argument is this. Language is indeed public; and it is not a matter of meanings-as-introspectable-entities, private objects, privileged access, or any of the Cartesian paraphernalia. The point, however, is that, when we understand someone else or ourselves, what we require—among other things—is a knowledge of intentional contents. Knowledge of those contents is not equivalent to knowledge of the matching of public behavior with stimuli nor to the matching of utterances with conditions in the world. We see this most obviously in the first-person case, and our neglect of the first-person case leads us to have a false model of the understanding of language. We think, mistakenly, that understanding a speaker is a matter of constructing a "theory," that the theory is based on "evidence," and that the evidence must be "empirical."

ACKNOWLEDGMENTS

I am indebted to a large number of people for comments and criticism of earlier drafts of this paper. I especially want to thank Noam Chomsky, Dagfinn Føllesdal, Ernest Lepore, Brian McLaughlin, George Myro, Dagmar Searle, and Bruce Vermazen.

NOTES

1. *Word and Object* (Cambridge, Mass.: MIT Press; New York: Wiley, 1960), p. 39.
2. "Review of B. F. Skinner's *Verbal Behavior*," in Jerry Fodor and Jerrold Katz, eds., *The Structure of Language* (Englewood Cliffs, N.J.: Prentice-Hall, 1964), pp. 547–578.
3. In the Chinese room argument, the man in the room

follows a computer program that makes his verbal behavior indistinguishable from that of a Chinese speaker, but he still does not understand Chinese. He satisfies the behavioral criterion for understanding without actually understanding. Thus, the refutation of strong AI is a fortiori a refutation of behaviorism. [See my "Minds, Brains, and Programs," *Behavioral and Brain Sciences,* III (1980): 417–457; and *Minds, Brains, and Science* (Cambridge, Mass.: Harvard, 1984).]

4. In what sense exactly can two translations be inconsistent? We cannot simply say that they have different *meanings,* for that would seem to imply the existence of determinate meanings. Rather, we must say that they are inconsistent in the sense that one system of translation will accept translations that the other system would reject [Quine, "Reply to Harman," *Synthese,* XIX, 1–2 (December 1968): 267–269; also, Word and Object, pp. 73–74].

5. Sometimes Quine talks about behavior *simpliciter,* sometimes about *dispositions* to behavior. I think the notion of dispositions to behavior is the one he prefers.

6. "The Inscrutability of Reference," *Southwestern Journal of Philosophy,* X (1979): 7–19, reprinted in *Inquiries into Truth and Interpretation* (New York: Oxford, 1984), pp. 227–241; page references are to this version.

7. "Only in the Context of a Sentence Do Words Have Any Meaning," *Midwest Studies in Philosophy,* II: *Studies in the Philosophy of Language* (1977).

8. Cf., for example, his "Quine's Empirical Assumptions," *Synthese,* XIX, 1–2 (December 1968): 53–68.

9. *Theories and Things* (Cambridge, Mass.: Harvard University Press, 1981), p. 23.

10. *Ontological Relativity and Other Essays* (New York: Columbia University Press, 1969), pp. 47–48.

11. Ibid., p. 47.

12. Ibid.

13. One of the most puzzling aspects of this whole literature is the remarks people make about the ability to speak two or more languages and to translate from one to the other. Quine speaks of the "traditional equations" (*Word and Object,* p. 28) for translating from one language into another. But, except for a few odd locutions, tradition has nothing to do with it. (It is a tradition, I guess, to translate Frege's *Bedeutung* as 'reference', even though it doesn't really mean that in German.) When I translate 'butterfly' as *papillon,* for example, there is no tradition involved at all; or, if there is, I certainly know nothing of it. I

translate 'butterfly' as *papillon* because that is what 'butterfly' means in French. Similarly, Michael Dummett speaks of "conventions" for translating from one language to another [see "The Significance of Quine's Indeterminacy Thesis," *Synthese,* XXVII, 3/4 (July/August 1974): 351–397]. But the point is that, if you know what the words mean, there isn't any room for further conventions. By convention, the numeral '2' stands for the number two in the Arabic notation, 'II' stands for the same number in the Roman notation. But, for these very reasons, we don't need a further convention that '2' can be translated as 'II'.

14. I argue elsewhere that the functioning of a speaker's meaning is also relative to a whole Network of intentional states and a Background of preintentional capacities. I believe that this relativity is vastly more radical than has been generally appreciated and, indeed, more radical than Quine's indeterminacy thesis, but it is irrelevant to this part of the indeterminacy dispute. [See my *Intentionality: An Essay in the Philosophy of Mind* (New York: Cambridge, 1983), chaps. 1 and 5.]

15. Davidson, *Inquiries into Truth and Interpretation,* p. 230.

16. Ibid., p. 235; my italics.

17. Ibid.; my italics.

18. Kirk Ludwig has pointed out to me that this seems to lead to a pragmatic paradox, since it looks as if, in order to state the thesis, we have to specify distinctions that, the thesis says, cannot be specified.

19. Here is an example of such undetermination from real life. Until he was in middle age, a friend of mine thought that the Greek expression *hoi polloi* as used in English meant the elite of rich people, but that it was characteristically used ironically. Thus, if he saw a friend in a low-class bar he might say, "I see you have been hobnobbing with the hoi polloi." Since he spoke ironically and interpreted other people as speaking ironically, there were no behavioral differences between his use and the standard use. Indeed, he might have gone his whole life with this semantic eccentricity undetected. All the same, there are very definite facts about what he meant.

20. "Radical Interpretation," *Dialectica,* XXVII (1973): 313–328, reprinted in *Inquiries into Truth and Interpretation,* pp. 125–139.

21. Pike's work appears to be the original inspiration for the idea of radical translation (see Quine, *Word and Object,* p. 28).

22. *Theories and Things,* p. 1.

SUGGESTED FURTHER READING

Davidson, Donald, *Essays on Truth and Interpretation* (Oxford: Clarendon Press, 1984).

Hirsh, Jr., E. D., *Validity in Interpretation* (New Haven: Yale University Press, 1967).

Iseminger, Gary, ed., *Intention and Interpretation* (Philadelphia: Temple University Press, 1992).

Levinson, Sanford and Steven Mailloux, eds., *Interpreting Law and Literature* (Evanston: Northwestern University Press, 1991).

Levy, Edwin, "Competing Radical Translations," Boston *Studies in Philosophy of Science* 8 (1971): 590–605.

Massey, G. J., "Indeterminacy, Inscrutability, and Ontological Relativity," *American Philosophical Quarterly,* Monograph 12 (1978): 43–55.

Mueller-Vollmer, Kurt, ed., *The Hermeneutics Reader* (New York: Continuum, 1994).

Quine, W. V., *Word and Object* (Cambridge: MIT Press, 1960).

Quine, W. V., *Ontological Relativity and Other Essays* (New York: Columbia University Press, 1969).

VIII THE NATURE OF LANGUAGE

The issue of what the nature of language is can be approached from many different perspectives and can be motivated by different worries. Three are represented in this section.

First, in the latter half of the twentieth century, the approach favored by most philosophers who wondered about the issue was to consider whether human languages are or can be private. The locus classicus for the view that private languages are possible has been some chapters in John Locke's *Essay Concerning Human Understanding*, first published in 1690. Locke does not explicitly ask whether languages are private, but the theory of meaning that he develops has the consequence that language is private. Locke's view can be summarized in the following syllogism:

Minor: All meanings of words are ideas.
Major: All ideas are private.

All meanings of words are private.

Locke holds the minor premise, because ideas seem to him to be the only things that could serve as meanings. Since people must know the meanings of the words they use, and since, according to Locke, the only things that people know are ideas, the meanings of words must be ideas. In coming to this conclusion, Locke had considered and rejected the possibilities that meanings were either properties (qualities) of things in the world or ideas in someone else's mind: "A Man cannot make his Words the Signs either of Qualities in Things, or of Conceptions in the Mind of another, whereof he has none in his own" (*Essay Concerning Human Understanding*, III.ii.2). The reason is that if a person were to try to have his words signify either something in a physical object or in another's mind, then the speaker would mean by his words something of which he had no knowledge (since all that a person knows are his own ideas). And for a speaker to use signs "of he knows not what . . . is in Truth for him [to use] Signs of nothing" (*Essay*, III.ii.2).

Locke clearly holds that the proper and immediate signification of meaningful words is the idea that the word stands for in the speaker and in the speaker alone. A word cannot signify both an idea of the speaker and an idea in someone else's mind, according to Locke; for then the word would both immediately signify the speaker's idea and not immediately signify the speaker's own idea (because it signifies an idea in another person's mind). Implicit in this argument is the premise that a word can immediately signify only one thing.

According to Locke, each person has her own mind, and the ideas in that mind are unique to that person, and accessible only to that person. The limited accessibility of ideas is much more important to this issue than the uniqueness of the ideas. As John Cook pointed out in an article titled "Wittgenstein on Privacy," a person's shadow is unique to that person, but many people have cognitive access to it, in the sense that many people can see it or stand on it, or draw its outline. What makes communication problematic on Locke's theory of meaning is the fact that no one has access to any ideas other than her own because no one can look into the mind of another.

The purpose of language according to Locke is to make each person's private, invisible thoughts known to others. According to him, a speaker utters a word, say, 'red', by which he signifies his own idea of redness with the intention of getting the audience to think of red also. Opponents of Locke's theory of language can exploit this statement of the purpose of language in order to demonstrate the impossibility of a private language. They can argue that by Locke's own account of meaning and his own reasoning about why a word must signify only the speaker's idea, no one can ever know anyone else's ideas. Recall that Locke had said that a word cannot signify an idea in another person's mind because no one can ever have that idea in his own mind. Jones's ideas belong only to Jones, and Smith can never have them. If this is true, then the purpose Locke states for language, that it is to make each person's private, invisible ideas known to others, cannot be achieved. Smith can never have Jones's ideas in his mind. That is one objection to the idea of a private language.

Here is another objection to Locke's explanation of the nature of language. If it were correct, then no one could ever know that he had successfully communicated anything. The reason is this. Suppose the speaker immediately signifies by the word 'red' some idea to which only he has access, and suppose that his utterance of the word 'red' causes the audience to think of some idea. Since the speaker cannot see into the mind of the audience and does not have any other access to it, there is never any way for the speaker to know whether he has succeeded in communicating. But since any reasonable person would concede that speakers are at least sometimes sure that their attempt to communicate has succeeded, Locke's view of the nature of language must be wrong.

These objections to the notion of a private language are simple and straightforward. Much more subtle reasoning was developed by Ludwig Wittgenstein in his *Philosophical Investigations* (1954). This explains in part why scholars do not agree about what he meant by a private language or how he argued for his view.

For the purposes of discussion, let us define a private language as one in which the meanings of the words refer to an entity that only the speaker could have access to, and suppose that each person's pain is something to which only the person with that pain can have cognitive access (a dubious assumption). Wittgenstein's argument that the meaning of the word 'pain' cannot be a sensation to which only the speaker has access depends on the idea that a language is something that can be used for communication. If the audience could never have access to the speaker's pain and the pain is the meaning of 'pain', then the audience could never know the meaning of 'pain' and communication would necessarily fail. In "Wittgenstein on Privacy," John Cook emphasized that Wittgenstein's argument assumed that people do communicate about pains. This is important because many critics of Wittgenstein reason in this way: the meaning of 'pain' is the speaker's pain; Wittgenstein holds that if such is the case, talk about pain is impossible; but talk about pain is not impossible; therefore, Wittgenstein's view is mistaken. What these critics do not understand is that Wittgenstein is developing a kind of reductio ad absurdum argument against them. He agrees that talk about pain is not impossible and agrees that if the meaning of 'pain' is a private sensation of pain, then such talk is impossible. He concludes that the meaning of 'pain' is not a private sensation of pain. In other words, Wittgenstein assumes that 'pain'-language is used to communicate and then tries to show that the meaning of 'pain' cannot be a pain of which no other person can have knowledge. His view is consistent with the proposition that individuals have and feel pains, and consistent with the proposition that all individuals feel the same thing when they feel the same pain. But these matters are independent of the issue about the nature of language.

There are many confusions surrounding the ways in which sensations are and are not private and how the way in which they are private may affect the nature of language. Cook had an elegant refutation of the view that since no one can feel another person's sensation, no one can know what sensation that person is experiencing. He pointed out that if such an argument were valid, then so is this one: since no one can have another person's shadow, no one can know anything about that person's shadow.

A defender of the private language view might respond that Wittgenstein nevertheless ignores an important difference between a pain and a shadow. A pain is private, whereas a shadow is public. However, the alleged privacy of pain is ultimately irrelevant. The issue of whether language is private or not does not hang on whether pains or sensations are private or not. The nature of language can be misdescribed even if public objects are the objects of reference. Wittgenstein's argument would be similar even if someone held that the meaning of 'red' is the experience of seeing red. It is a fact that many people can see the same red object, say, a candle, and it is the publicness of at least some red objects, their accessibility to speaker and audience, that is crucial to the meaning of 'red'.

If someone were to reply that 'red' has a dual meaning, a public redness and the private redness (the sensation of red that is unique to each person), Wittgenstein would point out that the private redness is superfluous so far as the semantic issue is concerned. Suppose a person had a different qualitative sensation each time he saw a red object but that he used the word 'red' in all observable ways as the other members of the linguistic community did. Then it would be true to say that he knew what the word 'red' meant or knew the meaning of the word 'red'. This shows the superfluity or irrelevance of the private sensation so far as the meaning of the word 'pain' is concerned. Again, this does not mean that sensations play no role in language.

So far, the discussion has focused on the nature of the object of meaning or reference, and nothing has been said about whether there is only one or many speakers of the language. The question about private languages has been in effect, "Can the meaning of a word be identified with a private entity?" The discussion can be focused in a very different way so that the relevant question is, "Can a human language be spoken by only one person?" For the purposes of answering this question, one can assume that the alleged objects of meaning are not private in the sense that only one person could have access to them. And the question also does not concern how a sole individual might learn a language. To make both of these points clear, consider whether Robinson Crusoe, who was raised an English speaker, could continue to say such things as, "There's a coconut" and mean that there is a coconut; or whether, if all but one member of a linguistic community died, the sole surviving member would have a language.

Wittgenstein, I think, would answer these questions in the negative and would deny that there could be a language spoken only by one person. One reason has to do with the connection between language and rules. Linguistic communication, he believes, is rule-governed behavior, and it does not make sense to say that someone is following a rule unless there is some way of judging whether the rule has been followed or broken. The speaker himself cannot be the final arbiter of this. The judge of whether a rule has been followed or not, like any standard of evaluation, must be separate from and independent of the matter to be decided. A speaker may think that he knows that he is following a rule, but there is a difference between thinking that one is doing something and doing it. The argument here might be presented in the following form:

1. Speaking a language requires following rules.
2. Following rules requires a (nontrivial) method of determining when rules are followed or broken.
3. A (nontrivial) method of determining when rules are broken requires a judge, not identical to the speaker.

Therefore,

4. There can be no judge, not identical with the user, if there is only one person to speak a language.

A. J. Ayer was not persuaded. In "Can There Be a Private Language?" he said that there is nothing privileged about the publicness of the meaning-verification that Wittgenstein seems to require. All justification and verification of whatever sort must end somewhere. Further, all justification must end with some sense perception—for example, seeing or hearing the judgment of other people that one has or has not followed a rule of speaking correctly—so one may just as well end with one's own private sensation. (As part of an objection to Ayer's view, consider this line of reasoning: every judicial decision must end with some person's decision, so one may just as well end with the village idiot's decision.)

Saul Kripke in "On Rules and Private Language" in effect responds to Ayer by saying that Wittgenstein recognizes that all verification ends somewhere and that one might always doubt the veracity of one's perceptions. According to Kripke, Wittgenstein is in effect trying to circumvent a problem that can be called "a skeptical paradox." Indeed, Wittgenstein says, "this was our paradox: no course of action could be determined by a rule, because every course of action can be made to accord with the rule" (*Philosophical Investigations,* paragraph 201). In other words, since any action can be interpreted to satisfy any rule, any appeal to a rule is vacuous. Kripke illustrates the point by taking the rule of addition as his example. The function expressed by 'plus' or '+' determines the value for an infinite number of pairs of numbers; for example, $129 + 52 = 181$. Corresponding to this mathematical function is, or so it seems, a mental fact that a person has and uses to compute this sum and all others. However, this position does not seem to provide an answer to the skeptical question; How do you know that the mental fact you used to get the answer 181 is the rule that you used in the past? Perhaps the rule that you used in the past would yield the result 24.

Notice that the skeptical question is asking for a mental fact to account for a person's arithmetic performance. Kripke's Wittgenstein argues that there is no such mental fact. It is logically possible that whenever a person used 'plus' or '+' in the past she was actually denoting the function that might be called 'quus', and which may defined as follows:

$x + y = x + y$ if $x , y < 51$ and $= 5$ otherwise.

The fact that the skeptic was asking for a mental fact to justify the arithmetic performance leaves open the possibility that some nonmental fact, say, the arithmetic function of addition itself, explains the performance. But this will not work. The arithmetic function remains the same whether a person adds correctly or incorrectly. It appears that a solution to the skeptical question requires a mental fact; and yet no mental fact seems adequate. To say that the mental fact is that one should do the same thing with 129 and 52 that one had done before is too vague and consistent with 'plus' meaning 'quus'. And to say that the mental fact is the rule that 129 + 52 equals 181 is simply false, because, by supposition, the person never had this thought before being presented with the problem.

According to Kripke, the kind of skepticism that Wittgenstein is trying to overcome may be called 'Humean'. David Hume denied that there was any observable connection to be discovered between cause and effect and between past instances of kind K and future instances of K. The Wittgensteinian skeptic denies that any discoverable connection can be found between past and present uses of a word.

Further, a satisfactory answer to the skeptic must satisfy two conditions. First, it must say what it is about a person's mental state that makes a person mean plus and not quus. Second, it must explain why this fact justifies the answer that 181 is the sum of 129 plus 52. It cannot be an accident that the person's mental state gives the right answer. The first condition is descriptive. The second is normative. Kripke claims that Wittgenstein's solution to the skeptical challenge is a skeptical solution. (In contrast, a "straight" solution to a skeptical problem is one that shows that the original skepticism is unjustified.) It turns out that the first condition that the skeptic laid down is mistaken. There need not be any mental fact that makes 'plus' mean addition. Just as Hume claimed that the idea of a necessary connection came from the "feeling of customary transition," Wittgenstein claims that no mental fact makes 'plus' mean addition.

The proper way to understand the meaning of '+' ('plus'), like many other words, is to understand its "role and utility in our lives." This understanding provides not "*truth* conditions," but "assertibility conditions." So, not only is there no mental or "internal" fact that determines what '+' means, there is no "external" fact that does so either.

It seems that according to Kripke, there is a fact of the matter that '+' means addition (plus), but it is not what we would think of as a mathematical fact; it is a complex behavioral fact about a community: "the success of the practices . . . depends on the brute empirical fact that we agree with each other in our responses." There is no further fact of the matter. One may well find this unsatisfying. One may object by asking, 'In virtue of what does the community behave as it does? Does there not need to be some fact, independent of the community, that causes the community to act as it does? And if there is such a fact about the community wouldn't it be plausible that the individual somehow shares in that fact?' But Kripke does not discuss this objection.

Although it is not clear how Ayer would have responded to Kripke, it is clear that he disagreed with Wittgenstein on other matters. According to Ayer, it is a merely contingent matter whether one or many people speak a language, and he appealed to the possible existence of a real Robinson Crusoe to make the point. If Crusoe says, "That's a coconut" upon seeing a coconut, why isn't it true that he means that that's a coconut? Or if he says, "I have a pain," why isn't it true that he means that he has a pain? Ayer correctly recognized that it is not significant whether material objects or sensations are the alleged meanings of terms. If a person is alone, then for all practical purposes one object is no more private than any other. Nonetheless, there is a reply to Ayer. He confuses Crusoe's vocalizations (that is, the production of sounds using human vocal chords), "That's a coconut," and "I have a pain," which are isomorphic or isophonic with English, with genuine communicative instances of English. If a voice synthesizer randomly fit together sounds until it emitted the sound, "I have a pain," it would not follow that the voice synthesizer meant that it had a pain. It is tendentious or question-begging for Ayer to argue that, since a scenario can be constructed that involves Crusoe producing noises that sound like English, therefore English is being spoken. Ayer has shown only that Crusoe's ability to vocalize remains the same after the shipwreck as before, not that these vocalizations continue to count as a communicative use of language. Crusoe would not be ordering or questioning or promising by means of any of his utterances, I would maintain, because there is no one to be ordered, questioned, or promised except, dubiously, himself. And if he could not be doing any of these things what sense does it make to say that he is stating or asserting that there's a coconut or that he is in pain? For the point and purpose of describing something is to inform someone of the described situation. Since Crusoe lacks such a purpose, he is going through the motions of language without speaking one. It is also useful to recall Austin's observation in "Performative Utterances" that one just cannot make a statement about anything at any time.

Another way to put the foregoing point is to say that if there is a private descriptive language, then there is a private performative language. One can easily describe a 'private marriage' ceremony with Crusoe mouthing the words, 'I take this woman to be my wife', and to the extent possible, performing acts analogous to marital acts—for example, making his own breakfast and worrying about mortgage payments. But he still wouldn't be married.

In addition to the acoustic identity between Crusoe's utterances and English, another possible source for Ayer's confusion on this point may be that he subconsciously thought of himself and his readers as Crusoe's audience. Ayer, who constructs the scenario, gives the impression that he understands what Crusoe is saying because he recognizes Crusoe's vocalizations as English and he knows what he wants Crusoe to mean by them. But Crusoe is not talking to Ayer, and it is illegitimate for Ayer to think of himself as part of Crusoe's audience. As Kripke says, "*if* we think of Crusoe as following rules, we are taking him into our community and applying our criteria for rule following to him." Crusoe is alone; his utterances cannot serve any function that language must have in order to deserve the name, and, for all that Crusoe knows, his utterances do not have the purpose or regularity one must know they have in order to count as part of language.

None of this is meant to deny that Crusoe retains a language in latency. He retains the psychological and linguistic wherewithal to speak with others if he were presented with the right sort of context, say, a group of rescuers. But that kind of latent ability to use language is different from an actual use.

In "Truth Rules, Hoverflies, and the Kripke-Wittgenstein Paradox," Ruth Millikan takes up the challenge of the Kripke-Wittgenstein paradox. She gives a nonskeptical solution. The meaning of a word is normative. If something has a meaning, then there is "a standard from which the facts, or one's dispositions, can diverge." She explains a way of measuring up to that standard or following a rule that does not involve representing that rule: it is to have an unexpressed purpose to follow a rule and to succeed in this purpose. These unexpressed purposes are biological in the same way that the heart, the eye-blink reflex, and the human brain have purposes. As a matter of fact, creatures that have these purposes survive and proliferate; so these purposes accord with evolutionary design. Millikan explains that although male hoverflies do not calculate the complex mathematics of intercepting female hoverflies, their behavior conforms to this rule and has caused their survival and proliferation. Of course, other rules would describe the behavior of the male hoverflies ("quoverfly" rules), but these rules would not explain the biological purpose, as the genuine rule does. The normative element, then, of the hoverfly rule is its biological purposiveness; and the same can be said of rules of meaning. Linguistic competence is competence in the biological sense that Millikan describes: "to mean to follow a certain rule is to have a purpose and to follow it."

The second of the three approaches to language that are contained in this section thinks of language as a formal system that correlates sentences with meanings in a systematic way. These correlations can be represented as ordered pairs consisting of sentences as the first members and meanings (sets of possible worlds) as the second. David Lewis, who is sympathetic to this goal, nonetheless thinks it can be coupled with a view something like Wittgenstein's. According to this latter view, language is a social phenomenon, in which utterances initiate behavior and allow people to understand the beliefs and desires of each other. Lewis suggests a synthesis of these two perspectives according to which humans use the formal system as a means of communication. This is possible because members of a community share two conventions: truth and trustfulness. Speakers of indicative sentences try to tell the truth and their audiences trust that they will. Speakers of imperative sentences trust that their audiences will make the sentences true, while the audiences try to do so. Lewis's article is a powerful attempt to reconcile the Wittgensteinian and Austinian view of language with the formal view of logicians and many linguists.

The third approach to the nature of language is due to the linguist Noam Chomsky, who rejects both Lewis's characterization of language and the attempt at synthesis, at least insofar as linguistics is concerned. On Chomsky's view, language is a certain component of the human brain, and linguistics is a branch of brain science. For this reason, language is objectively real, and theories about it are true or false in the same sense that any scientific theory is. Since brain science is in its infancy, linguistic theory is still relatively naive, and the abstractness of its descriptions of the brain are relatively low level. Contemporary linguistics is to an adequate theory of the brain as eighteenth century chemistry is to contemporary chemistry.

Another consequence of identifying language with a structure of the brain is that there is an objectively true description of it, at least in general. The apparently great differences between English, Finnish, and Japanese are probably not very great as they exist in the brains of English, Finnish, and Japanese speakers. Putting the point picturesquely, he says that, viewed by an angel, all human languages would look identical. What he means is that, viewed from afar, apparently large differences between, say, English and Japanese speakers are in fact very small differences. He points out that biologists have discovered that very minor differences at the microscopic level of genetic components generate apparently large differences at the macroscopic level of biological form and behavior. Moreover, the ordinary idea that English, Finnish, and Japanese are different "languages" does not have any scientific validity. There are no sharp or principled borders between one so-called language and another. The German spoken near the Dutch border is more easily understood by Dutch speakers than by German speakers in certain remote areas. All of these considerations are connected with Chomsky's belief that there is, for all human languages, a universal grammar, which is a component of the brain of every normal human being. (One might object to Chomsky that from an angel's point of view, there may be no difference between humans and gorillas; but that does not mean that there are not important differences. Why is the angel's view better than a closer one?)

Chomsky contrasts his view that language is a "subsystem of the mind/brain," which he dubs "I-language" (intensional language), with several other competing views. The most important of these is the view he attributes to David Lewis, according to which human language is "E-language" (extensional language), that is, an infinite set of strings of symbols for which there is an infinite number of possible grammars. On such a view, language is thought of as a mathematical entity. One objection to this way of construing human language is that its determinate set of symbols does not correspond to the utterances of human speakers, which include semigrammatical and other sorts of borderline cases. Another problem is that its view of semantics as relating syntactic structures (strings of words or other symbols) with models, usually set theoretic models, is mistaken. Semantics is the study of the relation between language and the world, not some mental or otherwise artificial representational device.

Another consequence of Chomsky's view is that he has no sympathy with the Wittgensteinian view, as interpreted by Anthony Kenny, that to know a language is to be able or to have a disposition to speak, read, understand talk, and so on. Chomsky points out that a speaker can improve his ability to speak and write without changing his knowledge of language, and that one's ability to use language can be lost, perhaps from an injury, and then regained by taking a drug without ever having lost that very language at all. Since language is a component of the brain, it is also not essentially tied to communication. Linguistic communication is merely one of several uses to which language can be put: it can also be used to remember things, to make private computations, and to write personal poetry.

Contradicting Quine's view in "Two Dogmas of Empiricism," Chomsky argues that it is obvious that there are determinate semantic relations and analytic sentences if one thinks about certain sentences that have a relational structure and involve intentional activities, for example, 'If John persuaded Bill to go to college, then Bill went to college'. Thus, there is a legitimate distinction to be made between truths of meaning and truths of fact.

42 Of Words

JOHN LOCKE

I. OF WORDS OR LANGUAGE IN GENERAL

1. God, having designed man for a sociable creature, made him not only with an inclination, and under a necessity to have fellowship with those of his own kind, but furnished him also with language, which was to be the great instrument and common tie of society. Man, therefore, had by nature his organs so fashioned, as to be fit to frame articulate sounds, which we call words. But this was not enough to produce language; for parrots, and several other birds, will be taught to make articulate sounds distinct enough, which yet by no means are capable of language.

2. Besides articulate sounds, therefore, it was further necessary that he should be able to use these sounds as signs of internal conceptions; and to make them stand as marks for the ideas within his own mind, whereby they might be made known to others, and the thoughts of men's minds be conveyed from one to another.

3. But neither was this sufficient to make words so useful as they ought to be. It is not enough for the perfection of language, that sounds can be made signs of ideas, unless those signs can be so made use of as to comprehend several particular things: for the multiplication of words would have perplexed their use, had every particular thing need of a distinct name to be signified by. To remedy this inconvenience, language had yet a further improvement in the use of *general terms,* whereby one word was made to mark a multitude of particular existences: which advantageous use of sounds was obtained only by the difference of the ideas they were made signs of: those names becoming general, which are made to stand for *general ideas,* and those remaining particular, where the ideas they are used for are *particular.*

4. Besides these names which stand for ideas, there be other words which men make use of, not to signify any idea, but the want or absence of some ideas, simple or complex, or all ideas together; such as are *nihil* in Latin, and in English, *ignorance* and *barrenness.* All which negative or privative words cannot be said properly to belong to, or signify no ideas: for then they would be perfectly insignificant sounds; but they relate to positive ideas, and signify their absence.

II. OF THE SIGNIFICATION OF WORDS

1. Man, though he have great variety of thoughts, and such from which others as well as himself might receive profit and delight; yet they are all within his own breast, invisible and hidden from others, nor can of themselves be made to appear. The comfort and advantage of society not being to be had without communication of thoughts, it was necessary that man should find out some external sensible signs,

From *An Essay Concerning Human Understanding* (1690), Book III.

whereof those invisible ideas, which his thoughts are made up of, might be made known to others. For this purpose nothing was so fit, either for plenty or quickness, as those articulate sounds, which with so much ease and variety he found himself able to make. Thus we may conceive how *words,* which were by nature so well adapted to that purpose, came to be made use of by men as the signs of their ideas; not by any natural connexion that there is between particular articulate sounds and certain ideas, for then there would be but one language amongst all men; but by a voluntary imposition, whereby such a word is made arbitrarily the mark of such an idea. The use, then, of words, is to be sensible marks of ideas; and the ideas they stand for are their proper and immediate signification.

2. The use men have of these marks being either to record their own thoughts, for the assistance of their own memory; or, as it were, to bring out their ideas, and lay them before the view of others: words, in their primary or immediate signification, stand for nothing but *the ideas in the mind of him that uses them,* how imperfectly soever or carelessly those ideas are collected from the things which they are supposed to represent. When a man speaks to another, it is that he may be understood: and the end of speech is, that those sounds, as marks, may make known his ideas to the hearer. That then which words are the marks of are the ideas of the speaker: nor can any one apply them as marks, immediately, to anything else but the ideas that he himself hath: for this would be to make them signs of his own conceptions, and yet apply them to other ideas; which would be to make them signs and not signs of his ideas at the same time; and so in effect to have no signification at all. Words being voluntary signs, they cannot be voluntary signs imposed by him on things he knows not. That would be to make them signs of nothing, sounds without signification. A man cannot make his words the signs either of qualities in things, or of conceptions in the mind of another, whereof he has none in his own. Till he has some ideas of his own, he cannot suppose them to correspond with the conceptions of another man; nor can he use any signs for them: for thus they would be the signs of he knows not what, which is in truth to be the

signs of nothing. But when he represents to himself other men's ideas by some of his own, if he consent to give them the same names that other men do, it is still to his own ideas; to ideas that he has, and not to ideas that he has not.

3. This is so necessary in the use of language, that in this respect the knowing and the ignorant, the learned and the unlearned, use the words they speak (with any meaning) all alike. They, in every man's mouth, stand for the ideas he has, and which he would express by them. A child having taken notice of nothing in the metal he hears called *gold,* but the bright shining yellow colour, he applies the word gold only to his own idea of that colour, and nothing else; and therefore calls the same colour in a peacock's tail gold. Another that hath better observed, adds to shining yellow great weight: and then the sound 'gold', when he uses it, stands for a complex idea of a shining yellow and a very weighty substance. Another adds to those qualities fusibility: and then the word 'gold' signifies to him a body, bright, yellow, fusible, and very heavy. Another adds malleability. Each of these uses equally the word 'gold', when they have occasion to express the idea which they have applied it to: but it is evident that each can apply it only to his own idea; nor can he make it stand as a sign of such a complex idea as he has not.

4. But though words, as they are used by men, can properly and immediately signify nothing but the ideas that are in the mind of the speaker; yet they in their thoughts give them a secret reference to two other things.

First, *They suppose their words to be marks of the ideas in the minds also of other men, with whom they communicate:* for else they should talk in vain, and could not be understood, if the sounds they applied to one idea were such as by the hearer were applied to another, which is to speak two languages. But in this men stand not usually to examine, whether the idea they, and those they discourse with have in their minds be the same: but think it enough that they use the word, as they imagine, in the common acceptation of that language; in which they suppose that the idea they make it a sign of is precisely the same to which the understanding men of that country apply that name.

5. Secondly, Because men would not be

thought to talk barely of their own imagination, but of things as really they are; therefore they often suppose the *words to stand also for the reality of things.* But this relating more particularly to substances and their names, as perhaps the former does to simple ideas and modes, we shall speak of these two different ways of applying words more at large, when we come to treat of the names of mixed modes and substances in particular: though give me leave here to say, that it is a perverting the use of words, and brings unavoidable obscurity and confusion into their signification, whenever we make them stand for anything but those ideas we have in our own minds.

6. Concerning words, also, it is further to be considered:

First, that they being immediately the signs of men's ideas, and by that means the instruments whereby men communicate their conceptions, and express to one another those thoughts and imaginations they have within their own breasts; there comes, by constant use, to be such a connexion between certain sounds and the ideas they stand for, that the names heard, almost as readily excite certain ideas as if the objects themselves, which are apt to produce them, did actually affect the senses. Which is manifestly so in all obvious sensible qualities, and in all substances that frequently and familiarly occur to us.

7. Secondly, That though the proper and immediate signification of words are ideas in the mind of the speaker, yet, because by familiar use from our cradles, we come to learn certain articulate sounds very perfectly, and have them readily on our tongues, and always at hand in our memories, but yet are not always careful to examine or settle their significations perfectly; it often happens that men, even when they would apply themselves to an attentive consideration, do set their thoughts more on words than things. Nay, because words are many of them learned before the ideas are known for which they stand: therefore some, not only children but men, speak several words no otherwise than parrots do, only because they have learned them, and have been accustomed to those sounds. But so far as words are of use and signification, so far is there a constant connexion between the sound and the idea,

and a designation that the one stands for the other; without which application of them, they are nothing but so much insignificant noise.

8. Words, by long and familiar use, as has been said, come to excite in men certain ideas so constantly and readily, that they are apt to suppose a natural connexion between them. But that they signify only men's peculiar ideas, and that *by a perfect arbitrary imposition,* is evident, in that they often fail to excite in others (even that use the same language) the same ideas we take them to be signs of: and every man has so inviolable a liberty to make words stand for what ideas he pleases, that no one hath the power to make others have the same ideas in their minds that he has, when they use the same words that he does. And therefore the great Augustus himself, in the possession of that power which ruled the world, acknowledged he could not make a new Latin word: which was as much as to say, that he could not arbitrarily appoint what idea any sound should be a sign of, in the mouths and common language of his subjects. It is true, common use, by a tacit consent, appropriates certain sounds to certain ideas in all languages, which so far limits the signification of that sound, that unless a man applies it to the same idea, he does not speak properly: and let me add, that unless a man's words excite the same ideas in the hearer which he makes them stand for in speaking, he does not speak intelligibly. But whatever be the consequence of any man's using of words differently, either from their general meaning, or the particular sense of the person to whom he addresses them; this is certain, their signification, in his use of them, is limited to his ideas, and they can be signs of nothing else.

III. OF GENERAL TERMS

1. All things that exist being particulars, it may perhaps be thought reasonable that words, which ought to be conformed to things, should be so too,—I mean in their signification: but yet we find quite the contrary. The far greatest part of words that make all languages are general terms: which has not been the effect of neglect or chance, but of reason and necessity.

2. First, It is impossible that every particular

thing should have a distinct peculiar name. For, the signification and use of words depending on that connexion which the mind makes between its ideas and the sounds it uses as signs of them, it is necessary, in the application of names to things, that the mind should have distinct ideas of the things, and retain also the particular name that belongs to every one, with its peculiar appropriation to that idea. But it is beyond the power of human capacity to frame and retain distinct ideas of all the particular things we meet with: every bird and beast men saw; every tree and plant that affected the senses, could not find a place in the most capacious understanding. If it be looked on as an instance of a prodigious memory, that some generals have been able to call every soldier in their army by his proper name, we may easily find a reason why men have never attempted to give names to each sheep in their flock, or crow that flies over their heads; much less to call every leaf of plants, or grain of sand that came in their way, by a peculiar name.

3. Secondly, If it were possible, it would yet be useless; because it would not serve to the chief end of language. Men would in vain heap up names of particular things, that would not serve them to communicate their thoughts. Men learn names, and use them in talk with others, only that they may be understood: which is then only done when, by use or consent, the sound I make by the organs of speech, excites in another man's mind who hears it, the idea I apply it to in mine, when I speak it. This cannot be done by names applied to particular things; whereof I alone having the ideas in my mind, the names of them could not be significant or intelligible to another, who was not acquainted with all those very particular things which had fallen under my notice.

4. Thirdly, But yet, granting this also feasible, (which I think is not,) yet a distinct name for every particular thing would not be of any great use for the improvement of knowledge: which, though founded in particular things, enlarges itself by general views; to which things reduced into sorts, under general names, are properly subservient. These, with the names belonging to them, come within some compass, and do not multiply every moment, beyond what either the

mind can contain, or use requires. And therefore, in these, men have for the most part stopped: but yet not so as to hinder themselves from distinguishing particular things by appropriated names, where convenience demands it. And therefore in their own species, which they have most to do with, and wherein they have often occasion to mention particular persons, they make use of proper names; and there distinct individuals have distinct denominations.

5. Besides persons, countries also, cities, rivers, mountains, and other the like distinctions of place have usually found peculiar names, and that for the same reason; they being such as men have often an occasion to mark particularly, and, as it were, set before others in their discourses with them. And I doubt not but, if we had reason to mention particular horses as often as we have to mention particular men, we should have proper names for the one, as familiar as for the other, and Bucephalus would be a word as much in use as Alexander. And therefore we see that, amongst jockeys, horses have their proper names to be known and distinguished by, as commonly as their servants: because, amongst them, there is often occasion to mention this or that particular horse when he is out of sight.

6. The next thing to be considered is,—How general words come to be made. For, since all things that exist are only particulars, how come we by general terms; or where find we those general natures they are supposed to stand for? Words become general by being made the signs of general ideas: and ideas become general, by separating from them the circumstances of time and place, and any other ideas that may determine them to this or that particular existence. By this way of abstraction they are made capable of representing more individuals than one; each of which having in it a conformity to that abstract idea, is (as we call it) of that sort. . . .

9. That this is the way whereby men first formed general ideas, and general names to them, I think is so evident, that there needs no other proof of it but the considering of a man's self, or others, and the ordinary proceedings of their minds in knowledge. And he that thinks *general natures or notions* are anything else but such abstract and partial ideas of more complex

ones, taken at first from particular existences, will, I fear, be at a loss where to find them. For let any one reflect, and then tell me, wherein does his idea of *man* differ from that of *Peter* and *Paul,* or his idea of *horse* from that of *Bucephalus,* but in the leaving out something that is peculiar to each individual, and retaining so much of those particular complex ideas of several particular existences as they are found to agree in? Of the complex ideas signified by the names *man* and *horse,* leaving out but those particulars wherein they differ, and retaining only those wherein they agree, and of those making a new distinct complex idea, and giving the name *animal* to it, one has a more general term, that comprehends with man several other creatures. Leave out of the idea of *animal,* sense and spontaneous motion, and the remaining complex idea, made up of the remaining simple ones of body, life, and nourishment, becomes a more general one, under the more comprehensive term, *vivens.* And, not to dwell longer upon this particular, so evident in itself; by the same way the mind proceeds to *body, substance,* and at last to *being, thing,* and such universal terms, which stand for any of our ideas whatsoever. To conclude: this whole mystery of genera and species, which make such a noise in the schools, and are with justice so little regarded out of them, is nothing else but *abstract ideas,* more or less comprehensive, with names annexed to them. In all which this is constant and unvariable, That every more general term stands for such an idea, and is but a part of any of those contained under it. . . .

11. To return to general words: it is plain, by what has been said, that *general* and *universal* belong not to the real existence of things; but are the inventions and creatures of the understanding, made by it for its own use, and concern only signs, whether words or ideas. Words are general, as has been said, when used for signs of general ideas, and so are applicable indifferently to many particular things; and ideas are general when they are set up as the representatives of many particular things: but universality belongs not to things themselves, which are all of them particular in their existence, even those words and ideas which in their signification are general. When therefore we quit particulars, the generals that rest are only creatures of our own making; their general nature being nothing but the capacity they are put into, by the understanding, of signifying or representing many particulars. For the signification they have is nothing but a relation that, by the mind of man, is added to them.

12. The next thing therefore to be considered is, What kind of signification it is that general words have. For, as it is evident that they do not signify barely one particular thing; for then they would not be general terms, but proper names, so, on the other side, it is as evident they do not signify a plurality; for *man* and *men* would then signify the same; and the distinction of numbers (as the grammarians call them) would be superfluous and useless. That then which general words signify is a *sort* of things; and each of them does that, by being a sign of an abstract idea in the mind; to which idea, as things existing are found to agree, so they come to be ranked under that name, or, which is all one, be of that sort. Whereby it is evident that the *essences* of the sorts, or, if the Latin word pleases better, *species* of things, are nothing else but these abstract ideas. For the having the essence of any species, being that which makes anything to be of that species; and the conformity to the idea to which the name is annexed being that which gives a right to that name; the having the essence, and the having that conformity, must needs be the same thing: since to be of any species, and to have a right to the name of that species, is all one. As, for example, to be a *man,* or of the *species* man, and to have right to the *name* man, is the same thing. Again, to be a man, or of the species man, and have the *essence* of a man, is the same thing. Now, since nothing can be a man, or have a right to the name man, but what has a conformity to the abstract idea the name man stands for, nor anything be a man, or have a right to the species man, but what has the essence of that species; it follows, that the abstract idea for which the name stands, and the essence of the species, is one and the same. From whence it is easy to observe, that the essences of the sorts of things, and, consequently, the sorting of things, is the workmanship of the understanding that abstracts and makes those general ideas.

43 On Rules and Private Language

SAUL KRIPKE

. . . A common view of the 'private language argument' in *Philosophical Investigations* assumes that it begins with section 243, and that it continues in the sections immediately following.[1] This view takes the argument to deal primarily with a problem about 'sensation language'. Further discussion of the argument in this tradition, both in support and in criticism, emphasizes such questions as whether the argument invokes a form of the verification principle, whether the form in question is justified, whether it is applied correctly to sensation language, whether the argument rests on an exaggerated scepticism about memory, and so on. Some crucial passages in the discussion following §243—for example, such celebrated sections as §258 and §265—have been notoriously obscure to commentators, and it has been thought that their proper interpretation would provide the key to the 'private language argument'.

In my view, the real "private language argument" is to be found in the sections *preceding* §243. Indeed, in §202 *the conclusion is already stated explicitly:* "Hence it is not possible to obey a rule 'privately': otherwise thinking one was obeying a rule would be the same thing as obeying it." I do not think that Wittgenstein here thought of himself as *anticipating* an argument he was to give in greater detail later. On the contrary, the crucial considerations are all contained in the discussion leading up to the conclusion stated in §202. The sections following §243 are meant to be read in the light of the preceding discussion; difficult as they are in any case, they are much less likely to be understood if they are read in isolation. The 'private language argument' as applied to *sensations* is only a special case of much more general considerations about language previously argued; sensations have a crucial role as an (apparently) convincing *counterexample* to the general considerations previously stated. Wittgenstein therefore goes over the ground again in this special case, marshalling new specific considerations appropriate to it. It should be borne in mind that *Philosophical Investigations* is not a systematic philosophical work where conclusions, once definitely established, need not be reargued. Rather the *Investigations* is written as a perpetual dialectic, where persisting worries, expressed by the voice of the imaginary interlocutor, are never definitively silenced. Since the work is not presented in the form of a deductive argument with definitive theses as conclusions, the same ground is covered repeatedly, from the point of view of various special cases and from different angles, with the hope that the entire process will help the reader see the problems rightly.

The basic structure of Wittgenstein's approach can be presented briefly as follows: A certain problem, or in Humean terminology, a

From *On Rules and Private Language* (Cambridge: Harvard University Press, 1982). Copyright © 1982 by Saul A. Kripke. Reprinted by permission of the author. Also by permission of Basil Blackwell Ltd.

'sceptical paradox', is presented concerning the notion of a rule. Following this, what Hume would have called a 'sceptical solution' to the problem is presented. There are two areas in which the force, both of the paradox and of its solution, are most likely to be ignored, and with respect to which Wittgenstein's basic approach is most likely to seem incredible. One such area is the notion of a mathematical rule, such as the rule for addition. The other is our talk of our own inner experience, of sensations and other inner states. In treating both these cases, we should bear in mind the basic considerations about rules and language. Although Wittgenstein has already discussed these basic considerations in considerable generality, the structure of Wittgenstein's work is such that the special cases of mathematics and psychology are not simply discussed by citing a general 'result' already established, but by going over these special cases in detail, in the light of the previous treatment of the general case. By such a discussion, it is hoped that both mathematics and the mind can be seen rightly: since the temptations to see them wrongly arise from the neglect of the same basic considerations about rules and language, the problems which arise can be expected to be analogous in the two cases. In my opinion, Wittgenstein did not view his dual interests in the philosophy of mind and the philosophy of mathematics as interests in two separate, at best loosely related, subjects, as someone might be interested both in music and in economics. Wittgenstein thinks of the two subjects as involving the same basic considerations. For this reason, he calls his investigation of the foundations of mathematics "analogous to our investigation of psychology" (p. 232). It is no accident that essentially the same basic material on rules is included in both *Philosophical Investigations* and in *Remarks on the Foundations of Mathematics,*[2] both times as the basis of the discussions of the philosophies of mind and of mathematics, respectively, which follow.

In the following, I am largely trying to present Wittgenstein's argument, or, more accurately, that set of problems and arguments which I personally have gotten out of reading Wittgenstein. With few exceptions, I am *not* trying to present views of my own; neither am I trying to endorse or to criticize Wittgenstein's approach. In some cases, I have found a precise statement of the problems and conclusions to be elusive. Although one has a strong sense that there is a problem, a rigorous statement of it is difficult. I am inclined to think that Wittgenstein's later philosophical style, and the difficulty he found (see his preface) in welding his thought into a conventional work presented with organized arguments and conclusions, is not simply a stylistic and literary preference, coupled with a *penchant* for a certain degree of obscurity,[3] but stems in part from the nature of his subject.

I suspect—for reasons that will become clearer later—that to attempt to present Wittgenstein's argument precisely is to some extent to falsify it. Probably many of my formulations and recastings of the argument are done in a way Wittgenstein would not himself approve. So the present paper should be thought of as expounding neither 'Wittgenstein's' argument nor 'Kripke's': rather Wittgenstein's argument as it struck Kripke, as it presented a problem for him.

As I have said, I think the basic 'private language argument' *precedes* section 243, though the sections following 243 are no doubt of fundamental importance as well. I propose to discuss the problem of 'private language' initially without mentioning these latter sections *at all*. Since these sections are often thought to be the 'private language argument', to some such a procedure may seem to be a presentation of Hamlet without the prince. Even if this is so, there are many other interesting characters in the play.

. . . In §201 Wittgenstein says, "this was our paradox: no course of action could be determined by a rule, because every course of action can be made to accord with the rule." In this section of the present essay, in my own way I will attempt to develop the "paradox" in question. The "paradox" is perhaps the central problem of *Philosophical Investigations*. Even someone who disputes the conclusions regarding 'private language', and the philosophies of mind, mathematics, and logic, that Wittgenstein draws from his problem, might well regard the problem itself as an important contribution to philoso-

phy. It may be regarded as a new form of philosophical scepticism.

Following Wittgenstein, I will develop the
problem initially with respect to a mathematical
example, though the relevant sceptical problem
applies to all meaningful uses of language. I,
like almost all English speakers, use the word
"plus" and the symbol '+' to denote a well-
known mathematical function, addition. The
function is defined for all pairs of positive integers. By means of my external symbolic representation and my internal mental representation, I 'grasp' the rule for addition. One point is
crucial to my 'grasp' of this rule. Although I
myself have computed only finitely many sums
in the past, the rule determines my answer for
indefinitely many new sums that I have never
previously considered. This is the whole point
of the notion that in learning to add I grasp a
rule: my past intentions regarding addition
determine a unique answer for indefinitely
many new cases in the future.

Let me suppose, for example, that '68 + 57' is
a computation that I have never performed
before. Since I have performed—even silently
to myself, let alone in my publicly observable
behavior—only finitely many computations in
the past, such an example surely exists. In fact,
the same finitude guarantees that there is an
example exceeding, in both its arguments, all
previous computations. I shall assume in what
follows that '68 + 57' serves for this purpose as
well.

I perform the computation, obtaining, of
course, the answer '125'. I am confident, perhaps after checking my work, that '125' is the
correct answer. It is correct both in the arithmetical sense that 125 is the sum of 68 and 57,
and in the metalinguistic sense that "plus," as I
intended to use that word in the past, denoted a
function which, when applied to the numbers I
called "68" and "57," yields the value 125.

Now suppose I encounter a bizarre sceptic.
This sceptic questions my certainty about my
answer, in what I just called the 'metalinguistic'
sense. Perhaps, he suggests, as I used the term
"plus" in the past, the answer I intended for
'68 + 57' should have been '5'! Of course the
sceptic's suggestion is obviously insane. My
initial response to such a suggestion might be
that the challenger should go back to school and

learn to add. Let the challenger, however, continue. After all, he says, if I am now so confident
that, as I used the symbol '+', my intention was
that '68 + 57' should turn out to denote 125, this
cannot be because I explicitly gave myself
instructions that 125 is the result of performing
the addition in this particular instance. By
hypothesis, I did no such thing. But of course
the idea is that, in this new instance, I should
apply the very same function or rule that I
applied so many times in the past. But who is to
say what function this was? In the past I gave
myself only a finite number of examples instantiating this function. All, we have supposed,
involved numbers smaller than 57. So perhaps
in the past I used "plus" and '+' to denote a
function which I will call 'quus' and symbolize
by '⊕'. It is defined by:

$$x \oplus y = x + y \text{ if } x, y < 57 = 5 \text{ otherwise.}$$

Who is to say that this is not the function I previously meant by '+'?

The sceptic claims (or feigns to claim) that
I am now misinterpreting my own previous
usage. By "plus," he says, *I always meant* quus;[4]
now, under the influence of some insane frenzy,
or a bout of LSD, I have come to misinterpret
my own previous usage.

Ridiculous and fantastic though it is, the
sceptic's hypothesis is not logically impossible.
To see this, assume the common sense hypothesis that by '+' I *did* mean addition. Then it
would be *possible,* though surprising, that under
the influence of a momentary 'high', I should
misinterpret all my past uses of the plus sign as
symbolizing the quus function, and proceed, in
conflict with my previous linguistic intentions,
to compute 68 plus 57 as 5. (I would have made
a mistake, not in mathematics, but in the supposition that I had accorded with my previous linguistic intentions.) The sceptic is proposing that
I have made a mistake precisely of this kind, but
with a plus and quus reversed.

Now if the sceptic proposes his hypothesis
sincerely, he is crazy; such a bizarre hypothesis
as the proposal that I always meant quus is
absolutely wild. Wild it indubitably is, no doubt
it is false; but if it is false, there must be some
fact about my past usage that can be cited to
refute it. For although the hypothesis is wild, it
does not seem to be a priori impossible.

Of course this bizarre hypothesis, and the references to LSD, or to an insane frenzy, are in a sense merely a dramatic device. The basic point is this. Ordinarily, I suppose that, in computing '68 + 57' as I do, I do not simply make an unjustified leap in the dark. I follow directions I previously gave myself that uniquely determine that in this new instance I should say '125'. What are these directions? By hypothesis, I never explicitly told myself that I should say '125' in this very instance. Nor can I say that I should simply 'do the same thing I always did,' if this means 'compute according to the rule exhibited by my previous examples.' That rule could just as well have been the rule for quaddition (the quus function) as for addition. The idea that in fact quaddition *is* what I meant, that in a sudden frenzy I have changed my previous usage, dramatizes the problem.

In the discussion below the challenge posed by the sceptic takes two forms. First, he questions whether there is any *fact* that I meant plus, not quus, that will answer his sceptical challenge. Second, he questions whether I have any reason to be so confident that now I should answer '125' rather than '5'. The two forms of the challenge are related. I am confident that I should answer '125' because I am confident that this answer also accords with what I *meant*. Neither the accuracy of my computation nor of my memory is under dispute. So it ought to be agreed that *if* I meant plus, then unless I wish to change my usage, I am justified in answering (indeed compelled to answer) '125', not '5'. An answer to the sceptic must satisfy two conditions. First, it must give an account of what fact it is (about my mental state) that constitutes my meaning plus, not quus. But further, there is a condition that any putative candidate for such a fact must satisfy. It must, in some sense, show how I am justified in giving the answer '125' to '68 + 57'. The 'directions' mentioned in the previous paragraph, that determine what I should do in each instance, must somehow be "contained" in any candidate for the fact as to what I meant. Otherwise, the sceptic has not been answered when he holds that my present response is arbitrary. Exactly how this condition operates will become much clearer below, after we discuss Wittgenstein's paradox on an intuitive level, when we consider various philosophical theories

as to what the fact that I meant plus might consist in. There will be many specific objections to these theories. But all fail to give a candidate for a fact as to what I meant that would show that only '125', not '5', is the answer I 'ought' to give.

The ground rules of our formulation of the problem should be made clear. For the sceptic to converse with me at all, we must have a common language. So I am supposing that the sceptic, provisionally, is not questioning my *present* use of the word "plus"; he agrees that, according to my *present* usage, '68 plus 57' denotes 125. Not only does he agree with me on this, he conducts the entire debate with me in my language as I *presently* use it. He merely questions whether my present usage agrees with my past usage, whether I am *presently* conforming to my *previous* linguistic intentions. The problem is not "How do I know that 68 plus 57 is 125?", which should be answered by giving an arithmetical computation, but rather "How do I know that '68 plus 57', as I *meant* 'plus' in the past, should denote 125?" If the word "plus" as I used it in the past, denoted the quus function, not the plus function ('quaddition' rather than addition), then my *past* intention was such that, asked for the value of '68 plus 57', I should have replied '5'.

I put the problem in this way so as to avoid confusing questions about whether the discussion is taking place 'both inside and outside language' in some illegitimate sense.[5] If we are querying the meaning of the word "plus," how can we use it (and variants, like 'quus') at the same time? So I suppose that the sceptic assumes that he and I agree in our *present* uses of the word "plus": we both use it to denote addition. He does *not*—at least initially—deny or doubt that addition is a genuine function, defined on all pairs of integers, nor does he deny that we can speak of it. Rather he asks why I now believe that by "plus" in the *past,* I meant addition rather than quaddition. If I meant the former, then to accord with my previous usage I should say '125' when asked to give the result of calculating '68 plus 57'. If I meant the latter, I should say '5'.

The present exposition tends to differ from Wittgenstein's original formulations in taking somewhat greater care to make explicit a distinction between use and mention, and between questions about present and past usage. About the present example Wittgenstein might simply ask, "How do I know that I should respond '125' to the query '68 + 57'?" or "How do I know that '68 + 57' comes out 125?" I have found that when the problem is formulated this way, some listeners hear it as a sceptical problem about *arithmetic:* "How do I know that 68 + 57 is 125?" (Why not answer this question with a mathematical proof?) At least at this stage, scepticism about arithmetic should not be taken to be in question: we may assume, if we wish, that 68 + 57 *is* 125. Even if the question is reformulated 'metalinguistically' as "How do I know that 'plus', as I use it, denotes a function that, when applied to 68 and 57, yields 125?", one may answer, "Surely I know that 'plus' denotes the plus function and accordingly that '68 plus 57' denotes 68 plus 57. But if I know arithmetic, I know that 68 plus 57 is 125. So I know that '68 plus 57' denotes 125!" And surely, if I use language at all, I cannot doubt coherently that "plus," as I now use it, denotes plus! Perhaps I cannot (at least at this stage) doubt this about my *present* usage. But I can doubt that my *past* usage of "plus" denoted plus. The previous remarks—about a frenzy and LSD—should make this quite clear.

Let me repeat the problem. The sceptic doubts whether any instructions I gave myself in the past compel (or justify) the answer '125' rather than '5'. He puts the challenge in terms of a sceptical hypothesis about a change in my usage. Perhaps when I used the term "plus" in the *past,* I always meant quus: by hypothesis I never gave myself any explicit directions that were incompatible with such a supposition.

Of course, ultimately, if the sceptic is right, the concepts of meaning and of intending one function rather than another will make no sense. For the sceptic holds that no fact about my past history—nothing that was ever in my mind, or in my external behavior—establishes that I meant plus rather than quus. (Nor, of course, does any fact establish that I meant quus!) But if this is correct, there can of course be no fact about which function I meant, and if there can be no fact about which particular function I meant in the *past,* there can be none in the *pres-*

ent either. But before we pull the rug out from under our own feet, we begin by speaking as if the notion that at present we mean a certain function by "plus" is unquestioned and unquestionable. Only past usages are to be questioned. Otherwise, we will be unable to *formulate* our problem.

Another important rule of the game is that there are no limitations, in particular, no *behaviorist* limitations, on the facts that may be cited to answer the sceptic. The evidence is not to be confined to that available to an external observer, who can observe my overt behavior but not my internal mental state. It would be interesting if nothing in my external behavior could show whether I meant plus or quus, but something about my inner state could. But the problem here is more radical. Wittgenstein's philosophy of mind has often been viewed as behavioristic, but to the extent that Wittgenstein may (or may not) be hostile to the 'inner', no such hostility is to be assumed as a premise; it is to be argued as a conclusion. So whatever 'looking into my mind' may be, the sceptic asserts that even if God were to do it, he still could not determine that I meant addition by "plus."

This feature of Wittgenstein contrasts, for example, with Quine's discussion of the 'indeterminacy of translation'.[6] There are many points of contact between Quine's discussion and Wittgenstein's. Quine, however, is more than content to assume that only behavioral evidence is to be admitted into his discussion. Wittgenstein, by contrast, undertakes an extensive introspective[7] investigation, and the results of the investigation, as we shall see, form a key feature of his argument. Further, the way the sceptical doubt is presented is not behavioristic. It is presented from the 'inside'. Whereas Quine presents the problem about meaning in terms of a linguist, trying to guess what someone *else* means by his words on the basis of his behavior, Wittgenstein's challenge can be presented to me as a question about *myself:* was there some past fact about me—what I 'meant' by plus—that mandates what I should do now?

To return to the sceptic. The sceptic argues that when I answered '125' to the problem '68 + 57', my answer was an unjustified leap in the dark; my past mental history is equally compatible with the hypothesis that I meant quus, and therefore should have said '5'. We can put the problem this way: When asked for the answer to '68 + 57', I unhesitatingly and automatically produced '125', but it would seem that if previously I never performed this computation explicitly I might just as well have answered '5'. Nothing justifies a brute inclination to answer one way rather than another. . . . Wittgenstein has invented a new form of scepticism. Personally I am inclined to regard it as the most radical and original sceptical problem that philosophy has seen to date, one that only a highly unusual cast of mind could have produced. Of course he does not wish to leave us with his problem, but to solve it: the sceptical conclusion is insane and intolerable. It is his solution, I will argue, that contains the argument against 'private language'; for allegedly, the solution will not admit such a language. But it is important to see that his achievement in posing this problem stands on its own, independently of the value of his own solution of it and the resultant argument against private language. For, if we see Wittgenstein's problem as a real one, it is clear that he has often been read from the wrong perspective. Readers, my previous self certainly included, have often been inclined to wonder: "How can he prove private language impossible? How can I possibly have any difficulty identifying my own sensations? And if there were a difficulty, how could 'public' criteria help me? I must be in pretty bad shape if I needed external *help* to identify my own sensations!" But if I am right, a proper orientation would be the opposite. The main problem is *not,* "How can we show private language—or some other special form of language—to be *impossible?*"; rather it is, "How can we show any *language* at all (public, private, or what-have-you) to be *possible?*"[8] It is not that calling a sensation 'pain' is easy, and Wittgenstein must invent a difficulty.[9] On the contrary, Wittgenstein's main problem is that it appears that he has shown *all* language, *all* concept formation, to be impossible, indeed unintelligible.

It is important and illuminating to compare Wittgenstein's new form of scepticism with the classical scepticism of Hume; there are important analogies between the two. Both develop a sceptical paradox, based on questioning a certain *nexus* from past to future. Wittgenstein questions the nexus between past 'intention' or 'meanings' and present practice: for example, between my past 'intentions' with regard to 'plus' and my present computation '68 + 57 = 125'. Hume questions two other nexuses, related to each other: the causal nexus whereby a past event necessitates a future one, and the inductive inferential nexus from the past to the future.

The analogy is obvious. It has been obscured for several reasons. First, the Humean and the Wittgensteinian problems are of course distinct and independent, though analogous. Second, Wittgenstein shows little interest in or sympathy with Hume: he has been quoted as saying that he could not read Hume because he found it "a torture".[10] Furthermore, Hume is the prime source of some ideas on the nature of mental states that Wittgenstein is most concerned to attack.[11] Finally (and probably most important), Wittgenstein never avows, and almost surely would not avow, the label 'sceptic', as Hume explicitly did. Indeed, he has often appeared to be a 'common-sense' philosopher, anxious to defend our ordinary conceptions and dissolve traditional philosophical doubts. Is it not Wittgenstein who held that philosophy only states what everyone admits?

Yet even here the difference between Wittgenstein and Hume should not be exaggerated. Even Hume has an important strain, dominant in some of his moods, that the philosopher never questions ordinary beliefs. Asked whether he "be really one of those sceptics, who hold that all is uncertain," Hume replies "that this question is entirely superfluous, and that neither I, nor any other person, was ever sincerely and constantly of that opinion."[12] Even more forcefully, discussing the problem of the external world: "We may well ask, *What causes induce us to believe in the existence of body? but 'tis in vain to ask, Whether there be body or not?* That is a point, which we must take for granted in all our reasonings."[13] Yet this oath of fealty to common sense begins a section that otherwise looks like an argument that the common conception of material objects is irreparably incoherent!

When Hume is in a mood to respect his professed determination never to deny or doubt our common beliefs, in what does his 'scepticism' consist? First, in a sceptical account of the causes of these beliefs; and second, in sceptical analyses of our common notions. In some ways Berkeley, who did not regard his own views as sceptical, may offer an even better analogy to Wittgenstein. At first blush, Berkeley, with his denial of matter, and of any objects 'outside the mind' seems to be *denying* our common beliefs; and for many of us the impression persists through later blushes. But not for Berkeley. For him, the impression that the common man is committed to matter and to objects outside the mind derives from an erroneous metaphysical interpretation of common talk. When the common man speaks of an 'external material object' he does not really mean (as we might say *sotto voce*) an *external material object* but rather he means something like 'an idea produced in me independently of my will'.[14]

Berkeley's stance is not uncommon in philosophy. The philosopher advocates a view apparently in patent contradiction to common sense. Rather than repudiating common sense, he asserts that the conflict comes from a philosophical misinterpretation of common language—sometimes he adds that the misinterpretation is encouraged by the 'superficial form' of ordinary speech. He offers his own analysis of the relevant common assertions, one that shows that they do not really say what they seem to say. For Berkeley this philosophical strategy is central to his work. To the extent that Hume claims that he merely analyses common sense and does not oppose it, he invokes the same strategy as well. The practice can hardly be said to have ceased today.[15]

Personally I think such philosophical claims are almost invariably suspect. What the claimant calls a 'misleading philosophical misconstrual' of the ordinary statement is probably the natural and correct understanding. The real misconstrual comes when the claimant continues, "All the ordinary man really means is . . ." and gives a sophisticated analysis compatible with his own philosophy. Be this as it may, the important point for present purposes is that Wittgenstein makes a Berkeleyan claim of this kind. For—as we shall see—his solution to his own sceptical problem begins by agreeing with the sceptics that there is no 'superlative fact' (§192) about my mind that constitutes my meaning addition by "plus" and determines in advance what I should do to accord with this meaning. But, he claims (in §§183–93), the appearance that our ordinary concept of meaning demands such a fact is based on a philosophical misconstrual—albeit a natural one—of such ordinary expressions as "he meant such-and-such," "the steps are determined by the formula," and the like. How Wittgenstein construes these expressions we shall see presently. For the moment let us only remark that Wittgenstein thinks that any construal that looks for something in my present mental state to differentiate between my meaning addition or quaddition, or that will consequently show that in the future I should say '125' when asked about '68 + 57', is a misconstrual and attributes to the ordinary man a notion of meaning that *is* refuted by the sceptical argument. "We are," he says in §194—note that Berkeley could have said just the same thing!— "like savages, primitive people, who hear the expressions of civilized men, put a false interpretation on them, and then draw the queerest conclusions from it." Maybe so. Personally I can only report that, in spite of Wittgenstein's assurances, the 'primitive' interpretation often sounds rather good to me . . .

In his *Enquiry,* after he has developed his "Sceptical Doubts Concerning the Operations of the Understanding," Hume gives his "Sceptical Solution of These Doubts." What is a 'sceptical' solution? Call a proposed solution to a sceptical philosophical problem a *straight* solution if it shows that on closer examination the scepticism proves to be unwarranted; an elusive or complex argument proves the thesis the sceptic doubted. Descartes gave a 'straight' solution in this sense to his own philosophical doubts. An a priori justification of inductive reasoning, and an analysis of the causal relation as a genuine necessary connection or nexus between pairs of events, would be straight solutions of Hume's problems of induction and causation, respectively. A *sceptical* solution of a sceptical philosophical problem begins on the contrary by conceding that the sceptic's negative assertions are unanswerable. Nevertheless our ordinary practice or belief is justified because—contrary appearances notwithstanding—it need not require the justification the sceptic has shown to be untenable. And much of the value of the sceptical argument consists precisely in the fact that he has shown that an ordinary practice, if it is to be defended at all, cannot be defended in a certain way. A sceptical solution may also involve—in the manner suggested above—a sceptical analysis or account of ordinary beliefs to rebut their *prima facie* reference to a metaphysical absurdity.

The rough outlines of Hume's sceptical solution to his problem are well known.[16] Not an a priori argument, but custom, is the source of our inductive inferences. If *A* and *B* are two types of events which we have seen constantly conjoined, then we are conditioned—Hume is a grandfather of this modern psychological notion—to expect an event of type *B* on being presented with one of type *A*. To say of a particular event *a* that it caused another event *b* is to place these two events under two types, *A* and *B*, which we expect to be constantly conjoined in the future as they were in the past. The idea of necessary connection comes from the 'feeling of customary transition' between our ideas of these event types.

The philosophical merits of the Humean solution are not our present concern. Our purpose is to use the analogy with the Humean solution to illuminate Wittgenstein's solution to his own problem. For comparative purposes one further consequence of Hume's sceptical solution should be noted. Naively, one might suppose that whether a particular event *a* causes another particular event *b*, is an issue solely involving the events *a* and *b* alone (and their relations), and involves no other events. If Hume is right, this is not so. Even if God were to look at the events, he would discern nothing relating them other than that one succeeds the other. Only when the particular events *a* and *b* are thought of as subsumed under two respective event types, *A* and *B*, which are related by a generalization that *all* events of type *A* are followed by events of type *B*, can *a* be said to 'cause' *b*. When the events *a* and *b* are considered by themselves alone, no causal notions are applicable. This Humean conclusion might be called: the impossibility of private causation.

Can one reasonably protest: surely there is nothing the event *a* can do with the *help* of other events of the same type that it cannot do by itself! Indeed, to say that *a*, by itself, is a sufficient cause of *b* is to say that, had the rest of the universe been removed, *a* still would have produced *b!* Intuitively this may well be so, but the intuitive objection ignores Hume's sceptical argument. The whole point of the sceptical argument is that the common notion of one event 'producing' another, on which the objection relies, is in jeopardy. It appears that there is no such relation as 'production' at all, that the causal relation is fictive. After the sceptical argument has been seen to be unanswerable on its own terms, a sceptical solution is offered, containing all we can salvage of the notion of causation. It just is a feature of this analysis that causation makes no sense when applied to two isolated events, with the rest of the universe removed. Only inasmuch as these events are thought of as instances of event types related by a regularity can they be thought of as causally connected. If two particular events were somehow so *sui generis* that it was logically excluded that they be placed under any (plausibly natural) event types, causal notions would not be applicable to them.

Of course I am suggesting that Wittgenstein's argument against private language has a structure similar to Hume's argument against private causation. Wittgenstein also states a sceptical paradox. Like Hume, he accepts his own sceptical argument and offers a 'sceptical solution' to overcome the appearance of paradox. His solution involves a sceptical interpretation of what is involved in such ordinary assertions as "Jones means addition by '+'." The impossibility of private language emerges as a corollary of his sceptical solution of his own paradox, as does the impossibility of 'private causation' in Hume. It turns out that the sceptical solution does not allow us to speak of a single individual, considered by himself and in isolation, as ever meaning anything. Once again an objection based on an intuitive feeling that no one else can affect what I mean by a given symbol ignores the sceptical argument that undermines any such naive intuition about meaning.

I have said that Wittgenstein's solution to his problem is a sceptical one. He does not give a 'straight' solution, pointing out to the silly sceptic a hidden fact he overlooked, a condition in the world which constitutes my meaning addition by "plus." In fact, he agrees with his own hypothetical sceptic that there is no such fact, no such condition in either the 'internal' or the 'external' world. Admittedly, I am expressing Wittgenstein's view more straightforwardly than he would ordinarily allow himself to do. For in denying that there is any such fact, might we not be expressing a philosophical thesis that doubts or denies something everyone admits? We do not wish to doubt or deny that when people speak of themselves and others as meaning something by their words, as following rules, they do so with perfect right. We do not even wish to deny the propriety of an ordinary use of the phrase "the fact that Jones meant addition by such-and-such a symbol," and indeed such expressions do have perfectly ordinary uses. We merely wish to deny the existence of the 'superlative fact' that philosophers misleadingly attach to such ordinary forms of words, not the propriety of the forms of words themselves.

It is for this reason that I conjectured above that Wittgenstein's professed inability to write a work with conventionally organized arguments and conclusions stems at least in part, not from personal and stylistic proclivities, but from the nature of his work. Had Wittgenstein—contrary to his notorious and cryptic maxim in §128— stated the outcomes of his conclusions in the form of definite theses, it would have been very difficult to avoid formulating his doctrines in a form that consists in apparent sceptical denials of our ordinary assertions. Berkeley runs into similar difficulties. Partly he avoids them by stating his thesis as the denial of the existence of 'matter', and claiming that 'matter' is a bit of philosophical jargon, not expressive of our common-sense view. Nevertheless he is forced at one point to say—apparently contrary to his usual official doctrine—that he denies a doctrine "strangely prevailing amongst men."[17] If, on the other hand, we do not state our conclusions in the form of broad philosophical theses, it is easier to avoid the danger of a denial of any ordinary belief, even if our imaginary interlocuter (e.g. §189; see also §195)[18] accuses us of doing so. Whenever our opponent insists on the perfect propriety of an ordinary form of expression (e.g. that "the steps are determined by the formula," "the future application is already present"), we can insist that if these expressions are properly understood, we agree. The danger comes when we try to give a precise formulation of exactly what it is that we *are* denying—*what* 'erroneous interpretation' our opponent is placing on ordinary means of expression. It may be hard to do this without producing yet another statement that, we must admit, is *still* 'perfectly all right, properly understood'.

So Wittgenstein, perhaps cagily, might well disapprove of the straightforward formulation given here. Nevertheless I choose to be so bold as to say: Wittgenstein holds, with the sceptic, that there is no fact as to whether I mean plus or quus. . . . Let me, then, summarize the 'private language argument' as it is presented in this essay. (1) We all suppose that our language expresses concepts—"pain," "plus," "red"—in such a way that, once I 'grasp' the concept, all future applications of it are determined (in the sense of being uniquely *justified* by the concept grasped). In fact, it seems that no matter what is in my mind at a given time, I am free in the future to interpret it in different ways—for example, I could follow the sceptic and interpret "plus" as "quus." In particular, this point applies if I direct my attention to a sensation and name it; nothing I have done determines future applications (in the justificatory sense above). Wittgenstein's scepticism about the determination of future usage by the past contents of my mind is analogous to Hume's scepticism about the determination of the future by the past (causally and inferentially). (2) The paradox can be resolved only by a 'sceptical solution of these doubts', in Hume's classic sense. This means that we must give up the attempt to find any fact about me in virtue of which I mean "plus" rather than "quus," and must then go on in a certain way. Instead we must consider how we actually use: (i) the categorical assertion that an individual is following a given rule (that he means addition by 'plus'); (ii) the conditional assertion that "if an individual follows such-and-such a rule, he must do so-and-so on a given occasion" (e.g., "if he means addition by '+', his answer to '68 + 57' should be '125' "). That is to say, we must look at the circumstances under which these assertions are introduced into discourse, and their role and utility in our lives. (3) As long as we consider a single individual in isolation, all we can say is this: An individual often does have the experience of being confident that he has 'got' a certain rule (sometimes that he has grasped it "in a flash"). It is an empirical fact that, after that experience, individuals often are disposed to give responses in concrete cases with complete confidence that proceeding this way is 'what was intended'. We cannot, however, get any further in explaining on this basis the use of the conditionals in (ii) above. Of course, dispositionally speaking, the subject is indeed determined to respond in a certain way, say, to a given addition problem. Such a disposition, together with the appropriate 'feeling of confidence', could be present, however, even if he were not really following a rule at all, or even if he were doing the 'wrong' thing. The justificatory element of our use of conditionals such as (ii) is unexplained. (4) If we take into account the fact that the individual is in a community, the picture changes and the role of (i) and (ii) above becomes apparent. When the community accepts a particular conditional (ii), it accepts its *contraposed* form: the failure of an individual to come up with the particular responses the community regards as right leads the community to suppose that he is not following the rule. On the other hand, if an individual passes enough tests, the community (endorsing assertions of the form (i)) accepts him as a rule follower, thus enabling him to engage in certain types of interactions with them that depend on their reliance on his responses. Note that this solution explains how the assertions in (i) and (ii) are introduced into language; it does *not* give conditions for these statements to be true. (5) The success of the practices in (3) depends on the brute empirical fact that we agree with each other in our responses. Given the sceptical argument in (1), this success cannot be explained by 'the fact that we all grasp the same concepts'. (6) Just as Hume thought he had demonstrated that the causal relation between two events is unintelligible unless they are subsumed under a regularity, so Wittgenstein thought that the considera-

tions in (2) and (3) above showed that all talk of an individual following rules has reference to him as a member of a community, as in (3). In particular, for the conditionals of type (ii) to make sense, the community must be able to judge whether an individual is indeed following a given rule in particular applications, i.e. whether his responses agree with their own. In the case of avowals of sensations, the way the community makes this judgement is by observing the individual's behavior and surrounding circumstances.

A few concluding points regarding the argument ought to be noted. First, following §243, a 'private language' is usually defined as a language that is logically impossible for anyone else to understand. The private language argument is taken to argue against the possibility of a private language in this sense. This conception is not in error, but it seems to me that the emphasis is somewhat misplaced. What is really denied is what might be called the 'private model' of rule following, that the notion of a person following a given rule is to be analyzed simply in terms of facts about the rule follower and the rule follower alone, without reference to his membership in a wider community. (In the same way, what Hume denies is the private model of causation: that whether one event causes another is a matter of the relation between these two events alone, without reference to their subsumption under larger event types.) The impossibility of a private language in the sense just defined does indeed follow from the incorrectness of the private model for language and rules, since the rule following in a 'private language' could only be analyzed by a private model, but the incorrectness of the private model is more basic, since it applies to all rules. I take all this to be the point of §202.

Does this mean that Robinson Crusoe, isolated on an island, cannot be said to follow any rules, no matter what he does?[19] I do not see that this follows. What does follow is that *if* we think of Crusoe as following rules, we are taking him into our community and applying our criteria for rule following to him.[20] The falsity of the private model need not mean that a *physically isolated* individual cannot be said to follow rules; rather that an individual, *considered in isolation* (whether or not he is physically isolated), cannot be said to do so. Remember that Wittgenstein's theory is one of assertability conditions. Our community can assert of any individual that he follows a rule if he passes the tests for rule following applied to any member of the community.

Finally, the point just made in the last paragraph, that Wittgenstein's theory is one of assertability conditions, deserves emphasis. Wittgenstein's theory should not be confused with a theory that, for any m and n, the value of the function we mean by "plus," *is* (by definition) the value that (nearly) all the linguistic community would give as the answer. Such a theory would be a theory of the *truth* conditions of such assertions as "By 'plus' we mean such-and-such a function," or "By 'plus' we mean a function, which, when applied to 68 and 57 as arguments, yields 125 as value." (An infinite, exhaustive totality of specific conditions of the second form would determine which function was meant, and hence would determine a condition of the first form.) The theory would assert that 125 is the value of the function meant for given arguments, if and only if '125' is the response nearly everyone would give, given these arguments. Thus the theory would be a social, or community-wide, version of the dispositional theory, and would be open to at least some of the same criticisms as the original form. I take Wittgenstein to deny that he holds such a view, for example, in *Remarks on the Foundations of Mathematics,* v, §33 [vii, §40]: "Does this mean, e.g., that the definition of the same would be this: same is what all or most human beings take for the same?—Of course not."[21] (See also *Philosophical Investigations,* p. 226, "Certainly the propositions, 'Human beings believe that twice two is four' and 'Twice two is four' do not mean the same"; and see also §§240–1.) One must bear firmly in mind that Wittgenstein has no theory of truth-conditions—necessary and sufficient conditions—for the correctness of one response rather than another to a new addition problem. Rather he simply points out that each of us *automatically* calculates new addition problems (without feeling the need to check with the community whether our procedure is proper); that the community feels entitled to correct a deviant calculation; that in practice

such deviation is rare, and so on. Wittgenstein thinks that these observations about sufficient conditions for justified assertion are enough to illuminate the role and utility in our lives of assertion about meaning and determination of new answers. What follows from these assertability conditions is *not* that the answer everyone gives to an addition problem is, by definition, the correct one, but rather the platitude that, if everyone agrees upon a certain answer, then no one will feel justified in calling the answer wrong.

Obviously there are countless relevant aspects of Wittgenstein's philosophy of mind that I have not discussed.[22] About some aspects I am not clear, and others have been left untouched because of the limits of this essay.[23] In particular, I have not discussed numerous issues arising out of the paragraphs *following* §243 that are usually called the 'private language argument', nor have I really discussed Wittgenstein's attendant positive account of the nature of sensation language and of the attribution of psychological states. Nevertheless, I do think that the basic 'private language argument' precedes these passages, and that only with an understanding of this argument can we begin to comprehend or consider what follows. That was the task undertaken in this essay.

NOTES

1. Unless otherwise specified (explicitly or contextually), references are to *Philosophical Investigations.* The small numbered units of the Investigations are termed 'sections' (or 'paragraphs'). Page references are used only if a section reference is not possible, as in the second part of the *Investigations.* Throughout I quote the standard printed English translation (by G. E. M. Anscombe) and make no attempt to question it except in a very few instances. *Philosophical Investigations* has undergone several editions since its first publication in 1953 but the paragraphing and pagination remain the same. The publishers are Basil Blackwell, Oxford and Macmillan, New York.

   This essay does not proceed by giving detailed exegesis of Wittgenstein's text but rather develops the arguments in its own way. I recommend that the reader reread the *Investigations* in the light of the present exegesis and see whether it illuminates the text.

2. Basil Blackwell, Oxford: 1956. In the first edition of *Remarks on the Foundation of Mathematics* the editors assert (p. vi) that Wittgenstein appears originally to have intended to include some of the mate-

rial on mathematics in *Philosophical Investigations*. The third edition (1978) includes more material than earlier editions and rearranges some of the sections and divisions of earlier editions. When I wrote the present work, I used the first edition. Where the references differ, the equivalent third edition reference is given in square brackets.

3. Personally I feel, however, that the role of stylistic considerations here cannot be denied. It is clear that purely stylistic and literary considerations meant a great deal to Wittgenstein. His own stylistic preference obviously contributes to the difficulty of his work as well as to its beauty.

4. Perhaps I should make a remark about such expressions as "By 'plus' I meant quus (or plus)," "By 'green' I meant green," etc. I am not familiar with an accepted felicitous convention to indicate the object of the verb 'to mean'. There are two problems. First, if one says, "By 'the woman who discovered radium' I meant the woman who discovered radium," the object can be interpreted in two ways. It may stand for a woman (Marie Curie), in which case the assertion is true only if 'meant' is used to mean referred to (as it can be used); or it may be used to denote the *meaning* of the quoted expression, not a woman, in which case the assertion is true with 'meant' used in the ordinary sense. Second, as is illustrated by 'referred to', 'green', 'quus', etc. above, as objects of 'meant', one must use various expressions as objects in an awkward manner contrary to normal grammar. (Frege's difficulties concerning unsaturatedness are related.) Both problems tempt one to put the object in quotation marks, like the subject; but such a usage conflicts with the convention of philosophical logic that a quotation denotes the expression quoted. Some special 'meaning marks', as proposed for example by David Kaplan, could be useful here. If one is content to ignore the first difficulty and always use 'mean' to mean denote (for most purposes of the present paper, such a reading would suit at least as well as an intensional one; often I speak as if it is a *numerical function* that is meant by plus), the second problem might lead one to nominalize the objects—'plus' denotes the plus function, 'green' denotes greenness, etc. I contemplated using italics ("'plus' means plus"; "'mean' may mean *denote*"), but I decided that normally (except when italics are otherwise appropriate, especially when a neologism like 'quus' is introduced for the first time), I will write the object of 'to mean' as an ordinary roman object. The convention I have adopted reads awkwardly in the written language but sounds rather reasonable in the spoken language.

Since use-mention distinctions are significant for the argument as I give it, I try to remember to use quotation marks when an expression is mentioned. However, quotation marks are also used for other purposes where they might be invoked in normal non-philosophical English writing (for example, in the case of "'meaning marks'" in the previous paragraph, or "'quasi-quotation'" in the next sentence). Readers familiar with Quine's 'quasi-quotation' will be aware that in some cases I use ordinary quotation where logical purity would require that I use quasi-quotation or some similar device. I have not tried to be careful about this matter, since I am confident that in practice readers will not be confused.

5. I believe I got the phrase "both inside and outside language" from a conversation with Rogers Albritton.

6. See W. V. Quine, *Word and Object* (MIT, The Technology Press, Cambridge, Massachusetts: 1960) especially chapter 2, "Translation and Meaning" (pp. 26–79). See also *Ontological Relativity and Other Essays* (Columbia University Press, New York and London: 1969), especially the first three chapters (pp. 1–90); and see also "On the Reasons for the Indeterminacy of Translation," *The Journal of Philosophy*, vol. 67 (1970), pp. 178–83.

7. I do not mean the term 'introspective' to be laden with philosophical doctrine. Of course much of the baggage that has accompanied this term would be objectionable to Wittgenstein in particular. I simply mean that he makes use, in his discussion, of our own memories and knowledge of our 'inner' experiences.

8. So put, the problem has an obvious Kantian flavor.

9. See especially the discussions of 'green' and 'grue' above, [not reprinted in this volume] which plainly could carry over to pain (let 'pickle' apply to pains before *t*, and tickles thereafter!); but it is clear enough by now that the problem is completely general.

10. Karl Britton, "Portrait of a Philosopher," *The Listener*, LIII, no. 1372 (June 16, 1955), p. 1072, quoted by George Pitcher, *The Philosophy of Wittgenstein* (Prentice Hall, Englewood Cliffs, N.J.: 1964), p. 325.

11. Much of Wittgenstein's argument can be regarded as an attack on characteristically Humean (or classical empiricist) ideas. Hume posits an introspectible qualitative state for each of our psychological states (an 'impression'). Further, he thinks that an appropriate 'impression' or 'image' can constitute an 'idea', without realizing that an image in no way tells us how it is to be applied. Of course the Wittgensteinian paradox is, among other things, a strong protest against such suppositions.

12. David Hume, *A Treatise of Human Nature*, ed. L. A. Selby-Bigge, Clarendon Press, Oxford: 1888), Book I, part IV, section I (p. 183 in the Selby-Bigge edition).

13. Hume, ibid., Book I, part IV, Section II (p. 187 in the Selby-Bigge edition). Hume's occasional affinities to 'ordinary language' philosophy should not be overlooked. Consider the following: "Those philosophers, who have divided human reason into *knowledge and probability,* and have defined the first to be *that evidence, which arises from the comparison of ideas,* are obliged to comprehend all our arguments from causes or effects under the general term of probability. But tho' everyone be free to use his terms in what sense he pleases . . . 'tis however certain, that in common discourse we readily affirm, that many arguments from causation exceed proba-

bility, and may be received as a superior kind of evidence. One would appear ridiculous, who would say, that 'tis only probable the sun will rise tomorrow, or that all men must dye . . ." (ibid., Book I, part III, section XI, p. 124 in the Selby-Bigge edition).

14. George Berkeley, *The Principles of Human Knowledge*, §29–34. Of course the characterization may be oversimplified, but it suffices for present purposes.

15. It is almost 'analytic' that I cannot produce a common contemporary example that would not meet with vigorous opposition. Those who hold the cited view would argue that, in this case, their analyses of ordinary usage are really correct. I have no desire to enter into an irrelevant controversy here, but I myself find that many of the 'topic-neutral' analyses of discourse about the mind proposed by contemporary materialists are just the other side of the Berkeleyan coin.

16. Writing this sentence, I find myself prey to an appropriate fear that (some) experts in Hume and Berkeley will not approve of some particular thing that I say about these philosophers here. I have made no careful study of them for the purpose of this paper. Rather a crude and fairly conventional account of the 'rough outlines' of their views is used for purposes of comparison with Wittgenstein.

17. Berkeley, *The Principles of Human Knowledge*, 4. Of course Berkeley might mean that the prevalence of the doctrine stems from the influence of philosophical theory rather than common sense, as indeed he asserts in the next section.

18. §189: "But *are* the steps then *not* determined by the algebraic formula?" In spite of Wittgenstein's interpretation within his own philosophy of the ordinary phrase "the steps are determined by the formula", the impression persists that the interlocutor's characterization of his view is really correct. See §195: "But I don't mean that what I do now (in grasping a sense) determines the future use *causally* and as a matter of experience, but that in a queer way, the use itself is in some sense present," which are the words of the interlocutor, and the bland reply. 'But of course it is, 'in *some* sense'! Really the only thing wrong with what you say is the expression "in a queer way". The rest is all right; and the sentence only seems queer when one imagines a different language-game for it from the one in which we actually use it."

19. See . . . A. J. Ayer, "Can There Be a Private Language?" *Proceedings of the Aristotelian Society Supplementary Volume* 28 (1954). Ayer assumes that the 'private language argument' excludes Crusoe from language [and] takes this alleged fact to be fatal to Wittgenstein's argument. . . . Others, pointing out that a 'private language' is one that others cannot understand (see the preceding paragraph in the text), see no reason to think that the 'private language argument' has anything to do with Crusoe (as long as we could understand his language). My own view of the matter, as explained very briefly in the text, differs somewhat from all these opinions.

20. If Wittgenstein would have any problem with Crusoe, perhaps the problem would be whether we have any 'right' to take him into our community in this way, and attribute our rules to him. See Wittgenstein's discussion of a somewhat similar question in §§199–200, and his conclusion, "Should we still be inclined to say they were playing a game? What right would one have to say so?"

21. Although, in the passage in question, Wittgenstein is speaking of a particular language-game of bringing something else and bringing the same, it is clear in context that it is meant to illustrate his general problem about rules. The entire passage is worth reading for the present issue.

22. [. . .] As members of the community correct each other, might a given individual correct himself? Some question such as this was prominent in earlier discussions of verificationist versions of the private language argument. Indeed, in the absence of Wittgenstein's sceptical paradox, it would appear that an individual remembers his own 'intentions' and can use one memory of these intentions to correct another mistaken memory. In the presence of the paradox, any such 'naive' ideas are meaningless. Ultimately, an individual may simply have conflicting brute inclinations, while the upshot of the matter depends on his will alone. The situation is not analogous to the case of the community, where distinct individuals have distinct and independent wills, and where, when an individual is accepted into the community, others judge that they can rely on his response (as was described in the text above). No corresponding relation between an individual and himself has the same utility. Wittgenstein may be indicating something like this in §268.

23. I might mention that, in addition to the Humean analogy emphasized in this essay, it has struck me that there is perhaps a certain analogy between Wittgenstein's private language argument and Ludwig von Mises's celebrated argument concerning economic calculation under socialism. (See e.g., his *Human Action*, 2d ed., Yale University Press, New Haven: 1963, chapter 26, pp. 698–715, for one statement.) According to Mises, a rational economic calculator (say, the manager of an industrial plant) who wishes to choose the most efficient means to achieve given ends must compare alternative courses of action for cost effectiveness. To do this, he needs an array of prices (e.g. of raw materials, or machinery) set by *others*. If *one* agency set *all* prices, it could have no rational basis to choose between alternative courses of action. (Whatever seemed to it to be right would be right, so one cannot talk about right.) I do not know whether the fact bodes at all ill for the private language argument, but my impression is that although it is usually acknowledged that Mises's argument points to a real difficulty for centrally planned economies, it is now almost universally rejected as a theoretical proposition.

44 Truth Rules, Hoverflies, and the Kripke-Wittgenstein Paradox

RUTH GARRETT MILLIKAN

[T]he sceptical argument that Kripke attributes to Wittgenstein, and even the 'sceptical solution', are of considerable importance regardless of whether they are clearly Wittgenstein's. The naturalistically inclined philosopher, who rejects Brentano's irreducibility and yet holds intentionality to be an objective feature of our thoughts, owes a solution to the Kripke-Wittgenstein paradox.[1]

The challenge is a welcome one. Although I will argue that the Kripke-Wittgenstein paradox is not a problem for naturalists only, I will propose a naturalist solution to it. (Should the Kripke-Wittgenstein paradox prove to be soluble from a naturalist standpoint but intractable from other standpoints, that would, I suppose, constitute an argument for naturalism.) Then I will show that the paradox and its solution have an important consequence for the theories of meaning and truth. The Kripke-Wittgenstein arguments which pose the paradox also put in question Dummett's and Putnam's view of language understanding. From this view it follows that truth rules must be "verificationist rules" that assign assertability conditions to sentences, rather than "realist rules" that assign correspondence truth conditions. The proposed solution to the paradox suggests another view of language understanding, according to which a speaker can express, through his language practice, a grasp of correspondence truth rules. This will block one route of Putnam's famous retreat from realism:

The point is that Dummett and I *agree* that you can't treat understanding a sentence (in general) as knowing its truth conditions; because it then becomes unintelligible what *that* knowledge *in turn* consists in. We both *agree* that the theory of understanding has to be done in a verificationist way . . . conceding that *some* sort of verificationist semantics must be given as our account of understanding. . . . I have given Dummett all he needs to demolish metaphysical realism . . . a picture I was wedded to![2]

(By "metaphysical realism" Putnam means, roughly, the traditional correspondence theory of truth.) Elsewhere I have argued that the distinction Putnam draws between "metaphysical realism" and "internal realism" is illusory, that naturalist arguments for correspondence truth are, inevitably, arguments for truth as correspondence to theory-independent objects, and that there is nothing incoherent in this notion of correspondence.[3] So in giving a naturalist argument to show that grasping correspondence truth rules is no more problematic than grasping verificationist ones, I take myself to be defending the strongest possible kind of correspon-

From *Philosophical Review* 99 (3) (July 1990). Copyright © 1990 by *Philosophical Review*. Reprinted with the permission of the publisher and the author.

dence theory of truth and the most flatfooted interpretation possible of the truth-conditions approach to semantics.

I. THE KRIPKE-WITTGENSTEIN PARADOX

The Kripke-Wittgenstein paradox, as Kripke explains it, is an apparent dead end we encounter when trying to explain what it is that constitutes a person's meaning something by a word. Kripke takes addition as his central example: what constitutes my meaning addition by "plus" or "+"? "Although I myself have computed only finitely many sums in the past, the rule for addition determines my answer for indefinitely many new sums that I have never previously considered. This is the whole point of the notion that in learning to add I grasp a rule: my past intentions regarding addition determine a unique answer for indefinitely many cases in the future."[4] What is it to "grasp" such a rule? What is it for me to have grasped a rule that determines that $68 + 57$ yields the answer 125, in the case that I have never happened to add 68 to 57? No such rule is determined merely by extrapolation from previous cases in which I have applied "+" to pairs of numbers; there are always infinitely many functions that accord with a given finite list of such argument-argument-value trios. For example, the "quus" rule might accord:

$$x \text{ quus } y = x + y, \text{ if } x, y < 57$$
$$= 5 \text{ otherwise}[5]$$

Nor (and this is more obviously a Wittgensteinian theme) can we suppose that my meaning addition by "+" consists in my having given myself general directions for what to do when encountering "+." To give myself general directions would be to lay down a rule of procedure for myself. What then constitutes my meaning by this set of instructions, by this laid-down rule, one procedure rather than another? Certainly this set of instructions does not include a thought of each of the infinitely many sums there are. And my past performances when having this set of instructions in mind do not exemplify a unique general procedure but many such possible procedures. Supplementing the instructions

with another set of instructions explaining how to follow the first set leads only to a regress. How then is the correct interpretation of the instructions in my mind determined?

Changing the example, Kripke writes

It has been supposed that all I need to do to determine my use of the word 'green' is to have an image, a sample, of green that I bring to mind whenever I apply the word in the future. When I use this to justify my application of 'green' to a new object, should not the sceptical problem be obvious to any reader of Goodman? Perhaps by 'green', in the past I meant *grue*, and the color image, which indeed was grue, was meant to direct me to apply the word 'green' to *grue* objects always. If the *blue* object before me now is grue, then it falls in the extension of 'green,' as I meant it in the past. It is no help to suppose that in the past I stipulated that 'green' was to apply to all and only those things 'of the same color as' the sample. The sceptic can reinterpret 'same color' as same *schmolor*, where things have the same schmolor if . . . [6]

Now it is true that arguments of this sort take hold only if we reject the possibility that intentionality is a *sui generis* feature given to consciousness.[7] We must assume that what comes before the mind, whatever it is that enters or informs consciousness when one means something, does not *itself* determine a use for itself, a purpose for itself, a particular kind of connection that it is to have with one's activities. Rather, whatever comes before the mind is, in this respect, not different from any other item standing alone: "And can't it be clearly seen here that it is absolutely inessential for the picture to exist in his imagination rather than as a drawing or model in front of him? . . . "[8] Wittgenstein argues against the possibility that intentionality is a *sui generis* feature, by showing, for each of a series of cases, that the results of introspection when one means, understands or is guided in accordance with rules, are not the only or the final criteria that we use to determine what we mean or when we understand or are being so guided. What lies before consciousness does not determine its own significance; knowing what one means is not a matter, merely, of apprehending the contents of one's mind. In short, meaning is neither a state of awareness nor an epistemological given. It does not occur encapsulated within consciousness; it is not a state that simply *shows* its content or its significance. If there is such a thing as meaning something, say, meaning addition, its nature must lie in part in what is *not* simply given to consciousness.

Nor is it merely because the object thought of or meant is external to mind that meaning has an ingredient not given to consciousness. Meaning to perform a mental activity like adding in the head, that is, having intentions about one's own thoughts, is fully infected with this non-given ingredient. Thus the problem posed is no different for the purest idealist than for the metaphysical realist. Nor is it only "naturalistically inclined philosophers" who need a solution to the Kripke-Wittgenstein paradox. It is anyone who has been convinced by Wittgenstein to doubt Brentano—or, say, convinced after Sellars to reject epistemological "givenness" in *all* of its multifarious forms.

Could it be that the non-given ingredient that pins down what rule I intend to follow for "+" is the *disposition* I have to proceed in a certain way when encountering "+"? Setting aside the problem of what Wittgenstein may have intended as an answer to this question, surely Kripke is right to answer no. Kripke gives two main reasons for his answer. First, people are in fact disposed to make mistakes in arithmetic. Second, the addition function applies to numbers of any magnitude, but "some pairs of numbers are simply too large for my mind—or my brain—to grasp."[9] Nor will it help to take into account dispositions I may have to correct myself or to accept correction from others. Some of my dispositions are dispositions to miscorrect myself. (I often do this when trying to add long columns of figures.) And there are surely conditions under which I would be disposed to accept miscorrection from others.

Kripke concludes, or he claims that Wittgenstein concludes, that there is, indeed, *no fact to the matter of what I mean by* "+." This conclusion is what I am calling the "Kripke-Wittgenstein paradox."[10] Wittgenstein, Kripke claims, offers only a "sceptical solution" to this paradox, a solution that "begins . . . by conceding that the sceptic's negative assertions are unanswerable."[11] I propose to offer a "straight solution" to this paradox, one that "shows that

on closer examination the scepticism proves to be unwarranted."[12]

Kripke distills the essence of the failure of dispositional accounts to capture the nature of rule following thus:

A candidate for what constitutes the state of my meaning one function, rather than another, by a given function sign, ought to be such that, whatever in fact I (am disposed to) do, there is a unique thing that I *should* do. Is not the dispositional view simply an equation of performance and correctness? Assuming determinism, even if I mean to denote *no* number theoretic function in particular by the sign '*', then to the same extent as it is true for '+', it is true here that for any two arguments m and n, there is a uniquely determined answer p that I would give. (I choose one at random, as we would normally say, but causally the answer is determined.) The difference between this case and the case of the '+' function is that in the former case, but not in the latter, my uniquely determined answer can properly be called 'right' or 'wrong'.[13]

The fundamental problem . . . is . . . : whether my actual dispositions are 'right' or not, is there anything that mandates what they *ought* to be?[14]

The problem is to account for the *normative* element that is involved when one means to follow a rule, to account for there being a *standard* from which the facts, or one's dispositions, can diverge.

II. GENERAL FORM OF THE SOLUTION

In the case of meaning, the normative element seems to be the same as the purposive element: to mean to follow a certain rule is to have as a purpose to follow it. Whether my actual dispositions are "right" or "wrong" depends on whether they accord with what I have purposed. The possible divergence of fact from a standard is, in this case, simply the failure to achieve a purpose.

Now having as one's purpose to follow a rule might involve having a representation of that purpose in mind, for example, in one's language of thought. But as Wittgenstein observed, any such representation would itself stand in need of interpretation. It would stand in need of a prior rule governing how it was to be taken, that is,

how it was to guide one. And that one was to follow this prior rule could not *also* be a represented purpose, not without inviting a regress.
To understand what it is to have an explicit purpose that one represents to oneself we must first
understand what it is to have a purpose the content of which is *not* represented. Basic or root
purposes must be *unexpressed* purposes.

"Intend" strongly suggests an explicitly represented purpose, that is, a purpose that is
thought about. So let me use the verb "to purpose" (with a voiced "s"; yes, it *is* in the dictionary) to include this more basic way of having a purpose. We can then put matters this way:
root purposing is unexpressed purposing; our
job is to discover in what this purposing consists. Let us also distinguish among three ways
of conforming to a rule: (1) merely coinciding
with a rule (this is the way in which we conform
to "quus" rules and to rules to which we have
mere dispositions to conform), (2) purposefully
following an explicit or expressed rule, and (3)
purposefully conforming to an implicit or unexpressed rule. Way (3) involves having an unexpressed purpose to follow a rule and *succeeding*
in this purpose. It is the same as displaying a
competence in conforming to the unexpressed
rule or displaying an *ability* to conform to it.
Another way to explain our task, then, is to say
that we need to learn what a competence in conforming to an unexpressed rule consists in, and
how it differs from a mere disposition to coincide with the rule.

My thesis will be that the unexpressed purposes that lie behind acts of explicit purposing
are biological purposes; a competence to conform to an unexpressed rule is a biological competence. By a biological purpose I mean the sort
of purpose the heart has, or those of the eyeblink
reflex, and the human brain. The purposes of
these are functions that they have historically
performed which have accounted for their continued proliferation. Biological purposes are,
roughly, functions fulfilled in accordance with
evolutionary design. It does not follow that
capacities to perform biological functions are,
in general, innate. For example, it is surely in
accordance with evolutionary design that the
newly hatched chick follows its mother about,
but the chick is not born with that disposition. It

is not born knowing which *is* its mother, but
must imprint on her first. Yet the imprinting, and
hence the following, both take place in accordance with evolutionary design. (Later in this
paper I will devote considerable space to clarifying how even quite novel biological purposes
can emerge as a result of experience and
learning.)[15]

Suppose that explicit intending involves
something like representing, imaging, or saying
something to oneself and then using, or reacting
to, or being guided by this representation in a
purposeful way, that is, in a way that expresses
a competence. My thesis, then, is that the purpose that informs this reacting, that makes it
into a competence, is a biological purpose. Similarly, if knowing a language involves having a
competence in following certain rules for construction and interpretation of sentences, the
purpose that informs this competence, I will
argue, is a biological purpose.

III. PURPOSIVE RULE FOLLOWING; COMPETENCE TO FOLLOW A RULE

Let me begin with a very simple example of an
organism that displays a competence in conforming to a rule. According to the biologists
Collett and Land,

Males of many species of hoverfly spend much of the
day hovering in one spot, thus keeping their flight
muscles warm and primed so that they are ready to
dart instantly after any passing female that they sight.
This chasing behavior is on such a hair-trigger that all
manner of inappropriate targets elicit pursuit (peb-
bles, distant birds, and midges so small as to be
scarcely visible to a human observer) as well as a very
occasional female. Although selective pressures have
favored a speedy response above careful evaluation of
the suitability of the target . . . the response itself is
precisely tailored to optimize the capture of objects
which are roughly the same size and speed as a con-
specific.[16]

Rather than turning toward the target in order to
track it, the hoverfly turns away from the target
and accelerates in a straight line so as to intercept it. Given that (1) female hoverflies are of
uniform size, hence are first detected at a
roughly uniform distance (about .7 m), (2)

females cruise at a standard velocity (about 8m/sec), and (3) males accelerate at a constant rate (about 30-35m/sec^2), the geometry of motion dictates that to intercept the female the male must make a turn that is 180° away from the target minus about 1/10 of the vector angular velocity (measured in degrees per second) of the target's image across his retina. The turn that his *body* must make, given as a function of the angle off center of the target's image on his retina, equals the (signed) angle of the image minus 1/10 its vector angular velocity, plus or minus 180°. According to Collett and Land, whether it is dried peas, male hoverflies, female hoverflies or flying blocks of wood that he spots, that is exactly the rule to which the hoverfly conforms. Taking note that this rule is not about how the hoverfly should behave in relation to distal objects, but rather about how he should react to a proximal stimulus, to a moving spot on his retina, let us call this rule "the proximal hoverfly rule."

I have chosen the proximal hoverfly rule as my first example of rule following because it seems so unlikely that the hoverfly calculates over any inner representation of this rule in order to follow it. Rather, the hoverfly has an unexpressed biological purpose to conform to this rule. That is, the hoverfly has within him a genetically determined mechanism of a kind that historically proliferated in part *because* it was responsible for producing conformity to the proximal hoverfly rule, hence for getting male and female hoverflies together. This mechanism may account for various other dispositions of the hoverfly, for example, causing him to attract predators by his conspicuous darting movements, or causing characteristic uniform mathematically describable patterns to play on his retina as he turns after the female. But mentioning these latter dispositions does not help to explain why the mechanism has survived, why it has proliferated in the species. Conformity to the proximal hoverfly rule, on the other hand, has helped to explain the reproductive success of (virtually) every ancestor hoverfly, hence to explain the continued presence of the mechanism in the species. Conformity to the proximal hoverfly rule, then—not attracting predators or producing certain patterns on the retina—is a

biological purpose of this mechanism, hence of the hoverfly. For similar reasons, a biological function of the heart is to pump blood but not also, say, to make a jazzy sound, and a biological function of the eyeblink reflex is to cover the eyes momentarily, but not also to swing the eyelashes in a graceful arc away from entanglement with the eyebrows, nor to point with them at the navel.

The hoverfly displays a *competence* in conforming to the proximal hoverfly rule when his coinciding with it has a "normal explanation," that is, an explanation that accords with the historical norm. That his behavior coincides with the rule must be explained in the same way, or must fit the same explanation schema, that accounted in the bulk of cases for the historic successes of his ancestors in conforming to the rule. Presumably this normal explanation makes reference to the way the hoverfly's nervous system is put together, how it works, how it is hooked to his retina and muscles, etc. If the hoverfly ends up coinciding with the rule not because his nerves and muscles work in a normal way but only because the wind serendipitously blows him around to face the right direction, he fails to express a competence.[17]

Not just anything a human effects is a human action. Effects that are actions must be intended, or at least foreseen, and must be generated from intentions in a normal way. Effects of human bodily movements that are not actions are called "accidental." Similarly, not just any process that originates in an animal's organs or behavioral systems is a biological activity. Biological activities are only those that express competencies. They correspond to normally fulfilled biological purposes, that is, to what the animal does in accordance with evolutionary design. Conversely, behavior that fails to express a competence corresponds to what an animal effects, biologically, only by accident. Thus the heart's saying pit-a-pat, the eyelashes' moving away from the eyebrows in a graceful arc and the hoverfly's coinciding, but due only to the wind, with the proximal hoverfly rule are not biological activities, but biological accidents.

To say that a given male hoverfly has a biological purpose to conform to the proximal hoverfly rule is very different from saying either that he himself has a history of having conformed to it (perhaps he has just reached adolescence) or that he has a disposition to conform to it. The normal hoverfly has a disposition to dart off when it sees a flying bird—and also a disposition to squash when stepped on—but these dispositions do not correspond to biological purposes or to competences. Conversely, male hoverflies that are crippled or blind have no disposition to conform to the proximal hoverfly rule, but still it is one of their biological purposes to do so. As male members of the hoverfly species, conforming is the biological norm, the standard for them.[18]

To say that the hoverfly has as a biological purpose to follow the proximal hoverfly rule is also quite different from saying that this rule is the only rule that fits all past instances of hoverfly turns, say, that resulted in hoverfly procreation. Suppose it were so that never in history had a male hoverfly spotted a female that happened to approach him at such an angle as to produce an image on his retina with a clockwise angular velocity between 500° and 510° per second. Then the proximal *quoverfly* rule, "If the vector angular velocity of the target's image is *not* counterclockwise and between 500° and 510° per second, make a turn that equals the (signed) angle of the image minus 1/10 its vector angular velocity, plus or minus 180°; at ease otherwise," fits all past actual cases of successful female encounters. But it is not a rule the hoverfly has as a biological purpose to follow. For it is not because their behavior coincided with *that* rule that the hoverfly's ancestors managed to catch females, hence to proliferate. In saying that, I don't have any particular theory of the nature of explanation up my sleeve. But surely, on any reasonable account, a complexity that can simply be dropped from the explanans without affecting the tightness of the relation of explanans to explanandum is not a *functioning* part of the explanation. For example, my coat does not keep me warm because it is fur-lined *and red,* nor because it is fur-lined *in the winter,* but just because it is fur-lined. (True, I am making the assumption that the qualifications and additions that convert the proximal hoverfly rule into the proximal quoverfly rule are objectively qualifications and additions rather than simplifi-

cations. This assumption rests upon a metaphysical distinction between natural properties and kinds and artificially synthesized grue-like properties and kinds or, what is perhaps the same, depends upon there being a difference between natural law and mere *de facto* regularity. But my project is to solve the Kripke-Wittgenstein paradox, not to defend commonsense ontology. Nor should either of these projects be confused with solving Goodman's paradox.)[19]

To say that the hoverfly has as a biological purpose to follow the proximal hoverfly rule is also quite different from saying that this rule is the only rule that fits the actual dispositions of normal hoverflies or of past hoverflies that managed to procreate. Suppose that, given the principles in accordance with which the hoverfly's turn-angle-determining devices work, engineering constraints necessitated a mechanism normal for hoverflies with a blind spot for clockwise angular velocities between 500° and 510° per second. These particular velocities produce no reaction at all on the part of the male. Then the same proximal quoverfly rule mentioned above fits the actual-dispositions of all normal hoverflies, but it still would not be a rule that the hoverfly has as a biological purpose to follow. The hoverfly's biological purposes include the expression only of dispositions that have helped to account for the proliferation of his ancestors. By hypothesis, the disposition to rest at ease when the target's image is counterclockwise and between 500° and 510° per second did not help the hoverfly's ancestors to propagate. It was only the times that the proximal hoverfly rule was obeyed that the ancestors procreated. So the hoverfly resting at ease behind his blind spot is not displaying a competence. It is conformity to the proximal hoverfly rule, not the quoverfly rule, that he biologically purposes, even if normal hoverflies are not especially accurate in fulfilling this natural purpose, in conforming to this ideal.

IV. PROXIMAL VS. DISTAL RULES

My plan, as I have indicated, is slowly to make plausible the claim that the normative element that is involved when one means to follow a rule is biological purposiveness. Meaning to follow a rule differs from having a disposition to coincide with a rule, in the same way that the hoverfly's biologically purposing to follow the proximal hoverfly rule differs from having a disposition to coincide with it. That is how I aim to solve the Kripke-Wittgenstein paradox concerning what *constitutes* rule following. At the same time, however, I wish to build a case that language understanding or language competency is competency in the biological sense. And I wish to argue that it is possible to have a biological competence to follow correspondence truth rules, hence that a "realist" theory of language understanding is possible on the biological model. To gain this latter end, we need to discuss distal as well as proximal rules.

Conforming to the proximal hoverfly rule is a means, for the hoverfly, of following a less proximal, or more distal rule: "If you see a female, catch it." Call this "the distal hoverfly rule." To say that conformity to the proximal hoverfly rule is a means to conformity to the distal rule is the same as to say that the mechanism that has historically accounted for the overwhelming majority of ancestor hoverflies' successes at conformity to the distal hoverfly rule begins with conformity to the proximal rule. That is, the normal explanation for conformity to the distal rule contains the specification that the hoverfly first conform to the proximal rule.

Now whether the hoverfly succeeds in following the proximal hoverfly rule depends, for the most part, only upon whether his insides are working right, that is, on whether he is a normal healthy member of his species. But whether, or how often, he manages to conform to the distal hoverfly rule depends upon more. It depends upon conditions that are outside his body and over which he has no control, such as how hard the wind is blowing, whether the females that pass by are in fact of normal size, traveling at the normal speed and, perhaps, whether they are willing. Without doubt, then, hoverflies are worse at conforming to the distal than to the proximal hoverfly rule. That is, their competence or ability to conform to the distal rule is less reliable than their competence or ability to conform to the proximal rule. But that the hoverfly may not be very reliable in his conformity

to the distal hoverfly rule bears not at all upon whether it is one of his biological purposes to conform. Compare: it is a biological purpose of the sperm to swim until it reaches an ovum. That is what it has a tail for. But very few sperm actually achieve this biological end because ova are in such short supply. Reaching an ovum is a purpose of the sperm since it is only because ancestor sperm reached ova that they reproduced, thus proliferating the tail. Similarly, it was only when ancestor hoverflies conformed to the distal hoverfly rule that they *became* ancestors.

Turning the coin over, the hoverfly is very reliable in his coincidence with this "overkill rule": "Dart off after everything that flies by you subtending about .5° on your retina, whether it's male, female, animate or inanimate, bird, plane or Superman." But this overkill rule does not correspond to any biological purpose of the hoverfly. True, conforming to the proximal hoverfly rule is one of the hoverfly's biological purposes, and conforming to this rule will *result* in his coinciding with the overkill rule if there are objects other than female hoverflies flying about him (even if there are not). But it is not coinciding with the overkill rule that has helped to account for hoverfly proliferation. Only the times when the distal hoverfly rule was obeyed did hoverfly ancestors procreate.[20] It is conformity to the distal hoverfly rule that explains the ancestor hoverflies' *successes*. As the hoverfly chases after a distant bird, he expresses no competence except, of course, competence to conform to the proximal hoverfly rule. Conformity to the distal hoverfly rule, not to the overkill rule, is what he biologically purposes, though at the moment he is accidentally, that is, nonbiologically, doing something else.

That is how purposes inform the rule-following behavior of the hoverfly, how norms, standards, or ideals apply to his behaviors, hence how the hoverfly comes to display competences or abilities to conform to rules rather than mere dispositions to coincide with them.[21] But the unexpressed rules that humans purposively conform to, at least most of those that they purposively conform to when using inner or outer language, are not rules that they are genetically hard-wired to follow, but rules that they have learned. How then can humans bio-logically purpose to follow such rules? Before turning directly to the problem of human rule following, let us examine a more simple case of learned biological purposes, of learned compe-tence-the case of a simpler animal that learns to follow rules.

V. LEARNED OR DERIVED RULES AND COMPETENCES

If a rat becomes ill within a few hours after eat-ing a specific food, it will later shun all foods that taste the same. For example, if the rat eats soap and soon becomes ill, thereafter it will refuse to eat soap. Although the rat may have dragged certain nesting materials home or explored new territory just before becoming ill, it will not on that account shun that kind of nest-ing material or that territory. Nor will it shun foods that merely look the same or that are found in the same place as the food eaten prior to illness.[22] It thus appears that a quite specific mechanism is harbored in the rat, a proper func-tion of which is to produce conformity to the specialized rule "If ingestion of a substance is followed by illness, do not ingest any substance with that taste again." Call this rule the "proxi-mal rat rule." Clearly, following the proximal rat rule is a biological means to following a more distal rat rule, say, "Do not eat poisonous sub-stances"; helping to produce conformity to this rule is a further proper function of the relevant inborn mechanisms in the rat.

Now the proximal rat rule, like the proximal hoverfly rule, tells the animal what to do given certain experiential contingencies. There is a difference, however, in the normal manner of executing these two rules. When the hoverfly conforms to his rule, nothing in his body under-goes a permanent change, but this is not so in the case of the rat. Suppose, for example, that the rat has just become ill after eating soap. In order to conform to the proximal rat rule, in order to avoid henceforth what tastes like soap, the rat's nervous system must first conform to certain preliminary "rules," rules that dictate that a certain sort of permanent change take place in it. The rat, we say, must "learn" in order to conform to his rule. But the fact that the rat's

evolutionary history dictates that it is normal for him to undergo learning in order to follow his rule rather than following it directly does not affect the biological status of the rule. That he should follow his rule is one of his biological purposes for exactly the same reason that the hoverfly's rule following is biologically pur-posed. Conformity to the rat rule is what his ancestor rats had in common in those cases in which possession of the relevant inborn mecha-nisms aided them to flourish and proliferate, so it is what the mechanism, hence the rat, biolog-ically purposes.

Now the rat that conforms to the proximal rat rule, if he ever becomes ill after eating, ends by conforming to a *derived* proximal rat rule, say, the rule "Do not eat what tastes like soap." Indeed, if a rat becomes ill after eating soap, it immediately becomes one of his biological pur-poses to follow the rule "Do not eat what tastes like soap." For that he is to follow this derived rule is logically entailed by the proximal rat rule plus the premise that he has in fact become ill after eating soap. Similarly, the hoverfly that currently has an image of appropriate size tra-versing his retina at a 60° angle with an angular velocity of 100° per second currently has as a biological purpose to make a turn of 130°. Notice that the hoverfly has this biological pur-pose quite independently of whether or not any hoverfly has ever been in exactly this experien-tial position before. It is theoretically possible, even if unlikely, that no hoverfly has ever had exactly *this* biological purpose before. This is similar to our rat who is sick after eating soap. It is now one of his biological purposes to fol-low the derived proximal rat rule "Do not eat what tastes like soap" even if it should be true that no other rat in history has ever become sick after eating soap, hence true that no rat in his-tory has ever had this particular biological pur-pose before.

In this manner, animals that learn can acquire biological purposes that are peculiar to them as individuals, tailored to their own peculiar cir-cumstances or peculiar histories.[23] Although biological purposes are functions fulfilled in accordance with evolutionary design, they need not be innately given purposes. Similarly, bio-logical competences need not be innate. A proper biological activity of an animal can be something that experience has prompted or "taught" the animal to do, experience coupled with an innate mechanism for being guided to learn by experience.

Nor is there need for such mechanisms to be as specialized as the mechanism that conforms the rat to the proximal rat rule. Not long ago many learning theorists believed that all animal learning took place in accordance with principles that were not species specific but universal. Suppose that this were true. Suppose that every species learned in accordance with the principles of one person's favorite general theory of operant conditioning, so that no reference to the particular evolutionary niche of a species was ever needed to explain how its learning mechanisms had historically enhanced its fitness. Then there would have to be some rarefied hypergeneral explanation of how and why these learning principles worked. Such an explanation might make reference, for example, to specific principles of generalization and discrimination used in differentiating stimuli and in projecting what is to count as "the same" behavior again, that is, reference to universal proximal rules followed during learning. It would have to tell how and why these particular ways of generalizing and discriminating effected, often enough, isolation or zeroing in on sufficiently reliable causes of reinforcement, and in what universal manner (!) reinforcers are connected with the well-being of animals. Thus it would tell *how* possession of the universal mechanism had normally, that is, historically, enhanced fitness in animals generally. Specific applications of this general explanation schema to individual animals in individual circumstances would then determine which among the various effects of their motions were the proximal and distal biological activities of these individuals, as they learned and applied their learning. Such applications would determine, for example, what specific reliable causes of reinforcement were purposefully being zeroed in on by particular animals at particular times, that is, what these animals were "trying" to learn and, after they learned it, what the specific goals of their learned behaviors were.

Now it is important to note that to fulfill a biological purpose is not always to take a step towards flourishing or propagating; it is not always good for an animal to fulfill its biologically determined goals. For example, a rat might come to have as a biological purpose to follow the derived rule "Do not eat what tastes like soap" even if it were true (I suspect it is true) that soap does not *make* rats sick or does not poison them. Suppose, rather, that the rat eats soap and then becomes ill due to a bout with Rattus enteritis. Still, in order to conform to the proximal rat rule, he must now conform to the derived proximal rule "Do not eat what tastes like soap," for this derived rule is entailed by the proximal rat rule given his situational experience. Yet following this derived rule may, in fact, have no tendency to bring him into conformity with the more distal rat rule "Do not eat poisonous substances." So it can happen that the rat acquires a biological purpose and acquires a competence to conform to a derived rule which does not further the end that is this rule's own *raison d'être*. Indeed, the rat *could* acquire a derived purpose and a competence to behave in a manner that was actually detrimental to him, say, a competence to follow the rule "Do not eat what tastes like corn" when, in fact, unless he eats corn, given his circumstances, he will starve. Compare: the hoverfly, dutifully conforming to the proximal hoverfly rule (the rule that tells how he is to react to a moving image on his retina) may thereby dart off after a bird, who would not otherwise have spotted the hoverfly, hence would not have *eaten* him. Thus it is that an individual may have a biological purpose and a competence to follow a derived rule that has no tendency to further the interests either of the individual or of his species and, more specifically, no tendency to produce conformity to more distal rules toward which following it was, biologically, supposed to be a means.[24]

What an animal is doing in accordance with evolutionary design need not be anything that any member of its species has ever done before. And it need not be anything that is good for the animal to do. So surely it need not be anything that common sense would call "natural" for it to do. Consider a circus poodle riding a bicycle. It is performing what common sense would call a most "unnatural" act. Yet it is one of the dog's biological purposes to perform that act. Biologically, the (typical circus) dog's distal action is procurement of his dinner. The dog harbors within him an intricate mechanism, operating in accordance with certain largely unknown but surely quite definite and detailed principles, in accordance with which dogs have been designed to develop perceptual, cognitive and motor skills and to integrate them so as to effect procurement of dinner in their individual environments. Living in an unusual environment, the circus dog acquires unusual purposes and competences when he applies his "dog rules" to his environment. But, although he may be making the audience laugh by accident, he is certainly not balancing on that bicycle by accident. He is balancing purposefully or in accordance with evolutionary design—in accordance with another application of the same general principles that procured his ancestors' dinners during evolutionary history.

VI. HUMAN RULE FOLLOWING

Humans are very sophisticated creatures, so we tell ourselves. We not only learn but learn new ways to learn, develop new concepts, and so forth. Further, much of our behavior results not just from learning but from theoretical and practical inference. But there must still be a finite number of inborn mechanisms, operating in accordance with a finite number of natural principles, having a finite number of biologically proper functions, that account for our dispositions to do these things. Coordinately, there must be a finite number of proximal and distal "Homo sapiens rules" that we have as biological purposes to follow, and there must be mechanisms to implement these rules built into the basic body and brain of normal persons.

Consider then any bit of human behavior produced by biologically well-functioning behavior-regulating systems, by systems that are not broken or jammed. (Behavior that results from malfunction is, of course, overwhelmingly unlikely to bear fruit of any interesting kind.) There will be a way of describing this behavior that captures its aspect as a *biological* activity, a description that tells what

proximal and distal biological purposes, and what biological competences if any, the behavior expresses. This will be so even if the behavior is totally unique, or systematically self-destructive, or not "natural" by any commonsense standards. But of course there will also be numerous ways of describing the behavior that fail to express its biological purposiveness, many "quus-like" descriptions—as "pointing toward the navel with the eyelashes" quus-describes the eyeblink reflex. So the question arises, what is the relation of *ordinary* human purposes, of human intentions and meanings, to biological purposes? Are descriptions of human intentional actions quus-descriptions from the standpoint of evolutionary design? Do ordinary human intentions merely, accidentally, *cohabit* with biological purposes?

Surely a naturalist must answer no. Ordinary human purposes, ordinary intentions, can only be a *species* of biological purpose. To suppose otherwise would be to suppose that the whole mechanism of human belief, desire, inference, concept formation, etc., the function of which culminates in the formation and execution of human intentions, is, as functioning in this capacity, an epiphenomenon of biology, an accidental by-product of systems that nature designed for other purposes. And what would these other purposes be?[25]

This accords with conclusions we reached earlier on the nature of explicit intentions. Explicitly meaning or intending, if this requires representing what one intends, presupposes a prior purposing: purposing to let the representation guide one in a certain way. This is true whether we are talking about representation in an inner medium, say, in a "language of thought," or representation in a public medium—talking, say, about the use of "plus." But this prior purposing cannot be analyzed as the original explicit purposing was analyzed without regress. Rather, a prior unexpressed purposing must be assumed. The reasonable conclusion seems to be that ordinary explicit intending rests on biological purposing—biologically purposing to be guided by, to react this way rather than that to, one's representations. Whether this biological purposing is innate (compare Fodor's version of the "language of thought") or whether it is derived via learning, mechanisms of concept formation, etc., it must *ultimately* derive its content from the details of our evolutionary history.

So unless doing arithmetic results from a total breakdown of the cognitive systems (in which case there may be nothing you purpose when you encounter "plus": how you react to it is accidental under every description) then *whatever* you mean to do when you encounter "plus," that content has been determined by your experience coupled with evolutionary design. But, reasonably, whatever you mean by "plus" is the same as what other people mean who are endowed with the same general sort of cognitive equipment and have been exposed to the same sort of training in arithmetic. This meaning has been determined by the application of *Homo sapiens* rules of some kind to experience. It is likely that these are extremely abstract general purpose *Homo sapiens* rules, in accordance with which human concept formation takes place, and it is likely that the explanation of the efficacy of these rules makes reference to very deep and general principles of ontology. But it is not my task to speculate about the precise form these *Homo sapiens* rules take, or about how the experience of standard training in arithmetic elicits from them the capacity to mean plus. Speculation about the specific forms that our most fundamental cognitive capacities take is the psychologist's job.[26]

I believe that these considerations constitute, albeit in very rough and broad outline, the solution to the Kripke-Wittgenstein paradox.

VII. TRUTH RULES: VERIFICATIONIST OR CORRESPONDENCE?

I have sketched a theory about meaning in the sense of purposing—both expressed and unexpressed purposing. It remains to connect this theory with the theory of semantic meaning.

Truth rules are rules that project, from the parts and structure of sentences in a language, the conditions under which these sentences would be true. Such rules express, of course, an aspect of the meaning of the sentences. The question is whether the conditions referred to by truth rules are to be understood in a "realist"

way as correspondence truth conditions, or in a "verificationist" way as assertability conditions. Dummett's concern about truth rules is this: whatever connection there is between sentences and that which determines their truth has to be a connection that is established via the actual employment of the language. Whatever form truth rules take, realist or verificationist, the *practical* abilities of speakers who understand a language must reflect these rules, indeed, must determine their content. Hence an analysis of the structure of the abilities required for language use and understanding should reveal the kind of rules truth rules are. But, Dummett argues, the only truth rules we could possibly exhibit a practical grasp of are verificationist truth rules.

In Section VIII below, I will claim that Dummett's argument hangs on treating language abilities or competencies, hence the following of language rules, as mere dispositions, or alternatively (perhaps), as taking place wholly within consciousness, and I will add to the arguments already piled up by Wittgenstein and Kripke against the adequacy of this sort of treatment. In the present section, however, I wish to propose a positive thesis. My claim will be that if we interpret rule following and, in general, purposes and competencies in the biological way, then we can see how, on the contrary, reference to correspondence truth rules might *easily* fall out of an analysis of language competence.

We begin by observing that whatever the content of truth rules may be, realist or verificationist, the intent or purpose of anyone engaged in making sincere assertions in a language must be to conform their sentences to these rules. The sincere speaker purposes to make assertions that are true. It follows that the *way* that the actual practice of a language embodies truth rules is that these are the rules in accordance with which the competent speaker (or thinker), when sincere, purposes to make (or think) assertions. These are rules that he is, as it were, *trying to* follow insofar as he is sincerely speaking (or thinking) *that* language. On the bottom layer at least (perhaps the layer that governs the language of thought) these rules must of course be unexpressed rules. But precisely because truth rules are at bottom unexpressed rules, introspection can give us no handle on what kind of rules they are. Rather, it is necessary to develop a *theory* about truth rules, an explanatory hypothesis about what rules we are purposing to follow when we make sincere assertions.

Assuming a biological standpoint, the question whether truth rules are realist or verificationist can be expressed by asking how "proximal" vs. "distal" truth rules are. The proximal hoverfly rule was a rule about how the hoverfly was to respond to a moving image on his retina, that is, roughly, to sensory stimulations. The distal hoverfly rule was a rule about how the hoverfly was to end up interacting with his more removed environment, namely, with females that entered his life at a distance. "Verificationist" truth rules, as Putnam and Dummett envision these, would be rules that governed responses to prior thoughts and, as Dummett has put it, "bare sense experiences," hence would be proximal rules.[27] "Realist" or correspondence rules, on the other hand, would for the most part be distal rules, rules that governed the manner in which assertions were to correspond to affairs that lie, very often, well beyond the interface of body and world. Convinced by Wittgenstein and Kripke that purposing to follow a rule is not something encapsulated *within* consciousness, we are not compelled to suppose that truth rules have to be rules about what is to happen either in the mind or at the interface between mind, or body, and world. So let us ask what it would be like if truth rules were distal correspondence rules.

The first thing to note is that if truth rules were distal rules they would surely have to be *backed* by proximal rules, rules about how to respond to our thoughts (inference) and to the immediate fruits of our perceptual explorations (perceptual judgment). They would have to be *backed* by rules that determined assertability conditions, the innermost of these conditions being within the mind or brain or at the interface of mind or brain and world. Call these back-up rules "proximal assertability rules." Proximal assertability rules would concern the most proximal conditions under which we should say or think certain things. Conformity to these rules would have, as a biological purpose, to effect conformity to distal rules, that is, to correspondence truth rules.

These truth rules would concern distal conditions under which we should say or think certain things. The truth rules might imply directives with this sort of form: if you have reason to speak (think) about the weather in Atlanta, say (think) "It is snowing in Atlanta" when and only when it is snowing in Atlanta; if you have reason to speak (think) about the color of snow, say (think) "Snow is white" if and only if snow is white. For a simple biological model here, compare worker honeybees. They (biologically) purpose to follow rules of this kind: when dancing, angle the axis of your dance 10° off the vertical if and only if there is a good supply of nectar 10° off a direct line from hive to sun. (Proposals concerning how humans might *learn* how to (purpose to) conform to distal correspondence truth rules are detailed in *LTOBC*.)[28]

Conforming to the proximal hoverfly rule and the proximal rat rule often fails to bring hoverflies and rats into conformity to the distal hoverfly and rat rules. Similarly, conforming to proximal assertability rules might often fail to bring humans into conformity to truth rules. One can unknowingly say what is false even though one has good evidence for what one says. And one frequently fails to say what is true, indeed, to say anything at all, because one lacks any evidence at all, either for or against. Also, whether conformity to the proximal hoverfly and rat rules helps to produce conformity to the distal hoverfly and rat rules on this or that occasion often depends upon factors in the hoverfly's or rat's external environment over which it has no control. Similarly, whether conformity to proximal assertability rules would bring us into conformity to truth rules in this case or that might depend upon factors over which we had no control. For example, circumstances responsible for most perceptual illusions are circumstances outside the observer which, normally, he neither controls nor needs to control. Nor is not having enough evidence either to affirm or to deny a proposition typically something that it is within one's control to remedy. The principles in accordance with which biological devices perform functions that are proper to them always refer, in the end, to conditions external to these devices. These are conditions that have *historically* been present often enough to enable a critical proportion of ancestors of those devices to perform these functions, or to perform them a critical proportion of the time, but that cannot be counted on always to be present. All biological devices are fallible devices, even when normal and healthy.[29]

It follows that the proximal assertability rules for a sentence would not *define* its semantics, for they would not determine what its truth conditions were. Rather, following proximal assertability rules would be means that were, merely, approximations to the end that was following correspondence truth rules—more or less helpful and more or less reliable means to that end. Let us reflect for a moment upon certain consequences of this model.

If proximal assertability rules were rules that we followed only as a more or less reliable means to following distal truth rules, then it would not at least be obvious that those who shared a language in the sense of having competences to abide by the same truth rules would have any need to share proximal assertability rules as well. The male hoverfly follows the distal rule "If you see a female, catch it" by following the proximal hoverfly rule. The male housefly follows the same distal rule by tracking the female rather than by plotting an interception path, employing different proximal means to the same distal end. Now consider how many different ways there are to make a map of a city: for example, by walking about with a yardstick, paper and pencil, by working from aerial photographs, by using surveyors' instruments, etc. Might there not also be various ways to make sentences that map onto the world in accordance with the same truth rules? Is there really any reason to suppose that only one set of proximal assertability rules could effect a reasonably reliable competence to conform to a given set of distal correspondence rules? Consider, for example, how many ways there are to tell whether a solution is acid or whether it has iodine in it. Consider how many alternative visual and tactile clues we use, on one occasion or another, to perceive depth. And consider: were the proximal assertability rules that Helen Keller used when she spoke English the same as those that you use? If not, does it follow that she did not really speak English after all?

Indeed, there is a sense, there is a way of individuating rules, in which it is impossible for people to share proximal assertability rules. Proximal assertability rules that I conform to correlate happenings at the periphery of my nervous system or body with sentences. Proximal assertability rules that you conform to correlate happenings at the periphery of your nervous system or body with sentences. For us to "share a set of proximal assertability rules" could not, of course, be for me to purpose to correlate happenings at the periphery of *your* body with *my* sentences. If I purposed to do that, I would be purposing to conform to a distal rule, not a proximal rule. We could "share proximal assertability rules" only in the sense that our rules ran parallel. But it is not immediately obvious what the point of running parallel to one another with language might be. Why would you take any interest in the sentences I uttered, if these correlated only with what was happening at the ends of my afferent nerves? Only if the proximal assertability rules that you and I used effected relatively reliable conformity to the same *distal* correspondence rules would there be any point in talking to one another. But if agreement is effected on the distal level, what need would there be for agreement on the proximal level? Hence what reason is there to assume, say with Quine, that comparison of only proximal rules *ought* to yield determinate translation between idiolects?[30]

VIII. CAUSES OF VERIFICATIONIST MYOPIA

Given a biological approach, then, there are reasons to think that truth rules may be distal correspondence rules, hence that classical truth conditions may do work for semantics. But Putnam and Dummett claim that any such view is unintelligible. Why?

Although there are passages in both Dummett and Putnam that could be given a less sympathetic reading, the reason is not (or at least is not simply) that these philosophers take understanding to be something that must transpire before consciousness. A more explicit theme is that understanding a language is a practical ability, constituted by a set of *dispositions,* in this case, learned responses: "Now when someone learns a language, what he learns is a practice; he learns to respond, verbally and nonverbally, to utterances and to make utterances of his own" (Dummett),[31] "language understanding [is] ... an activity involving 'language entry rules' (procedures for subjecting some sentences to stimulus control), procedures for deductive and inductive inference and 'language exit rules' ..." (Putnam).[32] It follows, Putnam and Dummett now agree, that if a language is characterized by certain truth rules, this fact must be one that shows up in the speech dispositions of the language users. And it follows that if there are no *dispositions* to recognize correspondence truth conditions, sentences can not have correspondence truth conditions.

Putnam's phrase "language entry rules" is a reference to Sellars, but, of course, many other central figures have also held that understanding a language must yield to a dispositional analysis, among them Quine, Davidson, many would say Wittgenstein, and, in the philosophy of mind (re: inner language), the functionalists. Despite this distinguished advocacy, surely Kripke's remark about illegitimate "equation of performance with correctness" is applicable here. To be competent in a language involves that one have a practical grasp of its truth rules. About that everyone agrees. But "true" is clearly a *normative* notion. "True" is how my sincerely uttered sentences are *when they come out right,* when they are, using Kripke's expression, as they "ought to be," when I achieve what I purpose in sincerely uttering them. And no mere set of dispositions, no mere performance, determines a measuring "ought," a standard or norm. No set of dispositions, then, could determine truth rules.

Nor is the normative ingredient in truth provided by the fact that the dispositions that constitute competence in a language must agree with a public norm. Compare games. Consider first a case in which I intend to play the same game as the others do, say, the one they call "chess," but I mistakenly play by different rules than the others. This is a case of playing wrongly in the sense that I have not played the game I intended, or, perhaps, the one others expected me to. Similarly, if I intend to use the same language as the others, but in fact adopt

different truth rules, then I speak wrongly, for I have not spoken the language I intended, or that others expected me to. This is called "not knowing the language" or "making mistakes in the language." Second, consider a case in which I have no intention to play with the chess pieces as the others do nor do the others expect me to. Then playing by different rules is just playing a different game. It is neither playing chess wrongly nor doing anything else wrongly. The linguistic parallel to this is called "speaking a *different* language." But speaking wrongly in the sense of speaking *falsely* is still a *third* possibility. Speaking falsely is not just a way of being out of step, nor is it just marching to the beat of a different drummer. Suppose we call it a "rule" of chess that you are supposed to checkmate your opponent. Then speaking falsely is like failing to checkmate the opponent. Better, it is like failing to pick up one straw without moving the others when playing jackstraws. Just as learning the rules better is not the cure for losing at chess or jackstraws, learning the community's language better is not the cure for bad judgment. And just as whether one succeeds at jackstraws, that is, at not moving the other sticks, does not depend on any agreement with the community, neither does whether one succeeds in speaking truth in one's language. To purpose to follow certain truth rules is to set a standard for *oneself*—a standard that one may fail to meet.

It is because purposes set standards that "true" is a normative notion and that no set of dispositions could determine truth rules. Similarly, although Dummett and Putnam are right that semantic meaning must be resident somehow in language competence, no set of dispositions equals a competence. First, a disposition does not express a competence unless it is a disposition informed by a purpose. My disposition to fall if left unsupported is no competence, nor is the hoverfly's disposition to chase birds. Conversely, having a competence does not, in general, imply that one has any particular dispositions. If I know how to A—say, to sharpen a drill bit—it doesn't follow that I have a disposition to succeed in A-ing if I try. Perhaps my hands are too cold, or the only grindstone available is not the kind I am practiced at using, or you insist on joggling my elbow. Though I know how to walk, sometimes I trip when I try. Recall the hoverfly, who exhibits a competence whenever he conforms to the distal hoverfly rule in a normal way, yet, due to the inconstancy of conditions outside him, often does not manage to conform to it at all. Nor are there specified conditions under which a person must succeed in order to know how. If I can only sharpen the bit using one sharpening tool whereas you know how to use another, then normal conditions for exercise of my ability to sharpen a drill bit will be different from normal conditions for exercise of yours; each may fail where the other succeeds. Knowing how to do A entails, at best, only that there are *some* normal conditions under which one succeeds in doing A.

Now there is an evident reason why knowing how to A does not, in general, entail having any simple disposition to succeed in A-ing. The reason is that most know-how involves *distal* action, and there is no such thing as a simple *disposition* to involvement with anything distal. How one interacts with things at a distance always depends upon what lies in between, on surrounding conditions. Simple dispositions can concern only reactions to and actions upon that which *touches* one or, perhaps, what is inside one. It follows that to assimilate language competence to a set of dispositions directly begs the question against distal truth rules. There is no need for tortuous arguments to demonstrate that truth rules must then be verificationist. On a dispositional account, to "grasp" correspondence truth rules for each sentence in one's language would be to have a "capacity ... to evince recognition of the truth of the sentence when and only when the relevant condition is fulfilled" (Dummett).[33] But if a "recognitional capacity" is a disposition, it must be a disposition to respond to a proximal stimulus, there being no such thing as a disposition to respond to something distal. And dispositions to respond to proximal stimuli with sentences could correspond, at best, to assertability conditions, certainly not to distal correspondence truth conditions. Q.E.D.

Compare the hoverfly. Assuming that his insides are working right, what he has a *disposition* to do is, at best, to conform to the proximal hoverfly rule. Does it follow that he has no ability to catch females?

It is significant, I think, how close the dispositional view of language understanding is to the more classical view that understanding takes place wholly within consciousness. On the classical view, understanding must ultimately involve relations only to things that touch the mind. On the dispositional view, understanding still involves only what touches the mind or, say, the nervous system. It is easy, then, to slip back and forth between two ways of interpreting the Dummett-Putnam attack upon realist truth.[34] Yet what Kripke has shown is that *neither* view of language understanding is a tenable view. Hence, whatever may be said for or against the positive theory of rule following that I have offered, the verificationist vision is surely unnecessarily nearsighted. If Kripke (and Kripke's Wittgenstein) are right, then *whatever* the status of rule following, we have no reason to think that the following of correspondence truth rules is any more *problematic* than is the following of verificationist truth rules.

On the other hand, perhaps what is most puzzling about the following of any kind of language rules is how one could "know" these rules without having a prior language, a prior way of "meaning" or thinking of these rules. Yet surely even the medium of thought, even whatever is currently before the mind or in the head, stands in need of interpretation. Knowing the rules is not a disposition, nor can it be explained in the end by reference to prior representations of the rules. The biological account agrees with both of these considerations.

ACKNOWLEDGMENTS

Earlier versions of this paper were read at the University of Wisconsin (Madison), Western Michigan University, the University of Maryland, Trinity University, the University of New England (Australia), Australian National University, Monash University and Vanderbilt University. I am grateful to the members of these departments, to Margaret Gilbert and John Troyer, and to unknown referees for *The Philosophical Review,* for helpful comments and suggestions.

NOTES

1. Brian Loar, "Critical Review of Saul Kripke's *Wittgenstein on Rules and Private Language," Noûs* 19 (1985), p. 280.
2. Hilary Putnam, "Realism and Reason," in *Meaning and the Moral Sciences* (London, England: Rout-

ledge and Kegan Paul, 1978). Michael Dummett's statement is in "What Is a Theory of Meaning?" in Samuel Guttenplan, ed., *Mind and Language* (Oxford, England: Clarendon Press of Oxford University Press, 1975), pp. 97–139, and in "What is a Theory of Meaning? (II)," in Gareth Evans and John McDowell, eds., *Truth and Meaning: Essays in Semantics* (Oxford, England: Clarendon Press of Oxford University Press, 1976), pp. 67–137.

3. In "Metaphysical Antirealism?" *Mind* 95 (1986), pp. 417–431; reprinted in *The Philosopher's Annual* Vol. IX-1986 (Atascadero, Calif.: Ridgeview Publishing Co., 1988).

4. S. Kripke, *Wittgenstein on Rules and Private Language* [hereafter WORPL] (Cambridge, Mass.: Harvard University Press, 1982), p. 7.

5. Ibid., p. 9.

6. Ibid., p. 20. Kripke's ellipsis points at the end; Kripke's footnotes omitted.

7. Loar claims that Kripke has not demonstrated that intentionality is not this. Kripke's text does however contain several footnotes commenting on the relevant arguments in Wittgenstein's text. I mention these arguments below.

8. L. Wittgenstein, *Philosophical Investigations* (New York, N.Y.: The Macmillan Company, 1953), Paragraph 141.

9. *WORPL*, pp. 26–27.

10. Kripke places a great deal of emphasis on the failure to find anything that "justifies" my proceeding as I do when I follow a rule, and he seems to think of a "justification" as something that must be, by its very nature, open to or within consciousness. Similarly: "Even now as I write, I feel confident that there is something *in my mind* [italics mine]—the meaning I attach to the 'plus' sign-that *instructs* me [italics Kripke's] what I ought to do in all future cases" (*WORPL*, pp. 21–22). And "The idea that we lack 'direct' access to the facts whether we mean plus or quus is bizarre in any case. Do I not know, directly, and with a fair degree of certainty, that I mean plus?" (*WORPL*, p. 40). Indeed, many passages in Kripke's essay suggest that what bothers him the most is not that nothing seems to determine what rule I am following, but that nothing *before my mind* determines it. The feeling is conveyed that Kripke finds the real blow to be that the intentionality involved in rule following does not reside *within* consciousness. If *that* is what Kripke takes to be the root "Wittgenstein paradox," then all will agree that Wittgenstein made no attempt to give a "straight solution" to it. Nor will I. On the other hand, if that were the main paradox, no one would ever have supposed that a dispositional account would be a "straight solution" to it and Kripke's discussion of dispositional accounts should have been placed not with his account of "Wittgenstein's paradox" but with his discussion of "Wittgenstein's sceptical solution," that is, as an account of what Kripke believed this skeptical solution was not.

Margaret Gilbert suggests (in conversation) that one paradox may be that meaning strikes one as being something that can be fully constituted at a given time t, whether or not meaning is something that happens within consciousness. And, to be sure, dispositions are usually taken to exist at given times so that a dispositional account might be viewed as an attempt at a straight solution to Gilbert's paradox. Gilbert's paradox, if one finds it paradoxical, is another that I will not attempt to solve. I will merely try to show how there is a fact to the matter of what I mean by "+."

11. *WORPL*, p. 66.

12. Ibid.

13. Ibid., p. 24; footnotes omitted.

14. Ibid., p. 57.

15. Full details of the notion of biological function that I rely on in this paper are given under the label "proper functions" in my *Language, Thought, and Other Biological Categories* [hereafter LTOBC] (Cambridge, Mass.: Bradford Books/The MIT Press, 1984), Chapters 1–2. See also my "In Defense of Proper Functions," *Philosophy of Science* 56 (1989), pp. 288–302.

16. "How Hoverflies Compute Interception Courses," *Journal of Comparative Physiology* 125 (1978), pp. 191–204.

17. For a full discussion of normal ("Normal") explanations for performance of proper functions, see *LTOBC*, Chapters 1 and 2, and my "Biosemantics," *The Journal of Philosophy* 86 (1989), pp. 281–297.

18. On the proper functions of imperfect members of a biological category, see *LTOBC*, Chapters 1 and 2.

19. Goodman's paradox is a paradox in epistemology. Kripke, on the other hand, is concerned not about how we could know or discover what someone means by "plus" but about what this determinate meaning *consists* in. Note too that assuming common-sense ontology does nothing, by itself, toward solving Goodman's paradox, which concerns how we can *know* or reasonably guess which entities are the basic ontological ones, *supposing* there to be such.

20. More precisely, only the distal hoverfly rule would be mentioned in giving a "most proximate normal explanation" of the function of the hoverfly's turning mechanism. See *LTOBC*, and the discussion of "normal explanations" in my "Biosemantics."

21. Notice that it is the reference to evolutionary *history* that has been doing all of the work in explaining how norms come to apply to the activities of an animal, in explaining how there can be a standard from which the facts of individual behavior diverge. I defend the position that function always derives from history in "In Defense of Proper Functions."

22. The reference is to studies by John Garcia. A bibliography of his papers may be found in *The American Psychologist* 35 (1980), pp. 41–43.

23. A much more detailed discussion of "derived proper functions" may be found in *LTOBC*, Chapter 2, and in my "Thoughts Without Laws: Cognitive Science

With Content," *The Philosophical Review* 95 (1986), pp. 47–80.

24. For further details on conflicting proper functions, see *LTOBC,* Chapter 2, and my "Thoughts Without Laws."

25. For a more detailed defense of this claim, see my "Biosemantics."

26. But, people still persist in asking, How do you know that we really *do* end up meaning *plus* by "plus"? How do you know we don't mean *quus?* Because if we meant quus then "plus" would mean quus, and the way to *say* that we all meant quus would be "we all mean quus"—which is what I said. Compare Donald Davidson, "Knowing One's Own Mind," *Proceedings and Addresses of the American Philosophical Association* 60 (1987), pp. 441–458, and Tyler Burge, "Individualism and Self Knowledge," *Journal of Philosophy* 60 (1988), pp. 649–663.

27. "What Is a Theory of Meaning? (II)," p. 111.

28. Chapters 9, 17 and 18.

29. For amplification of this very crucial theme, see my "Thoughts Without Laws" and "Biosemantics."

30. For further discussion of the relation of proximal assertability rules to truth rules see my "The Price of Correspondence Truth," *Noûs* 20 (1986), pp. 453–468, and also *LTOBC,* especially Chapters 8 and 9. Proximal assertability rules are close relatives of what I there called "intensions." (In this essay I am not emphasizing that perception characteristically is an activity involving overt exploration, a fact that was in the foreground when I spoke of intensions in *LTOBC.* Thus the notion "proximal assertability rules" is a somewhat duller tool than I intended "intensions" to be in LTOBC.)

31. "What Is a Theory of Meaning? (II)," p. 82.

32. "Realism and Reason," p. 110.

33. "What Is a Theory of Meaning? (II)," pp. 80–81.

34. I will not attempt to prove that Dummett and Putnam themselves do some sliding, but on Putnam, see *LTOBC,* Epilogue.

45 Languages and Language

DAVID LEWIS

I. THESIS

What is a language? Something which assigns meanings to certain strings of types of sounds or of marks. It could therefore be a function, a set of ordered pairs of strings and meanings. The entities in the domain of the function are certain finite sequences of types of vocal sounds, or of types of inscribable marks; if σ is in the domain of a language £, let us call σ a *sentence* of £. The entities in the range of the function are meanings; if σ is a sentence of £, let us call £(σ) the *meaning of* σ in £. What could a meaning of a sentence be? Something which, when combined with factual information about the world—or factual information about *any* possible world— yields a truth-value. It could therefore be a function from worlds to truth-values—or more simply, a set of worlds. We can say that a sentence σ is true in a language £ at a world w if and only if w belongs to the set of worlds £(σ). We can say that σ is true in £ (without mentioning a world) if and only if our actual world belongs to £(σ). We can say that σ is *analytic* in £ if and only if every possible world belongs to £(σ). And so on, in the obvious way.

II. ANTITHESIS

What is language? A social phenomenon which is part of the natural history of human beings; a sphere of human action, wherein people utter strings of vocal sounds, or inscribe strings of marks, and wherein people respond by thought or action to the sounds or marks which they observe to have been so produced.

This verbal activity is, for the most part, rational. He who produces certain sounds or marks does so for a reason. He knows that someone else, upon hearing his sounds or seeing his marks, is apt to form a certain belief or act in a certain way. He wants, for some reason, to bring about that belief or action. Thus his beliefs and desires give him a reason to produce the sounds or marks, and he does. He who responds to the sounds or marks in a certain way also does so for a reason. He knows how the production of sounds or marks depends upon the producer's state of mind. When he observes the sounds or marks, he is therefore in a position to infer something about the producer's state of mind. He can probably also infer something about the conditions which caused that state of

From *Language, Mind and Knowledge,* Keith Gunderson, ed. (Minneapolis: University of Minnesota Press, 1975), pp. 3–35. Copyright © 1981 by University of Minnesota Press. © 1983 by David Lewis. Reprinted by permission of the author. AUTHOR'S NOTE: This paper was originally prepared in 1968 and was revised in 1972. The 1968 draft appears in Italian translation as "Lingue e ligua," *Versus* 4 (1973): 2–21.

mind. He may merely come to believe these conclusions, or he may act upon them in accordance with his other beliefs and his desires.

Not only do both have reasons for thinking and acting as they do; they know something about each other, so each is in a position to replicate the other's reasons. Each one's replication of the other's reasons forms part of his own reason for thinking and acting as he does; and each is in a position to replicate the other's replication of his own reasons. Therefore the Gricean mechanism[1] operates: X intends to bring about a response on the part of Y by getting Y to recognize that X intends to bring about that response; Y does recognize X's intention, and is thereby given some sort of reason to respond just as X intended him to.

Within any suitable population, various regularities can be found in this rational verbal activity. There are regularities whereby the production of sounds or marks depends upon various aspects of the state of mind of the producer. There are regularities whereby various aspects of responses to sounds or marks depend upon the sounds or marks to which one is responding. Some of these regularities are accidental. Others can be explained, and different ones can be explained in very different ways.

Some of them can be explained as conventions of the population in which they prevail. Conventions are regularities in action, or in action and belief, which are arbitrary but perpetuate themselves because they serve some sort of common interest. Past conformity breeds future conformity because it gives one a reason to go on conforming; but there is some alternative regularity which could have served instead, and would have perpetuated itself in the same way if only it had got started.

More precisely: a regularity R, in action or in action and belief, is a *convention* in a population P if and only if, within P, the following six conditions hold. (Or at least they almost hold. A few exceptions to the "everyone"s can be tolerated.)

(1) Everyone conforms to R.

(2) Everyone believes that the others conform to R.

(3) This belief that the others conform to R gives everyone a good and decisive reason to conform to R himself. His reason may be that, in

particular, those of the others he is now dealing with conform to R; or his reason may be that there is general or widespread conformity, or that there has been, or that there will be. His reason may be a practical reason, if conforming to R is a matter of acting in a certain way; or it may be an epistemic reason, if conforming to R is a matter of believing in a certain way. First case: according to his beliefs, some desired end may be reached by means of some sort of action in conformity to R, provided that the others (all or some of them) also conform to R; therefore he wants to conform to R if they do. Second case: his beliefs, together with the premise that others conform to R, deductively imply or inductively support some conclusion; and in believing this conclusion, he would thereby conform to R. Thus reasons for conforming to a convention by believing something—like reasons for belief in general—are believed premises tending to confirm the truth of the belief in question. Note that I am *not* speaking here of practical reasons for acting so as to somehow produce in oneself a certain desired belief.

(4) There is a general preference for general conformity to R rather than slightly-less-than-general conformity—in particular, rather than conformity by all but any one. (This is not to deny that some state of *widespread* nonconformity to R might be even more preferred.) Thus everyone who believes that at least almost everyone conforms to R will want the others, as well as himself, to conform. This condition serves to distinguish cases of convention, in which there is a predominant coincidence of interest, from cases of deadlocked conflict. In the latter cases, it may be that each is doing the best he can by conforming to R, given that the others do so; but each wishes the others did not conform to R, since he could then gain at their expense.

(5) R is not the only possible regularity meeting the last two conditions. There is at least one alternative R' such that the belief that the others conformed to R' would give everyone a good and decisive practical or epistemic reason to conform to R' likewise; such that there is a general preference for general conformity to R' rather than slightly-less-than-general conformity to R'; and such that there is normally no way

of conforming to R and R' both. Thus the alternative R' could have perpetuated itself as a convention instead of R; this condition provides for the characteristic arbitrariness of conventions.

(6) Finally, the various facts listed in conditions (1) to (5) are matters of *common* (or *mutual*) knowledge: they are known to everyone, it is known to everyone that they are known to everyone, and so on. The knowledge mentioned here may be merely potential: knowledge that would be available if one bothered to think hard enough. Everyone must potentially know that (1) to (5) hold; potentially know that the others potentially know it; and so on. This condition ensures stability. If anyone tries to replicate another's reasoning, perhaps including the other's replication of his own reasoning, . . . , the result will reinforce rather than subvert his expectation of conformity to R. Perhaps a negative version of (6) would do the job: no one disbelieves that (1) to (5) hold, no one believes that others disbelieve this, and so on.

This definition can be tried out on all manner of regularities which we would be inclined to call conventions. It is a convention to drive on the right. It is a convention to mark poisons with skull and crossbones. It is a convention to dress as we do. It is a convention to train beasts to turn right on "gee" and left on "haw." It is a convention to give goods and services in return for certain pieces of paper or metal. And so on.

The common interests which sustain conventions are as varied as the conventions themselves. Our convention to drive on the right is sustained by our interest in not colliding. Our convention for marking poisons is sustained by our interest in making it easy for everyone to recognize poisons. Our conventions of dress might be sustained by a common aesthetic preference for somewhat uniform dress, or by the low cost of mass-produced clothes, or by a fear on everyone's part that peculiar dress might be thought to manifest a peculiar character, or by a desire on everyone's part not to be too conspicuous, or—most likely—by a mixture of these and many other interests.

It is a platitude—something only a philosopher would dream of denying—that there are conventions of language, although we do not find it easy to say what those conventions are. If

we look for the fundamental difference in verbal behavior between members of two linguistic communities, we can be sure of finding something which is arbitrary but perpetuates itself because of a common interest in coordination. In the case of conventions of language, that common interest derives from our common interest in taking advantage of, and in preserving, our ability to control others' beliefs and actions to some extent by means of sounds and marks. That interest in turn derives from many miscellaneous desires we have; to list them, list the ways you would be worse off in Babel.

III. SYNTHESIS

What have languages to do with language? What is the connection between what I have called *languages,* functions from strings of sounds or of marks to sets of possible worlds, semantic systems discussed in complete abstraction from human affairs, and what I have called *language,* a form of rational, convention-governed human social activity? We know what to *call* this connection we are after: we can say that a given language £ is *used by,* or is a (or the) language *of,* a given population P. We know also that this connection holds by virtue of the conventions of language prevailing in P. Under suitably different conventions, a different language would be used by P. There is some sort of convention whereby P uses £—but what is it? It is worthless to call it a convention to use £, even if it can correctly be so described, for we want to know what it is to use £.

My proposal[2] is that the convention whereby a population P uses a language £ is a convention of *truthfulness* and *trust* in £. To be truthful in £ is to act in a certain way: to try never to utter any sentence of £ that are not true in £. Thus it is to avoid uttering any sentence of £ unless one believes it to be true in £. To be trusting in £ is to form beliefs in a certain way: to impute truthfulness in £ to others, and thus to tend to respond to another's utterance of any sentence of £ by coming to believe that the uttered sentence is true in £.

Suppose that a certain language £ is used by a certain population P. Let this be a perfect case of normal language use. Imagine what would go on; and review the definition of a convention to verify that there does prevail in *P* a convention of truthfulness and trust in £.

(1) There prevails in *P* at least a regularity of truthfulness and trust in £. The members of *P* frequently speak (or write) sentences of £ to one another. When they do, ordinarily the speaker (or writer) utters one of the sentences he believes to be true in £; and the hearer (or reader) responds by coming to share that belief of the speaker's (unless he already had it), and adjusting his other beliefs accordingly.

(2) The members of *P* believe that this regularity of truthfulness and trust in £ prevails among them. Each believes this because of his experience of others' past truthfulness and trust in £.

(3) The expectation of conformity ordinarily gives everyone a good reason why he himself should conform. If he is a speaker, he expects his hearer to be trusting in £; wherefore he has reason to expect that by uttering certain sentences that are true in £ according to his beliefs—by being truthful in £ in a certain way—he can impart certain beliefs that he takes to be correct. Commonly, a speaker has some reason or other for wanting to impart some or other correct beliefs. Therefore his beliefs and desires constitute a practical reason for acting in the way he does: for uttering some sentence truthfully in £.

As for the hearer: he expects the speaker to be truthful in £, wherefore he has good reason to infer that the speaker's sentence is true in £ according to the speaker's beliefs. Commonly, a hearer also has some or other reason to believe that the speaker's beliefs are correct (by and large, and perhaps with exceptions for certain topics); so it is reasonable for him to infer that the sentence he has heard is probably true in £. Thus his beliefs about the speaker give him an epistemic reason to respond trustingly in £.

We have coordination between truthful speaker and trusting hearer. Each conforms as he does to the prevailing regularity of truthfulness and trust in £ because he expects complementary conformity on the part of the other.

But there is also a more diffuse and indirect sort of coordination. In coordinating with his present partner, a speaker or hearer also is coor-

dinating with all those whose past truthfulness and trust in £ have contributed to his partner's present expectations. This indirect coordination is a four-way affair: between present speakers and past speakers, present speakers and past hearers, present hearers and past speakers, and present hearers and past hearers. And whereas the direct coordination between a speaker and his hearer is a coordination of truthfulness with trust for a single sentence of £, the indirect coordination with one's partner's previous partners (and with *their* previous partners, etc.) may involve various sentences of £. It may happen that a hearer, say, has never before encountered the sentence now addressed to him; but he forms the appropriate belief on hearing it—one such that he has responded trustingly in £—because his past experience with truthfulness in £ has involved many sentences grammatically related to this one.

(4) There is in *P* a general preference for general conformity to the regularity of truthfulness and trust in £. Given that most conform, the members of P want all to conform. They desire truthfulness and trust in £ from each other, as well as from themselves. This general preference is sustained by a common interest in communication. Everyone wants occasionally to impart correct beliefs and bring about appropriate actions in others by means of sounds and marks. Everyone wants to preserve his ability to do so at will. Everyone wants to be able to learn about the parts of the world that he cannot observe for himself by observing instead the sounds and marks of his fellows who have been there.

(5) The regularity of truthfulness and trust in £ has alternatives. Let £' be any language that does not overlap £ in such a way that it is possible to be truthful and trusting simultaneously in £ and in £', and that is rich and convenient enough to meet the needs of *P* for communication. Then the regularity of truthfulness and trust in £' is an alternative to the prevailing regularity of truthfulness and trust in £. For the alternative regularity, as for the actual one, general conformity by the others would give one a reason to conform; and general conformity would be generally preferred over slightly-less-than-general conformity.

(6) Finally, all these facts are common knowledge in *P*. Everyone knows them, everyone knows that everyone knows them, and so on. Or at any rate none believes that another doubts them, none believes that another believes that another doubts them, and so on.

In any case in which a language £ clearly is used by a population *P*, then, it seems that there prevails in *P* a convention of truthfulness and trust in £, sustained by an interest in communication. The converse is supported by an unsuccessful search for counterexamples: I have not been able to think of any case in which there is such a convention and yet the language £ is clearly not used in the population *P*. Therefore I adopt this definition, claiming that it agrees with ordinary usage in the cases in which ordinary usage is fully determinate:

> a language £ is *used by* a population *P* if and only if there prevails in *P* a convention of truthfulness and trust in £, sustained by an interest in communication.

Such conventions, I claim, provide the desired connection between languages and language-using populations.

Once we understand how languages are connected to populations, whether by conventions of truthfulness and trust for the sake of communication or in some other way, we can proceed to redefine relative to a population all those semantic concepts that we previously defined relative to a language. A string of sounds or of marks is a sentence of *P* if and only if it is a sentence of some language £ which is used in *P*. It has a certain meaning in *P* if and only if it has that meaning in some language £ which is used in *P*. It is true in *P* at a world w if and only if it is true at w in some language £ which is used in *P*. It is true in *P* if and only if it is true in some language £ which is used in *P*.

The account just given of conventions in general, and of conventions of language in particular, differs in one important respect from the account given in my book *Convention*.[3]

Formerly, the crucial clause in the definition of convention was stated in terms of a conditional preference for conformity: each prefers to conform if the others do, and it would be the same for the alternatives to the actual conven-

tion. (In some versions of the definition, this condition was subsumed under a broader requirement of general preference for general conformity.) The point of this was to explain why the belief that others conform would give everyone a reason for conforming likewise, and so to explain the rational self-perpetuation of conventions. But a reason involving preference in this way must be a practical reason for acting, not an epistemic reason for believing. Therefore I said that conventions were regularities in action alone. It made no sense to speak of believing something in conformity to convention. (Except in the peculiar case that others' conformity to the convention gives one a practical reason to conform by acting to somehow produce a belief in oneself; but I knew that this case was irrelevant to ordinary language use.) Thus I was cut off from what I now take to be the primary sort of conventional coordination in language use: that between the action of the truthful speaker and the responsive believing of his trusting hearer. I resorted to two different substitutes.

Sometimes it is common knowledge how the hearer will want to act if he forms various beliefs, and we can think of the speaker not only as trying to impart beliefs but also as trying thereby to get the hearer to act in a way that speaker and hearer alike deem appropriate under the circumstances that the speaker believes to obtain. Then we have speaker-hearer coordination of action. Both conform to a convention of truthfulness for the speaker plus appropriate responsive action by the hearer. The hearer's trustful believing need not be part of the content of the convention, though it must be mentioned to explain why the hearer acts in conformity. In this way we reach the account of "signaling" in *Convention*, chapter IV.

But signaling was all too obviously a special case. There may be no appropriate responsive action for the hearer to perform when the speaker imparts a belief to him. Or the speaker and hearer may disagree about how the hearer ought to act under the supposed circumstances. Or the speaker may not know how the hearer will decide to act; or the hearer may not know that he knows; and so on. The proper hearer's response to consider is *believing*, but that is not ordinarily an action. So in considering language use in general, in *Convention,* chapter V, I was forced to give up on speaker-hearer coordination. I took instead the diffuse coordination between the present speaker and the past speakers who trained the present hearer. Accordingly, I proposed that the convention whereby a population P used a language £ was simply a convention of truthfulness in £. Speakers conform; hearers do not, until they become speakers in their turn, if they ever do.

I think now that I went wrong when I went beyond the special case of signaling. I should have kept my original emphasis on speaker-hearer coordination, broadening the definition of convention to fit. It was Jonathan Bennett[4] who showed me how that could be done: by restating the crucial defining clause not in terms of preference for conformity but rather in terms of reasons for conformity—practical or *epistemic* reasons. The original conditional preference requirement gives way now to clause (3): the belief that others conform gives everyone a reason to conform likewise, and it would be the same for the alternatives to the actual convention. Once this change is made, there is no longer any obstacle to including the hearer's trust as part of the content of a convention.

(The old conditional preference requirement is retained, however, in consequence of the less important clause (4). Clause (3) as applied to practical reasons, but not as applied to epistemic reasons, may be subsumed under (4).)

Bennett pointed out one advantage of the change: suppose there is only one speaker of an idiolect, but several hearers who can understand him. Shouldn't he and his hearers comprise a population that uses his idiolect? More generally, what is the difference between (a) someone who does not utter sentences of a language because he does not belong to any population that uses it, and (b) someone who does not utter sentences of the language although he does belong to such a population because at present—or always, perhaps—he has nothing to say? Both are alike, so far as action in conformity to a convention of truthfulness goes. Both are vacuously truthful. In *Convention,* I made it a condition of truthfulness in £ that one sometimes does utter sentences of £, though not that

one speaks up on any particular occasion. But that is unsatisfactory: what degree of truthful talkativeness does it take to keep up one's active membership in a language-using population? What if someone just never thought of anything worth saying?

(There is a less important difference between my former account and the present one. Then and now, I wanted to insist that cases of convention are cases of predominant coincidence of interest. I formerly provided for this by a defining clause that seems now unduly restrictive: in any instance of the situation to which the convention applies, everyone has approximately the same preferences regarding all possible combinations of actions. Why *all?* It may be enough that they agree in preferences to the extent specified in my present clause (4). Thus I have left out the further agreement-in-preferences clause.)

IV. OBJECTIONS AND REPLIES

Objection: Many things which meet the definition of a language given in the thesis—many functions from strings of sounds or of marks to sets of possible worlds—are not really possible languages. They could not possibly be adopted by any human population. There may be too few sentences, or too few meanings, to make as many discriminations as language-users need to communicate. The meanings may not be anything language-users would wish to communicate about. The sentences may be very long, impossible to pronounce, or otherwise clumsy. The language may be humanly unlearnable because it has no grammar, or a grammar of the wrong kind.

Reply: Granted. The so-called languages of the thesis are merely an easily specified superset of the languages we are really interested in. A language in a narrower and more natural sense is any one of these entities that could possibly—possibly in some appropriately strict sense—be used by a human population.

Objection: The so-called languages discussed in the thesis are excessively simplified. There is no provision for indexical sentences, dependent on features of the context of their utterance: for instance, tensed sentences, sentences with personal pronouns or demonstratives, or anaphoric sentences. There is no provision for ambiguous sentences. There is no provision for nonindicative sentences: imperatives, questions, promises and threats, permissions, and so on.

Reply: Granted. I have this excuse: the phenomenon of language would be not too different if these complications did not exist, so we cannot go too far wrong by ignoring them. Nevertheless, let us sketch what could be done to provide for indexicality, ambiguity, or nonindicatives. In order not to pile complication on complication we shall take only one at a time.

We may define an *indexical language* £ as a function that assigns sets of possible worlds not to its sentences themselves, but rather to sentences paired with possible occasions of their utterance. We can say that σ is true in £ at a world w on a possible occasion o of the utterance of σ if and only if w belongs to £(σ,o). We can say that σ is true in £ on o (without mentioning a world) if and only if the world in which o is located—our actual world if o is an actual occasion of utterance of σ, or some other world if not—belongs to £(σ,o). We can say that a speaker is truthful in £ if he tries not to utter any sentence σ of £ unless σ would be true in £ on the occasion of his utterance of σ. We can say that a hearer is trusting in £ if he believes an uttered sentence of £ to be true in £ on its occasion of utterance.

We may define an *ambiguous language* £ as a function that assigns to its sentences not single meanings, but finite sets of alternative meanings. (We might or might not want to stipulate that these sets are nonempty.) We can say that a sentence σ is true in £ at w under some meaning if and only if w belongs to some member of £(σ). We can say that σ is true in £ under some meaning if and only if our actual world belongs to some member of £(σ). We can say that someone is (minimally) truthful in £ if he tries not to utter any sentence σ of £ unless σ is true in £ under some meaning. He is trusting if he believes an uttered sentence of £ to be true in £ under some meaning.

We may define a *polymodal language* £ as a function which assigns to its sentences meanings containing two components: a set of worlds, as before; and something we can call a *mood:* indicative, imperative, etc. (It makes no difference what things these are—they might, for instance, be taken as code numbers.) We can say that a sentence σ is indicative, imperative, etc., in £ according as the mood-component of the meaning £(σ) is indicative, imperative, etc. We can say that a sentence σ is true in £, regardless of its mood in £, if and only if our actual world belongs to the set-of-worlds-component of the meaning £(σ). We can say that someone is truthful in £ with respect to indicatives if he tries not to utter any indicative sentence of £ which is not true in £; truthful in £ with respect to imperatives if he tries to act in such a way as to make true in £ any imperative sentence of £ that is addressed to him by someone in a relation of authority to him; and so on for other moods. He is trusting in £ with respect to indicatives if he believes uttered indicative sentences of £ to be true in £; trusting in £ with respect to imperatives if he expects his utterance of an imperative sentence of £ to result in the addressee's acting in such a way as to make that sentence true in £, provided he is in a relation of authority to the addressee; and so on. We can say simply that he is truthful and trusting in £ if he is so with respect to all moods that occur in £. It is by virtue of the various ways in which the various moods enter into the definition of truthfulness and of trust that they deserve the familiar names we have given them. (I am deliberating stretching the ordinary usage of "true," "truthfulness," and "trust" in extending them to nonindicatives. For instance, truthfulness with respect to imperatives is roughly what we might call *obedience* in £.)

Any natural language is simultaneously indexical, ambiguous, and polymodal; I leave the combination of complications as an exercise. Henceforth, for the most part, I shall lapse into ignoring indexicality, ambiguity, and nonindicatives.

Objection: We cannot always discover the meaning of a sentence in a population just by looking into the minds of the members of the population, no matter what we look for there. We may also need some information about the causal origin of what we find in their minds. So, in particular, we cannot always discover the meaning of a sentence in a population just by looking at the conventions prevailing therein. Consider an example: What is the meaning of the sentence "Mik Karthee was wise" in the language of our 137th-century descendants, if all we can find in any of their minds is the inadequate dictionary entry: "Mik Karthee: controversial American politician of the early atomic age"? It depends, we might think, partly on which man stands at the beginning of the long causal chain ending in that inadequate dictionary entry.

Reply: If this doctrine is correct, I can treat it as a subtle sort of indexicality. The set of worlds in which a sentence σ is true in a language £ may depend on features of possible occasions of utterance of σ. One feature of a possible occasion of utterance—admittedly a more recondite feature than the time, place, or speaker—is the causal history of a dictionary entry in a speaker's mind.

As with other kinds of indexicality, we face a problem of nomenclature. Let a *meaning₁* be that which an indexical language £ assigns to a sentence σ on a possible occasion o of its utterance: £(σ, o), a set of worlds on our account. Let a *meaning₂* be that fixed function whereby the meaning₁ in £ of a sentence σ varies with its occasions of utterance. Which one is a meaning? That is unclear—and it is no clearer which one is a sense, intension, interpretation, truth-condition, or proposition.

The objection says that we sometimes cannot find the meaning₁ of σ on o in *P* by looking into the minds of members of *P*. Granted. But what prevents it is that the minds do not contain enough information about o: in particular, not enough information about its causal history. We have been given no reason to doubt that we can find the meaning₂ of σ in *P* by looking into minds; and that is all we need do to identify the indexical language used by *P*.

An exactly similar situation arises with more familiar kinds of indexicality. We may be unable to discover the time of an utterance of a tensed sentence by looking into minds, so we may know the meaning₂ of the sentence uttered in the speaker's indexical language without knowing its meaning₁ on the occasion in question.

Objection: It makes no sense to say that a mere string of sounds or of marks can bear a meaning or a truth-value. The proper bearers of meanings and truth-values are particular speech acts.

Reply: I do not say that a string of types of sounds or of marks, by itself, can bear a meaning or truth-value. I say it bears a meaning and truth-value relative to a language, or relative to a population. A particular speech act by itself, on the other hand, can bear a meaning and truth-value, since in most cases it uniquely determines the language that was in use on the occasion of its performance. So can a particular uttered string of vocal sounds, or a particular inscribed string of marks, since in most cases that uniquely determines the particular speech act in which it was produced, which in turn uniquely determines the language.

Objection: It is circular to give an account of meanings in terms of possible worlds. The notion of a possible world must itself be explained in semantic terms. Possible worlds are models of the analytic sentences of some language, or they are the diagrams or theories of such models.[5]

Reply: I do not agree that the notion of a possible world ought to be explained in semantic terms, or that possible worlds ought to be eliminated from our ontology and replaced by their linguistic representatives—models or whatever.

For one thing, the replacement does not work properly. Two worlds indistinguishable in the representing language will receive one and the same representative.

But more important, the replacement is gratuitous. The notion of a possible world is familiar in its own right, philosophically fruitful, and tolerably clear. Possible worlds are deemed mysterious and objectionable because they raise questions we may never know how to answer: are any possible worlds five-dimensional? We seem to think that we do not understand possible worlds at all unless we are capable of omniscience about them—but why should we think that? Sets also raise unanswerable questions, yet most of us do not repudiate sets.

But if you insist on repudiating possible worlds, much of my theory can be adapted to meet your needs. We must suppose that you have already defined truth and analyticity in some base language—that is the price you pay for repudiating possible worlds—and you want to define them in general, for the language of an arbitrary population *P*. Pick your favorite base language, with any convenient special properties you like: Latin, Esperanto, Begriffsschrift, Semantic Markerese, or what have you. Let's say you pick Latin. Then you may redefine a language as any function from certain strings of sound or of marks to sentences of Latin. A sentence σ of a language £ (in your sense) is true, analytic, etc., if and only if £(σ) is true, analytic, etc., in Latin.

You cannot believe in languages in my sense, since they involve possible worlds. But I can believe in languages in your sense. And I can map your languages onto mine by means of a fixed function from sentences of Latin to sets of worlds. This function is just the language Latin, in my sense. My language £ is the composition of two functions: your language £, and my language Latin. Thus I can accept your approach as part of mine.

Objection: Why all this needless and outmoded hypostasis of meanings? Our ordinary talk about meaning does not commit us to believing in any such entities as meanings, any more than our ordinary talk about actions for the sake of ends commits us to believing in any such entities as sakes.

Reply: Perhaps there are some who hypostatize meanings compulsively, imagining that they could not possibly make sense of our ordinary talk about meaning if they did not. Not I. I hypostatize meanings because I find it convenient to do so, and I have no good reason not to. There is no point in being a part-time nominalist. I am persuaded on independent grounds that I ought to believe in possible worlds and possible beings therein, and that I ought to believe in sets of things I believe in. Once I have these, I have all the entities I could ever want.

Objection: A language consists not only of sentences with their meanings, but also of constituents of sentences—things sentences are made of—with their meanings. And if any language is to be learnable without being finite, it must somehow be determined by finitely many of its constituents and finitely many operations on constituents.

Reply: We may define a class of objects called *grammars*. A grammar Γ is a triple comprising (1) a large finite *lexicon of elementary constituents* paired with meanings; (2) a finite set of *combining operations* which build larger constituents by combining smaller constituents, and derive a meaning for the new constituent out of the meanings of the old ones; and (3) a *representing operation* which effectively maps certain constituents onto strings of sounds or of marks. A grammar Γ generates a function which assigns meanings to certain constituents, called *constituents in* Γ. It generates another function which assigns meanings to certain strings of sounds or of marks. Part of this latter function is what we have hitherto called a language. A grammar uniquely determines the language it generates. But a language does not uniquely determine the grammar that generates it, not even when we disregard superficial differences between grammars.

I have spoken of meanings for constituents in a grammar, but what sort of things are these? Referential semantics tried to answer that question. It was a near miss, failing because contingent facts got mixed up with the meanings. The cure, discovered by Carnap,[6] is to do referential semantics not just in our actual world but in every possible world. A meaning for a name can be a function from worlds to possible individuals; for a common noun, a function from worlds to sets; for a sentence, a function from worlds to truth-values (or more simply, the set of worlds where that function takes the value truth). Other derived categories may be defined by their characteristic modes of combination. For instance, an adjective combines with a common noun to make a compound common noun; so its meaning may be a function from common-noun meanings to common-noun meanings, such that the meaning of an adjective-plus-common-noun compound is the value of this function when given as argument the meaning of the common noun being modified. Likewise a verb phrase takes a name to make a sentence; so its meaning may be a function that takes the meaning of the name as argument to give the meaning of the sentence as value. An adverb (of one sort) takes a verb phrase to make a verb phrase, so its meaning may be a function from verb-phrase meanings to verb-phrase meanings. And so on, as far as need be, to more and more complicated derived categories.[7]

If you repudiate possible worlds, an alternative course is open to you: let the meanings for constituents in a grammar be phrases of Latin, or whatever your favorite base language may be.

A grammar, for us, is a semantically interpreted grammar—just as a language is a semantically interpreted language. We shall not be concerned with what are called grammars or languages in a purely syntactic sense. My definition of a grammar is meant to be general enough to encompass transformational or phrase-structure grammars for natural language[8] (when provided with semantic interpretations) as well as systems of formation and valuation rules for formalized languages. Like my previous definition of a language, my definition of a grammar is too general: it gives a large superset of the interesting grammars.

A grammar, like a language, is a set-theoretical entity which can be discussed in complete abstraction from human affairs. Since a grammar generates a unique language, all the semantic concepts we earlier defined relative to a language £—sentencehood, truth, analyticity, etc.—could just as well have been defined relative to a grammar Γ. We can also handle other semantic concepts pertaining to constituents, or to the constituent structure of sentences.

We can define the meaning in Γ, denotation in Γ, etc., of a subsentential constituent in Γ. We can define the meaning in Γ, denotation in Γ, etc., of a *phrase:* a string of sounds or of marks representing a subsentential constituent in Γ via the representing operation of Γ. We can define something we may call the *fine structure of meaning* in Γ of a sentence or phrase: the manner in which the meaning of the sentence or phrase is derived from the meanings of its constituents and the way it is built out of them. Thus we can take account of the sense in which, for instance, different analytic sentences are said to differ in meaning.

Now the objection can be restated: what ought to be called a language is what I have hitherto called a grammar, not what I have hitherto called a language. Different grammar, different language—at least if we ignore superficial differences between grammars. Verbal disagreement aside, the place I gave to my so-called languages ought to have been given instead to my so-called grammars. Why not begin by saying what it is for a grammar Γ to be used by a population P? Then we could go on to define sentencehood, truth, analyticity, etc., in P as sentencehood, truth, analyticity, etc., in whatever grammar is used by P. This approach would have the advantage that we could handle the semantics of constituents in a population in an exactly similar way. We could say that a constituent or phrase has a certain meaning, denotation, etc., in P if it has that meaning, denotation, etc., in whatever grammar is used by P. We could say that a sentence or phrase has a certain fine structure of meaning in P if it has it in whatever grammar is used by P.

Unfortunately, I know of no promising way to make objective sense of the assertion that a grammar Γ is used by a population P whereas another grammar Γ', which generates the same language as Γ, is not. I have tried to say how there are facts about P which objectively select the languages used by P. I am not sure there are facts about P which objectively select privileged grammars for those languages. It is easy enough to define truthfulness and trust in a grammar, but that will not help: a convention of truthfulness and trust in Γ will also be a convention of truthfulness and trust in Γ' whenever Γ and Γ' generate the same language.

I do not propose to discard the notion of the meaning in P of a constituent or phrase, or the fine structure of meaning in P of a sentence. To propose that would be absurd. But I hold that these notions depend on our methods of evaluating grammars, and therefore are no clearer and no more objective than our notion of a best grammar for a given language. For I would say that a grammar Γ is used by P if and only if Γ is a best grammar for a language £ that is used by P in virtue of a convention in P of truthfulness and trust in £; and I would define the meaning in P of a constituent or phrase, and the fine structure of meaning in P of a sentence, accordingly.

The notions of a language used by P, of a meaning of a sentence in P, and so on, are independent of our evaluation of grammars. Therefore I take these as primary. The point is not to refrain from ever saying anything that depends on the evaluation of grammars. The point is to do so only when we must, and that is why I have concentrated on languages rather than grammars.

We may meet little practical difficulty with the semantics of constituents in populations, even if its foundations are as infirm as I fear. It may often happen that all the grammars anyone might call best for a given language will agree on the meaning of a given constituent. Yet there is trouble to be found: Quine's examples of indeterminacy of reference[9] seem to be disagreements in constituent semantics between alternative good grammars for one language. We should regard with suspicion any method that purports to settle objectively whether, in some tribe, "gavagai" is true of temporally continuant rabbits or timeslices thereof. You can give their language a good grammar of either kind—and that's that.

It is useful to divide the claimed indeterminacy of constituent semantics into three separate indeterminacies. We begin with undoubted objective fact: the dependence of the subject's behavioral output on his input of sensory stimulation (both as it actually is and as it might have been) together with all the physical laws and anatomical facts that explain it. (a) This information either determines or underdetermines the subject's system of propositional attitudes: in particular, his beliefs and desires. (b) These propositional attitudes either determine or underdetermine the truth conditions of full sentences—what I have here called his language. (c) The truth-conditions of full sentences either determine or underdetermine the meanings of subsentential constituents—what I have here called his grammar.

My present discussion has been directed at the middle step, from beliefs and desires to truth conditions for full sentences. I have said that the former determine the latter—provided (what need not be the case) that the beliefs and desires of the subject and his fellows are such as to comprise a fully determinate convention of truthfulness and trust in some definite language. I have said nothing here about the determinacy of the first step; and I am inclined to share in Quine's doubts about the determinacy of the third step.

Objection: Suppose that whenever anyone is party to a convention of truthfulness and trust in any language £, his competence to be party to that convention—to conform, to expect conformity, etc.—is due to his possession of some sort of unconscious internal representation of a grammar for £. That is a likely hypothesis, since it best explains what we know about linguistic competence. In particular, it explains why experience with some sentences leads spontaneously to expectations involving others. But on that hypothesis, we might as well bypass the conventions of language and say that £ is used by P if and only if everyone in P possesses an internal representation of a grammar for £.

Reply: In the first place, the hypothesis of internally represented grammars is not an explanation—best or otherwise—of anything. Perhaps it is *part* of some theory that best explains what we know about linguistic competence; we can't judge until we hear something about what the rest of the theory is like.

Nonetheless, I am ready enough to believe in internally represented grammars. But I am much less certain that there are internally represented grammars than I am that languages are used by populations; and I think it makes sense to say that languages might be used by populations even if there were no internally represented by grammars. I can tentatively agree that £ is used by P if and only if everyone in P possesses an internal representation of a grammar for £, if that is offered as a scientific hypothesis. But I cannot accept it as any sort of analysis of "£ is used by P," since the analysandum clearly could be true although the analysans was false.

Objection: The notion of a convention of truthfulness and trust in £ is a needless complication. Why not say, straightforwardly, that £ is used by P if and only if there prevails in P a convention to bestow upon each sentence of £ the meaning that £ assigns to it? Or, indeed, that a grammar Γ of £ is used by P if and only if there prevails in P a convention to bestow upon each constituent in Γ the meaning that Γ assigns to it?

Reply: A convention, as I have defined it, is a regularity in action, or in action and belief. If that feature of the definition were given up, I do not see how to salvage any part of my theory of conventions. It is essential that a convention is a regularity such that conformity by others gives one a reason to conform; and such a reason must either be a practical reason for acting or an epistemic reason for believing. What other kind of reason is there?

Yet there is no such thing as an action of bestowing a meaning (except for an irrelevant sort of action that is performed not by language-users but by creators of language) so we cannot suppose that language-using populations have conventions to perform such actions. Neither does bestowal of meaning consist in forming some belief. Granted, bestowal of meaning is conventional in the sense that it depends on convention: the meanings would have been different if the conventions of truthfulness and trust had been different. But bestowal of meaning is not an action done in conformity to a convention, since it is not an action, and it is not a belief-formation in conformity to a convention, since it is not a belief-formation.

Objection: The beliefs and desires that constitute a convention are inaccessible mental entities, just as much as hypothetical internal representations of grammars are. It would be best if we could say in purely behavioristic terms what it is for a language £ to be used by a population P. We might be able to do this by referring to the way in which members of P would answer counterfactual questionnaires; or by referring to the way in which they would or would not assent to sentences under deceptive sensory stimulation; or by referring to the way in which they would intuitively group sentences into similarity-classes; or in some other way.

Reply: Suppose we succeeded in giving a behavioristic operational definition of the relation "£ is used by P." This would not help us to understand what it is for £ to be used by P; for we would have to understand that already, and also know a good deal of common-sense psychology, in order to check that the operational definition was a definition of what it is supposed to be a definition of. If we did not know what it meant for £ to be used by P, we would not know what sort of behavior on the part of members of P would indicate that £ was used by P.

Objection: The conventions of language are nothing more nor less than our famously obscure old friends, the rules of language, renamed.

Reply: A convention of truthfulness and trust in £ might well be called a rule, though it lacks many features that have sometimes been thought to belong to the essence of rules. It is not promulgated by any authority. It is not enforced by means of sanctions except to the extent that, because one has some sort of reason to conform, something bad may happen if one does not. It is nowhere codified and therefore is not "laid down in the course of teaching the language" or "appealed to in the course of criticizing a person's linguistic performance."[10] Yet it is more than a mere regularity holding "as a rule"; it is a regularity accompanied and sustained by a special kind of system of beliefs and desires.

A convention of truthfulness and trust in £ might have as consequences other regularities which were conventions of language in their own right: specializations of the convention to certain special situations. (For instance, a convention of truthfulness in £ on weekdays.) Such derivative conventions of language might also be called rules; some of them might stand a better chance of being codified than the overall convention which subsumes them.

However, there are other so-called rules of language which are not conventions of language and are not in the least like conventions of language: for instance, "rules" of syntax and semantics. They are not even regularities and cannot be formulated as imperatives. They might better be described not as rules, but as clauses in the definitions of entities which are to be mentioned in rules: clauses in the definition of a language £, of the act of being truthful in £, of the act of stating that the moon is blue, etc.

Thus the conventions of language might properly be called rules, but it is more informative and less confusing to call them conventions.

Objection: Language is not conventional. We have found that human capacities for language acquisition are highly specific and dictate the form of any language that humans can learn and use.

Reply: It may be that there is less conventionality than we used to think: fewer features of language which depend on convention, more which are determined by our innate capacities and therefore are common to all languages which are genuine alternatives to our actual language. But there are still conventions of language; and there are still convention-dependent features of language, differing from one alternative possible convention of language to another. That is established by the diversity of actual languages. There are conventions of language so long as the regularity of truthfulness in a given language has even a single alternative.

Objection: Unless a language-user is also a set-theorist, he cannot expect his fellows to conform to a regularity of truthfulness and trust in a certain language £. For to conform to this regularity is to bear a relation to a certain esoteric entity: a set of ordered pairs of sequences of sound-types or of mark-types and sets of possible worlds (or something more complicated still, if £ is a natural language with indexicality, ambiguity, and nonindicatives). The common man has no concept of any such entity. Hence he can have no expectations regarding such an entity.

Reply: The common man need not have any concept of £ in order to expect his fellows to be truthful and trusting in £. He need only have suitable particular expectations about how they might act, and how they might form beliefs, in various situations. He can tell whether any actual or hypothetical particular action or belief-formation on their part is compatible with his expectations. He expects them to conform to a regularity of truthfulness and trust in £ if any particular activity or belief-formation that would fit his expectations would fall under what we—but not *he*—could describe as conformity to that regularity.

It may well be that his elaborate, infinite system of potential particular expectations can only be explained on the hypothesis that he has some unconscious mental entity somehow analogous to a general concept of £—say, an internally represented grammar. But it does not matter whether this is so or not. We are concerned only to say what system of expectations a normal member of a language-using population must have. We need not engage in psychological speculation about how those expectations are generated.

Objection: If there are conventions of language, those who are party to them should know what they are. Yet no one can fully describe the conventions of language to which he is supposedly a party.

Reply: He may nevertheless know what they are. It is enough to be able to recognize conformity and nonconformity to his convention, and to be able to try to conform to it. We know ever so many things we cannot put into words.

Objection: Use of language is almost never a rational activity. We produce and respond to utterances by habit, not as the result of any sort of reasoning or deliberation.

Reply: An action may be rational, and may be explained by the agent's beliefs and desires, even though that action was done by habit, and the agent gave no thought to the beliefs or desires which were his reason for acting. A habit may be under the agent's rational control in this sense: if that habit ever ceased to serve the agent's desires according to his beliefs, it would at once be overridden and corrected by conscious reasoning. Action done by a habit of this sort is both habitual and rational. Likewise for habits of believing. Our normal use of language is rational, since it is under rational control.

Perhaps use of language by young children is not a rational activity. Perhaps it results from habits which would not be overridden if they ceased to serve the agent's desires according to his beliefs. If that is so, I would deny that these children have yet become party to conventions of language, and I would deny that they have yet become normal members of a language-using population. Perhaps language is first acquired and afterward becomes conventional. That would not conflict with anything I have said. I am not concerned with the way in which language is acquired, only with the condition of a normal member of a language-using population when he is done acquiring language.

Objection: Language could not have originated by convention. There could not have been an agreement to begin being truthful and trusting in a certain chosen language, unless some previous language had already been available for use in making the agreement.

Reply: The first language could not have originated by an agreement, for the reason given. But that is not to say that language cannot be conventional. A convention is so-called because of the way it persists, not because of the way it originated. A convention need not originate by convention—that is, by agreement—though many conventions do originate by agreement, and others could originate by agreement even if they actually do not. In saying that language is convention-governed, I say nothing whatever about the origins of language.

Objection: A man isolated all his life from others might begin—through genius or a miracle—to use language, say to keep a diary. (This would be an accidentally private language, not the necessarily private language Wittgenstein is said to have proved to be impossible.) In this case, at least, there would be no convention involved.

Reply: Taking the definition literally, there would be no convention. But there would be something very similar. The isolated man conforms to a certain regularity at many different times. He knows at each of these times that he has conformed to that regularity in the past, and he has an interest in uniformity over time, so he continues to conform to that regularity instead of to any of various alternative regularities that would have done about as well if he had started out using them. He knows at all times that this is so, knows that he knows at all times that this is so, and so on. We might think of the situation as one in which a convention prevails in the population of different time-slices of the same man.

Objection: It is circular to define the meaning in *P* of sentences in terms of the beliefs held by members of *P*. For presumably the members of *P* think in their language. For instance, they hold beliefs by accepting suitable sentences of their language. If we do not already know the meaning in *P* of a sentence, we do not know what belief a member of *P* would hold by accepting that sentence.

Reply: It may be true that men think in language, and that to hold a belief is to accept a sentence of one's language. But it does not follow that belief should be analyzed as acceptance of sentences. It should not be. Even if men do in fact think in language, they might not. It is at least possible that men—like beasts—might hold beliefs otherwise than by accepting sentences. (I shall not say here how I think belief should be analyzed.) No circle arises from the contingent truth that a member of *P* holds beliefs by accepting sentences, so long as we can specify his beliefs without mentioning the sentences he accepts. We can do this for men, as we can for beasts.

Objection: Suppose a language £ is used by a population of inveterate liars, who are untruthful in £ more often than not. There would not be even a regularity—still less a convention, which implies a regularity—of truthfulness and trust in £.

Reply: I deny that £ is used by the population of liars. I have undertaken to follow ordinary usage only where it is determinate; and, once it is appreciated just how extraordinary the situation would have to be, I do not believe that ordinary usage is determinate in this case. There are many similarities to clear cases in which a language is used by a population, and it is understandable that we should feel some inclination to classify this case along with them. But there are many important differences as well.

Although I deny that the population of liars *collectively* uses £, I am willing to say that each liar *individually* may use £, provided that he falsely believes that he is a member—albeit an exceptional, untruthful member—of a population wherein there prevails a convention of truthfulness and trust in £. He is in a position like that of a madman who thinks he belongs to a population which uses £, and behaves accordingly, and so can be said to use £, although in reality all the other members of this £-using population are figments of his imagination.

Objection: Suppose the members of a population are untruthful in their language £ more often than not, not because they lie, but because they go in heavily for irony, metaphor, hyperbole, and such. It is hard to deny that the language £ is used by such a population.

Reply: I claim that these people *are* truthful in their language £, though they are not *literally truthful* in £. To be literally truthful in £ is to be truthful in another language related to £, a language we can call literal-£. The relation between £ and literal-£ is as follows: a good way to describe £ is to start by specifying literal-£ and then to describe £ as obtained by certain systematic departures from literal-£. This two-stage specification of £ by way of literal-£ may turn out to be much simpler than any direct specification of £.

Objection: Suppose they are often untruthful in £ because they are not communicating at all. They are joking, or telling tall tales, or telling white lies as a matter of social ritual. In these situations, there is neither truthfulness nor trust in £. Indeed, it is common knowledge that there is not.

Reply: Perhaps I can say the same sort of thing about this non-serious language use as I did about nonliteral language use. That is: their seeming untruthfulness in nonserious situations is untruthfulness not in the language £ that they actually use, but only in a simplified approximation to £. We may specify £ by first specifying the approximation language, then listing the signs and features of context by which nonserious language use can be recognized, then specifying that when these signs or features are present, what would count as untruths in the approximation language do not count as such in £ itself. Perhaps they are automatically true in £, regardless of the facts; perhaps they cease to count as indicative.

Example: what would otherwise be an untruth may not be one if said by a child with crossed fingers. Unfortunately, the signs and features of context by which we recognize nonserious language use are seldom as simple, standardized, and conventional as that. While they must find a place somewhere in a full account of the phenomenon of language, it may be inexpedient to burden the specification of £ with them.

Perhaps it may be enough to note that these situations of non-serious language use must be at least somewhat exceptional if we are to have anything like a clear case of use of £; and to recall that the definition of a convention was loose enough to tolerate some exceptions. We could take the nonserious cases simply as violations—explicable and harmless ones—of the conventions of language.

There is a third alternative, requiring a modification in my theory. We may say that a *serious communication situation* exists with respect to a sentence σ of £ whenever it is true, and common knowledge between a speaker and a hearer, that (a) the speaker does, and the hearer does not, know whether σ is true in £; (b) the hearer wants to know; (c) the speaker wants the hearer to know; and (d) neither the speaker nor the hearer has other (comparably strong) desires as to whether or not the speaker utters σ. (Note that when there is a serious communication situation with respect to σ, there is one also with respect to synonyms or contradictories in £ of σ, and probably also with respect to other logical relatives in £ of σ.) Then we may say that the convention whereby P uses £ is a convention of truthfulness and trust in £ in serious communication situations. That is: when a serious communication situation exists with respect to σ, then the speaker tries not to utter σ unless it is true in £, and the hearer responds, if σ is uttered, by coming to believe that σ is true in £. If that much is a convention in P, it does not matter what goes on in other situations: they use £.

The definition here given of a serious communication resembles that of a signaling problem in *Convention,* chapter IV, the difference being that the hearer may respond by belief-formation only, rather than by what speaker and hearer alike take to be appropriate action. If this modification were adopted, it would bring my general account of language even closer to my account in *Convention* of the special case of signaling.

Objection: Truthfulness and trust cannot be a convention. What could be the alternative to uniform truthfulness—uniform untruthfulness, perhaps? But it seems that if such untruthfulness were not intended to deceive, and did not deceive, then it too would be truthfulness.

Reply: The convention is not the regularity of truthfulness and trust *simpliciter*. It is the regularity of truthfulness and trust in some particular language £. Its alternatives are possible regularities of truthfulness and trust in other languages. A regularity of uniform untruthfulness and non-trust in a language £ can be redescribed as a regularity of truthfulness and trust in a different language anti-£ complementary to £. Anti-£ has exactly the same sentences as £, but with opposite truth conditions. Hence the true sentences of anti-£ are all and only the untrue sentences of £.

There is a different regularity that we may call a regularity of truthfulness and trust *simpliciter*. That is the regularity of being truthful and trusting in whichever language is used by one's fellows. This regularity neither is a convention nor depends on convention. If any language whatever is used by a population *P*, then a regularity (perhaps with exceptions) of truthfulness and trust *simpliciter* prevails in *P*.

Objection: Even truthfulness and trust in £ cannot be a convention. One conforms to a convention, on my account, because doing so answers to some sort of interest. But a decent man is truthful in £ if his fellows are, whether or not it is in his interest. For he recognizes that he is under a moral obligation to be truthful in £: an obligation to reciprocate the benefits he has derived from others' truthfulness in £, or something of that sort. Truthfulness in £ may bind the decent man against his own interest. It is more like a social contract than a convention.

Reply: The objection plays on a narrow sense of "interest" in which only selfish interests count. We commonly adopt a wider sense. We count also altruistic interests and interests springing from one's recognition of obligations. It is this wider sense that should be understood in the definition of convention. In this wider sense, it is nonsense to think of an obligation as outweighing one's interests. Rather, the obligation provides one interest which may outweigh the other interests.

A convention of truthfulness and trust in £ is sustained by a mixture of selfish interests, altruistic interests, and interests derived from obligation. Usually all are present in strength; perhaps any one would be enough to sustain the convention. But occasionally truthfulness in £ answers only to interests derived from obligation and goes against one's selfish or even altruistic interests. In such a case, only a decent man will have an interest in remaining truthful in £. But I dare say such cases are not as common as moralists might imagine. A convention of truthfulness and trust among scoundrels might well be sustained—with occasional lapses—by selfish interests alone.

A convention persists because everyone has reason to conform if others do. If the convention is a regularity in action, this is to say that it persists because everyone prefers general conformity rather than almost-general conformity with himself as the exception. A (demythologized) social contract may also be described as a regularity sustained by a general preference for general conformity, but the second term of the preference is different. Everyone prefers general conformity over a certain state of general nonconformity called the state of nature. This general preference sets up an obligation to reciprocate the benefits derived from others' conformity, and that obligation creates an interest in conforming which sustains the social contract. The objection suggests that, among decent men, truthfulness in £ is a social contract. I agree; but there is no reason why it cannot be a social contract and a convention as well, and I think it is.

Objection: Communication cannot be explained by conventions of truthfulness alone. If I utter a sentence σ of our language £, you—expecting me to be truthful in £—will conclude that I take σ to be true in £. If you think I am well informed, you will also conclude that probably σ is true in £. But you will draw other conclusions as well, based on your legitimate assumption that it is for some good reason that I chose to utter σ rather than remain silent, and rather than utter any of the other sentences of £ that I also take to be true in £. I can communicate all sorts of misinformation by exploiting your beliefs about my conversational purposes, without ever being untruthful in £. Communication depends on principles of helpfulness and relevance as well as truthfulness.

Reply: All this does not conflict with anything I have said. We do conform to conversational regularities of helpfulness and relevance. But these regularities are not independent conventions of language; they result from our convention of truthfulness and trust in £ together with certain general facts—not dependent on any convention—about our conversational purposes and our beliefs about one another. Since they are byproducts of a convention of truthfulness and trust, it is unnecessary to mention them separately in specifying the conditions under which a language is used by a population.

Objection: Let £ be the language used in P, and let £− be some fairly rich fragment of £. That is, the sentences of £− are many but not all of the sentences of £ (in an appropriate special sense if £ is infinite); and any sentence of both has the same meaning in both. Then £− also turns out to be a language used by P; for by my definition there prevails in P a convention of truthfulness and trust in £−, sustained by an interest in communication. Not one but many—perhaps infinitely many—languages are used by P.

Reply: That is so, but it is no problem. Why not say that any rich fragment of a language used by P is itself a used language?

Indeed, we will need to say such things when P is linguistically inhomogeneous. Suppose, for instance, that P divides into two classes: the learned and the vulgar. Among the learned there prevails a convention of truthfulness and trust in a language £; among P as a whole there does not, but there does prevail a convention of truthfulness and trust in a rich fragment £− of £. We wish to say that the learned have a common language with the vulgar, but that is so only if £−, as well as £, counts as a language used by the learned.

Another case: the learned use $£_1$, the vulgar use $£_2$, neither is included in the other, but there is extensive overlap. Here $£_1$ and $£_2$ are to be the most inclusive languages used by the respective classes. Again we wish to say that the learned and the vulgar have a common language: in particular, the largest fragment common to $£_1$ and $£_2$. That can be so only if this largest common fragment counts as a language used by the vulgar, by the learned, and by the whole population.

I agree that we often do not count the fragments; we can speak of *the* language of P, meaning by this not the one and only thing that is a language used by P, but rather the most inclusive language used by P. Or we could mean something else: the union of all the languages used by substantial subpopulations of P, provided that some quite large fragment of this union is used by (more or less) all of P. Note that the union as a whole need not be used at all, in my primary sense, either by P or by any subpopulation of P. Thus in my example of the last paragraph, *the* language of P might be taken either as the largest common fragment of £1 and £2 or as the union of £1 and £2.

Further complications arise. Suppose that half of the population of a certain town uses English, and also uses basic Welsh; while the other half uses Welsh, and also uses basic English. The most inclusive language used by the entire population is the union of basic Welsh and basic English. The union of languages used by substantial subpopulations is the union of English and Welsh, and the proviso is satisfied that some quite large fragment of this union is used by the whole population. Yet we would be reluctant to say that either of these unions is the language of the population of the town. We might say that Welsh and English are the two languages of the town, or that basic English and basic Welsh are. It is odd to call either of the two language-unions a language; though once they are called that, it is no further oddity to say that one or the other of them is the language of the town. There are two considerations. First: English, or Welsh, or basic English, or basic Welsh, can be given a satisfactory unified grammar; whereas the language- unions cannot. Second: English, or Welsh, or basic Welsh, or basic English, is (in either of the senses I have explained) the language of a large population outside the town; whereas the language-unions are not. I am not sure which of the two considerations should be emphasized in saying when a language is the language of a population.

Objection: Let £ be the language of P; that is, the language that ought to count as the most inclusive language used by P. (Assume that P is linguistically homogenous.) Let £+ be obtained by adding garbage to £: some extra sentences, very long and difficult to pronounce, and hence never uttered in P, with arbitrary chosen meanings in £+. Then it seems that £+ is a language used by P, which is absurd.

A sentence never uttered at all is *a fortiori* never uttered untruthfully. So truthfulness-as-usual in £ plus truthfulness-by-silence on the garbage sentences constitutes a kind of truthfulness in £+; and the expectation thereof constitutes trust in £+. Therefore we have a prevailing regularity of truthfulness and trust in £+. This regularity qualifies as a convention in *P* sustained by an interest in communication.

Reply: Truthfulness-by-silence is truthfulness, and expectation thereof is expectation of truthfulness; but expectation of truthfulness-by-silence is not yet trust. Expectation of (successful) truthfulness—expectation that a given sentence will not be uttered falsely—is a necessary but not sufficient condition for trust. There is no regularity of trust in £+, so far as the garbage sentences are concerned. Hence there is no convention of truthfulness and trust in £+, and £+ is not used by *P.*

For trust, one must be able to take an utterance of a sentence as evidence that the sentence is true. That is so only if one's degree of belief that the sentence will be uttered falsely is low, not only absolutely, but as a fraction of one's degree of belief—perhaps already very low—that the sentence will be uttered at all. Further, this must be so not merely because one believes in advance that the sentence is probably true: one's degree of belief that the sentence will be uttered falsely must be substantially lower than the product of one's degree of belief that the sentence will be uttered times one's prior degree of belief that it is false. A garbage sentence of £+ will not meet this last requirement, not even if one believes to high degrees both that it is true in £+ and that it never will be uttered.

This objection was originally made, by Stephen Schiffer, against my former view that conventions of language are conventions of truthfulness. I am inclined to think that it succeeds as a counterexample to that view. I agree that £+ is not used by *P,* in any reasonable sense, but I have not seen any way to avoid conceding that £+ is a possible language—it might really be used—and that there does prevail in *P* a convention of truthfulness in £+, sustained by an interest in communication. Here we have another advantage of the present account over my original one.

Objection: A sentence either is or isn't analytic in a given language, and a language either is or isn't conventionally adopted by a given population. Hence there is no way for the ana-

lytic–synthetic distinction to be unsharp. But not only can it be unsharp; it usually is, at least in cases of interest to philosophers. A sharp analytic-synthetic distinction is available only relative to particular rational reconstructions of ordinary language.

Reply: One might try to explain unsharp analyticity by a theory of degrees of convention. Conventions do admit of degree in a great many ways: by the strengths of the beliefs and desires involved, and by the fraction of exceptions to the many almost-universal quantifications in the definition of convention. But this will not help much. It is easy to imagine unsharp analyticity even in a population whose conventions of language are conventions to the highest degree in every way.

One might try to explain unsharp analyticity by recalling that we may not know whether some worlds are really possible. If a sentence is true in our language in all worlds except some worlds of doubtful possibility, then that sentence will be of doubtful analyticity. But this will not help much either. Unsharp analyticity usually seems to arise because we cannot decide whether a sentence would be true in some bizarre but clearly possible world.

A better explanation would be that our convention of language is not exactly a convention of truthfulness and trust in a single language, as I have said so far. Rather it is a convention of truthfulness and trust in whichever we please of some cluster of similar languages: languages with more or less the same sentences, and more or less the same truth-values for the sentences in worlds close to our actual world, but with increasing divergence in truth-values as we go to increasingly remote, bizarre worlds. The convention confines us to the cluster, but leaves us with indeterminacies whenever the languages of the cluster disagree. We are free to settle these indeterminacies however we like. Thus an ordinary, open-textured, imprecise language is a sort of blur of precise languages—a region, not a point, in the space of languages. Analyticity is sharp in each language of our cluster. But when different languages of our cluster disagree on the analyticity of a sentence, then that sentence is unsharply analytic among us.

Rational reconstructions have been said to be

irrelevant to philosophical problems arising in ordinary, unreconstructed language. My hypothesis of conventions of truthfulness and trust in language-clusters provides a defense against this accusation. Reconstruction is not—or not always—departure from ordinary language. Rather it is selection from ordinary language: isolation of one precise language, or of a subcluster, out of the language-cluster wherein we have a convention of truthfulness and trust.

Objection: The thesis and the antithesis pertain to different subjects. The thesis, in which languages are regarded as semantic systems, belongs to the philosophy of artificial languages. The antithesis, in which language is regarded as part of human natural history, belongs to the philosophy of natural language.

Reply: Not so. *Both* accounts—just like almost any account of almost anything—can most easily be applied to simple, artificial, imaginary examples. Language-games are just as artificial as formalized calculi.

According to the theory I have presented, philosophy of language is a single subject. The thesis and antithesis have been the property of rival schools; but in fact they are complementary essential ingredients in any adequate account either of languages or of language.

NOTES

1. H. P. Grice, "Meaning," *Philosophical Review,* 66(1957):377–388.
2. This proposal is adapted from the theory given in Erik Stenius, "Mood and Language-Game," *Synthese,* 17(1967):254–274.

3. (Harvard University Press, Cambridge, Mass.: 1969). A similar account was given in the original version of this paper, written in 1968.
4. Personal communication, 1971. Bennett himself uses the broadened concept of convention differently, wishing to exhibit conventional meaning as a special case of Gricean meaning. See his "The Meaning-Nominalist Strategy," *Foundations of Language,* 10(1973):141–168.
5. Possible worlds are taken as models in S. Kripke, "A Completeness Theorem in Modal Logic," *Journal of Symbolic Logic,* 24(1959):1–15; in Carnap's recent work on semantics and inductive logic, discussed briefly in sections 9, 10, and 25 of "Replies and Systematic Expositions," *The Philosophy of Rudolf Carnap,* ed. P. Schilpp; and elsewhere. Worlds are taken as state descriptions—diagrams of models—in Carnap's earlier work: for instance, section 18 of *Introduction to Semantics.* Worlds are taken as complete, consistent novels—theories of models—in R. Jeffrey, *The Logic of Decision,* section 12.8.
6. "Replies and Systematic Expositions," section 9.v. A better-known presentation of essentially the same idea is in S. Kripke, "Semantical Considerations on Modal Logic," *Acta Philosophica Fennica,* 16(1963):83–94.
7. See my "General Semantics," *Synthese,* 22 (1970): 18–67.
8. For a description of the sort of grammars I have in mind (minus the semantic interpretation) see N. Chomsky, *Aspects of the Theory of Syntax,* and G. Harman, "Generative Grammars without Transformation Rules," *Language,* 37 (1963):597–616. My "constituents" correspond to semantically interpreted deep phrase-markers, or sub-trees thereof, in a transformational grammar. My "representing operation" may work in several steps and thus subsumes both the transformational and the phonological components of a transformational grammar.
9. W. V. Quine, "Ontological Relativity," *Journal of Philosophy,* 65(1968):185–212; *Word and Object,* pp. 68–79.
10. P. Ziff, *Semantic Analysis,* pp. 34–35.

46 Language and Problems of Knowledge

NOAM CHOMSKY

Before entering into the question of language and problems of knowledge, it may be useful to clarify some terminological and conceptual issues concerning the concepts "language" and "knowledge" which, I think, have tended to obscure understanding and to engender pointless controversy.

To begin with, what do we mean by "language"? There is an intuitive common-sense concept that serves well enough for ordinary life, but it is a familiar observation that every serious approach to the study of language departs from it quite sharply. It is doubtful that the common-sense concept is even coherent, nor would it matter for ordinary purposes if it were not. It is, in the first place, an obscure sociopolitical concept, having to do with colors on maps and the like, and a concept with equally obscure normative and teleological elements, a fact that becomes clear when we ask what language a child of five, or a foreigner learning English, is speaking—surely not my language, nor any other language, in ordinary usage. Rather we say that the child and foreigner are "on their way" to learning English, and the child will "get there," though the foreigner probably will not, except partially. But if all adults were to die from some sudden disease, and children of five or under were to survive, whatever it is that they were speaking would become a typical human language, though one that we say does

not now exist. Ordinary usage breaks down at this point, not surprisingly: its concepts are not designed for inquiry into the nature of language.

Or consider the question of what are called "errors." Many, perhaps most speakers of what we call "English" believe that the word "livid," which they have learned form the phrase "livid with rage," means "red" or "flushed." The dictionary tells us that it means "pale." In ordinary usage, we say that the speakers are wrong about the meaning of this word of their language, and we would say this even if 95%, or perhaps 100% of them made this "error." On the other hand, if dictionaries and other normative documents were destroyed with all memory of them, "livid" would then mean "flushed" in the new language. Whatever all this might mean, it plainly has nothing to do with an eventual science of language, but involves other notions having to do with authority, class structure, and the like. Unless the concept of "community norms" or "conventions" is clarified in some manner yet to be addressed—if this is possible at all in a coherent way—one should be cautious about accepting arguments concerning meaning that make free use of such ideas, taking them to be clear enough; they are not. We understand this easily enough in connection with pronunciation; thus to say that the pronunciation of one dialect is "right" while that of another is "wrong" makes as much sense as saying that it

This is a slightly revised version of a paper delivered at a conference in Madrid, April 28, 1986. Copyright © 1990 Noam Chomsky. Reprinted by permission of Noam Chomsky.

is "right" to talk Spanish and "wrong" to talk English. Such judgments, whatever their status, plainly have nothing to do with the study of language and mind, or human biology; or more accurately, they have to do with some vastly broader inquiry into the interaction of cognitive systems, some complex that is well beyond our current grasp and that we are unlikely ever to comprehend unless the elements that enter into it are identified and understood. The question of "error of interpretation" or "misuse" has much the same status.

Note that a person can be mistaken about his or her own language. Thus if "livid" in fact means "flushed" in my current language, and I tell you that it means "pale" in my language, then I am wrong, just as I would be wrong if I told you, perhaps in honest error, that in my language "whom" is always used for a direct object, not "who," or if I were to deny some feature of the urban dialect that I speak natively. Judgments about oneself are as fallible as any others, but that is not what is at issue here.

All of this is, or should be, commonplace. Correspondingly, every serious approach to the study of language departs from the common-sense usage, replacing it by some technical concept. The choices have generally been questionable ones. The general practice has been to define "language" as what I have called elsewhere "E-language," where "E" is intended to suggest "extensional" and "externalized." The definition is "extensional" in that it takes language to be a set of objects of some kind, and it is "externalized" in the sense that language, so defined, is external to the mind/brain. Thus a set, however chosen, is plainly external to the mind/brain.

As a side comment, let me say that I will use mentalistic terminology freely, but without any dubious metaphysical burden; as I will use the terms, talk about mind is simply talk about the brain at some level of abstraction that we believe to be appropriate for understanding crucial and essential properties of neural systems, on a par with discussion in nineteenth-century chemistry of valence, benzene rings, elements, and the like, abstract entities of some sort that one hoped would be related, ultimately, to the then-unknown physical entities. To say that the

world includes elements with valence of two which therefore behave in a certain way, or benzene rings, etc., is to say that whatever the elementary constituents of the world may be, their properties are such that they are correctly described in these terms at this level of abstraction. To say that the world includes such abstract entities as neural nets (it is the abstract structure that we take to be roughly invariant through time or among individuals, not the molecules, specific orientations, etc.) or mental representations is to say something similar about the brain. Mentalistic inquiry, so understood, is justified insofar as it yields insight and theoretical understanding of phenomena that concern us, and from another point of view, insofar as it facilitates inquiry into brain mechanisms. Just as nineteenth-century chemistry provided a guide to subsequent investigations of more "fundamental" physical entities, so one can expect the same to be true of the brain sciences, which have little idea what to seek without some awareness of the properties of the yet-to-be-discovered mechanisms. Mentalism, in short, is just normal scientific practice, and an essential step towards integrating the study of the phenomena that concern us into the more "fundamental" natural sciences. I might add that it is generally pointless to demand too much clarity in these matters. As the history of physics and even mathematics shows, clarity about foundational issues (e.g., in mathematics, the notions of limit or even proof) develops as a result of inquiry and is not a necessary preliminary to it; foundational questions and questions of conceptual clarity are often premature, and can often be approached and settled only as research progresses without too much concern about exactly what one is talking about.

A typical formulation of a notion of E-language is the definition of "language" by the distinguished American linguist Leonard Bloomfield as "the totality of utterances that can be made in a speech community," the latter another abstract entity, assumed to be homogeneous.[1] Another approach, based ultimately on Aristotle's conception of language as a relation of sound and meaning, is to define "language" as a set of pairs (s, m), where s is a sentence or utterance, and m is a meaning, perhaps represented as some kind of set-theoretical object in a system of possible worlds, a proposal developed by David Lewis among others. There are other similar proposals.

Under any of these proposals, a grammar will be a formal system of some kind that enumerates or "generates" the set chosen to be "the language," clearly an infinite set for which we seek a finite representation.

The concept "E-language" and its variants raise numerous questions. In the first place, the set is ill defined, not simply in the sense that it may be vague, with indeterminate boundaries, but in a deeper sense. Consider what are sometimes called "semi-grammatical sentences," such as "the child seems sleeping." Is this in the language or outside it? Either answer is unacceptable. The sentence clearly has a definite meaning. An English speaker interprets it in a definite way, quite differently from the interpretation that would be given by a speaker of Japanese. Hence it cannot simply be excluded from the set "E-English," though it is plainly not well formed. But speakers of English and Japanese will also differ in how they interpret some sentence of Hindi—or for that matter how they will interpret a wide variety of noises—so then all languages and a vast range of other sounds also fall within English, a conclusion that makes no sense. It is doubtful that there is any coherent solution to this range of problems. The fact is that a speaker of English, Japanese, or whatever, has developed a system of knowledge that assigns a certain status to a vast range of physical events, and no concept of E-language, nor any construct developed from it, is likely to be able to do justice to this essential fact.

A second problem has to do with choice of grammar. Evidently, for any set there are many grammars that will enumerate it. Hence it has commonly been argued, most notably by W. V. Quine, that choice of grammar is a matter of convenience, not truth, like the choice of "a grammar" for the well-formed sentences of arithmetic in some notation. But now we face real questions about the subject matter of the study of language. Clearly, there is some fact about the mind/brain that differentiates speakers of English from speakers of Japanese, and

there is a truth about this matter, which is ultimately a question of biology. But sets are not in the mind/brain, and grammars can be chosen freely as long as they enumerate the E-language, so the study of E-language, however constructed, does not seem to bear on the truth about speakers of English and Japanese; it is not, even in principle, part of the natural sciences, and one might argue that it is a pointless pursuit, a kind of chasing after shadows. Many philosophers—W. V. Quine, David Lewis, and others—have concluded that linguists must be in error when they hold that they are concerned with truths about the mind/brain, though clearly there are such truths about language for someone to be concerned with; they also hold that puzzling philosophical problems are raised by the claim that grammars are "internally represented" in some manner. Others (Jerrold Katz, Scott Soames, and others) have held that linguistics is concerned with some Platonic object that we may call "P-language," and that P-English is what it is independently of what may be true about the psychological states or brains of speakers of English. One can see how these conclusions might be reached by someone who begins by construing language to be a variety of E-language.

There is little point arguing about how to define the term "linguistics," but it is plain that there is an area of investigation, let us call it "C-linguistics" (cognitive linguistics) which is concerned with the truth about the mind/brains of the people who speak C-English and C-Japanese, suitably idealized. This subject belongs strictly within the natural sciences in principle, and its links to the main body of the natural sciences will become more explicit as the neural mechanisms responsible for the structures and principles discovered in the study of mind come to be understood. As I noted earlier, the status of this study of language and mind is similar to that of nineteenth-century chemistry or pre-DNA genetics; one might argue that it is similar to the natural sciences at every stage of their development. In any event, C-linguistics raises no philosophical problems that do not arise for scientific inquiry quite generally. It raises numerous problems of fact and interpretation, but of a kind familiar in empirical inquiry.

The status of P-linguistics, or of the study of E-language generally, is quite different. Thus the advocates of P-linguistics have to demonstrate that in addition to the real entities C-English, C-Japanese, etc., and the real mind/brains of their speakers, there are other Platonic objects that they choose to delineate somehow and study. Whatever the merits of this claim, we may simply put the matter aside, noting that people may study whatever abstract object they construct. This still leaves the apparent problem noted by Quine, Lewis, and others who argue that it is "folly" to claim that one of a set of "extensionally equivalent systems of grammar" that enumerate the same E-language is correctly attributed to the speaker-hearer as a property physically encoded in some manner, whereas another one merely happens to enumerate the E-language but is not a correct account of the speaker's mind/brain and system of knowledge. Plainly this conclusion cannot be correct, given that, as they agree, there is surely some truth about the mind/brain and the system of knowledge represented in it, so some error must have crept in along the way.

Note that the question is not one of metaphysical realism, or of choice of theory in science. Take whatever view one wants on these matters, and it is still alleged that some further philosophical problem, or "folly," arises in the case of attribution of one grammar but not another extensionally equivalent one to a speaker-hearer, a conclusion that is transparently in error, but seems to be as well founded as the correct conclusion that there is no "true" grammar of arithmetic. So we seem to be left with a puzzle.

A third class of problems that arise from the study of E-language has to do with the properties of these sets. Sets have formal properties, so it seems to be meaningful to ask whether human E-languages have certain formal properties: are they context-free, or recursive, or denumerable? All of these choices have been affirmed, and denied, but the point is that the questions are taken seriously, though it is far from clear that the questions are even meaningful. The answers are also thought to have some crucial bearing on questions of parsing and learnability, but quite wrongly, for reasons discussed years ago.[2]

All of this is, in my view, quite confused and pointless, because the notion of E-language is an artifact, with no status in an eventual science of language. E-languages can be selected one way or another, or perhaps better, not at all, since there appears to be no coherent choice and the concept appears to be useless for any empirical inquiry. In particular, it is quite mistaken to hold, as many do, that an E-language is somehow "given," and that there is no particular problem in making sense of the idea that a person uses a particular E-language, but that in contrast there are serious problems if not pure folly in the contention that a particular "grammar" for that E-language, but not some other one, is in fact used by the speaker. Clearly infinite sets are not "given." What is given to the child is some finite array of data, on the basis of which the child's mind develops some system of knowledge X, where X determines the status of arbitrary physical objects, assigning to some of them a phonetic form and meaning. With a different finite array of data—from Japanese rather than English, for example—the system of knowledge attained will differ, and the question of what the systems in the mind/brain really are is as meaningful as any other question of science. As for the E-language, it does raise innumerable problems, probably unanswerable ones, since whatever it is, if anything, it is more remote from mechanisms and at a higher level of abstraction than the internally represented system of knowledge, the "correct grammar" that is alleged to raise such difficulties.

The source of all of these problems resides in an inappropriate choice of the basic concept of the study of language, namely "language." The only relevant notion that has a real status is what is usually called "grammar." Here again we find an unfortunate terminological decision, which has undoubtedly been misleading. Guided by the misleading and inappropriate analogy to formal languages, I and others have used the term "language" to refer to some kind of E-language, and have used the term "grammar" with systematic ambiguity—a fact that has always been spelled out clearly, but has nevertheless caused confusion: the term "grammar" has been used to refer to the linguist's theory, or to the subject matter of that theory. A better usage would be to restrict the term "grammar" to the theory of the language, and to understand the language as what we may call "I-language," where "I" is to suggest "intensional" and "internalized." The I-language is what the grammar purports to describe: a system represented in the mind/brain, ultimately in physical mechanisms that are now largely unknown, and is in this sense *internalized*; a system that is *intensional* in that it may be regarded as a specific function considered in intension—that is, a specific characterization of a function—which assigns a status to a vast range of physical events, including the utterance "John seems to be sleeping," the utterance "John seems sleeping," a sentence of Hindi, and probably the squeaking of a door, if we could do careful enough experiments to show how speakers of English and Japanese might differ in the way they "hear" this noise.

As contrasted with E-language, however construed, I-languages are real entities, as real as chemical compounds. They are in the mind, ultimately the brain, in the same sense as chemical elements, organic molecules, neural nets, and other entities that we construct and discuss at some appropriate abstract level of discussion are in the brain. They are what they are, and it is a problem of science to discover the true account of what they are, the grammar for the speaker in question. The story presented by many philosophers is entirely backwards. It is the E-language, not the I-language (the "grammar," in one of the two senses in which this systematically ambiguous phrase has been used), that poses philosophical problems, which are probably not worth trying to solve, since the concept is of no interest and has no status. It may, indeed, be pure "folly" to construct and discuss it, to ask what formal properties E-languages have, and so on. I suspect it is. In particular, the analogy to formal systems of arithmetic and so is largely worthless, and should be discarded, though other analogies to arithmetic and logic, as systems of mentally represented knowledge, are quite definitely worth pursuing, and raise quite interesting questions, yet to be seriously explored. The debates of the past generation about these matters seem to me a classic example of the philosophical errors that arise from misinterpreting concepts of ordinary language—in this case, developing a useless, perhaps quite senseless concept, and assuming erroneously that it is the relevant scientific notion that corresponds to, or should replace, some concept of ordinary language—a source of philosophical error that was clearly exposed in the eighteenth-century critique of the theory of ideas, if not earlier, and has more recently been brought to general attention by Wittgenstein.

Let us now use the term "language" to refer to I-language, and the term "grammar" to refer to the theory of an I-language. What about the term "universal grammar," recently resurrected and given a sense that is similar to the traditional one, but not identical, since the entire framework of thinking has been radically modified? The term "universal grammar" has also been used with systematic ambiguity, to refer to the linguist's theory and to its subject matter. In keeping with our effort to select terms so as to avoid pointless confusion, let us use the term "universal grammar" to refer to the linguist's theory only. The topic of universal grammar is, then, the system of principles that specify what it is to be a human language. This system of principles is a component of the mind/brain prior to the acquisition of a particular language. It is plausible to suppose that this system constitutes the initial state of the language faculty, considered to be a subsystem of the mind/brain.

This initial state, call it S_0, is apparently a common human possession to a very close approximation, and also appears to be unique to humans, hence a true species property. It is what it is, and theories concerning it are true or false. Our goal is to discover the true theory of universal grammar, which will deal with the factors that make it possible to acquire a particular I-language and that determine the class of human I-languages and their properties. Looked at from a certain point of view, universal grammar describes a "language acquisition device," a system that maps data into language (I-language). A theory of universal grammar, like a particular proposed grammar, is true or false in whatever sense any scientific theory can be true or false. For our purposes, we may accept the normal reaalist assumptions of the practicing scientist, in this connection. Whatever problems may arise are not specific to this enterprise, and are surely far better studied in connection with the more developed natural sciences.

Crucially, (I-)languages and S_0 are real entities, the basic objects of study for the science of language, though it may be possible to study more complex abstractions, such as speech or language communities; any further such inquiry will surely have to presuppose grammars of (I-) language and universal grammar, and always has in practice, at least tacitly, even when this is explicitly denied, another confusion that I will not pursue here. An I-language—henceforth, simply "a language"—is the state attained by the language faculty under certain external conditions. I doubt very much that it makes any sense to speak of a person as *learning* a language. Rather, a language grows in the mind/brain. Acquiring language is less something that a child does than something that happens to the child, like growing arms rather than wings, or undergoing puberty at a certain stage of maturation. These processes take place in different ways depending on external events, but the basic lines of development are internally determined. The evidence seems to me overwhelming that this is true of language growth.

Let us now consider the question of knowledge. The language a person has acquired underlies a vast range of knowledge, both "knowledge-how" and "knowledge-that." A person whose mind incorporates the language English (meaning, a particular I-language that falls within what is informally called "English") knows how to speak and understand a variety of sentences, knows that certain sounds have certain meanings, and so on. These are typical cases of knowing-how and knowing-what, ordinary propositional knowledge in the latter case, and this of course does not exhaust the range of such knowledge. It seems entirely reasonable to think of the language as a system that is internalized in the mind/brain, yielding specific cases of propositional knowledge or knowledge how to do so and so. We now have to consider at least three aspects of knowledge: (1) the internalized system of knowledge of the language, (2) knowing how to speak and understand, and (3) knowledge that sentences mean what they do (etc.).

It is common among philosophers, particu-

larly those influenced by Wittgenstein, to hold that "knowledge of language is an ability," which can be exercised by speaking, understanding, reading, talking to oneself: "to know a language just is to have the ability to do these and similar things,"[3] and indeed more generally knowledge is a kind of ability. Some go further and hold that an ability is expressible in dispositional terms, so that language becomes, as Quine described it, "a complex of present dispositions to verbal behavior." If we accept this further view, then two people who are disposed to say different things under given circumstances speak different languages, even if they are identical twins with exactly the same history, who speak the same language by any sensible criteria we might establish. There are so many well-known problems with this conception that I will simply drop it, and consider the vaguer proposal that knowledge of language is a practical ability to speak and understand (Michael Dummet, Anthony Kenny, and others, in one or another form).

This radical departure from ordinary usage is, in my view, entirely unwarranted. To see how radical is the departure from ordinary usage, consider the consequences of accepting it, now using "ability" in the sense of ordinary usage. In the first place, ability can improve with no change in knowledge. Thus suppose Jones takes a course in public speaking or in composition, improving his ability to speak and understand, but learning nothing new about his language. The language that Jones speaks and understands is exactly what it was before, and his knowledge of language has not changed, but his abilities have improved. Hence knowledge of language is not to be equated with the ability to speak, understand, etc.

Similarly, ability to use langauge can be impaired, and can even disappear, with no loss of knowledge of language at all. Suppose that Smith, a speaker of English, suffers Parkinson's disease, losing entirely the ability to speak, understand, etc. Smith then does not have "the ability to do these and similar things," and therefore does not have knowledge of English, as the term is defined by Kenny, Dummett, and others. Suppose that use of the chemical L-Dopa can restore Smith's ability completely, as has been claimed (it does not matter whether the facts just noted are accurate; since we are dealing with a conceptual question, it is enough that they could be, as is certainly the case). Now what has happened during the recovery of the ability? On the assumption in question, Smith has recovered knowledge of English from scratch with a drug, after having totally lost that knowledge. Curiously, Smith recovered knowledge of *English,* not of *Japanese,* though no evidence was available to choose between these outcomes; he regained knowledge of his original English with no experience at all. Had Smith been a speaker of Japanese, he would have recovered Japanese with the same drug. Evidently, something remained fully intact while the ability was totally lost. In normal usage, as in our technical counterpart to it, we would say that what remained fully intact was "possession of the language," knowledge of English, showing again that knowledge cannot be reduced to ability.[4]

Note that there are cases where we would say that a person retains an ability but is incapable of exercising it, say a swimmer who cannot swim because his legs and arms are tied. But that is surely an entirely different kind of case than the one we are now considering, where the ability is lost but the knowledge is retained.

To sustain the thesis that knowledge is ability, we would have to invent some new concept of ability, call it "K-ability," which we understand in the sense of knowledge. Then we could say that Jones, who improved his ability to speak with no change in his knowledge of English, retained his K-ability to speak (etc.) without change; and Smith fully retained his K-ability while entirely losing his ability to use English, in the normal sense of "ability." Plainly this is pointless. The invented concept K-ability is invested with all the properties of knowledge, and diverges radically from the quite useful ordinary concept of ability. It is true that knowledge is K-ability, since we have defined the novel invented term "K-ability" to have the properties of knowledge, but that is hardly an interesting conclusion.

Exactly this tack is taken by Anthony Kenny, in the face of conceptual arguments such as those just reviewed. Thus in the case of the patient with Parkinson's disease, Kenny says that he did indeed have the ability to use the language when he had no ability to use the language, thus shifting to "K-ability," plainly, since the ability was totally lost.[5] Crucially, K-ability diverges radically from ability, and is like knowledge, as we can see from the fact that a person may have entirely lost the ability to speak and understand while entirely retaining the K-ability, can improve the ability with the K-ability unmodified, etc.

Kenny also assumes that there is a contradiction between my conclusion concerning the person who has lost the ability while retaining the knowledge and my statement elsewhere (which he accepts) that there might in principle be a "Spanish pill" that would confer knowledge of Spanish on a person who took it. There is no inconsistency. The issue in connection with aphasia or Parkinson's disease has nothing to do with a pill for acquiring a certain language; rather, the point is that the person in the *Gedankenexperiment* reacquires ability to use *exactly the same language that he had* (knowledge of which he never lost); the same dose of L-dopa restores ability to speak English to the English speaker and ability to speak Japanese to the Japanese speaker; it is not an "English pill." The same holds true of the person whose ability changes while his knowledge—or K-ability, if one prefers—remains constant.

It is curious that this attempt to maintain a clearly untenable thesis by inventing a new term "ability" that is used in the sense of "knowledge" and is radically different from "ability" in its normal sense is presented in the spirit of Wittgenstein, who constantly inveighed against such procedures and argued that they are at the root of much philosophical error, as in the present case.

Note that essentially the same arguments show that knowing-how cannot be explained in terms of ability, unless we adopt the same pointless procedure just discussed. Suppose a person knows how to ride a bicycle, loses this ability under some kind of brain injury, and then recovers it through administration of a drug, or when the effects of the injury recede. The person has made a transition from full ability, to no ability, to recovery of the original ability—not some other one. The argument is the same as before. Knowing-how is not simply a matter of ability, nor, surely, is knowing-that, contrary to much widely accepted doctrine. In fact, it is quite clear from closer investigation of the concept "knowing how." Rather, knowing-how involves a crucial cognitive element, some internal representation of a system of knowledge.[6] Since this matter is not germane here, I will not pursue it.

Could we say, then, that knowing how to speak and understand a language is in no formal way different from knowing how to ride a bicycle, as is commonly alleged, so that we need not be driven to assume a mentally-represented system of knowledge in the case of language? There are at least two fundamental problems with this line of argument. First, knowing-how in general involves a cognitive element, as just noted. Secondly, the "just like" argument is quite empty. We might as well say that there is no real problem in accounting for the ability that some people have to write brilliant poetry or wonderful quartets, or to discover deep theorems or scientific principles; it is just like knowing how to ride a bicycle. What possible point can there be to such proposals?

In any particular case, we have to discover what kind of cognitive structure underlies knowing how to do so-and-so or knowing that such-and-such.[7] In pursuing such inquiry, we rely entirely on "best theory" arguments, and we discover, not surprisingly, that very different kinds of systems, cognitive or other, are involved. To say that it is all just "knowing how," hence unproblematic, is merely a form of anti-intellectualism, little more than an expression of lack of curiosity about features of the world, in this case, central features of human nature and human life.

In summary, to try to sustain the principle that knowing how to speak and understand a language reduces to a network of abilities, one has to use the term "ability" in some novel technical sense—in fact, a sense invested with all the properties of knowlege. Plainly this is pointless.

A rather striking feature of the widespread conception of language as a system of abilities, or a habit system of some kind, or a complex of dispositions, is that it has been completely unproductive. It led precisely nowhere. One

cannot point to a single result or discovery about language, even of the most trivial kind, that derives from this conception. Here one must be a bit more precise. There was, in fact, a discipline that did obtain empirical results and that professed this doctrine, namely, American structural linguistics for many years. But the actual work carried out, and even the technical theories developed, departed from the doctrine at every crucial point. Thus, there is no relation between, say, the procedures of phonemic analysis devised and the concept of language as a habit system.[8] This latter belief did influence applied disciplines such as language teaching, very much to their detriment. But linguistics itself was essentially unaffected, except insofar as it was impoverished in vision and concerns by the doctrine it professed.

One might draw an analogy to operationalism in the sciences. This doctrine, widely professed at one time, undoubtedly had an influence in psychology. Namely, to the extent that it was followed in practice, it seriously impoverished the discipline. The principles were also professed in physics for a time, but I suspect that they had little impact there, since the scientists who professed the principles generally continued to do their work in utter contradiction to them, quite wisely. (We omit examples that are discussed in the standard literature; see, e.g., the reference in note 2.)

The central problem of the theory of language is to explain how people can speak and understand new sentences, new in their experience or perhaps in the history of the language. The phenomenon is not an exotic one, but is the norm in the ordinary use of language, as Descartes and his followers stressed in their discussion of what we may call "the creative aspect of language use," that is, the commonplace but often neglected fact that the normal use of language is unbounded in scope, free from identifiable stimulus control, coherent and appropriate to situations that evoke but do not cause it (a crucial distinction), arousing in listeners thoughts that they too might express in the same or similar ways. It is surprising how rarely the phenomenon was seriously addressed in the linguistics of the past century, until the mid-1950s at least, in part, perhaps, because of the conception of language as a system of habits, dispositions or abilities, Otto Jesperson being a rare and notable exception. When the question was addressed, the conventional answer was that new forms are produced and understood "by analogy" with familiar ones. (But this explanation in empty until an account is given of analogy, and none exists.)

In the past few years it has been shown that a wide range of phenomena from typologically quite different languages can be explained on the assumption that the language faculty of the mind/brain carries out digital computations following very general principles, making use of representations of a precisely determined sort, including empty categories of several kinds. This work then provides evidence, quite strong evidence I believe, for some rather striking and surprising conclusions: that the language faculty, part of the mind/brain, is in crucial part a system of digital computation of a highly restricted character, with simple principles that interact to yield very intricate and complex results. This is a rather unexpected property of a biological system. One must be alert to the possibility that the conclusion is an artifact, resulting from our mode of analysis, but the evidence suggests quite strongly that the conclusion reflects reality.

As far as I am aware, there is only one other known biological phenomenon that shares the properties of discrete infinity exhibited by language, and that involves similar principles of digital computation: namely, the human number faculty, also apparently a species property, essentially common to the species and unique to it, and, like human language, unteachable to other organisms, which lack the requisite faculties. There are, for example, numerous animal communication systems, but they are invariably finite (the calls of apes) or continuous (the "language" of bees, continuous in whatever sense we can say this of a physical system; the human gestural system; etc.). Note that the difference between human languages and these communication systems is not one of "more" or "less," but one of difference in quality; indeed, it is doubtful that any sense can be given to the idea that human language is a communication system, though it can be used for communication

along with much else. These observations suggest that at some remote period of evolutionary history, the brain developed a certain capacity for digital computation, for employing recursive rules and associated mental representations, thus acquiring the basis for thought and language in the human sense, with the arithmetical capacity perhaps latent as a kind of abstraction from the language faculty, to be evoked when cultural conditions allowed, much later, in fact never in the case of some societies, so it appears. Notice that there is surely no reason to suppose that every trait is specifically selected.

The phenomena of the languages of the world appear to be highly diverse, but, increasingly, it has been shown that over a large and impressive range they can be accounted for by the same principles, which yield highly varied results as the properties of lexical items vary from language to language. Thus in Spanish, there are clitic pronouns, including the reflexive, while in English there are not, so that the forms of English and Spanish, say in causative constructions, look quite different. But the principles that govern them appear to be essentially the same, their consequences differing by virtue of a lexical property of the pronominal system: in Spanish, but not in English, there is a system of pronouns that are lexically marked as affixes, and therefore must attach to other elements. The manner in which these affixes attach, and the targets to which they adjoin, are determined by the very same principles that determine the formation of complex syntactic constructions such as operator-variable constructions and others, so it now appears.

In other languages, many more items are identified in the lexicon as affixes, and the same syntactic principles determine complex morphological forms that reflect in another way the same underlying and near universal underlying structures.[9] Thus in Japanese, the causative element is not a verb, like Spanish *hacer* or English *make,* but rather an affix, so a verb must move from the embedded clause to attach to it, yielding what appears to be a monoclausal causative as distinct from the English-Spanish biclausal causative; in Spanish too there is a reflection of the same process when *se* raises to the main verb in the sentence "Juan se hizo afeitar," as if *hizo-afeitar* were a single word. The point is that as lexical items vary, the very same principles determine a wide range of superficially different complex phenomena in typologically quite different languages.

The principles of universal grammar are fixed as constituent elements of the language faculty, but languages plainly differ. How do they differ? One way has already been noted: they differ in properties of lexical items, though here too the options are narrowly constrained by general principles. Beyond that, it seems that the principles allow for a limited range of variation. That variation is limited has often been explicitly denied. The leading American linguist Edward Sapir held that languages can vary "without assignable limit," and Martin Joos put forth what he called the "Boasian" view, referring to Franz Boas, one of the founders of modern linguistics: namely, that "languages could differ from each other without limit and in unpredictable ways." Such views echo William Dwight Whitney, who greatly influenced Ferdinand de Saussure, and who emphasized "the infinite diversity of human speech."

Such views perhaps appeared tenable in some form if one regarded language as a habit system, a network of practical abilities, a complex of dispositions, and the like. In that case, language would be constrained only by whatever general conditions constrain the development of abilities and habits in general, by what are sometimes called "generalized learning mechanisms," if these exist. But this conception does not allow one even to approach the essential features of normal language use, as has been demonstrated beyond reasonable doubt in my view; and as already noted, the conception has been entirely unproductive.

Assuming without further discussion that this conception must be abandoned, the question of language variation will take on a new form in the context of a general revision of the framework of inquiry into problems of natural language. A conceptual change of this nature was proposed about thirty years ago, reviving in a new form some long-forgotten approaches to the study of natural language. This rather sharp conceptual change underlies the research program that has been given the name "generative grammar," referring to the fact that the grammar—or as we are now more properly calling it "the language"—generates an unbounded range of specific consequences, assigning a status to every expression and thus providing the mechanisms for the creative aspect of language use. The central questions of the study of language, conceived along the lines of the earlier discussion, now become the following:

(1) (i) What is the system of knowledge attained by a person who speaks and understands a language?
(ii) How is that knowledge acquired?
(iii) How is that knowledge put to use?

The last question has two aspects, the production problem and the perception problem. The second question, how language is acquired, is a variant of what we might call "Plato's problem," raised for example when Socrates demonstrated that a slave boy with no training in geometry in fact knew geometry, perhaps the first psychological (thought-)experiment. The problem is not a trivial one: people know a great deal more than can possibly be accounted for in terms of the standard paradigms of epistemology (or perhaps more accurately, what they know is different from what one might expect in these terms), language being a striking example. The production problem might be called "Descartes's problem," referring to one of the central Cartesian criteria for the existence of other minds: namely, when experiment demonstrates that another creature that resembles us exhibits the creative aspect of language use, then it would only be reasonable to attribute to the creature a mind like ours. In more recent years, a similar idea has been called "the Turing Test." This problem, one aspect of more general problems concerning will and choice, remains beyond the scope of serious human inquiry in fact, and may be so in principle, rather as Descartes suggested. In any event, having nothing to say about it, I will put it aside, keeping just to the perception problem, or what is sometimes called "the parsing problem" (restricting attention to certain computational aspects).

These questions were posed as constituting the research program of generative grammar about thirty years ago, along with an argument to the effect that prevailing answers to them in terms of habit systems and the like were completely unacceptable for reasons already briefly discussed. What alternative, then, can we propose? I will keep to the terminology suggested above, departing from earlier usage.

The first proposal was that a language is a rule system, where the kinds of rules and their interrelations are specified by universal grammar. In one familiar conception, the rules included context-free rules, lexical rules, transformational rules, phonological rules (in a broad sense), and what were misleadingly called "rules of semantic interpretation" relating syntactic structures to representations in a system sometimes called "LF," suggesting "logical form" but with certain qualifications. This term "rules of semantic interpretation" is misleading, as David Lewis among others has pointed out, because these rules relate syntactic objects, mental representations. They relate syntactic structures and LF-representations, which are syntactic objects. The term "semantics" should properly be restricted to the relation between language and the world, or to use of language, some might argue. The criticism is accurate, but it applies far more broadly. In fact, it applies in exactly the same form to what Lewis and others call "semantics," where "meanings" are set-theoretic objects of some sort: models, "pictures," situations and events, or whatever. These are mental representations,[10] not elements of the world, and the problem arises of how they are related to the world. It is often assumed that the relation is trivial, something like incorporation, so that it is unnecessary to provide a justification for these particular systems of mental representation, but it is easy to show that this cannot be true unless we trivialize our conception of what the world is by restricting attention to something like what Nelson Goodman calls "versions," all mental representations, abandoning (perhaps as meaningless) the question of why one collection of "versions" is jointly acceptable or "right" and others not, that is, not pursuing the commonsense answer: that certain versions are jointly "right" because of their accord with reality. But if we take this tack, which I do not suggest, semantics disappears and we are only studying various systems of mental representation. In fact, much of what is called "semantics" is really the study of the syntax of mental representations. It is a curious fact that those who correctly call their work in this area "syntax" are said to be avoiding semantics, while others who incorrectly describe their studies of syntax as "semantics" are said to be contributing to semantics.[11]

Adopting this conception of language, a language is a complex of rules of the permitted format, interconnected in a way permitted by universal grammar. In contrast to the conception of language in terms of habit systems or abilities, this was an extremely productive idea, which led quickly to a vast increase in the range of phenomena brought under investigation, with many discoveries about facts of language, even quite simple ones, that had never been noted or explored. Furthermore, the array of phenomena discovered and investigated were made intelligible at some level, by providing partial rule systems that accounted for their properties. The depth of explanation, however, could never really be very great. Even if appropriate rule systems could be constructed, and even if these systems were found to be restricted in type, we would always want to know why we have these kinds of rules and not others. Thus, languages typically have rules that allow the direct object of a verb to function as its subject, though it is still being interpreted as the object; but the converse property does not exist. Or consider again causative constructions, say, the form that we can give in abstract representation as (2), where the element CAUSE may be a word as in Spanish-English or an affix as in Japanese:

(2) problems CAUSE [that Y lies]

The principles of universal grammar permit a realization of this abstract form as something like (3), where CAUSE is an affix, or with CAUSE-*lie* associated in a closely linked verb sequence as in Spanish:

(3) problems CAUSE-lie Y

But the form (4) does not underlie a possible realization as (5):

(4) [that Y lies] CAUSE problems
(5) Y CAUSE-lie problems

Subject-object asymmetries of this sort are found very widely in language. They reflect in part the fact that subject-verb-object sentences are not treated in natural language as two-term relations as is familiar in logical analysis, but rather in the more traditional terms of Aristotelian logic and the universal grammar of the pre-modern period, as subject-predicate structures with a possibly complex predicate. In part, the asymmetries appear to follow from a newly discovered principle governing empty categories of the sort illustrated earlier. But whatever the explanation, problems of this nature abound, and an approach in terms of rule systems leaves them unsolved, except in a rather superficial way. From another point of view, there are simply too many possible rule systems, even when we constrain their form, and we thus do not achieve a convincing answer to our variant of Plato's problem.

Recognition of these facts has been at the core of the research program of the past twenty-five years. The natural approach has been to abandon the rules in favor of general principles, so that the question of why we have one choice of rules rather than another simply does not arise. Thus if there are no rules for the formation of passive constructions, or interrogatives, or relative clauses, or phrase structure, and no rules that change grammatical functions such as causative and others, then the question why we have certain rules, not others, does not arise. Increasingly, it has become clear that rules are simply epiphenomena, on a par with sentences in the sense that they are simply "projected" from the (I-) language, viewed in a certain way. But as distinct from sentences, which exist in mental representation and are realized in behavior, there is no reason to believe that rules of the familiar form exist at all, they have no status in linguistic theory and do not constitute part of mental representation or enter into mental computations, and we may safely abandon them, so it appears. We are left with general principles of universal grammar.

If there were only one possible human language, apart from lexical variety, we would then have a simple answer to our variant of Plato's problem: universal grammar permits only one realization apart from lexicon, and this is the language that people come to know when they acquire appropriate lexical items through experience in some manner. But clearly the variety of languages is greater than this, so this cannot be the complete story—though it is probably closer to true than has been thought in the past. Thus in languages such as English or Spanish, verbs and prepositions precede their objects, and the same is true of adjectives and nouns, as in such expressions as "proud of Mary" (where "Mary" is the object of "proud" with a semantically empty preposition *of* introduced automatically as a kind of case-marker for reasons determined by universal grammar) and "translation of the book" with a similar analysis. The categories noun, verb, adjective, and preposition (more generally, adposition) are the *lexical categories*. The general principles of universal grammar determine the kinds of phrases in which they appear as *heads*. The lexical entry itself determines the number and category of the *complements* of these heads and their semantic roles, and the general principles of phrase structure determine a limited range of other possibilities.

There is, however, an option left underdetermined by the principles of universal grammar. English and Spanish settle this option by placing the head invariably *before* its complements. We may say that they choose the "head-initial" value of the "head parameter." In Japanese, in contrast, verbs, adpositions, adjectives, and nouns *follow* their complements. The range of phrase structures in the two languages is very similar, and accords with quite general principles of universal grammar, but the languages differ in one crucial choice of the head parameter: the language may choose either the "head-initial" or the "head-final" value of this parameter. In fact, this is only the simplest case, and there is a very limited range of further options depending on directionality of assignment of abstract case and semantic roles, a matter that has been explored by Hilda Koopman, Lisa Travis, and others, but we may put these further complexities aside.

A crucial fact about the head parameter is that its value can be determined from very simple data. There is good reason to believe that this is true of all parameters; we must deal with the crucial and easily demonstrated fact that what a person knows is vastly underdetermined by available evidence, and that much of this knowledge is based on no direct evidence at all. Empty categories and their properties provide a dramatic example of this pervasive phenomenon, almost entirely ignored in earlier work. Thus a person is provided with no direct evidence about the position and various properties of elements that have no physical realization. There is little doubt that this problem of "poverty of stimulus" is in fact the norm rather than the exception. It must be, then, that the values of parameters are set by the kinds of simple data that are available to the child, and that the rich, complex, and highly articulated system of knowledge that arises, and is shared with others of somewhat different but equally impoverished experience, is determined in its basic features by the principles of the initial state S_0 of the language faculty. Languages may appear to differ, but they are cast in the same mold. One might draw an analogy to the biology of living organisms. Apparently, the biochemistry of life is quite similar from yeasts to humans, but small changes in timing of regulatory mechanisms of the cells and the like can yield what to us seem to be vast phenomenal differences, the difference between a whale and a butterfly, a human and a microbe, and so on. Viewed from an angel's point of view, with numerous other possible though not actual physical worlds under consideration, all life might appear identical apart from trivialities. Similarly, from an angel's point of view, all languages would appear identical, apart from trivialities, their fundamental features determined by facts about human biology.

The language itself (again, as always, in the sense of I-language) may be regarded as nothing more than an array of choices for the various parameters, selected in accord with whatever options universal grammar permits. Since there are a finite number of parameters, each finite-valued (probably two-valued), it follows that there are a finite number of possible languages. One can see at once why questions concerning the formal properties of natural languages are largely irrelevant; there are few questions of mathematical interest to raise concerning finite sets.

Here a qualification is necessary. We are separating out the lexicon (to which I will briefly return), a system that in principle can extend without bound though with sharp constraints in many languages (thus in English, we may always add another monomorphemic name of arbitrary length), and we are considering only what we might call "core language," to be distinguished from a "periphery" of marked and specifically learned exceptions; irregular verbs, idioms, and the like. These may presumably vary without bound apart from time and memory limitations, though surely in a manner that is sharply constrained in type. It is the core language that is nothing other than an array of values for parameters. I assume, of course, that the distinction between core and periphery is a real-world distinction, not a matter of convenience or pragmatic choice, except insofar as this is true of theories in chemistry and other branches of natural science, a consideration irrelevant here. For obvious reasons, the periphery is of much less interest for the basic psychological-biological questions to which linguistics is directed, if conceived along the lines of the previous discussion, and I will ignore it here.

Keeping to the core, then, there are finitely many possible languages. What a person knows, when that person speaks and understands a language, is a vocabulary and a particular array of values of parameters: an I-language. Once the parameters are set and lexical items acquired, the entire system functions, assigning a status to a vast range of expressions in a precise and explicit manner, even those that have never been heard or produced in the history of language (and well beyond, as noted earlier). Others understand what we say, because they have the same biological nature and sufficiently similar experience with simple utterances.

Turning to Plato's problem, a language is acquired by determining the values of the parameters of the initial state on the basis of simple data, and then the system of knowledge is represented in the mind/brain and is ready to function—though it might not function if the person lacks the ability to use it, perhaps because of some brain injury or the like. As for the parsing problem, it presumably should be solved along such lines as these: the hearer identifies words, and on the basis of their lexical properties, projects a syntactic structure as determined by principles of universal grammar and the values of the parameters. Connections and associations among these elements, including the empty categories that are forced to appear, are determined by other principles of universal grammar, perhaps parametrized. Thus given the sentence "a quién se hizo Juan afeitar," the mind of the speaker of Spanish automatically assigns a structure with two empty categories, one the subject of "afeitar," another its object. Principles of universal grammar then produce a contradiction, in the manner informally described earlier, and the sentence receives no coherent interpretation, though of course it has a status; thus the Spanish speaker assigns to it a lexical and syntactic structure, and might even be able to "force" a certain meaning, if the sentence were produced by a foreigner, by me for example. A monolingual speaker of English will also assign a certain status to this expression, at least in some kind of phonetic representation, very likely considerably more.

The abandonment of rule systems in favor of a principles-and-parameters approach, which has been gradually developing over the past twenty-five years and has been achieved to a substantial extent only in the past half-dozen years, has been extremely productive. It has, once again, led to a vast leap in empirical coverage, with entirely new empirical materials discovered in well-studied languages, and with languages of great typological variety incorporated within essentially the same framework. The depth of explanation has also advanced considerably, as it has become possible to explain why there are processes described by certain rules but not others. The principles now being developed yield very sharp and surprising predictions about languages of varied types, predictions which sometimes prove accurate, and sometimes fail in highly instructive ways. My guess is that we are at the beginning of a radically new and highly productive phase in the study of language.

The shift of perspective from rule systems to a principles-and-parameters approach might be regarded as a second major conceptual change

in the development of generative grammar, the first being the conceptual change noted earlier as part of the so-called "cognitive revolution," from a conception of language as a system of habits or abilities to a mentalistic approach that regards language as a computational system of the mind/brain—a step towards integrating the study of language to the natural sciences, for the reasons discussed earlier. The second shift of perspective is more theory-internal than the first, but is in a sense a much sharper break from the tradition, for two reasons. One is that the "cognitive revolution" of the 1950s was in many respects a rediscovery in different terms of ideas and insights that had been developed long before, both in psychology and the study of language, during the seventeenth century "cognitive revolution." A second is that the rule system developed in early generative grammar were in certain respects a formalization, in a different framework, of traditional notions about the way sentences are constructed and interpreted. The shift to a principles-and-parameters approach introduces ideas that have only a remote resemblance to those of the traditional or modern study of language, and the basic notion of the discipline and the ways in which problems are formulated and addressed take on a considerably different form as well.

The principles-and-parameters approach yields a rather new way of thinking about questions of typology and comparative-historical linguistics. Consider again the analogy of speciation in biology. Apparently, small changes in the way fixed mechanisms function can produce large-scale phenomenal differences, yielding different species of organisms. In general, a slight change in the functioning of a rigidly structured and intricate system can yield very complex and surprising clusters of changes as its effects filter through the system. In the case of language, change of a single parameter may yield a cluster of differences which, on the surface, appear disconnected, as its effects filter through the invariant system of universal grammar. There is reason to believe that something of the sort is correct. Thus, among the Romance languages, French has a curious status. It differs from the other Romance languages in a cluster of properties, and it appears that these differences emerged fairly recently, and at about the same time. It may be that one parameter was changed—the null subject parameter that permits subject to be suppressed, some have speculated—yielding a cluster of other modifications through the mechanical working of the principles of universal grammar, and giving French something of the look of a Germanic language. At the same time, French and Spanish share certain features distinguishing them from Italian, and there are numerous other complexities as we look at the actual languages, or "dialects" as they are called. Similarly, we find most remarkable similarities among languages that have no known historical connection, suggesting that they have simply set crucial parameters the same way. These are essentially new questions, which can now be seriously formulated for the first time and perhaps addressed.

As conceptions of language have changed over the years, so has the notion of what counts as a "real result." Suppose we have some array of phenomena in some language. In the era of structural-descriptive linguistics, a result consisted in a useful arrangement of the data. As Zellig Harris put it in the major theoretical work of structural linguistics, a grammar provides a compact one-one representation of the phenomena in a corpus of data. Some, for example Roman Jakobson, went further in insisting on conformity to certain general laws, particularly in phonology, but in very limited ways.

Under the conception of language as a rule system, this would no longer count as a significant result; such a description poses rather than solves the problem at hand. Rather, it would be necessary to produce a rule system of the permitted format that predicts the data in question and in nontrivial cases, infinitely more. This is a much harder task, but not a hopeless one; there are many possible rule systems, and, with effort, it is often possible to find one that satisfies the permitted format, if this is not too restricted.

Under the more recent principles-and-parameters approach, the task becomes harder still. A rule system is simply a description: it poses rather than solves the problem, and a "real result" consists of a demonstration that the phenomena under investigation, and countless others, can be explained by selecting properly the

values of parameters in a fixed and invariant system of principles. This is a far harder problem, made still more difficult by the great expansion of empirical materials in widely differing languages that have come to be partially understood, and to which any general theory must be responsible. Where the problem can be solved, we have results of some depth, well beyond anything imaginable earlier. It is an important fact that the problem is now intelligibly formulable, and that solutions are being produced over an interesting range, while efforts to pursue this inquiry are unearthing a large mass of new and unexplored phenomena in a wide variety of languages that pose new challenges, previously unknown.

This discussion has been based on the assumption that lexical items are somehow learned and available, suggesting that apart from parameter-setting, language acquisition as well as parsing and presumably the creative use of language (in the unlikely event that we can come to understand anything about this matter) are to a large extent determined by properties of the lexicon. But acquisition of lexical items poses Plato's problem in a very sharp form. As anyone who has tried to construct a dictionary or to work in descriptive semantics is aware, it is a very difficult matter to describe the meaning of a word, and such meanings have great intricacy and involve the most remarkable assumptions, even in the case of very simple concepts, such as what counts as a possible "thing." At peak periods of language acquisition, children are "learning" many words a day, meaning that they are in effect learning words on a single exposure. This can only mean that the concepts are already available, with all or much of their intricacy and structure predetermined, and the child's task is to assign labels to concepts, as might be done with very simple evidence.

Many have found this conclusion completely unacceptable, even absurd; it certainly departs radically from traditional views. Some, for example Hilary Putnam, have argued that it is entirely implausible to suppose that we have "an innate stock of notions" including *carburetor, bureaucrat,* etc.[12] If he were correct about this, it would not be particularly to the point, since the problem arises in a most serious way in connection with simple words such as "table," "person," "chase," "persuade," etc. But his argument for the examples he mentions is not compelling. It is that to have given us this innate stock of notions, "evolution would have had to be able to anticipate all the contingencies of future physical and cultural environments. Obviously it didn't and couldn't do this." A very similar argument had long been accepted in immunology; namely, the number of antigens is so immense, including even artificially synthesized substances that had never existed in the world, that it was considered absurd to suppose that evolution had provided "an innate stock of antibodies"; rather, formation of antibodies must be a kind of "learning process" in which the antigens played an "instructive role." But this assumption has been challenged, and is now widely assumed to be false. Niels Kaj Jerne won the Nobel Prize for his work challenging this idea, and upholding his own conception that an animal "cannot be stimulated to make specific antibodies, unless it has already made antibodies of this specificity before the antigen arrives," so that antibody formation is a selective process in which the antigen plays a selective and amplifying role.[13] Whether or not Jerne is correct, he certainly could be, and the same could be true in the case of word meanings, the argument being quite analogous.

Furthermore, there is good reason to suppose that the argument is at least in substantial measure correct, even for such words as *carburetor* and *bureaucrat,* which, in fact, pose the familiar problem of poverty of stimulus if we attend carefully to the enormous gap between what we know and the evidence on the basis of which we know it. The same is true of technical terms of science and mathematics, and it is quite surely the case for the terms of ordinary discourse. However surprising the conclusion may be that nature has provided us with an innate stock of concepts, and that the child's task is to discover their labels, the empirical facts appear to leave open few other possibilities. Other possibilities (say, in terms of "generalized learning mechanisms") have not, to my knowledge, been coherently formulated, and if they are some day formulated, it may well be that the apparent issue will dissolve.

To the extent that anything is understood about lexical items and their nature, it seems that they are based on conceptual structures of a very specific and closely integrated type. It has been argued plausibly that concepts of a locational nature, including goal and source of action, object moved, place, etc., enter widely into lexical structure, often in quite abstract ways. In addition, notions like actor, recipient of action, event, intention, and others are pervasive elements of lexical structure, with their specific properties and permitted interrelations. Consider, say, the words *chase* or *persuade*. Like their Spanish equivalents, they clearly involve a reference to human intention. To chase Jones is not only to follow him, but to follow him with the intent of staying on his path, perhaps to catch him. To persuade Smith to do something is to cause him to decide or intend to do it; if he never decides or intends to do it, we have not succeeded in persuading him. Furthermore, he must decide or intend by his own volition, not under duress; if we say that the police persuaded Smith to confess by torture, we are using the term ironically. Since these facts are known essentially without evidence, it must be that the child approaches language with an intuitive understanding of concepts involving intending, causation, goal of action, event, and so on, and places the words that are heard in a nexus that is permitted by the principles of universal grammar, which provide the framework for thought and language, and are common to human languages as conceptual systems that enter into various aspects of human life.

Notice further that we appear to have connections of meaning, analytic connections, in such cases as these; we have a rather clear distinction between truths of meaning and truths of fact. Thus, if John persuaded Bill to go to college, then Bill at some point decided or intended to go to college; otherwise, John did not persuade Bill to do so. This is a truth of meaning, not of fact. The a priori framework of human thought, within which language is acquired, provides necessary connections among concepts, reflected in connections of meaning among words, and more broadly, among expressions involving these words. Syntactic relations provide a rich array of further examples. It appears, then, that one of the central conclusions of modern philosophy is rather dubious: namely, the contention, often held to have been established by work of Quine and others, that one can make no principled distinction between questions of fact and questions of meaning, that it is a matter of more or less deeply held belief. Philosophers have, I think, been led to this dubious conclusion, which is held by some (e.g., Richard Rorty) to have undermined centuries of thought, by concentrating on an artificially narrow class of examples, in particular, on concepts that have little or no relational structure: such sentences as "cats are animals." Here, indeed, it is not easy to find evidence to decide whether the sentence is true as a matter of meaning or fact, and there has been much inconclusive debate about the matter. When we turn to more complex categories with an inherent relational structure such as *persuade* or *chase,* or to more complex syntactic constructions, there seems little doubt that analytic connections are readily discerned.

Furthermore, the status of a statement as a truth of meaning or of empirical fact can and must be established by empirical inquiry, and considerations of many sorts may well be relevant; for example, inquiry into language acquisition and variation among languages. The question of the existence of analytic truths and connections, therefore, is an empirical one, to be settled by empirical inquiry that goes well beyond the range of evidence ordinarily brought to bear. Suppose that two people differ in their intuitive judgments as to whether I can persuade John to go to college without his deciding or intending to do so. We are by no means at an impasse. Rather, we can construct conflicting theories and proceed to test them. One who holds that the connection between *persuade* and *decide* or *intend* is conceptual will proceed to elaborate the structure of the concepts, their primitive elements, and so on, and will seek to show that other aspects of the acquisition and use of language can be explained in terms of the very same assumptions about the innate structure of the language faculty, in the same language and others, and that the same concepts play a role in other aspects of thought and understanding. One who holds that the connec-

tion is one of deeply held belief, not connection of meaning, has the task of developing a general theory of belief fixation that will yield the right conclusions in these and numerous other cases. One who holds that the connection is based on the "semantic importance" of sentences relating *persuade* and *decide* or *intend* (i.e., that these sentences play a prominent role in inference, or serve to introduce the term *persuade* to the child's vocabulary, and thus are more important than others for communication[14]) faces the task of showing that these empirical claims, which appear to lack any plausibility, are in fact true. The first task seems far more promising to me, but it is a matter of empirical inquiry, not pronouncements on the basis of virtually no evidence. The whole matter requires extensive rethinking, and much of what has been generally assumed for the past several decades about these questions appears to be dubious at best. There is, it seems clear, a rich conceptual structure determined by the initial state of the language faculty (perhaps drawing from the resources of other genetically determined faculties of mind), waiting to be awakened by experience, much in accord with traditional rationalistic conceptions and even, in some respects, the so-called "empiricist" thought of James Harris, David Hume, and others.

I think we are forced to abandon many commonly accepted doctrines about language and knowledge. There is an innate structure that determines the framework within which thought and language develop, down to quite precise and intricate details. Language and thought are awakened in the mind, and follow a largely predetermined course, much like other biological properties. They develop in a way that provides a rich structure of truths of meaning. Our knowledge in these areas, and I believe elsewhere—even in science and mathematics— is not derived by induction, by applying reliable procedures, and so on; it is not grounded or based on "good reasons" in any useful sense of these notions. Rather, it grows in the mind, on the basis of our biological nature, triggered by appropriate experience, and in a limited way shaped by experience that settles options left open by the innate structure of mind. The result is an elaborate structure of cognitive systems,

systems of knowledge and belief, that reflects the very nature of the human mind, a biological organ like others, with its scope and limits. This conclusion, which seems to me well-supported by the study of language and I suspect holds far more broadly, perhaps universally in domains of human thought, compels us to rethink fundamental assumptions of modern philosophy and of our general intellectual culture, including assumptions about scientific knowledge, mathematics, ethics, aesthetics, social theory and practice, and much else, questions too broad and far-reaching for me to try to address here, but questions that should, I think, be subjected to serious scrutiny from a point of view rather different from those that have conventionally been assumed.

NOTES

1. For references, here and below, see my *Knowledge of Language: Its Nature, Origin and Use* (New York: Praeger, 1986).

2. For discussion, see my *Aspects of the Theory of Syntax* (Cambridge: MIT Press, 1965). Here the concept of E-language is put to the side, and the object of inquiry is taken to be (1) the set of potential utterances $s_1, s_2, \ldots$ made available by universal phonetics (a part of universal grammar, UG); (2) the set of potential structural descriptions $SD_1, SD_2, \ldots$ made available by UG; (3) the set of potential grammars $G_1, G_2, \ldots$ made available by UG; a function f provided by UG that associates a set of SD's with each pair (s_i, G_j), and an "evaluation metric" provided by UG that orders grammars and thus determines their accessibility, given data. UG is understood to be the initial stage of the language faculty, a genetically determined species property, and a particular G_i is understood to be the steady state attained by the language faculty, given linguistic data, what I will call below a particular I-language. As discussed there, however, one chooses to define E-language, if at all, the formal properties of such sets (i.e., the "generative capacity" of grammars) is a matter of no clear relevance to questions of learnability, or surely parsability, given that as was well-known, languages do not meet this condition.

3. Anthony Kenny, *The Legacy of Wittgenstein* (Oxford: Basil Blackwell, 1984), p. 138. Elsewhere Kenny speaks of "the futility of [my] attempt to separate knowledge of English from the ability to use—the mastery of—the language." But to deny his identification of knowledge with ability is not to hold that knowledge can be "separated" from ability, whatever that means exactly.

4. Suppose that someone prefers to say that the knowl-

edge of English was indeed lost, but that something else was retained. Then that "something else" is the only matter of interest for the new theory that will replace the old theory of knowledge, and the same conclusions follow: the only concept of significance, which plays the role of the now abandoned notion "knowledge," is this "possession of language" that cannot be identified with ability to speak and understand. Clearly there is no point in these moves.

5. He also invests the invented concept of K-ability with curious properties, holding that had the patient not recovered, he would not have had the K-ability when he lost the ability; but since the concept is invented, he may give it whatever properties he likes. To be precise, Kenny is not discussing the example given here but one that is identical in all relevant respects: an aphasic who loses all ability to use language and then recovers the ability in full when the effects of the injury recede. He also shifts from "ability" to "capacity," saying that when the person lacked the ability he had the capacity, thus using "capacity" in the sense of "knowledge" or "K-ability." In my *Rules and Representations* (New York: Columbia University Press, 1980), to which he refers in this connection, I pointed out that "capacity" is often used in a much looser sense than "ability," so that a shift to "capacity" may disguise the inaccuracy of a characterization of knowledge in terms of ability. Kenny's discussion is also marred in other respects. Thus he notes that my usage of mentalistic terminology is quite different from his, but then criticizes my usage because it would be nonsensical on his assumptions, which is correct but hardly relevant, since I was precisely challenging these assumptions, for the reasons reviewed here.

6. See my "Knowledge of Language," in K. Gunderson, ed., *Language, Mind and Knowledge* (Minneapolis: University of Minnesota Press, 1975).

7. If there is one. Note that I have not tried to establish that this must always be the case but rather that it is in the case of language; or that knowledge can never be reduced to ability, but rather that it cannot be in general, and in particular cannot be in the case of knowledge of language.

8. One cannot speak of strict inconsistency, since the concept of language as a habit system was regarded as a matter of fact, while the procedures of linguistic analysis devised by many of the more sophisticated theorists were regarded as simply a device, one among many, with no truth claim.

9. For very important recent discussion of this matter, see Mark Baker, *A Theory of Grammatical Function* (Chicago: University of Chicago Press, 1988).

10. At least, if we are doing C-linguistics, with empirical content. If not, then further clarification is required. The inquiry is in any event not semantics in the sense of empirical semantics, a study of relations between the language and something extralinguistic.

11. On a personal note, my own work, from the beginning, has been largely concerned with the problem of developing linguistic theory so that the represen-

tations provided in particular languages will be appropriate for explaining how sentences are used and understood, but I have always called this "syntax," as it is, even though the motivation is ultimately semantic; see, e.g., my *Logical Structure of Linguistic Theory* (1955–56; published in part in 1975, New York: Plenum), *Syntactic Structures* (The Hague: Mouton, 1957). This work is correctly described as syntax, but it deals with questions that others incorrectly term "semantic," and it is, I suspect, one crucial way to study semantics.

12. See Putnam, "Meaning and Our Mental Life," manuscript, 1985.
13. For discussion in a linguistic-cognitive context, see my *Rules and Representations* (New York: Columbia University Press, 1980), 136f.; and Jerne's Nobel Prize lecture, "The Generative Grammar of the Immune System," *Science* 229.1057–9, September 13, 1985.
14. The proposal of Paul M. Churchland, *Scientific Realism and the Plasticity of Mind* (Cambridge University Press, 1979; 1986, 51f.).

SUGGESTED FURTHER READING

Ayer, A.J., "Can There Be a Private Language?" *Proceedings of the Aristotelian Society Supplementary Volume* 28 (1954).

Baker, G. P. and P. M. S. Hacker, *Skepticism, Rules and Language* (New York: Basil Blackwell, 1984).

Kenny, Anthony, "Cartesian Privacy," in *Wittgenstein: The Philosophical Investigations,* ed. George Pitcher (Garden City, N.Y.: Anchor Books, 1966), pp. 352–370.

Lewis, David, *Convention* (Cambridge: Harvard University Press, 1969).

Lewis, David, *Counterfactuals* (Cambridge: Harvard University Press, 1973).

Ludlow, Peter, "Noam Chomsky," in *Companion to Analytic Philosophy,* ed. A. P. Martinich and David Sosa (Oxford: Blackwell Publishers, 2001).

Millikan, Ruth, *Language, Thought and Other Biological Categories* (Cambridge: MIT Press, 1984).

Millikan, Ruth, *White Queen Psychology and Other Essays for Alice* (Cambridge: MIT Press, 1993).

Pinker, Steven, *The Language Instinct* (New York: William Morrow, 1994).

Rhees, Rush, "Can There Be a Private Language?" *Proceedings of the Aristotelian Society Supplementary Volume* 28 (1954): 77–94.

Strawson, P. F., "Review of *Philosophical Investigations,*" *Mind* 63 (1954): 70–99.

Winch, Peter, "Facts and Superfacts," *Philosophical Quarterly* 33 (1983): 398–404.